CLASS 10

CBSE

QUESTION & CONCEPT BANK

CHAPTER-WISE & TOPIC-WISE

MATHEMATICS

BASIC

EDITION : Third

Published By: Physicswallah Limited

Physics Wallah Publication

ISBN : 978-93-7818-471-0

MRP : 675/-

Mobile App: Physics Wallah (Available on Play Store)

Website: www.pw.live

Youtube Channel: Physics Wallah - Alakh Pandey

Alakh Pandey - Class 10

Physics Wallah Foundation

NCERT Wallah

Email: publication@pw.live

SKU Code: BKP2603216361

PREFACE

In this era of cutthroat competition among Class 10th aspirants for great marks in Board Exams, only a few are prepared enough to achieve it. During the preparation, a student needs the most relevant study material to cover all topics, practice efficiently, and excel in Board exams and other 10th level competitive exams.

While there is an abundance of study materials available in the market, what we felt was missing was a self-driven and well-planned study material. We have addressed this issue by introducing the CBSE Class 10th Question Concept Bank.

CBSE Class 10th Question & Concept Bank is a book that covers all the important concepts and theories, along with a rich amount of practice questions. This book is designed to provide you with the perfect guidance you need. The study material is consistent with the syllabus offered in NCERT Books and has been curated by the **Physics Wallah Editorial Team** under the careful observation of Physics Wallah Faculties.

Their invaluable contributions have enriched the very essence of our books.

This book consists of the following features:

The content is made in such a way that you can invest your time to make a strong fundamental that will get compounded and will pay you the interest in every upcoming year of your competitive exam's preparation and board exam preparation.

This will help you stay ahead of your competitors.

Our content will help you secure excellent marks in CBSE Class 10th Board Exam.

Following are the different sections that we have provided to develop your skills:

In Theory:

- Concept Maps
- Important Terms
- Important Concepts
- Important Derivations
- Important Formulas
- Real Life Applications
- Different Problem Types
- Memes

In Questions (Competency Based):

- Multiple Choice Questions
- Assertion and Reason
- Subjective Questions (with VSA, SA, LA and Case Based Questions as per Latest Board Exam Pattern)
- NCERT and NCERT Exemplar Questions
- Mistake 101: What not to do!
- Nailing the Right Answer
- Key Takeaways
- Answer Keys & Explanations with Marking Scheme as per Latest CBSE Board Pattern
- Topper's Explanations

Includes Questions & Explanations from:

Sample Question Paper issued by CBSE – **(CBSE SQP)**

Competency Focused Practice Questions issued by CBSE – **(CFPQ)**

Previous Year Questions in CBSE Board Exams

A step to make our book even better for our students:

Provide your valuable feedback
or
Report the Error

View Errata
(Error Correction from our end)

SYLLABUS ISSUED BY CBSE

Units	Unit Name	Marks
I	NUMBER SYSTEMS	06
II	ALGEBRA	20
III	COORDINATE GEOMETRY	06
IV	GEOMETRY	15
V	TRIGONOMETRY	12
VI	MENSURATION	10
VII	STATISTICS & PROBABILITY	11
	Total	**80**

S. No.	Content	Competencies	Explanation
	UNIT I: NUMBER SYSTEM		
1.	**REAL NUMBERS** 1. Fundamental Theorem of Arithmetic statements after reviewing work done earlier and after illustrating and motivating through examples 2. Proofs of irrationality of $\sqrt{2}$, $\sqrt{3}$, $\sqrt{5}$.	• Develops understanding of numbers, including the set of real numbers and its properties. • Extends understanding the of powers (radical powers) and exponents. • Applies Fundamental Theorem of Arithmetic to solve problems related to real life contexts.	• Describes Fundamental Theorem of Arithmetic with examples • Prove algebraically the Irrationality of numbers like $\sqrt{2}$, $\sqrt{3}$, $\sqrt{5}$, $3 + 2\sqrt{5}$ etc.
	UNIT II: ALGEBRA		
1.	**POLYNOMIALS** 1. Zeroes of a polynomial 2. Relationship between zeroes and coefficient of quadratic polynomials	• Develops a relationship between algebraic and graphical methods of finding the zeroes of a polynomial	• Find the zeroes of polynomial graphically and algebraically and verifying the relation between zeroes and coefficient of quadratic polynomials
2.	**PAIR OF LINEAR EQUATIONS IN TWO VARIABLES** 1. Pair of linear equations in two variables and graphical method of their solution, consistency/ inconsistency. 2. Algebraic conditions for number of solutions. 3. Solution of a pair of linear equations in two variables algebraically by substitution, by elimination. Simple situational problems.	• Describes plotting a. pair of linear equations and graphically finding the solution. • Models and solves contextualised problems equations using (e.g.. simultaneous linear equations in two variables).	• Find the solution of pair of linear equations in two variables graphically and algebraically (substitution and elimination method).
3.	**QUADRATIC EQUATIONS** 1. Standard form of a quadratic equation $ax^2 + bx + c = 0, (a \neq 0)$. 2. Solutions of quadratic equations (only real roots) by factorisation, and by using quadratic formula. Relationship between discriminant and nature of roots. 3. Situational problems based on quadratic equations related to day-to - day activities to be incorporated.	• Demonstrates strategies of finding roots and determining the nature of roots of a quadratic equation.	• Solves Quadratic equations using factorisation and quadratic formula. • Determines the nature of roots using discriminant. • Formulates and solves problems based on real life context.

4.	**ARITHMETIC PROGRESSIONS** 1. Motivation for studying Arithmetic Progression 2. Derivation of the nth term and sum of the first n terms of AP and their application in solving daily life problems.	• Develops strategies to apply the concept of A.P. to daily life situations.	• Applies concepts of AP to find the nth term and sum of n terms. • Application of AP in real life problems
	UNIT III: COORDINATE GEOMETRY		
1.	**COORDINATE GEOMETRY** 1. **Review:** Concepts of coordinate geometry. Distance formula. Section formula (internal division).	• Derive formulae to establish relations for geometrical shapes in the context of a coordinate plane, such as finding the distance between two given points, to determine the coordinates of a point between any two given points.	• Solve problems using distance formula and section formula
	UNIT IV: GEOMETRY		
1.	**TRIANGLES** Definitions, examples, counter examples of similar triangles. 1. (Prove) If a line is drawn parallel to one side of a triangle to intersect the other two sides in distinct points, the other two sides are divided in the same ratio. 2. State (without proof) If a line divides two sides of a triangle in the same ratio, the line is parallel to the third side. 3. State (without proof) if in two triangles, the corresponding angles are equal, their corresponding sides are proportional and the triangles are similar. 4. State (without proof) if the corresponding sides of two triangles are proportional, their corresponding angles are equal and the two triangles are similar. 5. State (without proof) if one angle of a triangle is equal to one angle of another triangle and the sides including these angles are proportional the two triangle are similar.	• Works out ways to differentiate between congruent and similar figures. • Establishes properties for similarity of two triangles logically using different geometric criteria established earlier such as, Basic Proportionality Theorem, etc.	• Prove Basic Proportionality theorem and applying the theorem and its converse in solving questions. • Prove similarity of triangles different using similarity criteria.
2.	**CIRCLES** Tangent to a circle at point of contact. 1. (Prove) The tangent at any point of a circle is perpendicular to the radius through the point of contact. 2. (Prove) The lengths of tangents drawn from an external point to a circle are equal.	• derives proofs of theorems related to the tangents of circles.	• Prove the theorems based on the tangent to a circle. • Applies the concept of tangents of circle to solve various problems.
	UNIT V: TRIGONOMETRY		
1.	**INTRODUCTION TO TRIGONOMETRY** 1. Trigonometric ratios of an acute angle of a right-angled triangle. Proof of their existence (well defined) 2. Motivate the ratios whichever are defined at 0° and 90° Values of the trigonometric ratios of 30°, 45° and 60°. 3. Relationships between the ratios.	• Understands the definitions of the basic trigonometric functions (including the introduction of the sine and cosine functions).	• Evaluates trigonometric ratios • Describes trigonometric ratios of standard angles and solving related expressions
2.	**TRIGONOMETRIC IDENTITIES** 1. Proof and applications of the identity $\sin^2 A + \cos^2 A = 1$. 2. Only simple identities to be given.	• Uses Trigonometric identities to solve problems.	• Proves trigonometric identities using $\sin^2 A + \cos^2 A = 1$ and other identities
3.	**HEIGHTS AND DISTANCES: Angle of elevation, Angle of Depression.** 1. Simple problems on heights and distances. Problems should not involve more than two right triangles. Angles of elevation/depression should be only 30°, 45° and 60°.	• Applies Trigonometric ratios in solving problems in daily life contexts like finding heights of different structures or distance from them.	• Find heights and distances in real life word problems using trigonometric ratios

	UNIT VI: MENSURATION		
1.	**AREAS RELATED TO CIRCLES** 1. Area of sectors and segments of a circle. 2. Problems based on areas and perimeter / circumference of the above said plane figures. (In calculating area of segment of a circle, problems should be restricted to central angle of 60°, 90° and 120° only.	• Derives and uses. formulae to calculate areas of plane figures.	• Visualises and evaluates areas of sector and segment of a circle.
2.	**SURFACE AREAS AND VOLUMES** 1. Surface areas and volumes of combinations of any two of the following: cubes, cuboids, spheres, hemispheres and right circular cylinders/cones.	• Visualises and uses mathematical thinking to discover formulae to calculate surface areas and volumes of solid objects (cubes, cuboids, spheres, hemispheres, right circular cylinders/cones, and their combinations).	• Evaluates the surface areas and volumes of combinations of solids by visualisation
	UNIT VII: STATISTICS AND PROBABILITY		
1.	**STATISTICS** 1. Mean, median and mode of grouped data (bimodal situation to be avoided).	• Calculates mean, median and mode for different sets of data related with real life contexts.	• Computes the mean of a grouped frequency distribution using direct, assumed mean and step deviation method. • Computes the median and mode of grouped frequency distribution by algebraic method
2.	**PROBABILITY** 1. Classical definition of probability. 2. Simple problems on finding the probability of an event.	• Applies concepts from probability to solve problems on the likelihood of everyday events.	• Determines the probabilities in simple real-life problems

MATHEMATICS-Basic (QUESTION PAPER DESIGN)

CLASS–X

Time: 3 Hours **Max. Marks: 80**

S.No.	Typology of Questions	Total Marks	% Weightage (approx.)
1.	**Remembering:** Exhibit memory of previously learned material by recalling facts, terms, basic concepts, and answers. **Understanding:** Demonstrate understanding of facts and ideas by organizing, comparing, translating, interpreting, giving descriptions, and stating main ideas	60	75
2.	**Applying:** Solve problems to new situations by applying acquired knowledge, facts, techniques and rules in a different way.	12	15
3.	**Analysing:** Examine and break information into parts by identifying motives or causes. Make inferences and find evidence to support generalizations **Evaluating:** Present and defend opinions by making judgments about information, validity of ideas, or quality of work based on a set of criteria. **Creating:** Compile information together in a different way by combining elements in a new pattern or proposing alternative solutions	8	10
	Total	**80**	**100**

INTERNAL ASSESSMENT	20 MARKS
Pen Paper Test and Multiple Assessment (5+5)	10 Marks
Portfolio	05 Marks
Lab Practical (Lab activities to be done from the prescribed books)	05 Marks

Chapter-wise Weightage and Trend Analysis of
CBSE Past 5 Years' Papers

MATHEMATICS					
CHAPTERS	2022	2023	2024	2025	2026
Real Numbers	–	6	6	6	6
Polynomials	–	2	5	4	3
Pair of Linear Equations in Two Variables	–	5	6	6	5
Quadratic Equations	4	8	4	5	7
Arithmetic Progressions	6	5	5	5	5
Triangles	–	7	8	8	9
Coordinate Geometry	–	6	6	6	6
Introduction to Trigonometry	–	6	7	6	7
Some Applications of Trigonometry	7	6	5	6	5
Circles	6	8	7	7	6
Areas Related to Circles	–	5	5	4	5
Surface Areas and Volumes	4	5	5	6	5
Statistics	8	6	7	6	7
Probability	–	5	4	5	4

**The marks allotment mentioned above is chapter-wise and includes internal choice questions as well. Therefore, the total might not match the Maximum Marks of the respective Previous Year Paper.*

Question Typology

YEAR	Objective Questions		Subjective Questions			
	MCQs	A/R	VSA	SA	LA	Case Based type
2026	18	2	5	6	4	3
2025	18	2	5	6	4	3
2024	18	2	5	6	4	3
2023	18	2	5	6	4	3
2022	–	–		10	2	2

Evolving Trends in CBSE Exam Patterns

2022

- Question paper contains 14 questions
- It was a descriptive paper which contains very short question (2 marks), short questions (3 marks), long questions (4 marks), and two case studies.
- Internal choice has given in section A, B and C.

2023

- Rationalised Content Onwards
- Assertion/Reason questions are introduced from this year onwards.
- 3 case based questions with internal choices are added.
- The number of sections in the paper increased to 5 sections (A, B, C, D and E) compared to 2022.
- Competancy based questions are increased in number.
- Internal choice has given in section B,C,D and E
- MCQ (1 Mark), VSA (2 Marks), SA (3 Marks), LA (5 Marks), Case Based (4 Marks) 2023 onwards,

2024

- No changes in exam pattern

2025

- No changes in exam pattern

2026

- 50% competency based questions is asked in exam pattern.

HOW TO USE THIS BOOK

This book is structured to support your learning journey of preparing for your board exams through a variety of engaging and informative elements. Here's how to make the most of it:

CBSE Solved Paper of 2026 with Handwritten Style Answer: *Get yourself updated with the latest Board Question Papers. With handwritten answers, learn the practical application of concepts and effective answering techniques to achieve higher scores.*

CBSE Solved Paper

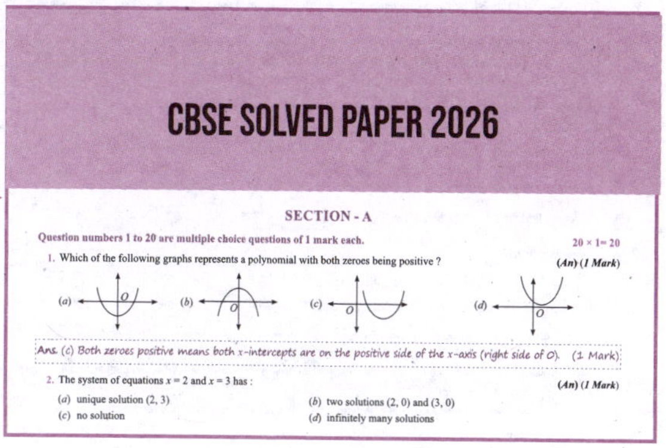

At the start of every chapter, you'll find a thoughtfully chosen image and a quote that captures the main idea and motivation of the topic. This approach aims to get your interest and give you a glimpse of the theme ahead.

Before diving into the details, we outline the syllabus and analyze the weightage given to each topic over the past five years. This helps you prioritize your study focus based on the significance of each section.

Preview

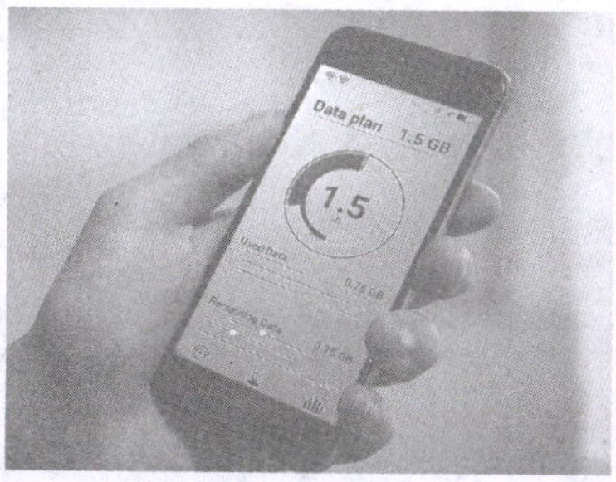

"Smartphone uses real numbers to calculate the amount of data you have used. If your data plan includes 1.5 GB of data per day, and you've used 0.75 GB, the phone calculates the remaining data using subtraction in the set of real numbers."

SYLLABUS & WEIGHTAGE

List of Concept Names	Years				
	2021	2022	2023	2024	2025
The Fundamental Theorem of Arithmetic (Fundamental Theorem of Arithmetic - statements after reviewing work done earlier and after illustrating and motivating through examples)	Exam not Conducted	–	2 Q (1 M each) 1 Q (4 M)	1 Q (2 M) 1 Q (3 M)	1 Q (2 M)
Revisiting Irrational Numbers (Proofs of irrationality of $\sqrt{2}, \sqrt{3}, \sqrt{5}$)		–	–	1 Q (1 M) 1 Q (2 M)	1 Q (1 M) 1 Q (3 M)

Concept Map

The concept map appears to be a comprehensive study aid that outlines key concepts in a structured format, featuring definitions, diagrams, and processes. For a student, it would serve as a visual summary, making complex ideas more accessible and aiding in revision and understanding of concept for their curriculum.

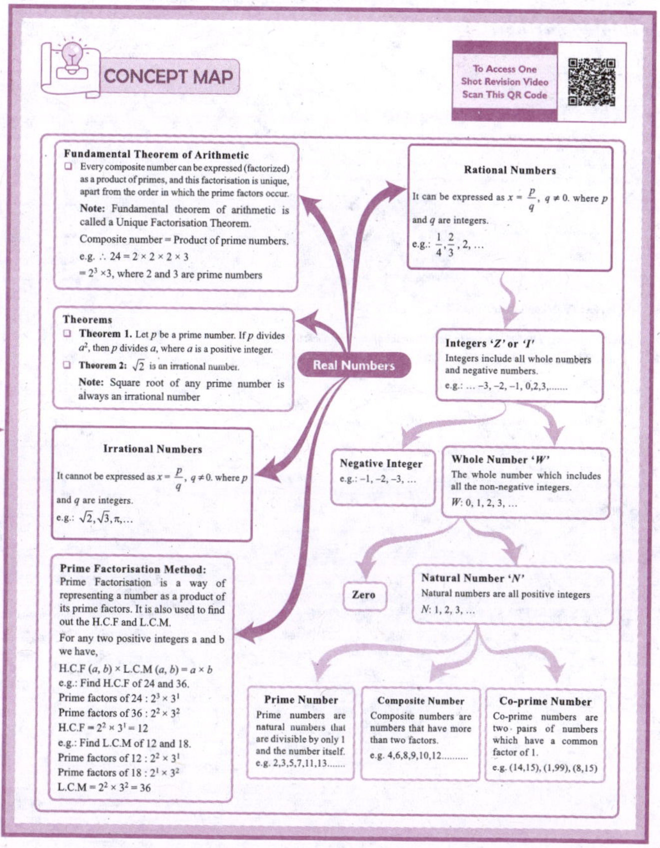

Important Terms:

Important terms often serve as foundational concepts upon which more complex ideas are built. Introducing them early ensures students have a solid understanding before delving into more advanced topics.

Important Concepts:

Familiarizing with key concepts in advance helps prepare cognitive framework for processing and integrating new information. By highlighting important concepts upfront, students are better equipped to identify connections and relationships between various ideas presented in the chapter.

1 GEOMETRICAL MEANING OF THE ZEROES OF A POLYNOMIAL

Important Terms

- **Polynomial:** Polynomial has two words, Poly (meaning "many") and Nomial (meaning "terms"). A polynomial is defined as an expression that includes variables, constants, and exponents.
- **General form of the Polynomial:** $p(x) = a_n x^n + a_{(n-1)} x^{(n-1)} + a_{(n-2)} x^{(n-2)} + \ldots + a_1 x^1 + a_0$. (where n is a whole number and $a_0, a_1, a_2, \ldots, a_n$ are real numbers) is called a polynomial in one variable x of degree n.
- **Degree of the Polynomial:** The highest power of the variable x in the given polynomial $p(x)$, is known as the degree of the polynomial.
- **Linear Polynomial:** If the degree of the given polynomial is one then, it is known as the linear polynomial. *e.g.*, $2x - 3$, $x + 5$
- **Quadratic Polynomial:** If the degree of the given polynomial is two then, it is known as the quadratic polynomial. *e.g.*, $2x^2 - 3$, $x^2 + \sqrt{3}\,x + 5$, $\frac{y}{5} + y^2 - \sqrt{2}$, etc.
- **Cubic Polynomial:** If the degree of the given polynomial is three then, it is known as the cubic polynomial.
- *e.g.*, $2 - x^3$, x^3, $3 - x^2 + x^3$, $3x^3 - 2x^2 + x - 1$, etc.
- **The value of $p(x)$ at $x = k$:** If $p(x)$ is a polynomial in x, and if k is any real number, then the value obtained by replacing x by k in $p(x)$, is called the value of $p(x)$ at $x = k$, and is denoted by $p(k)$.
- **Zero of a Polynomial $p(x)$:** If $p(k) = 0$, then the real number k is said to be a zero of a polynomial $p(x)$.
- **Zero of the Linear Polynomial:** If k is a zero of $p(x) = ax + b$, then $p(k) = ak + b = 0$, *i.e.*, $k = -\frac{b}{a}$.

Important Concepts

- **Geometrical Meaning of the Zeroes of a Polynomial:**

  (*i*) The linear polynomial $ax + b$, $a \neq 0$, has exactly one zero, namely, $\left(-\frac{b}{a}, 0\right)$.

  (*ii*) The zeroes of a quadratic polynomial $ax^2 + bx + c$, $a \neq 0$, are precisely the x-coordinates of the points where the parabola $(ax^2 + bx + c)$ representing $y = ax^2 + bx + c$ intersects the x-axis.

  Equation $y = ax^2 + bx + c$ has one of the two shapes either open upwards like ∪ or open downwards like ∩ depending on whether $a > 0$ or $a < 0$. (These curves are called parabolas.)

  From our observation about the shape of the graph of $y = ax^2 + bx + c$, the following three cases arise:

Case (*i*): Here, the graph cuts x-axis at two distinct points A and A'.

The x-coordinates of A and A' are the two zeroes of the quadratic polynomial $ax^2 + bx + c$ in this case (see Fig. *i* & *ii*)

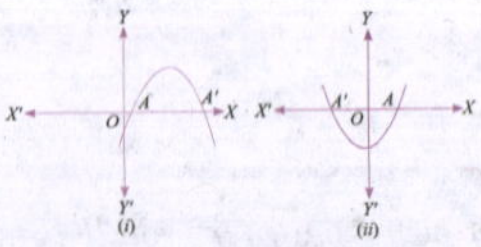

(*i*) (*ii*)

Important Derivations:

Derivations bridge the gap between theoretical concepts and their practical application, showing students how abstract ideas translate into real-world scenarios.

Important Formulas:

Introducing important formulas upfront brings clarity to the chapter's objectives, guiding students' focus towards essential mathematical principles that will be explored further.

Important Derivations

- **Theorem 1:** Let p be a prime number. If p divides a^2, then p divides a, where a is a positive integer.

  Proof: Let the prime Factorisation of a be as follows:

  $a = p^1, p^2, \ldots p^n$, where $p^1, p^2, \ldots, p^n$ are primes, not necessarily distinct.

  Therefore, $a^2 = (p^1, p^2, \ldots p^n)(p^1 \cdot p^2 \ldots p^n) = (p^1)^2, (p^2)2 \ldots (p^n)^2$.

  Now, we are given that p divides a^2. Therefore, from the Fundamental Theorem of Arithmetic, it follows that p is one of the prime factors of a^2. However, using the uniqueness part of the Fundamental Theorem of Arithmetic, we realize that the only prime factors of a^2 are $p^1, p^2, \ldots, p^n$. So p is one of $p^1, p^2, \ldots, p^n$.

  Now, since $a = p^1, p^2, \ldots p^n$.

  p divides a.

Important Formulas

Cube

- Area of four walls = Lateral surface area = $4a^2$
- Total surface area (T.S.A) of the cube = $6a^2$
- Length of diagonal of the cube = $\sqrt{3}a$

Cuboid

- Area of four walls of a room = Lateral surface area = $2h(l + b)$
- Total surface area (T.S.A) of the cuboid = $2(lb + bh + lh)$
- Length of diagonal of the cuboid = $\sqrt{l^2 + b^2 + h^2}$

Sphere

- Surface area (S.A.) of the sphere = $4\pi r^2$

Hemisphere

- Curved surface area (C.S.A.) of the hemisphere = $2\pi r^2$
- Total surface area (T.S.A.) of the hemisphere = $3\pi r^2$

Right Circular Cylinder

- Area of each end of the cylinder = πr^2
- Curved surface area (C.S.A) of the cylinder = (circumference of circle × height of cylinder) = $2\pi rh$
- Total surface area (T.S.A) of the cylinder = $2\pi r(h + r)$

Cone

- Slant Height $(l) = \sqrt{(r^2 + h^2)}$
- Curved surface area (C.S.A.) of cone = πrl
- Total surface area (T.S.A) of cone = $\pi r(r + l) = \pi r(r + \sqrt{(h^2 + r^2)})$

Real Life Applications

Here are some real-life applications of real numbers:

1. Banking and Finance:

- **Interest rates:** Real numbers are used to represent interest rates on loans and investments.
- **Account balances:** Real numbers are used to represent the balances in bank accounts, investments, and financial transactions.

Different Problem Types

Type I: Expressing a Positive Integer as a Product of its Prime Factors

Suppose we need to find the prime factorisation of 176

Solution:

Step I: Divide the given number by the smallest prime number 2.

Here, we divide 176 by 2 ⇒ $176 \div 2 = 88$

Step II: Again, divide the quotient of step 1 by the smallest prime number 2.

So, 88 is again divided by 2 ⇒ $88 \div 2 = 44$

Step III: Repeat the process, until the quotient becomes 1.

Now, again divide 44 by 2 ⇒ $44 \div 2 = 22$

22 is divisible by 2. So, divide it again by 2 ⇒ $22 \div 2 = 11$

As 11 is a prime number, divide it by 11 to get 1 ⇒ $11 \div 11 = 1$

2	176
2	88
2	44
2	22
11	11
	1

Step IV: Finally, multiply all the prime factors that are the divisors. Prime factorisation of 176 is $2 \times 2 \times 2 \times 2 \times 11 = 2^4 \times 11$

Memes

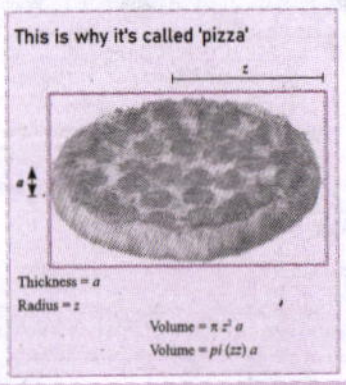

Real Life Applications:

Connecting abstract math to real scenarios deepens comprehension and aids in problem-solving.

Learning how math connects with other subjects shows that it's useful in many areas and helps us understand different topics better.

Different Problem Types:

Presenting different types of problems encourages critical thinking and creativity by challenging students to approach each problem uniquely, analyse it, develop strategies, and adapt their approaches to find solutions.

Different problem types challenge students to analyse problems from diverse angles, fostering critical thinking skills essential for problem-solving.

Memes:

Memes are a popular form of internet humour and culture. With creativity we have captured students' attention to make them more receptive to the material that follows.

Memorable memes help students retain and recall key mathematical ideas more effectively during studying and assessments

COMPETENCY BASED SOLVED EXAMPLES

Multiple Choice Questions **(1 M)**

1. **If the H.C.F of 360 and 64 is 8, then their L.C.M is:** (An) (CBSE, 2023)
   (a) 2480 (b) 2780 (c) 512 (d) 2880

Sol. We are given:
H.C.F (360, 64) = 8
The formula to find L.C.M using H.C.F and product of the numbers is:
$\text{L.C.M. } (a, b) = \frac{a \times b}{\text{H.C.F}(a, b)}$
Substituting the given values:
$a = 360, b = 64$
$\text{L.C.M } (360, 64) = \frac{360 \times 64}{8} = \frac{23040}{8} = 2880$

2. **The least number that is divisible by all the natural numbers from 1 to 10 (both inclusive) is** (An) (NCERT Exemplar)
   (a) 10 (b) 100 (c) 504 (d) 2520

Sol. The least number divisible by all the numbers from 1 to 10 will be the L.C.M of the following number: 1, 2, 3, 4, 5, 6, 7, 8, 9 & 10.
Prime factorisation of these numbers are $1 = 1, 2 = 2, 3 = 3, 4 = 2 \times 2, 5 = 5, 6 = 2 \times 3, 7 = 7, 8 = 2 \times 2 \times 2, 9 = 3 \times 3, 10 = 2 \times 5$
So, the L.C.M of these number is
$1 \times 2 \times 2 \times 2 \times 3 \times 3 \times 5 \times 7 = 2520$

Key Takeaways
Check that the correct option should be divisible by all the natural numbers 1–10 as the L.C.M is the lowest common multiple.

3. **120 can be expressed as a product of its prime factors as** (An) (CBSE, 2020)
   (a) $5 \times 8 \times 3$ (b) 15×2^3
   (c) $10 \times 2^2 \times 3$ (d) $5 \times 2^3 \times 3$

Sol. Let's find the prime factors of 120:
$120 = 2 \times 60 = 2 \times 2 \times 30$
$= 2 \times 2 \times 2 \times 15 = 2 \times 2 \times 2 \times 3 \times 5$
So, the prime factorization of 120 is $2^3 \times 3 \times 5$.

4. **If two positive integers a and b are written as $a = x^3y^2$ and $b = xy^3$; x, y are prime numbers, then H.C.F (a, b) is** (An) (CBSE SQP, 2023)
   (a) xy (b) xy^2 (c) x^3y^3 (d) x^2y^2

Sol. It is given that, $a = x^3y^2$ and $b = xy^3$, where x and y are prime numbers.
$\text{L.C.M } (a, b) = \text{L.C.M } (x^3y^2, xy^3)$
= The highest of powers of x and $y = x^3y^3$
$\text{H.C.F } (a, b) = \text{H.C.F } (x^3y^2, xy^3)$
The lowest of powers of x and $y = xy^2$
Hence, $\text{H.C.F}(a, b) = xy^2$ and $\text{L.C.M}(a, b) = x^3y^3$.

5. **The L.C.M of smallest two-digit composite number and smallest composite number is** (An) (CBSE SQP, 2023)
   (a) 12 (b) 4 (c) 20 (d) 44

Sol. By prime factorisation, we get;
$4 = 1 \times 2 \times 2$
$10 = 1 \times 2 \times 5$
Now, L.C.M of 4, $10 = 2 \times 2 \times 5 = 20$
Therefore, the L.C.M of the smallest two-digit composite number and the smallest composite number is 20.

Key Takeaways
The smallest 2-digit number = 10 and the smallest composite number = 4

6. **If two positive integers a and b can be expressed as $p = ab^2$ and $q = a^3b$; a, b being prime numbers, then L.C.M (p, q) is** (Ap) (NCERT Exemplar)
   (a) ab (b) a^2b^2 (c) a^3b^2 (d) a^3b^3

Sol. Let's express each polynomial as a product of the power of irreducible factors.
$p = ab^2 = a \times b^2, q = a^3b = a^3 \times b$
To find the L.C.M, raise each irreducible factor to the greatest exponent.
$\therefore \text{ L.C.M} = a^3 \times b^2 = a^3b^2$

Mistakes 101 : What not to do!
Sometimes, students take the term with the lower power from numbers to calculate the L.C.M of numbers.

7. **The ratio between the L.C.M and H.C.F of 5, 15, 20 is** (Ap)
   (a) 9 : 1 (b) 4 : 3
   (c) 11 : 1 (d) 12 : 1

Sol. Prime factorisations are:
$5 = 5^1, 15 = 3^1 \times 5^1, 20 = 2^2 \times 5^1$
$\text{L.C.M } (5, 15, 20) = 2^2 \times 3^1 \times 5^1 = 60$
$\text{H.C.F } (5, 15, 20) = 5^1 = 5$
$\text{Ratio} = \frac{\text{LCM}}{\text{HCF}} = \frac{60}{5} = 12$
Ratio = 12 : 1

CBSE Class – X Mathematics 46

Solved Examples

For each topic, solved examples are provided including tagging of Competencies, PYQs, CBSE SQPs etc that exemplify how to approach and solve questions. This section is designed to reinforce your learning and improve problemsolving skills.

MISCELLANEOUS EXERCISE

Multiple Choice Questions **(1 M)**

1. The solution of equations $x - y = 2$ and $x + y = 4$ is: (CBSE SQP, 2023)
   (a) 3 and 1 (b) 4 and 3 (c) 5 and 1 (d) –1 and –3
2. If a pair of linear equations is inconsistent then their graph lines will be
   (a) parallel (b) always coincident
   (c) always intersecting (d) intersecting or coincident
3. If $2x - 3y = 7$ and $(a + b)x - (a + b - 3)y = 4a + b$ have an infinite number of solutions then
   (a) $a = 5, b = 1$ (b) $a = -5, b = 1$
   (c) $a = 5, b = -1$ (d) $a = -5, b = -1$

ANSWER KEYS

Multiple Choice Questions
1. (a) 2. (a) 3. (d) 4. (a) 5. (d) 6. (c) 7. (c) 8. (c) 9. (a) 10. (c)
11. (a) 12. (c) 13. (a) 14. (c)

Assertion and Reason
1. (b) 2. (a) 3. (d) 4. (c)

Case Based Questions

Case Based-II
(i) (c) (ii) (b) (iii) (a) (iv) (c) (v) (d)

Case Based-V
(i) (d) (ii) (c) (iii) (b) (iv) (d) (v) (c)

HINTS & EXPLANATIONS

Multiple Choice Questions

1. (a) Given: $x - y = 2$ ... (i)
   $x + y = 4$ ... (ii)
   Adding eqn. (i) and (ii), we get $2x = 6 \Rightarrow x = 3$
   Put the value of x in equation (i), we get
   $3 - y = 2 \Rightarrow y = 1$
   Hence, $x = 3, y = 1$
2. (a) A pair of linear equations is inconsistent when there is no solution to the pair, which is possible if there is no common points in the lines represented by the pair of linear equations, which is possible if the lines are parallel.
3. (d) We have,
   $2x - 3y = 7$ ... (i)
   and $(a + b)x - (a + b - 3)y = 4a + b$ ... (ii)
   $\Rightarrow a_1 = 2,\ b_1 = -3,\ c_1 = -7$
   $a_2 = a + b, b_2 = -a - b + 3$ and $c_2 = -4a - b$

For infinite number of solutions,
$\frac{a_1}{a_2} = \frac{b_1}{b_2} = \frac{c_1}{c_2} \Rightarrow \frac{2}{a+b} = \frac{-3}{-(a+b-3)} = \frac{-7}{-(4a+b)}$
$\Rightarrow \frac{2}{a+b} = \frac{3}{a+b-3} = \frac{7}{4a+b}$
For $\frac{2}{a+b} = \frac{3}{a+b-3}$
$\Rightarrow 2a + 2b - 6 = 3a + 3b \Rightarrow a + b = -6$ ... (i)
For $\frac{3}{a+b-3} = \frac{7}{4a+b}$
$\Rightarrow 12a + 3b = 7a + 7b - 21 \Rightarrow 5a - 4b = -21$ ... (ii)
Adding eqn (i) and eqn (ii) by multiplying eqn (i) by 4.
$4(a + b) + 5b - 4b = -6 \times 4 + (-21)$
$\Rightarrow 9a = -45 \Rightarrow a = -5$
Substituting this in eqn (i)
$-5 + b = -6$
$b = -6 + 5 = -1$
Hence, $a = -5$ and $b = -1$

At the end of each chapter, you'll find additional exercises intended to test your grasp of the material. These are great for revision and to prepare for exams.

Answer Key and Explanations including Topper's Explanations, Mistake 101, Nailing the right answer and Key takeaway to know how to write the ideal answer.

Answer Key

MOCK TEST PAPER-1

Time allowed : 3 hours **Maximum Marks : 80**

GENERAL INSTRUCTIONS:

Read the following instructions very carefully and follow them:

(i) *This question paper contains **38** questions. **All** questions are compulsory.*
(ii) *Question Paper is divided into 5 Sections-**Section A, B, C, D and E.***
(iii) *In **Section A question number 1 to 18 are** Multiple Choice Questions **(MCQs)** and question number **19 & 20** are Assertion-Reason based **questions of 1 mark each.***
(iv) *In **Section-B question number 21 to 25 are** Very Short Answer (VSA) type **questions of 2 marks each.***
(v) *In **Section-C question number 26 to 31 are** Short Answer (SA) type **questions carrying 3 marks each.***
(vi) *In **Section-D question number 32 to 35 are** Long Answer (LA) type **questions carrying 5 marks each.***
(vii) *In **Section-E question number 36 to 38 are** Case Study based **questions carrying 4 marks each. Internal choice is provided in 2 marks question in each case-study.***
(viii) ***There is no overall choice. However, an internal choice has been provided in 2 questions in Section B, 2 questions in Section C, 2 questions in Section D and 3 questions in Section E.***
(ix) ***Draw neat figures wherever required. Take π = 22/7 wherever required if not stated.***
(x) ***Use of calculators is NOT allowed.***

SECTION - A

Section - A consists of Multiple Choice type questions of 1 mark each.

1. The least number that is divisible by all the natural numbers from 1 to 10 (both inclusive) is
   (a) 10 (b) 100 (c) 504 (d) 2520
2. If the zeroes of the quadratic polynomial $ax^2 + bx + c, c \neq 0$ are equal, then
   (a) c and a have opposite signs (b) c and b have same sign
   (c) c and a have same sign (d) c and b have opposite sign
3. The given pair of linear equations $x + 2y - 5 = 0$ and $-3x - 6y + 15 = 0$ have
   (a) Exactly one solution (b) Exactly two solutions
   (c) Infinitely many solutions (d) No solution
4. If $ax^2 + bx + c = a(x - p)^2$, the relation among a, b and c is:
   (a) $abc = 1$ (b) $a + c - 2b = 0$
   (c) $b^2 - ac = 0$ (d) $b^2 = 4ac$
5. If the numbers $n - 2$, $4n - 1$ and $5n + 2$ are in AP then value of n is
   (a) 1 (b) 4 (c) –4 (d) –2

Mock Test

Mock Test Papers: Test your preparedness with our Mock Test Papers designed to mirror the format and difficulty of real exams. Use the detailed explanations to identify areas of strength and opportunities for improvement.

CONTENTS

Upcoming CBSE SQPs/APQs can be accessed through this QR

Questions have been categorized according to the Bloom's Taxonomy (as per CBSE Board).
The following abbreviations have been used in the book:

(*Un*) - Understanding (*Re*) - Remembering (*Ap*) - Applying
(*An*) - Analysing (*Cr*) - Creating (*Ev*) - Evaluating

CBSE SOLVED PAPER 2026

Time allowed : 3 hours	Maximum Marks : 80

GENERAL INSTRUCTIONS:

Read the following instructions very carefully and strictly follow them:

(i) *This question paper contains **38** questions. **All** questions are **compulsory**.*

(ii) *This question paper is divided into **five** Sections - **A**, **B**, **C**, **D** and **E**.*

(iii) *In **Section A**, Question numbers **1** to **18** are Multiple Choice Questions (MCQs) and question numbers **19** and **20** are Assertion-Reason based questions of **1** mark each.*

(iv) *In **Section B**, Question numbers **21** to **25** are Very Short Answer (VSA) type questions, carrying **2** marks each.*

(v) *In **Section C**, Question numbers **26** to **31** are Short Answer (SA) type questions, carrying **3** marks each.*

(vi) *In **Section D**, Question numbers **32** to **35** are Long Answer (LA) type questions carrying **5** marks each.*

(vii) *In **Section E**, Question numbers **36** to **38** are **Case Study based** Questions carrying **4** marks each. Internal choice is provided in **2** marks questions in each case study.*

(viii) *There is no overall choice. However, an internal choice has been provided in **2** questions in Section **B**, **2** questions in Section **C**, **2** questions in Section **D** and **3** questions in Section **E**.*

(ix) *Draw neat diagrams wherever required. Take $\pi = \frac{22}{7}$ wherever required, if not stated.*

(x) *Use of calculator is **not allowed**.*

SECTION - A

Question numbers 1 to 20 are multiple choice questions of 1 mark each. **20 × 1= 20**

1. Which of the following graphs represents a polynomial with both zeroes being positive ? ***(An) (1 Mark)***

(*a*) 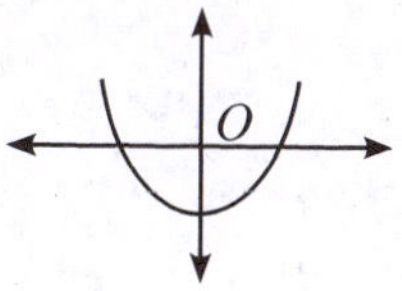
(*b*) 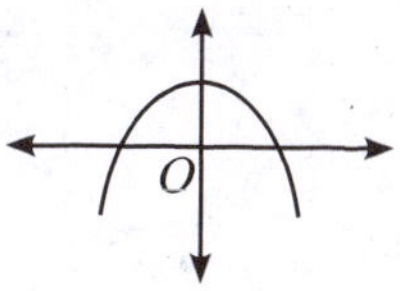
(*c*) 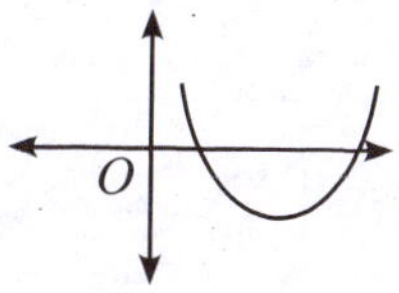
(*d*) 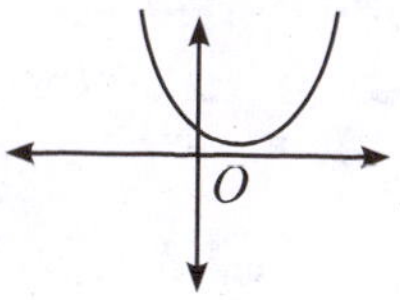

Ans. (c) Both zeroes positive means both x-intercepts are on the positive side of the x-axis (right side of O). (1 Mark)

2. The system of equations $x = 2$ and $x = 3$ has: ***(An) (1 Mark)***

(*a*) unique solution (2, 3)
(*b*) two solutions (2, 0) and (3, 0)
(*c*) no solution
(*d*) infinitely many solutions

Ans. (c) Vertical lines $x = 2$ and $x = 3$ are parallel, so they never intersect. Therefore, the system has no solution. (1 Mark)

3. If the numbers $1 - a$, $3 - a$ and $5 - a$ are in A.P., then the common difference is: ***(Un) (1 Mark)***

(*a*) $1 - a$
(*b*) $-2 + a$
(*c*) 2
(*d*) $2 - a$

Ans. (c) Numbers $1 - a$, $3 - a$, $5 - a$ in A.P.

$a_1 = 1 - a$, $a_2 = 3 - a$, $a_3 = 5 - a$

The common difference: $d = a_2 - a_1 = (3 - a) - (1 - a) = 2$ (1 Mark)

4. Which of the following statements is not true ? **(An) (1 Mark)**

(a) $\sin 0° = \cos 0°$ (b) $\tan 30° = \cot 60°$ (c) $\sin 30° = \cos 60°$ (d) $\sin 45° = \frac{1}{\sec 45°}$

Ans. (a) Check each option: (a) $\sin 0° = 0$, $\cos 0° = 1 \Rightarrow$ not equal $\Rightarrow$ not true.

(b) $\tan 30° = \frac{1}{\sqrt{3}}, \cot 60° = \frac{1}{\sqrt{3}} \Rightarrow$ true

(c) $\sin 30° = \frac{1}{2}, \cos 60° = \frac{1}{2} \Rightarrow$ true

(d) $\sin 45° = \frac{1}{\sqrt{2}}, \frac{1}{\sec 45°} = \frac{1}{\sqrt{2}} \Rightarrow$ true (1 Mark)

5. If $\tan \theta - \cot \theta = 0$, then the value of θ is: **(Ap) (1 Mark)**

(a) 30° (b) 45° (c) 60° (d) 90°

Ans. (b) $\tan\theta - \cot\theta = 0 \Rightarrow \tan\theta = \cot\theta \Rightarrow \tan\theta = \frac{1}{\tan\theta}$

$\Rightarrow \tan^2\theta = 1 \Rightarrow \tan\theta = 1$

$\therefore \theta = 45°$ (1 Mark)

6. In the adjoining figure, the angle of elevation of the point C from the point B, is: **(Ap) (1 Mark)**

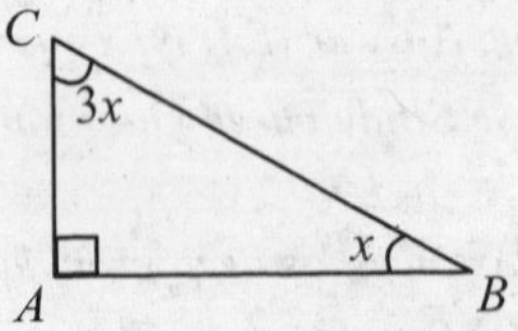

(a) 30° (b) 45° (c) 22.5° (d) 67.5°

Ans. (c)

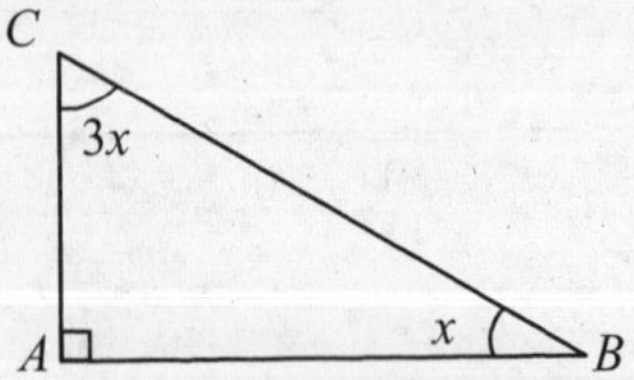

Angle of elevation from point B to point C is the angle at B in triangle ABC, i.e. $\angle B = x$.

In triangle ABC,

$\angle A = 90°$, $\angle B = x$, $\angle C = 3x$

$\angle A + \angle B + \angle C = 180°$ (Angle sum property)

$\Rightarrow 90° + x + 3x = 180° \Rightarrow 90° + 4x = 180°$

$\Rightarrow 4x = 90° \Rightarrow x = 22.5°$ (1 Mark)

7. In the adjoining figure, the slant height of the conical part is: **(Ap) (1 Mark)**

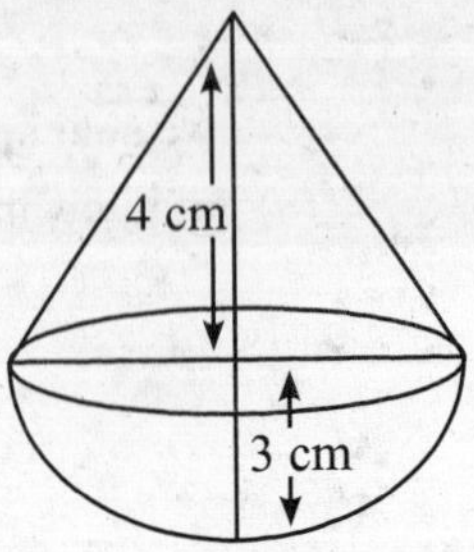

(a) 4 cm (b) 7 cm (c) 5 cm (d) 25 cm

Ans. (c)

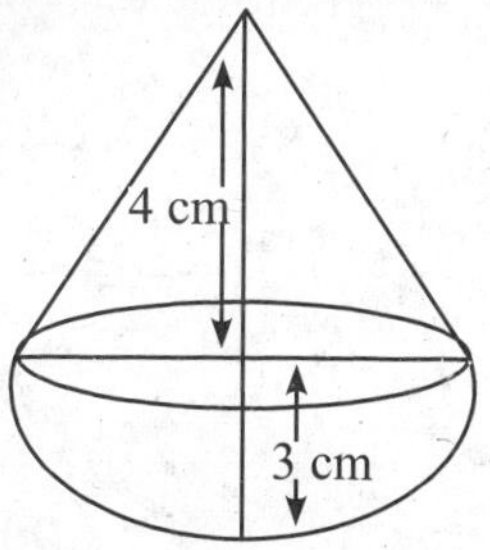

Height of cone $h = 4$cm, radius $r = 3$ cm.

Slant height formula: $l = \sqrt{r^2 + h^2}$

$l = \sqrt{3^2 + 4^2} = \sqrt{9+16} = \sqrt{25} = 5$ cm

(1 Mark)

8.

Class	0 – 10	10 – 20	20 – 30	30 – 40	40 – 50
Frequency	3	5	7	9	11

The upper limit of the median class of the above data is: ***(Ev) (1 Mark)***

(*a*) 10 (*b*) 20 (*c*) 30 (*d*) 40

Ans. (d) Class and frequency:

Class	f	cf
0 – 10	3	3
10 – 20	5	8
20 – 30	7	15
30 – 40	9	24
40 – 50	11	35

$N = 35$ so $\frac{N}{2} = 17.5$

therefore median class = 30 – 40

Upper limit of median class = 40

(1 Mark)

9. If for a data, median is 5 and mode is 4, then mean is equal to: ***(Ap) (1 Mark)***

(*a*) 7 (*b*) 11 (*c*) $\frac{11}{2}$ (*d*) $\frac{14}{3}$

Ans. (c) Given: Median = 5, Mode = 4

Using Mode = 3 Median – 2 Mean

$\Rightarrow 4 = 3 \times 5 - 2 \times \text{Mean}$

$\Rightarrow 4 = 15 - 2 \times \text{Mean}$

$\Rightarrow 2 \times \text{Mean} = 15 - 4 = 11$

$\Rightarrow \text{Mean} = \frac{11}{2}$

(1 Mark)

10. The HCF of $3^7.7^3$ and $3^3.7^7$ is: ***(Ap) (1 Mark)***

(*a*) 1 (*b*) 3.7 (*c*) $3^3.7^3$ (*d*) $3^7.7^7$

Ans. (c) First number: $3^7.7^3$

Second number: $3^3.7^7$

For HCF we take least power of both numbers

$\therefore$ HCF = $3^3.7^3$

(1 Mark)

11. A letter is selected from the letters of the word FEBRUARY. The probability that it is a vowel is: ***(Ap) (1 Mark)***

(*a*) $\frac{1}{8}$ (*b*) $\frac{2}{8}$ (*c*) $\frac{3}{8}$ (*d*) $\frac{3}{7}$

Ans. (c) Word: FEBRUARY

letters F, E, B, R, U, A, R, Y

Vowels: E, U, A → 3 vowels

Total letters = 8

Probability $= \frac{3}{8}$ (1 Mark)

12. Which of the following numbers will not end with 0 for any natural number n? **(An) (1 Mark)**

(a) $4n$ (b) 4^n (c) $3^n + 1$ (d) 10^{n+1}

Ans. (b) From each option: (a) $4n$

If n is a multiple of 5, then $4n$ will be divisible by 10.

So it can end with 0.

(b) 4^n

Powers of 4 follow this unit digit pattern:

4, 6, 4, 6, ...

So it never ends with 0.

(c) $3^n + 1$

Powers of 3 follow this unit digit pattern:

3, 9, 7, 1, 3, 9, 7, 1, ...

Adding 1 gives:

4, 0, 8, 2, 4, 0, 8, 2, ...

So sometimes it ends with 0.

(d) 10^{n+1}

Any power of 10 always ends with 0. (1 Mark)

13. The system of linear equations $px + qy = r$ and $p_1x + q_1y = r_1$ has a unique solution, if: **(Ap) (1 Mark)**

(a) $pq \neq p_1q_1$ (b) $pp_1 \neq qq_1$ (c) $pq_1 \neq qp_1$ (d) $pqr \neq p_1q_1r_1$

Ans. (c) $px + qy = r$

$a_1 = p, b_1 = q, c_1 = -r$

$p_1x + q_1x = r_1$

$a_2 = p_1, b_2 = q_1, c_2 = -r_1$

For unique solution:

$\frac{a_1}{a_2} \neq \frac{b_1}{b_2}$

$\frac{p}{p_1} \neq \frac{q}{q_1} \Rightarrow pq_1 \neq qp_1$ (1 Mark)

14. Which of the following equations is/are **not** quadratic? **(An) (1 Mark)**

$q_1 : (x-1)^2 = x^2$, $q_2 : (x-1)^3 = x^3$

$q_3 : (x+1)^3 = 3x^2$, $q_4 : \left(\sqrt{x}+1\right)^2 = 2\sqrt{x}$

(a) q_1, q_3 and q_4 (b) q_2 and q_3 (c) q_2, q_3 and q_4 (d) q_1 and q_4

Ans. (a) $q_1 : (x-1)^2 = x^2 \Rightarrow x^2 - 2x + 1 = x^2 \Rightarrow -2x + 1 = 0$

It is linear not quadratic

$q_2 : (x-1)^3 = x^3 \Rightarrow x^3 - 3x^2 + 3x - 1 = x^3$

$\Rightarrow -3x^2 + 3x - 1 = 0$ → quadratic

$q_3 : (x+1)^3 = 3x^2 \Rightarrow x^3 + 3x^2 + 3x + 1 = 3x^2$

$\Rightarrow x^3 + 3x + 1 = 0 \rightarrow$ cubic

It is not quadratic

$q_4 : (\sqrt{x}+1)^2 = 2\sqrt{x} \Rightarrow x + 2\sqrt{x} + 1 = 2\sqrt{x}$

$\Rightarrow x + 1 = 0 \rightarrow$ linear

$\therefore$ It is not quadratic equation.

Hence, q_1, q_3, q_4 are not quadratic equations. (1 Mark)

15. The discriminant of the quadratic equation $ax^2 + x + a = 0$ is: **(Ap) (1 Mark)**

(*a*) $\sqrt{1-4a^2}$ (*b*) $1 - 4a^2$ (*c*) $4a^2 - 1$ (*d*) $\sqrt{4a^2 - 1}$

Ans. (*b*) Given quadratic equation: $ax^2 + x + a = 0$

Compare with standard form: $Ax^2 + Bx + C = 0$

So, $A = a$, $B = 1$, $C = a$

The discriminant $D = B^2 - 4AC$

$\Rightarrow D = 1^2 - 4(a)(a) \Rightarrow D = 1 - 4a^2$ (1 Mark)

16. The coordinates of opposite vertices of the square *ABCD* are *A* (– 5, 0) and *C* (0, 5). The length of a diagonal of the square *ABCD* is: **(Ev) (1 Mark)**

(*a*) 5 units (*b*) 10 units (*c*) $\sqrt{10}$ units (*d*) $\sqrt{50}$ units

Ans. (*d*) Coordinates of opposite vertices of square ABCD are A(–5, 0) and C(0, 5).

Distance between two points (x_1, y_1) and (x_2, x_2) is given by: $d = \sqrt{(x_2 - x_1)^2 + (y_2 - y_1)^2}$

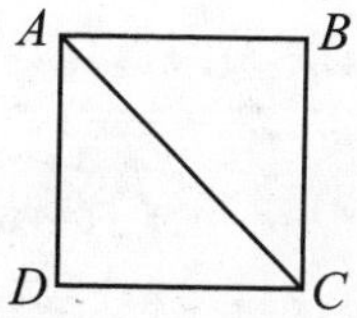

Here A(–5, 0), C(0, 5):

$\therefore AC = \sqrt{[(0-(-5)]^2 + (5-0)^2} = \sqrt{25+25} = \sqrt{50}$ units (1 Mark)

17. In the adjoining figure, $\Delta PQT \sim \Delta RST$. Which of the following is true? **(An) (1 Mark)**

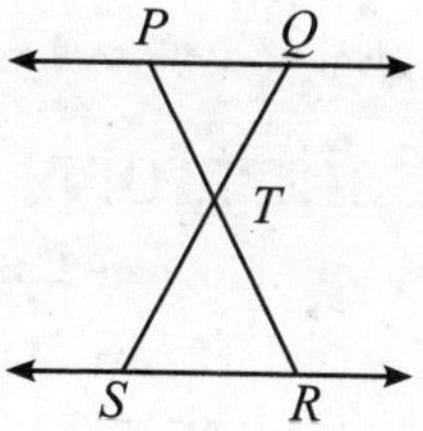

(*a*) $\frac{PQ}{ST} = \frac{QT}{RS}$

(*b*) $QT \,.\, RT = PT \,.\, ST$

(*c*) $PQ \,.\, PT = RS \,.\, RT$

(*d*) $\frac{PQ}{PT} = \frac{RT}{RS}$

Ans. (*b*) Given: $\Delta PQT \sim \Delta RST$

So, $\frac{PQ}{RS} = \frac{QT}{ST} = \frac{PT}{RT}$

From $\frac{QT}{ST} = \frac{PT}{RT} \Rightarrow QT \times RT = PT \times ST$ (1 Mark)

18. In the adjoining figure, if $EA \parallel SR$ and $PE = x$ cm, then the value of $5x$ is: **(Ap) (1 Mark)**

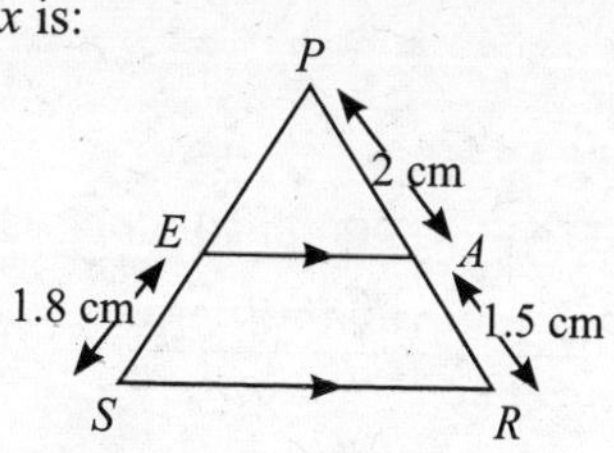

(*a*) 2.4 cm

(*b*) 12 cm

(*c*) 1.35 cm

(*d*) 6.75 cm

Ans. (*b*) PE = x, ES = 1.8, PA = 2 cm, AR = 1.5 cm

Δ PSR, with EA || SR

By BPT:

$$\frac{PE}{ES}=\frac{PA}{AR} \Rightarrow \frac{x}{1.8}=\frac{2}{1.5}$$

$$\Rightarrow x=1.8\times\frac{2}{1.5} \Rightarrow x=1.8\times\frac{4}{3} \Rightarrow x = 2.4$$

$\therefore 5x = 5 \times 2.4 = 12$ (1 Mark)

Directions : Question numbers 19 and 20 are Assertion and Reason based questions. Two statements are given, one labelled as Assertion (A) and the other is labelled as Reason (R). Select the correct answer to these questions from the codes (a), (b), (c) and (d) as given below:

(*a*) Both, Assertion (A) and Reason (R) are true and Reason (R) is the correct explanation of Assertion (A).

(*b*) Both, Assertion (A) and Reason (R) are true, but Reason (R) is not the correct explanation of Assertion (A).

(*c*) Assertion (A) is true, but Reason (R) is false.

(*d*) Assertion (A) is false, but Reason (R) is true.

19. Assertion (A): From a bag containing 5 red balls, 2 white balls and 3 green balls, the probability of drawing a non-white ball. is $\frac{4}{5}$

Reason (R): For any event E, $P(E) + P$ (not E) = 1 ***(Ev) (1 Mark)***

Ans. (a) Assertion (A): From a bag with 5 red, 2 white, 3 green balls,

Total balls = 5 + 2 + 3 = 10

White ball = 2

P(non-white) $=\frac{8}{10}=\frac{4}{5}$ – True.

Reason (R): P (E) + P (not E) = 1 (1 Mark)

Hence both, Assertion (A) and Reason (R) are true and Reason (R) is the correct explanation of Assertion (A).

20. Assertion (A): $7 \times 2 + 3$ is a composite number.

Reasion (R): A composite number has more than two factors. ***(Ap) (1 Mark)***

Ans. (d) Assertion (A): $7 \times 2 + 3 = 14 + 3 = 17$

17 is prime, not composite $\Rightarrow$ False.

Reason (R): A composite number has more than two factors $\Rightarrow$ True. (1 Mark)

SECTION – B

Question numbers 21 to 25 are very short answer type questions of 2 marks each. **5 × 2 = 10**

21. A box consists of 60 wall clocks, out of which 40 are good, 15 have minor defects and the remaining are broken. A trader will reject the box, if the clock taken out from the box is broken. The trader randomly takes out one clock from the box. What is the probability that: ***(An) (2 Marks)***

(*i*) the box will be rejected?

(*ii*) the clock taken out of the box has minor defect?

Ans. Given: Total clocks = 60

Good = 40

Minor defect = 15

Broken = 60 – 40 – 15 = 5

(i) Probability box rejected = probability clock is broken

$$\text{Probability} = \frac{\text{Number of favourable outcomes}}{\text{Total number of outcomes}}$$

$P(\text{reject})=\frac{5}{60}=\frac{1}{12}$ (1 Mark)

(ii) Probability clock has minor defect

Using above formula again

$P(\text{minor defect}) = \frac{15}{60} = \frac{1}{4}$ **(1 Mark)**

22. *A* point *P* divides a line segment *OR* in the ratio 2 : 1. If the coordinates of *O* are (0, 0) and that of *P* are (– 2, – 3), find the coordinates of *R*. ***(Ap) (2 Marks)***

Ans.

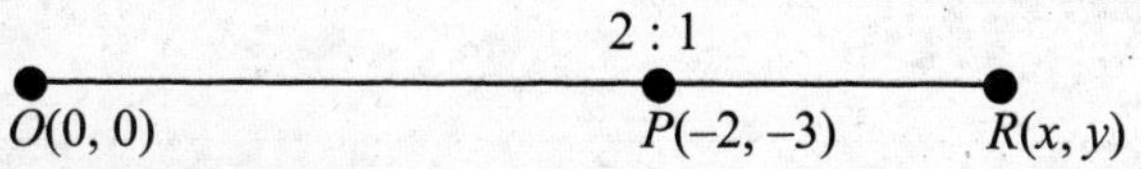

Given: Point P divides OR in ratio 2 : 1, O (0, 0), P (–2, –3)

Let, coordinates of R (x, y)

Using section formula: $\left(\frac{mx_2+nx_1}{m+n}, \frac{my_2+ny_1}{m+n}\right)$

On putting the values of m = 2, n = 1, $x_1 = 0$ and $y_1 = 0$

$P(-2,-3) = P\left(\frac{2\times x+1\times 0}{2+1}, \frac{2\times y+1\times 0}{2+1}\right)$ **(1 Mark)**

On comparing the coordinates

$\Rightarrow \frac{2\times x+1\times 0}{2+1} = \frac{2x}{3} = -2 \Rightarrow 2x = -6 \Rightarrow x = -3$

Now, $\frac{2\times y+1\times 0}{3} = \frac{2y}{3} = -3 \Rightarrow 2y = -9 \Rightarrow y = -\frac{9}{2} = -4.5$

$\therefore$ R (–3, – 4.5)

Hence coordinates of R is (–3, – 4.5) **(1 Mark)**

23. (*a*) One zero of a quadratic polynomial is twice the other. If the sum of zeroes is (– 6), find the polynomial. ***(Ap) (2 Marks)***

OR

(*b*) If one zero of the polynomial $x^2 - 5x - c$ is (–1), find the value of *c*. Also, find the other zero. ***(Ap) (2 Marks)***

Ans. (a) According to given conditions let the zeroes be α and 2α.

Sum of zeroes = –6

$\Rightarrow \alpha + 2\alpha = -6 \Rightarrow 3\alpha = -6 \Rightarrow \alpha = -2$ **(½ Mark)**

So the zeroes are –2 and –4.

Product of zeroes: (–2)(–4) = 8 **(½ Mark)**

Required quadratic polynomial using sum and product of zeroes is given by: x^2 – (sum of zeroes)x + (product of zeroes)

$= x^2 - (-6)x + 8 = x^2 + 6x + 8$

Hence required polynomial is $x^2 + 6x + 8$. **(1 Mark)**

OR

(b) Given polynomial is $x^2 - 5x - c$

Since –1 is a zero, substitute x = –1 in given polynomial

$(-1)^2 - 5(-1) - c = 0$

$\Rightarrow 1 + 5 - c = 0 \Rightarrow 6 - c = 0 \Rightarrow c = 6$ **(1 Mark)**

Put c in polynomial: $x^2 - 5x - 6$

By middle term factorisation

$\Rightarrow x^2 - 6x + x - 6 = 0 \Rightarrow x(x-6) + 1(x-6) = 0 \Rightarrow (x+1)(x-6) = 0 \Rightarrow x - 6 = 0 \Rightarrow x = 6$

Hence the value of c is 6 and other zero is 6 **(1 Mark)**

24. In the adjoining figure, $VW \parallel YZ$, $XV = \frac{3}{2}VY$, and WX = 4 cm. Find the length of XZ. **(An) (2 Marks)**

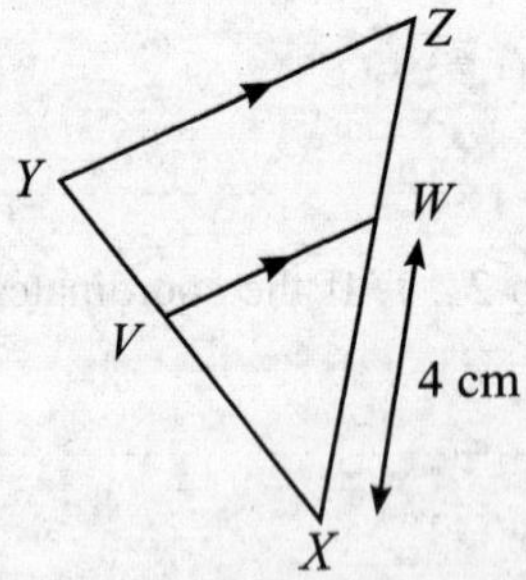

Ans. Given $XV = \frac{3}{2}VY$, then $\frac{XV}{VY} = \frac{3}{2}$.

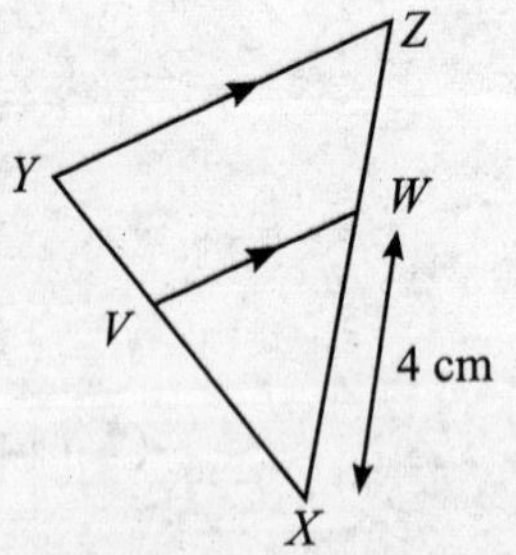

By the Basic Proportionality Theorem (Thales's Theorem), since

$VW \parallel YZ$:

$\frac{XV}{VY} = \frac{XW}{WZ}$ (1 Mark)

XW = 4, so $\frac{4}{WZ} = \frac{3}{2} \Rightarrow WZ = \frac{4 \times 2}{3} = \frac{8}{3}$ cm

Then $XZ = XW + WZ = 4 + \frac{8}{3} = \frac{12}{3} + \frac{8}{3} = \frac{20}{3}$ cm

Hence the length of XZ is $\frac{20}{3}$ cm (1 Mark)

25. (*a*) Evaluate : $\sin^2 30° - \cos^2 45° + \cot^2 60°$. **(Ev) (2 Marks)**

OR

(*b*) If $\sin(A + 2B) = 2\cos 60°$ and $A = 3B$, find the measures of A and B. **(Ev) (2 Marks)**

Ans. (a) As we know $\sin 30° = \frac{1}{2} \Rightarrow \sin^2 30° = \frac{1}{4}$

$\cos 45° = \frac{1}{\sqrt{2}} \Rightarrow \cos^2 45° = \frac{1}{2}$

$\cot 60° = \frac{1}{\sqrt{3}} \Rightarrow \cot^2 60° = \frac{1}{3}$

Put the above values in given expression (1 Mark)

$\therefore \sin^2 30° - \cos^2 45° + \cot^2 60° = \frac{1}{4} - \frac{1}{2} + \frac{1}{3} = \frac{3-6+4}{12} = \frac{1}{12}$ (1 Mark)

OR

(b) Given: $\sin(A + 2B) = 2\cos 60°$ and $A = 3B$

$\sin(A + 2B) = 2\cos 60° = 2\left(\frac{1}{2}\right) = 1$ (1 Mark)

$\Rightarrow \sin(A + 2B) = 1 \Rightarrow A + 2B = 90°$ (since $\sin 90° = 1$) .

Now putting $A = 3B$ in this equation

$(A + 2B) = 3B + 2B = 90° \Rightarrow 5B = 90° \Rightarrow B = 18°$ (½ Mark)

$\therefore A = 3 \times 18° = 54°$ (½ Mark)

Hence values of A and B are 54° and 18° respectively.

SECTION – C

Question numbers 26 to 31 are short answer type questions of 3 marks each. $6 \times 3 = 18$

26. In the adjoining figure, AB is the diameter of the circle with centre O. Two tangents p and q are drawn to the circle at the points A and B respectively. Prove that $p \parallel q$. Further, a line CD touches the circle at E and $\angle BCD = 110°$. Find the measure of $\angle ADC$.

(An) (3 Marks)

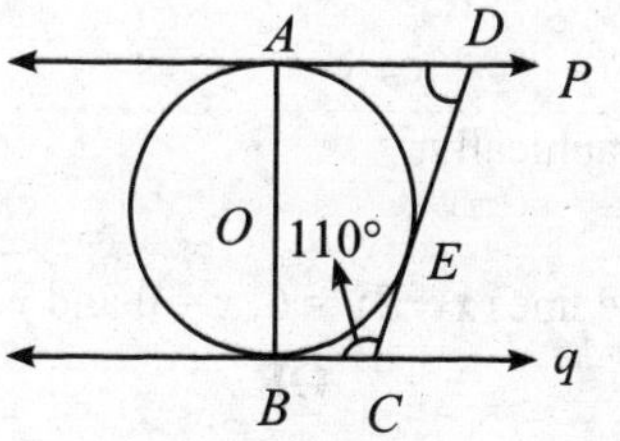

Ans. Given: AB is the diameter of the circle with centre O. Two tangents p and q are drawn to the circle at the points A and B respectively.

CD touches the circle at E and $\angle BCD = 110°$.

To prove: $p \parallel q$ and find $\angle ADC$

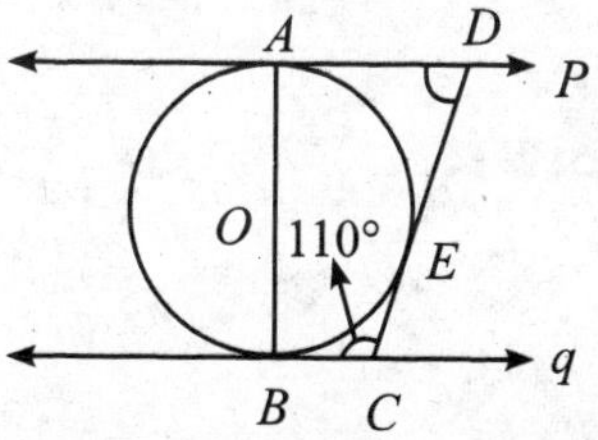

Proof: p is the tangent to the circle at point A.

$\therefore \angle OAD = 90°$ [Tangent is perpendicular to the radius through the point of contact]

Similarly, q is the tangent to the circle at point B.

$\therefore \angle OBC = 90°$ (½ Mark)

Since AB is a diameter, OA and OB are collinear.

Thus $\angle OAD = \angle OBC = 90°$, and these are alternate interior angles with respect to line AB and tangents p and q.

Hence $p \parallel q$. (1 Mark)

In quadrilateral ABCD:

$\angle DAB = 90°$ (tangent at A $\perp$ to radius OA)

$\angle ABC = 90°$(tangent at B $\perp$ to radius OB) (½ Mark)

$\angle BCD = 110°$ (given)

Sum of angles in quadrilateral = 360°:

$90° + 90° + 110° + \angle ADC = 360°$

$\Rightarrow 290° + \angle ADC = 360° \Rightarrow \angle ADC = 70°$ (1 Mark)

27. Given that $\sqrt{3}$ is an irrational number, prove that $2-5\sqrt{3}$ is also an irrational number. ***(Ev) (3 Marks)***

Ans. Let us assume that $2-5\sqrt{3}$ is rational.

Then we can write:

$2-5\sqrt{3}=\frac{p}{q}$, where $q\neq 0$, p, q are integers.

$\Rightarrow -5\sqrt{3}=\frac{p}{q}-2 \Rightarrow -5\sqrt{3}=\frac{p-2q}{q}$

$\Rightarrow 5\sqrt{3}=-\frac{p-2q}{q} \Rightarrow \sqrt{3}=-\frac{p-2q}{5q}$ (1 Mark)

Here p and q are integers, so $-\frac{p-2q}{5q}$ is an integer.

Thus $-\frac{p-2q}{5q}$ is a rational number. (1 Mark)

This implies $\sqrt{3}$ is rational, which contradicts the given fact that $\sqrt{3}$ is irrational.

Therefore, our assumption that $2-5\sqrt{3}$ is rational is wrong.

Hence $2-5\sqrt{3}$ is an irrational number. (1 Mark)

28. (*a*) solve the following system of equations graphically:

$x + 3y = 6$ and $2x - 3y = 12$

Also, find the area of the triangle formed by the lines $x + 3y = 6$, $x = 0$ and $y = 0$. **(Ev) (3 Marks)**

OR

(*b*) One of the supplementary angles exceeds the other by 120°. Express the given information as a system of linear equations in two variables. Hence, find the measure of both the angles. **(Ap) (3 Marks)**

Ans. (a) Given equations: $x + 3y = 6$ ..... (i)

$2x - 3y = 12$ ..... (ii)

From (i)

$x + 3y = 6$

If $x = 0$

$0 + 3y = 6 \Rightarrow y = 2$

Point: (0, 2)

If $y = 0$

$x + 3(0) = 6 \Rightarrow x = 6$

Point: (6, 0)

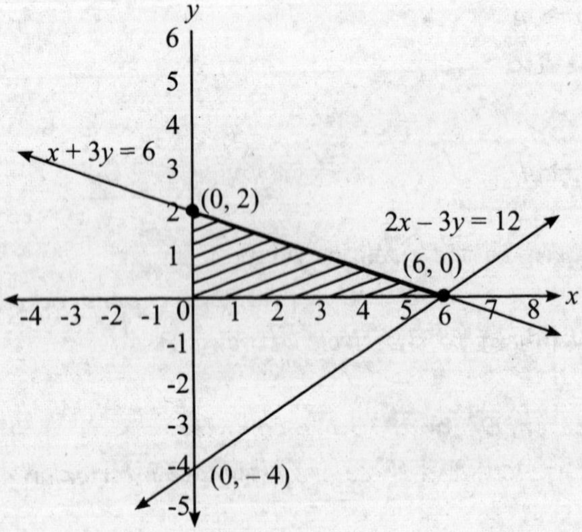

(1 Mark)

x	0	6
y	2	0

From (ii)

$2x - 3y = 12$

If $y = 0$

$2x - 3(0) = 12 \Rightarrow x = 6$

Point: (6, 0)

If $x = 0$

$2(0) - 3y = 12 \Rightarrow y = -4$ (½ Mark)

Point: (0, – 4)

x	0	6
y	– 4	0

So intersection point of both lines = (6, 0) (½ Mark)

Triangle with $x = 0$, $y = 0$ and this line: having vertices (0, 0), (0, 2), (6, 0)

We get, Base = 6, height = 2

$\therefore$ area of triangle $= \frac{1}{2} \times$ base $\times$ height $= \frac{1}{2} \times 6 \times 2 = 6$ sq units. (1 Mark)

OR

(b) Let the two angles be x and y.

ATQ

Since they are supplementary:

$x + y = 180°$ (½ Mark)

And one angle exceeds the other by 120°:

$x - y = 120°$ (½ Mark)

Add the two equations:

$(x + y) + (x - y) = 180° + 120° \Rightarrow 2x = 300° \Rightarrow x = 150°$ (1 Mark)

Substitute x in $x + y = 180°$:

$150° + y = 180° \Rightarrow y = 30°$ (1 Mark)

Hence the 2 angles are150° and 30°

29. If the point $D(x, y)$ is equidistant from the points $E(0, 3)$ and $F(3, 0)$, prove that $x = y$. Hence, find the x coordinate of the point D, if ΔDEF is an equilateral triangle. ***(Ap) (3 Marks)***

Ans. Given D(x, y) is equidistant from E(0, 3) and F(3, 0)

So, distance will be equal

$\therefore$ DE = DF

Using distance formula: $d = \sqrt{(x_2 - x_1)^2 + (y_2 - y_1)^2}$

$\Rightarrow \sqrt{(x-0)^2 + (y-3)^2} = \sqrt{(x-3)^2 + (y-0)^2}$

$\Rightarrow x^2 + (y - 3)^2 = (x - 3)^2 + y^2$

$\Rightarrow x^2 + y^2 - 6y + 9 = x^2 - 6x + 9 + y^2$

$\Rightarrow -6y = -6x$

$\Rightarrow x = y$ (1 Mark)

Now, if ΔDEF is an equilateral triangle:

Length $EF = \sqrt{(3-0)^2 + (0-3)^2} = \sqrt{9+9} = \sqrt{18} = 3\sqrt{2}$

Since triangle is equilateral,

DE = EF

$3\sqrt{2} = \sqrt{x^2 + (x-3)^2}$ $(\because x = y)$

$\Rightarrow x^2 + (x - 3)^2 = 18 \Rightarrow x^2 + x^2 - 6x + 9 = 18$

$\Rightarrow 2x^2 - 6x - 9 = 0$ (1 Mark)

$\Rightarrow x^2 - 3x - 4.5 = 0$

Now on comparing with equation $ax^2 + bx + c = 0$ we get $a = 1$, $b = -3$, $c = -4.5$

Using quadratic formula: $x = \dfrac{-b \pm \sqrt{b^2 - 4ac}}{2a}$

$\therefore x = \dfrac{3 \pm \sqrt{9+18}}{2} \Rightarrow x = \dfrac{3 \pm \sqrt{27}}{2} \Rightarrow x = \dfrac{3 \pm 3\sqrt{3}}{2}$ (1 Mark)

30. (*a*) Prove that: $\dfrac{\sin A - \tan A}{\sin A + \tan A} = \dfrac{1 - \sec A}{1 + \sec A}$ ***(Ap) (3 Marks)***

OR

(*b*) If $\sin x = p$, then prove that: ***(Ap) (3 Marks)***

(*i*) $\cot x = \dfrac{\sqrt{1-p^2}}{p}$

(*ii*) $\dfrac{1 + \tan^2 x}{1 + \cot^2 x} = \dfrac{p^2}{1 - p^2}$

Ans. (a) We need to prove $\dfrac{\sin A - \tan A}{\sin A + \tan A} = \dfrac{1 - \sec A}{1 + \sec A}$

In LHS = $\dfrac{\sin A - \tan A}{\sin A + \tan A} = \dfrac{\sin A - \dfrac{\sin A}{\cos A}}{\sin A + \dfrac{\sin A}{\cos A}}$ $\left(\because \tan A = \dfrac{\sin A}{\cos A}\right)$ (1 Mark)

$$=\frac{\sin A\left(1-\frac{1}{\cos A}\right)}{\sin A\left(1+\frac{1}{\cos A}\right)} \quad \left(\because \sec A=\frac{1}{\cos A}\right)$$ (1 Mark)

$$=\frac{1-\sec A}{1+\sec A} = \text{RHS}$$ (1 Mark)

Thus LHS = RHS.

OR

(b) (i) Given: $\sin x = p$

$\because \cos^2 x = 1 - \sin^2 x = 1 - p^2$ (½ Mark)

$\Rightarrow \cos x = \sqrt{1-p^2}$

Now, $\cot x = \frac{\cos x}{\sin x} = \frac{\sqrt{1-p^2}}{p}$

$\therefore \cot x = \frac{\sqrt{1-p^2}}{p}$ (1 Mark)

(ii) As we know $1+\tan^2 x = \sec^2 x = \frac{1}{\cos^2 x} = \frac{1}{1-p^2}$

and $1+\cot^2 x = \text{cosec}^2 x = \frac{1}{\sin^2 x} = \frac{1}{p^2}$ (½ Mark)

$\therefore \frac{1+\tan^2 x}{1+\cot^2 x} = \frac{\frac{1}{1-p^2}}{\frac{1}{p^2}} = \frac{p^2}{1-p^2}$ (1 Mark)

31. Prove that the lengths of tangents drawn from an external point to a circle are equal. ***(Ap) (3 Marks)***

Ans. Given: Two tangents PQ and PR are drawn from a point P to a circle having centre O.

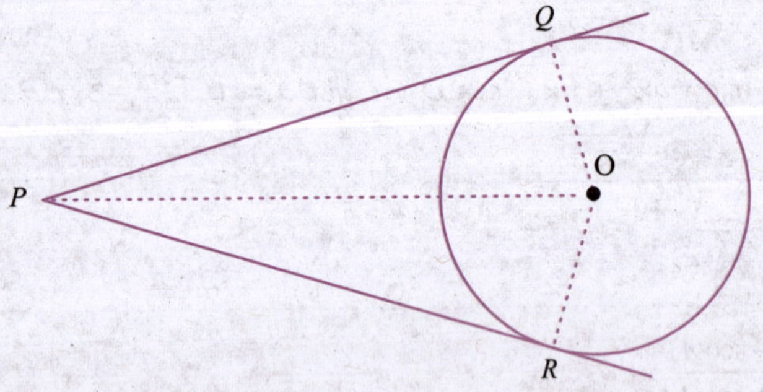

To prove: PQ = PR

Construction: Join OP, OQ and OR.

Proof: PQ is a tangent at Q and OQ is the radius.

$\therefore OQ \perp PQ$ [tangent is $\perp$ to the radius]

Similarly, $OR \perp PR$ (1 Mark)

In the right triangle OPQ and OPR, we have

OQ = OR [radii of the same circle]

OP = OP [common]

$\angle OQP = \angle ORP$ [90° each]

$\therefore \Delta OPQ \cong \Delta OPR$ [by RHS-congruence] (1 Mark)

Hence, PQ = PR. [by C.P.C.T] (1 Mark)

SECTION – D

Question numbers 32 to 35 are long answer type questions of 5 marks each. $4 \times 5 = 20$

32. Find the median and the mode for the following data: **(Ap) (5 Marks)**

Class	Frequency
0 – 20	15
20 – 40	18
40 – 60	21
60 – 80	29
80 – 100	17

Ans. (1 Mark)

Class	f	cf
0–20	15	15
20–40	18	33
40–60	21	54
60–80	29	83
80–100	17	100

Total (N) = 100

$\Rightarrow \frac{N}{2} = 50.$

$\therefore$ Median class = 40 – 60

Here $l = 40$, $Cf = 33$, $f = 21$, $h = 20$ (½ Mark)

$\because$ Median $= l + \frac{\frac{N}{2} - cf}{f} \times h$ (½ Mark)

Median $= 40 + \frac{50-33}{21} \times 20 = 40 + \frac{17}{21} \times 20$

Median $= 40 + \frac{340}{21} = 40 + 16.19 = 56.19$ (1 Mark)

Now, highest frequency = 29 in class 60 – 80

$\therefore$ Modal class = 60 – 80.

Here $l = 60, f_1 = 29, f_0 = 21, f_2 = 17, h = 20$: (½ Mark)

Mode $= l + \frac{f_1 - f_0}{2f_1 - f_0 - f_2} \times h$ (½ Mark)

Mode $= 60 + \frac{29-21}{2 \times 29 - 21 - 17} \times 20 = 60 + \frac{8}{58-38} \times 20$

$\Rightarrow$ Mode = 60 + 8 = 68 (1 Mark)

Hence median and mode of the data is 56.19 and 60 respectively.

33. (*a*) Express $\frac{24}{18-x} - \frac{24}{18+x} = 1$ as a quadratic equation in standard form and find discriminant of the quadratic equation, so obtained. Also find the roots of the equation. **(Ap) (5 Marks)**

OR

(*b*) The sum of squares of two positive numbers is 100. If one number exceeds the other by 2, find the numbers. **(Ev) (5 Marks)**

Ans. (a) Given: $\frac{24}{18-x} - \frac{24}{18+x} = 1$

$\Rightarrow \frac{24(18+x) - 24(18-x)}{(18-x)(18+x)} = 1$

$\Rightarrow \frac{24[18+x-18+x]}{324-x^2}=1 \quad [\because a^2 - b^2 = (a+b)(a-b)]$

$\Rightarrow \frac{24\times 2x}{324-x^2}=1 \Rightarrow \frac{48x}{324-x^2}=1$ **(1 Mark)**

$\Rightarrow 48x = 324 - x^2$

$x^2 + 48x - 324 = 0$

On comparing with standard form $ax^2 + bx + c = 0$

We get $a = 1$, $b = 48$, $c = -324$

$\because$ Discriminant $D = b^2 - 4ac$ **(1 Mark)**

$\Rightarrow D = 482 - 4(1)(-324)$

$\Rightarrow D = 2304 + 1296$

$\Rightarrow D = 3600$ **(1 Mark)**

Using quadratic formula:

$x = \frac{-b \pm \sqrt{D}}{2a}$ **(1 Mark)**

$\Rightarrow x = \frac{-48 \pm 60}{2}$

$\Rightarrow x = \frac{-48+60}{2} = \frac{12}{2} = 6$ or $x = \frac{-48-60}{2} = \frac{-108}{2} = -54$

Hence the roots are 6 and −54. **(1 Mark)**

OR

(b) Let the smaller number be x.

Then the larger number is $x + 2$ **(1 Mark)**

Given: sum of squares of 2 numbers is 100

$x^2 + (x+2)^2 = 100$ **(1 Mark)**

$\Rightarrow x^2 + x^2 + 4x + 4 = 100$

$\Rightarrow 2x^2 + 4x + 4 = 100$

$\Rightarrow 2x^2 + 4x - 96 = 0$

$\Rightarrow x^2 + 2x - 48 = 0$ **(1 Mark)**

$\Rightarrow x^2 + 8x - 6x - 48 = 0$

$\Rightarrow x(x+8) - 6(x+8) = 0$

$\Rightarrow (x-6)(x+8) = 0$

$x = 6$ or $x \neq -8$ (Positive number only) **(1 Mark)**

Other number: $x + 2 = 6 + 2 = 8$

Hence the smaller and larger numbers are 6 and 8 respectively **(1 Mark)**

34. In the adjoining figure, $IE \parallel TR$ and $\frac{GI}{IT} = \frac{1}{2}$. Find $\frac{TR}{IE}$. **(Cr) (5 Marks)**

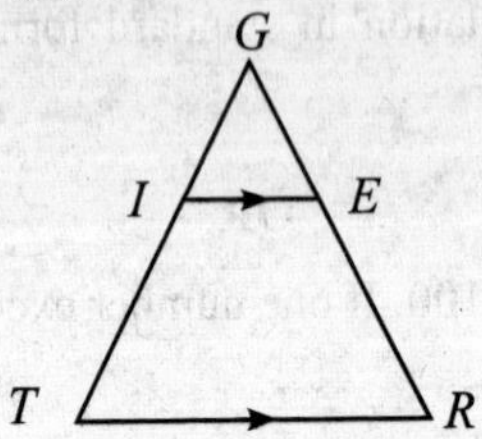

Ans. Given: $IE \parallel TR$ and $\frac{GI}{IT} = \frac{1}{2}$

To find: $\frac{TR}{IE}$

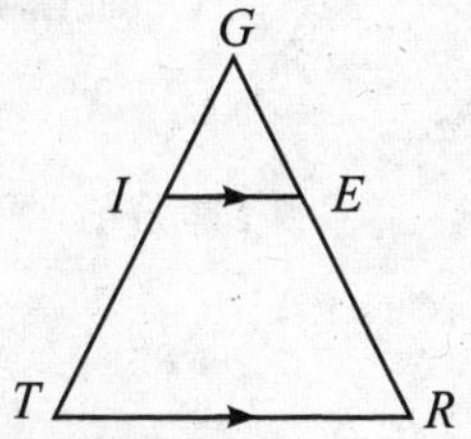

Now, in ΔGIE and ΔGTR:

$\angle G$ is common.

$IE \parallel TR \Rightarrow \angle GIE = \angle GTR$ (corresponding angles) (½ Mark)

Thus by AA similarity:

$\Delta GIE \sim \Delta GTR$ (½ Mark)

So the ratio of corresponding sides is equal (1 Mark)

$\frac{GI}{GT} = \frac{IE}{TR}$ ...(i) (½ Mark)

$\because \frac{GI}{IT} = \frac{1}{2} \Rightarrow IT = 2GI$ (½ Mark)

$\therefore GT = GI + IT = GI + 2GI = 3GI$ (1 Mark)

From (i)

$\frac{GI}{GT} = \frac{GI}{3GI} = \frac{1}{3}$

Thus, $\frac{IE}{TR} = \frac{1}{3} \Rightarrow \frac{TR}{IE} = 3$ (1 Mark)

35. (*a*) In lhe adjoining figure, ΔOAB is an equilateral triangle and the area of the shaded region is 750π cm^2. Find the perimeter of the shaded region. ***(An) (5 Marks)***

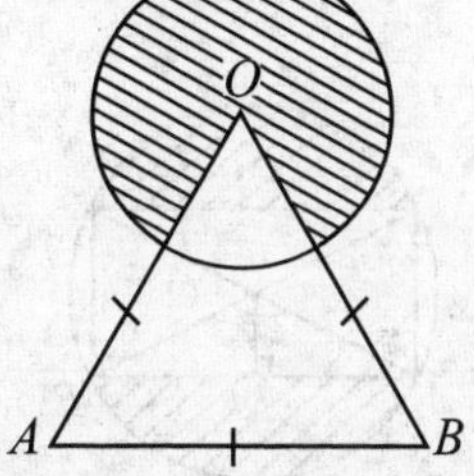

OR

(*b*) O and O' are the centres of the circles of radius r as shown in figures (*i*) and (*ii*) respectively. ***(Cr) (5 Marks)***

(*i*)

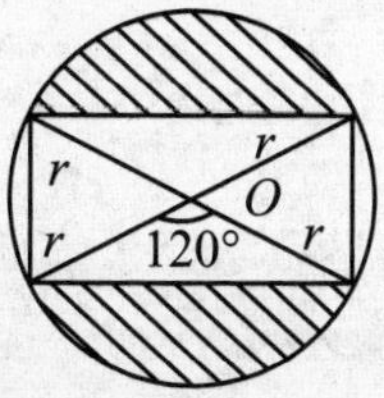

(*ii*)

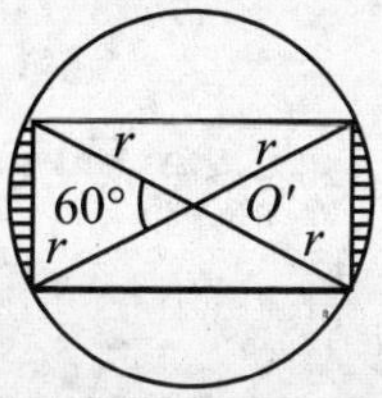

Find the ratio of area of shaded region in figure (*i*) to that of area of shaded region in figure (*ii*).

Ans. (a)

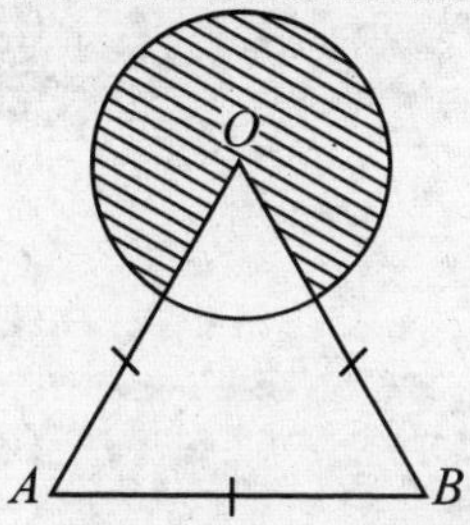

Since ΔOAB is an equilateral triangle,

$\angle AOB = 60°$ (1 Mark)

Area of shaded region $= \pi r^2 - \frac{\theta}{360°} \times \pi r^2 = 750\pi$ (1 Mark)

$\Rightarrow \pi r^2 - \frac{60}{360}\pi r^2 = 750\pi$

$\Rightarrow \pi r^2 - \frac{1}{6}\pi r^2 = 750\pi$

$\Rightarrow \frac{5}{6}\pi r^2 = 750\pi$

$\Rightarrow \frac{5}{6}r^2 = 750$

$\Rightarrow r^2 = \frac{750 \times 6}{5}$

$\Rightarrow r^2 = 900$

$\Rightarrow r = 30$ (1 Mark)

Perimeter consists of: Remaining arc of 300° + Two radii

Remaining arc length:

$\frac{300°}{360°} \times 2\pi r = \frac{5}{6} \times 2\pi(30) = 50\pi$ (½ Mark)

Two radii = 2r = 60 (½ Mark)

Perimeter of shaded region = $50\pi + 60$cm (1 Mark)

OR

(b) Figure (i)

Area of segment = Area of sector OAB – Area of ΔOAB.

Sector angle = 120°

Area of sector $OAB = \frac{120}{360} \times \pi r^2 = \frac{1}{3}\pi r^2$. (½ Mark)

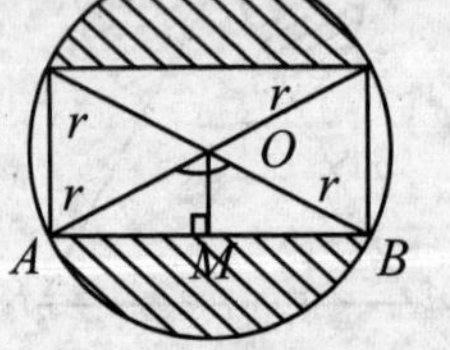

In $\Delta OAB, OA = OB = r, \angle AOB = 120°$.

Draw $OM \perp AB$ so M is midpoint of AB and $\angle AOM = 60°$.

In right triangle OMA:

$\cos 60° = \frac{OM}{OA} = \frac{OM}{r} \Rightarrow OM = r\cos 60° = \frac{r}{2}$

$\sin 60° = \frac{AM}{OA} = \frac{AM}{r} \Rightarrow AM = r\sin 60° = \frac{\sqrt{3}}{2}r$

So $AB = 2AM = \sqrt{3}r$ (½ Mark)

Area of ΔOAB:

$\frac{1}{2} \times AB \times OM = \frac{1}{2} \times (\sqrt{3}r) \times \frac{r}{2} = \frac{\sqrt{3}}{4}r^2$ (1 Mark)

$\text{Area(i)} = 2\left(\frac{\pi r^2}{3} - \frac{\sqrt{3}}{4}r^2\right) = \frac{2\pi r^2}{3} - \frac{\sqrt{3}}{2}r^2$ (½ Mark)

Figure (ii)

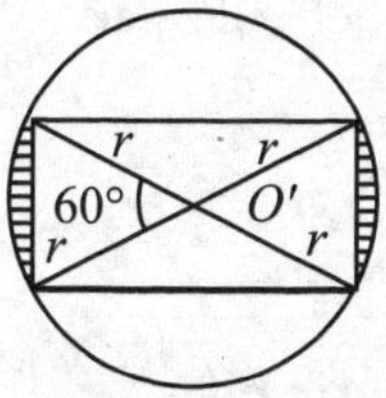

When a chord subtends 60° at the centre, the triangle formed by the two radii and the chord becomes an equilateral triangle.

Area of sector $= \frac{60}{360}\pi r^2 = \frac{\pi r^2}{6}$ (½ Mark)

Area of equilateral triangle (side = r) $= \frac{\sqrt{3}}{4}r^2$ (½ Mark)

Area of one segment $= \frac{\pi r^2}{6} - \frac{\sqrt{3}}{4}r^2$

Area (ii) $= 2\left(\frac{\pi r^2}{6} - \frac{\sqrt{3}}{4}r^2\right) = \frac{\pi r^2}{3} - \frac{\sqrt{3}}{2}r^2$ (½ Mark)

$$\frac{\text{Area (i)}}{\text{Area (ii)}} = \frac{r^2\left(\frac{2\pi}{3} - \frac{\sqrt{3}}{2}\right)}{r^2\left(\frac{\pi}{3} - \frac{\sqrt{3}}{2}\right)} = \frac{r^2\left(\frac{4\pi - 3\sqrt{3}}{6}\right)}{r^2\left(\frac{2\pi - 3\sqrt{3}}{6}\right)} = \frac{4\pi - 3\sqrt{3}}{2\pi - 3\sqrt{3}}$$ (1 Mark)

SECTION – E

Question numbers 36 to 38 are case-based questions of 4 marks each. $3 \times 4 = 12$

36. As a part of school project, Mishika and Sahaj created a bird-bath from the cylindrical log of wood by scooping out the hemispherical depression from one end of the cylinder as shown in the figure given. Cylinder has a length 2 m out of which 0.6 m is in earth and the diameter is 1.4 m.

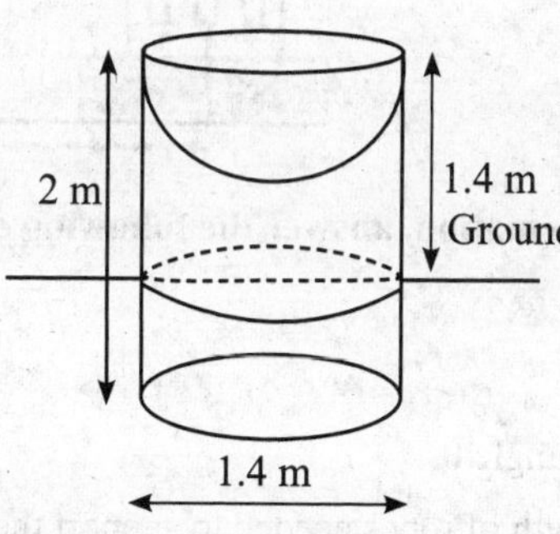

On the basis of the above information, answer the following questions: ***(An)***

(*i*) Write the radius of the hemispherical depression. **(*1 Mark*)**

(*ii*) Find the volume of water that can be filled in the hemispherical depression in terms of π. **(*1 Mark*)**

(*iii*) (*a*) Find the total surface area of log of wood above the ground after making the bird-bath. **(*2 Marks*)**

OR

(*iii*) (*b*) Compute the volume of log of wood above the ground after making the bird-bath.. **(*2 Marks*)**

Ans. Given: Cylinder length = 2m, diameter = 1.4 m ⇒ radius r = 0.7 m

Length above ground = 2 − 0.6 = 1.4 m

Hemispherical depression at one end.

(i) Radius of hemispherical depression = radius of cylinder = 0.7 m (1 Mark)

(ii) Volume of water in hemispherical depression $=\frac{2}{3}\pi r^3$

$$=\frac{2}{3}\pi(0.7)^3=\frac{2}{3}\pi(0.343)=\frac{0.686}{3}\pi=0.228\pi \text{ m}^3$$ (1 Mark)

(iii) (a) Curved surface area of cylinder above ground

$$2\pi rh=2\pi(0.7)(1.4)=1.96\pi$$ (½ Mark)

Curved surface area of hemisphere $=2\pi r^2=2\pi(0.49)=0.98\pi$ (½ Mark)

Total surface area above ground after making bird-bath $=1.96\pi+0.98\pi=2.94\pi m^2$ (1 Mark)

OR

(iii) (b) Volume of cylinder above ground $=\pi r^2 h=\pi(0.49)(1.4)=0.686\pi \text{ m}^3$ (½ Mark)

Volume of hemisphere removed $=\frac{2}{3}\pi r^3=\frac{2}{3}\pi(0.343)=\frac{0.686}{3}\pi \text{ m}^3$ (½ Mark)

Volume of log above ground after making bird-bath:

$$=0.686\pi-\frac{0.686}{3}\pi=0.686\pi\left(1-\frac{1}{3}\right)=0.686\pi\times\frac{2}{3}$$

$$=\frac{1.372}{3}\pi=0.457\pi \text{ m}^3$$ (1 Mark)

37. A flagstaff, 7 .32 m long is fitted at the top of l0 m tall building. The flagstaff is supported by the ropes which are tied to the point P on the ground which is x m away from the base of the building. It is given that l_1 is the length of rope from point P to the base of the flagstaff and l_2 is the length of rope from point P to the top of flagstaff. Rope l_1 makes an angle of 30° with the horizontal and θ be the angle which rope l_2 makes with the horizontal as shown in the figure.

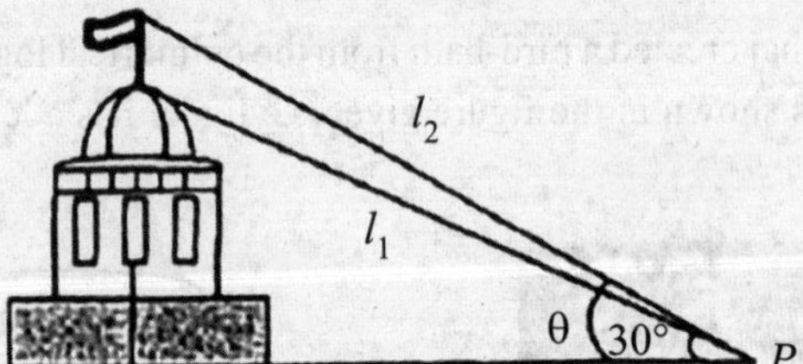

Based on the above information, answer the following questions : ***(Ev)***

(Use $\sqrt{2}=1.4$ and $\sqrt{3}=1.732$)

(*i*) Find the value of x. ***(1 Mark)***

(*ii*) Find the measure of angle θ. ***(1 Mark)***

(*iii*) (*a*) Find the total length of ropes needed to support the flagstaff. ***(2 Marks)***

OR

(*iii*) (*b*) Which rope is longer l_1 and l_2 and by how much? ***(2 Marks)***

Ans. Given: Building height, BC = 10 m

Flagstaff length, AC = 7.32 m

Total height of flagstaff top, AB = 10 + 7.32 = 17.32 m

Rope l_1 from point P to base of flagstaff (at height 10 m)

Rope l_2 from point P to top of flagstaff (at height 17.32 m)

l_1 makes angle 30° with horizontal

l_2 makes angle θ with horizontal

distance from building to P, BP = x

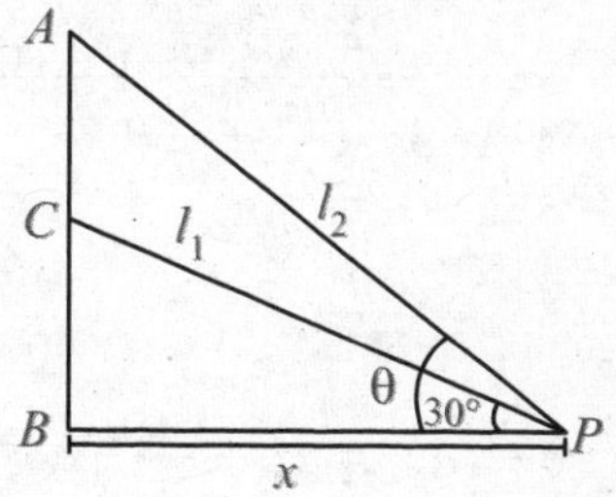

(i) From rope l_1: In ΔCBP

$\because \tan\theta = \frac{BC}{BP} \Rightarrow \tan 30° = \frac{10}{x}$

$\Rightarrow \frac{1}{\sqrt{3}} = \frac{10}{x} \Rightarrow x = 10\sqrt{3} = 10 \times 1.732 = 17.32\,m$ **(1Mark)**

(ii) From rope l_2: In ΔABP

$\because \tan\theta = \frac{AB}{BP} = \frac{17.32}{x} = \frac{17.32}{17.32} = 1 \Rightarrow \theta = 45°$ **(1Mark)**

(iii) (a) In ΔCBP From rope l_1: $\sin 30° = \frac{BC}{PC} = \frac{10}{l_1}$

$\frac{1}{2} = \frac{10}{l_1} \Rightarrow l_1 = 20\,m$ **(1Mark)**

In ΔABP From rope l_2: $\sin 45° = \frac{AB}{AP} = \frac{17.32}{l_2}$

$\frac{1}{\sqrt{2}} = \frac{17.32}{l_2} \Rightarrow l_2 = 17.32 \times \sqrt{2}$

$\Rightarrow l_2 = 17.32 \times 1.4 = 24.248\,m$

The total length of ropes needed to support the flagstaff

= 20 + 24.248 = 44.248 m. **(1 Mark)**

OR

(iii) (b) from above part l_2 = 24.248 m, l_1 = 20m $\Rightarrow l_2 > l_1$ **(1Mark)**

Difference = 24.248 − 28 = 4.248 m

Hence rope l_2 is longer than rope l_1 by 4.248 m **(1Mark)**

38. A watermelon vendor arranged the watermelons similar to shown in the adjoining picture:

The number of watermelons in subsequent rows differ by '*d*'. The bottom most row has 101 watermelons and the top most row has 1 watermelon. There are 21 rows from bottom to top.

Based on the information given above, answer the following questions: ***(Ap)***

(*i*) Find the value of '*d*'. ***(1 Mark)***

(*ii*) How many watermelons will be there in the 15th row from the bottom? ***(1 Mark)***

(*iii*) (*a*) Find the total number of watermelons from bottom to top. ***(2 Marks)***

OR

(*iii*) (*b*) If the number of watermelons in the nth row from top is equal to number of watermelons in the nth row from bottom, find the value of n. **(2 Marks)**

Ans. Given: Watermelons arranged in rows, each row differs by d.

Bottommost row = 101 watermelons

Topmost row = 1 watermelon

Number of rows = 21

(i) Watermelons are in 21 rows. Bottom row $(a_1) = 101$.

Top row $(a_{21}) = 1$

$\therefore\ a_{21} = a + (21 - 1)d \Rightarrow 1 = 101 + 20d \Rightarrow -100 = 20d \Rightarrow d = -5$ (1 Mark)

(ii) 15th row from bottom $(a_{15}) = a + (15 - 1)d = 101 + 14(-5) = 101 - 70 = 31$ (1 Mark)

(iii) (a) Total number of watermelons: $S_n = \frac{n}{2}(a+l)$ (1 Mark)

$= \frac{21}{2}(101+1) = \frac{21}{2} \times 102 = 21 \times 51 = 1071$

Hence, the total number of watermelons = 1071 (1Mark)

OR

(b) From top: first term $a' = 1$, common difference $d' = 5$ (increasing) and n^{th} term from top $= a' + (n - 1)d'$ $= 1 + (n - 1) \times 5$

From bottom: first term $a = 101$, common difference $d = -5$ (decreasing) and n^{th} term from bottom $= 101 + (n - 1)(-5) = 101 - 5(n - 1)$ (1 Mark)

According to given condition both n^{th} term are equal

$\therefore 1 + 5(n - 1) = 101 - 5(n - 1)$

$\Rightarrow 1 + 5n - 5 = 101 - 5n + 5$

$\Rightarrow 5n - 4 = 106 - 5n$

$\Rightarrow 10n = 110 \Rightarrow n = 11$ (1 Mark)

CBSE SOLVED PAPER 2025

Time allowed : 3 hours **Maximum Marks : 80**

GENERAL INSTRUCTIONS:

Read the following instructions very carefully and strictly follow them:

(i) *This question paper contains* ***38*** *questions.* ***All*** *questions are compulsory.*

(ii) *Question Paper is divided into* ***FIVE*** *Sections-****SECTION A, B, C, D*** *and* ***E.***

(iii) *In Section -****A****, question numbers* ***1*** *to* ***18*** *are Multiple Choice Questions (MCQs) and question numbers* ***19*** *&* ***20*** *are Assertion-Reason based questions of* ***1*** *mark each.*

(iv) *In Section-****B****, question numbers* ***21*** *to* ***25*** *are Very Short Answer (VSA) type questions of* ***2*** *marks each.*

(v) *In Section-****C****, question numbers* ***26*** *to* ***31*** *are Short Answer (SA) type questions carrying* ***3*** *marks each.*

(vi) *In Section-****D****, question numbers* ***32*** *to* ***35*** *are Long Answer (LA) type questions carrying* ***5*** *marks each.*

(vii) *In Section-****E****, question numbers* ***36*** *to* ***38*** *are* **case - based integrated units** *of assessment questions carrying* ***4*** *marks each. Internal choice is provided in 2 marks question in each case-study.*

(viii) *There is no overall choice. However, an internal choice has been provided in* ***2*** *questions in Section-****B****,* ***2*** *questions in Section-****C****,* ***2*** *questions in Section-****D*** *and* ***3*** *questions of* ***2*** *marks in Section-****E****.*

(ix) *Draw neat figures wherever required. Take π = 22/7 wherever required if not stated.*

(x) *Use of calculators is* ***NOT allowed.***

SECTION – A

(20 × 1 = 20)

(Multiple Choice Questions)

Section - A consists of 20 Multiple Choice Questions of 1 mark each.

1. In two concentric circles centred at *O*, a chord *AB* of the larger circle touches the smaller circle at *C*. If $OA = 3.5$ cm, $OC = 2.1$ cm, then *AB* is equal to *(1 M)*

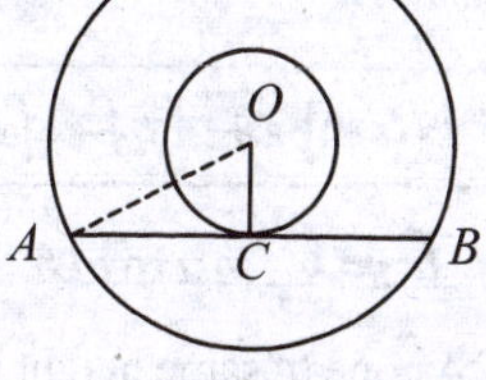

(*a*) 5.6 cm (*b*) 2.8 cm (*c*) 3.5 cm (*d*) 4.2 cm

1. (a) Given, OA = 3.5 cm, OC = 2.1 cm

Since AB is tangent to the smaller circle at C, OC is perpendicular to AB. Thus, triangle OAC is a right angled triangle at C.

Using Pythagoras theorem in $\triangle OAC$,

$$OA^2 = OC^2 + AC^2$$
$$\Rightarrow (3.5)^2 = (2.1)^2 + AC^2$$
$$\Rightarrow 12.25 = 4.41 + AC^2$$
$$\Rightarrow AC^2 = 12.25 - 4.41 = 7.84$$
$$\Rightarrow AC = \sqrt{7.84} = 2.8 \text{ cm}$$

$\because$ AB is a chord and C is the midpoint (as OC is perpendicular to AB).

$\therefore$ AB = 2 AC

Hence, AB = 2 × 2.8 = 5.6 cm.

2. Three coins are tossed together. The probability that at least one head comes up, is *(1 M)*

(*a*) $\frac{3}{8}$ (*b*) $\frac{7}{8}$ (*c*) $\frac{1}{8}$ (*d*) $\frac{3}{4}$

2. (b) When three coins are tossed, the total number of possible outcomes is $2^3 = 8$

And, The outcomes are HHH, HHT, HTH, THH, HTT, THT, TTH, TTT.

The number of favorable outcomes for at least one head = 7

Hence, the probability of getting at least one head

$$= \frac{\text{Number of favorable outcomes}}{\text{Total number of outcomes}} = \frac{7}{8}$$

3. The volume of air in a hollow cylinder is 450 cm³. A cone of same height and radius as that of cylinder is kept inside it. The volume of empty space in the cylinder is *(1 M)*

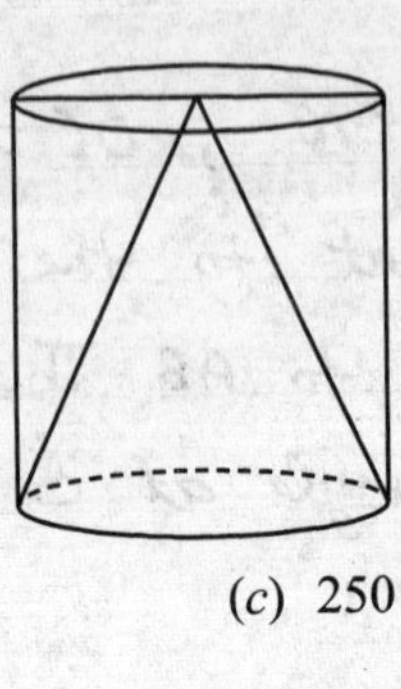

(*a*) 225 cm³ (*b*) 150 cm³ (*c*) 250 cm³ (*d*) 300 cm³

3. (d) Volume of the cylinder ($V_{cylinder}$) = 450 cm^3

Volume of the Cone with the same height and radius as the cylinder is,

$$V_{cone} = \frac{1}{3} V_{cylinder} = \frac{1}{3} \times 450$$

$$= 150\ cm^3$$

Hence, volume of the empty space in the cylinder is

$$V_{empty} = V_{cylinder} - V_{cone} = 450 - 150 = 300\ cm^3.$$

4. If the length of the shadow of a tower is $\sqrt{3}$ times its height, then the angle of elevation of the sun is *(1 M)*

(*a*) 45° (*b*) 30° (*c*) 60° (*d*) 0°

4. (b) Let the height of the tower = h

Then, length of the shadow = $\sqrt{3}h$

In the right triangle formed by the tower,

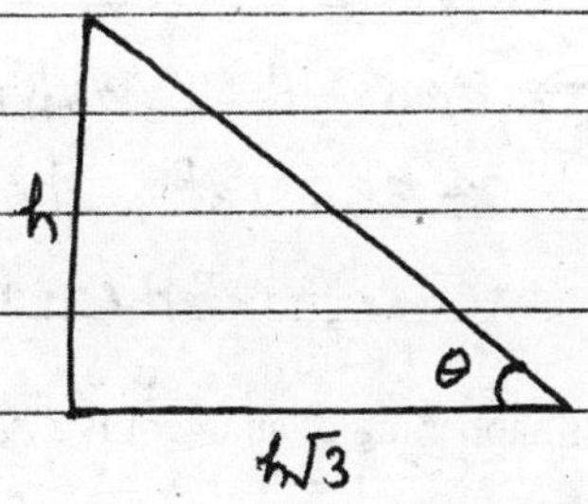

$$\tan\theta = \frac{\text{Height of the tower}}{\text{Length of the shadow}}$$

$$\Rightarrow \tan\theta = \frac{h}{h\sqrt{3}} = \frac{1}{\sqrt{3}} = \tan 30°$$

Hence, $\theta = 30°$

5. 22nd term of the *A.P.* : $\frac{3}{2}, \frac{1}{2}, \frac{-1}{2}, \frac{-3}{2}$, ... is *(1 M)*

(*a*) $\frac{45}{2}$ (*b*) – 9 (*c*) $\frac{-39}{2}$ (*d*) – 21

5. (c) Given A.P. is $\frac{3}{2}, \frac{1}{2}, -\frac{1}{2}, -\frac{3}{2}, ...$

First term $a = \frac{3}{2}$

Common difference $d = a_2 - a_1 = \frac{1}{2} - \frac{3}{2} = -1$

Since, the nth term of an A.P. is given by

$$a_n = a + (n-1)d$$

Hence, the 22nd term is

$$a_{22} = \frac{3}{2} + (22-1)(-1) = \frac{3}{2} + 21(-1)$$

$$\Rightarrow a_{22} = \frac{3}{2} - 21 = \frac{3-42}{2} = -\frac{39}{2}.$$

6. In the given graph, the polynomial $p(x)$ is shown. Number of zeroes of $p(x)$ is *(1 M)*

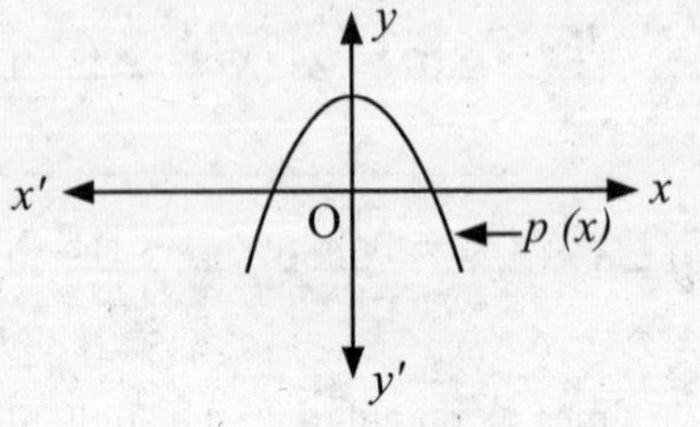

(*a*) 3 (*b*) 2 (*c*) 1 (*d*) 4

6. (b) The number of zeroes of a polynomial $p(x)$ is equal to the number of times the graph of $p(x)$ intersects the x-axis.

$\Rightarrow$ From the graph, the polynomial $p(x)$ intersects the x-axis at two distinct points.

Hence, the number of zeroes of $p(x)$ is 2.

7. If probability of happening of an event is 57%, then probability of non-happening of the event is *(1 M)*

(*a*) 0.43 (*b*) 0.57 (*c*) 53% (*d*) $\frac{1}{57}$

7. (a) Probability of happening of an event $P(E) = 57\%$

$= 0.57.$

Probability of non-happening of an event $P(\bar{E}) = 1 - P(E)$

Hence, $P(\bar{E}) = 1 - 0.57 = 0.43.$

8. OAB is sector of a circle with centre O and radius 7 cm. If length of arc $\widehat{AB} = \frac{22}{3}$ cm then $\angle AOB$ is equal to *(1 M)*

(*a*) $\left(\frac{120}{7}\right)^\circ$ (*b*) 45° (*c*) 60° (*d*) 30°

8. (C) Given, radius $(r) = 7$ cm, length of arc $(\widehat{AB}) = \frac{22}{3}$ cm.

The length of an arc is given by

$$\text{Arc length} = \frac{\theta}{360^\circ} \times 2\pi r$$

Where θ is the angle in degrees.

According to given information,

$$\frac{22}{3} = \frac{\theta}{360^\circ} \times 2 \times \frac{22}{7} \times 7$$

$$\Rightarrow \frac{22}{3} = \frac{\theta}{360^\circ} \times 44$$

$$\Rightarrow \theta = \frac{22}{3} \times \frac{360^\circ}{44}$$

$$\Rightarrow \theta = 60^\circ$$

9. If the sum of first n terms of an *A.P.* is given by $S_n = \frac{n}{2}(3n+1)$, then the first term of the *A.P.* is *(1 M)*

(*a*) 2 (*b*) $\frac{3}{2}$ (*c*) 4 (*d*) $\frac{5}{2}$

9. (a) Given, the sum of first n terms of an A.P.

$$S_n = \frac{n}{2}(3n+1)$$

The first term a of the A.P. is given by S_1.

For n = 1,

$$S_1 = \frac{1}{2}(3 \times 1 + 1) = \frac{1}{2} \times 4 = 2.$$

Hence, the first term (a) = 2.

10. To calculate mean of a grouped data, Rahul used assumed mean method. He used $d = (x - A)$ where A is assumed mean. Then $\bar{x}$ is equal to *(1 M)*

(*a*) $A + \bar{d}$ (*b*) $A + h\bar{d}$ (*c*) $h(A + \bar{d})$ (*d*) $A - h\bar{d}$

10. (a) In the assumed mean method, the mean $\bar{x}$ is calculated using the formula $\bar{x} = A + \bar{d}$

Where, A is the assumed mean and $\bar{d}$ is the mean of the deviations $d = (x - A)$

Hence, the correct expression for the mean is $A + \bar{d}$.

11. The point (3, – 5) lies on the line $mx - y = 11$ The value of m is *(1 M)*

(*a*) 3 (*b*) – (*c*) 8 (*d*) 2

11. (d) Given, the point (3, −5) lies on the line $mx - y = 11$.

Then, $m(3) - (-5) = 11$

$\Rightarrow 3m + 5 = 11$

$\Rightarrow 3m = 11 - 5 = 6$

$\Rightarrow m = \frac{6}{3} = 2$

Hence, $m = 2$.

12. If $\sqrt{3}\sin\theta = \cos\theta$, then value of θ is (1 M)

(*a*) $\sqrt{3}$ (*b*) 60° (*c*) $\frac{1}{\sqrt{3}}$ (*d*) 30°

12. (d) Given equation, $\sqrt{3}\sin\theta = \cos\theta$

Divide both sides by $\cos\theta$,

$\Rightarrow \sqrt{3}\frac{\sin\theta}{\cos\theta} = \frac{\cos\theta}{\cos\theta}$

$\Rightarrow \sqrt{3}\tan\theta = 1$ $\left(\because \tan\theta = \frac{\sin\theta}{\cos\theta}\right)$

$\Rightarrow \tan\theta = \frac{1}{\sqrt{3}} = \tan 30°$ $\left(\because \tan 30° = \frac{1}{\sqrt{3}}\right)$

Hence, $\theta = 30°$

13. *ABCD* is a rectangle with its vertices at (2, − 2), (8, 4) (4, 8) and (−2,2) taken in order. Length of its diagonal is (1 M)

(*a*) $4\sqrt{2}$ (*b*) $6\sqrt{2}$ (*c*) $4\sqrt{26}$ (*d*) $2\sqrt{26}$

13. (d) Given vertices of rectangle ABCD in order are

A(2, −2), B(8, 4), C(4, 8), D(−2, 2)

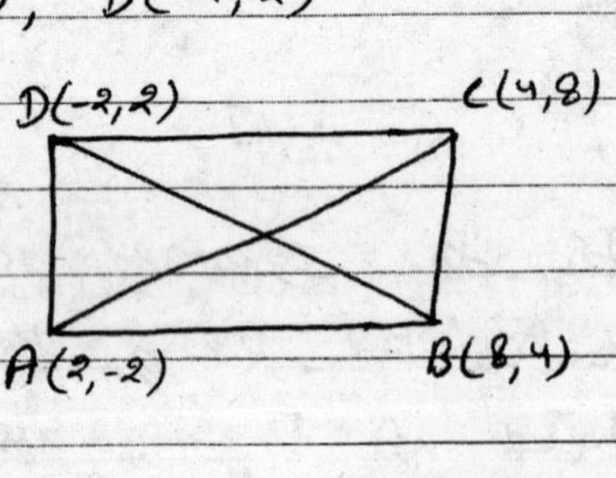

In a rectangle both diagonals are equal.

Now, the length of the diagonal AC is equal to the distance between point A(2, −2) & C(4, 8)

Using distance formula,

$$\text{Distance} = \sqrt{(x_2 - x_1)^2 + (y_2 - y_1)^2}$$

Hence, the length of diagonal $= \sqrt{(4-2)^2 + (8-(-2))^2}$

$= \sqrt{2^2 + 10^2} = \sqrt{4 + 100} = \sqrt{104} = 2\sqrt{26}$.

14. Two dice are rolled together. The probability of getting a sum more than 9 is *(1 M)*

(a) $\frac{5}{6}$ (b) $\frac{5}{18}$ (c) $\frac{1}{6}$ (d) $\frac{1}{2}$

14. (c) Total number of possible outcomes when two dice are rolled $= 6 \times 6 = 36$.

Favorable outcomes where the sum is more than 9 are
(4,6), (5,5), (6,4), (5,6), (6,5), (6,6)

$\Rightarrow$ Number of favorable outcomes = 6

Hence, Probability = $\frac{\text{Number of favorable outcomes}}{\text{Total number of possible outcomes}}$

$= \frac{6}{36} = \frac{1}{6}$.

15. If ΔABC, $DE \parallel BC$. If $AE = (2x + 1)$ cm, $EC = 4$ cm, $AD = (x + 1)$ cm and $DB = 3$ cm, then value of x is *(1 M)*

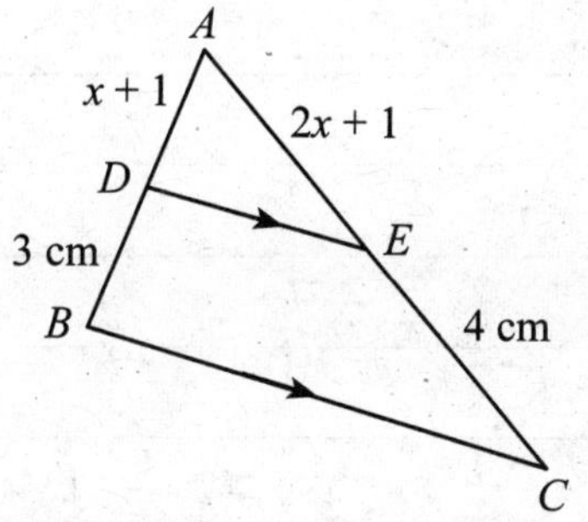

(a) 1 (b) $\frac{1}{2}$ (c) -1 (d) $\frac{1}{3}$

15. (b)

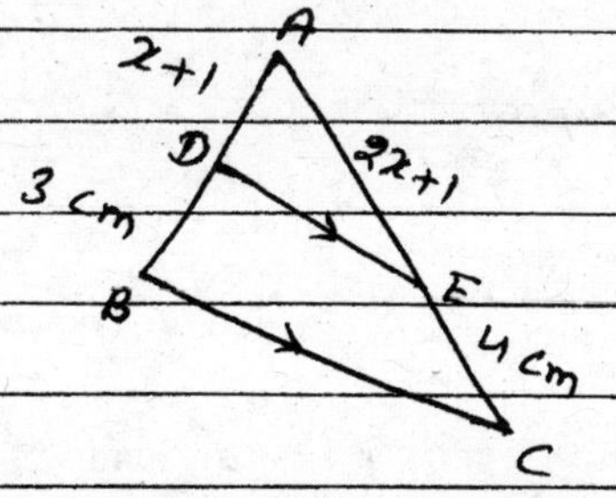

Given, $DE \parallel BC$ in $\triangle ABC$,

By Basic proportionality theorem,

$\frac{AD}{DB} = \frac{AE}{EC}$

$\Rightarrow \frac{x+1}{3} = \frac{2x+1}{4}$

$\Rightarrow 4(x+1) = 3(2x+1)$

$\Rightarrow 4x + 4 = 6x + 3$

$\Rightarrow 6x - 4x = 4 - 3$

$\Rightarrow 2x = 1$

$\Rightarrow x = \frac{1}{2}$.

16. The value of k for which the system of equations $3x - 7y = 1$ and $kx + 14y = 6$ is inconsistent, is (1 M)

(a) -6 (b) $\frac{2}{3}$ (c) 6 (d) $\frac{-3}{2}$

16. (a) Given equations are $3x - 7y = 1$ and $kx + 14y = 6$.

Since, for the system of equations to be inconsistent, the ratios of the coefficients must satisfy

$$\frac{a_1}{a_2} = \frac{b_1}{b_2} \neq \frac{c_1}{c_2}$$

Now, for the given equations,

$a_1 = 3,\ b_1 = -7,\ c_1 = -1$

$a_2 = k,\ b_2 = 14,\ c_2 = -6$

Hence, $\frac{3}{k} = \frac{-7}{14}$

$\Rightarrow \frac{3}{k} = \frac{-1}{2}$

$\Rightarrow k = -6$

Check, $k = -6$, $\frac{3}{-6} = \frac{-7}{14} \neq \frac{-1}{-6}$

$\Rightarrow -\frac{1}{2} = \frac{-1}{2} \neq \frac{1}{6}$ (Varified).

17. In the given figure, PA is tangent to a circle with centre O. If $\angle APO = 30°$ and $OA = 2.5$ cm, then OP is equal to (1 M)

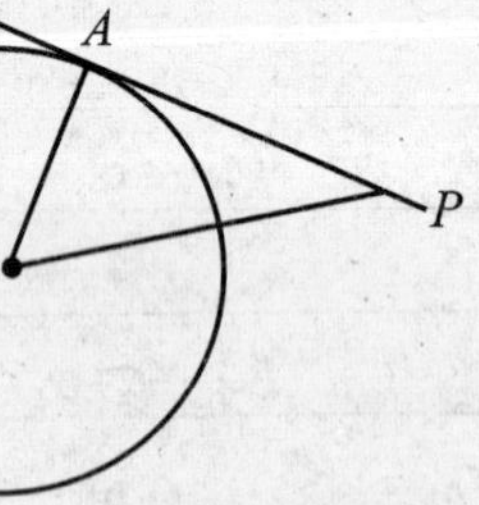

(a) 2.5 cm (b) 5 cm (c) $\frac{5}{\sqrt{3}}$ cm (d) 2 cm

17. (b) Given, PA is tangent to the circle with centre O,

$\angle APO = 30°$, and $OA = 2.5$ cm.

In right ΔOAP,

Since PA is tangent, $\angle OAP = 90°$,

$$\sin 30° = \frac{OA}{OP}$$

$\Rightarrow \frac{1}{2} = \frac{OA}{OP}$

Hence, $OP = 2 \times OA = 2 \times 2.5 = 5$ cm.

18. Two identical cones are joined as shown in the figure. If radius of base is 4 cm and slant height of the cone is 6 cm, then height of the solid is *(1 M)*

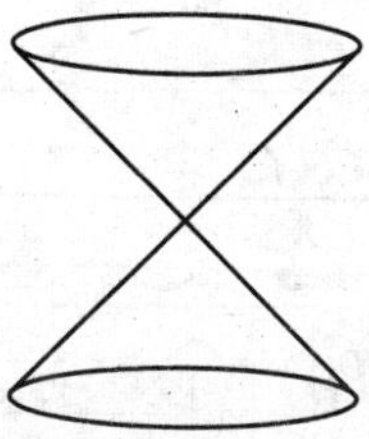

(*a*) 8 cm (*b*) $4\sqrt{5}$ cm (*c*) $2\sqrt{5}$ cm (*d*) 12 cm

18. (b) Given, radius $(r) = 4$ cm and slant height $(l) = 6$ cm.

Height (h) of one cone,

$h = \sqrt{l^2 - r^2} = \sqrt{6^2 - 4^2} = \sqrt{36-16} = \sqrt{20}$

$\Rightarrow h = 2\sqrt{5}$ cm.

Since, two identical cones are joined,

Hence, the total height of the solid is $2h = 2 \times 2\sqrt{5}$

$= 4\sqrt{5}$ cm.

(Assertion – Reason based question)

DIRECTIONS: In question numbers 19 and 20, a statement of Assertion (A) is followed by a statement of Reason (R). Choose the correct option:

(*a*) Both Assertion (A) and Reason (R) are true and Reason (R) is correct explanation of Assertion (A).

(*b*) Both Assertion (A) and Reason (R) are true, but Reason (R) is not correct explanation for Assertion (A).

(*c*) Assertion (A) is true, but Reason (R) is false.

(*d*) Assertion (A) is false, but Reason (R) is true.

19. Assertion (A) : $(a+\sqrt{b}).(a-\sqrt{b})$ is a rational number, where a and b are positive integers.

Reason (R) : Product of two irrationals is always rational. *(1 M)*

19. (c) Assertion (A): $(a+\sqrt{b}).(a-\sqrt{b}) = a^2 - b$, which is a rational number since a and b are positive integers.

Hence, Assertion (A) is true.

Reason (R): The product of two irrational numbers is not always rational. For example, $\sqrt{2}.\sqrt{3} = \sqrt{6}$ which is irrational.

Hence, Reason (R) is false.

20. Assertion (A) : $\Delta ABC \sim \Delta PQR$ such that $\angle A = 65°$, $\angle C = 60°$. Hence $\angle Q = 55°$.

Reason (R) : Sum of all angles of a triangle is 180°. *(1 M)*

20. (b) Assertion (A): Given, $\Delta ABC \sim \Delta PQR$, $\angle A = 65°$, $\angle C = 60°$

In ΔABC, $\angle A + \angle B + \angle C = 180°$

$\Rightarrow \angle B = 180° - \angle A - \angle C = 180° - 65° - 60°$

$\Rightarrow \angle B = 55°$

$\because \Delta ABC \sim \Delta PQR$

$\therefore \angle B = \angle Q = 55°$

Hence, Assertion (A) is true.

Reason (R): The sum of all angles in a triangle is 180°.

This is a fundamental property and is true.

But, Reason (R) does not correctly explain Assertion (A)

SECTION – B

(Very Short Answer Type Questions) **(5 × 2 = 10)**

Q. Nos. 21 to 25 are Very Short Answer type questions of 2 marks each.

21. A box contains 120 discs, which are numbered from 1 to 120. If one disc is drawn at random from the box, find the probability that *(2 M)*

(*a*) it bears a 2-digit number

(*b*) the number is a perfect square.

21. Total number of discs = 120

(a) 2-digit numbers range from 10 to 99.

$\Rightarrow$ Number of 2-digit number = 90.

$\because$ Probability $= \dfrac{\text{Number of favorable outcomes}}{\text{Total number of possible outcomes}}$

Hence, the probability of drawing a 2-digit number

$= \dfrac{90}{120} = \dfrac{3}{4}$.

(b) Perfect squares between 1 and 120 are 1, 4, 9, 16, 25, 36, 49, 64, 81, 100.

$\Rightarrow$ Number of perfect squares = 10.

Hence, Probability of drawing a perfect square $= \dfrac{10}{120} = \dfrac{1}{12}$.

22. (a) Evaluate : $\frac{\cos 45°}{\tan 30° + \sin 60°}$ (2 M)

OR

(b) Verify that $\sin 2A = \frac{2\tan A}{1+\tan^2 A}$, for $A = 30°$ (2 M)

22. (a) $\because \cos 45° = \frac{1}{\sqrt{2}}$, $\tan 30° = \frac{1}{\sqrt{3}}$, $\sin 60° = \frac{\sqrt{3}}{2}$

$\therefore \frac{\cos 45°}{\tan 30° + \sin 60°} = \frac{\frac{1}{\sqrt{2}}}{\frac{1}{\sqrt{3}} + \frac{\sqrt{3}}{2}} = \frac{\frac{1}{\sqrt{2}}}{\frac{2+3}{2\sqrt{3}}} = \frac{\frac{1}{\sqrt{2}}}{\frac{5}{2\sqrt{3}}}$

$\Rightarrow \frac{1}{\sqrt{2}} \times \frac{2\sqrt{3}}{5} = \frac{2\sqrt{3}}{5\sqrt{2}}$

Rationalize the denominator,

$\Rightarrow \frac{2\sqrt{3}}{5\sqrt{2}} \times \frac{\sqrt{2}}{\sqrt{2}} = \frac{2\sqrt{6}}{10} = \frac{\sqrt{6}}{5}$

OR

(b) For $A = 30°$,

LHS,

$\sin 2A = \sin 2 \times 30° = \sin 60° = \frac{\sqrt{3}}{2}$.

RHS, $\frac{2\tan A}{1+\tan^2 A} = \frac{2\tan 30°}{1+\tan^2 30°} = \frac{2 \times \frac{1}{\sqrt{3}}}{1+\left(\frac{1}{\sqrt{3}}\right)^2} = \frac{\frac{2}{\sqrt{3}}}{1+\frac{1}{3}}$

$\Rightarrow \frac{\frac{2}{\sqrt{3}}}{\frac{4}{3}} = \frac{2}{\sqrt{3}} \times \frac{3}{4} = \frac{6}{4\sqrt{3}} = \frac{3}{2\sqrt{3}}$

Rationalize the denominator,

$\Rightarrow \frac{3}{2\sqrt{3}} \times \frac{\sqrt{3}}{\sqrt{3}} = \frac{3\sqrt{3}}{6} = \frac{\sqrt{3}}{2}$

Hence, LHS = RHS (Verified)

23. (a) Solve the quadratic equation $\sqrt{3}x^2 + 10x + 7\sqrt{3} = 0$ using quadratic formula. (2 M)

OR

(b) find the nature of roots of the equation $4x^2 - 4a^2x + a^4 - b^4 = 0, b \neq 0$ (2 M)

23(a) Given quadratic equation is $\sqrt{3}x^2 + 10x + 7\sqrt{3} = 0$.

So, the coefficients are $a = \sqrt{3}$, $b = 10$, $c = 7\sqrt{3}$.

$\because$ Quadratic formula is $x = \dfrac{-b \pm \sqrt{b^2 - 4ac}}{2a}$

$\therefore$ Roots are $x = \dfrac{-10 \pm \sqrt{(10)^2 - 4.\sqrt{3}.7\sqrt{3}}}{2\sqrt{3}} = \dfrac{-10 \pm \sqrt{100 - 84}}{2\sqrt{3}}$

$\Rightarrow x = \dfrac{-10 \pm \sqrt{16}}{2\sqrt{3}} = \dfrac{-10 \pm 4}{2\sqrt{3}}$

$\Rightarrow x_1 = \dfrac{-10+4}{2\sqrt{3}} = \dfrac{-6}{2\sqrt{3}} = -\dfrac{3}{\sqrt{3}} = -\sqrt{3}$

& $x_2 = \dfrac{-10-4}{2\sqrt{3}} = \dfrac{-14}{2\sqrt{3}} = \dfrac{-7}{\sqrt{3}}$

OR

(b) Given quadratic equation is $4x^2 - 4a^2x + a^4 - b^4 = 0$.

So, the coefficients are $a = 4$, $b = -4a^2$, $c = a^4 - b^4$

Now, discriminate $D = b^2 - 4ac = (-4a^2)^2 - 4 \times 4 \times (a^4 - b^4)$

$\Rightarrow D = 16a^4 - 16a^4 + 16b^4 = 16b^4$

Since $b \neq 0$, $D = 16b^4 > 0$

Hence, the equation has real and distinct roots.

24. Using prime factorisation, find the HCF of 180, 140 and 210. *(2 M)*

24. Prime factorisation of 180,

$180 = 2^2 \times 3^2 \times 5$

Prime factorisation of 140,

$140 = 2^2 \times 5 \times 7$

Prime factorisation of 210,

$210 = 2 \times 3 \times 5 \times 7$

Since, HCF is the product of the lowest powers of the common prime factors.

Hence, HCF $= 2 \times 5 = 10$.

25. The perimeters of two similar triangles are 22 cm and 33 cm respectively. If one side of first triangle is 9 cm, then find the length of corresponding side of the second triangle. *(2 M)*

25. Given, perimeters of two similar triangles are 22 cm and 33 cm

$\because$ Both are similar triangles.

$\therefore$ Ratio of perimeters = Ratio of corresponding sides $= \frac{22}{33} = \frac{2}{3}$

Let the corresponding side of the second triangle be x,

then, $\frac{9}{x} = \frac{2}{3}$

Hence, $x = \frac{9 \times 3}{2} = \frac{27}{2} = 13.5$ cm.

SECTION – C

(Short Answer Type Questions) **(6 × 3 = 18)**

Q. Nos. 26 to 31 are Short Answer type questions of 3 marks each.

26. Given that $\sqrt{5}$ is an irrational number, prove that $2+3\sqrt{5}$ is an irrational number. *(3 M)*

26. Assume $2+3\sqrt{5}$ is rational. Then it can be expressed as $\frac{p}{q}$, where p and q are integers with no common factor and $q \neq 0$.

$\Rightarrow 2+3\sqrt{5} = \frac{p}{q}$

$\Rightarrow 3\sqrt{5} = \frac{p}{q} - 2$

$\Rightarrow \sqrt{5} = \frac{p-2q}{3q}$

Since $\sqrt{5}$ is irrational, the right-hand side must also be irrational. However, $\frac{p-2q}{3q}$ is rational, leading to a contradiction.

Hence, $2+3\sqrt{5}$ must be irrational.

27. (*a*) Find the *A.P.* whose third term is 16 and seventh term exceeds the fifth term by 12. Also, find the sum of first 29 terms of the *A.P.* *(3 M)*

OR

(*b*) Find the sum of first 20 terms of an *A.P.* whose n^{th} term is given by $a_n = 5 + 2n$. Can 52 be a term of this *A.P.*? *(3 M)*

27(a) Let the first term be a and common difference be d.

$\because$ n^{th} term of an A.P., $a_n = a + (n-1)d$

where a is the first term and d is the common dif

Given, third term $a_3 = 16$

$\Rightarrow a + 2d = 16$ ----- (1)

& Seventh term exceeds fifth term by 12

$\Rightarrow a_7 = a_5 + 12$

$\Rightarrow a + 6d = (a + 4d) + 12$

$\Rightarrow 2d = 12 \Rightarrow d = 6$

From equation (1),

$\Rightarrow a + 2(6) = 16 \Rightarrow a = 4$

Hence, A.P. is 4, 10, 16, 22, ----

$\because$ Sum of the first n terms of an A.P.,

$$S_n = \frac{n}{2}[2a + (n-1)d]$$

Where a is the first term, d is the common differen

$\because$ Sum of first 29 terms S_{29}

$\Rightarrow \frac{29}{2}[2(4) + (29-1)(6)] \Rightarrow \frac{29}{2}[8 + (28 \times 6)]$

$\Rightarrow \frac{29}{2}(8 + 168) \Rightarrow \frac{29}{2} \times 176 \Rightarrow 29 \times 88 = 2552.$

OR

(b) Given, n^{th} term $a_n = 5 + 2n$

$\Rightarrow$ First term $a_1 = 5 + 2(1) = 7$

$\Rightarrow$ Second term $a_2 = 5 + 2(2) = 9$

Then, common difference $(d) = a_2 - a_1 = 9 - 7 = 2.$

$\because$ Sum of the first n terms of an A.P.,

$$S_n = \frac{n}{2}[2a + (n-1)d]$$

Where a is the first term, d is the common difference.

$\because$ Sum of first 20 terms $S_{20} = \frac{20}{2}[2(7) + (20-1)(2)]$

$= 10[14 + 38] = 10 \times 52$

$\Rightarrow S_{20} = 520.$

Now, check if 52 is a term of the A.P.,

$$a_n = 5 + 2n = 52$$

$$\Rightarrow 2n = 47 \Rightarrow n = 23.5$$

Since n must be an integer, 52 is not a term of the A.P.

28. Prove that $\frac{\sin\theta}{1+\cos\theta} + \frac{1+\cos\theta}{\sin\theta} = 2\text{cosec}\theta$. *(3 M)*

28. LHS,

$$\frac{\sin\theta}{1+\cos\theta} + \frac{1+\cos\theta}{\sin\theta}$$

$$\Rightarrow \frac{\sin^2\theta + (1+\cos\theta)^2}{\sin\theta(1+\cos\theta)}$$

$$\Rightarrow \frac{\sin^2\theta + 1 + \cos^2\theta + 2\cos\theta}{\sin\theta(1+\cos\theta)}$$

$$\Rightarrow \frac{1+1+2\cos\theta}{\sin\theta(1+\cos\theta)} \quad [\because \sin^2\theta + \cos^2\theta = 1]$$

$$\Rightarrow \frac{2+2\cos\theta}{\sin\theta(1+\cos\theta)} = \frac{2(1+\cos\theta)}{\sin\theta(1+\cos\theta)} = \frac{2}{\sin\theta}$$

$$\Rightarrow 2\text{cosec}\theta \quad [\because \text{cosec}\theta = \frac{1}{\sin\theta}]$$

= RHS.

Hence proved.

29. Find length and breadth of a rectangular park whose perimeter is 100 m and area is 600 m². *(3 M)*

29. Let length be l and breadth be b.

Given, Perimeter = 100

$$\Rightarrow 2(l+b) = 100$$

$$\Rightarrow l + b = 50 \quad \text{---- (1)}$$

and area = 600

$\Rightarrow l \times b = 600$ --- (2)

From eqⁿ (1), $b = 50 - l$

Substitute b in equation (2), $l(50-l) = 600$

$\Rightarrow 50l - l^2 = 600$

$\Rightarrow l^2 - 50l + 600 = 0$

$\Rightarrow l^2 - 20l - 30l + 600 = 0$

$\Rightarrow l(l-20) - 30(l-20) = 0$

$\Rightarrow (l-20)(l-30) = 0$

$\Rightarrow l - 20 = 0$ or $l - 30 = 0$

$\Rightarrow l = 20$ or $l = 30$

If $l = 30$, then $b = 50 - 30$ $\Rightarrow b = 20$

If $l = 20$, then, $b = 50 - 20$ $\Rightarrow b = 30$

Hence, Length = 30 m, Breadth = 20 m.

30. *AB* and *CD* are diameters of a circle with centre *O* and radius 7 cm. If $\angle BOD = 30°$, then find the area and perimeter of the shaded region. *(3 M)*

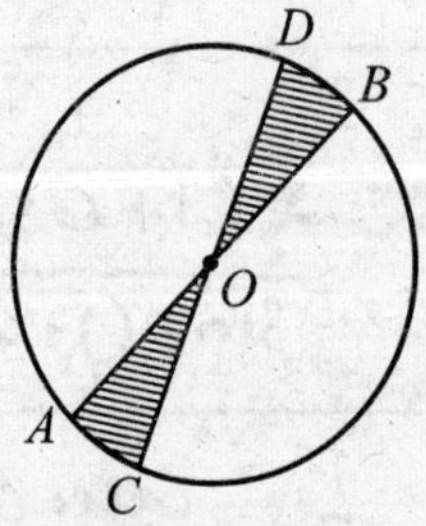

30. Given, radius (r) = 7cm and $\angle BOD = 30°$

Area of Sector BOD $= \frac{\theta}{360°} \times \pi r^2 = \frac{30°}{360°} \times \frac{22}{7} \times (7)^2$

$= \frac{1}{12} \times 22 \times 7 = \frac{77}{6}$ cm²

$\because \angle BOD = \angle AOC$ [vertically opposite angles]

$\therefore$ Area of Sector BOD = Area of Sector AOC

Hence, total shaded area = 2 × area of sector BOD

$= 2 \times \frac{77}{6} = \frac{77}{3}\ cm^2$

Now, Arc length BD $= \frac{\theta}{360^\circ} \times 2\pi r = \frac{30^\circ}{360^\circ} \times 2 \times \frac{22}{7} \times 7 = \frac{11}{3}$ cm

∵ Arc length BD = Arc length AC

Hence, total perimeter $= \overset{\frown}{AC} + OC + OA + \overset{\frown}{BD} + OB + OD$

$= 2(\overset{\frown}{BD}) + 4OC$ [∵ $\overset{\frown}{AC} = \overset{\frown}{BD}$, $OC = OA = OB = OD =$ radius]

$= 2\left(\frac{11}{3}\right) + 4(7) = \frac{22}{3} + 28$

$= \frac{22+84}{3} = \frac{106}{3}$ cm

31. (*a*) α, β are zeroes of the polynomial $3x^2 - 8x + k$. Find the value of *k*, if $\alpha^2 + \beta^2 = \frac{40}{9}$. (3 M)

OR

(*b*) Find the zeroes of the polynomial $2x^2 + 7x + 5$ and verify the relationship between its zeroes and coefficients. (3 M)

31. (a) Given, polynomial $3x^2 - 8x + k$ with zeroes α and β.

So, the coefficients are $a = 3$, $b = -8$, $c = k$.

Sum of zeroes, $\alpha + \beta = \frac{-b}{a} = \frac{8}{3}$

Product of zeroes, $\alpha\beta = \frac{c}{a} = \frac{k}{3}$

Now Given, $\alpha^2 + \beta^2 = \frac{40}{9}$

$\Rightarrow \alpha^2 + \beta^2 = (\alpha+\beta)^2 - 2\alpha\beta$

$\Rightarrow \frac{40}{9} = \left(\frac{8}{3}\right)^2 - 2 \times \frac{k}{3}$

$\Rightarrow \frac{40}{9} = \frac{64}{9} - \frac{2k}{3}$

$\Rightarrow \frac{2k}{3} = \frac{64}{9} - \frac{40}{9} = \frac{64-40}{9} = \frac{24}{9} = \frac{8}{3}$

$\Rightarrow 2k = 8$

$\Rightarrow k = 4$

OR

(b) Given, polynomial is $2x^2+7x+5$.

Finding roots,

$$2x^2+7x+5=0$$

$$\Rightarrow 2x^2+2x+5x+5=0$$

$$\Rightarrow 2x(x+1)+5(x+1)=0$$

$$\Rightarrow (x+1)(2x+5)=0$$

$\Rightarrow x+1=0$ or $2x+5=0$

$\Rightarrow x=-1$ $\quad x=-\frac{5}{2}$

Hence, the roots are $-1, -\frac{5}{2}$.

Now, Sum of zeroes $=-1+\left(-\frac{5}{2}\right)=\frac{-2-5}{2}=\frac{-7}{2}$

and $\frac{-b}{a}=\frac{-7}{2}$

product of zeroes $=(-1)\left(-\frac{5}{2}\right)=\frac{5}{2}$.

and $\frac{c}{a}=\frac{5}{2}$

$\Rightarrow$ Sum of zeroes $=\frac{-b}{a}$

& Product of zeroes $=\frac{c}{a}$

Hence, varified.

SECTION – D

(Long Answer Type Questions) **(4 × 5 = 20)**

Q. Nos 32 to 35 are Long Answer type questions of 5 marks each.

32. Find 'mean' and 'mode' marks of the following data: *(5 M)*

Marks	0–5	5–10	10–15	15–20	20–25	25–30
Number of Students	2	3	8	15	14	8

32.

Marks	Midpoint (x_i)	Number of students (f_i)	$f_i x_i$
0-5	2.5	2	5
5-10	7.5	3	22.5
10-15	12.5	8	100
15-20	17.5	15	262.5
20-25	22.5	14	315
25-30	27.5	8	220
Total		$\Sigma f_i = 50$	$\Sigma f_i x_i = 925$

$$\text{Mean} = \frac{\Sigma f_i x_i}{\Sigma f_i}$$

$$\Rightarrow \text{Mean} = \frac{925}{50} = 18.5$$

Since, the highest frequency is 18, therfore, the Modal class is 15-20.

Here, $l = 15$, $f_1 = 15$, $f_0 = 8$, $f_2 = 14$, $h = 5$

$$\because \quad \text{Mode} = l + \left(\frac{f_1 - f_0}{2f_1 - f_0 - f_2}\right) \times h$$

$$\therefore \quad \text{Mode} = 15 + \left(\frac{15-8}{2 \times 15 - 8 - 14}\right) \times 5$$

$$= 15 + \frac{7}{8} \times 5$$

$$= 15 + \frac{35}{8} = 15 + 4.375$$

$$= 19.375$$

Hence, Mean = 18.5, mode = 19.375

33. (*a*) Solve the following pair of linear equations by graphical method: (5 M)

$2x + y = 9$ and $x - 2y = 2$

OR

(*b*) Nidhi received simple interest of ₹ 1,200 when invested ₹ x at 6% p.a. and ₹ y at 5% p.a. for 1 year. Had she invested ₹ x at 3% p.a. and ₹ y at 8% p.a. for that year, she would have received simple interest of ₹ 1,260. Find the values of x and y. (5 M)

33(a). For Equation, $2x+y=9$

x	0	4.5
y	9	0

For Equation, $x-2y=2$

x	0	2
y	-1	0

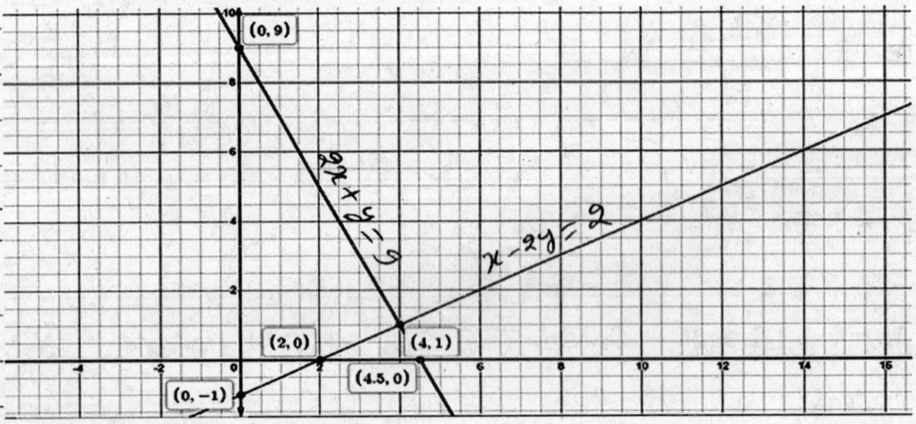

∵ The lines intersect at $x=4, y=1$.

Hence, the point of intersection is $(4, 1)$.

OR

33. (b) First investment Scenario,

$$\frac{x \times 6 \times 1}{100} + \frac{y \times 5 \times 1}{100} = 1200$$

$$\Rightarrow 0.06x + 0.05y = 1200 \quad \text{---(1)}$$

Second investment Scenario,

$$\frac{x \times 3 \times 1}{100} + \frac{y \times 8 \times 1}{100} = 1260$$

$$\Rightarrow 0.03x + 0.08y = 1260 \quad \text{---(2)}$$

multiply equation (1) by 3 and equation (2) by 6,

$$0.18x + 0.15y = 3600 \quad \text{----(1a)}$$

$$0.18x + 0.48y = 7560 \quad \text{---(2a)}$$

Subtract equation (1a) from equation (2a),

$0.33y = 3960$

$\Rightarrow y = 12,000$

Substitute $y = 12,000$ into equation (1)

$0.06x + 0.05 \times 12,000 = 1200$

$\Rightarrow 0.06x + 600 = 1200$

$\Rightarrow 0.06x = 600$

$\Rightarrow x = 10,000$

Hence, $x = 10,000$, $y = 12,000$

34. (*a*) The given figure shows a circle with centre *O* and radius 4 cm circumscribed by ΔABC. *BC* touches the circle at *D* such that $BD = 6$ cm, $DC = 10$ cm. Find the length of *AE*. *(5 M)*

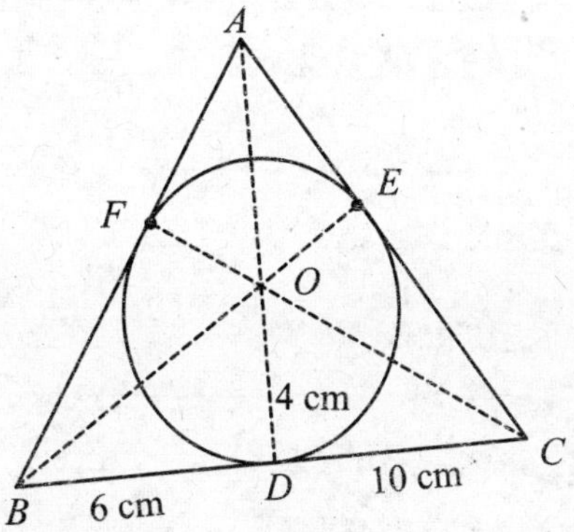

OR

(*b*) *PA* and *PB* are tangents drawn to a circle with centre *O*.
If $\angle AOB = 120°$ and $OA = 10$ cm, then

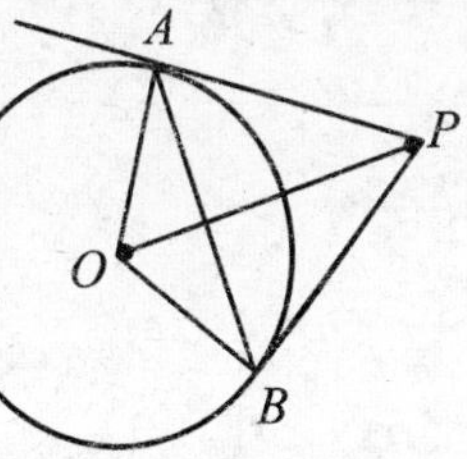

(*i*) Find $\angle OPA$. *(1 M)*
(*ii*) Find the perimeter of ΔOAP. *(3 M)*
(*iii*) Find the length of chord *AB*. *(1 M)*

34. (a) Given, $BD = 6$ cm, $DC = 10$ cm, and radius$(r) = 4$ cm.

$BC = BD + DC = 6 + 10 = 16$ cm.

Since, the lengths of two tangents drawn from an external point to a circle are equal.

Let $AE = AF = x$, $BF = BD = 6cm$ and $CE = CD = 10cm$

Perimeter of $\triangle ABC$,

$$AB + BC + CA = (x+6) + 16 + (x+10) = 2x + 32$$

Semi-perimeter (S),

$$S = \frac{2x+32}{2} = x+16$$

Area of $\triangle ABC$,

Using Heron's formula,

$$\text{Area} = \sqrt{S(S-a)(S-b)(S-c)}$$

$$= \sqrt{(x+16)(x+16-(x+6))(x+16-16)(x+16-(x+10))}$$

$$= \sqrt{(x+16)(10)(x)(6)}$$

$$= \sqrt{60x(x+16)} \quad \text{---- (1)}$$

Using radius,

$$\text{Area} = r \times S$$

$$= 4 \times (x+16) \quad \text{--- (2)}$$

From equation (1) & (2),

$$\sqrt{60x(x+16)} = 4(x+16)$$

$$\Rightarrow 60x(x+16) = 16(x+16)^2$$

$$\Rightarrow 60x = 16(x+16) \quad [\because x \neq -16]$$

$$\Rightarrow 60x = 16x + 256$$

$$\Rightarrow 60x - 16x = 256$$

$$\Rightarrow 44x = 256$$

$$\Rightarrow x = \frac{256}{44} = \frac{64}{11}$$

Hence, $AE = \frac{64}{11}$ cm

OR

(b) Given, $OA = 10cm$, $\angle AOB = 120°$.

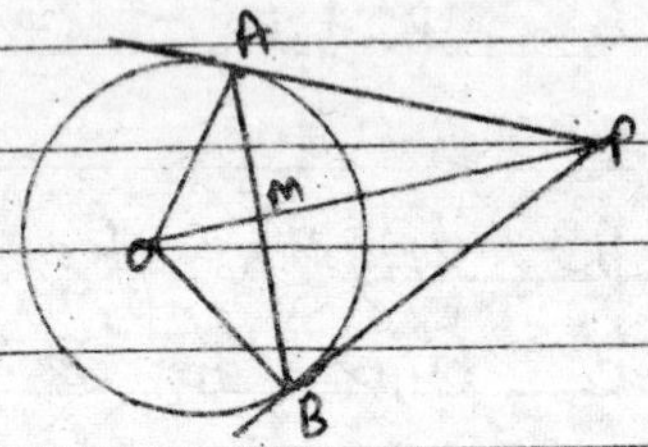

$\because$ PA and PB are tangents.

$\therefore \angle OAP = 90°$

(i) In $\triangle OAP$,

$\angle OAP = 90°$

$\angle AOP = 60°$ $[\because \angle AOB = 120°$ & OP bisects it

Hence, $\angle OPA = 180° - 90° - 60° = 30°$

(ii) In $\triangle OAP$,

$OA = 10$ cm

$\Rightarrow AP = OA \tan(\angle AOP) = OA \times \tan 60° = OA \times \sqrt{3}$

$\Rightarrow AP = 10 \times \sqrt{3} = 10\sqrt{3}$ cm

$\Rightarrow OP = \frac{OA}{\cos(\angle AOP)} = \frac{10}{\cos(60°)} = \frac{10}{1/2} = \frac{10 \times 2}{1} = 20$ cm.

Hence, perimeter $= OA + AP + OP$

$= 10 + 10\sqrt{3} + 20 = (30 + 10\sqrt{3})$ cm

(iii) $\because$ OP is perpendicular bisector of AB.

$\therefore AB = 2AM$.

In $\triangle OMA$,

$AM = OA \sin 60° = 10 \times \frac{\sqrt{3}}{2} = 5\sqrt{3}$ cm.

Hence, chord $AB = 2 \times 5\sqrt{3} = 10\sqrt{3}$ cm.

35. A drone is flying at a height of h metres. At an instant it observes the angle of elevation of top of an industrial turbine as 60° and angle of depression of foot of the turbine as 30°. If height of turbine is 200 metres, find the value of h and the distance of drone from the turbine. (Use $\sqrt{3} = 1.73$) *(5 M)*

35. Given, Height of turbine = 200 metres,

Angle of elevation to top = 60°,

Angle of depression to foot = 30°,

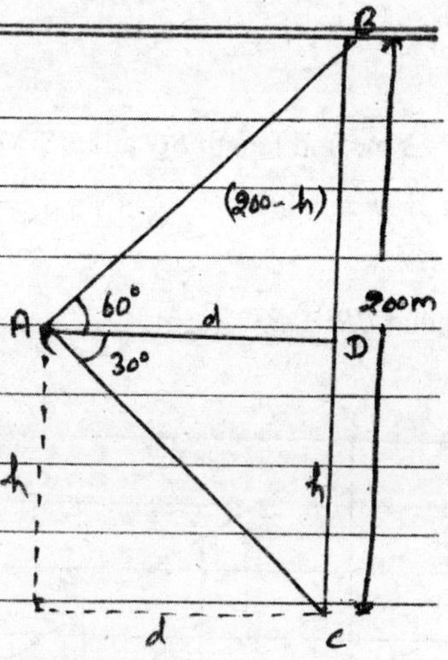

Let, height of drone = h metres,

Distance of drone from turbine = d metres

In $\triangle ADC$,

$\tan 30° = \frac{h}{d} \Rightarrow \frac{1}{\sqrt{3}} = \frac{h}{d} \Rightarrow d = h\sqrt{3}$ ---- (1)

In $\triangle ADB$,

$$\tan 60^\circ = \frac{200-h}{d} \Rightarrow \sqrt{3} = \frac{200-h}{d}$$

$$\Rightarrow \sqrt{3} = \frac{200-h}{h\sqrt{3}}$$ [From equation (1), $d = h\sqrt{3}$]

$\Rightarrow 3h = 200 - h \Rightarrow 4h = 200$

$\Rightarrow h = 50$ metres

Now, distance $d = h\sqrt{3} = 50 \times 1.73 = 86.5$ Metres

Hence, Height of drone $h = 50$ metres,

Distance from turbine $d = 86.5$ metres.

SECTION – E

(Case-study based Questions)

Q. Nos 36 to 38 are Case study based Questions of 4 marks each. **(3 × 4 = 12)**

36.

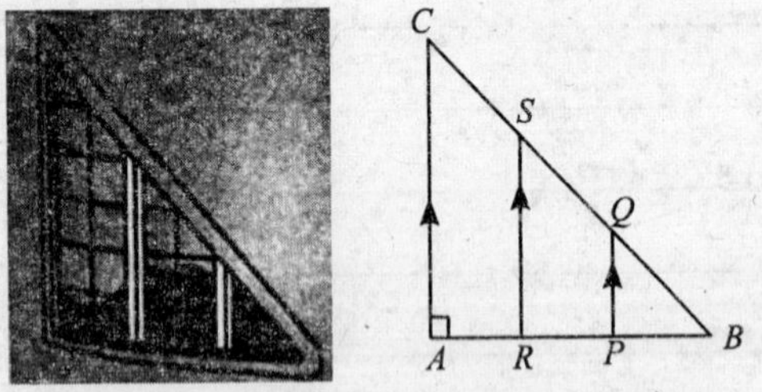

A triangular window of a building is shown above, Its diagram represents a ΔABC with $\angle A = 90^\circ$ and $AB = AC$. Points P and R trisect AB and $PQ \parallel RS \parallel AC$.

Based on the above, answer the following questions:

(*i*) Show that $\Delta BPQ \sim \Delta BAC$. (1 M)

(*ii*) Prove that $PQ = \frac{1}{3} AC$. (1 M)

(*iii*) (*a*) If $AB = 3$ m, find length BQ and BS. Verify that $BQ = \frac{1}{2} BS$. (2 M)

OR

(*iii*) (*b*) Prove that $BR^2 + RS^2 = \frac{4}{9} BC^2$. (2 M)

36.

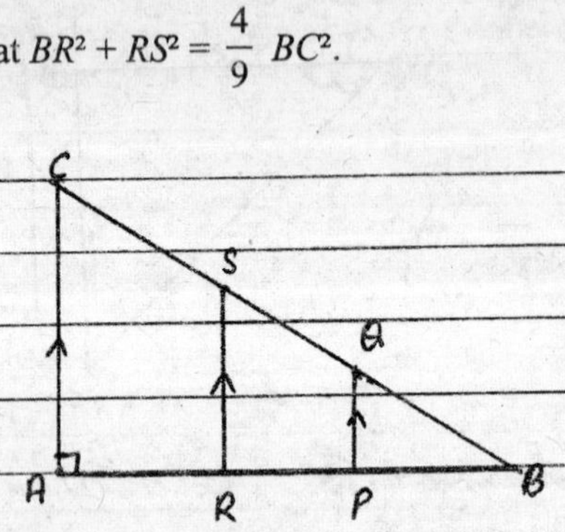

(i) Given, $AB = AC$ and $\angle A = 90^\circ$,

Point P and R trisects AB.

So $AR = RP = PB = \frac{AB}{3}$.

$PQ \parallel AC$ and $RS \parallel AC$

So $\angle BPQ = \angle BAC$ and $\angle BQP = \angle BCA$.

Now, In $\triangle BPQ$ and $\triangle BAC$,

$\angle BPQ = \angle BAC = 90°$

$\angle ABC = \angle PBQ$ (Common angle)

Hence, By AA Similarity,

$\triangle BPQ \sim \triangle BAC$.

(ii) $\because \triangle BPQ \sim \triangle BAC$,

$\therefore \frac{PQ}{AC} = \frac{BP}{BA} = \frac{1}{3}$

Hence, $PQ = \frac{1}{3} AC$.

(iii) (a) Given, $AB = 3m$,

then $BP = RP = AR = \frac{3}{3} = 1m$

$\Rightarrow BR = BP + RP = 2m$.

Now, In $\triangle ABC$,

$PQ \parallel AC$ & $SR \parallel AC$

Using Thale's theorem,

$\frac{BQ}{BC} = \frac{BP}{BA}$ & $\frac{BS}{BC} = \frac{BR}{BA}$

$\Rightarrow BQ = BC \times \frac{1}{3}$ & $BS = BC \times \frac{2}{3}$

$\Rightarrow BQ = \frac{BC}{3}$ & $BS = \frac{2}{3} BC$

Now, Using Pythagoras' theorem in $\triangle ABC$,

$AB^2 + AC^2 = BC^2$

$\Rightarrow 2AB^2 = BC^2$ $[\because AB = AC]$

$\Rightarrow BC^2 = 2 \times (3)^2$

$\Rightarrow BC = 3\sqrt{2}$ m.

So, $BQ = \frac{3\sqrt{2}}{3} = \sqrt{2}$ m

& $BS = \frac{2}{3} \times 3\sqrt{2} = 2\sqrt{2}$ m

And $BQ = \sqrt{2} = \frac{2\sqrt{2}}{2} = \frac{BS}{2}$

$\Rightarrow BQ = \frac{1}{2} BS$ (verified)

OR

(b) $\because$ $AC \parallel RS$ & $\angle CAB = 90°$

$\therefore$ $\angle SRB = 90°$

Using Pythagoras' theorem in $\triangle BRS$,

$BR^2 + RS^2 = BS^2$ ---- (1)

And In $\triangle ABC$, $AC \parallel RS$

Using Thales's theorem,

$\frac{BS}{BC} = \frac{BR}{AB}$

$\Rightarrow BS = BC \times \frac{BR}{AB} = BC \times \frac{2}{3}$ $\left[\because BR = \frac{2}{3} AB\right]$

$\Rightarrow BS = \frac{2}{3} BC$

From equation (1),

$BR^2 + RS^2 = \frac{4}{9} BC^2$.

Hence, proved.

37. Gurveer and Arushi built a robot that can paint a path as it moves on a graph paper. Some co-ordinate of points are marked on it. It starts from (0, 0), moves the points listed in order (in straight lines) and ends at (0, 0).

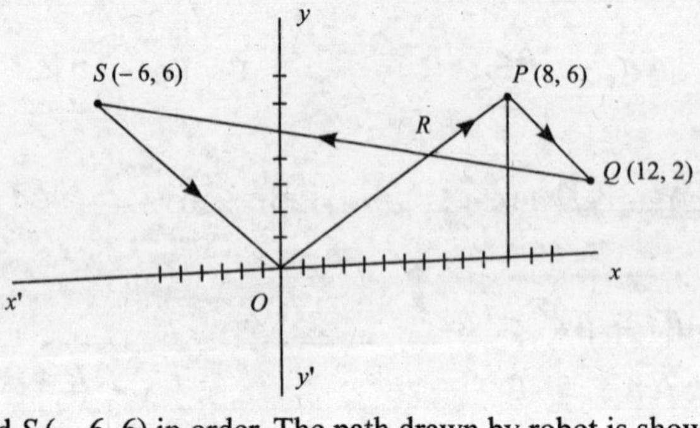

Arushi entered the points P (8, 6), Q (12, 2) and S (– 6, 6) in order. The path drawn by robot is shown in the figure. Based on the above, answer the following questions:

(*i*) Determine the distance OP. (1 M)

(*ii*) QS is represented by equation $2x + 9y = 42$. Find the co-ordinates of the point where it intersects y – axis. (1 M)

(*iii*) (*a*) Point R (4, 8, y) divides the line segment OP in a certain ratio, find the ratio. Hence, find the value of y. (2 M)

OR

(*iii*) (*b*) Using distance formula, show that $\frac{PQ}{OS} = \frac{2}{3}$. (2 M)

37. (i) Given, Coordinates of O (0, 0),

Coordinates of P (8, 6)

$\because$ The distance between two points (x_1, y_1) and (x_2, y_2) is $\sqrt{(x_2-x_1)^2+(y_2-y_1)^2}$

$\therefore \quad OP = \sqrt{(8-0)^2+(6-0)^2} = \sqrt{64+36} = \sqrt{100} = 10$ units

(ii) Given, Equation of QS is $2x+9y=42$.

$\because$ Intersection with y-axis occurs when $x=0$.

$\therefore \quad 2(0)+9y=42$

$\Rightarrow 9y=42 \Rightarrow y=\frac{42}{9}=\frac{14}{3}$

Hence, Intersection point is $\left(0, \frac{14}{3}\right)$.

(iii) (a) Let the ratio be $k:1$.

Using section formula for x-coordinate,

$$4.8 = \frac{k \times 8 + 1 \times 0}{k+1}$$

$\Rightarrow 4.8(k+1) = 8k \Rightarrow 4.8k + 4.8 = 8k$

$\Rightarrow 3.2k = 4.8$

$\Rightarrow k = 1.5$

Ratio $= 1.5:1$ or $3:2$

Now, Using section formula for y-coordinates,

$$y = \frac{1.5 \times 6 + 1 \times 0}{1.5+1} = \frac{9}{2.5} = 3.6$$

OR

(b) Given, Coordinates of P(8, 6), Q(12, 2), O(0, 0), S(-6, 6)

Distance $PQ = \sqrt{(12-8)^2+(2-6)^2} = \sqrt{16+16} = 4\sqrt{2}$

Distance $OS = \sqrt{(-6-0)^2+(6-0)^2} = \sqrt{36+36} = 6\sqrt{2}$

Ratio $= \frac{PQ}{OS} = \frac{4\sqrt{2}}{6\sqrt{2}} = \frac{4}{6} = \frac{2}{3}$

Hence, Proved.

38.

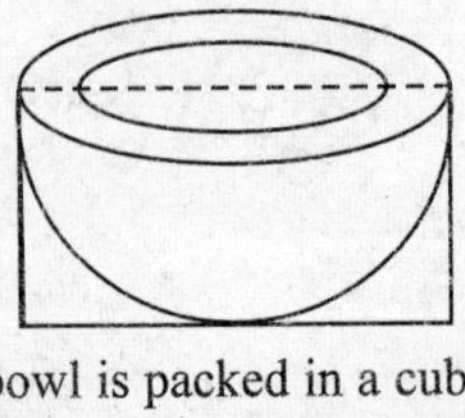

A hemispherical bowl is packed in a cuboidal box. The bowl just fits in the box. Inner radius of the bowl is 10 cm. Outer radius of the bowl is 10.5 cm.

Based on the above, answer the following questions:

(*i*) Find the dimensions of the cuboidal box. (1 M)

(*ii*) Find the total outer surface area of the box. (1 M)

(*iii*) (*a*) Find the difference between the capacity of the bowl and the volume of the box. (use π 3.14) (2 M)

OR

(*iii*) (*b*) the inner surface of the bowl and the thickness is to be painted. Find the area to be painted. (2 M)

38. (i) ∵ Inner radius of bowl = 10 cm,

Outer radius of bowl = 10.5 cm

∴ Outer diameter of the bowl = $2 \times 10.5 = 21$ cm

& Height of the bowl = 10.5 cm

Hence, Dimensions of the box is 21 cm × 21 cm × 10.5 cm.

(ii) ∵ Surface area $= 2(lb + bh + hl)$

Where, $l = 21$ cm, $b = 21$ cm, $h = 10.5$ cm

Hence, Surface area $= 2(21 \times 21 + 21 \times 10.5 + 10.5 \times 21)$

$= 2(441 + 220.5 + 220.5)$

$= 2(882)$

$= 1764 \text{ cm}^2$

(iii) (a) Volume of the bowl $= \frac{2}{3}\pi r^3 = \frac{2}{3} \times 3.14 \times 10^3 = 2093.33$ c

Volume of box $= l \times b \times h = 21 \times 21 \times 10.5 = 4630.5 \text{ cm}^3$

Hence, Difference $= 4630.5 - 2093.33 = 2537.17 \text{ cm}^3$

OR

(b) Inner surface area of the bowl $= 2\pi r^2 = 2 \times 3.14 \times 10^2$

$= 628 \text{ cm}^2$

Thickness area $= \pi R^2 - \pi r^2$

$= 3.14 \times 10.5^2 - 3.14 \times 10^2$

$= 3.14(110.25 - 100)$

$= 3.14 \times 10.25 = 32.185 \text{ cm}^2$

Hence, Total area to be painted $= 628 + 32.185$

$= 660.185 \text{ cm}^2$

CBSE SOLVED PAPER 2024

Time allowed : 3 hours	Maximum Marks : 80

GENERAL INSTRUCTIONS:

Read the following instructions very carefully and follow them:

(i) *This question paper contains **38** questions. **All** questions are compulsory.*

(ii) *Question Paper is divided into 5 Sections-**Section A, B, C, D and E.***

(iii) *In **Section A question number 1 to 18 are** Multiple Choice Questions **(MCQs)** and question number **19 & 20 are** Assertion-Reason based **questions of 1 mark each.***

(iv) *In **Section-B question number 21 to 25 are** Very Short Answer (VSA) type **questions of 2 marks each.***

(v) *In **Section-C question number 26 to 31 are** Short Answer (SA) type **questions carrying 3 marks each.***

(vi) *In **Section-D question number 32 to 35 are** Long Answer (LA) type **questions carrying 5 marks each.***

(vii) *In **Section-E question number 36 to 38 are** Case Study based questions **carrying 4 marks each. Internal choice is provided in 2 marks question in each case-study.***

(viii) ***There is no overall choice. However, an internal choice has been provided in 2 questions in Section B, 2 questions in Section C, 2 questions in Section D and 3 questions in Section E.***

(ix) ***Draw neat figures wherever required. Take $\pi = 22/7$ wherever required if not stated.***

(x) ***Use of calculators is NOT allowed.***

SECTION - A

Section - A consists of Multiple Choice type questions of 1 mark each.

1. In the given figure, tangents *PA* and *PB* drawn from *P* to circle are inclined to each other at an angle of 80°. The measure of $\angle PAB$ is *(1 M)*

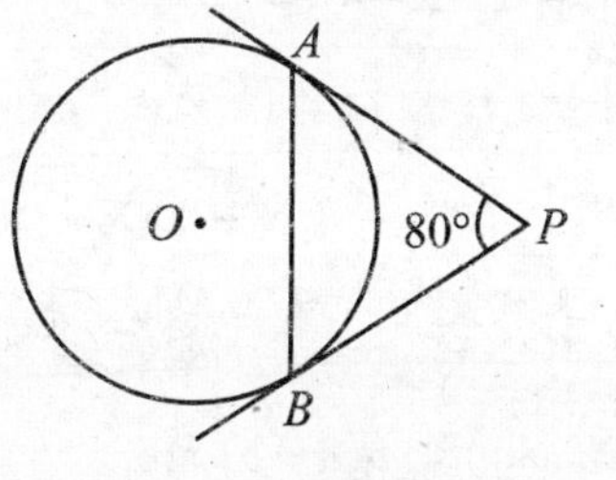

(*a*) 80° (*b*) 60 (*c*) 50° (*d*) 40°

1. (C) Given $\angle APB = 80°$

Since the lengths of the two tangents drawn from external point are equal.

$\therefore$ PA = PB

$\Rightarrow \angle PAB = \angle PBA$

Therefore, $\angle PAB + \angle PBA + 80° = 180°$

$2\angle PAB = 100$

$\angle PAB = 50°$

2. The value(s) of k for which the quadratic equation $5x^2 - 9kx + 5 - 0$ has real and equal roots, is/are (1 M)

(a) $\frac{-10}{9}$ (b) $\pm\frac{9}{10}$ (c) $\frac{10}{9}$ (d) $\pm\frac{10}{9}$

2. (D) Given, quadratic equation is $5x^2 - 9kx + 5 = 0$

for real and equal roots, $b^2 = 4ac$

$\Rightarrow 81k^2 = 4 \times 5 \times 5$

$\Rightarrow k^2 = \frac{100}{81} \Rightarrow k = \pm\frac{10}{9}$

3. The distance between the points $A(-1, 5)$ and $B(6, -2)$ is (1 M)

(a) $2\sqrt{7}$ (b) $7\sqrt{2}$ (c) 49 (d) 14

3. (B) Here given points are $A(-1,5)$ and $B(6,-2)$

Distance between AB is $= \sqrt{[6-(-1)]^2 + [-2-5]^2}$

$= \sqrt{49+49}$

$= 7\sqrt{2}$

4. A quadratic polynomial whose zeroes are 3 and –2, is (1 M)

(a) $x^2 - x - 6$ (b) $x^2 + x - 6$ (c) $2x^2 - x - 6$ (d) $2x^2 + x + 6$

4. (A) We know that for given roots $\alpha = 3$ and $\beta = -2$.

Sum of roots $= \alpha + \beta = 3 - 2 = 1$

product of roots $= \alpha\beta = -6$

Substituting them in the standard quadratic equation i.e $x^2 - (\alpha+\beta)x + \alpha\beta = 0$

$x^2 - 1x - 6 = 0 \Rightarrow x^2 - x - 6 = 0$.

5. The lines represented by linear equations $x = a$ and $y = b(a \neq b)$ are (1 M)

(a) intersecting at (a, b). (b) intersecting at (b, a). (c) parallel. (d) coincident.

5. (A) The equations are $x = a$ and $y = b$.

The graph of $x = a$ is parallel to y-axis and $y = b$ is parallel to x-axis.

$\therefore$ the angle between them is 90°, i.e they intersect at (a, b).

6. If in the given figure, $DE \parallel BC$. If BC. If $AD = 2.8\,\text{cm}, DB = 2.1\,\text{cm}$ and $EC = 4.8$ cm , then the value of x is (1 M)

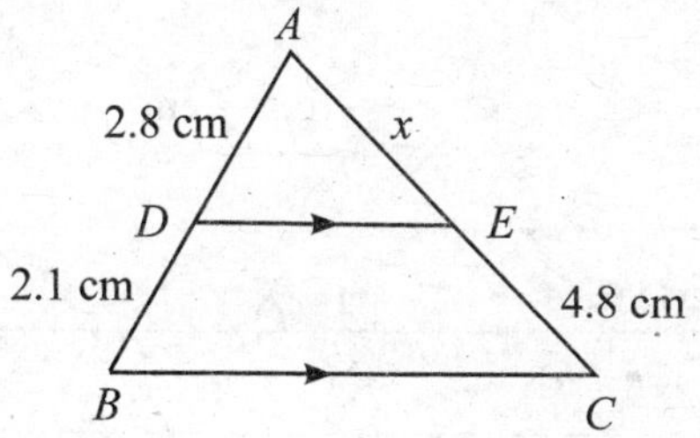

(*a*) 3.6 cm (*b*) 2.4 cm (*c*) 6.4 cm (*d*) 4.8 cm

6. (C) Given DE∥BC and AD = 2.8, DB = 2.1 and EC = 4.8

$\Rightarrow \frac{AD}{DB} = \frac{AE}{EC} \Rightarrow \frac{2.8}{2.1} = \frac{x}{4.8} \Rightarrow x = 6.4$ cm.

7. In a right-angled triangle $ABC, \angle A = 90^\circ$ and $AB = AC$. The value of sin C is (1 M)

(*a*) 0 (*b*) $\frac{\sqrt{3}}{2}$ (*c*) $\frac{1}{2}$ (*d*) $\frac{1}{\sqrt{2}}$

7. (D) Here we have, AB = AC, ∠A = 90°

$\Rightarrow \angle B = \angle C$

Therefore, $\angle B + \angle C + \angle A = 180^\circ$

$\Rightarrow 2\angle C + 90^\circ = 180^\circ$

$\Rightarrow \angle C = 45^\circ$

Hence $\sin C = \sin 45^\circ = \frac{1}{\sqrt{2}}$.

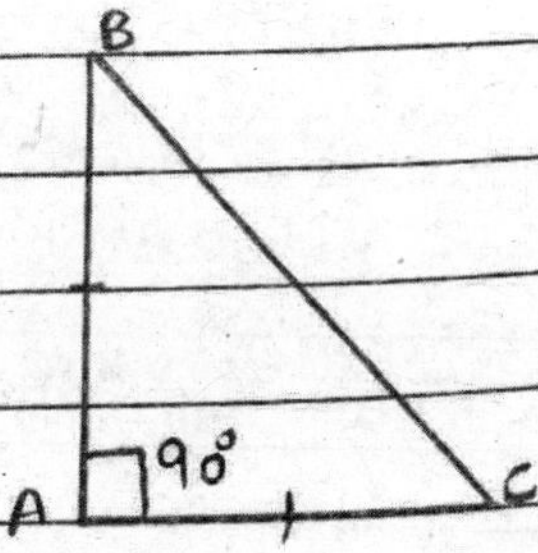

8. A die is thrown once. The probability of getting a number less than 6, is (1 M)

(*a*) 0 (*b*) $\frac{5}{6}$ (*c*) $\frac{1}{6}$ (*d*) 1

8. (B). Numbers of dice less than 6 are 1, 2, 3, 4, 5.
Hence probability of getting numbers less than 6 is $\frac{5}{6}$.

9. From an external point P, a tangent PA is drawn to a circle. The number of tangents through P parallel to PA is (1 M)

(*a*) 2 (*b*) more than 2 (*c*) 1 (*d*) 0

9. (D) If a tangent is drawn from an external point to a circle, then there can be only one tangent that touches the circle at that point.
Hence zero parallel tangents can be drawn.

10. If the volume of a sphere is $\frac{11}{21}$ cm^3, then the radius of the sphere is *(1 M)*

(*a*) 2 cm (*b*) 4 cm (*c*) $\frac{1}{2}$ cm (*d*) $\frac{1}{4}$ cm

10. (C). Volume of sphere $= \frac{4}{3}\pi r^3$

$\therefore$ According to question: $\frac{4}{3}\pi r^3 = \frac{11}{21}$

$\Rightarrow r^3 = \frac{11}{21} \times \frac{3}{4} \times \frac{7}{22} \Rightarrow r^3 = \frac{1}{8} \Rightarrow r = \frac{1}{2}$ cm.

11. In the given figure, graph of a polynomial $f(x)$ is shown. The number of zeroes of polynomial $f(x)$ is *(1 M)*

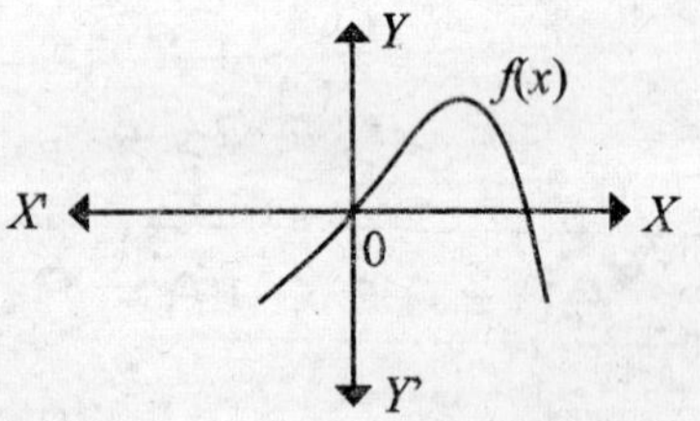

(*a*) 3 (*b*) 1 (*c*) 0 (*d*) 2

11. (D) The graph of the given polynomial function ($f(x)$) cuts the x-axis at two points. Hence two zeroes.

12. In the given figure, two concentric circles of radii 5 cm and 3 cm have their centre *O*. *OAB* is a sector of outer circle making an angle of 60° at the centre while *OCD* is the sector of smaller circle. The area of the shaded region is *(1 M)*

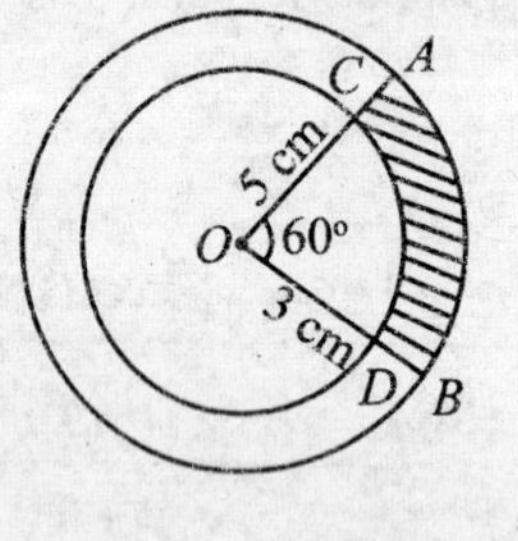

(*a*) $\frac{7\pi}{2}$ cm^2 (*b*) $\frac{8\pi}{3}$ cm^2 (*c*) $\frac{25\pi}{6}$ cm^2 (*d*) $\frac{3\pi}{2}$ cm^2

12. (B) Required Area = Area of OAB − Area of OCD

$= \frac{\pi \times (5)^2 \times 60}{360} - \frac{\pi \times (3)^2 \times 60°}{360}$

$= \frac{\pi}{6}[25 - 9] = \frac{8\pi}{3}$ cm^2

13. If the mean and median of a data are 10 and 11 respectively, then mode of the data is *(1 M)*

(*a*) 12 (*b*) 8 (*c*) 20 (*d*) 13

13. (D) We know the formula for the relation between mean, median and mode is

Mode = 3median − 2mean

⇒ Mode = $3 \times 11 - 2 \times 10 = 33 - 20 = 13$.

14. Two fair coins are tossed together. The probability of getting 2 heads, is *(1 M)*

(*a*) $\frac{1}{2}$ (*b*) $\frac{3}{4}$ (*c*) $\frac{1}{4}$ (*d*) $\frac{3}{8}$

14. (C) Sample space = {HH, TT, HT, TH}

Favourable outcomes = {HH}

P(getting 2 heads) = $\frac{1}{4}$

15. If $\cos A = \frac{1}{2}$, then $\tan A$ is equal to *(1 M)*

(*a*) $\frac{1}{\sqrt{3}}$ (*b*) $\sqrt{3}$ (*c*) 3 (*d*) $\frac{3}{2}$

15. (B) Given $\cos A = \frac{1}{2}$

⇒ $\angle A = 60°$

Therefore. $\tan 60° = \sqrt{3}$

16. From a solid cube of side 14 cm , a sphere of maximum diameter is carved out. The radius of sphere is *(1 M)*

(*a*) 7 cm (*b*) 14 cm (*c*) $\frac{7}{2}$ cm (*d*) $\sqrt{14}$ cm

16. (A) Given that the length of cube is 14cm, the diameter of the sphere will also be 14 cm.

Therefore, radius of sphere is $\frac{14}{2} = 7$ cm.

17. The common difference of an A.P. whose n^{th} term is given by $a_n = 5n - 1$, is (1 M)

(a) 1 (b) 6 (c) 5 (d) 4

17. (C) Given $a_n = 5n - 1$.

$\Rightarrow a_{n+1} = 5(n+1) - 1$

Common difference $d = 5(n+1) - 1 - [5n - 1]$

$= 5n + 5 - 1 - 5n + 1$

$= 5$

18. If for a distribution, $\sum_1^n f_i x_i = 132 + 5p, \sum_1^n f_i = 20$ and the mean of the distribution is 8.1, then the value of p is (1 M)

(a) 3 (b) 6 (c) 4 (d) 6

18. (B) Given: $\sum_1^n f_i x_i = 132 + 5p$, $\sum_1^n f_i = 20$, mean $= 8.1$

Then,

$\text{Mean} = \dfrac{\sum_1^n f_i x_i}{\sum_1^n f_i}$

$8.1 = \dfrac{132 + 5p}{20}$

$162 = 132 + 5p \Rightarrow p = 6.$

DIRECTIONS: In question numbers **19** and **20**, a statement of **Assertion (A)** is followed by a statement of **Reason (R)**. Choose the correct option from the following:

(a) Both Assertion (A) and Reason (R) are true. Reason (R) is the correct explanation of Assertion (A).

(b) Both Assertion (A) and Reason (R) are true. Reason (R) is not the correct explanation of Assertion (A).

(c) Assertion (A) is true, but Reason (R) is false.

(d) Assertion (A) is false, but Reason (R) is true.

19. **Assertion (A):** The distance of $P(a,b)$ from origin is $a^2 + b^2$.

Reason (R): The distance between two point $A(x_1, y_1)$ and $B(x_2, y_2)$ is $\sqrt{(x_2 - x_1)^2 + (y_2 - y_1)^2}$ (1 M)

19. (C) Assertion: Let origin $O(0,0)$

Distance of point $P(a,b)$ from $O(0,0)$ is

$\sqrt{(0-a)^2 + (0-b)^2} = \sqrt{a^2 + b^2}$

Reason is correct as distance between

$A(x_1, y_1)$ and $B(x_2, y_2)$ is given as $\sqrt{(x_2 - x_1)^2 + (y_2 - y_1)^2}$

Hence Assertion (A) is false, but Reason (R) is true

20. Assertion (A): $\sqrt{2}\left(5-\sqrt{2}\right)$ is an irrational number.

Reason (R): Product of two irrational numbers is always irrational. *(1 M)*

20. (C) Assertion: We can simplify $\sqrt{2}(5-\sqrt{2})$ by distributing $\sqrt{2}$ into parentheses: $\sqrt{2}(5-\sqrt{2}) = 5\sqrt{2}-(\sqrt{2})^2 = 5\sqrt{2}-2$.
Since $5\sqrt{2}-2$ can not be expressed as a ratio of two integers, it is irrational.
Reason: This statement is false: the product of two irrational numbers can be a rational number eg. $\sqrt{3}\times\sqrt{3} = 3$ is a rational Number.
Hence Assertion (A) is true, but Reason (R) is false.

SECTION - B

Q. No. 21 to 25 are Very Short Answer type questions of 2 marks each.

21. (*a*) If $Q\ (0, 2)$ is equidistant from $P\ (5,-3)$ and $R\ (x,-7)$, find the value(s) of x. *(2 M)*

OR

(*b*) If $A(1,1)$ and $B(7,9)$ are the end points of a diameter of a circle, then find the co-ordinates of the centre of the circle. *(2 M)*

21. (a) Since $Q(0,2)$ is equidistant from $P(5,-3)$ and $R(x,7)$

Therefore, $PQ = QR$

$\Rightarrow \sqrt{(5-0)^2+(-3-2)^2} = \sqrt{(x-0)^2+(7-2)^2}$

$\Rightarrow \sqrt{25+25} = \sqrt{x^2+25}$

$\Rightarrow 50 = x^2+25$ [Sq. Both the sides]

$\Rightarrow x = \pm 5$

Therefore x can take two values i.e 5 and -5.

22. Evaluate : $4\sin^2 60^\circ \tan^2 45^\circ - 2\sec^2 30^\circ \tan^2 60^\circ$ *(2 M)*

22. $4\sin^2 60^\circ \tan^2 45^\circ - 2\sec^2 30^\circ \tan^2 60^\circ$

$\Rightarrow 4\left(\frac{\sqrt{3}}{2}\right)^2 \times (1)^2 - 2\times\left(\frac{2}{\sqrt{3}}\right)^2 \times (\sqrt{3})^2$

$\Rightarrow 4\times\frac{3}{4}\times 1 - 2\times\frac{4}{3}\times 3$

$\Rightarrow 3 - 8 = -5$

Hence, -5 is the answer.

23. (*a*) Prove that $-7-2\sqrt{3}$ is an irrational number, given that $\sqrt{3}$ is an irrational number. (2 M)

OR

(*b*) Explain why $(7 \times 11 \times 13 + 12 \times 11)$ is not a prime number. (2 M)

23. (b) $7 \times 11 \times 13 + 2 \times 11$ (given)

$\Rightarrow (7 \times 11 \times 13) + (2 \times 11)$

$\Rightarrow (1001) + 22$

$\Rightarrow 1023 = 3 \times 341$

So, 1023 is not a prime number because it is divisible by number other than 1 and itself. Specifically, it can be divided evenly by 3 and 341.

24. Find the ratio in which the *Y*-axis divides the line segment joining the points *A* (5,– 6) and *B* (–1,– 4). Also, find the point of intersection. (2 M)

24. Let the point $A(5,-6)$, $B(-1,-4)$ and $P(0,y)$

Point P is on y-axis, hence its x-coordinate is 0

So, it is of the form $P(0,y)$

Let the ratio k : 1

using section formula $x = \frac{m_1x_2 + m_2x_1}{m_1 + m_2}$

$\Rightarrow 0 = \frac{-k+5}{k+1} \Rightarrow k = 5$

Again $y = \frac{m_1y_2 + m_2y_1}{m_1 + m_2} = \frac{-4k-6}{k+1} = \frac{-20-6}{6} = \frac{-13}{3}$

For k = 5

Hence, the coordinates of point $P\left(0, -\frac{13}{3}\right)$

25. There are 80 cards numbered from 1 to 80 . One card is drawn at random from them. Find the probability that the number on the selected card is not divisible by 8. (2 M)

25. There are total 80 cards.

Number of cards divisible by 8 are 10. i.e

8, 16, 24, 32, 40, 48, 56, 64, 72, 80.

Number of cards not divisible by 8 are 80 − 10 = 70.

Therefore,

$\text{Probability} = \frac{\text{Total fav. outcomes}}{\text{Total Number of outcomes}} = \frac{70}{80} = \frac{7}{8}$.

SECTION - C

Q. No. 26 to 31 are Short Answer type questions of 3 marks each.

26. Find LCM and HCF of two numbers 336 and 54, using prime-factorisation method. *(3 M)*

26. Factorrs of 336 are :

$336 = 2 \times 2 \times 2 \times 2 \times 3 \times 7$

$= 2^4 \times 3 \times 7$

factor of 54 are :

$54 = 2 \times 3 \times 3 \times 3 = 2 \times 3^3$

$H.C.F\ (336, 54) = 2^1 \times 3^1 = 2 \times 3 = 6$

$L.C.M\ (336, 54) = 2^4 \times 3^3 \times 7 = 3024$

27. The altitude of a right-angled triangle is 7 cm less than its base. If its hypotenuse is 17 cm long, then *(3 M)*

(*i*) represent the above information in the form of a quadratic equation;

(*ii*) find the length of the sides of the triangle.

27. (i) In ΔABC using pythgoras Theorem, we get,

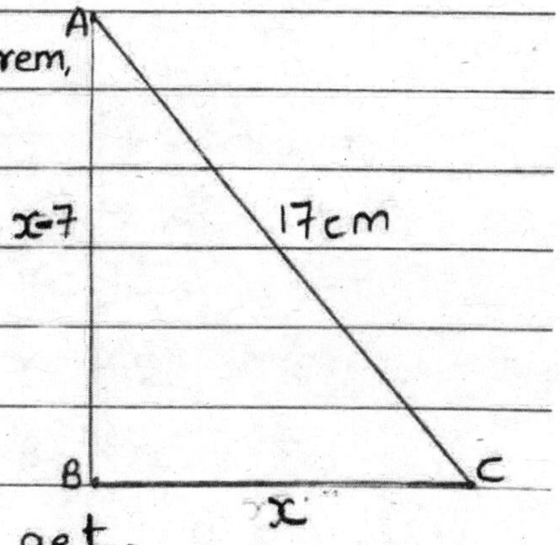

$(AB)^2 + (BC)^2 = (AC)^2$

$\Rightarrow (x-7)^2 + x^2 = (17)^2$

$\Rightarrow x^2 + 49 - 14x + x^2 = 289$

$\Rightarrow 2x^2 - 14x - 240 = 0$. (eq.)

(ii) Solving the obtained eq. we get,

$\Rightarrow 2x^2 - 14x - 240 = 0$

$\Rightarrow 2x^2 - 30x + 16x - 240 = 0$

$\Rightarrow 2x[x-15] + 16[x-15] = 0$

$\Rightarrow (x-15)(2x+16)$

$\Rightarrow x = 15$ or $x = \frac{-16}{2} \Rightarrow x = -8$ (Side can't be negative).

$\therefore$ Altitude $AB = 15 - 7 = 8$ cm, $BC = 15$

28. (*a*) A vessel is in the form of a hollow hemisphere surmounted by a hollow cylinder. The diameter of the hemisphere is 14 cm and the total height of the vessel is 13 cm. Find the inner surface area of the vessel. *(3 M)*

OR

(*b*) A solid toy is in the form of a hemisphere surmounted by a right circular cone. The height of the cone is 2 cm and the diameter of the base is 4 cm. Determine the volume of the toy. *(3 M)*

28. (b) Volume of toy = Vol. of Cone + Vol. of Hemisphere

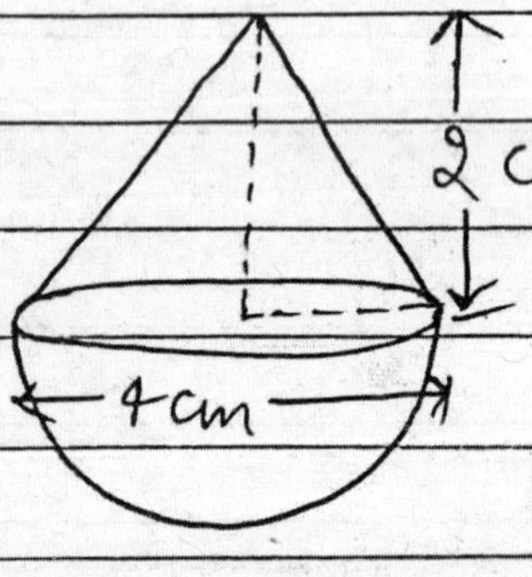

$= \frac{1}{3}\pi r^2 h + \frac{2}{3}\pi r^3$

$= \frac{1}{3}\pi r^2 (h + 2r)$

$= \frac{1}{3} \times \frac{22}{7} \times 2^2 (2 + 2 \times 2)$

$= \frac{1}{3} \times \frac{22}{7} \times 4 \times 6 = 25.14 \text{ cm}^3$

29. Find the zeroes of the quadratic polynominal $5x^2 + 3x - 2$ and verify the relationship between the zeroes and the co-efficients. *(3 M)*

29. Given quadratic equation is $5x^2 + 3x - 2 = 0$

For solving the values of x,

$\Rightarrow 5x^2 + 3x - 2 = 0$

$\Rightarrow 5x^2 + 5x - 2x - 2 = 0$

$\Rightarrow 5x[x+1] - 2[x+1] = 0$

$\Rightarrow (5x - 2)(x + 1)$

$\Rightarrow x = \frac{2}{5}$ or $x = -1$

Verification:

Sum of zeroes $= \alpha + \beta = \frac{2}{5} - 1 = \frac{-3}{5}$ or $\frac{-\text{coefficient of } x}{\text{coefficient of } x^2}$

Product of zeroes $= \alpha\beta = \frac{2}{5} \times (-1) = \frac{-2}{5}$ or $\frac{\text{Constant term}}{\text{Coeff. of } x^2}$

So, the relationship between the zeroes and the coefficients is verified.

30. In the given figure, $\angle ABC = \angle ACB$ and $\frac{BC}{BE} = \frac{BD}{AC}$ (3 M)

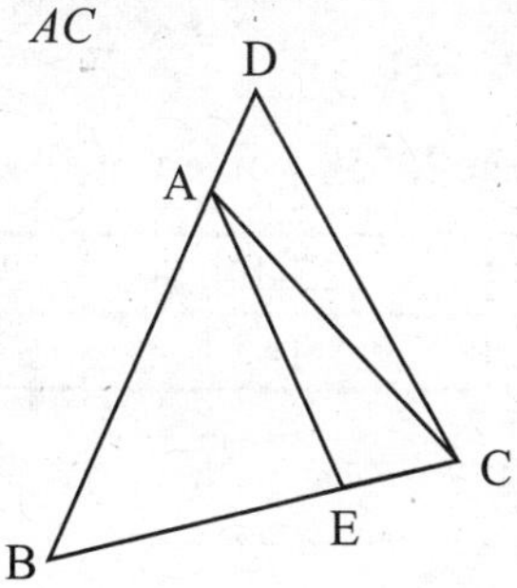

Show that $\Delta ABE \sim \Delta DBC$ and $AE \parallel DC$.

30. Given $\angle ABC = \angle ACB$ and $\frac{BC}{BE} = \frac{BD}{AC}$.

To proove: $\Delta ABE \sim \Delta DBC$ and $AC \parallel DC$

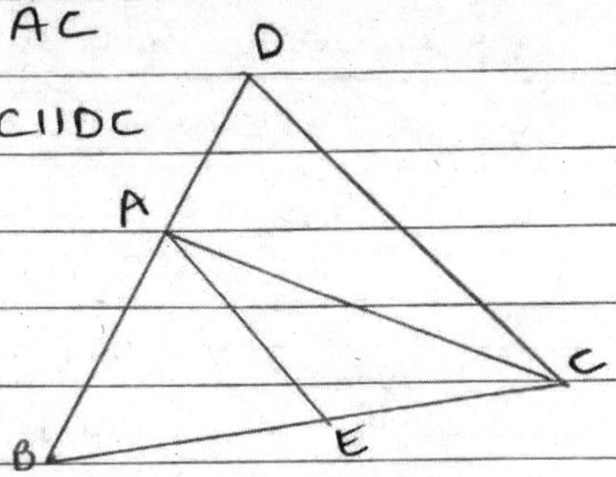

Proof: In ΔABC.

$\angle ABC = \angle ACB$.

$\therefore AB = AC$ ---① [opp. angles]

In ΔABE and ΔDBC

$\angle B = \angle B$ (common)

We have given $\frac{BC}{BE} = \frac{BD}{AC}$ $\left[\therefore \frac{BC}{BE} = \frac{BD}{BA} \text{ from ①}\right]$

$\Delta ABE \sim \Delta DBC$ (By SAS)

$AE \parallel DC$ ($\angle BAE = \angle BDC$ are corresponding)

31. (*a*) Prove that $(\sin\theta + \text{cosec}\theta)^2 + (\cos\theta + \sec\theta)^2 = 7 + \tan^2\theta + \cot^2\theta$ (3 M)

OR

(*b*) If $\cos A = \frac{5}{13}$, then verify that $\frac{\cos A}{1-\tan A} + \frac{\sin A}{1-\cot A} = \cos A + \sin A$. (3 M)

31. (a) To proove:

$(\sin\theta + \text{cosec}\theta)^2 + (\cos\theta + \sec\theta)^2 = 7 + \tan^2\theta + \cot^2\theta$.

$\text{LHS} = (\sin\theta + \text{cosec}\theta)^2 + (\cos\theta + \sec\theta)^2$

$= \sin^2\theta + \text{cosec}^2\theta + 2\sin\theta \cdot \text{cosec}\theta + \cos^2\theta + \sec^2\theta + 2\cos\theta\sec\theta$

$= (\sin^2\theta + \cos^2\theta) + 1 + \cot^2\theta + 2 + 1 + \tan^2\theta + 2$

$= 1 + 6 + \tan^2\theta + \cot^2\theta$

$= 7 + \tan^2\theta + \cot^2\theta$

$= \text{RHS}$.

Hence proved.

Q. No. 32 to 35 are Long Answer type questions of 5 marks each.

32. Consider the following distribution of hourly wages of 50 workers of a factory: *(5 M)*

Hourly wages (in ₹)	100–120	120–140	140–160	160–180	180–200
Number of workers	12	14	8	6	10

Find the mean and the median of the above data.

32. Let us find the class mark for each interval by using the relation :

$$x_i = \frac{\text{Upper Class Limit} + \text{lower class limit}}{2}$$

Class size of data = 20.

Daily wages in (Rs.)	Number of Workers (f_i)	x_i	$d_i = x_i - 150$	$u_i = \frac{x_i - 150}{h}$	$f_i u_i$
100-120	12	110	-40	-2	-24
120-140	14	130	-20	-1	-14
140-160	8	150	0	0	0
160-180	6	170	20	1	6
180-200	10	190	40	2	20
Total	50				-12

From the table we may observe that :

$h = 20,\ a = 150,\ \Sigma f_i = 50,\ f_i u_i = -12.$

Mean $\bar{x} = a + \left(\frac{\Sigma f_i u_i}{\Sigma f_i}\right) h$

Mean $= 150 + \left(\frac{-12}{50}\right) 20 = 150 - \frac{24}{5} = 150 - 4.8 = 145.2$

Median $= l + \frac{\frac{N}{2} - cf}{f} \times h = 120 + \frac{25 - 12}{14} \times 20 = 120 + 18.6 = 138.6.$

33. (*a*) In the given figure, *AB* is chord of length 6 cm of a circle of radius 5 cm. The tangents at *A* and *B* intersect at a point *P* Find the length of *PB*. (5 M)

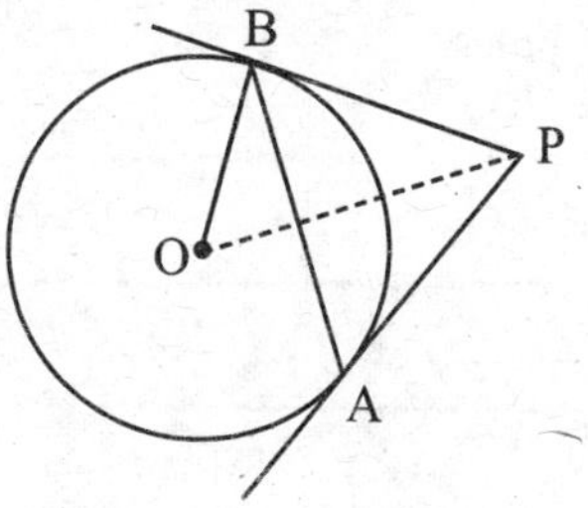

OR

(*b*) Prove that the parallelogram circumscribing a circle is a rhombus. Also, find area of the rhombus, if radius of circle is 3cm and length of one side of the rhombus is 10 cm. (5 M)

33. (b) Given ABCD be a parallelogram circumscribing a circle with the centre O.

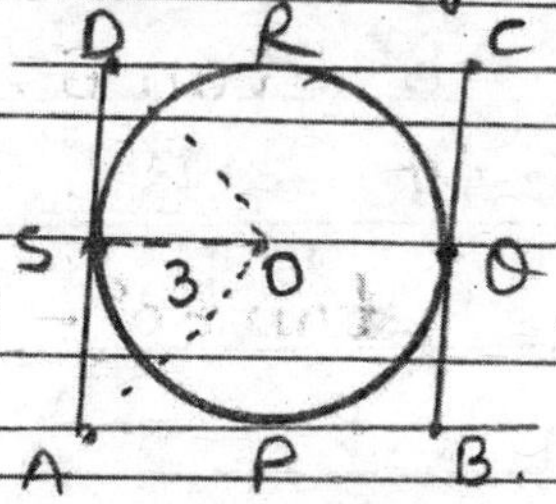

To prove: ABCD is a rhombus

We know tangents draw to a circle from an exterior point are equal in Length.

$\therefore$ AP = AS, BP = BQ, CR = CQ & DR = DS.

AP + BP + CR + DR = AS + BQ + CQ + DS

(AP + BP) + (CR + DR) = (AS + DS) + (BQ + CQ)

$\therefore$ AB + CD = AD + BC

or 2AB = 2AD (since AB = DC and AD = BC of parallelogram ABCD)

$\therefore$ AB = BC = DC = AD

Therefore ABCD is a rhombus.

Given r = 3 cm, side s = 10 cm

Let us construct DO and AO

In ΔDOA

SO = 3 cm radius and AD = 10 cm (side)

Area $= \frac{1}{2} \times$ Base(AD) $\times$ height (SO)

$= \frac{1}{2} \times 10 \times 3 = 15 cm^2$

Area of Rhombus ABCD $= 4 \times 15 = 60 cm^2$.

34. Two poles of equal height are standing opposite each other on either side of a road, which is 100 m wide. From a point somewhere between them on the road, the angles of elevation of the top of the poles are 60° and 30° respectively. Find the height of the poles and the distances of the point from the poles. (5 M)

34. In ΔAOC,

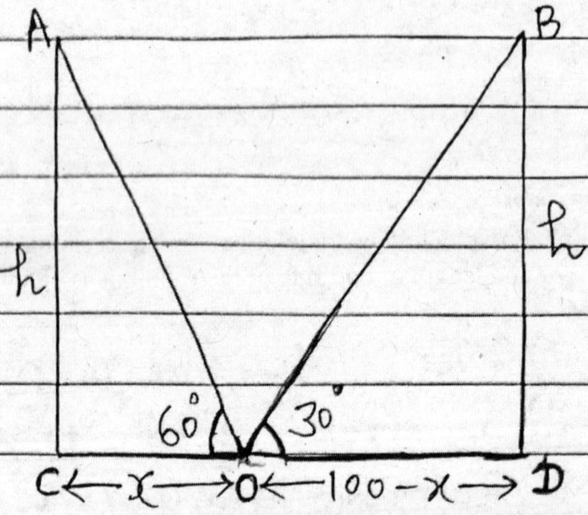

$\tan 60^\circ = \frac{h}{x}$

$\Rightarrow \sqrt{3} = \frac{h}{x} \Rightarrow x = \frac{h}{\sqrt{3}}$

In ΔBOD,

$\tan 30^\circ = \frac{h}{100-x}$

$\Rightarrow \frac{1}{\sqrt{3}} = \frac{h}{100-x} \Rightarrow 100 - x = \sqrt{3}h$

$\Rightarrow 100 - \frac{h}{\sqrt{3}} = \sqrt{3}h$

$\Rightarrow h\left(\frac{3+1}{\sqrt{3}}\right) = 100 \Rightarrow h = 25\sqrt{3}$ m

$\Rightarrow x = \frac{h}{\sqrt{3}} = \frac{25\sqrt{3}}{\sqrt{3}} = 25$m

$\therefore$ OC = 25m and OD = 75m

35. (*a*) Using graphical method, solve the following pair of equations : $x + 2y = 8$ and $3x - 2y = 12$ (5 M)

OR

(*b*) The sum of the digits of a 2 -digit number is 9 . Also, nine times this number is twice the number obtained by reversing the order of the digits. Find the number. (5 M)

35. (b) Let unit digit $= x$

Tens digit $= y$

Number will 10 times the tens digit + unit times the unit digit.

Hence number will $10y + x$.

Sum of digits are 9.

So that

$x+y = 9$ ......(1)

nine times this number is twice the number obtained by reversing the order of the digits.

$9(10y+x) = 2(10x+y)$

$90y + 9x = 20x + 2y$

$88y - 11x = 0$

Divide by 11 we get

$8y - x = 0$ ---- (2)

$x+y = 9$ ---- (1)

Adding both equations we get,

$9y = 9$

$y = 1$

Plug this value in equation first we get,

$x+y=9$, $x+1=9$, $x=8$.

So, our original number $10y+x = 10\times1+8 = 18$.

SECTION - E

Q. No. 36 to 38 are Case Study based questions of 4 marks each.

36. While preparing for a competitive examination. Akbar came across a match-stick pattern based question. The pattern is given below

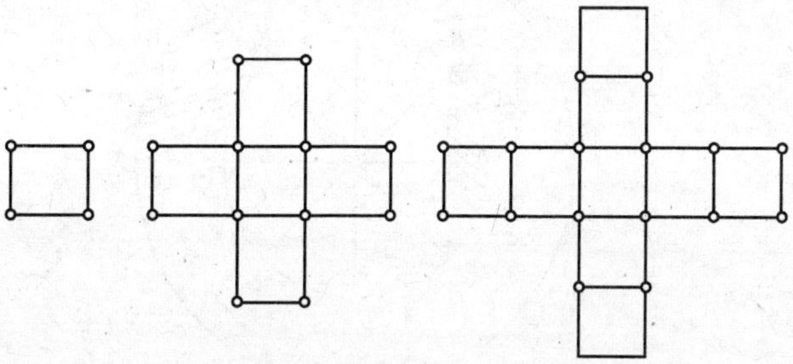

Fig. (1) Fig. (2) Fig. (3)

Based on the above information, answer the following questions :

(*i*) Write first term and common difference of the A.P. formed by number of squares in each figure. (1 M)

(*ii*) Write first term and common difference of the A.P. formed by (1 M)

(*iii*) (*a*) How many squares are there in Fig. (10) ? Also, write the number of sticks used in Fig. (10). (2 M)

OR

(*b*) If 88 sticks are used to make m^{th} figure (Fig. (m)), find the value of m. How many squares are formed in this figure? (2 M)

36. (i) Number of squares in fig (i), (ii) and (iii) are 1, 5, 9 respectively

Here $a = 1$, $d = 5 - 1 = 9 - 5 = 4$

It forms an A.P. where $a = 1$, $d = 4$

(ii) Number of sticks in fig (i), (ii) and (iii) are 4, 16, 28 respectively

$a' = 4$, $d' = 16 - 4 = 12$

First term $a' = 4$

Common difference $= 12$

(iii) (a) In 10th figure

Number of Square, $T_{10} = 1 + (10-1) \times 4$

$= 1 + 9 \times 4 = 1 + 36 = 37$

Number of sticks $T_{10}' = 4 + (10-1) \times 12$

$= 4 + 9 \times 12 = 4 + 108 = 112$

37. NSS (National Service Scheme) aims to connect the students to the community and to involve them in problem solving process. NSS symbol is based on the 'Rath' wheel of the Konark Sun Temple situated in Odisha. The wheel signifies the progress cycle of life. The diagrammatic representation of the symbol is given below :

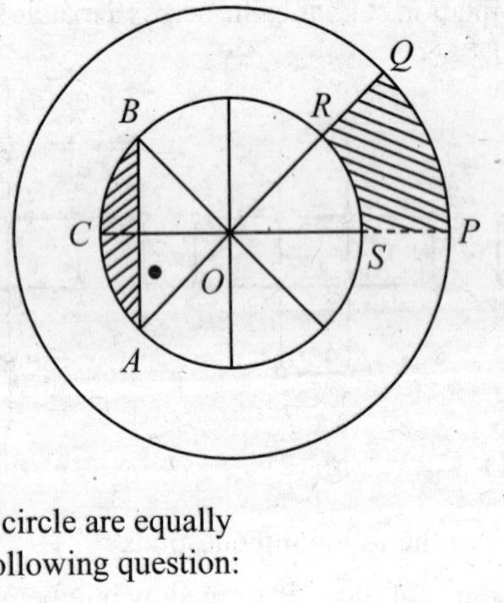

Observe the figure given as placed. Given the circle are equally

Based on the above information, answer the following question:

(*i*) Find $m\angle ROS$. (1 M)

(*ii*) Find the perimeter of sector *OPQ*. (1 M)

(*iii*) (*a*) Find the area of shaded region *PQRS*. (2 M)

OR

(*b*) Find the area of shaded region *ACB* i.e. the segment *ACB*. (2 M)

37. OP = 21 cm , OS = 10 cm

(i) m∠ROS

using area of sector $\frac{\theta}{360}\pi r^2$

as the given diameter of given inner circle are equally placed.

$\therefore \angle ROS = \frac{360°}{8} \Rightarrow 45°$

(ii) perimeter of sector OPQ

Length of arc PQ + OQ + OP $= \frac{45°}{360°} \times 2 \times \frac{22}{7} \times 21 + 21 + 21$

$= \frac{33}{2} + 42 = \frac{33 + 84}{2} = 58.5$ cm.

(iii) (a) Area of shaded region PQRS.

= Area of sector PQ − Area of sector OSR.

$= \frac{\theta}{360°}\pi\left((21)^2 - (10)^2\right) = \frac{45}{360°} \times \frac{22}{7} \times (441 - 100)$

$= \frac{3751}{28}$ cm^2.

38. In the figure given below, a folding table is shown :

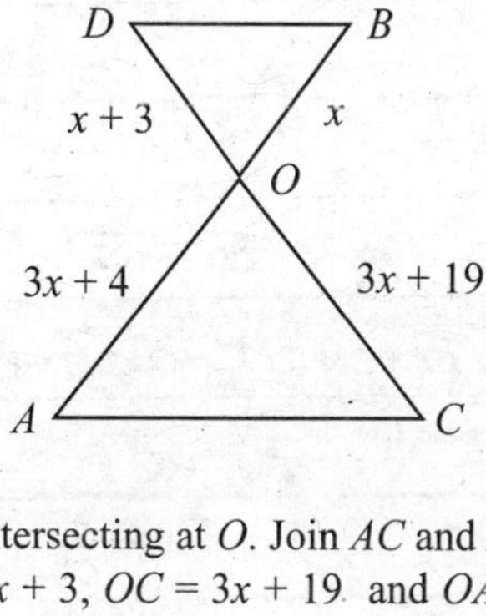

The legs of the table are represented by line segments AB and CD intersecting at O. Join AC and BD.
Considering table top is parallel to the ground, and $OB = x$, $OD = x + 3$, $OC = 3x + 19$ and $OA = 3x + 4$, answer the following questions :

(*i*) Prove that ΔOAC is similar to ΔOBD. (1 M)

(*ii*) Prove that $\frac{OA}{AC} = \frac{OB}{BD}$. (1 M)

(*iii*) (a) Observe the figure and find the value of x. Hence, find the length of OC. (2 M)

OR

(*iii*) (*b*) Observe the figure and find $\frac{BD}{AC}$. (2 M)

38.

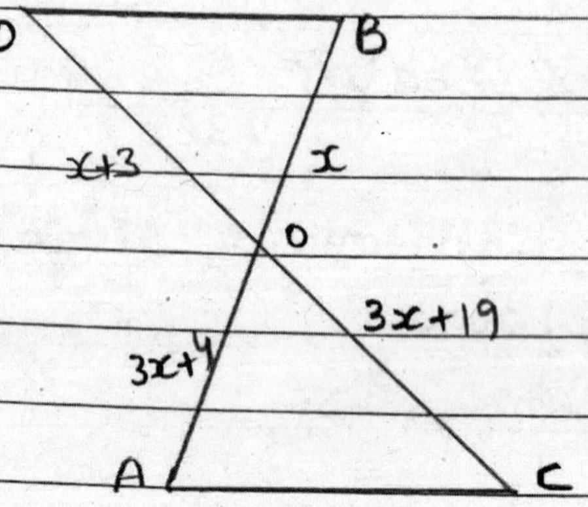

(i) If corresponding side of two similar triangle are in proportional than it is similar.

In ΔOAC and ΔOBD

$$\frac{OA}{OB} = \frac{OC}{OD} \quad --- \text{(I)}$$

$$\frac{3x+4}{x} = \frac{3x+19}{x+3} \quad --- \text{(II)}$$

$$3x^2+4x+9x+12 = 3x^2+19x$$

$$12 = 6x \Rightarrow x = 2.$$

putting $x = 2$ in eq. (I).

$$\frac{3\times2+4}{2} = \frac{3\times2+19}{5}$$

$$\frac{10}{2} = \frac{25}{5}$$

$5 = 5$ $\therefore$ it is similar.

(ii) as we proved above $\Delta OAC \sim \Delta OBD$.

$$\therefore \frac{OA}{AC} = \frac{OB}{BD}$$ [corresponding side of similar Δ are in proportn]

(iii) (a). $x = 2$ $\therefore$ $OC = 25$ cm.

❑❑❑

REAL NUMBERS

1

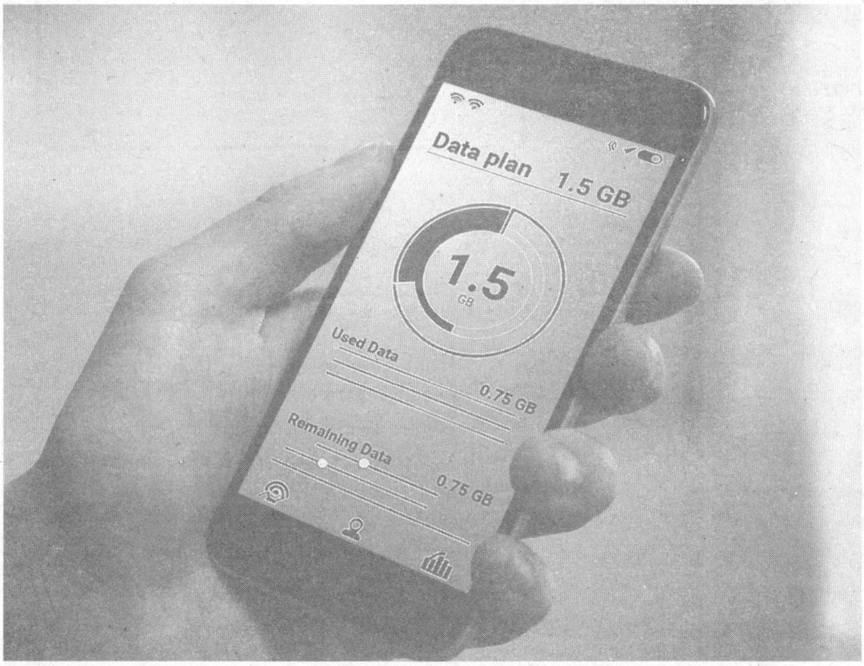

"Smartphone uses real numbers to calculate the amount of data you have used. If your data plan includes 1.5 GB of data per day, and you've used 0.75 GB, the phone calculates the remaining data using subtraction in the set of real numbers."

SYLLABUS & WEIGHTAGE

List of Concept Names	Years				
	2021	2022	2023	2024	2025
The Fundamental Theorem of Arithmetic (Fundamental Theorem of Arithmetic - statements after reviewing work done earlier and after illustrating and motivating through examples)	Exam not Conducted	–	2 Q (1 M each) 1 Q (4 M)	1 Q (2 M) 1 Q (3 M)	1 Q (2 M)
Revisiting Irrational Numbers (Proofs of irrationality of $\sqrt{2}, \sqrt{3}, \sqrt{5}$)		–	–	1 Q (1 M) 1 Q (2 M)	1 Q (1 M) 1 Q (3 M)

CONCEPT MAP

To Access One Shot Revision Video Scan This QR Code

Real Numbers

The Fundamental Theorem of Arithmetic:

- Every composite number can be expressed (factorized) as a product of primes, and this factorisation is unique, apart from the order in which the prime factors occur.

  Note: Fundamental theorem of arithmetic is called a Unique Factorisation Theorem.

  Composite number = Product of prime numbers.

  e.g. ∴ $24 = 2 \times 2 \times 2 \times 3$

  $= 2^3 \times 3$, where 2 and 3 are prime numbers

Theorems:

- **Theorem 1:** Let p be a prime number. If p divides a^2, then p divides a, where a is a positive integer.
- **Theorem 2:** $\sqrt{2}$ is an irrational number.

  Note: Square root of any prime number is always an irrational number

Irrational Numbers:

It cannot be expressed as $x = \frac{p}{q}$, $q \neq 0$. where p and q are integers.

e.g.: $\sqrt{2}, \sqrt{3}, \pi, \ldots$

Prime Factorisation Method:

Prime Factorisation is a way of representing a number as a product of its prime factors. It is also used to find out the H.C.F and L.C.M.

For any two positive integers a and b we have,

H.C.F $(a, b) \times$ L.C.M $(a, b) = a \times b$

e.g.: Find H.C.F of 24 and 36.

Prime factors of 24 : $2^3 \times 3^1$

Prime factors of 36 : $2^2 \times 3^2$

H.C.F $= 2^2 \times 3^1 = 12$

e.g.: Find L.C.M of 12 and 18.

Prime factors of 12 : $2^2 \times 3^1$

Prime factors of 18 : $2^1 \times 3^2$

L.C.M $= 2^2 \times 3^2 = 36$

Rational Numbers:

It can be expressed as $x = \frac{p}{q}$, $q \neq 0$. where p and q are integers.

e.g.: $\frac{1}{4}, \frac{2}{3}, 2, \ldots$

Integers 'Z' or 'I':

Integers include all whole numbers and negative numbers.

e.g.: … –3, –2, –1, 0,2,3,.......

Negative Integer:

e.g.: –1, –2, –3, …

Whole Number 'W':

The whole number which includes all the non-negative integers.

W: 0, 1, 2, 3, …

Zero

Natural Number 'N':

Natural numbers are all positive integers

N: 1, 2, 3, …

Prime Number:

Prime numbers are natural numbers that are divisible by only 1 and the number itself.

e.g. 2, 3, 5, 7, 11, 13.....

Composite Number:

Composite numbers are numbers that have more than two factors.

e.g. 4, 6, 8, 9, 10, 12....

Co-prime Number:

Co-prime numbers are two pairs of numbers which have a common factor of 1.

e.g. (14,15), (1,99), (8,15)

1 THE FUNDAMENTAL THEOREM OF ARITHMETIC

Important Terms

- **Prime Number:** The number which is divisible by either 1 or itself is called a prime number. For e.g. 2, 3, 5, 7 etc. This implies Prime numbers have only two factors i.e., 1 and itself.

  Note: 2 is the smallest Prime number. It is the only even prime number.
- **Composite Number:** The number which has more than two factors is known as a composite number. For e.g. 4, 6, 8, 10 etc.

  Note: (*i*) 1 is neither a prime nor a composite number.

  (*ii*) Smallest composite even number is 4 and smallest composite odd number is 9.

Tricks to Avoid Confusion About Numbers

Odd: 1 2 3	3 is a odd number which is not divisible by 2	
Even: 1 2 3 4	4 is an even number which is divisible by 2	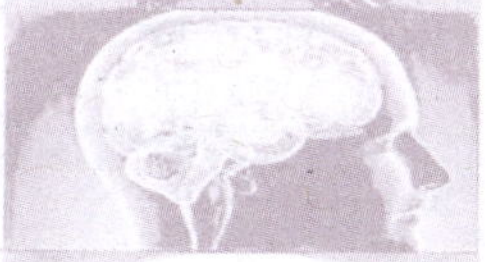
Prime: 1 2 3 4 5	5 is a prime number which is divisible by 1 and itself only	
Composite: 1 2 3 4 5 6 7 8 9	9 is a composite number which is divisible by 1, 3 and 9	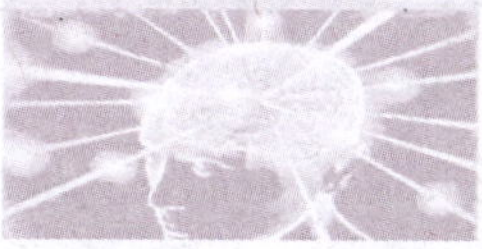

- **Co-prime Number:** Co-prime numbers are numbers that have only one prime factor of 1. This means that a number is said to co-prime when its greatest divisor is 1.
- **Factor of Number:** If a number divides another number exactly (without leaving any remainder), then the number which divides, is called a factor of the number that has been divided. For e.g. 1, 2, 3, 4, 6, 8, 12 and 24 are the factors of 24.
- **Factor Tree:** It is a chain of factors of a number, which is represented in the form of a tree.
- **Prime Factorisation:** Prime Factorisation is a way of representing a number as a product of its prime factors. And it is also used to find out the H.C.F and L.C.M.
- **H.C.F:** The H.C.F defines the greatest factor present in between given two or more numbers.

  Note: H.C.F of two or more prime numbers is always 1.

  H.C.F of 60 and 72 = $2 \times 2 \times 3 = 12$
- **L.C.M:** L.C.M is the Least Common Multiple of the given numbers.

  L.C.M. of 60 and 72 = $2 \times 2 \times 2 \times 3 \times 3 \times 5 = 360$

Important Formulas

- For any two positive integers a and b we have,

  H.C.F $(a, b) \times$ L.C.M $(a, b) = a \times b$.
- H.C.F $(p, q, r) \times$ L.C.M $(p, q, r) \neq p \times q \times r$, where p, q, r are positive integers. However, the following results hold good for three numbers p, q and r:

$$\text{LCM}(p,q,r) = \frac{p.q.r.\,\text{HCF}(p,q,r)}{\text{HCF}(p,q).\,\text{HCF}(q,r).\,\text{HCF}(p,r)}$$

$$\text{HCF}(p, q, r) = \frac{p.q.r.\,\text{LCM}(p,q,r)}{\text{LCM}(p,q).\,\text{LCM}(q,r).\,\text{LCM}(p,r)}$$

Important Concepts

- **The Fundamental Theorem of Arithmetic:** Every composite number can be expressed (factorized) as a product of primes, and this factorisation is unique, apart from the order in which the prime factors occur.

  Note: Fundamental theorem of arithmetic is called a Unique Factorisation Theorem.

  Composite number = Product of prime numbers.

  For example:

  (*i*) $2 \times 11 = 22$ is the same as $11 \times 2 = 22$.

  (*ii*) 6 can be written as 2×3 or 3×2, where 2 and 3 are prime numbers.

  (*iii*) 15 can be written as 3×5 or 5×3, where 3 and 5 are prime numbers.

  The prime Factorisation of a natural number is unique, except to the order of its factors. e.g., 12 detained by multiplying the prime numbers 2, 2 and 3 together,

  $12 = 2 \times 2 \times 3$

  We would probably write it as

  $12 = 2^2 \times 3$
- **Prime Factorisation Method to find H.C.F and L.C.M:**

  (*i*) Find all the prime factors of given numbers.

  e.g. $1296 = 2 \times 2 \times 2 \times 2 \times 3 \times 3 \times 3 \times 3 = 2^4 \times 3^4$

  $2520 = 2 \times 2 \times 2 \times 3 \times 3 \times 5 \times 7 = 2^3 \times 3^2 \times 5 \times 7$

  (*ii*) H.C.F of two or more numbers = Product of the smallest power of each common prime factor, present in the numbers.

  $\therefore$ H.C.F (1296, 2520) = $2^3 \times 3^2 = 72$

  (*iii*) L.C.M of two or more numbers = Product of the greatest power of each prime factor, present in the numbers.

  $\therefore$ L.C.M (1296, 2520) = $2^4 \times 3^4 \times 5 \times 7 = 45360$

Real Life Applications

Here are some real-life applications of real numbers:

1. Banking and Finance:

- **Interest rates:** Real numbers are used to represent interest rates on loans and investments.
- **Account balances:** Real numbers are used to represent the balances in bank accounts, investments, and financial transactions.

2. Computer Science:

- **Algorithms and programming:** Real numbers are used in computer programming for various applications, including simulations, graphics, and scientific computations.

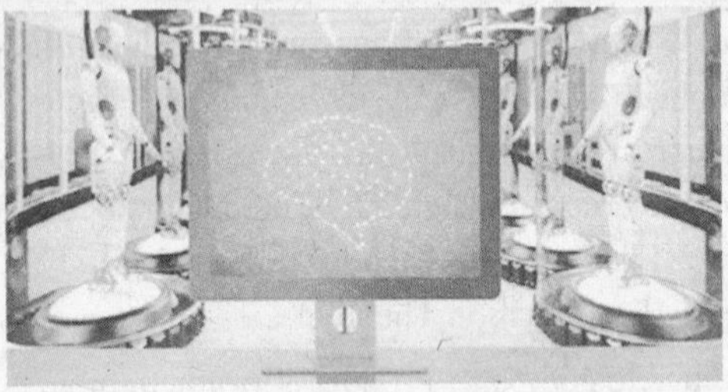

3. Economics:

- **Price indices:** Real numbers are used to represent price indices, inflation rates, and economic indicators in the field of economics.

Different Problem Types

Type I: Expressing a Positive Integer as a Product of its Prime Factors

Suppose we need to find the prime factorisation of 176

Solution:

Step I: Divide the given number by the smallest prime number 2.

Here, we divide 176 by 2.

$\Rightarrow 176 \div 2 = 88$

Step II: Again, divide the quotient of step I by the smallest prime number 2.

So, 88 is again divided by 2.

$\Rightarrow 88 \div 2 = 44$

Step III: Repeat the process, until the quotient becomes 1.

Now, again divide 44 by 2.

$\Rightarrow 44 \div 2 = 22$

22 is divisible by 2. So, divide it again by 2.

$\Rightarrow 22 \div 2 = 11$

As 11 is a prime number, divide it by 11 to get 1.

$\Rightarrow 11 \div 11 = 1$

2	176
2	88
2	44
2	22
11	11
	1

Step IV: Finally, multiply all the prime factors that are the divisors.

Prime factorisation of 176 is $2 \times 2 \times 2 \times 2 \times 11 = 2^4 \times 11$

Example: Find the prime factorisation of 980.

Solution: Prime factorisation of 980:

2	980
2	490
5	245
7	49
7	7
	1

$\Rightarrow 980 = 2 \times 2 \times 5 \times 7 \times 7 = 2^2 \times 5 \times 7^2$

Type II: Finding the H.C.F and L.C.M of Positive Integers

Suppose we need to find the H.C.F and L.C.M of 144, 180 and 192.

Solution:

Step I: Find Prime Factorization

First, we'll find the prime factorization of each number:

$144 = 2 \times 2 \times 2 \times 2 \times 3 \times 3 = 2^4 \times 3^2$

$180 = 2 \times 2 \times 3 \times 3 \times 5 = 2^2 \times 3^2 \times 5^1$

$192 = 2 \times 2 \times 2 \times 2 \times 2 \times 2 \times 3 = 2^6 \times 3^1$

Step II: Find H.C.F (Highest Common Factor)

We identify the common prime factors with the lowest power.

$144 = 2^4 \times 3^2$

$180 = \textcircled{2^2} \times 3^2 \times 5^1$

$192 = 2^6 \times \textcircled{3^1}$

$\Rightarrow$ Lowest power with common prime factors: 2^2, 3^1

Hence, H.C.F $= 2^2 \times 3^1 = 12$

Step III: Find L.C.M (Lowest Common Multiple)

We identify the common prime factors with the highest power.

$144 = 2^4 \times \textcircled{3^2}$

$180 = 2^2 \times 3^2 \times \textcircled{5^1}$

$192 = \textcircled{2^6} \times 3^1$

$\Rightarrow$ Highest power with common prime factors: $2^6, 3^2, 5^1$

Hence, L.C.M = $2^6 \times 3^2 \times 5^1 = 2880$

Example: Find the H.C.F and L.C.M of 20 and 12 by the prime factorisation method.

Solution: Prime factorisation of 20 = $2 \times 2 \times 5 = 2^2 \times 5$

Prime factorisation of 12 = $2 \times 2 \times 3 = 2^2 \times 3$

Lowest power with common prime factors: 2^2

Hence, H.C.F = $2^2 = 4$

Highest power with common prime factors: $2^2, 3^1, 5^1$

Hence, L.C.M = $2^2 \times 3^1 \times 5^1 = 60$

Type III: Finding the H.C.F and L.C.M of Polynomial

Suppose we need to find the H.C.F of $48x^5y^2$ and $112x^3y$, where x, y are prime numbers.

Solution:

Step I: Find Prime Factorization

Prime factorization of $48x^5y^2 = 2^4 \times 3^1 \times x^5 \times y^2$

Prime factorization of $112x^3y = 2^4 \times 7^1 \times x^3 \times y$

Step II: Find H.C.F (Highest Common Factor)

We identify the common prime factors with the lowest power.

$48x^5y^2 = 2^4 \times 3^1 \times x^5 \times y^2$

$112x^3y = \textcircled{2^4} \times 7^1 \times \textcircled{x^3} \times \textcircled{y}$

Lowest power with common prime factors: $2^4, x^3, y$

Hence, H.C.F = $2^4 \times x^3 \times y = 16x^3y$

Step III: Find L.C.M (Lowest Common Multiple)

We identify the common prime factors with the highest power.

$48x^5y^2 = 2^4 \times 3^1 \times \textcircled{x^5} \times \textcircled{y^2}$

$112x^3y = \textcircled{2^4} \times 7^1 \times x^3 \times y$

$\Rightarrow$ Highest power with common prime factors: $2^4, x^5, y^2$

Other prime factor with highest power: $3^1, 7^1$

Hence, L.C.M = $2^4 \times 3^1 \times 7^1 \times x^5 \times y^2 = 16 \times 3 \times 7 \times x^5 \times y^2 = 336x^5y^2$

Example: Find the H.C.F and L.C.M of $8x^2y^2$, $12x^3y^2$ and $24x^4y^3z^2$, where x, y are prime numbers.

Solution: Express each polynomial as a product of powers of irreducible factors.

$8x^2y^2 = 2^3 \times x^2 \times y^2$

$12x^3y^2 = 2^2 \times 3^1 \times x^3 \times y^2$

$24x^4y^3z^2 = 2^3 \times 3^1 \times x^4 \times y^3 \times z^2$

Hence, H.C.F is $2^2 \times x^2 \times y^2 = 4x^2y^2$

And the L.C.M is $2^3 \times 3^1 \times x^4 \times y^3 \times z^2 = 24x^4y^3z^2$

COMPETENCY BASED SOLVED EXAMPLES

Multiple Choice Questions (1 M)

1. If the H.C.F of 360 and 64 is 8, then their L.C.M is: *(An)* **(CBSE, 2023)**

(*a*) 2480 (*b*) 2780 (*c*) 512 (*d*) 2880

Sol. We are given:

H.C.F (360, 64) = 8

The formula to find L.C.M using H.C.F and product of the numbers is:

$$\text{L.C.M. } (a, b) = \frac{a \times b}{\text{H.C.F}(a,b)}$$

Substituting the given values:

$a = 360$, $b = 64$

$$\text{L.C.M } (360, 64) = \frac{360 \times 64}{8} = \frac{23040}{8} = 2880$$

2. The least number that is divisible by all the natural numbers from 1 to 10 (both inclusive) is *(An)* **(NCERT Exemplar)**

(*a*) 10 (*b*) 100 (*c*) 504 (*d*) 2520

Sol. The least number divisible by all the numbers from 1 to 10 will be the L.C.M of the following number: 1, 2, 3, 4, 5, 6, 7, 8, 9 & 10.

Prime factorisation of these numbers are $1 = 1$, $2 = 2$, $3 = 3$, $4 = 2 \times 2$, $5 = 5$, $6 = 2 \times 3$, $7 = 7$, $8 = 2 \times 2 \times 2$, $9 = 3 \times 3$, $10 = 2 \times 5$

So, the L.C.M of these number is

$1 \times 2 \times 2 \times 2 \times 3 \times 3 \times 5 \times 7 = 2520$

Key Takeaways

Check that the correct option should be divisible by all the natural numbers 1–10 as the L.C.M is the lowest common multiple.

3. 120 can be expressed as a product of its prime factors as *(An)* **(CBSE, 2020)**

(*a*) $5 \times 8 \times 3$ (*b*) 15×2^3

(*c*) $10 \times 2^2 \times 3$ (*d*) $5 \times 2^3 \times 3$

Sol. Let's find the prime factors of 120:

$120 = 2 \times 60 = 2 \times 2 \times 30$

$= 2 \times 2 \times 2 \times 15 = 2 \times 2 \times 2 \times 3 \times 5$

So, the prime factorization of 120 is $2^3 \times 3 \times 5$.

4. If two positive integers *a* and *b* are written as $a = x^3y^2$ and $b = xy^3$; *x*, *y* are prime numbers, then H.C.F (*a*, *b*) is *(An)* **(CBSE SQP, 2023)**

(*a*) xy (*b*) xy^2 (*c*) x^3y^3 (*d*) x^2y^2

Sol. It is given that, $a = x^3y^2$ and $b = xy^3$, where *x* and *y* are prime numbers.

L.C.M (a, b) = L.C.M (x^2y^2, xy^3)

= The highest of powers of *x* and $y = x^3y^3$

H.C.F (a, b) = H.C.F (x^2y^2, xy^3)

The lowest of powers of *x* and $y = xy^2$

Hence, H.C.F$(a, b) = xy^2$ and L.C.M$(a, b) = x^3y^3$.

5. The L.C.M of smallest two-digit composite number and smallest composite number is *(An)* **(CBSE SQP, 2023)**

(*a*) 12 (*b*) 4 (*c*) 20 (*d*) 44

Sol. By prime factorisation, we get;

$4 = 1 \times 2 \times 2$

$10 = 1 \times 2 \times 5$

Now, L.C.M of 4, $10 = 2 \times 2 \times 5 = 20$

Therefore, the L.C.M of the smallest two-digit composite number and the smallest composite number is 20.

Key Takeaways

The smallest 2-digit number = 10 and the smallest composite number = 4

6. If two positive integers *a* and *b* can be expressed as $p = ab^2$ and $q = a^3b$; *a*, *b* being prime numbers, then L.C.M (*p*, *q*) is *(Ap)* **(NCERT Exemplar)**

(*a*) ab (*b*) a^2b^2 (*c*) a^3b^2 (*d*) a^3b^3

Sol. Let's express each polynomial as a product of the power of irreducible factors.

$p = ab^2 = a \times b^2$, $q = a^3b = a^3 \times b$

To find the L.C.M, raise each irreducible factor to the greatest exponent.

$\therefore$ L.C.M $= a^3 \times b^2 = a^3b^2$

Mistakes 101 : What not to do!

Sometimes, students take the term with the lower power from numbers to calculate the L.C.M of numbers.

7. The ratio between the L.C.M and H.C.F of 5, 15, 20 is *(Ap)*

(*a*) 9 : 1 (*b*) 4 : 3

(*c*) 11 : 1 (*d*) 12 : 1

Sol. Prime factorisations are:

$5 = 5^1$, $15 = 3^1 \times 5^1$, $20 = 2^2 \times 5^1$

L.C.M $(5, 15, 20) = 2^2 \times 3^1 \times 5^1 = 60$

H.C.F $(5, 15, 20) = 5^1 = 5$

$$\text{Ratio} = \frac{\text{LCM}}{\text{HCF}} = \frac{60}{5} = 12$$

Ratio = 12 : 1

Nailing the Right Answer

Student should remember, the greatest possible of any two or three numbers can be determined using H.C.F.

8. Prime factors of 98 are ***(Ap)***

(*a*) 2×7^3 (*b*) 3×7^3 (*c*) 2×7^2 (*d*) 2×7^5

Sol. $98 = 2 \times 49$

Now, we continue factoring 49:

$49 = 7 \times 7$

Since both factors are 7, we have:

$98 = 2 \times 7 \times 7$

Thus, the prime factorisation of 98 is $2 \times 7 \times 7$ i.e., 2×7^2.

9. The H.C.F and the L.C.M of 12, 21, 15 respectively are ***(An)***

(*a*) 3, 140 (*b*) 12, 420 (*c*) 3, 420 (*d*) 420, 3

Sol. Prime factor of given number is

$12 = 2 \times 2 \times 3$

$15 = 3 \times 5$

$21 = 3 \times 7$

H.C.F = Product of smallest power of each common prime factor = $3 \times 1 = 3$

L.C.M = Product of greatest power of each prime factor = $2^2 \times 3 \times 5 \times 7 = 4 \times 3 \times 5 \times 7 = 420$

Hence, the H.C.F and L.C.M of 12, 21, 15 are 3 and 420 respectively.

10. The greatest number which when divides 1251, 9377 and 15628 leaves remainder 1, 2 and 3 respectively is ***(An)***

(*a*) 575 (*b*) 750

(*c*) 450 (*d*) 625

Sol. Numbers are: (1251 – 1), (9377 – 2) and (15628 – 3) or 1250, 9375 and 15625.

Required number is the H.C.F of 1250, 9375 and 15625.

Now, $1250 = 2 \times 5^4$

$9375 = 3 \times 5^5$

$15625 = 5^6$

H.C.F $= 5^4 = 625$

$\therefore$ 625 is the largest number that divides 1251, 9377 and 15628 leaving remainders 1, 2 and 3 respectively.

Mistakes 101 : What not to do!

Students often make mistakes in remainder value problems. To avoid errors, find differences between numbers and remainders, then apply the H.C.F concept.

11. If the L.C.M of *P* and 18 is 36 and the H.C.F of *P* and 18 is 2, then *P* equals: ***(Ap)***

(*a*) 2 (*b*) 3

(*c*) 1 (*d*) 4

Sol. We know that:

L.C.M $(P, 18) \times$ H.C.F $(P, 18) = P \times 18$

Given values: $36 \times 2 = P \times 18$

$72 = 18P$

Dividing both sides by 18, we get

$$P = \frac{72}{18} = 4$$

So, $P = 4$

12. If two positive integers *a* and *b* can be expressed as $p = ab^2$ and $q = a^3b$: *a*, *b* being prime numbers, then L.C.M (*p*, *q*) is ***(Ev)***

(*a*) ab (*b*) a^2b^2

(*c*) a^3b^2 (*d*) a^3b^3

Sol. Given, $p = a \times b \times b$; $q = a \times a \times a \times b$ Therefore L.C.M of p and $q = a^3b^2$.

13. Product of two numbers is 48. If their L.C.M. is 12 then then H.C.F. is equal to ***(Ap)***

(*a*) 4 (*b*) 12

(*c*) 48 (*d*) 2

Sol. $\text{H.C.F.} = \frac{\text{Product}}{\text{L.C.M.}} = \frac{48}{12} = 4$

14. H.C.F of two prime numbers is ***(Un)***

(*a*) 0 (*b*) 1

(*c*) 2 (*d*) 3

Sol. The H.C.F (Highest Common Factor) of two prime numbers is always 1.

This is because prime numbers are divisible only by 1 and themselves. Therefore, the only common factor between two distinct prime numbers is 1.

15. L.C.M of 6, 72 and 120 is ***(Ap)***

(*a*) 360 (*b*) 260

(*c*) 180 (*d*) None of these

Sol. Prime factorisation of 6, 72 and 120 are:

$6 = 2 \times 3$,

$72 = 2^3 \times 3^2$,

$120 = 2^3 \times 3 \times 5$

$\therefore$ L.C.M $(6, 72, 120) = 2^3 \times 3^2 \times 5 = 360$

Answer Key

1. (d)	2. (d)	3. (d)	4. (b)	5. (c)
6. (c)	7. (d)	8. (c)	9. (c)	10. (d)
11. (d)	12. (c)	13. (a)	14. (b)	15. (a)

Assertion and Reason **(1 M)**

Direction: In the following questions, a statement of Assertion (A) is followed by a statement of Reason (R). Mark the correct choice as.

(*a*) Both Assertion (A) and Reason (R) are true, and Reason (R) is the correct explanation of Assertion (A).

(*b*) Both Assertion (A) and Reason (R) are true, but Reason (R) is not the correct explanation of Assertion (A).

(*c*) Assertion (A) is true, but Reason (R) is false.

(*d*) Assertion (A) is false, but Reason (R) is true.

1. A number q is prime factorised as $3^2 \times 7^2 \times b$, where b is a prime number other than 3 and 7.
Assertion (A): q is definitely an odd number.
Reason (R): $3^2 \times 7^2$ is an odd number. *(An)*

Sol. $q = 3^2 \times 7^2 \times b$, where b is a prime number.
Possible prime numbers for b are 2, 5, 11, ...
We know that
Square of an odd number is odd.
$\therefore$ 3^2 and 7^2 are odd numbers
and the product of two odd numbers is odd.
$\therefore$ $3^2 \times 7^2$ is odd number.
Reason (R) is correct.
If $b = 2$, then
$(3^2 \times 7^2) \times (2)$ = odd number × even number = even number
Assertion (A) is false.
Assertion (A) is false but Reason is true.

2. Assertion (A): 5^n can never end with digit '0' for any Natural number n.
Reason (R): The prime factorisation of 5^n does not contain the prime numbers 2 and 5. *(An)*

Sol. If a number 5^n for any natural number n has to end With digit '0', then it would be divisible by 2 and 5 both, i.e., the prime factorisation of 5^n must contain the prime 2 and 5.
The prime factorisation of 5^n contains only 5, so, The there is not natural number 5 for which 5^n ends with the digit Zero.

3. Assertion (A): The H.C.F of two numbers is 145 and their L.C.M is 2175. If one number is 725, then the Other number is 425. *(Un)*
Reason (R): H.C.F × L.C.M = product of two given numbers.

Sol. We have been given,
H.C.F of the number = 145.
L.C.M of the number = 2175.
First number = 725.
We know,
The product of the numbers ($a \times b$) = H.C.F. × L.C.M.
Reason (R) is true.
Substituting the given values in above,
Let the second number be x,
$725 \times x = 145 \times 2175$
$\Rightarrow x = \frac{(145 \times 2175)}{725} \Rightarrow x = 435$
Therefore, the second number is 435.
Assertion (A) is false.
Hence, Assertion (A) is false but Reason is true.

Answer Key

1. (*d*) 2. (*a*) 3. (*d*)

Subjective Questions

Very Short Answer Type Questions (1 or 2 M)

1. Find the L.C.M of 150 and 200. *(Ap)* **(CBSE, 2020)**

Sol. To find the L.C.M (Least Common Multiple) of 150 and 200, we'll first find the prime factorization of both numbers.
Prime factorization of 150:
$150 = 2 \times 3 \times 5^2$ *(½ M)*
Prime factorization of 200:
$200 = 2^3 \times 5^2$ *(½ M)*
Now, to find the L.C.M, we need to take the highest power of each prime factor that appears in the factorization of either number:
L.C.M (150, 200) = $2^3 \times 3 \times 5^2$
L.C.M (150, 200) = $8 \times 3 \times 25$
L.C.M (150, 200) = 600
So, the L.C.M of 150 and 200 is 600. *(1 M)*

2. Explain why $7 \times 11 \times 13 + 13$ and $7 \times 6 \times 5 \times 4 \times 3 \times 2 \times 1 + 5$ are composite numbers. *(An)* **(NCERT Intext)**

Sol. It can be observed that
$7 \times 11 \times 13 + 13 = 13 \times (7 \times 11 + 1) = 13 \times (77 + 1)$
$= 13 \times 78 = 13 \times 13 \times 6$ *(½ M)*
The given expression has 6 and 13 as its factors. Therefore, it is a composite number.
$7 \times 6 \times 5 \times 4 \times 3 \times 2 \times 1 + 5 = 5 \times (7 \times 6 \times 4 \times 3 \times 2 \times 1 + 1)$
$= 5 \times (1008 + 1) = 5 \times 1009$ *(½ M)*
1009 cannot be factorised further. Therefore, the given expression has 5 and 1009 as its factors. Hence, it is a composite number. *(1 M)*

3. Express 729 as its prime factor *(Un)*

Sol. *(1 M)*

3	729
3	243
3	81
3	27
3	9
	3

Prime factor of 729 = $3 \times 3 \times 3 \times 3 \times 3 \times 3$ *(1 M)*

4. **Explain why $17 \times 11 \times 2 + 17 \times 11 \times 5$ is a composite number?** *(An)*

Sol. $17 \times 11 \times 2 + 17 \times 11 \times 5$

$= 17 \times 11 \times (2 + 5) = 17 \times 11 \times 7$ *(1 M)*

Since, $17 \times 11 \times 2 + 17 \times 11 \times 5$ can be expressed as a product of primes, therefore, it is a composite number. *(1 M)*

Short Answer Type Questions (2 or 3 M)

1. **Check whether 6^n can end with the digit '0' (zero) for any natural number n.** *(An)* **(CBSE, 2020)**

Sol. To determine whether 6^n can end with the digit '0' for any natural number n, we need to analyze the prime factorization of 6.

The prime factorization of 6 is 2×3. When you raise 6 to any power, it's essentially multiplying 6 by itself that many times. In other words, 6^n will always contain factors of both 2 and 3. *(1 M)*

To end with the digit '0', a number needs to be divisible by 10, which means it needs to have a factor of 2 and a factor of 5. *(½ M)*

Since 6^n only has factors of 2 and 3, it can never end with the digit '0' for any natural number n. Therefore, 6^n cannot end with the digit '0'. *(½ M)*

2. **Given that H.C.F (306, 657) = 9. Find L.C.M (306, 657).** *(Ap)*

Sol. Given that H.C.F (306, 657) = 9, As we know that,

H.C.F × L.C.M = Product of numbers *(1 M)*

$\therefore\ 9 \times \text{L.C.M} = 306 \times 657$

$\Rightarrow \text{L.C.M} = \dfrac{306 \times 657}{9} = 22338$ *(1 M)*

3. **Consider the numbers 4^n, where n is a natural number. Check whether there is any value of n for which 4^n ends with the digit zero.** *(An)* **(NCERT Intext)**

Sol. If the number 4^n, for any n, were to end with the digit zero, then it would be divisible by 5. That is, the prime factorisation of 4^n would contain the prime 5. This is not possible because $4^n = (2 \times 2)^n$; so the only prime in the factorisation of 4^n is 2. So, the uniqueness of the Fundamental Theorem of Arithmetic guarantees that there are no other primes in the factorisation of 4^n. So, there is no natural number n for which 4^n ends with the digit zero. *(3 M)*

4. **Find the H.C.F of the numbers 540 and 630, using prime factorization method.** *(Ap)* **(CBSE, 2023)**

Sol. To find the H.C.F of 540 and 630 using prime factorization:

Prime factorization of $540 = 2^2 \times 3^3 \times 5$ *(½ M)*

Prime factorization of $630 = 2 \times 3^2 \times 5 \times 7$ *(½ M)*

The common prime factors are 2, 3 and 5.

$\text{H.C.F} = 2^1 \times 3^2 \times 5^1 = 2 \times 9 \times 5 = 90$

So, the H.C.F of 540 and 630 is 90.

5. **Find H.C.F and L.C.M of 404 and 96 and verify that H.C.F × L.C.M = Product of the two given numbers.** *(Ev)*

Sol. Let $a = 404$ and $b = 96$

Expressing the number as a product of prime number

$404 = 2 \times 2 \times 101$ *(½ M)*

$96 = 2 \times 2 \times 2 \times 2 \times 2 \times 3$ *(½ M)*

$\therefore$ L.C.M of 404 and 96 is $2 \times 2 \times 2 \times 2 \times 2 \times 101 \times 3 = 9696$

$\therefore$ H.C.F of 404 and 96 is $2 \times 2 = 4$ *(1 M)*

Now, H.C.F × L.C.M $= 4 \times 9696 = 38784$

Product of two given numbers $404 \times 96 = 38784$

Hence H.C.F × L.C.M = Product of two given numbers. *(1 M)*

6. **Can the number 6^n, n being a natural number, end with the digit 5? Give reason.** *(An)* **(NCERT Intext)**

Sol. Let $x = 6^n = (2 \times 3)^n$ *(1 M)*

Here in our given number 6^n there are only two prime factors of 6 which are 2 and 3. *(1 M)*

To end the number 6^n with digit 5 there should be a factor of 5 but we don't have any factor in the form of 5 hence it will never end with 5 for any value of n. *(1 M)*

2 REVISITING IRRATIONAL NUMBERS

Important Terms

- **Real Numbers:** Real numbers are the set of all positive and negative integers, along with zero. For e.g., –3, –1, 0, 1, 2, 3 etc. It is denoted by R.

  Note: A number, which is either rational or irrational, is called a real number.

- **Rational Numbers:** The numbers which can be expressed as p/q, where p and q are integers and $q \neq 0$, are known as rational numbers and it is denoted by Q. For e.g. 5, –7, 5/9, –3/7, etc.
- **Irrational Numbers:** The numbers which cannot be expressed as p/q, where p and q are integers and $q \neq 0$, are known as irrational numbers. It is denoted by R\\$Q$. For e.g. $\sqrt{2}, \pi, -\frac{\sqrt{3}}{\sqrt{5}}$ etc.

Not everyone will get this

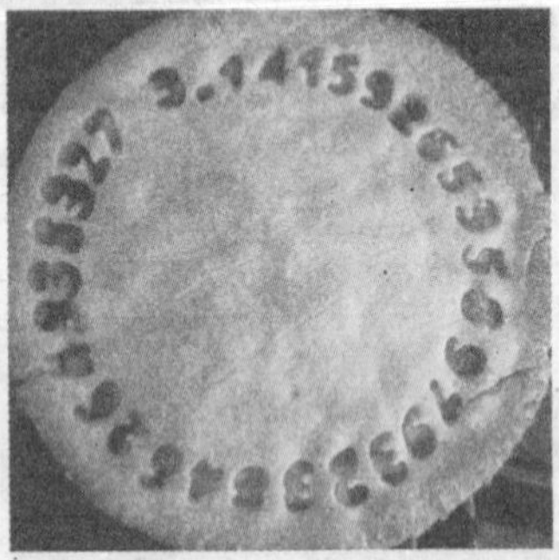

Important Derivations

- **Theorem 1:** Let p be a prime number. If p divides a^2, then p divides a, where a is a positive integer.

  Proof: Let the prime Factorisation of a be as follows:

  $a = p^1, p^2, \ldots p^n$, where $p^1, p^2, \ldots, p^n$ are primes, not necessarily distinct.

  Therefore, $a^2 = (p^1, p^2, \ldots p^n)(p^1, p^2 \ldots p^n) = (p^1)^2, (p^2)2 \ldots (p^n)^2$.

  Now, we are given that p divides a^2. Therefore, from the Fundamental Theorem of Arithmetic, it follows that p is one of the prime factors of a^2. However, using the uniqueness part of the Fundamental Theorem of Arithmetic, we realize that the only prime factors of a^2 are $p^1, p^2, \ldots, p^n$. So p is one of $p^1, p^2, \ldots, p^n$.

  Now, since $a = p^1, p^2, \ldots p^n$.

  p divides a.

- **Theorem 2:** $\sqrt{2}$ is an irrational number.

  Proof: Let's assume, to the contrary, that $\sqrt{2}$ is rational.

  Then $\sqrt{2} = a/b$, where a and b are co-prime.

  So, $\sqrt{2}b = a$.

  On squaring both sides, we get

  $a^2 = (\sqrt{2}b)^2$

  Therefore, 2 divides a^2.

  This implies that 2 divides a.

  So, we can write $a = 2c$ for some integer c.

  Again on squaring both sides, we get

  $a^2 = 4c^2$

  $\Rightarrow 2b^2 = 4c^2$ $\quad [\because a^2 = 2b^2]$

  $\Rightarrow b^2 = 2c^2$

  This means that 2 divides b^2 and therefore 2 divides b (again using Theorem 3).

  Therefore, a and b have at least 2 as a common factor.

  But this contradicts the fact that a and b do not have a common factor other than 1.

  This contradiction has arisen because of our wrong assumption that $\sqrt{2}$ is a rational number.

  So, we conclude that $\sqrt{2}$ is an irrational number.

Important Concepts

- **Method of Finding Irrationality of Numbers:** We know that, a number is an irrational number, if it cannot be written or expressed in the form p/q, where p, q are integers and $q \neq 0$, Infact, for any prime number. p, $\sqrt{q}$ is an irrational number. To prove the irrationality of the numbers, we use the method of contradiction.

Different Problem Types

Type I: Prove that $\sqrt{p}$ is an Irrational Number, Where p is a Prime Number

Proof: Let us assume that $\sqrt{p}$ is rational and its simplest form be $\frac{a}{b}$, where a and b are co-prime positive integers and $b \neq 0$.

So, $\sqrt{p} = \frac{a}{b}$

On squaring both the sides, we get

$p = \frac{a^2}{b^2}$

$\Rightarrow pb^2 = a^2$ ... (*i*)

Thus, p divides a^2.

$\Rightarrow p$ divides a ... (*ii*)

So, we can write $a = pc$ for some integer c.

On squaring both the sides, we get

$a^2 = p^2 c^2$

$\Rightarrow pb^2 = p^2 c^2$ [From (*i*)]

$\Rightarrow b^2 = p c^2$

Thus, p divides b^2.

$\Rightarrow p$ divides b ... (*iii*)

From eq. (*ii*) and (*iii*), we get p as a common factor of a and b.

But this contradicts the fact that a and b are co-primes. This contradiction has arisen due to our wrong assumption.

Thus, $\sqrt{p}$ is irrational.

Example: Prove that $\sqrt{7}$ is an irrational number.

Solution: Let's assume, to the contrary, that $\sqrt{7}$ is rational.

Then $\sqrt{7} = a/b$, where a and b are co-prime.

So, $\sqrt{7}b = a$.

On squaring both sides, we get

$a^2 = (\sqrt{7}b)^2$

Therefore, 7 divides a^2.

This implies that 7 divides a.

So, we can write $a = 7c$ for some integer c.

Again on squaring both sides, we get

$a^2 = 49c^2$

$\Rightarrow 7b^2 = 49c^2 \Rightarrow b^2 = 7c^2$ [$\because a^2 = 2b^2$]

This means that 7 divides b^2 and therefore 7 divides b (again using Theorem 3).

Therefore, a and b have at least 7 as a common factor.

But this contradicts the fact that a and b do not have a common factor other than 1.

This contradiction has arisen because of our wrong assumption that $\sqrt{7}$ is a rational number.

Thus, $\sqrt{7}$ is an irrational number.

Type II: Prove that $m \pm \sqrt{n}$ is Irrational, Where n is a Prime Number

Suppose we need to prove that $4 - \sqrt{5}$ is an irrational number.

Solution:

Step I: Assume $4 - \sqrt{5}$ is a rational number.

Let us assume to the contrary that $4 - \sqrt{5}$ is rational. Then, there exist co-prime positive integers a and b such that

$4 - \sqrt{5} = \frac{a}{b}$

Step II: Now, isolate $\sqrt{5}$.

$\Rightarrow 4 - \frac{a}{b} = \sqrt{5} \Rightarrow \frac{4b - a}{b} = \sqrt{5}$

$\Rightarrow \sqrt{5}$ is rational. [$\therefore$ a, b are integers $\because \frac{4b - a}{b}$ is a rational number]

This contradicts the fact that $\sqrt{5}$ is an irrational number. So, our assumption is incorrect. Hence, $4 - \sqrt{5}$ is an irrational number.

Example: Prove that $3 + 2\sqrt{5}$ is irrational. (NCERT Intext)

Solution: Let us assume to the contrary that $3 + 2\sqrt{5}$ is rational. Then there exist co-prime positive integers and such that

$3 + 2\sqrt{5} = \frac{a}{b}$

$\Rightarrow 2\sqrt{5} = \frac{a}{b} - 3 \Rightarrow \sqrt{5} = \frac{a - 3b}{2b} \Rightarrow \sqrt{5}$ is rational

$\left[\because a, b \text{ are integers} \therefore \frac{a - 3b}{2b} \text{ is a rational}\right]$

This contradicts the fact that $\sqrt{5}$ is irrational. So, our supposition is incorrect. Hence, $3 + 2\sqrt{5}$ is an irrational number.

COMPETENCY BASED SOLVED EXAMPLES

Multiple Choice Questions (1 M)

1. Which of the following is not irrational? *(Un)*

(*a*) $(2-\sqrt{3})^2$ (*b*) $(\sqrt{2}+\sqrt{3})^2$

(*c*) $(\sqrt{2}-\sqrt{3})(\sqrt{2}+\sqrt{3})$ (*d*) $\frac{2\sqrt{7}}{7}$

Sol. $(\sqrt{2}-\sqrt{3})(\sqrt{2}+\sqrt{3})=\left(\sqrt{2}\right)^2-\left(\sqrt{3}\right)^2$

$=2-3=-1$ $[\because (a-b)(a+b)=a^2-b^2]$

Mistakes 101 : What not to do!

Students often make mistakes when applying basic formulas. Take your time, understand the concepts, and practice to improve accuracy.

2. The product of a non-zero rational and an irrational number is *(Re)* (NCERT Exemplar)

(*a*) always irrational (*b*) always rational

(*c*) rational or irrational (*d*) one

Sol. Let r be a rational number, and i be an irrational number.

We'll choose $r=\frac{2}{3}$ and $i=\sqrt{2}$ for this example.

Now, the product of r and i is $\frac{2}{3}\cdot\sqrt{2}$ which is an irrational number.

3. The sum of a rational and irrational number is: *(An)*

(*a*) Rational (*b*) Irrational

(*c*) both of above (*d*) None of above

Sol. Let a be a rational number, and b be an irrational number.

We'll choose $a=\frac{1}{2}$ and $b=\sqrt{2}$ for this example.

Now, the sum of a and b is $\frac{1}{2}+\sqrt{2}$ which is an irrational number.

4. $\pi-\frac{22}{7}$ **is:** *(An)*

(*a*) a rational number (*b*) a prime number

(*c*) an irrational number (*d*) an even number

Sol. π is an irrational number because it cannot be written as $\frac{p}{q}$ form.

Irrational number – Rational number = Irrational number

This expression is a combination of a rational number $\left(\frac{22}{7}\right)$ and an irrational number (π).

Hence $\pi-\frac{22}{7}$ is an irrational number.

Nailing the Right Answer

Students should know that π is an irrational number because it cannot be expressed in the form of p/q.

Answer Key

1. (*c*) 2. (*a*) 3. (*b*) 4. (*c*)

Assertion and Reason (1 M)

Direction: In the following questions, A statement of Assertion (A) is followed by a statement of Reason (R). Mark the correct choice as.

(*a*) Both Assertion (A) and Reason (R) are true, and Reason (R) is the correct explanation of Assertion (A).

(*b*) Both Assertion (A) and Reason (R) are true, but Reason (R) is not the correct explanation of Assertion (A).

(*c*) Assertion (A) is true, but Reason (R) is false.

(*d*) Assertion (A) is false, but Reason (R) is true.

1. Assertion (A): There lies exactly one rational number between 2023 and 2024.

Reason (R): There are infinitely many rational- numbers between two rational numbers. *(An)*

Sol. There exists infinite rational numbers between two rational numbers. 2023 and 2024 are also rational numbers. Hence, There lies infinite rational numbers between 2023 and 2024. Assertion (A) is false, but reason (R) is true.

Answer Key

1. (*d*)

Subjective Questions

Very Short Answer Type Questions (1 or 2 M)

1. Prove that (3– $\sqrt{5}$) is an irrational number. *(Ev)*

Sol. Let us assume that $3-\sqrt{5}$ is a rational number.

Then, there exist coprime integers p, q, $q\neq 0$ such that

$3-\sqrt{5}=\frac{p}{q}\Rightarrow\sqrt{5}=3-\frac{p}{q}$

Here, $3-\frac{p}{q}$ is a rational number, but $\sqrt{5}$ is a irrational number. *(1 M)*

But, a irrational cannot be equal to a rational number.

This is a contradiction. Thus, our assumption is wrong.

Therefore $3-\sqrt{5}$ is an irrational number. *(1 M)*

2. If m is a rational number and n is an irrational number, then will $m+n$ and mn be rational or irrational numbers? *(An)*

Sol. Given:

m is a rational number

n is an irrational number

Let's consider $m+n$:

Since m is rational and n is irrational, the sum $m+n$ can be written as:

$m+n$ = Rational + Irrational = Irrational *(1 M)*

The sum of a rational and an irrational number is always an irrational number.

Now, let's consider mn:

Since m is rational and n is irrational, the product mn can be written as:

mn = Rational × Irrational = Irrational *(1 M)*

The product of a rational and an irrational number is always an irrational number.

Therefore, both $m+n$ and mn are irrational numbers.

Short Answer Type Questions (2 or 3 M)

1. Prove that $\sqrt{3}$ is an irrational number. *(Ev)*

Sol. Let us make an assumption on the contrary that $\sqrt{3}$ is a rational number. Therefore, there must exist positive integers a and b for which $\sqrt{3}=\frac{a}{b}$ where, a and b, are co-prime i.e., their H.C.F is 1

Now, $\sqrt{3}=\frac{a}{b} \Rightarrow 3=\frac{a^2}{b^2} \Rightarrow 3b^2=a^2$ *(1 M)*

$\Rightarrow$ 3 divides a^2 [$\because$ 3 divides $3b^2$]

$\Rightarrow$ 3 divides a ... (i)

$\Rightarrow$ $a=3c$ for some integer c

$\Rightarrow a^2=9c^2 \Rightarrow 3b^2=9c^2 \Rightarrow b^2=3c^2$ *(1 M)*

$\Rightarrow$ 3 divides b^2 [$\because$ 3 divides $3c^2$]

$\Rightarrow$ 3 divides b ... (ii)

Therefore, a and b have at least 3 as a common factor.

But this contradicts the fact that a and b do not have a common factor other than 1.

This contradiction has arisen because of our wrong assumption that $\sqrt{3}$ is a rational number.

Thus, $\sqrt{3}$ is an irrational number. *(1 M)*

Topper's Explanation **(CBSE 2019)**

19. Let us assume, if possible, that $\sqrt{3}$ is rational

Then, $\sqrt{3}$ can be expressed as $\frac{p}{q}$ where $q \neq 0$ and p, q are coprimes [HCF(p, q) = 1]

$\therefore \sqrt{3}=\frac{p}{q}$ [p, q ∈ Z ; HCF(p, q) = 1]

On squaring both sides,

$3=\frac{p^2}{q^2}$

$\Rightarrow p^2=3q^2$. —— ①

3 divides p^2

∴ 3 divides p.

Then, p can be written as;

p = 3a for some integer 'a'

On squaring,

$p^2=9a^2$

Put $p=3q^2$ from ①

$\Rightarrow 3q^2=9a^2$

$\Rightarrow q^2=3a^2$.

3 divides q^2

∴ 3 divides q.

∴ 3 divides both p and q, 3 is a common factor of p and q.

But, p and q are co-primes.

Therefore, our assumption is wrong

∴ $\sqrt{3}$ is irrational.

2. Show that $5+2\sqrt{7}$ is an irrational number, where $\sqrt{7}$ is given to be an irrational number. *(Cr)*

Sol. Given: $\sqrt{7}$ is irrational number

Assume $5+2\sqrt{7}$ is rational number then

$5+2\sqrt{7}=\frac{a}{b}; b \neq 0$ *(½ M)*

$\Rightarrow 2\sqrt{7}=\frac{a}{b}-5=\frac{a-5b}{b} \Rightarrow \sqrt{7}=\frac{a-5b}{2b}a$ *(1 M)*

Since, a and b are integers, so $\frac{a-5b}{2b}$ is rational number, but $\sqrt{7}$ is an irrational number. So equality can not exist.

Our assumption is not true. *(1 M)*

Hence, $5+2\sqrt{7}$ is an irrational number *(½ M)*

Topper's Explanation **(CBSE 2020)**

Let us assume to the contrary that $5+2\sqrt{7}$ is rational.

Then $5+2\sqrt{7}$ is of the form $\frac{p}{q}$ where p and q are co primes and $q \neq 0$.

$\frac{p}{q}=5+2\sqrt{7}$

$\frac{p}{q}-5=2\sqrt{7}$

$\frac{p-5q}{2q}=\sqrt{7}$

$\frac{p-5q}{2q}$ is rational as p and q are integers

This contradicts the given fact that $\sqrt{7}$ is irrational.

∴ Our assumption is wrong

$5+2\sqrt{7}$ is irrational //

Proved.

3. Prove that $4+2\sqrt{3}$ is an irrational number, given that $\sqrt{3}$ is an irrational number. *(Cr)* **(CBSE, 2023)**

Sol. Assume $4+2\sqrt{3}$ is rational. That means it can be expressed as a fraction in the form $\frac{p}{q}$, where *p* and *q* are intergers with no common factors other than 1 and $q \neq 0$. *(½ M)*

So, we have: $4+2\sqrt{3} = \frac{p}{q}$

Rearranging this equation:

$$2\sqrt{3} = \frac{p}{q} - 4 \quad (½ M)$$

$$2\sqrt{3} = \frac{p-4q}{q}$$

$$\sqrt{3} = \frac{p-4q}{2q} \quad (1 M)$$

Since $\sqrt{3}$ is irrational, and the right-hand side is rational (because it's a fraction of integers), this leads to contradiction. The sum of a rational number and an irrational number cannot be rational. Therefore, our assumption that $4+2\sqrt{3}$ is rational is false.

Hence $4+2\sqrt{3}$ is irrational number. *(1 M)*

Mistakes 101 : What not to do!

Hey students! Be cautious not to assume a number is irrational. Prove it by showing it can't be expressed as a fraction (*p*/*q*). Look for contradictions!

4. Given that $\sqrt{3}$ is an irrational number, show that $5+2\sqrt{3}$ is an irrational number. *(Cr)* **(CBSE, 2020)**

Sol. Assume $5+2\sqrt{3}$ is rational. That means it can be expressed as a fraction in the form $\frac{p}{q}$, where *p* and *q* are integers with no common factors other than 1 and $q \neq 0$. *(½ M)*

So, we have:

$$5+2\sqrt{3} = \frac{p}{q}$$

Rearranging this equation:

$$2\sqrt{3} = \frac{p}{q} - 5 \quad (½ M)$$

$$2\sqrt{3} = \frac{p-5q}{q} \quad (1 M)$$

$$\sqrt{3} = \frac{p-5q}{2q}$$

Since $\sqrt{3}$ is irrational, and the right-hand side is rational (because it's a fraction of integers), this leads to contradiction.

The sum of a rational number and an irrational number cannot be rational. Therefore, our assumption that $5+2\sqrt{3}$ is rational is false. *(½ M)*

Hence $5+2\sqrt{3}$ is irrational. *(½ M)*

MISCELLANEOUS EXERCISE

Multiple Choice Questions (1 M)

1. If H.C.F (306, 1314) = 18, then L.C.M (306, 1314) is
   (*a*) 22330 (*b*) 22335
   (*c*) 22338 (*d*) 22336
2. If $a = 2^3 \times 3$, $b = 2 \times 3 \times 5$, $c = 3^p \times 5$ and L.C.M $(a, b, c) = 2^3 \times 3^2 \times 5$, then $p =$
   (*a*) 6 (*b*) 4 (*c*) 9 (*d*) 2
3. H.C.F of two numbers is 27 and their L.C.M is 162. If one of the number is 54, then the other number is **(CBSE, 2020)**
   (*a*) 36 (*b*) 35
   (*c*) 9 (*d*) 81
4. Find the number of natural numbers lying between 200 and 400 which are divisible by 4 and 5.
   (*a*) 10 (*b*) 11
   (*c*) 9 (*d*) None of these
5. Find the largest number which will divide 398, 436 and 542 and leave 7, 11 and 15 as remainders, respectively.
   (*a*) 17 (*b*) 16 (*c*) 20 (*d*) 19
6. The smallest number by which $\sqrt{27}$ should be multiplied so as to get a rational number is
   (*a*) $\sqrt{27}$ (*b*) $3\sqrt{3}$
   (*c*) $\sqrt{3}$ (*d*) 3
7. Two runners *P* and *Q* stop after 3 hrs and 5 hrs respectively while running. After ab hours (where *ab* is a two digit number) both of them will pause together for the first time, if they started running at the same time. Find the value of $a + b$.
   (*a*) 5 (*b*) 6 (*c*) 8 (*d*) 7
8. Given that H.C.F (156, 78) = 78, L.C.M (156, 78) is **(CBSE, 2020)**
   (*a*) 156 (*b*) 78 (*c*) 156×78 (*d*) 156×2

Assertion and Reason (1 M)

Direction: In the following questions, a statement of Assertion (A) is followed by a statement of Reason (R). Mark the correct choice as.

(*a*) Both Assertion (A) and Reason (R) are true, and Reason (R) is the correct explanation of Assertion (A).
(*b*) Both Assertion (A) and Reason (R) are true, but Reason (R) is not the correct explanation of Assertion (A).
(*c*) Assertion (A) is true, but Reason (R) is false.
(*d*) Assertion (A) is false, but Reason (R) is true.

1. **Assertion (A):** The H.C.F of two numbers is 5 and their product is 150. Then their L.C.M is 40.
   Reason (R): For any two positive integers *a* and *b*, H.C.F $(a, b) \times$ L.C.M $(a, b) = a \times b$. **(CBSE SQP, 2023)**
2. **Assertion (A):** 2 is an example of a rational number.
   Reason (R): The square roots of all positive integers are irrational numbers.
3. **Assertion (A):** If the H.C.F of two numbers is 5 and their product is 150, then their L.C.M is 40.
   Reason (R): For any two positive integers *p* and *q*, H.C.F $(p, q) \times$ L.C.M $(p, q) = p \times q$

Subjective Questions

Very Short Answer Type Questions (1 or 2 M)

1. Find the L.C.M and the H.C.F of the following integers by applying the prime factorisation method 12, 15, 21.
2. Explain why $7 \times 11 \times 13 + 13$ and $7 \times 6 \times 5 \times 4 \times 3 \times 2 \times 1 + 5$ are composite numbers.
3. Three people running around a rectangular track, can complete one turn in 2, 4 and 5.5 hours respectively. When will they meet at the starting point?
4. Explain why $17 \times 11 \times 2 + 17 \times 11 \times 5$ is a composite number?
5. There is a number 6^n, where *n* is a natural number. Check if there is any value of $n \in N$ exists, for which 6^n is divisible by 7.
6. Find the least possible positive value of *P*, if the square of a number '*P*' is the sum of the square of the other two numbers '*Q*' and '*R*' where $5Q = 12R$ and *Q*, *R* are positive integers.
7. Find a number which is greater than 3 and when it gets divided by 4, 5 and 6 always leaves 3 as remainder.
8. Given that H.C.F (306, 657) = 9, find L.C.M (306, 657). **(NCERT Intext)**
9. If the H.C.F of 408 and 1032 is expressible in the form $1032 \times 2 + 408 \times p$, then find the value of *p*

Short Answer Type Questions (2 or 3 M)

1. If $\sqrt{2}$ is given as an irrational number, then prove that $(7-2\sqrt{2})$ is an irrational number. **(CBSE, 2020)**
2. Prove that $\sqrt{2}$ is an irrational number.
3. In a school 437 girls and 342 boys have been divided into groups, so that each group has the same number of students and no group has boys and girls mixed. What is the least number of groups needed?

4. Pooja multiplied a number 484 with a certain number to obtain the result 3823*a*. Find the value of *a*.

5. If the L.C.M and H.C.F of two numbers are 168 and 28 respectively, then find the number of possible such pairs.

6. Three people running around a rectangular track can complete one turn in 2, 4 and 5.5 hours respectively. When will they meet at the starting point?

7. Find H.C.F of 44, 96 and 404 by prime factorisation method. Hence find their L.C.M. **(CBSE, 2020)**

8. Four bells ring at an interval of 4, 7, 12 and 14 seconds respectively. If the four bells begin to ring at 12 O'clock when will this next ring together and how often will they do so in the next 14 minutes.

9. Prove that $\sqrt{2}+\sqrt{5}$ is irrational.

10. Find the largest number which when divided 445, 572 and 699 leave remainders 4, 5 and 6 respectively.

Long Answer Type Questions (4 or 5 M)

1. Prove that $\sqrt{7}+\sqrt{11}$ is an irrational number.

2. What is the minimum possible sum of the numbers, if the L.C.M and the H.C.F of two numbers are 924 and 7 respectively?

Case Based Questions

Case Based-I: A seminar is being conducted by an Educational Organisation, where the participants will be educators of different subjects. The number of participants in Hindi, English and Mathematics are 60, 84 and 108 respectively.

(CBSE QB)

(*i*) In each room the same number of participants are to be seated and all of them being in the same subject, hence maximum number participants that can accommodated in each room are

(*a*) 14 (*b*) 12
(*c*) 16 (*d*) 18

(*ii*) What is the minimum number of rooms required during the event?

(*a*) 11 (*b*) 31
(*c*) 41 (*d*) 21

(*iii*) The L.C.M of 60, 84 and 108 is

(*a*) 3780 (*b*) 3680
(*c*) 4780 (*d*) 4680

(*iv*) The product of H.C.F and L.C.M of 60, 84 and 108 is

(*a*) 55360 (*b*) 35360
(*c*) 45500 (*d*) 45360

(*v*) 108 can be expressed as a product of its primes as

(*a*) $2^3 \times 3^2$ (*b*) $2^3 \times 3^3$
(*c*) $2^2 \times 3^2$ (*d*) $2^2 \times 3^3$

Case Based-II: Teacher made a project on real numbers where she explained about H.C.F and L.C.M to find the relationship between different numbers and their general forms to students. Also, she explained that the product of two positive integers is equal to the product of their H.C.F and L.C.M.

Based on the above information, answer the following questions:

(*i*) If two positive integers *x* and *y* are expressible in terms of prime as $x = p^2q^3$ and $y = p^3q$, then which of the following is true?

(*a*) H.C.F = $pq^2 \times$ L.C.M
(*b*) L.C.M = $pq^2 \times$ H.C.F
(*c*) L.C.M = $p^2q \times$ H.C.F
(*d*) H.C.F = $p^2q \times$ L.C.M

(*ii*) Find the largest possible positive integer that will divide 398, 542 leaving remainder 7, 15 respectively.

(*a*) 3 (*b*) 1
(*c*) 34 (*d*) 17

(*iii*) Find the least positive integer which on adding 1 is exactly divisible by 126 and 600

(*a*) 12000 (*b*) 12599
(*c*) 12601 (*d*) 12500

(*iv*) If *A*, *B* and *C* are three rational numbers such that $85C - 340A = 109$, $425A + 85B = 146$, then the sum of *A*, *B* and *C* is divisible by

(*a*) 3 (*b*) 6
(*c*) 7 (*d*) 9

Case Based-III: A school Principal wants to address the students of classes eighth to tenth on the importance of personal hygiene. He asks the teacher in charge of the school to arrange all the students of eighth, ninth and tenth classes in a single hall. There are 84 students from eighth class, 63 students from ninth and 42 students from tenth class.

Based on the above information, answer the following questions:

(*i*) What is the minimum number of rows in which the students can be seated such that students belonging to the same class are seated in the same row?

(*ii*) Three numbers are in the ratio of 3 : 4 : 5 and their L.C.M is 2400. The H.C.F of the numbers is:

OR

The product of two numbers is 2028 and their H.C.F is 13. The L.C.M of the numbers is:

(*iii*) Realizing that the hall can accommodate more students, the school Principal now wants to include 98 students of class seventh also. What will be the number of students and minimum number of rows such that students belonging to the same class are seated in the same row?

Case Based-IV: In a classroom activity on real numbers, the students have to pick a number card from a pile of cards. If it is not a rational number then the student needs to frame a question for the rest of the class. The number cards picked up by the first 5 students and their questions on the numbers for the rest of the class are as shown below.

Based on the above information, answer the following questions:

(*i*) Aman picked up $\sqrt{8}$ and his question was - which of the following is true about $\sqrt{8}$?

(*a*) It is a natural number
(*b*) It is an irrational number
(*c*) It is a rational number
(*d*) None of these

(*ii*) Shreya picked up a card and her question was which of the following is not irrational?

(*a*) $3-4\sqrt{5}$ (*b*) $\sqrt{7}-6$
(*c*) $22+2\sqrt{9}$ (*d*) $4\sqrt{11}-6$

(*iii*) Ankita Picked up $\frac{1}{\sqrt{5}}$ and her question was: $\frac{1}{\sqrt{5}}$ is ___ number

(*a*) a whole (*b*) A rational
(*c*) An irrational (*d*) A natural

(*iv*) Aakash picked up $\sqrt{6}$ and his question was - which of the following is not irrational?

(*a*) $15+3\sqrt{6}$ (*b*) $\sqrt{24-9}$
(*c*) $5\sqrt{150}$ (*d*) None of these

Case Based-V: To enhance the reading skills of grade *X* students, the school nominates you and two of your friends to set up a class library. There are two sections- section *A* and Section *B* of grade *X*. There are 32 students in section A and 36 students in section B.

(CBSE QB)

(*i*) What is the minimum number of books you will acquire for the class library, so that they can be distributed equally among students of section *A* or section *B*?

(*a*) 144 (*b*) 128
(*c*) 288 (*d*) 272

(*ii*) If the product of two positive integers is equal to the product of their H.C.F (32, 36) is

(*a*) 2 (*b*) 4
(*c*) 6 (*d*) 8

(*iii*) 36 can be expressed as a product of its primes as

(*a*) $2^2 \times 3^2$ (*b*) $2^1 \times 3^3$
(*c*) $2^3 \times 3^1$ (*d*) $2^0 \times 3^0$

(*iv*) $7 \times 11 \times 13 \times 15 + 15$ is a

(*a*) Prime number
(*b*) Composite number
(*c*) Neither prime nor composite
(*d*) None of the above

(*v*) If *p* and *q* are positive integers such that $p = ab^2c$ and $q = a^2bc^3$, where *a*, *b* and *c* are prime numbers, then the L.C.M (p, q) is

(*a*) abc (*b*) $a^2b^2c^3$
(*c*) a^3b^2 (*d*) a^3b^3c

ANSWER KEYS

Multiple Choice Questions

1. (*c*) 2. (*d*) 3. (*d*) 4. (*c*) 5. (*a*) 6. (*c*) 7. (*b*) 8. (*a*)

Assertion and Reason

1. (*d*) 2. (*c*) 3. (*d*)

Case Based Questions

Case Based-I

(*i*) (*b*) (*ii*) (*d*) (*iii*) (*a*) (*iv*) (*d*) (*v*) (*d*)

Case Based-II

(*i*) (*b*) (*ii*) (*d*) (*iii*) (*b*) (*iv*) (*a*)

Case Based-IV

(*i*) (*b*) (*ii*) (*c*) (*iii*) (*c*) (*iv*) (*d*)

Case Based-V

(*i*) (*c*) (*ii*) (*b*) (*iii*) (*a*) (*iv*) (*b*) (*v*) (*b*)

HINTS & EXPLANATIONS

Multiple Choice Questions

1. (*c*) Given, H.C.F (306, 1314) = 18

we know, H.C.F (a, b) × L.C.M $(a, b) = a \times b$

$\therefore$ H.C.F (306, 1314) × L.C.M (306, 1314) = 306 × 1314

$$\text{L.C.M }(306, 1314) = \frac{306 \times 1314}{18} = 22338$$

2. (*d*) Given: $a = 2^3 \times 3$

$b = 2 \times 3 \times 5$

$c = 3^p \times 5$ and L.C.M $(a, b, c) = 2^3 \times 3^2 \times 5$

The highest power of 3 in the given L.C.M is 2.

$\therefore p = 2$

3. (*d*) Given: H.C.F = 27, L.C.M = 162, and $a = 54$

$$\text{L.C.M} = \frac{a \times b}{\text{H.C.F}} \Rightarrow 162 = \frac{54 \times b}{27}$$

$$\Rightarrow 162 \times 27 = 54 \times b \Rightarrow b = \frac{4374}{54} = 81$$

So, the other number is $b = 81$.

4. (*c*) Number which is divisible by 4 and 5 is the number divisible by 20.

So total numbers between 200 and 400 which are divisible by 20 is 9 (excluding 200 and 400 i.e., 220 ... 380 = (9) terms.

$\therefore$ there are 9 natural numbers between 200 and 400, which are divisible by 4 and 5.

5. (*a*) We have to find the largest number that will divide 398, 436 and 542 leaving the remainder 7, 11 and 15 respectively. Hence, we need to find the H.C.F of three numbers (398 – 7), (436 – 11) and (542 – 15).

Hence, 398 – 7 = 391

436 – 11 = 425

542 – 15 = 527

Now, the H.C.F (391, 425, 527) = 17

$\therefore$ The largest number is 17

6. (*c*) $\sqrt{27} = \sqrt{3 \times 3 \times 3} = 3\sqrt{3}$

where $\sqrt{3}$ is irrational and it becomes rational if it multiple by itself.

Hence, the smallest number by which we have to multiply is $\sqrt{3}$.

7. (*b*) For finding the time, when both runners will meet, we need to find the L.C.M of 3 and 5.

L.C.M (3, 5) = 3 × 5 = 15 hrs.

As *ab* is two digit number

$\therefore a = 1$ & $b = 5 \Rightarrow a + b = 1 + 5 = 6$

8. (*a*) Given that the H.C.F of 156 and 78 is 78, we can use the formula:

$$\text{L.C.M }(a, b) = \frac{a \times b}{\text{H.C.F}(a, b)}$$

Substituting the given values:

$a = 156$

$b = 78$

H.C.F (156, 78) = 78

L.C.M (156, 78) = $\frac{156 \times 78}{78}$ = 156

Assertion and Reason

1. (*d*) **Assertion:** Given that H.C.F = 5
L.C.M = 40
Product of numbers = 150
We know that,
H.C.F × L.C.M = Product of numbers
H.C.F × L.C.M = 5 × 40
= 200 is not equal to the product
So, Assertion is false
Reason: For any two positive integers a and b, H.C.F (a, b) × L.C.M $(a, b) = a \times b$.
Hence, Assertion is false but reason is true.

2. (*c*) **Assertion (A):**
The statement is true. The number 2 is a rational number because it can be expressed as a fraction, $\frac{2}{1}$, where both the numerator and denominator are integers, and the denominator is not zero.
Reason (R):
The statement is false. The square root of 4 is 2, which is a rational number. In general, the square of perfect squares (integers that are squares of other integers) are rational.
Assertion (A) is true, but Reason (R) is false.

3. (*d*) **Assertion (A):**
Given H.C.F = 5 and the product of the two numbers = 150.
We know that H.C.F × L.C.M = $p \times q$.
$\Rightarrow 5 \times$ L.C.M = 150 $\Rightarrow$ L.C.M = $\frac{150}{5} = 30$
The L.C.M is found to be 30, not 40. Therefore, Assertion (A) is false.
Reason (R):
- The statement is true. For any two positive integers p and q, H.C.F (p, q) × L.C.M $(p, q) = p \times q$ is a valid relationship.

Assertion (A) is false, but Reason (R) is true.

Subjective Questions

Very Short Answer Type Questions

1. Prime Factorisation of 12 = $2^2 \times 3$
Prime Factorisation of 15 = 3 × 5
Prime Factorisation of 21 = 3 × 7 *(1 M)*
H.C.F (12, 15, 21) = 3
L.C.M (12, 15, 21) = $2^2 \times 3 \times 5 \times 7 = 420$. *(1 M)*

2. We have, 7 × 11 × 13 + 13 = 13(7 × 11 + 1) = 13 × 78
So, it is the product of more than two prime numbers. Hence, it is a composite number. *(1 M)*
Now, 7 × 6 × 5 × 4 × 3 × 2 × 1 + 5 = 5 (7 × 6 × 4 × 3 × 2 + 1) = 5 × 1009
It is the product of prime numbers 5 and 1009. Hence, it is a composite number. *(1 M)*

3. As we know that,
2 hours = 120 minutes
4 hours = 240 minutes
5.5 hours = 330 minutes
i.e. 120 min, 240 min and 330 min. *(1 M)*
We need to find the time after which all the three people will meet again at the starting point. For this, there will be a number that is divisible by 120, 240 and 330 and that will be the time when all the three meet again at the starting point. To find this we have to take L.C.M of all three numbers.
L.C.M. (120, 240 and 330) = 2640 minutes
Time = $\frac{2640}{60}$ hours = 44 hours. *(1 M)*

4. 17 × 11 × 2 + 17 × 11 × 5
= 17 × 11 × (2 + 5) = 17 × 11 × 7 *(1 M)*
Since, 17 × 11 × 2 + 17 × 11 × 5 can be expressed as a product of primes, therefore, it is a composite number. *(1 M)*

5. The prime factorisation of number 6:
6 = 2 × 3
$\therefore 6^n = 2^n \times 3^n$ *(1 M)*
For the number 6^n to be divisible by 7, the prime factorisation of 6^n should not contain the prime number 7.
$\therefore 6^n$ is not divisible by 7. *(1 M)*

6. It is given that $P^2 = Q^2 + R^2$
Also, $\frac{Q}{R} = \frac{12}{5}$ (Given : $5Q = 12R$) *(1 M)*
Therefore, the least possible values of Q and R are 12 and 5 respectively. Hence
$P^2 = 12^2 + 5^2$
$\Rightarrow P^2 = 169 \Rightarrow P = 13$ *(1 M)*

7. Required number = L.C.M (4, 5 and 6) + 3 *(1 M)*
= 60 + 3 = 63 *(1 M)*

8. H.C.F (a, b) × L.C.M $(a, b) = ab$
$\Rightarrow$ L.C.M $(a, b) = \frac{ab}{\text{H.C.F.}(a, b)}$ *(1 M)*
$\therefore$ L.C.M (306, 657) $= \frac{306 \times 657}{9} = 34 \times 657 = 22338$ *(1 M)*

9. H.C.F of 408 and 1032 is 24.
1032 × 2 + 408 × (p) = 24 $\Rightarrow 408p = 24 - 2064$ *(1 M)*
$\therefore p = -5$ *(1 M)*

Short Answer Type Questions

1. Assume $7 - 2\sqrt{2}$ is rational. That means it can be expressed as a fraction in the form $\frac{p}{q}$, where p and q are integers with no common factors other than 1 and $q \neq 0$. *(½ M)*

So, we have:

$$7-2\sqrt{2}=\frac{p}{q}$$

Rearranging this equation:

$$2\sqrt{2}=7-\frac{p}{q}$$ (½ M)

$$2\sqrt{2}=\frac{7q-p}{q}$$

$$\sqrt{2}=\frac{7q-p}{2q}$$ (1 M)

Since $\sqrt{2}$ is irrational, and the right-hand side is rational (because it's a fraction of integers), this leads to a contradiction.

The difference of a rational number and an irrational number cannot be rational. Therefore, our assumption that $7-2\sqrt{2}$ is rational is false. (½ M)

Hence, $7-2\sqrt{2}$ is irrational. (½ M)

2. Let us assume, to the contrary, that $\sqrt{2}$ is rational.
So, we can find integers r and s ($\neq 0$) such that

$$\sqrt{2}=\frac{r}{s}$$ (½ M)

Suppose r and s have a common factor other than 1. Then, we divide by common factor to get $\sqrt{2}=\frac{a}{b}$, where a and b are co-prime

So, $b\sqrt{2}=a$ (½ M)

Squaring on both sides and rearranging, we get $2b^2 = a^2$.
Therefore, 2 divides a^2.
Now, it follows that 2 divides a. (½ M)
So, we can write $a = 2c$ for some integer c.
Substituting for a, we get $2b^2 = 4c^2$, that is $b^2 = 2c^2$
This means that 2 divides b^2, and so 2 divides b.
Therefore, a and b have at least 2 as a common factor (½ M)
But this contradicts the fact that a and b have no common factors other than 1

This contradiction has arisen because of our incorrect assumption that $\sqrt{2}$ is a rational number. (½ M)

So, we conclude that $\sqrt{2}$ is an irrational number. (½ M)

3. To find the maximum number of students in a group, we need to find H.C.F of 437 and 342. (1 M)

H.C.F (437, 342) = 19 (1 M)

$\therefore$ Number of groups $= \frac{437}{19}+\frac{342}{19} = 41$ groups (1 M)

4. Since 3823a is obtained after multiplying 484 with a certain number.

It is clear that 3823a is divisible by 484. Therefore 484 is a factor of 3823a. (1 M)

The prime factorisation of number 484:

$484 = 2 \times 2 \times 11 \times 11$

Hence the number 484 has only 2 prime factors i.e., 2 and 11.

Therefore, $3823a$ is divisible by both 2 and 11. (½ M)

Also, we know that if the last digit of a whole number is even, then the entire number is divisible by 2.

The last digit of given number is 'a', so we can take any value from 0, 2, 4, 6 or 8 for 'a'.

So, the possible numbers are 38230, 38232, 38234, 38236 and 38238. (½ M)

Out of all these numbers, only 38236 is divisible by 11.

Therefore, the value of a is 6. (1 M)

5. Let the two numbers be a and b.
Since their H.C.F is 28,
$\therefore a = 28x, b = 28y$, such that x, y are co-primes. (½ M)
As, we already know that,
L.C.M × H.C.F = $a \times b$ (½ M)
$168 \times 28 = 28x \times 28y$
$xy = 6$ (1 M)
$\Rightarrow xy = 1 \times 6$ or $xy = 2 \times 3$
$\therefore$ Only two pairs of numbers are there. (1 M)

6. As we know that,

2 hours = 120 minutes

4 hours = 240 minutes

5.5 hours = 330 minutes

i.e., 120 min, 240 min and 330 min. (1 M)

We need to find the time after which all the three people will meet again at the starting point. For this, there will be a number that is divisible by 120, 240 and 330 and that will be the time when all the three meet again at the starting point. (1 M)

To find this we have to take L.C.M of all three numbers.

L.C.M (120, 240 and 330) = 2640 minutes

Time = 2640/60 hours

= 44 hours. (1 M)

7. Prime factorization of 44 : $44 = 2^2 \times 11$

Prime factorization of 96 : $96 = 2^5 \times 3$

Prime factorization of $404 = 2^2 \times 101$ (1 M)

The H.C.F is the product of the lowest powers of the common prime factors, which is $2^2 = 4$. (½ M)

L.C.M $= 2^5 \times 3^1 \times 11^1 \times 101^1 = 106656$ (½ M)

So, the H.C.F of 44, 96, and 404 is 4 and their L.C.M is 106656. (1 M)

8. First we need to find the L.C.M of 4, 7, 12, 14.

Now, factors of $4 = 2 \times 2$, factors of $7 = 1 \times 7$

Factors of $12 = 2 \times 2 \times 3$ and factors of $14 = 2 \times 7$ (1 M)

So, the L.C.M of 4, 7, 12, 14 is 84 (1 M)

So all the three bells will rang together after 84 seconds . i.e, 12:01:24 (1 M)

9. Let us assume to the contrary that $\sqrt{2}+\sqrt{5}$ is rational. Then, there exists positive integers a and b such that

$\sqrt{2}+\sqrt{5}=\frac{a}{b}$, a and b are co-prime, $b \neq 0$ (1 M)

$$\Rightarrow \frac{a}{b} - \sqrt{2} = \sqrt{5} \Rightarrow \left(\frac{a}{b} - \sqrt{2}\right)^2 = \left(\sqrt{5}\right)^2$$

$$\Rightarrow \frac{a^2}{b^2} + 2 - 2.\frac{a}{b}.\sqrt{2} = 5 \Rightarrow \frac{a^2}{b^2} + 2 - \frac{2\sqrt{2}a}{b} = 5 \quad (1\ M)$$

$$\Rightarrow \frac{a^2}{b^2} - \frac{2\sqrt{2}a}{b} = 3 \Rightarrow \frac{a^2 - 2\sqrt{2}ab}{b^2} = 3 \Rightarrow a^2 - 2\sqrt{2}ab = 3b^2$$

$$\Rightarrow 2\sqrt{2}ab = a^2 - 3b^2 \Rightarrow \sqrt{2} = \frac{a^2 - 3b^2}{2ab} \quad (1\ M)$$

$\Rightarrow \sqrt{2}$ is a rational number.

[$\because$ a, b, 2 and 3 are integers. So, $\frac{a^2 - 3b^2}{2ab}$ is rational.]

This contradicts the fact that $\sqrt{2}$ is irrational. So, our assumption is wrong.

Hence, $\sqrt{2} + \sqrt{5}$ is irrational. Proved. *(1 M)*

10. $445 - 4 = 441$

$572 - 5 = 567$

$699 - 6 = 693$ *(½ M)*

H.C.F of 441, 567 and 693 is,

$441 = 3 \times 3 \times 7 \times 7$

$567 = 3 \times 3 \times 3 \times 3 \times 7$

$693 = 3 \times 3 \times 7 \times 11$ *(1 M)*

The common factors are $3 \times 3 \times 7 = 63$. *(½ M)*

$\therefore$ H.C.F (441, 567, 693) = 63

Hence, 63 is the required number. *(1 M)*

Long Answer Type Questions

1. Let us assume, to the contrary, that $\sqrt{7} + \sqrt{11}$ be a rational number $\frac{a}{b}$ (a, b are integers, $b \neq 0$) *(½ M)*

$$\therefore \sqrt{7} + \sqrt{11} = \frac{a}{b}$$

On squaring both sides:

$$7 + 11 + 2\sqrt{77} = \frac{a^2}{b^2} \quad (1\ M)$$

$$\Rightarrow \sqrt{77} = \frac{1}{2}\left(\frac{a^2}{b^2} - 18\right) \Rightarrow \sqrt{77} = \frac{a^2 - 18b^2}{2b^2} \quad (1\ M)$$

As a and b are integers,

$\therefore \frac{a^2 - 18b^2}{2b^2}$ is a rational number, *(½ M)*

$\Rightarrow \sqrt{77}$ is a rational number. *(½ M)*

But this contradicts the fact that $\sqrt{77}$ is irrational.

$\therefore$ Our assumption is wrong. *(½ M)*

Hence $\sqrt{7} + \sqrt{11}$ is an irrational number. *(1 M)*

2. Given: L.C.M = 924 and H.C.F = 7

Let the two numbers be $7a$ and $7b$, where 7 is the H.C.F of $7a$ and $7b$,

i.e., a and b are co-primes. *(1 M)*

L.C.M = 924 ; $7ab = 924$; $ab = 132$

$\Rightarrow ab = 1 \times 132$ *(1 M)*

$= 3 \times 44 = 4 \times 33 = 11 \times 12$

$\therefore$ The minimum possible sum= $(Ha + Hb)$ [H = H.C.F] *(1 M)*

$= 7 \times 11 + 7 \times 12 = 161$ *(1 M)*

Therefore, the correct answer is 161. *(1 M)*

Case Based Questions

Case Based-I

(*i*) (*b*) Given the number of students in each subject are Hindi = 60, English = 84, Mathematics = 108.

The prime factors of each subject students are

$60 = 2 \times 2 \times 3 \times 5 = 2^2 \times 3 \times 5$

$84 = 2 \times 2 \times 3 \times 7 = 2^2 \times 3 \times 7$

$108 = 2 \times 2 \times 3 \times 3 \times 3 = 2^2 \times 3^3$

The maximum number of participants that can accommodated in each room = H.C.F (60, 84, 108)

= Product of the smallest power of each common prime factor involved in the numbers = $2^2 \times 3 = 12$

(*ii*) (*d*) The minimum number of rooms required during the event is

$$\frac{\text{Total number of participants}}{12} = \frac{252}{12} = 21$$

(*iii*) (*a*) L.C.M of (60, 84, 108)

= Product of the greatest power of each prime factor involved in the numbers with highest power

$= 2^2 \times 3^3 \times 5 \times 7 = 4 \times 27 \times 35 = 3780$

(*iv*) (*d*) Now, H.C.F (60, 84, 108) × L.C.M (60, 84, 108)

$= 12 \times 3780 = 45360$

(*v*) (*d*) Number 108 can be expressed as a product of its prime as $2^2 \times 3^3$.

Case Based-II

(*i*) (*b*) We have,

$x = p^2q^3$ and $y = p^3q$

$\because$ p^2q *is* common in both numbers.

So, H.C.F $(x, y) = p^2q$

Also, L.C.M $(x, y) = p^3 \times q^3 = p^3q^3$

Thus, L.C.M $= p^3q^3 = p^2q \times pq^2$ = H.C.F $\times\, pq^2$

(*ii*) (*d*) Required number = H.C.F ((398 – 7), (542 – 15))

= H.C.F (391, 527)

$\because$ $527 = 391 \times 1 + 136$

$391 = 136 \times 2 + 119$

$136 = 119 \times 1 + 17$

$119 = 17 \times 7 + 0$

$\because$ Remainder, $r = 0$

$\therefore$ H.C.F (391, 527) = 17

(*iii*) (*b*) Required number = L.C.M (126, 600) – 1

Now, $126 = 2 \times 3 \times 3 \times 7$

$600 = 2 \times 2 \times 2 \times 3 \times 5 \times 5$

$\therefore$ L.C.M $= 2 \times 2 \times 2 \times 3 \times 3 \times 5 \times 5 \times 7 = 12600$

$\therefore$ Required number = 12600 – 1 = 12599

(*iv*) (*a*) We have,

$85C - 340A = 109$ ... (*i*)

$425A + 85B = 146$ ... (*ii*)

$\Rightarrow (425 - 340)A + 85B + 85C = 255$

[Adding (*i*) and (*ii*)]

$\Rightarrow 85A + 85B + 85C = 255$

$\Rightarrow A + B + C = \frac{255}{85} = 3$, which is a prime number

So, it is only divisible.

Case Based-III

(*i*) As we have to find the minimum number of rows, we have to first take the H.C.F of 84, 63 and 42.

$84 = 2^2 \times 3 \times 7$

$63 = 3^2 \times 7$

$42 = 2 \times 3 \times 7$

$\therefore$ H.C.F $= 3 \times 7 = 21$

So, 21 students of each class can be seated in one row. That means there will be 4 rows for class eighth, 3 rows for class ninth and 2 rows for class tenth.

Total number of rows = 4 + 3 + 2 = 9

(*ii*) Let the numbers be $3x$, $4x$ and $5x$

Their L.C.M $= 3 \times 4 \times 5 \times x = 60x = 2400$

$x = 40$.

Thus, the numbers are 120, 160 and 200. To find their H.C.F, we find their prime factors:

$120 = 2^3 \times 3 \times 5$

$160 = 2^5 \times 5$; $200 = 2^3 \times 5^2$

$\therefore$ H.C.F $= 2^3 \times 5 = 40$

OR

Given H.C.F = 13 and product of two number = 2028

We know that

H.C.F × L.C.M = product of two numbers.

13 × L.C.M = 2028

$\Rightarrow$ L.C.M $= \frac{2028}{13} = 156$.

(*iii*) Number of students of same class in one row = 7, minimum number of rows = 41

We will now calculate the H.C.F of 42, 63, 84 and 98.

$42 = 2 \times 3 \times 7$

$63 = 3^2 \times 7$

$84 = 2^2 \times 3 \times 7$

$98 = 2 \times 7^2$

$\therefore$ H.C.F = 7

So, 7 students of each class can now be seated in one row. That means there will be 12 rows for class eighth, 9 rows for class ninth, 6 rows for class tenth and 14 rows for class seventh.

Total number of rows = 12 + 9 + 6 + 14 = 41

Case Based-IV

(*i*) (*b*) We have,

$\sqrt{8} = 2\sqrt{2}$

$\because$ $\sqrt{2}$ is irrational no. and 2 is rational no. and product of rational and irrational number is an irrational.

So, $2\sqrt{2}$ i.e., $\sqrt{8}$ is an irrational no.

(*ii*) (*c*) $22 + 2\sqrt{9}$ is not irrational as,

$22 + 2\sqrt{9} = 22 + 2 \times 3 = 28$, which is rational.

(*iii*) (*c*) $\because$ $\sqrt{5}$ is irrational number and 1 is rational no. Also division of rational and irrational no. is irrational.

So, $\frac{1}{\sqrt{5}}$ is an irrational number

(*iv*) (*d*) For (*a*): $\sqrt{6}$ is irrational

$\Rightarrow 3\sqrt{6}$ is irrational $\Rightarrow 15 + 3\sqrt{6}$ is irrational

For (*b*): $\sqrt{24 - 9} = \sqrt{15}$

$\because$ 15 is not a perfect square. So, $\sqrt{15}$ i.e., $\sqrt{24-9}$ is irrational.

For (*c*): $5\sqrt{150} = 25\sqrt{10}$

Since, 10 is not a perfect square.

So, $\sqrt{10}$ is irrational $\Rightarrow 25\sqrt{10}$ is irrational.

Case Based-V

(*i*) (*c*) Given, number of students in section $A = 32$ and number of students in section $B = 36$

The minimum number of books acquire for the class library

= L.C.M of (32, 36) $= 2 \times 2 \times 2 \times 2 \times 2 \times 3 \times 3$

$= 2^5 \times 3^2 = 32 \times 9 = 288$

(*ii*) (*b*) Given, product of the two numbers

= L.C.M × H.C.F

$\therefore$ 32 × 36 = L.C.M (32, 36) × H.C.F (32, 36)

$\Rightarrow$ 32 × 36 = 288 × H.C.F (32, 36)

$\Rightarrow$ H.C.F (32, 36) $= \frac{32 \times 36}{288} = 4$

(*iii*) (*a*) The prime factors of 36 are

$36 = 2 \times 2 \times 3 \times 3 = 2^2 \times 3^2$

(*iv*) (*b*) $7 \times 11 \times 13 \times 15 + 15 = 15015 + 15 = 15030$

Hence, it is a composite number.

(*v*) (*b*) Given, $p = ab^2c$ and $q = a^2bc^3$

L.C.M (p, q) = Product of the greatest power of each prime factor involved in the numbers, with highest power $= a^2 \times b^2 \times c^3$

❑❑❑

POLYNOMIALS

2

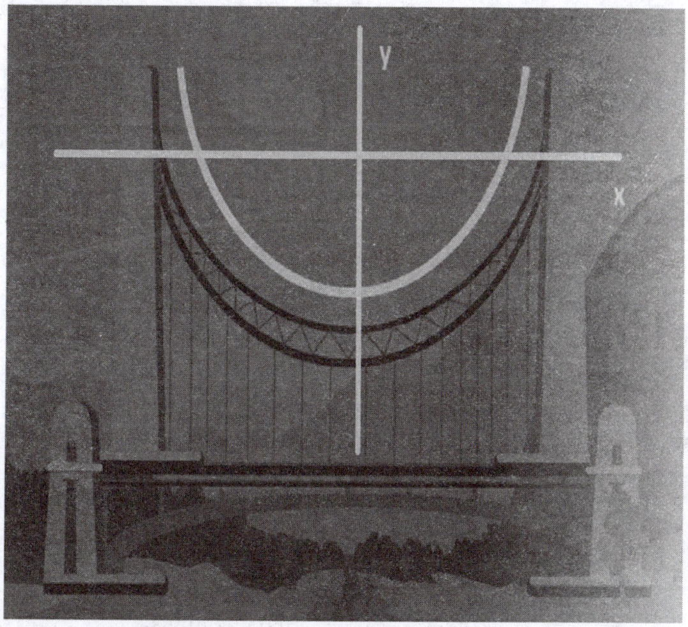

"Polynomials are used in roller coaster designs, hill slopes, bridges, and mountain ranges. Engineers use polynomial equations, especially in bridge design, to ensure strength and stability."

SYLLABUS & WEIGHTAGE

List of Concept Names	Years				
	2021	2022	2023	2024	2025
Geometrical Meaning of the Zeroes of a Polynomial (Zeroes of a polynomial)	Exam not Conducted	–	1 Q (1 M)	1 Q (1 M)	1 Q (1 M)
Relationship Between Zeroes and Coefficients of a Polynomial (Relationship between zeroes and coefficients of quadratic/cubic Polynomials)		–	1 Q (1 M) 1 Q (3 M)	1 Q (1 M) 1 Q (3 M)	2 Q (3 M each)

CONCEPT MAP

To Access One Shot Revision Video Scan This QR Code

Polynomial: A polynomial is defined as an expression that includes variables, constants and exponents.

Types of Polynomial

Linear Polynomial:
$p(x) = ax + b, a \neq 0$

Quadratic Polynomial:
$p(x) = ax^2 + bx + c, a \neq 0$

Cubic Polynomial:
$p(x) = ax^3 + bx^2 + cx + d, a \neq 0$

Degree of Polynomial:
Highest power of the variable is known as the degree of the polynomial.

Formation of Quadratic and Cubic Polynomial:

1. Quadratic polynomial having α and β as its zeroes is given by $p(x) = k\{x^2 - (\alpha + \beta)x + \alpha\beta\}$, where k is any non-zero real number.
2. Cubic polynomial having α, β, and γ as its zeroes is given by $p(x) = k\{x^3 - (\alpha + \beta + \gamma)x^2 + (\alpha\beta + \beta\gamma + \gamma\alpha)x - \alpha\beta\gamma\}$, where k is any non-zero real number.

General form:
$p(x) = a_0x^n + a_1x^{n-1} + a_2x^{n-2} + a_3x^{n-3} + ... + a_{n-1}x^1 + a_n$,
where all the powers are non-negative integers and $a_0, a_1, ... a_n, \in R$

Zeroes of Polynomials:
The value of x where the graph intersect x-axis

Zeroes of Linear Polynomial:
If k is zero of $p(x) = ax + b, a \neq 0$
i.e. $p(k) = ak + b = 0$
$$\therefore k = \frac{-b}{a} = \frac{-\text{Constant term}}{\text{Coefficient of } x}$$

Zeroes of Quadratic Polynomial:
If α and β are zeroes of quadratic polynomial $p(x) = ax^2 + bx + c, a \neq 0$
$$\alpha + \beta = \frac{-b}{a} = \frac{-\text{Coefficient of } x}{\text{Coefficient of } x^2}$$
$$\text{and } \alpha \cdot \beta = \frac{c}{a} = \frac{\text{Constant term}}{\text{Coefficient of } x^2}$$

Zeroes of Cubic Polynomial:
If α, β, and γ are the zeroes of the cubic polynomial $p(x) = ax^3 + bx^2 + cx + d$, then,
$$\alpha + \beta + \gamma = \frac{-b}{a} = -\frac{\text{Coefficient of } x^2}{\text{Coefficient of } x^3}$$
$$\alpha\beta + \beta\gamma + \gamma\alpha = \frac{c}{a} = \frac{\text{Coefficient of } x}{\text{Coefficient of } x^3}$$
$$\alpha\beta\gamma = \frac{-d}{a} = -\frac{\text{Constant term}}{\text{Coefficient of } x^3}.$$

1 GEOMETRICAL MEANING OF THE ZEROES OF A POLYNOMIAL

Important Terms

- **Polynomial:** Polynomial has two words, Poly (meaning "many") and Nomial (meaning "terms"). A polynomial is defined as an expression that includes variables, constants, and exponents.
- **General form of the Polynomial:** $p(x) = a_n x^n + a_{(n-1)} x^{(n-1)} + a_{(n-2)} x^{(n-2)} + \ldots + a_1 x^1 + a_0$. (where n is a whole number and $a_0, a_1, a_2, \ldots, a_n$ are real numbers) is called a polynomial in one variable x of degree n.
- **Degree of the Polynomial:** The highest power of the variable x in the given polynomial $p(x)$, is known as the degree of the polynomial.
- **Linear Polynomial:** If the degree of the given polynomial is one then, it is known as the linear polynomial. *e.g.*, $2x - 3, x + 5$
- **Quadratic Polynomial:** If the degree of the given polynomial is two then, it is known as the quadratic polynomial. *e.g.*, $2x^2 - 3, x^2 + \sqrt{3}\,x + 5, \frac{y}{5} + y^2 - \sqrt{2}$, etc.
- **Cubic Polynomial:** If the degree of the given polynomial is three then, it is known as the cubic polynomial.

  e.g., $2 - x^3, x^3, 3 - x^2 + x^3, 3x^3 - 2x^2 + x - 1$, etc.
- **The value of $p(x)$ at $x = k$:** If $p(x)$ is a polynomial in x, and if k is any real number, then the value obtained by replacing x by k in $p(x)$, is called the value of $p(x)$ at $x = k$, and is denoted by $p(k)$.
- **Zero of a Polynomial $p(x)$:** If $p(k) = 0$, then the real number k is said to be a zero of a polynomial $p(x)$.
- **Zero of the Linear Polynomial:** If k is a zero of $p(x) = ax + b$, then $p(k) = ak + b = 0$, *i.e.*, $k = -\frac{b}{a}$.

Important Concepts

- **Geometrical Meaning of the Zeroes of a Polynomial:**
  (*i*) The linear polynomial $ax + b, a \neq 0$, has exactly one zero, namely, $\left(-\frac{b}{a}, 0\right)$.
  (*ii*) The zeroes of a quadratic polynomial $ax^2 + bx + c, a \neq 0$, are precisely the x-coordinates of the points where the parabola $(ax^2 + bx + c)$ representing $y = ax^2 + bx + c$ intersects the x-axis.

Equation $y = ax^2 + bx + c$ has one of the two shapes either open upwards like ∪ or open downwards like ∩ depending on whether $a > 0$ or $a < 0$. (These curves are called parabolas.)

From our observation about the shape of the graph of $y = ax^2 + bx + c$, the following three cases arise:

Case (*i*): Here, the graph cuts x-axis at two distinct points A and A'. The x-coordinates of A and A' are the two zeroes of the quadratic polynomial $ax^2 + bx + c$ in this case (see Fig. *i* & *ii*)

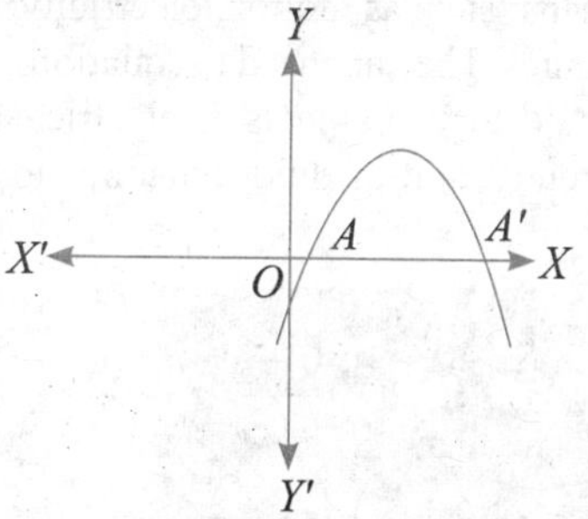

(*i*)

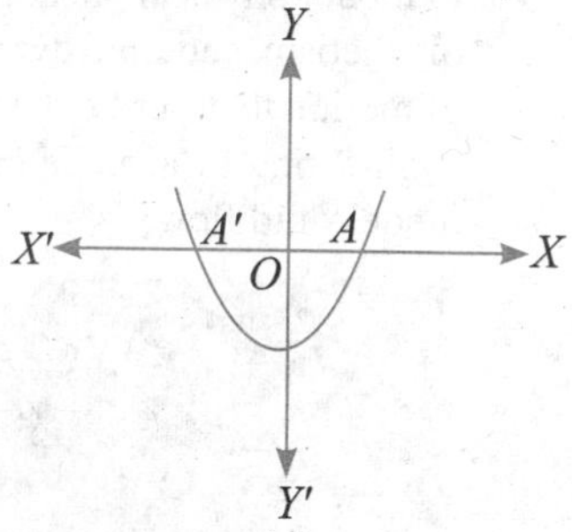

(*ii*)

Case (*ii*): Here, the graph cuts the x-axis at exactly one point, *i.e.*, at two coincident points. So, the two points A and A' of Case (*i*) coincide here to become one point A (see Fig. *iii* & *iv*).

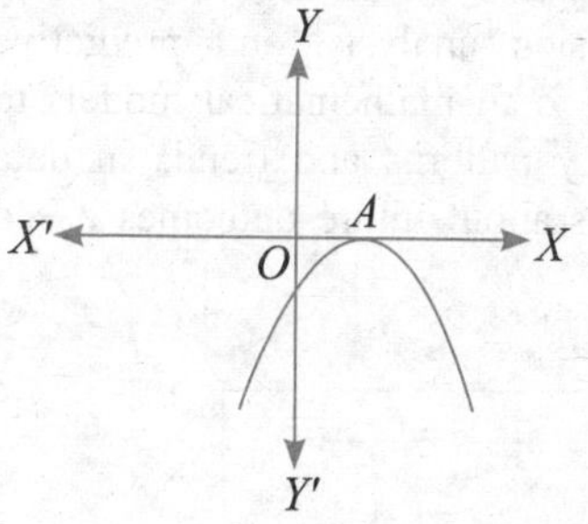

(*iii*)

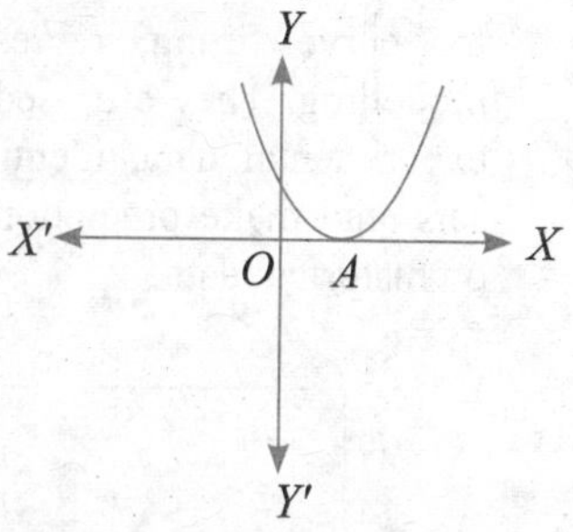

(*iv*)

Case (*iii*): Here, the graph is either completely above the x-axis or completely below the x-axis. So, it does not cut the x-axis at any point (see Fig. *v* & *vi*).

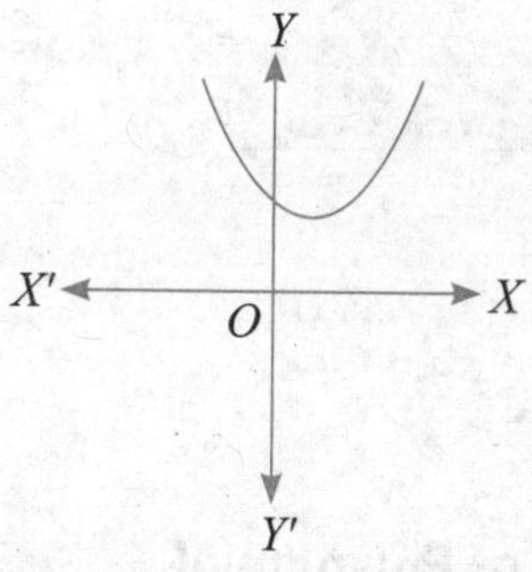

(*v*)

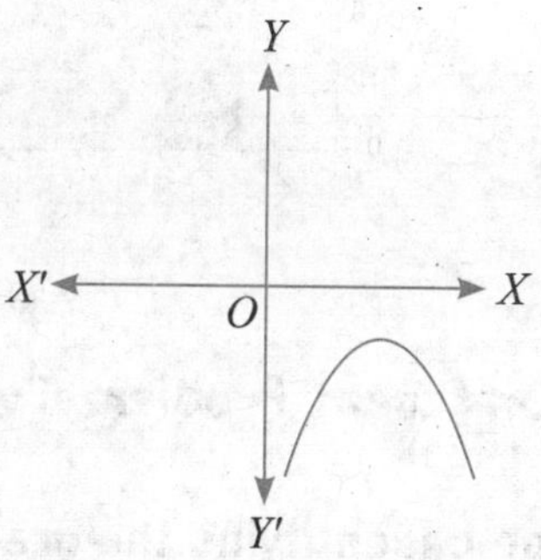

(*vi*)

So, the quadratic polynomial $ax^2 + bx + c$ has no zero in this case.

Remark: In general, given a polynomial $p(x)$ of degree n, the graph of $y = p(x)$ intersects the x-axis at most n points. Therefore, a polynomial $p(x)$ of degree n has at most n zeroes.

Quadratic Polynomial $f(x) = ax^2 + bx + c$

When $a > 0$

When $a < 0$

Real Life Applications

- Polynomials are widely used in engineering and physics to model physical phenomena, such as motion, electricity, magnetism, and fluid dynamics. They are used in equations of motion to describe the trajectory of objects, in electrical engineering to analyze circuits, and in fluid dynamics to model fluid flow.

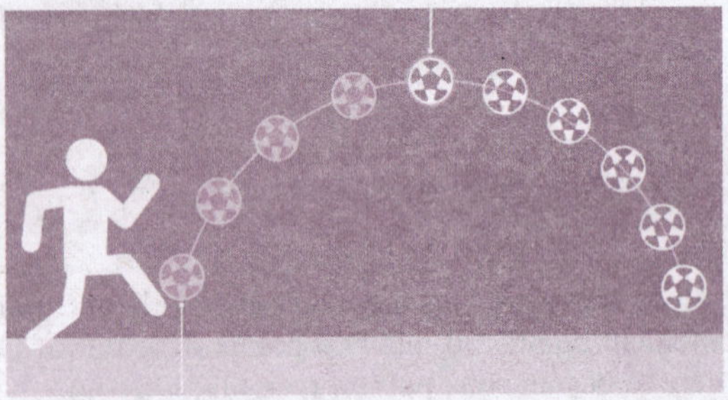

- Polynomials are used in data analysis and machine learning for curve fitting, regression analysis, and predictive modelling. They are used to fit mathematical models to experimental data, identify patterns and trends in data sets, and make predictions about future outcomes based on historical data.

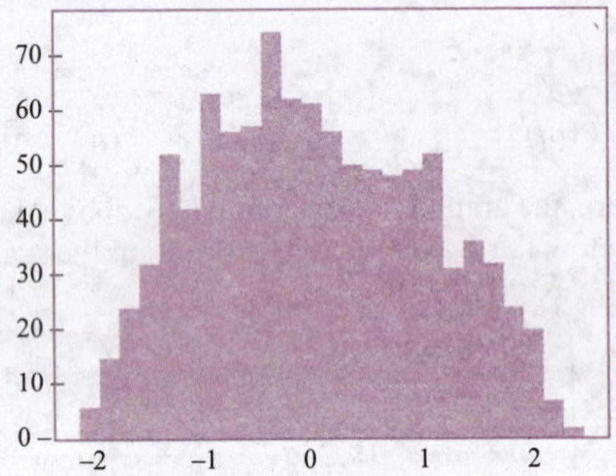

Different Problem Types

Type I: Identifying the graph of Polynomial

Step I: Shape of the Graph: If the graph forms a U-shaped curve, it indicates a quadratic polynomial.

Step II: Linearity: Linear polynomials form a straight line on the graph.

Step III: Neither Linear nor Quadratic: If the graph doesn't follow a straight line or a U-shaped curve, it's neither linear nor quadratic.

This suggests the function may be of a higher degree polynomial or a different type of function altogether.

Example: Identify the type of graphs:

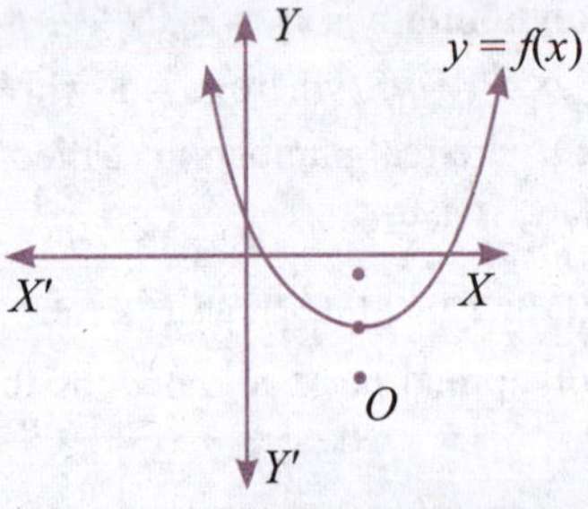

(i)

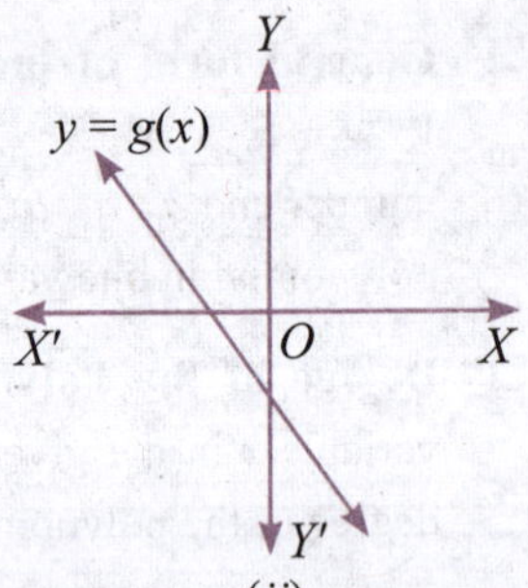

(ii)

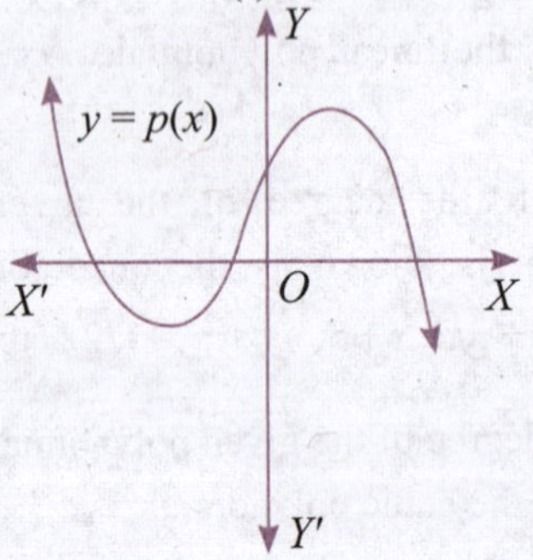

(iii)

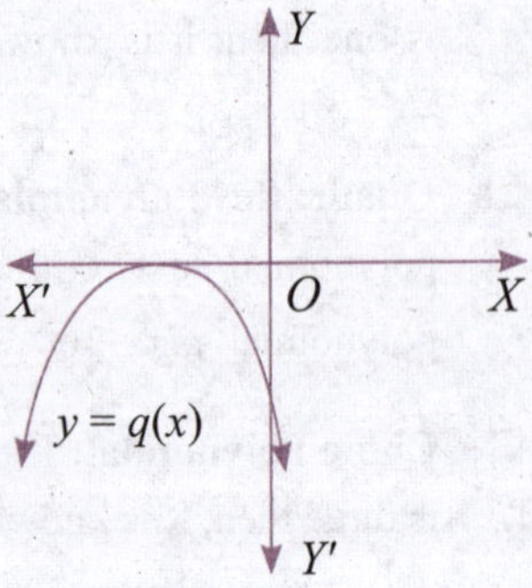

(iv)

Solution:

(i) The graph is a U-shaped curve, indicating a quadratic polynomial with a positive coefficient for the term with the highest power.

(ii) The graph is a straight line, suggesting a linear polynomial.

(iii) In this case, the function doesn't follow a straight line or a U-shaped curve, so it's neither linear nor quadratic polynomial.

(iv) The graph forms a downward-facing U-shaped curve, indicating a quadratic polynomial with a negative coefficient for the term with the highest power.

Type II: Finding the Number of Zeroes using the graph of the given polynomial:

Step I: Look for points on the graph where the polynomial intersects the x-axis. These points represent the zeroes or roots of the polynomial.

Example: The graphs of $y = p(x)$ are given in the figure below, for some polynomials $p(x)$. Find the number of zeroes of $p(x)$, in each case.

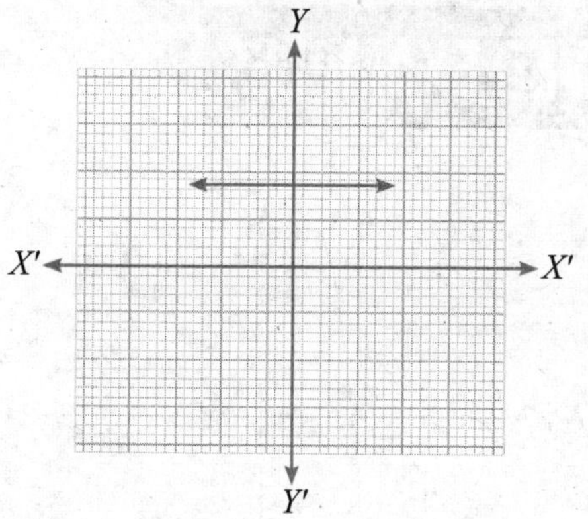

(i)

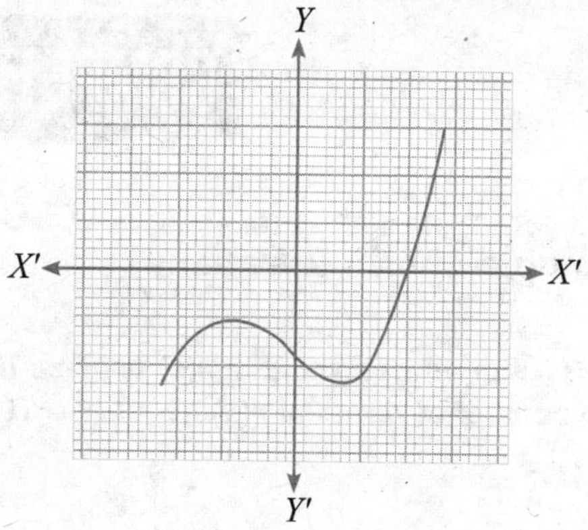

(ii)

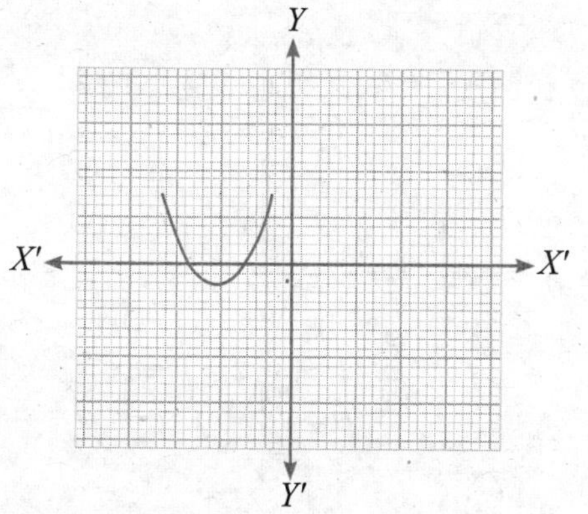

(iii)

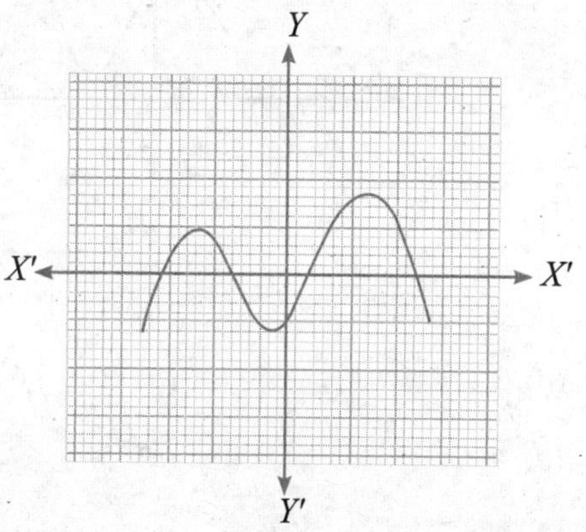

(iv)

Solution:

(*i*) The first graph has 0 zeroes, as the line does not intersect the x-axis.

(*ii*) The second graph has 1 zero, as the line intersects the x-axis once.

(*iii*) The third graph has 2 zeroes, as the line intersects the x-axis twice.

(iv) The fourth graph has 4 zeroes, as the line intersects the x-axis four times.

COMPETENCY BASED SOLVED EXAMPLES

Multiple Choice Questions

(1 M)

1. **Graph of a polynomial $p(x)$ is given in the figure. The number of zeroes of $p(x)$ is:** (*Un*) (CBSE, 2023)

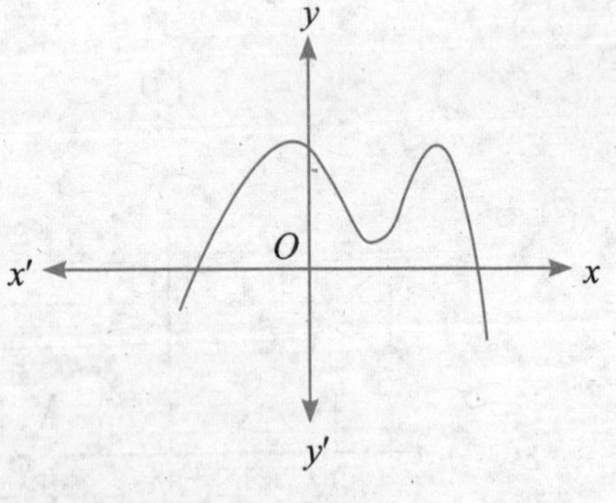

(*a*) 2 (*b*) 3

(*c*) 4 (*d*) 5

Sol. Here the graph of polynomial touches the x-axis 2 times.

Number of zeroes of polynomial = 2

2. **Which of the following could be the graph of the polynomial?**

$(x-1)^2(x+2)$? (*Cr*)

(*a*)

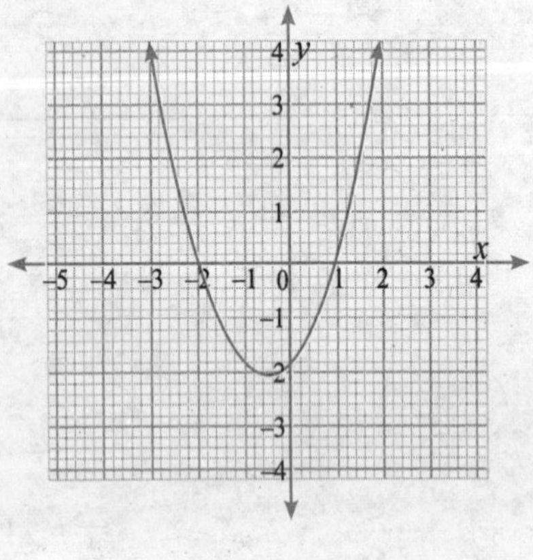

(*b*)

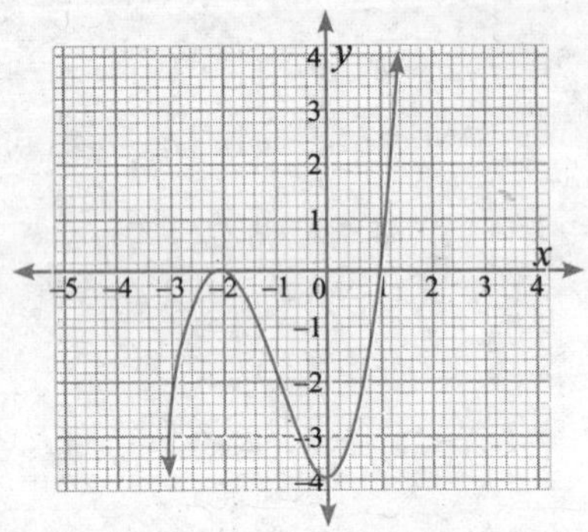

(*c*)

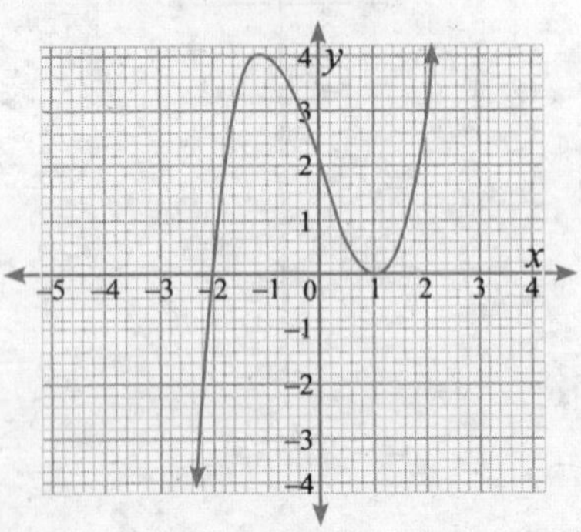

(*d*)

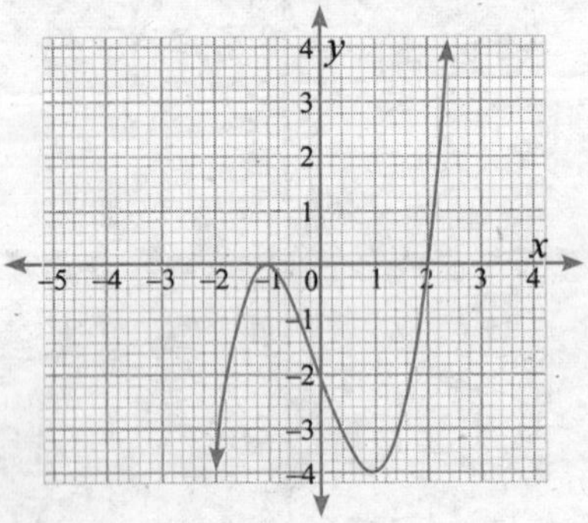

Sol. Let the polynomial be

$f(x) = (x-1)^2(x+2)$

Next, we find $f(0)$

$f(0) = (0-1)^2(0+2) = 2$

So $f(0) = 2$ is only satisfied in the options (*c*).

3. **Which of the following is not the graph of a quadratic polynomial?** (*Un*) (NCERT Exemplar)

(*a*)

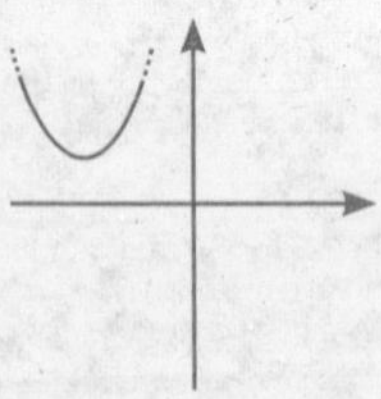

(*b*)

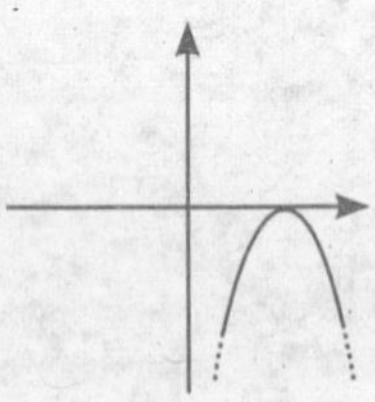

(*c*)

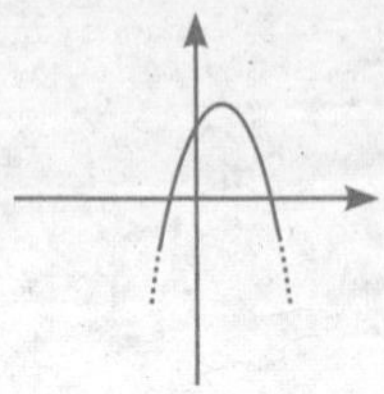

(*d*)

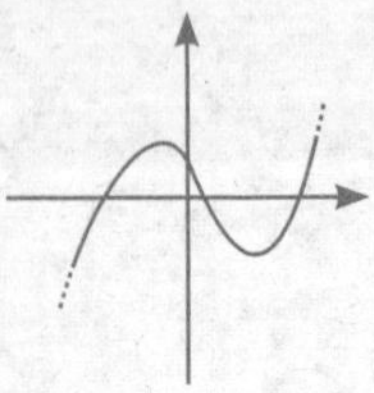

Sol. Graph '*d*' intersects at three points on the *X*–axis so the number of roots of the polynomial is 3, Hence it is a cubic polynomial rest other graphs are of quadratic polynomial.

4. **The maximum number of zeroes a cubic polynomial can have, is** *(Re)* (CBSE, 2020)

(a) 1 (b) 4

(c) 2 (d) 3

Sol. A cubic polynomial is of the form $ax^3 + bx^2 + cx + d$, where a, b, c and d are constants, and $a \neq 0$.

By the Fundamental Theorem of Algebra, any polynomial of degree n has exactly n complex roots, counting multiplicity. So, a cubic polynomial can have a maximum of 3 zeroes. This is consistent with its degree, which is 3.

5. **The graph of a polynomial $P(x)$ cuts the x-axis at 3 points and touches it at 2 other points. The number of zeroes of $P(x)$ is** *(Un)*

(a) 1 (b) 2

(c) 3 (d) 5

Sol. $P(x)$ cuts x–axis at 3–points & touches x–axis at 2–points.

we know, number of zeroes of a polynomial

= no. of times graph touches the x–axis

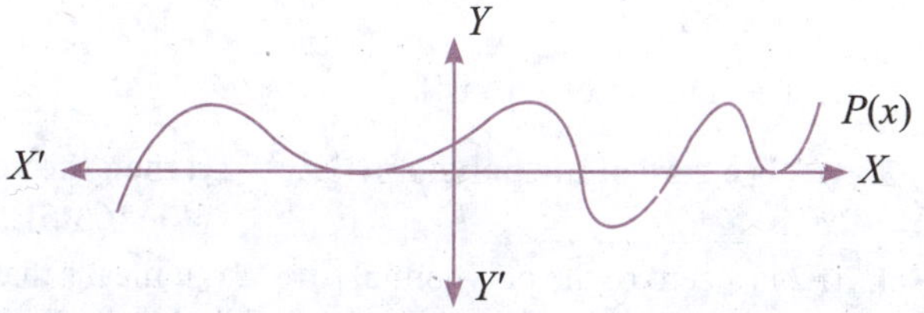

∴ No. of zeroes of $P(x) = 5$.

6. $f(y) = \sqrt{2}y^3 + 4y^6 + \frac{5}{4}y^2 - 3$, **find out the degree of this polynomial** *(Cr)*

(a) 5 (b) 2

(c) 6 (d) 3

Sol. The degree of the polynomial is the highest power of the variable y in the given polynomial $f(y)$.

Hence, degree of this polynomial is 6.

Mistakes 101 : What not to do!

Students may incorrectly identify the degree of a polynomial, leading to errors in the classification and analysis of the polynomial's behaviour.

7. **Number of zeroes of the polynomial p(x) shown in figure, are** *(An)* (CBSE, 2020)

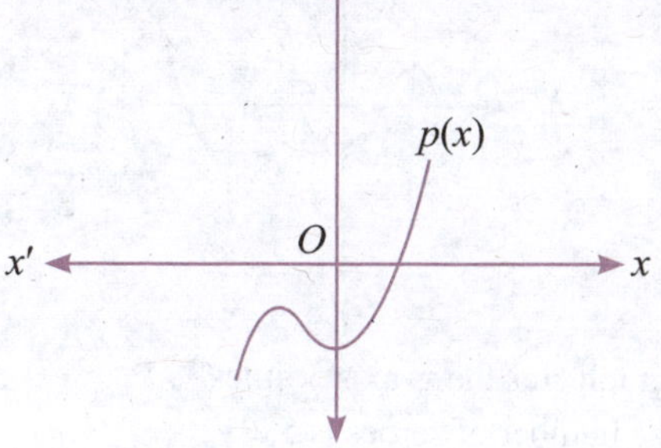

(a) 3 (b) 2

(c) 1 (d) 0

Sol. Here the graph of polynomial touches the x-axis 1 time.

Number of zeroes of polynomial = 1

8. **If one zero of a quadratic polynomial $(kx^2 + 3x + k)$ is 2, then the value of k is** *(Ev)* (CBSE, 2020)

(a) $\frac{5}{6}$ (b) $-\frac{5}{6}$

(c) $\frac{6}{5}$ (d) $-\frac{6}{5}$

Sol. If one zero of the quadratic polynomial $kx^2 + 3x + k$ is 2, then it means that when we substitute $x = 2$ into the polynomial, the result is 0.

So, let's substitute $x = 2$ into the polynomial:

$\Rightarrow k(2)^2 + 3(2) + k = 0 \Rightarrow 4k + 6 + k = 0$

$\Rightarrow 5k + 6 = 0 \Rightarrow k = -\frac{6}{5}$.

Answer Key

1. (a)	2. (c)	3. (d)	4. (d)
5. (d)	6. (c)	7. (c)	8. (d)

Assertion and Reason

(1 M)

Direction: In the following questions, a statement of Assertion (A) is followed by a statement of Reason (R). Mark the correct choice as.

(a) Both Assertion (A) and Reason (R) are true, and Reason (R) is the correct explanation of Assertion (A).

(b) Both Assertion (A) and Reason (R) are true, but Reason (R) is not the correct explanation of Assertion (A).

(c) Assertion (A) is true, but Reason (R) is false.

(d) Assertion (A) is false, but Reason (R) is true.

1. **Assertion (A): $p(x) = 8x^3 + 6x^2 + 5x + 3$ is a polynomial of degree 3.**

   Reason (R): The highest power of x in a polynomial $p(x)$ is the degree of the polynomial. *(Un)*

Sol. To determine the degree of a polynomial, we look at the term with the highest power of x. In this case, the highest power of x is 3, so the degree of the polynomial is indeed 3. The degree of a polynomial is determined by the term with the highest power of x. Therefore, both Assertion (A) and Reason (R) are true, and Reason (R) provides a valid explanation for Assertion (A).

2. **Assertion (A): The graph of $y = f(x)$ is shown in figure for the polynomial $f(x)$. The number of zeroes of $f(x)$ is 3.**

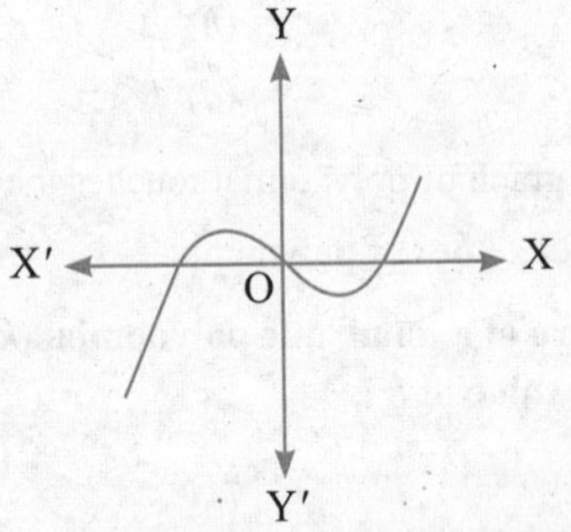

Reason (R): The number of zeroes of the polynomial $f(x)$ is the number of points at which $f(x)$ cuts or touches the x-axis. *(Re)*

Sol. In the given graph $y = f(x)$ cuts the x-axis 3 times. Therefore, the number of zeroes of $f(x)$ is 3.

Also, Reason states that, Zeroes of a polynomial are the values of x for which $f(x) = 0$ which corresponds to the points where the graph of the polynomial intersects or touches the x-axis.

Hence, Both Assertion (A) and Reason (R) are true, and Reason (R) is the correct explanation of Assertion (A).

3. Assertion (A): $p(x) = x^2 + 5x + 6$ is quadratic polynomial.

Reason (R): A quadratic polynomial is $p(x) = ax^2 + bx + c$, where a, b, c are real numbers and $a \neq 0$. *(Un)*

Sol. A quadratic polynomial is defined as a polynomial of degree 2. The polynomial given, $p(x) = x^2 + 5x + 6$, has the highest power of x as 2 , making it a quadratic polynomial.

$ax^2 + bx + c = 0$ is the standard form of a quadratic polynomial, where a represents the coefficient of the quadratic term, b represents the coefficient of the linear term, and c represents the constant term. The condition $a \neq 0$ ensures that the polynomial is indeed quadratic and not linear. Therefore, both Assertion (A) and Reason (R) are true, and Reason (R) provides a valid explanation for Assertion (A).

4. Assertion (A): $3x^3 + 3x^2 + 3x + 3$ is a cubic polynomial.

Reason (R): If the number '3' is multiplied with each term of a polynomial then it is called as cubic polynomial. *(Ap)*

Sol. A cubic polynomial is defined as a polynomial of degree 3, meaning the highest power of the variable is 3. In the given polynomial, the highest power of x is 3, which makes it a cubic polynomial.

Multiplying each term of a polynomial by a constant does not change its degree. The degree of a polynomial is solely determined by the highest power of the variable present in the polynomial.

Hence Assertion (A) is True but Reason (R) is False.

Answer Key

1. (a) 2. (a) 3. (a) 4. (c)

Subjective Questions

Very Short Answer Type Questions (1 or 2 M)

1. Find the number of zeroes of the polynomial $y = f(x)$ *(Ap)*

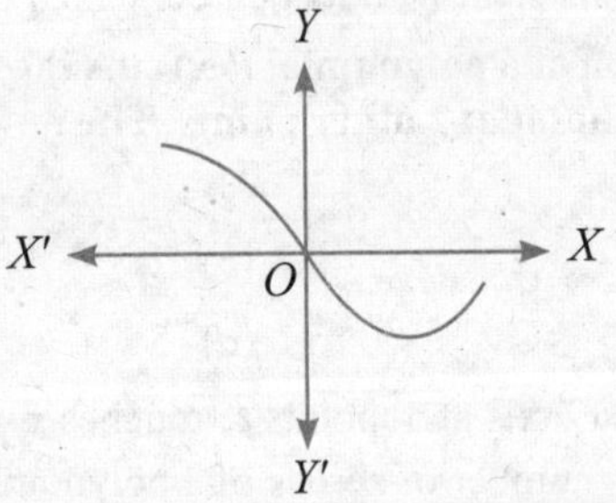

Sol. The numbers of times the graph touches/intersects the x–axis is 1. *(1 M)*

$\therefore$ The number of zero is 1. *(1 M)*

2. If 2 is a zero of the polynomial $ax^2 - 2x$, then the value of 'a' is __________. *(Ev)* **(CBSE, 2020)**

Sol. If 2 is a zero of the polynomial $ax^2 - 2x$, it means that when we substitute $x = 2$ into the polynomial, the result is 0.

So, let's substitute $x = 2$ into the polynomial:

$\Rightarrow a(2)^2 - 2(2) = 0$ *(½ M)*

$\Rightarrow 4a - 4 = 0 \Rightarrow 4a = 4 \Rightarrow a = 1$ *(½ M)*

3. Find the number of zeroes of $y = f(x)$ *(Re)*

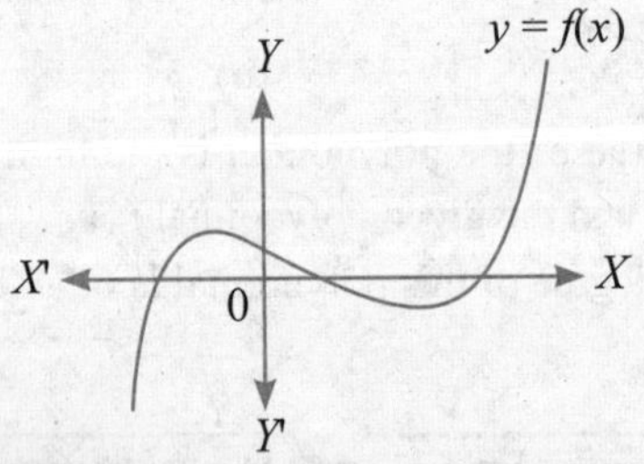

Sol. The number of times $y = f(x)$ touches/intersects the x–axis is 3. *(1 M)*

$\therefore$ The number of zeroes is 3 *(1 M)*

4. Identify the number of zeroes of the polynomial represented by the graph shown below. *(Un)*

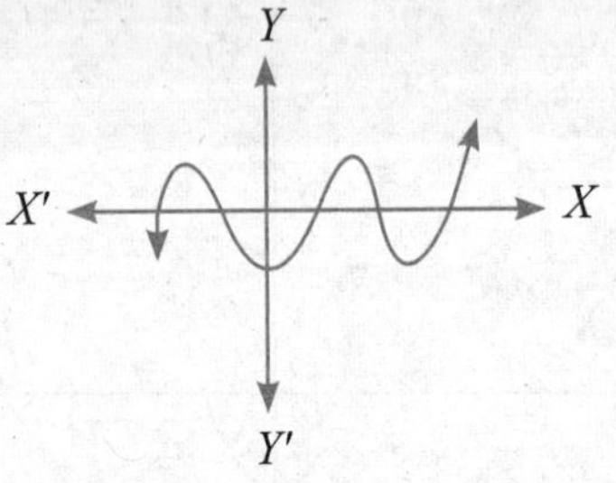

Sol. The graph cuts the x–axis 5 times. *(1 M)*

So, the number of zeroes is 5. *(1 M)*

5. **Identify the number of zeroes of the polynomial represented by the graph shown below.** *(Cr)*

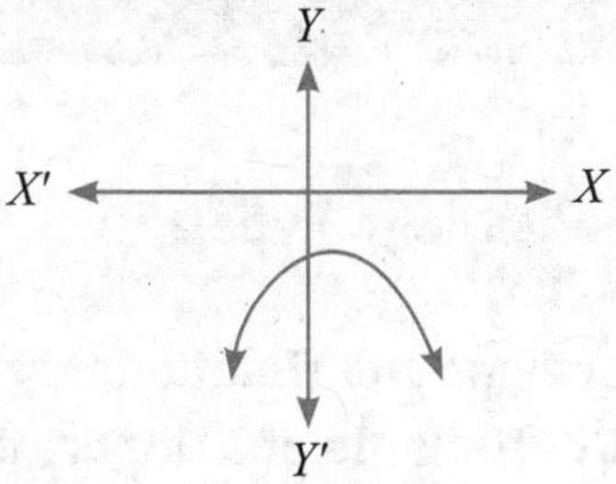

Sol. The graph does not intersect the x–axis. *(1 M)*

So, the number of zeroes is 0. *(1 M)*

6. **If $x = 1$ is a zero of the polynomial $f(x) = x^2 - 5x + k$, then find the value of k.** *(Re)*

Sol. Given polynomial $f(x) = x^2 - 5x + k$

At $x = 1$,

$f(1) = 1^2 - 5\times1 + k = 0$ *(1 M)*

$\Rightarrow k - 4 = 0 \Rightarrow k = 4$ *(1 M)*

7. **If $x = 3$ is one zero of the quadratic polynomial $x^2 - 2kx - 6$, then find the value of k.** *(Un)*

Sol. Given quadratic polynomial

$p(x) = x^2 - 2kx - 6$

At $x = 3$

$p(3) = 3^2 - 2k.3 - 6 = 0$ *(1 M)*

$\Rightarrow 9 - 6k - 6 = 0 \Rightarrow 3 - 6k = 0 \Rightarrow 6k = 3$

$\Rightarrow k = \dfrac{1}{2}$ *(1 M)*

Short Answer Type Questions (2 or 3 M)

1. **The graphical representation of quadratic polynomial $y = ax^2 + bx + c$ is shown in the given figure. Does it have (*i*) any solution (*ii*) zero(s)?** *(Re)*

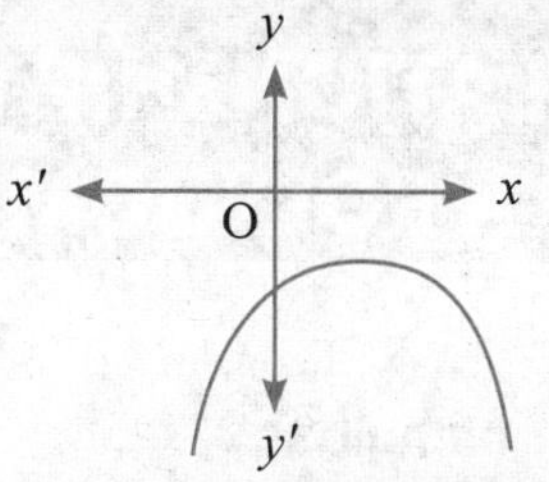

Sol. (*i*) There are infinite many solutions because there are infinite points that satisfy the equation $y = ax^2 + bx + c$. *(1½ M)*

(*ii*) There is no zero because graphically there is no point of intersection of x–axis and the curve. *(1½ M)*

2. **If each one of the following graphs is the graph of a polynomial, then identify which one corresponds to a linear polynomial and which one corresponds to a quadratic polynomial?** *(An)*

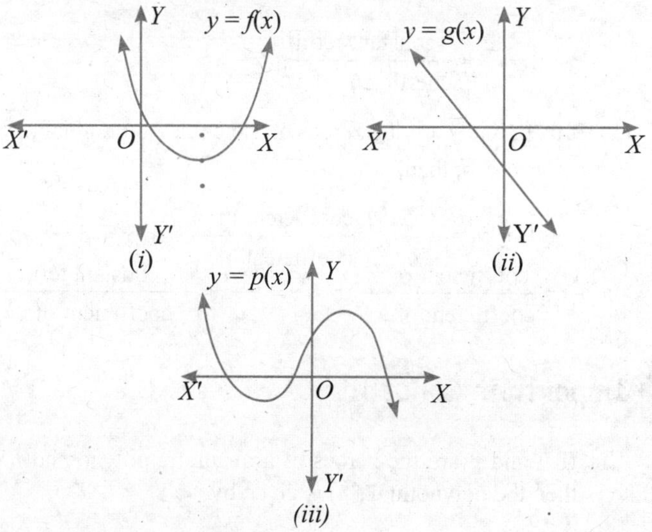

Sol. (*i*) We observe that the graph $y = f(x)$ is a parabola opening upwards. Therefore, $f(x)$ is a quadratic polynomial in which the coefficient of x^2 is positive. *(1 M)*

(*ii*) We find that the graph $y = g(x)$ is a straight line. So, $g(x)$ is a linear polynomial. *(1 M)*

(*iii*) Here, $p(x)$ is neither linear nor quadratic. *(1 M)*

2 RELATIONSHIP BETWEEN ZEROES AND COEFFICIENTS OF A POLYNOMIAL

Important Formulas

Relationship between Zeroes and Coefficients of a Polynomial:

In general,

(*i*) If α and β are the zeroes of the quadratic polynomial $p(x) = ax^2 + bx + c, a \neq 0$, then

$$\alpha + \beta = -\frac{b}{a} = -\frac{\text{coefficient of } x}{\text{coefficient of } x^2} \text{ and}$$

$$\alpha\beta = \frac{c}{a} = \frac{\text{constant term}}{\text{coefficient of } x^2}.$$

(*ii*) If α, β, and γ are the zeroes of the cubic polynomial $ax^3 + bx^2 + cx + d$, then,

$$\alpha + \beta + \gamma = -\frac{b}{a} = -\frac{\text{coefficient of } x^2}{\text{coefficient of } x^3}, \alpha\beta + \beta\gamma + \gamma\alpha = \frac{c}{a} = \frac{\text{coefficient of } x}{\text{coefficient of } x^3}, \alpha\beta\gamma = \frac{-d}{a} = -\frac{\text{constant term}}{\text{coefficient of } x^3}.$$

Important Concepts

- If α and β are the zeroes of a quadratic polynomial $f(x)$, then the polynomial $f(x)$ is given by

  $f(x) = k\{x^2 - (\alpha + \beta)x + \alpha\beta\}$

  OR

  $f(x) = k\{x^2 - (\text{Sum of the zeroes})\, x + \text{Product of the zeroes}\}$

  where k is any non-zero real number.
- Cubic polynomial having α, β, and γ as its zeroes is given by

  $f(x) = k\{x^3 - (\alpha + \beta + \gamma)x^2 + (\alpha\beta + \beta\gamma + \gamma\alpha)x - \alpha\beta\gamma\}$, where k is any non-zero real number.

Real Life Applications

Weekends are meant to be spent doing something exciting and adventurous. One such adventure that is sure to get your adrenaline pumping is a roller coaster ride at an adventure park. The thrill of the ride, the wind in your hair, and the screams of excitement all around you make for an unforgettable experience.

You all must have seen the roller coaster ride, then a doubt must have come in your mind that how was such a perfect architecture made?

You noticed that the shape resembles a curve about which you had studied in mathematics. The shape of the roller coaster ride is a parabola and it is represented by a polynomial. So polynomials are used in structure of roller coaster ride

Different Problem Types

Type I: On Verifying the Relationship Between the Zeroes and Coefficients of a Quadratic Polynomial

Step I: Find the Zeroes: To find the zeroes of the polynomial, set the polynomial equal to zero and solve for x.

Step II: Verify the Relationship:

- **Sum of Zeroes:** Check if the sum of the Zeroes $(\alpha + \beta)$ is equal to the negation of the coefficient of the linear term divided by the coefficient of the quadratic term $\left(-\frac{b}{a}\right)$.
- **Product of Zeroes:** Check if the product of the Zeroes $(\alpha \cdot \beta)$ is equal to the constant term divided by the coefficient of the quadratic term $\left(\frac{c}{a}\right)$.

Find the Zeroes of the quadratic polynomial $x^2 + 7x + 12$, and verify the relation between the zeroes and its coefficients.

Solution: We have,

$f(x) = x^2 + 7x + 12 = x^2 + 4x + 3x + 12 = x(x + 4) + 3(x + 4) = (x + 4)(x + 3)$

The zeroes of $f(x)$ are given by $f(x)=0$.

Now, $f(x) = 0$

$x^2 + 7x + 12 = 0 \Rightarrow (x + 4)(x + 3) = 0 \Rightarrow x + 4 = 0$ or, $x + 3 = 0$ $\Rightarrow x = -4$ or, $x = -3$

Thus, the zeroes of $f(x) = x^2 + 7x + 12$ are -4 and -3.

Now, Sum of the zeroes $= \alpha + \beta = (-4) + (-3) = -7$ and, $-\frac{\text{Coefficient of } x}{\text{Coefficient of } x^2} = -\frac{7}{1} = -7$.

$\therefore$ Sum of the zeroes $= -\frac{\text{Coefficient of } x}{\text{Coefficient of } x^2}$

Product of the zeroes $= \alpha\beta = (-4)\times(-3) = 12$ and, $\frac{\text{Constant term}}{\text{Coefficient of } x^2} = \frac{12}{1} = 12$

Type II: On Finding a Quadratic Polynomial When The Sum and Product of its Zeroes are Given

Step I: Identify Given Information: Begin by identifying the given information in the problem. Note down the sum (S) and product (P) of the zeroes of the quadratic polynomial.

Step II: Write equations based on the sum and product of the zeroes. i.e., $k\{x^2 - (\text{sum of the zeroes})x + \text{Product of the zeroes}\}$, where k is a constant.

Example: Find a quadratic polynomial each with the given numbers as the sum and product of its Zeroes respectively are $\frac{1}{4}$, –1.

Solution: We know that a quadratic polynomial is when the sum and product of its zeroes are given by

$f(x) = k\{x^2 -$ (Sum of the zeroes) x + Product of the zeroes$\}$, where k is a constant. We have, Sum = $\frac{1}{4}$ and Product = –1. So, required quadratic polynomial $f(x)$ is given by

$$f(x) = k\left(x^2 - \frac{1}{4}x - 1\right)$$

Type III: On Finding an Unknown When a Relation Between Zeroes and Coefficients is Given

Step I: Begin by identifying the relation provided between the zeroes and coefficients of the quadratic equation.

Step II: Write down the equations based on the given relation, expressing the coefficients (a, b, c) of the quadratic equation in terms of the unknown variable you need to find.

Step III: Solve the equation derived in step II to find the value of the unknown variable.

Step IV: Interpret the results in the context of the problem.

Example: If α and β are the zeroes of the polynomial $f(x) = x^2 - 5x + k$ such that $\alpha - \beta = 1$, find the value of k.

Solution: It is given that α and β are the zeroes of the polynomial $f(x) = x^2 - 5x + k$.

$$\therefore \alpha + \beta = -\left(\frac{-5}{1}\right) = 5 \text{ and } \alpha\beta = \frac{k}{1} = k$$

Now, $\alpha - \beta = 1$ [Given]

$\Rightarrow (\alpha - \beta)^2 = 1 \Rightarrow (\alpha + \beta)^2 - 4\alpha\beta = 1 \Rightarrow 25 - 4k = 1 \Rightarrow 24 = 4k$

$\Rightarrow k = 6$

Hence, the value of k is 6.

COMPETENCY BASED SOLVED EXAMPLES

Multiple Choice Questions

(1 M)

1. **If α and β are the zeroes of $(2x^2 + 5x - 9)$, then the value of αβ is** *(Ev)* **(CBSE, 2020)**

(a) $-\frac{5}{2}$ (b) $\frac{5}{2}$ (c) $-\frac{9}{2}$ (d) $\frac{9}{2}$

Sol. Product of the roots: $\alpha\beta = \frac{c}{a} = \frac{-9}{2}$

2. **A quadratic polynomial, whose zeroes are –3 and 4, is** *(Ap)* **(NCERT Exemplar)**

(a) $x^2 - x + 12$ (b) $x^2 + x + 12$

(c) $\frac{x^2}{2} - \frac{x}{2} - 6$ (d) $2x^2 + 2x - 24$

Sol. Sum of zeroes, $\alpha + \beta = -3 + 4 = 1$

Product of zeroes, $\alpha\beta = -3 \times 4 = -12$

$\therefore$ Quadratic Polynomial $= x^2 - (\alpha + \beta)x + \alpha\beta$

$= x^2 - x - 12 = \frac{x^2}{2} - \frac{x}{2} - 6$

3. **A quadratic polynomial, the sum of whose zeroes is 0 and one zero is 4, is** *(Un)*

(a) $x^2 - 16$ (b) $x^2 + 16$

(c) $x^2 + 4$ (d) $x^2 - 4$

Sol. Let the other zero be α.

$\therefore \alpha + 4 = 0 \Rightarrow \alpha = -4$

$\therefore$ Product of Zeroes $= 4\alpha = 4 \times -4 = -16$

Required quadratic polynomial

$= x^2 -$ (sum of Zeroes) $x +$ product of Zeroes

$= x^2 - 0 \cdot x + (-16) = x^2 - 16$

Key Takeaways

Quadratic equation in the form of roots is given as:

$x^2 - (\alpha + \beta)x + (\alpha\beta) = 0$

4. **If $f(t) = 2t^2 - 8 - 8t$ and m, n are the zeroes of the polynomial, then the value of $m^2 - 2mn + n^2$ is** *(Un)*

(a) 0 (b) 32

(c) 4 (d) 16

Sol. Given $f(t) = 2t^2 - 8t - 8$

$\therefore m + n = \frac{-(-8)}{2} = 4$

and $mn = \frac{-8}{2} = -4$

$(m - n)^2 = (m + n)^2 - 4mn = 16 + 16 = 32$

$\therefore m^2 - 2mn + n^2 = (m - n)^2 = 32$

5. **The quadratic polynomial, the sum of whose zeroes is –5 and their product is 6, is** *(Re)*

(a) $x^2 + 5x + 6$ (b) $x^2 - 5x + 6$

(c) $x^2 - 5x - 6$ (d) $-x^2 + 5x + 6$

Sol. Let α and β be the zeroes of polynomial

$\therefore$ Given $\alpha + \beta = -5$ and $\alpha\beta = 6$

We know that

$p(x) = x^2 - (\alpha + \beta)x + \alpha\beta = x^2 - (-5)x + 6$

$p(x) = x^2 + 5x + 6$

6. **If one of the zeroes of the quadratic polynomial $x^2 + 3x + k$ is 2, then the value of k is** *(Cr)*

(a) 10 (b) –10

(c) –7 (d) –2

Sol. Given quadratic polynomial is $x^2 + 3x + k$

Let α, β be the zeroes

We have from given quadratic polynomial

$\alpha + \beta = -3$ and $\alpha \cdot \beta = k$

Given one zeroes is 2

Let $\alpha = 2$

$\therefore 2 + \beta = -3 \Rightarrow \beta = -5$

$k = \alpha\beta = (2)(-5) = -10$

Mistakes 101 : What not to do!

Students may misuse or overlook factorization techniques, leading to incomplete factorization or incorrect solutions to polynomial equations.

7. **The zeroes of the polynomial $x^2 - 3x - m(m + 3)$ are** *(Ev)*

(a) $m, m + 3$ (b) $-m, m + 3$

(c) $m, -(m + 3)$ (d) $-m, -(m + 3)$

Sol. Given, $x^2 - 3x - m(m + 3)$ is the quadratic polynomial.

Now, $x^2 - 3x - m(m + 3) = 0$

$\Rightarrow x^2 - (3 + m - m)x - m(m + 3) = 0$

[by middle term factorization]

$\Rightarrow x^2 - (m + 3)x + mx - m(m + 3) = 0$

$\Rightarrow x(x - (m + 3)) + m(x - (m + 3)) = 0$

$\Rightarrow (x + m)(x - (m + 3)) = 0$

$\Rightarrow x + m = 0$ or $x - (m + 3) = 0$

$\Rightarrow x = -m$ or $x = m + 3$

$\therefore$ The zeroes are, $-m$ and $m + 3$.

8. **A quadratic polynomial, the product and sum of whose zeroes are 5 and 8 respectively is** *(Un)*

(a) $k[x^2 - 8x + 5]$ (b) $k[x^2 + 8x + 5]$

(c) $k[x^2 - 5x + 8]$ (d) $k[x^2 + 5x + 8]$

Sol. Given, sum of zeroes = 8

and product of zeroes = 5

We know, if α & β be the zero of polynomial $p(x)$, then

$p(x) = k[x^2 - (\text{sum of the zeroes})\, x + \text{product of the zeroes}]$

where k is any non–zero real number

$p(x) = k[x^2 - 8x + 5]$

9. If the zeroes of the quadratic polynomial $ax^2 + bx + c$, $c \neq 0$ are equal, then *(Ap)*

(*a*) c and a have opposite signs

(*b*) c and b have same sign

(*c*) c and a have same sign

(*d*) c and b have opposite sign

Sol. Given polynomial $ax^2 + bx + c, c \neq 0$

Let α and β be the zeroes of polynomial.

It is given that both the zeroes are equal i.e., either both the zeroes have negative sign or positive sign.

$\Rightarrow \alpha\beta$ must be positive

$\therefore \alpha\beta = \frac{c}{a}$ (positive) i.e., c and a must have same sign.

In quadratic polynomial. Coefficient of x^2 and constant term have the same sign i.e. 'c' and 'a' have the same sign. While 'b', the coefficient of x can be positive or negative but not zero.

Answer Key

1. (*c*) 2. (*c*) 3. (*a*) 4. (*b*) 5. (*a*)
6. (*b*) 7. (*b*) 8. (*a*) 9. (*c*)

Assertion and Reason

(1 M)

Direction: In the following questions, a statement of Assertion (A) is followed by a statement of Reason (R). Mark the correct choice as.

(*a*) Both Assertion (A) and Reason (R) are true, and Reason (R) is the correct explanation of Assertion (A).

(*b*) Both Assertion (A) and Reason (R) are true, but Reason (R) is not the correct explanation of Assertion (A).

(*c*) Assertion (A) is true, but Reason (R) is false.

(*d*) Assertion (A) is false, but Reason (R) is true.

1. Assertion (A): The number of zeroes of a given polynomial $p(x)$ is equal to the number of intersection points of the graph of $y = p(x)$ at x-axis.

Reason (R): The number of zeroes of polynomial $p(x) = x^2 + 7x + 10$ is 2. *(Re)*

Sol. Assertion: Number of zeroes = Number of intersection point at x–axis

Reason:

$p(x) = x^2 + 7x + 10 = 0 \Rightarrow x^2 + 5x + 2x + 10 = 0$

$\Rightarrow x(x + 5) + 2(x + 5) = 0 \Rightarrow (x + 5)(x + 2) = 0$

$\therefore x = -2, -5$

Both assertion (A) and reason(R) are true but reason is not correct explanation of the assertion.

2. Assertion (A): If the product of zeroes of quadratic polynomial $x^2 + 3x + 5(k + 1)$ is -10 then the value of k is -3.

Reason (R): Product of zeroes of quadratic polynomial $ax^2 + bx + c$ is $\frac{c}{a}$. *(Re)*

Sol. Assertion: Given $5(k + 1) = -10 \Rightarrow 5k = -15 \Rightarrow k = -3$

Reason : Product of zeroes $= \frac{c}{a} = \frac{\text{constant term}}{\text{coefficient of } x^2}$

Therefore, Both Assertion and Reason are True, and Reason is correct explanation of A

3. Assertion (A): A quadratic polynomial, whose sum of zeroes is 8 and their product is 12, is $x^2 - 8x + 12$.

Reason (R): If α and β are zeroes of quadratic polynomial $f(x)$, then the polynomial is given by $f(x) = x^2 - (\alpha\beta)x + (\alpha + \beta)$. *(Un)*

Sol. Assertion: Given $\alpha + \beta = 8$ and $\alpha.\beta = 12$

$\therefore p(x) = x^2 - (\alpha + \beta)\,x + \alpha\beta = x^2 - 8x + 12$

Therefore assertion is true but reason is false.

Answer Key

1. (*b*) 2. (*a*) 3. (*c*)

Subjective Questions

Very Short Answer Type Questions

(1 or 2 M)

1. $p(x) = 2x^2 - 6x - 3$. The two zeroes are of the form: $\frac{3 \pm \sqrt{k}}{2}$; Where k is a real number

Use the relationship between the zeroes and coefficients of a polynomial to find the value of k. Show your steps. **(*Cr*) (CBSE CFPQ, 2023)**

Sol. Given polynomial, $p(x) = 2x^2 - 6x - 3$

When the given polynomial is compared with the standard form, we get $a = 2$, $b = -6$, $c = -3$ *(½ M)*

The two zeroes of the given polynomial are $\alpha, \beta = \frac{3 \pm \sqrt{k}}{2}$ *(½ M)*

We need to find the value of k,

Using the relationship between the zeroes and the coefficients of a polynomial, we get

The product of zeroes $= c/a$,

$\frac{3 + \sqrt{k}}{2} \times \frac{3 - \sqrt{k}}{2} = \frac{-3}{2}$ *(½ M)*

Using the identity $a^2 - b^2 = (a + b)(a - b) \Rightarrow \frac{9 - k}{4} = \frac{-3}{2}$

On cross–multiplication, we get $18 - 2k = -12$

Transposing the constant to one side, we get

$2k = 30$ *(½ M)*

Hence, the value of k is 15

Nailing the Right Answer

Students should recognize that polynomial equations may have complex roots, which occur in conjugate pairs if the coefficients are real, treat complex roots appropriately when solving polynomial equations.

2. Find the value for which one root of the quadratic equation $px^2 - 14x + 8 = 0$ is 6 times the other. *(Un)*

Sol. The given quadratic equation is $px^2 - 14x + 8 = 0$

Let the root be "α" then other root will be 6α

Sum of the roots $= \frac{-b}{a}$ *(½ M)*

$\Rightarrow \alpha + 6\alpha = \frac{-(-14)}{p} \Rightarrow 7\alpha = \frac{14}{p}$

$\therefore \alpha = \frac{2}{p}$ ... (i) *(½ M)*

$\Rightarrow$ Product of the roots $= \frac{c}{a} \Rightarrow \alpha \cdot 6\alpha = \frac{8}{p} \Rightarrow 6\alpha^2 = \frac{8}{p}$

$\Rightarrow 6\left(\frac{2}{p}\right)^2 = \frac{8}{p}$ [From (i)] *(½ M)*

$\Rightarrow 6 \times \frac{4}{p^2} = \frac{8}{p}$

$\therefore p = 3$ *(½ M)*

Topper's Explanation ***(CBSE 2019)***

Let α and β be the roots of given quadratic equation

$\beta = 6\alpha$

Here, $a = p$ $b = -14$, $c = 8$.

$\alpha + \beta = \frac{-(-14)}{p} = \frac{-b}{a}$

$7\alpha = \frac{14}{p}$

$\alpha = \frac{2}{p}$ —①

Also, $\alpha\beta = \frac{8}{p} = \frac{c}{a}$

$\alpha \times 6\alpha = \frac{8}{p}$

$6\alpha^2 = \frac{8}{p}$

from ①

$6\left(\frac{2}{p}\right)^2 = \frac{8}{p}$

$\frac{6 \times 4}{p^2} = \frac{8}{p}$

$\frac{6}{p^2} = \frac{2}{p}$

$\frac{6}{2} = \frac{p^2}{p}$

$\therefore p = 3$

Key Takeaways

Relationship between the roots of a quadratic equation and the coefficients is $\alpha + \beta = -\frac{b}{a}$, $\alpha\beta = \frac{c}{a}$

3. Find the value of 'k' such that the polynomial $p(x) = 3x^2 + 2kx + x - k - 5$ has the sum of zeroes equal to half of their product. *(Ev)* **(CBSE, 2023)**

Sol. Sum of the roots $(\alpha + \beta) = -\frac{2k+1}{3}$

Product of the roots $(\alpha\beta) = \frac{-k-5}{3}$ *(½ M)*

$\alpha + \beta = \frac{\alpha\beta}{2} \Rightarrow -\frac{2k+1}{3} = \frac{-k-5}{6}$ *(½ M)*

$\Rightarrow -2(2k+1) = -(k+5) \Rightarrow -4k - 2 = -k - 5$

$\Rightarrow -4k + k = -5 + 2 \Rightarrow -3k = -3 \Rightarrow k = 1$ *(1 M)*

4. In the quadratic polynomial $t^2 - 16$, sum of the zeroes is ________. *(Ap)* **(CBSE, 2020)**

Sol. In a quadratic polynomial $ax^2 + bx + c$, the sum of the roots $(\alpha + \beta)$ is given by $-\frac{b}{a}$.

In the given polynomial $t^2 - 16$, we have $a = 1$ and $b = 0$

So, the sum of the roots is $-\frac{b}{a} = \frac{-0}{1} = 0$

Therefore, the sum of the zeroes is 0. *(1 M)*

5. Find the quadratic polynomial if the sum and Product of its zeroes are 2 and 1 respectively. *(Ap)*

Sol. If the roots are α and β then quadratic polynomial is given as

$f(x) = k(x^2 - (\alpha + \beta)x + \alpha\beta)$ *(1 M)*

where k is any constant

Here $\alpha + \beta = 2$, $\alpha\beta = 1$

$\therefore f(x) = k\left(x^2 - 2x + 1\right)$ *(1 M)*

Short Answer Type Questions (2 or 3 M)

1. If α, β are zeroes of quadratic polynomial $5x^2 + 5x + 1$, find the value of *(Un)*

I. $\alpha^2 + \beta^2$ **II. $\alpha^{-1} + \beta^{-1}$**

Sol. $P(x) = 5x^2 + 5x + 1$

$\alpha + \beta = \frac{-b}{a} = \frac{-5}{5} = -1$ *(½ M)*

$\alpha\beta = \frac{c}{a} = \frac{1}{5}$ *(½ M)*

I. $\alpha^2 + \beta^2 = (\alpha + \beta)^2 - 2\alpha\beta = (-1)^2 - 2\left(\frac{1}{5}\right)$ *(½ M)*

$= 1 - \frac{2}{5} = \frac{3}{5}$ *(½ M)*

II. $\alpha^{-1} + \beta^{-1} = \frac{1}{\alpha} + \frac{1}{\beta}$ *(½ M)*

$= \frac{(\alpha + \beta)}{\alpha\beta} = \frac{(-1)}{\frac{1}{5}} = -5$ *(½ M)*

2. Find the zeroes of the polynomial $x^2+\frac{1}{6}x-2$, and verify the relation between the coefficients and the zeroes of the polynomial. (*Ev*) (NCERT Exemplar)

Sol. $x^2+\frac{1}{6}x-2=\frac{1}{6}(6x^2+x-12)=\frac{1}{6}[6x^2+9x-8x-12]$ (½ M)

$=\frac{1}{6}[3x(2x+3)-4(2x+3)]=\frac{1}{6}(3x-4)(2x+3)$ (½ M)

Hence, $\frac{4}{3}$ and $-\frac{3}{2}$ are the zeroes of the given polynomial. (½ M)

The given polynomial is $x^2+\frac{1}{6}x-2$ (½ M)

The sum of zeroes $=\frac{4}{3}+\frac{-3}{2}=\frac{-1}{6}=-\frac{\text{Coefficient of } x}{\text{Coefficient of } x^2}$ (½ M)

The product of zeroes $=\frac{4}{3}\times\frac{-3}{2}=-2=\frac{\text{Constant term}}{\text{Coefficient of } x^2}$ (½ M)

3. If the product of zeroes of the polynomial ax^2-6x-6 is 4, find the value of a. Find the sum of zeroes of the polynomial. (*Ev*)

Sol. Let α, β be the zeroes of a given polynomial

$p(x)=ax^2-6x-6$.

Then, $\alpha\beta=\frac{-6}{a}\Rightarrow 4=\frac{-6}{a}\Rightarrow a=\frac{-6}{4}=\frac{-3}{2}$ (1½ M)

Now, sum of zeroes $=\frac{6}{a}=\frac{6}{\left(\frac{-3}{2}\right)}=\frac{2\times 6}{-3}=-4$ (1½ M)

4. If the zeroes of the polynomial x^2+px+q are double than the zeroes of $2x^2-5x-3$, find the value of p and q. (*Ev*)

Sol. Let α, β be the zeroes of $2x^2-5x-3$

$\therefore \alpha+\beta=\frac{5}{2}, \alpha\beta=\frac{-3}{2}$ (1 M)

It is given that 2α and 2β are zeroes of x^2+px+q

$\therefore 2\alpha+2\beta=-p\Rightarrow 2\times(\alpha+\beta)=-p$

$\Rightarrow 2\times\frac{5}{2}=-p\Rightarrow p=-5$ (1 M)

and $2\alpha\times 2\beta=q\Rightarrow 4\alpha\beta=q$

$\Rightarrow 4\times\left(\frac{-3}{2}\right)=q\Rightarrow q=-6$ (1 M)

5. If one zero of the polynomial $2x^2+3x+\lambda$ is 1/2, find the value of λ and the other zero. (*An*)

Sol. Let, the zero of $2x^2+3x+\lambda$ be 1/2 and β.

Product of zeroes $=\frac{c}{a},\Rightarrow\frac{1}{2}\times\beta=\frac{\lambda}{2}$ (1 M)

$\Rightarrow\beta=\lambda$

and sum of zeroes $=-\frac{b}{a}\Rightarrow\frac{1}{2}+\beta=-\frac{3}{2}$ (1 M)

$\Rightarrow\beta=-\frac{3}{2}-\frac{1}{2}=-2$

Hence $\lambda=\beta=-2$

Thus, the other zero is –2. (1 M)

6. Find the value of k such that the polynomial $x^2-(k+6)x+2(2k-1)$ has sum of its Zeroes equal to half of their product. (*Un*)

Sol. Given quadratic polynomial

$p(x)=x^2-(k+6)x+2(2k-1)$ ...(*i*) (½ M)

we know that

$p(x)=x^2-(\alpha+\beta)x+\alpha\beta$ ...(*ii*) (½ M)

comparing (*i*) & (*ii*), we get

$\alpha+\beta=k+6$

and $\alpha\beta=2(2k-1)$ (1 M)

given that

$\alpha+\beta=\frac{1}{2}\alpha\beta\Rightarrow k+6=\frac{1}{2}\times 2(2k-1)\Rightarrow k=7$ (1 M)

7. If α and β are the zeroes of the polynomial $f(x)=5x^2-7x+1$, then find the value of $\left(\frac{\alpha}{\beta}+\frac{\beta}{\alpha}\right)$. (*Ap*) (CBSE, 2020)

Sol. Sum of roots $\alpha+\beta=\frac{7}{5}$ (½ M)

Product of roots $=\alpha\beta=\frac{1}{5}$ (½ M)

$\frac{\alpha}{\beta}+\frac{\beta}{\alpha}=\frac{\alpha^2+\beta^2}{\alpha\beta}=\frac{(\alpha+\beta)^2-2\alpha\beta}{\alpha\beta}$ (1 M)

Now, substituting the known values:

$\frac{\alpha^2+\beta^2}{\alpha\beta}=\frac{\left(\frac{7}{5}\right)^2-2.\frac{1}{5}}{\frac{1}{5}}$

$=\frac{\frac{49}{25}-\frac{2}{5}}{\frac{1}{5}}=\frac{\frac{49-10}{25}}{\frac{1}{5}}=\frac{\frac{39}{25}}{\frac{1}{5}}=\frac{39}{5}$

So, $\frac{\alpha}{\beta}+\frac{\beta}{\alpha}=\frac{39}{5}$. (1 M)

8. Find a quadratic polynomial, the sum and product of whose zeroes are $\sqrt{2}$ and $-\frac{3}{2}$, respectively. Also find its zeroes. (*Ev*) (NCERT Exemplar)

Sol. A quadratic polynomial, the sum and product of whose zeroes are $\sqrt{2}$ and $-\frac{3}{2}$ is $x^2-\sqrt{2}x-\frac{3}{2}$ (1 M)

$x^2-\sqrt{2}\,x-\frac{3}{2}=\frac{1}{2}[2x^2-2\sqrt{2}x-3]$

$=\frac{1}{2}[2x^2+\sqrt{2}x-3\sqrt{2}x-3]$

$= \frac{1}{2}[\sqrt{2}x(\sqrt{2}x+1)-3(\sqrt{2}x+1)]$

$= \frac{1}{2}[\sqrt{2}x+1][\sqrt{2}x-3]$ (1 M)

Hence, the zeroes are $-\frac{1}{\sqrt{2}}$ and $\frac{3}{\sqrt{2}}$. (1 M)

9. If α, β, and γ are the zeroes of the polynomial $f(x) = x^3 - px^2 + qx - r$. Then find $\frac{1}{\alpha\beta}+\frac{1}{\beta\gamma}+\frac{1}{\gamma\alpha}$. *(Cr)*

Sol. Given $f(x) = x^3 - px^2 + qx - r$

We have

$\alpha+\beta+\gamma = p$ (1 M)

and $\alpha\beta\gamma = r$ (1 M)

Now $\frac{1}{\alpha\beta}+\frac{1}{\beta\gamma}+\frac{1}{\gamma\alpha} = \frac{\gamma+\alpha+\beta}{\alpha\beta\gamma} = \frac{p}{r}$ (1 M)

Mistakes 101 : What not to do!

Students may rely too heavily on memorised formulas or techniques without understanding the underlying concepts, leading to errors in application or difficulty adapting to new problem scenarios.

10. If α and β are the zeroes of the quadratic polynomial $f(t) = t^2 - 5t + 3$, then the value of $\alpha^4\beta^3 + \alpha^3\beta^4$. *(Un)*

Sol. Given, $f(t) = t^2 - 5t + 3$

Given α, β are zeroes

$\therefore \alpha + \beta = 5$

and $\alpha\beta = 3$ (1 M)

Now $\alpha^4\beta^3 + \alpha^3\beta^4 = \alpha^3\beta^3(\alpha+\beta)$ (1 M)

$= (3)^3 (5) = 27 \times 5 = 135$ (1 M)

Long Answer Type Questions (4 or 5 M)

1. If m and n are the zeroes of the polynomial $3x^2 + 11x - 4$, find the value of $m/n + n/m$. *(An)*

Sol. Given $p(x) = 3x^2 + 11x - 4$

Sum of zeroes, $m+n = -\frac{11}{3}$ (1 M)

Product of zeroes, $mn = \frac{-4}{3}$ (1 M)

Now $\frac{m}{n}+\frac{n}{m} = \frac{m^2+n^2}{mn} = \frac{(m+n)^2-2mn}{mn}$ (1 M)

$$= \frac{\left(-\frac{11}{3}\right)^2 - \left(\frac{-4}{3}\right)\times 2}{\frac{-4}{3}} = \frac{\frac{121}{9}+\frac{8}{3}}{\frac{-4}{3}}$$ (1 M)

$$= \frac{\frac{121+24}{9}}{\frac{-4}{3}} = \frac{-145}{12}$$ (1 M)

2. If α and β are the zeroes of the quadratic polynomial $p(s) = 3s^2 - 6s + 4$, then find the value of $\frac{\alpha}{\beta}+\frac{\beta}{\alpha}+2\left(\frac{1}{\alpha}+\frac{1}{\beta}\right)+3\alpha\beta$. *(Un)*

Sol. Since α and β are the zeroes of the polynomial $p(s) = 3s^2 - 6s + 4$,

$\therefore \alpha+\beta = \frac{-(-6)}{3} = 2$ and $\alpha\beta = \frac{4}{3}$ (1 M)

Given,

$$\frac{\alpha}{\beta}+\frac{\beta}{\alpha}+2\left(\frac{1}{\alpha}+\frac{1}{\beta}\right)+3\alpha\beta = \frac{\alpha^2+\beta^2}{\alpha\beta}+2\left(\frac{\beta+\alpha}{\alpha\beta}\right)+3\alpha\beta$$ (1 M)

$$= \frac{(\alpha+\beta)^2-2\alpha\beta}{\alpha\beta}+\frac{2(\alpha+\beta)}{\alpha\beta}+3\alpha\beta$$ (1 M)

$$= \frac{(2)^2-2\times\frac{4}{3}}{\frac{4}{3}}+\frac{2\times 2}{\frac{4}{3}}+3\times\frac{4}{3}$$ (1 M)

$$= \frac{4-\frac{8}{3}}{\frac{4}{3}}+\frac{4}{\frac{4}{3}}+\frac{12}{3} = 1+3+4 = 8$$ (1 M)

3. If α and β are the zeroes of the polynomial $ax^2 + bx + c$, find a polynomial whose zeroes are $\left\{\frac{1}{a\alpha+b} \text{ and } \frac{1}{a\beta+b}\right\}$. *(An)*

Sol. As α and β are the zeroes of the polynomial $ax^2 + bx + c$

$\therefore \alpha+\beta = \frac{-b}{a}$ and $\alpha\beta = \frac{c}{a}$ ... (i) (½ M)

Since $\frac{1}{a\alpha+b}$ and $\frac{1}{a\beta+b}$ are the zeroes of the required polynomial.

∴ sum of the zeroes

$$= \frac{1}{a\alpha+b}+\frac{1}{a\beta+b} = \frac{a\beta+b+a\alpha+b}{(a\alpha+b)(a\beta+b)}$$ (½ M)

$$= \frac{a(\alpha+\beta)+2b}{a^2\alpha\beta+ab(\alpha+\beta)+b^2}$$ (½ M)

$$= \frac{a\times\left(\frac{-b}{a}\right)+2b}{a^2\times\left(\frac{c}{a}\right)+ab\times\left(\frac{-b}{a}\right)+b^2}$$ [using eq. (i)]

$$= \frac{-b+2b}{ac-b^2+b^2} = \frac{b}{ac}$$ (1 M)

Product of the zeroes

$$= \left(\frac{1}{a\alpha+b}\right)\left(\frac{1}{a\beta+b}\right) = \frac{1}{a^2\alpha\beta+ab(\alpha+\beta)+b^2}$$ (½ M)

$$= \frac{1}{a^2\times\frac{c}{a}+ab\times\left(\frac{-b}{a}\right)+b^2}$$ [using eq. (i)] (½ M)

$$= \frac{1}{\frac{a^2c-ab^2+b^2a}{a}} = \frac{1}{\frac{a^2c}{a}} = \frac{1}{ac}$$ (1 M)

Hence, the required polynomial is given by x^2 – (sum of zeroes) x + product of zeroes = $x^2 - \left(\frac{b}{ac}\right)x + \frac{1}{ac}$ *(½ M)*

Nailing the Right Answer

Utilize algebraic manipulation techniques to simplify polynomial expressions, rearrange terms, or combine like terms. This can often lead to a more manageable expression or reveal patterns that aid in solving the problem.

4. If α and β are the zeroes of the quadratic polynomial $f(x) = x^2 - px + q$. Prove that

$$\frac{\alpha^2}{\beta^2}+\frac{\beta^2}{\alpha^2}=\frac{p^4}{q^2}-\frac{4p^2}{q}+2$$ **(Re)**

Sol. $f(x) = x^2 - px + q$

Here, $\alpha + \beta = p$

and $\alpha\beta = q$ *(1 M)*

Let us consider.

$$\text{L.H.S} = \frac{\alpha^2}{\beta^2}+\frac{\beta^2}{\alpha^2} = \frac{\alpha^4+\beta^4}{\alpha^2\beta^2} = \frac{(\alpha^2+\beta^2)^2-2\alpha^2\beta^2}{\alpha^2\beta^2}$$ *(1 M)*

$$= \frac{\left((\alpha+\beta)^2-2\alpha\beta\right)^2-2(\alpha\beta)^2}{(\alpha\beta)^2} = \frac{(p^2-2q)^2-2q^2}{q^2}$$ *(1 M)*

$$= \frac{p^4+4q^2-4p^2q-2q^2}{q^2} = \frac{p^4-4p^2q+2q^2}{q^2}$$ *(1 M)*

$$= \frac{p^4}{q^2}-\frac{4p^2}{q}+2 = \text{R.H.S.}$$ *(1 M)*

Nailing the Right Answer

Before attempting to solve a polynomial question, carefully read and understand the problem statement. Identify the given information, what is being asked, and any constraints or conditions provided.

MISCELLANEOUS EXERCISE

Multiple Choice Questions

(1 M)

1. If one of the zeroes of the quadratic polynomial $(k-1)x^2 + kx + 1$ is -3, then the value of k is **(NCERT Exemplar)**

(a) $\frac{4}{3}$ (b) $\frac{-4}{3}$

(c) $\frac{2}{3}$ (d) $\frac{-2}{3}$

2. If α, β are the zeroes of the polynomial $p(x) = 4x^2 - 3x - 7$, then $\left(\frac{1}{\alpha} + \frac{1}{\beta}\right)$ is equal to:

(a) $\frac{7}{3}$ (b) $\frac{-7}{3}$

(c) $\frac{3}{7}$ (d) $\frac{-3}{7}$

3. The zeroes of a polynomial if two zeroes equal but have opposite sign for $f(x) = x^3 - 3x^2 - 16x + 48$ is

(a) 4, – 4, – 3 (b) – 4, 4, 2

(c) 3, 4, – 4 (d) 4, – 4, 3

4. The zeroes of a polynomial $f(t) = t^3 - kt^2 + mt - n$ are 'a', 'b' and 'c'. The value of $\frac{1}{ca} + \frac{1}{ab} + \frac{1}{bc}$ is.

(a) $\frac{k}{n}$ (b) $\frac{m}{n}$

(c) $\frac{-k}{n}$ (d) $\frac{-m}{n}$

5. If one zero of the polynomial $(3x^2 + 8x + k)$ is the reciprocal of the other, then value of k is **(CBSE, 2020)**

(a) 3 (b) –3

(c) $\frac{1}{3}$ (d) $-\frac{1}{3}$

6. If $x = 3$ is one of the roots of the quadratic equation $x^2 - 2kx - 6 = 0$, then the value of k is **(CBSE SQP, 2023)**

(a) $-\frac{1}{2}$ (b) $\frac{1}{2}$

(c) 3 (d) 2

7. If $\alpha\beta = 5$, here 'α' and 'β' are the zeroes of $mx^2 - 5 + 3x$, then the value of 'm' is

(a) 1 (b) 5

(c) – 1 (d) None of these

8. If one zero is negative of other of a quadratic polynomial $g(x) = 3x^2 - 27ax + 9$, then the value of 'a' is.

(a) 9 (b) – 9

(c) 0 (d) None of these

9. If the sum of zeroes is equal to the product of zeroes for a polynomial $y(t) = nt^2 - 2t + 6n$, then the value of 'n' is.

(a) $\frac{2}{6}$ (b) $\frac{1}{3}$

(c) $\frac{3}{9}$ (d) All of these

10. If one zero of the quadratic polynomial, $(k-1)x^2 + kx + 1$ is -4 then the value of k is **(CBSE, 2020)**

(a) $-\frac{5}{4}$ (b) $\frac{5}{4}$

(c) $-\frac{4}{3}$ (d) $\frac{4}{3}$

Assertion and Reason

(1 M)

Direction: In the following questions, a statement of Assertion (A) is followed by a statement of Reason (R). Mark the correct choice as.

(a) Both Assertion (A) and Reason (R) are true, and Reason (R) is the correct explanation of Assertion (A).

(b) Both Assertion (A) and Reason (R) are true, but Reason (R) is not the correct explanation of Assertion (A).

(c) Assertion (A) is true, but Reason (R) is false.

(d) Assertion (A) is false, but Reason (R) is true.

1. **Assertion (A):** The graph $y = f(x)$ is shown in figure, for the polynomial $f(x)$. The number of zeroes of $f(x)$ is 5.

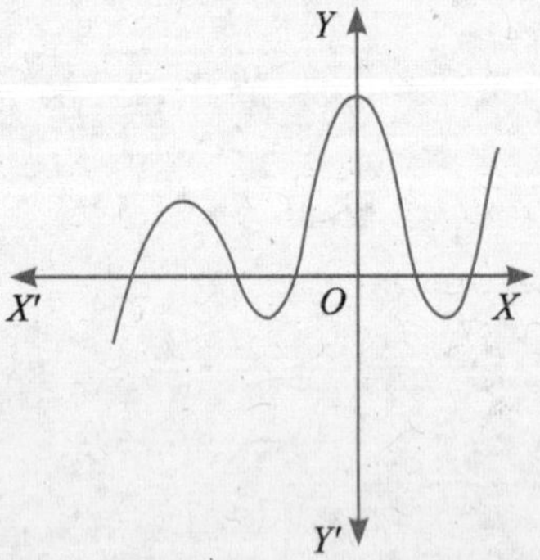

Reason (R): The number of zero of the polynomial $f(x)$ is the number of points at which $f(x)$ cuts or touches the y-axis.

2. **Assertion (A):** $(2-\sqrt{3})$ is one zero of the quadratic polynomial, then the other zero will be $(2+\sqrt{3})$.

Reason (R): Irrational zeroes always occur in pairs.

3. **Assertion (A):** The sum and product of the zeroes of a quadratic polynomial are $-\frac{1}{4}$ and $\frac{1}{4}$ respectively.

Then the quadratic polynomial is $2x^2 + \frac{x}{2} + \frac{1}{2}$.

Reason (R): The quadratic polynomial whose sum and product of zeroes are given is x^2 – (sum of zeroes). x + product of zeroes.

4. **Assertion (A):** Polynomial $x^2 + 4x$ has two real zeroes.

   Reason (R): Zeroes of the polynomial $x^2 + ax$ $(a \neq 0)$ are 0 and a. **(CBSE, 2023)**

5. **Assertion (A):** If one zero of polynomial $p(x) = (k+4)x^2 + 13x + 3k$ is reciprocal of other, then $k = 2$.

   Reason (R): If $(x - \alpha)$ is a factor of $p(x)$, then $p(\alpha) = 0$ i.e. α is a zero of $p(x)$.

Subjective Questions

Very Short Answer Type Questions (1 or 2 M)

1. Find a quadratic polynomial, the sum and product of whose zeroes are – 3 and 2, respectively. **(NCERT Intext)**
2. If α, β and γ are the zeroes of the polynomial $x^3 - 3x^2 + x + 1$, find the value of $\alpha + \beta + \gamma$.
3. If $x = 2$ & $x = 0$ are the zeroes of the polynomial $f(x) = 2x^3 - 5x^2 + ax + b$, then find the value of $a + b$.
4. If $x = 3$ is a root of $f(x) = x^3 - 4x^2 + 6k$, then find the value of k.

Short Answer Type Questions (2 or 3 M)

1. Find the zeroes of the quadratic polynomial $x^2 + 7x + 10$, and verify the relationship between the zeroes and the coefficients **(NCERT Intext)**
2. If α and β are the zeroes of the quadratic polynomial $ax^2 - bx + c$, then find the value of $\alpha^2 - \beta^2$.
3. Find a cubic polynomial whose zeroes are 1, 2 and –3.
4. Find the zeroes of the quadratic polynomial $4s^2 - 4s + 1$ and verify the relationship between the zeroes and the coefficients. **(CBSE SQP, 2023)**

Long Answer Type Questions (4 or 5 M)

1. If α and β are the zeroes of the quadratic polynomial $f(x) = ax^2 + bx + c$, then calculate the value of $\frac{\alpha^2}{\beta} + \frac{\beta^2}{\alpha}$.
2. If α and β are the zeroes of the polynomial $f(x) = x^2 - 3x + k$ such that $\alpha - \beta = 1$, find the value of k.
3. If α, β are the zeroes of the polynomial $f(x) = 2x^2 + 5x + k$ satisfying the relation $\alpha^2 + \beta^2 + \alpha\beta = \frac{21}{4}$, then find the value of k.
4. Verify that $\frac{1}{2}$, 1, and – 2 are zeroes of cubic polynomial $2x^3 + x^2 - 5x + 2$. Also, verify the relationship between the zeroes and their coefficients.
5. If α and β are the zeroes of the polynomial $x^2 + 4x + 3$, form the polynomial whose zeroes are $1 + \frac{\beta}{\alpha}$ and $1 + \frac{\alpha}{\beta}$.

Case Based Questions

Case Based-I: An object is projected into the air, subjected only to acceleration due to gravity, the path followed by an object is a parabola, represented by a polynomial If the polynomial $p(t) = -2t^2 + 7t + 4$ is representing the distance covered, then answer the following questions.

(*i*) Name and degree of given polynomial is
   (*a*) cubic, 2 (*b*) cubic, 3
   (*c*) biquadratic, 4 (*d*) quadratic, 2

(*ii*) The factors of the given polynomial are:
   (*a*) $(2t - 1)(t - 4)$ (*b*) $(-2t - 1)(t - 4)$
   (*c*) $(-2t - 1)(-t - 4)$ (*d*) None of these

(*iii*) The number of real zeroes of the given polynomial are:
   (*a*) 0 (*b*) 1
   (*c*) 2 (*d*) 3

(*iv*) The graph of the given polynomial cuts x-axis at:
   (*a*) $\frac{1}{2}, 4$ (*b*) $\frac{1}{2}, -4$
   (*c*) $-\frac{1}{2}, -4$ (*d*) $-\frac{1}{2}, 4$

Case Based-II: In our day to day life we see polynomials everywhere like in a football match, the path of the football in a kick is parabolic, represented by a quadratic polynomial.

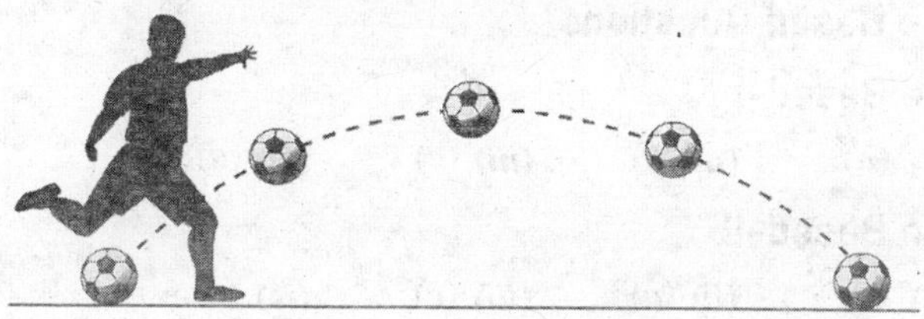

(i) In the standard form of a quadratic polynomial $ax^2 + bx + c$, a, b, and c are:

(a) All are rationals

(b) All are irrationals

(c) All are real numbers

(d) All are real numbers provided $a \neq 0$

(ii) Minimum/Maximum value of the polynomial $p(x) = ax^2 + bx + c$ exists at $x =$

(a) $-\frac{b}{2a}$ (b) $\frac{b}{2a}$ (c) $\frac{-D}{4a}$ (d) $\frac{D}{4a}$

(iii) Minimum/Maximum value of the polynomial $p(x) = ax^2 + bx + c$ is:

(a) $-\frac{b}{2a}$ (b) $\frac{b}{2a}$ (c) $\frac{-D}{4a}$ (d) $\frac{D}{4a}$

(iv) The graph of the quadratic polynomial $p(x) = ax^2 + bx + c$ cuts y-axis at:

(a) a (b) b

(c) c (d) None of these

Case Based-III: The skipping rope while skipping looks like a form of parabola. It is a natural example of parabolic shape which is represented by a quadratic polynomial. Similarly there are other examples as well related to polynomials.

(i) Find the value of x for which the graph of $p(x) = x^2 - 2$, intersects the x-axis.

(ii) If α and $\frac{1}{\alpha}$ are the zeroes of the quadratic polynomial $p(x) = 3x^2 - 2x + 5k$, then find the value of k:

OR

Find quadratic polynomial having sum and product of zeroes as α and $\frac{-1}{\alpha}$ respectively:

(iii) If α and β are the zeroes of the polynomial $p(x) = ax^2 + bx + c$, then find $\alpha^2\beta + \beta^2\alpha$

ANSWER KEYS

Multiple Choice Questions

1. (a) 2. (d) 3. (d) 4. (a) 5. (a) 6. (b) 7. (c) 8. (c) 9. (d) 10. (b)

Assertion and Reason

1. (c) 2. (a) 3. (a) 4. (a) 5. (b)

Case Based Questions

Case Based-I

(i) (d) (ii) (b) (iii) (c) (iv) (d)

Case Based-II

(i) (d) (ii) (a) (iii) (c) (iv) (c)

HINTS & EXPLANATIONS

Multiple Choice Questions

1. (*a*) Put $x = -3$ in the given polynomial $(k-1)x^2 + kx + 1$

$(k-1)(-3)^2 + k(-3) + 1 = 0 \Rightarrow (k-1)9 - 3k + 1 = 0$

$\Rightarrow 9k - 9 - 3k + 1 = 0 \Rightarrow 6k - 8 = 0 \Rightarrow k = \frac{8}{6} = \frac{4}{3}$

2. (*d*) Given $p(x) = 4x^2 - 3x - 7$

From the given equation $\alpha + \beta = \frac{+3}{4}, \alpha\beta = \frac{-7}{4}$

Therefore,

$$\frac{1}{\alpha} + \frac{1}{\beta} = \frac{\alpha+\beta}{\alpha\beta} = \frac{\frac{3}{4}}{\frac{-7}{4}} = -\frac{3}{7}$$

3. (*d*) Given $f(x) = x^3 - 3x^2 - 16x + 48$

Given two zeroes are equal but opposite sign

Let $a, -a$ & c are zeroes of $f(x)$

$$\therefore\ a + (-a) + c = \frac{-\text{coefficient of } x^2}{\text{coefficient of } x^3} = \frac{-(-3)}{1} \Rightarrow c = 3$$

$$\text{and } a(-a) \times c = \frac{-\text{Constant term}}{\text{Coefficient of } x^3} = \frac{-48}{1}$$

$\Rightarrow a^2c = 48 \Rightarrow a^2 \cdot 3 = 48 \Rightarrow a^2 = 16 \Rightarrow a = \pm 4$

$\therefore$ Zeroes are $a, -a, c = 4, -4, 3$

4. (*a*) Given a, b & c are zeroes of $f(t) = t^3 - kt^2 + mt - n$

$$\therefore\ a + b + c = \frac{-\text{coefficient of } t^2}{\text{coefficient of } t^3} = k$$

$$\text{and } abc = \frac{-\text{Constant term}}{\text{Coefficient of } t^3} = n$$

$$\therefore\ \frac{1}{ca} + \frac{1}{ab} + \frac{1}{bc} = \frac{a+b+c}{abc} = \frac{k}{n}$$

5. (*a*) Let's denote the roots of the polynomial $3x^2 + 8x + k$ as α and $\frac{1}{\alpha}$.

Let's solve this equation:

$\alpha + \frac{1}{\alpha} = -\frac{8}{3}$

$\alpha^2 + 1 = -\frac{8}{3}\alpha$

$3\alpha^2 + 3 = -8\alpha$

$3\alpha^2 + 8\alpha + 3 = 0$

Comparing this with the given polynomial $3x^2 + 8x + k$, we see that $k = 3$.

6. (*b*) Given $x = 3$ is one root of the quadratic equation $x^2 - 2kx - 6 = 0$. So, $x = 3$ will satisfy the equation.

Thus,

$(3)^2 - 2k \times 3 - 6 = 0 \Rightarrow 9 - 6k - 6 = 0$

$\Rightarrow 3 - 6k = 0 \Rightarrow 3 = 6k \Rightarrow k = \frac{1}{2}$

7. (*c*) Given $p(x) = mx^2 + 3x - 5$ and $\alpha\beta = 5$

We have from the polynomial

$\alpha\beta = \frac{-5}{m} \Rightarrow 5 = \frac{-5}{m} \Rightarrow m = -1$

8. (*c*) Given $g(x) = 3x^2 - 27ax + 9$

Let α is zero of the polynomial then other will be $-\alpha$

$\therefore$ Sum of zeroes $= \frac{-b}{a} \Rightarrow \alpha - \alpha = \frac{-(-27a)}{3} \Rightarrow a = 0$

9. (*d*) Given $y(t) = nt^2 - 2t + 6n$

Let α, β be the zeroes

Given $\alpha + \beta = \alpha\beta$

$\Rightarrow \frac{-(-2)}{n} = \frac{6n}{n} \Rightarrow \frac{2}{n} = 6 \Rightarrow n = \frac{1}{3}$

10. (*b*) So, let's substitute $x = -4$ into the polynomial:

$(k-1)(-4)^2 + k(-4) + 1 = 0$

$(k-1)(16) + (-4k) + 1 = 0$

$16k - 16 - 4k + 1 = 0$

$12k - 15 = 0$

$12k = 15$

$k = \frac{15}{12} = \frac{5}{4}$

So, the value of k is $\frac{5}{4}$

Assertion and Reason

1. (*c*) Assertion (A) is true but reason (R) is false.

As the number of zeroes of a polynomial $f(x)$ is the number of points at which $f(x)$ cuts (intersects) the x–axis and the number of zeroes in the given figure is 5. So A is correct but R is incorrect.

2. (*a*) Both assertion (A) and reason (R) are true and reason (R) is the correct explanation of assertion (A).

As irrational zeroes always occur in pairs therefore, if one zero is $(2-\sqrt{3})$ then the other will be $(2+\sqrt{3})$.

3. (*a*) Both assertion (A) and reason (R) are true and reason (R) is the correct explanation of assertion (A).

Sum of zeroes $= -\frac{1}{4}$ and

product of zeroes $= \frac{1}{4}$

Quadratic polynomial be $x^2 - \left(-\frac{1}{4}\right)x + \frac{1}{4}$

$$\Rightarrow x^2 + \frac{1}{4}x + \frac{1}{4} \Rightarrow \frac{1}{2}\left(2x^2 + \frac{x}{2} + \frac{1}{2}\right)$$

So, both A and R are correct and R explains A.

4. (*a*) **Assertion (A):** Polynomial $x^2 + 4x$ has two real zeroes.

This assertion is correct. The polynomial $x^2 + 4x$ can be factored as $x(x + 4)$, and its zeroes are $x = 0$ and $x = -4$, both of which are real numbers.

Reason (R): Zeroes of the polynomial $x^2 + ax$ are 0 and a.

This reason is also correct. For the polynomial $x^2 + ax$, if we set it equal to zero, we can factor out an x to get $x(x + a)$, which means its zeroes are $x = 0$ and $x = -a$. So, if $a = 4$, then the zeroes would indeed be $x = 0$ and $x = -4$.

Both Assertion (A) and Reason (R) are true, and Reason (R) is the correct explanation for Assertion (A).

5. (*b*) Both assertion (A) and reason (R) are true but reason (R) is not the correct explanation of assertion (A).

Reason is true.

Let $\alpha, \frac{1}{\alpha}$ be the zeroes of $p(x)$, then

$$\alpha \times \frac{1}{\alpha} = \frac{3k}{k+4} \Rightarrow 1 = \frac{3k}{k+4} \Rightarrow k + 4 = 3k \Rightarrow k = 2$$

Assertion and reason are true but Reason is not correct explanation for Assertion.

Subjective Questions

Very Short Answer Type Questions

1. Let the quadratic polynomial be $ax^2 + bx + c$, and its zeroes be α and β. We have

$\alpha + \beta = -3 = \frac{-b}{a}$, (½ M)

and $\alpha\beta = 2 = \frac{c}{a}$ (½ M)

If $a = 1$, then $b = 3$ and $c = 2$. (½ M)

So, one quadratic polynomial which fits the given conditions is $x^2 + 3x + 2$. (½ M)

2. Sum of zeroes i.e. $\alpha + \beta + \gamma = -\frac{\text{Coefficient of } x^2}{\text{Coefficient of } x^3}$ (1 M)

$= -\frac{(-3)}{1} = 3$ (1 M)

3. If 2 and 0 are the zeroes of the polynomial, then by using factor theorem

$f(2) = f(0) = 0$

$f(2) = 2(2)^3 - 5(2)^2 + a(2) + b = 0$

$\Rightarrow 16 - 20 + 2a + b = 0 \Rightarrow 2a + b = 4$ ... (*i*)

Also $f(0) = 2(0)^3 - 5(0)^2 + a(0) + b \Rightarrow 0 = b$ (1 M)

By putting $b = 0$ in (*i*), we get

$2a = 4 \Rightarrow a = 2$

So, $a + b = 2 + 0 = 2$ (1 M)

4. Given, $x = 3$ is a root of $f(x)$

$\Rightarrow f(3) = 0 \Rightarrow (3)^3 - (4).(3)^2 + 6k = 0$ (1 M)

$\Rightarrow -9 + 6k = 0 \Rightarrow k = \frac{9}{6} = \frac{3}{2}$ (1 M)

Short Answer Type Questions

1. We have

$x^2 + 7x + 10 = (x + 2)(x + 5)$ (½ M)

So, the value of $x^2 + 7x + 10$ is zero when $x + 2 = 0$ or $x + 5 = 0$, i.e., when $x = -2$ or $x = -5$. Therefore, the zeroes of $x^2 + 7x + 10$ are -2 and -5 . Now, (½ M)

sum of zeroes =

$-2 + (-5) = -(7) = \frac{-(7)}{1} = \frac{-(\text{Coefficient of } x)}{\text{Coefficient of } x^2}$, (1 M)

Product of zeroes =

$(-2) \times (-5) = 10 = \frac{10}{1} = \frac{\text{Constant term}}{\text{Coefficient of } x^2}$. (1 M)

2. Since α and β are the zeroes of polynomial $ax^2 - bx + c$

$\therefore \alpha + \beta = -\left(\frac{-b}{a}\right) = \frac{b}{a}, \ \alpha\beta = \frac{c}{a}$ (1 M)

$\alpha^2 - \beta^2 = (\alpha + \beta)(\alpha - \beta) = \frac{b}{a}\sqrt{(\alpha - \beta)^2}$

$= \frac{b}{a}\sqrt{\alpha^2 + \beta^2 - 2\alpha\beta} = \frac{b}{a}\sqrt{\alpha^2 + \beta^2 + 2\alpha\beta - 4\alpha\beta}$ (1 M)

$= \frac{b}{a}\sqrt{(\alpha + \beta)^2 - 4\alpha\beta} = \frac{b}{a}\sqrt{\left(\frac{b}{a}\right)^2 - 4\frac{c}{a}}$

$= \frac{b}{a}\sqrt{\frac{b^2 - 4ac}{a^2}} = \frac{b\sqrt{b^2 - 4ac}}{a^2}$ (1 M)

3. Given 1, 2 and –3 are the zeroes of the cubic polynomial.

Sum of zeroes $= 1 + 2 + (-3) = 0$ (1 M)

Sum of product of zeroes taken two at a time $= 1(2) + 2(-3) + (-3)(1) = -7$

Product of zeroes $= 1 \times 2 \times (-3) = -6$ (1 M)

We know that cubic polynomial can be written as x^3 – (sum of zeroes) x^2 + (sum of product of zeroes taken two at a time)x – (product of zeroes) $= x^3 - 0x^2 + (-7)x - (-6)$

$\therefore x^3 - 7x + 6$ is the required cubic polynomial. (1 M)

4. $p(s) = 4s^2 - 4s + 1$

$4s^2 - 2s - 2s + 1 = 0$

$2s(2s - 1) - 1(2s - 1) = 0$

$(2s - 1)(2s - 1) = 0$

$s = \frac{1}{2}, s = \frac{1}{2}$ (1 M)

$a = 4, b = -4, c = 1 \quad \alpha = \frac{1}{2},\ \beta = \frac{1}{2}$

$\Rightarrow \alpha + \beta = \frac{-b}{a} \Rightarrow \frac{1}{2} + \frac{1}{2} = \frac{-(4)}{4}$

$\Rightarrow \frac{1+1}{2} = \frac{+4}{4} \Rightarrow 1 = 1$ (1 M)

$\alpha\beta = \frac{c}{a} \Rightarrow \left(\frac{1}{2}\right)\left(\frac{1}{2}\right) = \frac{1}{4} \Rightarrow \frac{1}{4} = \frac{1}{4}$ (1 M)

Long Answer Type Questions

1. $f(x) = ax^2 + bx + c$

$\therefore \alpha + \beta = -\frac{b}{a}$ and $\alpha\beta = \frac{c}{a}$ (1 M)

We have,

$\frac{\alpha^2}{\beta} + \frac{\beta^2}{\alpha} = \frac{\alpha^3 + \beta^3}{\alpha\beta}$ (½ M)

$= \frac{(\alpha+\beta)^3 - 3\alpha\beta(\alpha+\beta)}{\alpha\beta}$ (1 M)

$= \frac{\left(-\frac{b}{a}\right)^3 - 3\left(\frac{c}{a}\right)\left(-\frac{b}{a}\right)}{\frac{c}{a}}$ (½ M)

$= \frac{\frac{-b^3}{a^3} + 3\frac{bc}{a^2}}{\frac{c}{a}}$ (1 M)

$\therefore \left(\frac{\alpha^2}{\beta}\right) + \left(\frac{\beta^2}{\alpha}\right) = \frac{3abc - b^3}{a^2c}$ (1 M)

2. Since α and β are the zeroes of the polynomial $f(x) = x^2 - 3x + k$

$\therefore \alpha + \beta = -\frac{\text{Coefficient of } x}{\text{Coefficient of } x^2} = \frac{-(-3)}{1} = 3$ (1 M)

and $\alpha\beta = \frac{\text{Constant term}}{\text{Coefficient of } x^2} = k$ (1 M)

Given, $\alpha - \beta = 1$

Squaring on both sides, we get

$\Rightarrow (\alpha - \beta)^2 = (1)^2$

$\Rightarrow \alpha^2 - 2\alpha\beta + \beta^2 = 1$ (1 M)

$\left[\begin{array}{l}(a+b)^2 = a^2 + b^2 + 2ab \\ (a+b)^2 - 2ab = a^2 + b^2\end{array}\right]$

$\Rightarrow \{(\alpha + \beta)^2 - 2\alpha\beta\} - 2\alpha\beta = 1$ (1 M)

$\Rightarrow (\alpha + \beta)^2 - 4\alpha\beta = 1 \Rightarrow (3)^2 - 4 \times k = 1$

$\Rightarrow 4k = 8 \Rightarrow k = 2$

Therefore, the value of k is 2. (1 M)

3. Since α and β are the zeroes of the polynomial $f(x) = 2x^2 + 5x + k$.

$\therefore \alpha + \beta = \frac{-5}{2}$ and $\alpha\beta = \frac{k}{2}$ (1 M)

Now, $\alpha^2 + \beta^2 + \alpha\beta = \frac{21}{4}$ (1 M)

$\Rightarrow (\alpha^2 + \beta^2 + 2\alpha\beta) - \alpha\beta = \frac{21}{4}$ (1 M)

$\Rightarrow (\alpha + \beta)^2 - \alpha \times \beta = \frac{21}{4}$ (1 M)

$\Rightarrow \frac{25}{4} - \frac{k}{2} = \frac{21}{4}$ $\left[\because \alpha + \beta = \frac{-5}{2} \text{ and } \alpha\beta = \frac{k}{2}\right]$

$\Rightarrow -\frac{k}{2} = -1 \Rightarrow k = 2$ (1 M)

4. $f(x) = 2x^3 + x^2 - 5x + 2$

$f\left(\frac{1}{2}\right) = 2\left(\frac{1}{2}\right)^3 + \left(\frac{1}{2}\right)^2 - 5\left(\frac{1}{2}\right) + 2 = \frac{1}{4} + \frac{1}{4} - \frac{5}{2} + 2 = 0$ (1 M)

$f(1) = 2(1)^3 + (1)^2 - 5(1) + 2 = 2 + 1 - 5 + 2 = 0$

$f(-2) = 2(-2)^3 + (-2)^2 - 5(-2) + 2$

$= -16 + 4 + 10 + 2 = 0$ (1 M)

Let $\alpha = \frac{1}{2}$, $\beta = 1$ and $\gamma = -2$

Now, Sum of zeroes $= \alpha + \beta + \gamma = \frac{1}{2} + 1 - 2 = -\frac{1}{2}$

Also, sum of zeroes $= -\frac{\text{Coefficient of } x^2}{\text{Coefficient of } x^3} = -\frac{1}{2}$

So, sum of zeroes $= \alpha + \beta + \gamma = -\frac{(\text{Coefficient of } x^2)}{\text{Coefficient of } x^3}$

Sum of product of zeroes taken two at a time $= \alpha\beta + \beta\gamma + \gamma\alpha$

$= \frac{1}{2} \times 1 + 1 \times (-2) + (-2) \times \frac{1}{2} = -\frac{5}{2}$ (1 M)

Also, $\alpha\beta + \beta\gamma + \gamma\alpha = \frac{\text{Coefficient of } x}{\text{Coefficient of } x^3} = \frac{-5}{2}$

So, sum of product of zeroes taken two at a time

$= \alpha\beta + \beta\gamma + \gamma\alpha = \frac{\text{Coefficient of } x}{\text{Coefficient of } x^3}$ (1 M)

Now, Product of zeroes $= \alpha\beta\gamma = \left(\frac{1}{2}\right)(1)(-2) = -1$

Also, Product of zeroes $= -\frac{\text{Constant term}}{\text{Coefficient of } x^3} = \frac{-2}{2} = -1$

$\therefore$ Product zeroes $= \alpha\beta\gamma = -\frac{\text{Constant term}}{\text{Coefficient of } x^3}$ (1 M)

5. Since α and β are the zeroes of the polynomial $x^2 + 4x + 3$.

Then, $\alpha + \beta = -4$, $\alpha\beta = 3$ (1 M)

For the required polynomial, sum of the zeroes

$= 1 + \frac{\beta}{\alpha} + 1 + \frac{\alpha}{\beta} = \frac{\alpha\beta + \beta^2 + \alpha\beta + \alpha^2}{\alpha\beta}$ (½ M)

$= \frac{\alpha^2 + \beta^2 + 2\alpha\beta}{\alpha\beta} = \frac{(\alpha+\beta)^2}{\alpha\beta} = \frac{(-4)^2}{3} = \frac{16}{3}$ (1 M)

Product of the zeroes $= \left(1 + \frac{\beta}{\alpha}\right)\left(1 + \frac{\alpha}{\beta}\right)$ (½ M)

$= 1 + \frac{\alpha}{\beta} + \frac{\beta}{\alpha} + \frac{\alpha\beta}{\alpha\beta} = 2 + \frac{\alpha^2 + \beta^2}{\alpha\beta} = \frac{2\alpha\beta + \alpha^2 + \beta^2}{\alpha\beta}$

$= \frac{(\alpha + \beta)^2}{\alpha\beta} = \frac{(-4)^2}{3} = \frac{16}{3}$ *(1 M)*

The required polynomial is $k(x^2$ – (sum of zeroes) x + product of zeroes)

$\Rightarrow k\left(x^2 - \frac{16}{3}x + \frac{16}{3}\right)$ *(1 M)*

Case Based Questions

Case Based-I

(i) (*d*) Quadratic, 2

(ii) (*b*) Given $p(t) = -2t^2 + 7t + 4 \Rightarrow p(t) = -2t^2 + 8t - t + 4$

$\Rightarrow p(t) = -2t(t-4) - 1(t-4) \Rightarrow p(t) = (t-4)(-2t-1)$

(iii) (*c*) We have $p(t) = 0$

$\therefore t = \frac{-1}{2}, 4$

No. of real zeroes = 2

(iv) (*d*) Since the zeroes of the polynomial are $t = \frac{-1}{2}$ and $t = 4$.

Therefore the graph cuts the x–axis at $\frac{-1}{2}$ and 4.

Case Based-II

(i) (*d*) In quadratic polynomial $p(x) = ax^2 + bx + c$; $a, b, c \in R$ and $a \neq 0$

i.e; All are real provided $a \neq 0$ because if $a = 0$, then $p(x)$ no longer remains a quadratic polynomial.

(ii) (*a*) $p(x) = ax^2 + bx + c$

$\Rightarrow p(x) = a\left[x^2 + \frac{b}{a}x + \frac{c}{a}\right]$

$\Rightarrow p(x) = a\left[x^2 + 2 \times x \times \frac{b}{2a} + \left(\frac{b}{2a}\right)^2 + \frac{c}{a} - \left(\frac{b}{2a}\right)^2\right]$

$\Rightarrow p(x) = a\left[\left(x + \frac{b}{2a}\right)^2 + \frac{4ac - b^2}{4a^2}\right]$

$\Rightarrow p(x) = a\left(x + \frac{b}{2a}\right)^2 - \frac{(b^2 - 4ac)}{4a}$

$\Rightarrow p(x) = a\left(x + \frac{b}{2a}\right)^2 - \frac{D}{4a}$ where D denotes discriminant

Now minimum value of $p(x)$ occur for $x + \frac{b}{2a} = 0$

i.e., $x = \frac{-b}{2a}$

(iii) (*c*) Maximum/Minimum value $= \frac{-D}{4a}$ at $x = -\frac{b}{2a}$ depends upon sign of a.

(iv) (*c*) At y–axis, $x = 0$

$\therefore$ for $x = 0$, $p(0) = a(0)^2 + b(0) + c = c$

$\therefore$ Graph cuts y–axis at 'c'.

Case Based-III

(i) $p(x) = x^2 - 2$

To find zeroes: $p(x) = x^2 - 2 = 0$

$\Rightarrow x^2 - 2 = 0 \Rightarrow x = \pm\sqrt{2}$

$\Rightarrow$ Graph intersects x–axis at $x = -\sqrt{2}$ and $x = \sqrt{2}$

(ii) Here $a = 3$, $b = -2$, $c = 5k$

$p(x) = 3x^2 - 2x + 5k$

Given zeroes are α and $\frac{1}{\alpha}$

Product of zeroes $= \alpha \cdot \frac{1}{\alpha} = 1 \Rightarrow \frac{c}{a} = 1$

$\Rightarrow \frac{5k}{3} = 1 \Rightarrow k = \frac{3}{5}$

OR

Required quadratic polynomial having sum of zeroes = α and product of zeroes $= \frac{-1}{\alpha}$ is given by:

$p(x) = k[x^2$ – (sum of zeroes)x + Product of zeroes]

$p(x) = k\left[x^2 - \alpha x - \frac{1}{\alpha}\right]; k \neq 0, k \in R.$

(iii) Since α and β are zeroes of $p(x) = ax^2 + bx + c$

$\therefore \alpha + \beta = -\frac{b}{a}$ & $\alpha\beta = \frac{c}{a}$

Now

$\alpha^2\beta + \beta^2\alpha = \alpha\beta(\alpha + \beta) = \frac{c}{a} \times \left(\frac{-b}{a}\right) = -\frac{bc}{a^2}$

❑❑❑

PAIR OF LINEAR EQUATIONS IN TWO VARIABLES

3

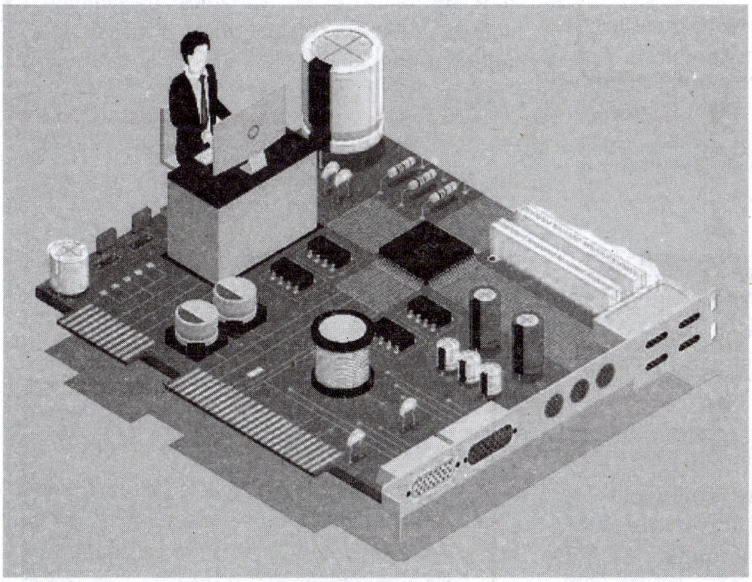

"In electrical circuits, engineers use pairs of linear equations to analyze and understand how currents and voltages behave. By solving these equations, engineers can determine the electrical flow at different points in the circuit, aiding in design and troubleshooting."

SYLLABUS & WEIGHTAGE

List of Concept Names	Years				
	2021	**2022**	**2023**	**2024**	**2025**
Pair of Linear Equations in Two Variables and Graphical Method for its Solutions (Pair of linear equations in Two variables and graphical method for their solution, consistency /inconsistency)	Exam not Conducted	–	2 Q (1 M each) 1 Q (3 M)	1 Q (1 M) 1 Q (5 M)	2 Q (1 M each) 1 Q (5 M)
Algebraic Methods of Solving a Pair of Linear Equations (Algebraic conditions for number of solutions. Solution of a pair of liner equations in two variables algebraically by substitution, by elimination. Simple situational problems.)		–	1 Q (3 M)	1 Q (5 M)	1 Q (5 M)

CONCEPT MAP

To Access One Shot Revision Video Scan This QR Code

Pair of Linear Equations in Two Variables

Solution: The value of the two variables which satisfy both the linear equations in the two variables

Algebraic Method

Substitution Method:
To find the solution using this method we substitute value of one variable (in terms of another variable) from one equation to another equation.

Example: $7x - 15y = 2$ … (*i*)
$x + 2y = 3$ … (*ii*)

Sol. From equation (*ii*), $x = 3 - 2y$ … (*iii*)
Substitute value of x in eq. (*i*)
$7(3 - 2y) - 15y = 2$
$-29y = -19 \Rightarrow y = \frac{19}{29}$
$\therefore$ In eq. (*iii*) $x = 3 - 2\left(\frac{19}{29}\right) = \left(\frac{49}{29}\right)$

Elimination Method:
To find the solution using this method we eliminate one of the variables by adding/ subtracting both equation after, if necessary, multiplying the equation by appropriate numbers.

Example: $2x + 3y = 8$ … (*i*)
$4x + 6y = 7$ … (*ii*)

Sol. From equation (*i*) × 2 – eq. (*ii*) × 1, we have
$(4x - 4x) + (6y - 6y) = 16 - 7$
$0 = 9$, which is a false statement
The pair of equation has no solution

Definition: A collection of two linear equations in the same two variables.

General from:
$a_1x + b_1y + c_1 = 0$, $a_2x + b_2y + c_2 = 0$
Where, a_1, a_2, a_3, b_1, b_2 & b_3 are real numbers such that
a_1 & b_1 and a_2 & b_2 can not be equal to zero simultaneously.

Graphical Representation and Nature of equations/ solutions

S. No.	Pair of Lines	$\frac{a_1}{a_2}$	$\frac{b_1}{b_2}$	$\frac{c_1}{c_2}$	Compare the Ratios	Graphical Representation		Algebraic Interpretation
1.	$x - 2y = 0$ $3x + 4y - 20 = 0$	$\frac{1}{3}$	$\frac{-2}{4}$	$\frac{0}{-20}$	$\frac{a_1}{a_2} \neq \frac{b_1}{b_2}$	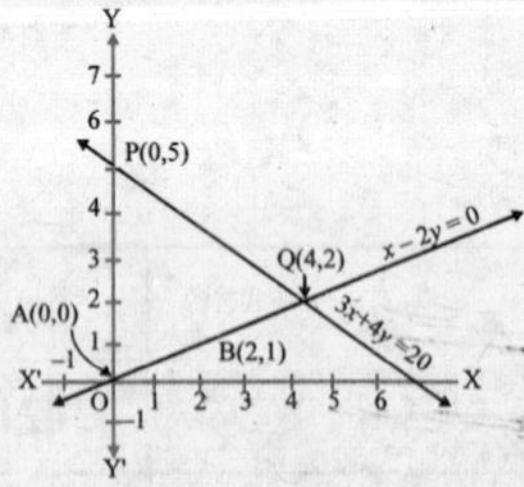	Intersecting Lines	Exactly one solution-consistent (Unique)
2.	$2x + 3y - 9 = 0$ $4x + 6y - 18 = 0$	$\frac{2}{4}$	$\frac{3}{6}$	$\frac{-9}{-18}$	$\frac{a_1}{a_2} = \frac{b_1}{b_2} = \frac{c_1}{c_2}$	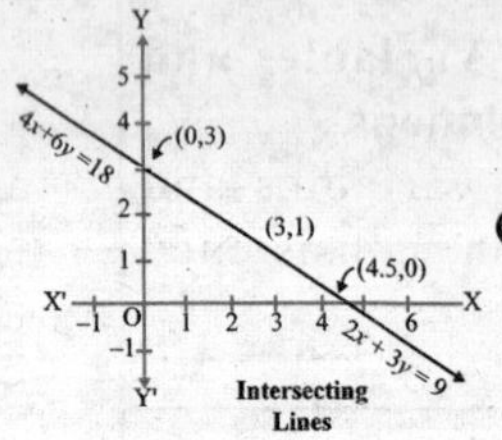	Coincident Lines	Infinitely many solutions-consistent (Dependent)
3.	$x + 2y - 4 = 0$ $2x + 4y - 12 = 0$	$\frac{1}{2}$	$\frac{2}{4}$	$\frac{-4}{-12}$	$\frac{a_1}{a_2} = \frac{b_1}{b_2} \neq \frac{c_1}{c_2}$	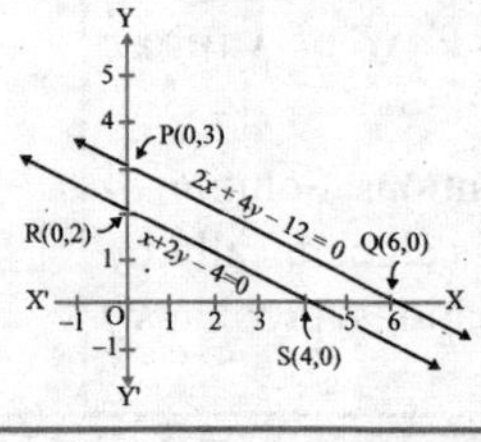	Parallel Lines	No solutions-Inconsistent

1 PAIR OF LINEAR EQUATIONS IN TWO VARIABLES AND GRAPHICAL METHOD FOR ITS SOLUTIONS

Important Terms

- **Linear equation in Two Variables:**

  A linear equation in two variables x and y is represented by the equation $ax + by + c = 0$, where a, b, and c are real numbers and both a and b can not be zero.

  Examples: $4x + 5y = 3$

  $3p + 2q = 0$ is a linear equation in two variables p and q.

  Note: The condition that both a and b can not be equal to zero in the definition can also be written as $a^2 + b^2 \neq 0$.

- **Solution of linear equations in Two Variables:**

  The solutions of a linear equation in two variables are the values of x & y which satisfy the linear equation in two variables.

  Examples: $4x + 5y = 3$ is a linear equation whose solutions are $(-13, 11)$, $(-3, 3)$ ...etc.

- **Pair of Linear Equations in Two Variables:**

  The collection of two linear equations in the same two variables is known as pair of linear equations in two variables.

  The general form of a pair of linear equations in two variables is written as,

  $a_1 x + b_1 y + c_1 = 0$ and $a_2 x + b_2 y + c_2 = 0$

  Where a_1, b_1, c_1, a_2, b_2, and c_2 are real numbers such that both a_1 and b_1 and both a_2 and b_2 can not be equal to zero.

  Examples: $4x + 5y = 3$ and $3x + 2y = 0$

- **Solution of a pair of linear equations in Two Variables:**

  Examples: $4x + 5y = 3$ and $3x + 2y = 0$. The solutions of a pair of linear equations in two variables are the values of x & y which satisfy both the given pair of linear equations.

  E.g.: Let $4x - y = 4$ & $3x + 2y = 14$ is a pair of linear equations.

  then, $x = 2$ and $y = 4$ is a solution of the linear equations

- **Consistent Pair of Linear Equations:**

  If a pair of linear equations has one or more than one solution then the pair of linear equations is called consistent.

Types of consistent pair of linear equations:

- **Independent Pair of Linear Equations:**

  A pair of linear equations that has a unique solution is known as independent pair of linear equations.

- **Dependent Pair of Linear Equations:**

  A pair of linear equations that has more than one or infinitely many solutions is known as dependent pair of linear equations.

- **Inconsistent Pair of Linear Equations:**

  If a pair of linear equations does not have a solution then the pair of linear equations is called in consistent.

Important Concepts

Graphical Method for Solution of a Pair of Linear Equations:

Consider a pair of linear equations in two variables:

$a_1 x + b_1 y + c_1 = 0$ and $a_2 x + b_2 y + c_2 = 0$

Where a_1, b_1, c_1, a_2, b_2, and c_2 are real numbers such that both a_1 and b_1 and both a_2 and b_2 can not be equal to zero.

To find the solution to the above pair of linear equations draw both lines, on the same graph paper, represented by the above linear equations.

Then, follow the cases given below.

(*i*) If, in the graph, the lines drawn are intersecting lines then the intersection point of these lines will be the solution of the pair of linear equations. This solution will be unique.

(*ii*) If, in the graph, the lines drawn are coincident lines then there will be infinitely many common points on the lines and hence there will be infinitely many solutions to the given pair of equations.

(*iii*) If, in the graph, the lines drawn are parallel lines then there will be no common points on the lines and hence there will be no solution to the given pair of equations.

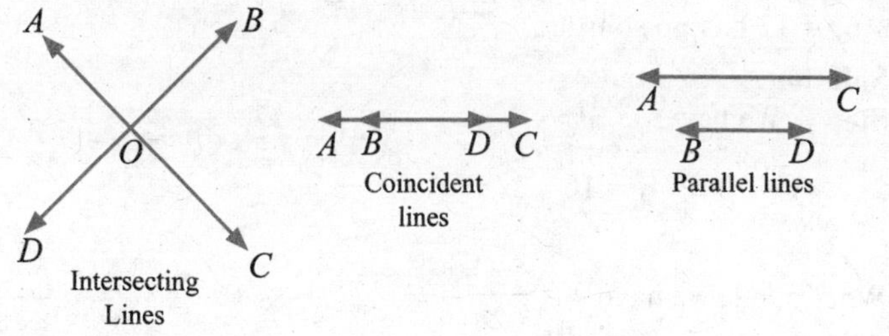

Important Formulas

Algebraic condition for nature of lines and the number of solutions:

Pair of linear equations $a_1x + b_1y + c_1 = 0$ $a_2x + b_2y + c_2 = 0$	Algebraic conditions	Graphical representation	Algebraic interpretation
Consistent (Independent)	$\frac{a_1}{a_2} \neq \frac{b_1}{b_2}$	Intersecting lines	Exactly one solution (unique solution)
Consistent (Dependent)	$\frac{a_1}{a_2} = \frac{b_1}{b_2} = \frac{c_1}{c_2}$	Coincident lines	Infinitely many solutions – dependent
In-consistent	$\frac{a_1}{a_2} = \frac{b_1}{b_2} \neq \frac{c_1}{c_2}$	Pair of parallel lines	No solution

Real Life Applications

Pair of linear equation in two variables is used to solve various age related problems. E.g.

Suppose that age of a father and a son are such that the age of the father is 4 times that of the son. Also, the age of the father will be 3 times that of the son after 10 *years*.

Then in this case we can find the age of the father and son by assuming the present age of the father *x years* and present age of the son *y years*. And then we can represent the above problem into pair of linear equations and after solving it we can get the required ages.

Different Problem Types

Type I: Determining the Solution of the Pair of Linear Polynomials while Graphing them.

Show graphically that the system of equations $2x + 4y = 10$, $3x + 6y = 12$ has no solution.

Solution:

Step I: We have,

$$2x + 4y = 10 \Rightarrow 4y = 10 - 2x \Rightarrow y = \frac{5-x}{2}$$

When $x = 1$, we have $y = \frac{5-1}{2} = 2$

When $x = 3$, we have $y = \frac{5-3}{2} = 1$

Step II: Now, we have the following table:

x	1	3
y	2	1

Step III: Plot the points $A(1, 2)$ and $B(3, 1)$ on a graph paper. Join A and B and extend it on both sides to obtain the graph of $2x + 4y = 10$ as shown below

We have, $3x + 6y = 12 \Rightarrow 6y = 12 - 3x \Rightarrow y = \frac{4-x}{2}$

When $x = 2$, we have $y = \frac{4-2}{2} = 1$

When $x = 0$, we have $y = \frac{4-0}{2} = 2$

Step IV: Here, we have the following table:

x	2	0
y	1	2

Step V: Plot the points $C(2, 1)$ and $D(0, 2)$ on the same graph paper. Join C and D and extend it on both sides to obtain the graph of $3x + 6y = 12$.

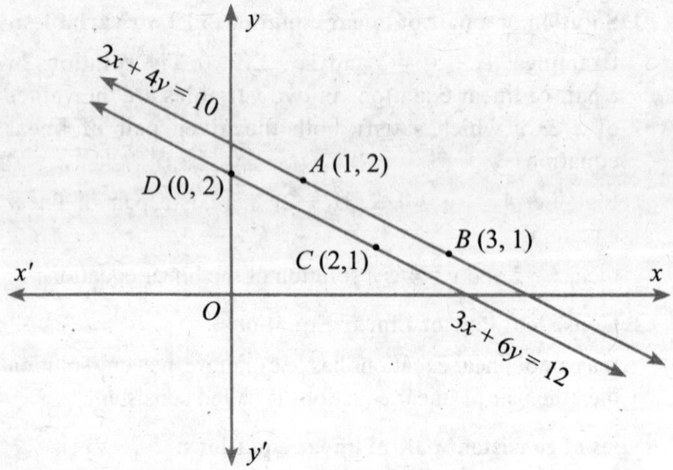

We find the lines represented by equations $2x + 4y = 10$ and $3x + 6y = 12$ are parallel. So, the two lines have no common point. Hence, the given system of equations has no solution.

COMPETENCY BASED SOLVED EXAMPLES

Multiple Choice Questions

(1 M)

1. The given pair of linear equations $x + 2y - 5 = 0$ and $-3x - 6y + 15 = 0$ have *(An)*

(*a*) Exactly one solution (*b*) Exactly two solutions

(*c*) Infinitely many solutions (*d*) No solution

Sol. Given, $x + 2y - 5 = 0$ and $-3x - 6y + 15 = 0$

Here, $a_1 = 1,\ b_1 = 2,\ c_1 = -5$

$a_2 = -3,\ b_2 = -6,\ c_2 = 15$

Now, $\frac{a_1}{a_2} = -\frac{1}{3}, \frac{b_1}{b_2} = -\frac{1}{3}, \frac{c_1}{c_2} = -\frac{1}{3}$

It implies that

$\frac{a_1}{a_2} = \frac{b_1}{b_2} = \frac{c_1}{c_2}$

So given pair of liner of linear have infinite many

2. For what value of k will the equations $x + 2y + 7 = 0$, $2x + ky + 14 = 0$ represents coincident lines? *(Ap)*

(*a*) 6 (*b*) 4

(*c*) 3 (*d*) 2

Sol. For coincident lines,

$$\frac{a_1}{a_2} = \frac{b_1}{b_2} = \frac{c_1}{c_2} \Rightarrow \frac{1}{2} = \frac{2}{k} = \frac{7}{14}$$

$$\Rightarrow \frac{1}{2} = \frac{2}{k} \Rightarrow k = 4$$

3. The value of k for which the equations $3x - y + 8 = 0$ and $6x - ky = -16$ represent coincident lines, is *(Ap)*(CBSE,2020)

(*a*) $-\frac{1}{2}$ (*b*) $\frac{1}{2}$

(*c*) 2 (*d*) –2

Sol. $3x - y = -8$ ...(*i*)

$6x - ky = -16$ ...(*ii*)

Here, $a_1 = 3,\ b_1 = -1,\ c_1 = 8$

$a_2 = 6,\ b_2 = -k,\ c_2 = 16$

$$\Rightarrow \frac{a_1}{a_2} = \frac{b_1}{b_2} = \frac{c_1}{c_2} \Rightarrow \frac{3}{6} = \frac{-1}{-k} = \frac{8}{16}, \Rightarrow \frac{1}{2} = \frac{1}{k} = \frac{1}{2}$$

So, $k = 2$

4. If a pair of linear equations is consistent, then the lines represented by them are *(Un)*(CBSE, 2020)

(*a*) parallel (*b*) intersecting or coincident

(*c*) always coincident (*d*) always intersecting

Sol. intersecting or coincident If a pair of linear equations is consistent, then the lines represented by them are intersecting or coincident.

5. The value of k for which the system of equation $x + y - 4 = 0$ and $2x + ky = 3$, has no solution, is *(Ap)*

(*a*) –2 (*b*) –3 (*c*) 3 (*d*) 2

Sol. For no solution,

$$\frac{a_1}{a_2} = \frac{b_1}{b_2} \neq \frac{c_1}{c_2} \Rightarrow \frac{1}{2} = \frac{1}{k} \neq \frac{-4}{-3} \Rightarrow k = 2$$

6. A pair of linear equations which has unique solution $x = 2, y = -3$ is: *(An)*(NCERT Exemplar)

(*a*) $x + y = -1$, $2x - 3y = -5$ (*b*) $2x + 5y = -11$, $4x + 10y = -22$

(*c*) $2x - y = 1$, $3x + 2y = 0$ (*d*) $x - 4y - 14 = 0$, $2x - y + 13 = 0$

Sol. $2x + 5y = -11$ and $4 + 10y = -22$

Put $x = 2$ and $y = -3$ in both equations,

LHS $= 2x + 5y = 2 \times 2 + 5 \times (-3)$

$= 4 - 15 = -11 =$ RHS

LHS $= 4x + 10y = 4(2) + 10(-3)$

$= 8 - 30 = -22 =$ RHS

7. Two lines are given to be parallel. The equation of one of the lines is $3x - 2y = 5$. The equation of the second line can be *(Cr)*

(*a*) $9x + 8y = 7$ (*b*) $-12x - 8y = 7$

(*c*) $-12x + 8y = 7$ (*d*) $12x + 8y = 7$

Sol. We have,

$3x - 2y = 5$

$\because$ For two lines to be parallel $\frac{a_1}{a_2} = \frac{b_1}{b_2} \neq \frac{c_1}{c_2}$

(*a*) $9x + 8y = 7$

$$\Rightarrow \frac{a_1}{a_2} = \frac{3}{9} = \frac{1}{3}, \frac{b_1}{b_2} = \frac{-2}{8} = \frac{-1}{4}, \Rightarrow \frac{a_1}{a_2} \neq \frac{b_1}{b_2}$$

So, (*a*) is not parallel.

(*b*) $-12x - 8y = 7$

$$\Rightarrow \frac{a_1}{a_2} = \frac{3}{-12} = \frac{-1}{4}, \frac{b_1}{b_2} = \frac{-2}{-8} = \frac{1}{4} \Rightarrow \frac{a_1}{a_2} \neq \frac{b_1}{b_2}$$

So, (*b*) is also not parallel

(*c*) $-12x + 8y = 7$

$$\Rightarrow \frac{a_1}{a_2} = \frac{3}{-12} = \frac{-1}{4}, \frac{b_1}{b_2} = \frac{-2}{8} = \frac{-1}{4}$$

$$\& \frac{c_1}{c_2} = \frac{-5}{-7} = \frac{5}{7} \Rightarrow \frac{a_1}{a_2} = \frac{b_1}{b_2} \neq \frac{c_1}{c_2}$$

So, (*c*) is parallel to the given line.

(*d*) $12x + 8y = 7$

$$\Rightarrow \frac{a_1}{a_2} = \frac{3}{12} = \frac{1}{4}, \frac{b_1}{b_2} = \frac{-2}{8} = \frac{-1}{4} \Rightarrow \frac{a_1}{a_2} \neq \frac{b_1}{b_2}$$

So, (*d*) is not parallel.

Answer Key

1. (c) 2. (b) 3. (c) 4. (b) 5. (d)
6. (b) 7. (c)

Assertion and Reason

(1 M)

Direction: In the following questions, a statement of Assertion (A) is followed by a statement of Reason (R). Mark the correct choice as:

(*a*) Both Assertion (A) and Reason (R) are true and Reason (R) is the correct explanation of Assertion (A).

(*b*) Both Assertion (A) and Reason (R) are true but Reason (R) is not the correct explanation of Assertion (A).

(*c*) Assertion (A) is true but Reason (R) is false.

(*d*) Assertion (A) is false but Reason (R) is true.

1. **Assertion (A):** If $x = 3x$, $y = 1$ is the solution of the line $2x + y - q^2 - 3 = 0$, then the value of $q = \pm 2$.
   Reason (R): The solutions of the line will satisfy the equation of the line. *(An)*

Sol. It is given that, $x = 3$ and $y = 1$ is the solution of line $2x + y - q^2 - 3 = 0$

Therefore,

$\Rightarrow 2 \times 3 + 1 - q^2 - 3 = 0 \Rightarrow 6 + 1 - 3 - q^2 = 0$

$\Rightarrow 4 - q^2 = 0 \Rightarrow q = \sqrt{4}$

$\Rightarrow q = \pm 2$

2. **Assertion (A): If $x = 3$, $y = 1$ is the solution of the line $2x + y - q^2 - 3 = 0$, then the value of $q = \pm 2$.**
   Reason (R): The solutions of the line will satisfy the equation of the line. *(Un)*

Sol. It is given that, $x = 3$ and $y = 1$ is the solution of line $2x + y - q^2 - 3 = 0$

Therefore,

$\Rightarrow 2 \times 3 + 1 - q^2 - 3 = 0 \Rightarrow 6 + 1 - 3 - q^2 = 0$

$\Rightarrow 4 - q^2 = 0 \Rightarrow q = \pm 2$

Hence, both A and R are true and R explains A.

3. **Assertion (A): The value of k for which the system of equations $kx - y = 2$, $6x - 2y = 3$ has a unique solution is 3.**
   Reason (R): The system of linear equations $a_1x + b_1y + c_1 = 0$ and $a_2x + b_2y + c_2 = 0$ has a unique solution if $\frac{a_1}{a_2} \neq \frac{b_1}{b_2}$. *(Cr)*

Sol. If system of linear equations has a unique solution, then

$\frac{k}{6} \neq \frac{-1}{-2} \Rightarrow \frac{k}{6} \neq \frac{1}{2} \Rightarrow k \neq 3$

Hence, A is false but R is true.

Answer Key

1. (c) 2. (a) 3. (d)

Subjective Questions

Very Short Answer Type Questions

(1 or 2 M)

1. **Given below is a non-linear equation.**

$$\frac{3(x+y)+7(x-y)}{x^2-y^2} = 12$$

Garima has reduced it to a linear equation in two variables. Shown below are her steps.

Step 1: $\frac{3(x+y)+7(x-y)}{(x+y)(x-y)} = 12$

Step 2: $\frac{3}{(x+y)} + \frac{7}{(x-y)} = 12$

Step 3: Takes $\frac{1}{(x+y)} = a$ and $\frac{1}{(x-y)} = b$

Step 4: $3a + 7b = 12$

However, she has made a mistake in one step. Identify the erroneous step and complete the solution. *(Cr)* **(CBSE CFPQ,2023)**

Sol. Given below is a non - linear equation.

$$\frac{3(x+y)+7(x-y)}{x^2-y^2} = 12$$

However,

$$\frac{3(x+y)+7(x-y)}{x^2-y^2} = 12$$

$$\Rightarrow \frac{3(x+y)+7(x-y)}{(x+y)(x-y)} = 12 \quad (1\ M)$$

$$\Rightarrow \frac{3(x+y)}{(x+y)(x-y)} + \frac{7(x-y)}{(x+y)(x-y)} = 12$$

$$\Rightarrow \frac{3}{x-y} + \frac{7}{x+y} = 12$$

Hence, Step 2 is incorrect. *(1 M)*

2. **Does the following system of linear equations is consistent?**
   $2x + 3y = 7$
   $3x - y = 5$ *(Un)*

Sol. We have,

$2x + 3y = 7$

$3x - y = 5$

$\therefore a_1 = 2,\ b_1 = 3$ and $c_1 = -7$

$a_2 = 3,\ b_2 = -1$ and $c_2 = -5$

$\therefore \frac{a_1}{a_2} = \frac{2}{3}$ and $\frac{b_1}{b_2} = \frac{3}{-1}$ *(1 M)*

Thus, $\frac{a_1}{a_2} \neq \frac{b_1}{b_2}$

$\therefore$ Lines are intersecting.

Hence, system of linear equation is consistent. *(1 M)*

Short Answer Type Questions (2 or 3 M)

1. Find the solution of the following pair of linear equations using graphical method. *(Un)*

$x + y = 4$ and $3x + 2y = 11$

Sol. $x + y = 4$ ... (i)

and $3x + 2y = 11$ ... (ii)

To obtain the equivalent geometric representation, we find two points on the line representing each equation. i.e., we find two solutions of each equation.

These solutions are given below in the table.

For $x + y = 4$

x	1	3
y	3	1

For $3x + 2y = 11$

x	3	1
y	1	4

(1 M)

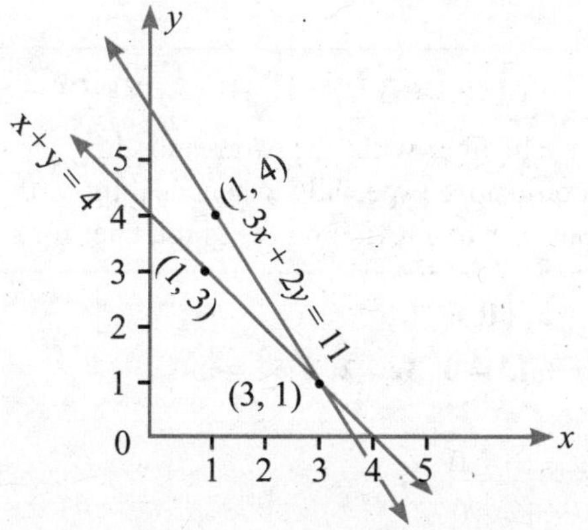

(1 M)

The given equations representing two lines, intersect each other at a unique point (3, 1). Hence, the equations are consistent with a unique solution. (1 M)

Mistakes 101 : What not to do!

When graphing equations, students might make errors in plotting points or drawing lines accurately, leading to incorrect interpretations of intersections or solutions.

2. The two circles represent the ordered pairs, (a, b), which are solutions of the respective equations. The circles are divided into 3 regions P, Q and R as shown.

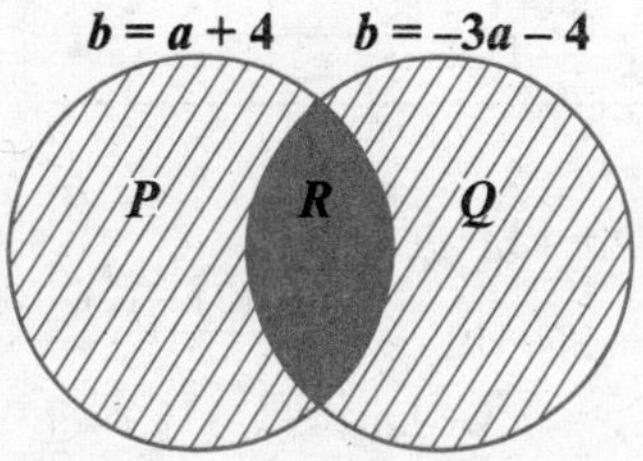

Write one ordered pair each belonging to P, Q and R. Show your work. *(An)* (CBSE CFPQ,2023)

Sol. In the figure above, the equation for region P is $b = a + 4$

Thus, when $a = 1$, $b = 5$

Ordered pair for region P is (1, 5) (½ M)

The equation for region Q is $b = -3a - 4$ (½ M)

Thus, when $a = -1$, $b = -1$

$\therefore$ Ordered pair for region Q is $(-1, -1)$ (½ M)

The point of intersection of the two circles belong to region R

$\Rightarrow a + 4 = -3a - 4$ (½ M)

$\Rightarrow 4a = -8 \Rightarrow a = -2 \Rightarrow b = -2 + 4 = 2$

$\therefore$ Ordered pair for region R is $(-2, 2)$ (1 M)

Key Takeaways

Developing skills to interpret graphs of linear equations accurately aids in understanding the relationship between variables and identifying solutions graphically.

3. Draw the graphs of the pair of linear equations $x - y + 2 = 0$ and $4x - y - 4 = 0$. Calculate the area of the triangle formed by the lines so drawn and the x-axis. *(Ap)* (NCERT Exemplar)

Sol. For drawing the graphs of the given equations. we find two solutions of each of the equations, which are given below.

x	0	–2
$y = x + 2$	2	0

x	0	1
$y = 4x - 4$	–4	0

(1 M)

Plot the points A (0, 2), B (–2, 0), P (0, –4) and Q (1, 0) on the graph paper, and join the points to form the lines AB and PQ as shown below.

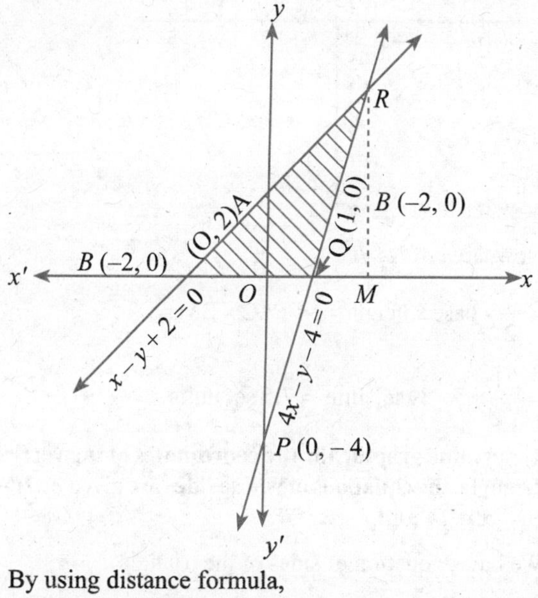

(1 M)

By using distance formula,

$AB = \sqrt{(1-(-2))^2} = 3$ units (½ M)

Area of triangle $= \frac{1}{2} \times 3 \times 4 = 6$ square units (½ M)

4. Draw the graphs of the following equations on the same graph paper:

$2x + 3y = 12$ and $x - y = 1$

Find the coordinates of the vertices of the triangle formed by the two straight lines on the y-axis and also determine the are of this triangle. *(Cr)*

Sol. We have, $2x + 3y = 12 \Rightarrow y = \frac{12-2x}{3}$

Now, if, $x = 0$, then, $y = \frac{12-2(0)}{3} = 4$

If $x = 3$ then, $y = \frac{12-2(3)}{3} = 2$ *(1 M)*

x	0	3
y	4	2
Coordinates	(0, 4)	(3, 2)

x	0	–1
y	–1	–2
Coordinates	(0, –1)	(–1, –2)

Also, $x - y = 1 \Rightarrow y = x - 1$

Now, if, $x = 0$, then, $y = 0 - 1 = -1$

If $x = -1$ then $y = -1 - 1 = -2$ *(1 M)*

We polt the points on a graph paper and draw the lines. The triangle formed by these two lines and the y-axis has been shaded. Vertices of the triangle are A(0, 4), B(3, 2) and C(0, –1).

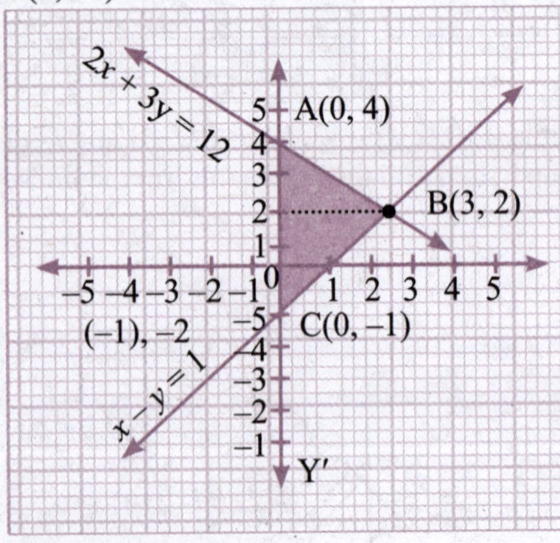

Now, area of ΔABC

$= \frac{1}{2} \times \text{base} \times \text{height} = \frac{1}{2} \times AC \times BM$

$= \left(\frac{1}{2} \times 5 \times 3\right)$ sq. unit = 7.5 sq. units *(1 M)*

5. Determine graphically the coordinates of the vertices of a triangle, the equations of whose sides are given by $2y - x = 8$, $5y - x = 14$ and $y - 2x = 1$. *(Cr)* **(CBSE 2020)**

Sol. We have, equation of sides of the triangle

$2y - x = 8$ ... *(i)*

$5y - x = 14$ ... *(ii)*

and $y - 2x = 1$ ... *(iii)*

Now,

For *(i)*			For *(ii)*			For *(iii)*		
x	0	–8	*x*	1	6	*x*	0	–1
y	4	0	*y*	3	4	*y*	1	–1

(1 M)

Now, plotting these points and then drawing lines we get,

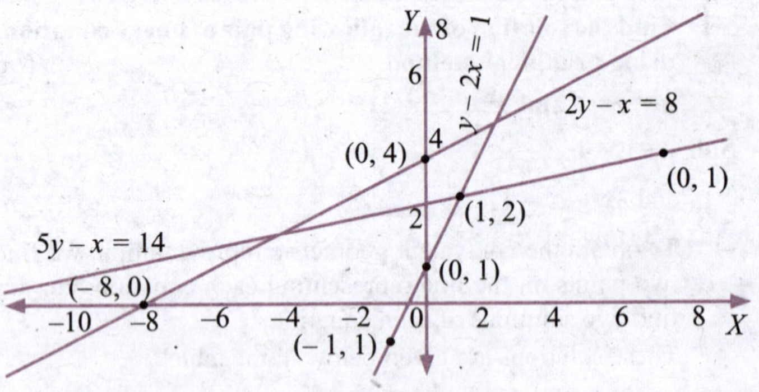

(1 M)

From the graph, it can be seen that the lines interesect each other at points (–4, 2), (2, 5) and (1, 3).

Thus, (–4, 2), (2, 5) and (1, 3) are the coordinates of vertices of the triangle. *(1 M)*

Nailing the Right Answer

Label each line with the corresponding equation to avoid confusion, especially when dealing with multiple equations or when revisiting the graph later for reference.

6. Solve graphically

$2x + 3y + 13 = 0$; $3x - 2y + 12 = 0$ *(Ev)*

Sol. We have,

$2x + 3y + 13 = 0$

$3x - 2y + 12 = 0$

Now,

$2x - 3y + 13 = 0 \Rightarrow 2x - 3y + 13$

$\Rightarrow x = \frac{3y-13}{2}$ *(1 M)*

When $y = 1$, we have

$x = \frac{3 \times 3 - 13}{2} = -5$

When $y = -3$, we have

$x = \frac{3 \times 3 - 13}{2} = -2$

Thus, we have the following table giving points on the line $2x - 3y + 13 = 0$ *(1 M)*

x	–5	–2
y	1	3

Now,

$3x - 2y + 12 = 0$

$\Rightarrow 3x - 2y + 12 \Rightarrow x = \frac{(2y-12)}{3}$

When $y = 0$, we have

$x = \frac{2 \times 0 - 12}{3} = -14$

When $y = 3$, we have

$x = \frac{2 \times 3 - 12}{3} = -2$

Thus, we have the following table giving points on the line $3y - 2y - 12 = 0$

x	-5	-2
y	1	3

Graph of the given equations are:

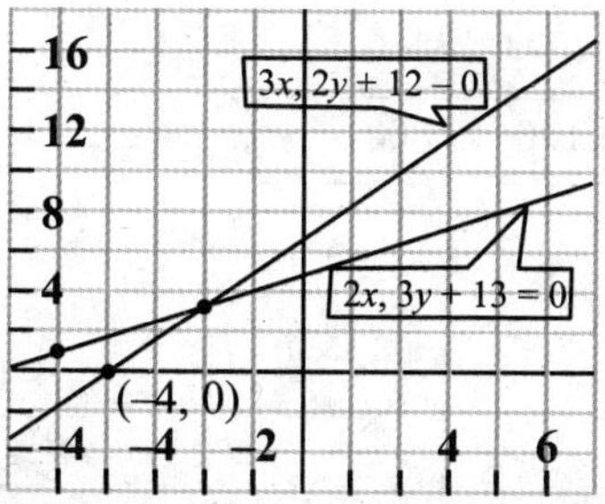

Clearly, two lines interesect at – (–4,0) *(1 M)*

7. Half the perimeter of a rectangular garden, whose length is 4 m more than its width, is 36 m. Find the dimensions of the garden. **(*Cr*) (NCERT Intext)**

Sol. Let us suppose, the width of the garden = x m and the length of the garden = y m. It is given that length of rectangular garden is 4 m more than its width.

$\therefore y = 4 + x$

$\Rightarrow y - x = 4$ ... (i) *(½ M)*

Also, half of the perimeter of rectangular garden is 36m.

$\therefore \frac{1}{2}$ [2(Length + Breadth)] = 36

$\Rightarrow y + x = 36$ ... (ii) *(½ M)*

For, $y - x = 4$ or $y = x + 4$

The solution table is

x	0	12	8
$y = x + 4$	4	16	12

For, $y + x = 36$ or $y = 36 - x$

The solution table is

x	0	16	36
$y = 36 - x$	36	20	0

(½ M)

Now, let us plot the graph

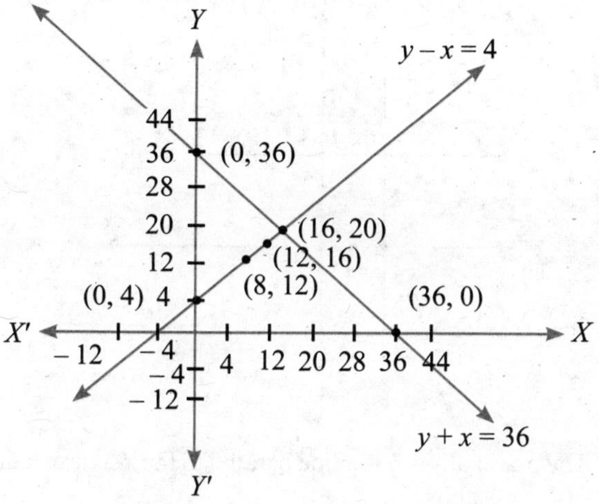

(1 M)

As we can see from the graph that the lines intersects each other at a point (16, 20). So, the solution of equations (i) and (ii) is $x = 16$ and $y = 20$

Therefore, the width of the garden is 16 m and length is 20 m. *(½ M)*

Nailing the Right Answer

Check if the point where the lines meet fits into both equations.

8. A music store sold 7 violins in one week for a total of ₹1500. Two different types of violins were sold. One type cost ₹200 and the other type cost ₹300. Represent this situation algebraically and graphically. **(*Cr*)**

Sol. Let us suppose, A and B are the two types of violins.

Number of violins of type A + Number of violins of type B = Total number of violins sold

And,

(Price of type A violin) (Number of type A violins) + (Price of type B violin) (Number of type B violins) = Total sales

Let,

Number of type A violins = x

Number of type B violins = y *(½ M)*

Total number of violins sold = 7

Price of type A violin= ₹ 200 (per violin)

Price of type B violin = ₹ 300 (per violin)

Total sales = ₹ 1500

Now, according to the question,

Algebraically,

$x + y = 7$ ... (i)

$200x + 300y = 1500$ ... (ii) *(½ M)*

Now, graphically

$x + y = 7$

$\Rightarrow y = 7 - x$

x	0	7
y	7	0

Hence, points are (0,7) and (7,0)

$200x + 300y = 1500$

$\Rightarrow 2x + 3y = 15 \Rightarrow y = \frac{15 - 2x}{3}$

x	0	3
y	5	3

Hence, points are (0,5) and (3,3)

(½ M)

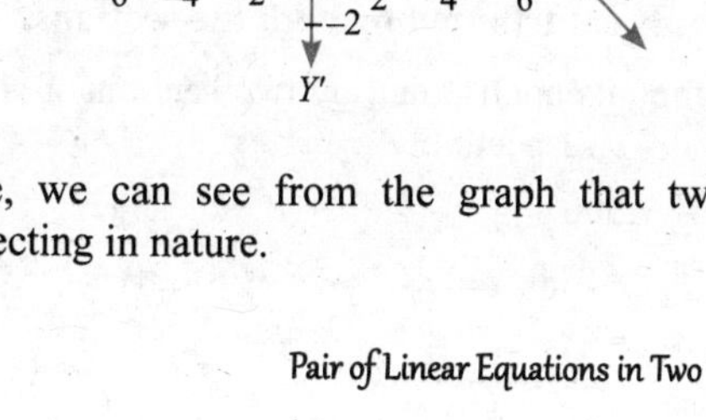

(1 M)

Hence, we can see from the graph that two lines are intersecting in nature. *(½ M)*

Long Answer Type Questions (4 or 5 M)

1. Solve graphically the following system of linear equations: $2x + y = 6$, $x - 2y + 2 = 0$. Find the vertices of the triangle formed by the above two lines and the x-axis. Also, find the area of the triangle. *(An)*

Sol. The given equations are:

$2x + y = 6$ ... (*i*)

$\Rightarrow y = 6 - 2x$

Hence table of solutions for (*i*)

x	1	2
$y = 6 - 2x$	4	2

Therefore, points are (1, 4) and (2, 2) *(½ M)*

$x - 2y + 2 = 0$ ... (*ii*)

$\Rightarrow y = \dfrac{x+2}{2}$

Table for solutions for (*ii*)

x	0	2
$y = \dfrac{x+2}{2}$	1	2

Hence, points are (0, 1) and (2, 2) *(½ M)*

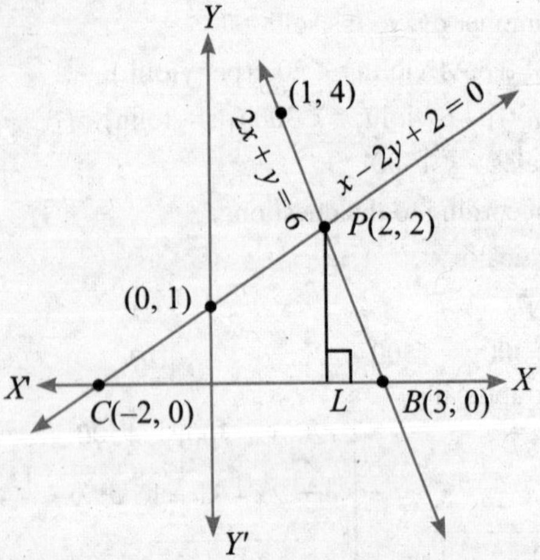

(1 M)

As we can see from the graph that the two straight lines intersect at $P(2, 2)$.

Therefore, $x = 2$, $y = 2$ is the solution of the given system. *(1 M)*

Vertices of the triangle are $P(2, 2)$, $B(3, 0)$ and $C(-2, 0)$ *(½ M)*

Now, $PL \perp BC$, $BC = 5$ units and $PL = 2$ units *(½ M)*

$\therefore$ area of $\Delta PBC = \dfrac{1}{2}(5 \times 2) = 5$ sq. units. *(1 M)*

2. For Joshimath Subsidence victims two sections *A* and *B* of class *X* contributed ₹1,500. If the contribution of *X-B* was ₹100 more than that of *X-A*, find graphically the amounts contributed by both the sections. *(Un)*

Sol. Let amounts contributed by two sections *X-A* and *X-B* are ₹ x and ₹ y respectively.

$x + y = 1{,}500$ ... (*i*)

and $y - x = 100$ ... (*ii*) *(1 M)*

From (*i*), $y = 1500 - x$

x	0	1500
y	1500	0

(½ M)

From (*ii*), $y = 100 + x$

x	0	700
y	100	800

(½ M)

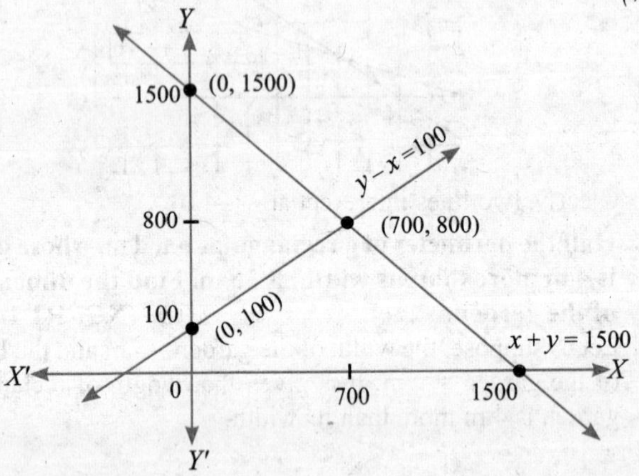

(1 M)

$\because$ The lines intersect each other at point (700, 800).

So, $x = 700$ and $y = 800$. *(1 M)*

$\therefore$ *X-A* and *X-B* contributed ₹700 and ₹800 respectively. *(1 M)*

Nailing the Right Answer

Draw perpendicular lines from the intersection point to each axis for precise coordinate reading.

3. Draw the graphs of the lines $x = -2$ and $y = 3$. Write the vertices of the figure formed by these lines, the x-axis and the y-axis. Also, find the area of the figure. *(Ap)* **(NCERT Exemplar)**

Sol. We know the graph of $x = -2$ is a line parallel to y-axis at a distance of 2 units to the left of it.

So, the line l is the graph of $x = -2$ *(½ M)*

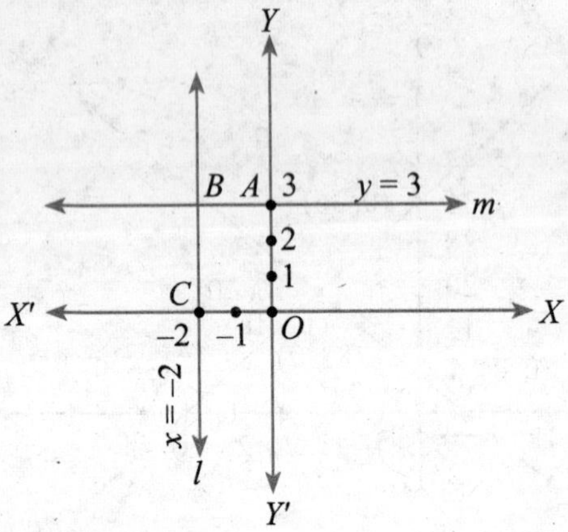

(½ M)

The graph of $y = 3$ is a line parallel to the x-axis at a distance of 3 units above it.

So, the line m is the graph of $y = 3$

The figure enclosed by the lines $x = -2$, $y = 3$ the x-axis and the y-axis is $OABC$, which is a rectangle.

A is a point on the y-axis at a distance of 3 units above the x-axis. So, the coordinates of A are (0, 3); *(½ M)*

C is a point on the x-axis at a distance of 2 units to the left of y-axis. So, the coordinates of C are (–2, 0) *(½ M)*

B is the solution of the pair of equations $x = -2$ and $y = 3$ So, the coordinates of B are (–2, 3) *(½ M)*

So, the vertices of the rectangle $OABC$ are O (0, 0), A(0, 3) B (–2, 3), C(– 2,0) *(½ M)*

The length and breadth of this rectangle are 2 units and 3 units, respectively. *(1 M)*

As the area of a rectangle = length × breadth,
the area of rectangle $OABC = 2 \times 3 = 6$ sq. units. *(1 M)*

4. Draw the graphs of the equations $x - y + 1 = 0$ and $3x + 2y - 12 = 0$. Determine the coordinates of the vertices of the triangle formed by these lines and the x-axis, and shade the triangular region. **(*An*) (NCERT Intext)**

Sol. $x - y + 1 = 0$ or $y = x + 1$

x	0	1	2
y	1	2	3

(1 M)

$3x + 2y - 12 = 0$

$$\Rightarrow x = \frac{12 - 2y}{3}$$

x	4	2	0
y	0	3	6

(1 M)

Hence, the graphic representation is as follows.

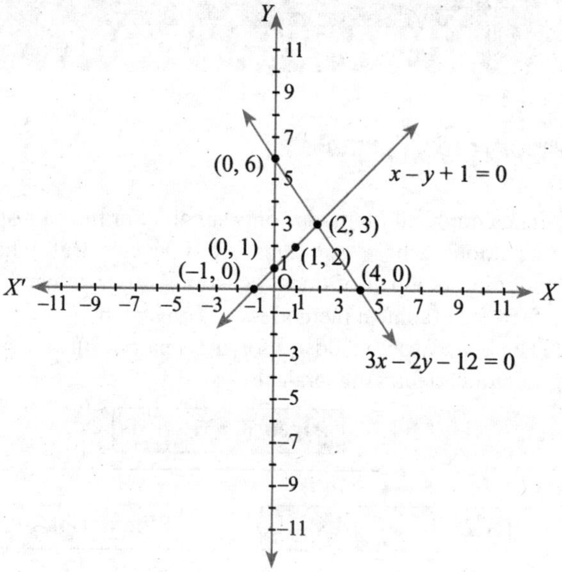

(2 M)

From the figure, it can be observed that these lines are intersecting each other at point, (2, 3) and x-axis at (–1, 0) and (4, 0). Therefore, the vertices of the triangle are (2, 3), (–1, 0) and (4,0). *(1 M)*

Key Takeaways

If both the lines intersect at a point, then there exists a unique solution to the pair of linear equations. In such a case, the pair of linear equations is said to be consistent.

2 ALGEBRAIC METHODS OF SOLVING A PAIR OF LINEAR EQUATIONS

Important Terms

- The Graphical Method is only suitable for the pair of linear equations whose solutions are integers. But when the solution of a pair of linear equations is non-integral values then the graphical method is not convenient.
- There are two methods of solving a pair of linear equations in two variables algebraically.

Algebraic Method → **Substitution Method**, **Elimination Method**

- **Substitution Method:**
  A pair of linear equations in two variables x and y can be solved by substitution method by using the following steps:
  Step I: Consider any one of the linear equations in the pair as suitable and then find the value of one variable in terms of another variable. Let's say we are finding value of y in terms of x.
  Step II: Substitute the value of y, obtained in step-I, in the other equation and simplify it to get a linear equation in x. Then, find the value of x.
  If in this case the variables are cancelled out and we get a statement with no variable then if the statement is correct then the pair of linear equations has infinitely many solutions and if the statement is not correct then the pair of linear equations has no solution.
  Step III: Substitute the value of x in step-I and then find the value of y.
  NOTE: This method is known as substitution method because in this method we substitute the value of a variable in terms of another variable in another equation.
- **Elimination method:**
  A pair of linear equation in two variables x and y can be solved by elimination method, by using the following steps:
  Step I: Make the coefficients of one of the variables i.e. either x or y, in the both equations numerically equal and to do so multiply these equations by some suitable non-zero constant.
  Step II: If the numerically equal coefficients are opposite in sign, then add the new equations otherwise subtract them.
  If in step-II, you get a statement with no variable, which is correct then the original pair of equations has infinitely many solutions.
  If in step-II, you get a statement with no variable, which is incorrect then the original pair of equations has no solution i.e the given system is inconsistent.
  Step III: Substitute the value of the variable obtained in step-II in either of the original equations to get the value of another variable.

Important Concepts

- Equation of the form $ax + by = c$ and $bx + ay = d$, where $a \neq b$.
- Use the following procedure to solve this type of pair of linear equations.
  Step I: Add the given equations and from it obtain an equation of the form $x + y = u$
  Step II: Subtract the given equations and from it obtain an equation of the form $x - y = v$ ($or -x + y = v$)
- Now, $x + y = u$ and $x - y = v$ ($or -x + y = v$) can be solved easily by adding.

Backbenchers after learning linear equations

no study	=	fail
+ study	=	no fail
no study + study	=	fail + no fail
study (no + 1)	=	fail (no + 1)
∴ study	=	fail

Real Life Applications

Pair of linear equation in two variables is used to solve many types of time, speed and distance related problems. E.g.

Suppose that A boat goes 30 km upstream (against the current/stream) and 44 km downstream (with the current/stream) in 10 hours. In 13 hours, it can go 40 km upstream and 55 km down-stream.

If we have to find the speed of the boat in still water and the speed of the stream then we can find these using pair of linear equation in two variables by assuming the speeds of the boat and the stream x km/h and y km/h respectively and then we can represent the above problem into Pair of linear equations and after solving it we can get the required speeds.

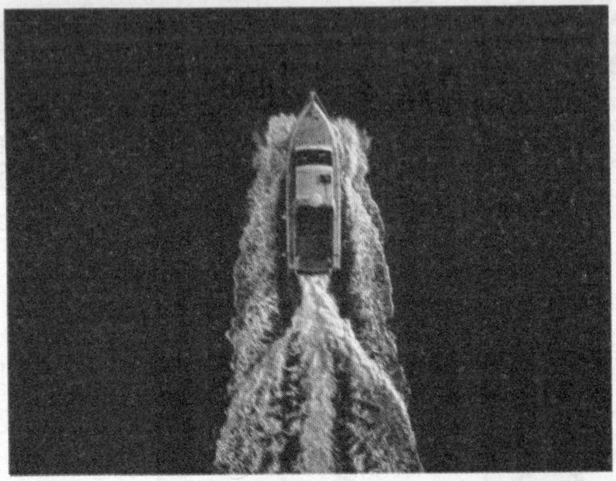

Different Problem Types

Type I: Solving Simultaneous Linear Equation in Two Variables Using Elimination:

Solve the following systems of linear equations by using the method of elimination by equating the coefficients:

$3x + 2y = 11, 2x + 3y = 4$

Solution:

Step I: The given systems of equations is

$3x + 2y = 11$ ....(*i*)

$2x + 3y = 4$ ....(*ii*)

Step II: Multiplying (*i*) by 3 and (*ii*) by 2, we get

$9x + 6y = 33$ ....(*iii*)

$4x + 6y = 8$ ....(*iv*)

Step III: Subtracting (*iv*) from (*iii*), we get

$5x = 25 \Rightarrow x = 5$

Step IV: Substituting $x = 5$ equation in (*i*), we get

$15 + 2y = 11 \Rightarrow 2y = -4 \Rightarrow y = -2$

Hence, the solution of the given system of equations is

$x = 5,\ y = -2$

Type II: Solving Simultaneous Linear Equation in Two Variables Using Substitution Method:

Solve the following pair of equations by substitution method:

$x + y = 5$ ... (*i*)

$2x - 3y = 4$ ... (*ii*)

Solution:

Step I: We pick either of the equations and write one variable in terms of the other.

Let us consider Equation (*ii*): $2x - 3y = 4 \Rightarrow x = \left(\frac{4+3y}{2}\right)$

Step II: Substitute the value of x in Equation (*i*). We get

i.e., $\left(\frac{4+3y}{2}\right) + y = 5 \Rightarrow \left(\frac{4+3y+2y}{2}\right) = 5 \Rightarrow 4 + 5y = 2 \times 5$

$\Rightarrow 4 + 5y = 10 \Rightarrow 5y = 10 - 4 \Rightarrow 5y = 6 \Rightarrow y = \frac{6}{5}$

Step III: Substituting this value of y in Equation (*i*), we get

$x + \frac{6}{5} = 5 \Rightarrow x = 5 - \frac{6}{5} \Rightarrow x = \frac{5 \times 5 - 6}{5} \Rightarrow x = \frac{25-6}{5} \Rightarrow x = \frac{19}{5}$

Therefore, the solution is $x = \frac{19}{5}, y = \frac{6}{5}$.

COMPETENCY BASED SOLVED EXAMPLES

Multiple Choice Questions

(1 M)

1. If 2 is subtracted from the numerator and 1 is added to the denominator, a fraction becomes $\frac{1}{2}$ but when 4 is added to the numerator and 3 is subtracted from the denominator, it becomes $\frac{3}{2}$, then find the fraction: (*Re*)

(*a*) $\frac{12}{11}$ (*b*) $\frac{8}{11}$ (*c*) $\frac{7}{11}$ (*d*) $\frac{13}{13}$

Sol. Let us suppose, the fraction be $\frac{x}{y}$

Now, according to given conditions,

$\frac{x-2}{y+1} = \frac{1}{2}$

$\Rightarrow 2(x - 2) = 1\ (y + 1)$

$\Rightarrow 2x - 4 = y + 1$

$\Rightarrow 2x - y = 5$ ... (*i*)

Again, according to question

$\frac{x+4}{y-3} = \frac{3}{2} \Rightarrow 2(x + 4) = 3\ (y - 3)$

$\Rightarrow 2x + 8 = 3y - 9 \Rightarrow 2x - 3y = -17$ ... (*ii*)

Subtracting eqn. (*ii*) from eqn. (*i*)

$(2x - y) - (2x - 3y) = 5 - (-17)$

$\Rightarrow 2y = 22 \Rightarrow y = 11 \Rightarrow 2x - 11 = 5$ ...[From (*i*)]

$\Rightarrow 2x = 16 \Rightarrow x = 8$

Substitute the value of x in eq. (*i*), we get

$y = 2 \times 8 - 5 = 11$

Hence, the required fraction is $\frac{8}{11}$.

Mistakes 101 : What not to do!

Skipping algebraic steps like combining terms or distributing can cause errors in solutions

2. Aruna has only ₹ 1 and ₹ 2 coins with her. If the total number of coins that she has is 50 and the amount of money with her is ₹ 75, then the number of ₹ 1 and ₹ 2 coins are, respectively (*Un*) **(NCERT Exemplar)**

(*a*) 35 and 15 (*b*) 35 and 20

(*c*) 15 and 35 (*d*) 25 and 25

Sol. Let the no. of ₹ 1 & ₹ 2 coins are x and y respectively.

Then, according to the question,

$x + y = 50$ ... (*i*)

and $x \times 1 + 2 \times y = 75 \Rightarrow x + 2y = 75$ ... (*ii*)

Substracting eqn. (*i*) from eqn. (*ii*) we get, $y = 25$

Substituting this value in eqn. (*i*) we get,

$x + 25 = 50 \Rightarrow x = 25$

Thus, number of ₹ 1 and ₹ 2 coins are 25 and 25 respectively.

3. For what value of *k*, do the equations $3x - y + 18 = 0$ and $6x - ky = -16$ represent coincident lines? *(Cr)* (NCERT Exemplar)

(a) $\frac{1}{2}$ (b) $-\frac{1}{2}$ (c) 2 (d) –2

Sol. $3x - y = -18$ ... (i)

$6x - ky = -16$ ... (ii)

For coincident lines,

$$\frac{a_1}{a_2} = \frac{b_1}{b_2} = \frac{c_1}{c_2} \Rightarrow \frac{3}{6} = \frac{-1}{-k} = \frac{-8}{-16}$$

On solving, we get, $k = 2$

4. The father's age is six times his son's age. After four years, the age of the father will be four times his son's age. Find the present ages, of the son and the father, in years. *(Ev)*

(a) 8 and 32 (b) 5 and 30

(c) 6 and 36 (d) 3 and 24

Sol. Let the present age of father and his son are x years and y years respectively.

Then, according to the question,

$x = 6y$ ...(i)

and $(x + 4) = 4(y + 4)$

$\Rightarrow x - 4y = 12$ ...(ii)

Substituting the value of x from eqn (i) in equation (ii) we get,

$6y - 4y = 12$

$\Rightarrow 2y = 12$

$y = 6$

$x = 6y = 6 \times 6 = 36$ [from eqn (i)]

Thus, the present age of father and his son are 36 years and 6 years respectively.

Answer Key

1. (b) 2. (d) 3. (c) 4. (c)

Assertion and Reason

(1 M)

Direction: In the following questions, a statement of Assertion (A) is followed by a statement of Reason (R). Mark the correct choice as:

(a) Both Assertion (A) and Reason (R) are true and Reason (R) is the correct explanation of Assertion (A).

(b) Both Assertion (A) and Reason (R) are true but Reason (R) is not the correct explanation of Assertion (A).

(c) Assertion (A) is true but Reason (R) is false.

(d) Assertion (A) is false but Reason (R) is true.

1. Assertion (A): The pair of linear equations $5x + 4y = 3$ and $10x + 8y = -1$ has no solution because after elimination we get, $0 = -7$

Reason (R): If we get an equation free from variable in elimination/substitution method and if the obtained equation is not true then the pair of linear equations has no solution. *(Re)*

Sol. Assertion: $5x + 4y = 3$ ... (i)

$10x + 8y = -1$ ... (ii)

Now (ii) $-2\times$ (i) $\Rightarrow 10x + 8y - 2(5x + 4y) = -1 - 2 \times 3 \Rightarrow 0 + 0 = -7 \Rightarrow 0 = -7$, which is not true

∴ The pair of linear equation has no solution.

Reason: Reason is true by theory.

Also, Reason is correct explanation of the Assertion

2. Assertion (A): To find the value of *x* in pair of linear equations.

$2x - 5y = 3$ and $3x + 5y = 3$

we should add both the given equation

Reason (R): In substitution method we remove one of the variables by addition or substraction. *(Re)*

Sol. Assertion: Assertion is true because when we add both the equation then the y- term in the equation will be eliminated and then we can find the value of *x* as shown below

$(2x - 5y) + (3x + 5y) = 3 + 3$

$\Rightarrow 5x + 0y = 6 \Rightarrow x = \frac{6}{5}$

Reason: Reason is wrong because in substitution method we substitute value of one variable (in terms of another variable) from one equation in another equation to get value of another variable

Hence, Assertion is true but Reason is wrong.

Answer Key

1. (a) 2. (c)

Subjective Questions

Very Short Answer Type Questions

(1 or 2 M)

1. The difference between two numbers is 26 and the larger number exceeds thrice of the smaller number by 4. Find the numbers. *(Ev)*(CBSE, 2020)

Sol. Let the larger number be *y* and the smaller number be *x*.

According to question,

$y - x = 26$ ...(i)

and $y = 3x + 4$ ...(ii)

Substituting the value of y from equation (*ii*) in equation (*i*), we get *(1 M)*

$3x + 4 - x = 26$

or $2x = 26 - 4$

or $2x = 22$

or $x = 11$

Putting this value of x in equation (1), we get

or $y - 11 = 26$

or $y = 26 + 11 = 37$ *(1M)*

2. If $x = a$ and $y = b$ is the solution of the pair of equations $x - y = 2$ and $x + y = 4$, find the value of a and b.

(*Ev*) [NCERT Exemplar]

Sol. $\because x = a$ and $y = b$ is solution of the equations

$x - y = 2$ and $x + y = 4$

$\therefore\ a - b = 2$ ... (*i*)

$a + b = 4$ ... (*ii*)

Now, adding eqn. (*i*) and eqn. (*ii*) we get,

$2a = 6 \Rightarrow a = 3$ *(1 M)*

Substituting this value in eqn. (*ii*) we get,

$3 + b = 4 \Rightarrow b = 1$

$\therefore a = 3$ and $b = 1$ *(1 M)*

3. If the ratio of incomes of P and Q is 5 : 6 and the ratio of their expenditure is 9 : 11. If each of them saves ₹ 1000, then find the algebraic representation of the problem. **(*Un*)**

Sol. Let us suppose, income of P = ₹$5x$

and, income of Q = ₹$6x$

Let, expenditure of P = ₹$9y$

And, expenditure of Q = ₹$11y$

As we know,

Income – Expenditure = Saving *(1 M)*

Now, according to given conditions,

$5x - 9y = 1000$ ... (*i*)

$6x - 11y = 1000$ ... (*ii*) *(1 M)*

4. Find whether the following pair of linear equations is consistent or inconsistent:

$3x + 2y = 8$

$6x - 4y = 9$ **(*An*)(CBSE SQP, 2023)**

Sol. $3x + 2y = 8$

$6x - 4y = 9$

$a_1 = 3, a_2 = 4, c_2 = 9$ *(1 M)*

$$\frac{a_1}{a_2} = \frac{3}{6} = \frac{1}{2} \quad \frac{b_1}{b_2} = \frac{2}{-4} = \frac{-1}{2} \quad \frac{c_1}{c_2} = \frac{8}{9}$$

$$\frac{a_1}{a_2} \neq \frac{b_1}{b_2} \neq \frac{c_1}{c_2}$$

The given pair of lines is consistent. *(1 M)*

5. Shown below are lines l_1: $2x - 5y - 27 = 0$ and l_2: $7x - y + 14 = 0$.

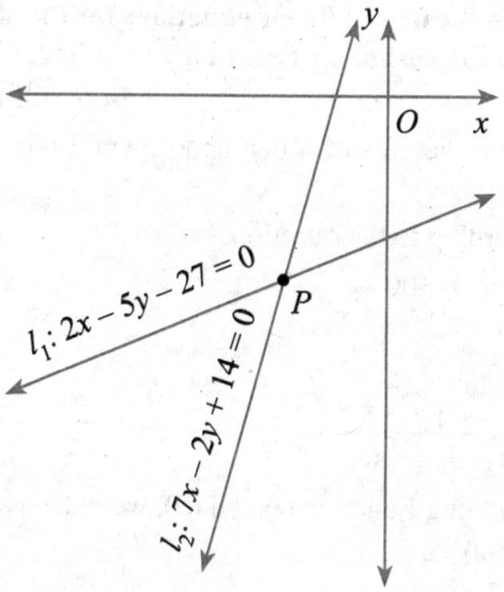

Write the equation of a line l_3, in two variables, such that it intersects l_1 and l_2 exactly at one point, *P*. Show your work. **(*Ap*) (CBSE CFPQ,2023)**

Sol. The given equations are:

$2x - 5y - 27 = 0$ ... (*i*)

$7x - 2y + 14 = 0$ ... (*ii*)

Multiplying equation (*i*) by 2 and equation (*ii*) by –5 we get:

$4x - 10y - 54 = 0$ ... (*iii*)

$-35x + 10y - 70 = 0$ ... (*iv*)

Adding equation (*iii*) & (*iv*) we get

$-31x - 124 = 0 \Rightarrow -x - 4 = 0 \Rightarrow x = -4$ *(1M)*

Subtituting $x = -4$ in equation (*i*) we get:

$-8 - 5y - 27 = 0 \Rightarrow -5y - 35 = 0 \Rightarrow y = -7$

$\therefore$ Coordinates of point $P = (-4, -7)$

$\because$ The line l_3 passes through point P

$\therefore$ Equation of line l_3 is $x + y + 11 = 0$ *(1 M)*

Short Answer Type Questions (2 or 3 M)

1. Solve the following pair of equations by substitution method:

$x - y = 12$

$2x = 2y - 7$ **(*Un*)**

Sol. $x - y = 12$ ... (*i*)

$2x = 2y - 7$ ... (*ii*)

Let us consider the equation (*i*):

$x - y = 12 \Rightarrow x = 12 + y$ ... (*iii*) *(1 M)*

Substituting the value of x in equation (*ii*), we get

$2(12 + y) = 2y - 7 \Rightarrow 24 + 2y = 2y - 7 \Rightarrow 24 = -7$ *(1 M)*

This is the case of a variable being cancelled out

Since $24 = -7$ is an incorrect statement.

Therefore, we conclude that the pair of equations has no solutions. *(1 M)*

2. **The cost of 4 pens and 4 pencil boxes is ₹ 100. Three times the cost of a pen is ₹ 15 more than the cost of a pencil box. Form the pair of linear equations for the above situation. Find the cost of a pen and a pencil box.**

(*An*) (NCERT Exemplar)

Sol. Taking the cost of a pen and a pencil box be ₹ x and ₹ y respectively.

According to the question,

$4x + 4y = 100$

$\Rightarrow x + y = 25$ ... (*i*) (½ M)

and

$3x = y + 15$

$\Rightarrow 3x - y = 15$ ... (*ii*) (½ M)

On adding Equation (*i*) and (*ii*), we get,

$4x = 40$

$\Rightarrow x = 10$ (½ M)

Putting $x = 10$, in Eq. (*i*) we get

$y = 25 - 10 = 15$ (½ M)

So, the cost of a pen = Rs. 10, and,

The cost of a pencil box = Rs. 15 (*1 M*)

3. **Solve the following pair of equations by substitution method:**

$2x - 4y = 2$

$4x - 8y = 4$ **(*Un*)**

Sol. $2x - 4y = 2$ ... (*i*)

$4x - 8y = 4$ ... (*ii*)

Consider the equation (*i*):

$2x - 4y = 2 \Rightarrow x = \frac{2+4y}{2} = 1 + 2y$ ... (*iii*) (*1 M*)

Substituting the value of x in equation (*ii*), we get

$4(1 + 2y) - 8y = 4$

$\Rightarrow 4 + 8y - 8y = 4 \quad \Rightarrow \quad 4 = 4$ (*1 M*)

This is the case of a variable being cancelled out and since $4 = 4$ is a correct statement.

Therefore, we conclude that the pair of equations has infinite solutions. (*1 M*)

Nailing the Right Answer

Sometimes, it's helpful to solve for one variable in one equation, then plug that expression into the other equation. This makes solving easier.

4. **The ratio of incomes of two persons is 9 : 7 and the ratio of their expenditure is 4 : 3. If each of them manages to save ₹ 2000 per month, find their monthly incomes.**

(*Re*)

Sol. Let the income of two people be ₹ $9x$ and ₹ $7x$ and their expenditures be ₹ $4y$ and ₹ $3y$ respectively. (½ M)

Then the equation formed for the given situations are given by:

$9x - 4y = 2000$ ...(*i*)

and $7x - 3y = 2000$ ...(*ii*) (½ M)

Multiply equation (*i*) by 3 and equation (*ii*) by 4 to make the coefficient of y equal. Then we get the equations:

$3(9x - 4y) = 3(2000) \Rightarrow 27x - 12y = 6000$ ... (*iii*)

$4(7x - 3y) = 4(2000) \Rightarrow 28x - 12y = 8000$ ... (*iv*)

(½ M)

Subtract Equation (*iii*) from equation (*iv*) to eliminate y, because the coefficients of y are the same. So, we get

$28x - 12y - (27x - 12y) = 8000 - 6000$

$\Rightarrow x = 2000$ (½ M)

Substituting this value of x in equation (*i*), we get

$\Rightarrow 9(2000) - 4y = 2000$

$\Rightarrow 18000 - 4y = 2000 \Rightarrow -4y = 2000 - 18000$

$\Rightarrow -4y = -16000 \quad \Rightarrow y = \frac{-16000}{-4} \Rightarrow y = 4000$ (½ M)

Hence, the solution of the equations is $x = 2000$, $y = 4000$.

Therefore, the monthly incomes of two persons are ₹ 18000 and ₹ 14000 respectively. (½ M)

Nailing the Right Answer

Assign variables to represent unknown quantities in ratio equations consistently. Use meaningful variables that reflect the quantities being compared in the ratios.

5. **In a competitive examination, one mark is awarded for each correct answer while $\frac{1}{2}$ mark is deducted for every wrong answer. Jayanti answered 120 questions and got 90 marks. How many questions did she answer correctly?**

(*Cr*) (NCERT Exemplar)

Sol. Taking the number of questions attempted correctly = x

Number of questions answered = 120

And, wrong answer attempted = $(120 - x)$ (½ M)

Marks awarded for right answer = $1 \times x = x$ marks (½ M)

Marks deducted for $(120 - x)$ wrong answer = $1/2\ (120 - x)$

(½ M)

Therefore,

$x - \frac{1}{2}(120 - x) = 90$ (½ M)

$x + \frac{x}{2} = 90 + 60 \Rightarrow \frac{3x}{2} = 150 \Rightarrow x = 100$

Hence she answered 100 questions correctly. (*1 M*)

6. **Use elimination method to find all possible solutions of the following pair of linear equations:** **(*Un*)**

$3x + 4y = 8$

$6x + 8y = 7$

Sol. We have $3x + 4y = 8$ ... (*i*)

$6x + 8y = 7$ ... (*ii*)

Multiply Equation (*i*) by 2 and Equation (*ii*) by 1 to make the coefficients of x equal. Then we get the equations as:

$6x + 8y = 16$ ... (*iii*)

$6x + 8y = 7$ ... (*iv*) (*1 M*)

Subtracting Equation (*iv*) from Equation (*iii*),

$(6x + 8y) - (6x + 8y) = 16 - 7$

i.e., $0 = 9$, which is a false statement. (*1 M*)

Therefore, the pair of equations has no solution. (*1 M*)

7. Find the solution of the pair of equations $\frac{x}{10} + \frac{y}{5} - 1 = 0$ and $\frac{x}{8} + \frac{y}{6} = 15$

Hence, find λ, if $y = \lambda x + 5$. (*Cr*) **(NCERT Exemplar)**

Sol. Given equations are

$\frac{x}{10} + \frac{y}{5} - 1 = 0$ (multiply by 20)

$2x + 4y = 20$ ... (*i*)

$\frac{x}{8} + \frac{y}{6} = 15$ (multiply by 24)

$3x + 4y = 360$ ... (*ii*)

On solving, equation (*i*) and (*ii*),

$x = 340$ (*1 M*)

Now,

$x + 2y = 10 \Rightarrow 340 + 2y = 10$ [$x = 340$]

$2y = 10 - 340 \Rightarrow 2y = -330 \Rightarrow y = -165$ (*1 M*)

Now,

$y = \lambda x + 5$ [Given]

$-165 = \lambda(340) + 5$ [$y = -165$ and $x = 340$]

$-\lambda\,(340) = 5 + 165 \Rightarrow -\lambda\,(340) = 170 \Rightarrow \lambda = -\frac{1}{2}$

The solution of the given pair of equations is $x = 340$, $y = -165$ and $\lambda = -\frac{1}{2}$ (*1 M*)

8. The coach of a cricket team buys 4 bats and 1 ball for Rs. 2050. Later, she buys 3 bats and 2 balls for Rs. 1600. Find the cost of each bat and each ball.

(*An*) **(CBSE SQP,2023)**

Sol. Let cost of one bat be Rs x

Let cost of one ball be Rs y (*½ M*)

ATQ

$4x + 1y = 2050$ ...(1)

$3x + 2y = 1600$ ...(2) (*½ M*)

from (1) $4x + 1y = 2050$ (2)

$y = 2050 - 4x$ (*½ M*)

Substiture value of y in (2)

$[3x + 2(2050 - 4x) = 1600]$

$3x + 4100 - 8x = 1600$

$-5x = -2500$

$x = 500$ (*½ M*)

Substiture value of x in (1)

$4x + 1y = 2050$

$4(500) + y = 2050$

$2000 + y = 2050$

$y = 50$

9. Solve of x and y

$\frac{2}{x} + \frac{3}{y} = 13$ **and** $\frac{5}{x} - \frac{4}{y} = -2$ **(*Ev*)(CBSE, 2020)**

Sol. $\frac{2}{y} + \frac{3}{y} = 13$ and $\frac{5}{x} - \frac{4}{x} = -2$

Let $\frac{1}{x} = p$ and $\frac{1}{y} = q$

then given equations can be written as:

$2p + 3q = 13$

$2p + 3q - 13 = 0$ ...(*i*)

and

$5p - 4q = -2$

$5p - 4q + 2 = 0$ ...(*ii*) (*1 M*)

Using cross-multiplication method, we get

$\frac{p}{6-52} = \frac{q}{-65-4} = \frac{1}{-8-15}$

$\Rightarrow \frac{p}{-46} = \frac{q}{-69} = \frac{1}{-23}$

$\Rightarrow \frac{p}{-46} = \frac{-1}{-23}$ and $\frac{q}{-69} = \frac{1}{-23}$ (*1 M*)

$\Rightarrow p = \frac{-46}{-23}$ and $q = \frac{-69}{-23}$

$\Rightarrow p = 2$ and $q = 3$

$\Rightarrow \frac{1}{x} = 2$ and $\frac{1}{y} = 3$

$\Rightarrow x = \frac{1}{2}$ and $y = \frac{1}{3}$ (*1 M*)

10. There are some students in the two examination halls *A* and *B*. To make the number of students equal in each hall, 10 students are sent from *A* to *B*. But if 20 students are sent from *B* to *A*, the number of students in *A* becomes double the number of students in *B*. Find the number of students in the two halls. (*Ev*) **[NCERT Exemplar]**

Sol. Let the number of students in *A* and *B* are x and y respectively. (*½ M*)

Now, according to the question,

$x - 10 = y + 10 \Rightarrow x - y = 20$ ... (*i*) (*½ M*)

Also, $x + 20 = 2(y - 20)$

$\Rightarrow x - 2y = -60$ ... (*ii*) (*½ M*)

Substracting eqn. (*ii*) from eqn. (*i*) we get,

$(x - y) - (x - 2y) = 20 - (-60)$

$\Rightarrow -y + 2y = 80 \Rightarrow y = 80$ (*½ M*)

$\Rightarrow x - 80 = 20$ [From eqn. (*i*)]

$\Rightarrow x = 20 + 80 = 100$ (*½ M*)

Thus, the number of students in hall *A* and *B* are 100 and 80 respectively. (*½ M*)

11. Rahul has a total of 50 notes of ₹100 and ₹200. If Rahul has a total of ₹6000 then how many notes of each denomination ₹100 and ₹200 Rahul has? *(Un)*

Sol. Let the number of notes of ₹ 100 and ₹ 200 be x and y respectively, (½ M)

Then, according to the question

$x + y = 50$ ... (*i*) (½ M)

and $100x + 200y = 6000$ ... (*ii*) (½ M)

Subtracting equation (*i*), after multiplying it by 100, from eqn. (*ii*) we get,

$(100x + 200y) - 100(x + y) = 6000 - 100 \times 50$

$\Rightarrow 200y - 100y = 6000 - 5000 \Rightarrow 100y = 1000 \Rightarrow y = 10$ (½ M)

From (*i*)...

$x + 10 = 50 \Rightarrow x = 40$ (½ M)

Thus, Rahul has 40 notes of 100 and 10 notes of 200. (½ M)

12. A two-digit number is such that when its ones and tens digits are interchanged then the 4 times of the number obtained is equal to 7 times the original number. Also, the digits at one's place and at ten's place differ by 3, where the digit at ones place is greater than the digit at tens place. Find the original number. *(An)*

Sol. Let the ones and ten's digits of the required no. are x and y.

Now, the required no. = $10y + x$

The number after reversing its digit = $10x + y$ (½ M)

∴ According to the question,

$4(10x + y) = 7(10y + x) \Rightarrow 40x + 4y = 70y + 7x$

$\Rightarrow 33x - 66y = 0 \Rightarrow x - 2y = 0$ ... (*i*) (½ M)

Also,

∵ The difference between units and tens digit is 3.

$\therefore x - y = 3 \Rightarrow x = 3 + y$ ... (*ii*) (½ M)

Substituting $x = 3 + y$ in eqn. (*i*) we get,

$3 + y - 2y = 0 \Rightarrow 3 - y = 0 \Rightarrow y = 3$ (½ M)

Substituting this value in (*ii*)

$x = 3 + 3 = 6$ (½ M)

∴ Required no. is 36. (½ M)

13. Solve $2x + 3y = 11$ and $2x - 4y = -24$ and hence find the value of 'm' for which $y = mx + 3$. *(An)* **(NCERT Intext)**

Sol. $2x + 3y = 11$ ... (*i*)

$2x - 4y = -24$ ... (*ii*)

From equation (*i*), we obtain

$$x = \frac{11-3y}{2} \quad \text{... (iii)} \quad (½ M)$$

Substituting this value in equation (*ii*), we obtain

$$2\left(\frac{11-3y}{2}\right) - 4y = -24 \quad (½ M)$$

$11 - 3y - 4y = -24 \Rightarrow -7y = -35$

$y = 5$ ... (*iv*) (1 M)

Putting this value of y in equation (*iii*), we obtain

$$x = \frac{11-3\times 5}{2} = -\frac{4}{2} = -2 \quad (½ M)$$

Hence, $x = -2$, $y = 5$

Also, $y = mx + 3 \Rightarrow 5 = -2m + 3 \Rightarrow -2m = 2 \Rightarrow m = -1$ (½ M)

Long Answer Type Questions (4 or 5 M)

1. Susan invested certain amount of money in two schemes *A* and *B*, which offer interest at the rate of 8% per annum and 9% per annum, respectively. She received ₹ 1860 as annual interest. However, had she interchanged the amount of investments in the two schemes, she would have received ₹ 20 more as annual interest. How much money did she invest in each scheme? *(Re)* **[NCERT Exemplar]**

Sol. Let the amount invested in scheme *A* and *B* are ₹x and ₹y.

According to question,

Annual interest = ₹1860

$$\Rightarrow 8\% \text{ of } x + 9\% \text{ of } y = 1860 \Rightarrow \frac{8x}{100} + \frac{9y}{100} = 1860$$

$\Rightarrow 8x + 9y = 186000$ ... (*i*) (1 M)

Also, Annual interest after interchanging the investments in the two schemes = 1860 + 20

$$\Rightarrow 8\% \text{ of } y + 9\% \text{ of } x = 1880 \Rightarrow \frac{8}{100}y + \frac{9}{100}x = 1880$$

$\Rightarrow 8y + 9x = 188000$ ... (*ii*) (1 M)

Adding (*i*) and (*ii*)

$17x + 17y = 374000 \Rightarrow x + y = 22000$ ... (*iii*) (½ M)

Subtracting eqn. (*i*) and eqn. (*ii*) we get,

$x - y = 2000$ (½ M)

Adding eqn. (*iii*) and eqn. (*iv*)

$(x + y) + (x - y) = 22000 + 2000$ (½ M)

$\Rightarrow 2x = 24000 \Rightarrow x = 12000$ (½ M)

Substituting this value in equation (*iii*)

$12000 + y = 22000 \Rightarrow y = 10000$ (½ M)

Thus, she invested ₹12000 in scheme *A* and ₹10000 in scheme *B*. (½ M)

2. Ananya had red, blue and yellow marbles in the ratio 4 : 5: 3. She gave all her red marbles and some blue marbles to Neha. The ratio of the number of blue marbles and yellow marbles left with Ananya was 7 : 9.

If Ananya gave 20 marbles to Neha, how many of them are red marbles? Show your work.

(Ap) **(CBSE CFPQ, 2023)**

Sol. Let the number of red marbles with Ananya = $4x$ (½ M)

Number of blue marbles = $5x$ (½ M)

and number of yellow marbles = $3x$ (½ M)

Number of red marbles given to Neha = $4x$ (½ M)

Let number of blue marbles given to Neha = y (½ M)

$\therefore$ According to question,

$4x + y = 20$ ... (*i*) (½ M)

Also, $\frac{5x - y}{3x} = \frac{7}{9} \Rightarrow 45x - 9y = 21x$

$\Rightarrow 24x - 9y = 0$ ... (*ii*) (½ M)

Multiplying equation (*i*) by –6 we get

$-24x - 6y = -120$ ... (*iii*) (½ M)

Adding equation (*ii*) & (*iii*) we

$-15y = -120 \Rightarrow y = 8$ (½ M)

Now, substituting $y = 8$ in equation (*i*) we get

$4x = 12$ (½ M)

$\therefore$ Number of red marbles = 12

3. Determine, algebraically, the vertices of the triangle formed by the lines (*An*) (NCERT Exemplar)

$3x - y = 3$, $2x - 3y = 2$, $x + 2y = 8$

Sol. $3x - y = 3$ ... (*i*)

$2x - 3y = 2$ ... (*ii*)

$x + 2y = 8$ ... (*iii*)

If the equation of the line (*i*), (*ii*) and (*iii*) represent the side of a ΔABC.

Then, on solving (*i*) and (*ii*),

[Multiplying eq. (*i*) by 3 and then subtract eq. (*ii*)]

$(9x - 3y) - (2x - 3y) = 9 - 2$ (½ M)

$7x = 7 \Rightarrow x = 1$

Putting, $x = 1$ in eq. (*i*),

We get, $3 \times 1 - y = 3 \Rightarrow y = 0$

Therefore, the coordinates of point B are (1, 0) (1 M)

On solving lines (*ii*) and (*iii*),

[Multiplying eq (*iii*) by 2 and then subtract eq (*ii*)]

$(2x + 4y) - (2x - 3y) = 16 - 2$ (½ M)

$7y = 14 \Rightarrow y = 2$

Putting, $y = 2$ in eq (*iii*),

$x + 2 \times 2 = 8 \Rightarrow x + 4 = 8 \Rightarrow x = 4$

Therefore, the coordinates of point C are (4, 2). (1 M)

On solving lines (*iii*) and (*i*),

[Multiplying in eq (*i*) by 2 and then add eq (*iii*)]

$(6x - 2y) + (x + 2y) = 6 + 8$

$7x = 14 \Rightarrow x = 2$

Putting $x = 2$ in eq (*i*) we get

$3 \times 2 - y = 3 \Rightarrow y = 3$

Hence, the coordinates of point A are (2, 3) (1 M)

Therefore, the vertices of the ΔABC formed by the given lines are $A(2, 3)$, $B(1, 0)$, $C(4, 2)$. (1 M)

4. The present age of a father is three years more than three times the age of his son. Three years hence the father's age will be 10 years more than twice the age of the son. Determine their present ages. **(*An*)**

Sol. Let, present age of son = x

And, present age of father = $3x + 3$ (1 M)

3 years later, age of son = $x + 3$

Age of father = $3x + 3 + 3 = 3x + 6$ ... (*i*) (1 M)

According to the given condition,

Age of father = $10 + 2(x + 3)$ (1 M)

$\therefore$ $3x + 6 = 10 + 2(x + 3) \Rightarrow 3x + 6 = 10 + 2x + 6$

$\Rightarrow 3x - 2x = 10 + 6 - 6 \Rightarrow x = 10$ (1 M)

$\therefore$ Present age of son = 10 years

Present age of father = $3x + 3 = 3 \times 10 + 3 = 33$ years (1 M)

5. The difference of two natural numbers is 5 and the difference of their reciprocals is 1/10. Find the numbers. **(CBSE, 2020)**

Sol. Given

Difference of the two natural numbers = 5

Difference of their reciprocal $= \frac{1}{10}$

Let the two natural number be N_1 and N_2.

Therefore,

$N_1 - N_2 = 5$ ...(*i*)

$\frac{1}{N_2} - \frac{1}{N_2} = \frac{1}{10}$ ...(*ii*)

Considering (*ii*)

$\frac{1}{N_2} - \frac{1}{N_2} = \frac{1}{10}$

$\Rightarrow \frac{N_1 - N_2}{N_1 N_2} = \frac{1}{10}$

$\Rightarrow \frac{5}{N_1 N_2} = \frac{1}{10}$ [From (*i*)]

$\Rightarrow N_1 N_2 = 50$ ...(*iii*)

Since, $(a + b)^2 = (a - b)^2 + 4ab$

Therefore,

$(N_1 + N_2)^2 = (N_1 - N_2)^2 + 4N_1 N_2$

$\Rightarrow (N_1 + N_2)^2 = 5^2 + 4 \times 50$ [From (*i*) and (*ii*)]

$\Rightarrow (N_1 + N_2)^2 = 225$

$\Rightarrow (N_1 + N_2 = 15$ ...(*iv*)

Adding (*i*) and (*iv*), we get

$2N_1 = 20$

$\Rightarrow N_1 = 10$

Putting then value of N_1 in (*iv*)

$N_2 = 5$

MISCELLANEOUS EXERCISE

Multiple Choice Questions

(1 M)

1. The solution of equations $x - y = 2$ and $x + y = 4$ is: **(CBSE SQP, 2023)**

   (a) 3 and 1 (b) 4 and 3 (c) 5 and 1 (d) –1 and –3

2. If a pair of linear equations is inconsistent then their graph lines will be

   (a) parallel (b) always coincident

   (c) always intersecting (d) intersecting or coincident

3. If $2x - 3y = 7$ and $(a + b)x - (a + b - 3)y = 4a + b$ have an infinite number of solutions then

   (a) $a = 5, b = 1$ (b) $a = -5, b = 1$

   (c) $a = 5, b = -1$ (d) $a = -5, b = -1$

4. The system $x + 2y = 3$ and $5x + ky + 7 = 0$ has no solution when

   (a) $k = 10$ (b) $k \neq 10$

   (c) $k = -73$ (d) $k = -21$

5. The pair of equations $x + 2y + 5 = 0$ and $-3x - 6y + 1 = 0$ have **(CBSE SQP, 2023)**

   (a) A unique solution

   (b) Exactly two solution

   (c) Infinitely many solution

   (d) No solution

6. If the lines represented by given pair of equations,

   $3x + 2ky = 2$

   $2x + 5y + 1 = 0$

   are parallel, then the value of k is

   (a) 3/5 (b) 2/5 (c) 15/4 (d) 3/2

7. Two numbers are in the ratio 5 : 6. If 8 is subtracted from each of the numbers, the ratio becomes 4 : 5. Then, find the numbers:

   (a) 36, 44 (b) 42, 48 (c) 40, 48 (d) 44, 50

8. Rakhi has only ₹ 5 and ₹ 10 coins with her. If the total number of coins that she has is 50 and the amount of money with her is ₹ 400, then the number of ₹ 5 and ₹ 10 coins is, respectively

   (a) 35 and 15 (b) 35 and 20

   (c) 20 and 30 (d) 25 and 25

9. In a competitive examination, one mark is awarded for each correct answer while 1/2 mark is deducted for every wrong answer. Priya answered 120 questions and got 90 marks. How many questions did she answer correctly?

   (a) 100 (b) 74 (c) 90 (d) 60

10. A shopkeeper gives books on rent for reading. She takes a fixed charge for the first two days, and an additional charge for each day thereafter. Preeti paid ₹ 22 for a book kept for six days, while Ritu paid ₹ 16 for the book kept for four days, then the charge for each extra day is:

    (a) ₹ 5 (b) ₹ 8 (c) ₹ 3 (d) ₹ 2

11. Find the value of x, if $\frac{x}{a}+\frac{y}{b}=a+b$ and $\frac{x}{a^2}+\frac{y}{b^2}=2$.

    (a) a^2 (b) b^2 (c) a^2b^2 (d) ab

12. Shyam has some cows and some hens in his shed. The total number of legs is 92 and total number of heads is 29. Find the number of cows in shed?

    (a) 15 (b) 14 (c) 17 (d) 19

13. 2 tables and 3 chairs together cost ₹ 2000 whereas 3 tables and 2 chairs together cost ₹ 2500. Find the total cost of 1 table and 5 chairs.

    (a) ₹ 1700 (b) ₹ 1500 (c) ₹ 1300 (d) ₹ 1450

14. Find the value of (x, y) $x > 0, y > 0$, for the pair of equation

    $$\frac{2}{\sqrt{x}}+\frac{3}{\sqrt{y}}=2, \quad \frac{4}{\sqrt{x}}-\frac{9}{\sqrt{y}}=-1$$

    (a) (2, 3) (b) (3, 2) (c) (4, 9) (d) (4, – 9)

Assertion and Reason

(1 M)

Direction: In the following questions, a statement of Assertion (A) is followed by a statement of Reason (R). Mark the correct choice as:

(a) Both Assertion (A) and Reason (R) are true and Reason (R) is the correct explanation of Assertion (A).

(b) Both Assertion (A) and Reason (R) are true but Reason (R) is not the correct explanation of Assertion (A).

(c) Assertion (A) is true but Reason (R) is false.

(d) Assertion (A) is false but Reason (R) is true.

1. **Assertion (A):** If $k = 2$, then $x + y - 4 = 0$ and $2x + ky - 3 = 0$ has no solution.

   Reason (R): $a_1x + b_1y + c_1 = 0$ and $a_2x + b_2y + c_2 = 0$ are consistent if $\frac{a_1}{a_2} \neq \frac{b_1}{b_2}$.

2. **Assertion (A):** Given pair of linear equations: $9x + 3y + 12 = 0$, $18x + 6y + 24 = 0$ have infinitely many solutions.

   Reason (R): Pair of linear equations $a_1x + b_1y + c_1 = 0$ and $a_2x + b_2y + c_2 = 0$ have infinitely many solutions, if

   $$\frac{a_1}{a_2}=\frac{b_1}{b_2}=\frac{c_1}{c_2}$$

3. **Assertion (A):** If after substituting the value of one variable in terms of another variable, from one equation in another equation we get an equation free from variable. Then, the pair of equations does not have any solution.

Reason (R): In substitution method, if we get an equation free from variable, after substitution, and the equation is incorrect than the pair of equation does not have my solution.

4. **Assertion (A):** While solving a pair of linear equation by elimination method, if we get $5 = 11$

   Then, the pair of linear equations has no solution.

   Reason (R): In elimination method, if we get a statement free from variable and the statement is true then the pair of linear equations has no solution.

Subjective Questions

Very Short Answer Type Questions (1 or 2 M)

1. For what values of p does the pair of equations $4x + py + 8 = 0$ and $2x + 2y + 2 = 0$ have a unique solution?
2. Find the number of solutions of the following pair of linear equations: $x + 2y - 8 = 0$ and $2x + 4y = 16$
3. Write whether the following pair of linear equations is consistent or not: $x + y = 14$ and $x - y = 4$
4. A cottage industry produces a certain number of pottery articles in a day. It was observed on a particular day that the cost of production of each article (in rupees) was 3 more than twice the number of articles produced on that day. If the total cost of production on that day was ₹ 90, find the number of articles produced and the cost of each article.
5. Find the value of c, for which the pair of equations $cx - y = 2$ and $6x - 2y = 3$ will have infinitely many solution.
6. If cost of 5 books and 7 pens together is ₹79, whereas the cost of 7 books and 5 pens together is ₹77. Write a linear equation in two variables to represent this statement.

Short Answer Type Questions (2 or 3 M)

1. Solve the following system of equations graphically $x + 3y = 6$ and $2x - 3y = 12$ and hence find the value of a if $4x + 3y = a$.
2. Ramila went to a stationary stall and purchased 2 pencils and 3 erasers for ₹9. Her friend Sonali saw the new variety of pencils and erasers with Ramila and she also bought 4 pencils and 6 arasers of same kind for ₹18. Represent this situation algebraically and graphically.
3. The larger of two supplementary angles exceed the smaller by 18°. Find the angles.
4. Solve the following pair of linear equations using the substitution method

   $3.5x + 2.5y = 9.5$ and $7.5x + 2.5y = 12.5$
5. Solve the following pair of linear equations by elimination method:

   $a - b = 5$ and $\frac{a}{5} + \frac{b}{4} = 20$
6. Anu had some chocolates, and he divided them into two lots A and B. He sold the first lot at the rate of ₹2 for 3 chocolates and the second lot at the rate of ₹1 per chocolate, and got a total of ₹40. If he had sold the first lot at the rate of ₹1 per chocolate, and the second lot at the rate of ₹4 for 5 chocolates, his total collection would have been ₹46. Find the total number of chocolates he had.
7. In a class there are certain number of benches, if 3 students sit on each bench then 9 students do not get any seat, but if 4 students sit on each bench then one bench remains unused. Express the statement in equation.
8. The area of a rectangle gets reduced by 9 square units if its length is reduced by 5 units and its breadth is increased by 3 units. If we increase the length by 3 units and the breadth by 2 units, the area increases by 67 square units. Find the dimensions of the rectangle.
9. In an examination, you are awarded 3 marks for the correct answer and –1 mark for the incorrect answer then the total marks obtained by you is 50. If you were awarded 2 marks for the correct answer and –0.5 marks for the incorrect answer then total marks obtained by you would have 40. Then find the total number of questions in the examinations.
10. If $2x + y = 23$ and $4x - y = 19$, find the value of $(5y - 2x)$ and $\left(\frac{y}{x} - 2\right)$

Long Answer Type Questions (4 or 5 M)

1. A rectangular park is to be designed whose breadth is 3 m less than its length. Its area is to be 4 square metres more than the area of a park that has already been made in the shape of an isosceles triangle with its base as the breadth of the rectangular park and of altitude 12 m. Find the length and breadth of the park.
2. Solve the following system of linear equations graphically;

   $3x + y - 11 = 0$; $x - y - 1 = 0$

   Shade the region bounded by these lines and y-axis. Then, determine the areas of the region bounded by these lines and y-axis.
3. For what values of m and n the following system of linear equations has infinitely many solutions.

   $3x + 4y = 12$ and $(m + n)x + 2(m - n)y = 5m - 1$
4. The difference of the digits of two digit number is 3. If this number is added to the number obtained by interchanging the digits, the sum is 99. Find the number?
5. By using substitution method, solve the following system of equations:

   $2x - 3y - 1 = 0$ and $\frac{x+(3x+2y)}{x-(3x+2y)} = -3$
6. A shopkeeper sells a saree at 8% profit and a sweater at 10% discount, thereby, getting a sum ₹1008. If she had sold the saree at 10% profit and the sweater at 8% discount, she would have got ₹1028. Find the cost price of the saree and the list price (price before discount) of the sweater.

Case Based Questions

Case Based-I: Mr. RK Agrawal is the owner of a famous amusement park in Delhi. The ticket charge for the park is ₹ 150 for children and ₹ 400 for adults.

Generally, he does not go to the park and it is managed by a team of staff. One day Mr. Agrawal decided to randomly check the park and went there. When he checked the cash counter, he found that 480 tickets were sold and ₹ 134500 was collected

(i) Let the number of children visited be x and the number of adults visited be y. What is the pair of equations that models the problem?

(ii) How many children visited the park?

OR

How much money would have been collected if 300 children and 350 adults had visited the park?

(iii) How much more/less would have been collected if the price of the ticket for children and adult had ₹200 and ₹300 respectively.

Case Based-II: Jodhpur is the second-largest city in the Indian state of Rajasthan and officially the second metropolitan city of the state. Jodhpur was historically the capital of the Kingdom of Marwar, which is now part of Rajasthan. Jodhpur is a popular tourist destination, featuring many palaces, forts, and temples, set in the stark landscape of the Thar Desert. It is popularly known as the "Blue City" among the people of Rajasthan and all over India. The old city circles the Mehrangarh Fort and is bounded by a wall with several gates. The city has expanded greatly outside the wall, though, over the past several decades. Jodhpur is also known for the rare breed of horses known as Marwari or Malani, which are only found here.

Last year we visited Jodhpur in a group of 25 friends. When we went to Mehrangarh Fort we found the following fare for the ride:

Ride	Normal Hours Fare	Peak Hours Fare
Horse	₹50	3 Times
Elephant	₹100	2 Times

Some people choose to ride on a horse and the rest choose to ride on an elephant. Each rides for only one times.

(i) First day we rode in normal hours and we paid ₹ 1950 for the ride. Let x be the number of horses hired and y be the number of elephants hired. Which of the following is the correct system of equations that models the problem?

(a) $50x + 100y = 1950$
$3x + 2y = 25$

(b) $150x + 200y = 1950$
$3x + 2y = 25$

(c) $50x + 100y = 1950$
$x + y = 25$

(d) $150x + 200y = 1950$
$x + y = 25$

(ii) How many horses were hired?

(a) 14 (b) 11
(c) 12 (d) None of these

(iii) How many elephants were hired?

(a) 14 (b) 11
(c) 12 (d) None of these

(iv) Next day we rode in peak hours, then how much total fare was paid by our group?

(a) ₹ 2500 (b) ₹ 3200
(c) ₹ 4450 (d) None of these

(v) What was the increase in total fare because of the peak hour ride?

(a) ₹ 4450 (b) ₹ 3200 (c) ₹ 1250 (d) ₹ 2500

Case Based-III: Two schools '*P*' and '*Q*' decided to award prizes to their students for two games of Hockey ₹ x per student and Cricket ₹ y per student. School '*P*' decided to award a total of ₹ 9,500 for the two games to 5 and 4 students respectively; while school '*Q*' decided to award ₹ 7,370 for the two games to 4 and 3 students respectively.

Based on the above information, answer the following questions:

(i) Represent the following information algebraically (in terms of x and y).

(ii) What is the prize amount for hockey?

OR

Prize amount on which game is more and by how much?

(iii) What will be the total prize amount if there are 2 students each from two games?

Case Based-IV: Dhoni is a former Indian cricketer and captain of the Indian national cricket team. He is known for his powerful and innovative batting, and he has scored many boundaries throughout his career. He has a particular penchant for hitting sixes, and he is one of the most successful finishers in limited-overs cricket. Dhoni has hit a total of 359 fours and 209 sixes in One Day Internationals (ODIs), and 78 fours and 16 sixes in Twenty20 Internationals (T20Is). Some of his most memorable boundary shots include the helicopter shot, which he invented himself, and his signature flick shot over the leg side.

In on of the matches he scored 98 runs only in boundaries.

Some of the boundaries were fours (4 runs each) and some of the boundaries were sixes (6 runs each).

If the number of sixes made was two less than that of fours answer the following questions.

(*i*) What is the algebraic representation of the above problem?

(*ii*) How many fours did he make?

OR

How many sixes did he make?

(*iii*) What are total number of boundaries scored by Dhoni?

Case Based-V: A book store shopkeeper gives books on rent for reading. He has variety of books in his store related to fiction, stories and quizzes etc. He takes a fixed charge for the first two days and an additional charge for subsequent day. Amruta paid ₹ 22 for a book and kept for 6 days; while Radhika paid ₹ 16 for keeping the book for 4 days. **(CBSE Term-I, 2022)**

Assume that the fixed charge be ₹ x and additional charge (per day) be ₹ y.

Based on the above information, answer any four of the following questions:

(*i*) The situation of amount paid by Radhika, is algebraically represented by

(*a*) $x - 4y = 16$ (*b*) $x + 4y = 16$

(*c*) $x - 2y = 16$ (*d*) $x + 2y = 16$

(*ii*) The situation of amount paid by Amruta, is algebraically represented by

(*a*) $x - 2y = 11$ (*b*) $x - 2y = 22$

(*c*) $x + 4y = 22$ (*d*) $x - 4y = 11$

(*iii*) What are the fixed charges for a book?

(*a*) ₹ 9 (*b*) ₹ 10 (*c*) ₹ 13 (*d*) ₹ 15

(*iv*) What are the additional charges for each subsequent day for a book?

(*a*) ₹ 6 (*b*) ₹ 5 (*c*) ₹ 4 (*d*) ₹ 3

(*v*) What is the total amount paid by both, if both of them have kept the book for 2 more days?

(*a*) ₹ 35 (*b*) ₹ 52 (*c*) ₹ 50 (*d*) ₹ 58

ANSWER KEYS

Multiple Choice Questions

1. (*a*) 2. (*a*) 3. (*d*) 4. (*a*) 5. (*d*) 6. (*c*) 7. (*c*) 8. (*c*) 9. (*a*) 10. (*c*)
11. (*a*) 12. (*c*) 13. (*a*) 14. (*c*)

Assertion and Reason

1. (*b*) 2. (*a*) 3. (*d*) 4. (*c*)

Case Based Questions

Case Based-II

(*i*) (*c*) (*ii*) (*b*) (*iii*) (*a*) (*iv*) (*c*) (*v*) (*d*)

Case Based-V

(*i*) (*d*) (*ii*) (*c*) (*iii*) (*b*) (*iv*) (*d*) (*v*) (*c*)

HINTS & EXPLANATIONS

Multiple Choice Questions

1. (*a*) Given: $x - y = 2$ ... (*i*)

$x + y = 4$ ... (*ii*)

Adding eqn. (*i*) and (*ii*), we get $2x = 6 \Rightarrow x = 3$

Put the value of x in equation (*i*), we get

$3 - y = 2 \Rightarrow y = 1$

Hence, $x = 3, y = 1$

2. (*a*) A pair of linear equations is inconsistent when there is no solution to the pair, which is possible if there is no common points in the lines represented by the pair of linear equations, which is possible if the lines are parallel.

3. (*d*) We have,

$2x - 3y = 7$ ... (*i*)

and $(a + b)x - (a + b - 3)y = 4a + b$ ... (*ii*)

$\Rightarrow a_1 = 2,\ b_1 = -3,\ c_1 = -7$

$a_2 = a + b,\ b_2 = -a - b + 3$ and $c_2 = -4a - b$

For infinite number of solutions,

$$\frac{a_1}{a_2} = \frac{b_1}{b_2} = \frac{c_1}{c_2} \Rightarrow \frac{2}{a+b} = \frac{-3}{-(a+b-3)} = \frac{-7}{-(4a+b)}$$

$$\Rightarrow \frac{2}{a+b} = \frac{3}{a+b-3} = \frac{7}{4a+b}$$

For $\frac{2}{a+b} = \frac{3}{a+b-3}$

$\Rightarrow 2a + 2b - 6 = 3a + 3b \Rightarrow a + b = -6$ ... (*i*)

For $\frac{3}{a+b-3} = \frac{7}{4a+b}$

$\Rightarrow 12a + 3b = 7a + 7b - 21 \Rightarrow 5a - 4b = -21$ ... (*ii*)

Adding eqn (*i*) and eqn (*ii*) by multiplying eqn (*i*) by 4.

$4(a + b) + 5b - 4b = -6 \times 4 + (-21)$

$\Rightarrow 9a = -45 \Rightarrow a = -5$

Substituting this in eqn (*i*)

$-5 + b = -6$

$b = -6 + 5 = -1$

Hence, $a = -5$ and $b = -1$

4. (*a*) We have,

$x + 2y = 3$ and $5x + ky + 7 = 0$

$\Rightarrow a_1 = 1, b_1 = 2, c_1 = -3, a_2 = 5, b_2 = k$ and $c_2 = 7$

For no solution,

$$\frac{a_1}{a_2} = \frac{b_1}{b_2} \neq \frac{c_1}{c_2}$$

$$\Rightarrow \frac{1}{5} = \frac{2}{k} \neq \frac{-3}{7} \Rightarrow \frac{1}{5} = \frac{2}{k} \text{ and } \frac{2}{k} \neq \frac{-3}{7}$$

$$\Rightarrow k = 10 \text{ and } k \neq -\frac{14}{3}$$

$\therefore k = 10$

5. (*d*) Given: pair of equation $x + 2y + 5 = 0$

and $-3x - 6y + 1 = 0$

Comparing pair of equation with $a_1x + b_1y + c_1 = 0$ and $a_2x + b_2y + c_2 = 0$, we get

Now, $a_1 = 1, a_2 = -3, b_1 = 2, b_2 = -6, c_1 = 5\ c_2 = 1$

$$\frac{a_1}{a_2} = \frac{1}{-3}, \frac{b_1}{b_2} = \frac{1}{-3}, \frac{c_1}{c_2} = \frac{5}{1} \Rightarrow \frac{a_1}{a_2} = \frac{b_1}{b_2} \neq \frac{c_1}{c_2}$$

Hence, no solution.

6. (*c*) As, we know that for parallel lines $\frac{a_1}{a_2} = \frac{b_1}{b_2} \neq \frac{c_1}{c_2}$

Hence,

$$\Rightarrow \frac{3}{2} = \frac{2k}{5} \quad \Rightarrow k = \frac{15}{4}$$

7. (*c*) According to given conditions,

$\frac{x}{y} = \frac{5}{6} \Rightarrow 6x - 5y = 0$ ... (*i*)

and, $\frac{x-8}{y-8} = \frac{4}{5} \Rightarrow 5(x - 8) = 4(y - 8) \Rightarrow 5x - 4y = 8$ ... (*ii*)

Using equation (*i*), we get

$6x - 5y = 0 \quad \Rightarrow x = \frac{5y}{6}$ ... (*iii*)

On putting value of x in eq. (*ii*), we get

$$5x - 4y = 8 \Rightarrow 5\left(\frac{5y}{6}\right) - 4y = 8$$

$$\Rightarrow \frac{25y}{6} - 4y = 8 \Rightarrow \frac{y}{6} = 8 \Rightarrow y = 48$$

Now, using eq. (*iii*), we get

$x = \frac{5y}{6} = \frac{5 \times 48}{6}$ $(\because y = 48)$

$\Rightarrow x = 40$

Hence, $x = 40$ and $y = 48$.

8. (*c*) Let the number of ₹5 and ₹10 coins are x and y respectively.

Then, according to the question,

$x + y = 50$ ... (*i*)

and $5 \times x + 10 \times y = 400 \Rightarrow 5x + 10y = 400$ ... (*ii*)

Subtracting eqn (*i*) from eqn (*ii*) after multiplying eqn (*i*) by 5 we get,

$(5x + 10y) - 5(x + y) = 400 - 250 = 150 \Rightarrow y = 30$

Substituting this in eqn (*i*)

$x + 30 = 50 \Rightarrow x = 20$

Thus, the required no. of ₹5 and ₹10 coins are 20 and 30 respectively.

9. (*a*) Let the number of currect answer given by Priya = x and the number of wrong answer given by Priya = y

Now,

$\because$ Total number of question = 120

$\therefore\ x + y = 120$ ... (*i*)

Also, the marks received by Priya = 90

$\Rightarrow x \times 1 - y \times \frac{1}{2} = 90 \Rightarrow 2x - y = 180$ ... (*ii*)

Adding equations (*i*) and (*ii*) we get,

$(x + y) + (2x - y) = 120 + 180 \Rightarrow 3x = 300 \Rightarrow x = 100$

Thus, 100 questions was correctly answered by Priya.

10. (*c*) Let, fixed charges be ₹x and charges for each extra day be ₹y

According to given conditions,

$x + 4y = 22$ ... (*i*)

$x + 2y = 16$ ... (*ii*)

On subtracting eq. (*ii*) from (*i*), we obtain

$y =$ ₹3

Hence charge for each extra day is ₹3.

11. (*a*) It is given that,

$\frac{x}{a} + \frac{y}{b} = a + b$ ... (*i*)

and $\frac{x}{a^2} + \frac{y}{b^2} = 2$ ... (*ii*)

On dividing eq. (*i*) by b, we get

$\frac{x}{ab} + \frac{y}{b^2} = \frac{a+b}{b}$ ... (*iii*)

On subtracting eq. (*iii*) from (*ii*), we get

$$\frac{x}{a^2} + \frac{y}{b^2} - \left(\frac{x}{ab} + \frac{y}{b^2}\right) = 2 - \frac{a+b}{b}$$

$$\Rightarrow \frac{x}{a^2} + \frac{y}{b^2} - \frac{x}{ab} - \frac{y}{b^2} = \frac{2b - a - b}{b} \Rightarrow \frac{x}{a^2} - \frac{x}{ab} = \frac{b-a}{b}$$

$$\Rightarrow \frac{bx - ax}{a^2 b} = \frac{b-a}{b} \Rightarrow \frac{x(b-a)}{a^2 b} = \frac{b-a}{b} \Rightarrow x = \frac{a^2 b}{b} = a^2$$

12. (*c*) Let the number of cows and hens are x and y respectively.

$\because$ A cow and a hen, each have only one head.

So, the total no. of cows and hens = 29

($\because$ total no. of head = 29)

$\Rightarrow x + y = 29$ ... (*i*)

$\because$ A cow has 4 legs and a hen has 2 legs.

So, the total no. of legs in the shed = $4x + 2y$

$\Rightarrow 92 = 4x + 2y \Rightarrow 2x + y = 46$ ... (*ii*)

Subtracting (*i*) from eqn (*ii*) we get,

$(2x + y) - (x + y) = 46 - 29 \Rightarrow x = 17$

$\therefore$ The number of cows in the shed = 17

13. (*a*) Let the price of a tables and a chair are ₹x and ₹y respectively.

So, the total cost of 2 tables and 3 chairs = $2x + 3y$

$\Rightarrow 2000 = 2x + 3y \Rightarrow 2x + 3y = 2000$ ... (*i*)

Also, the total cost of 3 tables and 2 chairs = $3x + 2y$

$\Rightarrow 2500 = 3x + 2y \Rightarrow 3x + 2y = 2500$ ... (*ii*)

Adding eqn (*i*) and (*ii*)

$5x + 5y = 4500 \Rightarrow x + y = 900$ ... (*iii*)

Again, subtracting eqn (*i*) from eqn (*ii*) we get,

$x - y = 500$ ... (*iv*)

Adding eqn (*iii*) and eqn (*iv*)

$(x + y) + (x - y) = 900 + 500$

$\Rightarrow 2x = 1400 \Rightarrow x = 700$

Substituting this value in equation (*iii*)

$700 + y = 900 \Rightarrow y = 200$

$\therefore$ Total cost of 1 table and 5 chairs = $x + 5y$

= $700 + 200 \times 5$ = ₹1700

14. (*c*) We have,

$\frac{2}{\sqrt{x}} + \frac{3}{\sqrt{y}} = 2$ ... (*i*)

and $\frac{4}{\sqrt{x}} - \frac{9}{\sqrt{y}} = -1$ ... (*ii*)

Adding eqn (*i*) and eqn (*ii*) after multiplying eqn (*i*) by 3

$$\left(\frac{6}{\sqrt{x}} + \frac{9}{\sqrt{y}}\right) + \left(\frac{4}{\sqrt{x}} - \frac{9}{\sqrt{y}}\right) = 2 \times 3 - 1$$

$$\Rightarrow \frac{10}{\sqrt{x}} = 5 \Rightarrow \sqrt{x} = 2 \Rightarrow x = 4$$

$$\frac{2}{\sqrt{4}} + \frac{3}{\sqrt{y}} = 2 \Rightarrow 1 + \frac{3}{\sqrt{y}} = 2 \Rightarrow \frac{3}{\sqrt{y}} = 1$$

$$\Rightarrow \sqrt{y} = 3 \Rightarrow y = 9$$

Assertion and Reason

1. (*b*) Both assertion (A) and reason (R) are true but reason (R) is not the correct explanation of assertion (A).

For no solution,

$$\frac{1}{2} = \frac{1}{k} \neq \frac{-4}{-3} \text{ i.e.,} \frac{4}{3} \Rightarrow k = 2 \left[\frac{1}{2} \neq \frac{4}{3} \text{holds}\right]$$

Hence, assertion is true.

Reason is also true by definition but it is incorrect explanation of the assertion

2. (*a*) Both assertion (A) and reason (R) are true and reason (R) is the correct explanation of assertion (A).

For infinitely many solutions, $\frac{a_1}{a_2} = \frac{b_1}{b_2} = \frac{c_1}{c_2}$

From the given equations, we have

$$\frac{9}{18} = \frac{3}{6} = \frac{12}{24} \Rightarrow \frac{1}{2} = \frac{1}{2} = \frac{1}{2} \text{ i.e.,} \frac{a_1}{a_2} = \frac{b_1}{b_2} = \frac{c_1}{c_2}$$

Hence, both A and R are true and R explains A.

3. (*d*) A: The assertion is wrong because in that case the pair of linear equations has infinitely many solutions if the obtained equation is correct and has no solution, if the obtained equation is incorrect.

R: Reason is true

Hence, Assertion is wrong but Reason is true.

4. (*c*) A: The statement, 5 = 11 is a wrong statement

$\therefore$ The pair of linear equations has no solution.

R: The reason is wrong because if statement obtained is true then the pair of linear equation has infinitely many solutions instead of no solution.

Hence, the assertion is true but the reason is not true.

Subjective Questions

Very Short Answer Type Questions

1. We have,

$4x + py + 8 = 0$ ... (*i*)

$2x + 2y + 2 = 0$ ... (*ii*)

$\Rightarrow a_1 = 4, b_1 = p, c_1 = 8, a_2 = 2, b_2 = 2$, and $c_2 = 2$

Now, for unique solution

$\frac{a_1}{a_2} \neq \frac{b_1}{b_2} \Rightarrow \frac{4}{2} \neq \frac{p}{2}$ (1 M)

$\Rightarrow p \neq 4$

Thus, for any value of p except 4 the given pair of linear equations has unique solution. (1 M)

2. We have,

$x + 2y - 8 = 0$ ... (*i*)

and $2x + 4y - 16 = 0$ ... (*ii*)

$\Rightarrow a_1 = 1, b_1 = 2, c_1 = -8, a_2 = 2, b_2 = 4$ and $c_2 = -16$

$\Rightarrow \frac{a_1}{a_2} = \frac{1}{2}, \frac{b_1}{b_2} = \frac{2}{4} = \frac{1}{2}$ *and* $\frac{c_1}{c_2} = \frac{-8}{-16} = \frac{1}{2}$ (1 M)

$\Rightarrow \frac{a_1}{a_2} = \frac{b_1}{b_2} = \frac{c_1}{c_2}$

Hence, the pair of linear equations have infinitely many solution. (1 M)

3. We have,

$x + y = 14$ ... (*i*)

$x - y = 4$ ... (*ii*)

$\Rightarrow a_1 = 1, b_1 = 1, c_1 = -14, a_2 = 1, b_2 = -1$ and $c_2 = -4$

$\Rightarrow \frac{a_1}{a_2} = \frac{1}{1} = 1, \frac{b_1}{b_2} = \frac{1}{-1} = -1, \frac{c_1}{c_2} = \frac{-14}{-2} = \frac{7}{2}$ (1 M)

Thus, $\frac{a_1}{a_2} \neq \frac{b_1}{b_2}$

Hence, the pair of linear equation is consistent and has unique solution. (1 M)

4. Let the number of articles produced in a day be x.

$\therefore$ Cost of production of each article = ₹ $(2x + 3)$ ... (*i*)

Given, total cost of production is ₹ 90

No. of articles × Cost of production of each article = Total Cost

$\therefore x(2x + 3) = 90 \Rightarrow 2x^2 + 3x - 90 = 0$

$\Rightarrow 2x^2 + 15x - 12x - 90 = 0$ (1 M)

$\Rightarrow (2x + 15)(x - 6) = 0 \Rightarrow x = \frac{-15}{2}$ or $x = 6$

As the number of articles produced can not be negative. Therefore, x can only be 6.

Hence, number of articles produced = 6

From equation (*i*), Cost of each article = $(2 \times 6) + 3$ = ₹15 (1 M)

5. We have,

$cx - y = 2 \Rightarrow cx - y - 2 = 0$

and $6x - 2y = 3 \Rightarrow 6x - 2y - 3 = 0$

$\Rightarrow a_1 = c, b_1 = -1, c_1 = -2, a_2 = 6, b_2 = -2$ and $c_3 = -3$

$\because$ For infinitely many solutions

$\frac{a_1}{a_2} = \frac{b_1}{b_2} = \frac{c_1}{c_2}$

But, $\because \frac{b_1}{b_2} = \frac{-1}{-2} = \frac{1}{2}$ and $\frac{c_1}{c_2} = \frac{-2}{-3} = \frac{2}{3}$ (1 M)

So, $\frac{b_1}{b_2} \neq \frac{c_1}{c_2}$

Thus, the lines represented by the pair of equations do not coincide for any value of c.

Hence, the pair of linear equations can not have infinitely many solution for any value of c. (1 M)

6. Let us suppose, cost of a book = ₹x

And, cost of a pen = ₹y (1 M)

According to question,

Given, cost of 5 books and 7 pens together is ₹79.

$\therefore 5x + 7y = 79$

Given, cost of 7 books and 5 pens together is ₹77.

$\therefore 7x + 5y = 77$ (1 M)

Short Answer Type Questions

1. We have,

$x + 3y = 6 \Rightarrow x = 6 - 3y$

x	0	6
y	2	0
(x, y)	(0, 2)	(6, 0)

and $2x - 3y = 12$ (½ M)

$\Rightarrow 3y = 2x - 12 \Rightarrow y = \frac{2x - 12}{3}$

x	0	6
y	–4	0
(x, y)	(0, –4)	(6, 0)

(½ M)

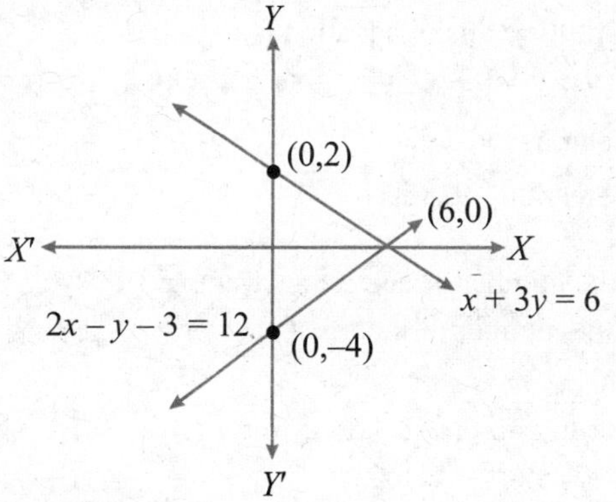

(1 M)

Clearly two lines Intersect at $P(6,0)$

Hence $x = 6, y = 0$ is the solution of the system of equations. (½ M)

Given equation,

$4x + 3y = a$

but $x = 6$ and $y = 0 \Rightarrow 4 \times 6 + 3 \times 0 = a \Rightarrow 24 = a$

$\therefore\ a = 24$ (½ M)

2. Let the cost of one pencil = ₹ x

and the cost of one eraser = ₹y (½ M)

According to the question,

$2x + 3y = 9$ ... (*i*)

and $4x + 6y = 18$ ... (*ii*) (½ M)

So, algebraic representation of the situation is

$2x + 3y = 9$ and $4x + 6y = 18$ (½ M)

For Graphical representation,

$2x + 3y = 9$ and $4x + 6y = 18$

$\Rightarrow 3y = 9 - 2x$ and $6y = 18 - 4x$

$\Rightarrow\ y = \dfrac{9-2x}{3}$ and $y = \dfrac{18-4x}{6}$

x	–3	0
y	5	3
(x, y)	(–3, 5)	(0, 3)

x	–3	0
y	5	3
(x, y)	(–3, 5)	(0, 3)

(1 M)

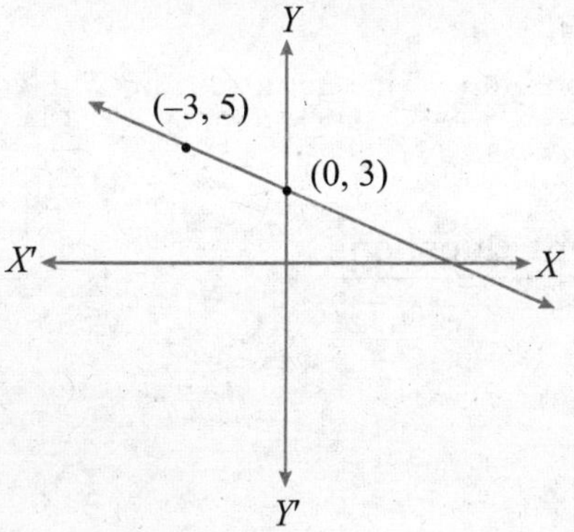

(½ M)

This is the required graphical representation.

3. Let x and y are two supplementary angles such that $x > y$ (½ M)

So, $x + y = 180°$ ... (*i*) (½ M)

Also, ∵ their difference is 18°

So, $x - y = 18°$ ... (*ii*) (½ M)

Adding eqn (*i*) and eqn (*ii*)

$(x + y) + (x - y) = 180° + 18°$

$\Rightarrow 2x = 198° \Rightarrow x = 99°$ (½ M)

From eqn (*i*)

$99° + y = 180° \Rightarrow y = 180° - 99° = 81°$ (½ M)

Hence, two supplementary angles are 99° and 81°. (½ M)

4. We have,

$3.5x + 2.5y = 9.5$ ... (*i*)

$7.5x + 2.5y = 12.5$ ... (*ii*)

Solving the first equation for y, we get:

$y = \dfrac{(9.5-3.5x)}{2.5}$ ... (*iii*) (1 M)

Substituting this expression for y in the second equation, we get:

$7.5x + 2.5\left(\dfrac{(9.5-3.5x}{2.5}\right) = 12.5 \Rightarrow 7.5x + 9.5 - 3.5x = 12.5$

$\Rightarrow x = \dfrac{3}{4}$ (1 M)

Substituting this value of x in the eqn (*iii*)

$y = \dfrac{9.5 - 3.5 \times \frac{3}{4}}{2.5} = \dfrac{38-10.5}{10} = \dfrac{27.5}{10} = \dfrac{11}{4}$

Therefore, the solution to the pair of equations is $x = \dfrac{3}{4}$ and $y = \dfrac{11}{4}$. (1 M)

5. (*i*) We have,

$a - b = 5$ ... (*i*)

$\dfrac{a}{5} + \dfrac{b}{4} = 20$ ... (*ii*)

Multiply the first equation by 5 and the second equation by 20 to get:

$5(a - b) = 5 \times 5 \Rightarrow 5a - 5b = 25$

$20\left(\dfrac{a}{5} + \dfrac{b}{4}\right) = 20 \times 20 \Rightarrow 4a + 5b = 400$ (1 M)

Now we can add these two equations to eliminate b:

$9a = 425 \Rightarrow a = \dfrac{425}{9}$ (1 M)

Substituting this value of a into the first equation, we get:

$a - b = 5$

$\Rightarrow \dfrac{425}{9} - b = 5 \Rightarrow b = \left(\dfrac{425}{9}\right) - 5$

$b = \left(\dfrac{425-45}{9}\right) \Rightarrow b = \dfrac{380}{9}$

Therefore, the solution to the pair of linear of equations is

$a = \dfrac{425}{9}$ and $b = \dfrac{380}{9}$ (1 M)

6. Let the number of chocolates in lot A be x

And let the number of chocolates in lot B be y

$\therefore$ Total number of chocolates $= x + y$

Price of 1 chocolate $= ₹\ \frac{2}{3}$, so for x chocolates $= \frac{2}{3}x$ and

price of y chocolates at the rate of ₹1 per chocolate $= y$

$\therefore$ By the given condition $= \frac{2}{3}x + y = 40.$ (1 M)

$\Rightarrow 2x + 3y = 120$ ... (i)

Similarly $x + \frac{4}{5}y = 46$

$\Rightarrow 5x + 4y = 230$ ... (ii) (1 M)

Solving (i) and (ii) we get

$x = 30$ and $y = 20$

$\therefore x + y = 30 + 20 = 50$

So, Anu had 50 chocolates. (1 M)

7. Let the total number of students in class $= x$

And, number of benches $= y$ (½ M)

It is given that if three students sit on each bench, nine students will be left. So we can deduce that the number of students is nine more than three times the number of benches.

$\therefore$ Total number of students $= 3y + 9$

$\Rightarrow x = 3y + 9$ ... (i) (½ M)

Also, it is given that if four students sit on each bench, one bench will be left. So we can deduce that the number of students is 4 less than four times the number of benches.

$\therefore$ Total number of students $= 4y - 4$

$\Rightarrow x = 4y - 4$ ... (ii) (½ M)

From (i) & (ii)

$3y + 9 = 4y - 4 \Rightarrow y = 13$ (½ M)

Also, $x = 4 \times 13 - 4 = 48$ (From (ii) (½ M)

$\therefore$ Number of students $= 48$

and number of benches $= 13$ (½ M)

8. Let the length of the rectangle $= x$ units

and the breadth of the rectangle $=$ y units

$\therefore$ Area of the rectangle $= xy$ square units (½ M)

$\because$ Area decreases by 9 unit^2 its length and breadth are reduced by 5 units and increased by 3 units respectively.

So, $(x - 5)(y + 3) = xy - 9 \Rightarrow xy + 3x - 5y - 15 = xy - 9$

$\Rightarrow 3x - 5y = 6$ ... (i) (½ M)

Also, since, area increases by 67 unit^2 its length and breadth are increased by 3 units and 2 units respectively.

So, $(x + 3)(y + 2) = 67 + xy \Rightarrow xy + 2x + 3y + 6 = 67 + xy$

$\Rightarrow 2x + 3y = 61$ ... (ii) (½ M)

Adding equation (i) with (ii) after multiplying eqn (i) by 3 and eqn (ii) by 5.

$(9x - 15y) + (10x + 15y) = 18 + 305 \Rightarrow 19x = 323 \Rightarrow x = 17$

(½ M)

Substituting this in equation (i)

$3 \times 17 - 5 \times y = 6 \Rightarrow 5y = 51 - 6 = 45 \Rightarrow y = 9$ (½ M)

$\therefore$ Length $= 17$ units

and breadth $= 9$ units (½ M)

9. Let the number of correct answer $= x$

and the number of incorrect answer $= y$ (½ M)

Then,

According to the question,

$3x - y = 50$ ... (i) (½ M)

and $2x - 0.5y = 40$ ... (ii) (½ M)

Subtracting eqn (i) from eqn (ii) after multiplying eqn (ii) by 2.

$2(2x - 0.5y) - (3x - y) = 40 \times 2 - 50 \Rightarrow x = 80 - 50 = 30$

(½ M)

Now, substituting this value in equation (i) we get,

$3 \times 30 - y = 50 \Rightarrow 90 - y = 50 \Rightarrow y = 90 - 50 = 40$ (½ M)

Thus, total number of question in the examinations

$= 30 + 40 = 70$ (½ M)

10. Let L be the length of the rectangle.

So, breadth of the rectangle $= L - 3$

Area of the rectangle $= L\ \ L - 3$ ...(i)

Base of the isosceles triangle $= L - 3$

Altitude of the isosceles triangle $= 12$ m

Area of the isosceles triangle $= \frac{1}{2}(L2)(L-3)$ ...(ii)

Given that

$L(L-3)\frac{1}{2}(L2)(L-3)-4$

Or, $L^2 - 3L = 6L - 18 + 4$

Or, $L^2 - 9L + 14 = 0$

Or, $L^2 - 7L - 2L + 14 = 0$

Or, $L(L - 7)(L - 7) = 0$

Or, $(L - 7)(L - 2) = 0$

So, $L = 7$m 3m = 4m

Length and breadth of the rectangle are 7m and 4m respectively.

Long Answer Type Questions

1. We have,

$x = 3$ ... (i)

$x = 5$ ... (ii)

and $2x - y - 4 = 0$ ... (iii)

$\Rightarrow x = \frac{y+4}{2}$ (½ M)

x	2	3
y	0	2

(1 M)

Graph of the equations (i), (ii) and (iii) is

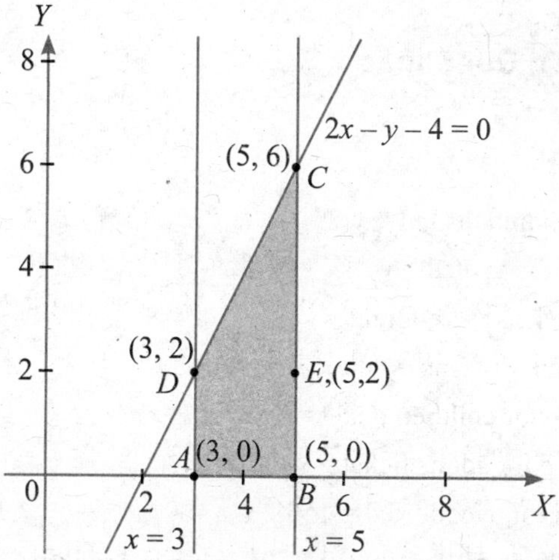

(1 M)

Thus the lines intersect each other at points $A(3, 0)$, $B(5, 0)$, $C(5, 6)$, $D(3, 2)$. (1 M)

Area of the quadrilateral $ABCD$ = Area of square $ABED$ + Area of ΔDEC (½ M)

$= 2 \times 2 + \frac{1}{2} \times 2 \times 4 = 8$ sq. units. (1 M)

2. The given equations are:

$3x + y - 11 = 0$ and $x - y - 1 = 0$

For equation, $3x + y - 11 = 0 \Rightarrow y = -3x + 11$

The solution table is

x	2	3
$y = -3x + 11$	5	2

(1 M)

For equation, $x - y - 1 = 0 \Rightarrow y = x - 1$

The solution table is:

x	–1	3
$y = x - 1$	–2	2

(1 M)

Now, let us plot the graph:

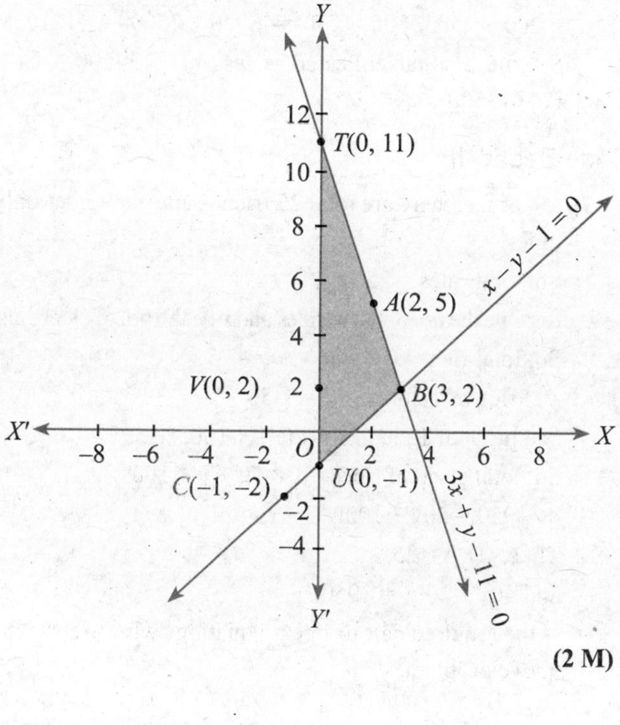

(2 M)

As it can be seen that the two lines intersect at point $B(3, 2)$. Therefore, $x = 3$ and $y = 2$.

The area bounded by the lines represented by the given equations and y-axis is shaded, as shown in graph.

Area of the shaded region is,

$\Rightarrow$ Area of $\Delta BUT = \frac{1}{2} \times$ base $\times$ height

$= \frac{1}{2} \times (TU \times VB) = \frac{1}{2} \times 12 \times 3 = 18$ sq. units.

Therefore, required area = 18 sq. units. (1 M)

3. We have, $3x + 4y = 12 \Rightarrow 3x + 4y - 12 = 0$

and $(m + n)x + 2(m - n)y = 5m - 1$

$\Rightarrow (m + n)x + 2(m - n)y - (5m - 1) = 0$

$\Rightarrow a_1 = 3, b_1 = 4, c_1 = -12, a_2 = m + n, b_2 = 2(m - n)$, and $c_2 = -(5m - 1)$ (1 M)

Now, for infinitely many solutions,

$\frac{a_1}{a_2} = \frac{b_1}{b_2} = \frac{c_1}{c_2} \Rightarrow \frac{3}{m+n} = \frac{4}{2(m-n)} = \frac{-12}{-(5m-1)}$ (1 M)

For, $\frac{3}{m+n} = \frac{4}{2(m-n)}$

$\Rightarrow m - 5n = 0$ ... (i) (½ M)

For, $\frac{4}{2(m-n)} = \frac{12}{5m-1}$

$\Rightarrow m - 6n = -1$ ... (ii) (½ M)

Subtracting eqn (ii) from eqn (i)

$(m - 5n) - (m - 6n) = 0 - (-1)$

$\Rightarrow -5n + 6n = 1 \Rightarrow n = 1$ (1 M)

Substituting this in eqn (i)

$m - 5 \times 1 = 0 \Rightarrow m = 5$

Thus, $m = 5$ and $n = 1$ (1 M)

4. Let us suppose, 'x' be the unit's digit of the required two digit number and let 'y' be the ten's digit of the two digit number.

So, two digit number = $10y + x$

Now, the number obtained by interchanging the digits = $10x + y$ (½ M)

Acc. to question,

$(10y + x) + (10x + y) = 99 \Rightarrow 11x + 11y = 99$

$\Rightarrow 11(x + y) = 99$

$\Rightarrow x + y = 9$ ... (i) (½ M)

If $x > y$, then $x - y = 3$ ... (ii) (½ M)

On adding eq. (i) and (ii), we obtain

$2x = 12 \Rightarrow x = 6$ (½ M)

Now, on substituting the value of x in eq. (ii), we get

$x - y = 3 \Rightarrow 6 - y = 3 \Rightarrow y = 6 - 3 = 3$ (½ M)

Hence, two digit number = $10y + x$

$= (10 \times 3) + 6 = 36$ (½ M)

if $x < y$ then $y - x = 3$ ... (iii) (½ M)

On adding eq. (*i*) and (*iii*), we get

$2y = 12 \Rightarrow y = 6$ (½ M)

On substituting value of y in eq. (*i*), we get

$x + y = 9 \Rightarrow x + 6 = 9 \Rightarrow x = 3$ (½ M)

hence, the two digit number

$= 10 \times y + x = (10 \times 6) + 3 = 63$ (½ M)

5. $2x - 3y = 1$ ... (*i*)

and $\frac{x+(3x+2y)}{x-(3x+2y)} = -3$

On applying Componendo and Dividendo to both the sides, we get

$$\frac{x+(3x+2y)+x-(3x+2y)}{x+(3x+2y)-x+(3x+2y)} = \frac{-3+1}{-3-1}$$ (1 M)

$$\Rightarrow \frac{2x}{6x+4y} = \frac{-2}{-4} \Rightarrow \frac{x}{3x+2y} = \frac{1}{2}$$ (½ M)

$\Rightarrow 2x = 3x + 2y \Rightarrow 2x - 3x - 2y = 0$

$\Rightarrow x + 2y = 0$ ... (*ii*) (1 M)

On multiplying eq. (*ii*) by 2 and then subtracting from eq. (*i*),

$-7y = 1$

$$\Rightarrow y = -\frac{1}{7}$$ (1 M)

On substituting the value of y in (*i*), we get

$$2x - 3\left(\frac{-1}{7}\right) = 1 \Rightarrow 2x + \frac{3}{7} = 1$$ (½ M)

$$\Rightarrow 2x = \frac{1}{1} - \frac{3}{7} = \frac{4}{7} \Rightarrow x = \frac{2}{7}$$

Therefore, $x = \frac{2}{7}$ and $y = \frac{-1}{7}$ (1 M)

6. Let the C.P. of a saree = ₹x

and the M.P. of a sweater = ₹y (1 M)

Now, according to the question,

x + 8% of $x + y$ – 10% of y = 1008 (½ M)

$$\Rightarrow x \times \frac{108}{100} + y \times \frac{90}{100} = 1008 \Rightarrow 6x + 5y = 56 \times 100$$

$\Rightarrow 6x + 5y = 5600$ ... (*i*) (½ M)

Also, x + 10% $x + y$ – 8% of y = 1028 (½ M)

$$\Rightarrow x \times \frac{110}{100} + y \times \frac{92}{100} = 1028$$

$\Rightarrow 55x + 46y = 51400$ ... (*ii*) (½ M)

Subtracting eqn (*i*) from eqn (*ii*) after multiplying eqn (*i*) by 9

$(55x + 46y) - 9(6x + 5y) = 51400 - 9 \times 5600$

$\Rightarrow x + y = 51400 - 50400 = 1000$ (1 M)

Thus, the cost price (C.P.) of the saree and list price (M.P.) of the sweater = $x + y$ = ₹1000. (1 M)

Case Based Questions

Case Based-I

(*i*) No. of children visited = x

No. of adults visited = y

∵ 480 tickets were found

So, total no. of visits = 480 ⇒ $x + y = 480$ ... (*i*)

∵ charge for children ticket = ₹150

and charge for adults ticket = ₹400

So, total charge collected = $150 \times x + 400 \times y$

$\Rightarrow 134500 = 150x + 400y \Rightarrow 150x + 400y = 134500$ ... (*ii*)

Thus, the problem can be modeled by,

$x + y = 480$ and $150x + 400y = 134500$

(*ii*) Subtracting eqn (*i*) from eqn (*ii*) after multiplying it by 400

$(150x + 400y) - 400(x + y) = 134500 - 400 \times 480$

$\Rightarrow -250x = 134500 - 192000 \Rightarrow -250x = -57500$

$\Rightarrow x = 230$

Substituting this in equation (*i*) we get

$230 + y = 480 \Rightarrow y = 480 - 230 = 250$

Thus 230 children visited the park.

OR

The money would have collected if 300 children and 350 adults had visited the park

$= 300 \times 150 + 350 \times 400 = 45000 + 140000$ = ₹185000

(*iii*) Charge of 1 children ticket = ₹200

Charge of 1 adult ticket = ₹300

Total charge collected = 200 × no. of children visited + 300 × no. of adults visited

$= 200 \times 230 + 300 \times 250 = 46000 + 75000$ = ₹121000

So, the amount collected is less by ₹134500 – ₹121000 i.e. ₹13500.

Case Based-II

(*i*) (*c*) Since, there are total 25 friends and each rides only one times.

So, total rides = 25.

Let x be the no. of horse rides and y be the no. of elephants ride.

So, total ride = $x + y \Rightarrow x + y = 25$

∵ Price of 1 horse ride = ₹ 50

and price of 1 elephant ride = ₹ 100

So, total price of rides = $x \times 50 + y \times 100$

$\Rightarrow 1950 = 50x + 100y$

Thus, $x + y = 25$ ... (*i*)

and $50x + 100y = 1950$ ... (*ii*)

Is the required pair of linear equations which represents the above problem.

(*ii*) (*b*) Substracting eqn (*ii*) from eqn (*i*) after multiplying eqn (*i*) by 100.

$100(x + y) - (50x + 100y) = 25 \times 100 - 1950$

$\Rightarrow 50x = 550 \Rightarrow x = 11$

Thus, the no. of horses hired = 11

(*iii*) (*a*) From eqn (*i*)

$11 + y = 25 \Rightarrow y = 25 - 11 = 14$

Thus, the no. of elephants hired = 14

(*iv*) (*c*) Price of 1 horse ride in peak hour = 50 × 3 = ₹150

Price of 1 elephant ride in peak hour = 100 × 2 = ₹200

∴ Total amount paid by the group

$= 150x + 200y = 150 \times 11 + 200 \times 14 = 1650 + 2800 =$ ₹4450

(*v*) (*d*) Total increase in fare due to peak hours

= ₹4450 – ₹1950 = ₹2500

Case Based-III

(*i*) Given, Hockey ₹ x per student and cricket ₹ y per student. For school '*P*', the total prize amount for hockey and cricket is ₹9500. The number of students awarded for hockey and cricket are 5 and 4 respectively.

Hence, $5x + 4y = 9500$ ...(*i*)

For school 'Q', the total prize amount for hockey and cricket is ₹7370. The number of students awarded are 4 and 3 respectively.

Hence, $4x + 3y = 7370$ ... (*ii*)

(*ii*) Given equations are:

$$5x + 4y = 9500 \,|\times 3$$
$$4x + 3y = 7370 \,|\times 4$$

$$15x + 12y = 28500$$
$$\underset{-}{16x} + \underset{-}{12y} = \underset{-}{29480}$$
$$-x = -980 \quad \text{(on subtracting)}$$

Hence, prize amount for hockey is ₹980

OR

On substituting the value of x in (*i*), we get

$$5(980) + 4y = 9500 \Rightarrow y = \frac{9500 - 4900}{4} = \frac{4600}{4} = 1150$$

Hence, prize amount of cricket is more by 1150 – 980 = ₹170

(*iii*) If there are 2 students each from two games, then total prize money = $2x + 2y = 2(980) + 2(1150) =$ ₹4260

Case Based-IV

(*i*) Let the number of fours made by Dhoni = x

and let the number of sixes made by Dhoni = y

∴ Total runs scores by making fours = $4x$

& total runs scores by making sixes = $6y$

∵ total runs scored = 98 runs

$\Rightarrow 4x + 6y = 98 \Rightarrow 2x + 3y = 49$ ... (*i*)

Number of sixes made was two less than that of fours

∴ $x - y = 2$ ... (*ii*)

Thus, the algebraic representation of the above problem is $2x + 3y = 49$ & $x - y = 2$

(*ii*) Adding both equations after multiplying eq^n (*ii*) by 3.

$(2x + 3y) + 3(x - y) = 49 + 2 \times 3$

$\Rightarrow 5x = 55 \Rightarrow x = 11$

∴ The number of fours made = 11

OR

Substituting $x = 11$ in eq^n (*ii*)

$11 - y = 2 \Rightarrow y = 11 - 2 = 9$

Thus, the no. of sixes made = 9.

(*iii*) Total number of boundaries scored by Dhoni will be Sum of sixes + sum of fours i.e., $x + y = 11 + 9 = 20$.

Case Based-V

(*i*) (*d*) Let the fixed charge for first two days be x and the additional charges thereafter be y.

Radhika kept the book for 4 days and paid ₹16

The algebraic equation is: $x + 2y = 16$

(*ii*) (*c*) Let the fixed charge for first two days be x and the additional charges thereafter be y.

Amrulta kept the book for 6 days and paid ₹22

∴ The algebraic equation is: $x + 4y = 22$

(*iii*) (*b*) The two equations are

$x + 2y = 16$ ... (*i*)

$x + 4y = 22$ ... (*ii*)

Now, 2 × (*i*) – (*ii*), gives

$x = 10$

∴ The fixed charger is ₹ 10.

(*iv*) (*d*) The two equations are

$x + 2y = 16$ ... (*i*)

$x + 4y = 22$ ... (*ii*)

Solving, (*i*) and (*ii*), we get

$\Rightarrow 2y = 6 \Rightarrow y = 3$

The additional charges are ₹3.

(*v*) (*c*) If Radhika Kept the book for two more days, she would have paid = 10 + 4(3)

= 10 + 12 = ₹22.

If Amrita kept the book for two more days, she would have paid = 22 + 2(3)

= 22 + 6 = ₹28

The total amount paid by both = ₹(22 + 28) = ₹50

QUADRATIC EQUATIONS

4

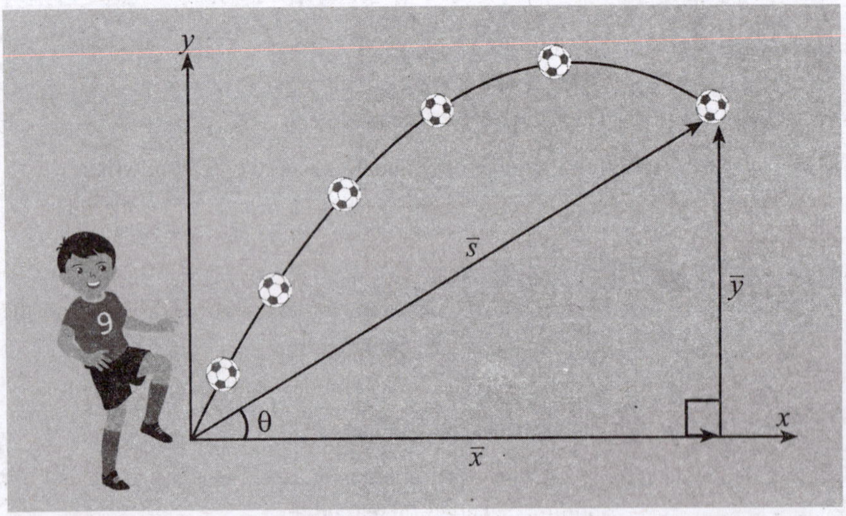

"Quadratic equations can predict the trajectory of objects such as balls in sports like basketball, soccer, and golf. This information helps athletes make strategic decisions during game play."

SYLLABUS & WEIGHTAGE

List of Concept Names	Years				
	2021	2022	2023	2024	2025
Introduction to Quadratic Equations (Standard form of a quadratic equation $ax^2 + bx + c = 0$, $(a \neq 0)$.)	Exam not Conducted	–	1 Q (1 M)	–	–
Methods of Solving a Quadratic Equation (Solutions of quadratic equations (only real roots) by factorization, and by using quadratic formula.)		2 Q (2 M each)	2 Q (1 M each) 1 Q (2 M)	–	1 Q (2 M)
Nature of Roots of a Quadratic Equation (Relationship between discriminant and nature of roots.)		1 Q (2 M)	1 Q (2 M)	1 Q (1 M)	1 Q (2 M)
Word Problems Based on Quadratic Equation Related to Day to Day Activities (Situational problems based on quadratic equations related to day to day activities to be incorporated.)		–	–	1 Q (3 M)	1 Q (3 M)

CONCEPT MAP

To Access One Shot Revision Video Scan This QR Code

Factorisation Method:
In this method ($ax^2 + bx + c = 0$) can be expressible as the product of two linear expressions, say $(px + q)$ and $(rx + s)$, where p, q, r are real numbers such that $p \neq 0, r \neq 0$.
Then $ax^2 + bx + c = 0 \Rightarrow (px + q)(rx + s) = 0$

$(px + q) = 0$ or $(rx + s) = 0 \Rightarrow x = \dfrac{-q}{p}$ or $x = \dfrac{-s}{r}$

Quadratic Formula:
For $ax^2 + bx + c = 0$, $D = b^2 - 4ac$,

$$x = \frac{-b \pm \sqrt{D}}{2a}$$

Method of finding solution

An equation of the form $ax^2 + bx + c = 0$ where a, b, c are real numbers and $a \neq 0$. is called a quadratic equation in x.

Solution of Roots of Quadratic Equation:
A real number α is called a root of the quadratic equation $ax^2 + bx + c = 0$, $a \neq 0$ if $a\alpha^2 + b\alpha + c = 0$.

Quadratic Equation

Application:
- Speed = $\dfrac{\text{Distance}}{\text{Time}}$
- Area of figures
- Volume of water = flow rate × time
- Number of ages

Nature of roots:
$ax^2 + bx + c = 0, a \neq 0$, where $D = (b^2 - 4ac)$ and the roots are given by $\alpha = \dfrac{-b + \sqrt{D}}{2a}$ and $\beta = \dfrac{-b - \sqrt{D}}{2a}$

Case I:
When $D > 0$, roots are real, distinct and given by $\alpha = \dfrac{-b + \sqrt{D}}{2a}$ and $\beta = \dfrac{-b - \sqrt{D}}{2a}$

Case II:
When $D = 0$, roots are real and equal and roots are given by $\alpha = \dfrac{-b}{2a}$ and $\beta = \dfrac{-b}{2a}$

Case III:
When $D < 0$, roots are imaginary.

1 INTRODUCTION TO QUADRATIC EQUATIONS

Important Terms

- **Quadratic Equation:** A quadratic equation in x is of the form $ax^2 + bx + c = 0$, where a, b and c are real numbers and $a \neq 0$.
- **Coefficients of a Quadratic Equation:** The constants a, b and c is called the coefficients of quadratic equation, where coefficient of x^2, coefficient of x and constant term are a, b and c respectively.
- **Standard form of a Quadratic Equation:** A quadratic equation in x is of the form $ax^2 + bx + c = 0$, where a, b and c are real numbers and $a \neq 0$.

  So, $ax^2 + bx + c = 0$ is the standard form of a quadratic equation.

Important Concepts

- A quadratic equation has two and only two roots.
- A quadratic equation can not have more than two different roots.

Real Life Applications

All of us enjoyed playing video games as kids. Do you recall the android game Hill Climb Racing, in which you could play the role of a stunt driver without really driving a car?

You drive up and down a hill in this game while gathering cash and fuel tanks. The game has separate onscreen controls for the brake and the gas. Holding down the gas pedal will boost your car up the hill. You must have noticed that as you drive up a hill, it takes more efforts to reach the top, therefore you have to hold the gas pedal constantly. However, you don't need to exert any effort when going down the hill.

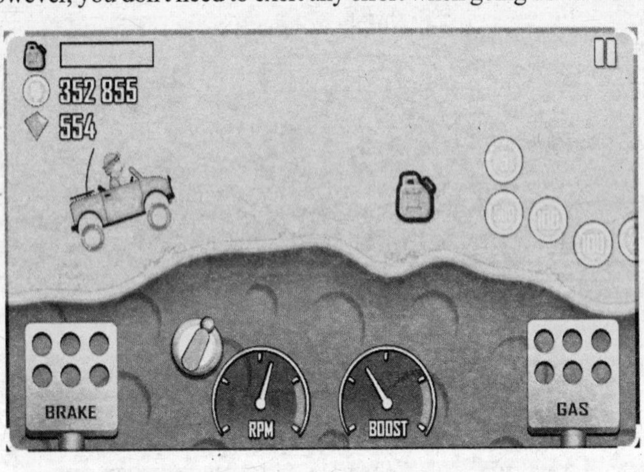

When you first start playing the game, the slopes are simple; but, as you go, the slopes get harder. Do you ever wonder how slopes are designed in games to vary in difficulty? So using a quadratic equation, game developers may create a difficulty level of slope with the help of quadratic equations.

Different Problem Types

Type I: Formation of Quadratic Equations from Algebraic Word Problems

To form quadratic equations from algebraic word problems, first translate the problem into an algebraic expression using variables.

Next, set up an equation based on the relationships described in the problem. This often involves identifying squared terms or products of variables that lead to a quadratic equation, typically in the form $ax^2 + bx + c = 0$.

Represent the following situation mathematically:

John and Jivanti together have 45 marbles. Both of them lost 5 marbles each, and the product of the number of marbles they now have is 124. We would like to find out how many marbles they had to start with.

Solution: We will systematically address this problem through the following steps:

Step I: Assign the variable x to the number of marbles John had initially.

Step II: To find out how many marbles Jivanti had, subtract John's marbles from the total, which is $45 - x$.

Step III: Calculate the new amount of marbles John has after losing 5, which is $x - 5$.

Step IV: Calculate the new amount of marbles Jivanti has after losing 5, which simplifies from $45 - x - 5$ to $40 - x$.

Step V: The product of the remaining marbles for John and Jivanti is then $(x - 5)(40 - x)$.

Step VI: Expand this product to get a quadratic expression: $40x - x^2 - 200 + 5x$, and simplify it to $-x^2 + 45x - 200$.

Step VII: Since the product of their marbles is known to be 124, set the quadratic expression equal to 124: $-x^2 + 45x - 200 = 124$.

Step VIII: Rearrange this equation by bringing all terms to one side to get the quadratic equation in standard form:

$$-x^2 + 45x - 324 = 0.$$

Step IX: Finally, the quadratic equation $x^2 - 45x + 324 = 0$ represents the mathematical model of the problem.

Example: Represent the following situations mathematically:

A cottage industry produces a certain number of toys in a day. The cost of production of each toy (in rupees) was found to be 55 minus the number of toys produced in a day. On a particular day, the total cost of production was 750. We would like to find out the number of toys produced on that day.

Solution: Let the number of toys produced on that day be x.

Thus, the cost of production (in rupees) of each toy that day $= 55 - x$.

So, the total cost of production (in rupees) that day = $x \times (55 - x)$.

Therefore, we have the equation $x \times (55-x) = 750 \Rightarrow 55x - x^2 = 750$.

Rearranging the terms, we get, $-x^2+55x-750=0 \Rightarrow x^2-55x+750=0$.

Hence, the number of toys produced that day satisfies the quadratic equation $x^2 - 55x + 750 = 0$, which is the required representation of the problem mathematically.

Type II: On Determining Whether a Given Equation is Quadratic or Not

To figure out if an equation is quadratic, check if it has a term with a variable squared (like x^2), but no higher powers like x^3. A quadratic equation usually looks like $ax^2 + bx + c = 0$, where a, b, and c are numbers and a is not zero.

Check whether the following is the quadratic equation:

(*i*) $(x - 2)^2 + 1 = 2x - 3$

Solution: (*i*) We will systematically address this problem through the following steps:

Step I: L.H.S $= (x - 2)^2 + 1 = x^2 - 4x + 4 + 1 = x^2 - 4x + 5$.

Step II: The equation $(x- 2)^2 + 1 = 2x - 3$ can be rewritten by substituting the expanded form of the LHS, leading to $x^2 - 4x + 5 = 2x - 3$.

Step III: To simplify, subtract $2x$ and add 3 to both sides of the equation, which gives $x^2 - 6x + 8 = 0$.

Step IV: The resulting equation is in the form $ax^2 + bx + c = 0$, which is the standard form of a quadratic equation. Hence, the given equation is a quadratic equation.

Example: Which of the following are quadratic equations, give reason:

(*i*) $4x^2 - 5x + 13 = 0$ **(*ii*)** $x(x + 1) = x^2 + 5$

(*iii*) $2x + \frac{5}{x}$ **(*iv*)** $x^2 + \frac{2}{x^2} = 2$

Solution: (*i*) Since, $4x^2 - 5x + 13 = 0$ is of the form $ax^2 + bx + c = 0$ and it has highest power of x is 2.

$\Rightarrow 4x^2 - 5x + 13 = 0$ is a quadratic equation.

(*ii*) $x(x + 1) = x^2 + 5 \Rightarrow x^2 + x = x^2 + 5 \Rightarrow x - 5 = 0$

Here the coefficient of x^2 is 0, so it is a linear equation, not a quadratic equation.

It is not of the form $ax^2 + bx + c = 0$

Therefore, the given equation is not a quadratic equation.

(*iii*) $2x + \frac{5}{x} = x^2 \Rightarrow 2x^2 + 5 = x^3$

In this expression the highest power of x is 3. So, it is a cubic and not a quadratic equation because a quadratic equation has highest power of 2.

(*iv*) $x^2 + \frac{2}{x^2} = \Rightarrow x^4 + 2 = 2x^2$

$\Rightarrow x^4 - 2x^2 + 2 = 0$; Here power of x is 4 so it is biquadratic and not a quadratic equations

COMPETENCY BASED SOLVED EXAMPLES

Multiple Choice Questions (1 M)

1. Which of the following is a quadratic equation? (*An*)

(*a*) $x^3 + 5x^2 + x + 3 = 0$ (*b*) $4x^2 - 3x - 5 = 0$

(*c*) $x + 5 = 0$ (*d*) $4x^5 = 0$

Sol. Option (*a*): $x^3 + 5x^2 + x + 3 = 0$

$\because$ The degree of the equation is 3

$\therefore$ It is not a quadratic equation.

Option (*b*): $4x^2 - 3x - 5 = 0$

$\because$ The degree of the equation is 2

Hence, $4x^2 - 3x - 5 = 0$ is a quadratic equation.

Option (*c*): $x + 5 = 0$

$\because$ The degree of the equation is 1

$\therefore x + 5 = 0$ is not a quadratic equation.

Option (*d*): $4x^5 = 0$

$\because$ The degree of the equation is 5

$\therefore 4x^5 = 0$ is not a quadratic equation.

2. Which of the following is not a quadratic equation? (*An*)

(*a*) $2x^2 - x + 3 = 0$ (*b*) $4x^2 - 3x = 0$

(*c*) $x^3 - 5x + 3 = 0$ (*d*) $4x^2 = 0$

Sol. Option (*a*): $2x^2 - x + 3 = 0$ has degree = 2

$\therefore 2x^2 - x + 3 = 0$ is a quadratic equation.

Option (*b*): $4x^2 - 3x = 0$ has degree = 2

$\therefore 4x^2 - 3x = 0$ is a quadratic equation.

Option (*c*): $x^3 - 5x + 3 = 0$ has degree = 3

So, $x^3 - 5x + 3 = 0$ is not a quadratic equation.

Option (*d*): $4x^2 = 0$ has degree = 2

$\therefore 4x^2 = 0$ is a quadratic equation.

3. Degree of the quadratic equation is always (*Un*)

(*a*) 1 (*b*) 2 (*c*) 3 (*d*) 4

Sol. Degree of the quadratic equation is always 2.

4. The coefficient of x^0 in the quadratic equation $x(x - 1) - 5 = 0$ is: (*Cr*)

(*a*) 5 (*b*) –5 (*c*) 1 (*d*) 1/2

Sol. We have, $x(x - 1) - 5 = 0 \Rightarrow x^2 - x - 5 = 0$. The coefficient of x^0 means constant term, i.e. –5

5. $ax^2 + bx + c = 0$ will be a quadratic equation when: (*Ap*)

(*a*) $c \neq 0$ (*b*) $a \neq 0$

(*c*) $b^2 = 4ac$ (*d*) $b \neq 0$

Sol. $ax^2 + bx + c = 0$ will be a quadratic equation only when $a \neq 0$.

6. **Which of the following is a quadratic equation?** (*Cr*)

(*a*) $x^2 + 2x + 1 = (4 - x)^2 + 3$

(*b*) $-2x^2 = (5 - x)\left(2x - \frac{2}{5}\right)$

(*c*) $(k + 1)x^2 + \frac{3}{2}x = 7$, where $k = -1$

(*d*) $x^3 - x^2 = (x - 1)^3$

Sol. We have a quadratic equation: $ax^2 + bx + c = 0, a \neq 0$

(*a*) $x^2 + 2x + 1 = (4 - x)^2 + 3$

$x^2 + 2x + 1 = 16 - 8x + x^2 + 3$

$10x - 18 = 0$, degree is 1

$\therefore$ This is linear equation.

(*b*) $-2x^2 = (5 - x)(2x - \frac{2}{5})$

$-2x^2 = 10x - 2x^2 - 2 + \frac{2}{5}x$

$52x - 10 = 0$, Here degree is 1

$\therefore$ This is also a linear equation.

(*c*) $(k + 1)x^2 + \frac{3}{2}x = 7$,

As $k = -1$

$(-1 + 1)x^2 + \frac{3}{2}x = 7$

$3x - 14 = 0$, Here degree is 1

$\therefore$ This is a linear equation.

(*d*) $x^3 - x^2 = (x - 1)^3$

$x^3 - x^2 = x^3 - 3x^2 + 3x - 1$

$2x^2 - 3x + 1 = 0$, Here degree is 2

$\therefore$ Above equation represents a quadratic equation.

Key Takeaways

If an equation doesn't contain a term with x^2, it cannot be considered quadratic because it lacks the characteristic of a quadratic term. Instead, it might be a linear equation (degree 1) or a higher-order polynomial equation.

7. **If $ax^2 + bx + c = a(x - p)^2$, the relation among *a*, *b* and *c* is:** (*Un*)

(*a*) $abc = 1$ (*b*) $a + c - 2b = 0$

(*c*) $b^2 - ac = 0$ (*d*) $b^2 = 4ac$

Sol. We have, $ax^2 + bx + c = a(x - p)^2$

$ax^2 + bx + c = ax^2 + ap^2 - 2apx$

On comparing coefficients, we get $-2ap = b$

$\Rightarrow p = -\frac{b}{2a}$ ... (*i*)

and $c = ap^2$ ... (*ii*)

from equation (*i*) and (*ii*), we get

$\Rightarrow c = a\frac{b^2}{4a^2} \Rightarrow b^2 = 4ac$

Nailing the Right Answer

Identify Key Components: Start by identifying the quadratic equation's key components: the coefficient of the squared term (*a*), the linear term (*b*), and the constant term (*c*).

Mistakes 101 : What not to do!

Students may overlook common factors or skip steps while factoring quadratic expressions, resulting in incorrect factors and solutions.

8. **Which of the following is the standard form of a quadratic equation?** (*An*)

(*a*) $ax^2 + bx + c = 0$ (*b*) $cx + ax^2 + b = 0$

(*c*) $cx^2 + a + bx = 0$ (*d*) None of these.

Sol. Standard form of a quadratic equation is $ax^2 + bx + c = 0$.

9. **What is the coefficient of x^2 in the quadratic equation $2x^2 - 5x + 3 = 0$?** (*An*)

(*a*) 2 (*b*) –5

(*c*) 3 (*d*) None of the above

Sol. Given, $2x^2 - 5x + 3 = 0$

$\therefore$ Coefficient of x^2 in the given quadratic equation is 2.

10. **Which of the following equations is a quadratic equation?** (*Ap*)

(*a*) $3x + 3 = 0$ (*b*) $x^3 + x^2 + x + 1 = 0$

(*c*) $-4x^2 + 6x - 1 = 0$ (*d*) $5x + 4 = 0$

Sol. Clearly, $-4x^2 + 6x - 1 = 0$ has a degree 2. So, it is a quadratic equation.

11. **Which of the following is not a quadratic equation?** (*Un*)

(*a*) $-2x^2 + 3x + 1 = 0$ (*b*) $4x^2 - 8x = 0$

(*c*) $3x - 1 = 0$ (*d*) $x^2 - 2x - 3 = 0$

Sol. Option (*a*), (*b*), (*d*) has degree 2

So, these are quadratic equations.

But option (*c*) $3x - 1 = 0$ has degree 1

So, $3x - 1 = 0$ is not a quadratic equation.

12. **Sum of coefficients of x^2, x and constant term in quadratic equation $4x^2 + 3x + 2 = 0$?** (*Cr*)

(*a*) 9 (*b*) 8 (*c*) 7 (*d*) 6

Sol. The quadratic equation $4x^2 + 3x + 2 = 0$ can be written in the standard form as $ax^2 + bx + c = 0$, where $a = 4$, $b = 3$ and $c = 2$.

The sum of the coefficients of x^2, x and the constant term is given by $a + b + c$.

Substituting the values of a, b and c, we get:

$a + b + c = 4 + 3 + 2 = 9$

Key Takeaways

The sum of the coefficients of a quadratic equation is given by $a + b + c$.

Answer Key

1. (b) 2. (c) 3. (b) 4. (b) 5. (b)
6. (d) 7. (d) 8. (a) 9. (a) 10. (c)
11. (c) 12. (a)

Assertion and Reason

(1 M)

Direction: In the following questions, A statement of Assertion (A) is followed by a statement of Reason (R). Mark the correct choice as.

(*a*) Both Assertion (A) and Reason (R) are true, and Reason (R) is the correct explanation of Assertion (A).

(*b*) Both Assertion (A) and Reason (R) are true, but Reason (R) is not the correct explanation of Assertion (A).

(*c*) Assertion (A) is true, but Reason (R) is false.

(*d*) Assertion (A) is false, but Reason (R) is true.

1. Assertion (A): An equation of the form $ax^2 + bx + c = 0$, where $a = 0$, is not a quadratic equation.

Reason (R): In a quadratic equation, the coefficient of x^2 must be non-zero, since the degree of the equation is two. *(Re)*

Sol. A: $ax^2 + bx + c = 0$ and $a = 0$

Then $ax^2 + bx + c = 0$ becomes $bx + c$ which is not a quadratic equation.

$\therefore$ Assertion is true.

R: For a quadratic equation, the coefficient of x^2 i.e., a must be non-zero i.e., $a \neq 0$.

Since, the degree of the equation is 2.

Hence, assertion is true and reason is also true, and reason is the correct explanation of assertion.

2. Assertion (A): An equation of the form $3x + 2 = 0$ is not a quadratic equation.

Reason (R): In a quadratic equation, the degree of the variable should be exactly two. *(Un)*

Sol. A: $3x + 2 = 0$ has degree = 1

So, $3x + 2 = 0$ is not *a* quadratic equation.

R: For quadratic equation degree of the variable must be 2.

Hence, assertion & reason both are true and reason is the correct explanation of assertion.

Mistakes 101 : What not to do!

Students might incorrectly equate roots obtained from factoring or the quadratic formula with the actual solutions to the equation without verifying them.

3. Assertion (A): The sum of the coefficients of x^2, x and the constant term in the quadratic equation $x^2 + 13x + 36 = 0$ is 50.

Reason (R): The sum of the coefficients of any quadratic equation in standard form $ax^2 + bx + c = 0$ is given by $a + b + c$. *(Re)*

Sol. A: $x^2 + 13x + 36 = 0$, sum of the coefficient of x^2, coefficient of x and coefficient of constant

$= 1 + 13 + 36 = 50$

R: $ax^2 + bx + c = 0$, sum of the coefficient of x^2, coefficient of x and coefficient of x^0 (constant term)

$= a + b + c$

Hence, assertion & reason both are true and reason is the correct explanation of assertion.

Answer Key

1. (a) 2. (a) 3. (a)

Subjective Questions

Very Short Answer Type Questions

(1 or 2 M)

1. Which of the following are quadratic equations? *(Un)*

(*i*) $2x^2 - 3\sqrt{2}x + 6 = 0$

(*ii*) $3x^2 - 2\sqrt{x} + 8 = 0$

Sol. (*i*) Clearly, $2x^2 - 3\sqrt{2}x + 6$ has a degree 2

$\therefore 2x^2 - 3\sqrt{2}x + 6 = 0$ is a quadratic equation *(1 M)*

(*ii*) $3x^2 - 2\sqrt{x} + 8 = 0$ is not of the form $ax^2 + bx + c = 0$.

$\therefore 3x^2 - 2\sqrt{x} + 8 = 0$ is not a quadratic equation. *(1 M)*

2. The sum of a fraction and 7 times of its reciprocal is $\frac{45}{96}$. Represent the above statement in the form of a quadratic equation. *(Ap)*

Sol. Let the fraction be x. Then, according to the question,

$$x + \frac{7}{x} = \frac{45}{96}$$ *(1 M)*

$\Rightarrow 96x^2 - 45x + 672 = 0$ *(1 M)*

This is the required quadratic equation.

3. Write the standard form of quadratic equation for the given expression: $(x - 7)(x - 8) = 0$. *(Un)*

Sol. Let us convert the given equation into the standard form of quadratic equation ($ax^2 + bx + c = 0$)

$\therefore (x - 7)(x - 8) = 0$ *(1 M)*

$\Rightarrow x^2 - 7x - 8x + 56 = 0 \Rightarrow x^2 - 15x + 56 = 0$ *(1 M)*

Key Takeaways

To find the standard for of quadratic equation solve the given equation and compare it with its standard form i.e., $ax^2 + b + c = 0$.

4. Represent the given situation in the form of a quadratic equation.

"The product of 2 consecutive positive integers is 306."

(Cr) **(NCERT Intext)**

Sol. Let, the two consecutive positive integers be x and $x + 1$.

Then, according to the question,

$x(x + 1) = 306$

$x^2 + x = 306$

$x^2 + x - 306 = 0$

It is of the form $ax^2 + bx + c = 0$ which is the required quadratic equation. *(1 M)*

5. A rectangular garden has an area of 120 square meters. If the length is 4 meters more than twice the width, Represent it in the form of a quadratic equation. ***(Re)***

Sol. Let x be the width of the rectangular garden. Then, the length is $2x + 4$. *(1 M)*

Since the area of the rectangular garden is 120 square meters, we can write the equation:

$x(2x + 4) = 120 \Rightarrow 2x^2 + 4x - 120 = 0$ *(1 M)*

Short Answer Type Questions (2 or 3 M)

1. Write the standard form of quadratic equation for given expression: $(x - 12)(8 - x) = 0$ ***(Un)***

(*i*) Write coefficients of x^2, x, and constant term

(*ii*) Find sum and product of coefficients of x^2, x and constant term respectively.

Sol. The given expression can be written as: $(x - 12)(8 - x) = 0$

Expanding the expression, we get: $8x - x^2 - 96 + 12x = 0$

i.e., $20x - x^2 - 96 = 0$ *(1 M)*

Rearranging terms, we get the quadratic equation in standard form: $-x^2 + 20x - 96 = 0$

(*i*) The coefficients of x^2, x and the constant term are -1, 20 and -96, respectively. *(1 M)*

(*ii*) The sum of the coefficients of x^2, x and the constant term $= -1 + 20 - 96 = -77$ *(½ M)*

The product of the coefficients of x^2, x and the constant term $= (-1) \times 20 \times (-96) = 1920$ *(½ M)*

2. Represent the following situations in the form of quadratic equation:

Rohan's mother is 26 years older than him. The product of their ages (in years) 3 years from now will be 360. We would like to find Rohan's present age. ***(An)* (NCERT Intext)**

Sol. Let's take Rohan's age $= x$ years.

Hence, his mother's age $= x + 26$

3 years from now, Rohan's age $= x + 3$ *(1 M)*

Age of Rohan's mother will $= x + 26 + 3 = x + 29$ *(1 M)*

The product of their ages 3 years from now will be 360 so that

$(x + 3)(x + 29) = 360 \Rightarrow x^2 + 29x - 3x + 87 = 360$

$\Rightarrow x^2 + 32x + 87 - 360 = 0 \Rightarrow x^2 + 32x - 273 = 0$ *(1 M)*

Long Answer Type Questions (4 or 5 M)

1. Represent the following situations in the form of quadratic equation:

A train travels a distance of 480 km at a uniform speed. If the speed had been 8 km/h less, then it would have taken 3 hours more to cover the same distance. We need to find the speed of the train. ***(An)* (NCERT Intext)**

Sol. Distance travelled by train = 480 km

Let the speed of train be x kmph.

Time taken for the journey $= \dfrac{480}{x}$ *(1 M)*

Given speed is decreased by 8 kmph

Hence the new speed of train $= (x - 8)$ kmph *(1 M)*

Time taken for the journey $= \dfrac{480}{x-8}$ *(1 M)*

According to the question, $\dfrac{480}{x-8} - \dfrac{480}{x} = 3$ *(1 M)*

$\Rightarrow \dfrac{480(x-x+8)}{x(x-8)} = 3 \Rightarrow \dfrac{480}{3} \times 8 = x^2 - 8x$

$\Rightarrow 1280 = x^2 - 8x \Rightarrow x^2 - 8x - 1280 = 0$ *(1 M)*

2 | METHODS OF SOLVING A QUADRATIC EQUATION

Important Concepts

- **Roots of a Quadratic Equation:** we say that $x = \alpha$ (where α is a real number) is a solution of quadratic equation $ax^2 + bx + c = 0$, $a \neq 0$, if $a(\alpha)^2 + b(\alpha) + c = 0$.
- **Factorisation Method:** We use the following steps:

  Step I: Write the given equation in standard form i.e. $ax^2 + bx + c = 0$ and find the values of a, b and c.

  Step II: Calculate the product of a and c, then write it as ac, sum of its two factors such that their sum is equal to b. i.e. $ac = p \times q$ and $p + q = b$ Where, p and q are factors of ac.

  Step III: Put the value of b, obtained in step II in the given equation.

  Step IV: Write the equation in the form of a product of linear factors.

  Step V: Now, equate each factor to zero to get the desired roots.
- **Quadratic Formula (Shridharacharya Formula):** The roots of a quadratic equation $ax^2 + bx + c = 0$ are given by

$$\frac{-b \pm \sqrt{b^2 - 4ac}}{2a}.$$

Me: How do I get a job? How do I pay taxes? How do I buy a new house?

School:

This is called the quadratic formula or Shridharacharya's rule. Thus, $ax^2 + bx + c = 0$ has two roots α and β, given by

$$\alpha = \frac{-b + \sqrt{b^2 - 4ac}}{2a} \text{ and } \beta = \frac{-b - \sqrt{b^2 - 4ac}}{2a}.$$

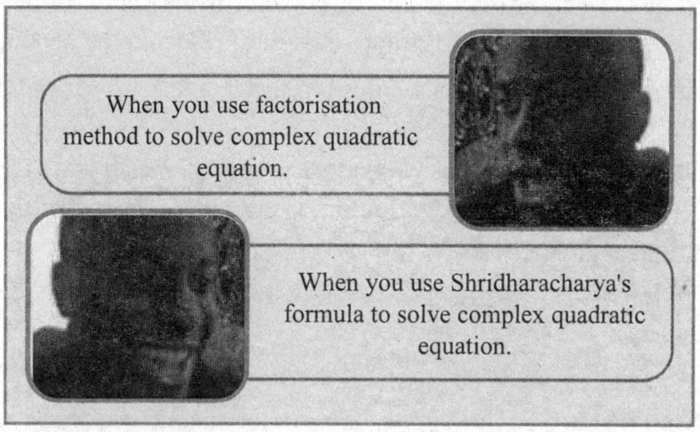

- If α and β are the roots of $ax^2 + bx + c = 0$ then we say that $x = \alpha, \beta$ satisfies the equation $ax^2 + bx + c = 0$ or $x = \alpha, \beta$ are solution of the equation $ax^2 + bx + c = 0$.
- The roots of a quadratic equation $ax^2 + bx + c = 0$ are called the zeros of the polynomial $ax^2 + bx + c$.
- If α be a root of the quadratic equation $ax^2 + bx + c = 0$ then $(x - \alpha)$ is a factor of corresponding quadratic expression $ax^2 + bx + c$.

Real Life Applications

In order to determine the distance and speed of an artillery launch to destroy an enemy camp, the military uses quadratic equations.

Different Problem Types

Type I: Determination of Roots of the Quadratic Equation by Factorisation Method

In the factorization method for determining roots of a quadratic equation, the equation is expressed in the form $ax^2 + bx + c = 0$. By factoring the equation into two linear expressions and setting each factor equal to zero, the roots of the quadratic equation can be easily identified by solving for x.

Find the roots of the equation $2x^2 - 5x + 3 = 0$, by factorisation.

Solution: We will systematically address this problem through the following steps:

Step I: First split the middle term $-5x$ into two terms, $-2x$ and $-3x$, because $-2x \times -3x = 6x^2$, which is the product of the coefficient of x^2 and the constant term.

Step II: Rewrite the quadratic equation $2x^2 - 5x + 3 = 0$ as $2x^2 - 2x - 3x + 3 = 0$.

Step III: Group the terms to factor by grouping: $(2x^2 - 2x)$ and $(-3x + 3)$.

Step IV: Factor out the common factor from each group: $2x(x - 1)$ from the first group and $-3(x - 1)$ from the second group.

Step V: Here$(x - 1)$ is a common factor and factor it out, yielding $(2x - 3)(x - 1) = 0$.

Step VI: Apply the zero-product property, which states that if the product of two factors is zero, at least one of the factors must be zero, to set $2x - 3 = 0$ and $x - 1 = 0$.

Step VII: Solve for x in each equation: From $2x - 3 = 0$,we get $x = \frac{3}{2}$; and from $x - 1 = 0$, we get $x = 1$.

Step VIII: Conclude that the roots of the quadratic equation $2x^2 - 5x + 3 = 0$ are $x = \frac{3}{2}$ and $x = 1$, since those are the values of x that make each factor equal to zero.

Example: Find the value of p, for which one root of the quadratic equation $px^2 - 14x + 8 = 0$ is 6 times the other.

Solution: Given, equation is $px^2 - 14x + 8 = 0$

Here $a = p, b = -14, c = 8$

Let one root $= \alpha$, then other root $= 6\alpha$

Sum of roots $= \frac{-b}{a}$

$$\therefore \alpha + 6\alpha = \frac{-(-14)}{p} \Rightarrow 7\alpha = \frac{14}{p} \Rightarrow \alpha = \frac{14}{p \times 7} \Rightarrow \alpha = \frac{2}{p}$$

$$\text{Products of roots} = \frac{c}{d} \Rightarrow (\alpha)(6\alpha) = \frac{8}{p} \Rightarrow 6\alpha^2 = \frac{8}{p} \quad \ldots (i)$$

Putting the value of α from eq. (*i*), wet get

$$6\left(\frac{2}{p}\right)^2 = \frac{8}{p} \Rightarrow 6 \times \frac{4}{p^2} = \frac{8}{p} \Rightarrow 24p = 8p^2 \Rightarrow 8p^2 - 24p = 0$$

$\Rightarrow 8p(p - 3) = 0 \Rightarrow$ Either $8p = 0 \Rightarrow p = 0$ or $p - 3 = 0 \Rightarrow p = 3$

For $p = 0$, given condition is not satisfied

[$\because$ leading coefficient can't be zero]

$\therefore p = 3$

Type II: On Determining Whether The Given Values are Solutions of The Given Equation or Not

To ascertain whether given values are solutions to an equation, substitute them into the equation and assess equality. For example, if presented with $ax^2 + bx + c = 0$, plug the values into the equation and verify if both sides match. If they do, the values are solutions; otherwise, they are not.

Determine whether the given values are solutions of the given equation or not: $3x^2 - 2x - 1 = 0, x = 1$

Solution: We will systematically address this problem through the following steps:

Step I: Substituting $x = 1$ on the L.H.S of the given equation, we get

L.H.S $= 3 \times 1^2 - 2 \times 1 - 1 = 0 =$ R.H.S.

So, x = 1 is a solution of the given equation.

Step II: Since the L.H.S equals the right-hand side (R.H.S) after substitution, $x = 1$ is indeed a solution to the equation $3x^2 - 2x - 1 = 0$.

Example: In each of the following determine whether the given values are solution of the given equation or not:
(*i*) $6x^2 - x - 2 = 0, x = -1/2, x = 2/3$, (*ii*) $x^2 - x + 1 = 0, x = 1, x = -1$, (*iii*) $x^2 + \sqrt{2}x - 4 = 0, x = \sqrt{2}, x = -2\sqrt{2}$

Solution: (*i*) Substituting $x = -\frac{1}{2}$ in the L.H.S of the given equation,

we get L.H.S $= 6 \times \left(-\frac{1}{2}\right)^2 - \left(-\frac{1}{2}\right) - 2 = \frac{6}{4} + \frac{1}{2} - 2 = 0 =$ R.H.S.

So, $x = -\frac{1}{2}$ is a solution of the given equation.

For $x = \frac{2}{3}$, we have

So, L.H.S $= 6 \times \left(\frac{2}{3}\right)^2 - \frac{2}{3} - 2 = 0 =$ R.H.S is also a solution of the given equation.

(*ii*) Substituting $x = 1$ on the L.H.S of the given equation, we get

L.H.S $= 1^2 - 1 + 1 = 1 \neq$ R.H.S

So, $x = 1$ is not a solution of the given equation.

Similarly, $x = -1$ is not a solution of the given equation.

(*iii*) Substituting $x = \sqrt{2}$ on the L.H.S of the given equation, we get

L.H.S $= (\sqrt{2})^2 + \sqrt{2} \times \sqrt{2} - 4 = 2 + 2 - 4 = 0 =$ R.H.S

So, $x = \sqrt{2}$ is solution of the given equation.

Substituting $x = -2\sqrt{2}$ on the L.H.S of the given equation, we get

L.H.S $= (-2\sqrt{2})^2 + \sqrt{2} \times (-2\sqrt{2}) - 4 = 8 - 4 - 4 = 0 =$ R.H.S

So, $x = -2\sqrt{2}$ is also a solution of the given equation.

Type III: On Determining an Unknown Involved in a Quadratic Equation When its Root(s) is (Are) Given

When tasked with determining an unknown in a quadratic equation with given roots, consider the general form $ax^2 + bx + c = 0$. By using the fact that the sum and product of roots are related to coefficients, the missing variable can be determined unveiling the quadratic equation's complete structure.

Determine the value of k for which the given value is a solution of the equation: $kx^2 + 2x - 3 = 0, x = 2$

Solution: We will systematically address this problem through the following steps:

Step I: Since $x = 2$ is a root of the equation. Therefore, it will satisfy the equation.

Step II: Substitute $x = 2$ in the equation, we get

$k(2)^2 + 2 \times 2 - 3 = 0 \Rightarrow 4k + 4 - 3 = 0 \Rightarrow 4k + 1 = 0$

Step III: Now, solve for $k \Rightarrow 4k + 1 = 0 \Rightarrow 4k = -1 \Rightarrow k = -\frac{1}{4}$

Therefore, for $x = 2$ to be a root of the equation, k must be $-\frac{1}{4}$.

Example: The altitude of a right triangle is 7 cm less than its base. If the hypotenuse is 13 cm, find the other two sides.

Solution: Let the base of the right triangle be 'x' cm.

Then, according to question, altitude of a right triangle = $(x - 7)$ cm

Given, hypotenuse = 13 cm

Now, by Pythagoras theorem

$(\text{Hypotenuse})^2 = (\text{Perpendicular})^2 + (\text{Base})^2$

$13^2 = (x-7)^2 + x^2 \Rightarrow 169 = x^2 + 49 - 14x + x^2 \Rightarrow 2x^2 - 14x + 49 - 169 = 0 \Rightarrow 2x^2 - 14x - 120 = 0$

or $x^2 - 7x - 60 = 0$

By factorisation method, $x^2 - 12x + 5x - 60 = 0$

$\Rightarrow x(x-12) + 5(x-12) = 0 \Rightarrow (x-12)(x+5) = 0 \Rightarrow x - 12 = 0$ or $x + 5 = 0 \Rightarrow x = 12$ or $x = -5$

But, length cannot be negative.

$\therefore x = 12$

Hence, base of a right triangle = 12 cm and altitude of a right triangle = $(12 - 7)$ cm = 5 cm

Type IV: Determination of roots of the Quadratic Equation by Quadratic Formula

The quadratic formula offers a systematic approach to determine the roots of a quadratic equation ($ax^2 + bx + c = 0$).

By applying the formula $x = \dfrac{-b \pm \sqrt{b^2 - 4ac}}{2a}$ =, where a, b and c are coefficients, one can efficiently find the solutions, unveiling the roots of the quadratic equations.

Solve the quadratic equation $x^2 - 7x + 12 = 0$ by using quadratic formula

Solution: We will systematically address this problem through the following steps:

Step I: Compare the given equation $x^2 - 7x + 12 = 0$ with the standard quadratic equation $ax^2 + bx + c = 0$, we get $a = 1$, $b = -7$, and $c = 12$.

Step II: Calculate the roots using the quadratic formula:

$$x = \frac{-b \pm \sqrt{b^2 - 4ac}}{2a}$$

Step III: Substitute the values of a, b, and c into the formula, we get $x = \dfrac{-(-7) \pm \sqrt{(-7)^2 - 4.1.12}}{2.1} \Rightarrow x = \dfrac{7 \pm \sqrt{49 - 48}}{2}$

$$\Rightarrow x = \frac{7 \pm 1}{2}$$

Step IV: Calculate the two roots: $x = \dfrac{7+1}{2}$ or $\dfrac{7-1}{2} \Rightarrow x = 4$ or 3

Therefore, the two roots of the equation $x^2 - 7x + 12 = 0$ are $x = 4$ and $x = 3$.

Example: Using quadratic formula, solve the following equation for x: $abx^2 + (b^2 - ac)x - bc = 0$

Solution: (*i*) We have, $abx^2 + (b^2 - ac)x - bc = 0$

$$\therefore x = \frac{-(b^2 - ac) \pm \sqrt{(b^2 - ac)^2 - 4(ab)(-bc)}}{2ab}$$

$$\Rightarrow x = \frac{-(b^2 - ac) \pm \sqrt{(b^2 - ac)^2 + 4ab^2c}}{2ab}$$

$$\Rightarrow x = \frac{-(b^2 - ac) \pm \sqrt{b^4 - 2ab^2c + a^2c^2 + 4ab^2c}}{2ab}$$

$$= \frac{-(b^2 - ac) \pm \sqrt{(b^2 + ac)^2}}{2ab} \Rightarrow x = \frac{-(b^2 - ac) \pm (b^2 + ac)}{2ab}$$

$$\Rightarrow x = \frac{-(b^2 - ac) + (b^2 + ac)}{2ab}, x = \frac{-(b^2 - ac) - (b^2 + ac)}{2ab}$$

$$\Rightarrow x = \frac{2ac}{2ab}, x = \frac{-2b^2}{2ab} \Rightarrow x = \frac{c}{b}, x = \frac{-b}{a}$$

COMPETENCY BASED SOLVED EXAMPLES

Multiple Choice Questions

(1 M)

1. **The discriminant of the quadratic equation $4x^2 - 6x + 3 = 0$**

(Ap) (CBSE, 2020)

(*a*) 12 (*b*) 84

(*c*) $2\sqrt{3}$ (*d*) -12

Sol. $D = b^2 - 4ac$

Where $a = 4$, $b = -6$, and $c = 3$.

Substitute these values into the formula:

$D = (-6)^2 - 4 \cdot 4 \cdot 3$

$\Rightarrow D = 36 - 48$

$\Rightarrow D = -12$

2. **The number of quadratic polynomials having zeroes -5 and -3 is/are:** (*Un*)

(*a*) 1

(*b*) 2

(*c*) 3

(*d*) more than 3

Sol. Given, the zeroes of the polynomial are -5 and -3.

As we know that the general form of the polynomial with zeroes α and β is given by:

$k[x^2 - (\alpha + \beta)x + \alpha\beta]$, where k is any real number

$= k[x^2 - (-5 - 3)x + (-5)(-3)] = k[x^2 + 8x + 15]$

k can take infinite value. Therefore, the number of polynomials having zeroes -5 and -3 is more than 3.

3. **A quadratic polynomial, the product and sum of whose zeroes are 5 and 8 respectively is** *(Re)*

(a) $k[x^2 - 8x + 5]$ (b) $k[x^2 + 8x + 5]$

(c) $k[x^2 - 5x + 8]$ (d) $k[x^2 + 5x + 8]$

Sol. Given, sum of zeroes = 8 and product of zeroes = 5

We know, a quadratic polynomial is,

$k\,[x^2 -$ (sum of zeroes) $x +$ (product of zeroes)]

$\therefore$ The quadratic poly is: $k\,[x^2 - 8x + 5]$

4. **Which of these is a quadratic equation having one of its roots as zero?** *(Ap)*

(i) $x^3 + x^2 = 0$ (ii) $x^2 - 2x = 0$ (iii) $x^2 - 9 = 0$

(a) only (i) (b) only (ii)

(c) only (i) and (ii) (d) only (ii) and (iii)

Sol. (i) $x^3 + x^2 = 0$ is a cubic equation.

(ii) $x^2 - 2x = 0 \Rightarrow x(x-2) = 0 \Rightarrow x = 0, 2$

(iii) $x^2 - 9 = 0 \Rightarrow (x+3)(x-3) = 0 \Rightarrow x = -3, 3$

Thus only (ii) is the correct option.

5. **If α, β are the zeros of the quadratic polynomial $p(x) = x^2 - (k+6)x + 2(2k-1)$, then the value of k, if $\alpha + \beta = \frac{1}{2}\alpha\beta$, is** *(Un)*

(a) –7 (b) 7

(c) –3 (d) 3

Sol. Given, $p(x) = x^2 - (k+6)x + 2(2k-1)$.

Let α and β are zeroes of $p(x)$.

$\therefore \alpha + \beta = k + 6$ [sum of roots of quadratic polynomial]

$\alpha\beta = 2(2k-1)$ [product of roots of quadratic polynomial]

Also given,

$$\alpha + \beta = \frac{1}{2}\alpha\beta \Rightarrow (k+6) = \frac{1}{2}\cdot 2(2k-1)$$

$$\Rightarrow k + 6 = 2k - 1 \Rightarrow 2k - k = 6 + 1 \Rightarrow k = 7$$

Answer Key

1. (d) 2. (d) 3. (a) 4. (b) 5. (b)

Assertion and Reason (1 M)

Direction: In the following questions, A statement of Assertion (A) is followed by a statement of Reason (R). Mark the correct choice as.

(a) Both Assertion (A) and Reason (R) are true, and Reason (R) is the correct explanation of Assertion (A).

(b) Both Assertion (A) and Reason (R) are true, but Reason (R) is not the correct explanation of Assertion (A).

(c) Assertion (A) is true, but Reason (R) is false.

(d) Assertion (A) is false, but Reason (R) is true.

1. **Assertion (A): If one root of the quadratic equation $6x^2 - x - k = 0$ is 2/3, then the value of k is 2.**

Reason (R): The quadratic equation $ax^2 + bx + c = 0$, $a \neq 0$ has almost two roots. *(An)*

Sol. A: We have, $6x^2 - x - k = 0$

As one root is $\frac{2}{3}$.

So, $6\times\left(\frac{2}{3}\right)^2 - \frac{2}{3} - k = 0 \Rightarrow k = \frac{8}{3} - \frac{2}{3} = \frac{6}{3} = 2$

$\therefore$ Assertion is true.

R: $ax^2 + bx + c = 0$, $a \neq 0$ has almost two roots.

$\therefore$ Reason is true but does not explain the assertion.

Thus, both A and R are true but R is not the correct explanation of A.

2. **Assertion (A): Values of x are $-a/2$, a for a quadratic equation $2x^2 + ax - a^2 = 0$.**

Reason (R): For quadratic equation $ax^2 + bx + c = 0$,

$$x = \frac{-b \pm \sqrt{b^2 - 4ac}}{2a}$$ *(Cr)*

Sol. Reason is correct as the formula to find roots of an equation is

$$x = \frac{-b \pm \sqrt{b^2 - 4ac}}{2a}$$

let us verify the reason on the equation $2x^2 + ax - a^2 = 0$

$$\because x = \frac{-b \pm \sqrt{b^2 - 4ac}}{2a}$$

on comparing, $a = 2$, $b = a$, $c = -a^2$

$$\therefore x = \frac{-(a) \pm \sqrt{a^2 - 4(2)(-a^2)}}{2(2)}$$

$$= \frac{-a \pm \sqrt{9a^2}}{4} = \frac{-a + 3a}{4}, \frac{-a - 3a}{4} = \frac{2a}{4}, \frac{-4a}{4} = \frac{a}{2}, -a$$

That means $-\frac{a}{2}$, a are not the zeroes.

Therefore, Assertion (A) is false but Reason (R) is true.

Answer Key

1. (b) 2. (d)

Subjective Questions

Very Short Answer Type Questions (1 or 2 M)

1. **Find the sum and product of the roots of the quadratic equation $2x^2 - 9x + 4 = 0$.** *(Re)*

Sol. $2x^2 - 9x + 4 = 0 \Rightarrow 2x^2 - 8x - x + 4 = 0$ (½ M)

$\Rightarrow 2x(x-4) - 1(x-4) = 0 \Rightarrow (2x-1)(x-4) = 0$

$\Rightarrow 2x - 1 = 0$ or $x - 4 = 0 \Rightarrow x = \frac{1}{2}$ or $x = 4$ (½ M)

Hence, sum of roots $= 4 + \frac{1}{2} = \frac{9}{2}$ (½ M)

Product of roots $= 4 \times \frac{1}{2} = 2$ (½ M)

2. **Find the roots of the quadratic equation $3x^2 - 4\sqrt{3}x + 4 = 0$.** *(Ev) (CBSE, 2020)*

Sol. To find both roots of the quadratic equation $3x^2 - 4\sqrt{3}x + 4 = 0$, we'll use the quadratic formula:

$$x = \frac{-b \pm \sqrt{b^2 - 4ac}}{2a}$$ (½ M)

Where $a = 3$, $b = -4\sqrt{3}$, and $c = 4$.

Substitute these values into the quadratic formula:

$$x = \frac{-(-4\sqrt{3} \pm \sqrt{(-4\sqrt{3})^2 - 4\cdot3\cdot4})}{2\cdot3}$$

$$x = \frac{4\sqrt{3} \pm \sqrt{48-48}}{6}$$ (½ M)

This simplifies to:

$$x_1 = \frac{4\sqrt{3}}{6} = \frac{2\sqrt{3}}{3}$$

$$x_2 = \frac{4\sqrt{3}}{6} = \frac{2\sqrt{3}}{3}$$ (½ M)

So, both roots of the quadratic equation $3x^2 - 4\sqrt{3}x + 4 = 0$ are $x = \frac{2\sqrt{3}}{3}$. This confirms that the quadratic equation has repeated roots. (½ M)

3. Find the value of k for which the roots of the equation $3x^2 - 10x + k = 0$ are reciprocal of each other. *(Ap)*

Sol. We have, equation $3x^2 - 10x + k = 0$

Given, roots are reciprocal of each other.

Consider, roots are α and $\frac{1}{\alpha}$

Here, on comparing with $ax^2 + bx + c = 0$, we get

$a = 3, b = -10, c = k$ *(1 M)*

Product of the roots $= \frac{c}{a}$

$\therefore \alpha \times \frac{1}{\alpha} = \frac{k}{3} \Rightarrow 1 = \frac{k}{3} \Rightarrow k = 3$

Hence, value of k is 3. *(1 M)*

4. If $x = 2$ and $m = 3$, the equation is $3x^2 - 2kx + 2m = 0$, find k. *(Un)*

Sol. Given, equation is $3x^2 - 2kx + 2m = 0$

Since, given $x = 2$ and $m = 3$ *(1 M)*

So, $3(2)^2 - 2k(2) + 2(3) = 0$

$\Rightarrow 12 - 4k + 6 = 0 \Rightarrow -4k + 18 = 0$

Hence, $k = \frac{9}{2}$. *(1 M)*

5. Calculate the roots of the quadratic equation $x^2 + 5x - (\alpha + 1)(\alpha + 6) = 0$, where α is a constant. *(Ap)*

Sol. Given, quadratic equation is:

$x^2 + 5x - (\alpha + 1)(\alpha + 6) = 0$

$\Rightarrow x^2 + (\alpha + 6)x - (\alpha + 1)x - (\alpha + 1)(\alpha + 6) = 0$ *(1 M)*

$\Rightarrow x[x + (\alpha + 6)] - (\alpha + 1)[x + (\alpha + 6)] = 0$

$\Rightarrow [x + (\alpha + 6)][x - (\alpha + 1)] = 0$

$\Rightarrow x + (\alpha + 6) = 0$ or $x - (\alpha + 1) = 0$

Hence, $x = -(\alpha + 6)$ or $x = (\alpha + 1)$ *(1 M)*

6. One of the solutions of the following equation is –7 where k is a constant.

$z^2 - kz - 28 = 0$

(i) Find the value of k.

(ii) Find the other solution.

Show your steps. *(Re)* **(CBSE CFPQ, 2023)**

Sol. (i) $z = (-7)$ (given)

So, value of k in equation will be (subsitute)

$\Rightarrow z^2 - kz - 28 = 0$ $(z = -7)$

$\Rightarrow (-7)^2 - (-7)k - 28 = 0 \Rightarrow 49 + 7k - 28 = 0$

$\Rightarrow 7k + 21 = 0 \Rightarrow k = -3$, *(1 M)*

(ii) By substituting $k = -3$ in given equation we get

$\Rightarrow z^2 - kz - 28 = 0 \Rightarrow z^2 - (-3)z - 28 = 0$

$\Rightarrow z^2 + 3z - 28 = 0 \Rightarrow z^2 + 7z - 4z - 28 = 0$ *(½ M)*

$\Rightarrow z(z + 7) - 4(z + 7) = 0 \Rightarrow (z - 4)(z + 7) = 0$

$\Rightarrow z = 4$ and $z = -7$

Thus, other solution of z is 4 *(½ M)*

7. Find the solutions of the quadratic equation $2x^2 - x - 6 = 0$. *(Un)*

Sol. By comparing the given equation $2x^2 - x - 6 = 0$

With $ax^2 + bx + c = 0$, we get $a = 2$, $b = -1$, $c = -6$

By using quadratic formula, we get

$$x = \frac{-b \pm \sqrt{b^2 - 4ac}}{2a} = \frac{1 \pm \sqrt{1+48}}{4} = \frac{1 \pm 7}{4}$$ *(1 M)*

$\Rightarrow x = \frac{1+7}{4}$ or $\frac{1-7}{4} \Rightarrow x = 2$ or $-\frac{3}{2}$

Hence, $x = 2$ or $-\frac{3}{2}$ is the solution. *(1 M)*

Nailing the Right Answer

If other methods are not feasible, resort to the quadratic formula. Be diligent in plugging in the correct coefficients and interpreting the results correctly.

Mistakes 101 : What not to do!

When using the quadratic formula, students may forget to take the square root of the discriminant or neglect to consider both positive and negative roots, resulting in incomplete solutions.

8. If α and β are the zeroes of $f(x) = 2x^2 + 5x + k$ such that $\alpha^2 + \beta^2 + \alpha\beta = \frac{21}{4}$, find the value of k *(An)*

Sol. $\alpha + \beta = -\frac{5}{2}$, $\alpha\beta = \frac{k}{2}$ *(½ M)*

$\alpha^2 + \beta^2 + \alpha\beta = \frac{21}{4} \Rightarrow (\alpha + \beta)^2 - \alpha\beta = \frac{21}{4}$ *(1 M)*

$\Rightarrow \frac{25}{4} - \frac{k}{2} = \frac{21}{4} \Rightarrow -\frac{k}{2} = -1$

$\therefore k = 2$ *(½ M)*

Short Answer Type Questions (2 or 3 M)

1. Find the roots of the quadratic equation $\sqrt{2}x^2 + 7x + 5\sqrt{2} = 0$, by factorisation method. *(Re)* **(NCERT Intext)**

Sol. Given, equation is:

$\sqrt{2}x^2 + 7x + 5\sqrt{2}$

Here, $a = \sqrt{2}, b = 7, c = 5\sqrt{2}$

Then,

$a\times c=\sqrt{2}\times 5\sqrt{2}=10=5\times 2=(p\times q)$ (1 M)

and $a + c = 5 + 2 = (p + q) = 7 = b$ (½ M)

$\therefore \sqrt{2}x^2+5x+2x+5\sqrt{2}=0$

$\Rightarrow x\left(\sqrt{2}x+5\right)+\sqrt{2}\left(\sqrt{2}x+5\right)=0$ (½ M)

$\Rightarrow\left(x+\sqrt{2}\right)\left(\sqrt{2}x+5\right)=0\Rightarrow x+\sqrt{2}=0$ or $\sqrt{2}x+5=0$

$\Rightarrow x=-\sqrt{2}$ or $x=\dfrac{-5}{\sqrt{2}}$

Hence, the required roots are $-\sqrt{2}$ or $\dfrac{-5}{\sqrt{2}}$. (1 M)

Nailing the Right Answer

Evaluate which method (factoring, or quadratic formula) would be most efficient and appropriate for solving the given quadratic equation.

2. Solve the following quadratic equation:
$6a^2x^2 - 7abx - 3b^2 = 0$ (Cr)

Sol. Given, quadratic equation is: $6a^2x^2 - 7abx - 3b^2 = 0$

On comparing the given equation with $Ax^2 + Bx + C = 0$, we get: $A = 6a^2$, $B = -7ab$, $C = -3b^2$

Then, discriminant $D = B^2 - 4AC$

$= (-7ab)^2 - 4 \times 6a^2 \times (-3b^2) = 49a^2b^2 + 72a^2b^2 = 121a^2b^2$ (1 M)

Then, roots of the equation, $x=\dfrac{-B\pm\sqrt{D}}{2A}$ (½ M)

$=\dfrac{-(-7ab)\pm\sqrt{121a^2b^2}}{2\times 6a^2}=\dfrac{7ab\pm 11ab}{12a^2}$

$=\dfrac{7ab+11ab}{12a^2}$ or $\dfrac{7ab-11ab}{12a^2}$ (½ M)

$=\dfrac{18ab}{12a^2}$ or $\dfrac{-4ab}{12a^2}=\dfrac{3b}{2a}$ or $\dfrac{-b}{3a}$

Hence, the roots of the given equation are $\dfrac{3b}{2a}$ or $\dfrac{-b}{3a}$. (1 M)

3. Find the value of $\dfrac{1}{(a\alpha+b)}+\dfrac{1}{(a\beta+b)}$ where α and β are the roots of equation $ax^2 + bx + c = 0$ (Ap)

Sol. Given equation $ax^2 + bx + c = 0$

Sum of roots $=\alpha+\beta=\dfrac{-b}{a}$

and Product of roots $=\alpha\beta=\dfrac{c}{a}$ (1 M)

Now, $\dfrac{1}{a\alpha+b}+\dfrac{1}{a\beta+b}$

$=\dfrac{a\beta+b+a\alpha+b}{(a\alpha+b)(a\beta+b)}=\dfrac{a(\alpha+\beta)+2b}{a^2\alpha\beta+ab(\alpha+\beta)+b^2}$ (1 M)

$=\dfrac{-\frac{b}{a}\times a+2b}{a^2\times\frac{c}{a}-\frac{b}{a}\times ab+b^2}=\dfrac{b}{ac-b^2+b^2}=\dfrac{b}{ac}$. (1 M)

4. If α and β are roots of the quadratic equation $x^2 - 7x + 10 = 0$, find the quadratic equation whose roots are α^2 and β^2. (Cr)

Sol. Given, α and β are the roots of $x^2 - 7x + 10 = 0$

$\Rightarrow x^2 - 7x + 10 = 0$

$\Rightarrow x^2 - 5x - 2x + 10 = 0$ (½ M)

$\Rightarrow x(x - 5) -2 (x - 5) = 0 \Rightarrow (x - 2) (x - 5) = 0$

$\Rightarrow x = 2$ and $x = 5$ (½ M)

$\therefore \alpha = 2$ and $\beta = 5$

Hence, $\alpha^2 = 4$ and $\beta^2 = 25$

Now, we need to find the quadratic equation having roots α^2 and β^2 i.e., 4 and 25. (½ M)

As we know, quadratic equation can be written as

x^2 – (sum of roots)x + product of roots = 0 (½ M)

$x^2 - (4 + 25)x + (4 \times 25) = 0$

$x^2 - 29x + 100 = 0$ (1 M)

5. Solve for x: $\dfrac{1}{x+4}-\dfrac{1}{x-7}=\dfrac{11}{30}, x\neq -4, 7.$ (Ap)

Sol. We have, $\dfrac{1}{x+4}-\dfrac{1}{x-7}=\dfrac{11}{30}$

$\Rightarrow\dfrac{x-7-x-4}{(x+4)(x-7)}=\dfrac{11}{30}$ (1 M)

$\Rightarrow\dfrac{-11}{(x+4)(x-7)}=\dfrac{11}{30}\Rightarrow\dfrac{-1}{(x+4)(x-7)}=\dfrac{1}{30}$

$\Rightarrow (x + 4)(x - 7) = - 30 \Rightarrow (x + 4)(x - 7) + 30 = 0$

$\Rightarrow x^2 + 4x - 7x - 28 + 30 = 0 \Rightarrow x^2 - 3x - 28 + 30 = 0$

$\Rightarrow x^2 - 3x + 2 = 0 \Rightarrow x^2 - 2x - x + 2 = 0$ (1 M)

$\Rightarrow x(x - 2) - 1(x - 2) = 0 \Rightarrow (x - 2) (x - 1) = 0$

$\Rightarrow x - 1 = 0$ or $x - 2 = 0 \Rightarrow x = 1$ or 2 (1 M)

6. Solve for x: $x^2 + 5x - (a^2 + a - 6) = 0$ (Un)

Sol. $x^2 + 5x - (a^2 + a - 6) = 0$

we know, for $px^2 + qx + r = 0$

$x=\dfrac{-b\pm\sqrt{b^2-4ac}}{2a}$ (½ M)

$a = 1, b = 5, c = -(a^2 + a - 6)$ (½ M)

Now,

$x=\dfrac{-5\pm\sqrt{5^2-4\times 1\times-(a^2+a-6)}}{2\times 1}$

$\Rightarrow x=\dfrac{-5\pm\sqrt{25+4a^2+4a-24}}{2}\Rightarrow x=\dfrac{-5\pm\sqrt{4a^2+4a+1}}{2}$

$\Rightarrow x=\dfrac{-5\pm\sqrt{(2a+1)^2}}{2}\Rightarrow x=\dfrac{-5\pm(2a+1)}{2}$ (1 M)

$\Rightarrow x=\dfrac{-5+2a+1}{2}=\dfrac{2a-4}{2}=a-2$ (Take '+')

$\Rightarrow x=\dfrac{-5-2a-1}{2}=\dfrac{-2a-6}{2}=-a-3=-(a+3)$ (Take '–')

$x = (a - 2), x = -(a + 3)$ (1 M)

7. If α, β are zeroes of quadratic polynomial $5x^2 + 5x + 1$, find the value of (Ap)

1. $\alpha^2 + \beta^2$ 2. $\alpha^{-1} + \beta^{-1}$

Sol. $P(x) = 5x^2 + 5x + 1$

$\alpha + \beta = \frac{-b}{a} = \frac{-5}{5} = -1$ (½ M)

$\alpha\beta = \frac{c}{a} = \frac{1}{5}$ (½ M)

$\alpha^2 + \beta^2 = (\alpha + \beta)^2 - 2\alpha\beta = (-1)^2 - 2\left(\frac{1}{5}\right)$ (½ M)

$= 1 - \frac{2}{5} = \frac{3}{5}$ (½ M)

$\alpha^{-1} + \beta^{-1} = \frac{1}{\alpha} + \frac{1}{\beta}$ (½ M)

$= \frac{(\alpha+\beta)}{\alpha\beta} = \frac{(-1)}{\frac{1}{5}} = -5$ (½ M)

8. Ayush used the quadratic formula to solve a quadratic equation in y to get: $y = \frac{7 \pm \sqrt{169}}{10}$

Write a quadratic equation Ayush could have been solving. Show your steps. **(Cr)**

Sol. Given that $y = \frac{7 \pm \sqrt{169}}{10} \Rightarrow y = \frac{7 \pm 13}{10}$

$\Rightarrow y = \frac{20}{10}, \frac{6}{10} \Rightarrow y = 2, \frac{-3}{5}$ (1 M)

The general form of the quadratic equation is $x^2 - (\alpha + \beta)x + \alpha\beta = 0$, where α and β are the roots of the equation.

Let $\alpha = 2$ and $\beta = \frac{-3}{5}$

The required equation is $y^2 - \left(2 + \left(\frac{-3}{5}\right)\right)y + 2\left(\frac{-3}{5}\right) = 0$

$\Rightarrow y^2 - \frac{7}{5}y - \frac{6}{5} = 0 \Rightarrow 5y^2 - 7y - 6 = 0$ (1 M)

Therefore, Ayush could have been solving the quadratic equation $5y^2 - 7y - 6 = 0$ (1 M)

Long Answer Type Questions (4 or 5 M)

1. Solve for x: $\frac{1}{x+1} + \frac{3}{5x+1} = \frac{5}{x+4}, x \neq -1, -\frac{1}{5}, -4$ **(An)**

Sol. Given, $\frac{1}{x+1} + \frac{3}{5x+1} = \frac{5}{x+4}$

$\Rightarrow \frac{1}{x+1} - \frac{5}{x+4} = \frac{-3}{5x+1} \Rightarrow \frac{(x+4) - 5(x+1)}{(x+1)(x+4)} = \frac{-3}{5x+1}$ (½ M)

$\Rightarrow \frac{x+4-5x-5}{x^2+5x+4} = \frac{-3}{5x+1} \Rightarrow \frac{(-4x-1)}{x^2+5x+4} = \frac{-3}{5x+1}$ (½ M)

$\Rightarrow (4x + 1)(5x + 1) = 3(x^2 + 5x + 4)$

$\Rightarrow 20x^2 + 4x + 5x + 1 = 3x^2 + 15x + 12$ (1 M)

$\Rightarrow 20x^2 - 3x^2 + 9x - 15x + 1 - 12 = 0$

$\Rightarrow 17x^2 - 6x - 11 = 0 \Rightarrow 17x^2 - 17x + 11x - 11 = 0$ (1 M)

$\Rightarrow 17x(x - 1) + 11(x - 1) = 0 \Rightarrow (x - 1)(17x + 11) = 0$ (1 M)

$\Rightarrow x - 1 = 0$ or $17x + 11 = 0$

Either $x = 1$ or $x = -11/17$ (1 M)

2. Solve for x: $\frac{1}{a+b+x} = \frac{1}{a} + \frac{1}{b} + \frac{1}{x}$; $a \neq b \neq 0$, $x \neq 0$, $x \neq -(a+b)$ **(Re)**

Sol. $\frac{1}{a+b+x} = \frac{1}{a} + \frac{1}{b} + \frac{1}{x} \Rightarrow \frac{1}{a+b+x} - \frac{1}{x} = \frac{1}{a} + \frac{1}{b}$ (1 M)

$\Rightarrow \frac{x-a-b-x}{x(a+b+x)} = \frac{a+b}{ab} \Rightarrow \frac{-(a+b)}{x(a+b+x)} = \frac{(a+b)}{ab}$ (1 M)

$\Rightarrow -ab = ax + bx + x^2 \Rightarrow x^2 + ax + bx + ab = 0$ (½ M)

$\Rightarrow x(x + a) + b(x + a) = 0$ (1 M)

$\Rightarrow (x + b)(x + a) = 0 \Rightarrow (x + a) = 0$ or $(x + b) = 0$ (½ M)

$\Rightarrow x = -a$ or $x = -b$

Hence, the values of x are $-a$ and $-b$. (1 M)

3. Given, Solve for x:

$\left(\frac{2x}{x-5}\right)^2 + 5\left(\frac{2x}{x-5}\right) - 24 = 0, x \neq 5$ **(Un)**

Sol. Let $\frac{2x}{(x-5)} = y$

$\Rightarrow y^2 + 5y - 24 = 0 \Rightarrow y^2 + 8y - 3y - 24 = 0$ (1 M)

$\Rightarrow y(y + 8) - 3(y + 8) = 0 \Rightarrow (y + 8)(y - 3) = 0$

$\Rightarrow y = 3$ or $y = -8$

Putting $y = 3$, we get (1 M)

$\frac{2x}{x-5} = 3 \Rightarrow 2x = 3x - 15 \Rightarrow x = 15$ (1 M)

Again, Putting $y = -8$, we get

$\frac{2x}{x-5} = -8$

$\Rightarrow 2x = -8x + 40 \Rightarrow 10x = 40 \Rightarrow x = 4$ (1 M)

$\therefore x = 15$ or 4 (1 M)

Mistakes 101 : What not to do!

Misplacement or omission of parentheses when simplifying or manipulating quadratic expressions can alter the equation's structure and lead to erroneous solutions.

4. Solve for x:

$\frac{x-1}{2x+1} + \frac{2x+1}{x-1} = 2$, **where** $x \neq -\frac{1}{2}, 1$. **(Un)**

Sol. Let $\frac{x-1}{2x+1} = y$

$\therefore y + \frac{1}{y} = 2$ (½ M)

$\Rightarrow y^2 + 1 = 2y \Rightarrow y^2 - 2y + 1 = 0 \Rightarrow y^2 - y - y + 1 = 0$ (1 M)

$\Rightarrow y(y - 1) - 1(y - 1) = 0 \Rightarrow (y - 1)(y - 1) = 0$ (½ M)

$\Rightarrow y = 1$ or 1 (1 M)

Now $\frac{x-1}{2x+1} = 1$ or $\frac{x-1}{2x+1} = 1$

$x - 1 = 2x + 1$ or $x - 1 = 2x + 1$ (½ M)

$-1 - 1 = 2x - x$ or $-1 - 1 = 2x - x$

$-2 = x$ or $-2 = x$ (½ M)

$x = -2$ or -2

$\therefore x = -2$ (1 M)

3 NATURE OF ROOTS OF A QUADRATIC EQUATION

Important Concepts

Let the given equation be $ax^2 + bx + c = 0$, where $a \neq 0$. Then, the discriminant is given by $D = b^2 - 4ac$, and the roots of the given equation are

$$\alpha = \frac{-b+\sqrt{D}}{2a} \text{ and } \beta = \frac{-b-\sqrt{D}}{2a}.$$

- **Case I:** When $D > 0$
  In this case, the roots are real and distinct. These roots are given by
  $$\alpha = \frac{-b+\sqrt{D}}{2a} \text{ and } \beta = \frac{-b-\sqrt{D}}{2a}.$$
- **Case II:** When $D = 0$
  In this case, the roots are real and equal.
  Each root $= \frac{(-b)}{2a}$.
- **Case III:** When $D < 0$
  In this case, the roots are imaginary, and we say that the given equation has no real roots.
- In this case $D > 0$, if D is a perfect square then roots are rational and if D is a non-perfect square then roots are irrational.
- If $a,b,c \in Q$ and $p+\sqrt{q}$ is one root of quadratic equation then the other root must be the conjugate i.e., $p-\sqrt{q}$ and vice-versa. Here p and q are real numbers.

Real Life Applications

You all enjoy going on a picnic. Consider that a few of your class's students had organised a picnic. As a result, you all came together to create the budget for food, which may be distributed equally among each student. The total budget for food was ₹ 2000. The cost of food for each member increased by ₹ 20 because of 5 students' absence to attend the picnic. So, are you able to find how many students attended the picnic and how much money each students paid for their food?

Yes, you can use a quadratic equation to solve it. You must first create an equation in the form of a quadratic before determining its roots.

Different Problem Types

Type I: On Determining the Discriminant of a Quadratic Equation

Find the discriminant of the quadratic equation $2x^2 - 4x + 3 = 0$

Solution: We will systematically address this problem through the following steps:

Step I: Since, the given quadratic equation is of the form $ax^2 + bx + c = 0$.

Step II: The given values of the coefficients in the equation, which are $a = 2$, $b = -4$, and $c = 3$.

Step III: Substitute the values of a, b, and c into the discriminant formula:

Step IV: Now, discriminant $D = b^2 - 4ac = (-4)^2 - 4 \times 2 \times 3 = 16 - 24 = -8$

Example: Find The discriminant of the quadratic equation $5x^2 - 12\sqrt{3}\,x + 7 = 0$

Solution: $\therefore D = b^2 - 4ac$ Here $a = 5, b = -12\sqrt{3}, c = 7$

$D = (-12\sqrt{3})^2 - 4 \times 7 \times 5 = 432 - 140 = 292$

Type II: On Determining the Nature of the Roots of a Given Quadratic Equation

Determine the nature of the roots of the quadratic equation $2x^2 + x - 1 = 0$

Solution: We will systematically address this problem through the following steps:

Step I: Since, the given quadratic equation is of the form $ax^2 + bx + c = 0$.

Step II: The given values of the coefficients in the equation, which are $a = 2$, $b = 1$, and $c = -1$.

Step III: Substitute the values of a, b and c into the discriminant formula:

Step IV: Now, discriminant $D = b^2 - 4ac = (1)^2 - 4 \times 2 \times (-1) = 1 + 8 = 9 > 0$

Step V: Since, $D > 0$ Hence, the given quadratic equation has two real roots.

Example 1: Find the roots of quadratic equation $2x^2 - 8x + 8 = 0$

Solution: We have, $2x^2 - 8x + 8 = 0$, Here $a = 2$, $b = -8$, $c = 8$

$\therefore D = b^2 - 4ac = (-8)^2 - 4 \times 2 \times 8 = 64 - 64 = 0$

Hence, the given quadratic equation has two equal real roots.

Example 2: Find the values of k for which the equation $x^2 - 8x + k = 0$ has distinct real roots.

Solution: The given equation is $x^2 - 8x + k = 0$

Here, $a = 1$, $b = -8$ and $c = k$

$\therefore D = (-8)^2 - 4 \times 1 \times k = 64 - 4k$

The given equation will have real and distinct roots, if

$D > 0 \Rightarrow 64 - 4k > 0 \Rightarrow 64 > 4k \Rightarrow 4k < 64 \Rightarrow k < \frac{64}{4} = 16$

Hence, the given equation will have distinct roots, if $k<16$.

Type III: On Determining Whether the Given Quadratic Equations have Real Roots and if So, Finding the Roots

Determine whether the given quadratic equation $9x^2 + 7x - 2 = 0$ have real roots and if so, find the roots.

Solution: We will systematically address this problem through the following steps:

Step I: Since, the given quadratic equation is of the form $ax^2 + bx + c = 0$.

Step II: The given values of the coefficients in the equation, which are $a = 9$, $b = 7$, and $c = -2$.

Step III: Substitute the values of a, b and c into the discriminant formula:

Step IV: Now, discriminant $D = b^2 - 4ac = (7)^2 - 4 \times 9 \times (-2) = 49 + 72 = 121 > 0$

Step V: Since, $D > 0$ Hence, the given quadratic equation has two real roots.

Step VI: Now, roots are given by

$$\alpha = \frac{-b+\sqrt{D}}{2\alpha} = \frac{-7+\sqrt{121}}{2\times 9} = \frac{-7+11}{18} = \frac{4}{18} = \frac{2}{9}$$

$$\text{and, } \beta = \frac{-b-\sqrt{D}}{2\alpha} = \frac{-7-\sqrt{121}}{2\times 9} = \frac{-7-11}{18} = -1$$

Example: Check whether the given quadratic equations have real roots and if so, find the roots.

(*i*) $3x^2 - 2x + \frac{1}{3} = 0$ (*ii*) $x^2 + x + 2 = 0$

Solution: (*i*) Here $a = 3$, $b = -2$ and $c = \frac{1}{3}$.

Therefore, discriminant $b^2 - 4ac = (-2)^2 - 4 \times 3 \times \frac{1}{3} = 4 - 4 = 0$.

Hence, the given quadratic equation has two equal real roots.

The roots are $\frac{-b}{2a}, \frac{-b}{2a}$, i.e., $\frac{2}{6}, \frac{2}{6}$, i.e., $\frac{1}{3}, \frac{1}{3}$.

(*ii*) Here $a = 1$, $b = 1$ and $c = 2$.

Therefore, discriminant $b^2 - 4ac = (1)^2 - 4 \times 1 \times 2 = 1 - 8 = -7 < 0$

Hence, the given quadratic equation has no real roots.

COMPETENCY BASED SOLVED EXAMPLES

Multiple Choice Questions

(1 M)

1. If the quadratic equation $9x^2 + bx + \frac{1}{4} = 0$ has equal roots, then the value of b is (*Re*) (CBSE, 2023)

(*a*) 0 (*b*) −3 only

(*c*) 3 only (*d*) ±3

Sol. Given the quadratic equation:

$$9x^2 + bx + \frac{1}{4} = 0$$

To have equal roots, the discriminant (D) should be equal to zero.

$D = q^2 - 4pr$

Where, $p = 9$, $q = b$ and $r = \frac{1}{4}$

Substituting these values into the formula:

$$D = b^2 - 4 \cdot 9 \cdot \frac{1}{4}$$

$D = b^2 - 9 \Rightarrow b^2 - 9 = 0 \Rightarrow b^2 = 9$

$\Rightarrow b^2 - 9 = 0 \Rightarrow b = \pm\sqrt{9} \Rightarrow b = \pm 3$

2. The discriminant of the quadratic equation $5x^2 - 12\sqrt{3}x + 7 = 0$ is: (*Un*)

(*a*) 572 (*b*) 292

(*c*) −572 (*d*) None of these

Sol. $\because D = b^2 - 4ac$ Here $a = 5$, $b = -12\sqrt{3}$, $c = 7$

$D = \left(-12\sqrt{3}\right)^2 - 4\times 7\times 5 = 432 - 140 = 292$

3. If the roots of quadratic equation $(a^2 + b^2)x^2 - 2(ac + bd)x + (c^2 + d^2) = 0$ are equal, then (*Cr*)

(*a*) $\frac{a}{d} = \frac{b}{c}$ (*b*) $\frac{a^2+b^2}{c^2} = \frac{b^2+c^2}{d^2}$

(*c*) $\frac{a}{b} = \frac{c}{d}$ (*d*) $\frac{a}{b} = \frac{d}{c}$

Sol. Here $A = (a^2 + b^2)$, $B = -2(ac + bd)$, $C = c^2 + d^2$

$\therefore D = B^2 - 4AC = 0$

We know $D = 0$ for equal roots

$\Rightarrow 4(ac + bd)^2 - 4 \times (c^2 + d^2)(a^2 + b^2) = 0$

$\Rightarrow 4(a^2c^2 + b^2d^2 + 2acbd) - 4(a^2c^2 + a^2d^2 + c^2b^2 + d^2b^2) = 0$

$\Rightarrow (ad - cb)^2 = 0 \Rightarrow ad = cb \Rightarrow \frac{a}{b} = \frac{c}{d}$

Nailing the Right Answer

Be mindful of the signs of coefficients and terms when applying solution methods, especially when using the quadratic formula or completing the square.

4. Aman solved a quadratic equation and found its roots to be real.
Which of these could represent the graph of the equation Aman solved? ***(Re)*** **(CBSE CFPQ, 2023)**

(*i*)

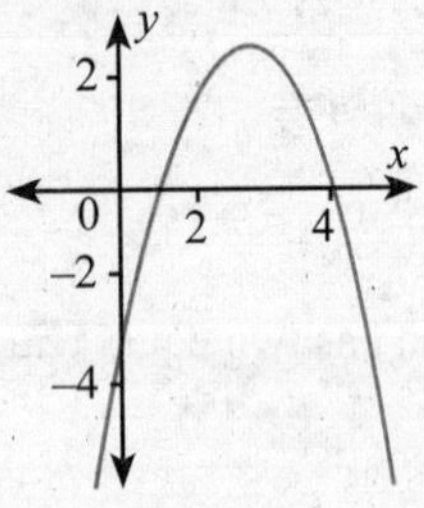

(*ii*)

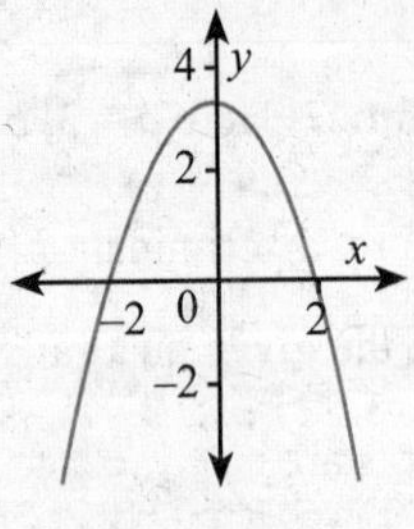

(*iii*)

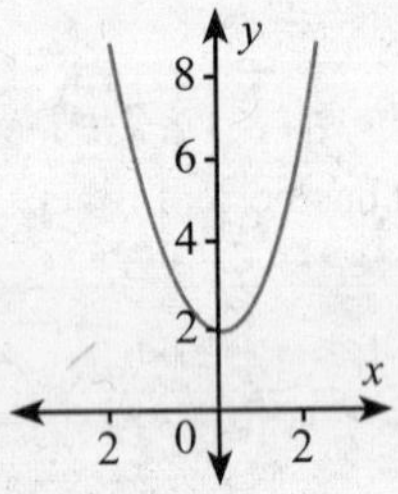

(*iv*)

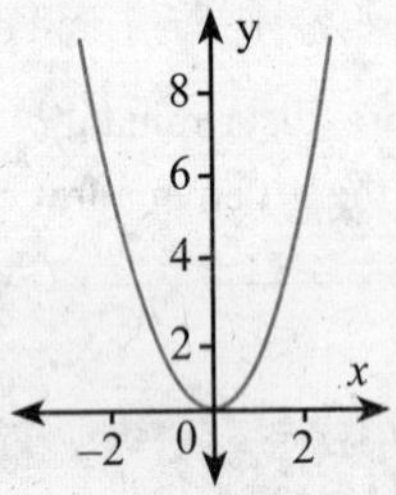

(*a*) Only (*iii*) (*b*) Only (*i*) and (*ii*)
(*c*) Only (*iii*) and (*iv*) (*d*) only (*i*), (*ii*) and (*iv*)

Sol. A quadratic equation has two real roots if the curve either intersects or touches the x-axis
A quadratics equation has no real root when the curve does not touch or intersect the x-axis

5. If the quadratic equation $ax^2 + bx + c = 0$ has two real and equal roots, then '*c*' is equal to: ***(Re)***

(*a*) $\frac{-b}{2a}$ (*b*) $\frac{b}{2a}$ (*c*) $\frac{-b^2}{4a}$ (*d*) $\frac{b^2}{4a}$

Sol. Given, quadratic equation is $ax^2 + bx + c = 0$
Condition for real and equal roots is $D = 0$
$\therefore b^2 - 4ac = 0$ $[\because D = b^2 - 4ac]$
$\Rightarrow b^2 = 4ac \Rightarrow c = \frac{b^2}{4a}$

6. Roots of quadratic equation $2x^2 - 4x + 3 = 0$ are ***(Un)*** **(CBSE, 2020)**

(*a*) real and equal (*b*) real and distinct
(*c*) not real (*d*) real

Sol. In our equation $2x^2 - 4x + 3 = 0$, $a = 2$, $b = -4$, and $c = 3$.
Let's calculate the discriminate:
$D = b^2 - 4ac \Rightarrow D = (-4)^2 - 4 \cdot 2 \cdot 3$
$\Rightarrow D = 16 - 24 \Rightarrow D = -8$
Since the discriminant D = –8 is negative, the roots of the quadratic equation $2x^2 - 4x + 3 = 0$ are complex. Therefore, the roots are not real.

7. The number of real roots of equation $(x + 1)^2 - x = 0$ is/are ***(An)***

(*a*) 1 (*b*) 2 (*c*) 3 (*d*) 0

Sol. We have, $(x + 1)^2 - x = 0$
$\Rightarrow x^2 + 1 + 2x - x = 0 \Rightarrow x^2 + x + 1 = 0$
$\because D = b^2 - 4ac = 1^2 - 4 \times 1 \times 1 = -3 < 0$ (No real roots)

8. If $x^2(a^2 + b^2) + 2x(ac + bd) + c^2 + d^2 = 0$ has no real roots, then ***(Ap)***

(*a*) $ad \neq bc$ (*b*) $ad < bc$
(*c*) $ad > bc$ (*d*) All of these

Sol. Given the equation has no real roots.
$\therefore D < 0$
$\therefore B^2 - 4AC < 0$
$\Rightarrow 2^2(ac + bd)^2 - 4(a^2 + b^2)(c^2 + d^2) < 0$
$\Rightarrow 4a^2c^2 + 4b^2d^2 + 8acbd < 4a^2c^2 + 4b^2d^2 + 4a^2d^2 + 4b^2c^2$
$\Rightarrow 2acbd < a^2d^2 + b^2c^2 \Rightarrow 2acbd < (ad - bc)^2 + 2acbd$
$\Rightarrow (ad - bc)^2 > 0$
Above relation will hold only for $ad \neq bc$.
$\Rightarrow ad \neq bc$, $ad < bc$ and $ad > bc$ are the correct.

Answer Key

1. (*d*) **2.** (*b*) **3.** (*c*) **4.** (*d*) **5.** (*d*)
6. (*c*) **7.** (*d*) **8.** (*d*)

Assertion and Reason (1 M)

Direction: In the following questions, A statement of Assertion (A) is followed by a statement of Reason (R). Mark the correct choice as.

(*a*) Both Assertion (A) and Reason (R) are true, and Reason (R) is the correct explanation of Assertion (A).
(*b*) Both Assertion (A) and Reason (R) are true, but Reason (R) is not the correct explanation of Assertion (A).
(*c*) Assertion (A) is true, but Reason (R) is false.
(*d*) Assertion (A) is false, but Reason (R) is true.

1. Assertion (A): $3x^2 - 6x + 3 = 0$ has repeated roots.
Reason (R): The quadratic equation $ax^2 + bx + c = 0$ have repeated roots if discriminant $D > 0$. ***(Cr)***

Sol. We have, $3x^2 - 6x + 3 = 0$
$\because D = b^2 - 4ac$
$\therefore D = (-6)^2 - 4(3)(3) = 36 - 36 = 0$
Thus, roots are repeated as $D = 0$.
Reason is false, as roots are equal or repeated for $D = 0$.
$\therefore$ Assertion (A) is true but reason (R) is false.

2. Assertion (A): The quadratic equation $x^2 + 2x + 2 = 0$ has no real roots.
Reason (R): If discriminant $D = b^2 - 4ac < 0$ then the roots of quadratic equation $ax^2 + bx + c = 0$ has no real roots. ***(Re)***

Sol. Discriminant, $D = b^2 - 4ac$

$= (2)^2 - 4 \times 1 \times 2 = -4 < 0$

$\therefore$ The equation has no real roots

Reason is also true and explains the assertion.

So, both A and R are true and R explains A.

3. **Assertion (A): The roots of the equation $7x^2 + x - 1 = 0$ are real and distinct**

Reason (R): If $b^2 - 4ac > 0$ then roots are real and distinct. *(Un)*

Sol. $7x^2 + x - 1 = 0$

Here $a = 7, b = 1, c = -1$

$\therefore D = b^2 - 4ac = 1^2 - 4 \times 7 \times -1 = 29 > 0$

Equation has real and distinct roots.

Reason is also true and explains the assertion.

So, both A and R are true and R explains A.

Answer Key

1. (c) 2. (a) 3. (a)

Subjective Questions

Very Short Answer Type Questions (1 or 2 M)

1. **Find the values of p for which the quadratic equation $x^2 - 2px + 1 = 0$ has no real roots.** *(Un)* **(CBSE, 2020)**

Sol. For the quadratic equation $x^2 - 2px + 1 = 0$ to have no real roots, its discriminant (D) must be negative:

$D = b^2 - 4ac < 0$

Given $a = 1, b = -2p$, and $c = 1$, let's compute the discriminant:

$D = (-2p)^2 - 4(1)(1)$

$D = 4p^2 - 4 < 0$ *(1 M)*

$\Rightarrow p^2 - 1 < 0 \Rightarrow (p - 1)(p + 1) < 0$

- When $p < -1$: Both $p - 1$ and $p + 1$ are negative, so their product is positive.
- When $-1 < p < 1$: $p - 1$ is negative, $p + 1$ is positive, so their product is negative.
- When $p > 1$: Both $p - 1$ and $p + 1$ are positive, so their product is positive.

So, the solution to p lies in the interval $-1 < p < 1$.

Therefore, the value of p for which the quadratic equation $x^2 - 2px + 1 = 0$ has no real roots is $p \in (-1, 1)$. *(1 M)*

2. **Find the value of p, for which the roots of the equation $(3p + 1)x^2 + (11 + p)x + 9 = 0$ are equal.** *(Re)*

Sol. Compare the given equation with $ax^2 + bx + c = 0$;

we get : $a = 3p + 1$, $b = 11 + p$ and $c = 9$

$D = b^2 - 4ac = (11 + p)^2 - 4(3p + 1) \times 9$

$= 121 + 22p + p^2 - 108p - 36 = p^2 - 86p + 85$ *(1 M)*

Since the roots are equal i.e., $D = 0$

$= p^2 - 85p - p + 85 = 0 = (p - 85)(p - 1) = 0$

$\Rightarrow (p - 85)(p - 1) = 0 \Rightarrow p = 85$ or $p = 1$ *(1 M)*

3. **For what value of k, $(4 - k)x^2 + (2k + 4)x + (8k + 1)$ is a perfect square?** *(Un)*

Sol. The given quadratic equation is

$(4 - k)x^2 + (2k + 4)x + (8k + 1) = 0.$

Comparing the given equation with $ax^2 + bx + c = 0$, we get $a = (4 - k)$, $b = (2k + 4)$ and $c = (8k + 1)$.

As the given equation is a perfect square, then

$D = b^2 - 4ac = 0$

$\Rightarrow (2k + 4)^2 - 4(4 - k)(8k + 1) = 0$ *(1 M)*

$\Rightarrow 4(k + 2)^2 - 4(4 - k)(8k + 1) = 0$

$\Rightarrow 4[(k + 2)^2 - (4 - k)(8k + 1)] = 0$

$\Rightarrow [(k^2 + 4k + 4) - (-8k^2 + 31k + 4)] = 0$

$\Rightarrow 9k^2 - 27k = 0 \Rightarrow 9k(k - 3) = 0$

i.e., $k = 0$ or $k = 3$

Hence, the given equation is a perfect square, if $k = 0$ or $k = 3$. *(1 M)*

4. **For what values of k, the roots of the equation $x^2 + 4x + k = 0$ are real?** *(An)*

Sol. Let $x^2 + 4x + k = 0$ be a quadratic equation.

Given, it has real roots.

$\therefore D \geq 0$

$\Rightarrow b^2 - 4ac \geq 0 \Rightarrow (4)^2 - 4(1)(k) \geq 0$ *(1 M)*

$\Rightarrow 16 - 4k \geq 0 \Rightarrow 16 \geq 4k \Rightarrow 4k \leq 16$

$\therefore k \leq 4$

Hence, the values of k must be less than or equal to 4. *(1 M)*

5. **Find the nature of the roots of the quadratic equation $7x^2 - 9x + 2 = 0$.** *(Cr)*

Sol. The given quadratic equation is $7x^2 - 9x + 2 = 0$.

Comparing with $ax^2 + bx + c = 0$, we get $a = 7$, $b = -9$ and $c = 2$

$D = b^2 - 4ac = (-9)^2 - 4(7)(2) = 81 - 56 = 25$ *(1 M)*

As $D > 0$ and a perfcet square. So roots are real, rational and distinct. *(1 M)*

6. **Find the values of p so that the equation $x^2 + 4px + p^2 - p + 2 = 0$ has equal roots.** *(Re)*

Sol. Comparing $x^2 + 4px + p^2 - p + 2 = 0$ with $ax^2 + bx + c = 0$, we get: $a = 1$, $b = 4p$ and $c = p^2 - p + 2$

Since, the roots are equal then the discriminant, $D = 0$

$\therefore b^2 - 4ac = 0$

$\Rightarrow (4p)^2 - 4(p^2 - p + 2) = 0 \Rightarrow 16p^2 - 4p^2 + 4p - 8 = 0$

$\Rightarrow 12p^2 + 4p - 8 = 0 \Rightarrow 3p^2 + p - 2 = 0$

$\Rightarrow 3p^2 + 3p - 2p - 2 = 0$ *(1 M)*

$\Rightarrow 3p(p + 1) - 2(p + 1) = 0 \Rightarrow (3p - 2)(p + 1) = 0$

$\Rightarrow p = -1$ or $\frac{2}{3}$ *(1 M)*

7. If p and q are positive, then find the nature of roots of the equation $x^2 - px - q = 0$. *(Un)*

Sol. The given quadratic equation is $x^2 - px - q = 0$

Comparing with $ax^2 + bx + c = 0$, we get $a = 1$, $b = -p$ and $c = -q$.

Here, $D = b^2 - 4ac$

$= (-p)^2 - 4(1)(-q) = p^2 + 4q$ *(1 M)*

Since $p, q > 0$

Therefore, discriminant $= p^2 + 4q > 0$

Hence, the roots are real and distinct. *(1 M)*

8. Find the nature of the roots of the equation $(b + c)x^2 - (a + b + c)x + a = 0$, $(a,b,c \in Q)$. *(Cr)*

Sol. The discriminant of the equation is $B^2 - 4AC$

$= [-(a + b + c)^2] - 4(b + c)(a)$ *(1 M)*

$= a^2 + b^2 + c^2 + 2ab + 2bc + 2ca - 4ab - 4ac$

$= a^2 + b^2 + c^2 - 2ab + 2bc - 2ca = (a - b - c)^2 > 0$

So, roots are real and distinct. *(1 M)*

9. The roots of the equation, $x^2 + bx + c = 0$ are equal if ___. *(Ev)* **(CBSE, 2020)**

Sol. $D = b^2 - 4ac$

For the equation $x^2 + bx + c = 0$, $a = 1$, $b = b$ and $c = c$.

For real and equal roots, $D = 0 \Rightarrow b^2 - 4ac = 0$ *(½ M)*

Substituting $a = 1$, $b = b$, and $c = c$:

$\Rightarrow b^2 - 4 \cdot 1 \cdot c = 0 \Rightarrow b^2 - 4c = 0 \Rightarrow b^2 = 4c$

So, the roots of the equation $x^2 + bx + c = 0$ are equal if $b^2 = 4c$. *(½ M)*

10. For what value(s) of a quadratic equation $30ax^2 - 6x + 1 = 0$ has no real roots? *(Un)*

Sol. Given, quadratic equation is $30ax^2 - 6x + 1 = 0$

On comparing this equation with $Ax^2 + Bx + C = 0$

we get $A = 30a$, $B = -6$, $C = 1$

For no real roots, $D < 0$

$B^2 - 4AC < 0 \Rightarrow (-6)^2 - 4(30a)\times(1) < 0$ *(1 M)*

$\Rightarrow 36 < 120a \Rightarrow 10a > 3 \Rightarrow a > 0.3$ *(1 M)*

Hence, the value of a should be greater than 0.3 for no real roots.

Short Answer Type Questions (2 or 3 M)

1. For what value of p, does the quadratic equation $px^2 + 2x + p = 0$ have real and equal roots? *(Ap)* **(CBSE, 2022)**

Sol. $D = b^2 - 4ac$

In this equation, $a = p$, $b = 2$, and $c = p$.

If the roots are real and equal, then $D = 0$, so:

$\Rightarrow b^2 - 4ac = 0$ *(1 M)*

Substituting $a = p$, $b = 2$, and $c = p$:

$\Rightarrow (2)^2 - 4(p)(p) = 0$

$\Rightarrow 4 - 4p^2 = 0$ *(½ M)*

$\Rightarrow p^2 = 1 \Rightarrow p = \pm 1$

So, the values of p for which the quadratic equation $px^2 + 2x + p = 0$ has real and equal roots are $p = 1$ and $p = -1$. *(½ M)*

2. Does there exist a quadratic equation whose coefficients are rational but both of its roots are irrational? Justify your answer. *(Un)* **(NCERT Exemplar)**

Sol. Yes, a quadratic equation having coefficients as rational number, has irrational roots, *(½ M)*

Taking example,

$2x^2 - 3x - 15 = 0$ has rational coefficients.

Now, calculating,

$D = b^2 - 4ac$ $(a = 2, b = -3, c = -15)$

$D = (-3)^2 - 4(2)(-15)$

$D = 129$ *(1 M)*

Roots of the equation can be given as:

$$x = \frac{-b \pm \sqrt{b^2 - 4ac}}{2a}$$

$$x = \frac{-(-3) \pm \sqrt{129}}{2 \times 2} \quad x = \frac{3 \pm \sqrt{129}}{4}$$ *(1 M)*

So, we can say that roots are irrational as $\sqrt{129}$ is irrational. *(½ M)*

3. For what value of k, the given quadratic equation $kx^2 - 6x - 1 = 0$ has no real roots? *(Un)*

Sol. We have, $kx^2 - 6x - 1 = 0$.

Here $a = k$, $b = -6$ and $c = -1$

For no real roots $D < 0$ *(1 M)*

$\Rightarrow b^2 - 4ac < 0 \Rightarrow (-6)^2 - 4 \times k \times -1 < 0$

$\Rightarrow 36 + 4k < 0 \Rightarrow 4k < -36 \Rightarrow k < -9$ *(1 M)*

So, for $k < -9$ the given equation has no solution. *(1 M)*

4. A train travels at a certain average speed for a distance of 63 km and then travels a distance of 72 km at an average speed of 6 km/h more than its original speed. If it takes 3 hours to complete the total journey, what is its original average speed? *(Re)* **(NCERT Exemplar)**

Sol. Let its original average speed be x km/h.

Therefore, $\frac{63}{x} + \frac{72}{x+6} = 3$ *(½ M)*

$\Rightarrow \frac{7}{x} + \frac{8}{x+6} = \frac{3}{9} = \frac{1}{3} \Rightarrow \frac{7(x+6)+8x}{x(x+6)} = \frac{1}{3}$ *(½ M)*

$\Rightarrow 21(x + 6) + 24x = x(x + 6) \Rightarrow 21x + 126 + 24x = x^2 + 6x$

$\Rightarrow x^2 - 39x - 126 = 0 \Rightarrow (x + 3)(x - 42) = 0$ *(½ M)*

$\Rightarrow x = -3$ or $x = 42$ *(½ M)*

Since x is the average speed of the train, x cannot be negative.

Therefore, $x = 42$.

So, the original average speed of the train is 42 km/h. *(1 M)*

5. If the quadratic equation $px^2 - 2\sqrt{5}px + 15 = 0$ has two equal roots, then find the value of p. *(Un)*

Sol. $D = 0$ (for equal roots)

$\Rightarrow (-2\sqrt{5}p)^2 - 4p \times 15 = 0$ *(1 M)*

$\Rightarrow 20p^2 - 60p = 0 \Rightarrow 20p(p - 3) = 0$ *(1 M)*

$\Rightarrow 20p = 0$ or $p = 3$

$\Rightarrow p = 0$ (invalid) [$\because$ Leading coefficient can't be zero]

$\therefore p = 3$ *(1 M)*

6. **Find the value of k, for which the quadratic equation $(k + 4)x^2 + (k + 1)x + 1 = 0$ has equal roots.** (*Cr*)

Sol. The given quadratic equation will have equal roots, when

$D = (k + 1)^2 - 4(k + 4)(1) = 0$ (*1 M*)

$\Rightarrow (k^2 + 2k + 1) - 4k - 16 = 0 \Rightarrow k^2 - 2k - 15 = 0$

$\Rightarrow k^2 - 5k + 3k - 15 = 0$ (*1 M*)

$\Rightarrow k(k - 5) + 3(k - 5) = 0 \Rightarrow (k - 5)(k + 3) = 0$

$\Rightarrow k - 5 = 0$ or $k + 3 = 0 \Rightarrow k = 5$ or $k = -3$

Thus, the possible value of k are 5 and -3. (*1 M*)

7. **If the equation $(1 + m^2)x^2 + 2mcx + c^2 - a^2 = 0$ has equal roots then show that $c^2 = a^2(1 + m^2)$.** (*An*)

Sol. Given, quadratic equation is:

$(1 + m^2)x^2 + 2mcx + c^2 - a^2 = 0$

On comparing it with $Ax^2 + Bx + C = 0$, we get $A = 1 + m^2$, $B = 2mc$, $C = c^2 - a^2$ (*1 M*)

The roots of the given equation are equal, then

Discriminant, $D = 0$

$\therefore B^2 - 4AC = 0$

$(2mc)^2 - 4 \times (1 + m^2) \times (c^2 - a^2) = 0$ (*1 M*)

$\Rightarrow 4m^2c^2 - 4(c^2 + c^2m^2 - a^2 - a^2m^2) = 0$

$\Rightarrow 4m^2c^2 - 4c^2 - 4c^2m^2 + 4a^2 + 4m^2a^2 = 0$

$\Rightarrow m^2a^2 + a^2 - c^2 = 0 \Rightarrow c^2 = m^2a^2 + a^2$

$\Rightarrow c^2 = a^2(1 + m^2)$ (*1 M*)

Hence, proved.

8. **For what positive values of k, does the quadratic equation $3x^2 - kx + 3 = 0$ not have real roots?** (*Un*)

Sol. Given, quadratic equation $3x^2 - kx + 3 = 0$ has no real roots.

On comparing the given equation with $ax^2 + bx + c = 0$, we have: $a = 3$, $b = -k$, $c = 3$

Then, discriminant, $D = b^2 - 4ac$

$\Rightarrow (-k)^2 - 4 \times 3 \times 3 \Rightarrow k^2 - 36$ (*1 M*)

But for no real roots, $D < 0$

Then $k^2 - 36 < 0 \Rightarrow k^2 < 36$ (*1 M*)

$\Rightarrow k < \pm 6 \Rightarrow k > -6$ or $k < 6$

Hence, for all $-6 < k < 6$, the given equation has no real roots. (*1 M*)

9. **Find the value of p for which the quadratic equation $(p + 1)x^2 - 6(p + 1)x + 3(p + 9) = 0$, $p \neq -1$, has equal roots. Hence, find the roots of the equation.** (*Cr*)

Sol. Given equation is:

$(p + 1)x^2 - 6(p + 1)x + 3(p + 9) = 0$ ... (*i*)

Since, the equation has equal roots

$\therefore$ Discriminant $= 0 \Rightarrow b^2 - 4ac = 0$ (*1 M*)

Here, $a = (p + 1)$, $b = -6(p + 1)$, $c = 3(p + 9)$

$\therefore [-6(p + 1)]^2 - 4 \times (p + 1) \times [3(p + 9)] = 0$

$\therefore (p + 1)[36(p + 1) - 12(p + 9)] = 0$

$\Rightarrow 36p + 36 - 12p - 108 = 0$

$\Rightarrow 24p - 72 = 0$ $[\because p \neq -1$ (Given)$]$

$\Rightarrow p = \frac{72}{24} = 3$ (*1 M*)

Putting $p = 3$ in equation (*i*), we get

$4x^2 - 24x + 36 = 0 \Rightarrow x^2 - 6x + 9 = 0$

$\Rightarrow (x - 3)^2 = 0 \Rightarrow x = 3, 3$ (*1 M*)

Hence, the value of p is 3 and the roots of the equation are 3 and 3.

10. **Find the value of 'k' so that the quadratic equation $3x^2 - 5x - 2k = 0$ has real and equal roots.** (*Ap*) **(CBSE, 2022)**

Sol. Given, quadratic equation is: $3x^2 - 5x - 2k = 0$

For real and equal roots, $b^2 - 4ac = 0$ (*½ M*)

Here, $a = 3$, $b = -5$, and $c = -2k$ (*½ M*)

$\therefore b^2 - 4ac = (-5)^2 - 4 \times 3 \times (-2k) = 0 \Rightarrow k = \frac{-25}{24}$ (*1 M*)

Long Answer Type Questions (4 or 5 M)

1. **If (-5) is a root of the quadratic equation $2x^2 + px - 15 = 0$ and the quadratic equation $p(x^2 + x) + k = 0$ has equal roots, then find the values of p and k.** (*An*)

Sol. Since, (-5) is a root of given quadratic equation

$2x^2 + px - 15 = 0$

$\therefore 2(-5)^2 + p(-5) - 15 = 0$ (*1 M*)

$50 - 5p - 15 = 0 \Rightarrow 5p = 35 \Rightarrow p = 7$ (*1 M*)

And $p(x^2 + x) + k = 0$ has equal roots $\Rightarrow px^2 + px + k = 0$

For equal roots, $D = 0$

So, $(b)^2 - 4ac = 0 \Rightarrow (p)^2 - 4p \times k = 0$ (*1 M*)

$\Rightarrow (7)^2 - 4 \times 7 \times k = 0 \Rightarrow 28k = 49 \Rightarrow k = \frac{49}{28} = \frac{7}{4}$ (*1 M*)

Hence, $p = 7$ and $k = \frac{7}{4}$. (*1 M*)

2. **Find the value of p for which the quadratic equation $(2p + 1)x^2 - (7p + 2)x + (7p - 3) = 0$ has equal roots. Also find these roots.** (*Re*)

Sol. $(2p + 1)x^2 - (7p + 2)x + (7p - 3) = 0$ ... (*i*)

$\because$ Above quadratic equation has equal roots,

$D = 0 \Rightarrow \{-(7p + 2)\}^2 - 4(2p + 1)(7p - 3) = 0$ (*1 M*)

$\Rightarrow 49p^2 + 4 + 28p - 4(14p^2 + p - 3) = 0$

$\Rightarrow 49p^2 + 4 + 28p - 56p^2 - 4p + 12 = 0$

$\Rightarrow -7p^2 + 24p + 16 = 0 \Rightarrow 7p^2 - 24p - 16 = 0$ (*1 M*)

$\Rightarrow 7p^2 - 28p + 4p - 16 = 0 \Rightarrow 7p(p - 4) + 4(p - 4) = 0$

$\Rightarrow (p - 4)(7p + 4) = 0 \Rightarrow (p - 4) = 0$ or $7p + 4 = 0$

$\Rightarrow p = 4$ or $p = -\frac{4}{7}$ (*1 M*)

When $p = -\frac{4}{7}$, the given quadratic equation (*i*) becomes

$$\left(-\frac{8}{7} + 1\right)x^2 - \left(-\frac{28}{7} + 2\right)x + \left(-\frac{28}{7} - 3\right) = 0$$

$\Rightarrow -x^2 + 14x - 49 = 0$

$\Rightarrow x^2 - 14x + 49 = 0 \Rightarrow (x - 7)^2 = 0 \Rightarrow x = 7, 7$ (*1 M*)

When $p = 4$, the given quadratic equation (*i*) becomes

$(8 + 1)x^2 - (28 + 2)x + (28 - 3) = 0 \Rightarrow 9x^2 - 30x + 25 = 0$

$\Rightarrow (3x - 5)^2 = 0 \Rightarrow x = \frac{5}{3}, \frac{5}{3}$

Hence, roots are 7, 7 or $\frac{5}{3}, \frac{5}{3}$. (*1 M*)

4 WORD PROBLEMS BASED ON QUADRATIC EQUATION RELATED TO DAY TO DAY ACTIVITIES

Important Concepts

Methods to Solve Word Problems:

Step I: Consider the first quantity as a variable 'x' and then find the other quantity in terms of 'x' by using the given condition.

Step II: Obtain a quadratic equation in terms of variable x, according to the condition given in the question.

Step III: Simplify the equation obtained in step II by any method like factorisation or quadratic formula to obtain the value(s) of variable x.

Step IV: Further check whether the value(s) of variable x, satisfies the given condition or not.

Real Life Applications

Quadratic equations can be applied to various scenarios, such as throwing a ball, shooting a cannon, diving from a platform and hitting a golf ball.

Different Problem Types

Type I: Applications of Quadratic Equations for Solving Problems on Numbers/Time and Distance/ Ages/ Geometry

Seven years ago, Varun's age was five times the square of Swati's age. Three years hence Swati's age will be two fifth of Varun's age. Find their present ages.

Solution:

Step I: Seven years ago, let Swati's age be x years. Then, seven years ago Varun's age was $5x^2$ years.

Step II: Swati's present age = $(x + 7)$ years, Varun's present age = $(5x^2 + 7)$ years

Three years hence, we have

Swati's age = $(x + 7 + 3)$ years = $(x + 10)$ years

Varun's age =$(5x^2 + 7 + 3)$ years = $(5x^2 + 10)$ years

Step III: It is given that three years hence Swati's age will be $\frac{2}{5}$ of Varun's age.

$\therefore\ x + 10 = \frac{2}{5}(5x^2 + 10) \Rightarrow x + 10 = 2x^2 + 4 \Rightarrow 2x^2 - x - 6 = 0$

$\Rightarrow 2x^2 - 4x + 3x - 6 = 0 \Rightarrow 2x(x - 2) + 3(x - 2) = 0 \Rightarrow x - 2 = 0 \Rightarrow x = 2$

Hence, Swati's present age = $(2 + 7)$ years = 9 years

Varun's present age = $(5 \times 4 + 7)$ years = 27 years

Example 1: The sum of two numbers is 15. If the sum of their reciprocals is $\frac{3}{10}$, find the numbers.

Solution: Let the required numbers be x and $15 - x$. Then, $\frac{1}{x} + \frac{1}{15-x} = \frac{3}{10}$

Simplifying the the Equation:

$\Rightarrow \frac{15-x+x}{x(15-x)} = \frac{3}{10} \Rightarrow \frac{15}{x(15-x)} = \frac{3}{10}$

Having derived the quadratic equation from the given information, our next objective is to find its roots.

$\Rightarrow x^2 - 10x - 5x + 50 = 0 \Rightarrow (x - 10)(x - 5) = 0$

$x - 10 = 0$ or, $x - 5 = 0 \Rightarrow x = 10$ or, $x = 5$

Hence, the two numbers are 10 and 5.

Example 2: A plane left 30 minutes later than the schedule time and in order to reach its destination 1500 km away in time it has to increase its speed by 250 km/hr from its usual speed. Find its usual speed.

Solution: Let the usual speed of the plane be x km/hr.

Then, Time taken to cover 1500 km with the usual speed = $\frac{1500}{x}$ hrs

Time taken to cover 1500 km with the speed of $(x + 250)$ km/hr $= \frac{1500}{x+250}$

$\therefore \frac{1500}{x} = \frac{1500}{x+250} + \frac{1}{2} \Rightarrow \frac{1500}{x} - \frac{1500}{x+250} = \frac{1}{2}$

$\Rightarrow \frac{1500x + 1500 \times 250 - 1500x}{x(x+250)} = \frac{1}{2} \Rightarrow \frac{1500 \times 250}{x^2 + 250x} = \frac{1}{2}$

$\Rightarrow 750000 = x^2 + 250x \Rightarrow 750000 = x^2 + 250x \Rightarrow x^2 + 250x - 750000 = 0 \Rightarrow x^2 + 1000x - 750x - 750000 = 0$

$\Rightarrow x(x + 1000) - 750(x + 1000) = 0 \Rightarrow (x + 1000)(x - 750) = 0$

$\Rightarrow x = -1000$ or, $x = 750 \Rightarrow x = 750$

[$\because$ speed cannot be negative]

Hence, the usual speed of the plane is 750 km/hr.

Example 3: The hypotenuse of a grassy land in the shape of a right triangle is 1 meter more than twice the shortest side. If the third side is 7 meters more than the shortest side, find the sides of the grassland.

Solution: Let the length of the shortest side be x metres. Then, by hypothesis Hypotenuse = $(2x + 1)$ metres, Third side = $(x + 7)$ metres.

By Pythagoras theorem, we have

$(\text{Hypotenuse})^2$ = Sum of the square of the remaining two sides

$\Rightarrow (2x + 1)^2 = x^2 + (x + 7)^2 \Rightarrow 4x^2 + 4x + 1 = 2x^2 + 14x + 49$

$\Rightarrow 2x^2 - 10x - 48 = 0 \Rightarrow x^2 - 5x - 24 = 0$

$\Rightarrow x^2 - 8x + 3x - 24 = 0 \Rightarrow (x - 8)(x + 3) = 0 \Rightarrow x = 8, -3 \Rightarrow x = 8$ [$\because x = -3$ is not possible]

Hence, the lengths of the sides of the grassy land are 8 meters, 17 meters and 15 meters.

COMPETENCY BASED SOLVED EXAMPLES

Multiple Choice Questions

(1 M)

1. **The sum of two numbers is 10 and their product is 21. Then two numbers are** ***(Un)***

(*a*) 3 and 7 (*b*) 5 and 5

(*c*) 6 and 4 (*d*) 5 and 3

Sol. Let the two numbers be x and y:

$\therefore x + y = 10$ ... (*i*)

and $xy = 21$ ... (*ii*)

$\therefore y = 10 - x$

Now, substitute this in eq. (*ii*)

$x(10 - x) = 21 \Rightarrow x = 3$ and 7

From eqn. (*i*)

$y = 7$

2. **The length of a rectangle is 4 cm more than twice its width, and the area of the rectangle is 48 cm². Then dimensions of the rectangle are** ***(Re)***

(*a*) 6 cm by 8 cm (*b*) 4 cm by 12 cm

(*c*) 5 cm by 10 cm (*d*) 3 cm by 16 cm

Sol. Let width = x

$\therefore$ Length = $(4 + 2x)$

According to the question. We get equation

$2x^2 + 4x = 48 \Rightarrow x = 4$ and $x = -6$

$\therefore$ width = 4 cm

Length = $4 + 2 \times 4 = 12$ cm.

3. **A boat travels 48 kilometers upstream in 6 hours. The same boat travels 72 kilometers downstream in 4 hours. The speed of the boat in still water and the speed of the current is** ***(Cr)***

(*a*) 10 km/h and 2 km/h (*b*) 12 km/h and 4 km/h

(*c*) 15 km/h and 3 km/h (*d*) 13 km/h and 5 km/h

Sol. Let the speed of boat in still water be x km/h and the speed of the current be y km/h

$\therefore$ Speed upstream = $(x - y)$ km/h = $\frac{48}{6} = 8$ km/h

Speed downstream = $(x + y)$ km/h = $\frac{72}{4} = 18$ km/h

$x - y = 8$ ... (*i*)

$x + y = 18$ ... (*ii*)

On adding equation (*i*) and (*ii*), we get

$2x = 26 \Rightarrow x = 13$ km/h

Form equation (*ii*), $y = 18 - x = 18 - 13$

= 5 km/h

Therefore, the speed of the boat in still water is 13 km/h and the speed of the current is 5 km/h.

4. **The sum of the ages of a father and son is 45 years. Five years ago, the product of their ages (in years) was 124. Then present age of the father is** ***(Re)***

(*a*) 40 years (*b*) 36 years

(*c*) 50 years (*d*) 55 years

Sol. Let the present age of the father be x years

Then, the present age of the son = $(45 - x)$

5 years ago, age of the father = $(x - 5)$ years

5 years ago, age of the son = $(45 - x - 5)$ years = $(40 - x)$ years

$\therefore (x - 5)(40 - x) = 124 \Rightarrow -x^2 + 45x - 200 = 124$

$\Rightarrow x^2 - 45x + 324 = 0 \Rightarrow x^2 - 36x - 9x + 324 = 0$

$\Rightarrow (x - 36)(x - 9) = 0 \Rightarrow x = 36$ or $x = 9$

$\Rightarrow x = 9$ (Rejected, because father's age can not be 9)

Hence, the present age of father is 36 years.

Answer Key

1. (*a*) 2. (*b*) 3. (*d*) 4. (*b*)

Assertion and Reason

(1 M)

Direction: In the following questions, A statement of Assertion (A) is followed by a statement of Reason (R). Mark the correct choice as.

(*a*) Both Assertion (A) and Reason (R) are true, and Reason (R) is the correct explanation of Assertion (A).

(*b*) Both Assertion (A) and Reason (R) are true, but Reason (R) is not the correct explanation of Assertion (A).

(*c*) Assertion (A) is true, but Reason (R) is false.

(*d*) Assertion (A) is false, but Reason (R) is true.

1. **Assertion (A): A train travels at a speed of 50 km/hour and takes 8 hours to cover a certain distance. If the train had traveled 50 km/hour faster, it would have taken only 4 hours to cover the same distance.**

Reason (R): The distance covered by the train can be represented by a quadratic equation. *(Un)*

Sol. Assertion: Let the distance covered by the train be x km

$\therefore x = 50$ km/h × 8 hours

= 400 km

Given, the train travels 50 km/h faster than its original speed.

$\therefore$ Speed = (50 + 50) km/h = 100 km/h

Time taken to cover 100 km/h = 4 hours

$\therefore$ Distance = 100 km/h × 4 hours = 400 km

Hence, assertion is true.

Also, reason is true and reason is the correct explanation of the assertion.

2. **Assertion (A): The area of a rectangular field is 240 square meters. If the length of the field is 4 meters more than twice its breadth, then the area of the field can be represented by a quadratic equation.**

Reason (R): The area of a rectangle can be represented by the quadratic equation. *(Cr)*

Sol. Assertion: Let breadth of the field = x meters

Length of the field = $(2x + 4)$ meters

Given, area = 240 m^2

$\therefore (2x + 4)x = 240$

$\Rightarrow 2x^2 + 4x - 240 = 0$

Hence, the area of the field can be represented by a quadratic equation.

$\therefore$ Assertion is true.

Reason is also true because the area of a rectangle can indeed be represented by a quadratic equation which will involve the product of length and breadth of the rectangle, which are both variables in this case.

$\therefore$ Reason is the correct explanation of the assertion.

3. **Assertion (A): A boat travels upstream with a speed of 6 km/h and downstream with a speed of 10 km/h. The speed of the boat in still water is 8 km/h.**

Reason (R): The speed of the current is 2 km/h. *(Re)*

Sol. The speed of the boat in still water can be found by using the formula: speed of boat in still water = (speed downstream + speed upstream)/2. Here, (10 + 6)/2 = 8 km/h.

Assertion is true. The speed of the current can be found by subtracting the speed upstream from the speed of the boat in still water. Here, 8 – 6 = 2 km/h.

Reason is true and reason is the correct explanation of assertion.

Answer Key

1. (a) 2. (a) 3. (a)

Subjective Questions

Very Short Answer Type Questions (1 or 2 M)

1. **When a marble is dropped from an initial height, d metres, with an initial speed, v m/s, the height of the marble at time t is represented by $h(t) = vt - 2t^2 + d$.**

A marble is dropped from a height of 48 m with an initial speed, 10 m/s. How long does it take for the marble to hit the ground? Show your steps and give valid reasons. *(Un)* **(CBSE CFPQ, 2023)**

Sol. Given:

Height = d metres = 48 m

Speed = v m/s = 10 m/s *(½ M)*

$h(t) = vt - 2t^2 + d$

By substituting value of 'd' and 'v' in equation we get

$h(t) = 10t - 2t^2 + 48 = -2t^2 + 10t + 48 = -2t^2 + 16t - 6t + 48$

$= -2t(t - 8) - 6(t - 8) = (-2t - 6)(t - 8) \Rightarrow t = \frac{6}{-2} = -3$

and $t = 8$ *(1 M)*

Since, time cannot be negative

$\therefore t = 8s$ *(½ M)*

2. **The sum of two numbers is 12 and their product is 35. What are the two numbers?** *(Re)*

Sol. Let the two numbers be x and y.

We know that:

$x + y = 12$ ... (*i*)

$xy = 35$ ... (*ii*)

From the equation (*i*), we get $y = 12 - x$. Substituting this into the equation (*ii*), we have:

$x(12 - x) = 35 \Rightarrow 12x - x^2 = 35$

$\Rightarrow x^2 - 12x + 35 = 0 \Rightarrow x^2 - 7x - 5x + 35 = 0$ *(1 M)*

$\Rightarrow (x - 7)(x - 5) = 0$

we get $x = 5$ or $x = 7$.

When $x = 5$, $y = 12 - 5 = 7$ and when $x = 7$, $y = 12 - 7 = 5$.

Therefore, the two numbers are 5 and 7. *(1 M)*

3. **The area of a rectangle is 40 square meters. If the length of the rectangle is 6 meters more than its width, what are the dimensions of the rectangle?** *(Cr)*

Sol. Let x meter be the width of the rectangle. Then, the length is $(x + 6)$ meter. We know that the area of the rectangle is 40 sq.m.

$\therefore x(x + 6) = 40 \Rightarrow x^2 + 6x - 40 = 0$

$\Rightarrow x^2 + 10x - 4x - 40 = 0$ *(1 M)*

$\Rightarrow (x + 10)(x - 4) = 0 \Rightarrow x + 10 = 0$ or $x - 4 = 0$

Solving for x, we get $x = 4$ or $x = -10$. Since the width cannot be negative, we have $x = 4$, length = $(x + 4) = 6 + 4$ = 10 meters. Therefore, the dimensions of the rectangle are 4 meters by 10 meters. *(1 M)*

Short Answer Type Questions (2 or 3 M)

1. A motor boat, whose speed is 15 *km/hr* in still water, goes 30 *km* downstream and comes back in 4 hours 30 minutes. Determine the speed of the stream. *(Re)*

Sol. Let the speed of the stream be x *km/hr*

$\Rightarrow$ The speed of the boat downstream = $(15 + x)$ *km/hr* and the speed of the boat upstream = $(15 - x)$ *km/hr*.

As we know, $\text{Time} = \dfrac{\text{Distance}}{\text{Speed}}$

Now, time taken to go 30 *km* downstream $= \dfrac{30}{15+x}$ *hrs* and

time taken to come back 30 *km* upstream $= \dfrac{30}{15-x}$ *hrs* *(1 M)*

Given: Total time for journey = 4 hours 30 minutes

$= 4\frac{1}{2}\ hrs = \frac{9}{2}\ hrs$

$\therefore\ \dfrac{30}{15+x} + \dfrac{30}{15-x} = 4\dfrac{1}{2}$ *(½ M)*

$\Rightarrow\ \dfrac{30(15-x)+30(15+x)}{(15+x)(15-x)} = \dfrac{9}{2}$

$\Rightarrow\ \dfrac{450-30x+450+30x}{225-x^2} = \dfrac{9}{2} \Rightarrow \dfrac{900}{225-x^2} = \dfrac{9}{2}$

$\Rightarrow\ 2 \times 900 = 9\,(225 - x^2) \Rightarrow 2 \times 100 = 225 - x^2$

$\Rightarrow\ x^2 = 225 - 200 \Rightarrow x^2 = 25 \Rightarrow x = \pm 5$ *(½ M)*

Neglecting $x = -5$, as speed cannot be negative.

$\therefore$ Speed of stream is 5 *km/hr.* *(1 M)*

2. A truck travels a distance of 300 *km* at a uniform speed. If the speed of the truck is increased by 5 *km/hr*, the journey would have taken two hours less. Find the original speed of the truck. *(An)*

Sol. Let the original speed of the truck be x *km/hr*.

In 1st case, Distance = 300 *km* and speed = x *km/hr*.

$\Rightarrow$ Time taken $= \dfrac{\text{distance}}{\text{speed}} = \dfrac{300}{x}$ *hrs.*

In 2nd case, Distance = 300 *km* and

speed = $(x + 5)$ *km/hr*.

$\Rightarrow$ Time taken $= \dfrac{\text{distance}}{\text{speed}} = \dfrac{300}{x+5}$ *hrs.*

According to the question,

$\dfrac{300}{x} - \dfrac{300}{x+5} = 2$ *(1 M)*

$\Rightarrow\ \dfrac{300(x+5)-300x}{x(x+5)} = 2 \Rightarrow \dfrac{300x+1500-300x}{x^2+5x} = 2$

$\Rightarrow\ 2(x^2 + 5x) = 1500 \Rightarrow x^2 + 5x - 750 = 0$

$\Rightarrow\ x^2 + 30x - 25x - 750 = 0$ *(½ M)*

$\Rightarrow\ (x + 30)(x - 25) = 0 \Rightarrow x + 30 = 0$ or $x - 25 = 0$

$\therefore\ x = -30$ or $x = 25$ *(1 M)*

Neglecting $x = -30$, as speed can't be negative

$\therefore$ Speed of truck is 25 *km/hr.* *(½ M)*

3. In a cinema hall, the number of columns was equal to the number of seats in each column. If the number of columns is doubled and the number of seats in each column is reduced by 5, then the total number of seats is increased by 375. How many columns were there? *(Ap)*

Sol. Let the number of columns be x

No. of seats in each columns = x

Total number of seats = Number of seats in each column × number of columns = $x \times x = x^2$ *(½ M)*

Now, the new no. of columns = $2x$ and the new no. of seats in each column = $x - 5$

The total number of seats now will be = $2x(x - 5)$.

According to the question:

$2x(x - 5) - x^2 = 375$ *(½ M)*

$\Rightarrow\ 2x^2 - 10x - x^2 = 375 \Rightarrow x^2 - 10x - 375 = 0$

$\Rightarrow\ x^2 - 25x + 15x - 375 = 0$ *(1 M)*

$\Rightarrow\ x(x - 25) + 15(x - 25) = 0 \Rightarrow (x - 25)(x + 15) = 0$

$\Rightarrow\ x - 25 = 0$ or $x + 15 = 0 \Rightarrow x = 25$ or $x = -15$

Neglecting $x = -15$, as number of column cannot be negative.

$\therefore$ Number of columns = 25 *(1 M)*

4. At present Asha's age (in years) is 2 more than the square of her daughter Nisha's age. When Nisha grows to her mother's present age, Asha's age would be one year less than 10 times the present age of Nisha. Find the present ages of both Asha and Nisha. *(Re)* **(NCERT Exemplar)**

Sol. Taking the present age of Asha = x years

The present age of her daughter Nisha = y years *(½ M)*

At Present, Asha's age, $x = (y^2) + 2$ ... *(i)*

Age of Nisha will be equal to age of her mother (x) after no of years Age of Mother – Age of Daughter *(½ M)*

$= (x - y) = (y^2 + 2 - y) = (y^2 - y + 2)$ years

$\therefore$ Age of (Nisha) daughter after $(y^2 - y + 2)$ years $= y^2 - y + 2 + y = (y^2 + 2)$ years

Age of Asha (mother) after $(y^2 - y + 2)$ years

$= x + y^2 - y + 2 = y^2 + 2 + y^2 - y + 2$ [From *(i)*]

$= 2y^2 - y + 4$ years *(½ M)*

After $(y^2 - y - 2)$ years, age of Asha $= 2y^2 - y + 4 = 10y - 1$

$\Rightarrow 2y^2 - y - 10y + 5 = 0 \Rightarrow 2y^2 - 11y + 5 = 0$

$\Rightarrow 2y^2 - 10y - 1y + 5 = 0 \Rightarrow 2y\,(y - 5) - 1\,(y - 5) = 0$

$\Rightarrow (y - 5)(2y - 1) = 0 \Rightarrow (y - 5) = 0$ or $2y - 1 = 0$

$\Rightarrow y = 5$ or $y = +\dfrac{1}{2}$ years *(½ M)*

From *(i)*, we have

$x = y^2 + 2$

Putting $y = 5$, we have

$\therefore\ x = (5)^2 + 2 = 25 + 2 = 27$

Mother's age can never be $\dfrac{1}{9}$ years, so it is not taken.

So, the ages of Asha and Nisha are 27 years and 5 years respectively. *(1 M)*

5. **A plane left 30 minutes late than its scheduled time and in order to reach the destination 1500 *km* away in time, it had to increase its speed by 100 *km/h* from the usual speed. Find its usual speed.** ***(Un)***

Sol. Let the usual speed of plane be x *km/h.*

Increased speed = $(x + 100)$*km/h.*

$\therefore$ Distance to cover = 1500 *km.*

Time taken by plane with usual speed $= \frac{1500}{x}$ *hrs.*

Time taken by plane with increased speed $= \frac{1500}{(100+x)}$ *hrs*

According to the question,

$\Rightarrow \frac{1500}{x} - \frac{1500}{(100+x)} = \frac{30}{60} = \frac{1}{2}$ *(1 M)*

$\Rightarrow \frac{1500\times100}{x^2+100x} = \frac{1}{2} \Rightarrow x^2 + 100x = 300000$

$\Rightarrow x^2 + 100x - 300000 = 0$

$\Rightarrow x^2 + 600x - 500x - 300000 = 0$ *(1 M)*

$\Rightarrow x(x + 600) - 500(x + 600) = 0 \Rightarrow (x + 600)(x - 500) = 0$

Either $x + 600 = 0$

$x = -600$ (Rejected), as speed can't be negative

or $x - 500 = 0$

$x = 500$

$\therefore$ Usual speed of plane = 500 *km/hr.* *(1 M)*

6. **The product of two successive integral multiples of 5 is 1050. Determine the multiples.** ***(Re)***

Sol. Let the two successive integral multiples of 5 be x and $(x + 5)$.

Then, according to question,

$\Rightarrow x(x + 5) = 1050$ *(½ M)*

$\Rightarrow x^2 + 5x - 1050 = 0 \Rightarrow x^2 + 35x - 30x - 1050 = 0$ *(½ M)*

$\Rightarrow x(x + 35) - 30(x + 35) = 0 \Rightarrow (x - 30)(x + 35) = 0$

$\Rightarrow x - 30 = 0$ or $x + 35 = 0 \Rightarrow x = 30$ or -35 *(1 M)*

When $x = 30$,

Multiples are 30 and 30 + 5 = 35

When $x = -35$,

Multiples are –35 and –35 + 5 = –30 *(1 M)*

7. **In a class test, the sum of Shrishti's marks in maths and science is 45. If she had 1 more mark in maths and 1 less in science, the product of marks would have been 500. Find her marks in maths and science.** ***(Cr)***

Sol. Let the Shrishti's marks in maths be x.

Then, her marks in science = $45 - x$

Now, according to the question,

$(x + 1)[(45 - x) - 1] = 500$ *(½ M)*

$(x + 1)(44 - x) = 500$

$\Rightarrow 44x + 44 - x^2 - x = 500 \Rightarrow x^2 - 43x + 456 = 0$

$\Rightarrow x^2 - 24x - 19x + 456 = 0$ *(½ M)*

$\Rightarrow x(x - 24) - 19(x - 24) = 0 \Rightarrow (x - 19)(x - 24) = 0$

$\therefore x = 19, 24$ *(1 M)*

If $x = 19$, then $(45 - x) = 45 - 19 = 26$

If $x = 24$, then $(45 - x) = 45 - 24 = 21$ *(1 M)*

Hence, she either got 19 marks in maths and 26 marks in science or 24 marks in maths and 21 marks in science.

8. **Find two consecutive odd positive integers, sum of whose squares is 290.** ***(Re)***

Sol. Let one of the odd positive integer be x then the other odd positive integer is $x + 2$ their sum of squares $= x^2 + (x + 2)^2$

$= x^2 + x^2 + 4x + 4$ *(1 M)*

$= 2x^2 + 4x + 4$

Given that their sum of squares = 290

$\Rightarrow 2x^2 + 4x + 4 = 290 \Rightarrow 2x^2 + 4x = 290 - 4 = 286$

$\Rightarrow 2x^2 + 4x - 286 = 0 \Rightarrow 2(x^2 + 2x - 143) = 0$

$\Rightarrow x^2 + 2x - 143 = 0 \Rightarrow x^2 + 13x - 11x - 143 = 0$ *(1 M)*

$\Rightarrow x(x + 13) - 11(x + 13) = 0 \Rightarrow (x - 11)(x + 13) = 0$

$\Rightarrow (x - 11) = 0$ or $(x + 13) = 0$ Therefore, $x = 11$ or -13

According to question, x is a positive odd integer.

Hence, We take positive value of x

So, $x = 11$ and $(x + 2) = 11 + 2 = 13$ *(1 M)*

Therefore, the odd positive integers are 11 and 13.

Long Answer Type Questions (4 or 5 M)

1. **The sum of the ages of a boy and his sister (in years) is 25 and product of their ages is 150 . Find their present ages.** ***(Ev)* (CBSE, 2022)**

Sol. Let boy's age be x year

then his sister's age be $(25 - x)$ years. *(1 M)*

$\therefore x(25 - x) = 150$

$\Rightarrow 25x - x^2 = 150$ *(1 M)*

$\Rightarrow x^2 - 25x = 150 = 0$

$x = \frac{25 \pm \sqrt{625-600}}{2}$ *(1 M)*

$= \frac{25\pm5}{2} = 15$ or 10

Hence, their present ages are 10 years or 15 years. *(1 M)*

2. **A motor boat whose speed is 18 km/h in still water takes 1 hour more to go 24 km upstream than to return downstream to the same spot. Find the speed of the stream.** ***(Un)* (CBSE SQP, 2023)**

Sol. Let the speed of the stream = x km/hr *(½ M)*

Speed of boat 18 km/hr

Upstream speed = $(18 - x)$ km/hr

Downstream speed = $(18 + x)$ km/hr

Time taken (upstream) $= \frac{24}{(18-x)}$

Time taken (downstream) $= \frac{24}{(18+x)}$

ATQ

$\frac{24}{(18-x)} = \frac{24}{(18+x)} + 1$ *(1 M)*

$$\Rightarrow \frac{24}{(18-x)} - \frac{24}{(18+x)} = 1$$

$\Rightarrow 24(18 + x) - 24(18 - x) = (18 - x)(18 + x)$

$\Rightarrow 24(18 + x - 18 + x) = (18)^2 - x^2$

$\Rightarrow 24(2x) = 324 - x^2 \Rightarrow 48 - 324 - x^2$

$\Rightarrow x^2 + 48x - 324 = 0$ *(1 M)*

$\Rightarrow x^2 - 6x + 54x - 324 = 0 \Rightarrow x(x - 6) + 54(x - 6) = 0$

$\Rightarrow (x - 6)(x + 54) = 0 \Rightarrow x - 6 = 0 \quad , \quad x + 54 = 0$

$\Rightarrow x = 6 \quad , \quad x = -54$ *(1 M)*

Speed cannot be negative

$\Rightarrow$ Speed of steam = 6 km/hr *(1 M)*

3. A rectangular park is to be designed whose breadth is 3m less than its length. Its area is to be 4 square metres more than the area of a park that has already been made in the shape of an isosceles triangle with its base as the breadth of the rectangular park and of altitude 12 m. Find the length and breadth of the park. ***(Ap)* (CBSE 2020)**

Sol. Let the length of the rectangular park be x *m* then, breadth be $(x - 3)$ m

$\therefore$ Area of rectangular park = $x(x - 3)m^2$ *(½ M)*

Area of isosceles triangular park $= \frac{1}{2}(x-3) \times 12\, m^2$

$= 6(x - 3)m^2$ *(1 M)*

According to the given condition,

$\Rightarrow x(x - 3) - 6(x - 3) = 4 \Rightarrow x^2 - 3x - 6x + 18 = 4$

$\Rightarrow x^2 - 9x + 14 = 0 \Rightarrow x^2 - 7x - 2x + 14 = 0$ *(1 M)*

$\Rightarrow (x - 2)(x - 7) = 0 \Rightarrow x = 2$ or 7 *(½ M)*

$\therefore x = 7$ m

(As breadth can't be negative)

and $x - 3 = (7 - 3)$m = 4m

Hence, length and breadth of the rectangular park is tm and 4m respectively. *(1 M)*

4. Rashmi can row her boat at a speed of 5 *km/h* in still water. If she takes 1 hour more to row the boat 5.25 *km* upstream than to return downstream, find the speed of the boat in upstream. ***(Re)***

Sol. Let the speed of the stream be x *km/h*

$\therefore$ Speed of the boat in upstream = $(5 - x)$ *km/h* *(½ M)*

Speed of the boat in downstream = $(5 + x)$ *km/h* *(½ M)*

We know, Time $= \frac{\text{Distance}}{\text{Speed}}$

Time for going 5.25 *km* upstream $= \frac{5.25}{5-x}$

Time for returning 5.25 *km* downstream $= \frac{5.25}{5+x}$ *(½ M)*

Therefore, according to the question,

$$\frac{5.25}{5-x} - \frac{5.25}{5+x} = 1$$ *(1 M)*

$$\Rightarrow \frac{525}{100}\left(\frac{1}{5-x} - \frac{1}{5+x}\right) = 1 \Rightarrow 21\left(\frac{5+x-5+x}{25-x^2}\right) = 4$$

$\Rightarrow 21(2x) = 4(25 - x^2) \Rightarrow 42x = 100 - 4x^2$

$\Rightarrow 2x^2 + 21x - 50 = 0$ *(1 M)*

$\Rightarrow 2x^2 + 25x - 4x - 50 = 0 \Rightarrow (2x + 25)(x - 2) = 0$

i.e., $x = 2$ or $-\frac{25}{2}$ *(½ M)*

Since, speed cannot be negative, so we reject $x = \frac{-25}{2}$.

Thus, the speed of the stream is 2 *km/h*.

And speed of the boat in upstream = $(5 - 2)$ *km/h*

= 3 *km/h*. *(1 M)*

5. At *t* minutes past 2 pm, the time needed by the minutes hand of a clock to show 3 pm was found to be 3 minutes less than $\frac{t^2}{4}$ minutes. Find *t*. ***(Cr)***

Sol. Time taken by the minute hand to travel from 2 pm to 3 pm = 60 minutes *(½ M)*

So, t minutes past 2, the time needed to show 3 pm is $(60 - t)$ *(½ M)*

According to given question,

$(60 - t) = \frac{t^2}{4} - 3$ *(½ M)*

$\Rightarrow 60 - t = \frac{t^2 - 12}{4} \Rightarrow 240 - 4t = t^2 - 12$ *(½ M)*

$\Rightarrow t^2 + 4t - 12 - 240 = 0 \Rightarrow t^2 + 4t - 252 = 0$ *(½ M)*

$\Rightarrow t^2 + 18t - 14t - 252 = 0$ *(1 M)*

$\Rightarrow t(t + 18) - 14(t + 18) = 0 \Rightarrow (t - 14)(t + 18) = 0$

$\Rightarrow t - 14 = 0$ or $t + 18 = 0$

$\therefore t = 14$ *(½ M)*

and $t = -18$ (since, time can not be negative, $t = -18$ is neglected)

Hence, value of time is 14 minutes. *(1 M)*

6. A two digit number is such that the product of its digits is 14 . If 45 is added to the number; the digits interchange their places. Find the number. ***(Un)* (CBSE, 2020)**

Sol. Given $xy = 14$ ...(i)

The number is $(10x + y)$

Given that when 45 is added to the number the digits gets interchanged.

Hence $10x + y + 45 = 10y + x$ *(1 M)*

$9x - 9y + 45 = 0$

$x - y + 5 = 0$ ...(ii) *(½ M)*

From (i) and (ii), we get

$x - (14/x) + 5 = 0$

$x^2 + 5x - 14 = 0$ *(½ M)*

$x^2 + 7x - 2x - 14 = 0$

$x(x + 7) - 2(x + 7) = 0$

$(x + 7)(x - 2) = 0$

$x = -7$ or $x = 2$ *(1 M)*

Since the digits cannot be negative, $x = 2$

$xy = 14$

Therefore, $y = 7$

The number is $10x + y = 27$ *(1 M)*

MISCELLANEOUS EXERCISE

Multiple Choice Questions

(1 M)

1. The discriminant of the quadratic equation $2x^2 - 4x + 3 = 0$ is **(CBSE, 2020)**
   (a) –8 (b) 10
   (c) 8 (d) $2\sqrt{2}$
2. The discriminant of the quadratic equation $5x^2 - 12\sqrt{3}x + 7 = 0$ is:
   (a) 572 (b) 292
   (c) –572 (d) None of these
3. The roots of quadratic equation $2x^2 - 12x + 15 = 0$ are
   (a) real (b) imaginary
   (c) equal (d) real & equal
4. Value(s) of k for which the quadratic equation $2x^2 - kx + k = 0$ has equal roots is **(CBSE SQP, 2023)**
   (a) 0 only (b) 4
   (c) 8 only (d) 0, 8

Assertion and Reason

(1 M)

Direction: In the following questions, A statement of Assertion (A) is followed by a statement of Reason (R). Mark the correct choice as.

(a) Both Assertion (A) and Reason (R) are true, and Reason (R) is the correct explanation of Assertion (A).

(b) Both Assertion (A) and Reason (R) are true, but Reason (R) is not the correct explanation of Assertion (A).

(c) Assertion (A) is true, but Reason (R) is false.

(d) Assertion (A) is false, but Reason (R) is true.

1. **Assertion (A):** If $5+\sqrt{7}$ is a root of a quadratic equation with rational coefficients, then its other root is $5-\sqrt{7}$.

   Reason (R): Surd roots of a quadratic equation with rational co-efficients occur in conjugate pairs.
2. **Assertion (A):** If roots of the equation $x^2 - bx + c = 0$ are two consecutive integers, then $b^2 - 4c = 1$.

   Reason (R): If a, b, c are odd integers then the roots of the equation $4abcx^2 + (b^2 - 4ac)x - b = 0$ are real and distinct.

Subjective Questions

Very Short Answer Type Questions

(1 or 2 M)

1. **If quadratic equation $3x^2 - 4x + k = 0$ has equal roots, then the value of k is________.** *(Ap)* **(CBSE, 2020)**
2. Find the nature of roots of quadratic equation $x^2 + x + 1 = 0$.
3. Solve $36x^2 - 676 = 0$.
4. Solve for x: $12abx^2 - (9a^2 - 8b^2)x - 6ab = 0$.
5. Value of the roots of the quadratic equation, $x^2 - x - 6 = 0$ are ______. **(CBSE, 2020)**

Short Answer Type Questions

(2 or 3 M)

1. A quilt maker has a rectangular quilt measuring 12 units by 8 units. He wants to add a border to it as shown in the figure below. He has 64 sq units of fabric for the border. **(CBSE CFPQ, 2023)**

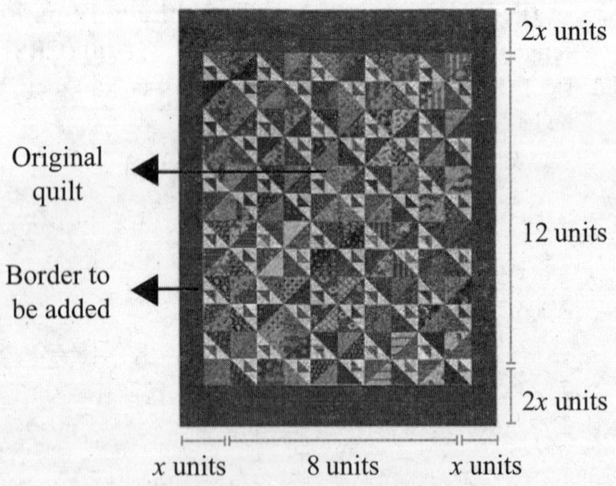

   (i) If x and $2x$ are the widths of the border as shown, frame a quadratic equation using the total area enclosed by the new quilt (with the border).

   (ii) Find the measures of the new quilt (with the border).
2. Find the number of real roots in quadratic equation $(x - 1)^2 + (x - 2)^2 + (x - 3)^2 = 0$.
3. Ekom is selling tickets for a ride on a giant wheel. If he charges ₹ 30, he will sell 40 tickets. For each ₹ 1 decrease in price, 9 more tickets would get sold. Represent the above problem in the form of a quadratic equation.
4. A fruit grower has 400 crates of apples ready for market and will have 15 more crates for each day the shipment is delayed. The price per crate decreases by ₹ 3. The present price is ₹ 70. Form a quadratic equation to represent the above situation.
5. The length of a rectangular park is 5 metres more than twice its breadth. If the area of the park is 250 sq m, find the length and breadth of the park. **(CBSE, 2022)**

Long Answer Type Questions

(4 or 5 M)

1. Two water taps together can fill a tank in $9\frac{3}{8}$ hours. The tap of larger diameter takes 10 hours less than the smaller one to fill the tank separately. Find the time in which each tap can separately fill the tank.

2. An express train takes 1 hour less than a passenger train to travel 132 *km* between Mysore and Bangalore (without taking into consideration the time they stop at intermediate stations). If the average speed of the express train is 11 *km/h* more than that of the passenger train, find the average speed of the two trains.

3. Sum of the areas of two squares is 468 m^2. If the difference of their perimeters is 24 *m*, find the sides of the two squares.

4. Out of a group of total students of class *x*, $\frac{7}{2}$ times the square root of the total number are playing cricket. The two remaining ones are playing badminton. Find the total number of students.

5. In the centre of a rectangular lawn of dimensions 50 *m* × 40 *m*, a rectangular pond has to be constructed so that the area of the grass surrounding the pond would be 1184 m^2 [see Fig.]. Find the length and breadth of the pond.

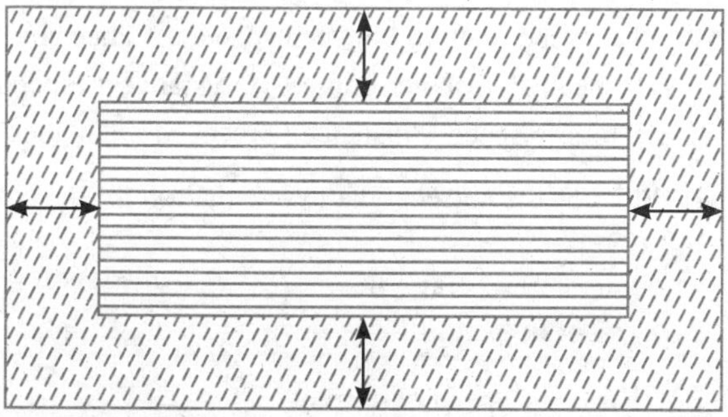

6. To fill a swimming pool two pipes are used. If the pipe of larger diameter is used for 4 hours and the pipe of smaller diameter for 9 hours, only half of the pool can be filled. Find how much long it would take for each pipe to fill the pool separately, if the pipe of smaller diameter takes 10 hours more than the pipe of larger diameter?

7. A train travels 360 km at a uniform speed. If the speed had been 5 km/h more, it would have taken 1 hour less for the same journey. Find the speed of the train.

(CBSE SQP, 2023)

Case Based Questions

Case Based-I: Suppose a company wants to construct a rectangular park. If length that is 25 meters longer than the width. The area of the park should be 600 square meters. To determine the length of the park, the company needs to solve a quadratic equation. Read the following and answer the questions.

(*i*) What is the quadratic equation that represents the area of the rectangular park?

(*ii*) What is the length of the rectangular park?

OR

What is the value of the discriminant of the quadratic equation?

(*iii*) What is the value of the coefficient of x^2 in the quadratic equation?

Case Based-II: The two gears shown in the figure resemble two circles which touch each other externally. The sum of their areas is 130π *sq. cm* and distance between their centres is 14 *cm*.

(*i*) Taking the radius of one circle to be *x cm*, the quadratic equation for the situation described above is

(*a*) $x^2 - 16x + 63 = 0$ (*b*) $x^2 - 16x - 63 = 0$

(*c*) $x^2 - 14x + 33 = 0$ (*d*) $x^2 + 14x - 33 = 0$

(*ii*) The roots of the quadratic equation $abx^2 + (b^2 - ac)x - bc = 0$ are

(*a*) Real and equal (*b*) Real and distinct

(*c*) No real roots exist (*d*) None of the above

(*iii*) The value of *p* for which the quadratic equation $x(x - 4) + p = 0$ has real and distinct roots, is

(*a*) $p < 4$ (*b*) $p > 4$

(*c*) $p < -4$ (*d*) $p > -4$

Case Based-III: Due to some technical problems, an aeroplane started late by one hour from its starting point. The pilot decided to increase the speed of the aeroplane by 100 *km/hr* from its usual speed, to cover a journey of 1200 *km* in time.

(*i*) The roots of the quadratic equation formed in this situation are

(*a*) Real and distinct (*b*) Real and equal

(*c*) No real roots exist (*d*) None of the above

(*ii*) The values of *k* for which the difference between the roots of the equation $x^2 + kx + 3 = 0$ is 2, is

(*a*) 0 (*b*) +2 (*c*) +4 (*d*) +8

(*iii*) The values of *m* and *n* if $x = 2$ and $x = 3$ are solutions of the equation $3x^2 - mx + 2n = 0$, are

(*a*) $m = 9, n = 15$ (*b*) $m = 15, n = 9$

(*c*) $m = 3, n = 6$ (*d*) $m = 6, n = 15$

Case Based-IV: Raj and Ajay are very close friends. Both the families decide to go to Ranikhet by their own cars. Raj's car travels at a speed of x km/h while Ajay's car travels 5 km/h faster than Raj's car. Raj took 4 hours more than Ajay to complete the journey of 400 km. **(CBSE QB)**

Based on above situation answer the following questions

(*i*) What will be the distance covered by Ajay's car in two hours?

(*a*) $2(x + 5)$ km (*b*) $(x - 5)$ km

(*c*) $2(x + 10)$ km (*d*) $(2x + 5)$ km

(*ii*) The quadratic equation in terms of speed of Raj's car is

(*a*) $x^2 - 5x - 500 = 0$ (*b*) $x^2 + 4x - 400 = 0$

(*c*) $x^2 + 5x - 500 = 0$ (*d*) $x^2 - 4x + 400 = 0$

(*iii*) What is the speed of Raj's car?

(*a*) 20 km/hour (*b*) 15 km/hour

(*c*) 25 km/hour (*d*) 10 km/hour

(*iv*) How much time Ajay took to travel 400 km?

(*a*) 20 hour (*b*) 40 hour

(*c*) 25 hour (*d*) 16 hour

(*v*) What is the speed of Ajay's car?

(*a*) 15 km/h (*b*) 20 km/h

(*c*) 25 km/h (*d*) 30 km/h

Case Based-V: The speed of a motor boat is 20 km/hr. For covering the distance of 15 km, the boat took 1 hour more for upstream than downstream. **(CBSE QB)**

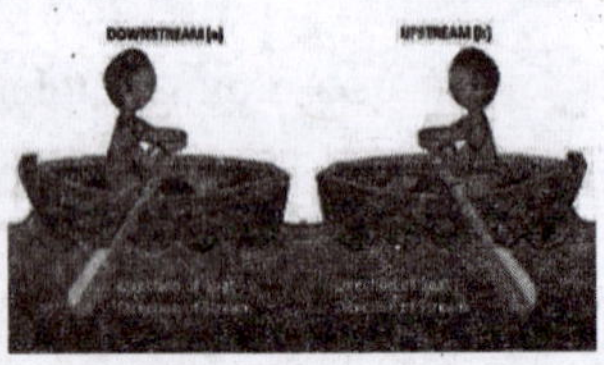

(*i*) Let speed of the stream be x km/hr then speed of the motorboat in upstream will be

(*a*) 20 km/h (*b*) $(20 + x)$ km/h

(*c*) $(20 - x)$ km/h (*d*) 2 km/h

(*ii*) What is the relation between speed, distance and time?

(*a*) speed = (distance)/time (*b*) distance = (speed)/time

(*c*) time = speed × distance (*d*) speed = distance × time

(*iii*) Which is the correct quadratic equation for the speed of the current?

(*a*) $x^2 + 30x - 200 = 0$ (*b*) $x^2 + 20x - 400 = 0$

(*c*) $x^2 + 30x - 400 = 0$ (*d*) $x^2 - 20x - 400 = 0$

(*iv*) What is the speed of current?

(*a*) 20 km/hour (*b*) 10 km/hour

(*c*) 15 km/hour (*d*) 25 km/hour

(*v*) How much time boat took in downstream?

(*a*) 90 minutes (*b*) 15 minutes

(*c*) 30 minutes (*d*) 45 minutes

ANSWER KEYS

Multiple Choice Questions

1. (*a*) **2.** (*b*) **3.** (*a*) **4.** (*d*)

Assertion and Reason

1. (*a*) **2.** (*b*)

Case Based Questions

Case Based-II

(*i*) (*c*) (*ii*) (*b*) (*iii*) (*a*)

Case Based-III

(*i*) (*a*) (*ii*) (*c*) (*iii*) (*b*)

Case Based-IV

(*i*) (*a*) (*ii*) (*c*) (*iii*) (*a*) (*iv*) (*d*) (*v*) (*c*)

Case Based-V

(*i*) (*c*) (*ii*) (*a*) (*iii*) (*c*) (*iv*) (*b*) (*v*) (*c*)

HINTS & EXPLANATIONS

Multiple Choice Questions

1. (*a*) $D = b^2 - 4ac$

   Where $a = 2$, $b = -4$, and $c = 3$.

   Substitute these values into the formula:

   $D = (-4)2 - 4 \cdot 2 \cdot 3$

   $\Rightarrow D = 16 - 24$

   $\Rightarrow D = -8$

2. (*b*) Given, $5x^2 - 12\sqrt{3}x + 7 = 0$

   On comparing with $ax^2 + bx + c = 0$

   we get: $a = 5$, $b = -12\sqrt{3}$ $c = 7$

   $D = b^2 - 4ac$

   $= \left(-12\sqrt{3}\right)^2 - 4 \times 5 \times 7 = 144 \times 3 - 140 = 432 - 140 = 292$

3. (*a*) Given, $2x^2 - 12x + 15 = 0$

   $D = b^2 - 4ac = (-12)^2 - 4(2)(15) = 144 - 120 = 24$

   As $D > 0$, the equation has distinct real roots

4. (*d*) Given: $2x^2 + kx + k = 0$

   On comparing with $ax^2 + bx + c = 0$, wet get

   $a = 2$, $b = -k$ and $c = k$

   For equal roots, the discriminant must be zero

   i.e., $D = b^2 - 4ac = 0$

   $\Rightarrow (-k)^2 - 4(2)\,k = 0$

   $\Rightarrow k^2 - 8k = 0$

   $\Rightarrow k(k - 8) = 0$

   $\therefore\ k = 0, 8$

Assertion and Reason

1. (*a*) If one root of a quadratic equation with rational coefficient is an irrational number, then the other root will be its irrational conjugate pair.

   If one root is $5 + \sqrt{7}$, then other root will be $5 - \sqrt{7}$.

   Hence, Assertion and Reason both are true and Reason is the correct explanation of Assertion.

2. (*b*) Assertion: Given equation $x^2 - bx + c = 0$

   Let α, β be two consecutive roots such that

   $|\alpha - \beta| = 1 \Rightarrow (\alpha + \beta)^2 - 4\alpha\beta = 1 \Rightarrow b^2 - 4c = 1$

   $\therefore$ Assertion is true.

   Reason: Given equation $4abcx^2 + (b^2 - 4ac)x - b = 0$

   $D = (b^2 - 4ac)^2 + 16ab^2c$

   $D = (b^2 + 4ac)^2 > 0$

   Hence, roots are real and distinct.

   $\therefore$ Reason is true and reason is not correct explanation of the assertion.

Subjective Questions

Very Short Answer Type Questions

1. $D = b^2 - 4ac$

   In the equation $3x^2 - 4x + k = 0$, $a = 3$, $b = -4$, and $c = k$.

   If the roots are equal, then $D = 0$, so: *(½ M)*

   $D = (-4)^2 - 4(3)(k) = 0$

   $\Rightarrow 16 - 12k = 0 \Rightarrow k = \frac{16}{12} \Rightarrow k = \frac{4}{3}$

   So, the value of k for which the equation $3x^2 - 4x + k = 0$ has equal roots is $k = \frac{4}{3}$. *(½ M)*

2. We have, $x^2 + x + 1 = 0$

   On comparing with $ax^2 + bx + c = 0$, we get

   $a = 1$, $b = 1$, $c = 1$

   $D = b^2 - 4ac = (1)^2 - 4 \times 1 \times 1 = 1 - 4 = -3$

   $D = -3$ *(1 M)*

   As, $D < 0$

   Hence, the equation has no real roots. *(1 M)*

3. We have, $36x^2 - 676 = 0$

   $\Rightarrow 36x^2 = 676 \Rightarrow x^2 = \frac{676}{36}$ *(1 M)*

   $\Rightarrow x = \pm\sqrt{\frac{676}{36}} \Rightarrow x = \pm\frac{26}{6} \Rightarrow x = \pm\frac{13}{3}$ *(1 M)*

   Thus, $x = \frac{13}{3}$ and $\frac{-13}{3}$ are solutions of the given equation.

4. The given quadratic equation is:

   $12abx^2 - (9a^2 - 8b^2)x - 6ab = 0$

   $\Rightarrow\ 12abx^2 - 9a^2x + 8b^2x - 6ab = 0$

   $\Rightarrow\ 3ax\,(4bx - 3a) + 2b\,(4bx - 3a) = 0$ *(1 M)*

   $\Rightarrow\ (4bx - 3a)\,(3ax + 2b) = 0$

   i.e., $4bx - 3a = 0$ or $3ax + 2b = 0$

   $\therefore\ x = \frac{3a}{4b}$ or $x = -\frac{2b}{3a}$ *(1 M)*

5. $x = \frac{-b \pm \sqrt{b^2 - 4ac}}{2a}$

   Where a = 1, $b = -1$, and $c = -6$.

   Substitute these values into the quadratic formula:

   $x = \frac{-(-1) \pm \sqrt{(-1)^2 - 4 \cdot 1 \cdot (-6)}}{2 \cdot 1}$ *(½ M)*

   $x = \frac{1 \pm \sqrt{1 + 24}}{2}$

   $x_1 = \frac{1+5}{2} = 3 \Rightarrow x_2 = \frac{1-5}{2} = -2$ *(½ M)*

Short Answer Type Questions

1. (*i*) The area of the original quilt as $12 \times 8 = 96$ sq units.

The area of the quilt with the border as $96 + 64 = 160$ sq units. (½ M)

A quadratic equation using the total area of the quilt as:

$(4x + 12)(2x + 8) = 160 \Rightarrow 8x^2 + 56x - 64 = 0$ (½ M)

(*ii*) The quadratic equation obtained in the previous step and finds the roots as (–8) and 1. (1 M)

$x \neq (-8)$ as length cannot be negative.

Hence, the value of x is 1 unit (½ M)

The length and breadth of the new quilt as 16 units and 10 units respectively. (½ M)

2. $(x - 1)^2 + (x - 2)^2 + (x - 3)^2 = 0$

$\Rightarrow x^2 - 2x + 1 + x^2 - 4x + 4 + x^2 - 6x + 9 = 0$

$\Rightarrow 3x^2 - 12x + 14 = 0$ (½ M)

On comparing with $ax^2 + bx + c = 0$, we get

Here $a = 3, b = -12, c = 14$

$\therefore D = b^2 - 4ac$ (1 M)

$= (-12)^2 - 4{\times}3{\times}14 = 144 - 168 = -24$ (½ M)

As, $D < 0$, Hence equation has no real roots. (1 M)

3. Let n denotes the number of ₹ 1 decrease.

Total revenue can be described as the product of price per ticket and the number of tickets sold.

Revenue = price per ticket × no. of tickets sold (1 M)

∴ The current revenue is $R = 30 \times 40$ because there are 40 tickets sold at price of ₹ 30 each.

According to the question,

The price decreases for each ₹ 1 decrement, the new price will be $(30 - n)$

For each ₹ 1 decrement, 9 more tickets would get sold. So, total tickets sold changes from 40 to $(40 + 9n)$

∴ New Revenue $= (30 - n)(40 + 9n)$ (1 M)

$= 1200 + 270n - 40n - 9n^2 = -9n^2 + 230n + 1200$ (1 M)

4. Let n denotes the number of days by which shipment get delayed.

Revenue = price per crates × No. of crates sold (1 M)

∴ The current revenue is $R = 70 \times 400$

According to the question,

For 1 day delay in the shipment, the price per crate will be decreased by ₹ 3. Therefore, The new price will be $(70 - 3n)$.

For each 1 day delay in the shipment, the grower needs to ship 15 more crates.

Therefore, the amount of crates will be $(400 + 15n)$.

∴ New revenue $= (70 - 3n)(400 + 15n)$ (1 M)

$= 28000 + 1050n - 1200n - 45n^2$

$= -45n^2 - 150n + 28000$ (1 M)

5. Let the breadth of the rectangular park be $x$cm.

Then, according to question

Length of the rectangular park be $2x + 5$ cm.

Also, given area of rectangular park = 250 cm²

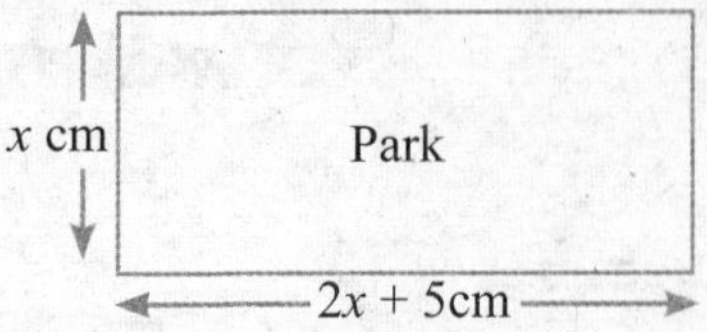

$\therefore 250 = x(2x + 5)$

$\Rightarrow 2x^2 + 5x - 250 = 0$

$\Rightarrow 2x^2 + 25x - 20x - 250 = 0$

$\Rightarrow x(2x + 25)(x - 10) = 0$ (1 M)

$\Rightarrow 2x + 25 = 0$ and $x - 10 = 0$

$\Rightarrow x = -\frac{25}{2}$ and $x = 10$

∴ Breadth, $x = 10$ cm..(∵ x can't be negative)

Now, Length $= 2(10) + 5 = 25$cm

Hence, thelength of the park is 25cm and breadth of the park is 10cm. (1 M)

Long Answer Type Questions

1. Let x hrs be the time taken by the smaller pipe to fill the tank.

∴ Time taken by the larger pipe to fill the tank will be $(x-10)$ hrs. If the smaller pipe takes x hours to fill the pool, it will fill $\frac{1}{x}$ hours part in 1 hour.

Similarly, if larger pipe takes $(x - 10)$ hours to fill the pool, it will fill $\frac{1}{x-10}$ part in 1 hour.

Therefore, in 1 hour both the pipe can fill $\frac{1}{x} + \frac{1}{x-10}$ part of tank. (1 M)

Now, it is given that

Time taken by both the taps to fill the tank

$= 9\frac{3}{8}\ hrs = \frac{75}{8}\ hrs$

Thus, in 1 hour both the taps together can fill $\frac{8}{75}$ part of the tank.

$\frac{1}{x} + \frac{1}{x-10} = \frac{8}{75}$ (1 M)

$\Rightarrow \frac{x-10+x}{x(x-10)} = \frac{8}{75} \Rightarrow \frac{2x-10}{x^2-10x} = \frac{8}{75}$

$\Rightarrow 75(2x - 10) = 8x^2 - 80x \Rightarrow 150x - 750 = 8x^2 - 80x$

$\Rightarrow 8x^2 - 230x + 750 = 0 \Rightarrow 8x^2 - 200x - 30x + 750 = 0$ (1 M)

$\Rightarrow 8x(x - 25) - 30(x - 25) = 0 \Rightarrow (x - 25)(8x - 30) = 0$

$\Rightarrow x = 25, 30/8$ (1 M)

Time taken by the smaller pipe cannot be 30/8 hours, as the time taken by the larger pipe will become negative.

Hence, the smaller tap takes 25 hrs and larger tap takes $(x - 10)$. i.e., $(25 - 10) = 15$ hrs to fill the tank. (1 M)

2. Let the average speed of a passenger train $= x$ *km/h*.

Then, the average speed of express train $= (x + 11)$ *km/h*

We know, Time $= \frac{\text{Distance}}{\text{Speed}}$

$\therefore$ Time taken by passenger train to cover 132 *km* $= \frac{132}{x}$ *hrs*

and time taken by express train to cover 132 *km* $= \frac{132}{x+11}$ *hrs*

(1 M)

According to the question, the time taken by the express train to cover 132 *km* is 1 hour less than the passenger train to cover the same distance.

$\therefore \frac{132}{x} - \frac{132}{x+11} = 1$ *(1 M)*

$\Rightarrow \frac{132(x+11-x)}{x(x+11)} = 1 \Rightarrow 132 \times 11 = x(x+11)$

$\Rightarrow x^2 + 11x - 1452 = 0 \Rightarrow x^2 + 44x - 33x - 1452 = 0$ *(1 M)*

$\Rightarrow (x+44)(x-33) = 0 \Rightarrow x = -44, 33$ *(1 M)*

Neglecting –44 as speed cannot be negative.

Therefore, the speed of the passenger train will be 33 *km/h* and thus, the speed of the express train will be (33 + 11) *km/h* = 44 *km/h*. *(1 M)*

3. Let the side of smaller square be x and that of larger square be y.
Therefore, their perimeter will be $4x$ and $4y$ respectively and area of the squares will be x^2 and y^2 respectively.
According to the question, difference of perimeter is 24 *m*.
$\therefore 4y - 4x = 24$ *(1 M)*
$\Rightarrow y - x = 6 \Rightarrow y = x + 6$
Also, sum of the areas of two squares is 468 m^2.
$\Rightarrow y^2 + x^2 = 468 \Rightarrow (6+x)^2 + x^2 = 468$ *(1 M)*
$\Rightarrow 36 + x^2 + 12x + x^2 = 468$
$\Rightarrow 2x^2 + 12x - 432 = 0 \Rightarrow x^2 + 6x - 216 = 0$
$\Rightarrow x^2 + 18x - 12x - 216 = 0$ *(1 M)*
$\Rightarrow x(x+18) - 12(x+18) = 0 \Rightarrow (x+18)(x-12) = 0$
$\Rightarrow x = -18, 12$ *(1 M)*
We know that side of a square cannot be negative.
Hence, the sides of the squares are 12 *m* and (12 + 6)*m* = 18*m*.
(1 M)

4. Let the number of students be x.
Number of students playing cricket $= \frac{7}{2}\sqrt{x}$
Number of students remaining = 2
According to the question,
$\Rightarrow x = \frac{7}{2}\sqrt{x} + 2$ *(1 M)*
$\Rightarrow x - 2 = \frac{7}{2}\sqrt{x}$
Squaring both sides, we get
$\Rightarrow (x-2)^2 = \left(\frac{7}{2}\right)^2 x \Rightarrow 4(x^2 - 4x + 4) = 49x$
$\Rightarrow 4x^2 - 16x + 16 = 49x$ *(1 M)*
$\Rightarrow 4x^2 - 65x + 16 = 0 \Rightarrow 4x^2 - 64x - x + 16 = 0$ *(1 M)*
$\Rightarrow 4x(x-16) - 1(x-16) = 0 \Rightarrow (x-16)(4x-1) = 0$
This gives $x = 16$ or $x = \frac{1}{4}$ *(1 M)*
We reject $x = \frac{1}{4}$ as number of students cannot be in fraction.
Hence, the total number of students is 16. *(1 M)*

5. Let the pond is constructed inside x meter, from all sides from the boundary of the lawn

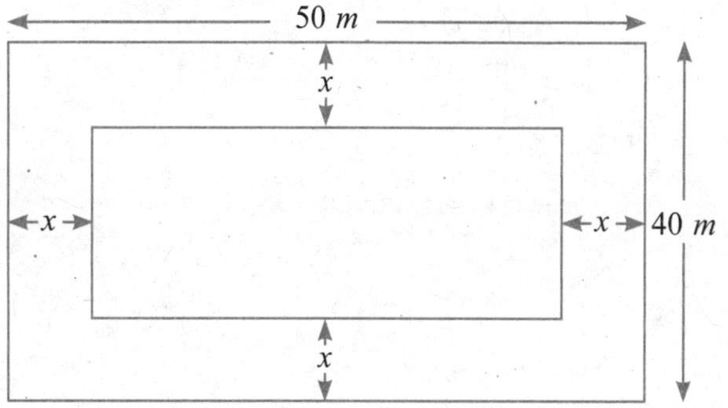

(1 M)

Then, Area of the grass surrounding the pond
= Area of the lawn – Area of the pond
$= 50 \times 40 - (50 - 2x)(40 - 2x)$
$= 2000 - 2000 - 4x^2 + 180x = -4x^2 + 180x$ *(1 M)*
Also, Area of the grass = 1184 m^2 (Given).
So, $-4x^2 + 180x = 1184 \Rightarrow x^2 - 45x + 296 = 0$
$\Rightarrow (x-37)(x-8) = 0 \Rightarrow x = 8$ or 37 *(1 M)*
$\because x = 37$ then length of the pond $= 50 - 37 \times 2 = -24 < 0$.
but length cannot be in negative. *(1 M)*
So, $x = 8$.
$\therefore$ Length and breadth of the pond are $(50 - 2 \times 8)$ i.e., 34 *m* and $(40 - 2 \times 8)$ i.e., 24 *m* respectively. *(1 M)*

6. Let x and y hours be the time taken by larger pipe and smaller pipe to fill the swimming pool respectively.
Given, $y - x = 10$ or $y = x + 10$
If smaller pipe takes x hours to fill the pool, it will fill $\frac{1}{x}$ part in 1 hour.
Similarly if larger pipe takes y hours to fill the pool, it will fill $\frac{1}{y}$ part in 1 hour. *(1 M)*
According to the question, if the larger pipe is used for 4 hours and the smaller pipe is used for 9 hours only half of the pool can be filled.
$\therefore 4 \times \frac{1}{x} + 9 \times \frac{1}{y} = \frac{1}{2}$ *(1 M)*
$\Rightarrow \frac{4}{x} + \frac{9}{y} = \frac{1}{2}$
Now putting $y = x + 10$
$\Rightarrow \frac{4}{x} + \frac{9}{x+10} = \frac{1}{2} \Rightarrow \frac{4(x+10)+9x}{x(x+10)} = \frac{1}{2}$
$\Rightarrow \frac{4x+40+9x}{x(x+10)} = \frac{1}{2} \Rightarrow \frac{13x+40}{x^2+10x} = \frac{1}{2} \Rightarrow 26x + 80 = x^2 + 10x$
$\Rightarrow x^2 - 16x - 80 = 0 \Rightarrow x^2 - 20x + 4x - 80 = 0$ *(1 M)*
$\Rightarrow x(x-20) + 4(x-20) = 0 \Rightarrow (x-20)(x+4) = 0$
$\Rightarrow x - 20 = 0$ or $x + 4 = 0$
i.e., $x = 20$ or -4 *(1 M)*
Neglecting –4, as time can't be negative.
$\therefore$ Time taken by larger pipe to fill the pool is 20 *hrs*.
Then time taken by smaller pipe will be 30 *hrs*. *(1 M)*

7. Let the speed of train be x km/hr (½ M)
distance = 360 km

$$\text{Speed} = \frac{\text{distance}}{\text{time}}$$

$$\text{Time} = \frac{360}{x}$$ (½ M)

New speed = $(x + 5)$ km/hr

$$\text{Time} = \frac{D}{5}$$

$$x+5 = \frac{360}{\left(\frac{360}{x}-1\right)}$$ (1 M)

$$\Rightarrow (x+5)\left(\frac{360}{x}-1\right) = 360$$

$\Rightarrow (x + 5)(360 - x) = 360 \Rightarrow -x^2 - 5x + 1800 = 0$ (1 M)

$\Rightarrow x^2 + 5x - 1800 = 0 \Rightarrow x^2 + 45x - 40x - 1800 = 0$

$\Rightarrow x(x + 45) - 40(x + 45) = 0 \Rightarrow (x + 45)(x - 40) = 0$ (1 M)

$x + 45 = 0$, $x - 40 = 0$

$x = -45$, $x = 40$

Speed cannot ne negative

Speed of train = 40 km/hr (1 M)

Case Based Questions

Case Based-I

(i) Let width of the park be x meters

Length = $(x + 25)$ meters

$\therefore$ Area = $x(x + 25)$

Given, area = 600 *sq.m*

$\therefore x(x + 25) = 600 \Rightarrow x^2 + 25x - 600 = 0$

$x^2 + 25x - 600 = 0$ represents the area of the rectangular park.

(ii) We have, $x^2 + 25x - 600 = 0 \Rightarrow x^2 + 40x - 15x - 600 = 0$

$\Rightarrow x(x + 40) - 15(x + 40) = 0 \Rightarrow (x - 15)(x + 40) = 0$

$\Rightarrow x = 15$ or $x = -40$

Neglecting $x = -40$, width can not be negative

$\therefore x = 15$

Hence, length of the rectangular park = $(x + 25)$ = $(15 + 25)$ = 40 meters.

OR

The discriminant of the quadratic equation is $b^2 - 4ac$. Substituting the values from the quadratic equation $x^2 + 25x - 600 = 0$, we get: $D = (25)^2 - 4(1)(-600) = 3025$

(iii) The coefficient of x^2 is 1.

Case Based-II

(i) (c) Here, the radius of one circle = x *cm*.

Then, the radius of the second circle = $(14 - x)$*cm*.

The area of the first circle = πx^2 cm^2 and area of the second circle = $\pi(14 - x)^2$ cm^2

According to the question, $\pi x^2 + \pi(14 - x)^2 = 130\pi$

$\Rightarrow \pi(x^2 + 196 - 28x + x^2) = 130\pi$

On solving, we get

$\Rightarrow 2x^2 - 28x + 196 = 130 \Rightarrow 2x^2 - 28x + 66 = 0$

$\Rightarrow x^2 - 14x + 33 = 0$

(ii) (b) $\because D = B^2 - 4AC = (b^2 - ac)^2 - 4(ab)(-bc)$

$= b^4 + a^2c^2 - 2ab^2c + 4ab^2c = b^4 + a^2c^2 + 2ab^2c$

$= (b^2)^2 + (ac)^2 + 2 \times b^2 \times ac$

$= (b^2 + ac)^2$, which is greater than zero

[Since, the square or every integer is always positive]

Hence, roots are real and distinct.

(iii) (a) The given equation can be written as $x^2 - 4x + p = 0$.

Now, for real and distinct roots, $D > 0$.

$\Rightarrow (-4)^2 - 4(1)(p) > 0 \Rightarrow 16 > 4p \Rightarrow p < 4$.

Case Based-III

(i) (a) Total distance = 1200 *km*

Let speed of the aeroplane = x *km/h*

Time taken to cover distance 1200 *km* = $\frac{1200}{x}$ *hr*

Now, speed increases by 100 *km/hr*.

So, New speed = $(x + 100)$ *km/hr*.

Also, aeroplane started late by 1 *hr*.

So, new time = $\left(\frac{1200}{x}-1\right)$ *hr*.

$\therefore$ According to the question,

$$(x+100)\left(\frac{1200}{x}-1\right) = 1200$$

$\Rightarrow (x + 100)(1200 - x) = 1200x$

$\Rightarrow 1200x - x^2 + 120000 - 100x = 1200x$

$\Rightarrow x^2 + 100x - 120000 = 0$

The quadratic equation formed in this situation is $x^2 + 100x - 120000 = 0$.

$\because$ Discriminant $D = (100)^2 - 4 \times 1 \times (-120000)$

$= 10000 + 480000 = 490000 > 0$

As $D > 0$, roots are real and distinct.

(ii) (c) The roots of the given quadratic equation $x^2 + kx + 3 = 0$ can be found by using the quadratic formula.

$$x = \frac{-b \pm \sqrt{b^2 - 4ac}}{2a} = \frac{-k \pm \sqrt{k^2 - 12}}{2}$$

The difference between the roots = 2

$$\Rightarrow \frac{-k+\sqrt{k^2-12}}{2} + \frac{k+\sqrt{k^2-12}}{2} = 2$$

$$\Rightarrow \frac{2\sqrt{k^2-12}}{2} = 2$$

Therefore, $\sqrt{k^2 - 12} = 2$

Squaring both sides, we get $k^2 - 12 = 4 \Rightarrow k^2 = 16$

$\Rightarrow k = \pm 4$

(*iii*) (*b*) It is given that $x = 2$ and $x = 3$ are solutions of the equation $3x^2 - mx + 2n = 0$.

Therefore, $3(2)^2 - 2m + 2n = 0$ ... (*i*)

and $3(3)^2 - 3m + 2n = 0$ ... (*ii*)

On solving equation (*i*), we get

$12 - 2m + 2n = 0 \Rightarrow 2m - 2n = 12 \Rightarrow m - n = 6$ ... (*iii*)

Now, on solving equation (*ii*), we get

$27 - 3m + 2n = 0 \Rightarrow 3m - 2n = 27$ ... (*iv*)

Solving the equations (*iii*) and (*iv*), we get

$m = 15, n = 9$.

Case Based-IV

We have speed of Raj's Car = x km/h

Therefore, speed of Ajay's Car = $(x + 5)$ km/h

Now, time taken to complete the journey by Raj = $\frac{400}{x}$

and Time taken to complete the journey by Ajay = $\frac{400}{x+5}$

According to question, Raj took 4 hours more than Ajay.

$\therefore \frac{400}{x} - \frac{400}{x+5} = 4 \Rightarrow 400\left(\frac{x+5-x}{x(x+5)}\right) = 4$

$\Rightarrow 500 = x(x + 5) = x^2 + 5x$

$\Rightarrow x^2 + 5x - 500 = 0 \Rightarrow x^2 + 25x - 20x - 500 = 0$

$\Rightarrow x(x + 25) - 20(x + 25) = 0 \Rightarrow (x + 25)(x - 25) = 0$

$\Rightarrow x = 20, x \neq -25$ (Because speed can never be negative)

$\therefore x = 20$ km/h

(*i*) (*a*) Distance covered by Ajay's car in two hours $=$ Speed $\times$ Time $= (x + 5) \times 2 = 2(x + 5)$km

(*ii*) (*c*) We get the quadratic equation $x^2 + 5x - 500 = 0$ for the speed of Raj's car.

(*iii*) (*a*) Speed of the Raj's car = x km/h = 20 km/h

(*iv*) (*d*) Time taken by Ajay to travel 400 km = $\frac{400}{x+5}$

$= \frac{400}{20+5} = \frac{400}{25} = 16$ hours

(*v*) (*c*) Speed of Ajay's car = $(x + 5)$ km/h = 20 + 5 = 25 km/h

Case Based-V

We have downstream speed of motor boat = $(20 + x)$km/h

and upstream speed of motor boat = $(20 - x)$km/h

Where x km/h is the speed of the stream.

We have, $\frac{15}{20-x} - \frac{15}{20+x} = 1 \Rightarrow \frac{15(20+x-20+x)}{(20-x)(20+x)} = 1$

$\Rightarrow 15 \times 2x = 400 - x^2 \Rightarrow x^2 + 30x - 400 = 0$

$\Rightarrow x^2 + 40x - 10x - 400 = 0 \Rightarrow x(x + 40) - 10(x + 40) = 0$

$\Rightarrow (x + 40)(x - 10) = 0 \Rightarrow x = 10$ $\{x \neq -40\}$

$\therefore x = 10$km/h ($\because$ Speed can never be negative)

(*i*) (*c*) Speed of the motor boat in upstream = $(20 - x)$km/h

(*ii*) (*a*) Relation between speed, distance and time is given by

Speed $= \frac{\text{distance}}{\text{time}}$

(*iii*) (*c*) The quadratic equation $x^2 + 30x - 400 = 0$ is for the speed of the current (Stream)

(*iv*) (*b*) Speed of the current = x km/h = 10 km/h

(*v*) (*c*) Time taken by boat in downstream = $\frac{15}{20+x}$h

$= \frac{15}{20+10} = \frac{15}{30} = \frac{1}{2}$hr = 30 minutes.

❑❑❑

ARITHMETIC PROGRESSIONS

5

"Arithmetic Progression is used in Pyramid-like patterns, where objects are increasing or decreasing in a constant manner like seats in a stadium or an auditorium. A situation might be that seats in each row are decreasing by 4 from the previous row."

SYLLABUS & WEIGHTAGE

List of Concept Names	Years				
	2021	2022	2023	2024	2025
Arithmetic Progressions and its nth Term (Motivation for studying Arithmetic Progression Derivation of the nth term)	Exam not Conducted	1 Q (4 M)	–	1 Q (1 M) 1 Q (4 M)	1 Q (1 M)
Sum of First n-Terms of An AP (Sum of the first n terms of AP and their application in solving daily life problems.)		1 Q (2 M)	1 Q (4 M)	–	1 Q (1 M) 2 Q (3 M)

CONCEPT MAP

To Access One Shot Revision Video Scan This QR Code

Arithmetic Progressions

Sum of nth term:

- When first term (a) and common difference (d) is given, then,

$$S_n = \frac{n}{2}[2a+(n-1)d]$$

- When first term (a) and last term (l) is given, then

$$S_n = \frac{n}{2}[a+l]$$

General form of an A.P.

$a, a+d, a+2d, ..., a+(n-1)d$

Common difference (d)

- The fixed number added in an arithmetic progression is the common difference i.e., difference between the two consecutive terms of an A.P. is called common difference.

$$d = a_n - a_{n-1}$$

- It can be positive, negative or zero.

Types of an A.P.:

Finite A.P.: An arithmetic progression (A.P) in which number of terms are finite is known as finite A.P.

$a_1, a_2, ...\ a_n$

Infinite A.P.: An arithmetic progression (A.P) in which number of terms are infinite is known as infinite A.P.

$a_1, a_2, a_3.............$

n^{th} term from end

$a_n = l-(n-1)\,d$

Here, l is last term and d is common difference

Definition:

A sequence of numbers in which each term is obtained by adding/subtracting a fixed number to the preceding term, except the first term is called an Arithmetic Progression.

n^{th} term of an A.P.

$a_n = a+(n-1)\,d$

Here, a is first term and d is common difference

Term:

Each number in the sequence of an A.P.

1 ARITHMETIC PROGRESSIONS AND ITS nth TERM

Important Terms

- **Sequence:** A systematic arrangement of numbers or terms according to some rule is called a sequence. Each of the numbers in a sequence are called terms of the sequence and is denoted by $a_1, a_2, a_3, \ldots$ etc.
- **Arithmetic Progression and its Common Difference:** A particular type of sequence in which each term, except first term goes ahead in a definite manner such that every term except first term is obtained by adding a fixed number (positive or negative or zero) to the preceding term. In this way we can define Arithmetic progression as below:

A sequence $a_1, a_2, a_3, \ldots\ldots\ldots a_n, \ldots\ldots$ is called an arithmetic progression, if there exists a constant number denoted by 'd' such that

$a_2 = a_1 + d; a_3 = a_2 + d; a_4 = a_3 + d; \ldots\ldots\ldots\ldots\ldots; a_n = a_{n-1} + d$

d may be positive or negative or zero and d is called common difference of respective Arithmetic Progression (AP).

For example 2, 5, 8, 11,...... are in AP with First term represented by $a = 2$, and common difference $d = 3$

- **General Form of an AP:** The general form of an AP can be written as: $\{a, a + d, a + 2d, a + 3d, \ldots\}$ where a is the first term and d is the common difference.

Arithmetic Progression:

Common Difference:

Arithmetic Progression after adding a Constant:

Common Difference:

Common Difference (Anil Kapoor) be like: Main Badalega nhi Mama

Important Formulas

- Common difference $d = a_2 - a_1 = a_3 - a_2 = \ldots\ldots\ldots\ldots = a_n - a_{n-1}$
- In an AP with first term a and common difference d, the nth term (or the general term) is given by

  $a_n = a + (n - 1)d.$
- The nth term of an AP from the end with first term a, common difference d and last term l is given by $a_n = l - (n - 1)\,d$.

Important Derivations

Derivations of Formula for n^{th} term of an AP

Let $a_1, a_2, a_3, \ldots$ be the terms of an AP whose first term is a_1 or just a and the common difference is d, then

the second term, $a_2 = a + d = a + (2 - 1)d$

the third term, $a_3 = a_2 + d = (a + d) + d = a + 2d = a + (3 - 1)d$

the fourth term, $a_4 = a_3 + d = (a + 2d) + d = a + 3d = a + (4 - 1)d$

Looking at the pattern, we can say that n^{th} term, $a_n = a + (n - 1)d$

Therefore, the nth term a_n of the AP with first term a and common difference d is given by $a_n = a + (n - 1)d$.

Important Concepts

- Common difference of an AP can be negative, zero or positive.
- In an AP, if some constant term is added or subtracted from each term, then the resulting sequence obtained is also an AP, having same common difference.
- In an AP, if each term is multiplied or divided by a non-zero constant k, then the resulting sequence obtained is also an AP, having common difference kd, where d is the common difference of the given AP
- If a, b and c are three consecutive terms of an AP, then the sum two numbers is twice the middle number i.e., $2b = a + c$.
- If there is an AP with n terms having a as first term and d as the common difference, then m^{th} term from the end is $(n - m + 1)^{th}$ term from the beginning.
- It is convenient to solve a problem if we select the terms as per the following table:

Number of Terms	Terms	Common Difference
3 terms	$a - d, a, a + d$	d
4 terms	$a - 3d, a - d, a + d, a + 3d$	$2d$
5 terms	$a - 2d, a - d, a, a + d, a + 2d$	d

Real Life Applications

Summer vacation is the favourite time of the year for all students, as it gives them a chance to relax and explore new things. Suppose this time you decided to visit your native place by train.

You noticed that there are 100 luggage bags in first carriage, 125 luggage bags in second carriage, 150 luggage bags in third carriage and so on. So, how many luggage bags will be there in the ninth carriage? Don't worry you can easily find the answer using n^{th} term of an AP.

Different Problem Types

Type I: Determining if Sequence Forms an Arithmetic Progression (AP)

Determine whether the following sequence forms an arithmetic progression (AP): 6, 12, 18, 24, 30..........

Solution:

Step I: Identify consecutive terms.

- Consecutive terms: 6, 12, 18, 24, 30, etc.

Step II: Calculate differences.

Differences:

- $12-6=6$
- $18-12=6$
- $24-18=6$
- $30-24=6$

Step III: Analysis

- Since the differences are all the same (6), the sequence has a constant difference between consecutive terms.

Step IV: Conclusion

- Therefore, the sequence 6, 12, 18, 24, 30, forms an arithmetic progression (AP).

Example 1: Determine whether the following sequence forms an arithmetic progression (AP): 10, 7, 4, 1, – 2, ...

Solution: Consecutive terms: 10, 7, 4, 1, – 2, etc.

Differences:

- $7-10=-3$
- $4-7=-3$
- $1-4=-3$
- $(-2)-1=-3$

Since the differences are all the same (-3), the sequence has a constant difference between consecutive terms.

Therefore, the sequence 10, 7, 4, 1, – 2, forms an arithmetic progression (AP).

Example 2: Given the sequence 1, 4, 9, 16, 25, determine whether it forms an arithmetic progression (AP). Provide reasoning for your answer.

Solution: Consecutive terms: 1, 4, 9, 16, 25, etc.

Differences:

- $4-1=3$
- $9-4=5$
- $16-9=7$
- $25-16=9$

Since the differences between consecutive terms are not constant, the sequence does not exhibit the characteristic property of an arithmetic progression (AP), which requires a constant difference between consecutive terms.

Therefore, the sequence 1, 4, 9, 16, 25....., does not form an arithmetic progression (AP).

Type II: Understanding Arithmetic Progressions (AP) & n^{th} term of AP

Reena applied for a job and got selected. She has been offered a job with a starting monthly salary of ₹8000, with an annual increment of ₹ 500 in her salary. What will be her salary (in ₹) for the 1st, 2nd, & 3rd years?

Solution:

Step I: Identify Given Information

- Starting salary (1st year) = ₹8000
- Annual increment = ₹500

Step II: Determine the Common Difference (d).

The common difference (d) in an arithmetic progression is the difference between consecutive terms. Here, d = ₹500.

Step III: Use the nth term of AP Formula to Find Salaries for Each Year. The formula to find the nth term (salary for the nth year) of an arithmetic progression is:

$a_n = a_1 + (n - 1)\, d$

Where:

- a_n = Salary for the nth year
- a_1 = Starting salary (Ist year)
- n = Year number
- d = Common difference

Step IV: Calculate Salaries for Each Year

- For the 1st year ($n = 1$):

$$a_1 = ₹8000 + (1 - 1)\,₹500 = ₹8000$$

- For the 2nd year ($n = 2$):

$$a_2 = ₹8000 + (2 - 1)\,₹500 = ₹8500$$

- For the 3rd year ($n = 3$):

$$a_3 = ₹8000 + (3 - 1)\,₹500 = ₹9000$$

Example 1: Find the 10th term of the AP: 3, 8, 13, ...

Solution:

Here, $a = 3, d = 8 - 3 = 5$ and $n = 10$.

We have $a_n = a + (n - 1)d$

So, $a_{10} = 3 + (10 - 1) \times 5 = 3 + 45 = 48$

Therefore, the 10th term of the given AP is 48.

Example 2: How many two-digit numbers are divisible by 3?

Solution: The list of two-digit numbers divisible by 3 is:

12, 15, 18, ... , 99

Here, $a = 12, d = 3, a_n = 99.$

As, $a_n = a + (n - 1)d,$

we have

$$99 = 12 + (n - 1) \times 3$$

$$87 = (n - 1) \times 3$$

$$n - 1 = \frac{87}{3} = 29$$

$$n = 29 + 1 = 30$$

So, there are 30 two-digit numbers divisible by 3.

Type III: Find the mth term from the last term of an AP

Find the 11th term from the last term (towards the first term) of the AP: 10, 7, 4, ..., –62.

Solution:

Step I: First calculate the first term, last term, common difference and n^{th} term

Here, $a = 10, d = 7 - 10 = -3, l = -62$, where $l = a + (n - 1)d,$

To find the 11th term from the last term, we will find the total number of terms in an AP.

Step II: Use formula for last term

So,

$$-62 = 10 + (n - 1)(-3)$$

$$-72 = (n - 1)(-3)$$

$$n - 1 = 24$$

$$n = 25$$

So, there are 25 terms in the given AP. The 11th term from the last term will be $n - m + 1 = 25 - 11 + 1$ i.e, 15th term from the beginning. So,

$$a_{15} = 10 + (15 - 1)(-3) = 10 - 42 = -32$$

i.e., the 11th term from the last term is –32.

Example : In an arithmetic progression (AP), the 5th term is 20, and the 9th term is the last term in on AP, which is 32. Determine the 7th term from the last term (towards the first term) of the AP.

Solution: Given;

5th term, $a_5 = 20 = a + 4d = 20$ ... (*i*)

9th term, $a_9 = 32$ (which is the last term in an AP)

$a + 8d = 32$ ... (*ii*)

On Solving eq. (*i*) and (*ii*), we get $d = 3$ and $a = 8$

Now we know that the last term (a_9) is 32 (given).

So, there are 9 terms in the arithmetic progression.

7th term from the last:

$a'_7 = a_{9-7+1} = a_3$

$a_3 = a_1 + (3 - 1)\,.\,d = 8 + 2\,.\,3 = 8 + 6 = 14$

Therefore, the 7th term from the last term (towards the first term) of the arithmetic progression is 14.

COMPETENCY BASED SOLVED EXAMPLES

Multiple Choice Questions

1. The first three terms in the sequences $a_n = n^2 + 1$ are *(Un)*

(a) 2, 5, 12 (b) 2, 5, 10

(c) 2, 6, 10 (d) None of these

Sol. It is given that, $a_n = n^2 + 1$.

On putting values of n as 1, 2, and 3 we get

$a_1 = 1^2 + 1 = 1 + 1 = 2$ $(n = 1)$

$a_2 = 2^2 + 1 = 4 + 1 = 5$ $(n = 2)$

$a_3 = 3^2 + 1 = 9 + 1 = 10$ $(n = 3)$

Therefore, the first three terms of the sequence defined by $a_n = n^2 + 1$ are 2, 5 and 10.

2. In an AP, if the first term is –2 and the common difference is also –2, then the first four terms of AP is: *(Un)*

(a) –1, –2, –3, –4 (b) –2, 4, –8, 16

(c) –2, –4, –6, –8 (d) –2, –4, –8, –16

Sol. Let us suppose, the first four terms of an AP be $a,\ a + d, a + 2d$ and $a + 3d$

It is given that, –2 is the first term and common difference is also −2. Hence, the AP would be:

$-2, (-2 - 2), [-2 + 2(-2)], [-2 + 3(-2)]$

$= -2, -4, -6, -8$

3. Two APs have the same common difference. The first term of one of these is –1 and that of the other is –8. The difference between their 4th terms is *(An) (CBSE SQP, 2023)*

(a) 1 (b) –7 (c) 7 (d) 9

Sol. The nth term (T_n) of an arithmetic progression can be found using the formula:

$$T_n = a + (n - 1)d$$

Where:

$T_n =$ n^{th} term; a = first term; d = common difference

n = term number

For the first AP with a first term of –1, let's calculate the 4th term:

$$T_4 = -1 + (4 - 1)\,d = -1 + 3d$$

For the second AP with a first term of –8, the 4th term would be:

$$T_4 = -8 + (4 - 1)\,d = -8 + 3d$$

Now, to find the difference between these two 4th terms, we subtract the second AP's 4th term from the first AP's 4th term:

$$\text{Difference} = (-1 + 3d) - (-8 + 3d) = -1 + 3d + 8 - 3d$$
$$= -1 + 8 = 7$$

4. If common difference of an A.P. is –6, then value of $a_{20} - a_{14}$ is: *(An) (CBSE, 2023)*

(a) 36 (b) 6

(c) –36 (d) –6

Sol. Given, $d = -6$

$a_{20} - a_{14} = a + 19d - (a + 13d) = a + 19d - a - 13d = 6d$

$= 6 \times -6 = -36$

Key Takeaways

n^{th} term of AP $= a + (n - 1)d$, where a is first term and d is the common difference

5. In an AP, if $a = 3.5, d = 0, n = 101$, then find the value of a_n. *(Ap)*

(a) 36 (b) 3.5

(c) 73 (d) 104.5

Sol. It is given that, $a = 3.5$, $d = 0$ and $n = 101$

Therefore, by using n^{th} term formula,

$a_n = a + (n - 1)d$

$a_{101} = 3.5 + (101 - 1) \times 0 = 3.5$

Hence, value of a_{101} is 3.5.

6. If the common difference of an AP is 5, then find the value of $a_{18} - a_{13}$. *(An) (NCERT Exemplar)*

(a) 10 (b) 20

(c) 25 (d) 30

Sol. Here, $a_{18} - a_{13} = a + 17d - a - 12d = 5d$

$= 5 \times 5 = 25$ $[\because d = 5]$

7. In an AP, if first two terms are –3 and 4 respectively, then the 21st term of an AP is *(Ev)*

(a) 21 (b) 137 (c) 143 (d) –143

Sol. It is given that,

First two terms of AP are –3 and 4

Here, $a = -3$ … (i)

and $a + d = 4$ … (ii)

$\Rightarrow -3 + d = 4 \Rightarrow d = 4 + 3 = 7$

Now, $a_{21} = a + (21 - 1)d$

$a_{21} = -3 + (20)7$ $[\because a = -3, d = 7]$

$a_{21} = 137$

Therefore, 21st term of AP is 137.

Mistakes 101 : What not to do!

Students make mistakes While applying the correct formula to calculate the unknown parameter.

8. Find the 7th term of an AP, if the 2nd term of AP is 13 and the 5th term is 25. *(An)*

(*a*) 30 (*b*) 33 (*c*) 37 (*d*) 46

Sol. It is given that,

$a_2 = 13$

$a_5 = 25$

Hence, by using n^{th} term formula, we have

$a + d = 13$ ... (*i*)

and $a + 4d = 25$ ... (*ii*)

On solving equations (*i*) and (*ii*), we get

$a = 9$ and $d = 4$

Now, $a_7 = a + (7 - 1)d$

$a_7 = 9 + 6 \times 4$

$a_7 = 9 + 24$

$a_7 = 33$

9. 26th term of the A.P. 7, 4, 1, –2, ... is *(Ev)*

(*a*) –68 (*b*) 68 (*c*) 34 (*d*) –34

Sol. First term = 7

Second term = 4

d = Second term – First term

$= 4 - 7 = -3$

n^{th} term in *AP* is given as:

$a_n = a + (n - 1)d$

26th term would be: $= 7 + (26 - 1) \times (-3) = -68$

10. Find the number of multiples of 4 between 10 and 250. *(Un)*

(*a*) 20 (*b*) 80 (*c*) 60 (*d*) 30

Sol. The first and last term which are the multiple of 4 and lies between 10 and 250 are 12 and 248. So, the arithmetic progression is 12, 16, 20, ..., 248.

Now, using general term formula of AP

$a_n = a + (n - 1)d$

$248 = 12 + (n - 1)4$

$236 = (n - 1)4$

$n - 1 = 59$

$n = 60$

11. Find the middle most term(s) of the AP: –11, –7, –3, ..., 49. *(Cr)*

(*a*) 14, 18 (*b*) 19, 23 (*c*) 17, 21 (*d*) 23, 25

Sol. From the given AP, we have

$a = -11$

$d = -7 - (-11) = 4$ $[\because a_2 - a_1 = d]$

and $a_n = 49$

Now, by using n^{th} term formula, we have

$a_n = a + (n - 1)d$

or $49 = -11 + (n - 1)4$

$\Rightarrow 49 + 11 = (n - 1)4 \Rightarrow 60 = (n - 1)4$

$\Rightarrow n = 16$

As value of n is an even number, hence, there will be two middle terms of the given AP, which are $\frac{16}{2}th$ and $\left(\frac{16}{2}+1\right)th$,

i.e. the 8th term and the 9th term.

Therefore,

$a_8 = a + 7d = -11 + 7 \times 4 = 17$

$a_9 = a + 8d = -11 + 8 \times 4 = 21$

Hence, 17 and 21 are the middle most terms of the given AP.

Nailing the Right Answer

Students should be familiar with all the formulas related to arithmetic progression.

12. Find the 20th term from the last term of the AP: 3, 8, 13, ..., 253. *(Ap)*

(*a*) 153 (*b*) 151 (*c*) 156 (*d*) 158

Sol. The given AP is 3, 8, 13...

Here, $a = 3$ and $d = 8 - 3 = 5$

The nth term of an AP from the end is

$a_n = l - (n - 1)\, d$

$\therefore a_{20} = 253 - (20 - 1)5$

$a_{20} = 253 - 95 = 158$

Key Takeaways

n^{th} term from the end $= l - (n - 1)d$, where l = Last term, d = common difference

Answer Key

1. (b)	2. (c)	3. (c)	4. (c)	5. (b)
6. (c)	7. (b)	8. (b)	9. (a)	10. (c)
11. (c)	12. (d)			

Assertion and Reason

Direction: **In the following questions, a statement of Assertion (A) is followed by a statement of Reason (R). Mark the correct choice as.**

(*a*) Both Assertion (A) and Reason (R) are true, and Reason (R) is the correct explanation of Assertion (A).

(*b*) Both Assertion (A) and Reason (R) are true, but Reason (R) is not the correct explanation of Assertion (A).

(*c*) Assertion (A) is true, but Reason (R) is false.

(*d*) Assertion (A) is false, but Reason (R) is true.

1. Assertion (A): 184 is the 50th term of the sequence 3, 7, 11,...

Reason (R): The nth term of AP is given by $a_n = a + (n - 1)d$. *(An)*

Sol. The given sequence is 3, 7, 11, ...

Here, $a = 3$ and $d = 7 - 3 = 4$

$\therefore a_{50} = a + (50 - 1)d = 3 + (49)4 = 199$

Hence, Assertion is false.

As we know Reason is true which denotes the formula for n^{th} term. Assertion (A) is false, but Reason (R) is true.

2. Assertion (A): **Common difference of the AP: –5, –1, 3, 7, is 4.**

Reason (R): **Common difference of the AP a, $a + d$, $a + 2d$,......., is given by d = 2nd term – 1st term.** *(Ap)*

Sol. Common difference is the difference between two successive terms in AP

$\therefore d$ = 2nd term – 1st term $= -1 - (-5) = -1 + 5 = 4$.

Therefore, both A and R are true and R is the correct explanation for A.

3. Assertion (A): **$-5, \frac{-5}{2}, 0, \frac{5}{2}$ is in Arithmetic Progression.**

Reason (R): **The terms of an Arithmetic Progression cannot have both positive and negative rational numbers.** *(Un)* (CBSE SQP, 2023)

Sol. Calculate the common difference (d):

d = Second term – First term

$$d = \left(-\frac{5}{2}\right) - (-5) = -\frac{5}{2} + 5 = \frac{5}{2}$$

Since the common difference $\left(\frac{5}{2}\right)$ is constant, the sequence forms an arithmetic progression.

Reason (R): It's incorrect because the terms of an arithmetic progression can indeed include both positive and negative rational numbers.

Assertion (A) is true but reason (R) is false.

Answer Key

1. (d) 2. (a) 3. (c)

Subjective Questions

Very Short Answer Type Questions (1 or 2 M)

1. **Write first three terms of a sequence where n^{th} term, $t_n = n^2 - 2^n$.** *(Un)*

Sol. It is given that, $t_n = n^2 - 2^n$

On putting values of n as 1, 2 and 3, we get

$t_1 = 1^2 - 2^1 = 1 - 2 = -1$ $(n = 1)$

$t_2 = 2^2 - 2^2 = 4 - 4 = 0$ $(n = 2)$ *(1 M)*

$t_3 = 3^2 - 2^3 = 9 - 8 = 1$ $(n = 3)$

Therefore, first three terms of sequence are –1, 0 and 1. *(1 M)*

2. **Find a and b so that the numbers a, 7, b, 23 are in A.P.** *(An)* (CBSE, 2022)

Sol. $\because$ Given terms are in AP.

$\therefore 7 - a = b - 7 = 23 - b$

$\Rightarrow b - 7 = 23 - b \Rightarrow 2b = 30 \Rightarrow b = 15$ *(1 M)*

Also, $7 - a = b - 7 \Rightarrow a + b = 14$

$\Rightarrow a = 14 - b = 14 - 15 = -1$

Hence, $a = -1$, $b = 15$ *(1 M)*

3. **The taxi fare after each km, when the fare is ₹15 for the first km and ₹8 for each additional km. Does the list of numbers involved here make an AP?** *(Cr)* (NCERT Intext)

Sol. Total fare for 1st km = ₹15 = a_1

Total fare for 2 km = ₹(15 + 8) = ₹23 = a_2

Total fare for 3 km = ₹(23 + 8) = ₹31 = a_3 *(1 M)*

Total fare for 4 km = ₹(31 + 8) = ₹39 = a_4

Now, $a_2 - a_1 = 23 - 15 = 8$, $a_3 - a_2 = 31 - 23 = 8$,

$a_4 - a_3 = 39 - 31 = 8$

Since, $a_2 - a_1 = a_3 - a_2 = a_4 - a_3 = 8$, so the numbers form an AP with common difference $d = 8$. *(1 M)*

4. **Determine the AP whose 3rd term is 5 and the 7th term is 9.** *(Ev)* (NCERT Intext)

Sol. We have, $a_3 = 5 \Rightarrow a + (3-1)d = 5 \Rightarrow a + 2d = 5$ ...(*i*)

Also, $a_7 = 9 \Rightarrow a + (7-1)d = 9 \Rightarrow a + 6d = 9$ ...(*ii*)

Subtracting (*ii*) from (*i*) we get, $-4d = -4 \Rightarrow d = 1$ *(1 M)*

Putting the value of $d = 1$ in (*i*) we get, $a + 2(1) = 5$

$\Rightarrow a = 5 - 2 = 3$

Hence, the required AP is: $a, a + d, a + 2d, \ldots$

$= 3, 3 + 1, 3 + 2(1), \ldots$ or $3, 4, 5, \ldots$ *(1 M)*

5. **Find the 10th term from the end of the AP 4, 9, 14, ..., 254.** *(Un)*

Sol. It is given that,

l = Last term = 254 and d = Common difference = 5

Using the formula of mth term from the end i.e., $l - (m - 1)d$.

$\therefore$ 10th term from the end

$= l - (10 - 1)\,d$ *(1 M)*

$= l - 9d = 254 - 9 \times 5 = 209$

Therefore, 10th term from the end of the given AP is 209. *(1 M)*

6. **Write first four terms of the AP where the first term a and the common difference d are given as, $a = 10$, $d = 10$.** *(An)* (NCERT Intext)

Sol. $a = 10$, $d = 10$

$\therefore a_1 = a = 10$

$a_2 = a_1 + d = 10 + 10 = 20$ *(1 M)*

$a_3 = a_2 + d = 20 + 10 = 30$

$a_4 = a_3 + d = 30 + 10 = 40$

First four terms of this AP are 10, 20, 30, and 40. *(1 M)*

7. **Find the number of terms in the AP: 7, 13, 19, ..., 205** *(Un)* (NCERT Intext)

Sol. The given AP is 7, 13, 19, …, 205

Here,

First term, $a = 7$ and

Common difference, $d = a_2 - a_1 = 13 - 7 = 6$

Let us suppose there are n terms in this AP

n^{th} term of an AP is given by:

$a_n = a + (n - 1)\,d$ *(1 M)*

$205 = 7 + (n - 1)\,6$ $[\because a_n = 205]$

$198 = (n - 1)\,6$

$33 = (n - 1)$

$n = 34$

Hence, there are 34 terms in the given AP *(1 M)*

8. Check whether –150 is a term of the AP 11, 8, 5, 2, … or not. *(Un)*

Sol. The given AP is 11, 8, 5, 2..

Therefore, First term, $a = 11$ and

Common difference, $d = a_2 - a_1 = 8 - 11 = -3$

Let us suppose –150 be the nth term of this AP, if it is, then

We know that n^{th} term of an AP is given by:

$a_n = a + (n-1)d$ *(1 M)*

$-150 = 11 + (n-1)(-3)$ $\quad [\because a = 11, d = -3 \ \& \ a_n = -150]$

$-150 = 11 - 3n + 3$

$-164 = -3n$

$n = \dfrac{164}{3}$

Here, n is no. of terms and no. of terms cannot be a fraction.

$\therefore$ –150 is not a term of this AP *(1 M)*

Short Answer Type Questions (2 or 3 M)

1. Find the 12th term from the end of the *AP*: –2, –4, –6, ..., – 100. *(Ev)* **(NCERT Exemplar)**

Sol. Here, $a = -2$; $d = -4 - (-2) = -4 + 2 = -2$ and, $l\ (a_n) = -100$

$\Rightarrow a_n = -100 \Rightarrow a + (n-1)d = -100 \Rightarrow -2 + (n-1)(-2) = -100$ *(1 M)*

$\Rightarrow -2 - 2n + 2 = -100 \Rightarrow -2n = -100 \Rightarrow n = 50$

$\therefore$ There are 50 terms in the given *AP*. *(1 M)*

Now, 12th term from the end $= (50 - 12 + 1)^{th}$ term $= 39^{th}$ term

$\therefore a_{39} = a + (39-1)d = -2 + (39-1)(-2) = -2 - 76 = -78$ *(1 M)*

Topper's Explanation **(CBSE 2016)**

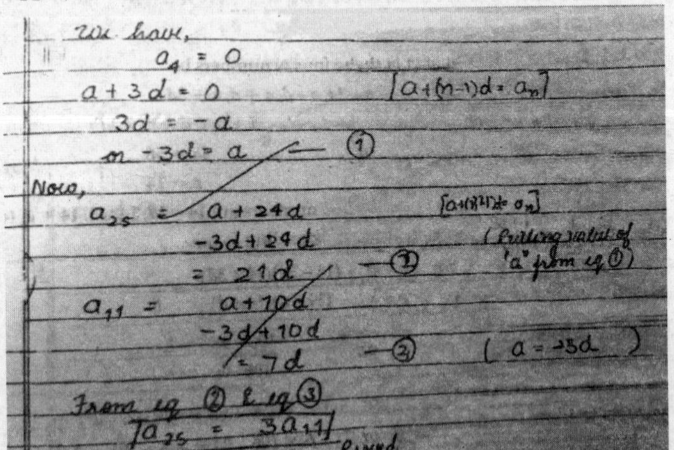

2. Which term of the AP 3, 15, 27, 39, … will be 120 more than its 21st term? *(Ap)*

Sol. Given sequence is 3, 15, 27, 39, ...

Here, first term $(a) = 3$

and common difference $(d) = 15 - 3 = 12$

Let m^{th} term be 120 more than 21st term.

$\therefore m^{th}$ term $= 21^{st}$ term $+ 120$

$a + (m-1)d = a + 20d + 120$ *(1 M)*

$(m-1)\,12 = 20(12) + 120$

$m - 1 = \dfrac{360}{12}$

$m = 30 + 1 = 31$ *(1 M)*

Hence, 31st term is 120 more than 21st term.

3. Show that $(a-b)^2$, (a^2+b^2) and $(a+b)^2$ are in AP *(Ev)*

Sol. The given terms are $(a-b)^2$, (a^2+b^2) and $(a+b)^2$.

In an AP, the difference of two adjacent terms is always constant.

Common difference, $d = a^2 + b^2 - (a-b)^2$

$= a^2 + b^2 - a^2 - b^2 + 2ab = 2ab$

Also, $d = (a+b)^2 - (a^2+b^2)$

$= a^2 + b^2 + 2ab - a^2 - b^2 = 2ab$ *(1 M)*

Since, common difference between two consecutive terms is constant. Hence, given terms are in AP *(1 M)*

4. Two APs have the same common difference. The difference between their 100th term is 100, what is the difference between their 1000th terms? *(Un)* **(NCERT Intext)**

Sol. Let us suppose, the first term of two APs be a_1 and a_1' respectively and the common difference between the terms of these AP's be d. *(½ M)*

We know that n^{th} term of an AP is given by:

$a_n = a + (n-1)d$

$\therefore$ For the first AP,

$a_{100} = a_1 + (100-1)d = a_1 + 99d$ … *(i)*

and $a_{1000} = a_1 + (1000-1)d$

$a_{1000} = a_1 + 999d$ … *(ii)* *(½ M)*

Therefore, for second AP,

$a_{100} = a_1' + (100-1)d = a_1' + 99d$ … *(iii)*

and $a_{1000} = a_1' + (1000-1)d = a_1' + 999d$ … *(iv)* *(½ M)*

It is given that, difference between 100th term of the two APs = 100

$\therefore (a_1 + 99d) - (a_1' + 99d) = 100$ (from *(i)* & *(iii)*)

$a_1 - a_1' = 100$ … *(iv)* *(½ M)*

Now, difference between 1000th terms of the two APs,

$(a_1 + 999d) - (a_1' + 999d) = a_1 - a_1'$ *(½ M)*

From equation *(iv)*,

This difference, $a_1 - a_1' = 100$

Therefore, the difference between 1000th terms of the two AP will also be 100. *(½ M)*

5. Which term of the sequence 4, 9, 14, 19, ... is 124? *(Un)*

Sol. The given sequence is an AP with first term $a = 4$ and common difference $d = 5$. *(½ M)*

Let n^{th} term of an AP be 124 *(½ M)*

$\therefore a_n = 124$

$a + (n-1)d = 124$ *(1 M)*

$\Rightarrow 4 + (n-1) \times 5 = 124$ $\quad (\because a = 4, d = 5)$

$\Rightarrow n = 25$

Therefore, 124 is the 25th term of the given sequence. *(1 M)*

6. **Show that the sequence log(a), log(ab), log(ab^2).... is an AP. Find its nth term.** *(Cr)*

Sol. In an AP, difference between terms should be same i.e., $a_2 - a_1 = a_3 - a_2$. *(½ M)*

We will first find the common difference,

$d = \log ab - \log a$ $[d = a_2 - a_1]$

$= \log\left(\frac{ab}{a}\right)$ $\left[\log a - \log b = \log \frac{a}{b}\right]$

$= \log b$ *(½ M)*

Also, $d = \log ab^2 - \log ab$ $[d = a_3 - a_2]$

$= \log\left(\frac{ab^2}{ab}\right) = \log b$ *(½ M)*

$\because a_2 - a_1 = a_3 - a_2$

Therefore, this sequence is an AP. *(½ M)*

Now, $a_n = a + (n - 1)d$

$= \log a + (n - 1)\log b$ *(½ M)*

$= \log a + \log b^{n-1}$ $[\because n \log a = \log a^n]$

$= \log (ab^{n-1})$ *(½ M)*

7. **Ramit is moving towards a stationary source of sound at a constant speed. At his initial position, he hears a pitch of 5 hertz.**

If the pitch from the source increases by 4 hertz for every 5 m Ramit travels, find the distance he would have travelled towards the source when the pitch is exactly 149 hertz. Show your steps. *(Ap)* **(CBSE CFPQ, 2023)**

Sol. An arithmetic progressions (AP) for the increase in pitch every 5 m as:

5 hertz, 9 hertz, 13 hertz, 17 hertz, ... *(½ M)*

The first term of the AP, a as 5 and the common difference, d as 4. *(½ M)*

The nth term of the AP when the pitch is exactly 149 hertz as: $5 + 4(n - 1) = 149 \Rightarrow n = 37$ *(1 M)*

The distance travelled by Ramit as $36 \times 5 = 180$ m. *(1 M)*

Long Answer Type Questions (4 or 5 M)

1. **In an A.P., if $S_n = 3n^2 + 5n$ and $a_k = 164$, find the value of k.** *(Ev)* **(CBSE, 2023)**

Sol. Given $S_n = 3n^2 + 5n \Rightarrow t_k = 164$ *(1 M)*

We have, $S_1 = 3(1)^2 + 5(1) = 8$

and $S_2 = 3(2)^2 + 5(2) = 22$ *(1 M)*

Now, $S_2 - S_1 = 22 - 8 = 14$

So, $t_1 = a = 8$ and $t_2 = 14$ *(1 M)*

$\Rightarrow d = t_2 - t_1 = 14 - 8 = 6$

Also, $t_n = a + (n - 1)d$

$\Rightarrow t_n = 8 + 6(n - 1) = 2 + 6n$ *(1 M)*

Also, $t_k = 164$

$\Rightarrow 2 + 6k = 164 \Rightarrow 6k = 162 \Rightarrow k = 27$ *(1 M)*

2. **If in an AP, the sum of three terms is –3 and their product is 8, then find these terms.** *(Ap)*

Sol. Let us suppose, three terms in AP be $a - d, a, a + d$ *(½ M)*

Hence, $a - d + a + a + d = -3$ *(½ M)*

$3a = -3$

$a = -1$ *(½ M)*

Also, $(a - d)\, a\, (a + d) = 8$ *(½ M)*

$a(a^2 - d^2) = 8$ $(\because a = -1)$

$\Rightarrow (-1)(1 - d^2) = 8 \Rightarrow 1 - d^2 = -8 \Rightarrow -d^2 = -8 - 1 \Rightarrow d^2 = 9$

$\Rightarrow d = \pm 3$ *(1 M)*

Therefore, if $a = -1$ and $d = 3$

First term of the AP will be $= a - d = -1 - 3 = -4$.

Second term of the AP will be $= a = -1$

Third term of the AP will be $= a + d = -1 + 3 = 2$ *(1 M)*

and, if $a = -1$ and $d = -3$

First term of the AP will be $= a - d = -1 - (-3) = 2$

Second term of the AP will be $= a = -1$

Third term of the AP will be $= a + d = -1 + (-3) = -4$ *(1 M)*

3. **If the 10th term of an AP is 52 and 16th term is 82, then find the 32nd term and the general term of AP.** **(Cr)**

Sol. Let us suppose, a be the first term and d be the common difference of the given AP *(½ M)*

As, $a_{10} = 52$ and $a_{16} = 82$ (given) *(½ M)*

Therefore, by using n^{th} term formula, we get

$a + (10 - 1)d = 52$ and $a + (16 - 1)\, d = 82$

$\Rightarrow a + 9d = 52$ ... (*i*)

and $a + 15d = 82$ ... (*ii*)

On subtracting eq.(*ii*) from (*i*), we get

$-6d = -30 \Rightarrow d = 5$ *(1 M)*

On putting value of d in eq. (*i*), we get

$a + 45 = 52 \Rightarrow a = 7$ *(1 M)*

Now, by using n^{th} term formula,

$a_{32} = a + (32 - 1)\, d = 7 + 31 \times 5 = 162$

and $a_n = a + (n - 1)\, d = 7 + (n - 1) \times 5 = 5n + 2$

Therefore, $a_{32} = 162$ *(1 M)*

$a_n = 5n + 2.$ *(1 M)*

2 SUM OF FIRST n-TERMS OF AN AP

Important Terms

- **Finite AP:** An arithmetic progression (AP) in which number of terms are finite is known as finite AP. Each Finite AP has a last term.
- **Infinite AP:** An arithmetic progression (AP) in which number of terms are infinite is known as infinite AP. Infinite AP does not have a last term.

Important Formulas

- The sum of first n-terms of an AP is given by

  $$S_n = \frac{n}{2}[2a+(n-1)d]$$

  Here a = first term, n = number of terms and d = common difference.
- If l is the last term of an AP., then sum of all terms is given by

  $$S_n = \frac{n}{2}[a+l]$$

Important Derivations

Derivation of Sum of First n-Terms of an AP

Let us suppose,

AP be $a, a + d, a + 2d, ... a + (n - 1)d$

Now, let S denote the sum of the first n terms of the AP, therefore we have

$S_n = a + (a + d) + (a + 2d) + ... + [a + (n - 1) d]$ ... (*i*)

Now, rewriting the above terms in reverse order, we get

$S_n = [a + (n - 1)d] + [a + (n - 2)d] + ... + (a + d) + a$ ... (*ii*)

On adding eq. (*i*) and (*ii*), we get

a	+	$a + (n-1)d$	=	$2a + (n-1)d$
+		+		
$a + d$	+	$a + (n-2)d$	=	$2a + (n-1)d$
+ ⋮ +		+ ⋮ +		⋮
$a + (n-2)d$	+	$a + d$	=	$2a + (n-1)d$
+		+		
$a + (n-1)d$	+	a	=	$2a + (n-1)d$
S_n	+	S_n	=	$n[2a + (n-1)d]$

(n times)

$$\Rightarrow 2S_n = n[2a + (n-1)d] \Rightarrow S_n = \frac{n}{2}[2a+(n-1)d]$$

Important Concepts

- The nth term of an AP is the difference of the sum to first n terms and the sum to first $(n - 1)$ terms of it, i.e., $a_n = S_n - S_{n-1}$.
- The sum of terms equidistant from the start and end of an AP is constant and is equal to the sum of the first and last term.
- Except the first term, any term of an AP is equal to the half of the sum of terms equidistant from the term. Suppose a_n is the term which is equidistant from the term a_{n-k} and a_{n+k}, then $a_n = \frac{1}{2}(a_{n-k} + a_{n+k})$, [where, $k < n$]
- Sum of first n natural numbers, i.e., $1 + 2 + 3 ... + n$

  $$\Rightarrow \sum_{r=1}^{n} r = \frac{n(n+1)}{2}$$

Find the sum of first 100 natural number.

9th Students

$1+2+3+4+5$ ...... $+99+100$

$= 3+3+4+$ .... $+ 99 + 100$

One eternity later

Ans. = 5050

10th Students

$1 + 2 + 3 + 4 +$ ..... $+ 99 + 100$

$= \frac{n(n+1)}{2} = \frac{100(101)}{2}$

$= 5050$

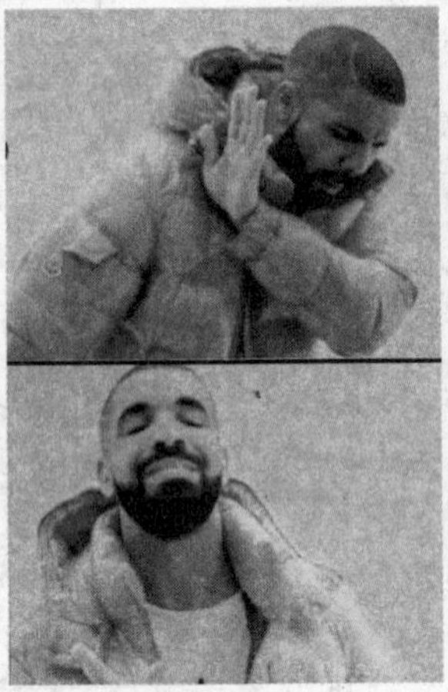

- Sum of first n even natural numbers, i.e., $2 + 4 + 6 + ... + n$

  $$\Rightarrow \sum_{r=1}^{n} 2r = n\,(n+1)$$

- Sum of first n odd natural numbers, i.e., $1 + 3 + 5 + ... + n$

  $$\Rightarrow \sum_{r=1}^{n} (2r-1) = n^2$$

Real Life Applications

What is your favourite sport? As an Indian, I bet around 90% of us will say cricket. All of us love to play and watch cricket. When you go to the stadium to watch a cricket match, you must have seen that seating arrangement is in ascending order.

Suppose that there are 150 seats in the first row, 200 seats in the second row, 250 seats in the third row and so on. If there are total 50 rows in the stadium, then what will be the seating capacity of the stadium? Don't worry you can easily find the answer, using sum of nth term of an AP.

Different Problem Types

Type I: Sum of n terms of Arithmetic Progression (AP) and its applications

Find the sum of the first 22 terms of the AP: 8, 3, –2, ...

Solution:

Step I: Calculate the first term, common difference and total number of terms in AP

Here, $a = 8$, $d = 3 - 8 = -5$, $n = 22$.

Step II: Apply the formula of sum of n terms of AP

We know that

$$S = \frac{n}{2}[2a + (n-1)d]$$

Therefore,

$$S = \frac{22}{2}[16 + 21(-5)] = 11(16 - 105) = 11(-89) = -979$$

So, the sum of the first 22 terms of the AP is –979.

Example 1: A sum of ₹700 is to be used to give seven cash prizes to students of a school for their overall academic performance. If each prize is ₹20 less than its preceding prize, find the value of each of the prizes.

Solution:

Let's denote the value of the first prize as x. We can represent the values of the prizes as an arithmetic progression (AP) with a common difference of –₹20.

The formula for the sum of the first n terms of an AP is given by:

$$S_n = \frac{n}{2}[2a + (n-1)d] \Rightarrow 700 = \frac{7}{2}[2x + (7-1)(-20)]$$

$$700 = 7x - 420$$

$$7x = 1120$$

$$x = 160$$

First prize: ₹160

Second prize: ₹160 – ₹20 = ₹140

Third prize: ₹140 – ₹20 = ₹120

Fourth prize: ₹120 – ₹20 = ₹100

Fifth prize: ₹100 – ₹20 = ₹80

Sixth prize: ₹80 – ₹20 = ₹60

Seventh prize: ₹60 – ₹20 = ₹40

Therefore, the values of the prizes are ₹160, ₹ 140 , ₹ 120 , ₹ 100, ₹ 80 , ₹ 60 , and ₹40, respectively.

Example 2: Find the sum of first 20 terms of the list of numbers whose n^{th} term is given by $a_n = 2 + 2n$

Solution:

As

$a_n = 2 + 2n$,

$a_1 = 2 + 2 = 4$

$a_2 = 2 + 2 \times 2 = 6$

$a_3 = 2 + 2 \times 3 = 8$

so,

List of numbers becomes 4, 6, 8, 10,...

Here, 6 – 4 = 8 – 6 = 10 – 8 = 2 and so on.

So, it forms an AP with common difference $d = 2$.

To find S_{20}, we have $n = 20$, $a = 4$, $d = 2$.

Therefore,

$$S_{20} = \frac{20}{2}[2 \times 4 + (20-1) \times 2] = 10[8 + 38] = 460$$

So, sum of first 20 terms of the list of numbers is 460.

COMPETENCY BASED SOLVED EXAMPLES

Multiple Choice Questions

(1 M)

1. **If the sum of the first n terms of an A.P. be $3n^2 + n$ and its common difference is 6, then its first term is:** *(Ev)*

   (a) 2 (b) 3

   (c) 1 (d) 4

Sol. Given, $S_n = 3n^2 + n$

First term, $S_1 = 3(1)^2 + 1 = 4$

2. **Find the sum of first five multiples of 3.** *(Ap)* **(NCERT Exemplar)**

   (a) 45 (b) 48

   (c) 23 (d) 75

Sol. The first five multiples of 3 are 3, 6, 9, 12 and 15 and there multiples form an AP

Here, $a = 3$

$d = 6 - 3 = 3$

and $n = 5$

and sum of n terms of an AP is given as

$$S_n = \frac{n}{2}[2a + (n-1)d]$$

$$\therefore S_n = \frac{5}{2}[2 \times 3 + (5-1)3]$$

$$S_n = \frac{5}{2}[6 + 12]$$

$$S_n = 45$$

Therefore, the sum of first five multiples of 3 is 45.

3. **Find the number of terms of the AP 17, 15, 13, 11, ... which are required to be added to get the sum 72.** *(An)*

   (a) 6 terms (b) 4 terms

   (c) 8 terms (d) 15 terms

Sol. From the given AP, we have

$a = 17$ and $d = 15 - 17 = -2$

Let the sum of n terms of AP be 72

i.e., $S_n = 72$

Sum of n terms of an AP is given by

$$S_n = \frac{n}{2}[2a+(n-1)d]$$

$$\Rightarrow \frac{n}{2}[2(17)+(n-1)(-2)] = 72 \qquad [\because a = 7, d = -2]$$

$\Rightarrow n[34 - 2n + 2] = 72 \times 2 \Rightarrow 34n - 2n^2 + 2n = 144$

$\Rightarrow n^2 - 18n + 72 = 0 \Rightarrow (n-6)(n-12) = 0$

$\Rightarrow n = 6$ and $n = 12$

Therefore, the sum of the first 6 terms = the sum of the first 12 terms = 72, which implies that the sum of the numbers from the 7th term to the 12th term is zero.

4. If a, b, c, d, e, f are in AP, then find the value of $(e - c)$. *(Ap)*

(*a*) $2(c - a)$ (*b*) $2(d - b)$

(*c*) $2(f - d)$ (*d*) $2(d - c)$

Sol. Let us suppose, x be the common difference between terms of AP, then

$a + x = b$ $[\because a_2 = a + d, a_3 = a + 2d, a_4 = a + 3d$ and so on$]$

$a + 2x = c$

$a + 3x = d$

$a + 4x = e$

$a + 5x = f$

Now, $e - c = (a + 4x) - (a + 2x) = 2x$

and $d - c = a + 3x - a - 2x = x$

Clearly, $e - c = 2(d - c)$

Hence, value of $(e - c)$ is $2(d - c)$.

5. If $S_n = nP + \dfrac{n(n-1)}{2}Q$, where S_n denotes the sum of the first n terms of an AP, then common difference is *(Un)*

(*a*) Q (*b*) $2P + 3Q$

(*c*) $Q + 2P$ (*d*) $2Q + P$

Sol. It is given that,

$$S_n = nP + \frac{n(n-1)Q}{2}$$

Now, $S_1 = (1)P + \dfrac{1(1-1)\,Q}{2} = P + 0 = P = a_1$

$$S_2 = 2(P) + \frac{2(2-1)Q}{2} = 2P + \frac{2Q}{2} = 2P + Q$$

As we know,

$a_n = S_n - S_{n-1}$

$\therefore a_2 = S_2 - S_1 = (2P + Q) - P = P + Q$

So, $d = a_2 - a_1 = (P + Q) - P = Q$

6. The sum of first n odd natural numbers is *(Ap)*

(*a*) $\dfrac{n^2}{2}$ (*b*) n^2

(*c*) $\dfrac{n^2+1}{2}$ (*d*) None of these

Sol. The sequence of odd natural numbers is 1, 3, 5, ...

Clearly, it forms an AP, having 1 as first term and 2 as common difference.

Also, sum of first n terms of an AP is given by

$$S_n = \frac{n}{2}[2a+(n-1)d]$$

Therefore, $S_n = \dfrac{n}{2}[2\times1+(n-1)2] = \dfrac{n}{2}[2+2n-2]$

$$= \frac{n}{2}\times 2n = n^2$$

7. Find the value of n, if $\dfrac{3+5+7+...+n \text{ terms}}{5+8+11+...+10 \text{ terms}} = 7$. *(An)*

(*a*) 35 (*b*) 24

(*c*) 39 (*d*) 40

Sol. It is given that,

$$\frac{3+5+7+...+n\text{ terms}}{5+8+11+...+10\text{ terms}} = 7$$

As, sum of n terms of an AP is given by

$$S_n = \frac{n}{2}[2a+(n-1)]d$$

Therefore,

$$\Rightarrow \frac{\frac{n}{2}[2(3)+(n-1)2]}{\frac{10}{2}[2(5)+(10-1)3]} = 7 \Rightarrow \frac{\frac{n}{2}[6+2n-2]}{\frac{10}{2}[10+9\times3]} = 7$$

$$\Rightarrow \frac{6n+2n^2-2n}{100+270} = 7 \Rightarrow 2(n^2+2n-1295) = 0$$

$\Rightarrow n^2 + 2n - 1295 = 0 \Rightarrow (n - 35)(n + 37) = 0$

Hence, value of n is 35.

8. Find the sum of all two digit numbers which when divided by 7 leaves 3 as remainder. *(Ev)*

(*a*) 444 (*b*) 582

(*c*) 676 (*d*) 777

Sol. The given AP can be written as

10, 17, 24, ..., 94

We see that 10, 17, 24, ..., 94 are in AP

Here $a = 10$, $d = 7$, $n = 13$ and $l = 94$

By using the formula

Hence, $S_n = \dfrac{n}{2}[a+l] = \dfrac{13}{2}[10+94]$

$$= \frac{13}{2}\times104 = 13 \times 52 = 676$$

Hence, the required sum is 676.

9. Find the sum of the series $85^2 - 83^2 + 84^2 - 82^2 + 83^2 - 81^2 + 82^2 - 80^2 + ...$ upto 15 terms. *(Ev)*

(*a*) 4825 (*b*) 4300

(*c*) 4620 (*d*) 4310

Sol. From the given series,

$S = (85 + 83)(85 - 83) + (84 + 82)(84 - 82) + (83 + 81)(83 - 81) + \ldots$ upto 15 terms

$S = 168 \times 2 + 166 \times 2 + 164 \times 2 + \ldots$ upto 15 terms

$S = 2[84 \times 2 + 83 \times 2 + 82 \times 2 + \ldots\ldots$ upto 15 terms]

$S = 4[84 + 83 + 82 + \ldots\ldots\ldots\ldots\ldots\ldots\ldots$ upto 15 terms]

This in an AP,

∴ Sum of n terms of an AP is given by,

$$S_n = \frac{n}{2}[2a+(n-1)d]$$

$$\Rightarrow S = 4 \times \frac{15}{2}[2 \times 84 + 14(-1)] \qquad [\because a = 84, d = -1]$$

$S = 15 \times 308 = 4620$

10. If the sum of first n terms of an AP is $(pn + qn^2)$, where p and q are real numbers, then the common difference of AP is ***(Un)***

(*a*) $p - 1$ (*b*) $p + q$

(*c*) $2p + 2q$ (*d*) $2q$

Sol. It is given that, sum of n terms = $pn + qn^2$

If, $n = 1$

$S_1 = p + q$

or, $a_1 = p + q$ ... (*i*)

Also, $S_2 = 2p + 4q$ ... (*ii*)

or, $a_2 = S_2 - S_1$

$= 2p + 4q - p - q$ (Using eq. (*i*) & (*ii*))

$= p + 3q$ ... (*iii*)

Now, $d = a_2 - a_1$

$\Rightarrow d = p + 3q - p - q$ (Using eq. (*iii*) & (*i*))

$\Rightarrow d = 2q$

11. If the 8th term of an arithmetic progression is 51 and 5th term is 33, then the sum of the first 10 terms of the arithmetic progression is ***(Ap)***

(*a*) 312 (*b*) 320

(*c*) 345 (*d*) 360

Sol. It is given that $a_8 = 51$ and $a_5 = 33$.

$a + 7d = 51$ ... (*i*)

$a + 4d = 33$ ... (*ii*)

On solving eq (*i*) and (*ii*), we get

$a = 9, d = 6$

Now, $S_n = \frac{n}{2}[2a + (n-1)d]$

$S_{10} = 5[2 \times 9 + 9 \times 6] = 360$

12. Find the sum of all the integers from 1 to 100 that are divisible by 2 or 5. ***(Cr)***

(*a*) 3000 (*b*) 3050

(*c*) 3600 (*d*) 3100

Sol. Sum of numbers between 1 to 100 which is divisible by 2

$$2 + 4 + 6 + 8 + \ldots\ldots + 100 = \frac{50}{2}(2 + 100) = 2550$$

Sum of numbers between 1 to 100 which is divisible by 5

$$5 + 10 + 15 + \ldots\ldots + 100 = \frac{20}{2}(5 + 100) = 1050$$

Sum of number between 1 to 100 which is divisible by both 2 and 5 *i.e.*, divisible by 10.

$$10 + 20 + \ldots\ldots + 100 = \frac{10}{2}(10 + 100) = 550$$

Therefore for sum of all integer between 1 to 100

$= 2550 + 1050 - 550 = 3050$

Answer Key

1. (d) 2. (a) 3. (a) 4. (d) 5. (a)
6. (b) 7. (a) 8. (c) 9. (c) 10. (d)
11. (d) 12. (b)

Assertion and Reason

(1 M)

Direction: In the following questions, a statement of Assertion (A) is followed by a statement of Reason (R). Mark the correct choice as.

(*a*) Both Assertion (A) and Reason (R) are true, and Reason (R) is the correct explanation of Assertion (A).

(*b*) Both Assertion (A) and Reason (R) are true, but Reason (R) is not the correct explanation of Assertion (A).

(*c*) Assertion (A) is true, but Reason (R) is false.

(*d*) Assertion (A) is false, but Reason (R) is true.

1. **Assertion (A): Sum of first hundred even natural numbers divisible by 5 is 500.** ***(An)***

   Reason (R): Sum of first n terms of an AP is given by $S_n = \frac{n}{2}[a + l]$, l is last term

Sol. First hundred even natural numbers divisible by 5 are 10, 20, 30, 40, 50..........1000

If last term is 1000, then sum of all these numbers can't be 500

Therefore, A is false but R is true.

2. **Assertion (A): Sum of all 11 terms of an AP whose middle most term is 30 is 330.**

   Reason (R): Sum of first n terms of an AP is given by $S_n = \frac{n}{2}[a + l]$, l is the middle term ***(Un)***

Sol. Middle most term $= \frac{n+1}{2} = \frac{11+1}{2} = 6^{th}$ term

$a_6 = a + 5d = 30$ ... (*i*)

Also, $S_{11} = \frac{n}{2}[2a+(n-1)d]$

$= \frac{11}{2}[2a+10d] = 11[a+5d] = 11 \times 30 = 330$ [From (*i*)]

Also, sum of first n terms of an AP is given by $S_n = \frac{n}{2}[a + l]$,

where l is last term not the middle term.

Therefore, A is true but R is false.

Answer Key

1. (d) 2. (c)

Subjective Questions

Very Short Answer Type Questions (1 or 2 M)

1. **If the sum of n terms of AP is $3n^2 + 5n$ and m^{th} term is 164, then find the value of m.** *(Ev)*

Sol. It is given that, $S_n = 3n^2 + 5n$

Now, $S_{n-1} = 3(n-1)^2 + 5(n-1) = 3(n^2 + 1 - 2n) + 5n - 5$

$= 3n^2 - n - 2$ *(1 M)*

$a_n = S_n - S_{n-1} = 3n^2 + 5n - (3n^2 - n - 2) = 6n + 2$

Given, $a_m = 164$

$6m + 2 = 164$

$m = 27$ *(1 M)*

2. **Find the sum of first 30 terms of the AP whose first term is –2 and common difference is 4.** *(An)*

Sol. Given, $a = -2$ and $d = 4$.

Sum of n terms of an AP is given by,

$S_n = \frac{n}{2}[2a + (n-1)d]$ *(1 M)*

$\therefore S_{30} = \frac{30}{2}[2 \times (-2) + (30-1) \times 4] = 15[-4 + (29 \times 4)]$

$= 15(-4 + 116) = 15 \times 112 = 1680$

Therefore, the sum of first 30 terms is 1680. *(1 M)*

3. **Find the sum of first 20 terms of AP 1, 4, 7, 10, ...** *(Ap)*

Sol. Here, $a = 1$ and $d = 3$

Now sum of n terms of an AP is given by formula,

$S_n = \frac{n}{2}\left[2a + (n-1)d\right]$ *(1 M)*

$\therefore S_{20} = \frac{20}{2}[2 \times 1 + (20-1)3]$

$S_{20} = 590$ *(1 M)*

4. **The nth term of an *AP* is $(7 - 4n)$, then what is its common difference?** *(Ev)* **(CBSE, 2020)**

Sol. n^{th} term $= a_n = 7 - 4n$

First term $= a_1 = 7 - 4(1) = 7 - 4 = 3$ *(1 M)*

Second term $a_2 = 7 - 4(2) = -1$

$\therefore$ Common difference = Second term – First term

$= (-1) - 3 = -4$ *(1 M)*

5. **In an AP if $a = 5, d = 3, a_n = 50$, find S_n.** *(Ap)* **(NCERT Intext)**

Sol. It is given that, $a = 5, d = 3, a_n = 50$

n^{th} term of an AP is given by:

$a_n = a + (n-1)d$ ... (*i*)

On putting the values of a, d and a_n in eq. (*i*), we get

$\Rightarrow 50 = 5 + (n-1) \times 3 \Rightarrow 3(n-1) = 45 \Rightarrow n = 16$ *(1 M)*

Also, sum of n terms of an AP is given by:

$S_n = \frac{n}{2}(a + a_n)$

$\therefore S_n = \frac{16}{2}(5 + 50) = 440 \quad [\because a_n = 50]$ *(1 M)*

Short Answer Type Questions (2 or 3 M)

1. **The first term of an AP is 5, the last term is 45 and the sum of all its terms is 400. Find the number of terms and the common difference of the AP** *(An)* **(NCERT Intext)**

Sol. First term $a = 5$, last term $l = 45$ and $S_n = 400$

Since, $S_n = \frac{n}{2}(a + l)$ *(½ M)*

$\Rightarrow 400 = \frac{n}{2}(5 + 45) \Rightarrow 400 = \frac{n}{2}(50)$

$\Rightarrow 400 = n(25) \Rightarrow n = 16$ *(1 M)*

Since, $l = a + (n-1)d$

$\Rightarrow 45 = 5 + (16 - 1)d$ *(½ M)*

$\Rightarrow 45 - 5 = (15)d \Rightarrow 40 = 15d$

$\Rightarrow d = \frac{40}{15} \Rightarrow d = \frac{8}{3}$ *(1 M)*

Key Takeaways

Sum of n terms, $S_n = \frac{n}{2}(a + l)$

2. **Find the sum of first 8 multiples of 3.** *(Ap)*

Sol. First, 8 multiples of 3 are {3, 6, 9, ..., 24} *(½ M)*

We can observe they are in AP with first term (a) = 3 and last term (l) = 24 and number of terms are 8.

$S_n = \frac{n}{2}(a + l)$ *(½ M)*

$\Rightarrow S_n = \frac{8}{2}(3 + 24)$

$S_8 = 4 \times (3 + 24) = 108$

Hence, the sum of the first 8 multiples of 3 is 108. *(1 M)*

3. **The first term of an AP is –5 and the last term is 45. If the sum of the terms of the AP is 120, then find the number of terms and the common difference.** *(Ev)*

Sol. Here, $a = -5$, $l = 45$ and $S_n = 120$

$S_n = 120 \Rightarrow \frac{n}{2}(a + l) = 120 \Rightarrow \frac{n}{2}(-5 + 45) = 120$ *(½ M)*

$\frac{n}{2} \times 40 = 120 \Rightarrow n = \frac{120 \times 2}{40} = 6$ *(½ M)*

Hence, number of terms = 6.

Now, $l = 45 \Rightarrow a_n = 45$ *(½ M)*

$\Rightarrow a + (n-1)d = 45 \Rightarrow -5 + (6-1)d = 45$ *(½ M)*

$\Rightarrow -5 + 5d = 45$

$\Rightarrow 5d = 50 \Rightarrow d = 10.$

Hence, common difference = 10. *(1 M)*

4. The exterior angles marked in each of the polygons below are in arithmetic progression.

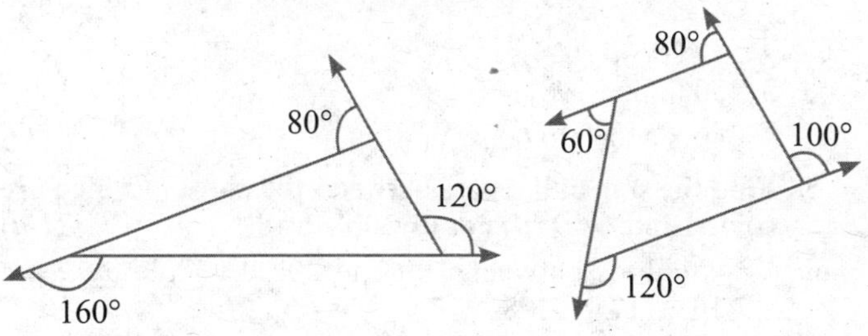

Minal drew one such polygon with n sides. The smallest exterior angle is 8° and each subsequent angle is 4° more than the previous angle.

Find the number of sides of the polygon that Minal had drawn. Show your steps. (*Ap*) **(CBSE CFPQ, 2023)**

Sol. The equation for the sum of the arithmetic progression as:

$\frac{n}{2}[16+4(n-1)] = 360$ *(1 M)*

$n^2 + 3n - 180 = 0$ *(½ M)*

Now, the roots of the above equation are 12, – 15 *(1 M)*

So, the number of sides of the polygon that Minal had drawn is 12. *(½ M)*

5. If the ratio of 11th term of an AP to its 18th term is 2 : 3, then find the ratio of the sum of first five terms to the sum of first 10 terms. **(*Un*)**

Sol. It is given that,

$\frac{a_{11}}{a_{18}} = \frac{2}{3}$ *(½ M)*

$\frac{a+10d}{a+17d} = \frac{2}{3}$ $[\because a_n = a + (n-1)d]$ *(½ M)*

$3a + 30d = 2a + 34d$

$3a - 2a = 34d - 30d$

$a = 4d$ *(½ M)*

Now, $S_n = \frac{n}{2}[2a+(n-1)d]$

$\frac{S_5}{S_{10}} = \frac{\frac{5}{2}\{2a+(5-1)d\}}{\frac{10}{2}\{2a+(10-1)d\}}$ *(½ M)*

$= \frac{1}{2}\left\{\frac{2a+4d}{2a+9d}\right\} = \frac{1}{2}\left\{\frac{2\times4d+4d}{2\times4d+9d}\right\}$ $[\because a = 4d]$

$= \frac{1}{2}\times\frac{12d}{17d} = \frac{6}{17}$

Therefore, $S_5 : S_{10} = 6 : 17$ *(1 M)*

6. Find the sum of all the three digit numbers which when divided by 5 leaves 3 as remainder. **(*Ap*)**

Sol. Smallest three digit number = 100.

As, 100 is completely divisible by 5.

Therefore, 103 is the first three digit number which will leave remainder 3 when divided by 5.

And, the largest 3 digit number which gives a remainder 3 when divided by 5 is 998

So, AP will be 103, 108, 113, ..., 998 *(1 M)*

$a + (n-1)d = a_n$

$103 + (n-1)5 = 998$ $(\because a = 103, d = 5, a_n = 998)$ *(½ M)*

$103 + 5n - 5 = 998$

$n = 180$

Therefore, number of terms $(n) = 180$ *(½ M)*

Now, sum $= \frac{n}{2}(a+\ell)$ *(½ M)*

$= \frac{180}{2}(103+998) = 90 \times 1101 = 99090$ *(½ M)*

7. Find the sum of last ten terms of the AP: 8, 10, 12, ... 126. **(*Ev*)**

Sol. Here, $a = 8$, $d = 10 - 8 = 2$ and $l\ (a_n) = 126$

$\Rightarrow a_n = 126 \Rightarrow a + (n-1)d = 126 \Rightarrow 8 + (n-1)(2) = 126$ *(1 M)*

$\Rightarrow 8 + 2n - 2 = 126 \Rightarrow 2n + 6 = 126$

$\Rightarrow 2n = 120 \Rightarrow n = 60$

Here, $a_{51} = a + (51-1)d = 8 + 50 \times 2 = 108$

$a_{52} = 8 + (52-1)(2) = 8 + 51 \times 2 = 8 + 102 = 110$ *(1 M)*

$\therefore$ Required sum = 108 + 110 + ... + 126

Here, $a = 108$; $d = 2$ and $l = 126$

Now, $S_{10} = \frac{10}{2}[108+126] = 5 \times 234 = 1170.$ *(1 M)*

Nailing the Right Answer

Students should carefully use the formula and input the value of '*n*' to understand the progression.

Long Answer Type Questions (4 or 5 M)

1. How many terms of the AP: 24, 21, 18, ... must be taken so that their sum is 78? **(*An*) (CBSE, 2020)**

Sol. Given that 24, 21, 18, ... is an AP.

Let n terms should be taken to make the sum 78 then *(1 M)*

24 + 21 + 18 + ...to n terms = 78

Here $a = 24$, $d = -3$, $S_n = 78$, $n = ?$

$S_n = \frac{n}{2}\{2a+(n-1d\}$ *(1 M)*

$\Rightarrow 78 = \frac{n}{2}\ \{2 \times 24 + (n-1)(-3)\}$

$\Rightarrow 156 = n(48 - 3n + 3) \Rightarrow 156 = n(51 - 3n)$ *(1 M)*

$\Rightarrow 3n^2 - 51n + 156 = 0 \Rightarrow 3(n^2 - 17n + 52) = 0$

$\Rightarrow (n-13)(n-4) = 0$

$\therefore n = 4, 13$ *(1 M)*

2. The sum of four consecutive numbers in an AP is 32 and the ratio of the product of the first and the last term to the product of two middle terms is 7 : 15. Find the numbers. **(*Cr*) (NCERT Exemplar)**

Sol. Let the 4 numbers which are in AP be

$a - 3d, a - d, a + d, a + 3d$ ... (*i*) *(½ M)*

Given, the sum of these terms = 32

$\Rightarrow (a-3d)+(a-d)+(a+d)+(a+3d)=32$ (½ M)

$\Rightarrow 4a = 32 \Rightarrow a = 8$ (½ M)

Given, the ratio of the product of the first and the last term to the product of two middle terms is 7 : 15

$$\frac{(a-3d)(a+3d)}{(a-d)(a+d)} = \frac{7}{15}$$ (½ M)

$$\frac{a^2-9d^2}{a^2-d^2} = \frac{7}{15}$$ (½ M)

$15a^2 - 135d^2 = 7a^2 - 7d^2$ (½ M)

$8a^2 = 128d^2$

$128d^2 = 512 \quad (\because a = 8)$

$d^2 = 4$

$d = \pm 2$ (½ M)

Putting the value $d = \pm 2$ and $a = 8$ in (*i*) we get the required number as 2, 6, 10, 14 (½ M)

3. If the ratio of the sums of first *n* terms of two A.P.'s is (7*n* + 1) : (4*n* + 27), find the ratio of their *m*th terms. (*Cr*)

Sol. Let, *a* and *A* be the first terms and *d* and *D* be the common difference of two A.P.'s (*1 M*)

Then, according to question,

$$\frac{S_n}{S'_n} = \frac{\frac{n}{2}[2a+(n-1)d]}{\frac{n}{2}[2A+(n-1)D]} = \frac{7n+1}{4n+27}$$ (*1 M*)

$$\Rightarrow \frac{2a+(n-1)d}{2A+(n-1)D} = \frac{7n+1}{4n+27}$$

$$\Rightarrow \frac{a+\left(\frac{n-1}{2}\right)d}{A+\left(\frac{n-1}{2}\right)D} = \frac{7n+1}{4n+27} \quad ...(i)$$ (*1 M*)

Putting, $\frac{n-1}{2} = m-1$ or, $n = 2m-1$ (*1 M*)

$$\frac{a+(m-1)d}{A+(m-1)D} = \frac{7(2m-1)+1}{4(2m-1)+27}$$

Hence, $\frac{a_m}{A_m} = \frac{14m-6}{8m+23}$ (*1 M*)

4. Find the sum of all odd numbers between 100 and 300. (*Ev*) (**CBSE, 2020**)

Sol. 101, 103, 105 … 299

First term = 101

Last term = 299

Common difference = 2 (*1 M*)

$299 = 101 + (n-1)\,2$

$\frac{198}{2} = (n-1)$

$n = 100$ (*1 M*)

$$S = \frac{100}{2}[2\times101+(100-1)2]$$

$$= \frac{50[202+99\times2]}{2} = \frac{50\times400}{2} = 10{,}000$$ (*1 M*)

$$S = \frac{100}{2}[2\times101\times(100-1)\times2]$$

$S = 50\,[202 + 99 \times 2]$

$S = 50\,[202 + 198]$

$S = 50 \times 400 = 20{,}000$ (*1 M*)

5. Find the sum of integers between 100 and 200 which are (*i*) divisible by 9 (*ii*) not divisible by 9. (*Un*)

Sol. (*i*) Numbers between 100 and 200 divisible by 9 are 108, 117, ... 198

Here, $a = 108$ and $d = 9$

$t_n = a+(n-1)d \Rightarrow 198 = 108 + (n-1)9$ (½ M)

$\Rightarrow 90 = (n-1)9 \Rightarrow 10 = n-1 \Rightarrow n = 11$ (*1 M*)

Now, $S_n = \frac{n}{2}[a+l]$ [$\because l = t_n$ = *last term*]

$= \frac{11}{2}[108+198] = \frac{11\times306}{2} = 11 \times 153 = 1683$ (*1 M*)

(*ii*) Total numbers between 100 and 200 are 99.

101, 102, ...199 (½ M)

Now, $S_n = \frac{n}{2}[a+l] = \frac{99}{2}[101+199] = \frac{99}{2}\times300$

$= 99 \times 150 = 14850$ (*1 M*)

$\therefore$ Sum of integers not divisible by 9 between 100 and 200

= Sum of all integers between 100 and 200 – Sum of integers divisible by 9 between 100 and 200

= 14850 – 1683 = 13167 (*1 M*)

6. A small terrace at a football ground comprises of 15 steps each of which is 50 m long and built of solid concrete. Each step has a rise of $\frac{1}{4}$ m and a tread of $\frac{1}{2}$ m. (see Fig.). Calculate the total volume of concrete required to build the terrace. (*Cr*) (**NCERT Intext**)

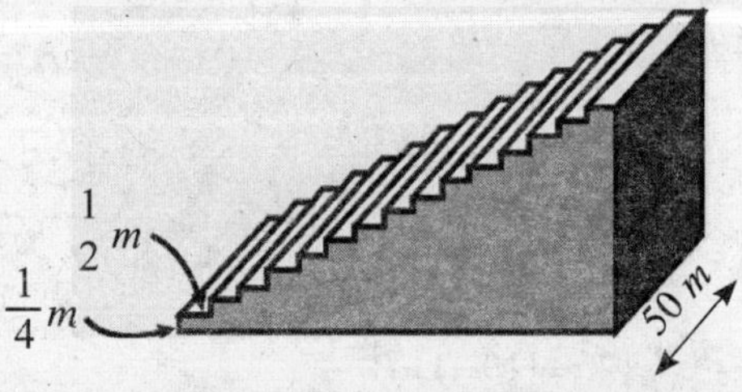

Sol. From the given figure, we can see that the height of first step is $\frac{1}{4}$ *m*, height of second step is $\frac{1}{4}+\frac{1}{4}=\frac{1}{2}m$ and that of third step is $\frac{1}{4}+\frac{1}{4}+\frac{1}{4}=\frac{3}{4}m$ (½ M)

Clearly, height of each step is increasing by $\frac{1}{4}m$.

Thus the height of steps form an AP: e.g.

$\frac{1}{4}, \frac{1}{2}, \frac{3}{4}, 1, ...$ (½ M)

Also, Volume of steps = Volume of Cuboid

= Length × Breadth × Height

Therefore,

Volume of concrete required to build the Ist step

$= \frac{1}{4}\times\frac{1}{2}\times50 = \frac{25}{4}$ (½ M)

Volume of concrete required to build the IInd step

$= \frac{1}{2} \times \frac{1}{2} \times 50 = \frac{50}{4}$ (½ M)

Volume of concrete required to build the IIIrd step

$= \frac{3}{4} \times \frac{1}{2} \times 50 = \frac{75}{4}$ (½ M)

Again, the volumes of concrete required to build the steps form an AP i.e.

$\frac{25}{4}, \frac{50}{4}, \frac{75}{4}, \ldots$ (½ M)

Here,

First term, i.e., $a = \frac{25}{4}$

Common difference, i.e., $d = \frac{50}{4} - \frac{25}{4} = \frac{25}{4}$ (½ M)

Now, sum of n terms of an AP is given by formula,

$S_n = \frac{n}{2}[2a + (n-1)d]$ (½ M)

$S_{15} = \frac{15}{2}\left(2 \times \frac{25}{4} + (15-1)\frac{25}{4}\right)$ (½ M)

$S_{15} = 15/2\ (100)$

$S_{15} = 750$

Therefore, the total volume of concrete required to build the terrace is 750 m^3. (½ M)

Key Takeaways

Sum of n terms $S_n = \frac{n}{2}[2a + (n-1)d]$

Where n = no of terms, a = first term and d = difference

7. 200 logs are stacked in the following manner: 20 logs in the bottom row, 19 in the next row, 18 in the row next to it and so on. In how many rows are the 200 logs placed and how many logs are in the top row? (*Cr*) (NCERT Intext)

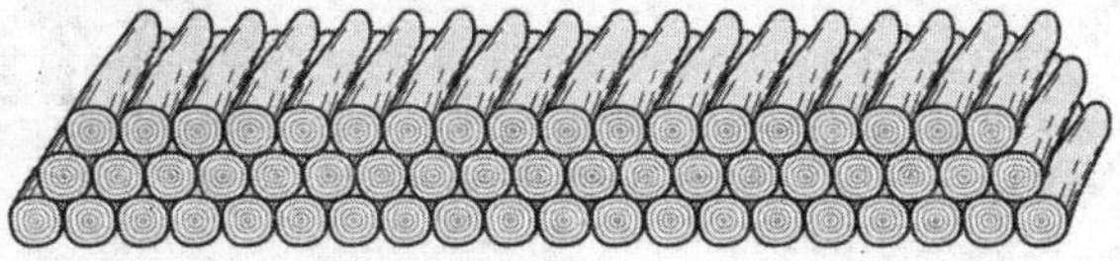

Sol. Here, we can see that the number of logs arranged in rows form an AP i.e., 20, 19, 18… (½ M)

Hence, for the given AP,

First term i.e., a is 20 and common difference,

$d = a_2 - a_1 = 19 - 20 = -1$ (½ M)

Now, let us assume a total of 200 logs is placed in 'n' number of rows.

Therefore, $S_n = 200$ (½ M)

We know that the sum of n terms of an AP is given by,

$S_n = \frac{n}{2}[2a + (n-1)d]$ (½ M)

$\therefore 200 = \frac{n}{2}[2(20) + (n-1)(-1)]$

$[\because S_n = 200, d = -1, a = 20]$ (½ M)

$400 = n(40 - n + 1)$

$400 = 41n - n^2 \Rightarrow n^2 - 41n + 400 = 0$

$\Rightarrow n^2 - 16n - 25n + 400 = 0$

$\Rightarrow n(n-16) - 25(n-16) = 0$ (½ M)

$\Rightarrow (n-16)(n-25) = 0$

i.e., $n - 16 = 0$ or $n - 25 = 0$

$n = 16$ or $n = 25$ (½ M)

Also, we know that the nth term of an AP is given by,

$a_n = a + (n-1)d$

$\therefore a_{16} = 20 + (16-1)(-1)$ $[\because a = 20, d = -1]$

$a_{16} = 5$ (½ M)

In the similar way,

$a_{25} = 20 + (25-1)(-1) = 20 + 24(-1) = 20 - 24 = -4$ (½ M)

As, the number of logs can never be negative, Hence, 200 logs can be placed in 16 number of rows and the number of logs present in the 16th row is 5. (½ M)

MISCELLANEOUS EXERCISE

Multiple Choice Questions

(1 M)

1. Find the 11th term of an AP $-5, -\frac{5}{2}, 0, \frac{5}{2}$.........

(a) –20 (b) 20

(c) –15 (d) 30

2. Two AP's have the same common difference. The first term of one of these is –1 and that of the other is –8, then find the difference between their 4th terms.

(a) –3 (b) –8

(c) 7 (d) –5

3. Find the value of n if the numbers $n-2$, $4n-1$ and $5n+2$ are in AP.

(a) 1 (b) 4

(c) –4 (d) –2

4. If 17th term of an AP exceeds its 10th term by 7, then common difference of the AP is

(a) 1 (b) 6

(c) 5 (d) 4

5. If $a-3d, a-d, a+d, a+3d$ are continuous terms of an AP., then find the common difference of AP

(a) d (b) $2d$

(c) $2a$ (d) $a-d$

6. In an AP, if 8th and 12th term are 39 and 59 respectively, then find the first term of AP.

(a) 3 (b) 6

(c) 4 (d) 1

7. If the first and third terms of AP, are 15 and 20 respectively then, the sum of the n terms of an AP is.

(a) $n[30+(n-1)5]$ (b) $\frac{n}{2}\left[30+(n-1)\frac{5}{2}\right]$

(c) $\frac{n}{2}\left[15+(n-1)\frac{5}{2}\right]$ (d) None of these

8. If a, b, c, d, e are in AP, then find the value of $a-3b+3c-d$.

(a) $a+b$ (b) $a-b$

(c) 0 (d) None of these

9. In an AP if 10th term is 25 and 14th term is 33, then determine the general term of an AP

(a) $3n+8$ (b) $2n+7$

(c) $2n+5$ (d) $3n+7$

10. If the first and third terms of AP are a^2+7 and $3a^2+4$ respectively, then the second term of AP is

(a) a^2 (b) $\frac{3}{2}+a^2$

(c) $3a^2+2$ (d) $2a^2+\frac{11}{2}$

11. The nth term of the A.P. $a, 3a, 5a,$ ...... is

(a) na (b) $(2n-1)a$

(c) $(2n+1)a$ (d) $2na$

12. If $\frac{1}{a}, \frac{1}{b}, \frac{1}{c}$ are in AP, then $\frac{b+a}{b-a}+\frac{b+c}{b-c}$ equals

(a) 1 (b) 2

(c) $\frac{b-c}{a-b}$ (d) $\frac{ab}{c}$

13. In an Arithmetic Progression, the sum of first 'n' terms is $\frac{3n^2}{2}+\frac{5n}{2}$. Then the 25th term will be:

(a) 75 (b) 74

(c) 76 (d) None of these

14. The angles of a pentagon are in arithmetic progression. The sum of the smallest and largest angle is

(a) 172° (b) 108°

(c) 180° (d) 216°

Assertion and Reason

(1 M)

Direction: In the following questions, a statement of Assertion (A) is followed by a statement of Reason (R). Mark the correct choice as:

(a) Both Assertion (A) and Reason (R) is true and Reason (R) is the correct explanation of Assertion (A).

(b) Both Assertion (A) and Reason (R) is true but Reason (R) is not the correct explanation of Assertion (A).

(c) Assertion (A) is true but Reason (R) is false.

(d) Assertion (A) is false but Reason (R) is true.

1. **Assertion (A):** Sum of first 10 terms of an AP –0.5, –1.0, –1.5, ... is –27.5.

Reason (R): Sum of n terms of an AP is given as $S_n=\frac{n}{2}[2a+(n-1)d]$, where a is first term and d is common difference.

2. **Assertion (A):** If $a_n - a_{n-1}$ is not independent of n, then the given sequence is an AP.

Reason (R): Common difference $d=a_n-a_{n-1}$ is independent of n or constant.

3. **Assertion (A):** If three consecutive terms $2m + 1$, $3m + 3$ and $5m - 1$ form an AP, then m is equal to 6.

Reason (R): In an AP $a, a + d, a + 2d$, ... the sum to n terms of the AP is given as, $S_n = \frac{n}{2}[2a+(n-1)d]$.

4. **Assertion (A):** If the sum of the first n terms of an AP is given by $S_n = 3n^2 - 4n$, then its nth term is $a_n = 6n - 7$.

Reason (R): n^{th} term of an AP whose sum to n terms is S_n is given by $a_n = S_n - S_{n-1}$.

Subjective Questions

Very Short Answer Type Questions (1 or 2 M)

1. Find the number of terms of an AP, if the nth term of the AP 8, 10, 12, 14, 16 ..... is 550.
2. Find $a_{30} - a_{20}$, for the AP –9, –14, –19, –24, ...
3. Find the 9th term from the end (towards the first term) of the AP: 5, 9, 13, ..., 185.
4. Find the common difference of an AP in which $a_{18} - a_{14} = 32$.
5. If 7 times the 7th term of an AP is equal to 11 times its 11th term, then find its 18th term.
6. Find the 25th term of the AP: $-5, \frac{-5}{2}, 0, \frac{-5}{2}$...
7. Is 144 a term of the AP: 3, 7, 11, ...? Justify your answer.
8. In an AP, if $a = 28$ and $d = -4$, then find the value of a_7.
9. The sum of the first two terms of an arithmetic progression is the same as the sum of the first seven terms of the same arithmetic progression.

   Can such an arithmetic progression exist? Justify your answer. **(CBSE CFPQ, 2023)**
10. Which term of the AP: 3, 8, 13, 18, … is 98?

Short Answer Type Questions (2 or 3 M)

1. Find the middle term of AP 6, 13, 20, ... 216.
2. In an AP, if the sum of three terms is 12 and the sum of the square of them is 56, then find the three numbers.
3. If first term of an AP is 5 and the sum of its first four terms is half the sum of the next four terms, then find the common difference of AP.
4. A positive integer has three digits, which are in AP and their sum is 15. The number obtained by reversing the digits is 594 less than the original number. Find the number.
5. If five times the fifth term of an AP is equal to 8 times its eight term, show that its 13th term is zero.
6. Sum of three numbers which forms an AP is 30 and their product is 910. Find the numbers.
7. In an AP, if sum of four consecutive numbers is 20 and the sum of their squares is 120, then find the four numbers of AP
8. If the sum of n terms of three arithmetic progression are S_1, S_2 and S_3. Also, the first term of each AP is 1 and the common differences are 1, 2 and 3 respectively then prove that $S_1 + S_3 = 2S_2$.
9. Find the largest negative term of the sequence 20, $19\frac{1}{4}$, $18\frac{1}{2}$, $17\frac{3}{4}$, ...
10. Prove that the common difference of an AP, the sum of whose n terms is S_n, is $S_n - 2S_{n-1} + S_{n-2}$.
11. If p^{th} and q^{th} term of an AP is q and p respectively, then prove that the rth term of AP is $p + q - r$.
12. Find the term of the AP, 51, 47, 43, ... which is a cube of itself?
13. A sum of ₹280 is to be used towards four prizes. If each prize after the first is ₹20 less than its preceding prize, find the value of each of the prizes.
14. A ladder has rungs 25 cm apart. (see Fig.). The rungs decrease uniformly in length from 45 cm at the bottom to 25 cm at the top. If the top and the bottom rungs are $2\frac{1}{2}m$ apart, what is the length of the wood required for the rungs? **(NCERT Intext)**

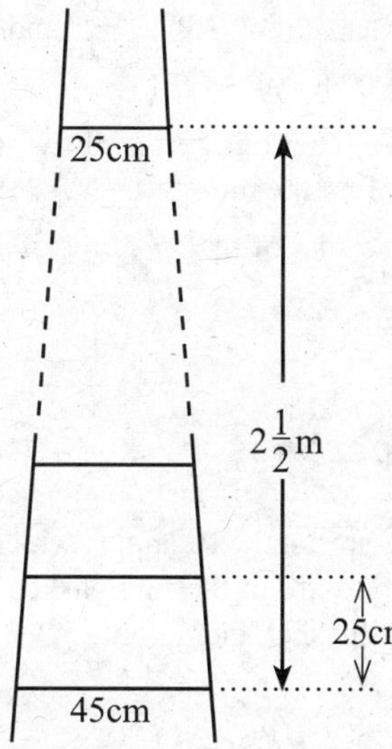

Long Answer Type Questions (4 or 5 M)

1. If a_1, a_2, a_3 ....a_n are in AP, then show that

$$\frac{1}{\sqrt{a_1}+\sqrt{a_2}}+\frac{1}{\sqrt{a_2}+\sqrt{a_3}}+......+\frac{1}{\sqrt{a_{n-1}}+\sqrt{a_n}} = \frac{n-1}{\sqrt{a_1}+\sqrt{a_n}}$$

2. A spiral is made up of successive semicircles, with centres alternately at A and B, starting with centre at A of radii 0.5 cm, 1.0 cm, 1.5 cm, 2.0 cm, ... as shown in figure. What is the total length of such a spiral made up of thirteen consecutive semicircles? (Take $\pi = 22/7$) **(NCERT Intext)**

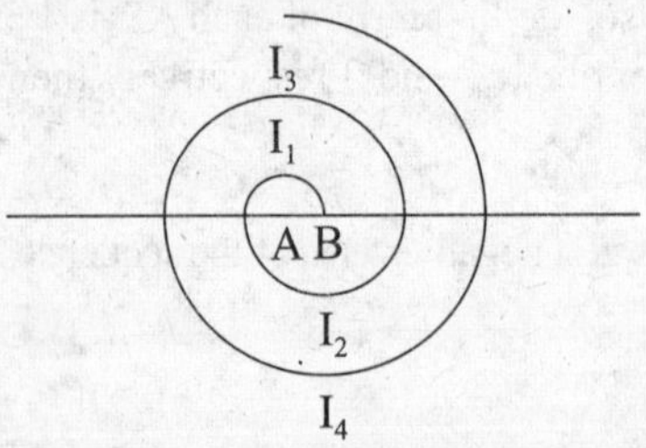

3. The houses of a row are numbered consecutively from 1 to 49. Show that there is a value of x such that the sum of the numbers of the houses preceding the house numbered x is equal to the sum of the numbers of the houses following it. Find this value of x. **(NCERT Intext)**

4. Priya is preparing for the Bicycle Marathon. Her racing bicycle has a device to calculate the number of kilometres she cycled. She decides to increase the distance she cycles everyday by a fixed number of kilometres.
   (i) On the first day Priya cycled 8 km. In 10 days she cycled a total of 170 km. How many kilometres did she cycle on the 3rd day?
   (ii) Priya plans to go on a cycle tour from Bangalore to Mangalore covering 425 km. She travels 20 km on day 1 and increases the distance covered each day by 5 km. In how many days will she reach her destination?
   (CBSE CFPQ, 2023)

5. If 10th and 20th term of an AP be $\frac{1}{20}$ and $\frac{1}{10}$ respectively, then find the 200th term of AP

6. If the ratio of the sum of n terms of two AP's is $(7n + 1) : (4n + 27)$, then find the ratio of their m^{th} terms.

7. Let S_n denote the sum of first 'n' terms of an AP if $S_{2n} = 3S_n$, then find the ratio $\frac{S_{3n}}{S_n}$.

Case Based Questions

Case Based-I: There are total 810 apples which are arranged in such a way that 5 apples are in the first basket, 12 in the second basket, 19 in the third basket and so on.

Based on the above information, answer the following questions:

(i) Find the number of apples in the 9th basket.

(ii) Find the sum of apples in the first 13 baskets.

OR

Find the sum of apples in the first 14 baskets.

(iii) In how many baskets are 810 apples kept?

Case Based-II: Your father wants to buy a flat and plans to take loan from a bank for that. He repays his total loan of ₹15,34,000 by paying every month starting with the first installment of ₹13000. Also he increases the installment by ₹1300 every month.

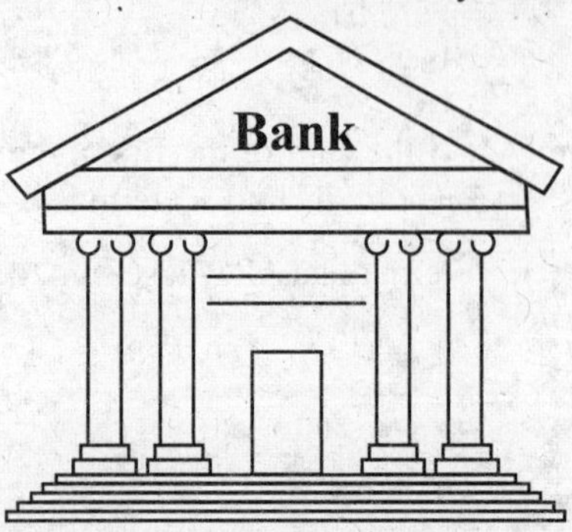

Based on the above information, answer the following questions:

(i) The amount paid by him in 20th installment is

(*a*) ₹ 38,700 (*b*) ₹ 37,700
(*c*) ₹ 36,000 (*d*) ₹ 39,900

(ii) The amount paid by him upto 30 installments is

(*a*) ₹ 5,20,000 (*b*) ₹ 95,500
(*c*) ₹ 9,55,500 (*d*) ₹ 8,55,000

(iii) The total number of installments he has to pay is

(*a*) 40 (*b*) 59
(*c*) 39 (*d*) 45

(iv) The ratio of the 1st installment to the 20th installment is

(*a*) 10 : 39 (*b*) 10 : 29
(*c*) 1 : 49 (*d*) 39 : 53

Case Based-III: A health camp was organized in a school for all the students and staff to spread awareness about health check-up and maintaining a healthy life.

In one such health camp, it is found out that the heights of a group of students in a class X form an arithmetic progression (AP). The height of the shortest student is 140 cm and the common difference is 4 cm.

Answer the following questions based on this information:

(i) What is the height of the 10th student in the class?

(*a*) 176 cm (*b*) 184 cm
(*c*) 196 cm (*d*) 204 cm

(ii) What is the sum of the heights of the first 20 students in the class?

(*a*) 3400 cm (*b*) 3560 cm
(*c*) 3800 cm (*d*) 4000 cm

(*iii*) If total number of students are 22, then the number of students in the class have a height greater than 180 cm is

(*a*) 10 (*b*) 11

(*c*) 13 (*d*) 7

(*iv*) What is the height of the shortest student in the class?

(*a*) 126 cm (*b*) 135 cm

(*c*) 139 cm (*d*) 140 cm

Case Based-IV: Manufacturing is emerging as an integral pillar in the country's economic growth, thanks to the performance of key sectors like automotive, engineering, chemicals, pharmaceuticals, and consumer durables. India is competitive manufacturing location due to the low cost of manpower and strong technical and engineering capabilities contributing to higher quality production runs.

A company produces shoes and sells it at a price that increases by ₹10 every month. In the first month, the company sold 500 units of the product at a price of ₹500 per unit.

Answer the questions based on the given information.

(*i*) What is the selling price of the product in the 10th month?

(*ii*) How much money did the company earn from selling the product in the first 6 months? (Assume they sell 500 units each month)

OR

How much money did the company earn from selling the product in the first 10 months? (Assume they sell 500 units each month)

(*iii*) In which month will the selling price of the product reach ₹ 800 per unit?

Case Based-V: An interior designer, Sana, hired two painters, Manan and Bhima to make paintings for her buildings. Both painters were asked to make 50 different paintings each.

The prices quoted by both the painters are given below:

- Manan asked for ₹6000 for the first painting, and an increment of ₹200 for each following painting.
- Bhima asked for ₹4000 for the first painting, and an increment of ₹400 for each following painting.

Answer the questions based on the given information.

(*i*) How much money did Manan get for his 25th painting? Show your work.

(*ii*) How much money did Bhima get in all? Show your work.

(*iii*) If both Manan and Bhima make paintings at the same pace, find the first painting for which Bhima will get more money than Manan. Show your steps.

OR

Sana's friend, Aarti hired Manan and Bhima to make paintings for her at the same rates as for Sana. Aarti had both painters make the same number of paintings, and paid them the exact same amount in total.

How many paintings did Aarti get each painter to make? Show your work.

ANSWER KEYS

Multiple Choice Questions

1. (*b*) **2.** (*c*) **3.** (*a*) **4.** (*a*) **5.** (*b*) **6.** (*c*) **7.** (*b*) **8.** (*c*) **9.** (*c*) **10.** (*d*)
11. (*b*) **12.** (*b*) **13.** (*c*) **14.** (*d*)

Assertion and Reason

1. (*a*) **2.** (*d*) **3.** (*b*) **4.** (*a*)

Case Based Questions

Case Based-II

(*i*) (*b*) (*ii*) (*c*) (*iii*) (*a*) (*iv*) (*b*)

Case Based-III

(*i*) (*a*) (*ii*) (*b*) (*iii*) (*b*) (*iv*) (*d*)

HINTS & EXPLANATIONS

Multiple Choice Questions

1. (*b*) The given AP is $-5, -\frac{5}{2}, 0, \frac{5}{2}$.........

Here, $a = -5$

and $d = \frac{-5}{2} - (-5)$ $[\therefore d = a_2 - a_1]$

$d = \frac{5}{2}$

By using n^{th} term formula, we get

$a_{11} = a + (11-1)d$

$a_{11} = -5 + 10 \times \frac{5}{2}$

$a_{11} = -5 + 25$

$a_{11} = 20$

Hence, value of a_{11} is 20.

2. (*c*) Let us suppose, a_1 and a' be the first terms of two AP's respectively and d be the common difference of both AP's.

Now, the 4th term of first AP is

$a_4 = a_1 + 3d$

and the 4th term of another AP is

$a'_4 = a' + 3d$

It is given that,

$a_1 = -1$ and $a' = -8$

Hence,

$a_4 - a_4' = (-1 + 3d) - (-8 + 3d)$

$a_4 - a_4' = -1 + 8 + 3d - 3d$

$a_4 - a_4' = 7$

3. (*a*) Let,

$a = n - 2;\ b = 4n - 1;\ c = 5n + 2$

Since the terms are in AP,

$\therefore 2b = a + c$

$\Rightarrow 2(4n - 1) = n - 2 + 5n + 2 \Rightarrow 8n - 2 = 6n$

$\Rightarrow 8n - 6n = 2 \Rightarrow n = 1$

Therefore, value of n is 1.

4. (*a*) It is given that

$a_{17} = a_{10} + 7$

$a + 16d = a + 9d + 7$

$7d = 7$

$d = 1$

5. (*b*) Let $a - 3d, a - d, a + d, a + 3d$ are continuous terms of an AP

Common difference, $d = (a - d) - (a - 3d)$

$= a - d - a + 3d = 2d$

6. (*c*) It is given that 8th and 12th term are 39 and 59 respectively.

$\therefore a + 7d = 39$ ... (*i*)

and $a + 11d = 59$ ... (*ii*)

On solving eq. (*i*) and (*ii*), we get $a = 4$ and $d = 5$

7. (*b*) It is given that,

$a_1 = 15$ ... (*i*)

and $a_3 = 20$

By using nth term formula, we have

$a_3 = 15 + 2d$ ... (*ii*)

$20 = 15 + 2d$ $[\because a = a_1 = 15]$

$20 - 15 = 2d$

$d = \frac{5}{2}$

Sum of n terms of AP is given by

$$S_n = \frac{n}{2}\left[2a + (n-1)\frac{5}{2}\right] = \frac{n}{2}\left[30 + (n-1)\frac{5}{2}\right]$$

8. (*c*) The given terms a, b, c, d and e are in AP

Let x be the common difference between terms of this AP

Then, $b = a + x,\ c = a + 2x,\ d = a + 3x,\ e = a + 4x$

Therefore, $a - 3b + 3c - d$

$= a - 3(a + x) + 3(a + 2x) - (a + 3x)$

$= a - 3a - 3x + 3a + 6x - a - 3x = 0$

9. (*c*) It is given that,

$a_{10} = 25$ and $a_{14} = 33$

By using n^{th} term formula, we have

$a + 9d = 25$ ... (*i*)

$a + 13d = 33$ ... (*ii*)

On solving eq. (*i*) and (*ii*) we get,

$d = 2$ and $a = 7$

Hence, general term

$a_n = a + (n-1)d = 7 + (n-1)2$ $[\because a = 7, d = 2]$

$= 7 + 2n - 2 = 2n + 5$

10. (*d*) It is given that,

$a_1 = a^2 + 7$ ... (*i*)

and $a_3 = 3a^2 + 4$

By using n^{th} term formula, we have

$a_1 + 2d = 3a^2 + 4$ ... (*ii*)

On solving eq. (*i*) and (*ii*), we get

$d = a^2 - \frac{3}{2}$

Now, the second term $a_2 = a_1 + d$

$= a^2 + 7 + a^2 - \frac{3}{2} = 2a^2 + \frac{11}{2}$

11. (*b*) The given *AP* is; $a, 3a, 5a$, ...

First term = a.

common difference = $3a - a = 2a$.

$\therefore$ The nth term $= a + (n-1)2a = a + 2an - 2a$.

$= 2an - a = a(2n - 1)$

12. (*b*) Here $\frac{1}{b} - \frac{1}{a} = \frac{1}{c} - \frac{1}{b}$

$\Rightarrow 2ac = ab + bc$ ... (*i*)

Now $\frac{b+a}{b-a}+\frac{b+c}{b-c}$

$$=\frac{(b+a)(b-c)+(b+c)(b-a)}{(b-a)(b-c)}$$

$$=\frac{2b^2-2ac}{b^2-(ab+bc)+ac}=\frac{2(b^2-ac)}{b^2-2ac+ac} \quad \text{(from } (i))$$

$$=\frac{2(b^2-ac)}{b^2-ac}=2$$

13. (*c*) As we know, $a_n = S_n - S_{n-1}$

$\therefore a_{25} = S_{25} - S_{24}$

$$=\frac{3(25)^2}{2}+\frac{5(25)}{2}-\frac{3(24)^2}{2}-\frac{5(24)}{2}\quad\left[\because S_n=\frac{3n^2}{2}+\frac{5n}{2}\right]$$

$$=\frac{3}{2}(25^2-24^2)+\frac{5}{2}(25-24)$$

$$a_{25}=\frac{3}{2}\times 49+\frac{5}{2}=\frac{152}{2}=76$$

14. (*d*) Let the angles of pentagon be $a-2d, a-d, a, a+d$ and $a+2d$.

$\therefore a-2d+a-d+a+a+d+a+2d = 540°$

$5a = 540$

$a = 108°$

Now, sum of smallest and largest angle be

$a-2d+a+2d = 2a = 216°$

Assertion and Reason

1. (*a*) Assertion, $S_{10}=\frac{10}{2}[2(-0.5)+(10-1)(-0.5)]$

$=5[-1.0+(9\times(-0.5))]=5[-1-4.5]=5(-5.5)=-27.5$

Reason is true as it represents the sum of n-terms

Both assertion (*A*) and reason (*R*) is true and reason (*R*) is the correct explanation of assertion (*A*).

2. (*d*) Common difference of an AP i.e., $d = a_n - a_{n-1}$ is constant that means it is independent of n.

Hence, Assertion is incorrect as it says that common difference is not independent of n and reason is true.

$\therefore$ Assertion is incorrect and Reason is correct.

3. (*b*) As $2m+1$, $3m+3$ and $5m-1$ form an AP,

Therefore, $(3m+3)-(2m+1) = (5m-1)-(3m+3)$

$m+2 = 2m-4$ $\quad [\because a_2 - a_1 = a_3 - a_2$ in an AP$]$

$\therefore m = 6$

As we know, sum of number of terms is denoted as

$$S_n=\frac{n}{2}[2a+(n-1)d]$$

Hence, both *A* and *R* is correct but *R* does not explain *A*.

4. (*a*) We know, $a_n = S_n - S_{n-1}$

$a_n = 3n^2 - 4n - 3(n-1)^2 + 4(n-1)$

$a_n = 6n - 7$

Both assertion (*A*) and reason (*R*) is true and reason (*R*) is the correct explanation of assertion (*A*).

Subjective Questions

Very Short Answer Type Questions

1. It is given that, $a_n = 550$

$\therefore a+(n-1)d = 550$

Here, $a = 8$ and $d = 2$

$8+(n-1)2 = 550$ *(1 M)*

$2(n-1) = 542$

$n-1 = 271$

$n = 272$ *(1 M)*

2. Here, $a = -9$ and

$d = a_2 - a_1 = -14-(-9) = -5$ *(1 M)*

$\therefore a_{30} - a_{20} = a+29d-a-19d$

$= 10d = 10(-5) = -50$ *(1 M)*

3. $l = 185, d = 4$

$l_9 = l-(n-1)d$ *(1 M)*

$l_9 = 185 - 8\times 4 = 153$ *(1 M)*

4. Given, $a_{18} - a_{14} = 32$

$\Rightarrow (a+17d)-(a+13d) = 32$ *(1 M)*

$\Rightarrow 17d - 13d = 32$ or $d = \frac{32}{4} = 8$ *(1 M)*

5. Given, $7a_7 = 11a_{11}$

$\Rightarrow 7(a+6d) = 11(a+10d)$ or $7a+42d = 11a+110d$ *(1 M)*

$\Rightarrow 4a+68d = 0$ or $a+17d = 0$

Now, $a_{18} = a+17d = 0$ *(1 M)*

6. Here, $a = -5$, $d = -\frac{5}{2}-(-5) = \frac{5}{2}$

We know, $a_{25} = a+(25-1)d$ *(1 M)*

$=(-5)+24\left(\frac{5}{2}\right) = -5+60 = 55$ *(1 M)*

7. Here, $a = 3$ and $d = 7-3 = 4$

Now, $a_n = a+(n-1)d$ *(½ M)*

$144 = 3+(n-1)4$

$\Rightarrow \frac{141}{4} = n-1 \Rightarrow n = \frac{145}{4}$ *(½ M)*

$\because n$ is in fraction. Therefore, 144 is not a term of an AP *(1 M)*

8. It is given that,

$a = 28, d = -4$ and $n = 7$

By using n^{th} term formula,

$a_n = a+(n-1)d$ *(1 M)*

$a_7 = 28+(7-1)(-4)$

$a_7 = 28+6(-4)$

$a_7 = 28-24$

$a_7 = 4$ *(1 M)*

9. According to the question, $S_2 = S_7$

$\frac{2}{2}(2a+d) = \frac{7}{2}(2a+6d)$ *(½ M)*

$2a + d = 7a + 21d$

$5a = -20d$

$a = -4d$

$a + 4d = 0$

$a_5 = 0$ (½ M)

yes, this type of AP exists.

let $a = 16$ then $d = -4$

i.e., 16, 12, 8, 4, 0, –4, –8

Justification: $S_2 = S_7 \Rightarrow 16 + 12 + 8 + 4 + 0 + (-4) + (-8)$

$\Rightarrow 28 = 28$ (1 M)

10. Here, $a = 3$ and $d = 8 - 3 = 5$

Since, $a_n = a + (n-1)d$ (1 M)

$98 = 3 + (n-1)5$

$\frac{95}{5} = (n-1)$

$n = 20$

Hence, 98 is the 20th term of an AP (1 M)

Short Answer Type Questions

1. From the given AP, we have

$a = 6$, $d = 7$ and $a_n = 216$ (½ M)

n^{th} term of an AP is given by

$a_n = a + (n-1)d$ (½ M)

On Putting the values of a, d and a_n, we get

$\therefore 216 = 6 + (n-1)7$ (½ M)

$210 = (n-1)7$

$30 = n - 1$

$n = 31$

Hence, total terms = 31 (½ M)

Now, middle term $= \frac{31+1}{2} = 16^{th}$ term (½ M)

$\therefore \quad a_{16} = a + 15d = 6 + 105 = 111$

Hence, middle term of the given AP is 111. (½ M)

2. Let us suppose, the three numbers of AP be $(a-d)$, a and $(a+d)$

It is given that,

$(a-d) + a + (a+d) = 12$

$\Rightarrow 3a = 12 \Rightarrow a = 4$ (1 M)

and it is also given that,

$(a-d)^2 + a^2 + (a+d)^2 = 56$

$\Rightarrow a^2 - 2ad + d^2 + a^2 + a^2 + 2ad + d^2 = 56$

$\Rightarrow 3a^2 + 2d^2 = 56 \Rightarrow 2d^2 = 56 - 3a^2$

$\Rightarrow 2d^2 = 56 - 3(4)^2$ $[\because a = 4]$

$\Rightarrow 2d^2 = 56 - 48 \Rightarrow 2d^2 = 8 \Rightarrow d^2 = 4$

$\Rightarrow d = \pm 2.$ (1 M)

If $d = 2$, then the numbers are $(4-2)$, 4, $(4+2)$ i.e., 2, 4, 6 $[\because a = 4]$ (½ M)

and,

If $d = -2$, then the number are $(4+2)$, 4, $(4-2)$ i.e., 6, 4, 2. $[\because a = 4]$ (½ M)

3. Let us suppose, d is the common difference of our AP

First term $(a) = 5$ (½ M)

So, first four terms = 5, $5 + d$, $5 + 2d$, $5 + 3d$

Next four terms = $5 + 4d$, $5 + 5d$, $5 + 6d$, $5 + 7d$ (1 M)

It is given that,

Sum of first 4 terms = Sum of next 4 terms/2

$\therefore 20 + 6d = \frac{20 + 22d}{2}$ (½ M)

$\Rightarrow 40 + 12d = 20 + 22d \Rightarrow -10d = -20 \Rightarrow d = 2$

Therefore, common difference = 2 (1 M)

4. Let digit at unit place be $(a - d)$

and digit at tenth place be (a)

and digit at hundredth place be $(a + d)$ (½ M)

It is given that,

$a - d + a + a + d = 15$

$3a = 15$

$a = 5$ (½ M)

Therefore, original number is $100(a + d) + 10a + a - d$

$= 100a + 100d + 11a - d = 111a + 99d$ ... (i) (½ M)

Now, new number obtained by reversing the digit

$= 100(a - d) + 10a + a + d = 100a - 100d + 11a + d$

$= 111a - 99d$ ... (ii) (½ M)

Now, according to the question,

$111a - 99d = 111a + 99d - 594$

$-99d - 99d = -594 \Rightarrow 594 = 198d \Rightarrow d = 3$ (½ M)

Hence, the original number $= 111(5) + 99(3)$

$= 555 + 297 = 852$ (½ M)

5. Let us suppose $a_1, a_2, a_3, \ldots, a_n, \ldots$ be an AP with its first term = a and common difference = d. (½ M)

According to the question,

$5a_5 = 8a_8$ [Given]

$\Rightarrow 5(a + 4d) = 8(a + 7d)$ $[\because a_n = a + (n-1)d]$ (1 M)

$\Rightarrow 5a + 20d = 8a + 56d \Rightarrow 5a - 8a = 56d - 20d$

$\Rightarrow 3a + 36d = 0 \Rightarrow 3(a + 12d) = 0$ (½ M)

$\Rightarrow a + 12d = 0 \Rightarrow a + (13 - 1)d = 0 \Rightarrow a_{13} = 0$

Hence, proved. (1 M)

6. Let us suppose, the three numbers in the AP be

$a - d, a, a + d$ (½ M)

It is given that, $(a - d) + a + (a + d) = 30$

$\Rightarrow 3a = 30 \Rightarrow a = 10$ (½ M)

It is also given that $(a - d)\,a(a + d) = 910$

$\Rightarrow a(a^2 - d^2) = 910$ $[\because (a - b)(a + b) = a^2 - b^2]$

Therefore, $10(10^2 - d^2) = 910$ $[\because a = 10]$ (½ M)

$\Rightarrow 100 - d^2 = 91 \Rightarrow d^2 = 100 - 91 \Rightarrow d^2 = 9 \Rightarrow d = \pm 3$ (½ M)

If $d = \pm 3$, then the numbers are 7, 10 and 13. (1 M)

7. Let us suppose, the four numbers be $(a - 3d)$, $(a - d)$, $(a + d)$, $(a + 3d)$. ... (i) (½ M)

It is given that, sum of four numbers = 20

Therefore,

$(a-3d)+(a-d)+(a+d)+(a+3d)=20$ (½ M)

$\Rightarrow 4a-4d+4d=20 \Rightarrow 4a=20 \Rightarrow a=5$ (½ M)

It is also given that sum of the squares = 120

Therefore,

$(a-3d)^2+(a-d)^2+(a+d)^2+(a+3d)^2=120$ (½ M)

After simplification, we will get

$\Rightarrow 4a^2+20d^2=120 \Rightarrow 4(a^2+5d^2)=120$

$\Rightarrow a^2+5d^2=30 \Rightarrow 25+5d^2=30$ [since, $a=5$]

$\Rightarrow 5d^2=5 \Rightarrow d=\pm 1$ (½ M)

Putting the values of $d=\pm 1$ and $a=5$ in (*i*), we get the required number as 2, 4, 6, 8. (½ M)

8. It is given that,

S_1 = Sum of n terms of an AP with first term 1 and common difference 1

Therefore, $S_1=\frac{n}{2}[2\times 1+(n-1)\,1]$

$\Rightarrow S_1=\frac{n}{2}[2+n-1] \Rightarrow S_1=\frac{n}{2}[n+1]$ (½ M)

And

S_2 = Sum of n terms of an AP with first term 1 and common difference 2

$\Rightarrow S_2=\frac{n}{2}[2\times 1+(n-1)\times 2]=n^2$ (½ M)

And S_3 = Sum of n terms of an AP with first term 1 and common difference 3

$\Rightarrow S_3=\frac{n}{2}[2\times 1+(n-1)\times 3]=\frac{n}{2}[2+3n-3]$

$=\frac{n}{2}(3n-1)$ (½ M)

Now, $S_1+S_3=\frac{n}{2}(n+1)+\frac{n}{2}(3n-1)$ (½ M)

$=\frac{n^2}{2}+\frac{n}{2}+\frac{3n^2}{2}-\frac{n}{2}$

$S_1+S_3=2n^2$ (½ M)

$\because S_2=n^2$

Clearly, $S_1+S_3=2S_2$. (½ M)

9. Clearly, the given sequence is an AP

So, first term i.e., $a=20$ and common difference i.e., $d=-\frac{3}{4}$ (½ M)

Let us suppose, a_n is the first negative term i.e., $a_n<0$

$\Rightarrow a+(n-1)d<0 \Rightarrow 20+(n-1)\left(-\frac{3}{4}\right)<0$ (½ M)

$\Rightarrow 20<(n-1)\frac{3}{4} \Rightarrow 80<3(n-1) \Rightarrow 80<3n-3$

$\Rightarrow 83<3n \Rightarrow n>\frac{83}{3}$ or $n>27\frac{2}{3}$ (1 M)

28 is the natural number just greater than $27\frac{2}{3}$.

Now, 28th term of the given sequence is the first negative term and we know that first negative term is the largest of all the negative terms.

$a_{28}=a+27d=20+27\left(-\frac{3}{4}\right)$

[$\because a=20$ and $d=\left(-\frac{3}{4}\right)$]

$=20-\frac{81}{4}=\frac{80-81}{4}=-\frac{1}{4}$ (1 M)

10. Let us suppose, T_n be the nth term of the AP and T_{n-1} is the $(n-1)^{th}$ term of AP

To find the nth term T_n, we will use formula of difference of sums i.e.,

$T_n=S_n-S_{n-1}$ (1 M)

where

S_n is the sum of first n terms of an AP

S_{n-1} is the sum of the first $(n-1)$ terms of an AP

Next, we find the $(n-1)^{th}$ term using the same formula

$T_{n-1}=S_{n-1}-S_{(n-1)-1}=S_{n-1}-S_{n-2}$ (1 M)

Now, the common difference of an AP,

$d=T_n-T_{n-1}$

$=S_n-S_{n-1}-(S_{n-1}-S_{n-2})=S_n-S_{n-1}-S_{n-1}+S_{n-2}$

$=S_n-2S_{n-1}+S_{n-2}$ (1 M)

11. It is given that,

$a_p=q$ and $a_q=p$ (½ M)

By using n^{th} term formula, we have

$a+(p-1)d=q$ ... (*i*)

and $a+(q-1)d=p$ ... (*ii*) (½ M)

On subtracting eq. (*ii*) from (*i*)

$pd-d-qd+d=q-p$

$d(p-q)=(q-p)$

$d=-1$ (½ M)

On putting value of d in (*i*),

$a+(p-1)(-1)=q$ (½ M)

$a-p+1=q$

$a=q+p-1$ (½ M)

Now, $a_r=a+(r-1)d=(q+p-1)+1-r$

[$\because a=q+p-1$ and $d=-1$]

$=p+q-r$ (½ M)

12. Let us suppose, x be the required term.

Therefore, $x^3=x \Rightarrow x^3-x=0 \Rightarrow x(x^2-1)=0$

or $x(x-1)(x+1)=0$ [$\because (a^2-b^2)=(a+b)(a-b)$]

Hence, $x=0$, 1 or -1 (½ M)

From the given AP sequence, we have

$a=51$ and $d=-4$ (½ M)

Now, by using n^{th} term formula,

$a_n=a+(n-1)d$

$a_n=51+(n-1)(-4)$

$a_n=51-4n+4=55-4n$ (½ M)

If $55-4n=0$

$\Rightarrow 4n=55$

$\Rightarrow n=\frac{55}{4}$, which is not a natural number. (½ M)

If $55 - 4n = 1$, then $4n = 54$ or $n = \frac{54}{4}$, which is also not a natural number. (½ M)

Now, if $55 - 4n = -1$, then $4n = 56$

$\Rightarrow 4n = 56 \Rightarrow n = \frac{56}{4} = 14$

Hence, 14th term of the AP is the cube of itself. (½ M)

13. Let 1st prize be ₹x

$\therefore$ The sequence in A.P. is

$x, x - 20, x - 40, x - 60$ (½ M)

Then $a = x$, $d = -20$, $S_n = 280$ and $n = 4$

$\therefore \; S_n = \frac{n}{2}[2a + (n-1)d]$ (½ M)

Hence, $S_4 = \frac{4}{2}[2x + 3(-20)]$ (½ M)

$280 = 2[2x - 60]$

$\Rightarrow 140 = 2x - 60$

Thus, $2x = 200$ or $x = 100$ (½ M)

The prizes are ₹100, ₹80, ₹60, ₹40. (1 M)

14. It is given that,

Distance between the rungs of the ladder = 25cm.

It is also given that, distance between the top rung and bottom rung of the ladder $= 2\frac{1}{2}$ m $= \frac{5}{2} \times 100$ cm $= 250$ cm

So, total number of rungs $= \frac{250}{25} + 1 = 11$ (½ M)

It is clear from the figure, that the length of rungs of ladder are decreasing from bottom to top. Hence, it can be concluded that the rungs are decreasing in an order of AP (½ M)

The length of the wood required for the rungs would be equal to the sum of the terms of AP so formed. (½ M)

Here, first term (a) = 45

Last term (l) = 25

Number of terms (n) = 11 (½ M)

As, sum of n terms of an AP is given by formula,

$S_n = \frac{n}{2}(a + l)$

Therefore, $S_{11} = \frac{11}{2}(45 + 25)$ (½ M)

$= \frac{11}{2}(70) = 385$ cm

Therefore, the length of the wood required for the rungs is 385cm. (½ M)

Long Answer Type Questions

1. It is given that, $a_1, a_2, a_3, \ldots a_n$ are in AP (½ M)

Now, taking

$$\text{L.H.S} = \frac{1}{\sqrt{a_1} + \sqrt{a_2}} + \frac{1}{\sqrt{a_2} + \sqrt{a_3}} + \ldots + \frac{1}{\sqrt{a_{n-1}} + \sqrt{a_n}}$$ (½ M)

$\therefore$ L.H.S = R.H.S

On rationalising the denominator, we get

$$= \frac{\sqrt{a_2} - \sqrt{a_1}}{a_2 - a_1} + \frac{\sqrt{a_3} - \sqrt{a_2}}{a_3 - a_2} + \ldots + \frac{\sqrt{a_n} - \sqrt{a_{n-1}}}{a_n - a_{n-1}}$$ (½ M)

As, $a_2 - a_1 = a_3 - a_2 = \ldots = a_n - a_{n-1} = d$ (½ M)

$$= \frac{\sqrt{a_2} - \sqrt{a_1}}{d} + \frac{\sqrt{a_3} - \sqrt{a_2}}{d} + \ldots + \frac{\sqrt{a_n} - \sqrt{a_{n-1}}}{d}$$ (½ M)

$$= \frac{\sqrt{a_2} - \sqrt{a_1} + \sqrt{a_3} - \sqrt{a_2} + \ldots + \sqrt{a_n} - \sqrt{a_{n-1}}}{d}$$

$$= \frac{1}{d}\left(\sqrt{a_n} - \sqrt{a_1}\right)$$ (1 M)

On rationalising the numerator, we get

$$= \frac{1}{d}\left(\frac{a_n - a_1}{\sqrt{a_n} + \sqrt{a_1}}\right)$$ (½ M)

$$= \frac{a + (n-1)d - a}{d\left(\sqrt{a_n} + \sqrt{a_1}\right)} \quad [\because a_n = a(n-1)d]$$ (½ M)

$$= \frac{n-1}{\sqrt{a_1} + \sqrt{a_n}} = \text{R.H.S}$$ (½ M)

$\therefore$ L.H.S. = R.H.S.

Hence proved.

2. We know,

Perimeter of a semi-circle $= \pi r$ (½ M)

Hence,

$P_1 = \pi(0.5) = \pi/2$ cm

$P_2 = \pi(1) = \pi$ cm

$P_3 = \pi(1.5) = 3\pi/2$ cm (1 M)

Here, P_1, P_2, P_3 are the lengths of the semi-circles.

Therefore, we obtain a sequence as follows

$\frac{\pi}{2}, \pi, \frac{3\pi}{2}, 2\pi\ldots$ (½ M)

Here, $P_1 = \frac{\pi}{2}$ cm $= a = a_1$,

$P_2 = \pi$ cm $= a_2$

and Common difference (d) $= P_2 - P_1$ or $a_2 - a_1$

$= \pi - \frac{\pi}{2} = \frac{\pi}{2}$ (½ M)

The sum of n terms of an AP is given by,

$S_n = \frac{n}{2}[2a + (n-1)d]$ (½ M)

Hence, sum of the length of 13 consecutive circles is,

$$S_{13} = \frac{13}{2}\left[2\left(\frac{\pi}{2}\right) + (13-1)\frac{\pi}{2}\right] \quad \left[\because a = \frac{\pi}{2} \text{ and } d = \frac{\pi}{2}\right]$$ (1 M)

$$= \frac{13}{2}[\pi + 6\pi] = \frac{13}{2}(7\pi)$$

$$= \frac{13}{2} \times 7 \times \frac{22}{7}$$

$= 143$ cm (½ M)

Therefore, the total length of such a spiral made up of thirteen consecutive semicircles is 143 cm. (½ M)

3. It is given that,

The houses of a row are numbered from 1, 2, 3, 4, 5.......49.

Hence, the houses numbered in a row form an AP (½ M)

Therefore,

First term, i.e., $a = 1$

Common difference, i.e., $d = 1$ (½ M)

Sum of n terms of AP = $\frac{n}{2}[2a + (n-1)d]$

Sum of number of houses preceding x houses = S_{x-1} (½ M)

$$S_{x-1} = \frac{x-1}{2}\left[2a+\left((x-1)-1)d\right)\right] = \frac{x-1}{2}\left[2(1)+(x-1-1)1\right]$$

$$= \frac{x-1}{2}[2+x-2] = \frac{x-1}{2}(x) \quad \text{...}(i) \ (1\ M)$$

According to the question,

Sum of number of houses following x^{th} house is $S_{49} - S_x$.

(½ M)

$$= \frac{49}{2}\left[2\times1+(49-1)\times1\right]-\frac{x}{2}\left[2\times1+(x-1)\times1\right]$$

$$= \frac{49}{2}[2+48]-\frac{x}{2}[2+x-1]$$

$$= \frac{49}{2}\times50-\frac{x}{2}[x+1] = 1225-\frac{x(x+1)}{2} \quad \text{...}(ii)\ (1\ M)$$

According to the given condition, eq.(i) and eq.(ii) must be equal to each other. Hence,

$$\frac{x(x-1)}{2} = 1225-\frac{x(x+1)}{2} \quad (½\ M)$$

$$\frac{x^2}{2}-\frac{x}{2} = 1225-\frac{x^2}{2}-\frac{x}{2}$$

$x^2 = 1225$

$x = \pm35$

The number of houses can never be negative. Therefore, the value of x is 35. (½ M)

4. (i) Applies the formula for the sum of n terms correctly and finds the value of the common difference d as 2. (1 M)

Either applies the formula for the nth term or generates the pattern with $a = 8$ and $d = 2$ to find the distance cycled on the 3rd day as 12 km. (1 M)

(ii) Applies the formula for the sum of n terms of AP and represents the given scenario mathematically as $n^2 + 7n - 170 = 0$. (1 M)

$\Rightarrow n^2 + 17n - 10n - 170 = 0 \Rightarrow n(n + 17) - 10(n + 17) = 0$

$\Rightarrow (n + 17)(n - 10) = 0$ (1 M)

$\Rightarrow n = 10, -17$ (not possible)

Hence, $n = 10$ days (1 M)

5. Given,

$$T_{10} = \frac{1}{20}$$

Let first term = a

common difference = d

$$\Rightarrow a+9d = \frac{1}{20} \quad \text{...}(i) \quad (1\ M)$$

$$T_{20} = \frac{1}{10}$$

$$\Rightarrow a+19d = \frac{1}{10} \quad \text{...}(ii) \quad (1\ M)$$

From equation (i) and (ii)

$$a = \frac{1}{200},\ d = \frac{1}{200} \quad (1\ M)$$

$$\therefore S_{200} = \frac{200}{2}\left[\frac{2}{200}+(200-1)\frac{1}{200}\right] \quad (1\ M)$$

$$= \frac{201}{2} = 100\frac{1}{2}$$

(1 M)

6. Let us suppose a_1, a_2 be the first terms and d_1, d_2 be the common differences of the two given AP's. (½ M)

Hence, the sum of their n^{th} terms is given as follows:

For $a = a_1$ & $d = d_1$:

$$S_n = \frac{n}{2}[2a_1 + (n-1)d_1] \text{ and} \quad \text{...}(i)$$

(½ M)

For $a = a_2$ & $d = d_2$:

$$S_{n'} = \frac{n}{2}[2a_2 + (n-1)d_2] \quad \text{...}(ii)\ (½\ M)$$

Now, on taking ratio of (i) and (ii), we get

$$\frac{S_n}{S_{n'}} = \frac{\frac{n}{2}[2a_1+(n-1)d_1]}{\frac{n}{2}[2a_2+(n-1)d_2]} \quad (½\ M)$$

$$= \frac{2a_1+(n-1)d_1}{2a_2+(n-1)d_2} \quad \text{...}(iii)\ (½\ M)$$

But,

$$\Rightarrow \frac{S_n}{S_{n'}} = \frac{7n+1}{4n+27} \quad \text{[given]} \quad \text{...}(iv)\ (½\ M)$$

Now, in order to find the ratio of the mth terms of the two given AP's, replace n by $(2m - 1)$ in eq. (iii) and (iv) as follows

Therefore,

$$\frac{2a_1+(2m-2)d_1}{2a_2+(2m-2)d_2} = \frac{7(2m-1)+1}{4(2m-1)+27} \quad (½\ M)$$

$$\frac{2\left[a_1+(m-1)d_1\right]}{2\left[a_2+(m-1)d_2\right]} = \frac{14m-7+1}{8m-4+27} \quad (½\ M)$$

$$\frac{a_1+(m-1)d_1}{a_2+(m-1)d_2} = \frac{14m-6}{8m+23} \quad (½\ M)$$

Therefore, the ratio of the mth terms of the two AP's is $(14m - 6) : (8m + 23)$ (½ M)

7. Let us suppose, a be the first term and d be the common difference of AP

It is given that,

$S_{2n} = 3S_n$ (½ M)

$$\therefore \frac{2n}{2}\left[2a+(2n-1)d\right] = \frac{3n}{2}\left[2a+(n-1)d\right] \quad (½\ M)$$

$\Rightarrow$ $2[2a + (2n - 1)d] = 3[2a + (n - 1)d]$ (½ M)

$\Rightarrow$ $4a + (4n - 2)d = 6a + (3n - 3)d$

$\Rightarrow$ $2a = (n + 1)d$ ... (i) (½ M)

Now, we need to find $\frac{S_{3n}}{S_n}$,

$$\therefore \frac{S_{3n}}{S_n} = \frac{\frac{3n}{2}[2a+(3n-1)d]}{\frac{n}{2}[2a+(n-1)d]}$$ (1 M)

$$= \frac{3[(n+1)d+(3n-1)d]}{[(n+1)d+(n-1)d]}$$ (½ M)

$(\because 2a=(n+1)d)$

$$= \frac{3\,(4nd)}{2nd} = 6$$

Hence, $\frac{S_{3n}}{S_n} = 6.$ (1 M)

Case Based Questions

Case Based-I

(i) It is given that,

No. of apples in Ist basket i.e., $a = 5$

No. of apples in IInd basket i.e., $a_2 = 12$

$\therefore d = a_2 - a_1 = 7$

Now, no. of apples in the 9th basket is

$a_9 = a + 8d = 5 + 8(7) = 61$

(ii) It is given that $a = 5$, $d = 7$

$$\therefore S_{13} = \frac{13}{2}[2\times5+(13-1)7] = \frac{13}{2}[10+12\times7]$$

$$= \frac{13}{2}\times94 = 13\times47 = 611$$

Hence, total no. of apples in first 13 baskets are 611.

OR

It is given that $a = 5, d = 7$

$$\therefore S_{14} = \frac{14}{2}[2\times5+(14-1)7] = \frac{14}{2}[10+13\times7]$$

$$= \frac{14}{2}\times101 = 7\times101 = 707$$

Hence, total no. of apples in first 14 baskets are 707.

(iii) Total no. of apples = 810 [Given]

Let total number of baskets be n.

$$\therefore S_n = \frac{n}{2}[2a+(n-1)d]$$

$\Rightarrow 810 \times 2 = n\,[2 \times 5 + (n - 1)7]$

$[\because S_n = 810,\ a = 5 \text{ and } d = 7]$

$1620 = 10n + 7n^2 - 7n$

$7n^2 + 3n - 1620 = 0$

On solving the equation, we get $n = 15$

Hence, 15 baskets are required to keep 810 apples.

Case Based-II

(i) (b) Since first installment is of ₹13000 and he increases the installment by ₹1300 every month., gives a sequence 13000, 14300, 15600, 16900, ...

Here, $a = 13000$, $d = 1300$

Amount paid by him in 20th installment will be

$a_{20} = a + 19d$

$= 13000 + 19 \times 1300 =$ ₹37,700

Hence, amount paid by him in 20th installment is ₹37,700.

(ii) (c) Amount paid upto 30 installments will be given as follows,

$$S_n = \frac{n}{2}[2a+(n-1)d]$$

$$S_{30} = \frac{30}{2}[2\times13{,}000+29\times1300]$$

$$S_{30} = \frac{30}{2}\times63700 = 15\times63700 = ₹955500$$

Hence, the amount paid by him upto 30th installment is ₹9,55,500.

(iii) (a) Let n be the number of installments

Total amount to be paid is ₹ 15,34,000

$$\Rightarrow \frac{n}{2}[2a+(n-1)d] = 15{,}34{,}000$$

$$\Rightarrow \frac{n}{2}[26{,}000+(n-1)1300] = 15{,}34{,}000$$

$$\Rightarrow n[26{,}000+(n-1)1300] = 15{,}34{,}000\times2$$

$$\Rightarrow 1300n[20+n-1] = 15{,}34{,}000\times2$$

$$\Rightarrow 20n+n^2-n = \frac{15{,}34{,}000\times2}{1300}$$

$\Rightarrow n^2 + 19n - 2360 = 0 \Rightarrow n^2 + 59n - 40n - 2360 = 0$

$\Rightarrow (n + 59)(n - 40) = 0$

i.e., $n = -59$ or 40

As number of installments cannot be negative.

Hence, total number of installments are 40.

(iv) (b) Ratio of 1st and 20th installment

$$= \frac{a_1}{a_{20}} = \frac{a_1}{a_1+19d} = \frac{13{,}000}{37700} = \frac{10}{29}$$

Ratio is 10:29.

Case Based-III

(i) (a) The heights of the students form an arithmetic progression with first term (a) = 140 cm and common difference (d) = 4 cm.

Now, the height of the 10th student, we can use the formula for n^{th} term of an AP:

$a_n = a + (n - 1)d$

$a_{10} = 140 + (10 - 1) \times 4 = 176$ cm

Therefore, the height of the 10th student is 176 cm.

(ii) (b) The sum of heights of the first 20 students,

$$S_n = \left(\frac{n}{2}\right)\times\left[2a+(n-1)d\right]$$

$$S_{20} = \left(\frac{20}{2}\right)\times\left[2(140)+(20-1)\times 4\right]$$

$S_{20} = 10 \times [280 + 76]$

$S_{20} = 3,560$

Therefore, the sum of heights of the first 20 students is 3,560 cm.

(iii) (b) To find the number of students with height greater than 180 cm, we need to find the term number (n) for which $a_n > 180$.

$\therefore a + (n-1)d > 180$

$140 + (n-1)4 > 180$

$n - 1 > 10$

$n > 11$

Since, total no. of students are 22. Hence, no. of students greater that 180 cm are 22 – 11 = 11.

(iv) (d) The height of the shortest student is simply the first term of the AP, which is 140 cm.

Case Based-IV

(i) The selling price of the product forms an arithmetic progression with first term (a) = ₹ 500 and common difference (d) = ₹ 10.

To find the selling price of the product in the 10th month,

$a_n = a + (n-1)d$

$a_{10} = 500 + (10-1)10 = 590$

Therefore, the selling price of the product in the 10th month is ₹590.

(ii) To find the money earned by the company from selling the single unit of shoes in the first 6 months each

$$S_n = \left(\frac{n}{2}\right)\times\left[2a+(n-1)d\right]$$

$$S_6 = \left(\frac{6}{2}\right)\times\left[2(500)+(6-1)\times 10\right]$$

$S_6 = 3 \times [1000 + 50]$

$S_6 = 3,150$

Therefore, the company earned ₹ 3,150 from selling the single unit of product in the first 6 months each.

Hence, to sell 500 unit, total money earned is 500 × 3150 = ₹15,75,000

OR

To find the money earned by the company from selling the single unit of shoes in the first 10 months each.

$$S_n = \left(\frac{n}{2}\right)\times\left[2a+(n-1)d\right]$$

$$S_{10} = \left(\frac{10}{2}\right)\times\left[2(500)+(10-1)\times 10\right]$$

$S_{10} = 5 \times [1000 + 90]$

$S_{10} = 5,450$

Therefore, the company earned ₹5,450 from selling the single unit of product in the first 10 months.

Hence, to sell 500 unit, total money earned is 500 × 5450 = ₹27,25,000

(iii) Here, $a_n = 800$, $a = 500$, $d = 10$

We know $a_n = a + (n-1)d$

$800 = 500 + (n-1)10$

$30 = n - 1$, $n = 31$

Therefore, the selling price will reach ₹ 800 per unit in the 31st month.

Case Based-V

(i) Note that the amounts Manan is paid for each painting forms an AP.

Takes $a = 6000$, $d = 200$ and $n = 25$

Amount = 6000 + (25 – 1)200 = ₹10800.

(ii) The total amount earned by Bhima as follows:

$$S_{50} = \frac{50}{2}\,[2(4000) + (50-1)\,)400] = 25\,(8000 + 19600)$$

= ₹6,90,000

(iii) Frame equation as follows:

$6000 + (n-1)200 = 4000 + (n-1)400 \Rightarrow n = 11$

Since they both earn the same amount for the 11th painting, as Bhima's increment is more, Bhima gets more money than Manan for the 12th painting.

OR

Assume that the number of paintings required is n.

Frame equation as follows:

S_n(Manan) = S_n(Bhima)

$$\Rightarrow \frac{n}{2}[2(6000) + (n-1)200] = \frac{n}{2}[2(4000) + (n-1)400]$$

On Solving the equation we get $n = 21$.

TRIANGLES

6

"Triangles are used in big buildings like skyscrapers that are exactly the same in size and shape which make the buildings strong and steady.. These triangles are called as congruent triangles."

SYLLABUS & WEIGHTAGE

List of Concept Names	Years				
	2021	2022	2023	2024	2025
Similar Figures and Similarity of Triangles Definitions, examples, counter examples of similar triangles. (*i*) (Prove) If a line is drawn parallel to one side of a triangle to intersect the other two sides in distinct points, the other two sides are divided in the same ratio. (*ii*) (Motivate) If a line divides two sides of a triangle in the same ratio, the line is parallel to the third side.	Exam not Conducted	–	1 Q (2 M) 1 Q (4 M)	1 Q (1 M) 1 Q (4 M)	1 Q (1 M) 1 Q (4 M)
Criteria for Similarity of Triangles (*i*) (Motivate) If in two triangles, the corresponding angles are equal, their corresponding sides are proportional and the triangles are similar. (*ii*) (Motivate) If the corresponding sides of two triangles are proportional, their corresponding angles are equal and the two triangles are similar. (*iii*) (Motivate) If one angle of a triangle is equal to one angle of another triangle and the sides including these angles are proportional, the two triangles are similar		–	1 Q (1 M)	1 Q (3 M)	1 Q (1 M) 1 Q (2 M)

CONCEPT MAP

To Access One Shot Revision Video Scan This QR Code

Triangles

Similarity of triangles

- Corresponding angles are congruent
- Corresponding sides are in same ratio

Congruent of Triangles

- Corresponding angles are congruent
- Corresponding sides are also congruent

Criteria for similarity of triangles

***AA* (Angle-Angle) criteria:** If two angles of one triangle are respectively equal to two angles of another triangle, then the two triangles are similar.

***AAA* (Angle-Angle-Angle):** If in two triangles, corresponding angles are equal, then their corresponding sides are in the same ratio and hence the two triangles are similar.

***SSS* (Side-Side-Side):** If in two triangles, sides of one triangle are proportional to (i.e., in the same ratio of) the sides of the other triangle, then their corresponding angles are equal and hence the two triangles are similar.

***SAS* (Side–Angle–Side):** If one angle of a triangle is equal to one angle of the other triangle and the sides including these angles are proportional, then the two triangles are similar.

Theorem

- If a line is drawn parallel to one side of a triangle to intersect the other two sides in distinct points, the other two sides are divided in the same ratio.
- If a line divides any two sides of a triangle in the same ratio, then the line is parallel to the third side.
- If in two triangles, corresponding angles are equal, then their corresponding sides are in the same ratio (or proportional) and hence the two triangles are similar.
- If in two triangles, sides of one triangle are proportional to (i.e., in the same ratio of) the sides of the other triangle, then their corresponding angles are equal and hence the two triangles are similar.
- If one angle of a triangle is equal to one angle of the other triangle and the sides including these angles are proportional, then the two triangles are similar.

Important Terms

- **Scale Factor:** The scale factor is the ratio of any two corresponding lengths in similar figures. It determines the relationship between the corresponding sides of the figures.
- **Corresponding Angles:** Corresponding angles are angles that occupy the same relative positions in two or more similar figures
- **Corresponding Sides:** Corresponding sides are sides that are in the same relative position in two or more similar figures.
- **Proportional:** Two quantities are proportional if they have a constant ratio. In the context of similar figures, corresponding sides are proportional, meaning their lengths are in the same ratio.
- **Congruent:** Two figures are said to be congruent if all the corresponding sides and all the corresponding angles are equal in measure.
- **Similar:** Two figures having the same shape but not necessarily the same size is known as similar.

1 SIMILAR FIGURES AND SIMILARITY OF TRIANGLES

Important Terms

- **Scale Factor:** The scale factor is the ratio of any two corresponding lengths in similar figures. It determines the relationship between the corresponding sides of the figures.
- **Corresponding Angles:** Corresponding angles are angles that occupy the same relative positions in two or more similar figures
- **Corresponding Sides:** Corresponding sides are sides that are in the same relative position in two or more similar figures.
- **Enlargement:** Enlargement is a transformation that increases the size of a figure without altering its shape
- **Reduction:** Reduction is a transformation that decreases the size of a figure without changing its shape.
- **Proportional:** Two quantities are proportional if they have a constant ratio. In the context of similar figures, corresponding sides are proportional, meaning their lengths are in the same ratio.
- **Congruent:** Two figures are said to be congruent if all the corresponding sides and all the corresponding angles are equal in measure.
- **Similar:** Two figures having the same shape but not necessarily the same size is known as similar.
- **Similar Polygons:** Two polygons of the same number of sides are similar, if (*i*) their corresponding angles are equal and (*ii*) their corresponding sides are in the same ratio (or proportion). e.g.

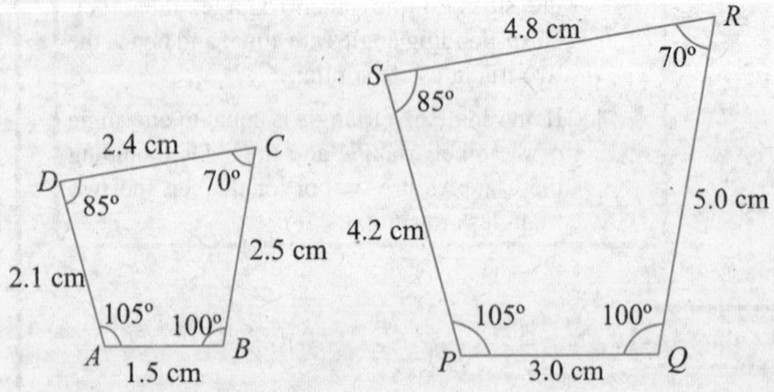

- **Similarity of Triangles:** Two triangles are similar, if (*i*) their corresponding angles are equal and (*ii*) their corresponding sides are in the same ratio (or proportion).

Important Derivations

Theorem 1: If a line is drawn parallel to one side of a triangle to intersect the other two sides in distinct points, the other two sides are divided in the same ratio. **(CBSE DL/ODL, 2024)**

Proof: We are given a triangle *ABC* in which a line parallel to side *BC* intersects other two sides *AB* and *AC* at *D* and *E* respectively.

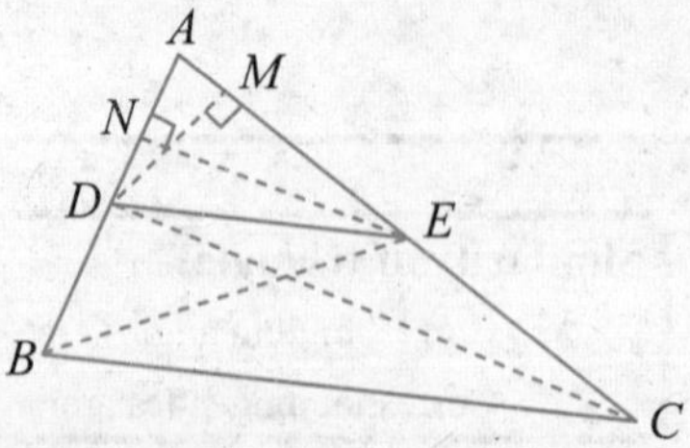

We need to prove that $\frac{AD}{DB} = \frac{AE}{EC}$.

Let us join *BE* and *CD* and then draw $DM \perp AC$ and $EN \perp AB$.

Now, area of $\Delta ADE = \frac{1}{2} \times \text{base} \times \text{height} = \frac{1}{2} \times AD \times EN$.

The area of ΔADE is denoted as $ar(\Delta ADE)$.

So, $ar(\Delta ADE) = \frac{1}{2} \times AD \times EN$

Similarly, $ar(\Delta BDE) = \frac{1}{2} \times BD \times EN$,

$ar(\Delta ADE) = \frac{1}{2} AE \times DM$ and $ar(\Delta DEC) = \frac{1}{2} EC \times DM$.

Therefore, $$\frac{ar(\Delta ADE)}{ar(\Delta BDE)} = \frac{\frac{1}{2} \times AD \times EN}{\frac{1}{2} \times DB \times EN} = \frac{AD}{DB} \quad \ldots (i)$$

and $$\frac{ar(\Delta ADE)}{ar(\Delta DEC)} = \frac{\frac{1}{2} \times AE \times DM}{\frac{1}{2} \times EC \times DM} = \frac{AE}{EC} \quad \ldots (ii)$$

Note that ΔBDE and ΔDEC are on the same base *DE* and between the same parallels *BC* and *DE*.

So, $ar(\Delta BDE) = ar(\Delta DEC)$ ... (*iii*)

Therefore, from (*i*), (*ii*) and (*iii*), we have: $\frac{AD}{DB} = \frac{AE}{EC}$

Topper's Explanation **(CBSE 2024)**

Statement: If a line is drawn parallel to one side of a triangle to intersect the other 2 sides at two distinct points, the other two sides are divided in the same ratio.

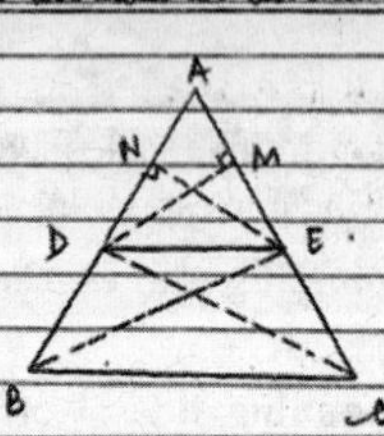

Given: ΔABC where $DE \parallel BC$ and DE intersects AB at D and intersects AC at E.

To prove: $\frac{AB}{BD} = \frac{AE}{EC}$

Construction: Draw $DM \perp AC$ and $EN \perp AB$. Join BE and AC.

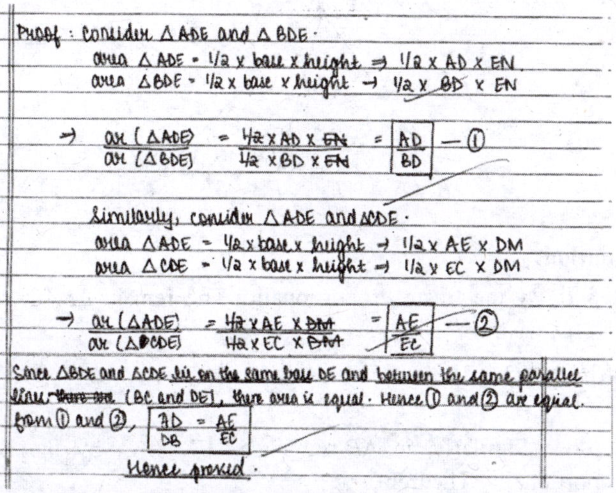
Proof : consider ΔADE and ΔBDE.
area $\Delta ADE = 1/2 \times$ base $\times$ height $\Rightarrow 1/2 \times AD \times EN$.
area $\Delta BDE = 1/2 \times$ base $\times$ height $\rightarrow 1/2 \times BD \times EN$

$\rightarrow \frac{ar(\Delta ADE)}{ar(\Delta BDE)} = \frac{1/2 \times AD \times EN}{1/2 \times BD \times EN} = \boxed{\frac{AD}{BD}}$ — ①

Similarly, consider ΔADE and ΔCDE.
area $\Delta ADE = 1/2 \times$ base $\times$ height $\rightarrow 1/2 \times AE \times DM$
area $\Delta CDE = 1/2 \times$ base $\times$ height $\rightarrow 1/2 \times EC \times DM$

$\rightarrow \frac{ar(\Delta ADE)}{ar(\Delta CDE)} = \frac{1/2 \times AE \times DM}{1/2 \times EC \times DM} = \boxed{\frac{AE}{EC}}$ — ②

Since ΔBDE and ΔCDE lie on the same base DE and between the same parallel lines (BC and DE), their area is equal. Hence ① and ② are equal.
from ① and ②, $\boxed{\frac{AD}{DB} = \frac{AE}{EC}}$
Hence proved.

Theorem 2: (Converse of Basic Proportionality theorem (BPT)). If a line divides any two sides of a triangle in the same ratio, then the line must be paralled to the third side.

Given: A ΔABC and a line l intersecting AB in D and AC in E,

such that $\frac{AD}{DB} = \frac{AE}{EC}$

To Prove: $l \parallel BC$ i.e. $DE \parallel BC$

Proof: If possible, let DE be not parallel to BC. Then, there must be another line parallel to BC. Let $DF \parallel BC$. Since $DF \parallel BC$. Therefore, from Basic Proportionality Theorem, we get

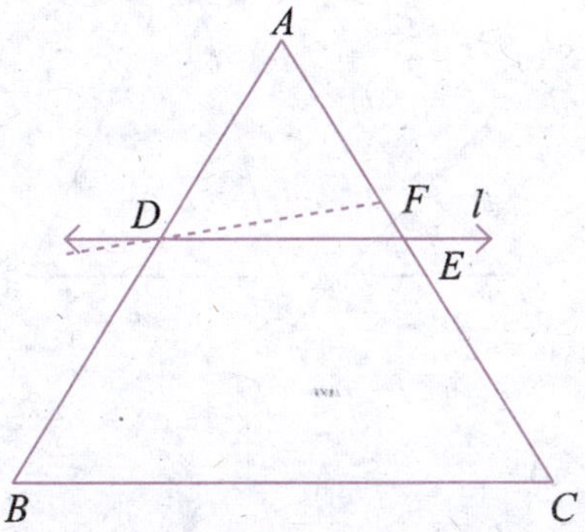

$$\frac{AD}{DB} = \frac{AF}{FC} \quad \ldots (i)$$

But $\frac{AD}{DB} = \frac{AE}{EC}$ (Given) $\ldots (ii)$

From (i) and (ii), we get $\frac{AF}{FC} = \frac{AE}{EC} \Rightarrow \frac{AF}{FC} + 1 = \frac{AE}{EC} + 1$

[Adding 1 on both sides]

$$\Rightarrow \frac{AF + FC}{FC} = \frac{AE + EC}{EC} \Rightarrow \frac{AC}{FC} = \frac{AC}{EC} \Rightarrow FC = EC$$

This is possible only when F and E coincide i.e. DF is the line l itself. But, $DF \parallel BC$. Hence, $l \parallel BC$.

Important Concepts

- All congruent figures are similar but the similar figures need not be congruent.
- If corresponding angles of two triangles are equal, then they are known as equiangular triangles.
- The ratio of any two corresponding sides in two equiangular triangles is always the same.
- Tell about Thales Theorem (Basic Proportionality Theorem)

Real Life Applications

- The concept of similar triangles is very important in our life. If we want to find the height of an object, say a building or a tower, we can find the desired height by measuring the length of the shadow and then using the shape where our edges are similar.

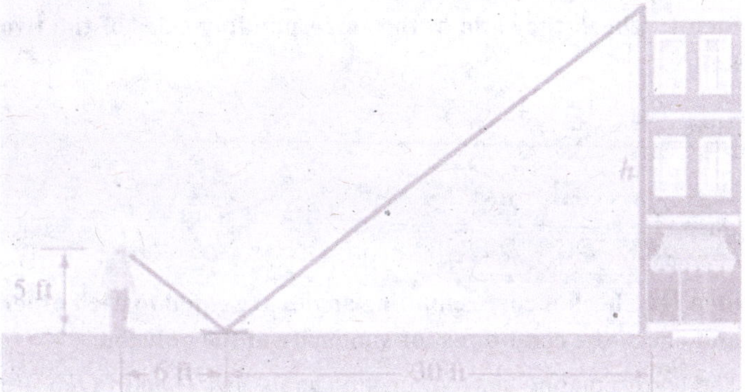

- Cohesion is an important mathematical concept for people to understand patterns in the environment. Integration builds on children's daily experiences and allows them to develop a perspective for geometric relationships.

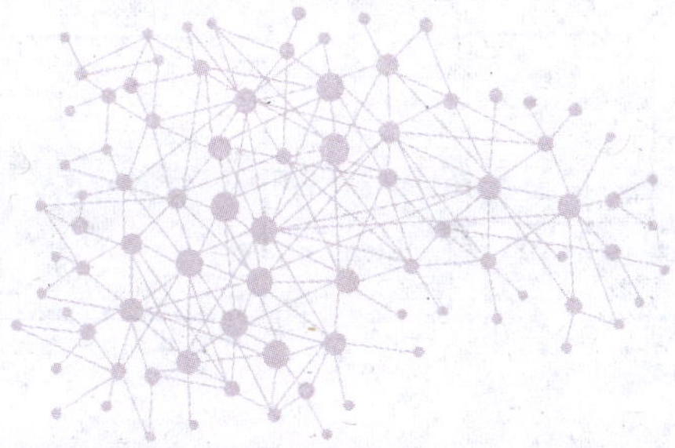

Different Problem Types

Type I: Understanding Similar Figures

Two similar figures have the same shape but not necessarily the same size. Therefore, all circles are similar. We can say that all congruent figures are similar but the similar figures need not be congruent.

State whether the following quadrilaterals are similar or not.

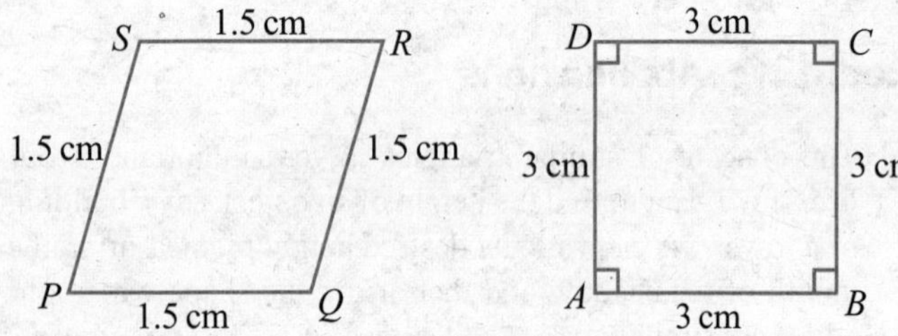

Solution:

Step I: Check the ratio of the corresponding sides of the two figures:

Here, $\frac{PQ}{AB} = \frac{1.5}{3} = \frac{1}{2}$

Also, $\frac{QR}{BC} = \frac{SR}{DC} = \frac{PS}{DA} = \frac{1.5}{3} = \frac{1}{2}$

Step II: Check if corresponding angles are equal to each other and check the conditions for similarity of the polygon:

The corresponding sides of quadrilaterals *ABCD* and *PQRS* are proportional but their corresponding angles are not equal. Hence, quadrilaterals *ABCD* and *PQRS* are not similar.

Example: Show that the following given figures are similar.

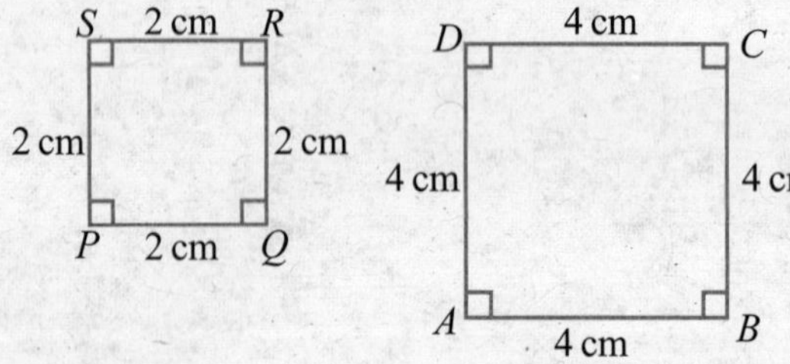

Solution:

Clearly, $\frac{AB}{PQ} = \frac{BC}{QR} = \frac{CD}{RS} = \frac{DA}{SP} = 2$

Also, $\angle A = \angle P$

$\angle B = \angle Q$

$\angle C = \angle R$

$\angle D = \angle S$

Thus the squares are similar figures as their corresponding sides are proportional and their corresponding angles are equal.

Type II: Understanding Similarity of Triangles

In the given figure, *DE* || *AC* and *DF* || *AE*.

Prove that $\frac{BF}{FE} = \frac{BE}{EC}$

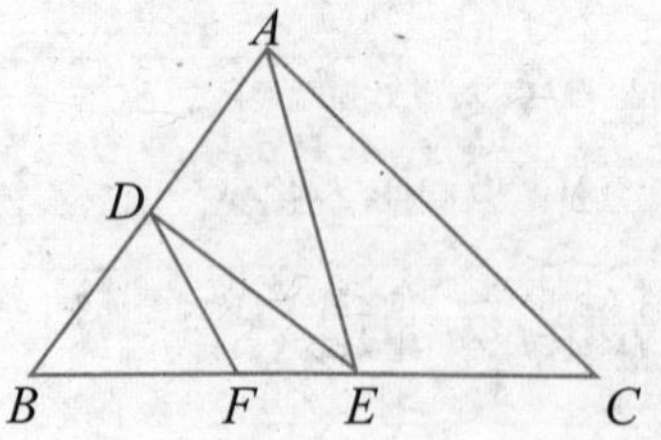

Solution:

Step I: By the Basic Proportionality Theorem in ΔBAC, since $DE \| AC$, we have

$\therefore \frac{BE}{EC} = \frac{BD}{AD}$ ... (*i*)

Step II: Similarly, in ΔBAE, since $DF \| AE$, by the Basic Proportionality Theorem,

$\therefore \frac{BF}{FE} = \frac{BD}{DA}$ ... (*ii*)

Step III: Combining equations (*i*) and (*ii*), we get: $\frac{BE}{EC} = \frac{BF}{FE}$. Hence, proved.

Example: In fig., $\angle 1 = \angle 2$ and $\angle 3 = \angle 4$. Show that $PT \cdot QR = PR \cdot ST$

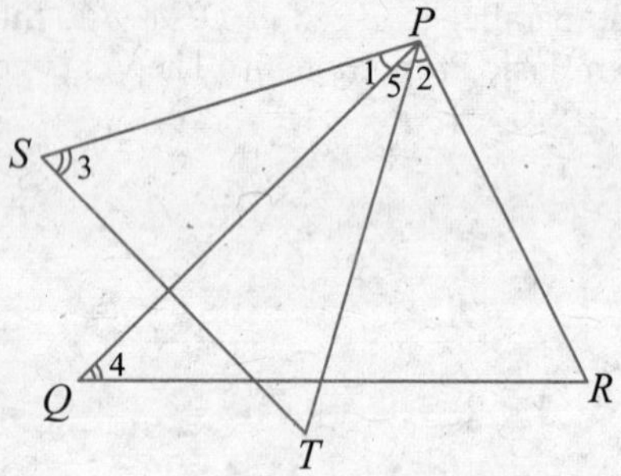

Solution:

$\angle 1 = \angle 2$ (Given)

$\Rightarrow \angle 1 + \angle 5 = \angle 2 + \angle 5$

or $\angle SPT = \angle QPR$

and $\angle 3 = \angle 4$ (Given)

$\Rightarrow \Delta PST \sim \Delta PQR$

$\Rightarrow \frac{ST}{QR} = \frac{PT}{PR}$

or $\frac{ST}{PT} = \frac{QR}{PR}$

$\Rightarrow PR \cdot ST = QR \cdot PT$

COMPETENCY BASED SOLVED EXAMPLES

Multiple Choice Questions

(1 M)

1. **All circles and squares are** *(Re)* (NCERT Intext)

   (*a*) Congruent (*b*) Similar

   (*c*) Both (*a*) and (*b*) (*d*) None of these

Sol. As we know that two similar figures have the same shape but not necessarily the same size. Same size means radii of the circles are equal and sides of the squares are equal. So, all circles and squares are similar, since the radii of all the circles and the sides of all the squares are not equal.

Key Takeaways

- ❑ Congruent shapes have the same size and shape.
- ❑ Similar shapes have the same shape but can be different in size.

2. **ΔPQR is shown below. ST is drawn such that $\angle PRQ = \angle STQ$.** *(Ev)*

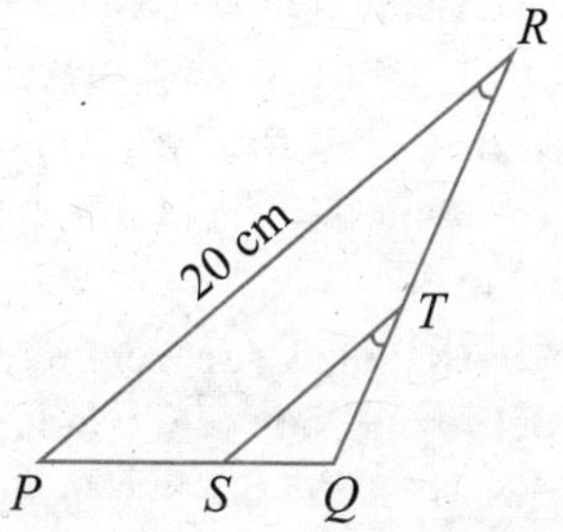

If ST divides QR in a ratio of 2 : 3, then what is the length of ST?

(*a*) $\frac{10}{3}$ cm (*b*) 8 cm

(*c*) 12 cm (*d*) $\frac{40}{3}$ cm

Sol. ΔPRQ is similar to ΔSTQ

All sides are proportional.

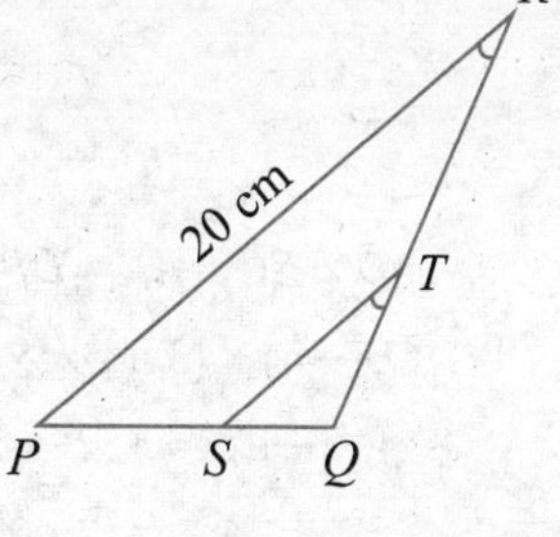

$$\frac{QT}{QR} = \frac{ST}{PR}$$

ST divides QR in the ratio 2:3.

$$\frac{2}{5} = \frac{ST}{20}$$

$ST = 8$ cm

3. **Identify the given geometry are:** *(Ap)*

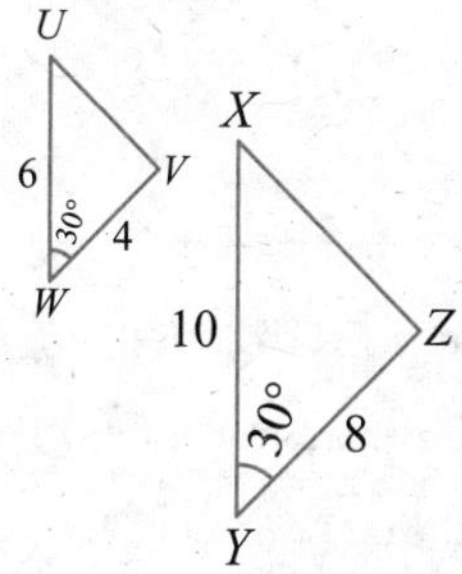

(*a*) Similar (*b*) Equal

(*c*) Congruent (*d*) None of these

Sol. As we know that the two triangles are similar if the ratio of their two corresponding sides are equal and also the angle formed by these two sides are equal.

$\angle W = \angle Y = 30°$ (given)

Now, we need to check whether the sides that include the angles are in proportion or not.

$$\frac{UW}{XY} = \frac{6}{10} = \frac{3}{5}$$

$$\frac{WV}{YZ} = \frac{4}{8} = \frac{1}{2}$$

The sides are not in proportion, so the triangles UVW and XYZ are not similar.

4. **In a ABC, AD is the bisector of $\angle BAC$. If $AB = 8$ cm, $BD = 6$ cm and $DC = 3$ cm. Then the value of AC is** *(Ev)*

   (*a*) 4 cm (*b*) 6 cm

   (*c*) 5 cm (*d*) 8 cm

Sol. Given, In a ΔABC, AD is the bisector of $\angle BAC$. $AB = 8$ cm and $DC = 3$ cm and $BD = 6$ cm.

We know that the internal bisector of angle of a triangle divides the opposite side internally in the ratio of the sides containing the angle.

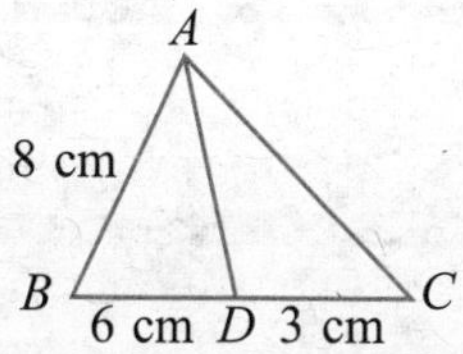

So, $\frac{AB}{AC} = \frac{BD}{DC}$

$$\frac{8}{AC} = \frac{6}{3}$$

$$AC = \frac{8 \times 3}{6}$$

$AC = 4$ cm.

5. Shown below is a rectangle *PQRS*. $\angle UTQ$ is a right angle.

(*Ap*) (CBSE CFPQ, 2023)

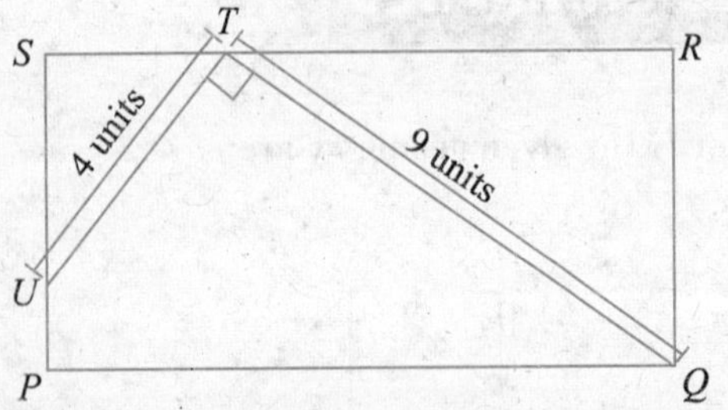

Which of these is TRUE about *UST* and *TRQ*?

(*a*) The perimeters are in the ratio 16:81.

(*b*) The ratio of $SUT{:}\angle RTQ$ is 4:9.

(*c*) The ratio of $US{:}TR$ is 4:9.

(*d*) The ratio of $US{:}QR$ is 4:9.

Sol. In the above figure let $\angle PQT = x°$

$\Rightarrow \angle RTQ = \angle PQT = x°$ (Alternate interior angles)

In ΔTRQ,

$\angle R = 90°, \angle RTQ = x°$

Also, $\angle STU + 90° + \angle RTQ = 180°$ (Linear Pair)

$\Rightarrow \angle STU + 90° + x° = 180° \Rightarrow \angle STU = 90° - x°$

In ΔUST,

$\angle S = 90°$ and $\angle SUT = x°$

Thereby, In ΔTRQ and ΔUST we get,

$\angle R = \angle S = 90°$ and $\angle RTQ = \angle SUT = x°$

Hence, $\Delta TRQ \sim \Delta UST$ (*AA* criterion)

Now we know that ratio of the corresponding sides of two similar triangles is equal.

$$\Rightarrow \frac{US}{TR} = \frac{4}{9}$$

Nailing the Right Answer

Students should meticulously examine provided data to identify similar triangles.

Answer Key

1. (*b*) 2. (*b*) 3. (*d*) 4. (*a*) 5. (*c*)

Assertion and Reason

(1 M)

Direction: **In the following questions, a statement of Assertion (A) is followed by a statement of Reason (R). Mark the correct choice as.**

(*a*) Both Assertion (A) and Reason (R) are true, and Reason (R) is the correct explanation of Assertion (A).

(*b*) Both Assertion (A) and Reason (R) are true, but Reason (R) is not the correct explanation of Assertion (A).

(*c*) Assertion (A) is true, but Reason (R) is false.

(*d*) Assertion (A) is false, but Reason (R) is true.

1. Assertion (A): **If in a ΔABC, a line $DE \parallel BC$, intersects AB in D and AC in E, then $\frac{AB}{AD} = \frac{AC}{AE}$.**

Reason (R): **If a line is drawn parallel to one side of a triangle intersecting the other two sides, then the other two sides are divided in the same ratio.** (*An*)

Sol. For Assertion

Since, $DE \parallel BC$ by Thale's Theorem

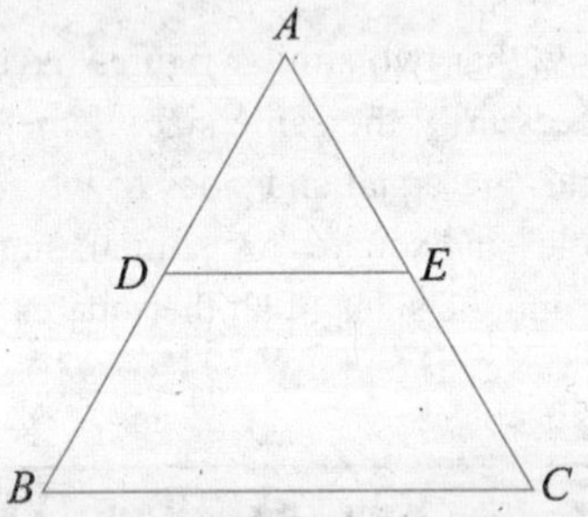

$$\frac{AD}{DB} = \frac{AE}{EC} \Rightarrow \frac{DB}{AD} = \frac{EC}{AE} \Rightarrow 1 + \frac{DB}{AD} = 1 + \frac{EC}{AE}$$

$$\Rightarrow \frac{AD+DB}{AD} = \frac{AE+EC}{AE} \Rightarrow \frac{AB}{AD} = \frac{AC}{AE}$$

Assertion is true

Reason is also true : This is Thale's Theorem

Both Assertion (A) and Reason (R) are true and Reason (R) is the correct explanation of Assertion (A).

2. Assertion (A): **In ΔABC, $DE \parallel BC$ such that $AD = (7x - 4)$ cm, $AE = (5x - 2)$cm, $DB = (3x + 4)$cm and $EC = 3x$ cm then x is equal to 4.**

Reason (R): **Pythagoras theorem says that if a line is drawn parallel to one side of a triangle intersecting the other two sides, then the other two sides are divided in the same ratio.** (*Ap*)

Sol. We have, $\frac{AD}{DB} = \frac{AE}{EC}$

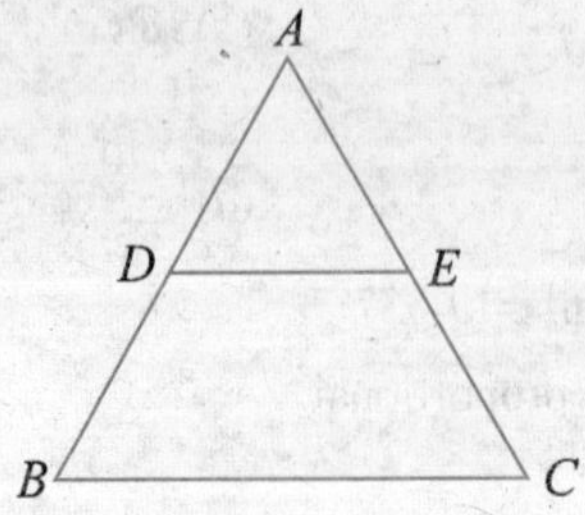

$AD \times EC = AE \times DB$

$(7x - 4) \times (3x) = (5x - 2)(3x + 4)$

$21x^2 - 12x = 15x^2 + 20x - 6x - 8 \Rightarrow 6x^2 - 26x + 8 = 0$

$\Rightarrow 3x^2 - 13x + 4 = 0 \Rightarrow 3x(x - 4) - 1(x - 4) = 0$

$\Rightarrow (3x - 1)(x - 4) = 0$

i.e., $x = 4$ or $\frac{1}{3}$

Assertion (A) is true.

The reason is incorrect. Pythagoras theorem deals with right-angled triangles, not the division of sides in triangles by a line drawn parallel to one side. The property described is actually Thales' theorem, which states that if a line is drawn parallel to one side of a triangle, it divides the other two sides proportionally.

Assertion (A) is true but Reason (R) is false.

Key Takeaways

- Pythagoras theorem: Applies to right-angled triangles, deals with side lengths.
- Thales' theorem: Involves proportional division of triangle sides by a line parallel to one side.
- Different theorems, Pythagoras for right triangles, Thales for proportional division.

Answer Key

1. (a) 2. (c)

Subjective Questions

Very Short Answer Type Questions (1 or 2 M)

1. Using Converse of basic proportionality theorem, prove that the line joining the mid-points of any two sides of a triangle is parallel to the third side. (Re)

Sol. Given: Let us assume ΔABC in which P is a mid-point of AB and Q is the mid-point of AC.

To prove: $PQ \parallel BC$

Proof: In ΔABC, P and Q are the mid-points of sides AB and AC respectively.

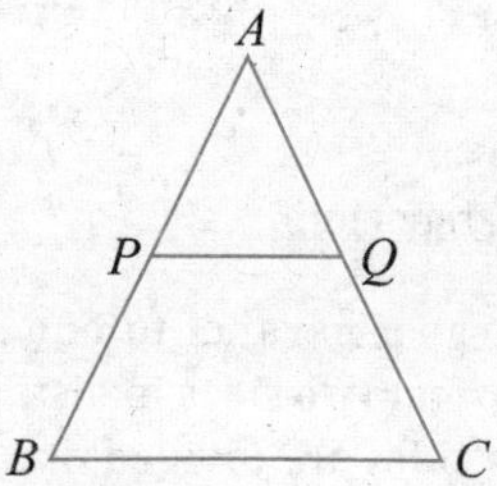

$\therefore AP = PB$ and $AQ = QC$ (1 M)

$\Rightarrow \frac{AP}{PB} = 1$ and $\frac{AQ}{QC} = 1 \Rightarrow \frac{AP}{PB} = \frac{AQ}{QC} = 1$

$\therefore PQ \parallel BC$ (By converse of BPT)

Hence proved. (1 M)

Short Answer Type Questions (2 or 3 M)

1. In ΔABC, DE is parallel to BC and intersects AB and AC at D and E respectively, then (Ap)

(i) $\frac{AB}{DB} = \frac{AC}{EC}$ **and**

(ii) $\frac{AB}{AD} = \frac{AC}{AE}$

Sol. Proof: (i) By proportionality Theorem $\frac{AD}{DB} = \frac{AE}{EC}$

On adding 1 to both sides (½ M)

$\frac{AD}{DB} + 1 = \frac{AE}{EC} + 1$ (1 M)

$\Rightarrow \frac{AD + DB}{DB} = \frac{AE + EC}{EC} \Rightarrow \frac{AB}{DB} = \frac{AC}{EC}$

(ii) $\frac{AD}{DB} = \frac{AE}{EC}$ (By Basic proportionality Theorem)

Taking inverse and then adding 1 to both sides

$1 + \frac{DB}{AD} = 1 + \frac{EC}{AE}$ (½ M)

$\Rightarrow \frac{AD + DB}{AD} = \frac{AE + EC}{AE} \Rightarrow \frac{AB}{AD} = \frac{AC}{AE}$ (1 M)

2. In the given figure, $AB \parallel CD$. Find the value of y. (Ev)

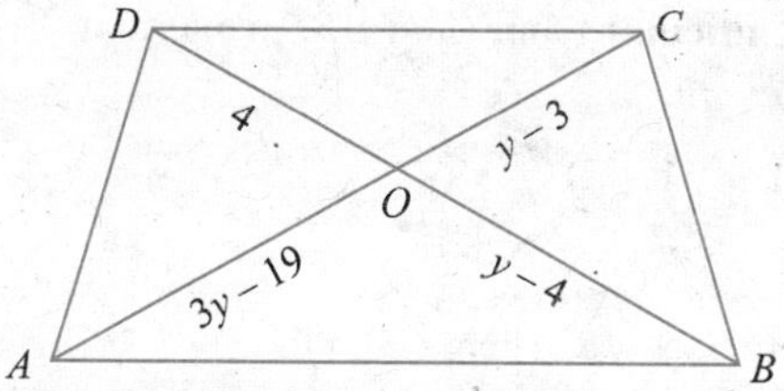

Sol. Since the diagonals of a trapezium divide each other proportionally.

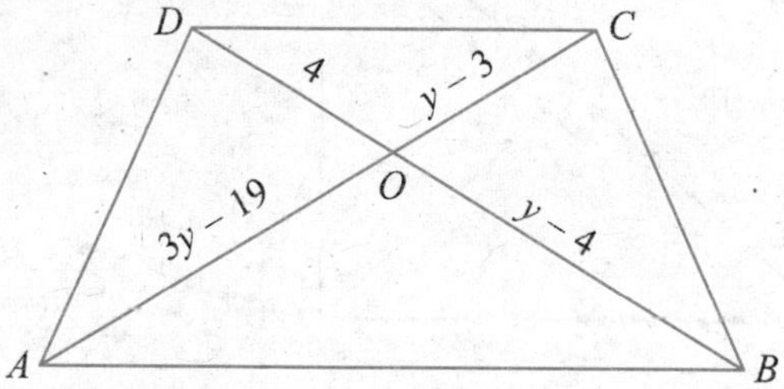

$\therefore \frac{AO}{OC} = \frac{BO}{OD}$ (1 M)

$\Rightarrow \frac{3y - 19}{y - 3} = \frac{y - 4}{4} \Rightarrow 12y - 76 = y^2 - 4y - 3y + 12$ (1 M)

$\Rightarrow y^2 - 19y + 88 = 0 \Rightarrow y^2 - 11y - 8y + 88 = 0$

$\Rightarrow y(y - 11) - 8(y - 11) = 0 \Rightarrow (y - 8)(y - 11) = 0$

$\Rightarrow y = 8$ or $y = 11$. (1 M)

3. Prove that the line segments joining the midpoints of the adjacent sides of a quadrilateral form a parallelogram. (Re)

Sol. Given: A quadrilateral $ABCD$ in which P, Q, R and S are the midpoints of AB, BC, CD and DA respectively.

To prove: $PQRS$ is a parallelogram.

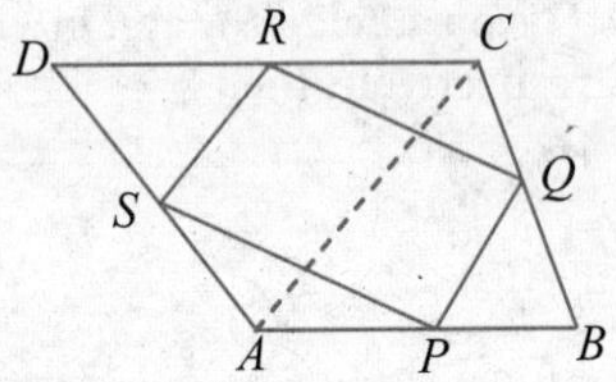

Construction: Join AC. *(1 M)*

Proof: In ΔABC, P and Q are the midpoints of sides AB and BC respectively.

[As we know that the line joining the mid-points of two sides of a triangle is parallel to the third side].

$\therefore PQ \parallel AC$ and $PQ = \frac{1}{2}$ AC ... (i) *(½ M)*

In ΔDAC, S and R are the midpoints of AD and CD respectively.

$\therefore SR \parallel AC$ and $SR = \frac{1}{2} AC$ ... (ii) *(½ M)*

From (i) and (ii), we get $PQ \parallel SR$ and $PQ = SR$

Similarly, by joining diagonals BD, we can show $PS \parallel QR$ and $PS = QR$

Since both pairs of opposite sides are parallel and equal

Hence, $PQRS$ is a parallelogram. *(1 M)*

Long Answer Type Questions (4 or 5 M)

1. ABC is a right triangle having a right-angled at C. Let BC = a, CA = b, AB = c and let p be the length of perpendicular from C on AB, prove that *(Ev)*

(i) $cp = ab$

(ii) $\frac{1}{p^2} = \frac{1}{a^2} + \frac{1}{b^2}$

Sol. (i) Let $CD \perp AB$. Then, $CD = p$.

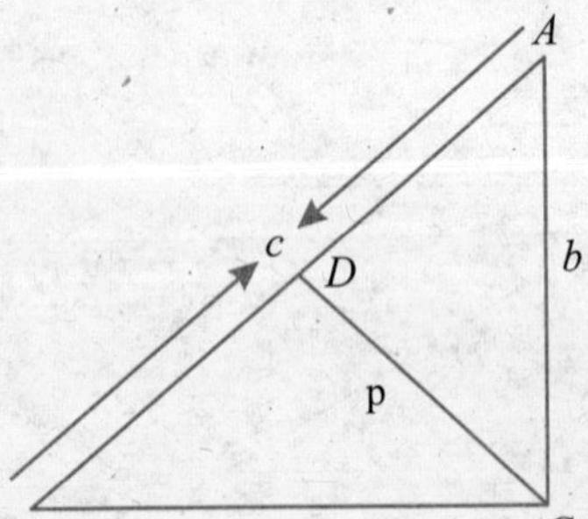

(1 M)

Area of $\Delta ABC = \frac{1}{2}$ (Base × Height) *(1 M)*

$= \frac{1}{2}(AB \times CD) = \frac{1}{2}cp$ *(½ M)*

Also,

Area of $\Delta ABC = \frac{1}{2}(BC \times AC) = \frac{1}{2}ab$

$\therefore \frac{1}{2}cp = \frac{1}{2}ab$

$\Rightarrow cp = ab$ [Hence proved] *(1 M)*

(ii) Since ΔABC is right triangle right-angled at C.

$\therefore AB^2 = BC^2 + AC^2$

$\Rightarrow c^2 = a^2 + b^2$

$\Rightarrow \left(\frac{ab}{p}\right)^2 = a^2 + b^2 \quad \left[\because cp = ab \Rightarrow c = \frac{ab}{p}\right]$ *(½ M)*

$\Rightarrow \frac{1}{p^2} = \frac{a^2+b^2}{a^2b^2} \Rightarrow \frac{1}{p^2} = \frac{1}{b^2} + \frac{1}{a^2}$ [Hence proved] *(1 M)*

2. The diagonals of a quadrilateral ABCD intersect each other at the point O such that $\frac{AO}{BO} = \frac{CO}{DO}$. Show that ABCD is a trapezium. **(Cr) (NCERT Intext)**

Sol. Given: Quadrilateral $ABCD$ where AC and BD intersects each other at O, such that

$\frac{AO}{BO} = \frac{CO}{DO}$.

To prove: $ABCD$ is a trapezium. *(½ M)*

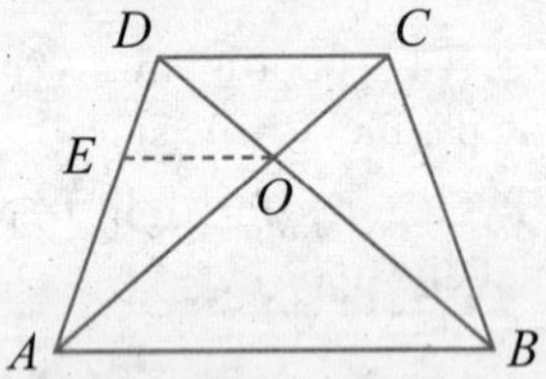

(½ M)

Construction: From the point O, draw a line EO touching AD at E such that $EO \parallel AB$. *(½ M)*

Proof: In ΔDAB, $EO \parallel AB$

$\frac{DE}{EA} = \frac{DO}{OB}$ (using BPT) ... (i) *(½ M)*

Also,

$\frac{AO}{BO} = \frac{CO}{DO}$ (given)

$\Rightarrow \frac{DO}{OB} = \frac{CO}{AO}$ ... (ii) *(½ M)*

From equation (i) and (ii), we get

$\frac{DE}{EA} = \frac{CO}{AO}$ *(½ M)*

In ΔACD,

$\frac{DE}{EA} = \frac{CO}{AO}$

$\therefore EO \parallel CD$ [by the converse of BPT] *(1 M)*

But $EO \parallel AB$

$\Rightarrow AB \parallel DC$

$\therefore ABCD$ is a trapezium. *(1 M)*

3. If a line is drawn parallel to one side of a triangle to intersect the other two sides in distinct points, prove that the other two sides are divided in the same ratio.

(Cr) (CBSE 2020)

Sol.

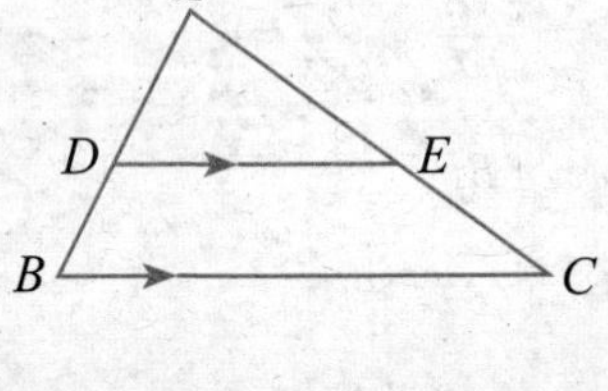

Given: In ΔABC, $DE \parallel BC$.

To prove: $\frac{AB}{PQ} = \frac{AD}{PM}$

Construction:

(i) Join BE and CD.

(ii) Draw $DM \perp AC$ and $EN \perp AB$.

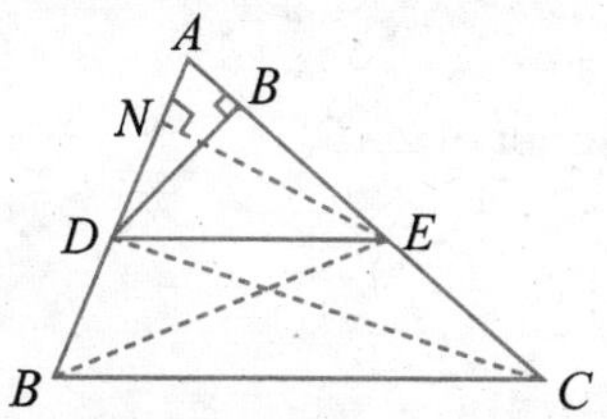

(1 M)

Proof:

$$\text{area } (\Delta ADE) = \frac{1}{2} \times \text{base} \times \text{height}$$

$$= \frac{1}{2} \times AD \times EN$$

and

$$\text{area } (\Delta BDE) = \frac{1}{2} \times BD \times EN \quad (1\ M)$$

Therefore,

$$\frac{\text{area } \Delta ADE}{\text{area } \Delta BDE} = \frac{\frac{1}{2} \times AD \times EN}{\frac{1}{2} \times BD \times EN} = \frac{AD}{BD} \quad \ldots (i)$$

Similarly,

$$\frac{\text{area } \Delta ADE}{\text{area } \Delta DEC} = \frac{\frac{1}{2} \times AE \times DM}{\frac{1}{2} \times EC \times DM} = \frac{AE}{EC} \quad \ldots (ii)\ (1\ M)$$

But area (ΔBDE) area (ΔDEC) ... (*iii*)

Triangles on the same base and between the same parallels are equal in area.

Therefore, from (*i*), (*ii*) and (*iii*) we get

$$\frac{AD}{DB} = \frac{AE}{EC} \quad (1\ M)$$

Hence proved.

4. In the figure, $DE \parallel OQ$ and $DF \parallel OR$. Show that $EF \parallel QR$.

(*Ev*) (NCERT Intext)

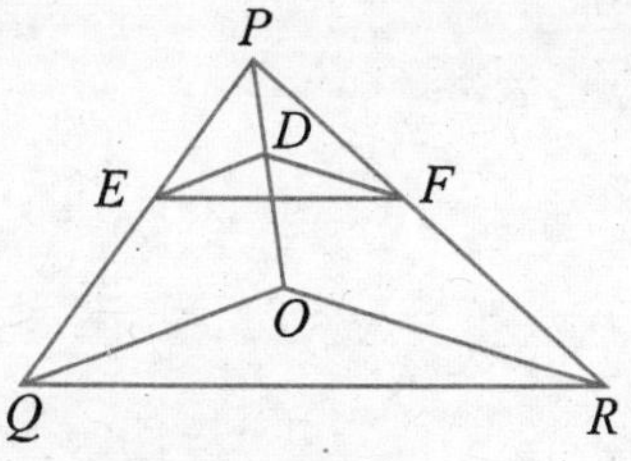

Sol. Given: $DE \parallel OQ$ and $DF \parallel OR$

To prove: $EF \parallel QR$

Proof: In ΔPQO, $DE \parallel OQ$ (1 M)

So by using Basic Proportionality Theorem, we get

$$\frac{PD}{DO} = \frac{PE}{EQ} \quad \ldots (i) \quad (1\ M)$$

Now in ΔPOR, $DF \parallel OR$ (given)

So by using Basic Proportionality Theorem, we get

$$\frac{PD}{DO} = \frac{PF}{FR} \quad \ldots (ii) \quad (1\ M)$$

From equation (*i*) and (*ii*), we get,

$$\frac{PE}{EQ} = \frac{PF}{FR} \quad (1\ M)$$

Therefore, by converse of Basic Proportionality Theorem,

$EF \parallel QR$. Hence proved. (1 M)

5. The bisector of the vertical angle of a triangle divides the base in the ratio of the other two sides. **(*Un*)**

Sol. Given: In ΔABC, AD is the bisector of $\angle A$.

To Prove: $\frac{BD}{DC} = \frac{AB}{AC}$

Construction: Draw CP parallel to AD to meet Ba produced at P.

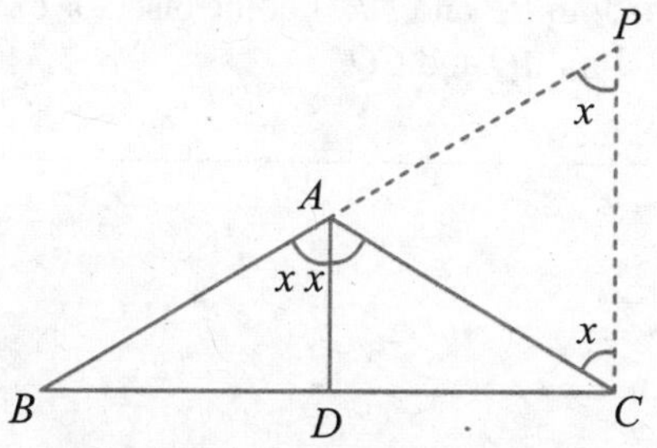

(1 M)

Proof: Let $\angle BAD = \angle DAC = x$

$\angle DAC = \angle ACP$ (alternate angles and $\overline{AB} \parallel \overline{CP}$)

$\angle BAD = \angle ACP$ (corresponding angles) (1 M)

But $\angle BAD = \angle DAC$ (given)

$\therefore \angle ACP = \angle APC$ (½ M)

In triangle APC,

$AC = AP$ (1 M)

(sides opposite to equal angles are equal)

In triangle BCP,

$$\frac{BD}{DC} = \frac{BA}{AC} \text{ (by basic proportionality theorem)} \quad (½\ M)$$

$$\Rightarrow \frac{BD}{DC} = \frac{BA}{AC}$$

Hence proved. (1 M)

6. In a quadrilateral $ABCD$, if bisectors of $\angle ABC$ and $\angle ADC$ meet on the diagonal AC, prove that bisectors of $\angle BAD$ and $\angle BCD$ will meet on the diagonal BD. *(Cr)*

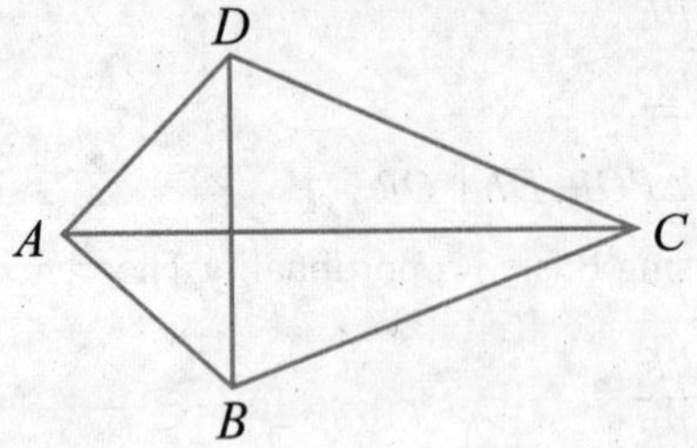

Sol.

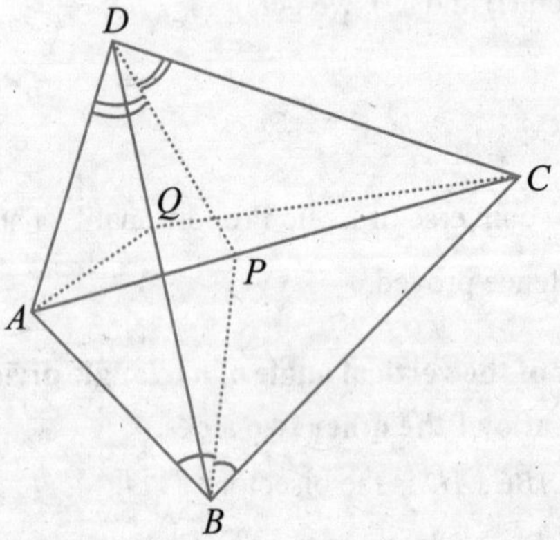

(1 M)

Given: $ABCD$ is a quadrilateral in which the bisectors of $\angle ABC$ and $\angle ADC$ meet on the diagonal AC at P. *(½ M)*

To prove: Bisector of $\angle BAD$ and $\angle BCD$ meet on diagonal BD.

Construction: Join BP and DP. Let the bisector of $\angle BAD$ meet BD at Q. Join AQ and CQ. *(½ M)*

Proof: In order to prove that the bisectors of $\angle BAD$ and $\angle BCD$ meet on the diagonal BD. It is sufficient to prove that CQ is the bisector of $\angle BCD$ for which we will prove that Q divides BD in the ratio $BC : DC$. *(1 M)*

In ΔABC, BP is the bisector of $\angle ABC$

$$\therefore \quad \frac{AB}{BC} = \frac{AP}{PC} \quad \ldots (i)$$

In ΔACD, DP is the bisector of $\angle ADC$

$$\therefore \quad \frac{AD}{DC} = \frac{AP}{PC} \quad \ldots (ii)$$

From (*i*) and (*ii*)

$$\frac{AB}{BC} = \frac{AD}{DC} \Rightarrow \frac{AB}{AD} = \frac{BC}{DC} \quad \ldots (iii) \quad (½ M)$$

In ΔABD, AQ is the bisector of $\angle BAD$ (by construction)

$$\Rightarrow \quad \frac{AB}{AD} = \frac{BQ}{DQ} \quad \ldots (iv)$$

From (*iii*) and (*iv*), we get

$$\Rightarrow \quad \frac{BC}{DC} = \frac{BQ}{DQ} \quad (½ M)$$

Thus, in ΔCBD, Q divides BD in the ratio $CB : BD$

$\therefore CQ$ is the bisector of $\angle BCD$

Hence, bisector of $\angle BAD$ and $\angle BCD$ meet on the diagonal BD at Q. *(1 M)*

Important Concepts

1. **Criteria for Similarity of Triangles:**

   (*i*) If in two triangles, corresponding angles are equal, then their corresponding sides are in the same ratio (or proportional) and hence the two triangles are similar.

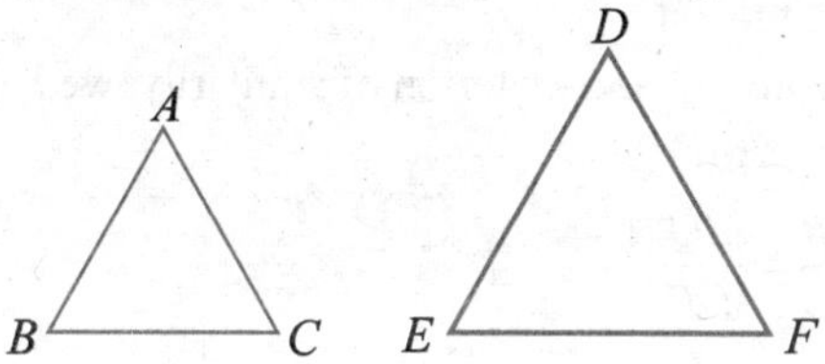

i.e., $\angle A = \angle D, \angle B = \angle E, \angle C = \angle F \Rightarrow \frac{AB}{DE} = \frac{AC}{DF} = \frac{BC}{EF}$

It is known as *AAA* similarity criterion.

   (*ii*) If in two triangles, sides of one triangle are proportional to (i.e., in the same ratio of) the sides of the other triangle, then their corresponding angles are equal and hence the two triangles are similar.

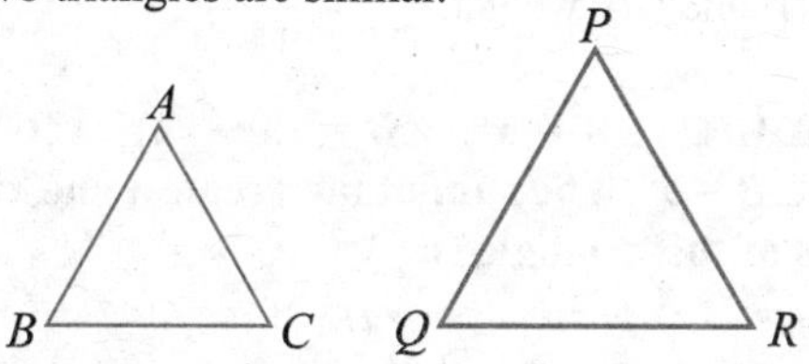

i.e., $\frac{AB}{PQ} = \frac{BC}{QR} = \frac{AC}{PR} \Rightarrow \angle A = \angle P, \angle B = \angle Q, \angle C = \angle R$

It is known as *SSS* similarity criterion.

   (*iii*) If one angle of a triangle is equal to one angle of the other triangle and the sides including these angles are in proportion, then the two triangles are similar.

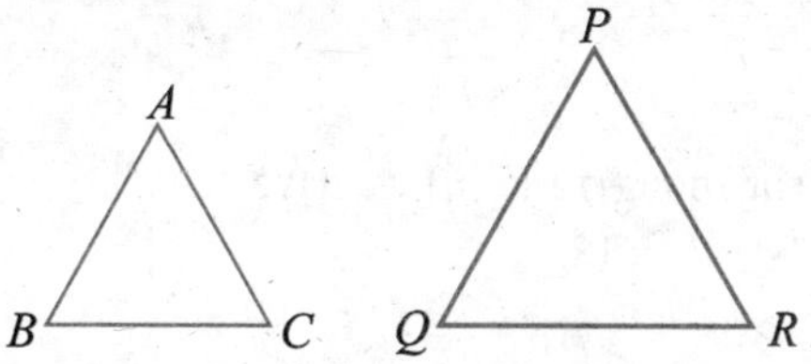

i.e., $\angle A = \angle P$ and $\frac{AB}{PQ} = \frac{AC}{PR} \Rightarrow \Delta ABC \sim \Delta PQR$

It is known as *SAS* similarity criterion.

Note:

- Two triangles are similar if one angle of one triangle is equal to one angle of the other and sides including these angles are proportional. This is referred to as *SAS* (Side-Angle-Side) criterion for similarity.
- Two triangles are similar if the three sides of one are proportional to the three sides of the other. This is usually referred to as *SSS* (Side-Side-Side) criterion.

Real Life Applications

- **Map Scaling:** When creating maps, cartographers use similar triangles to determine distances and scales. By comparing the lengths of corresponding sides in similar triangles on the map and the actual terrain, they can accurately represent the distances between different locations.

- **Architecture and Engineering:** Architects and engineers use similar triangles to scale down large structures for models. This ensures that the model accurately represents the proportions of the actual building.

Different Problem Types

Type I: Criteria for Similarity of Triangles

If $PQ \parallel RS$, prove that $\Delta POQ \sim \Delta SOR$.

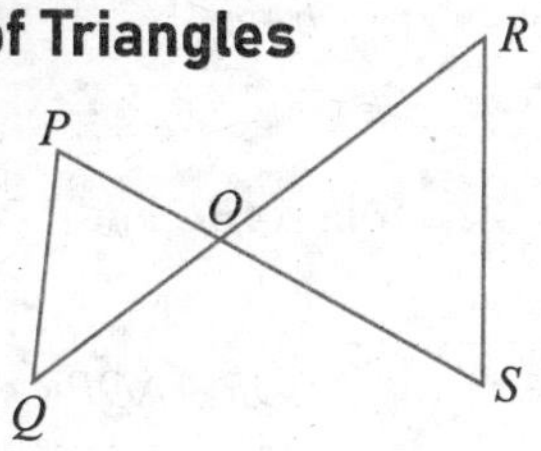

Solution: $PQ \| RS$

Step I: Corresponding angles due to parallel lines

So, $\angle P = \angle S$ (Given)

and $\angle Q = \angle R$ (Alternate angles)

Step II: Vertically Opposite Angles

Also, $\angle POQ = \angle SOR$ (Vertically opposite angles)

Step III: *AAA* Similarity Criterion

Therefore, $\Delta POQ \sim \Delta SOR$ (*AAA* similarity criterion)

Example: In the given figure, if $\Delta ABE \cong \Delta ACD$, show that $\Delta ADE \sim \Delta ABC$.

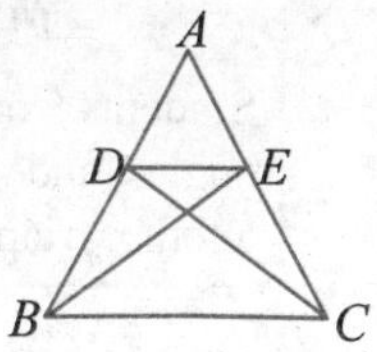

Solution:

Given, $\Delta ABE \cong \Delta ACD$

$AB = AC$ [By *C.P.C.T.*]

and $AE = AD$ [By *C.P.C.T.*]

$\therefore \frac{AB}{AC} = \frac{AD}{AE} = \frac{1}{1}$

and $\angle DAE = \angle BAC$ [Common]

$\therefore \Delta ADE \sim \Delta ABC$ [By *SAS* similarity]

Hence, proved.

COMPETENCY BASED SOLVED EXAMPLES

Multiple Choice Questions

(1 M)

1. In $\Delta ABC, DE \parallel AB$. If $AB = a, DE = x, BE = b$ and $EC = c$. Then x expressed in terms of a, b and c is: *(Ev)*

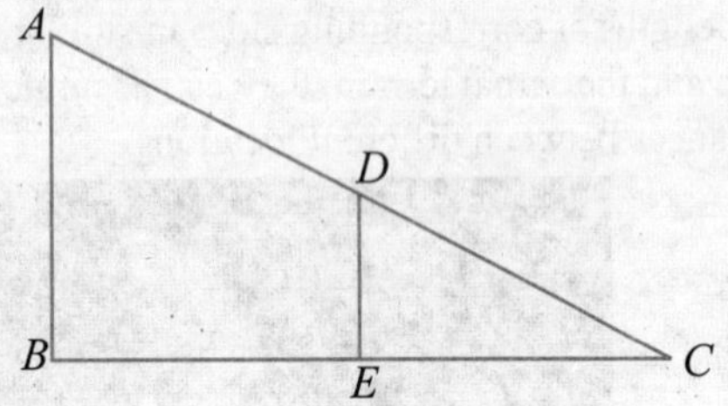

(a) $\frac{ac}{b}$ (b) $\frac{ac}{b+c}$

(c) $\frac{ab}{c}$ (d) $\frac{ab}{b+c}$

Sol. In ΔCDE and ΔCAB

$\angle C = \angle C$ [Common]

$\angle 1 = \angle 2$ [Corresponding angles as $DE \parallel AB$]

$\Delta CDE \sim \Delta CAB$ [By AA rule]

$\frac{DE}{AB} = \frac{CE}{BC}$ [Sides of similar triangles]

$\frac{x}{a} = \frac{c}{b+c}$

$x = \frac{ac}{b+c}$

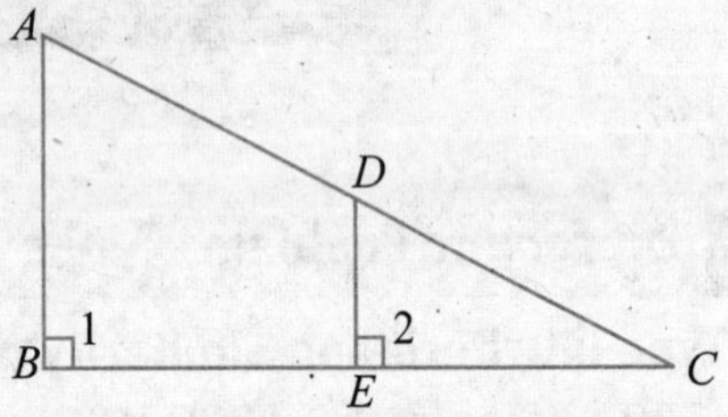

2. If in ΔABC and ΔPQR we have $\frac{AB}{QR} = \frac{BC}{PR} = \frac{CA}{PQ}$ than: ***(Un)* (CBSE SQP, 2023)**

(a) $\Delta PQR \sim \Delta QPR$ (b) $\Delta PQR \sim \Delta ABC$

(c) $\Delta CBA \sim \Delta PQR$ (d) $\Delta BCA \sim \Delta PQR$

Sol. Given, $\frac{AB}{QR} = \frac{BC}{PR} = \frac{CA}{PQ}$

Thus, $\Delta PQR \sim \Delta CAB$ (SSS rule)

Mistakes 101 : What not to do!

Students commonly make errors in determining which angles and sides of one triangle are equal to those of another triangle.

3. In ΔABC, DE is parallel to BC, with D on AB and E on AC. If $\frac{AD}{DB} = \frac{3}{4}$, then $\frac{BC}{DE}$ is *(Un)*

(a) 2 : 5 (b) 3 : 7

(c) 7 : 3 (d) 5 : 3

Sol. In ΔABC, we have

$DE \parallel BC \Rightarrow \frac{AB}{AD} = \frac{AC}{AE}$

Thus, in triangles ABC and ADE, we have

$\frac{AB}{AD} = \frac{AC}{AE}$

and, $\angle A = \angle A$

Therefore, by SAS-criterion of similarity, we have

$\Delta ABC \sim \Delta ADE$

$\Rightarrow \frac{AB}{AD} = \frac{BC}{DE}$ ... (i)

It is given that

$\frac{AB}{AD} = \frac{3}{4} \Rightarrow \frac{DB}{AD} = \frac{4}{3} \Rightarrow \frac{DB}{AD} + 1 = \frac{4}{3} + 1$

$\Rightarrow \frac{DB + AD}{AD} = \frac{7}{3} \Rightarrow \frac{AB}{AD} = \frac{7}{3}$ ... (ii)

From (i) and (ii), we get $\frac{BC}{DE} = \frac{7}{3}$

4. In a ΔABC, $\angle A = x°$, $\angle B = (3x - 2)°$, $\angle C = y°$. Also $\angle C - \angle B = 9°$. The sum of the greatest and the smallest angles of this triangle is *(Ev)*

(a) 107° (b) 135°

(c) 155° (d) 145°

Sol. In ΔABC, $\angle A + \angle B + \angle C = 180°$

$x° + (3x - 2)° + y° = 180°$

$4x + y = 182°$ ... (i)

$\angle C - \angle B = 9°$

$y° - (3x - 2)° = 9°$

$y - 3x + 2 = 9$

$y - 3x = 7$ ... (ii)

$y = 3x + 7$

From equation (i) and (ii) we have

$4x + (3x + 7) = 182$

$7x = 175$

$x = 25°$

Now, $y = 3 \times 25 + 7 = 82$

$\therefore \angle A = x° = 25°$

$\angle B = (3x - 2)° = (3 \times 25 - 2)° = 73°$

$\angle C = y° = 82°$

$\therefore$ The sum of the greatest and the smallest angles of this triangle = 25° + 82° = 107°.

5. Which of the following is NOT a similarity criterion *(An)*

(a) AA (b) SAS

(c) AAA (d) RHS

Sol. RHS is not a similarity citerion, it is a congruence criterion.

6. In fig., PA, QB and RC are each perpendicular to AC. If $x = 8$ cm and $z = 6$ cm, then y is equal to *(Ev)*

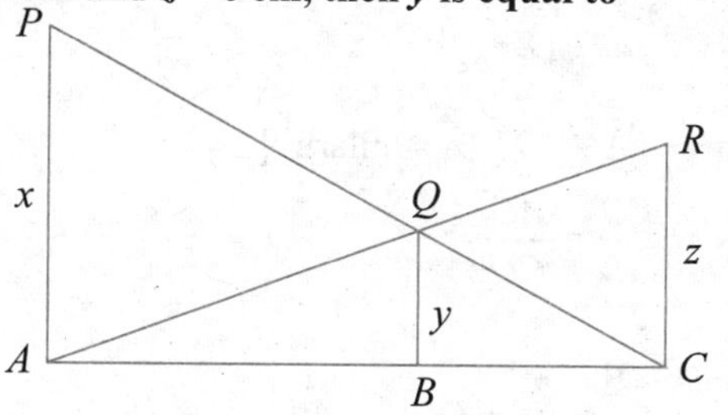

(a) $\frac{56}{7}$ cm (b) $\frac{7}{56}$ cm

(c) $\frac{25}{7}$ cm (d) $\frac{24}{7}$ cm

Sol. Given $x = 8$ cm and $z = 6$ cm

We have from the figure, $\frac{1}{y} = \frac{1}{x} + \frac{1}{z}$

Putting the value of x and z in the above equation we get,

$$\Rightarrow \frac{1}{y} = \frac{1}{8} + \frac{1}{6} \Rightarrow \frac{1}{y} = \frac{3+4}{24} = \frac{7}{24} \Rightarrow y = \frac{24}{7}$$

Answer Key

1. (b) 2. (a) 3. (c) 4. (a) 5. (d) 6. (d)

Assertion and Reason

(1 M)

Direction: In the following questions, a statement of Assertion (A) is followed by a statement of Reason (R). M the correct choice as.

(a) Both Assertion (A) and Reason (R) are true, and Reason (R) is the correct explanation of Assertion (A).

(b) Both Assertion (A) and Reason (R) are true, but Reason (R) is not the correct explanation of Assertion (A).

(c) Assertion (A) is true, but Reason (R) is false.

(d) Assertion (A) is false, but Reason (R) is true.

1. Assertion (A): ΔABC is an isosceles triangle right angled at C, then $AB^2 = 2AC^2$.

Reason (R): In right ΔABC, right angled at B, $AC^2 = AB^2 + BC^2$. *(An)*

Sol. We know that $AC^2 = AB^2 + BC^2$ by Pythagoras theorem.

Since the triangle is isosceles, we know that $AC = BC$. Therefore, we can substitute AC for BC in the above equation, we get

$2AC^2 = AB^2$

Therefore, Assertion is true.

The reason given, "In right ΔABC, right angled at B, $AC^2 = AB^2 + BC^2$," is a valid justification.

Both Assertion (A) and Reason (R) are true, and Reason (R) is the correct explanation of Assertion (A).

2. Assertion (A): ABC is an isosceles, right triangle, right angled at C. Then $AB^2 = 3AC^2$.

Reason (R): In an isosceles triangle ABC if $AC = BC$ and $AB^2 = 2AC^2$, then $\angle C = 90°$. *(Ap)*

Sol. In right angled ΔABC,

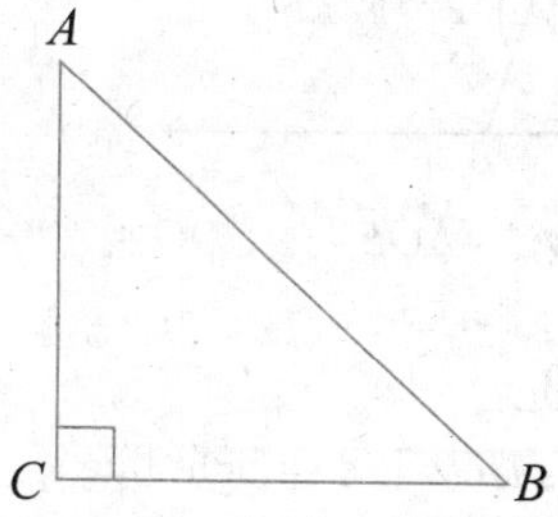

$AB^2 = AC^2 + BC^2$ (By Pythagoras Theorem)

$AB^2 = AC^2 + AC^2$ $[BC = AC]$

$AB^2 = 2AC^2$

Assertion is false.

Again since, $AB^2 = 2AC^2 = AC^2 + AC^2$

$AB^2 = AC^2 + BC^2$ ($AC = BC$ given)

$\angle C = 90°$

(By converse of Pythagoras Theorem)

Reason is true.

Answer Key

1. (a) 2. (d)

Subjective Questions

Very Short Answer Type Questions

(1 or 2 M)

1. E is a point on the side AD produced of a parallelogram $ABCD$ and BE intersects CD at F. Show that $\Delta ABE \sim \Delta CFB$. *(An)* **(NCERT Intext)**

Sol. Given: E is a point on the side AD produced of a parallelogram $ABCD$ and BE intersects CD at F.

To prove: $\Delta ABE \sim \Delta CFB$

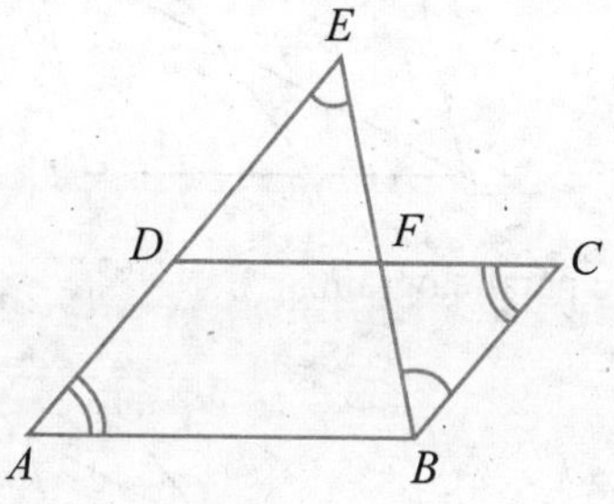

Proof: In ΔABE and ΔCFB, *(1 M)*

$\angle A = \angle C$ (Opposite angles of a parallelogram)

$\angle AEB = \angle CBF$ (Alternate interior angles as $AE \parallel BC$)

By AA similarity criterion, we have

$\Delta ABE \sim \Delta CFB$. *(1 M)*

2. In the figure, $\Delta ODC \sim \Delta OBA$, $\angle BOC = 125°$ and $\angle CDO = 70°$. Find $\angle DOC$, *(Un)* **(NCERT Intext)**

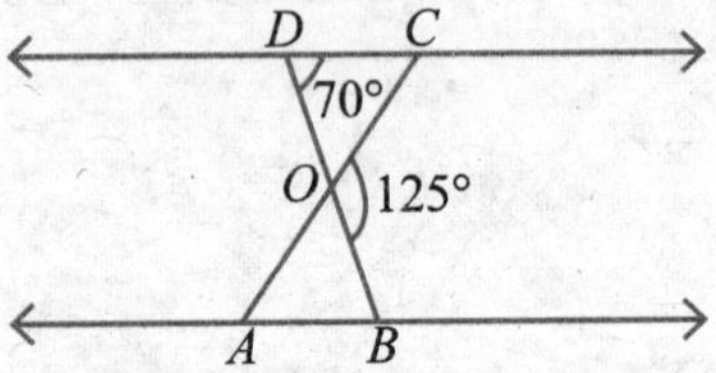

(1 M)

Sol. Given: $\Delta ODC \sim \Delta OBA$, $\angle CDO = 70°$ and $\angle BOC = 125°$

To find: $\angle DOC$

Solution: As DOB is a straight line.

Therefore, $\angle DOC + \angle COB = 180°$ [Linear pair]

$\Rightarrow \angle DOC = 180° - 125°$ (Given, $\angle BOC = 125°$)

$= 55°$ (1 M)

3. In the given figure, ABC and AMP are two right triangles, right angled at B and M respectively, prove that $\Delta ABC \sim \Delta AMP$ *(Ap)* **(NCERT Intext)**

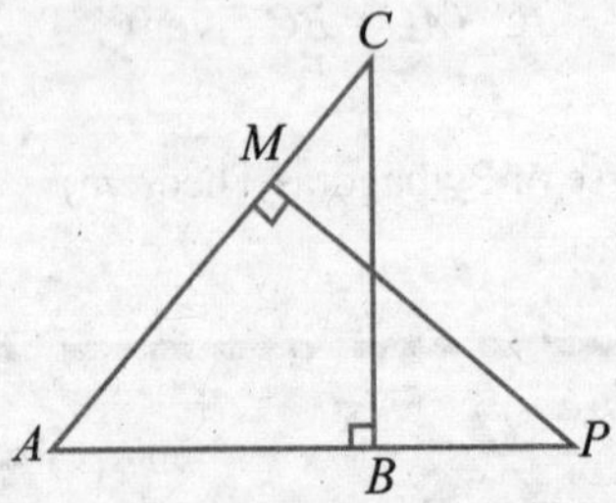

Sol. Given: We have ΔABC, right angled at B and ΔAMP, right angled at M.

To prove: $\Delta ABC \sim \Delta AMP$ (1 M)

Proof: In ΔABC and ΔAMP,

$\angle CAB = \angle MAP$ (common angle)

$\angle ABC = \angle AMP = 90°$

$\therefore \Delta ABC \sim \Delta AMP$ (AA similarity criterion) (1 M)

4. *ABCD* is a parallelogram. Point P divides AB in the ratio 2:3 and point Q divides DC in the ratio 4:1. Prove that OC is half of OA. *(Ap)* **(CBSE SQP, 2023)**

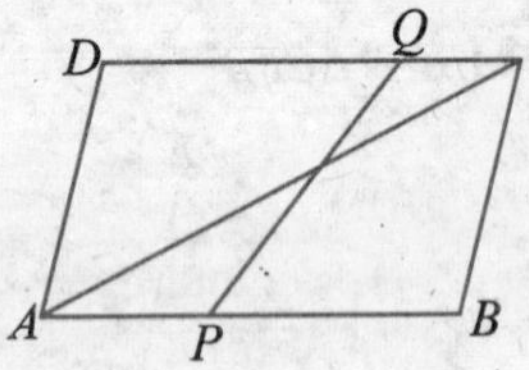

Sol. $ABCD$ is a parallelogram.

$AB = DC = a$

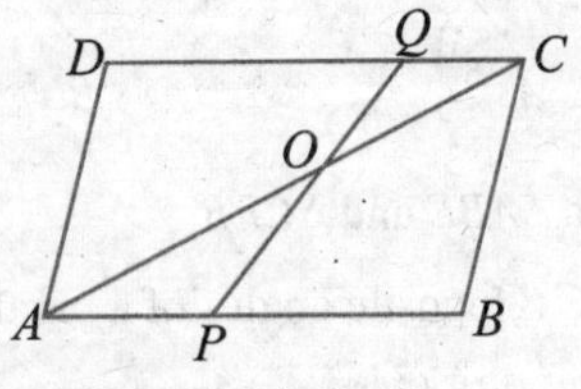

Point P divides AB in the ratio 2 : 3

$AP = \frac{2}{5}a$, $BP = \frac{3}{5}a$ (½ M)

point Q divides DC in the ratio 4:1.

$DQ = \frac{4}{5}a$, $CQ = \frac{1}{5}a$ (½ M)

$\Delta APO \sim \Delta CQO$ [AA similarity]

$\frac{AP}{CQ} = \frac{PO}{QO} = \frac{AO}{CO}$ (½ M)

$\frac{AO}{CO} = \frac{\frac{2}{5}a}{\frac{1}{5}a} = \frac{2}{1} \Rightarrow OC = \frac{1}{2}OA$ (½ M)

5. State pairs of triangles in the given figures are similar. Write the similarity criterion used by you for answering the question and also write the pairs of similar triangles in the symbolic form: *(Un)* **(NCERT Intext)**

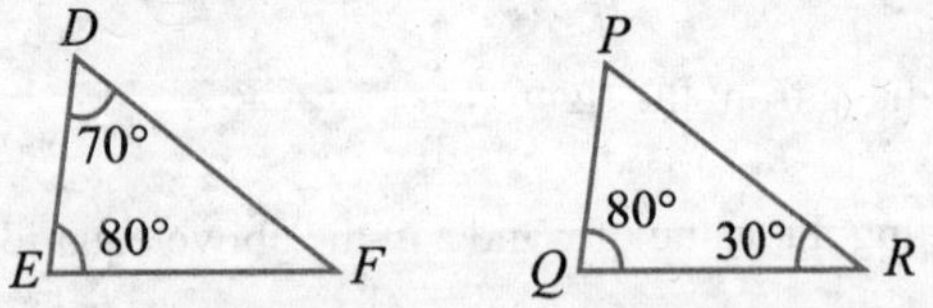

Sol. In ΔDEF

$\angle D + \angle E + \angle F = 180°$ (½ M)

(Sum of angles of a triangle is 180°.)

$70° + 80° + \angle F = 180°$

$150° + \angle F = 180°$

$\angle F = 180° - 150°$

$\angle F = 30°$ (½ M)

In ΔDEF and ΔPQR

$\angle E = \angle Q$

$\angle F = \angle R$

Therefore by AA similarity criterion,

$\Delta DEF \sim \Delta PQR$ (1 M)

Key Takeaways

The sum of the interior angle measures of a triangle always adds up to 180°.

Short Answer Type Questions (2 or 3 M)

1. In the given figure, E is a point on side CB produced of an isosceles triangle ABC with $AB = AC$. If $AD \perp BC$ and $EF \perp AC$, prove that $\Delta ABD \sim \Delta ECF$. *(Cr)*

Sol. Given: ABC is an isosceles triangle in which $AB = AC$. Also, $AD \perp BC$ and $EF \perp AC$.

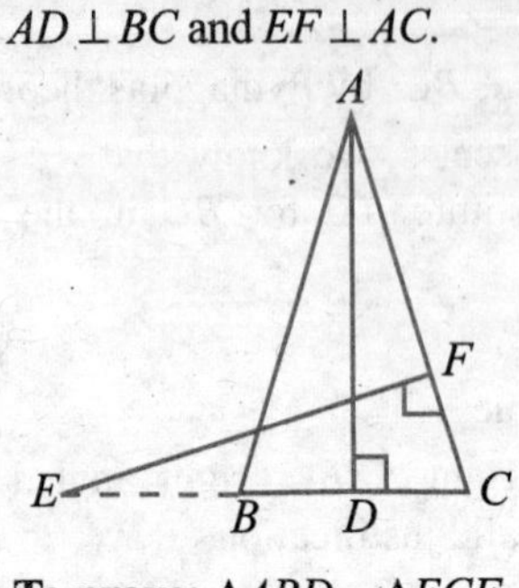

(1 M)

To prove: $\Delta ABD \sim \Delta ECF$

Proof: ABC is an isosceles triangle.

$AB = AC$ (given) *(½ M)*

$\therefore \angle ABD = \angle ECF$ (angles opposite to equal sides are equal)

In ΔABD and ΔECF,

$\angle ADB = \angle EFC$ (Each 90°)

$\angle ABD = \angle ECF$ (Proved above) *(½ M)*

$\therefore \Delta ABD \sim \Delta ECF$ (by AA similarity criterion) *(1 M)*

2. In Fig. 6, *DEFG* is a square in a triangle *ABC* right angled at A. Prove the *(An)* **(CBSE, 2020)**

Fig. 6

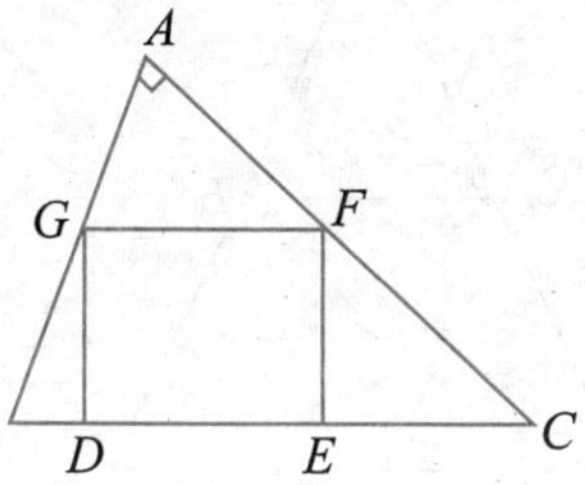

(*i*) $\Delta AGF \sim \Delta DBG$

(*ii*) $\Delta AGF \sim \Delta EFC$

Sol. (*i*) In ΔAGF, and ΔDBG, we have

$\angle GAF = \angle BDG$ [Each equal to 90°]

and, $\angle AGF = \angle DBG$ [Corresponding angles]

$\therefore \Delta AGF \sim \Delta DBG$ [By AA-criterion of similarity] *(1 M)*

(*ii*) In ΔAGF and ΔEFC, we have

$\angle FAG = \angle CEF$ [Each equal to 90°] *(1 M)*

and, $\angle AFG = \angle ECF$

$\therefore \Delta DBG \sim \Delta EFG$ [By AA-criterion of similatity] *(1 M)*

3. In Fig. if $AD = 6$cm, $DB = 9$cm, $AE = 12$cm and $\angle$ADE = 48°. Find $\angle$ABC.

(Cr) **(CBSE SQP, 2023)**

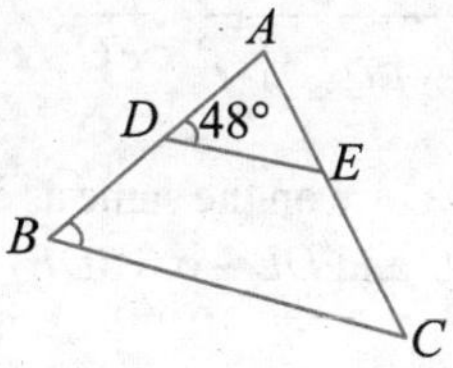

Sol. Given $AD = 6$cm, $DB = 9$cm

$AE = 8$cm $EC = 12$cm, $\angle ADE = 48$

To find:- $\angle ABC = ?$

Proof:

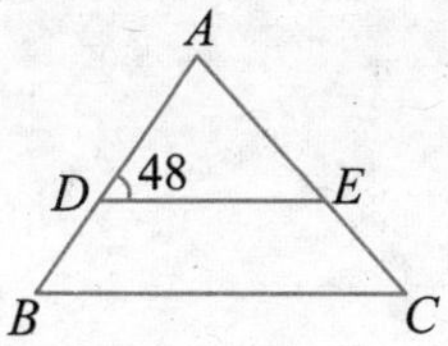

In ΔABC

Consider, $\dfrac{AD}{DB} = \dfrac{AE}{EC}$ *(1 M)*

$\dfrac{6}{9} = \dfrac{8}{12}$

$\dfrac{2}{3} = \dfrac{2}{3}$ *(1 M)*

$\dfrac{AD}{DB} = \dfrac{AE}{EC}$

DEIIBC (Converse of BPT)

$\angle ADE = \angle ABC$ (Corresponding angles) $\angle ABC = 48°$ *(1 M)*

4. In the given ΔABC, obtuse angled at B. If $AD \perp CB$ produced, then $AC^2 = AB^2 + BC^2 + 2BC \cdot BD$ *(Ap)*

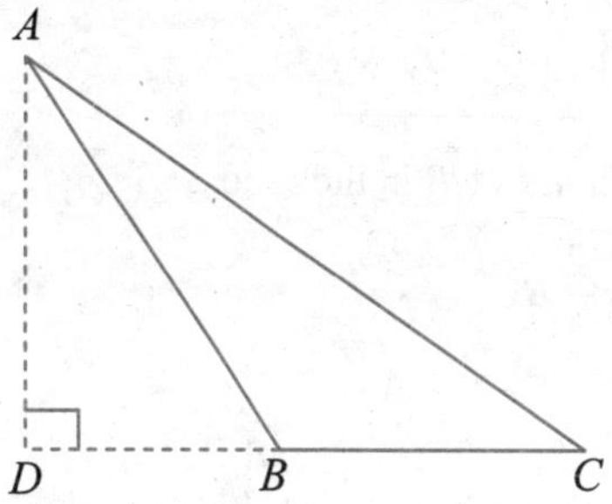

Sol. Given: In figure ABC, is a triangle in which $\angle ABC > 90°$ and $AD \perp CB$ produced.

To Prove: $AC^2 = AB^2 + BC^2 + 2BC \cdot BD$ *(½ M)*

Proof: In right triangle ABC,

$\because \angle D = 90°$

$\because AC^2 = AD^2 + DC^2$ (By Pythagoras theorem) *(½ M)*

$= AD^2 + (DB + BC)^2$

$= AD^2 + DB^2 + BC^2 + 2\, DB \cdot BC$

$= AB^2 + BC^2 + 2BC \cdot DB$ *(1 M)*

[$\because$ In right triangle ADB with $\angle D = 90°$, $AB^2 = AD^2 + DB^2$ (By Pythagoras theorem)] *(1 M)*

5. In Fig.,

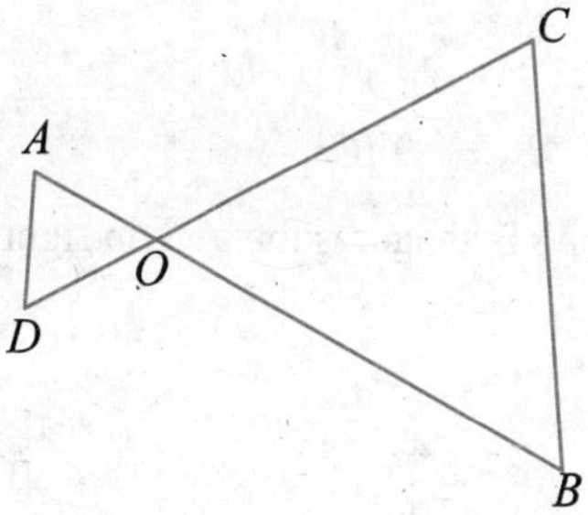

OA.OB = OC.OD.

Show that $\angle A = \angle C$ and $\angle B = \angle D$. *(An)*

Sol. $OA.OB = OC.OD$ (given)

So, $\dfrac{OA}{OC} = \dfrac{OD}{OB}$ ... (*i*) *(½ M)*

Also, we have

$\angle AOD = \angle COB$ (Vertically opposite angles) ... (*ii*) *(½ M)*

Therefore, from (*i*) and (*ii*),

$\Delta AOD \sim \Delta COB$ (*SAS* similarity criterion) *(1 M)*

So, $\angle A = \angle C$ and $\angle D = \angle B$

(Corresponding angles of similar triangles) *(1 M)*

Long Answer Type Questions (4 or 5 M)

1. In a right triangle ABC right-angled at C, P and Q are the points on the sides CA and CB respectively, which divide these sides in the ratio 2 : 1. Prove that *(Ap)*

(i) $9AQ^2 = 9AC^2 + 4BC^2$

(ii) $9BP^2 = 9BC^2 + 4AC^2$

(iii) $9(AQ^2 + BP^2) = 13AB^2$

Sol. It is given that P divides CA in the ratio 2 : 1. Therefore,

$CP = \frac{2}{3}AC$ ... (i) (½ M)

Also, Q divides CB in the ratio 2 : 1.

$\therefore QC = \frac{2}{3}BC$ ... (ii) (½ M)

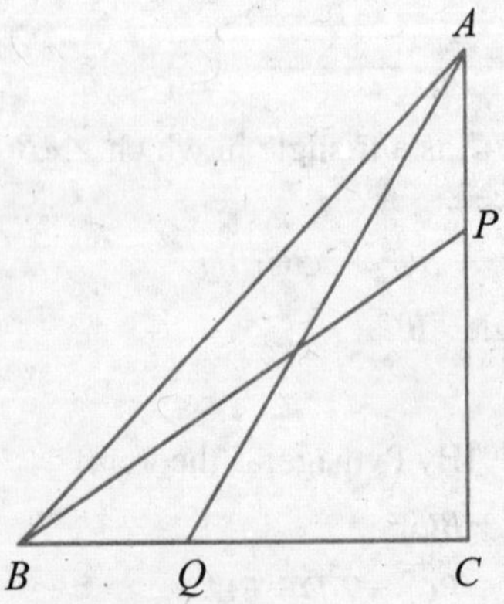

(1 M)

(i) Applying Pythagoras theorem in right-angled triangle ACQ, we have

$AQ^2 = QC^2 + AC^2$ (½ M)

$\Rightarrow AQ^2 = \frac{4}{9}BC^2 + AC^2$ [Using (ii)]

$\Rightarrow 9AQ^2 = 4BC^2 + 9AC^2$ ... (iii) (1 M)

(ii) Applying Pythagoras theorem in right triangle BCP, we have

$BP^2 = BC^2 + CP^2$

$\Rightarrow BP^2 = BC^2 + \frac{4}{9}AC^2$ [Using (i)] (½ M)

$\Rightarrow 9BP^2 = 9BC^2 + 4AC^2$ ... (iv)

(iii) Adding (iii) and (iv), we get

$9(AQ^2 + BP^2) = 13(BC^2 + AC^2)$

$\Rightarrow 9(AQ^2 + BP^2) = 13AB^2$ [$\because BC^2 = AC^2 + AB^2$]

[Hence proved] (1 M)

2. Prove that If a line is drawn parallel to one side of a triangle to intersect the other two sides in distinct points, the other two sides are divided in the same ratio.

In ΔPQR, S and T are points on PQ and PR respectively. $\frac{PS}{SQ} = \frac{PT}{TR}$ and $\angle PST = \angle PRQ$. Prove that PQR is an isosceles triangle. *(An)* **(CBSE SQP, 2023)**

Sol. Given $\Delta ABC = DE \parallel BC$

To prove $\frac{AD}{DB} = \frac{AE}{EC}$

Construction: join BE and CD (½ M)

Draw $DM \perp AC$ and $EN \perp CD$

Proof: or $\Delta ABC = \frac{1}{2} \times b \times h$

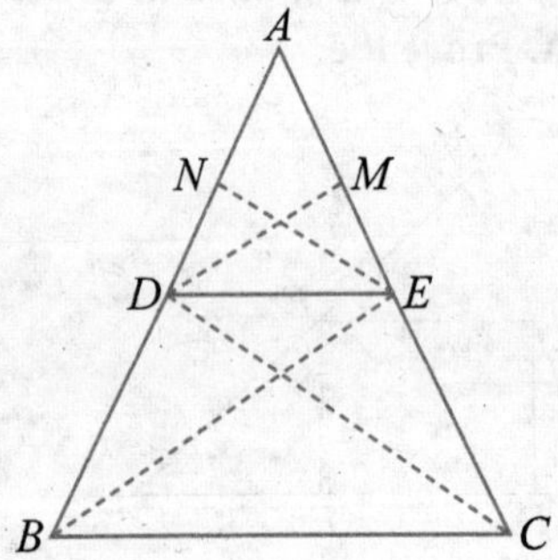

$\therefore = \frac{1}{2} \times AD \times EN$ ...(i)

Or $\Delta ABC = \frac{1}{2} \times DB \times EN$ ... (ii)

Divide eq^n (i) by (ii)

$\frac{\text{Or } \Delta ABC}{\text{Or } \Delta BDE} = \frac{\frac{1}{2} \times AD \times EN}{\frac{1}{2} \times DB \times EN} = \frac{AD}{DB}$ ... (A) (1 M)

Or $\Delta ABC = \frac{1}{2} \times AE \times DM$ ... (iii)

Or $\Delta DEC = \frac{1}{2} \times EC\ DM$ ... (iv)

Divide eqn (iii) by (iv)

$\frac{\text{Or } \Delta ADE}{\text{Or } \Delta DEC} = \frac{\frac{1}{2} \times AE \times DM}{\frac{1}{2} \times EC \times DM} = \frac{AE}{EC}$ (A) (1 M)

ΔBDE and ΔDEC are on the same as DE and between name parallel lines BC and DE – or (BDE) = or (DEC)

hence

$\frac{ar\ \Delta ADE}{ar \Delta BDE} = \frac{ar \Delta ADE}{ar \Delta DEC}$

$\frac{AD}{DB} = \frac{AE}{EC}$ **(from (A) and (B))**

Given

$\frac{PS}{PQ} = \frac{PT}{TR}$

$\angle PST = \angle PRQ$

To prove: PQR is an isosceles Δ^{le}

Proof: $\frac{PS}{PQ} = \frac{PT}{TR}$

$\angle PST = \angle PQR$ **(Corresponding angles)**

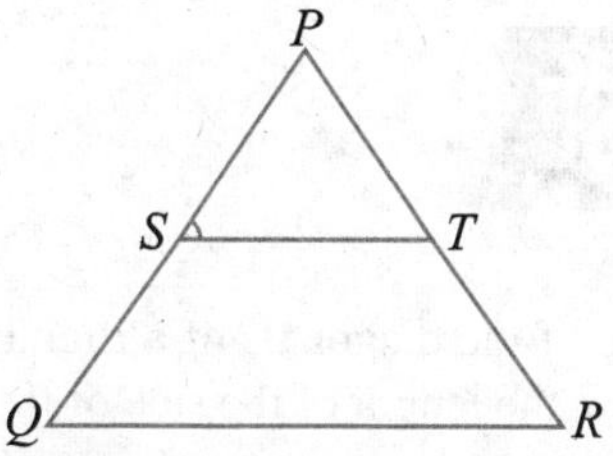

But $\angle PST = \angle PRQ$

$\angle PQR = \angle PRQ$

$PR = PQ$ (sides opposite to equal angles are equal)

$-\Delta PQR$ is isosceles Δ^{le}

3. In Fig, *OB* is the perpendicular bisector of the line segment *DE*, *FA* ⊥ *OB* and *FE* intersects *OB* at the point *C*. Prove that $\frac{1}{OA}+\frac{1}{OB}=\frac{2}{OC}$ (*Un*) (NCERT Exemplar)

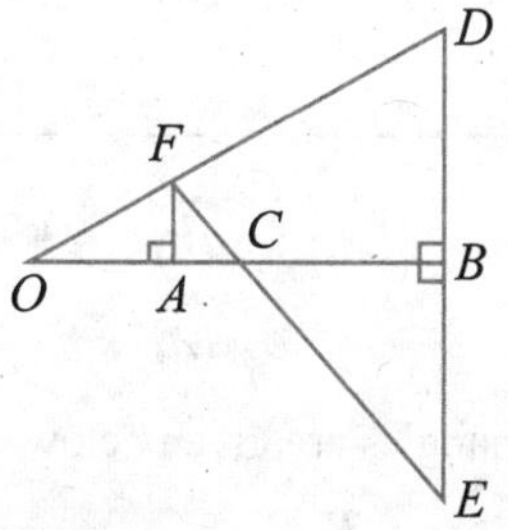

Sol. In ΔAOF and ΔBOD

$\angle O = \angle O$ (Same angle) and $\angle A = \angle B$ (each 90°)

Therefore, $\Delta AOF \sim \Delta BOD$ (*AA* similarity) (1 M)

So, $\frac{OA}{OB}=\frac{FA}{DB}$ … (*i*) (½ M)

Also, in ΔFAC and ΔEBC, $\angle A = \angle B$ (Each 90°) and $\angle FCA = \angle ECB$ (Vertically opposite angles).

Therefore, $\Delta FAC \sim \Delta EBC$ (AA similarity). (1 M)

So, $\frac{FA}{EB}=\frac{AC}{BC}$

But $EB = DB$ (*B* is mid-point of *DE*)

So, $\frac{FA}{DB}=\frac{AC}{BC}$ … (*ii*)

Therefore, from (*i*) and (*ii*), we have:

$\frac{AC}{BC}=\frac{OA}{OB}$ (1 M)

i.e., $\frac{OC-OA}{OB-OC}=\frac{OA}{OB}$

or $OB \cdot OC - OA \cdot OB = OA \cdot OB - OA \cdot OC$ (½ M)

or $OB \cdot OC + OA \cdot OC = 2OA \cdot OB$

or $(OB + OA) \cdot OC = 2OA \cdot OB$

or $\frac{1}{OA}+\frac{1}{OB}=\frac{2}{OC}$ (1 M)

[Dividing both the sides by $OA \cdot OB \cdot OC$]

Mistakes 101 : What not to do!

Students often make mistakes in identifying which sides and angles are equal to prove congruent triangles.

4. If *AD* and *PM* are medians of triangles *ABC* and *PQR*, respectively where $\Delta ABC \sim \Delta PQR$, prove that $\frac{AB}{PQ}=\frac{AD}{PM}$. (*Re*) (NCERT Intext)

Sol. Given: $\Delta ABC \sim \Delta PQR$

To prove: $\frac{AB}{PQ}=\frac{AD}{PM}$.

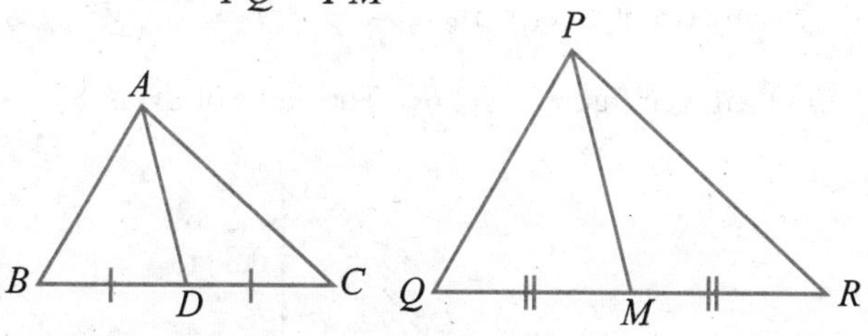

(1 M)

Proof: $\Delta ABC \sim \Delta PQR$

We know that the corresponding sides of similar triangles are in proportion.

$\therefore \frac{AB}{PQ}=\frac{AC}{PR}=\frac{BC}{QR}$ …(*i*) (1 M)

Also, $\angle A = \angle P$, $\angle B = \angle Q$, $\angle C = \angle R$ …(*ii*) (½ M)

Since *AD* and *PM* are medians,

$\therefore BD = \frac{BC}{2}$ and $QM = \frac{QR}{2}$ …(*iii*) (½ M)

From equations (*i*) and (*iii*), we get

$\frac{AB}{PQ}=\frac{BD}{QM}$ …(*iv*) (1 M)

In ΔABD and ΔPQM, $\angle B = \angle Q$ [using eq. (*ii*)]

From equation (*iv*), we have, $\frac{AB}{PQ}=\frac{BD}{QM}$

$\therefore \Delta ABD \sim \Delta PQM$ (SAS similarity criterion)

$\Rightarrow \frac{AB}{PQ}=\frac{BD}{QM}=\frac{AD}{PM}$ (by definition of similarity)

Hence proved (1 M)

MISCELLANEOUS EXERCISE

Multiple Choice Questions

(1 M)

1. ΔABC is an equilateral triangle with each side of length $2x$. If $AD \perp BC$, then the value of AD is

(*a*) $\sqrt{3}$ (*b*) $\sqrt{3}\,x$

(*c*) x (*d*) $2x$

2. Which of the following are DEFINITELY similar to each other? **(CBSE CFPQ, 2023)**

(*a*) any two rhombuses

(*b*) any two right triangles

(*c*) any two regular pentagons

(*d*) any two isosceles triangles

3. In the given figure, $DE \parallel BC$. The value of EC is

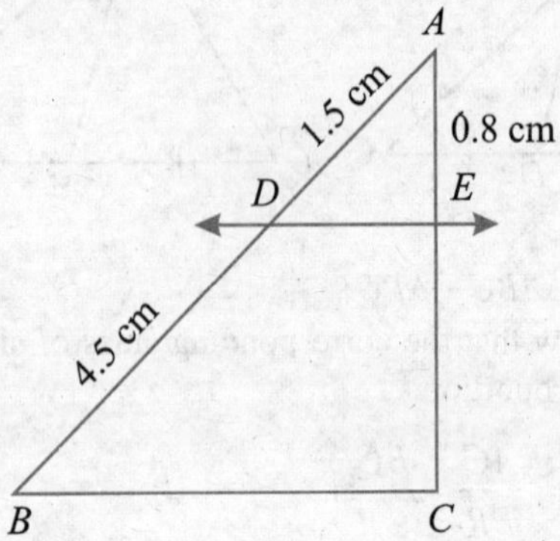

(*a*) 1.5 cm (*b*) 3 cm

(*c*) 2.4 cm (*d*) 1 cm

4. O is the point of intersection of two equal chords AB and CD such that $OB = OD$, then triangles OAC and ODB are

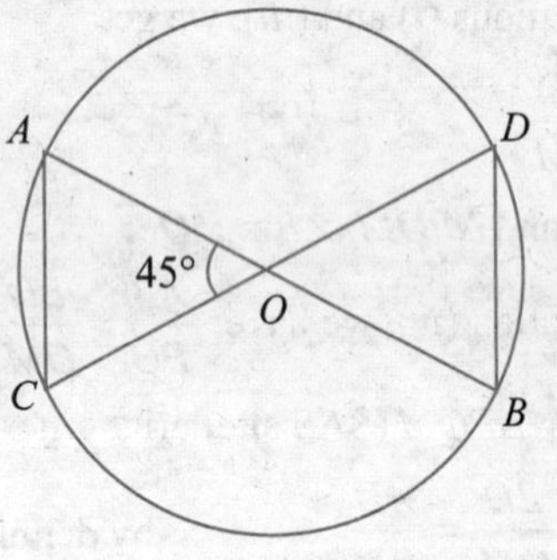

(*a*) Scalene (*b*) Isosceles but not similar

(*c*) Equilateral and similar (*d*) Isosceles and similar

5. D and E are respectively the midpoints on the sides AB and AC of a triangle ABC and $BC = 6$ cm. If $DE \parallel BC$, then the length of DE (in cm) is

(*a*) 2.5 (*b*) 3

(*c*) 5 (*d*) 6

6. The lengths of the diagonals of a rhombus are 40 cm and 30 cm. Then, the length of the side of the rhombus is

(*a*) 30 cm (*b*) 25 cm

(*c*) 20 cm (*d*) 27 cm

7. In the figure given below $DE \parallel BC$. If $AD = x$, $DB = x - 2$, $AE = x + 2$ and $EC = x - 1$, the value of x is:

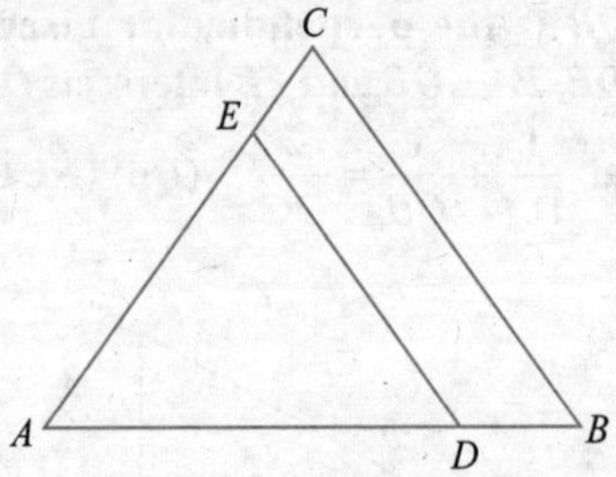

(*a*) 4 (*b*) 16

(*c*) 2 (*d*) 8

8. Two scalene triangles are given below.

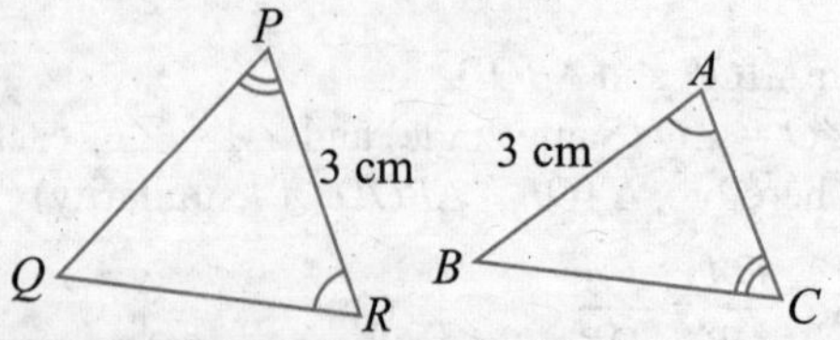

Anas and Rishi observed them and said the following:

Anas: ΔPQR is similar to ΔCBA

Rishi: ΔPQR is congruent to ΔCBA

Which of them is/are correct?

(*a*) Only Anas

(*b*) Only Rishi

(*c*) Both Anas and Rishi

(*d*) Neither of them, as two scalene triangles can never be similar or congruent.

9. In the given figure, $AD = 6$ cm, $AE = 9$ cm and $EC = 4$ cm, then the value of $2BD$ is

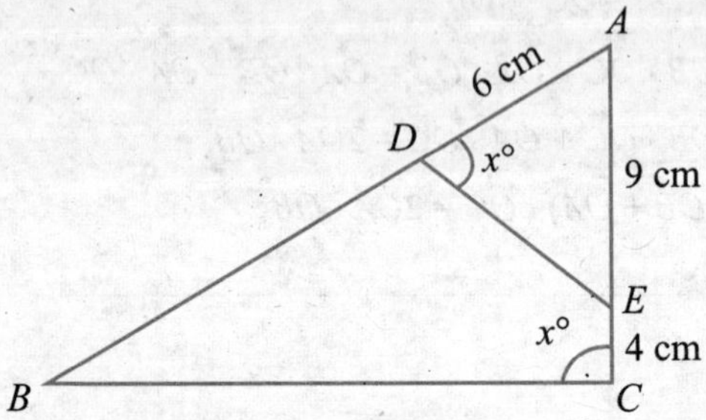

(*a*) 9 (*b*) 18

(*c*) 27 (*d*) 36

10. In an isosceles triangle ABC, with $AB = AC.BD$ is perpendicular from B to the side AC. If $BD^2 - CD^2 = KCD.AD$, then K is equal to

(a) 7 (b) 5

(c) 2 (d) 3

11. If E is a point on side CA of an equilateral ΔABC such that $BE \perp CA$, then $AB^2 + BC^2 + CA^2 =$

(a) $2BE^2$ (b) $3BE^2$

(c) $4BE^2$ (d) $\frac{4}{3}BE^2$

12. In the given figure, $AM : MC = 3 : 4$, $BP : PM = 3 : 2$ and $BN = 12$ cm. Then AN is equal to

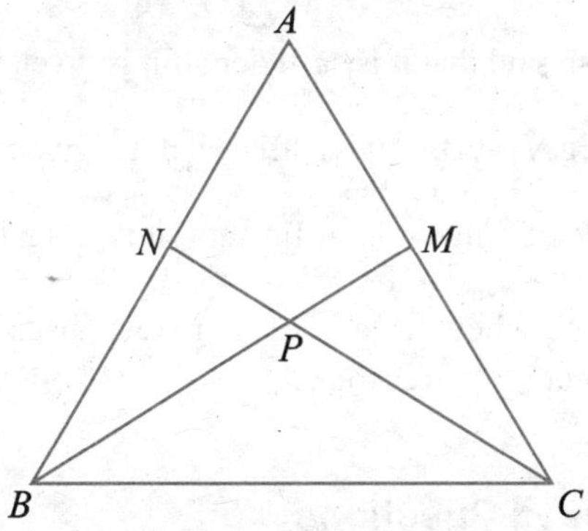

(a) 24 cm (b) 12 cm

(c) 24 cm (d) 22 cm

13. If $\Delta ABC \sim \Delta DEF$, $AB = 4$ cm, $DE = 6$ cm, $EF = 9$ cm and $FD = 12$ cm, the perimeter of ΔABC.

(a) 18 cm (b) 20 cm

(c) 19 cm (d) 22 cm

14. In ΔABC, DE is parallel to BC, with D on AB and E on AC. If $\frac{AD}{DB} = \frac{3}{4}$, then $\frac{BC}{DE}$ is

(a) 2 : 5 (b) 3 : 7

(c) 7 : 3 (d) 5 : 3

15. The bisectors of the angles B and C of a ΔABC, meet the opposite sides in D and E respectively and DE is parallel to BC. Then the triangle is

(a) Right-angled (b) Equilateral

(c) Isosceles (d) Scalene

Assertion and Reason

(1 M)

Direction: **In the following questions, a statement of Assertion (A) is followed by a statement of Reason (R). Mark the correct choice as.**

(a) Both Assertion (A) and Reason (R) are true, and Reason (R) is the correct explanation of Assertion (A).

(b) Both Assertion (A) and Reason (R) are true, but Reason (R) is not the correct explanation of Assertion (A).

(c) Assertion (A) is true, but Reason (R) is false.

(d) Assertion (A) is false, but Reason (R) is true.

1. **Assertion (A):** D and E are points on the sides AB and AC respectively of a ΔABC such $DE \parallel BC$ then the value of x is 4, when $AD = x$ cm, $DB = (x - 2)$ cm, $AE = (x + 2)$ cm and $EC = (x - 1)$ cm.

Reason (R): If a line is parallel to one side of a triangle then it divides the other two sides in the same ratio.

2. **Assertion (A):** D and E are points on the sides AB and AC respectively of a $AABC$ such that $AB = 10.8$cm, $AD = 6.3$cm, $AC = 9.6$cm and $EC = 4$cm then DE is parallel to BC.

Reason (R): If a line is parallel to one side of a triangle then it divides the other two sides in the same ratio.

Subjective Questions

Very Short Answer Type Questions

(1 or 2 M)

1. What are similar triangles, and how do you determine if two triangles are similar?

2. If Fig, $\angle D = \angle E$ and $\frac{AD}{DB} = \frac{AE}{EC}$. Prove that BAC is an isosceles triangle. **(NCERT Exemplar)**

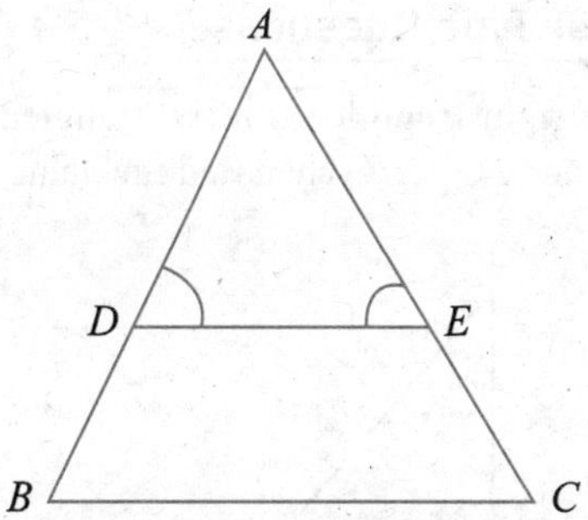

3. In figure, AD is a median of ΔABC and $AE \perp BC$. If $BC = a$, $CA = b$, $AB = c$, $AD = p$, $AE = h$ and $DE = x$. Then find the value of b^2 in terms p, a and x.

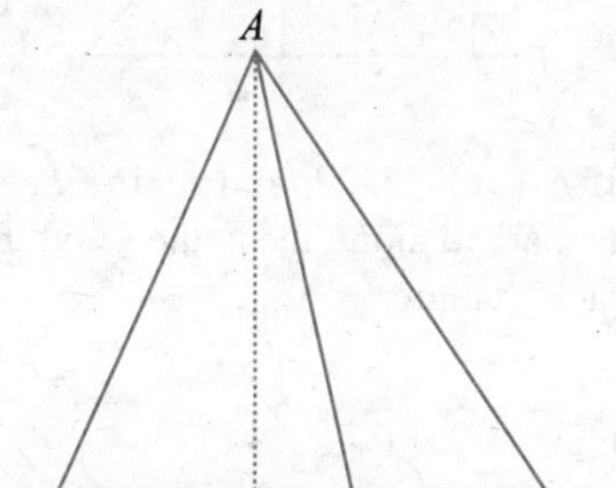

4. In the given, if $ABCD$ is a trapezium in which $AB \parallel CD \parallel EF$, then prove that $\frac{AE}{ED} = \frac{BF}{FC}$. **(CBSE SQP, 2023)**

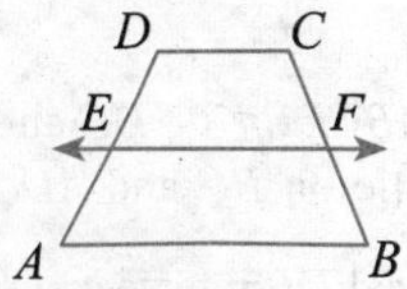

5. How are the perimeters of similar triangles related to each other?

Short Answer Type Questions (2 or 3 M)

1. In Fig., $DE \parallel AC$ and $DC \parallel AP$. Prove that $\frac{BE}{EC} = \frac{BC}{CP}$.

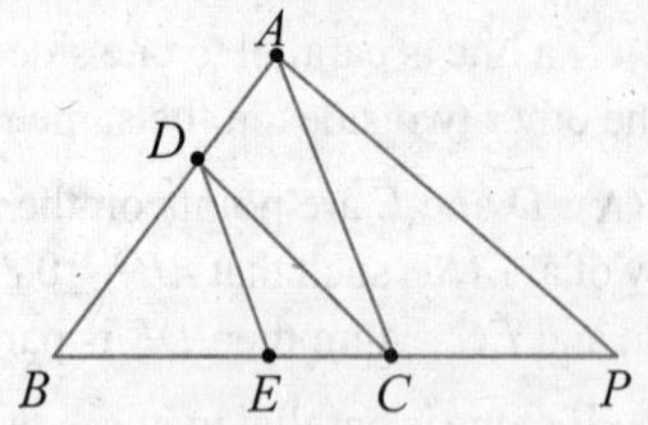

2. The areas of two similar triangles ΔABC and ΔDEF are 16 cm^2 and 36 cm^2 respectively.

   If $EF = 9$ cm, find BC.

3. If AD and PM are medians of triangles ABC and PQR, respectively where $\Delta ABC \sim \Delta PQR$, prove that $\frac{AB}{PQ} = \frac{AD}{PM}$

4. In an equilateral triangle ABC, AD is drawn perpendicular to BC meeting BC at D. Prove that $AD^2 = 3BD^2$.

Long Answer Type Questions (4 or 5 M)

1. ABC is a right triangle with right-angled at B. $BD \perp AC$, $DM \perp BC$ and $DN \perp AB$. Then find the value of DM^2.

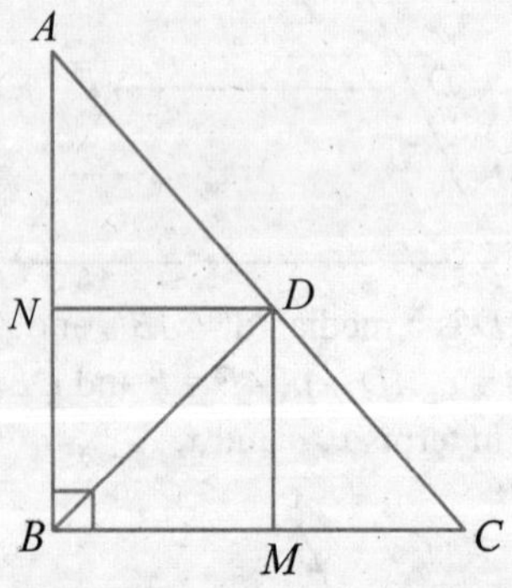

2. In Fig., if $\Delta ABC \sim \Delta DEF$ and their sides are of lengths (in cm) as marked along them, then find the lengths of the sides of each triangle.

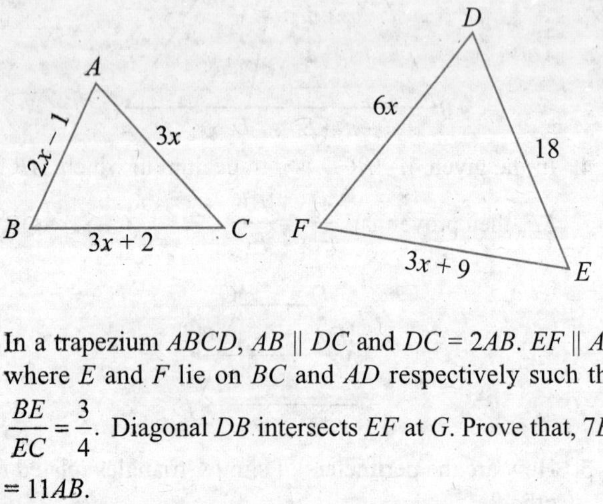

3. In a trapezium $ABCD$, $AB \parallel DC$ and $DC = 2AB$. $EF \parallel AB$, where E and F lie on BC and AD respectively such that $\frac{BE}{EC} = \frac{3}{4}$. Diagonal DB intersects EF at G. Prove that, $7EF = 11AB$.

4. In a mathematics class, a teacher drew the following figure where $\frac{TQ}{QR} = \frac{1}{3}$. She then asked, "What is the sufficient condition required to prove that $\Delta TQP \sim \Delta RQS$?"

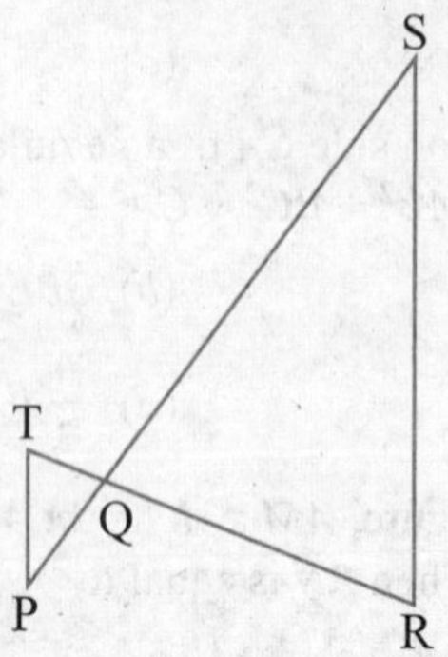

- Darsh said that it is sufficient if it is given that $\frac{TP}{SR} = \frac{1}{3}$.
- Bhargav said that it is sufficient if it is given that $\angle P = \angle S$.
- Tanvi said that it is sufficient if it is given that $\frac{PQ}{QS} = \frac{1}{3}$.

Examine whether each of their responses is correct or incorrect. Give reasons. **(CBSE CFPQ, 2023)**

Case Based Questions

Case Based-I: Aruna visited to her uncle's house. From a point A, where Aruna was standing, a bus and building come in a straight line as shown in the figure.

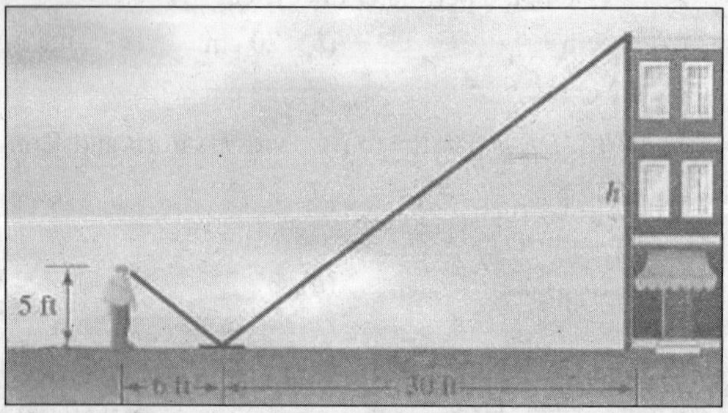

Based on the above information, answer the following questions.

(*i*) Which similarity criteria can be seen in this case, if bus and building are considered in a straight line?

(*ii*) If the distance between Aruna and the bus is twice as much as the height of the bus, then find the height of the bus.

OR

If the distance of Aruna from the building is twelve times the height of the bus, then find the ratio of the heights of bus and building.

(*iii*) What is the ratio of the distance between Aruna and the top of the bus to the distance between the tops of the bus and the building?

Case Based-II: Ankita wants to make a toran for Diwali using some pieces of cardboard. She cut some cardboard pieces as shown below. If the perimeter of ΔADE and ΔBCE are in the ratio 2 : 3, then answer the following questions.

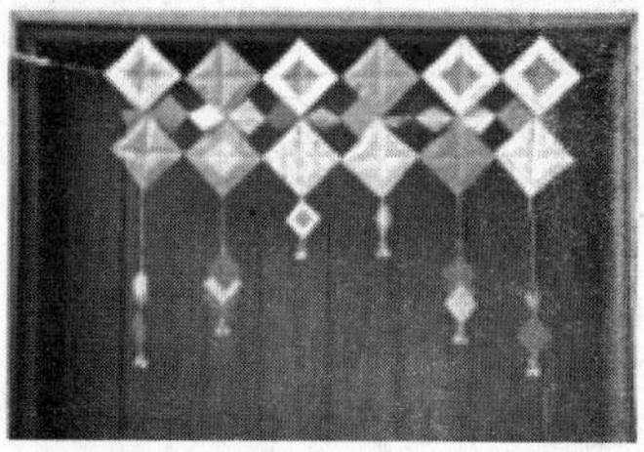

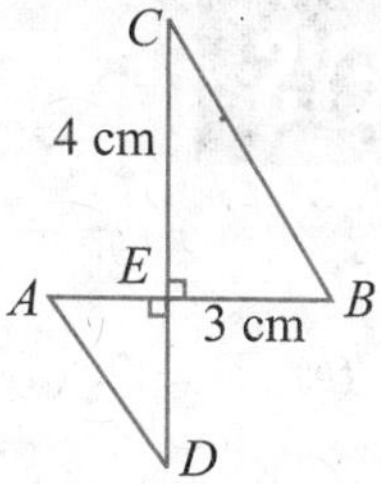

(*i*) If the two triangles here are similar by SAS similarity rule, then their corresponding proportional sides are

(*a*) $\frac{AE}{CE} = \frac{DE}{BE}$ (*b*) $\frac{BE}{AE} = \frac{CE}{DE}$

(*c*) $\frac{AD}{CE} = \frac{BE}{DE}$ (*d*) None of these

(*ii*) Length of $BC =$

(*a*) 3 cm (*b*) 4 cm

(*c*) 5 cm (*d*) None of these

(*iii*) Length of $AD =$

(*a*) $\frac{10}{3}$ cm (*b*) $\frac{9}{4}$ cm

(*c*) $\frac{9}{4}$ cm (*d*) $\frac{4}{3}$ cm

(*iv*) Length of $ED =$

(*a*) $\frac{4}{3}$ cm (*b*) $\frac{4}{3}$ cm

(*c*) $\frac{8}{3}$ cm (*d*) Can't be determined

Case Based-III: Class teacher drew the shape of a quadrilateral on board. Ankit observed the shape and explored it in his notebook in different ways as shown below.

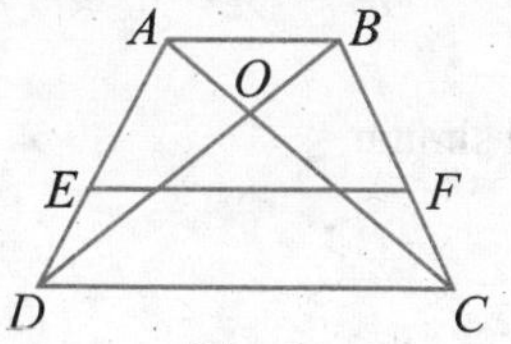

Fig. 1

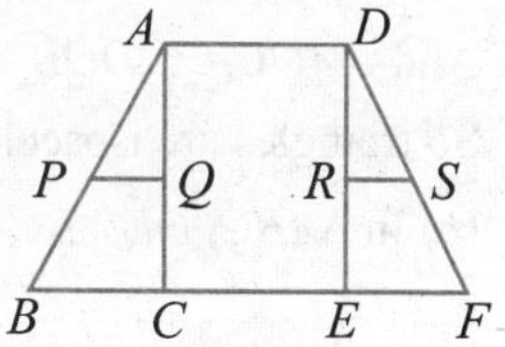

Fig. 2

Based on the above information, answer the following questions.

(*i*) In fig. 1, if $AB \parallel CD$, and $DO = 3x - 19$, $OB = x - 5$, $OC = x - 3$ and $AO = 3$, then find the value of x.

(*ii*) In fig. 1, if $OD = 3x - 1$, $OB = 5x - 3$, $OC = 2x + 1$ and $AO = 6x - 5$, then find the value of x

OR

In fig. 2, in ΔABC, if $PQ \parallel BC$ and $AP = 2.4$ cm, $AQ = 2$ cm, $QC = 3$ cm and $BC = 6$ cm, then find the value of $AB + PQ$.

(*iii*) In fig. 2, in ΔDEF, if $RS \parallel EF$, $DR = 4x - 3$, $DS = 8x - 7$, $ER = 3x - 1$ and $FS = 5x - 3$, then find the value of x

Case Based-IV: In the backyard of a house, Shikha has some empty space in the shape of a ΔPQR. She decided to make it a garden. She divided the whole space into three parts by making boundaries AB and CD using bricks to grow flowers and vegetables where $AB \parallel CD \parallel QR$ as shown in figure.

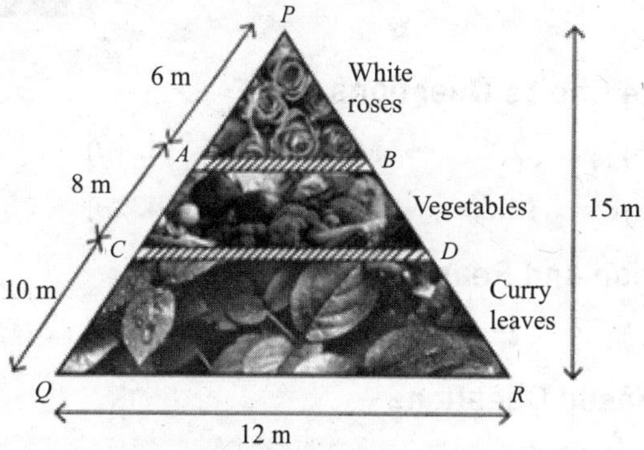

Based on the above information, answer the following questions.

(*i*) The length of AB is

(*a*) 3 m (*b*) 4 m

(*c*) 5 m (*d*) 6 m

(*ii*) The length of CD is

$\angle P = \angle P$ (common)

$\angle A = \angle Q$ (Corresponding angles)

By AA similarity criterion, $\Delta PAB \sim \Delta PQR$

$\therefore \frac{AB}{QR} = \frac{PA}{PQ} \Rightarrow \frac{AB}{12} = \frac{6}{24} \Rightarrow AB = 3\text{m}$

(*a*) 4 m (*b*) 5 m

(*c*) 6 m (*d*) 7 m

(*iii*) Area of whole empty land is

(*a*) 90 cm^2 (*b*) 60 m^2

(*c*) 32 m^2 (*d*) 72 m^2

Case Based-V: A farmer has a field in the shape of trapezium, whose map with scale 1 cm = 20 m, is given below:

The field is divided into four parts by joining the opposite vertices.

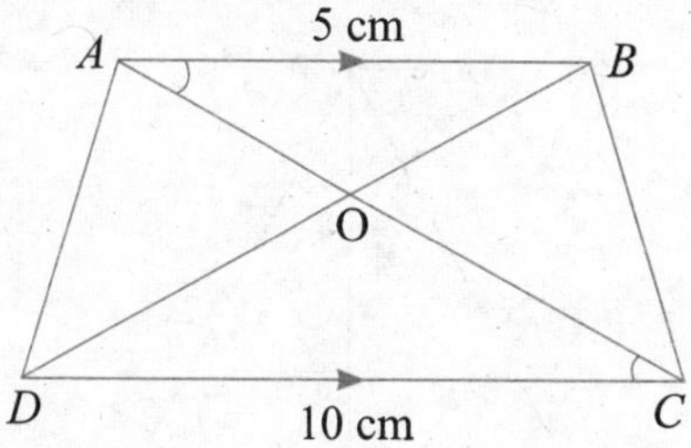

Based on the above information, answer any four of the following questions:

(*i*) The two triangular regions AOB and COD are

(*a*) Similar by AA criterion

(*b*) Similar by SAS criterion

(*c*) Similar by RHS criterion

(*d*) Not similar

(*ii*) If the ratio of the perimeter of ΔAOB to the perimeter of ΔCOD would have been 1 : 4, then

(*a*) $AB = 2\,CD$ (*b*) $AB = 4\,CD$

(*c*) $CD = 2\,AB$ (*d*) $CD = 4\,AB$

(*iii*) If in Δs AOD and BOC, $\frac{AO}{BC} = \frac{AD}{BO} = \frac{OD}{OC}$, then

(*a*) $\Delta AOD \sim \Delta BOC$ (*b*) $\Delta AOD \sim \Delta BCO$

(*c*) $\Delta ADO \sim \Delta BCO$ (*d*) $\Delta ODA \sim \Delta OBC$

ANSWER KEYS

Multiple Choice Questions

1. (*b*) **2.** (*c*) **3.** (*c*) **4.** (*d*) **5.** (*b*) **6.** (*b*) **7.** (*a*) **8.** (*a*) **9.** (*c*) **10.** (*c*)
11. (*c*) **12.** (*c*) **13.** (*a*) **14.** (*c*) **15.** (*c*)

Assertion and Reason

1. (*a*) **2.** (*b*)

Case Based Questions

Case Based-II

(*i*) (*b*) (*ii*) (*c*) (*iii*) (*a*) (*iv*) (*b*)

Case Based-IV

(*i*) (*a*) (*ii*) (*d*) (*iii*) (*a*)

Case Based-V

(*i*) (*b*) (*ii*) (*d*) (*iii*) (*b*)

HINTS & EXPLANATIONS

Multiple Choice Questions

1. (*b*) Given an equilateral triangle *ABC* in which,

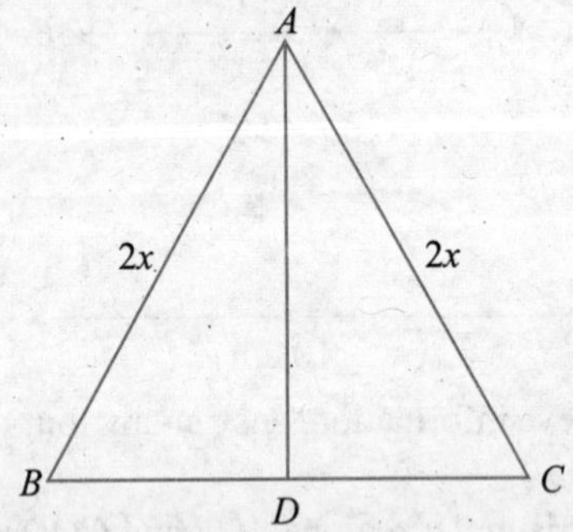

$AB = BC = CA = 2x$ and $AD \perp BC$

In an equilateral triangle, the altitude also bisects the side.

As, *AD* is perpendicular to *BC*.

Therefore, $BD = 1/2\ BC = x$

In ΔADB, $AB^2 = AD^2 + BD^2$ (By Pythagoras theorem)

$(2x)^2 = AD^2 + x^2$

$AD = \sqrt{3}x$

2. (*c*)

3. (*c*) Since, $DE \parallel BC$

$$\frac{AD}{DB} = \frac{AE}{EC} \Rightarrow \frac{1.5}{4.5} = \frac{0.8}{EC} \Rightarrow EC = 0.8 \times 3 = 2.4 \text{ cm}$$

4. (*d*) Given, *O* is the point of intersection of two equal chords *AB* and *CD* such that $OB = OD$,

As chords are equal and $OB = OD$, so *AO* will also be equal to *OC*

Also $\angle AOC = \angle DOB = 45°$ (corresponding angles)

Now in triangles *OAC* and *ODB* $\frac{AO}{OB} = \frac{OC}{OD}$

And $\angle AOC = \angle DOB = 45°$

So triangles are isosceles and similar

5. (*b*) In ΔABC, $DE \parallel BC$

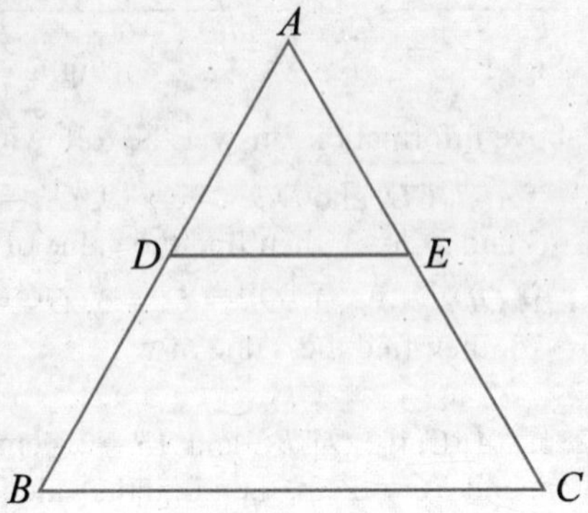

$$\frac{AD}{AB} = \frac{DE}{BC}$$ (By *BPT*)

$$\Rightarrow \frac{DE}{BC} = \frac{1}{2}$$ (*D* is the mid-point of *AB*)

$\therefore DE = 3$ cm

6. (*b*) $AC = 40$ cm and $BD = 30$ cm

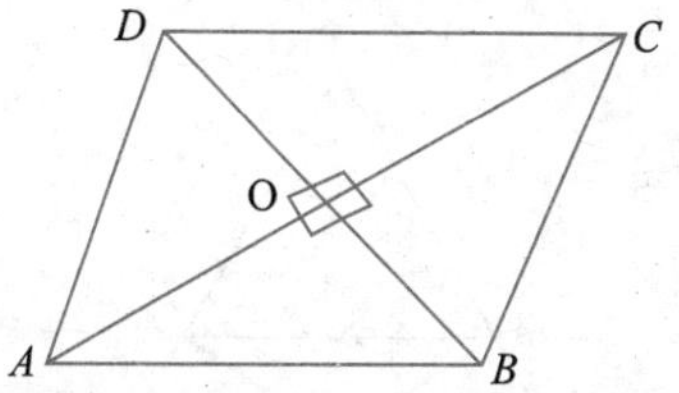

The diagonals of the rhombus bisect each other at right angle, so the side of the rhombus is the hypotenuse for the triangles formed.

$\therefore OC = \dfrac{AC}{2} = 20\,\text{cm}$

$OD = \dfrac{BD}{2} = 15\,\text{cm}$

Now, on applying pythagoras theorem in ΔOCD, we have

$OC^2 + OD^2 = CD^2$

$\left(\dfrac{40}{2}\right)^2 + \left(\dfrac{30}{2}\right)^2 = \text{Side}^2 \Rightarrow \text{Side}^2 = 20^2 + 15^2$

$\Rightarrow \text{Side}^2 = 400 + 225 = 625 \Rightarrow \text{Side} = 25$ cm

7. (*a*) In ΔABC, $DE \parallel BC$

$\therefore \dfrac{AD}{DB} = \dfrac{AE}{EC} \Rightarrow \dfrac{x}{2x-2} = \dfrac{x+2}{2x+1} \Rightarrow x = 4$

8. (*a*) When you apply *AA* rule to both triangles, you will find that both triangles are similar, *AA* rule does not see the placement of angles and we don't need a side to prove it. Also, It is obvious that any congruence rule such as *SSS* or *SAS* won't apply to these because only one side is given to be the same, Also if you get confused between *AAS* or *ASA* rule, See the placement of side. In the first triangle the side is between the angles but in the second triangle the side is not between them so it won't make them congruent.

9. (*c*) In ΔADE and ΔABC

$\angle A = \angle A$ (common)

$\angle ADE = \angle ACB$ (given)

$\therefore \Delta ADE \sim \Delta ACB$ (by *AA* similarity)

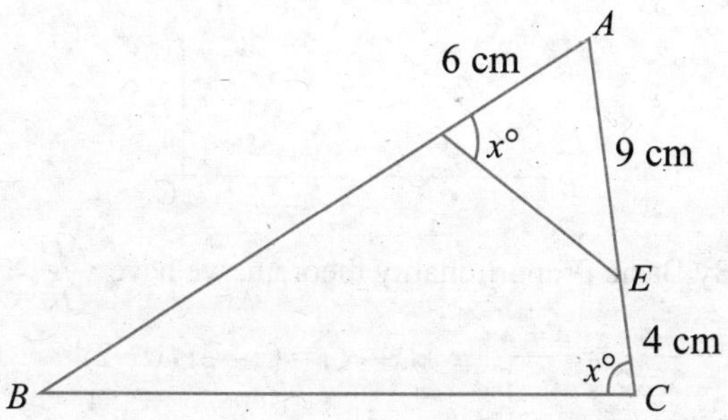

$\therefore \dfrac{AD}{AC} = \dfrac{AE}{AB} \Rightarrow AB = \dfrac{13 \times 9}{6}$

$= 19.5$ cm

Hence, $BD = AB - AD$

$= 19.5 - 6 = 13.5$ cm

$\therefore 2BD = 27$ cm

10. (*c*) Since triangle *ABD* is a right triangle, right angled at *D*

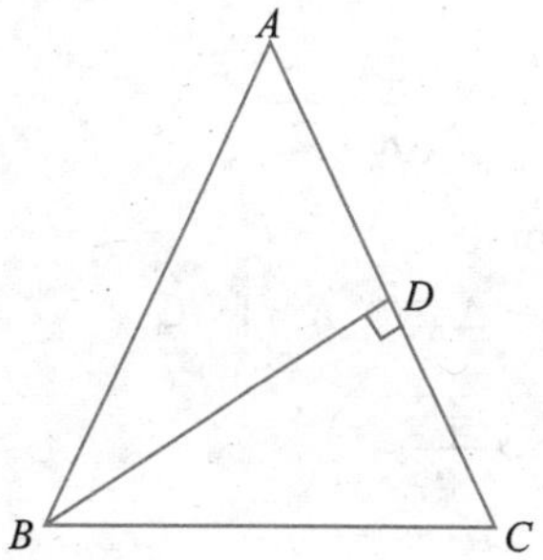

$\therefore AB^2 = AD^2 + BD^2$

$\Rightarrow AC^2 = AD^2 + BD^2$ $[\because AB = AC]$

$\Rightarrow (AD + CD)^2 = AD^2 + BD^2$

$\Rightarrow AD^2 + CD^2 + 2AD.CD = AD^2 + BD^2$

$\Rightarrow BD^2 - CD^2 = 2CD.AD$

Hence, the value of *k* is 2.

11. (*c*) Let $AB = BC = AC = x$

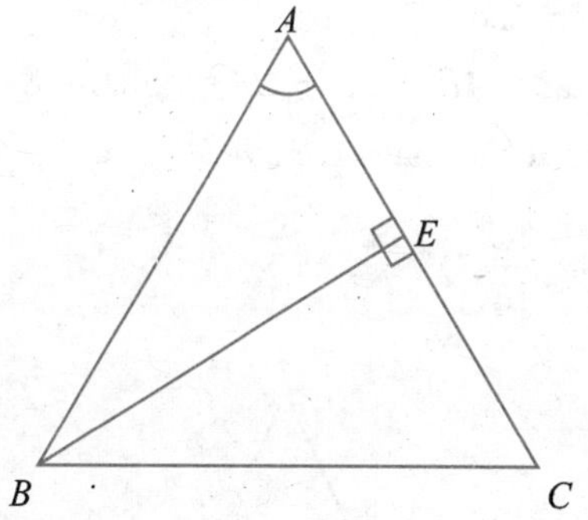

$EC = \dfrac{x}{2}$

now $BE = \sqrt{BC^2 - EC^2}$

$BE = \sqrt{x^2 - \dfrac{x^2}{4}} \Rightarrow BE^2 = \dfrac{3}{4}x^2 \Rightarrow x^2 = \dfrac{4}{3}BE^2$ ... (*i*)

$\therefore AB^2 + BC^2 + CA^2 = x^2 + x^2 + x^2 = 3x^2$

$= \left(\dfrac{4}{3}BE^2\right) = 4BE^2$ [Using (*i*)]

12. (*c*) Given, $AM : MC = 3 : 4$, $BP : PM = 3 : 2$ and $BN = 12$ cm

Draw *MR* parallel to *CN* which meets *AB* at the point *R*

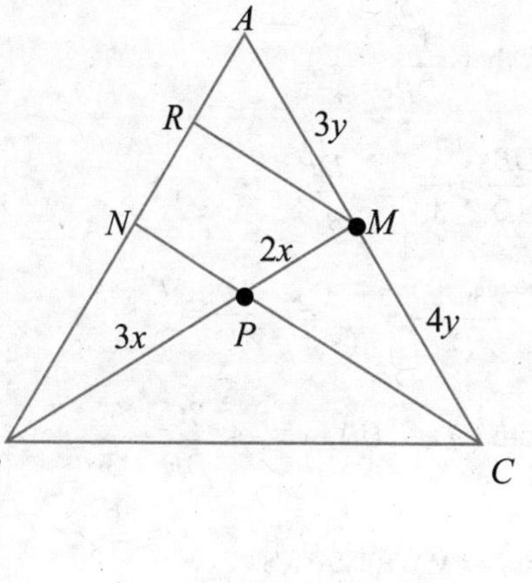

Consider ΔBMR. In this, we have $PN \parallel MR$ (By construction)

$\therefore \frac{BN}{NR} = \frac{BP}{PM} \Rightarrow \frac{12}{NR} = \frac{3}{2}$ (By BPT)

$\Rightarrow NR = 8$ cm

Now, consider ΔANC, $RM \parallel NC$ (by construction)

$\frac{AR}{RN} = \frac{AM}{MC} \Rightarrow \frac{AR}{8} = \frac{3}{4}$ (By BPT)

$\Rightarrow AR = 6$ cm

Thus, $AN = AR + RN = 6 + 18 = 24$ cm

13. (*a*) Given, $\Delta ABC \sim \Delta DEF$,

Also, $AB = 4$ cm, $DE = 6$ cm, $EF = 9$ cm and $FD = 12$ cm,

$\therefore \frac{AB}{DE} = \frac{BC}{EF} = \frac{AC}{DF} \Rightarrow \frac{4}{6} = \frac{BC}{9} = \frac{AC}{12}$

By solving above equations, we get

$BC = 6$ cm and $AC = 8$ cm

Perimeter $= AB + BC + CA = 4 + 6 + 8 = 18$ cm

14. (*c*) In ΔABC, we have $DE \parallel BC$.

$\Rightarrow \frac{AB}{AD} = \frac{AC}{AE}$ [By BPT]

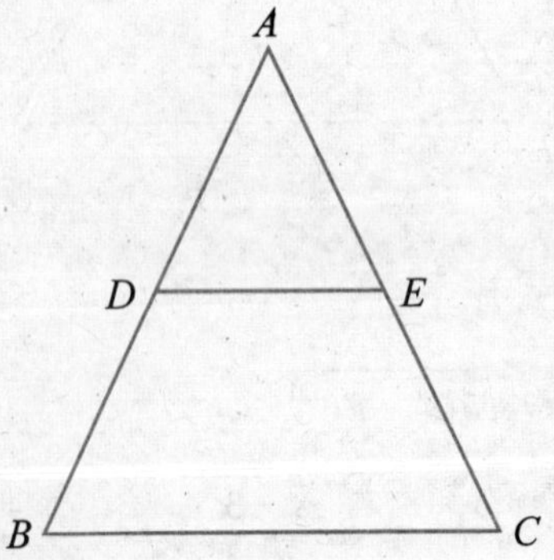

Now, in ΔABC and ΔADE

$\frac{AB}{AD} = \frac{AC}{AE}$ [Proved above]

and $\angle A = \angle A$ (common)

So, $\Delta ABC \sim \Delta ADE$ [by SAS criterion of similarity]

$\Rightarrow \frac{AB}{AD} = \frac{BC}{DE}$ ... (*i*)

Given that $\frac{AD}{DB} = \frac{3}{4}$

$\Rightarrow \frac{DB}{AD} = \frac{4}{3} \Rightarrow \frac{DB}{AD} + 1 = \frac{4}{3} + 1$

$\Rightarrow \frac{DB + AD}{AD} = \frac{7}{3} \Rightarrow \frac{AB}{AD} = \frac{7}{3}$ ... (*ii*)

$\therefore$ From (*i*) and (*ii*), we get $\frac{BC}{DE} = \frac{7}{3}$

15. (*c*)

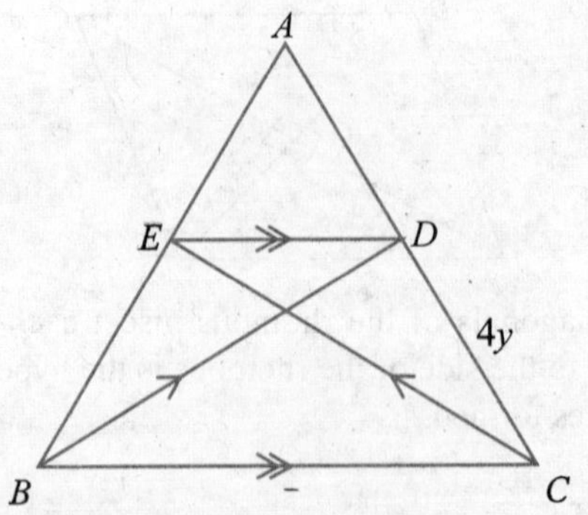

In ΔABC, BD is the bisector of $\angle B$.

$\therefore \frac{AB}{BC} = \frac{AD}{DC}$ ... (*i*) (By angle bisector theorem)

Also, in ΔABC, CE is the bisector of $\angle C$.

$\therefore \frac{AC}{BC} = \frac{AE}{BE}$ ... (*ii*) (By angle bisector theorem)

Now, in ΔABC, $DE \parallel BC$.

$\Rightarrow \frac{AE}{BE} = \frac{AD}{DC}$ [By BPT] ... (*iii*)

Now by using (*i*), (*ii*) and (*iii*)

$\frac{AB}{BC} = \frac{AC}{BC} \Rightarrow AB = AC$

Hence, ΔABC is an isosceles triangle.

Assertion and Reason

1. (*a*) We know that If a line is parallel to one side of a triangle then it divides *A* other two sides in the same ratio. This is Basic Proportionality theorem. So, Reason is correct.

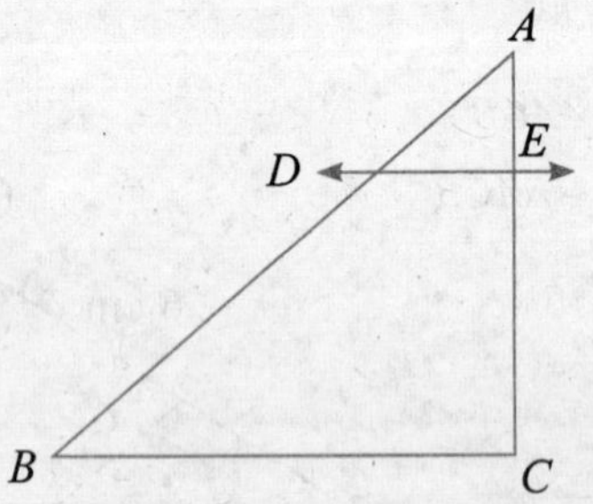

By Basic Proportionality theorem, we have $\frac{AD}{DB} = \frac{AE}{EC}$

$\Rightarrow \frac{x}{x-2} = \frac{x+2}{x-1} \Rightarrow x(x - 1) = (x - 2)(x + 2)$

$\Rightarrow x^2 - x = x^2 - 4 \Rightarrow x = 4$ cm

So, Assertion is correct

Reason (R) are true and reason (R) is the correct explanation of assertion (A).

2. (*b*) We know that If a line is parallel to one side of a triangle then it divides the other two sides in the same ratio. This is Basic Proportionality theorem. So, Reason is correct.

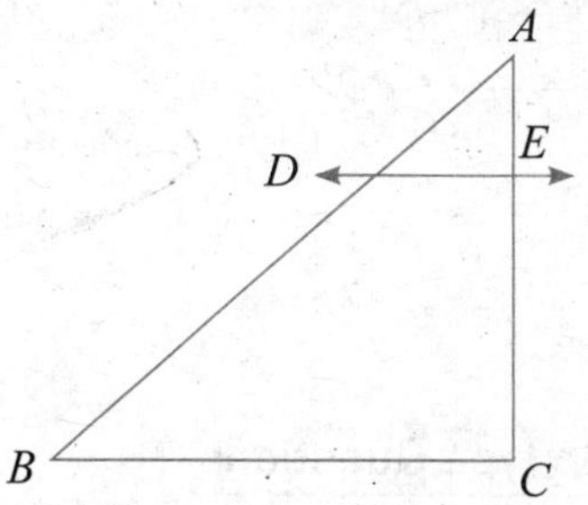

$DB = 10.8 - 6.3 = 4.5$ cm and $AE = 9.6 - 4 = 5.6$ cm

Now, $\frac{AD}{DB} = \frac{6.3}{4.5} = \frac{63}{45} = \frac{7}{5}$ and $\frac{AE}{EC} = \frac{5.6}{4} = \frac{56}{40} = \frac{7}{5}$

$\Rightarrow \frac{AD}{DB} = \frac{AE}{EC}$

By Converse of Basic Proportionality theorem, $DE \parallel BC$

So, Assertion is correct

But reason (R) is not the correct explanation of assertion (A).

Subjective Questions

Very Short Answer Type Questions

1. Two triangles are similar if their corresponding angles are congruent and the corresponding sides are in proportion. *(1 M)*
   There are a few ways to determine if two triangles are similar:
   Angle-Angle (AA) Similarity.
   Side-Side-Side (SSS) Similarity
   Side-Angle-Side (SAS) Similarity *(1 M)*

2. $\frac{AD}{DB} = \frac{AE}{EC}$ (Given)
   Therefore, $DE \parallel BC$ (Converse of Basic Proportionality Theorem) *(½ M)*
   So, $\angle D = \angle B$ and $\angle E = \angle C$ (Corresponding angles) ... (i)
   But $\angle D = \angle E$ (Given)
   Therefore, $\angle B = \angle C$ [From (i)] *(1 M)*
   So, $AB = AC$ (Sides opposite to equal angles)
   i.e., BAC is an isosceles triangle. *(½ M)*

Nailing the Right Answer

To prove an isosceles triangle, students must check for similar sides and angles.

3.

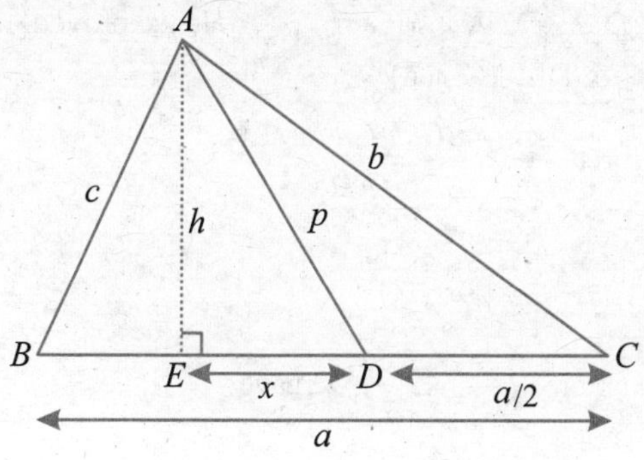

In right angled triangle AEC, applying Pythagoras theorem, we have

$AC^2 = AE^2 + EC^2$

$\Rightarrow b^2 = h^2 + \left(x + \frac{a}{2}\right)^2 = h^2 + x^2 + \frac{a^2}{4} + ax$ ... (i)

In right angled triangle AED, we have:

$AD^2 = AE^2 + ED^2 \Rightarrow p^2 = h^2 + x^2$ ... (ii)

Therefore, from (i) and (ii), we get

$b^2 = p^2 + ax + \frac{a^2}{4}$ *(1 M)*

4. Given, $AB \parallel CD \parallel EF$

To prove: $\frac{AB}{ED} = \frac{BF}{FC}$

Constant: Join BD which *(½ M)*

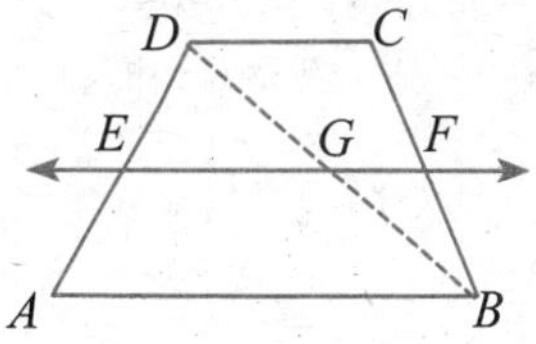

intersect EF at G.

Proof: in ΔABD

$EG \parallel AB$ ($EF \parallel AB$)

$\frac{AE}{ED} = \frac{BG}{GD}$ (by BPT) ... (i) *(½ M)*

In ΔDBC

$GF \parallel CD$ ($EF \parallel CD$)

$\frac{BE}{FD} = \frac{BF}{FC}$ (by BPT) ... (ii) *(½ M)*

from (i) and (ii)

$\frac{AE}{ED} = \frac{BF}{FC}$ *(½ M)*

5. If two triangles are similar, their corresponding sides are proportional. This means that the ratio of the lengths of any two corresponding sides is the same for both triangles. *(1 M)*
   Therefore, if the ratio of corresponding sides of two similar triangles is a:b, then the ratio of their perimeters will also be a:b. In other words, the perimeters of two similar triangles are in the same ratio as the lengths of their corresponding sides. *(1 M)*

Short Answer Type Questions

1. In ΔBPA
   $DC \parallel AP$
   By $BPT \Rightarrow \frac{BC}{CP} = \frac{BD}{DA}$ ... (i) *(1 M)*
   Now, In ΔBCA
   $PF \parallel AC$
   by $BPT \Rightarrow \frac{BE}{EC} = \frac{BD}{DA}$ ... (ii)
   From equation (i) and eqn (ii), we get

$\frac{BC}{CP} = \frac{BE}{EC}$ proved. *(1 M)*

2. **Given:** Let us assume ΔABC in which PQ is parallel to BC and P is a mid-point of AB.

To prove: Q is a mid point of AC.

Proof: In ΔABC, $PQ \parallel BC$. *(1 M)*

$\therefore \frac{AP}{PB} = \frac{AQ}{QC}$ (by BPT) *(1 M)*

$\Rightarrow \frac{AQ}{QC} = 1$ ($\because$ P is the mid-point of AB, $\therefore AP = PB$)

$\Rightarrow AQ = QC$

Hence, Q is the mid-point of AC. *(1 M)*

3. We know if one angle of a triangle is equal to one angle of the other triangle and the sides including these angles are proportional, then the two triangles are similar.

This is referred to as *SAS* criterion for two triangles.

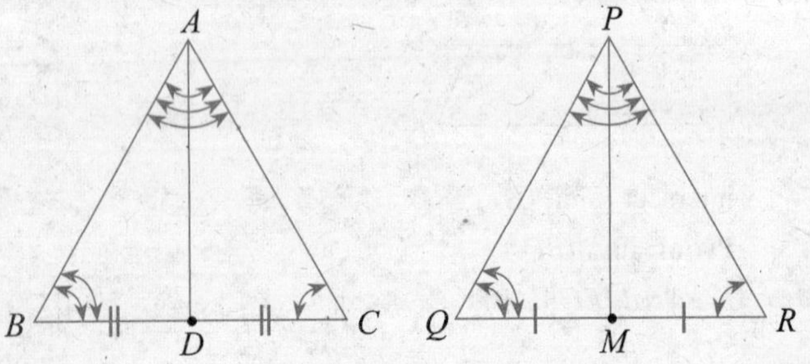

(1 M)

Given, $\Delta ABC \sim \Delta PQR$

$\Rightarrow \angle ABC = \angle PQR$ (corresponding angles) ... (*i*) *(½ M)*

$\Rightarrow AB/PQ = BC/QR$ (corresponding sides) *(½ M)*

$\Rightarrow AB/PQ = (BC/2)/(QR/2)$

$\Rightarrow AB/PQ = BD/QM$ (D and M are mid-points of BC and QR) ... (*ii*)

In ΔABD and ΔPQM,

$\angle ABD = \angle PQM$ (from i)

$AB/PQ = BD/QM$ (from ii)

$\Rightarrow \Delta ABD \sim \Delta PQM$ (SAS criterion)

$\Rightarrow AB/PQ = BD/QM = AD/PM$ (corresponding sides)

$\Rightarrow AB/PQ = AD/PM$

Hence proved. *(1 M)*

4. In ΔABD, form Pythagoras theorem,

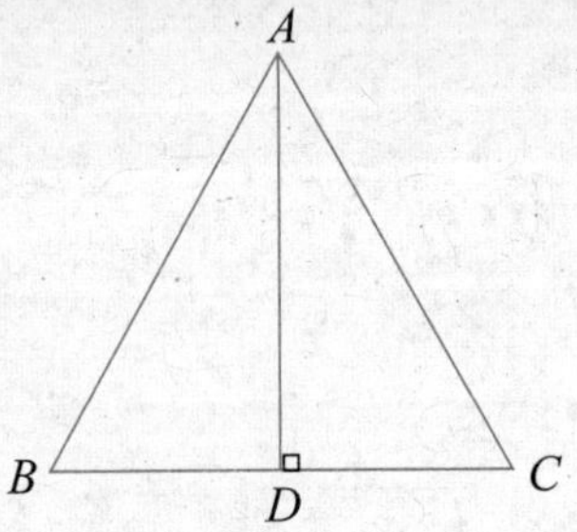

(1 M)

or, $AB^2 = AD^2 + BD^2$ *(1 M)*

or, $BC^2 = AD^2 + BD^2$, (as $AB = BC = CA$)

or, $(2BD)^2 = AD^2 + BD^2$,

($\perp$ is the median in an equilateral Δ)

$4BD^2 - BD^2 = AD^2$

$\therefore 3BD^2 = AD^2$.

Hence proved. *(1 M)*

Long Answer Type Questions

1.

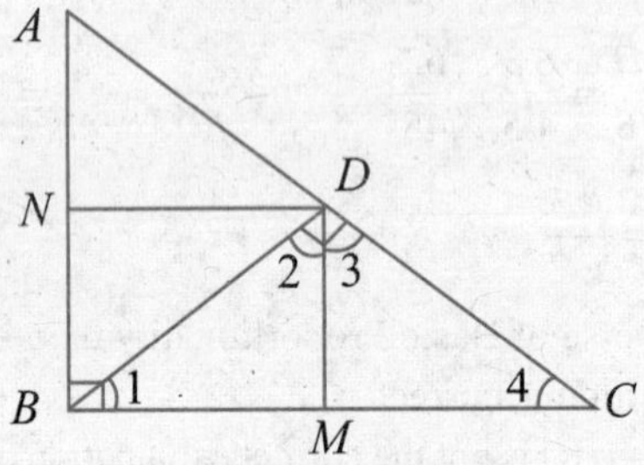

We have a right angled triangle ABC right angle at B and $BD \perp AC$ where D is the foot of the perpendicular on AC.

We have, $AB \perp BC$ and $DM \perp BC$ *(½ M)*

$\Rightarrow AB \parallel DM$

Similarly, we have $CB \perp AB$ and $DN \perp AB \Rightarrow CB \parallel DN$

Hence, quadrilateral $BMDN$ is a rectangle. *(½ M)*

$\therefore$ $BM = ND$ [opp. sides of a rectangle]

Now in ΔBMD, we have

$\angle 1 + \angle BMD + \angle 2 = 180°$ *(½ M)*

[Angle sum property of a triangle]

$\Rightarrow \angle 1 + 90° + \angle 2 = 180° \Rightarrow \angle 1 + \angle 2 = 90°$ ... (*i*)

Similarly, in ΔDMC, we have

$\angle 3 + \angle 4 = 90°$ ... (*ii*) *(½ M)*

Since $BD \perp AC$. Therefore,

$\angle 2 + \angle 3 = 90°$ ... (*iii*) *(½ M)*

On equating (*i*) and (*iii*), we get

$\angle 1 + \angle 2 = \angle 2 + \angle 3 \Rightarrow \angle 1 = \angle 3$

Now, on equating eq. (*ii*) and (*iii*), we get

$\angle 3 + \angle 4 = \angle 2 + \angle 3 \Rightarrow \angle 4 = \angle 2$ *(½ M)*

Thus, in ΔBMD and ΔDMC, we have

$\angle 1 = \angle 3$ and $\angle 2 = \angle 4$

So, by AA-criterion of similarity, we have

$\Delta BMD \sim \angle DMC$ *(1 M)*

$\Rightarrow \frac{BM}{DM} = \frac{MD}{MC}$ [by C.P.C.T.]

$\Rightarrow \frac{DN}{DM} = \frac{DM}{MC}$ [$\because BM = ND$]

$\Rightarrow DM^2 = DN \times MC$ [Hence proved] *(1 M)*

2. $\Delta ABC \sim \Delta DEF$ (Given)

Therefore, $\frac{AB}{DE} = \frac{BC}{EF} = \frac{CA}{FD}$ *(½ M)*

So, $\frac{2x-1}{18} = \frac{2x+2}{3x+9} = \frac{3x}{6x}$ *(½ M)*

Now, taking $\frac{2x-1}{18} = \frac{3x}{6x}$, we have

$$\frac{2x-1}{18}=\frac{1}{2}$$

or

$4x-2=18$

or

$x=5$ *(1 M)*

Therefore, $AB=2\times5-1=9$, $BC=2\times5+2=12$, $CA=3\times5=15$, $DE=18$, $EF=3\times5+9=24$ and $FD=6\times5=30$ *(1 M)*

Hence, $AB=9$ cm, $BC=12$ cm, $CA=15$ cm *(1 M)*

$DE=18$ cm, $EF=24$ cm and $FD=30$ cm *(1 M)*

Mistakes 101 : What not to do!

Students make errors when attempting to apply side-angle-side (SAS), angle-side-angle (ASA), and side-side-side (SSS) criteria to determine unknown parameters.

3. *(½ M)*

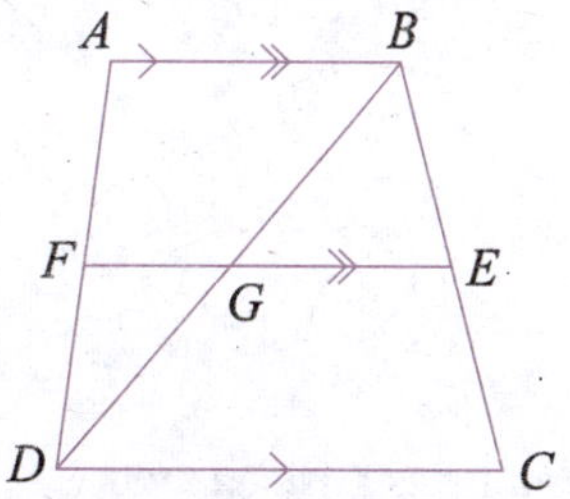

In trapezium $ABCD$, $AB \parallel DC$ and $DC = 2AB.BE$ 4

Also, $\frac{BE}{EC}=\frac{3}{4}$

In trapezium $ABCD$, $EF \parallel AB \parallel CD$

$\therefore \frac{AF}{FD}=\frac{BE}{EC}=\frac{3}{4}$ *(1 M)*

In ΔBGE and ΔBDC,

$\angle B=\angle B$ (Common)

$\angle BEG=\angle BCD$ (corresponding angles)

$\therefore \Delta BGE \sim \Delta BDC$ [AA similarity] *(1 M)*

or, $\frac{EG}{CD}=\frac{BE}{BC}$ ... (*i*)

As, $\frac{BE}{EC}=\frac{4}{3}$ or, $\frac{EC}{BE}=\frac{3}{4}$ or, $\frac{EC}{BE}+1=\frac{3}{4}+1$ *(½ M)*

or, $\frac{EC+BE}{BE}=\frac{7}{4}$ or, $\frac{BC}{BE}=\frac{7}{4}$ *or* $\frac{BE}{BC}=\frac{4}{7}$

From (*i*), $\frac{EG}{CD}=\frac{4}{7}$ or, $EG=\frac{4}{7}CD$ ... (*i*)

Similarly, $\Delta DGF \sim \Delta DBA$

$\frac{DF}{DA}=\frac{FG}{AB}$ *(½ M)*

or, $\frac{FG}{AB}=\frac{3}{7}$ or, $FG=\frac{4}{7}CD$ ... (*ii*)

$$\left[\because \frac{AF}{AD}=\frac{4}{7}=\frac{BE}{BC} \Rightarrow \frac{EC}{BC}=\frac{3}{7}=\frac{DF}{DA}\right]$$

Adding eqns. (*i*) and (*ii*),

$EG+FG=\frac{4}{7}CD+\frac{3}{7}AB$ *(½ M)*

or, $EF=\frac{4}{7}\times(2AB)+\frac{3}{7}AB=\frac{8}{7}AB+\frac{3}{7}AB=\frac{11}{7}AB$

$\therefore 7EF=11AB$.

Hence proved. *(1 M)*

4. Writes that Darsh's answer is incorrect. *(½ M)*

Writes that in order to apply any of the similarity criterion, atleast one more piece of information is necessary. *(½ M)*

Writes that Bhargav's answer is correct. *(½ M)*

Gives the following reason:

$\angle TQP=\angle RQS$ [Vertically opposite angles]

$\angle P=\angle S$ [Given]

$\angle T=\angle R$ [Angle sum property]

Hence, concludes that by AAA criterion of similarity of triangles, $\Delta TQP \sim \Delta RQS$. *(1½ M)*

Writes that Tanvi's answer is correct. *(½ M)*

Gives the following reason:

$\frac{TQ}{QR}=\frac{1}{3}$ [Given]

$\angle TQP=\angle RQS$ [Vertically opposite angles]

$\frac{PQ}{QS}=\frac{1}{3}$ [Given]

Hence, concludes that by SAS criterion of similarity of triangles, $\Delta TQP \sim \Delta RQS$. *(1½ M)*

Nailing the Right Answer

Students should be adept at applying side-angle-side (SAS), angle-side-angle (ASA), and side-side-side (SSS) criteria to prove congruent triangles.

Case Based Questions

Case Based-I

(*i*) In ΔABC and ΔADE,

$\angle A=\angle A$ (Common)

$\angle B=\angle D$ (Corresponding angles)

$\therefore \Delta ABC \sim \Delta ADE$ (by AA similarity criteria)

(*ii*) We have, $AB=2BC$

$\Rightarrow BC=\frac{25}{2}=12.5$ m

So, height of bus = 12.5 m

OR

We have, $AD = 12\ BC$

$\Rightarrow AD = 12 \times 12.5 = 150$ m

$\because \Delta ABC \sim \Delta ADE$

$\therefore \frac{AB}{AD} = \frac{BC}{DE} \Rightarrow \frac{BC}{DE} = \frac{25}{150} = \frac{1}{6}$

So, the ratio of heights of bus and building is 1 : 6.

(iii) Since, $\Delta ABC \sim \Delta ADE$

$\Rightarrow \frac{AB}{AD} = \frac{AC}{AE} \Rightarrow \frac{AC}{AE} = \frac{1}{6}$

$\Rightarrow \frac{AC}{AE - AC} = \frac{1}{6-1} \Rightarrow \frac{AC}{EC} = \frac{1}{5}$

$\therefore$ Required ratio = 1 : 5

Case Based-II

(i) (*b*) If ΔAED and ΔBEC, are similar by *SAS* similarity rule, then their corresponding proportional sides are $\frac{BE}{AE} = \frac{CE}{DE}$

(ii) (*c*) By Pythagoras theorem, we have

$BC = \sqrt{CE^2 + EB^2} = \sqrt{4^2 + 3^2} = \sqrt{16+9}$

$= \sqrt{25} = 5$ cm

(iii) (*a*) Since ΔADE and ΔBCE are similar.

$\therefore \frac{\text{Perimeter of } \Delta ADE}{\text{Perimeter of } \Delta BCE} = \frac{AD}{BC}$

$\Rightarrow \frac{2}{3} = \frac{AD}{5} \Rightarrow AD = \frac{5 \times 2}{3} = \frac{10}{3}$ cm

(iv) (*b*) $\frac{\text{Perimeter of } \Delta ADE}{\text{Perimeter of } \Delta BCE} = \frac{AE}{BE} \Rightarrow \frac{2}{3} BE = AE$

$\Rightarrow AE = \frac{2}{3}\sqrt{BC^2 - CE^2}$

Also, in ΔAED, $AE = \sqrt{AD^2 - DE^2}$

Case Based-III

(i) Since, $\Delta AOB \sim \Delta COD$ [By *AA* similarity criterion]

$\therefore \frac{AO}{OC} = \frac{BO}{OD} \Rightarrow \frac{3}{x-3} = \frac{x-5}{3x-19}$

$\Rightarrow 3(x - 19) = (x - 5)(x - 3)$

$\Rightarrow 9x - 57 = x^2 - 3x - 5x + 15 \quad \Rightarrow x^2 - 17x + 72 = 0$

$\Rightarrow (x - 8)(x - 9) = 0 \quad \Rightarrow x = 8$ or 9

(ii) Since, $\Delta AOB \sim \Delta COD$ [By *AA* similarity criterion]

$\therefore \frac{AO}{OC} = \frac{BO}{OD} \Rightarrow \frac{6x-5}{2x+1} = \frac{5x-3}{3x-1}$

$\Rightarrow (6x - 5) = (3x - 1) = (5x - 3)(2x + 1)$

$\Rightarrow 18x^2 - 6x - 15x + 5 = 10x^2 + 5x - 6x - 3$

$\Rightarrow 8x^2 - 20x + 8 = 0 \quad \Rightarrow 2x^2 - 5x + 2 = 0$

From options, $x = 2$ is the only value that satisfies this equation.

OR

Since $\Delta APQ \sim \Delta ABC$ [By *AA* similarity criterion]

$\therefore \frac{AP}{AB} = \frac{AQ}{AC} = \frac{PQ}{BC} \Rightarrow \frac{2.4}{AB} = \frac{2}{5} = \frac{PQ}{6}$

$\therefore AB = \frac{2.4 \times 5}{2} = 6$ cm and $PQ = \frac{2 \times 6}{5} = 2.4$ cm

$\therefore AB + PQ = 6 + 2.4 = 8.4$ cm

(iii) Since, $\Delta DRS \sim \Delta DEF$ [By *AA* similarity criterion]

$\therefore \frac{DE}{DR} = \frac{DF}{DS} \Rightarrow \frac{DE}{DR} - 1 = \frac{DF}{DS} - 1$

$\Rightarrow \frac{DE - DR}{DR} = \frac{DF - DS}{DS} \Rightarrow \frac{ER}{DR} = \frac{FS}{DS}$

$\Rightarrow \frac{DR}{ER} = \frac{DS}{FS} \Rightarrow \frac{4x-3}{3x-1} = \frac{8x-7}{5x-3}$

$\Rightarrow 20x^2 - 12x - 15x + 9 = 24x^2 - 8x - 21x + 7$

$\Rightarrow 4x^2 - 2x - 2 = 0 \quad \Rightarrow 2x^2 - x - 1 = 0$

Only option (1) i.e., $x = 1$ satisfies this equation.

Case Based-IV

(i) (*a*) In ΔPAB and ΔPQR,

(ii) (*d*) Similarly, ΔPCD and ΔPQR are similar.

$\therefore \frac{PC}{PQ} = \frac{CD}{QR} \Rightarrow \frac{14}{24} = \frac{CD}{12} \Rightarrow CD = 7\text{m}$

(iii) (*a*) Area of whole empty land

$= \frac{1}{2} \times \text{base} \times \text{height} = \frac{1}{2} \times 12 \times 15 = 90 \text{ m}^2$

Case Based-V

(i) (*b*) Similar by *SAS* criterion

(ii) (*d*) $CD = 4AB$

$\frac{\text{Perimeter of } \Delta AOB}{\text{Perimeter of } \Delta COD} = \frac{1}{4}$

Also, $\frac{\text{Perimeter of } \Delta AOB}{\text{Perimeter of } \Delta COD} = \frac{AB}{CD}$

$\Rightarrow \frac{1}{4} = \frac{AB}{CD} \Rightarrow CD = 4AB$

(iii) (*b*) $\Delta AOD \sim \Delta BCO$

❑❑❑

COORDINATE GEOMETRY

7

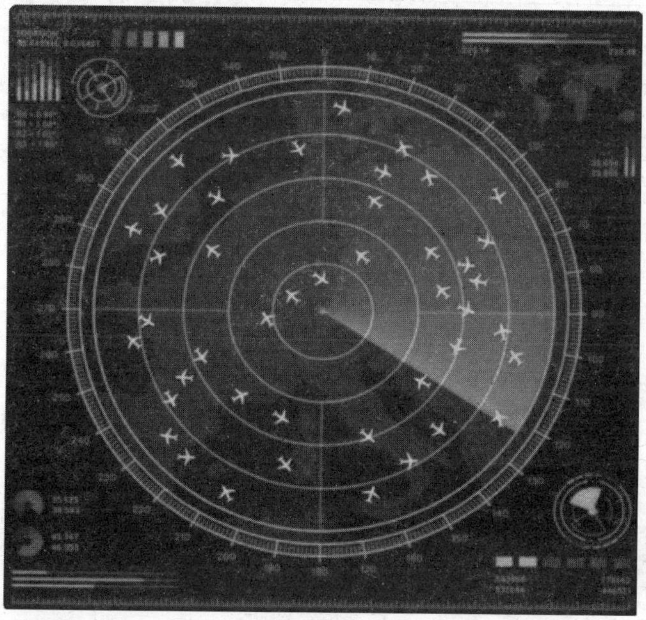

"Coordinate Geometry is used in air traffic controllers. Air traffic controllers keep an eye on every plane in the sky by using coordinates, which are like points on a map. They keep updating these points as the planes move, so they always know exact location where each plane is."

SYLLABUS & WEIGHTAGE

List of Concept Names	Years				
	2021	2022	2023	2024	2025
Distance Formula (Concepts of coordinate geometry, graphs of linear equations)	Exam not Conducted	–	1 Q (2 M) 1 Q (4 M)	2 Q (1 M each) 1 Q (2 M)	1 Q (4 M) 1 Q (1 M)
Section Formula (Section formula (in division), Mid-point formula)		–	1 Q (2 M)	1 Q (2 M)	–

CONCEPT MAP

To Access One Shot Revision Video Scan This QR Code

Coordinate Geometry

Centroid

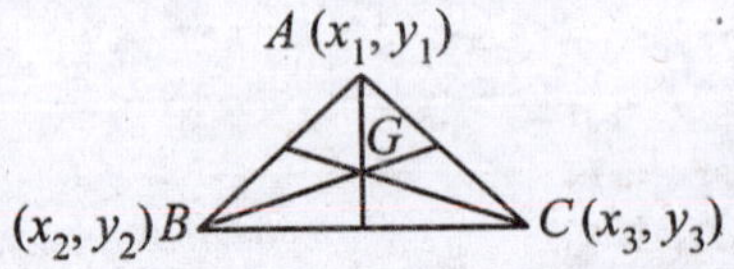

$$G = \left(\frac{x_1 + x_2 + x_3}{3}, \frac{y_1 + y_2 + y_3}{3}\right)$$

Example: Determine the centroid of a triangle whose vertices are (5, 3), (6, 1) and (7, 8)

Sol. Given parameters are,

$(x_1, y_1) = (5, 3)$, $(x_2, y_2) = (6,1)$

and $(x_3, y_3) = (7, 8)$

$$G = \left(\frac{x_1 + x_2 + x_3}{3}, \frac{y_1 + y_2 + y_3}{3}\right)$$

$$G = \left(\frac{5+6+7}{3}, \frac{3+1+8}{3}\right)$$

$$G = \left(\frac{18}{3}, \frac{12}{3}\right) = (6,4)$$

Coordinate axis

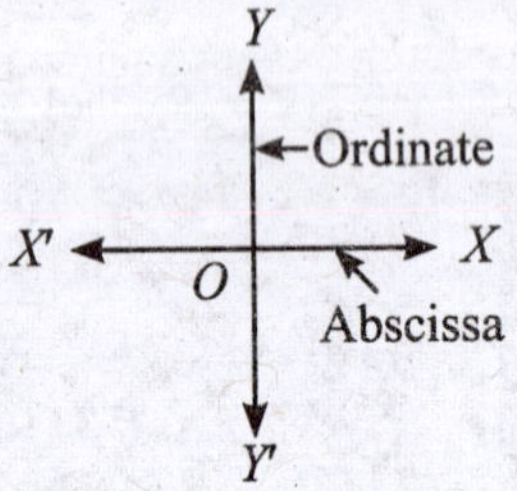

Horizontal = x-axis (Abscissa)

Vertical = y-axis (Ordinate)

Distance formula

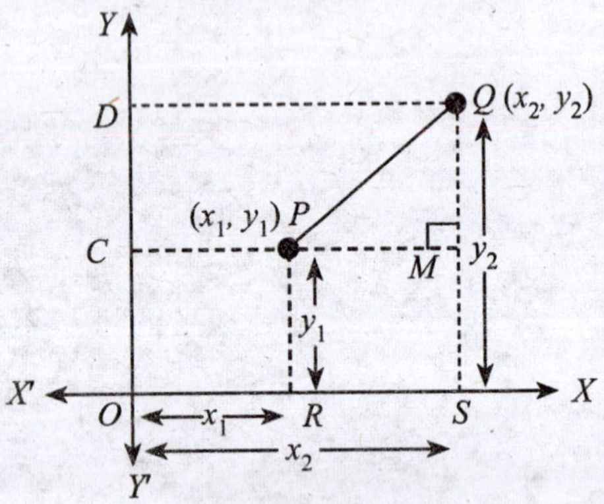

$$PQ = \sqrt{(x_2 - x_1)^2 + (y_2 - y_1)^2}$$

Example: Find the distance between the point $P(-5,7)$ and $Q(-1,3)$.

Sol. We have,

Distance formula: $d = \sqrt{(x_2 - x_1)^2 + (y_2 - y_1)^2}$

Given, $x_1 = -5, x_2 = -1, y_1 = 7, y_2 = 3$

So, $d = \sqrt{(-1-(-5))^2 + (3-7)^2} = \sqrt{(4)^2 + (-4)^2}$

$= \sqrt{16+16} = \sqrt{32} = 4\sqrt{2}$ units

Mid-point Line Segment

The mid-point of the line segment joining the points $P(x_1, y_1)$ and $Q(x_2, y_2)$ is $\left(\frac{x_1 + x_2}{2}, \frac{y_1 + y_2}{2}\right)$.

Example: Find the coordinates of mid-point of the line segment joining (4, –1) and (–2, –3).

Sol. Let the given points be $P(4, -1)$ and $Q(-2, -3)$

Since, the mid-point of the line segment joining the points $P(4, -1)$ and $Q(-2, -3)$

$$= \left(\frac{4-2}{2}, \frac{-1-3}{2}\right) = \left(\frac{2}{2}, \frac{-4}{2}\right) = (1, -2)$$

Section formula

The coordinates of the point $P(x, y)$ which divides the line segment joining the points $A(x_1, y_1)$ and $B(x_2, y_2)$ internally in the ratio $m_1 : m_2$ are $\left(\frac{m_1x_2 + m_2x_1}{m_1 + m_2}, \frac{m_1y_2 + m_2y_1}{m_1 + m_2}\right)$.

Example: Find the coordinates of the point which divides the line joining of (–1, 7) and (4, –3) in the ratio 2 : 3.

Sol. Let $P(x, y)$ be the required point. Thus, we have

$$x = \frac{m_1x_2 + m_2x_1}{m_1 + m_2} \text{ and } y = \frac{m_1y_2 + m_2y_1}{m_1 + m_2}$$

Therefore,

$$x = \frac{2 \times 4 + 3 \times (-1)}{2+3} = \frac{8-3}{5} = \frac{5}{5} = 1$$

$$y = \frac{2 \times (-3) + 3 \times 7}{2+3} = \frac{-6+21}{5} = \frac{15}{5} = 3$$

So, the coordinates of P are (1, 3).

1 DISTANCE FORMULA

Important Terms

- **Coordinate geometry:** The location of any point on a plane is expressed by a pair of values (x, y) and these pairs are known as the coordinates.
- **Abscissa:** The distance of a point from the y-axis is called its x-coordinate or abscissa.
- **Ordinate:** The distance of a point from the x-axis is called its y-coordinate, or ordinate.
- **Origin:** The point at which the axes intersect is known as the origin and generally it is denoted by O.

Important Formulas

- **Distance Formula:** The distance between $P(x_1, y_1)$ and $Q(x_2, y_2)$ is $\sqrt{(x_2 - x_1)^2 + (y_2 - y_1)^2}$.

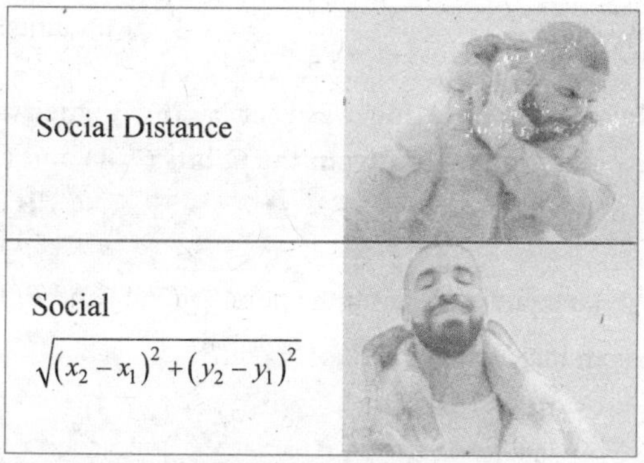

- **Distance from Origin:** The distance of a point $P(x,y)$ from origin is $\sqrt{x^2 + y^2}$.

Important Derivations

Distance Formula: The distance between two points (x_1, y_1) and (x_2, y_2) in a coordinate system is given by formula $\sqrt{(x_2 - x_1)^2 + (y_2 - y_1)^2}$. This is known as the distance formula.

Proof: Let $P(x_1, y_1)$ and $Q(x_2, y_2)$ are the two points. Draw the line PR and QS perpendicular to the x-axis. A perpendicular is drawn from point P on QS to meet at the point M.

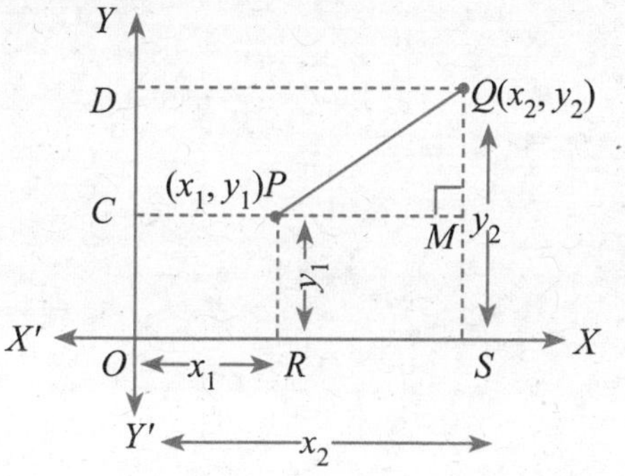

$\therefore$ OR $= x_1$, OS $= x_2$

$RS = x_2 - x_1 = PM$

$SQ = y_2$, $SM = PR = y_1$

$\therefore$ $QM = y_2 - y_1$

On applying the pythagoras theorem in ΔPMQ, we get

$$PQ^2 = PM^2 + QM^2$$

$$PQ2 = (x_2 - x_1)^2 + (y_2 - y_1)^2$$

$\Rightarrow$ $PQ = \sqrt{(x_2 - x_1)^2 + (y_2 - y_1)^2}$ [Since, distance can never be negative, only positive square root is taken.]

Important Concepts

Quadrants in Co-ordinate Geometry: A plane is divided into four parts known as quadrants by the axes of a two-dimensional Cartesian system. These quadrants are denoted by Roman Numerals (with the signs of the (x, y) coordinates).

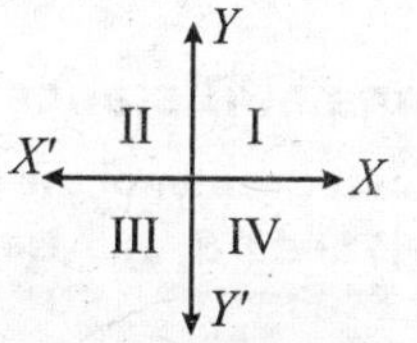

Quadrant	X-coordinate	Y-coordinate
First quadrant	+	+
Second quadrant	–	+
Third quadrant	–	–
Fourth quadrant	+	–

- The coordinate of a point on the x-axis are of the form $(x, 0)$ and that of the point on y-axis are $(0, y)$

Real Life Applications

The Global Positioning System (GPS) is a space based satellite navigation system that provides information of location and time all weather conditions.

In a GPS, the longitude and the latitude of a place are its coordinates. The distance between 2 places in GPS is found using the distance formula.

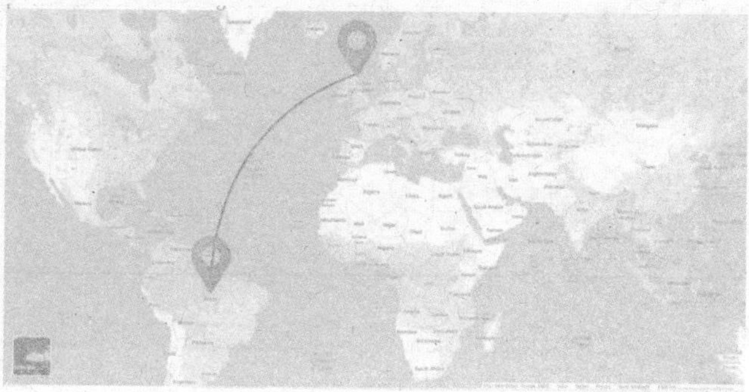

Different Problem Types

Type I: Distance Between Two Given Points:

Find the distance between the points $P(-6, 7)$ and $Q(-1, -5)$

Solution:

Step I: Find the differences between the x-coordinates and y-coordinates of the two points:

$$x_2 - x_1 = -1-(-6) = 5, y_2 - y_1 = -5-7 = -12$$

Step II: Square the differences obtained in the previous step and add them together.

$$5^2 + (-12)^2 = 25 + 144 = 169$$

Step III: Take the square root of the sum calculated in the previous step to obtain the distance between the two points:

$$PQ = \sqrt{169} = 13$$

Example: Find the distance between the points A (0, 6) and B (0, –2).

Solution: We have,

Distance formula: $d = \sqrt{(x_2 - x_1)^2 + (y_2 - y_1)^2}$

Given, $x_1 = 0, x_2 = 0, y_1 = 6, y_2 = -2$

So, $d = \sqrt{(0-0)^2 + (-2-6)^2} = \sqrt{(0)^2 + (-8)^2} = \sqrt{64} = 8$ units

Type II: Applications of Distance Formula:

Find the coordinates of the center of the circle passing through the points (0, 0), (–2, 1) and (–3, 2). Also, find its radius.

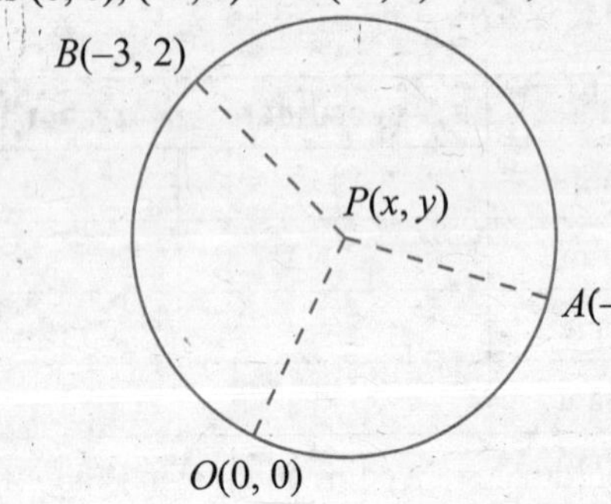

Solution:

Step I: Let $P(x, y)$ be the centre of the circle passing through the points $O(0, 0)$, $A(-2, 1)$ and $B(-3, 2)$. Then, $OP = AP = BP$

Step II: Since, $OP = AP$

$\Rightarrow OP^2 = AP^2$

$\Rightarrow x^2 + y^2 = (x+2)^2 + (y-1)^2$

$\Rightarrow x^2 + y^2 = x^2 + y^2 + 4x - 2y + 5$

$\Rightarrow 4x - 2y + 5 = 0$ ... (*i*)

Step III: Also, $OP = BP$

$\Rightarrow OP^2 = BP^2$

$\Rightarrow x^2 + y^2 = (x+3)^2 + (y-2)^2$

$\Rightarrow x^2 + y^2 = x^2 + y^2 + 6x - 4y + 13$

$\Rightarrow 6x - 4y + 13 = 0$ ... (*ii*)

On solving equations (*i*) and (*ii*), we get: $x = \frac{3}{2}$ and $y = \frac{11}{2}$.

Thus, the coordinates of the Center are $\left(\frac{3}{2}, \frac{11}{2}\right)$

Step IV:

$\therefore$ Radius $= OP = \sqrt{x^2 + y^2} = \sqrt{\frac{9}{4} + \frac{121}{4}} = \frac{1}{2}\sqrt{130}$ units.

Example: Find a relation between x and y such that the point (x, y) is equidistant from the points (7, 1) and (3, 5). **(NCERT Intext)**

Solution:

Let $P(x, y)$ be equidistant from the points $A(7, 1)$ and $B(3, 5)$.

We are given that $AP = BP$. So, $AP^2 = BP^2$

i.e., $(x-7)^2 + (y-1)^2 = (x-3)^2 + (y-5)^2$

i.e., $x^2 - 14x + 49 + y^2 - 2y + 1 = x^2 - 6x + 9 + y^2 - 10y + 25$

i.e., $x - y = 2$

Which is the required relation.

COMPETENCY BASED SOLVED EXAMPLES

Multiple Choice Questionc

(1 M)

1. **The distance of the point (– 1, 7) from x-axis is:** *(Ap)*

(*a*) –1 (*b*) 7 (*c*) 6 (*d*) $\sqrt{50}$

Sol. The distance of any point from x-axis is the y-coordinate. Therefore, the distance of the point (–1, 7) from x-axis is 7.

2. **The distance of the point (–6, 8) from origin is:** *(Ap)*

(*a*) 6 (*b*) –6 (*c*) 8 (*d*) 10

Sol. From the distance formula, we have

Distance of point (–6, 8) from $O(0, 0)$

$$= \sqrt{(8-0)^2 + (-6-0)^2} = \sqrt{64+36}$$

$$= \sqrt{100} = 10 \text{ unit}$$

3. **The distance between the points (3, –2) and (–3, 2) is** *(An)* (CBSE, 2020)

(*a*) $\sqrt{52}$ units (*b*) $4\sqrt{10}$ units

(*c*) $2\sqrt{10}$ units (*d*) 40 units

Sol. Distance $= \sqrt{(3+3)^2 + (-2-2)^2}$

$$= \sqrt{36+16} = \sqrt{52} \text{ units}$$

4. **The perimeter of a triangle with vertices (0, 4), (0, 0) and (3, 0) is** *(An)*(CBSE, 2020)

(*a*) $7+\sqrt{5}$ (*b*) 5

(*c*) 10 (*d*) 12

Sol. Let $A(4, 0)$ $B(0, 0)$ and $C(0, 3)$ be the vertices of the triangle. Using distance formula we have

$$AB = \sqrt{4^2 + O} = 4$$

$$BC = \sqrt{O + 3^2} = 3$$

$$CA = \sqrt{4^2 + 3^2} = 5$$

Clearly adding $AB + BC + CA$ = perimeter of Δ

$\Rightarrow$ Perimeter of $\Delta ABC = 3 + 4 + 5 = 12$ units

5. **If the distance between the points (2, –2) and (–1, x) is 5, then one of the values of x is** *(Ap)*(NCERT Exemplar)

(*a*) –4 (*b*) 2 (*c*) –3 (*d*) 1

Sol. By using distance formula,

$$\sqrt{(x_2 - x_1)^2 + (y_2 - y_1)^2} = 5 \quad (\because AB = 5)$$

Here $x_1 = -1, y_1 = x, x_2 = 2$ and $y_2 = -2$

$$\therefore \sqrt{(2+1)^2 + (-2-x)^2} = 5$$

$$\Rightarrow \sqrt{(3)^2 + (-2-x)^2} = 5$$

$$\Rightarrow \sqrt{9 + (-2-x)^2} = 5$$

On squaring both sides, we get

$$\Rightarrow 9 + (-2-x)^2 = 25$$

$$\Rightarrow (2+x)^2 = 16$$

$$\Rightarrow 2 + x = \pm 4$$

$$\Rightarrow x = 2, -6$$

6. **The distance between the points (m, –n) and (–m, n) is** *(Ap)*

(*a*) $\sqrt{m^2+n^2}$ (*b*) $m+n$

(*c*) $2\sqrt{m^2+n^2}$ (*d*) $\sqrt{2m^2+2n^2}$

Sol. Given points are (m, –n) and (–m, n)

Let, $x_1 = m, y_1 = -n$

$x_2 = -m, y_2 = n$

Distance between A and B

$$AB = \sqrt{(x_2 - x_1)^2 + (y_2 - y_1)^2}$$

$$\Rightarrow AB = \sqrt{(-m-m)^2 + (n-(-n))^2}$$

$$\Rightarrow AB = \sqrt{(-2m)^2 + (2n)^2}$$

$$\Rightarrow AB = 2\sqrt{m^2+n^2}$$

Mistakes 101 : What not to do!

In this type of problem, students often mistakenly enter incorrect coordinates into the formula.

7. **A point (x, y) is at a distance of 5 units from the origin. How many such points lie in the third quadrant?** *(An)*

(*a*) 0 (*b*) 1

(*c*) 2 (*d*) infinitely many

Sol. All the points at the distance of 5 units from the origin form a circle with radius 5 units. Therefore there are infinite points on the circle in 3rd quadrant.

8. **The coordinates of the centre of the circle, O, and a point on the circle, N, are shown in the figure below.** *(An)*

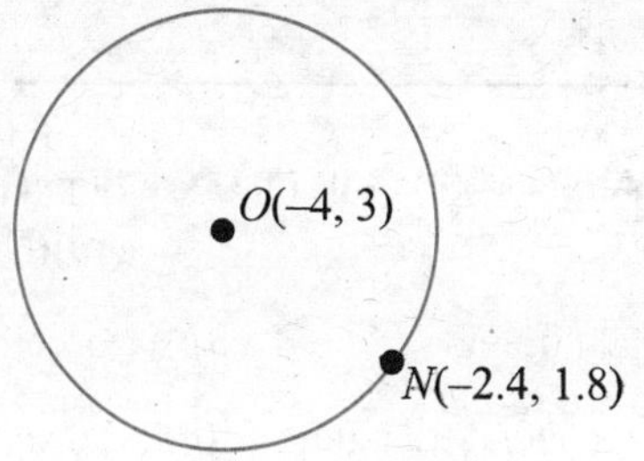

What is the radius of the circle?

(*a*) $\sqrt{0.4}$ units (*b*) 2 units

(*c*) 4 units (*d*) $\sqrt{42.4}$ units

Sol. Distance = $NO = \sqrt{(-2.4+4)^2+(1.8-3)^2}$

$= \sqrt{4} = 2$ units

9. The points (–1, –2), (1, 0), (–1, 2), (–3, 0) form a quadrilateral of type: **(*An*)**

(*a*) Square (*b*) Rectangle

(*c*) Parallelogram (*d*) Rhombus

Sol. Let $A(-1, -2)$, $B(1, 0)$, $C(-1, 2)$ and $D(-3, 0)$

Distance between two points (x_1, y_1) and (x_2, y_2) can be calculated using the formula $\sqrt{(x_2-x_1)^2+(y_2-y_1)^2}$

Distance between the points $A(-1, -2)$ and $B\ (1, 0)$

$= \sqrt{(1+1)^2+(0+2)^2} = \sqrt{8}$

Distance between the points $B(1, 0)$ and $C\ (-1, 2)$

$= \sqrt{(-1-1)^2+(2-0)^2} = \sqrt{8}$

Distance between the points $C(-1, 2)$ and $D(-3, 0)$

$= \sqrt{(-3+1)^2+(0-2)^2} = \sqrt{8}$

Distance between the points $A(-1, -2)$ and $D\ (-3, 0)$ =

$\sqrt{(-3+1)^2+(0+2)^2} = \sqrt{8}$

Since, length of the sides between all vertices are equal, they are the vertices of a square.

10. The distance between the points (*a*cosθ + *b*sinθ, 0) and (0, *a*sinθ – *b*cosθ), is **(*Ap*)**

(*a*) $a^2 + b^2$ (*b*) $a^2 - b^2$

(*c*) $\sqrt{a^2+b^2}$ (*d*) $\sqrt{a^2-b^2}$

Sol. By distance formula

$= \sqrt{(0-(a\cos\theta+b\sin\theta))^2+(a\sin\theta-b\cos-0)}$

$= \sqrt{\begin{array}{l}a^2\cos^2\theta+b^2\sin^2\theta+2ab\sin\theta\cos\theta+a^2\sin^2\theta+b^2\\ \qquad\qquad\cos^2\theta-2ab\sin\theta\cos\theta\end{array}}$

$= \sqrt{a^2+b^2}$

Nailing the Right Answer

Label intermediate steps in your calculation to keep track of each part of the process and ensure clarity in your solution.

11. The points (-4,0),(4,0),(0,3) are the vertices of a **(*An*)(NCERT Exemplar)**

(*a*) right triangle (*b*) isosceles triangle

(*c*) equilateral triangle (*d*) scalene triangle

Sol. Let $A(-4, 0)$, $B(4, 0)$, $C(0, 3)$ are the given vertices.

So, distancse between $A(-4, 0)$ and $B(4, 0)$.

$AB^2 = (4-(-4))^2 + (0-0)^2 = 64$

$\Rightarrow AB = \sqrt{64} = 8$

Now, distance between $B(4, 0)$ and $C(0, 3)$,

$BC^2 = (0-(4))^2 + (3-0)^2 = 25$

$\Rightarrow BC = \sqrt{25} = 5$

Now, distance between $A(-4, 0)$ and $C(0, 3)$

$AC^2 = (0-(-4))^2 + (3-0)^2 = 25$

$\Rightarrow AC = \sqrt{25} = 5$

As, $BC = AC$

ΔABC is an isosceles triangle because an isosceles triangle has two sides equal.

Key Takeaways

Follow the properties of the given triangle to prove with the given coordinates.

12. The distance of the point (3, 5) from *x*-axis (in units) is: **(*Un*)(CBSE SQP, 2023)**

(*a*) 3 (*b*) –3

(*c*) 5 (*d*) –5

Sol. The distance of point (3, 5) from the *x*-axis is equal to the ordinate of the given coordinates. So, the distance from *x*-axis is 5 units.

13. The distance between the points (c, 0) and (0, –c) is: **(*Un*)(CBSE, 2023)**

(*a*) $c\sqrt{2}$ units (*b*) 2*c* units

(*c*) $2\sqrt{c}$ units (*d*) *c* units

Sol. Distance between the point $A(x_1, y_1)$, $B(x_2, y_2)$ is

$AB = \sqrt{(x_2-x_1)^2+(y_2-y_1)^2}$

$AB = \sqrt{(0-c)^2+(-c-0)^2}$

$AB = \sqrt{2c^2} = c\sqrt{2}$ units

Answer Key

1. (*b*)	2. (*d*)	3. (*a*)	4. (*d*)	5. (*b*)
6. (*c*)	7. (*d*)	8. (*b*)	9. (*a*)	10. (*c*)
11. (*b*)	12. (*c*)	13. (*a*)		

Assertion and Reason (1 M)

Direction: In the following questions, a statement of Assertion (A) is followed by a statement of Reason (R). Mark the correct choice as.

(*a*) Both Assertion (A) and Reason (R) are true, and Reason (R) is the correct explanation of Assertion (A).

(*b*) Both Assertion (A) and Reason (R) are true, but Reason (R) is not the correct explanation of Assertion (A).

(*c*) Assertion (A) is true, but Reason (R) is false.

(*d*) Assertion (A) is false, but Reason (R) is true.

1. Assertion (A): **The distance point P(2, 3) from the x-axis is 3.**

   Reason (R): **The distance from x-axis is equal to its ordinate.**

Sol. Assertion (A): The distance between the point (2, 3) and x-axis can be determined by assuming a point (2, 0) on x-axis

$\therefore$ Distance between (2, 3) and (2, 0) $= \sqrt{(2-2)^2+(0-3)^2}$

$= \sqrt{3^2} = \sqrt{9} = 3$ (Ordinate)

Hence, Assertion is true

Reason (R): We know, the distance from x-axis is equal to its ordinate. Hence, reason is true.

Hence, Both Assertion (A) and Reason (R) are true, and Reason (R) is the correct explanation of Assertion (A).

2. Assertion (A): **The point (0, 3) lies on y-axis.**

   Reason (R): **The x-coordinate on the point on y-axis is not zero.**

Sol. Assertion (A): Since, x-coordinate of the point (0, 3) is zero.

We know that if the point lies on y-axis, its x-coordinate is 0.

So, point (0, 3) lies on y-axis.

Hence, Assertion is true.

Reason (R): Given reason is false.

Hence, Assertion (A) is true, but Reason (R) is false.

Answer Key

1. (*a*) 2. (*c*)

Subjective Questions

Very Short Answer Type Questions (1 or 2 M)

1. **Points $A(3, 1)$, $B(5, 1)$, $C(a, b)$ and $D(4, 3)$ are vertices of a parallelogram $ABCD$. Find the values of a and b.** *(Re)*(CBSE, 2019)

Sol. (*i*) Given points for A & B are $A(3, 1)$ and $C(a, b)$.

$\therefore$ The coordinates of the mid point of diagonal AC are $\left(\frac{3+a}{2}, \frac{1+b}{2}\right)$ (½ M)

(*ii*) Given points for B and D are $B(5, 1)$ and $D(4, 3)$.

$\therefore$ The coordinates of the mid point of diagonal BD are $\left(\frac{5+4}{2}, \frac{1+3}{2}\right) = \left(\frac{9}{2}, 2\right)$ (½ M)

(*iii*) Since the coordinates of the midpoint of diagonal AC are the same as the coordinates of the midpoint of diagonal BD

Therefore, $\left(\frac{3+a}{2}, \frac{1+b}{2}\right) = \left(\frac{9}{2}, 2\right)$

$\Rightarrow \frac{3+a}{2} = \frac{9}{2}$ and $\frac{1+b}{2} = 2$

$\Rightarrow 3 + a = 9$ and $1 + b = 4 \Rightarrow a = 9 - 3$ and $b = 4 - 1$

$\Rightarrow a = 6$ and $b = 3$

Hence, the value of a is 6 and the value of b is 3. (1 M)

Topper's Explanation *(CBSE 2019)*

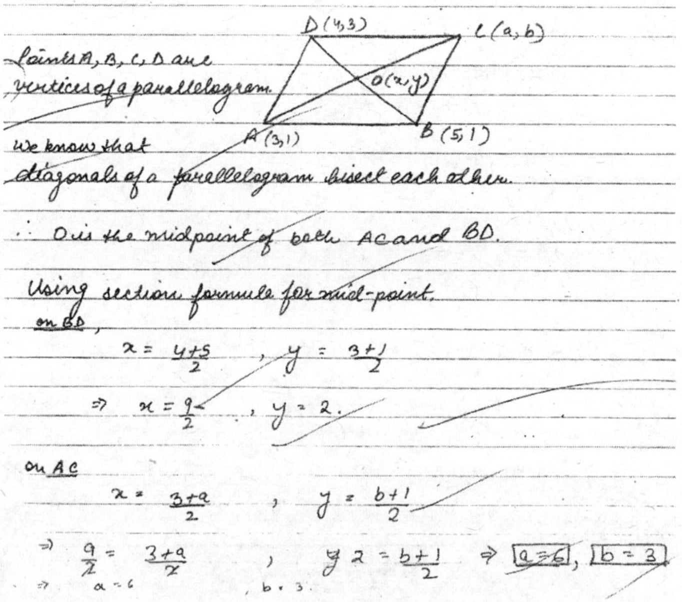

2. **Find the distance between the points A(a cos 35°, 0) and B(0, a cos 55°).** *(Ap)*

Sol. Distance between two points is given by

$= \sqrt{(x_2-x_1)^2+(y_2-y_1)^2}$ (½ M)

$= \sqrt{(0-a\cos 35°)^2+(a\cos 55°-0)^2}$ (½ M)

$= \sqrt{a^2\cos^2 35° + a^2\cos^2 55°}$

$= \sqrt{a^2\cos^2 35° + a^2\cos^2(90°-35°)}$

$= a\sqrt{\cos^2 35° + \sin^2 35°}$ $(\cos(90° - \theta) = \sin\theta)$

$= a$ units $(\because \sin^2\theta + \cos^2\theta = 1)$

(1 M)

3. **The line $x + 2y = 2$ forms a triangle *OPQ*, with the coordinate axes.** (*Un*)

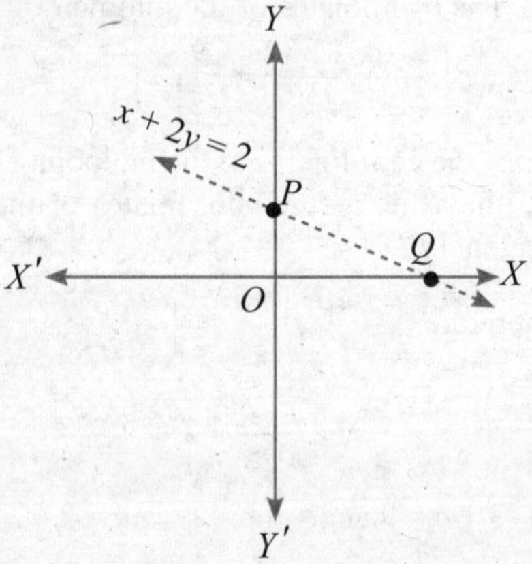

(*i*) **What are the coordinates of points *P* and *Q*?**

(*ii*) **What is the area of the triangle formed? Show your steps.**

Sol. (*i*) Since *P* & *Q* lies on line $x + 2y = 2$

Also *P* lies on *y*-axis, $\therefore x = 0$

and *Q* lies on *x*-axis, $\therefore y = 0$

$\Rightarrow$ For *P*, $0 + 2y = 2 \Rightarrow y = 1$

Hence $P(0, 1)$

For *Q*,

$x + 2 \times 0 = 2$

$\Rightarrow Q(2, 0)$ (*1 M*)

(*ii*) Area of $\Delta POQ = \frac{1}{2} \times OQ \times PO$

$= \frac{1}{2} \times 2 \times 1$

$= 1$ sq. unit. (*1 M*)

Key Takeaways

A point on the *x*-axis is of the form $(a, 0)$, and a point on the *y*-axis is of the form $(0, b)$

4. **Find the distance of a point $P(x, y)$ from the origin.** (*Cr*)

Sol. Let $O(0, 0)$ be the origin

By using distance formula.

$OP = \sqrt{(x-0)^2 + (y-0)^2}$ (*1 M*)

$= \sqrt{x^2 + y^2}$ (*1 M*)

5. **If the distances of $P(x, y)$ from $A(5, 1)$ and $B(-1, 5)$ are equal, then prove that $3x = 2y$.** (*Re*)

Sol. Since, *P* is the equidistant from *A* and *B*

By using distance formula.

$\therefore PA = PB \Rightarrow (PA)^2 = (PB)^2$

$\Rightarrow (x - 5)^2 + (y - 1)^2 = (x + 1)^2 + (y - 5)^2$ (*½ M*)

$\Rightarrow x^2 - 10x + 25 + y^2 - 2y + 1 = x^2 + 2x + 1 + y^2 - 10y + 25$

$\Rightarrow -10x - 2x - 2y + 10y = 0$ (*½ M*)

$\Rightarrow -12x + 8y = 0$

$\Rightarrow 12x = 8y \Rightarrow 3x = 2y$ (*1 M*)

Short Answer Type Questions (2 or 3 M)

1. **Find the points on *x*-axis which are at a distance of 5 units from the point $Q(-1, 4)$.** (*An*)

Sol. Let us suppose the point on *x*-axis be $P(x, 0)$.

$\therefore$ distance $PQ = 5$ units

We know that distance between two points $P(x_1, y_1)$ and $Q(x_2, y_2) = \sqrt{(x_2 - x_1)^2 + (y_2 - y_1)^2}$ (*½ M*)

Here, $x_1 = -1, y_1 = 4, x_2 = x$ and $y_2 = 0$.

$\Rightarrow \sqrt{(x-(-1))^2 + (0-4)^2} = 5$ (*1 M*)

Squaring on both sides, we get

$\Rightarrow (x + 1)^2 + (0 - 4)^2 = 25$ (*½ M*)

$\Rightarrow (x + 1)^2 + (-4)^2 = 25$

$\Rightarrow x^2 + 2x + 1 + 16 = 25$

$\Rightarrow x^2 + 2x - 8 = 0$

$\Rightarrow (x + 4)(x - 2) = 0$

$\Rightarrow x = 2, -4$

Hence, the required points on *x*-axis are $(2, 0)$ and $(-4, 0)$. (*1 M*)

2. **Find the point on *y*-axis which is equidistant from the points $(5, -2)$ and $(-3, 2)$.** (*Un*)

Sol. Let a point $P(0, y)$ on the *y*-axis, $A(5, -2)$ and $B(-3, 2)$ which is equidistant from *P*.

$\therefore PA = PB \Rightarrow (PA)^2 = (PB)^2$ (*½ M*)

By using distance formula.

$(0 - 5)^2 + (y + 2)^2 = (0 + 3)^2 + (y - 2)^2$

$\Rightarrow 25 + y^2 + 4y + 4 = 9 + y^2 - 4y + 4$ (*1 M*)

$8y = 9 - 25$ (*½ M*)

$8y = -16 \Rightarrow y = -2$

$\therefore$ the required point is $P(0, -2)$ (*1 M*)

Long Answer Type Questions (4 or 5 M)

1. **Find the centre of a circle passing through points $(6, -6)$, $(3, -7)$ and $(3, 3)$.** (*Ap*) **(NCERT Intext)**

Sol. Let us suppose, $P = (6, -6)$, $Q = (3, -7)$, $R = (3, 3)$ are the points on a circle.

If *O* is the centre of the circle, then $OP = OQ = OR$ (radii of the circle are equal). (*½ M*)

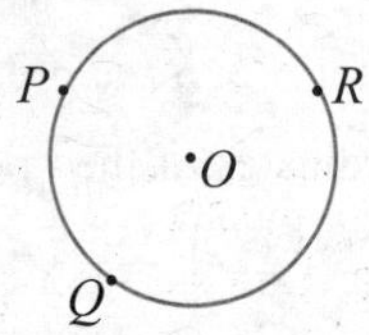

Let coordinates of $O = (x, y)$, then by using distance formula

$$= \sqrt{(x_2 - x_1)^2 + (y_2 - y_1)^2} \quad (½\ M)$$

$$OP = \sqrt{(x-6)^2 + (y+6)^2} \quad (½\ M)$$

$$OQ = \sqrt{(x-3)^2 + (y+7)^2}$$

$$OR = \sqrt{(x-3)^2 + (y+3)^2}$$

As, $OP = OQ$ (½ M)

$\therefore (x - 6)^2 + (y + 6)^2 = (x - 3)^2 + (y + 7)^2$

$\Rightarrow x^2 + 36 - 12x + y^2 + 36 + 12y = x^2 + 9 - 6x + y^2 + 49 + 14y$

$\Rightarrow x^2 + y^2 - 12x + 12y + 72 = x^2 + y^2 + 14y + 58 - 6x$

(½ M)

On simplifying the above equation, we get

$-6x = 2y - 14$ ... (i)

In the same way: $OQ = OR$

$(x - 3)^2 + (y + 7)^2 = (x - 3)^2 + (y - 3)^2$

$\Rightarrow (y + 7)^2 = (y - 3)^2$

$\Rightarrow y^2 + 14y + 49 = y^2 - 6y + 9$ (½ M)

$\Rightarrow 20y = -40$

or $y = -2$ (½ M)

On putting the value of y in equation (i), we get

$\Rightarrow -6x = 2y - 14$

$\Rightarrow -6x = -4 - 14 = -18$

$\Rightarrow x = 3$ (½ M)

Therefore, centre of the circle is located at point (3,–2).

(1 M)

Mistakes 101 : What not to do!

Neglecting to include negative signs in coordinate values when plotting points or calculating distances or slopes, resulting in errors in calculations or interpretations.

2. The two opposite vertices of a square are (–1, 2) and (3, 2). Find the coordinates of the other two vertices.

(Cr) (NCERT Intext)

Sol. Let us suppose $PQRS$ is a square, where $S(x_1, y_1)$ and $Q(x_2, y_2)$ are opposite vertices of a square. And point O is the point of intersection of PR and QS.

We know that the distance between two points (x_1, y_1) and (x_2, y_2) is given by the distance formula

$$d = \sqrt{(x_2 - x_1)^2 + (y_2 - y_1)^2} \quad (1\ M)$$

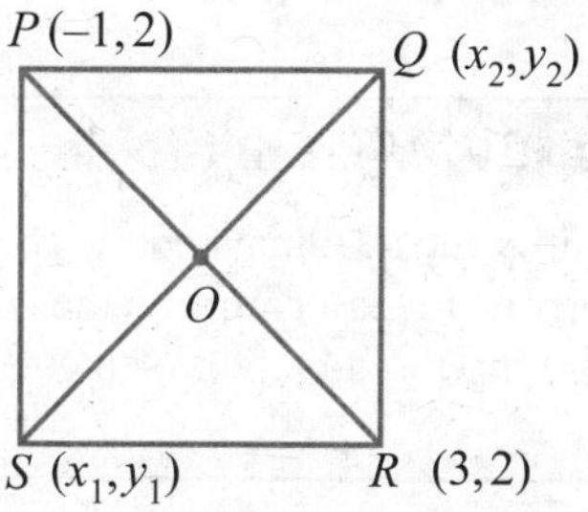

(½ M)

Distance between P and R is calculated by using distance formula.

$$PR = \sqrt{(3+1)^2 + (2-2)^2} \quad (½\ M)$$

$= 4 = QS$ [As diagonals of the square are equal]

We know that the sides of the square are equal to each other.

$\therefore PQ = QR$ (½ M)

$$\Rightarrow \sqrt{(x_2 - (-1))^2 + (y_2 - 2)^2} = \sqrt{(x_2 - 3)^2 + (y_2 - 2)^2}$$

$\Rightarrow (x_2 + 1)^2 = (x_2 - 3)^2$

$\Rightarrow x_2^2 + 1 + 2x_2 = x_2^2 + 9 - 6x_2 \Rightarrow x_2 = 1$ (½ M)

Let 'a' be the side of square.

In right angled triangle ΔPQR using pythagoras theorem, we get

$PQ^2 + QR^2 = PR^2$

$a^2 + a^2 = 4^2$

$2a^2 = 16$

$a^2 = 8$

$a = 2\sqrt{2}$ (½ M)

$\therefore PQ = 2\sqrt{2}$

$$\Rightarrow \sqrt{(x_2 - (-1))^2 + (y_2 - 2)^2} = 2\sqrt{2}$$

$(1 + 1)^2 + (y_2 - 2)^2 = 8$

$(y_2 - 2)^2 = 8 - 4$

$(y_2 - 2)^2 = 4$

$y_2 - 2 = 2$

$y_2 = 4$ (½ M)

Hence, the coordinates of Q are (1, 4).

As we know that diagonal of a square are equal and bisect each other.

$$\therefore \text{Coordinartes of } O = \left(\frac{3-1}{2}, \frac{2+2}{2}\right) = (1, 2)$$

Now, coordinates of S can be calculated, as follows:

As O is the mid-point of RS.

$$\therefore (1, 2) = \left(\frac{x_1 + 1}{2}, \frac{y_1 + 4}{2}\right) \quad (½\ M)$$

On equating x and y term, we get

$$1 = \frac{x_1 + 1}{2} \text{ and } 2 = \frac{y_1 + 4}{2}$$

$2 = x_1 + 1$ and $4 = y_1 + 4$

$x_1 = 1$ and $y_1 = 0$

Coordinates of S are (1, 0).

Hence, the required vertices are $S(1, 0)$ and $Q(1, 4)$. (½ M)

Mistakes 101 : What not to do!

Students may misidentify the quadrants on the coordinate plane, leading to errors in determining the signs of coordinates or interpreting the direction of movement of geometric objects.

3. Three players are standing on the circle at points $A(-5, 0)$, $B(1, 0)$ and $C(3, 4)$. A ball is placed at a point that is equidistant from all 3 players.

(*Cr*) (CBSE CFPQ, 2023)

(*i*) What are the coordinates of the ball?

(*ii*) The fourth player is standing at the point $D(-5, 4)$. Is he/she standing on the circle?

Show your steps and give valid reasons.

Sol. (*i*) Consider the coordinates of the ball as $O(x, y)$ and considering $OA = OB = OC$, apply distance formula and write the equations: *(1 M)*

$OA = OB \Rightarrow (x + 5)^2 + (y)^2 = (x - 1)^2 + (y)^2$ and

$OB = OC \Rightarrow (x - 1)^2 + (y)^2 = (x - 3)^2 + (y - 4)^2$

Simplifying the above equations to find the coordinates of the ball as $O(-2, 4)$. *(2 M)*

(*ii*) Consider O as the centre and finds the radius of the circle by finding either OA or OB or OC. *(1 M)*

$$OA = \sqrt{\{(-2+5)^2 + (4-0)\}^2} = \sqrt{25} = 5 \text{ units}$$

The distance between O and D as 3 units and the fourth player is not standing on the circle as the distance between the player and the centre of the circle is not equal to the radius of the circle. *(1 M)*

4. If the point $C(-1, 2)$ divides internally the line segment joining $A(2, 5)$ and $B(x,y)$ in the ratio 3 : 4, find the coordinates of B. **(*Ap*)**

Sol. Let the coordinates of B be (x, y). It is given that $AC : BC = 3 : 4$.

So, the coordinates of C are *(1 M)*

$$\left(\frac{3x+4\times2}{3+4}, \frac{3y+4\times5}{3+4}\right) = \left(\frac{3x+8}{7}, \frac{3y+20}{7}\right)$$

But, the coordinates of C are $(-1, 2)$ *(1 M)*

$$\frac{3x+8}{7} = -1 \text{ and } \frac{3y+20}{7} = 2$$

$x = -5$ and $y = -2$ *(1 M)*

Thus, the coordinates of B are $(-5, -2)$. *(1 M)*

2 SECTION FORMULA

Important Terms

- **Section Formula:** Section formula in coordinate geometry is used to find the ratio in which a line segment is divided by a point internally or externally.

  Coordinates of the point which divides the line-segment AB joining the points $A(x_1, y_1)$ and $B(x_2, y_2)$ internally in the ratio $m_1 : m_2$.
- **Mid Point:** Mid point is a point which equally divides line segment joining two points.
- **Internal Point:** A point P is called internal point if P divides AB in ratio $m:n$ internally.

Important Formulas

- **Section Formula:** The coordinates of the point $P(x, y)$ which divides the line segment joining the points $A(x_1, y_1)$ and $B(x_2, y_2)$ internally in the ratio $m_1 : m_2$ are $\left(\frac{m_1x_2+m_2x_1}{m_1+m_2}, \frac{m_1y_2+m_2y_1}{m_1+m_2}\right)$
- **Mid Point Formula:** The mid-point of the line segment joining the points $P(x_1, y_1)$ and $Q(x_2, y_2)$ is $\left(\frac{x_1+x_2}{2}, \frac{y_1+y_2}{2}\right)$

Important Concepts

- The midpoint divides a line segment in an equal ratio, that is, 1 : 1.
- The bisector of a line segment cuts it at its midpoint.
- We have, if P does not lie between A and B but lies on the line AB, outside the line segment AB, and $PA : PB = m_1 : m_2$, we say that P divides externally the line segment joining the points A and B.
- The ratio $m_1 : m_2$ can also be written as $\lambda : 1$, where $\lambda = \frac{m_1}{m_2}$.

Real Life Applications

The 90 mile straight section of highway lies between the towns of Balladonia and Caiguna in the Australian Outback.Some friends of ours recently drove this stretch of the Eyre Highway.

If their car started making some strange noises along this section of road, would they be better off heading back to Balladonia, or continuing onto Caiguna?

Well assuming there is a mechanic in each town, it would depend on whether they had crossed the halfway point, (or "Midpoint"), of their journey.

Different Problem Types

Type I: On Finding the Section Point When the Section Ratio is Given

Find the coordinates of the point which divides the line segment joining the points (6, 3) and (–4, 5) in the ratio 3 : 2 internally.

Solution:

Step I: Determine the coordinates of the two points (let's call them A and B) between which you want to find the intersection point.

$$A = (6, 3), B = (-4, 5)$$

Step II: Apply the section formula to find the coordinates of the intersection point

$$x = \frac{mx_2+nx_1}{m+n}, y = \frac{my_2+my_1}{m+n}$$

Therefore,

$$x = \frac{3\times(-4)+2\times6}{3+2} = 0,\ y = \frac{3\times5+2\times3}{3+2} = \frac{21}{5}$$

Step III: The resulting coordinates $P(x, y)$ represent the intersection point of the line segment AB, divided according to the given section ratio.

So, the coordinates of P are $(0, \frac{21}{5})$

Example: Find the coordinates of the point which divides the line joining of (–2, 2) and (2, 8) in the ratio 1 : 3.

Solution:

Let $P(x, y)$ be the required point. Thus, we have

$$x = \frac{m_1x_2+m_2x_1}{m_1+m_2} \text{ and } y = \frac{m_1y_2+m_2y_1}{m_1+m_2}$$

Therefore,

$$x = \frac{1\times2-2\times3}{1+3} = \frac{2-6}{4} = \frac{-4}{4} = -1$$

$$y = \frac{1\times8+3\times2}{1+3} = \frac{8+6}{4} = \frac{14}{4} = \frac{7}{2}$$

So, the coordinates of P are $(-1, \frac{7}{2})$.

Type II: On Finding the Section Ratio or an Endpoint of the Segment When the Section Point is Given

In what ratio does the x-axis divide the line segment joining the points (2, –3) and (5, 6)? Also, find the coordinates of the point of intersection.

Solution:

Step I: Assuming the desired ratio is $\lambda:1$, then the coordinates of the dividing point are as follows:

$$R\left(\frac{5\lambda+2}{\lambda+1},\frac{6\lambda-3}{\lambda+1}\right)$$

Step II: According to the questions let's draw the graph:

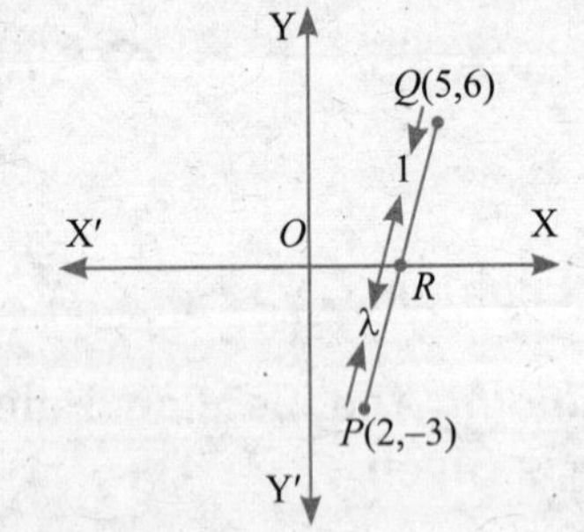

Step III: Solving for λ it is a point on x-axis on which y-coordinates of every point are zero.

$$\therefore \frac{6\lambda-3}{\lambda+1}=0 \Rightarrow \lambda=\frac{1}{2}$$

Thus, the required ratio is $\frac{1}{2}:1$ or, $1:2$.

Putting $\lambda = 1/2$ in the coordinates of R, we find that its coordinates are (3, 0).

Example: Find the ratio in which the line segment joining A(1, –5) and B(–4, 5) is divided by the x-axis. Also find the coordinates of the point of division.

Solution:

Let the required ratio be $k:1$. Then, the coordinates of the point of division is

$$P\left(\frac{-4k+1}{k+1},\frac{5k-5}{k+1}\right)$$

Since, this point lies on x-axis. Therefore its y-coordinate is zero.

i.e., $\frac{5k-5}{k+1}=0 \Rightarrow 5k-5=0$

$$\Rightarrow 5k=5 \text{ or } k=\frac{5}{5}=1$$

Thus, the required ratio is 1 : 1 and the point of division is

$$P\left(\frac{-4\times1+1}{1+1},\frac{5\times1-5}{1+1}\right)$$

i.e., $P\left(-\frac{3}{2},0\right)$

Type III: On finding the Unknown Vertex from Given Points:

The three vertices of a parallelogram taken in order are (–1,0), (3,1) an (2,2) respectively. Find the coordinates of the fourth vertex:

Solution:

Step I: Let $A(-1,0)$, $B(3,1)$, $C(2,2)$ are $D(x, y)$ be the vertices of a parallelogram ABC, taken in order.

Step II: Since, the diagonals of a parallelogram bisect each other.

$\therefore$ Coordinates of the mid-point of AC

$$\Rightarrow \left(\frac{-1+2}{2},\frac{0+2}{2}\right)=\left(\frac{3+x}{2},\frac{1+y}{2}\right)$$

$$\Rightarrow \left(\frac{1}{2},1\right)=\left(\frac{3+x}{2},\frac{y+1}{2}\right) \Rightarrow \frac{3+x}{2}=\frac{1}{2} \text{ and } \frac{y+1}{2}=1$$

$\therefore x=-2$ and $y=1$

Hence, the fourth vertex of the parallelogram is (–2, 1).

Example: If (1, 2), (4, y), (x, 6) and (3, 5) are the vertices of a parallelogram taken in order, find x and y.

Solution:

Let $A(1, 2)$, $B(4, y)$, $C(x, 6)$ and $D(3, 5)$ be the vertices of a parallelogram $ABCD$.

Since, the diagonals of a parallelogram bisect each other.

$$\therefore \left(\frac{x+1}{2},\frac{6+2}{2}\right)=\left(\frac{3+4}{2},\frac{5+y}{2}\right)$$

$$\Rightarrow \frac{x+1}{2}=\frac{7}{2} \Rightarrow x+1=7 \text{ or } x=6$$

$$\Rightarrow 4=\frac{5+y}{2} \text{ or } 5+y=8 \text{ or } y=8-5=3$$

Hence, $x = 6$ and $y = 3$.

COMPETENCY BASED SOLVED EXAMPLES

Multiple Choice Questions **(1 M)**

1. Find the coordinates of the points of trisection (i.e., points dividing in three equal parts) of the line segment joining the points $A(2,-2)$ and $B(-7, 4)$ *(Ap)* (NCERT Intext)

(*a*) (1, 0) and (–4, –2) (*b*) (–1, 0) and (4, 2)

(*c*) (1, 0) and (–4, 2) (*d*) (–1, 0) and (–4, 2)

Sol. Let P and Q be the points of trisection of AB i.e., $AP = PQ = QB$ (see Fig below)

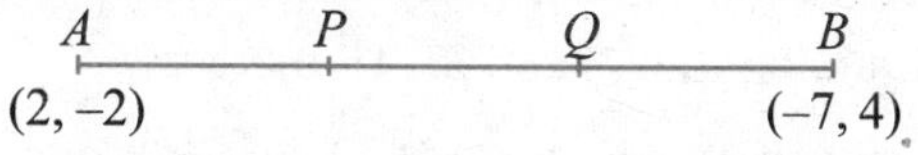

Therefore, P divides AB internally in the ratio 1:2. Therefore, the coordinates of P, by applying the section formula, are

$$\left(\frac{1(-7)+2(2)}{1+2}, \frac{1(4)+2(-2)}{1+2}\right), \text{i.e., } (-1, 0)$$

Now, Q also divides AB internally in the ratio 2 : 1. So, the coordinates of Q are

$$\left(\frac{2(-7)+1(2)}{1+2}, \frac{2(4)+1(-2)}{1+2}\right), \text{i.e., } (-4, 2)$$

Therefore, the coordinates of the points of trisection of the line segment joining A and B are (–1, 0) and (–4, 2).

2. What is the ratio in which the line segment joining (2, –3) and (5, 6) is divided by x-axis? *(Un)*

(*a*) 1 : 2 (*b*) 2 : 1

(*c*) 2 : 5 (*d*) 5 : 2

Sol. Let x-axis divides the line segment in the ratio K : 1 Then by using section formula,

$$P = \left(\frac{5K+2}{K+1}, \frac{6K-3}{K+1}\right)$$

$$\Rightarrow \frac{6K-3}{K+1} = 0 \Rightarrow K = \frac{1}{2},$$ Hence the ratio is 1 : 2.

3. The point which divides the line segment joining the points(7, –6) and (3, 4) in ratio 1 : 2 internally lies in the *(Ap)* (NCERT Exemplar)

(*a*) I quadrant (*b*) II quadrant

(*c*) III quadrant (*d*) IV quadrant

Sol. Let us suppose the point be (x, y)

Let points A and B have coordinates (x_1, y_1) and (x_2, y_2) respectively. $C(x, y)$ is the point dividing this line in the ratio $m : n$, then according to the sectional formula:

$$C(x, y) = \left(\frac{mx_2 + nx_1}{m+n}, \frac{my_2 + my_1}{m+n}\right)$$

Here the point (x, y) divides the line segment AB in the ratio 1 : 2.

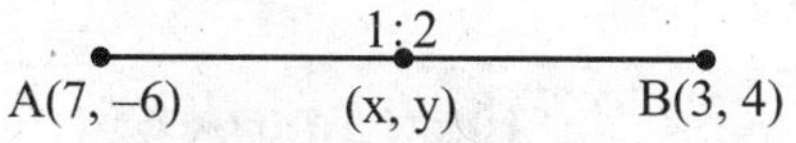

$$x = \frac{1(3)+2(7)}{1+2} \Rightarrow x = \frac{17}{3}$$

$$\text{and, } y = \frac{1(4)+2(-6)}{1+2} \Rightarrow y = -\frac{8}{3}$$

Hence, the required point is $\left(\frac{17}{3}, \frac{-8}{3}\right)$, which lies in fourth quadrant.

4. If the point $P(k, 0)$ divides the line segment joining the points $A(2, -2)$ and $B(-7, 4)$ in the ratio 1 : 2, then the value of k is *(Cr)*

(*a*) 1 (*b*) 2 (*c*) –2 (*d*) –1

Sol. Given $x_1 = 2, y_1 = -2$

$x_2 = -7, y_2 = 4$

By section formula we have

$$(x, y) = \left(\frac{mx_2 + nx_1}{m+n}, \frac{my_2 + ny_1}{m+n}\right)$$

$$(k, 0) = \left(\frac{1\times(-7)+2\times 2}{1+2}, \frac{1\times 4+2\times(-2)}{1+2}\right)$$

now comparing x-coordinate. we have,

$$k = \frac{-7+4}{3} = \frac{-3}{3} = -1$$

5. If the centroid of a triangle is (6, 6) and its orthocenter is (0, 0), then its circumcentre is *(Re)*

(*a*) (2, 2) (*b*) (1, 1)

(*c*) (6, 6) (*d*) (9, 9)

Sol. As we know that orthocenter, centroid and circumcentre are collinear and centroid divides the line in 2 : 1.

Here the coordinate of the centroid (C) is (6, 6) and orthocentre (O) is (0, 0)

Let us suppose, $P(x, y)$ is circumcentre.

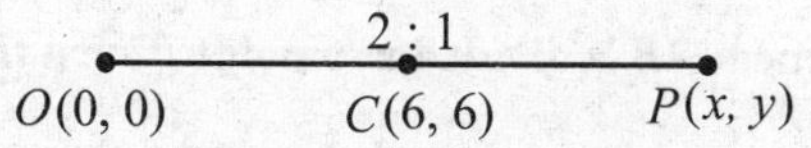

If points A and B have coordinates (x_1, y_1) and (x_2, y_2) respectively. $C(x, y)$ the point dividing this line in the ratio $m : n$, then according to the sectional formula:

$$C(x, y) = \left(\frac{mx_2 + nx_1}{m+n}, \frac{my_2 + ny_1}{m+n}\right)$$

Therefore, $6 = \dfrac{2 \times x + 1 \times 0}{2+1} \Rightarrow x = 9$

and $6 = \dfrac{2 \times y + 1 \times 0}{2+1} \Rightarrow y = 9$

$\therefore P(x, y) = (9, 9)$

Nailing the Right Answer

Determine the ratio in which the line segment is divided by the point whose coordinates are to be found. This ratio may be given explicitly or can be derived from the problem statement.

6. The coordinates of one end point of a diameter of a circle are (4, –1) and the coordinates of the centre of the circle are (1, –3). Find the coordinates of the other end of the diameter. *(Ap)*

(*a*) (–5, –2) (*b*) (2, –5)

(*c*) (5, 2) (*d*) (–2, –5)

Sol. Let us suppose *MN* be a diameter of the circle having its centre at *C*(1, –3), such that the coordinates of one end *M* is (4, –1).

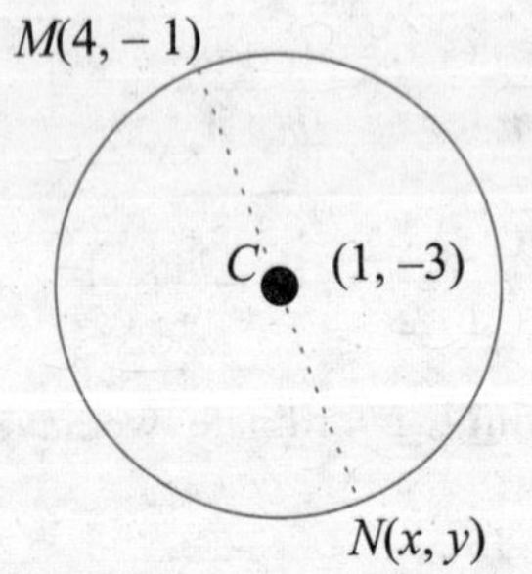

Let the coordinates of *N* be (*x*, *y*).

As, *C* is the mid point of line segment *MN*.

Here, the coordinates of *C* are $\left(\dfrac{x+4}{2}, \dfrac{y-1}{2}\right)$.

It is given that the coordinates of *C* are (1, –3)

$\therefore \dfrac{x+4}{2} = 1$ and $\dfrac{y-1}{2} = -3$

$\Rightarrow x + 4 = 2$ and $y - 1 = -6$

$\Rightarrow x = -2$ and $y = -5$

Hence, the coordinates of *N* are (–2, –5).

7. A segment *AB* is divided at a point *P* such that $\dfrac{PB}{AB} = \dfrac{3}{7}$, then the ratio of *AP* : *PB* is *(An)*

(*a*) 4 : 7 (*b*) 7 : 4

(*c*) 7 : 3 (*d*) 4 : 3

Sol. Given $\dfrac{PB}{AB} = \dfrac{3}{7}$

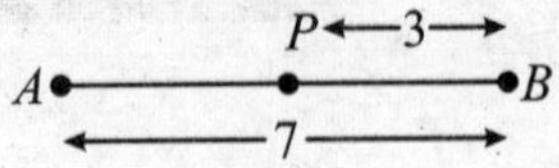

$\Rightarrow \dfrac{AB}{PB} = \dfrac{7}{3}$

$\Rightarrow \dfrac{AP + PB}{PB} = \dfrac{7}{3} \Rightarrow 3AP + 3PB = 7PB$

$\Rightarrow 3AP = 4PB$

Hence, $\dfrac{AP}{PB} = \dfrac{4}{3}$

8. In what ratio does the point $\left(\dfrac{-19}{3}, \dfrac{7}{3}\right)$ divide the line segment joining *A*(3, 7) and *B*(–11, 0)? *(Cr)*

(*a*) 1 : 2 (externally) (*b*) 1 : 2 (internally)

(*c*) 2 : 1 (externally) (*d*) 2 : 1 (internally)

Sol. Let the ratio in which the point $\left(\dfrac{-19}{3}, \dfrac{7}{3}\right)$ divides the line segment joining the points *A*(3, 7) and *B*(–11, 0) be *k* : 1,

Using section formula $x = \dfrac{mx_2 + nx_1}{m+n}$ and $y = \dfrac{my_2 + ny_1}{m+n}$

The points are *A*(3, 7) and *B*(–11, 0) and the ratio is *k* : 1

$\therefore x = \dfrac{k(-11) + 1(3)}{k+1} = \dfrac{-11k + 3}{k+1}$

$y = \dfrac{k(0) + 1(7)}{k+1} = \dfrac{7}{k+1}$

Since, the point is $\left(\dfrac{-19}{3}, \dfrac{7}{3}\right)$.

$\therefore \dfrac{7}{3} = \dfrac{7}{k+1}$

$\Rightarrow k + 1 = 3$

$\Rightarrow k = 2$

The ratio is 2 : 1 and it divides internally.

9. What will be the coordinates of *B*, if the point $C\left(\dfrac{29}{7}, \dfrac{46}{7}\right)$, divides the line segment joining *A*(5, 8) and *B*(*a*, *b*) in the ratio 2 : 5? *(Un)*

(*a*) $a = 2, b = 3$ (*b*) $a = -2, b = 3$

(*c*) $a = 2, b = -3$ (*d*) $a = -2, b = -3$

Sol. Using, section formula $x = \dfrac{mx_2 + nx_1}{m+n}$ and $y = \dfrac{my_2 + ny_1}{m+n}$

The point *C* divides are *A*(5, 8) and *B*(*a*, *b*) in the ratio 2 : 5

$\therefore x = \dfrac{2(a) + 5(5)}{2+5} = \dfrac{2a + 25}{7}$, $y = \dfrac{2(b) + 5(8)}{2+5} = \dfrac{2b + 40}{7}$

But the coordinates of C are $\left(\frac{29}{7}, \frac{46}{7}\right)$

Therefore, $\frac{2a+25}{7} = \frac{29}{7} \Rightarrow 2a + 25 = 29 \Rightarrow a = 2$

and $\frac{2b+40}{7} = \frac{46}{7} \Rightarrow 2b + 40 = 46 \Rightarrow b = 3$

10. The coordinates of a point A, where AB is diameter of a circle whose centre is (2, –3) and B is (1, 4), are: ***(Re)***

(*a*) (3, 0) (*b*) (0, –10)

(*c*) (3, –10) (*d*) (3, 4)

Sol. Let the co-ordinates of point A is (x, y)

Now, AB is the diameter of circle. So, mid-point of AB is the center of the circle.

Given, center $O(2, -3)$ and B is (1,4).

So, by using mid-point formula, we get:

$\therefore (2,-3) = \left(\frac{x+1}{2}, \frac{y+4}{2}\right)$

$\Rightarrow \frac{x+1}{2} = 2$ and $\frac{y+4}{2} = -3$

$\Rightarrow x + 1 = 4$ and $y + 4 = -6$

$\Rightarrow x = 3$ and $y = -10$

Therefore, the coordinates of A are (3, –10).

11. If $P\left(\frac{a}{3}, 4\right)$ is the mid-point of the line segment joining the points $Q(-6, 5)$ and $R(-2, 3)$, then the value of a is ***(Ap)* (NCERT Exemplar)**

(*a*) –4 (*b*) –12 (*c*) 12 (*d*) –6

Sol. It is given that $\left(\frac{a}{3}, 4\right)$ is the mid – point of the line segment QR joining the points $Q(-6, 5)$ and $R(-2, 3)$.

The coordinates of the mid-point (x_m, y_m) between the two points (x_1, y_1) and (x_2, y_2) is given by

$$(x_m, y_m) = \left(\frac{x_1+x_2}{2}, \frac{y_1+y_2}{2}\right)$$

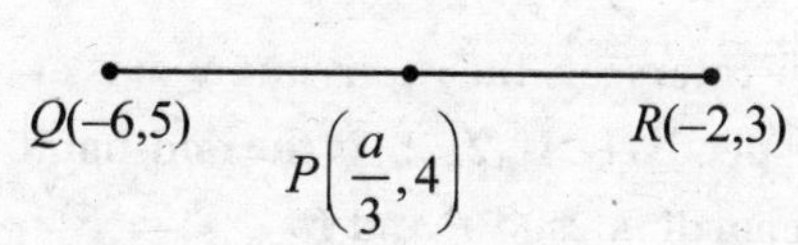

Hence, $\frac{-6-2}{2} = \frac{a}{3} \Rightarrow \frac{-8}{2} = \frac{a}{3} \Rightarrow -4 = \frac{a}{3} \Rightarrow a = -12$

Therefore, value of a is –12.

12. Three vertices of a parallelogram $ABCD$ are $A(1, 4)$, $B(-2, 3)$ and $C(5, 8)$. The ordinate of the fourth vertex D is ***(Cr)***

(*a*) 8 (*b*) 9 (*c*) 7 (*d*) 6

Sol. Let $A(1, 4)$, $B(-2, 3)$, $C(5, 8)$ and $D(a, b)$ are the vertices of a parallelogram.

Midpoint of diagonal $AC = \left(\frac{x_1+x_2}{2}, \frac{y_1+y_2}{2}\right)$

$= \left(\frac{1+5}{2}, \frac{4+8}{2}\right) = \left(\frac{6}{2}, \frac{12}{2}\right) = (3,6)$

Midpoint of diagonal BD

$= \left(\frac{x_1+x_2}{2}, \frac{y_1+y_2}{2}\right) = \left(\frac{-2+a}{2}, \frac{3+b}{2}\right)$

The diagonals of the parallelogram bisect each other. The diagonals share same mid-point.

$\therefore (3,6) = \left(\frac{-2+a}{2}, \frac{3+b}{2}\right)$

On comparing both sides, we get

$3 = \frac{-2+a}{2}$ and $6 = \frac{3+b}{2}$

In the question value of ordinate is asked,

$\Rightarrow 6 = \frac{3+b}{2}$

$\Rightarrow 12 = 3 + b$

$\Rightarrow b = 9$

13. If P(–1, 1) is the midpoint of the line segment joining $A(-3, b)$ and $B(1, b + 4)$, then b is equal to ***(Re)* (CBSE, 2022)**

(*a*) 1 (*b*) –1

(*c*) 2 (*d*) 0

Sol. The given parts are $A(-3, b)$ and $B(1, b + 4)$

$y = \frac{b+b+4}{2}$

$1 = \frac{2b+4}{2}$

$1 = b + 2$

$b = -1$

14. The line segment joining the points P(-3, 2) and Q(5, 7) is divided by the y-axis in the ratio ***(Un)***

(*a*) 3 : 1 (*b*) 3 : 4

(*c*) 3 : 2 (*d*) 3 : 5

Sol. Let the point on y-axis which divides the line PQ is $M(0, y)$ and the ratio be k : 1.

According to the section formula,

$$M(x, y) = \left(\frac{m_1x_2 + m_2x_1}{m_1 + m_2}, \frac{m_1y_2 + m_2y_1}{m_1 + m_2}\right)$$

$$M(0, y) = \left(\frac{5k + (-3)}{k+1}, \frac{k(7) + 1(2)}{k+1}\right)$$

On comparing, we get $0 = \dfrac{5k-3}{k+1}$

$\Rightarrow 5k - 3 = 0 \Rightarrow k = \dfrac{3}{5}$

Answer Key

1. (d) 2. (a) 3. (d) 4. (d) 5. (d)
6. (d) 7. (d) 8. (d) 9. (a) 10. (c)
11. (b) 12. (b) 13. (b) 14. (d)

Assertion and Reason (1 M)

Direction: **In the following questions, a statement of Assertion (A) is followed by a statement of Reason (R). Mark the correct choice as.**

(*a*) Both Assertion (A) and Reason (R) are true, and Reason (R) is the correct explanation of Assertion (A).

(*b*) Both Assertion (A) and Reason (R) are true, but Reason (R) is not the correct explanation of Assertion (A).

(*c*) Assertion (A) is true, but Reason (R) is false.

(*d*) Assertion (A) is false, but Reason (R) is true.

1. Assertion (A): **The co-ordinates of the point which divides the join of A(–5, 11) and B(4, –7) in the ratio 7 : 2 is (2, –3)**

Reason (R): **The coordinates of the point $P(x, y)$ which divides the line segment joining the points $A(x_1, y_1)$ and $B(x_2, y_2)$ in the ratio $m_1 : m_2$ is $\left(\dfrac{m_1x_2 + m_2x_1}{m_1 + m_2}, \dfrac{m_1y_2 + m_2y_1}{m_1 + m_2}\right)$** *(Re)*

Sol. We know that the coordinates of the point $P(x,y)$ which divides the line segment joining the points $A(x_1, y_1)$ and $B(x_2, y_2)$ in the ratio $m_1 : m_2$ is

$$\left(\frac{m_1x_2 + m_2x_1}{m_1 + m_2}, \frac{m_1y_2 + m_2y_1}{m_1 + m_2}\right)$$

So, Reason is correct.

Here, $x_1 = -5, y_1 = 11, x_2 = 4, y_2 = -7, m_1 = 7, m_2 = 2$

Now, x-coordinate $= \dfrac{m_1x_2 + m_2x_1}{m_1 + m_2}$

$$= \frac{(7\times4)+(2\times-5)}{7+2} = \frac{28-10}{9} = \frac{18}{9} = 2$$

and y-coordinate $= \dfrac{m_1y_2 + m_2y_1}{m_1 + m_2}$

$$= \frac{(7\times-7)+(2\times11)}{7+2} = \frac{-49+22}{9} = \frac{-27}{9} = -3$$

So, Assertion is also correct

Both Assertion (A) and Reason (R) are true, and Reason (R) is the correct explanation of Assertion (A).

Answer Key

1. (a)

Subjective Questions

Very Short Answer Type Questions (1 or 2 M)

1. Find the coordinates of a point A, where AB is diameter of a circle whose centre is (2, –3) and B is the point (1, 4). *(Un)*

Sol. Let the coordinates of $A(x, y)$.

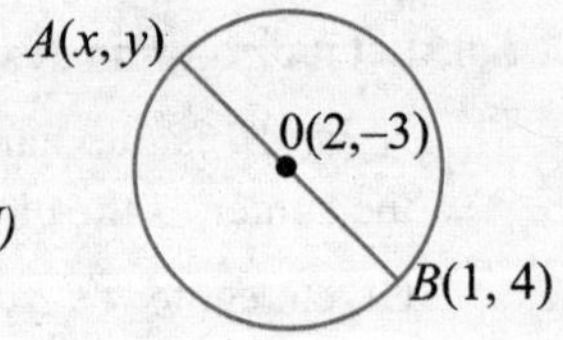

By mid point formula

$2 = \dfrac{x+1}{2}$ and $-3 = \dfrac{y+4}{2}$ *(1 M)*

$4 = x + 1$ and $-6 = y + 4$

$x = 3$ and $y = -10$

$\therefore A = (3, -10)$ *(1 M)*

2. If the point $R(-1, 2)$ divides the line segment joining $P(2, 5)$ and Q in ratio 3 : 4 internally, then find the coordinates of Q. *(Re)*

Sol. Let us suppose the coordinates of Q be (α, β).

As, $PR : RQ = 3 : 4$.

$R(x, y) = \left(\dfrac{mx_2 + nx_1}{m+n}, \dfrac{my_2 + ny_1}{m+n}\right)$ *(½ M)*

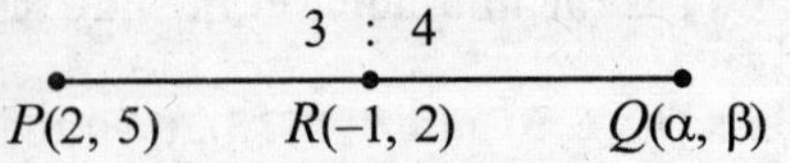

Therefore, the coordinates of R are:

Coordinates of $R = \left(\dfrac{3\alpha + 4\times2}{3+4}, \dfrac{3\beta + 4\times5}{3+4}\right)$

$= \left(\dfrac{3\alpha+8}{7}, \dfrac{3\beta+20}{7}\right)$ *(½ M)*

And, it is given that the coordinates of R are (–1, 2).

Therefore, $\dfrac{3\alpha+8}{7} = -1$ and $\dfrac{3\beta+20}{7} = 2$

$\Rightarrow \alpha = -5$ and $\beta = -2$

Hence, the coordinates of Q are (–5, –2). *(1 M)*

3. A line intersects the y-axis and x-axis at the points P and Q respectively. If (2, –5) is the mid-point of PQ, then find the coordinates of P and Q. *(Cr)*

Sol. Let $P(0, y)$ and $Q(x, 0)$, let $R = (2, -5)$ is the mid-point using mid point formula

$\dfrac{x+0}{2} = 2$ and $\dfrac{y+0}{2} = -5$ *(1 M)*

$x = 4$ and $y = -10$.

The required points are (4, 0) and (0, – 10). *(1 M)*

4 **Find the coordinates of the centre of the circle whose endpoints of a diameter are (0, 2), (3, 4).** *(Un)*

Sol. Given coordinates of endpoints of a diameter are:

$(0, 2) = (x_1, y_1)$

$(3, 4) = (x_2, y_2)$ *(½ M)*

Centre of the circle is the mid-point of diameter.

Coordinates of the centre of a circle

$$= \left(\frac{x_1+x_2}{2}, \frac{y_1+y_2}{2}\right)$$ *(½ M)*

$$= \left(\frac{0+3}{2}, \frac{2+4}{2}\right) = \left(\frac{3}{2}, \frac{6}{2}\right) = \left(\frac{3}{2}, 3\right)$$ *(1 M)*

Short Answer Type Questions (2 or 3 M)

1. **If (1, 0) is the midpoint of the line joining the points $A(-6, -5)$ and B, then find the coordinates of B.** *(Re)*

Sol. Given,

(1, 0) is the midpoint of A and B.

$A = (-6, -5) = (x_1, y_1)$ *(½ M)*

Let the coordinates of B are (a, b).

$(a,b) = (x_2, y_2)$

Using the midpoint formula,

$(x, y) = [(x_1 + x_2)/2, (y_1 + y_2)/2]$ *(1 M)*

$\Rightarrow (1,0) = [(a - 6)/2, (b - 5)/2]$

Now equating the x and y coordinates,

$$\Rightarrow \frac{a-6}{2} = 1 \text{ and } \frac{b-5}{2} = 0$$ *(½ M)*

$\Rightarrow a - 6 = 2$ and $b - 5 = 0$

$\Rightarrow a = 8$ and $b = 5$

Therefore, the coordinates of $B = (8, 5)$. *(1 M)*

Mistakes 101 : What not to do!

Students may overlook the midpoint formula, $(x_1 + x_2)/2$, $(y_1 + y_2)/2$, when trying to find the midpoint of a line segment, resulting in errors in determining the coordinates of the midpoint.

2. **Find the ratio in which $P(4, m)$ divides the line segment joining the points $A(2, 3)$ and $B(6, -3)$. Hence find m.** *(Cr)*

Sol. Let the ratio in which the point (4,1) divider the line segment Joining the points $A(2,3)$ and $B(6,-3)$. be $k : 1$

A(2,3) P(4,m) B(6,–3) *(½ M)*

$$\therefore 4 = \frac{k(6)+1(2)}{k+1}$$ *(½ M)*

$\Rightarrow 4k + 4 = 6k + 2$

$\Rightarrow 2 = 2k \Rightarrow k = 1$ *(½ M)*

$\therefore P$ divides the line segment in 1 : 1 ratio. *(½ M)*

Now put the value of k in y.

$$m = \frac{-3(1)+3(1)}{1+1} = \frac{-3+3}{2} = 0$$ *(1 M)*

3. **In Fig., arrangement of desks in a classroom is shown. Ashima, Bharti and Asha are seated at A, B and C respectively. Answer the following:**

(i) Find whether the girls are sitting in a line.

(ii) If A, B and C are collinear, find the ratio in which point B divides the line segment joining A and C.

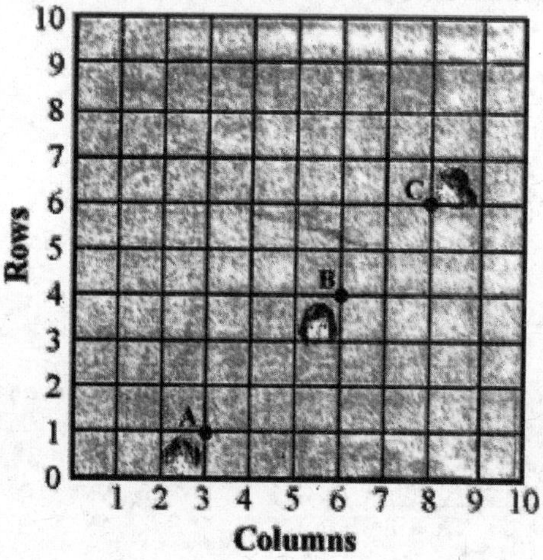

(Un) (CBSE, 2020)

Sol. (*i*) Using distance formula, we have

$$AB = \sqrt{(6-3)^2+(4-1)^2} = \sqrt{(3)^2+(3)^2}$$
$$= \sqrt{9+9} = \sqrt{18} = 3\sqrt{2} \text{ units}$$

$$BC = \sqrt{(8-6)^2+(6-4)^2} = \sqrt{(2)^2+(2)^2}$$
$$= \sqrt{4+4} = \sqrt{8} = 2\sqrt{2} \text{ units}$$ *(1 M)*

$$AC = \sqrt{(8-3)^2+(6-1)^2} = \sqrt{(5)^2+(5)^2}$$
$$= \sqrt{25+25} = \sqrt{50} = 5\sqrt{2} \text{ units}$$

$$\because AB + BC = 3\sqrt{2} + 2\sqrt{2} = 5\sqrt{2} = AC$$

$\therefore A$, B and C are collinear.

Thus, Ashima, Bharti and Camella are seated in a line *(1 M)*

(ii) Let $AB : BC = k : 1$

Using section formula, we get

$$6 = \frac{8k+3}{k+1}$$

$$k = \frac{3}{2} \text{ or Ratio} = 3 : 2$$ *(1 M)*

So, the point $\left(\frac{24}{11}, y\right)$ divides the line segment joining the points $P(2, -2)$ and $Q(3, 7)$ in the ratio 2 : 9.

$$y = \frac{7k-2}{k+1} \Rightarrow y = \frac{\frac{14}{9}-2}{\frac{2}{9}+1} \Rightarrow y = -\frac{4}{11} \quad \text{(1 M)}$$

4. Find the ratio in which the segment joining the points (1, 3) and (4, 5) is divided by *x* axis? Also find the coordinates of this point on *x*-axis. *(Ap)*

Sol. Let the point P is divide on the x-axis and its coordinates be $P(x, 0)$.

Let the ratio in which point *P* divider the line segment joining the points (1, –3) and (4, 5) be $k : 1$.

By section formula are have.

$$(x, 0) = \left(\frac{4k+1}{k+1}, \frac{5k-3}{k+1}\right) \quad \text{(1 M)}$$

Comparing the *y* coordinates from the above equations we get

$$\frac{5k-3}{k+1} = 0 \Rightarrow k = \frac{3}{5} \quad \text{(1 M)}$$

Now putting the value of k in *x* coordinate, we get

$$x = \frac{4\times\frac{3}{5}+1}{\frac{3}{5}+1} = \frac{17}{8}$$

5. On a golf course, three holes *A*(–6, –1), *B* and *C*(9, –4) lie on a straight line in that order. The distance between *B* and *C* is two times that between *B* and *A*.

Rahul strikes the ball, which is at point *P*(2, 3), such that it goes in the hole *B*.

(*i*) Find the coordinates of hole *B*.

(*ii*) Find the shortest distance covered by the ball.

Show your steps. *(Ap)* **(CBSE CFPQ, 2023)**

Sol. (*i*) Write that points *B* internally divides the line joining A and *C* in the ratio 1:2. (½ M)

Use the section formula to find the coordinates of hole *B* as:

$$\left(\frac{2(-6)+1(9)}{1+2}, \frac{2(-1)+1(-4)}{1+2}\right) \quad \text{(1 M)}$$

Evaluate the above expressions to find the coordinates of hole *B* as (–1,–2). (½ M)

(*ii*) The shortest distance covered by the ball as

$$\sqrt{\left[(2-(-1))^2+(3-(-2))^2\right]} = \sqrt{34} \text{ units} \quad \text{(1 M)}$$

Long Answer Type Questions (4 or 5 M)

1. If the point *C*(–1, 2) divides internally the line segment joining *A*(2, 5) and *B*(*x*,*y*) in the ratio 3 : 4, find the coordinates of *B*. *(Ap)*

Sol. Let the coordinates of *B* be (*x*, *y*). It is given that *AC* : *BC* = 3 : 4.

So, the coordinates of *C* are (1 M)

$$\left(\frac{3x+4\times 2}{3+4}, \frac{3y+4\times 5}{3+4}\right) = \left(\frac{3x+8}{7}, \frac{3y+20}{7}\right)$$

But, the coordinates of *C* are (–1, 2) (1 M)

$$\frac{3x+8}{7} = -1 \text{ and } \frac{3y+20}{7} = 2$$

$x = -5$ and $y = -2$ (1 M)

Thus, the coordinates of *B* are (–5, –2). (1 M)

2. Find the coordinates of the points of trisection of the line segment joining the points (8, 0) and (–6, 12). *(Un)*

Sol. Let *A*(8, 0) and *B*(–6, 12) be the given points.

Let the points of trisection be *P* and *Q* such that $AP = PQ = QB$. (1 M)

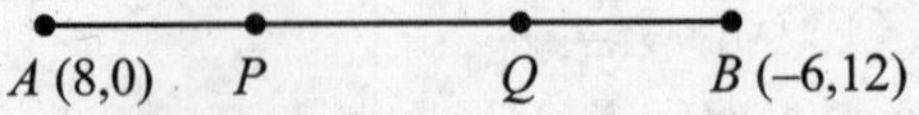

For point *P*:

$m_1 : m_2 = AP : PB = 1 : 2, (x_1, y_1) = (8,0)$ and $(x_2, y_2) = (-6,12)$. (½ M)

$$\therefore x = \frac{m_1x_2+m_2x_1}{m_1+m_2} = \frac{(1)(-6)+(2)(8)}{1+2} = \frac{-6+16}{3} = \frac{10}{3}$$

$$\therefore y = \frac{m_1y_2+m_2y_1}{m_1+m_2} = \frac{(1)(12)+2(0)}{1+2} = \frac{12+0}{3} = 4 \quad \text{(1 M)}$$

$$\therefore \text{Point } P = \left(\frac{10}{3}, 4\right) \quad \text{(½ M)}$$

For point *Q*:

$m_1 : m_2 = AQ : QB = 2 : 1, (x_1, y_1) = (8,0)$ and $(x_2, x_2) = (-6,12)$. (½ M)

$$\therefore x = \frac{m_1x_2+m_2x_1}{m_1+m_2} = \frac{(2)(-6)+(1)(8)}{2+1} = \frac{-12+8}{3} = \frac{-4}{3}$$

$$\therefore y = \frac{m_1y_2+m_2y_1}{m_1+m_2} = \frac{(2)(12)+(1)(0)}{1+2} = \frac{24+0}{3} = 8 \quad \text{(½ M)}$$

$$\therefore \text{Point } Q = \left(\frac{-4}{3}, 8\right) \quad \text{(1 M)}$$

Nailing the Right Answer

Utilize properties of coordinate geometry, such as the midpoint formula or properties of parallel and perpendicular lines, to derive or simplify calculations involving the section formula.

MISCELLANEOUS EXERCISE

Multiple Choice Questions (1 M)

1. The distance of the point (–4, 3) from y-axis is:

   (*a*) –4 (*b*) 4

   (*c*) 3 (*d*) 5

2. The line segment joining the points (3, –1) and (–6, 5) is trisected. The coordinates of point of trisection are

   (*a*) (3, 3) (*b*) (–3, 3)

   (*c*) (3, –3) (*d*) (–3, –3)

3. The line $3x + y - 9 = 0$ divides the line joining the points (1, 3) and (2, 7) internally in the ratio

   (*a*) 3 : 4 (*b*) 3 : 2

   (*c*) 2 : 3 (*d*) 4 : 3

4. If (a/3, 4) is the mid-point of the segment joining the points P(–6, 5) and R(–2, 3), then the value of 'a' is

   (*a*) 12 (*b*) –6

   (*c*) –12 (*d*) –4

5. If the point $C(k,4)$ divides the join of the points A(2,6) and B(5,1) in the ratio 2 : 3 then the value of k is

   (*a*) 16 (*b*) 28 / 5

   (*c*) 16 / 5 (*d*) 8 / 5

6. If the coordinates of one end of a diameter of a circle are (2,3) and the coordinates of its centre are (–2,5), then the coordinates of the other end of the diameter are

   (*a*) (–6,7) (*b*) (6,–7)

   (*c*) (4,2) (*d*) (5,3)

7. A relation between x and y such that the point (x,y) is equidistant from the point (1,5) and (–2,3) is

   (*a*) $2x + 4y = 13$ (*b*) $x + 2y = 14$

   (*c*) $x + y = 7$ (*d*) $x - 2y = 7$

8. The coordinates of mid-point P which divides the line joining the points $A(a + 2, b - 2)$ and $B(-a -2, b - 2)$ is

   (*a*) $(a, b - 2)$ (*b*) (0, –2)

   (*c*) $(0, b)$ (*d*) $(0, b -2)$

Assertion and Reason (1 M)

Direction: In the following questions, a statement of Assertion (A) is followed by a statement of Reason (R). Mark the correct choice as.

(*a*) Both Assertion (A) and Reason (R) are true, and Reason (R) is the correct explanation of Assertion (A).

(*b*) Both Assertion (A) and Reason (R) are true, but Reason (R) is not the correct explanation of Assertion (A).

(*c*) Assertion (A) is true, but Reason (R) is false.

(*d*) Assertion (A) is false, but Reason (R) is true.

1. **Assertion (A):** The point (0, 4) lies on y-axis.

   Reason (R): The x coordinate of the point on y-axis is zero

   (CBSE SQP, 2023)

2. **Assertion (A):** The point M(–1, 6) divides the line segment joining the points A(–3, 10) and B(6, –8) in the ratio 2 : 7 internally.

   Reason (R): Three points P, Q and R are collinear if area of $\Delta PQR = 0$.

Subjective Questions

Very Short Answer Type Questions (1 or 2 M)

1. Find the coordinates of the point which divides the line segment joining (–1, 3) and (4, –7) internally in the ratio 3 : 4.

2. If P(–2, 4), Q(0, 0) and R(4, 2) are the vertices of a ΔPQR, then find the length of median through the vertex P.

3. On the Cartesian plane, Q is the midpoint of the line segment PR. Find the value of x,y.

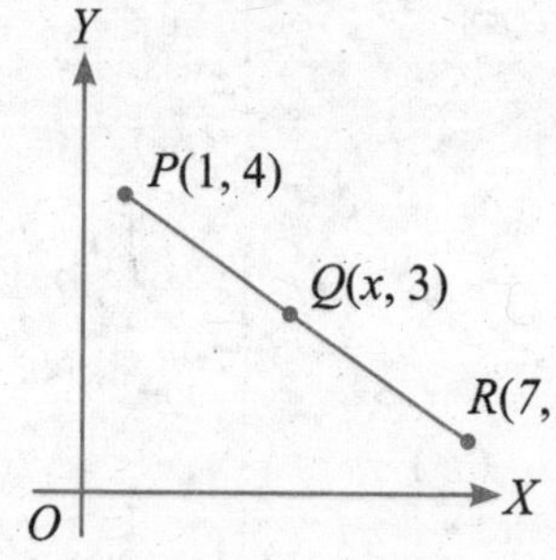

4. Find the distance of the point Z(–2.4, –1) from the origin.

Short Answer Type Questions (2 or 3 M)

1. Determine the ratio in which the line segment joining the points (1, –7) and (6, 4) is divided by x-axis.
2. Find the co-ordinates of the points which divide the line segment joining $P(-2, 2)$ and $Q(2, 8)$ into four equal parts.
3. If the line segment joining (2,3) and (–1,2) is divided internally in the ratio 3 : 4 by the line $x + 2y = k$, then find the value of k.
4. The mid-point of the line segment joining $(2a, 4)$ and $(-2, 2b)$ is $(1, 2a + 1)$. Find the value of a and b.

Long Answer Type Questions (4 or 5 M)

1. Coordinates of P and Q are (4, –3) and (–1,7) respectively. Find the abscissa of a point R on the line segment PQ such that $\frac{PR}{PQ} = \frac{3}{5}$
2. Preeti and Arun are both driving to their respective offices from the same home. Preeti drives towards the east at an average speed of 30 km per hour for 12 minutes and then towards the south at an average speed of 60 km per hour for 3 minutes. Arun drives towards the west at an average speed of 30 km per hour for 4 minutes and then towards the north at an average speed of 45 km per hour for 4 minutes.

   What is the straight-line distance between Preeti's office and Arun's office? Show your steps and represent the given scenario on the coordinate plane. **(CBSE CFPQ, 2023)**
3. Find the ratio in which the line $x - 3y = 0$ divides the line segment joining the points (–2, –5) and (6, 3). Find the coordinates of the point of intersection.

Case Based Questions

Case Based-I: Tharunya was thrilled to know that the football tournament is fixed with a monthly timeframe from 20th July to 20th August 2023 and for the first time in the FIFA Women's World Cup's history, two nations host in 10 venues. Her father felt that the game can be better understood if the position of players is represented as points on a coordinate plane.

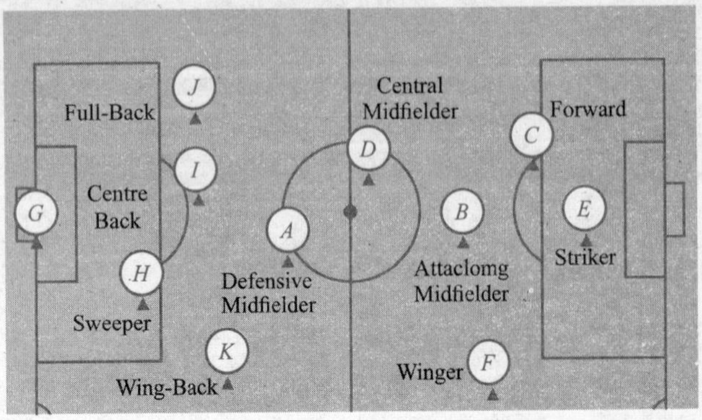

(CBSE SQP, 2023)

(*i*) At an instance, the midfielders and forward formed a parallelogram. Find the position of the central midfielder (D) if the position of other players who formed the parallelogram are :- $A(1,2)$, $B(4,3)$ and $C(6,6)$

(*ii*) Check if the Goal keeper $G(-3,5)$, Sweeper $H(3,1)$ and Wing-back $K(0,3)$ fall on a same straight line.

OR

Check if the Full-back $J(5, -3)$ and centre-back $I(-4,6)$ are equidistant from forward $C(0,1)$ and if C is the mid-point of IJ.

(*iii*) If Defensive midfielder $A(1,4)$, Attacking midfielder $B(2,-3)$ and Striker $E(a, b)$ lie on the same straight line and B is equidistant from A and E, find the position of E.

Case Based-II: Mehek and Neha are friends living on the same street in Kota. Neha's house is at the intersection of one street with another street on which there is a PW Vidyapeeth. They both study in the same PW Library and that is not far from Neha's house. Suppose the library is situated at the point O, i.e., the origin, Mehek's house is at A. Neha's house is at B and PW Vidyapeeth is at C. **(CBSE SQP, 2023)**

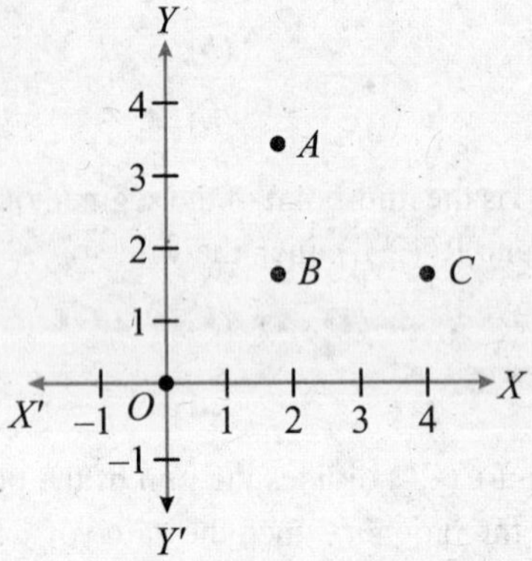

Based on the above information, answer the following questions.

(*i*) How far is Mehek's house from Neha's house?
(*a*) 3 units (*b*) 4 units
(*c*) 5 units (*d*) 2 units

(*ii*) How far is the PW Vidyapeeth from Neha's house?
(*a*) 3 units (*b*) 2 units
(*c*) 5 units (*d*) 4 units

(*iii*) How far is the PW Vidyapeeth from Mehek's house?
(*a*) 2 units (*b*) 3 units
(*c*) 4 units (*d*) None of these

(*iv*) How far is the PW Library from Mehek's house than Neha's house?
(*a*) $\sqrt{13}$ units (*b*) $\sqrt{2}$ units
(*c*) $\sqrt{13}+\sqrt{5}$ units (*d*) $\sqrt{13}-\sqrt{5}$ units

Case Based-III: Answer the questions based on the information given.

Show below is a map of Giri's neighbourhood.

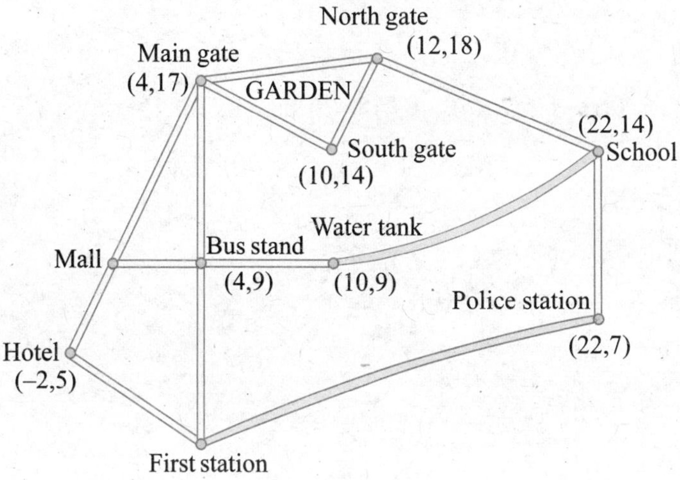

(CBSE CFPQ, 2023)

Giri did a survey of his neighbourhood and collected the following information.

* The hotel, mall and the main gate of the garden lie in a straight line.
* The distance between the hotel and the mall is half the distance between the mall and the main gate of the garden.
* The bus stand is exactly midway between the main gate of the garden and the fire station.
* The mall, bus stand and the water tank lie in a straight line.

(i) What is the x-coordinate of the mall's location?

(*a*) –8 (*b*) 0

(*c*) 1 (*d*) 2

(ii) What are the coordinates of the fire station?

(*a*) (0, 8) (*b*) (4, –17)

(*c*) (4, 1) (*d*) (4, 13)

(iii) What is the shortest distance between the water tank and the school?

(*a*) $\sqrt{13}$ units (*b*) $\sqrt{65}$ units

(*c*) 13 units (*d*) 169 units

(iv) How much more is the shortest distance of the school from the water tank then the distance of the school from the police station?

(*a*) 6 units (*b*) 7 units

(*c*) 13 units (*d*) 20 units

Case Based-IV: Anjali starts walking from her house to office. Instead of going to the office directly, she goes to a bank first, from there to her daughter's school and then reaches the office. (Assume that all distance covered are in straight lines). If the house is situated at (2, 4), bank at (5, 8), school at (13, 14) and office at (13, 26) and coordinates are in km.

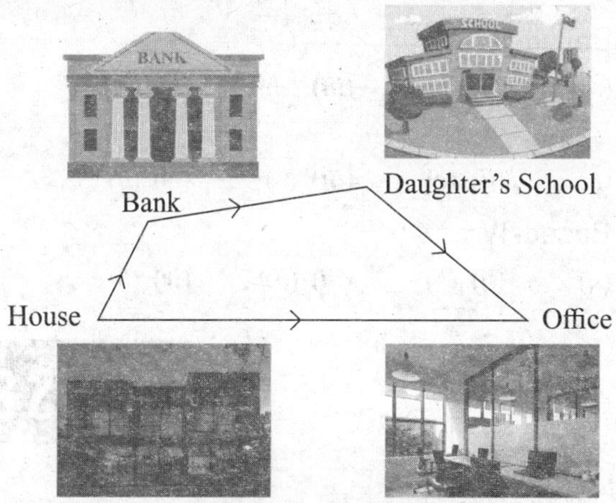

(i) The distance between house and bank is

(*a*) 5 (*b*) 10

(*c*) 15 (*d*) 23

(ii) The distance between Daughter's school and bank is

(*a*) 5 (*b*) 10

(*c*) 15 (*d*) 27

(iii) The distance between house and office is

(*a*) 28.4 (*b*) 24.6

(*c*) 24 (*d*) 26

(iv) The distance between Daughter's school and office is

(*a*) 21 (*b*) 22

(*c*) 23 (*d*) 24

ANSWER KEYS

Multiple Choice Questions

1. (*b*) **2.** (*b*) **3.** (*a*) **4.** (*c*) **5.** (*c*) **6.** (*a*) **7.** (*a*) **8.** (*d*)

Assertion and Reason

1. (*a*) **2.** (*b*)

Case Based Questions

Case Based-II

(*i*) (*d*) (*ii*) (*b*) (*iii*) (*d*) (*iv*) (*d*)

Case Based-III

(*i*) (*b*) (*ii*) (*c*) (*iii*) (*c*) (*iv*) (*a*)

Case Based-IV

(*i*) (*a*) (*ii*) (*b*) (*iii*) (*b*) (*iv*) (*b*)

HINTS & EXPLANATIONS

Multiple Choice Questions

1. (*b*) The distance of the point (x, y) from y-axis is its x-coordinate.

Hence, the distance of the point $(-4, 3)$ from y-axis is 4 units.

2. (*b*) Let the line segment PQ is trisected at A and D.

A divide the line PQ in 1 : 2 and B divide the line PQ in 2 : 1

Coordinates of A are $= \left(\frac{1(-6)+2(3)}{1+2}, \frac{1(5)+2(-1)}{1+2}\right)$

$= \left(\frac{-6+6}{3}, \frac{5-2}{3}\right) = (0,1)$

Coordinates of B are $= \left(\frac{2(-6)+1(3)}{2+1}, \frac{2(5)+1(-1)}{2+1}\right)$

$= \left(\frac{-12+3}{3}, \frac{10-1}{3}\right) = (-3,3)$

3. (*a*) Let the line $3x + y - 9 = 0$ divide the line segment joining $A(1, 3)$ ad $B(2, 7)$ in the ratio $K : 1$ at point C.

The coordinates of C are $\left(\frac{2K+1}{K+1}, \frac{7K+3}{K+1}\right)$

But the point C lies on the line $3x + y - 9 = 0$

$\therefore 3\left(\frac{2K+1}{K+1}\right) + \frac{7K+3}{K+1} - 9 = 0$

$\Rightarrow 6K + 3 + 7K + 3 - 9 - 9K = 0$

$\Rightarrow 4K - 3 = 0$

$\Rightarrow K = \frac{3}{4}$ $\therefore$ Required ratio $= 3:4$

4. (*c*) The mid-point

$= \left(\frac{-6-2}{2}, \frac{5+3}{2}\right)$

$\Rightarrow \left(\frac{a}{3}, 4\right) = (-4, 4)$

$\therefore \frac{a}{3} = -4 \Rightarrow a = -12$

5. (*c*) If $P(x,y)$ is the dividing point of the line joining AB then by section formula we have,

$x = \frac{m_1x_2 + m_2x_1}{m_1 + m_2}$ and $y = \frac{m_1y_2 + m_2y_1}{m_1 + m_2}$

$\Rightarrow \frac{2\times5+3\times2}{2+3} = k$

$\Rightarrow k = \frac{16}{5}$

6. (*a*) Let the diameter be AB whose Coordinates of centre and $B(-2,5)$ and $(2,3)$ respectively. let the coordinates of A be (x,y)

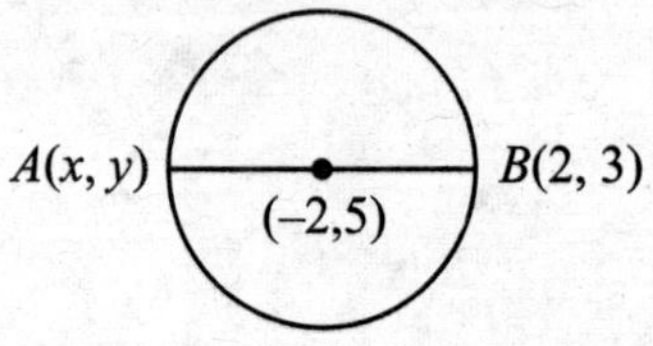

By Mid-point formula, we have

$$(-2,5) = \left(\frac{x+2}{2}, \frac{y+3}{2}\right)$$

$$\Rightarrow -2 = \frac{x+2}{2} \text{ and } 5 = \frac{y+3}{2}$$

$x = -6$ and $y = 7$.

$\therefore$ The coordinates of A is $(-6,7)$

7. (*a*) By distance formula

$$\sqrt{(x-1)^2+(y-5)^2} = \sqrt{(x+2)^2+(y-3)^2}$$

$$(x-1)^2 + (y-5)^2 = (x+2)^2 + (y-3)^2$$

$$x^2 - 2x + 1 + y^2 - 10y + 25 = x^2 + 4x + 4 + y^2 - 6y + 9$$

$$\therefore 2x + 4y = 13$$

8. (*d*) Mid-point of $AB = ((x_1 + x_2)/2, (y_1 + y_2)/2)$

$= ((a + 2 - a - 2)/2, (b - 2 + b - 2)/2)$

$= (0/2, (26 - 4)/2)$

$= (0, b - 2)$

Assertion and Reason

1. (*a*) The point (0, 4) lies on the Cartesian plane, where the horizontal line is the x-axis and the vertical line is the y-axis.

The x-coordinate represents the horizontal position of a point, and the y-coordinate represents the vertical position of a point.

The point (0, 4) has an x-coordinate of zero, which means that it lies on the y-axis, which is a vertical line passing through the origin (0, 0).

Therefore, the Assertion is true.

The Reason is also true because the x-coordinate of any point on the y-axis is always zero.

Moreover, the Reason correctly explains why the Assertion is true.

Hence, both A and R are true, and R is the correct explanation of A.

2. (*b*) Both assertion (A) and reason (R) are true but reason (R) is not the correct explanation of assertion (A).

As, point M divides the line segment AB in the ratio 2 : 7 internally, hence by using section formula, we get

$$-1 = \frac{k \times 6 + 1 \times (-3)}{k+1}$$

$$-1(k+1) = k \times 6 + 1 \times (-3)$$

$$-k - 1 = 6k - 3$$

$$7k = 2$$

$$\Rightarrow k = \frac{2}{7}$$

$\therefore$ Ratio is 2 : 7 internally.

Also, if ar $(\Delta PQR) = 0$, then P, Q, and R are collinear.

Subjective Questions

Very Short Answer Type Questions

1. We have $A(-1, 3)$ and $B(4, -7)$. Let a point $P(x, y)$ divide the line segment joining the point A and B in the ratio 3 : 4 internally.

Now according to the section formula, if a point P divides a line segment joining $A(x_1, y_1)$ and $B(x_2, y_2)$ in the ratio $m : n$ internally, then

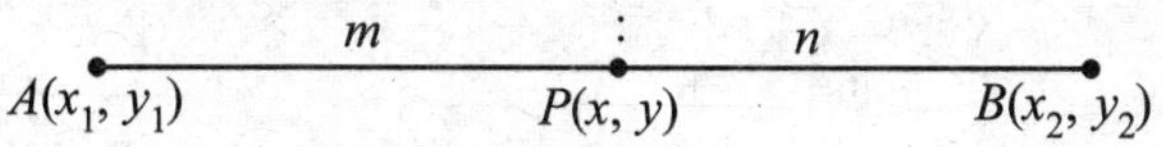

$$P(x, y) = \left(\frac{nx_1 + mx_2}{m+n}, \frac{ny_1 + my_2}{m+n}\right) \quad (½\ M)$$

$$P(x, y) = \left(\frac{4(-1)+3(4)}{3+4}, \frac{4(3)+3(-7)}{3+4}\right) = \left(\frac{8}{7}, -\frac{9}{7}\right) \quad (½\ M)$$

Therefore, co-ordinates of point P is $\left(\frac{8}{7}, -\frac{9}{7}\right)$. *(1 M)*

2. Let 'D' be the mid-point of the side 'QR'.

$$(x_m, y_m) = \left(\frac{x_1 + x_2}{2}, \frac{y_1 + y_2}{2}\right)$$

Let us now find its co-ordinates.

$$(x_D, y_D) = \left(\frac{0+4}{2}, \frac{0+2}{2}\right)$$

$$(x_D, y_D) = (2, 1) \quad (1\ M)$$

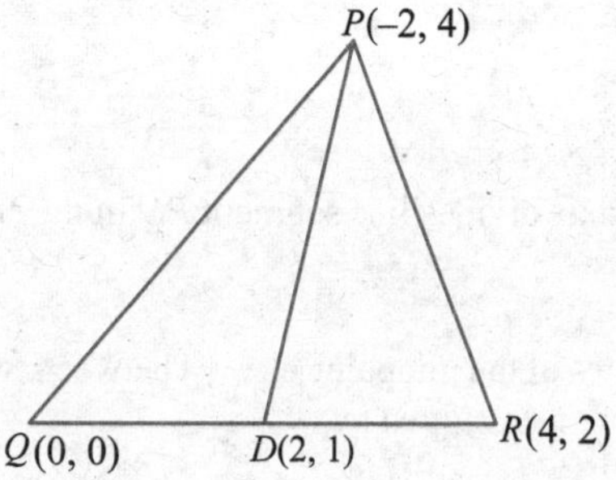

(½ M)

Therefore,

$$PD = \sqrt{(2+2)^2 + (1-4)^2} \quad (½\ M)$$

$$= \sqrt{4^2 + (-3)^2} = \sqrt{16+9} = \sqrt{25} = 5 \text{ units}$$

Hence, length of median PD is 5 units. *(1 M)*

3. Since, $Q(x, 3)$ is the midpoint of $P(1, 4)$ and $R(7, y)$

$$\therefore (x, 3) = \left(\frac{1+7}{2}, \frac{4+y}{2}\right) \quad (1\ M)$$

$$\Rightarrow x = \frac{8}{2} \text{ and } 3 = \frac{4+y}{2}$$

$\Rightarrow x = 4$ and $6 = 4 + y$

$\Rightarrow y = 6 - 4 = 2$

Hence, $x = 4$ and $y = 2$ *(1 M)*

4. Given that:s

The coordinates of a point Z are $(-2.4, -1)$.

To find out:

The distance OZ, when O is the origin.

We know that the distance of a point $Z(x,y)$ from the origin O is $d = \sqrt{x^2 + y^2}$ *(½ M)*

$\therefore OZ = \sqrt{(-2.4)^2 + (-1)^2}$

$= \sqrt{5.76 + 1}$ *(½ M)*

$= \sqrt{6.76}$

$= 2.6$ units

Hence, the distance of the point $Z(-2.4, -1)$ from the origin is 2.6 units. *(1 M)*

Short Answer Type Questions

1. According to the section formula, if a point C divides a line segment joining $A(x_1, y_1)$ and $B(x_2, y_2)$ in the ratio $k : 1$ internally, then

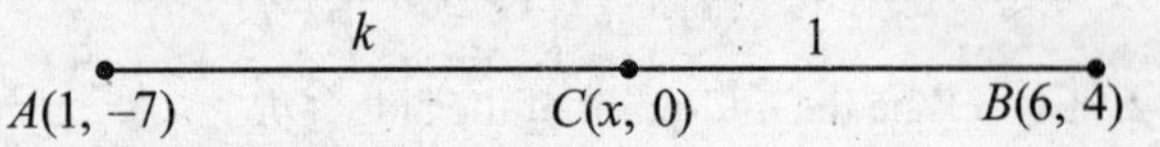

$C(x, 0) = C\left(\dfrac{6k+1}{k+1}, \dfrac{4k-7}{k+1}\right)$ *(1 M)*

By equating the y-coordinates of both the sides of the equation, we get

$\Rightarrow \dfrac{4k-7}{k+1} = 0$ *(1 M)*

$\Rightarrow 4k - 7 = 0$

$\Rightarrow 4k = 7 \Rightarrow k = \dfrac{7}{4}$

Hence, the x-axis divides line segment PQ in the ratio 7 : 4. *(1 M)*

2. The coordinates of the midpoint (x_m, y_m) between two points (x_1, y_1) and (x_2, y_2) is given by,

$(x_m, y_m) = \left(\dfrac{x_1 + x_2}{2}, \dfrac{y_1 + y_2}{2}\right)$ *(½ M)*

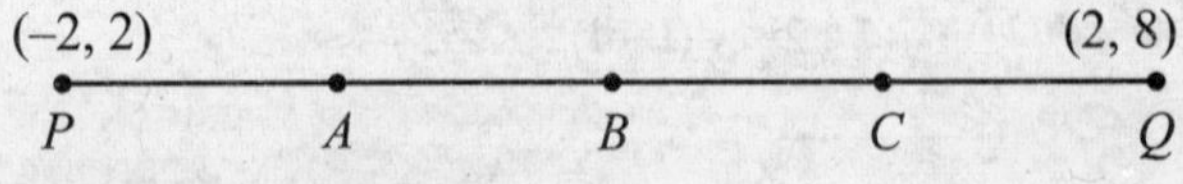

As, it is given that PQ is divided into four equal parts: therefore, $PA = AB = BC = CQ$

As, B is the mid-point of PQ.

$\therefore$ Co-ordinates of B are:

$\left(\dfrac{-2+2}{2}, \dfrac{2+8}{2}\right) = \left(\dfrac{0}{2}, \dfrac{10}{2}\right) = (0, 5)$ *(½ M)*

Now, A is the mid-point of PB

$\therefore$ Co-ordinates of A are:

$\left(\dfrac{-2+0}{2}, \dfrac{2+5}{2}\right) = \left(\dfrac{-2}{2}, \dfrac{7}{2}\right) = \left(-1, \dfrac{7}{2}\right)$ *(½ M)*

And C is the mid-point of BQ.

$\therefore$ Co-ordinates of C are:

$\left(\dfrac{0+2}{2}, \dfrac{5+8}{2}\right) = \left(\dfrac{2}{2}, \dfrac{13}{2}\right) = \left(1, \dfrac{13}{2}\right)$ *(½ M)*

Therefore, required co-ordinates of the points are:

$A\left(-1, \dfrac{7}{2}\right)$, $B(0, 5)$ and $C\left(1, \dfrac{13}{2}\right)$. *(1 M)*

3. If the line segment joining (x_1, y_1) and (x_2, y_2) is divide by internally in the ratio $m_1 : m_2$ then the intersection point is

$x = \dfrac{m_1x_2 + m_2x_1}{m_1 + m_2}$ and $y = \dfrac{m_1y_2 + m_2y_1}{m_1 + m_2}$ *(½ M)*

so,

$x = \dfrac{3 \times (-1) + 4 \times 2}{3+4} = \dfrac{5}{7}$ *(½ M)*

$y = \dfrac{3 \times (2) + 4 \times 3}{3+4} = \dfrac{18}{7}$ *(½ M)*

the obtained point $\left(\dfrac{5}{7}, \dfrac{18}{7}\right)$ lies on given equation of line.

so, this point must be satisfying the equation

$\therefore \dfrac{5}{7} + 2 \times \dfrac{18}{7} = k$ *(½ M)*

$\Rightarrow k = \dfrac{41}{7}$ *(1 M)*

4. Midpoint of two points $= \left(\dfrac{x_1 + x_2}{2}, \dfrac{y_1 + y_2}{2}\right)$ *(½ M)*

Given, midpoint of $(2a, 4)$ and $(-2, 2b) = (1, 2a + 1)$

$\Rightarrow \left(\dfrac{2a-2}{2}, \dfrac{4+2b}{2}\right) = (1, 2a+1)$ *(½ M)*

$\Rightarrow \dfrac{2a-2}{2} = 1; \dfrac{4+2b}{2} = 2a+1$

$\Rightarrow 2a - 2 = 2 \Rightarrow a = 2$ *(½ M)*

And, $\dfrac{4+2b}{2} = 2a+1$ *(½ M)*

$\Rightarrow \dfrac{4+2b}{2} = 2(2)+1 = 5$

$\Rightarrow 4 + 2b = 10$

$\Rightarrow 2b = 6 \Rightarrow b = 3$ *(½ M)*

$\therefore a = 2$ and $b = 3$ *(½ M)*

Long Answer Type Questions

1. Given $\dfrac{PR}{PQ} = \dfrac{3}{5}$

$\Rightarrow \dfrac{PQ}{PR} = \dfrac{5}{3}$ ...(*i*)

Here $PQ = PR + QR$ *(1 M)*

Substituting the value of PQ in (i) and subtracting 1 from both sides

$$\frac{PR+QR}{PR}-1=\frac{5}{3}-1 \quad (1\ M)$$

$$\therefore \frac{QR}{PR}=\frac{2}{3} \Rightarrow \frac{PR}{QR}=\frac{3}{2} \quad (½\ M)$$

So the ratio at which R divides PQ is 3 : 2

We know that if a point R(x,y) divides the line segment PQ joining the points $P(x_1, y_1)$ and $Q(x_2, y_2)$ in the ratio $m : n$ then by the section formula.

$$x=\frac{mx_2+nx_1}{m+n} \ \& \ y=\frac{my_2+ny_1}{m+n} \quad (1\ M)$$

As we are given the coordinates of P and Q

$$x=\frac{3\times(-1)+2\times 4}{3+2}, y=\frac{3\times 7+2\times(-3)}{3+2} \quad (½\ M)$$

$$\therefore x=1, y=3$$

So the abscissa of point R is 1 (1 M)

2. The distance travelled by Preeti towards the east as $\frac{30\times 12}{60}=6$ km. (½ M)

The distance travelled by Preeti towards the south as $\frac{60\times 3}{60}=3$ km. (½ M)

The distance travelled by Arun towards the west as $\frac{30\times 4}{60}=2$ (½ M)

The distance travelled by Arun towards the north as $\frac{45\times 4}{60}=3$ km. (½ M)

Represent the above scenario on a coordinate plane. The figure may look as follows:

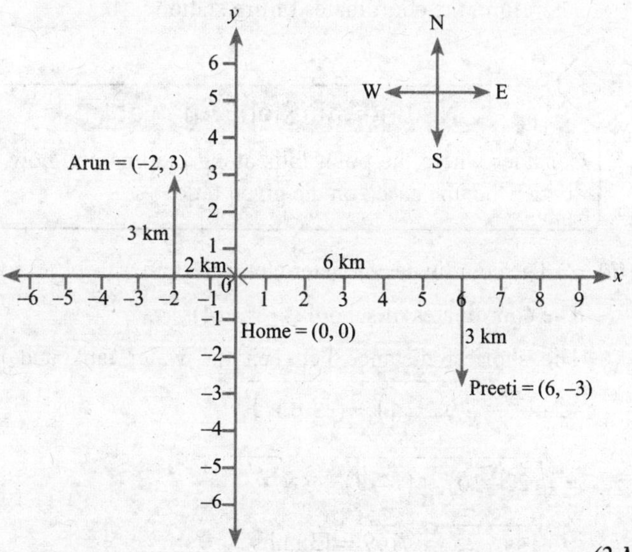

(2 M)

Coordinates of Preeti's office as (6, –3) and the coordinates of Arun's office as (–2, 3).

$\because$ distance between (x_1, y_1) and (x_2, y_2)

$$=\sqrt{(x_1-x_2)^2+(y_1-y_2)^2} \quad (½\ M)$$

$\therefore$ Distance between the two offices

$$=\sqrt{\{(6+2)^2+(-3-3)^2\}}=10\text{km} \quad (½\ M)$$

3. Let the given points be:

$A(-2, -5) = (x_1, y_1) \Rightarrow x_1 = -2, y_1 = -5$

$B(6, 3) = (x_2, y_2) \Rightarrow x_2 = 6, y_2 = 3$ (½ M)

Let the line $x - 3y = 0$ divides the line segment joining the points A and B in the ratio $k : 1$.

Using section formula,

By section formula, we have

$$P(x,y)=\left(\frac{kx_2+x_1}{k+1}, \frac{ky_2+y_1}{k+1}\right) \quad (½\ M)$$

Comparing the coordinates, we get

$$x=\frac{(6k-2)}{(k+1)} \text{ and } y=\frac{(3k-5)}{(k+1)} \quad (½\ M)$$

Here, the above point lies on the line $x - 3y = 0$.

Thus,

$$\left(\frac{6k-2}{k+1}\right)-3\left(\frac{3k-5}{k+1}\right)=0 \quad (½\ M)$$

$$\Rightarrow 6k-2-3(3k-5)=0 \Rightarrow 6k-2-9k+15=0$$

$$\Rightarrow -3k+13=0 \Rightarrow -3k=-13 \Rightarrow k=\frac{13}{3} \quad (½\ M)$$

Thus, the ratio in which the line $x - 3y = 0$ divides the line segment AB is 13 : 3.

Therefore,

$$x=\left(\frac{6(13/3)-2}{(13/3)+1}\right)=\frac{78-6}{13+3}=\frac{72}{16}=\frac{9}{2} \quad (1\ M)$$

$$\text{And } y=\frac{3\times\frac{13}{3}-5}{\frac{13}{3}+1}=\frac{39-15}{13+3}=\frac{24}{16}=\frac{3}{2} \quad (½\ M)$$

Therefore, the coordinates of the point of intersection $=\left(\frac{9}{2}, \frac{3}{2}\right)$. (1 M)

Case Based Questions

Case Based-I

(*i*) Let D be (a, b), then

Mid point of AC = Midpoint of BD

$$\left(\frac{1+6}{2}, \frac{2+6}{2}\right)=\left(\frac{4+a}{2}, \frac{3+b}{2}\right)$$

$4 + a = 7, 3 + b = 8$

$a = 3, b = 5$

Central midfielder is at (3, 5)

(ii) $GH = \sqrt{(-3-3)^2+(5-1)^2} = \sqrt{36+16} = \sqrt{52} = 2\sqrt{13}$

$GK = \sqrt{(0+3)^2+(3-5)^2} = \sqrt{9+4} = \sqrt{13}$

$HK = \sqrt{(3-0)^2+(1-3)^2} = \sqrt{9+4} = \sqrt{13}$

$GK + HK = GH \Rightarrow G, H$ & K lie on a same straight line

OR

$CJ = \sqrt{(0-5)^2+(1+3)^2} = \sqrt{25+16} = \sqrt{41}$

$CI = \sqrt{(0+4)^2+(1-6)^2} = \sqrt{16+25} = \sqrt{41}$

Full-back $J(5, -3)$ and centre-back $I(-4, 6)$ are equidistant from forward $C(0,1)$

Mid-point of $IJ = \left(\frac{5-4}{2}, \frac{-3+6}{2}\right) = \left(\frac{1}{2}, \frac{3}{2}\right)$

C is NOT the mid-point of IJ

(iii) A, B and E lie on the same straight line and B is equidistant from A and E

$\Rightarrow B$ is the mid-point of AE

$\left(\frac{1+a}{2}, \frac{4+b}{2}\right) = (2, -3)$

$1 + a = 4$; $a = 3$. $4 + b = -6$; $b = -10$

Hence, position of E is at $(3, -10)$.

Case Based-II

(i) (d) Mehek's house is at A and Mehek's house is at B.

$\therefore AB = \sqrt{(2-2)^2+(3-1)^2} = \sqrt{0+2^2} = 2$units.

(ii) (b) PW vidyapeeth is at C and Mehek's house is at B.

$\therefore BC = \sqrt{(4-2)^2+(1-1)^2} = \sqrt{2^2+0} = 2$units.

(iii) (d) PW vidyapeeth is at C and Mehek's house is at A

$\therefore AC = \sqrt{(4-2)^2+(1-3)^2} = \sqrt{2^2+(-2)^2} = \sqrt{4+4}$
$= \sqrt{8} = 2\sqrt{2}$

(iv) (d) Distance between PW library from Mehek's house.

$\therefore AO = \sqrt{(2-0)^2+(3-0)^2} = \sqrt{4+9} = \sqrt{13}$

and distance between PW library from Mehek's house

$\therefore BO = \sqrt{(2-0)^2+(1-0)^2} = \sqrt{4+1} = \sqrt{5}$

$\therefore$ Distance between PW Library from Mehek's house than Mehek's house $= \sqrt{13} - \sqrt{5}$ units.

Case Based-III

(i) (b) According to Question mall, Bus stand and water tank all lie on straight line.

Also mall divides Hotel & Main gate into 1:2 ratio.

$\therefore x = \frac{m_1x_2 + m_2x_1}{m_1 + m_2}$ $\left\{\begin{matrix} m_1 = 1, m_2 = 2 \\ x_1 = -2, x_2 = 4 \end{matrix}\right\}$

$\Rightarrow x = \frac{1\times 4 + 2\times(-2)}{1+2} \Rightarrow x = \frac{4-4}{3} = 0$

Key Takeaways

The equation of x-axis is $y = 0$ and the equation of y-axis is $x = 0$

Nailing the Right Answer

Apply the section formula to calculate the coordinates of the point that divides the line segment internally in the given ratio.

(ii) (c) The coordinates of main gate are (4, 17)

The coordinates of bus stand are (4, 9)

Let the coordinates of fire station be (x, y)

It is given that, the bus stand is exactly midway between the main gate of the garden and the fire station.

The coordinates of bus stand $= \left(\frac{x_1+x_2}{2}, \frac{y_1+y_2}{2}\right)$

$\Rightarrow (4, 9) = \left(\frac{x+4}{2}, \frac{y+17}{2}\right)$

By comparing x and y coordinates on both sides, we get:

$\frac{x+4}{2} = 4 \Rightarrow x + 4 = 8 \Rightarrow x = 4$

And, $\frac{y+17}{2} = 9 \Rightarrow y + 17 = 18 \Rightarrow y = 1$

Therefore, the coordinates of fire station is 4, 1

Nailing the Right Answer

Consider where the point falls along the line and how it divides the line based on the given ratio.

(iii) (c) The coordinates of water tank is (10, 9)

The coordinates of school is (22, 14)

The shortest distance between the water tank and the school $= \sqrt{(x_2-x_1)^2+(y_2-y_1)^2}$

$= \sqrt{(22-10)^2+(14.9)^2} = \sqrt{12^2+5^2}$

$= \sqrt{144+25} = \sqrt{169} = 13$ units

Therefore, the shortest distance between the water tank and the school 13 units.

(iv) (a) The coordinates of water tank is (10, 9)

The coordinates of school is (22, 14)

The shortest distance between the water tank and the school $= \sqrt{(x_2 - x_1)^2 + (y_2 - y_1)^2}$

$= \sqrt{(22-10)^2 + (14-9)^2} = \sqrt{12^2 + 5^2}$

$= \sqrt{144+25} = \sqrt{169} = 13$ units

From the figure, the coordinates school and police station are (22, 14) and (22, 7)

The distance between school and police station

$= \sqrt{(22-22)^2 + (7-14)^2}$

$= \sqrt{0^2 + (-7)^2}$

The difference = 13 – 7 = 6 units

Therefore, the shortest distance of the school from the water tank is 6 units more than the distance of the school from the police station.

Case Based-IV

(i) (a) Distance between two points $A(x_1, y_1)$ and $B(x_2, y_2)$ is given by distance formula:

$$AB = \sqrt{(x_2 - x_1)^2 + (y_2 - y_1)^2}$$

Therefore, distance between house and bank

$= \sqrt{(5-2)^2 + (8-4)^2} = \sqrt{(3)^2 + (4)^2}$

$= \sqrt{9+16} = \sqrt{25} = 5$ km

Hence, distance between house and bank is 5 km.

(ii) (b) Distance between bank and daughter's school

$= \sqrt{(13-5)^2 + (14-8)^2} = \sqrt{(8)^2 + (6)^2}$

$= \sqrt{64+36} = \sqrt{100} = 10$ km

Hence, distance between bank and daughter's school is 10 km.

(iii) (b) Distance between house to office,

$= \sqrt{(13-2)^2 + (26-4)^2} = \sqrt{(11)^2 + (22)^2}$

$= \sqrt{121+484} = \sqrt{605} = 24.59 = 24.6$ km

Hence, distance between house to office is 24.6 km.

(iv) (b) Distance between daughter's school and office, by distance formula we have

$= \sqrt{(13-13)^2 + (26-4)^2} = \sqrt{(0)^2 + (22)^2}$

$= \sqrt{(22)^2} = 22$ km

Hence, distance between daughter's school and office is 22 km.

❑❑❑

INTRODUCTION TO TRIGONOMETRY

8

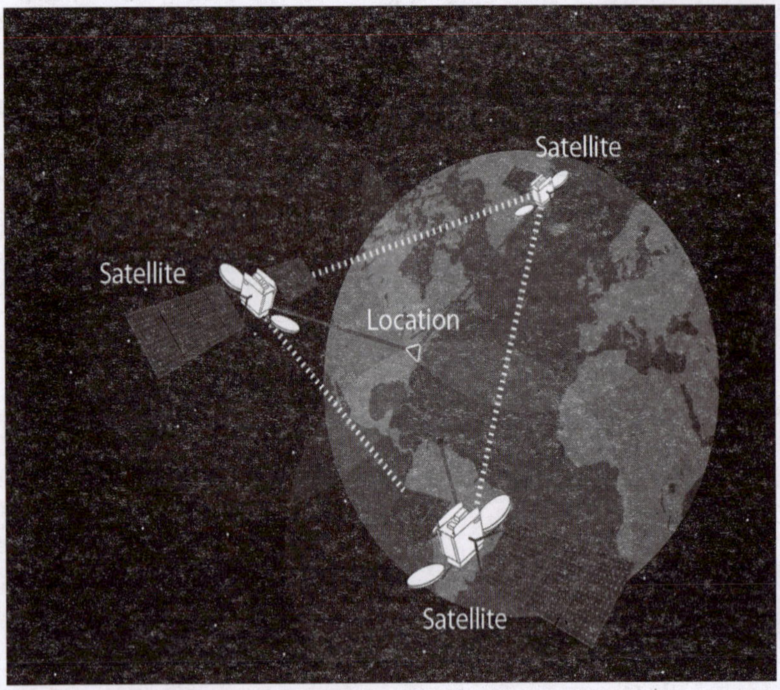

"Trilateration is a method used to find the location of a point by measuring distances from three known points. It is especially useful in GPS technology, where it helps determine a device's exact position by calculating the distance from satellites. This method uses basic trigonometry, involving the use of triangle properties."

SYLLABUS & WEIGHTAGE

List of Concept Names	Years				
	2021	2022	2023	2024	2025
Trigonometric Ratios and Some Specific Angles	Exam not Conducted	–	1 Q (1 M)	2 Q (1 M each) 1 Q (2 M) 1 Q (3 M)	2 Q (2 M each) 1 Q (1 M)
Trigonometric Identities		–	1 Q (2 M) 1 Q (3 M)	1 Q (3 M)	1 Q (3 M)

CONCEPT MAP

To Access One Shot Revision Video Scan This QR Code

Introduction to Trigonometry

Right angled triangle

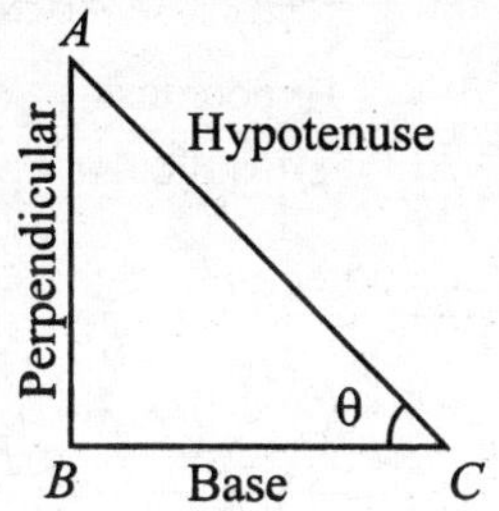

$$\sin\theta = \frac{AB}{AC}$$

$$\cos\theta = \frac{BC}{AC}$$

$$\tan\theta = \frac{AB}{BC}$$

$$\text{cosec}\ \theta = \frac{AC}{AB}$$

$$\sec\theta = \frac{AC}{BC}$$

$$\cot\theta = \frac{BC}{AB}$$

Trigonometric ratios and angles

$$\sin\theta = \frac{1}{\text{cosec}\,\theta} \Rightarrow \text{cosec}\,\theta = \frac{1}{\sin\theta}$$

$$\cos\theta = \frac{1}{\sec\theta} \Rightarrow \sec\theta = \frac{1}{\cos\theta}$$

$$\tan\theta = \frac{1}{\cot\theta} \Rightarrow \cot\theta = \frac{1}{\tan\theta}$$

Trigonometric Identities

$$\sin^2\theta + \cos^2\theta = 1$$

$$\sec^2\theta - \tan^2\theta = 1$$

$$\text{cosec}^2\theta - \cot^2\theta = 1$$

Trigonometric ratios of some specific angles.

θ	0°	30°	45°	60°	90°
sin	0	$\frac{1}{2}$	$\frac{1}{\sqrt{2}}$	$\frac{\sqrt{3}}{2}$	1
cos	1	$\frac{\sqrt{3}}{2}$	$\frac{1}{\sqrt{2}}$	$\frac{1}{2}$	0
tan	0	$\frac{1}{\sqrt{3}}$	1	$\sqrt{3}$	Not Defined
cosec	Not Defined	2	$\sqrt{2}$	$\frac{2}{\sqrt{3}}$	1
sec	1	$\frac{2}{\sqrt{3}}$	$\sqrt{2}$	2	Not Defined
cot	Not Defined	$\sqrt{3}$	1	$\frac{1}{\sqrt{3}}$	0

1 TRIGONOMETRIC RATIOS AND SOME SPECIFIC ANGLES

Important Terms

- **Right Angled triangle:** A triangle which has any one of the interior angle equal to 90° is called Right angled triangle.

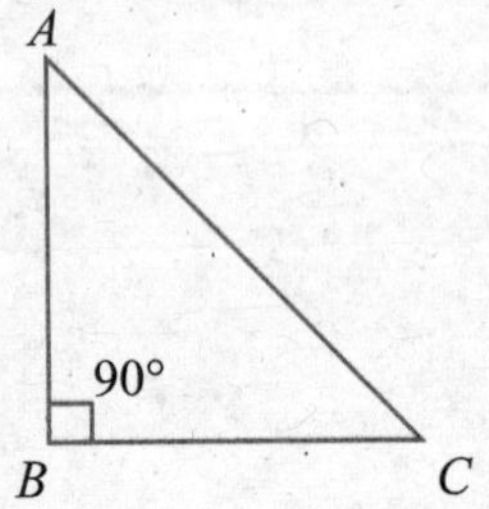

- **Hypotenuse:** The hypotenuse is the longest side of a right-angled triangle. It is represented by the side opposite to the right angle
- **Perpendicular:** Perpendicular is the side that makes right angle with the base of the triangle. The largest side which is opposite to the right-angle(90°) is known as the Hypotenuse.
- **Base:** A right triangle's base is one of the sides that adjoins the 90° angle
- **Trigonometric ratios of the angle:** The ratios of the sides of a right triangle with respect to its acute angles, called trigonometric ratios of the angle.

Note: All you have to remember is, this

- Side opposite to 90° is hypotenuse.
- Side opposite to the considered angle is perpendicular.
- The side which is left is the base.

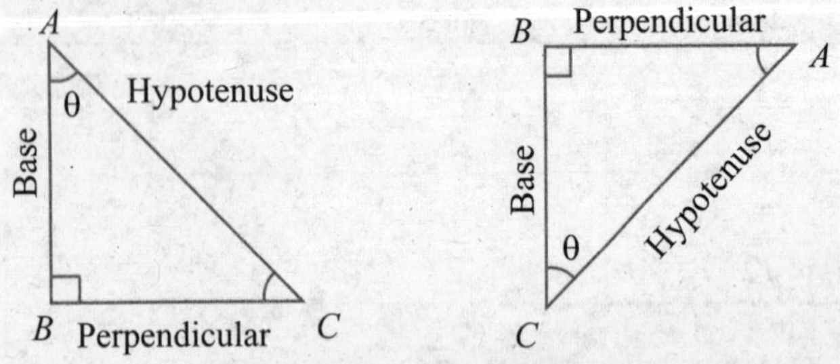

Here θ is the angle into consideration

Angles	Hypotenuse	Perpendicular	Base
for $\angle A$	AC	BC	AB
for $\angle C$	AC	AB	BC

Important Formulas

Trigonometric Ratios

The ratio of the sides of a right angle triangle with respect to acute angles are called "Trigonometric ratios of the angle".

- sine of θ, written as $\sin\theta = \dfrac{\text{Perpendicular}}{\text{Hypotenuse}} = \dfrac{p}{h}$
- cosine of θ, written as $\cos\theta = \dfrac{\text{Base}}{\text{Hypotenuse}} = \dfrac{b}{h}$
- tangent of θ, written as $\tan\theta = \dfrac{\text{Perpendicular}}{\text{Base}} = \dfrac{P}{b}$
- cosecant of θ, written as $\text{cosec}\theta = \dfrac{\text{Hypotenuse}}{\text{Perpendicular}} = \dfrac{h}{p}$
- secant of θ, written as $\sec\theta = \dfrac{\text{Hypotenuse}}{\text{Base}} = \dfrac{h}{\text{b}}$
- cotangent of θ, written as $\cot\theta = \dfrac{\text{Base}}{\text{Perpendicular}} = \dfrac{b}{p}$

Relation Between Trigonometric Ratio

- $\sin\theta = \dfrac{1}{\text{cosec}\theta} \Rightarrow \text{cosec}\theta = \dfrac{1}{\sin\theta}$
- $\cos\theta = \dfrac{1}{\sec\theta} \Rightarrow \sec\theta = \dfrac{1}{\cos\theta}$
- $\tan\theta = \dfrac{1}{\cot\theta} \Rightarrow \cot\theta = \dfrac{1}{\tan\theta}$
- We also observe that
- $\tan\theta = \dfrac{\sin\theta}{\cos\theta} \Rightarrow \cot\theta = \dfrac{\cos\theta}{\sin\theta}$

Important Concepts

- The values of the trigonometric ratios of an angle do not vary with the lengths of the sides of the triangle, if the angle remains the same
- The value of each of the trigonometric ratio of an angle does not depend on the size of the triangle. It depends only on the angle
- Each trigonometric ratio is a real number and has no unit.

In right angled ΔABC

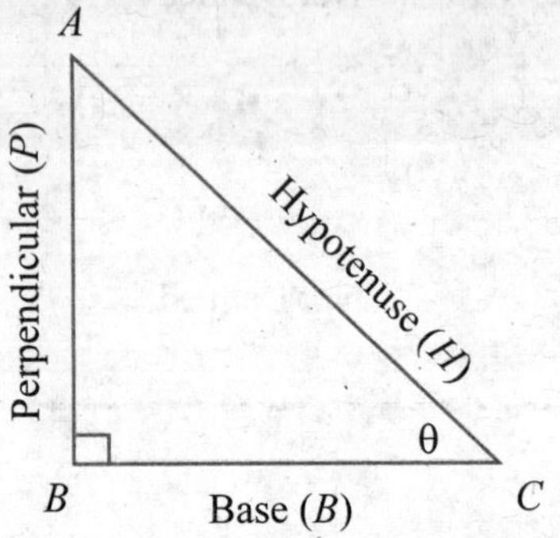

$\sin\theta = \frac{\text{Perpendicular}}{\text{Hypotenuse}} = \frac{P}{H} = \frac{\text{Pandit}}{\text{Har}}$ $\cos\theta = \frac{\text{Base}}{\text{Hypotenuse}} = \frac{B}{H} = \frac{\text{Badri}}{\text{Har}}$ $\tan\theta = \frac{\text{Perpendicular}}{\text{Base}} = \frac{P}{B} = \frac{\text{Prasad}}{\text{Bhole}}$

sin → $\frac{\text{Pandit}}{\text{Har}}$ cos → $\frac{\text{Badri}}{\text{Har}}$ tan → $\frac{\text{Prasad}}{\text{Bhole}}$

θ	0°	30°	45°	60°	90°
sin	0	$\frac{1}{2}$	$\frac{1}{\sqrt{2}}$	$\frac{\sqrt{3}}{2}$	1
cos	1	$\frac{\sqrt{3}}{2}$	$\frac{1}{\sqrt{2}}$	$\frac{1}{2}$	0
tan	0	$\frac{1}{\sqrt{3}}$	1	$\sqrt{3}$	Not Defined
cosec	Not Defined	2	$\sqrt{2}$	$\frac{2}{\sqrt{3}}$	1
sec	1	$\frac{2}{\sqrt{3}}$	$\sqrt{2}$	2	Not Defined
cot	Not Defined	$\sqrt{3}$	1	$\frac{1}{\sqrt{3}}$	0

Real Life Applications

Trigonometry to Measure Height of a Building or a Mountain

Trigonometry is used in calculating height and length of a building or a tower. The distance of a building from the viewpoint and the elevation angle can be found easily from the height and length of a building by using the trigonometric functions.

Angle of elevation and also in engineering. Trigonometry is used to calculate the forces and stresses on structures and machines.

Navigation:

- Navigators and pilots use trigonometry to calculate distances, angles, and bearings for navigation purposes.
- Trigonometric functions are applied in celestial navigation to determine the position of stars and planets.

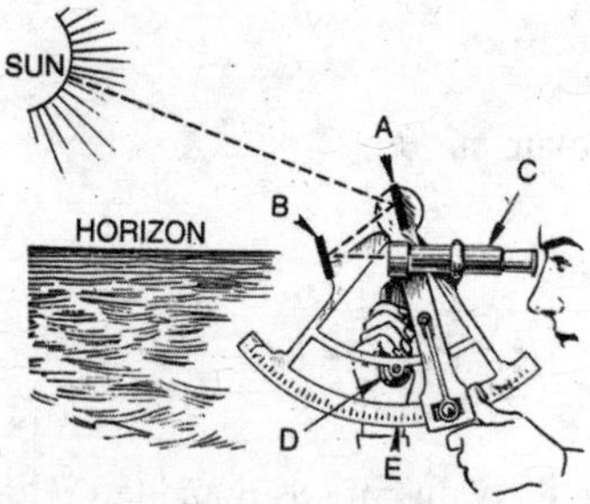

Different Problem Types

Type I: Finding Trigonometric Ratios of an Angle Given One Ratio

Given $\tan A = \frac{4}{3}$, find the other trigonometric ratios of angle A.

Solution: Given: $\tan A = \frac{4}{3}$

Step I: Find the Hypotenuse using the Pythagorean theorem:

Let's assume that the adjacent side is 3 units and the opposite side is 4 units. Then, using the Pythagorean theorem, we have:

$\text{Hypotenuse}^2 = (\text{Adjacent side})^2 + (\text{Opposite side})^2$

$\text{Hypotenuse}^2 = 3^2 + 4^2$

$\text{Hypotenuse}^2 = 25$

$\text{Hypotenuse} = \sqrt{25} = 5$

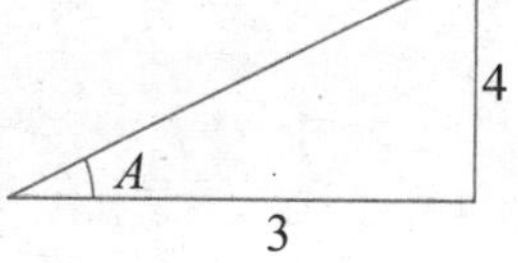

Step II: Find the other Trigonometric Ratios:

Now that we have the values of all three sides of the right triangle, we can find the other trigonometric ratios:

$$\sin A = \frac{\text{Opposite side}}{\text{Hypotenuse}} = \frac{4}{5},\ \cos A = \frac{\text{Adjacent}}{\text{Hypotenuse}} = \frac{3}{5}$$

$$\text{cosec } A = \frac{1}{\sin A} = \frac{1}{\frac{4}{5}} = \frac{5}{4}$$

$$\sec A = \frac{1}{\cos A} = \frac{1}{\frac{3}{5}} = \frac{5}{3},\ \cot A = \frac{1}{\tan A} = \frac{1}{\frac{4}{3}} = \frac{3}{4}$$

Therefore, the other trigonometric ratios of angle A are:

$$\sin A = \frac{4}{5}, \cos A = \frac{3}{5}, \text{cosec } A = \frac{5}{4}, \sec A = \frac{5}{3}, \cot A = \frac{3}{4}$$

Example: Given: $\sin B = \frac{5}{13}$, where B is an acute angle. Find $\cos B$ and $\tan B$.

Solution:

$$\cos B = \sqrt{1-(\sin B)^2} \Rightarrow \cos B = \sqrt{1-\left(\frac{5}{13}\right)^2}$$

$$\cos B = \sqrt{1-\frac{25}{169}} \Rightarrow \cos B = \frac{12}{13}$$

Now calculate $\tan B$

$$\tan B = \frac{\sin B}{\cos B} = \frac{\frac{5}{13}}{\frac{12}{13}} = \frac{5}{12}$$

Therefore, the value of $\cos B$ and $\tan B$ are:

$$\cos B = \frac{12}{13} \text{ and } \tan B = \frac{5}{12}$$

Type II: Solving a Trigonometric Expression with Angles

Evaluate the trigonometric expression

$$\frac{\cos^2(60°)-\sin^2(60°)}{\cos(30°)+\sin(30°)}$$

Solution:

Step I: Calculate the trigonometric functions at the given angles:

$$\cos(60°) = \frac{1}{2}, \sin(60°) = \frac{\sqrt{3}}{2}, \cos(30°) = \frac{\sqrt{3}}{2}, \sin(30°) = \frac{1}{2}$$

Step II: Substitute these values into the expression:

$$\frac{\left(\frac{1}{2}\right)^2-\left(\frac{\sqrt{3}}{2}\right)^2}{\frac{\sqrt{3}}{2}+\frac{1}{2}}$$

Step III: Simplify the terms inside the parentheses:

$$\frac{\frac{1}{4}-\frac{3}{4}}{\frac{\sqrt{3}}{2}+\frac{1}{2}}$$

Step IV: Combine the fractions in the numerator:

$$\frac{-\frac{2}{4}}{\frac{\sqrt{3}+1}{2}}$$

Step V: Simplify the fraction and the denominator:

$$\frac{-\frac{1}{2}}{\frac{\sqrt{3}+1}{2}} = \frac{-1}{\sqrt{3}+1} = \frac{-1}{\sqrt{3}+1}.\frac{\sqrt{3}-1}{\sqrt{3}-1} = \frac{-\sqrt{3}+1}{3-1} = \frac{-\sqrt{3}+1}{2}$$

Therefore, the simplified form of the given expression is $\frac{1-\sqrt{3}}{2}$.

Example: Given expression:

$$\frac{\cos^2(30°)-\sin^2(30°)}{\cos(45°)+\sin(45°)}$$

Solution: First, we evaluate the trigonometric functions at the specified angles:

$$\cos(30°) = \frac{\sqrt{3}}{2}, \sin(30°) = \frac{1}{2}, \cos(45°) = \frac{1}{\sqrt{2}}, \sin(45°) = \frac{1}{\sqrt{2}}$$

Now substitute these values into the expression:

$$\frac{\left(\frac{\sqrt{3}}{2}\right)^2-\left(\frac{1}{2}\right)^2}{\frac{1}{\sqrt{2}}+\frac{1}{\sqrt{2}}}$$

Simplifying further: $\frac{\frac{3}{4}-\frac{1}{4}}{\frac{2}{\sqrt{2}}} = \frac{\frac{2}{4}}{\sqrt{2}} = \frac{\frac{1}{2}}{\sqrt{2}} = \frac{1}{2\sqrt{2}}$

Therefore, the simplified form of the given expression is $\frac{1}{2\sqrt{2}}$.

COMPETENCY BASED SOLVED EXAMPLES

Multiple Choice Questionc

(1 M)

1. (sin 30° + cos 30°) – (sin 60° + cos 60°) *(Ev)* (NCERT Exemplar)

(a) –1 (b) 0 (c) 1 (d) $\frac{1}{2}$

Sol. (sin 30° + cos 30°) – (sin 60° + cos 60°)

$$= \frac{1}{2} + \frac{\sqrt{3}}{2} - \frac{\sqrt{3}}{2} - \frac{1}{2} = 0$$

2. Value of $\frac{\tan 30°}{\cot 60°}$ is: *(Ap)* (NCERT Exemplar)

(a) $\frac{1}{\sqrt{2}}$ (b) $\frac{1}{\sqrt{3}}$ (c) $\frac{\sqrt{3}}{2}$ (d) 1

Sol. $\frac{\tan 30°}{\cot 60°} = \frac{\frac{1}{\sqrt{3}}}{\frac{1}{\sqrt{3}}} = 1$

3. If the value of cos A = 4/5, then tan A = ? *(Un)*

(a) 1 (b) 3/4 (c) 4/3 (d) 4/5

Sol. Using trigonometric identity

$1 + \tan^2 A = \sec^2 A \Rightarrow \sec^2 A - 1 = \tan^2 A$

$$\Rightarrow \frac{1}{\cos^2 A} - 1 = \tan^2 A \Rightarrow \left(\frac{5}{4}\right)^2 - 1 = \tan^2 A$$

$$\Rightarrow \frac{9}{16} = \tan^2 A \Rightarrow \tan A = \frac{3}{4}$$

4. Given that: sin $A = a/b$, then cos$A$ = ? *(Ev)*

(a) $\frac{\sqrt{b^2 + a^2}}{b}$ (b) $\frac{\sqrt{b^2 - a^2}}{b}$

(c) $\frac{b^2}{a^2}$ (d) $\frac{a^2}{b^2}$

Sol. Given $\sin A = \frac{a}{b}$

As, $\sin A = \frac{\text{Perpendicular}}{\text{Hypotenuse}}$

∴ Perpendicular = ax; Hypotenuse = bx

Now, Base² + Perpendicular² = Hypotenuse²

Base² + $(ax)^2 = (bx)^2$

Base = $x\sqrt{b^2 - a^2}$

$$\cos A = \frac{\text{Base}}{\text{Hypotenuse}} = \frac{x\sqrt{b^2 - a^2}}{bx} = \frac{\sqrt{b^2 - a^2}}{b}$$

5. If sin A = 1/2 and cos B = 1/2, then $A + B$ = ? *(Un)*

(a) 45° (b) 30° (c) 60° (d) 90°

Sol. Since $\sin A = \frac{1}{2} \Rightarrow \sin A = \sin 30° \Rightarrow A = 30°$

$\cos B = \frac{1}{2} \Rightarrow \cos B = \cos 60° \Rightarrow B = 60°$

Therefore

$A + B = 30° + 60° \Rightarrow A + B = 90°$

6. If 4 tan A = 3, then $\frac{4\sin A - \cos A}{4\sin A + \cos A}$ = ? *(Cr)*

(a) $\frac{2}{3}$ (b) $\frac{1}{3}$ (c) $\frac{1}{2}$ (d) 1

Sol. $\frac{4\sin A - \cos A}{4\sin A + \cos A}$

Dividing numerator and denominator by cos A.

$$= \frac{\frac{4\sin A - \cos A}{\cos A}}{\frac{4\sin A + \cos A}{\cos A}} = \frac{4\tan A - 1}{4\tan A + 1} = \frac{3-1}{3+1} = \frac{2}{4} = \frac{1}{2}$$

7. If $\sin\theta = \frac{1}{3}$, then the value of $2\cot^2\theta + 2$ is *(An)*

(a) 6 (b) 1 (c) 18 (d) 10

Sol. $\sin\theta = \frac{1}{3} = \frac{P}{H}$

Let $H = 3k$, $P = k$

Using Pythagoras Theorem

$H^2 = P^2 + B^2$

$9k^2 = k^2 + B^2$

$B^2 = 8k^2$

$B = 2\sqrt{2}k$

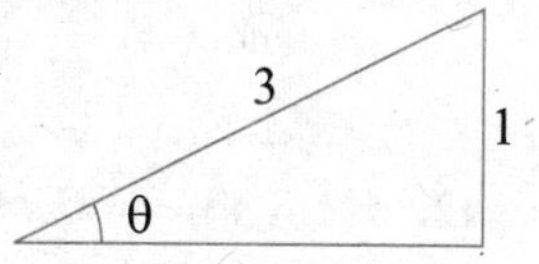

Therefore, $\cot\theta = \frac{B}{P} = \frac{2\sqrt{2}k}{1k} = 2\sqrt{2}$

Thus, $2\cot^2\theta + 2 = 2(2\sqrt{2})^2 + 2$

$= 2 \times 8 + 2 = 16 + 2 = 18$

8. In a ΔABC, right angled at B, AB = 24 cm and BC = 7 cm. Then the value of tan C is: *(Ev)*

(a) $\frac{12}{7}$ (b) $\frac{24}{7}$ (c) $\frac{7}{25}$ (d) $\frac{7}{24}$

Sol. AB = 24 cm and BC = 7 cm

$\tan C = \frac{\text{Perpendicular}}{\text{Base}}$

$\tan C = \frac{24}{7}$

9. (sin 30° + cos 60°) – (sin 60° + cos 30°) is equal to: (*Ap*)

(*a*) 0 (*b*) 1

(*c*) $1-\sqrt{3}$ (*d*) $1+\sqrt{3}$

Sol. $\sin 30° = \dfrac{1}{2}$, $\sin 60° = \dfrac{\sqrt{3}}{2}$, $\cos 30° = \dfrac{\sqrt{3}}{2}$ and $\cos 60° = \dfrac{1}{2}$

By substituting the values, we get:

$$\left(\frac{1}{2}+\frac{1}{2}\right)-\left(\frac{\sqrt{3}}{2}+\frac{\sqrt{3}}{2}\right)=1-\sqrt{3}$$

10. The value of $\dfrac{\sin 45°}{\cos 45°}$ is equal to: (*Re*)

(*a*) 0 (*b*) 1 (*c*) 2 (*d*) Not defined

Sol. $\sin 45° = \dfrac{1}{\sqrt{2}}$ and $\cos 45° = \dfrac{1}{\sqrt{2}}$

Hence, $\dfrac{\sin 45°}{\cos 45°} = 1$

11. If $\cos X = \dfrac{2}{3}$ then tan *X* is equal to: (*Ap*)

(*a*) $\dfrac{5}{2}$ (*b*) $\sqrt{\dfrac{5}{2}}$ (*c*) $\dfrac{\sqrt{5}}{2}$ (*d*) $\dfrac{5}{\sqrt{2}}$

Sol. Using Trigonometric Identities:

$1 + \tan^2 X = \sec^2 X$

And $\sec X = \dfrac{1}{\cos X} = \dfrac{1}{\frac{2}{3}} = \dfrac{3}{2}$

Hence,

$1 + \tan^2 X = \left(\dfrac{3}{2}\right)^2 = \dfrac{9}{4}$

$\Rightarrow \tan^2 X = \dfrac{9}{4} - 1 = \dfrac{5}{4} \Rightarrow \tan X = \dfrac{\sqrt{5}}{2}$

12. If $\cos A = \dfrac{4}{5}$ then the value of tan*A* is:

(*Ap*) (CBSE SQP, 2023)

(*a*) $\dfrac{3}{5}$ (*b*) $\dfrac{3}{4}$ (*c*) $\dfrac{4}{3}$ (*d*) $\dfrac{1}{8}$

Sol. Since $\cos\theta = \dfrac{4}{5}$ but $\cos\theta = \dfrac{AB}{AC}$

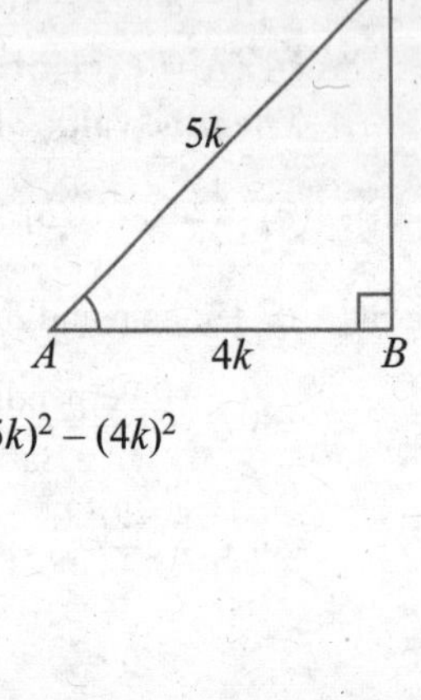

So, $\dfrac{AB}{AC} = \dfrac{4}{5}$

Thus, $AB = 4k$ and $AC = 5k$

Using Pythagoras theorem in triangle *ABC*, we have:

$AC^2 = AB^2 + BC^2$

$\Rightarrow BC^2 = AC^2 - AB^2 \Rightarrow BC^2 = (5k)^2 - (4k)^2$

$\Rightarrow BC^2 = 9k^2 \Rightarrow BC = 3k$

$\therefore \tan\theta = \dfrac{BC}{AB} = \dfrac{3}{4}$

13. In ΔABC right angled at *B*, sin*A* = 7/25, then the value of cos *C* is (*An*)

(*a*) 7/25 (*b*) 24/25

(*c*) 7/24 (*d*) 24/7

Sol. Given $\sin A = \dfrac{7}{25}$

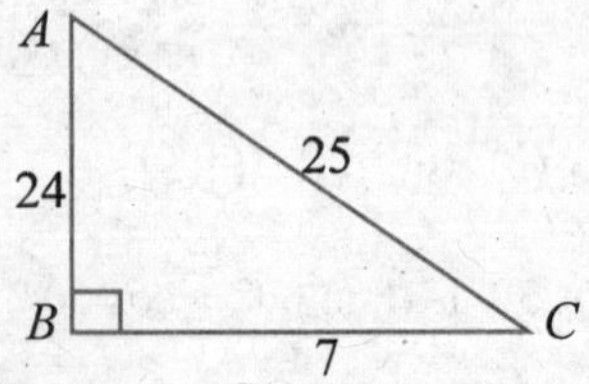

$\cos C = \dfrac{b}{h} = \dfrac{7}{25}$

14. In $\cot\theta = \dfrac{1}{\sqrt{3}}$, the value of $\sec^2\theta + \text{cosec}^2\theta$ is (*Ap*)

(*a*) 1 (*b*) $\dfrac{40}{9}$ (*c*) $\dfrac{38}{9}$ (*d*) $5\dfrac{1}{3}$

Sol. Given $\cot\theta = \dfrac{1}{\sqrt{3}}$

$\therefore \cot\theta = \cot 60° \Rightarrow \theta = 60°$

$\therefore \sec^2\theta + \text{cosec}^2\theta = \sec^2 60 + \text{cosec}^2 60$

$= (2)^2 + \left(\dfrac{2}{\sqrt{3}}\right)^2 = 4 + \dfrac{4}{3} = \dfrac{16}{3} = 5\dfrac{1}{3}$

15. The value of 2 sin² + 3 tan² 60° – cos² 45° is:

(*Ev*) (CBSE 2023)

(*a*) $3\sqrt{3}$ (*b*) $\dfrac{19}{2}$

(*c*) $\dfrac{9}{4}$ (*d*) 9

Sol. We know that $\sin 30° = \dfrac{1}{2}$, $\tan 60° = \sqrt{3}$ and $\cos 45° = \dfrac{1}{\sqrt{2}}$

$\therefore 2\sin^2 30° + 3\tan^2 60° - \cos^2 45°$

$= 2\left(\dfrac{1}{2}\right)^2 + 3\left(\sqrt{3}\right)^2 - \left(\dfrac{1}{\sqrt{2}}\right)^2$

$= 2\times\dfrac{1}{4} + 3\times 3 - \dfrac{1}{2} = \dfrac{1}{2} + 9 - \dfrac{1}{2} = 9$

Answer Key

1. (b)	**2.** (d)	**3.** (b)	**4.** (b)	**5.** (d)
6. (c)	**7.** (c)	**8.** (b)	**9.** (c)	**10.** (b)
11. (c)	**12.** (b)	**13.** (a)	**14.** (d)	**15.** (d)

Assertion and Reason (1 M)

Direction: In the following questions, a statement of assertion (*A*) is followed by a statement of reason (*R*). Mark the correct choice as:

(*a*) Both Assertion (*A*) and Reason (*R*) are true and Reason (*R*) is the correct explanation of Assertion (*A*).

(*b*) Both Assertion (*A*) and Reason (*R*) are true but Reason (*R*) is not the correct explanation of Assertion (*A*).

(*c*) Assertion (*A*) is true but Reason (*R*) is false.

(*d*) Assertion (*A*) is false but Reason (*R*) is true.

1. Assertion(A): The value of $2\tan^2 45° + \cos^2 30° - \sin^2 60°$ is 2.

Reason (R): Value of tan 45° = 1, $\cos 30° = \frac{\sqrt{3}}{2}$ and $\sin 60° = \frac{\sqrt{3}}{2}$. ***(Ap)***

Sol. From trigonometric table,

$\tan 45° = 1$, $\cos 30° = \frac{\sqrt{3}}{2}$ and $\sin 60° = \frac{\sqrt{3}}{2}$

Reason (R) is true.

$2\tan^2 45° + \cos^2 30° - \sin^2 60°$

$= 2(1)^2 + \left(\frac{\sqrt{3}}{2}\right)^2 - \left(\frac{\sqrt{3}}{2}\right)^2 = 2$

Assertion (A) is correct.

Both assertion (A) and reason (R) are true and reason (R) is the correct explanation of assertion (A).

2. Assertion (A): In a right angled triangle, if $\tan\theta = \frac{3}{4}$, the greatest side of the triangle is 5 units.

Reason (R): (greatest side)² = (hypotenuse)² = (perpendicular)² + (base)². ***(Re)***

Sol. $\tan\theta = \frac{3}{4} = \frac{\text{Perpendicular}}{\text{Base}}$

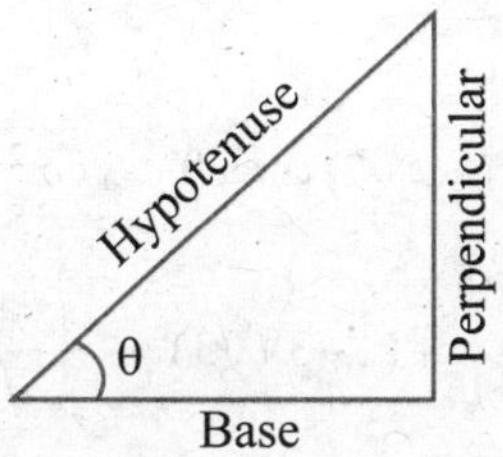

By Pythagoras' Theorem,

$(\text{Greatest Side})^2 = (\text{Perpendicular})^2 + (\text{Base})^2$

$\Rightarrow (\text{Hypotenuse})^2 = (\text{Perpendicular})^2 + (\text{Base})^2$

$\Rightarrow (\text{Hypotenuse})^2 = (3)^2 + (4)^2 = 25$

$\Rightarrow$ Hypotenuse = 5 Units

Both assertion (A) and reason (R) are true and reason (R) is the correct explanation of assertion (A).

Answer Key

1. (*a*) 2. (*a*)

Subjective Questions

Very Short Answer Type Questions (1 or 2 M)

1. Find the value of *x* if ***(Ev)***

$$2\,\text{cosec}^2 30° + x\sin^2 60° - \frac{3}{4}\tan^2 30° = 10$$

Sol. $2\,\text{cosec}^2 30° + x\sin^2 60° - \frac{3}{4}\tan^2 30° = 10$

$\Rightarrow 2(2)^2 + x\left(\frac{\sqrt{3}}{2}\right)^2 - \frac{3}{4}\left(\frac{1}{\sqrt{3}}\right)^2 = 10$ *(1 M)*

$\Rightarrow 2(4) + x\left(\frac{3}{4}\right) - \frac{3}{4}\left(\frac{1}{3}\right) = 10$ *(½ M)*

$\Rightarrow 8 + x\left(\frac{3}{4}\right) - \frac{1}{4} = 10 \Rightarrow 32 + x(3) - 1 = 40$

$\Rightarrow 3x = 9 \Rightarrow x = 3$ *(½ M)*

2. If $\tan(A+B) = \sqrt{3}$ and $\tan(A-B) = \frac{1}{\sqrt{3}}$, then the value of *A* is _____. ***(Ev)* (CBSE, 2020)**

Sol. Given, $\tan(A+B) = \sqrt{3}$ and $\tan(A-B) = \frac{1}{\sqrt{3}}$

Therefore, $A + B = 60°$ and $A - B = 30°$ *(½ M)*

Adding the two equations, we get $2A = 90°$

$\Rightarrow A = \frac{90°}{2} = 45°$ *(½ M)*

3. In ΔABC right angled at *B*, *AB* = 24 cm, *BC* = 7 cm. Determine: ***(Ap)***

(i) sin *A*, cos *A*

(ii) sin *C*, cos *C*

Sol. By Pythagoras' Theorem,

$AC^2 = AB^2 + BC^2 = (24)^2 + (7)^2 = 576 + 49 = 625$ *(1 M)*

$\Rightarrow AC = \sqrt{625} = 25$ cm

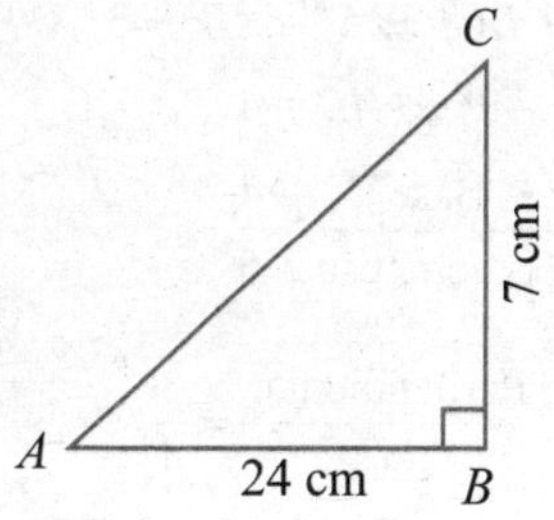

(i) $\sin A = \frac{BC}{AC} = \frac{7}{25}, \cos A = \frac{AB}{AC} = \frac{24}{25}$ (½ M)

(ii) $\sin C = \frac{AB}{AC} = \frac{24}{25}, \cos C = \frac{BC}{AC} = \frac{7}{25}$ (½ M)

4. If tan x = 3cot x, then find the value of x (*Ev*)

Sol. $\tan x = 3 \cot x$

$\Rightarrow \tan x = 3 \times \frac{1}{\tan x}$ (1 M)

$\Rightarrow \tan^2 x = 3$

$\Rightarrow \tan x = \sqrt{3} \Rightarrow \tan x = \tan 60° \Rightarrow x = 60°$ (1 M)

5. Evaluate: $\sin^2 60° + 2 \tan 45° - \cos^2 30°$. (*Ap*) (CBSE SQP, 2023)

Sol. $\sin^2 60° + 2 \tan 45° - \cos^2 30°$.

$= \left(\frac{\sqrt{3}}{2}\right)^2 + 2(1) - \left(\frac{\sqrt{3}}{2}\right)^2$ (1 M)

$= \frac{3}{4} + 2 - \frac{3}{4} = 2$ (1 M)

6. If the value of $\sin\theta = \frac{1}{2}$, then find the value of $3\cos\theta - 4\cos^3\theta$. (*Un*)

Sol. $\sin\theta = \frac{1}{2} \Rightarrow \theta = 30°$

$3 \cos 30° - 4 \cos^3 30°$ (1 M)

$= 3\left(\frac{\sqrt{3}}{2}\right) - 4\left(\frac{\sqrt{3}}{2}\right)^3 = \frac{\sqrt{3}}{2}\left[3 - 4 \times \frac{3}{4}\right] = 0$ (1 M)

Short Answer Type Questions (2 or 3 M)

1. If $\sin A = \frac{3}{5}$, find cos A and tan A. (*Un*)

Sol. Since $\sin A = \frac{\text{Perpendicular}}{\text{Hypotenuse}} = \frac{3}{5}$,

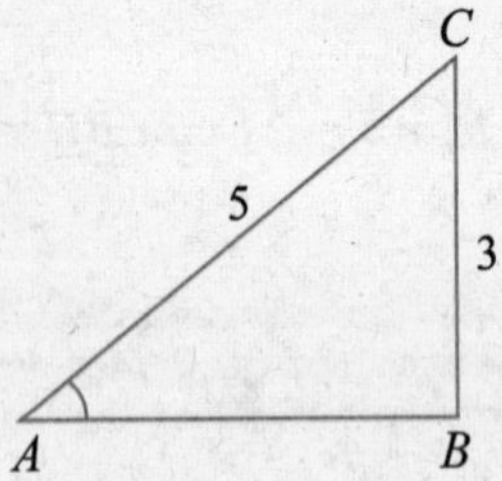

(1 M)

Perpendicular = BC = 3 units,
and Hypotenuse = AC = 5 units.
By Pythagoras theorem, we have

$AC^2 = AB^2 + BC^2 \Rightarrow 5^2 = AB^2 + 3^2$

$\Rightarrow AB^2 = 5^2 - 3^2 \Rightarrow AB = 4$ (1 M)

$\therefore \cos A = \frac{\text{Base}}{\text{Hypotenuse}} = \frac{4}{5}$ (½ M)

and $\tan A = \frac{\text{Perpendicular}}{\text{Base}} = \frac{3}{4}$ (½ M)

2. If $\sin A = \frac{1}{2}$, verify that $2\sin A \cos A = \frac{2\tan A}{1+\tan^2 A}$. (*Un*)

Sol. Given $\sin A = \frac{1}{2}$

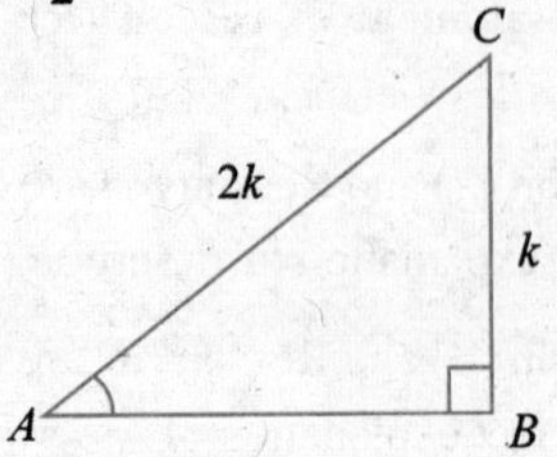

$\sin A = \frac{BC}{AC} = \frac{1}{2}$

Let $BC = k$ and $AC = 2k$

$\therefore AB = \sqrt{AC^2 - BC^2}$ (Pythagoras theorem)

$= \sqrt{(2k)^2 - k^2} = \sqrt{3}k$ (1 M)

Thus, $\cos A = \frac{AB}{AC} = \frac{\sqrt{3}k}{2k} = \frac{\sqrt{3}}{2}$ (1 M)

and $\tan A = \frac{BC}{AB} = \frac{k}{\sqrt{3}k} = \frac{1}{\sqrt{3}}$

$\therefore 2 \sin A \cos A = 2.\frac{1}{2}.\frac{\sqrt{3}}{2} = \frac{\sqrt{3}}{2}$ ... (*i*)

and $\frac{2\tan A}{1+\tan^2 A} = \frac{2\frac{1}{\sqrt{3}}}{1+\left(\frac{1}{\sqrt{3}}\right)^2}$ ... (*ii*)

$= \frac{\frac{2}{\sqrt{3}}}{1+\frac{1}{3}} = \frac{\frac{2}{\sqrt{3}}}{\frac{4}{3}} = \frac{2}{\sqrt{3}} \times \frac{3}{4} = \frac{\sqrt{3}}{2}$ (1 M)

Hence verified.

3. If $(x-2)\sin^2 30° + (x-3)\tan^2 60° - x\cos^2 45° = \frac{17}{4}$, find the value of x. (*Cr*)

Sol. $(x-2)\sin^2 30° + (x-3)\tan^2 60° - x\cos^2 45° = \frac{17}{4}$

$\Rightarrow (x-2)\left(\frac{1}{2}\right)^2 + (x-3)(\sqrt{3})^2 - x\left(\frac{1}{\sqrt{2}}\right)^2 = \frac{17}{4}$

$\Rightarrow \frac{x-2}{4} + 3(x-3) - \frac{x}{2} = \frac{17}{4}$ (1 M)

$\Rightarrow \frac{x-2}{4} + 3x - 9 - \frac{x}{2} = \frac{17}{4} \Rightarrow \frac{x-2+12x-36-2x}{4} = \frac{17}{4}$ (1 M)

$\Rightarrow (x-2) + 12x - 36 - 2x = 17$

$\Rightarrow x + 12x - 2x = 17 + 36 + 2$

$\Rightarrow 11x = 55 \Rightarrow x = 5$ (1 M)

4. Determine value of y such that $2 \operatorname{cosec}^2 30° + y \sin^2 60° = 11$. *(Un)*

Sol. $2 \operatorname{cosec}^2 30° + y \sin^2 60° = 11$

$$\Rightarrow 2(2)^2 + y\left(\frac{\sqrt{3}}{2}\right)^2 = 11 \quad (1\ M)$$

$$\Rightarrow 8 + \frac{3y}{4} = 11 \Rightarrow \frac{3y}{4} = 11 - 8 \Rightarrow \frac{3y}{4} = 3 \quad (1\ M)$$

$$\Rightarrow y = \frac{4}{3} \times 3 \Rightarrow y = 4 \quad (1\ M)$$

5. Find the value of A and B if,

$$\cos(3A + B) = \frac{1}{2} \text{ and } \sin(3A - B) = \frac{1}{2}. \quad (Cr)$$

Sol. $\cos(3A + B) = \frac{1}{2}$

or $\cos(3A + B) = \cos 60°$ $\left[\because \cos 60° = \frac{1}{2}\right]$

$\Rightarrow 3A + B = 60°$ ... (*i*) (1 M)

Similarly, $\sin(3A - B) = \frac{1}{2}$

$\Rightarrow \sin(3A - B) = \sin 30°$ $\left[\because \sin 30° = \frac{1}{2}\right]$

$\Rightarrow 3A - B = 30°$ ... (*ii*) (1 M)

Solving (*i*) and (*ii*), we get

$A = 15°$ and $B = 15°$ (1 M)

6. If $\sin\alpha = \frac{1}{2}$, then find the value of (3 cos –4 $\cos^2 \alpha$) *(Un)* **(CBSE, 2020)**

Sol. $\sin \alpha = \frac{1}{2} \Rightarrow \alpha = 30°$ (½ M)

$\therefore 3 \cos \alpha - 4 \cos^3 \alpha = 3 \cos 30° - 4 \cos^3 30°$

$$= 3\left(\frac{\sqrt{3}}{2}\right) - 4\left(\frac{\sqrt{3}}{2}\right)^3 = \frac{3\sqrt{3}}{2} - \frac{4(3\sqrt{3})}{8} \quad (1\ M)$$

$$= \frac{3\sqrt{3}}{2} - \frac{3\sqrt{2}}{2} = 0 \quad (½\ M)$$

7. *ABC* is a right angle triangle having a right angled at *B*, *AB* = 7 cm and (*AC* – *BC*) = 1 cm. Find the values of sin *C* and cos *C*. *(An)*

Sol. Consider ΔABC in which $\angle B = 90°$, $AB = 7$ cm and $(AC - BC) = 1$ cm.

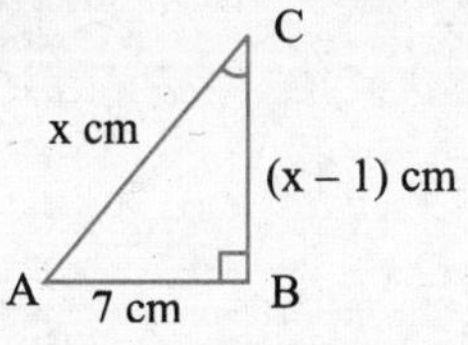

Let $AC = x$ cm.

Then, $BC = (x - 1)$ cm

By Pythagoras theorem, we have:

$AB^2 + BC^2 = AC^2$

$\Rightarrow (7)^2 + (x - 1)^2 = x^2 \Rightarrow 49 + x^2 - 2x + 1 = x^2$

$\Rightarrow 2x = 50 \Rightarrow x = 25$ (1 M)

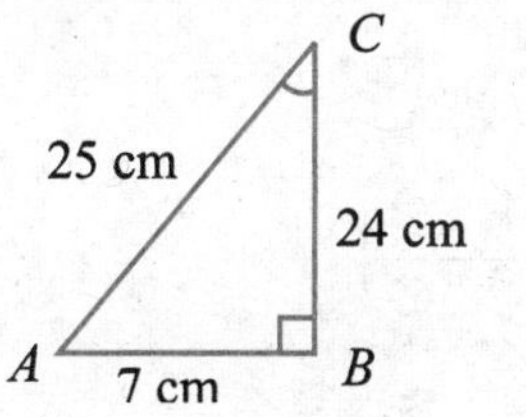

(1 M)

$$\therefore \sin C = \frac{AB}{AC} = \frac{7}{25} \text{ and } \cos C = \frac{BC}{AC} = \frac{24}{25} \quad (1\ M)$$

8. If $\operatorname{cosec} A = \sqrt{10}$, find the remaining trigonometric ratios. *(Ap)*

Sol. Since, $\operatorname{cosec} A = \frac{\text{Hypotenuse}}{\text{Perpendicular}} = \frac{\sqrt{10}}{1}$.

By Pythagoras theorem, we have

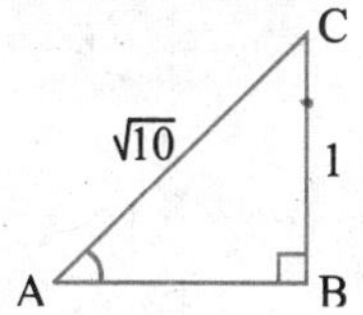

$AC^2 = AB^2 + BC^2$

$\Rightarrow (\sqrt{10})^2 = AB^2 + 1^2 \Rightarrow AB^2 = 10 - 1 = 9$

$\Rightarrow AB = \sqrt{9} = 3$ (½ M)

$$\therefore \sin A = \frac{\text{Perpendicular}}{\text{Hypotenuse}} = \frac{1}{\sqrt{10}}; \quad (½\ M)$$

$$\cos A = \frac{\text{Base}}{\text{Hypotenuse}} = \frac{3}{\sqrt{10}}; \quad (½\ M)$$

$$\tan A = \frac{\text{Perpendicular}}{\text{Base}} = \frac{1}{3}; \quad (½\ M)$$

$$\sec A = \frac{\text{Hypotenuse}}{\text{Base}} = \frac{\sqrt{10}}{3}; \quad (½\ M)$$

$$\text{and } \cot A = \frac{\text{Base}}{\text{Perpendicular}} = \frac{3}{1} = 3 \quad (½\ M)$$

9. The value of cot *B* is $\frac{12}{5}$, then find the value of $\tan^2 B - \sin^2 B$ *(Un)*

Sol. Since $\cot B = \frac{\text{Base}}{\text{Perpendicular}} = \frac{12}{5}$,

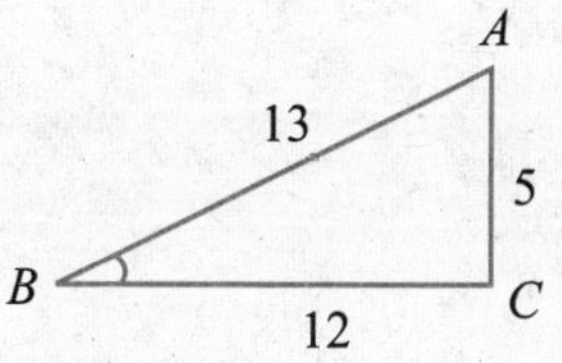

(1 M)

By Pythagoras theorem, we have

$AB^2 = BC^2 + AC^2$

$\Rightarrow AB^2 = 12^2 + 5^2 = 169 \Rightarrow AB = \sqrt{169} = 13$

$$\therefore \sin B = \frac{AC}{AB} = \frac{5}{13}, \tan B = \frac{AC}{BC} = \frac{5}{12} \quad (1\ M)$$

Now, $\tan^2 B - \sin^2 B = (\tan B)^2 - (\sin B)^2$

$$= \left(\frac{5}{12}\right)^2 - \left(\frac{5}{13}\right)^2 = \frac{25}{144} - \frac{25}{169}$$

$$= 25\left(\frac{1}{144} - \frac{1}{169}\right) = 25\left(\frac{169-144}{144\times169}\right)$$

$$= 25\frac{25}{144\times169} = \frac{25\times25}{144\times169} = \frac{5^2\times5^2}{12^2\times13^2} \quad (1\ M)$$

10. If $\tan(A+B) = \sqrt{3}$ and $\tan(A-B) = \frac{1}{\sqrt{3}}$, $0 < A+B \le 90°$, $A > B$, then find the values of A and B.

(*Ev*) (CBSE, 2020)

Sol. $\tan(A+B) = \sqrt{3}$

$\Rightarrow (A+B) = 60°$ ... (*i*) (½ M)

$\tan(A-B) = \frac{1}{\sqrt{3}}$

$\Rightarrow \tan(A-B) = \tan 30°$

$\Rightarrow (A-B) = 30°$ ... (*ii*) (½ M)

Adding (*i*) and (*ii*); we get,

$A + B + A - B = 60° + 30°$

$\Rightarrow 2A = 90°$

$\Rightarrow A = 45°$

Putting the value of A in equation (*i*),

$45° + B = 60°$

$\Rightarrow B = 60° - 45°$

$\Rightarrow B = 15°$

Thus, $A = 45°$ and $B = 15°$ (1 M)

Long Answer Type Questions (4 or 5 M)

1. If $\frac{\text{cosec}\,\theta + \cot\theta}{\text{cosec}\,\theta - \cot\theta} = \frac{81}{49}$, find $\frac{\cos\theta + \sin\theta}{\sin\theta - \cos\theta}$. **(*An*)**

Sol. $\frac{\text{cosec}\,\theta + \cot\theta}{\text{cosec}\,\theta - \cot\theta} = \frac{81}{49}$

$\Rightarrow 49\,\text{cosec}\,\theta + 49\cot\theta = 81\,\text{cosec}\,\theta - 81\cot\theta$

$\Rightarrow 49\cot\theta + 81\cot\theta = 81\,\text{cosec}\,\theta - 49\,\text{cosec}\,\theta$

$\Rightarrow 130\cot\theta = 32\,\text{cosec}\,\theta$ (½ M)

$\Rightarrow 130.\frac{\cos\theta}{\sin\theta} = 32.\frac{1}{\sin\theta} \Rightarrow 65\cos\theta = 16$

$\Rightarrow \cos\theta = \frac{16}{65} = \frac{\text{Base}}{\text{Hypotenuse}}$ (1 M)

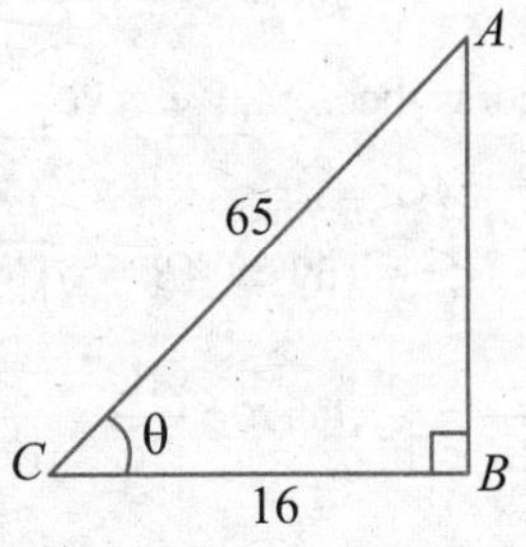

On applying Pythagoras theorem in ΔABC, we get

$AB^2 = AC^2 - BC^2 = 65^2 - 16^2$ (1 M)

$= (65+16)(65-16)$ $[a^2 - b^2 = (a-b)(a+b)]$

$= (81)(49)$

$AB = \sqrt{81\times49} = 9\times7 = 63$ (½ M)

$\therefore \sin\theta = \frac{AB}{AC} = \frac{63}{65}$ (1 M)

Required expression $= \frac{\cos\theta + \sin\theta}{\sin\theta - \cos\theta}$

$$= \frac{\frac{16}{65} + \frac{63}{65}}{\frac{63}{65} - \frac{16}{65}} = \frac{79}{65} \times \frac{65}{47} = \frac{79}{47} \quad (1\ M)$$

2. If $\tan\theta = \frac{2x(x+1)}{2x+1}$, find $\sin\theta$ and $\cos\theta$. **(*Cr*)**

Sol. $\tan\theta = \frac{P}{B} = \frac{2x(x+1)}{2x+1}$

Let P = perpendicular

$P = PM = 2x(x+1)$

B = Base $= OM = (2x+1)$

H = Hypotenuse $= OP = ?$

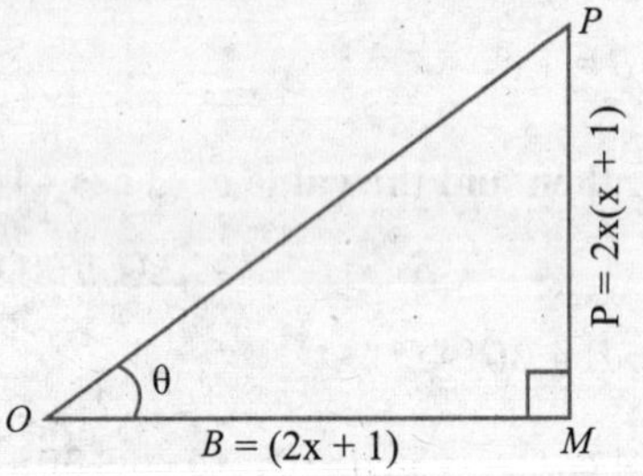

(1 M)

$\therefore \quad H^2 = P^2 + B^2$

$OP^2 = PM^2 + OM^2$

$OP^2 = [2x(x+1)]^2 + [(2x+1)]^2$ (1 M)

$OP^2 = [4x^2(x^2 + 2x + 1) + 4x^2 + 1 + 4x]$

$OP^2 = [4x^4 + 8x^3 + 4x^2 + 4x^2 + 1 + 4x]$

$OP^2 = [4x^4 + 4x^2 + 1 + 8x^3 + 4x + 4x^2]$

$OP^2 = [(2x^2)^2 + (2x)^2 + (1)^2 + 2.(2x^2).(2x) + 2.(2x).(1) + 2.(1).(2x^2)]$ (1 M)

Now, we know,

$a^2 + b^2 + c^2 + 2ab + 2bc + 2ca = (a+b+c)^2$

$\therefore OP^2 = [2x^2 + 2x + 1]^2$

$\Rightarrow OP = (2x^2 + 2x + 1)$ (1 M)

$\sin\theta = \frac{PM}{OP} = \frac{2x(x+1)}{2x^2+2x+1}$

and $\cos\theta = \frac{OM}{OP} = \frac{2x+1}{2x^2+2x+1}$ (1 M)

3. If the value of $\sec A = \frac{26}{10}$, then find the value of $\tan^2 A - \sin^2 A - \sin^4 A \sec^2 A$. *(Ap)*

Sol. Given, $\sec A = \frac{26}{10} = \frac{\text{Hypotenuse}}{\text{Base}}$

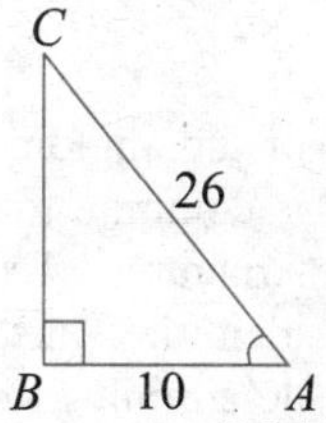

Using Pythagoras theorem,

$AC^2 = AB^2 + BC^2$

$BC^2 = 26^2 - 10^2 = 676 - 100 = 576$

$BC = 24$ units *(1 M)*

$\tan A = \frac{24}{10}$; $\sin A = \frac{24}{26}$ *(1 M)*

Now substitute the values

$\tan^2 A - \sin^2 A - \sin^4 A \times \sec^2 A$

$$= \left(\frac{24}{10}\right)^2 - \left(\frac{24}{26}\right)^2 - \left(\frac{24}{26}\right)^4 \times \left(\frac{26}{10}\right)^2$$ *(1 M)*

$$= \frac{24^2}{10^2} - \frac{24^2}{26^2} - \frac{24^4}{26^4} \times \frac{26^2}{10^2}$$

$$= 24^2\left(\frac{1}{10^2} - \frac{1}{26^2}\right) - \frac{24^4}{26^2 \times 10^2}$$ *(1 M)*

$$= 24^2\left(\frac{26^2 - 10^2}{26^2 \times 10^2}\right) - \frac{24^4}{26^2 \times 10^2}$$

$$= 24^2\left(\frac{24^2}{26^2 \times 10^2}\right) - \frac{24^4}{26^2 \times 10^2}$$ [now $26^2 - 10^2 = 24^2$]

$$= \frac{24^4}{26^2 \times 10^2} - \frac{24^4}{26^2 \times 10^2} = 0$$ *(1 M)*

4. Show that

$$\frac{4}{3}\cot^2 30^\circ + 3\sin^2 60^\circ - 2\operatorname{cosec}^2 60^\circ - \frac{3}{4}\tan^2 30^\circ = 3\frac{1}{3}.$$

(An)

Sol. $$\text{L.H.S} = \frac{4}{3}\cot^2 30^\circ + 3\sin^2 60^\circ - 2\operatorname{cosec}^2 60^\circ - \frac{3}{4}\tan^2 30^\circ$$

$$= \frac{4}{3} \times (\sqrt{3})^2 + 3 \times \left(\frac{\sqrt{3}}{2}\right)^2 - 2\left(\frac{2}{\sqrt{3}}\right)^2 - \frac{3}{4}\left(\frac{1}{\sqrt{3}}\right)^2$$ *(1 M)*

$$= \frac{4}{3} \times 3 + 3 \times \frac{3}{4} - 2 \times \frac{4}{3} - \frac{3}{4} \times \frac{1}{3}$$ *(1 M)*

$$= 4 + \frac{9}{4} - \frac{8}{3} - \frac{3}{12} = \frac{48 + 27 - 32 - 3}{12} = \frac{40}{12}$$ *(1 M)*

$$= \frac{40}{12} = \frac{10}{3} = 3\frac{1}{3} = \text{R.H.S.}$$ *(1 M)*

$\therefore$ L.H.S = R.H.S Hence proved *(1 M)*

2 TRIGONOMETRIC IDENTITIES

Important Terms

Trigonometric identities: Trigonometric ratios for some specific angles and establish some identities involving these ratios, called trigonometric identities.

Important Formulas

(*a*) $\sin^2\theta + \cos^2\theta = 1$

(*b*) $1 + \tan^2\theta = \sec^2\theta$

(*c*) $1 + \cot^2\theta = \text{cosec}^2\theta$

Important Derivations

❑ $\mathbf{\sin^2\theta + \cos^2\theta = 1}$

Proof:

Let *ABC* be a right angled triangle, right angled at *C* and $\angle B = \theta$.

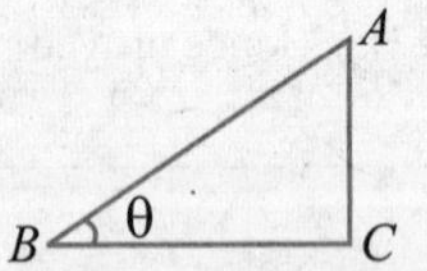

$$\sin\theta = \frac{AC}{AB}$$

$$\sin^2\theta = \frac{AC^2}{AB^2} \quad \ldots (i)$$

$$\cos\theta = \frac{BC}{AB}$$

$$\cos^2\theta = \frac{BC^2}{AB^2} \quad \ldots (ii)$$

On adding equations (*i*) and (*ii*), we get

$$\sin^2\theta + \cos^2\theta = \frac{AC^2}{AB^2} + \frac{BC^2}{AB^2} = \frac{AC^2 + BC^2}{AB^2}$$

$$\therefore \sin^2\theta + \cos^2\theta = \frac{AB^2}{AB^2} = 1$$

$$\left[AC^2 + BC^2 = AB^2 \text{ by Pythagoras theorem}\right]$$

Real Life Applications

Architecture: In architecture trigonometric identifies are found when especially developing large infrastructure. All identities of trigonometric are used to find either length of one or more side or the angle at which different materials should be placed at. It is common to find them when constructing blueprints for actual structures. (Examples of this are shown below.) Trigonometric identities like finding the sine of an angle will help when determining how much of a certain material is needed to use in order to construct the building and other example, Trigonometric identities are used in navigation to calculate the distance between two points, as well as the direction and angle of travel.

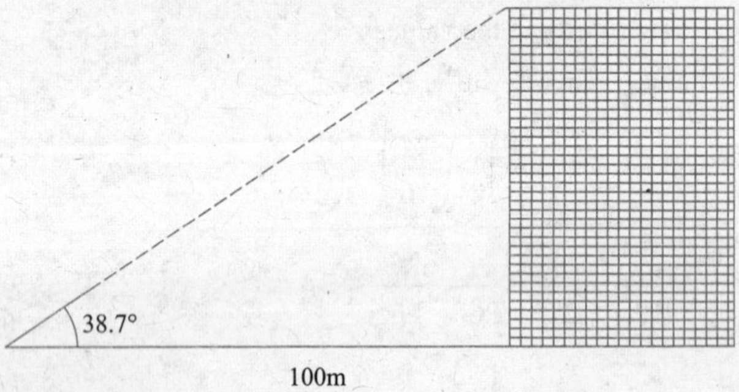

Different Problem Types

Type I: Simplifying a Trigonometric Expression with Trigonometric Identities

Solve the trigonometric expression

$$\frac{\sin^2 x}{\sec x - \text{cosec}\, x}$$

Solution: Given expression: $\dfrac{\sin^2 x}{\sec x - \csc x}$

Step I: Convert secant and cosecant to their reciprocal forms:

$$\frac{\sin^2 x}{\frac{1}{\cos x} - \frac{1}{\sin x}}$$

Step II: Find a common denominator for the fractions in the denominator: $\dfrac{\sin^2 x}{\frac{\sin x - \cos x}{\sin x \cos x}}$

Step III: Invert the denominator and multiply to simplify the expression: $\dfrac{\sin^2 x.\dfrac{\sin x \cos x}{\sin x - \cos x}}{1}$

Step IV: Simplify the expression: $\dfrac{\sin^3 x \cos x}{\sin x - \cos x}$

Therefore, the simplified form of the given expression is $\dfrac{\sin^3 x \cos x}{\sin x - \cos x}$

Example 1: **Find the value of** $\cos^2\theta + \dfrac{1}{1+\cot^2\theta}$

Solution:

$$\cos^2\theta + \frac{1}{1+\cot^2\theta} = \cos^2\theta + \frac{1}{1+\frac{\cos^2\theta}{\sin^2\theta}}$$

$$= \cos^2\theta + \frac{1}{\frac{\sin^2\theta+\cos^2\theta}{\sin^2\theta}} = \cos^2\theta + \frac{\sin^2\theta}{\sin^2\theta+\cos^2\theta} = \cos^2\theta + \sin^2\theta = 1$$

Example 2: **Prove that**

$$\frac{\sin\theta-\cos\theta}{\sin\theta+\cos\theta}+\frac{\sin\theta+\cos\theta}{\sin\theta-\cos\theta}=\frac{2}{1-2\cos^2\theta}$$

Solution: We have,

$$\text{L.H.S} = \frac{\sin\theta-\cos\theta}{\sin\theta+\cos\theta}+\frac{\sin\theta+\cos\theta}{\sin\theta-\cos\theta}$$

$$= \frac{(\sin\theta-\cos\theta)^2+(\sin\theta+\cos\theta)^2}{(\sin\theta+\cos\theta)(\sin\theta-\cos\theta)}$$

$$= \frac{\sin^2\theta+\cos^2\theta-2\sin\theta\cos\theta+\sin^2\theta+\cos^2\theta+2\sin\theta\cos\theta}{(\sin^2\theta-\cos^2\theta)}$$

$$= \frac{2\sin^2\theta+2\cos^2\theta}{\sin^2\theta-\cos^2\theta} = \frac{2(\sin^2\theta+\cos^2\theta)}{\sin^2\theta-\cos^2\theta}$$

$$= \frac{2}{1-\cos^2\theta-\cos^2\theta} = \frac{2}{1-2\cos^2\theta} = \text{R.H.S}$$

$\therefore$ L.H.S = R.H.S

Hence proved

COMPETENCY BASED SOLVED EXAMPLES

Multiple Choice Questions (1 M)

1. Shown below is a solved trigonometric problem. *(Ev)*

$$\frac{\operatorname{cosec}\theta+\cot\theta-1}{\operatorname{cosec}\theta-\cot\theta+1}$$

$$= \frac{\operatorname{cosec}\theta+\cot\theta-(\cot^2\theta-\operatorname{cosec}^2\theta)}{\operatorname{cosec}\theta-\cot\theta+1} \quad \textbf{(Step 1)}$$

$$= \frac{\cot\theta+\operatorname{cosec}\theta-(\cot\theta-\operatorname{cosec}\theta)(\cot\theta+\operatorname{cosec}\theta)}{\operatorname{cosec}\theta-\cot\theta+1} \quad \textbf{(Step 2)}$$

$$= \frac{(\cot\theta+\operatorname{cosec}\theta)(1-\cot\theta+\operatorname{cosec}\theta)}{\operatorname{cosec}\theta-\cot\theta+1} \quad \textbf{(Step 3)}$$

$= \cot\theta + \operatorname{cosec}\theta$ **(Step 4)**

In which step is there an error in solving?

(*a*) Step 1 (*b*) Step 2

(*c*) Step 3 (*d*) There is no error.

Sol. The expression in Step 1 is:

$$\frac{\operatorname{cosec}\theta+\cot\theta-1}{\operatorname{cosec}\theta-\cot\theta+1}=\frac{\operatorname{cosec}\theta+\cot\theta-(\cot^2\theta-\operatorname{cosec}^2\theta)}{\operatorname{cosec}\theta-\cot\theta+1}$$

This step incorrectly uses the identity

as we know $\operatorname{cosec}^2\theta - \cot^2\theta = 1$

$\therefore$ There is an error in solving in Step 1

Mistakes 101 : What not to do!

Students often make mistakes in using the correct formula in a given expression.

2. If $\sin A + \sin^2 A = 1$**, then** $\cos^2 A$ **= ?** *(Re)*

(*a*) $\sin A$ (*b*) $1 + \sin^2 A$

(*c*) 2 (*d*) $\sin^2 A$

Sol. Given

$\sin A + \sin^2 A = 1 \Rightarrow \sin A = 1 - \sin^2 A$

$\Rightarrow \sin A = \cos^2 A$

3. The value of $\cos^2\theta - \dfrac{1}{1+\tan^2\theta}$ **is** *(Ap)*

(*a*) $\sqrt{3}$ (*b*) 1 (*c*) 0 (*d*) $\frac{1}{2}$

Sol. $$\cos^2\theta - \frac{1}{1+\tan^2\theta} = \cos^2\theta - \frac{1}{1+\frac{\sin^2\theta}{\cos^2\theta}}$$

$$= \cos^2\theta - \frac{1}{\frac{\sin^2\theta+\cos^2\theta}{\cos^2\theta}} = \cos^2\theta - \frac{\cos^2\theta}{\sin^2\theta+\cos^2\theta}$$

$= \cos^2\theta - \cos^2\theta$ $[\because \sin^2\theta + \cos^2\theta = 1]$

$= 0$

4. If $\cot\theta + \tan\theta = x$ **and** $\sec\theta - \cos\theta = y$**, the value of** $(x^2y)^{2/3} - (xy^2)^{2/3}$ **is** *(An)*

(*a*) 0 (*b*) 1

(*c*) $\tan\theta$ (*d*) $\sec\theta$

Sol. Given: $\tan\theta + \cot\theta = x$

$$\Rightarrow \frac{\sin\theta}{\cos\theta}+\frac{\cos\theta}{\sin\theta} = x \Rightarrow \frac{\sin^2\theta+\cos^2\theta}{\cos\theta\sin\theta} = x$$

$$\Rightarrow x = \frac{1}{\sin\theta\cos\theta}$$

and $\sec\theta - \cos\theta = y$

$$\Rightarrow \frac{1}{\cos\theta} - \cos\theta = y \Rightarrow \frac{1-\cos^2\theta}{\cos\theta} = y \Rightarrow \frac{\sin^2\theta}{\cos\theta} = y$$

So, $(x^2y)^{2/3} - (xy^2)^{2/3}$

$$= \left\{\frac{1}{\cos^2\theta\sin^2\theta} \times \frac{\sin^2\theta}{\cos\theta}\right\}^{2/3} - \left\{\frac{1}{\cos\theta\sin\theta} \times \frac{\sin^4\theta}{\cos^2\theta}\right\}^{2/3}$$

$$= \left(\frac{1}{\cos^3\theta}\right)^{2/3} - \left(\frac{\sin^3\theta}{\cos^3\theta}\right)^{2/3} = \frac{1}{\cos^2\theta} - \frac{\sin^2\theta}{\cos^2\theta}$$

$$= \frac{1-\sin^2\theta}{\cos^2\theta} = \frac{\cos^2\theta}{\cos^2\theta} = 1 \qquad [\because 1-\sin^2\theta = \cos^2\theta]$$

5. If $\sin\theta + \cos\theta = p$ and $\sec\theta + \operatorname{cosec}\theta = q$, then the value of $q(p^2-1) - 2p$ is *(An)*

(*a*) $2q$ (*b*) 0

(*c*) 1 (*d*) $p - q$

Sol. $q(p^2 - 1) = (\sec\theta + \operatorname{cosec}\theta)\{(\sin\theta + \cos\theta)^2 - 1\} - 2p$

Applying $(a + b)^2$ and simplifying, we get

$$= \left(\frac{1}{\cos\theta} + \frac{1}{\sin\theta}\right)\{2\sin\theta\cos\theta\} - 2p$$

$$= \left(\frac{\sin\theta + \cos\theta}{\sin\theta\cos\theta}\right)(2\sin\theta\cos\theta) - 2(\sin\theta + \cos\theta) = 0$$

6. Given that $\sin\theta = \frac{a}{b}$, then $\cos\theta$ is. *(Ev)*

(*a*) $\frac{b}{\sqrt{b^2-a^2}}$ (*b*) $\frac{b}{a}$

(*c*) $\frac{\sqrt{b^2-a^2}}{b}$ (*d*) $\frac{a}{\sqrt{b^2-a^2}}$

Sol. $\sin\theta = \frac{a}{b} = \frac{\text{Perpendicular}}{\text{Hypotenuse}}$

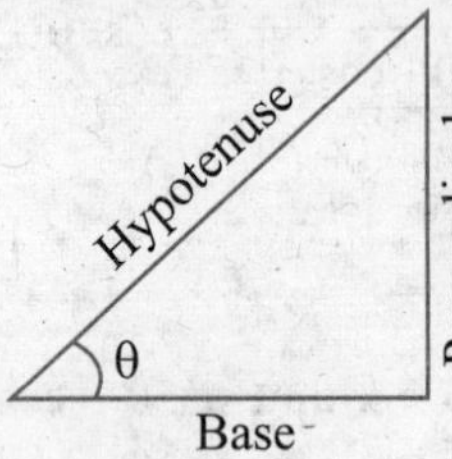

By Pythagoras' Theorem,

$\Rightarrow$ (Hypotenuse)^2 = (Perpendicular)^2 + (Base)^2

$\Rightarrow$ (Base)^2 = (Hypotenuse)^2 – (Perpendicular)^2

$\Rightarrow$ (Base)$^2 = (b)^2 - (a)^2$

$\Rightarrow$ Base $= \sqrt{b^2 - a^2}$

Hence, $\cos\theta = \frac{\text{Base}}{\text{Hypotenuse}} = \frac{\sqrt{b^2-a^2}}{b}$

7. $\frac{1-\cos\theta}{1+\cos\theta}$ is equal to *(Un)*

(*a*) $(\operatorname{cosec}\theta + \cot\theta)^2$ (*b*) $(\operatorname{cosec}\theta - \cot\theta)^2$

(*c*) $\operatorname{cosec}^2\theta + \cot^2\theta$ (*d*) None of these

Sol. $\frac{1-\cos\theta}{1+\cos\theta} = \frac{(1-\cos\theta)(1-\cos\theta)}{(1+\cos\theta)(1-\cos\theta)}$

$$= \frac{(1-\cos\theta)^2}{1-\cos^2\theta} = \frac{1+\cos^2\theta - 2\cos\theta}{\sin^2\theta}$$

On separating a denominator, we get

$$= \frac{1}{\sin^2\theta} + \frac{\cos^2\theta}{\sin^2\theta} - 2\frac{\cos\theta}{\sin\theta}\frac{1}{\sin\theta}$$

$= \operatorname{cosec}^2\theta + \cot^2\theta - 2\operatorname{cosec}\theta\cot\theta = (\operatorname{cosec}\theta - \cot\theta)^2$

8. Is expression $\frac{\tan x}{\frac{\sin^3 x}{\cos x} + \sin x\cos x} = 1$ true/false? *(Un)*

(*a*) true (*b*) false

(*c*) can't say (*d*) None of these

Sol. $\frac{\tan x}{\frac{\sin^3 x}{\cos x} + \sin x\cos x} = \frac{\tan x \times \cos x}{\sin^3 x + \sin x\cos^2 x}$

$$= \frac{\frac{\sin x}{\cos x} \times \cos x}{\sin x(\sin^2 x + \cos^2 x)} = \frac{\sin x}{\sin x \times 1} = 1$$

Hence, given expression is true.

9. $\frac{1}{\sec\theta - \tan\theta}$ is equal to *(Re)*

(*a*) $\sec\theta - \tan\theta$ (*b*) $\tan\theta$

(*c*) $\sec\theta + \tan\theta$ (*d*) $\sec\theta$

Sol. $\frac{1}{\sec\theta - \tan\theta} \times \frac{\sec\theta + \tan\theta}{\sec\theta + \tan\theta}$

$$= \frac{\sec\theta + \tan\theta}{\sec^2\theta - \tan^2\theta} = \sec\theta + \tan\theta$$

10. The value of $\sec^2 A\tan^2 B - \tan^2 A\sec^2 B$ is *(Ev)*

(*a*) $\tan^2 B - \tan^2 A$ (*b*) $\sec^2 B + \tan^2 A$

(*c*) $\tan^2 B - \sec^2 A$ (*d*) $\sec^2 B - \tan^2 A$

Sol. $(1 + \tan^2 A)\tan^2 B - \tan^2 A(1 + \tan^2 B)$

$= \tan^2 B + \tan^2 A\tan^2 B - \tan^2 A - \tan^2 A\tan^2 B$

$= \tan^2 B - \tan^2 A$

11. If θ is an acute angle and $\tan\theta + \cot\theta = 2$, then the value of $\sin^3\theta + \cos^3\theta$ is *(Un)*

(*a*) 1 (*b*) $\frac{1}{\sqrt{2}}$

(*c*) $\frac{\sqrt{2}}{2}$ (*d*) $\sqrt{2}$

Sol. Given θ is an acute angle.

$$\Rightarrow \tan\theta + \cot\theta = 2 \Rightarrow \tan\theta + \frac{1}{\tan\theta} = 2$$

$$\Rightarrow \frac{\tan^2\theta + 1}{\tan\theta} = 2 \Rightarrow \tan^2\theta - 2\tan\theta + 1 = 0$$

$$\Rightarrow (\tan\theta - 1)^2 = 0 \Rightarrow \tan\theta = 1 = \tan 45° \Rightarrow \theta = 45°$$

$$\therefore \sin^3\theta + \cos^3\theta = \sin^3 45 + \cos^3 45$$

$$= \left(\frac{1}{\sqrt{2}}\right)^3 + \left(\frac{1}{\sqrt{2}}\right)^3 = \frac{2}{2\sqrt{2}} = \frac{1}{\sqrt{2}}$$

12. If $a\cot\theta + b\,\text{cosec}\theta = p$ and $b\cot\theta + a\,\text{cosec}\theta = q$ then $p^2 - q^2 =$ *(Un)*

(*a*) $a^2 - b^2$ (*b*) $b^2 - a^2$

(*c*) $a^2 + b^2$ (*d*) $b - a$

Sol. Given $a\cot\theta + b\,\text{cosec}\theta = p$ and $b\cot\theta + a\,\text{cosec}\theta = q$

$\therefore p^2 - q^2 = (a\cot\theta + b\,\text{cosec}\theta)^2 - (b\cot\theta + a\,\text{cosec}\theta)^2 = a^2\cot^2\theta + b^2\text{cosec}^2\theta + 2ab\cot\theta\,\text{cosec}\theta - (b^2\cot^2\theta + a^2\text{cosec}^2\theta + 2ab\cot\theta\,\text{cosec}\theta)$

$= (a^2 - b^2)\cot^2\theta + (b^2 - a^2)\text{cosec}^2\theta$

$= (b^2 - a^2)(\text{cosec}^2\theta - \cot^2\theta) = (b^2 - a^2)\cdot 1 = (b^2 - a^2)$

13. $1 - \cos^2 A$ is equal to *(Ap)* **(CBSE SQP, 2023)**

(*a*) $\sin^2 A$ (*b*) $\tan^2 A$

(*c*) $1 - \sin^2 A$ (*d*) $\sec^2 A$

Sol. We know that,

$\sin^2 A + \cos^2 A = 1$

$\Rightarrow 1 - \cos^2 A = \sin^2 A$

Therefore, $1 - \cos^2 A$ is equals to $\sin^2 A$

Answer Key

1. (*a*)	2. (*a*)	3. (*c*)	4. (*b*)	5. (*b*)
6. (*c*)	7. (*b*)	8. (*a*)	9. (*c*)	10. (*a*)
11. (*b*)	12. (*b*)	13. (*a*)		

Assertion and Reason (1 M)

Direction: In the following questions, a statement of assertion (*A*) is followed by a statement of Reason (*R*). Mark the correct choice as:

(*a*) Both Assertion (*A*) and Reason (*R*) are true and Reason (*R*) is the correct explanation of Assertion (*A*).

(*b*) Both Assertion (*A*) and Reason (*R*) are true but Reason (*R*) is not the correct explanation of Assertion (*A*).

(*c*) Assertion (*A*) is true but Reason (*R*) is false.

(*d*) Assertion (*A*) is false but Reason (*R*) is true.

1. Assertion (A): If $k + 1 = \sec^2\theta(1 + \sin\theta)(1 - \sin\theta)$, then the value of k is 1.

Reason (R): If $\sin\theta + \cos\theta = \sqrt{3}$ then the value of $\tan\theta + \cot\theta$ is 1. *(Ap)*

Sol. Given

$k + 1 = \sec^2\theta\,(1 + \sin\theta)\,(1 - \sin\theta)$

or, $k + 1 = \sec^2\theta\,(1 - \sin^2\theta)$

or, $k + 1 = \sec^2\theta \,.\, \cos^2\theta)$ $[\because \sin^2\theta + \cos^2\theta = 1]$

or, $k + 1 = \sec^2\theta \times \dfrac{1}{\sec^2\theta}$

or, $k + 1 = 1$

or, $k = 1 - 1$

$\therefore k = 0$

$\therefore$ Assertion is false.

In case of reason:

Given $\sin\theta + \cos\theta = \sqrt{3}$

Squaring on both sides,

$(\sin\theta + \cos\theta)^2 = (\sqrt{3})^2$

$\Rightarrow \sin^2\theta + \cos^2\theta + 2\sin\theta\cos\theta = 3$

$\Rightarrow 1 + 2\sin\theta\cos\theta = 3$

$\Rightarrow 2\sin\theta\cos\theta = 2$

$\Rightarrow \sin\theta\cos\theta = 1$ ... (*i*)

$$\tan\theta + \cot\theta = \frac{\sin\theta}{\cos\theta} + \frac{\cos\theta}{\sin\theta}$$

$$= \frac{\sin^2\theta + \cos^2\theta}{\cos\theta\sin\theta} = \frac{1}{1} = 1$$

Reason is true

Hence Assertion (A) is false but Reason (R) is true

2. Assertion (A): If $\cos A + \cos^2 A = 1$ then $\sin^2 A + \sin^4 A = 2$.

Reason (R): $1 - \sin^2 A = \cos^2 A$, for any value of A. *(Ev)*

Sol. Given Assertion

$\cos A + \cos^2 A = 1$

$\cos A = 1 - \cos^2 A = \sin^2 A$

and $\sin^2 A + \sin^4 A = \cos A + \cos^2 A = 1$

$\therefore \sin^2 A + \sin^4 A = 1$

and reason $1 - \sin^2 A = \cos^2$ is true

Assertion (A) is false but reason (R) is true.

Answer Key

1. (*d*)	2. (*d*)

Subjective Questions

Very Short Answer Type Questions (1 or 2 M)

1. Find the value of $\left(\sin^2\theta + \dfrac{1}{1 + \tan^2\theta}\right)$ *(Ev)*

Sol. Here $\sin^2\theta + \dfrac{1}{1 + \tan^2\theta} = \sin^2\theta + \dfrac{1}{\sec^2\theta}$ *(1 M)*

$= \sin^2\theta + \cos^2\theta = 1$ *(1 M)*

2. **Find the value of $(1 + \tan^2\theta)(1 - \sin\theta)(1 + \sin\theta)$** *(An)*

Sol. $\therefore (1+\tan^2\theta)(1-\sin\theta)(1+\sin\theta)$

$= \sec^2\theta(1-\sin^2\theta)$ *(1 M)*

$= \sec^2\theta.\cos^2\theta = \sec^2\theta.\dfrac{1}{\sec^2\theta} = 1$ *(1 M)*

3. **Prove that $\dfrac{\cot A - \cos A}{\cot A + \cos A} = \dfrac{\operatorname{cosec} A - 1}{\operatorname{cosec} A + 1}$**

(An) (NCERT Intext)

Sol. $\text{L.H.S} = \dfrac{\cot A - \cos A}{\cot A + \cos A} = \dfrac{\dfrac{\cos A}{\sin A} - \cos A}{\dfrac{\cos A}{\sin A} + \cos A}$ *(1 M)*

$= \dfrac{\cos A\left(\dfrac{1}{\sin A} - 1\right)}{\cos A\left(\dfrac{1}{\sin A} + 1\right)} = \dfrac{\left(\dfrac{1}{\sin A} - 1\right)}{\left(\dfrac{1}{\sin A} + 1\right)} = \dfrac{\operatorname{cosec} A - 1}{\operatorname{cosec} A + 1} = \text{R.H.S}$

$\therefore$ L.H.S = R.H.S Hence proved *(1 M)*

4. **Show that $\sec^4\theta - \sec^2\theta = \tan^4\theta + \tan^2\theta$.** *(Ap)*

Sol. L.H.S. $= \sec^4\theta - \sec^2\theta = \sec^2\theta(\sec^2\theta - 1)$ *(1 M)*

$= (1 + \tan^2\theta)(1 + \tan^2\theta - 1) = \tan^4\theta + \tan^2\theta = \text{R.H.S}$

(1 M)

5. **Prove that $\dfrac{\operatorname{cosec}^2 x - \sin^2 x \cot^2 x - \cot^2 x}{\sin^2 x} = 1$,**

(An) (CBSE CFPQ, 2023)

Sol. Simplifies the given L.H.S as: $\dfrac{1 - \sin^2 x \cot^2 x}{\sin^2 x}$ *(1 M)*

Simplifies the above expression as:

$\operatorname{cosec}^2 x - \cot^2 x$ *(½ M)*

Simplifies the above expression as 1 and concludes that LHS = R.H.S. *(½ M)*

6. **Show that the value of $\dfrac{\sin\theta}{1 - \cos\theta} = \operatorname{cosec}\theta + \cot\theta$.** *(Ev)*

Sol. We have,

$\text{L.H.S} = \dfrac{\sin\theta}{(1-\cos\theta)} \times \dfrac{(1+\cos\theta)}{(1+\cos\theta)}$

$= \dfrac{\sin\theta(1+\cos\theta)}{1-\cos^2\theta} = \dfrac{\sin\theta(1+\cos\theta)}{\sin^2\theta}$ *(1 M)*

$[\because 1 - \cos^2\theta = \sin^2\theta]$

$= \dfrac{1+\cos\theta}{\sin\theta} = \dfrac{1}{\sin\theta} + \dfrac{\cos\theta}{\sin\theta} = \operatorname{cosec}\theta + \cot\theta = \text{R.H.S}$ *(1 M)*

$\therefore$ L.H.S = R.H.S Hence proved

7. **If $\sin\theta + \cos\theta = \sqrt{3}$, then prove that $\tan\theta + \cot\theta = 1$**

(Un) (NCERT Exemplar)

Sol. $\sin\theta + \cos\theta = \sqrt{3}$

$(\sin\theta + \cos\theta)^2 = 3$

or $\sin^2\theta + \cos^2\theta + 2\sin\theta\cos\theta = 3$ *(1 M)*

or $2\sin\theta\cos\theta = 2$

$\sin\theta\cos\theta = 1 = \sin^2\theta + \cos^2\theta$

or $1 = \dfrac{\sin^2\theta + \cos^2\theta}{\sin\theta\cos\theta}$

Therefore, $\tan\theta + \cot\theta = 1$ *(1 M)*

Hence proved.

8. **Prove that $\sin^6\theta + \cos^6\theta + 3\sin^2\theta\cos^2\theta = 1$**

(An) (NCERT Exemplar)

Sol. We know that $\sin^2\theta + \cos^2\theta = 1$

Therefore,

$(\sin^2\theta + \cos^2\theta)^3 = 1$ *(1 M)*

or, $(\sin^2\theta)^3 + (\cos^2\theta)^3 + 3\sin^2\theta\cos^2\theta(\sin^2\theta + \sin^2\theta) = 1$

or, $\sin^6\theta + \cos^6\theta + 3\sin^2\theta\cos^2\theta = 1$ *(1 M)*

Hence proved.

9. **Given $\tan\theta = \dfrac{1}{\sqrt{5}}$, what is the value of $\dfrac{\operatorname{cosec}^2\theta - \sec^2\theta}{\operatorname{cosec}^2\theta + \sec^2\theta}$**

(An)

Sol. Given $\tan\theta = \dfrac{1}{\sqrt{5}}$

and $\dfrac{\operatorname{cosec}^2\theta - \sec^2\theta}{\operatorname{cosec}^2\theta + \sec^2\theta} = \dfrac{(1+\cot^2\theta)-(1+\tan^2\theta)}{(1+\cot^2\theta)+(1+\tan^2\theta)}$ *(1 M)*

$= \dfrac{\cot^2\theta - \tan^2\theta}{2 + \cot^2\theta + \tan^2\theta}$ *(½ M)*

$= \dfrac{\dfrac{1}{\tan^2\theta} - \tan^2\theta}{2 + \dfrac{1}{\tan^2\theta} + \tan^2\theta} = \dfrac{5 - \dfrac{1}{5}}{2 + 5 + \dfrac{1}{5}} = \dfrac{\dfrac{24}{5}}{\dfrac{36}{5}} = \dfrac{2}{3}$ *(½ M)*

Short Answer Type Questions (2 or 3 M)

1. **If $\sin\theta + \cos\theta = \sqrt{3}$, then prove that $\tan\theta + \cot\theta = 1$.**

(An)

Sol. Given, $\sin\theta + \cos\theta = \sqrt{3}$,

Squaring

$\sin^2\theta + \cos^2\theta + 2\sin\theta.\cos\theta = 3$ *(1 M)*

$\Rightarrow 1 + 2\sin\theta.\cos\theta = 3 \Rightarrow 2\sin\theta.\cos\theta = 2$

$\Rightarrow \sin\theta\,.\,\cos\theta = 1$ *(1 M)*

Now L.H.S $= \tan\theta + \cot\theta = \dfrac{\sin\theta}{\cos\theta} + \dfrac{\cos\theta}{\sin\theta}$

$= \dfrac{\sin^2\theta + \cos^2\theta}{\sin\theta.\cos\theta} = \dfrac{1}{1} = 1 = \text{R.H.S}$

$\therefore$ L.H.S = R.H.S Hence proved *(1 M)*

2. **Prove that $(\operatorname{cosec}\theta - \cot\theta)^2 = \dfrac{1-\cos\theta}{1+\cos\theta}$**

(Ev) (CBSE SQP, 2023)

Sol. $(\operatorname{cosec}\theta - \cot\theta) = \dfrac{1-\cos\theta}{1+\cos\theta}$

LHS $= (\operatorname{cosec}\theta - \cot\theta)^2$

$$=\left(\frac{1}{\sin\theta}-\frac{\cos\theta}{\sin\theta}\right)^2$$ *(½ M)*

$$=\left(\frac{1-\cos\theta}{\sin\theta}\right)^2$$ *(½ M)*

$$=\frac{(1-\cos\theta)^2}{\sin^2\theta}=\frac{(1-\cos\theta)^2}{1-\cos^2\theta}$$ *(1 M)*

$$=\frac{(1-\cos\theta)^2}{(1-\cos\theta)(1+\cos\theta)}=\frac{1-\cos\theta}{1+\cos\theta}=\text{R.H.S}$$ *(1 M)*

Hence, L.H.S = R.H.S proved

3. Prove that: $\dfrac{2\cos^3\theta-\cos\theta}{\sin\theta-2\sin^3\theta}=\cot\theta$ ***(An)***

Sol. $\text{L.H.S}=\dfrac{2\cos^3\theta-\cos\theta}{\sin\theta-2\sin^3\theta}=\dfrac{\cos\theta(2\cos^2\theta-1)}{\sin\theta(1-2\sin^2\theta)}$ *(1 M)*

$$=\frac{\cos\theta(\cos 2\theta)}{\sin\theta(\cos 2\theta)}$$ *(½ M)*

$(\because \cos2\theta = 2\cos^2\theta - 1 = 1 - 2\sin^2\theta)$ *(½ M)*

$= \cot\theta$ = R.H.S.

∴ L.H.S. = R.H.S.

Hence, Proved *(1 M)*

Topper's Explanation ***(CBSE 2020)***

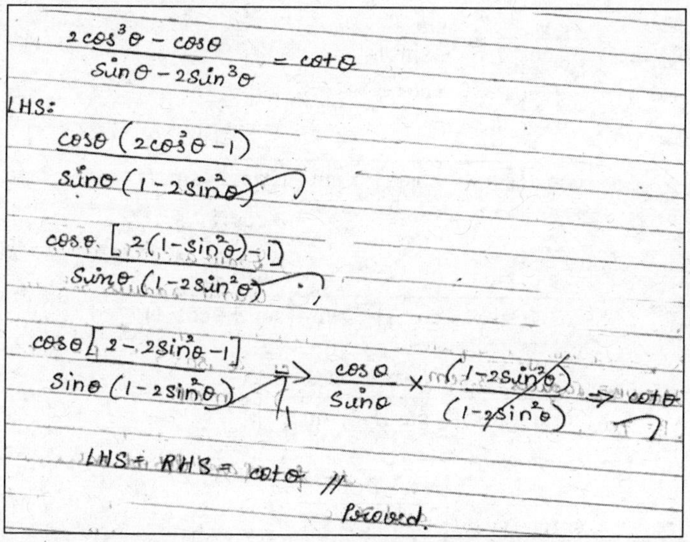

$\dfrac{2\cos^3\theta-\cos\theta}{\sin\theta-2\sin^3\theta}=\cot\theta$

LHS:

$\dfrac{\cos\theta\,(2\cos^2\theta-1)}{\sin\theta\,(1-2\sin^2\theta)}$

$\dfrac{\cos\theta\,[2(1-\sin^2\theta)-1]}{\sin\theta\,(1-2\sin^2\theta)}$

$\dfrac{\cos\theta\,[2-2\sin^2\theta-1]}{\sin\theta\,(1-2\sin^2\theta)} \Rightarrow \dfrac{\cos\theta}{\sin\theta}\times\dfrac{(1-2\sin^2\theta)}{(1-2\sin^2\theta)} \Rightarrow \cot\theta$

LHS = RHS = $\cot\theta$ //

Proved.

4. Prove that:

$(1 + \cot A + \tan A)(\sin A - \cos A) = \sin A \tan A - \cot A \cos A$. ***(Un)***

Sol. L.H.S. $= (1 + \cot A + \tan A)(\sin A - \cos A)$ *(1 M)*

$= \sin A - \cos A + \cot A \cdot \sin A - \cot A \cdot \cos A + \tan A \cdot \sin A - \tan A \cdot \cos A$

$= \sin A - \cos A + \dfrac{\cos A}{\sin A} \cdot \sin A - \cot A \cdot \cos A$ *(1 M)*

$+ \tan A \cdot \sin A - \dfrac{\sin A}{\cos A} \cdot \cos A$

$\sin A - \cos A + \cos A - \cot A\cdot\cos A + \tan A\cdot\sin A - \sin A$

$= \tan A \cdot \sin A - \cot A \cdot \cos A$ = R.H.S *(1 M)*

Hence proved

5. Prove that $\dfrac{\operatorname{cosec}\theta}{\operatorname{cosec}\theta-1}+\dfrac{\operatorname{cosec}\theta}{\operatorname{cosec}\theta+1}=2\sec^2\theta$

***(Ap)*(CBSE, 2020)**

Sol. L.H.S

$$=\frac{\operatorname{cosec}\theta}{\operatorname{cosec}\theta-0}+\frac{\operatorname{cosec}\theta}{\operatorname{cosec}\theta+1}$$

$$=\frac{\operatorname{cosec}\theta(\operatorname{cosec}\theta+1)+\operatorname{cosec}\theta(\operatorname{cosec}\theta-1)}{\operatorname{cosec}^2\theta-1}$$

$$=\frac{\operatorname{cosec}^2+\operatorname{cosec}\theta+\operatorname{cosec}^2\theta-\operatorname{cosec}\theta}{\operatorname{cosec}^2\theta-1}$$ *(1 M)*

$$=\frac{2\operatorname{cosec}^2\theta}{\cot^2\theta}\quad(\because \operatorname{cosec}^2\theta-1=\cot^2\theta)$$

$$=\frac{2}{\sin^2\theta}\times\frac{\sin^2\theta}{\cos^2\theta}\left(\because \operatorname{cosec}^2\theta=\frac{1}{\sin^2\theta}\text{ and }\cot^2\theta=\frac{\cos^2\theta}{\sin^2\theta}\right)$$

$$=\frac{2}{\cos^2\theta}$$ *(1 M)*

$$=2\sec^2\theta\left(\because \sec^2\theta=\frac{1}{\cos^2\theta}\right)=\text{R.H.S}$$

Hence proved. *(1 M)*

6. Prove that $(1 + \tan A - \sec A) \times (1 + \tan A + \sec A) = 2\tan A$. ***(Un)* (CBSE, 2020)**

Sol. Consider the L.H.S:

$(1 + \tan A - \sec A)(1 + \tan A + \sec A)$

$= [(1 + \tan A) - \sec A][(1 + \tan A) + \sec A]$ *(1 M)*

$= (1 + \tan A)^2 - \sec^2 A = 1 + 2\tan A + \tan^2 A - \sec^2 A$ *(1 M)*

$= 1 + 2\tan A + (-1) = 2\tan A$ = R.H.S

Hence proved. *(1 M)*

Long Answer Type Questions (4 or 5 M)

1. Prove that $\dfrac{\tan^2 A}{\tan^2 A-1}+\dfrac{\operatorname{cosec}^2 A}{\sec^2 A-\operatorname{cosec}^2 A}=\dfrac{1}{1-2\cos^2 A}$ ***(Cr)***

Sol. $\text{L.H.S}=\dfrac{\tan^2 A}{\tan^2 A-1}+\dfrac{\operatorname{cosec}^2 A}{\sec^2 A-\operatorname{cosec}^2 A}$

$\because \tan A=\dfrac{\sin A}{\cos A}, \operatorname{cosec} A=\dfrac{1}{\sin A}, \sec A=\dfrac{1}{\cos A}$ *(½ M)*

$$=\frac{\dfrac{\sin^2 A}{\cos^2 A}}{\dfrac{\sin^2 A}{\cos^2 A}-1}+\frac{\dfrac{1}{\sin^2 A}}{\dfrac{1}{\cos^2 A}-\dfrac{1}{\sin^2 A}}$$ *(½ M)*

$$=\frac{\dfrac{\sin^2 A}{\cos^2 A}}{\dfrac{\sin^2 A-\cos^2 A}{\cos^2 A}}+\frac{\dfrac{1}{\sin^2 A}}{\dfrac{\sin^2 A-\cos^2 A}{\sin^2 A\cos^2 A}}$$ *(½ M)*

$$=\frac{\sin^2 A}{\sin^2 A-\cos^2 A}+\frac{\cos^2 A}{\sin^2 A-\cos^2 A}$$ (½ M)

$$=\frac{\sin^2 A+\cos^2 A}{\sin^2 A-\cos^2 A}$$ (½ M)

$$=\frac{1}{\sin^2 A-\cos^2 A}\quad \because \sin^2 A+\cos^2 A=1$$ (1 M)

Since, $\sin^2 A = 1 - \cos^2 A$

$$=\frac{1}{1-\cos^2 A-\cos^2 A}$$ (½ M)

$$=\frac{1}{1-2\cos^2 A}=\text{R.H.S}$$ (1 M)

Hence, L.H.S. = R.H.S.

Hence proved.

2. Prove that: $\frac{\sin A-2\sin^3 A}{2\cos^3 A-\cos A}=\tan A$ *(An)*

Sol. L.H.S. $=\frac{\sin A-2\sin^3 A}{2\cos^3 A-\cos A}$ (1 M)

$$=\frac{\sin A}{\cos A}\left(\frac{1-2\sin^2 A}{2\cos^2 A-1}\right)$$ (1 M)

$$=\frac{\sin A}{\cos A}\cdot\frac{\{1-2(1-\cos^2 A)\}}{(2\cos^2 A-1)}$$ (1 M)

$$=\tan A\left(\frac{1-2+2\cos^2 A}{2\cos^2 A-1}\right)=\tan A\left(\frac{2\cos^2 A-1}{2\cos^2 A-1}\right)$$

$= \tan A =$ R.H.S (1 M)

Hence L.H.S = R.H.S proved. (1 M)

Nailing the Right Answer

In this type of problem, always remember to form a formula by taking the common trigonometric function.

3. If $\operatorname{cosec}\theta - \sin\theta = a$ and $\sec\theta - \cos\theta = b$, prove that $a^2b^2(a^2+b^2+3)=1$ *(Un)*

Sol. L.H.S $= a^2b^2(a^2+b^2+3)$

$= (\operatorname{cosec}\theta - \sin\theta)^2(\sec\theta-\cos\theta)^2$
$\{(\operatorname{cosec}\theta-\sin\theta)^2+(\sec\theta-\cos\theta)^2+3\}$ (1 M)

$$=\left(\frac{1-\sin^2\theta}{\sin\theta}\right)^2\left(\frac{1-\cos^2\theta}{\cos\theta}\right)^2\left\{\left(\frac{1-\sin^2\theta}{\sin\theta}\right)^2+\left(\frac{1-\cos^2\theta}{\cos\theta}\right)^2+3\right\}$$ (1 M)

$$=\left(\frac{\cos^2\theta}{\sin\theta}\right)^2\left(\frac{\sin^2\theta}{\cos\theta}\right)^2\left\{\left(\frac{\cos^2\theta}{\sin\theta}\right)^2+\left(\frac{\sin^2\theta}{\cos\theta}\right)^2+3\right\}$$

$$=\frac{\cos^4\theta}{\sin^2\theta}\times\frac{\sin^4\theta}{\cos^2\theta}\left\{\frac{\cos^4\theta}{\sin^2\theta}+\frac{\sin^4\theta}{\cos^2\theta}+3\right\}$$ (1 M)

$$=\cos^2\theta\times\sin^2\theta\left\{\frac{\cos^6\theta+\sin^6\theta+3\cos^2\theta\sin^2\theta}{\sin^2\theta\cos^2\theta}\right\}$$

$= \cos^6\theta + \sin^6\theta + 3\cos^2\theta\sin^2\theta$ (1 M)

$= (\cos^2\theta)^3 + (\sin^2\theta)^3 + 3\sin^2\theta\cos^2\theta(\sin^2\theta+\cos^2\theta)$

$= (\cos^2\theta + \sin^2\theta)^3$

[Using $a^3 + b^3 + 3ab(a+b) = (a+b)^3$]

$= 1^3 = 1 =$ R.H.S (1 M)

Hence proved.

4. Prove the following:

$$\frac{\tan A}{1-\cot A}+\frac{\cot A}{1-\tan A}=1+\tan A+\cot A$$ *(Cr)*

Sol. L.H.S. $=\frac{\tan A}{1-\cot A}+\frac{\cot A}{1-\tan A}$

$$=\frac{\frac{\sin A}{\cos A}}{1-\frac{\cos A}{\sin A}}+\frac{\frac{\cos A}{\sin A}}{1-\frac{\sin A}{\cos A}}$$ (1 M)

$$=\frac{\frac{\sin A}{\cos A(\sin A-\cos A)}}{\sin A}+\frac{\frac{\cos A}{\sin A(\cos A-\sin A)}}{\cos A}$$

$$=\frac{\sin^2 A}{\cos A(\sin A-\cos A)}-\frac{\cos^2 A}{\sin A(\sin A-\cos A)}$$ (1 M)

$$=\frac{1}{\sin A-\cos A}\left[\frac{\sin^2 A}{\cos A}-\frac{\cos^2 A}{\sin A}\right]$$ (½ M)

$$=\frac{1}{\sin A-\cos A}\left[\frac{\sin^3 A-\cos^3 A}{\sin A.\cos A}\right]$$ (1 M)

$$=\frac{1}{\sin A-\cos A}\times\frac{(\sin A-\cos A)(\sin^2 A+\cos^2 A+\sin A.\cos A)}{\sin A.\cos A}$$

$$=\frac{\sin^2 A}{\sin A.\cos A}+\frac{\cos^2 A}{\sin A.\cos A}+\frac{\sin A.\cos A}{\sin A.\cos A}$$ (½ M)

$$=\frac{\sin A}{\cos A}+\frac{\cos A}{\sin A}+1$$

$= \tan A + \cot A + 1 =$ R.H.S (1 M)

$\therefore$ L.H.S = R.H.S Hence proved.

MISCELLANEOUS EXERCISE

Multiple Choice Questions (1 M)

1. If $\sin\theta + \sin^2\theta + \sin^3\theta = 1$, the value of $\cos^6\theta - 4\cos^4\theta + 8\cos^2\theta$ is
   (*a*) 2 (*b*) 5
   (*c*) 3 (*d*) 4
2. If $x\sin^3\theta + y\cos^3\theta = \sin\theta \,.\, \cos\theta$ and $x\sin\theta = y\cos\theta$, the value of $x^2 + y^2$ is
   (*a*) $\sin\theta.\cos\theta$ (*b*) $\sec\theta$
   (*c*) 2 (*d*) 1
3. $8\cot^2 A - 8\,\text{cosec}^2 A$ is equal to **(CBSE 2020)**
   (*a*) 8 (*b*) $\frac{1}{8}$
   (*c*) –8 (*d*) $-\frac{1}{8}$
4. If $\sec\theta = 2$, evaluating $\frac{1-\tan\theta}{1+\cos\theta}$ gives
   (*a*) $-\sqrt{3}+5$ (*b*) $\sqrt{3}+1$
   (*c*) $\sqrt{3}-2$ (*d*) $\frac{\sqrt{3}+1}{2}$
5. If $\sqrt{3}\tan\theta = 3\sin\theta$, then the value of $\sin^2\theta - \cos^2\theta$
   (*a*) $\frac{1}{3}$ (*b*) $\frac{2}{3}$
   (*c*) $\frac{3}{5}$ (*d*) $\frac{2}{5}$
6. P and Q are acute angles such that $P > Q$.
   Which of the following is DEFINITELY true? **(CBSE CFPQ, 2023)**
   (*a*) $\sin P < \sin Q$ (*b*) $\tan P > \tan Q$
   (*c*) $\cos P > \cos Q$ (*d*) $\cos P > \sin Q$
7. The value of $(\sin 45° + \cos 45°)$ is **(NCERT Exemplar)**
   (*a*) $\frac{1}{\sqrt{2}}$ (*b*) $\sqrt{2}$
   (*c*) $\frac{\sqrt{3}}{2}$ (*d*) 1
8. $\frac{\cos^2\theta}{\sin^2\theta} - \frac{1}{\sin^2\theta}$, in simplified form, is:
   (*a*) $\tan^2\theta$ (*b*) $\sec^2\theta$
   (*c*) 1 (*d*) –1
9. $(\sec A + \tan A)(1 - \sin A)$ equals:
   (*a*) $\sec A$ (*b*) $\sin A$
   (*c*) $\text{cosec} A$ (*d*) $\cos A$
10. Choose the correct option $\frac{2\tan 30°}{1+\tan^2 30°} =$
    (*a*) sin 60° (*b*) cos 60°
    (*c*) tan 60° (*d*) sin 30°

Assertion and Reason (1 M)

Direction: In the following Questions, the Assertion and Reason have been put forward. Read the statements carefully and choose the correct alternative from the following:

(*a*) Both the Assertion (A) and the Reason (R) are correct and the Reason (R) is the correct explanation of the Assertion (A).
(*b*) The Assertion (A) and the Reason(R) are correct but the Reason (R is not the correct explanation of the Assertion (A).
(*c*) Assertion (A) is false but the Reason (R) is true.
(*d*) Assertion (A) is true and Reason (R) is false.

1. **Assertion (A):** The value of $\cos\theta = \frac{7}{2}$ is not possible.
   Reason (R): Hypotenuse is the largest side in any right angled triangle.
2. **Assertion (A):** The value of $\sec^2 30° - \cot^2 60°$ is 1.
   Reason (R): The value of $\sin 60° = \frac{\sqrt{3}}{2}$
3. **Assertion (A):** If $\cos A + \cos^2 A = 1$ then $\sin^2 A + \sin^4 A = 2$.
   Reason (R): $\sin^2 A + \cos^2 A = 1$, for any value of A.

Subjective Questions

Very Short Answer Type Questions (1 or 2 M)

1. If $5\tan\theta = 3$, then what is the value of $\left(\frac{5\sin\theta - 3\cos\theta}{4\sin\theta + 3\cos\theta}\right)$? **(CBSE 2020)**
2. Evaluate: $\frac{\cos 45°}{\sec 30° + \text{cosec} 30°}$
3. If $\sin\theta - \cos\theta = 0$ then find the value of $\sin^4\theta + \cos^4\theta$,

4. Show that

$(\sqrt{3}+1)(3-\cot 30°) = \tan^3 60° - 2\sin 60°$.

5. If $2\sin^2\theta - \cos^2\theta = 2$ then find the value of θ.

6. If $\sqrt{3}\sin\theta = \cos\theta$, find the value of $\dfrac{3\cos^2\theta + 2\cos\theta}{3\cos\theta + 2}$

7. Prove that $\sqrt{\dfrac{1-\sin\theta}{1+\sin\theta}} = \sec\theta - \tan\theta$. **(CBSE 2020)**

8. Prove that $\dfrac{1-\sin\theta}{1+\sin\theta} = (\sec\theta - \tan\theta)^2$

9. Prove that $(\sin^4\theta - \cos^4\theta + 1)\operatorname{cosec}^2\theta = 2$

(NCERT Exemplar)

Short Answer Type Questions (2 or 3 M)

1. Prove that: $\left(1+\dfrac{1}{\tan^2 A}\right)\left(1+\dfrac{1}{\cot^2 A}\right) = \dfrac{1}{\sin^2 A - \sin^4 A}$

(CBSE 2023)

2. Find the value of x

$\operatorname{cosec} 3x = \dfrac{\cot 30° + \cot 60°}{1 + \cot 30° \cot 60°}$

3. Prove that $\dfrac{\tan^2\theta}{1+\tan^2\theta} + \dfrac{\cot^2\theta}{1+\cot^2\theta} = 1$ **(CBSE 2020)**

4. Prove that $\sec A(1 - \sin A)(\sec A + \tan A) = 1$.

(CBSE SQP, 2023)

5. Show that $\dfrac{(1+\sin\theta)^2 + (1-\sin\theta)^2}{2\cos^2\theta} = \dfrac{1+\sin^2\theta}{1-\sin^2\theta}$

6. Prove that: $(\operatorname{cosec}\theta - \cot\theta)^2 = \dfrac{1-\cos\theta}{1+\cos\theta}$ **(CBSE 2020)**

Long Answer Type Questions (4 or 5 M)

1. If $\dfrac{1}{\sin\theta - \cos\theta} = \dfrac{\operatorname{cosec}\theta}{\sqrt{2}}$,

prove that $\left(\dfrac{1}{\sin\theta + \cos\theta}\right)^2 = \dfrac{\sec^2\theta}{2}$. **(CBSE CFPQ, 2023)**

2. If $\sec\theta + \tan\theta = p$, prove that $\sin\theta = \dfrac{p^2 - 1}{p^2 + 1}$

3. Prove that $\dfrac{\sin\theta}{(\sec\theta + \tan\theta - 1)} + \dfrac{\cos\theta}{(\operatorname{cosec}\theta + \cot\theta - 1)} = 1$

4. Prove that: $\dfrac{\sin\theta}{\cot\theta + \operatorname{cosec}\theta} = 2 + \dfrac{\sin\theta}{\cot\theta - \operatorname{cosec}\theta}$

Case Based Questions

Case Based-I: Puja and her father go to meet her friend Priya for a party. When they reached to Priya's place, Puja saw the roof of the house, which is triangular in shape. If she imagined the dimensions of the roof as given in the figure, then

(i) If D is the mid point of AC, then Find the value of BD.

(ii) Find the measure of $\angle A$ and $\angle C$

OR

Find the value of $\sin A + \cos C$.

(iii) Find the value of $\tan^2 C + \tan^2 A$.

We have, $AB = BC = 6\sqrt{2}$ m and $AC = 12$m.

Case Based-II: Amuk a Student of class 10th, has to make a project on introduction to trigonometry. She decides to make a bird house which is triangular in shape. She uses Cardboard to make the bird house as Considering the front side of the bird house as right angled at R.

Answer the following questions.

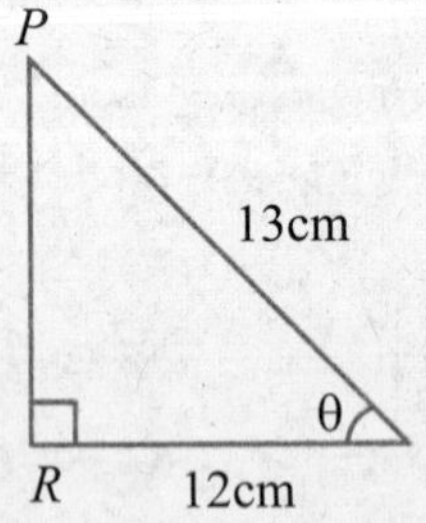

(i) If $\angle PQR = \theta$, then $\cos\theta$ is equal to

(a) $\dfrac{13}{12}$ (b) $\dfrac{12}{13}$

(c) $\dfrac{5}{13}$ (d) $\dfrac{13}{5}$

(ii) The value of $\sec\theta$ is

(a) $\dfrac{5}{13}$ (b) $\dfrac{13}{12}$

(c) $\dfrac{12}{13}$ (d) None of these

(*iii*) The value of $\frac{\tan\theta}{1+\tan^2\theta}$ is equal to

(*a*) $\frac{60}{169}$ (*b*) $\frac{60}{119}$

(*c*) $\frac{169}{60}$ (*d*) None of these

(*iv*) The value of $\cot^2\theta - \text{cosec}^2\theta$ = ?

(*a*) 1 (*b*) 2

(*c*) –1 (*d*) 2

Case Based-III: Three friends Ajay, Sonu, Monu are playing hide and Seek in a park. Ajay and Sonu hide in the Shrubs and Monu have to find both of them. If the positions of three friends are at *A*, *B* and *C* respectively as Diagram and forms a right angled triangle such that *AB* = 9M, *BC* = $3\sqrt{3}$ and $\angle B = 90°$, then answer the following questions.

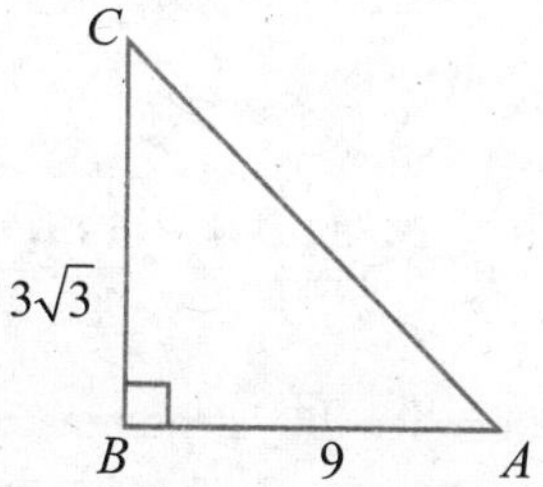

(*i*) The measure of $\angle A$ is

(*a*) 30° (*b*) 60°

(*c*) 90° (*d*) None of these

(*ii*) The Measure of $\angle C$ is

(*a*) 90° (*b*) 60°

(*c*) 30° (*d*) None of these

(*iii*) The length of *AC* is equal to

(*a*) $3\sqrt{3}$ (*b*) $4\sqrt{3}$

(*c*) $6\sqrt{3}$ (*d*) None of these

(*iv*) The value of cos 2*A* is equal to

(*a*) $\frac{\sqrt{3}}{2}$ (*b*) $\frac{1}{2}$

(*c*) $\frac{1}{\sqrt{2}}$ (*d*) 0

(*v*) The value of $\sin\left(\frac{c}{2}\right)$ is

(*a*) 0 (*b*) $\frac{1}{\sqrt{2}}$

(*c*) $\frac{\sqrt{3}}{2}$ (*d*) $\frac{1}{2}$

ANSWER KEYS

Multiple Choice Questions

1. (*d*) **2.** (*d*) **3.** (*c*) **4.** (*c*) **5.** (*a*) **6.** (*b*) **7.** (*b*) **8.** (*d*) **9.** (*d*) **10.** (*a*)

Assertion and Reason

1. (*a*) **2.** (*b*) **3.** (*c*)

Case Based Questions

Case Based-II

(*i*) (*b*) (*ii*) (*b*) (*iii*) (*a*) (*iv*) (*c*)

Case Based-III

(*i*) (*a*) (*ii*) (*b*) (*iii*) (*c*) (*iv*) (*b*) (*v*) (*d*)

HINTS & EXPLANATIONS

Multiple Choice Questions

1. (*d*) $\sin\theta + \sin^3\theta = 1 - \sin^2\theta = \cos^2\theta$

$\sin\theta\,(1 + \sin^2\theta) = \cos^2\theta$

On squaring both sides, we get

$\sin^2\theta\,(1 + \sin^2\theta)^2 = \cos^4\theta$

$\Rightarrow (1 - \cos^2\theta)(2 - \cos^2\theta)^2 = \cos^4\theta$

$\Rightarrow (1 - \cos^2\theta)(4 + \cos^4\theta - 4\cos^2\theta) = \cos^4\theta$

$\Rightarrow -\cos^6\theta + 4\cos^4\theta - 8\cos^2\theta + 4 = 0$

$\Rightarrow \cos^6\theta - 4\cos^4\theta + 8\cos^2\theta = 4$

2. (*d*) $x\sin^3\theta + y\cos^3\theta = \sin\theta\cos\theta$

$\Rightarrow (x\sin\theta)\sin^2\theta + (y\cos\theta)\cos^2\theta = \sin\theta\cos\theta$

$\Rightarrow x\sin\theta(\sin^2\theta) + x\sin\theta(\cos^2\theta) = \sin\theta\cos\theta$

$(\because y\cos\theta = x\sin\theta)$

$\Rightarrow x\sin\theta = \sin\theta\cos\theta \Rightarrow x = \cos\theta$

Now $x\sin\theta = y\cos\theta \Rightarrow \cos\theta\sin\theta = y\cos\theta \Rightarrow y = \sin\theta$

Therefore, $x^2 + y^2 = \cos^2\theta + \sin^2\theta = 1$

3. (*c*) $8\cot^2 A - 8\,\text{cosec}^2 A = 8\,[\cot^2 A - \text{cosec}^2 A]$

$= 8\,[-\{\text{cosec}^2 A - \cot^2 A\}] = 8\,[-1] = -8$

4. (*c*) We know that, $\sec^2\theta - \tan^2\theta = 1$

$\Rightarrow \tan^2\theta = \sec^2\theta - 1 \Rightarrow \tan^2\theta = 4 - 1$ [Given $\sec\theta = 2$]

$\Rightarrow \tan\theta = \sqrt{3}$

Now, $\dfrac{1-\tan\theta}{1+\tan\theta} = \dfrac{1-\sqrt{3}}{1+\sqrt{3}} \times \dfrac{1-\sqrt{3}}{1-\sqrt{3}} = \dfrac{1+3-2\sqrt{3}}{1-3}$

$= \dfrac{4-2\sqrt{3}}{-2} = \sqrt{3} - 2$

5. (*a*) $\dfrac{\sqrt{3}\sin\theta}{\cos\theta} = 3\sin\theta \Rightarrow \sec\theta = \sqrt{3}$

$\therefore \cos\theta = \dfrac{1}{\sqrt{3}} \Rightarrow \cos^2 = \dfrac{1}{3}$

$\sin^2\theta - \cos^2\theta = 1 - \cos^2\theta - \cos^2\theta = 1 - 2\cos^2\theta$

$[\because \sin^2\theta = 1 - \cos^2\theta]$

$= 1 - 2\left(\dfrac{1}{3}\right) = 1 - \dfrac{2}{3} = \dfrac{1}{3}$

6. (*b*) P and Q are acute angles such that $P > Q$

Let $P = 60°$ and $Q = 45°$

$\sin P = \sin 60° = \dfrac{\sqrt{3}}{2}$, $\sin Q = \sin 45° = \dfrac{1}{\sqrt{2}}$

$\cos P = \cos 60° = \dfrac{1}{2}$, $\cos Q = \cos 45° = \dfrac{1}{\sqrt{2}}$

$\tan P = \tan 60° = \sqrt{3}$, $\tan Q = \tan 45° = 1$

Using above information, $\tan P > \tan Q$ is true.

Hence, option (*b*) is correct.

Mistakes 101 : What not to do!

Students forgetting to assume a value based on given conditions can lead to an incorrect solution.

7. (*b*) To calculate $\sin 45° + \cos 45°$, we can use the fact that

$\sin 45° = \dfrac{1}{\sqrt{2}}$ and $\cos 45° = \dfrac{1}{\sqrt{2}}$

$\sin 45° + \cos 45° = \dfrac{1}{\sqrt{2}} + \dfrac{1}{\sqrt{2}} = \dfrac{1+1}{\sqrt{2}} = \dfrac{2}{\sqrt{2}}$

Now, to rationalize the denominator, we multiply the numerator and denominator by $\sqrt{2}$.

$\dfrac{2}{\sqrt{2}} \times \dfrac{\sqrt{2}}{\sqrt{2}} = \dfrac{2\sqrt{2}}{2} = \sqrt{2}$

So, $\sin 45° + \cos 45° = \sqrt{2}$

8. (*d*) $\dfrac{\cos^2\theta}{\sin^2\theta} - \dfrac{1}{\sin^2\theta} = \dfrac{\cos^2\theta - 1}{\sin^2\theta}$

$= \dfrac{-\sin^2\theta}{\sin^2\theta} = -1$ $[\because \sin^2\theta + \cos^2\theta = 1]$

9. (*d*) $(\sec A + \tan A)(1 - \sin A)$

$= \left(\dfrac{1}{\cos A} + \dfrac{\sin A}{\cos A}\right)(1 - \sin A) = \dfrac{(1+\sin A)}{\cos A}(1 - \sin A)$

$= \dfrac{(1-\sin^2 A)}{\cos A} = \dfrac{\cos^2 A}{\cos A} = \cos A$

10. (*a*) We know $\tan 30° = \dfrac{1}{\sqrt{3}}$

$\therefore \dfrac{2\tan 30°}{1+\tan^2 30°} = \dfrac{2(1/\sqrt{3})}{1+(1/\sqrt{3})^2}$

$= \dfrac{(2/\sqrt{3})}{(1+1/3)} = \dfrac{(2/\sqrt{3})}{(4/3)} = \dfrac{6}{4\sqrt{3}} = \dfrac{\sqrt{3}}{2} = \sin 60°$

Assertion and Reason

1. (*a*) **Assertion:** $\cos\theta = \frac{B}{H} = \frac{7}{2}$

Here, base is greater than the hypotenuse, which is not possible in any right triangle.

Both assertion (A) and reason (R) are true and reason (R) is the correct explanation of assertion (A).

2. (*b*) **Assertion:**

$$\sec^2 30° - \cot^2 60° = \left(\frac{2}{\sqrt{3}}\right)^2 - \left(\frac{1}{\sqrt{3}}\right)^2 = \frac{4}{3} - \frac{1}{3} = 1$$

Reason: $\sin 60° = \frac{\sqrt{3}}{2}$.

Both assertion (A) and reason (R) are true but reason (R) is not the correct explanation of assertion (A).

3. (*c*) **Assertion:** $\cos A + \cos^2 A = 1$

$\cos A = 1 - \cos^2 A = \sin^2 A$

$\sin^2 A + \sin^4 A = \cos A + \cos^2 A = 1$

Assertion (A) is false

Reason: $\sin^2 A + \cos^2 A = 1$

Reason is true.

Assertion (A) is false but Reason (R) is true.

Subjective Questions

Very Short Answer Type Questions

1. Given that 5 tan θ = 3

$\Rightarrow \tan\theta = \frac{3}{5} \Rightarrow \frac{\sin\theta}{\cos\theta} = \frac{3}{5}$ (½ M)

Let $\sin\theta = 3k$ and $\cos\theta = 5k$, where k is any integer.

Consider the given expression:

$$\frac{5\sin\theta - 3\cos\theta}{4\sin\theta + 3\cos\theta} = \frac{0}{27k}$$

$= 0$ (½ M)

2. $$\frac{\cos 45°}{\sec 30° + \text{cosec}\, 30°} = \frac{\frac{1}{\sqrt{2}}}{\frac{2}{\sqrt{3}} + 2} = \frac{\frac{1}{\sqrt{2}}}{\frac{2+2\sqrt{3}}{\sqrt{3}}}$$ (½ M)

$$= \frac{1}{\sqrt{2}} \times \frac{\sqrt{3}}{2+2\sqrt{3}}$$

$$= \frac{\sqrt{3}}{2\sqrt{2}(\sqrt{3}+1)}$$ (½ M)

Now, rationalize the terms we get,

$$= \frac{\sqrt{3}}{2\sqrt{2}(\sqrt{3}+1)} \times \frac{\sqrt{3}-1}{\sqrt{3}-1} = \frac{3-\sqrt{3}}{2\sqrt{2}(3-1)} = \frac{3-\sqrt{3}}{2\sqrt{2}(2)}$$

$$= \frac{3-\sqrt{3}}{2\sqrt{2}(2)} \times \frac{\sqrt{2}}{\sqrt{2}} = \frac{3\sqrt{2}-\sqrt{3}\sqrt{2}}{8} = \frac{3\sqrt{2}-\sqrt{6}}{8}$$ (*1 M*)

3. Given, $\sin\theta - \cos\theta = 0$

$\Rightarrow \sin\theta - \cos\theta \Rightarrow \frac{\sin\theta}{\cos\theta} = 1$

$\Rightarrow \tan\theta = 1 = \tan 45°$ (*1 M*)

$\Rightarrow \theta = 45°$

$\therefore \sin^4\theta + \cos^4\theta = \sin^4 45° + \cos^4 45°$

$$= \left(\frac{1}{\sqrt{2}}\right)^4 + \left(\frac{1}{\sqrt{2}}\right)^4 = \frac{1}{4} + \frac{1}{4} = \frac{2}{4} = \frac{1}{2}$$ (*1 M*)

4. L.H.S. $= (\sqrt{3}+1)(3-\cot 30°) = (\sqrt{3}+1)(3-\sqrt{3})$

$= 3\sqrt{3} - 3 + 3 - \sqrt{3} = 2\sqrt{3}$ (*1 M*)

R.H.S. $= \tan^3 60° - 2\sin 60° = (\sqrt{3})^3 - 2\frac{\sqrt{3}}{2}$

$= 3\sqrt{3} - \sqrt{3} = 2\sqrt{3}$ (*1 M*)

$\therefore$ L.H.S. = R.H.S.

Hence proved.

5. Given, $2\sin^2\theta - \cos^2\theta = 2 \Rightarrow 2\sin^2\theta - (1-\sin^2\theta) = 2$ (*1 M*)

$\Rightarrow 3\sin^2\theta - 1 = 2 \Rightarrow 3\sin^2\theta = 3 \Rightarrow \sin^2\theta = 1$

$\Rightarrow \sin\theta = 1 \Rightarrow \sin\theta = \sin 90° \Rightarrow \theta = 90°$ (*1 M*)

6. Given, $\sqrt{3}\sin\theta = \cos\theta$

$\Rightarrow \frac{\sin\theta}{\cos\theta} = \frac{1}{\sqrt{3}} \Rightarrow \tan\theta = \tan 30° \Rightarrow \theta = 30°$ (*1 M*)

Now, $\frac{3\cos^2\theta + 2\cos\theta}{3\cos\theta + 2}$

$$= \frac{\cos\theta(3\cos\theta+2)}{3\cos\theta+2} = \cos\theta = \cos 30° = \frac{\sqrt{3}}{2}$$ (*1 M*)

7. Consider the L.H.S:

$$\sqrt{\frac{1-\sin\theta}{1+\sin\theta}} = \sqrt{\frac{1-\sin\theta}{1+\sin\theta} \times \frac{1-\sin\theta}{1-\sin\theta}} = \sqrt{\frac{(1-\sin\theta)^2}{1^2 - \sin^2\theta}}$$ (*1 M*)

$$= \sqrt{\frac{(1-\sin\theta)^2}{\cos^2\theta}} = \frac{1-\sin\theta}{\cos\theta} = \frac{1}{\cos\theta} - \frac{\sin\theta}{\cos\theta}$$

$= \sec\theta - \tan\theta$ = R.H.S

Hence proved (*1 M*)

8. L.H.S. $= \frac{1-\sin\theta}{1+\sin\theta}$

$$= \frac{1-\sin\theta}{1+\sin\theta} \times \frac{1-\sin\theta}{1-\sin\theta}$$ [Rationalising the denominator] (*1 M*)

$$= \frac{(1-\sin\theta)^2}{1-\sin^2\theta} = \left(\frac{1-\sin\theta}{\cos\theta}\right)^2 = \left(\frac{1}{\cos\theta} - \frac{\sin\theta}{\cos\theta}\right)^2$$

$= (\sec\theta - \tan\theta)^2$ = R.H.S

$\therefore$ L.H.S = R.H.S (*1 M*)

Hence proved

9. L.H.S. = $(\sin^4\theta - \cos^4\theta + 1)\,\text{cosec}^2\theta$
$= [(\sin^2\theta - \cos^2\theta)(\sin^2\theta + \cos^2\theta) + 1]\text{cosec}^2\theta$
$= (\sin^2\theta - \cos^2\theta + 1)\text{cosec}^2\theta$ [Because $\sin^2\theta + \cos^2\theta = 1$] *(1 M)*
$= 2\sin^2\theta\,\text{cosec}^2\theta$ [Because $1 - \cos^2\theta = \sin^2\theta$]
$= 2 =$ RHS *(1 M)*
$\therefore$ L.H.S = R.H.S
Hence proved

Nailing the Right Answer

To prove trigonometric problems, students should use trigonometric formulas and relations carefully.

Short Answer Type Questions

1. $$\text{L.H.S} = \left(1+\frac{\cos^2 A}{\sin^2 A}\right)\left(1+\frac{\sin^2 A}{\cos^2 A}\right)$$ *(1 M)*

$$= \left(\frac{\sin^2 A+\cos^2 A}{\sin^2 A}\right)\left(\frac{\cos^2 A+\sin^2 A}{\cos^2 A}\right)$$

$$= \frac{1}{\sin^2 A}\times\frac{1}{\cos^2 A}$$ *(1 M)*

$$= \frac{1}{\sin^2 A(1-\sin^2 A)} = \frac{1}{\sin^2 A-\sin^4 A} = \text{R.H.S}$$ *(1 M)*

Hence, L.H.S = R.H.S proved.

2. Given, $$\text{cosec}3x = \frac{\cot 30^\circ + \cot 60^\circ}{1+\cot 30^\circ \cot 60^\circ}$$

$$\text{cosec}3x = \frac{\cot 30^\circ + \cot 60^\circ}{1+\cot 30^\circ \cot 60^\circ} = \frac{\sqrt{3}+\frac{1}{\sqrt{3}}}{1+\sqrt{3}\times\frac{1}{\sqrt{3}}} = \frac{\frac{(3+1)}{\sqrt{3}}}{2}$$

$$= \frac{4}{\sqrt{3}}\times\frac{1}{2} = \frac{2}{\sqrt{3}}$$ *(1 M)*

So, $\text{cosec}3x = \frac{2}{\sqrt{3}}$ *(1 M)*

we know $\frac{2}{\sqrt{3}} = \text{cosec}60^\circ$

$\Rightarrow \text{cosec}3x = \text{cosec }60^\circ \Rightarrow 3x = 60^\circ \Rightarrow x = 20^\circ$ *(1 M)*

3. Consider the L.H.S:

$$\frac{\tan^2\theta}{1+\tan^2\theta}+\frac{\cot^2\theta}{1+\cot^2\theta} = \frac{\tan^2\theta}{1+\tan^2\theta}+\frac{\frac{1}{\tan^2\theta}}{1+\frac{1}{\tan^2\theta}}$$ *(½ M)*

$$= \frac{\tan^2\theta}{1+\tan^2\theta}+\frac{\frac{1}{\tan^2\theta}}{\frac{1+\tan^2\theta}{\tan^2\theta}} = \frac{\tan^2\theta}{1+\tan^2\theta}+\frac{1}{1+\tan^2\theta}$$ *(½ M)*

$$= \frac{1+\tan^2\theta}{1+\tan^2\theta} = 1$$

L.H.S. = R.H.S *(1 M)*

4. $\sec A(1-\sin A)(\sec A+\tan A) = 1$

$$\text{L.H.S} = \frac{1}{\cos A}(1-\sin A)\left(\frac{1}{\cos A}+\frac{\sin A}{\cos A}\right)$$ *(1 M)*

$$= \frac{(1-\sin A)}{\cos A}\left(\frac{1+\sin A}{\cos A}\right) = \frac{(1-\sin A)(1+\sin A)}{\cos^2 A}$$ *(1 M)*

$$= \frac{1-\sin^2 A}{\cos^2 A}$$ $(1 - \sin^2 A = \cos^2 A)$

$$= \frac{\cos^2 A}{\cos^2 A} = 1$$

L.H.S. = R.H.S. *(1 M)*

5. $$\text{L.H.S.} = \frac{(1+\sin\theta)^2+(1-\sin\theta)^2}{2\cos^2\theta}$$ *(1 M)*

$$= \frac{(1+2\sin\theta+\sin^2\theta)+(1-2\sin\theta+\sin^2\theta)}{2\cos^2\theta}$$

$$= \frac{1+2\sin\theta+\sin^2\theta+1-2\sin\theta+\sin^2\theta}{2\cos^2\theta}$$

$$= \frac{2+2\sin^2\theta}{2\cos^2\theta}$$ *(1 M)*

$$= \frac{2(1+\sin^2\theta)}{2(1-\sin^2\theta)} = \frac{1+\sin^2\theta}{1-\sin^2\theta} = \text{R.H.S.}$$

$\therefore$ L.H.S = R.H.S
Hence proved. *(1 M)*

6. We have, L.H.S = $(\text{cosec }\theta - \cot\theta)^2$

$$= \left(\frac{1}{\sin\theta}-\frac{\cos\theta}{\sin\theta}\right)^2 = \left(\frac{1-\cos\theta}{\sin\theta}\right)^2$$ *(1 M)*

$$= \frac{(1-\cos\theta)^2}{\sin^2\theta} = \frac{(1-\cos\theta)^2}{1-\cos^2\theta}$$ $[\sin^2\theta = 1 - \cos^2\theta]$ *(1 M)*

$$= \frac{(1-\cos\theta)^2}{(1-\cos\theta)(1+\cos\theta)} = \frac{1-\cos\theta}{1+\cos\theta} = \text{R.H.S.}$$

Hence, L.H.S. = R.H.S proved *(1 M)*

Long Answer Type Questions

1. Squares both sides of the given equation as:

$$\frac{1}{\sin^2\theta+\cos^2\theta-2\sin\theta\cos\theta} = \frac{\text{cosec}^2\theta}{2}$$ *(½ M)*

Simplifies the above expression as:

$$\frac{2}{\text{cosec}^2\theta} = 1-2\sin\theta\cos\theta$$ *(1 M)*

Simplifies the above equation as:

$2\sin\theta\cos\theta = 1 - 2\sin^2\theta$ *(1 M)*

Squares the LHS of the equation to be proved as:

$$\frac{1}{\sin^2\theta+\cos^2\theta+2\sin\theta\cos\theta}$$ *(½ M)*

Uses step 3 and simplifies the above expression as:

$$\frac{1}{2-2\sin^2\theta}$$ (1 M)

Simplifies the above expression as:

$$\frac{1}{2\cos^2\theta}=\frac{\sec^2\theta}{2}$$

Concludes that LHS = RHS. (1 M)

2. R.H.S. $=\dfrac{p^2-1}{p^2+1}=\dfrac{(\sec\theta+\tan\theta)^2-1}{(\sec\theta+\tan\theta)^2+1}$ (1 M)

$$=\frac{\sec^2\theta+\tan^2\theta+2\sec\theta\tan\theta-1}{\sec^2\theta+\tan^2\theta+2\sec\theta\tan\theta+1}$$ (1 M)

$$=\frac{(\sec^2\theta-1)+\tan^2\theta+2\sec\theta\tan\theta}{\sec^2\theta+(1+\tan^2\theta)+2\sec\theta\tan\theta}$$ (1 M)

$$=\frac{\tan^2\theta+\tan^2\theta+2\sec\theta\tan\theta}{\sec^2\theta+\sec^2\theta+2\sec\theta\tan\theta}=\frac{2\tan^2\theta+2\sec\theta\tan\theta}{2\sec^2\theta+2\sec\theta\tan\theta}$$

$$=\frac{2\tan\theta(\tan\theta+\sec\theta)}{2\sec\theta(\sec\theta+\tan\theta)}=\frac{\tan\theta}{\sec\theta}$$ (1 M)

$$=\frac{2\tan\theta(\tan\theta+\sec\theta)}{2\sec\theta(\sec\theta+\tan\theta)}=\frac{\tan\theta}{\sec\theta}$$

$$=\frac{\frac{\sin\theta}{\cos\theta}}{\frac{1}{\cos\theta}}=\sin\theta=\text{L.H.S.}$$ (1 M)

$\therefore$ L.H.S = R.H.S Hence proved.

3. Given $\dfrac{\sin\theta}{(\sec\theta+\tan\theta-1)}+\dfrac{\cos\theta}{(\operatorname{cos}ec\theta+\cot\theta-1)}$

$$=\frac{\sin\theta}{\frac{1}{\cos\theta}+\frac{\sin\theta}{\cos\theta}-1}+\frac{\cos\theta}{\frac{1}{\sin\theta}+\frac{\cos\theta}{\sin\theta}-1}$$ (1 M)

$$=\frac{\sin\theta}{\frac{1+\sin\theta-\cos\theta}{\cos\theta}}+\frac{\cos\theta}{\frac{1+\cos\theta-\sin\theta}{\sin\theta}}$$

$$=\frac{\sin\theta\cos\theta}{1+\sin\theta-\cos\theta}+\frac{\sin\theta\cos\theta}{1+\cos\theta-\sin\theta}$$

$$=\sin\theta\cos\theta\left(\frac{1}{1+\sin\theta-\cos\theta}+\frac{1}{1+\cos\theta-\sin\theta}\right)$$ (1 M)

$$=\sin\theta\cos\theta\left(\frac{1+\cos\theta-\sin\theta+1+\sin\theta-\cos\theta}{(1+\sin\theta-\cos\theta)(1-\sin\theta+\cos\theta)}\right)$$

$$=\sin\theta\cos\theta\left(\frac{2}{[1+(\sin\theta-\cos\theta)](1-(\sin\theta-\cos\theta))}\right)$$ (1 M)

$$=\sin\theta\cos\theta\left(\frac{2}{(1)^2-(\sin\theta-\cos\theta)^2}\right)$$

$$=\sin\theta\cos\theta\left(\frac{2}{1-(\sin^2\theta+\cos^2\theta-2\sin\theta\cos\theta)}\right)$$ (1 M)

$$=\sin\theta\cos\theta\left(\frac{2}{1-(1-2\sin\theta\cos\theta)}\right)$$ $[\because \sin^2\theta+\cos^2\theta=1]$

$$=\sin\theta\cos\theta\left(\frac{2}{2\sin\theta\cos\theta}\right)=1=\text{R.H.S}$$ (1 M)

$\therefore$ L.H.S = R.H.S Hence proved.

4. L.H.S $=\dfrac{\sin\theta}{\cot\theta+\operatorname{cosec}\theta}$

$$=\frac{\sin\theta}{\frac{\cos\theta}{\sin\theta}+\frac{1}{\sin\theta}}=\frac{\sin^2\theta}{1+\cos\theta}$$ (1 M)

on rationalizing, we get

$$=\frac{\sin^2\theta}{1+\cos\theta}\times\frac{1-\cos\theta}{1-\cos\theta}=\frac{\sin^2\theta(1-\cos\theta)}{1-\cos^2\theta}$$ (½ M)

$$=\frac{(1-\cos\theta)\sin^2\theta}{\sin^2\theta}=1-\cos\theta$$ ... (*i*) (1 M)

$$\text{R.H.S}=2+\frac{\sin\theta}{\cot\theta-\operatorname{cosec}\theta}$$

$$=2+\frac{\sin\theta}{\frac{\cos\theta}{\sin\theta}-\frac{1}{\sin\theta}}=2+\frac{\sin^2\theta}{\cos\theta-1}$$ (1 M)

$$=2-\frac{\sin^2\theta}{1-\cos\theta}=2-\frac{1-\cos^2\theta}{1-\cos\theta}=2-\frac{(1-\cos\theta)(1+\cos\theta)}{1-\cos\theta}$$

$[\because a^2-b^2=(a-b)(a+b)]$

$=2-(1+\cos\theta)=2-1-\cos\theta=1-\cos\theta$ ... (*ii*)

From equation (*i*) and (*ii*), we get L.H.S = R.H.S

$$\frac{\sin\theta}{\cot\theta+\operatorname{cosec}\theta}=2+\frac{\sin\theta}{\cot\theta-\operatorname{cosec}\theta}$$ (1 M)

$\therefore$ L.H.S = R.H.S

Hence proved. (½ M)

Mistakes 101 : What not to do!

Students often make mistakes in using trigonometric ratios and formulas. Incorrect conversions can lead to inaccurate solutions.

Case Based Questions

Case Based-I

(i) D is mid point of AC.

$\therefore AD = DC = 6\text{m}$

Now, $AB^2 = BD^2 + AD^2$ ($\therefore \Delta ABD$ is a right triangle)

$\Rightarrow BD^2 = (6\sqrt{2})^2 - 6^2 = 72 - 36 = 36 \Rightarrow BD = 6$ m

(ii) In ΔABD, $\sin A = \dfrac{BD}{AB} = \dfrac{6}{6\sqrt{2}} = \dfrac{1}{\sqrt{2}}$

$\Rightarrow \sin A = \sin 45° \Rightarrow \angle A = 45°$

In ΔBDC, $\tan C = \dfrac{BD}{DC} = \dfrac{6}{6} \Rightarrow \tan C = 1 = \tan 45° \Rightarrow \angle C = 45°$

OR

$\sin A = \dfrac{1}{\sqrt{2}}, \cos C = \cos 45° = \dfrac{1}{\sqrt{2}}$

$\therefore \sin A + \cos C = \dfrac{1}{\sqrt{2}} + \dfrac{1}{\sqrt{2}} = \dfrac{2}{\sqrt{2}} = \sqrt{2}$

(iii) $\tan C = 1$ and $\tan A = \tan 45° = 1 \Rightarrow \tan^2 C + \tan^2 A = 1 + 1 = 2$

Case Based-II

(i) (*b*) $\therefore \Delta PQR$ is a right angled triangle

$\therefore PR^2 + RQ^2 = PQ^2$

$PR^2 = (13)^2 - (12)^2 = 169 - 144 = 25 \Rightarrow PR = 5$

$\cos\theta = \dfrac{QR}{PQ} = \dfrac{12}{13}$

(ii) (*b*) $\sec\theta = \dfrac{1}{\cos\theta} = \dfrac{13}{12}$

(iii) (*a*) $\tan\theta = \dfrac{PR}{RQ} = \dfrac{5}{12}$

$\therefore \dfrac{\tan\theta}{1+\tan^2\theta} \Rightarrow \dfrac{5/12}{1+\dfrac{25}{144}} = \dfrac{5/12}{169/144} = \dfrac{60}{169}$

(iv) (*c*) $\cot\theta = \dfrac{1}{\tan\theta} = \dfrac{12}{5}$ and $\text{cosec}\,\theta = \dfrac{PQ}{PR} = \dfrac{13}{5}$

$\therefore \cot^2\theta - \text{cos}\,ec^2\theta = \dfrac{144}{25} - \dfrac{169}{25} = -1$

Case Based-III

(i) (*a*) We have, $AB = 9$ m, $BC = 3\sqrt{3}$ m

in ΔABC we have

$\tan A = \dfrac{BC}{AB} = \dfrac{3\sqrt{3}}{9} = \dfrac{1}{\sqrt{3}} = \tan 30$

$\angle A = 30°$

(ii) (*b*) $\tan C = \dfrac{AB}{BC} = \dfrac{9}{3\sqrt{3}} = \sqrt{3}$

$\tan C = \tan 60° \Rightarrow \angle C = 60°$

(iii) (*c*) $\text{Sin } A = \dfrac{BC}{AC} \Rightarrow \sin 30° = \dfrac{BC}{AC}$

$\dfrac{1}{2} = \dfrac{3\sqrt{3}}{AC} \Rightarrow AC = 6\sqrt{3}\ m$

(iv) (*b*) $\angle A = 30°$

$\cos 2A = \cos(2\times 30°) = \cos 60° = \dfrac{1}{2}$

(v) (*d*) We have, $\angle C = 60°$

$\sin\left(\dfrac{C}{2}\right) = \sin\left(\dfrac{60}{2}\right) = \sin 30 = \dfrac{1}{2}$

❑❑❑

SOME APPLICATIONS OF TRIGONOMETRY

9

"In photography and filmmaking, trigonometry is used to calculate the right angles and distances from the camera to the subject. This application of trigonometry, specifically involving height and distance, allows photographers and filmmakers to enhance the perspective and depth, creating more engaging and visually compelling images."

SYLLABUS & WEIGHTAGE

List of Concept Names	Years				
	2021	2022	2023	2024	2025
Heights and Distances (Angle of elevation, Angle of Depression. Simple problems on heights and distances. Problems should not involve more than two right triangles. Angles of elevation/depression should be only 30°, 45° and 60°.)	Exam not Conducted	1 Q (3 M) 1 Q (4 M)	1 Q (1 M) 1 Q (4 M)	1 Q (5 M)	1 Q (1 M) 1 Q (5 M)

CONCEPT MAP

To Access One Shot Revision Video Scan This QR Code

Some Application of Trigonometry

Trigonometric ratios can be used to find the distances and heights of those objects for which direct measurement of lengths are not possible.

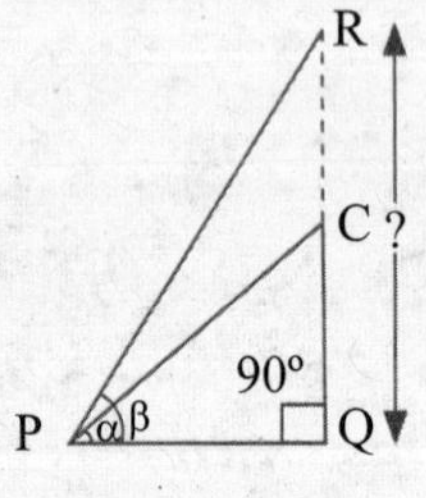

Find length QR

Distance between two points

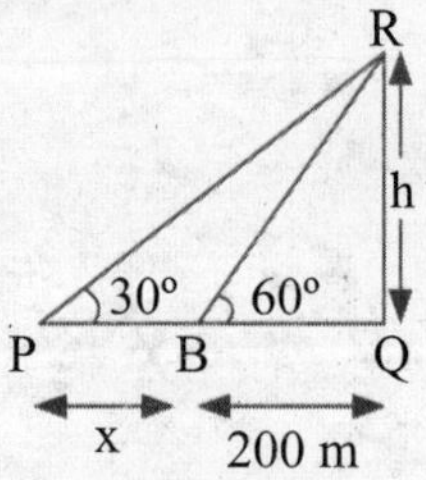

Find x and h

Angle of Elevation:

The angle of elevation of the point viewed is the angle formed by the line of sight with the horizontal when the point being viewed is above the horizontal level.

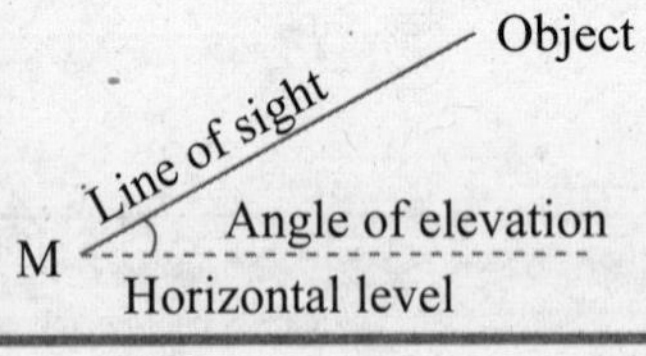

Angle of Depression:

The angle of depression of a point on the object being viewed is the angle formed by the line of sight with the horizontal when the point is below the horizontal level.

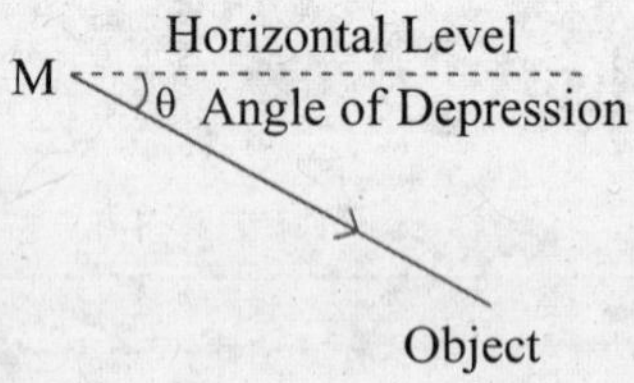

Line of Sight:

Line of sight is the line drawn from the eye of an observer to the point in the object viewed by the observer.

1 HEIGHTS AND DISTANCES

Important Terms

- **Horizontal Line:** A line parallel to horizontal plane is called horizontal line.
- **Line of Sight:** It is the line drawn from the eye of an observer to the point in the object viewed by the observer.
- **Angle of Elevation:** The angle of elevation of the point viewed is the angle formed by the line of sight with the horizontal when the point being viewed is above the horizontal level. This angle is formed when we raise our head to look at the object.

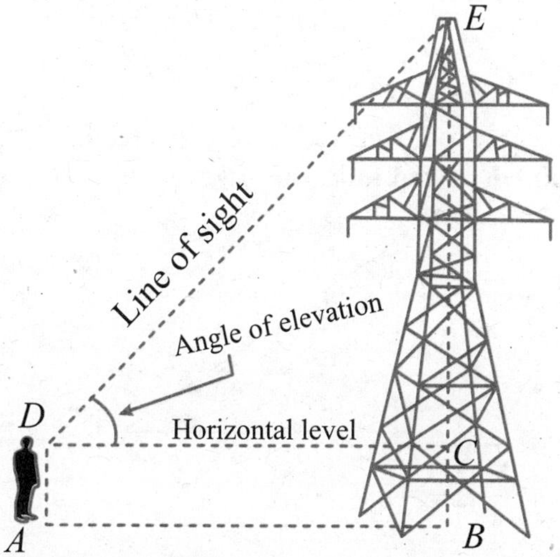

- **Angle of Depression:** The angle of depression of a point viewed is the angle formed by the line of sight with the horizontal when the point is below the horizontal level. This angle is formed when we lower our head to look at the point being viewed.

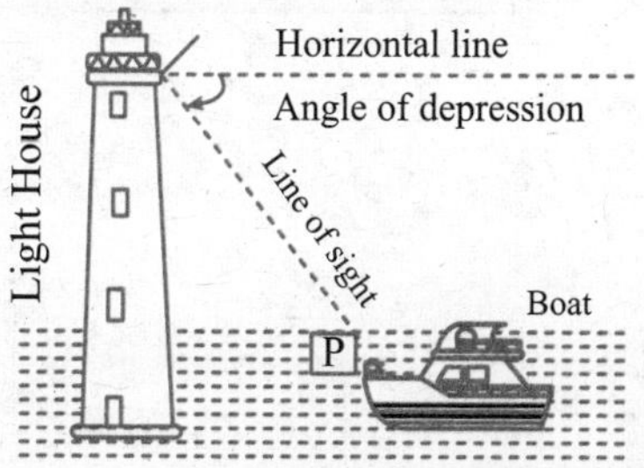

- **Theodolite:** Theodolite is an instrument which is used for measuring the angle of elevation or depression between an object and the eye of the observer.

Important Formulas

Value of Trigonometric Ratios of standard angles

$\angle A$	$0°$	$30°$	$45°$	$60°$	$90°$
$\sin A$	0	$\frac{1}{2}$	$\frac{1}{\sqrt{2}}$	$\frac{\sqrt{3}}{2}$	1
$\cos A$	1	$\frac{\sqrt{3}}{2}$	$\frac{1}{\sqrt{2}}$	$\frac{1}{2}$	0
$\tan A$	0	$\frac{1}{\sqrt{3}}$	1	$\sqrt{3}$	Not defined

Important Concepts

- The angle of elevation of the sun from the earth is called the sun's altitude. The sun's altitude is different at different times of the day.
- The observer is taken as a point unless the height of the observer is given.
- The angles of elevation and depression are always acute angles.
- If an observer moves towards the object, then angle of elevation increases and if moves away then angle of elevation decreases.
- The angle of elevation of a point P as seen from a point O is equal to the angle of depression of O as seen from P.

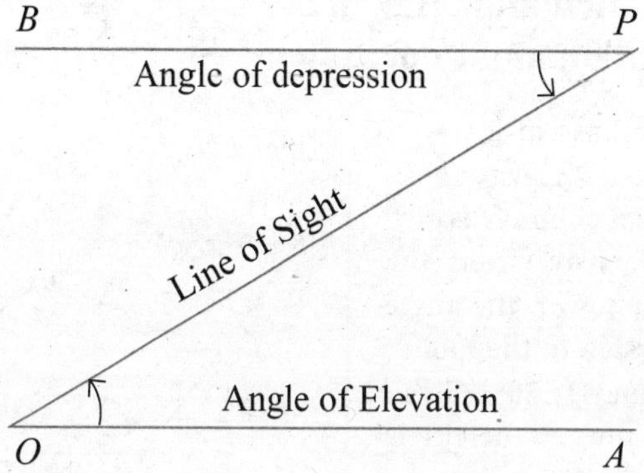

- If height of the object is doubled and distance between observer and foot (or base) of the object is also doubled, then angle of elevation remains same.
- The height of object above the water surface is equal to the depth of its image below the water surface.

Real Life Applications

Have you ever heard about Mt. Kailash? It is the striking peak standing in the remote south-west corner of Tibet in the Himalayan Mountains and is of great significance to Hinduism and witnesses a large crowd every year for Kailash Yatra with people coming from all over the world. There are numerous people who climb the highest peak in the world i.e., Mount Everest every year, but no one has been able to climb Mount Kailash till now.

So, have you ever thought that what will be the height of Mt. Kailash? How can we measure it? You can get the height of Mt. Kailash using trigonometry. Suppose you stand at point A which is 11.5 km from the foot of the Mt. Kailash and look at the top of Mount Kailash, that is your line of sight and with the help of theodolite find out that the angle of elevation is 30°. Now, you can use these values to get the height of Mt. Kailash.

Measuring the height of tall buildings

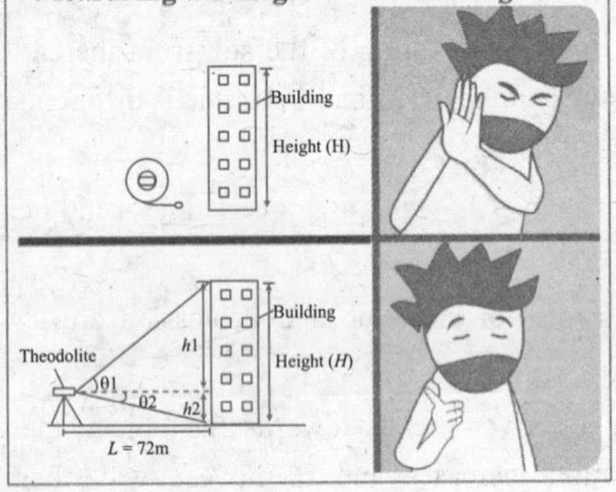

Different Problem Types

Type I: Calculating Height of a Object Using Angles of Elevation and Depression

From the base of a tower, the angle of elevation to the top of a chimney is 60°. Simultaneously, from the top of the tower, the angle of depression to the foot of the chimney is 30°. Given that the tower's height is 50 meters, determine the height of the chimney.

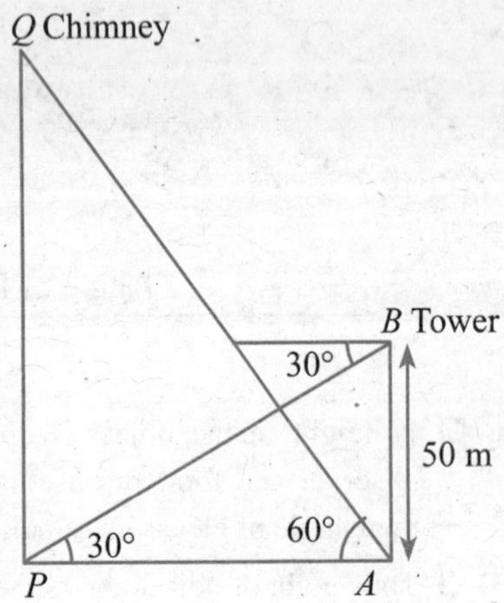

Solution:

Step I: Draw a diagram representing the situation described in the problem.

Let PQ be the chimney and AB be the tower.

We have,

$AB = 50\text{m}$, $\angle APB = 30°$ and $\angle PAQ = 60°$

Step II: Use trigonometric ratios based on the given angles:

In $\Delta\, ABP$,

$$\tan 30° = \frac{AB}{AP} \Rightarrow \frac{1}{\sqrt{3}} = \frac{50}{AP}$$

$$\Rightarrow AP = 50\sqrt{3}\text{ m}$$

Now, in $\Delta\, APQ$,

$$\tan 60° = \frac{PQ}{AP}$$

$$\Rightarrow \sqrt{3} = \frac{PQ}{50\sqrt{3}}$$

$$\therefore PQ = 150\text{ m}$$

So, the height of the chimney is 150m.

Example 1: Find the angle of depression of point P from point R in the following figure.

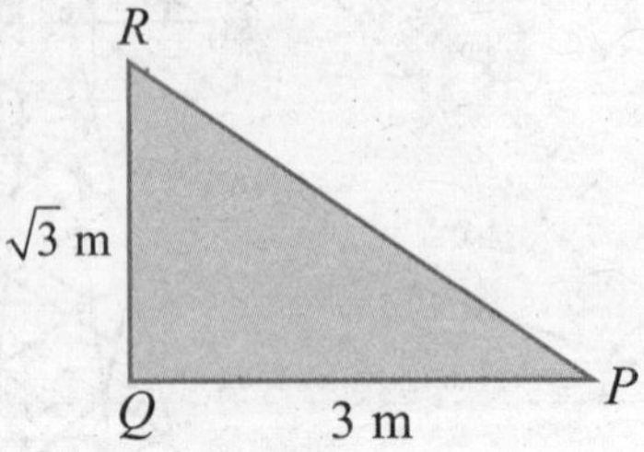

Solution: In right $\Delta\, PQR$

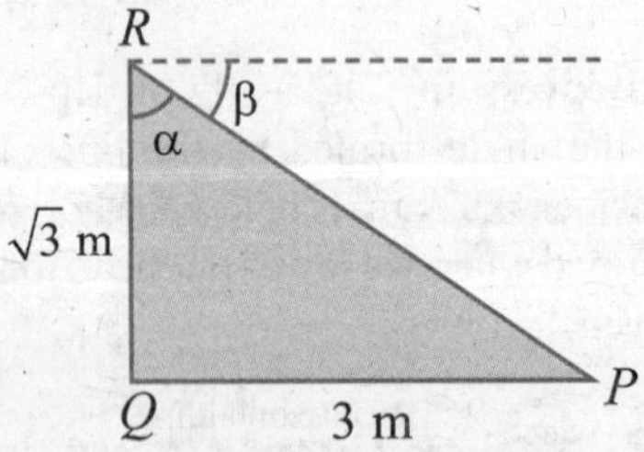

$$\tan \alpha = \frac{PQ}{QR}$$

$$\tan \alpha = \frac{3}{\sqrt{3}} = \sqrt{3}$$

$$\alpha = 60°$$

Hence, angle of depression $\beta = 90° - \alpha = 90° - 60° = 30°$

Example 2: A TV tower stands vertically on a bank of a canal. From a point on the other bank directly opposite the tower, the angle of elevation of the top of the tower is 60°. From another point 20 m away from this point on the line joining this point to the foot of the tower, the angle of elevation of the top of the tower is 30° (see Fig.). Find the height of the tower and the width of the canal.

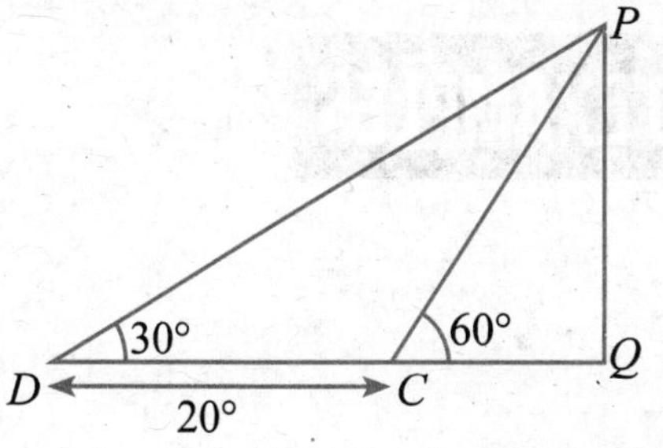

Solution: Let us suppose PQ be the height of the tower.

$$DC = 20 \text{ m (given)}$$

In right angled ΔPQD,

$$\tan 30° = \frac{PQ}{QD}$$

$$\frac{1}{\sqrt{3}} = \frac{PQ}{(20+QC)} \quad \left(\because \tan 30° = \frac{1}{\sqrt{3}}\right)$$

$$PQ = \frac{(20+QC)}{\sqrt{3}} \quad \ldots (i)$$

In right ΔPQC,

$$\tan 60° = \frac{PQ}{QC}$$

$$\sqrt{3} = \frac{PQ}{QC} \quad (\because \tan 60° = \sqrt{3})$$

$$\Rightarrow PQ = \sqrt{3}\, QC \quad \ldots (ii)$$

On putting value of equation (*i*) in (*ii*) we get

$$\sqrt{3}QC = \frac{(20+QC)}{\sqrt{3}}$$

$$3QC = 20 + QC$$

$$2QC = 20$$

$$QC = 10 \text{ m}$$

Putting the value of QC in equation (*ii*), we get

$$PQ = 10\sqrt{3} \text{ m}$$

Therefore, the height of the tower is $10\sqrt{3}$ m and the width of the canal is 10 m.

COMPETENCY BASED SOLVED EXAMPLES

Multiple Choice Questions **(1 M)**

1. The string of a kite in air is 50m long and it makes an angle of 60° with the horizontal. Assuming the string to be straight, the height of the kite from the ground is: *(An)* (CBSE, 2023)

(*a*) $50\sqrt{3}$ m (*b*) $\frac{100}{\sqrt{3}}$ m

(*c*) $\frac{50}{\sqrt{3}}$ m (*d*) $25\sqrt{3}$ m

Sol. Given,

Length of string (*AB*) of kite= 50 m

Angle of elevation = 60°

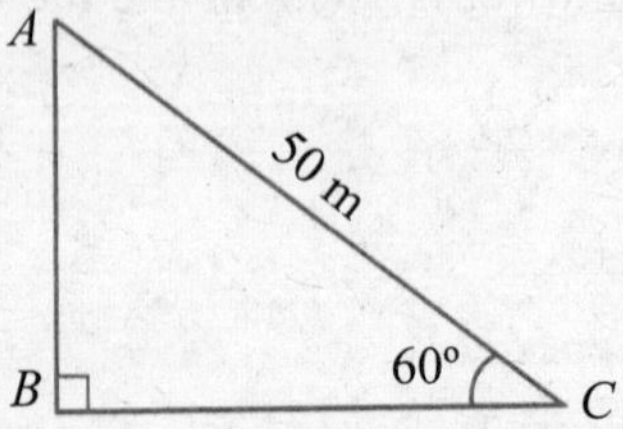

Consider ΔABC, as shown in the figure:

$$\sin 60° = \frac{AB}{AC} \Rightarrow \frac{\sqrt{3}}{2} = \frac{AB}{50}$$

$$\Rightarrow \frac{50\sqrt{3}}{2} = AB \Rightarrow AB = 25\sqrt{3} \text{ m}$$

Hence, the height of the kite is $25\sqrt{3}$ m .

2. When the sun's elevation is 30°, the shadow of a tower standing on a level plane is found to be 50 m longer than when it is 60°. Find the height of the tower. *(Un)*

(*a*) $5\sqrt{3}$ (*b*) $25\sqrt{3}$

(*c*) $15\sqrt{3}$ (*d*) $3\sqrt{3}$

Sol. Let us suppose, $AB = h$ be the height of the tower. Let $RA = x$ m

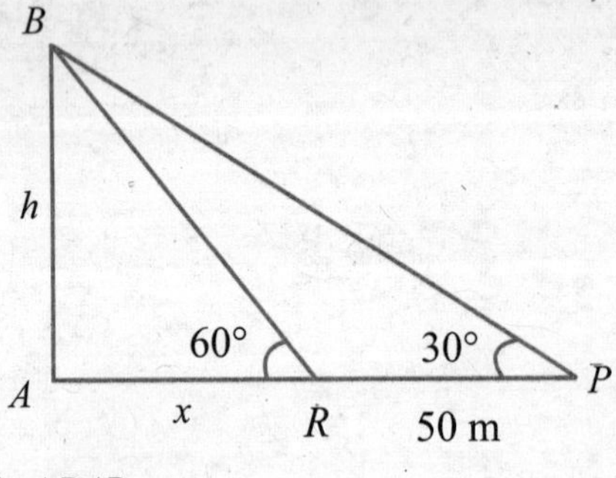

In right ΔBAR,

$$\tan 60° = \frac{BA}{RA}$$

$$\Rightarrow \sqrt{3} = \frac{h}{x} \quad (\because \tan 60° = \sqrt{3})$$

$$\Rightarrow x = \frac{h}{\sqrt{3}} \quad \text{... (i)}$$

In right ΔBAP,

$$\tan 30° = \frac{BA}{PA} \Rightarrow \frac{1}{\sqrt{3}} = \frac{h}{50+x} \quad (\because PA = PR + RA)$$

Using eq. (*i*), we get

$$\Rightarrow \frac{1}{\sqrt{3}} = \frac{h}{50+\frac{h}{\sqrt{3}}} \Rightarrow \frac{1}{\sqrt{3}}\left(50+\frac{h}{\sqrt{3}}\right) = h$$

$$\Rightarrow \frac{50}{\sqrt{3}} + \frac{h}{3} = h \Rightarrow \frac{50}{\sqrt{3}} = \frac{2h}{3} \Rightarrow h = 25\sqrt{3} \text{ m}$$

Therefore, the height of the tower is $25\sqrt{3}$ m .

Nailing the Right Answer

Students should observe the right triangle carefully in height and distance problems and apply trigonometric ratios accurately.

3. If a pole is 6 m high and it casts a shadow of length $2\sqrt{3}$ *m* on the ground, then the sun's elevation is *(An)* (NCERT Exemplar)

(*a*) 60° (*b*) 45° (*c*) 120° (*d*) 90°

Sol. It is given that the height of the pole is 6 m and it casts a shadow of length $2\sqrt{3}$ *m* on the ground. Therefore,

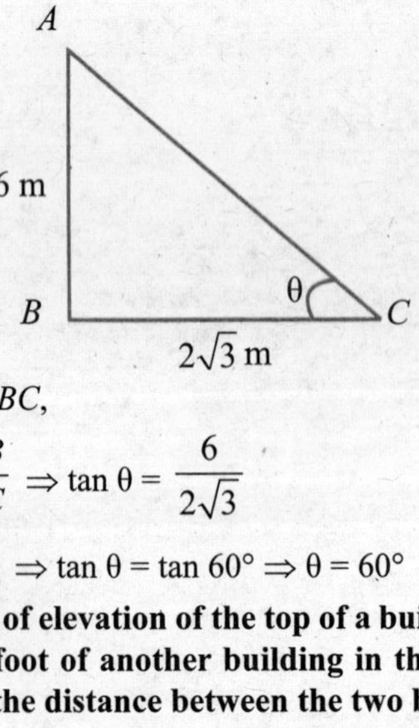

In right ΔABC,

$$\tan\theta = \frac{AB}{BC} \Rightarrow \tan\theta = \frac{6}{2\sqrt{3}}$$

$$\Rightarrow \tan\theta = \sqrt{3} \Rightarrow \tan\theta = \tan 60° \Rightarrow \theta = 60°$$

4. The angle of elevation of the top of a building 30 m high from the foot of another building in the same plane is 60°, then the distance between the two buildings is *(Cr)*

(*a*) $10\sqrt{3}$ m (*b*) $13\sqrt{3}$m

(*c*) $12\sqrt{3}$m (*d*) 48 m

Sol. Let us suppose, $AB = x$ be the distance between the two buildings.

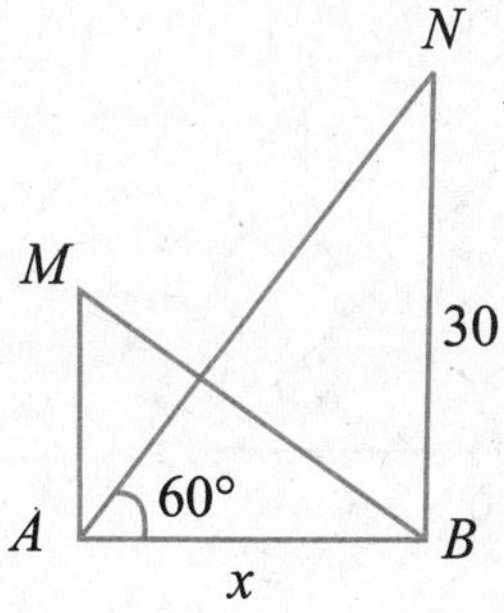

In right ΔABN,

$$\tan 60° = \frac{BN}{AB} \Rightarrow \sqrt{3} = \frac{30}{x} \qquad (\because \tan 60° = \sqrt{3})$$

$$\Rightarrow x = \frac{30}{\sqrt{3}} = 10\sqrt{3}\text{m}$$

Therefore, the distance between the two buildings is $10\sqrt{3}$m.

Mistakes 101 : What not to do!

Students may errors by misidentifying angles and misapplying concepts.

5. If the ratio of the length of a pole and its shadow is $1 : \sqrt{3}$, then the angle of elevation of the sun is **(*Ev*)**

(*a*) 120° (*b*) 45°

(*c*) 30° (*d*) 90°

Sol. Let us suppose $PQ = h$, be the height of the pole and let QR be its shadow of length $\sqrt{3}\,h$ meter.Let angle of elevation of the sun be 'θ'.

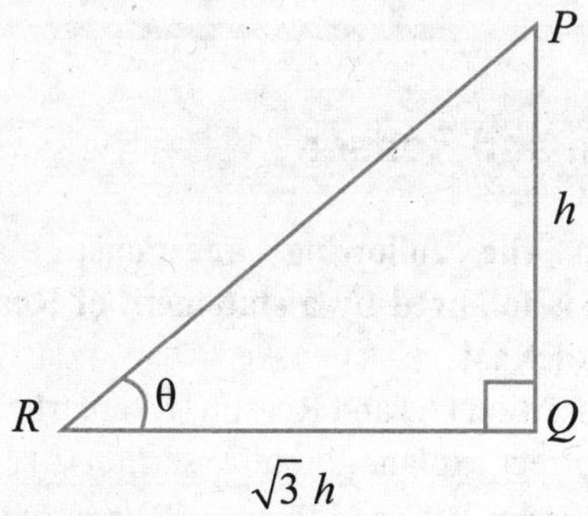

In right ΔPQR,

$$\tan\theta = \frac{PQ}{QR} \Rightarrow \tan\theta = \frac{h}{\sqrt{3}h}$$

$$\Rightarrow \tan\theta = \frac{1}{\sqrt{3}} \Rightarrow \theta = 30°$$

6. The line drawn from the eye of an observer to the point in the object viewed by the observer is said to be **(*Re*)**

(*a*) Horizontal level (*b*) Angle of depression

(*c*) Line of sight (*d*) None of the these

Sol. The line drawn from the eye of an observer to the point in the object viewed by the observer is called the "line of sight".

Mistakes 101 : What not to do!

Students frequently make errors by misunderstanding basic nomenclature and definitions of height and distance.

7. A wire connects the top of two poles of height 20 m and 14 m. Find the length of the wire if it makes an angle of 30° with the horizontal. **(*Ev*)**

(*a*) 12 m (*b*) 16 m

(*c*) 14 m (*d*) 6 m

Sol. Let us suppose, PQ and CD are the heights of two poles and PD is the length of a given wire.

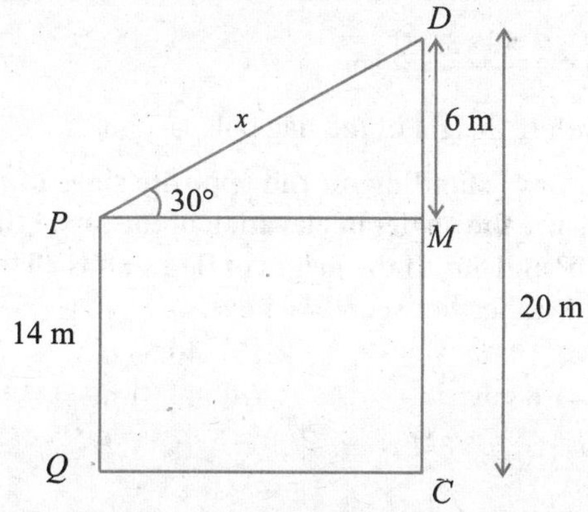

It is given that, $CD = 20$ m and $PQ = 14$ m

Let $PD = x$ m

Hence, $DM = (20 - 14)\text{m} = 6$ m

In right ΔPMD,

$$\frac{DM}{PD} = \sin 30° \Rightarrow \frac{1}{2} = \frac{6}{x} \qquad \left(\because \sin 30° = \frac{1}{2}\right)$$

$$\Rightarrow x = PD = 12 \text{ m}$$

Therefore, the length of the wire is 12m.

8. A tree which is 6 m tall casts a shadow of length 4 m on the ground. At the same time, a flag pole cast a shadow 50 m long. Find the height of the flag pole. **(*An*)**

(*a*) 75 m (*b*) 100 m (*c*) 80 m (*d*) 125 m

Sol. Let us suppose, PQ be the height of the tree and QR be its shadow.

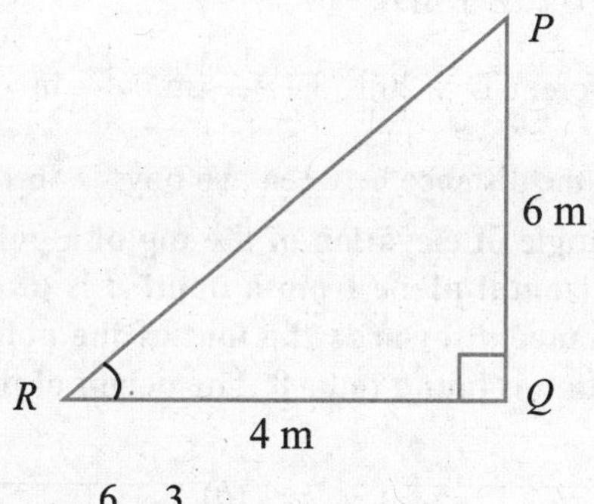

Here, $\tan\theta = \frac{6}{4} = \frac{3}{2}$

Now, let AB be the height of the flag pole and BC be its shadow.

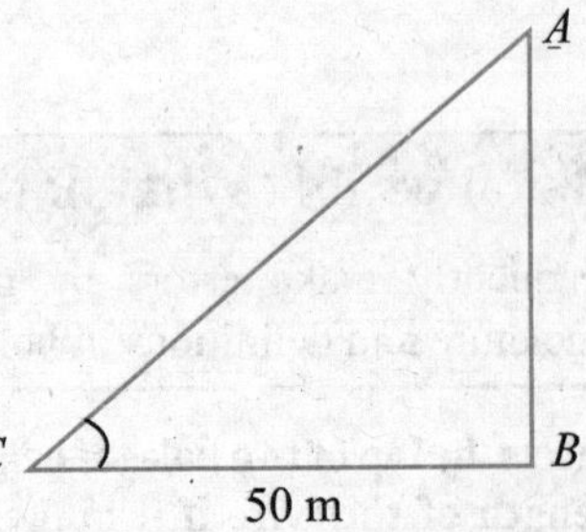

At the same time, the angle of elevation of tree and pole are equal.

$\therefore \angle PRQ = \angle ACB$

Now, in right ΔABC

$$\tan\theta = \frac{AB}{BC} \Rightarrow \frac{3}{2} = \frac{AB}{50} \qquad \left[\because \tan\theta = \frac{3}{2}\right]$$

$$\Rightarrow AB = \frac{50\times 3}{2} = 75\,\text{m}$$

Therefore, height of the flag pole is 75m.

9. Two boys standing on the opposite sides of a flag staff measure the angles of elevation of the top of the flag staff as 30° and 60°. If the height of flag staff is 20 m, then find the distance between two boys. ***(Un)***

(*a*) 46.19 m (*b*) 40.63 m
(*c*) 41.68 m (*d*) 43.81 m

Sol.

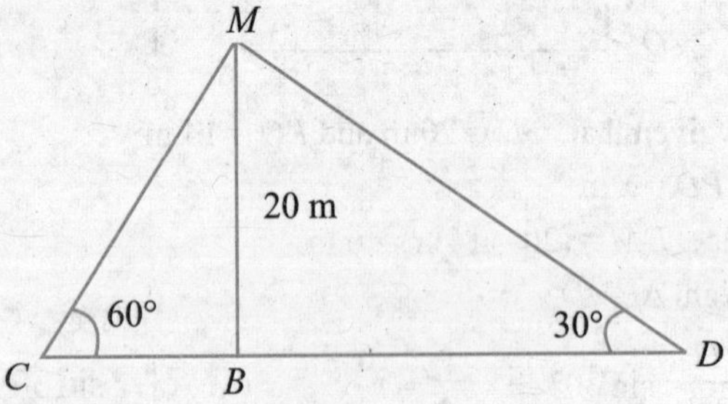

In right ΔMBC, $\tan 60° = \dfrac{MB}{BC}$

$$\tan 60° = \frac{20}{BC} \Rightarrow BC = \frac{20}{\sqrt{3}}$$

In right ΔMBD, $\tan 30° = \dfrac{MB}{BD}$

$$\tan 30° = \frac{20}{BD} \Rightarrow BD = 20\sqrt{3}$$

As, $CD = CB + BD$

Therefore, $CD = 20\left(\sqrt{3} + \dfrac{1}{\sqrt{3}}\right)\text{m} = \dfrac{80}{\sqrt{3}}\text{m} = 46.19$ m

Hence, the distance between two boys is 46.19 m.

10. The angle of elevation of the top of a pole standing on a horizontal plane from a point *A* is α. After walking a distance *d* towards the foot of the pole the angle of elevation is found to be β. The height of the pole is ***(Un)***

(*a*) $\dfrac{d}{\cot\alpha + \cot\beta}$ (*b*) $\dfrac{d}{\cot\alpha - \cot\beta}$

(*c*) $\dfrac{d}{\tan\alpha - \tan\beta}$ (*d*) $\dfrac{d}{\tan\alpha + \tan\beta}$

Sol.

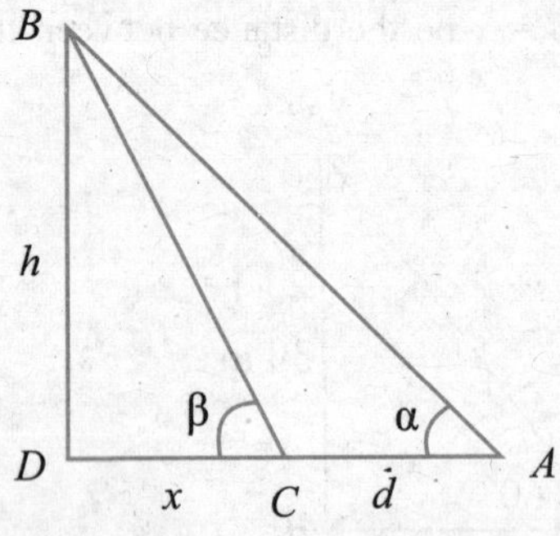

In ΔBDC,

$$\tan\beta = \frac{BD}{DC}$$

$$\tan\beta = \frac{h}{x}$$

$$\Rightarrow x = h\cot\beta \qquad \ldots (i)$$

In ΔBDA,

$$\tan\alpha = \frac{BD}{DA}$$

$$\tan\alpha = \frac{h}{x+d},\ x + d = h\cot\alpha$$

$$h\cot\beta + d = h\cot\alpha \qquad \text{[using eq. (i)]}$$

$$d = h(\cot\alpha - \cot\beta)$$

$$h = \frac{d}{\cot\alpha - \cot\beta}$$

Therefore, the height of the pole is $\dfrac{d}{\cot\alpha - \cot\beta}$.

Answer Key

1. (d)	2. (b)	3. (a)	4. (a)	5. (c)
6. (c)	7. (a)	8. (a)	9. (a)	10. (b)

Assertion and Reason (1 M)

Direction: In the following questions, a statement of Assertion (A) is followed by a statement of Reason (R). Mark the correct choice as:

(*a*) Both Assertion (A) and Reason (R) are true and Reason (R) is the correct explanation of Assertion (a).

(*b*) Both Assertion (A) and Reason (R) are true but Reason (R) is not the correct explanation of Assertion (A).

(*c*) Assertion (A) is true but Reason (R) is false.

(*d*) Assertion (A) is false but Reason (R) is true.

1. Assertion (A): **The line of sight is the line drawn from the eye of an observer to the point in the object viewed by the observer.**

   Reason (R): **Trigonometric ratios are used to find height or length of an object.** ***(An)***

Sol. Assertion (A) is true because the line of sight is indeed the line from an observer's eye to the object being viewed. Reason (R) is true as well since trigonometric ratios are indeed used to find the height or length of an object by leveraging angles and distances.

Both assertion (A) and reason (R) are true but reason (R) is not the correct explanation of assertion (A).

2. Assertion (A): **If the length of shadow of a vertical pole is equal to its height, then the angle of elevation of the sun is 45°.**

Reason (R): **According to Pythagoras theorem, $h^2 = l^2 + b^2$, where h = hypotenuse, l = length and b = base** (Ap)

Sol. Using trigonometric ratios, specifically the tangent ratio, we can relate the angle of elevation θ to the height of the pole and the length of its shadow:

$$\tan\theta = \frac{h}{l}$$

Since $l = h$, we have:

$$\tan(\theta) = \frac{h}{h} = 1$$

$\Rightarrow \tan\theta = \tan 45° \Rightarrow \theta = 45°$

Thus, the angle of elevation of the sun is indeed 45° when the length of the shadow of a vertical pole is equal to its height.

Assertion (A) is true.

The Pythagorean theorem states that in a right triangle, the square of the length of the hypotenuse is equal to the sum of the squares of the lengths of the other two sides.

Reason (R) is also true.

Both assertion (A) and reason (R) are true but reason (R) is not the correct explanation of assertion (A).

3. Assertion (A): **In the given figure, if BC = 20 m, then height AB is 11.56 m.**

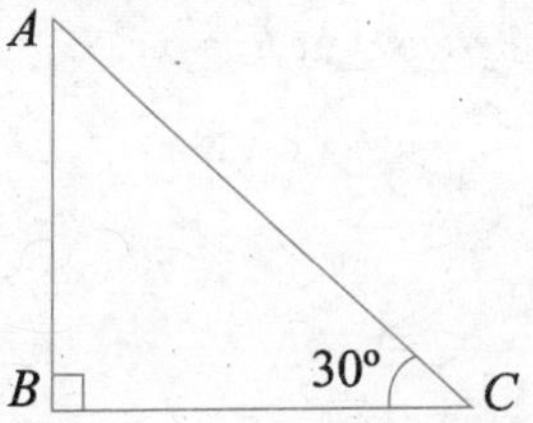

Reason (R): **$\tan\theta = AB/BC$ = perpendicular/base, where θ is the angle $\angle ACB$** (Ap)

Sol. In right ΔABC,

$$\tan\theta = \frac{AB}{BC} \Rightarrow \tan 30° = \frac{AB}{20}$$

$$\therefore AB = \frac{20}{\sqrt{3}} \approx 11.56 m$$

Hence, assertion is true.

Reason is also correct

Both assertion (A) and reason (R) are true and reason (R) is the correct explanation of assertion (A)

Answer Key

1. (b) 2. (b) 3. (a)

Subjective Questions

Very Short Answer Type Questions (1 or 2 M)

1. **Shown below is a rectangular tub of water of depth 34 cm. An object O is at the bottom of the tub. The image of the object is formed at I for an observer at Q.**

(*Note: The figure is not to scale.*)

Find the distance by which the object seems to be moved for the observer. Show your work and give valid reasons.

(Note: Take $\sqrt{2}$ = 1.4, $\sqrt{3}$ = 1.7) (An) **(CBSE CFPQ, 2023)**

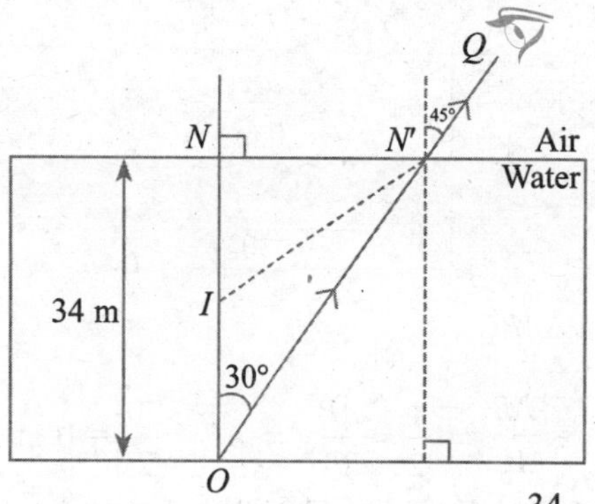

Sol. The length NN' in $\Delta NON'$ as 34tan 30° = $\frac{34}{\sqrt{3}}$ cm. (½ M)

Corresponding angles are equal and find the measure of $\angle NIN'$ as 45°. (½ M)

The depth NI in $\Delta NIN'$ as $\frac{34}{\sqrt{3}} \div \tan 45° = \frac{34}{\sqrt{3}}$ cm. (½ M)

The distance by which the object seemed to be moved for the observer as $34 - \frac{34}{\sqrt{3}} = 34 \times \frac{0.7}{1.7} = 14$ cm. (½ M)

2. **The angle of elevation of the top of the tower AB from a point C on the ground, which is 60 m away from the foot of the tower, is 30°, as shown in Fig. Find the height of the tower.** (Ap) **(CBSE, 2020)**

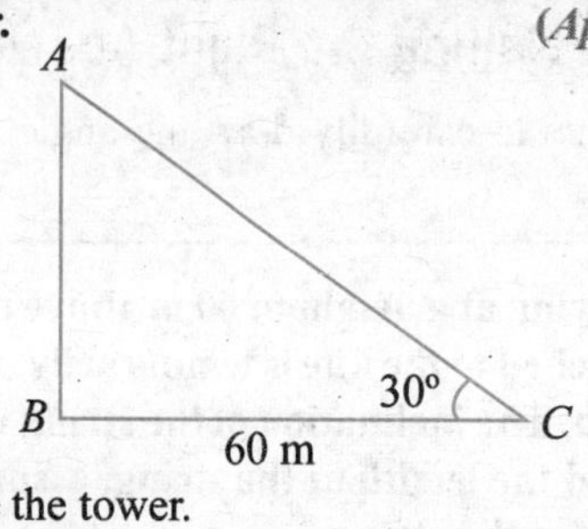

Sol. Let AB be the tower.

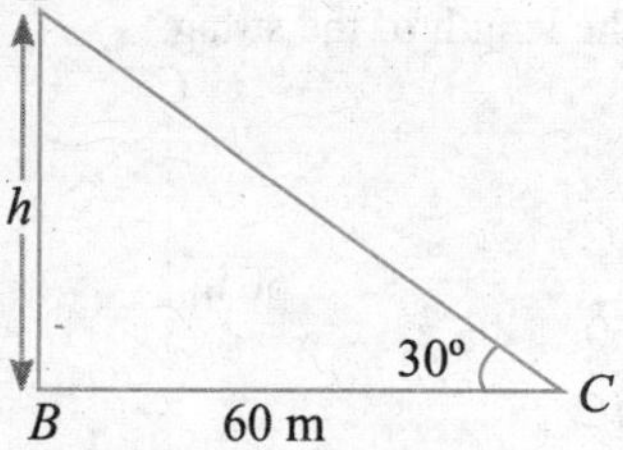

In ΔABC, (1 M)

$$\tan 30° = \frac{h}{60} \Rightarrow \frac{1}{\sqrt{3}} = \frac{h}{60} \Rightarrow h = 20\sqrt{3} \text{ m}$$ (1 M)

3. **A circus artist is climbing a 20 m long rope, which is tightly stretched and tied from the top of a vertical pole to the ground. Find the height of the pole, if the angle made by the rope with the ground level is 30°.** **(*An*) (NCERT Intext)**

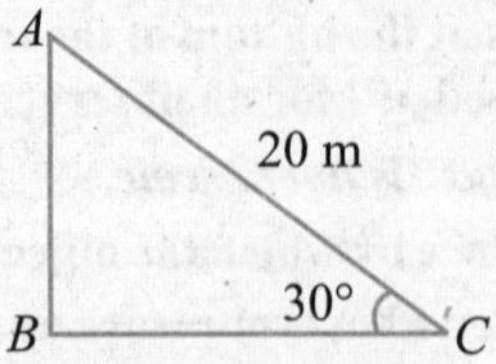

Sol. Let AB be the vertical pole and AC be 20m long rope tied to point C.

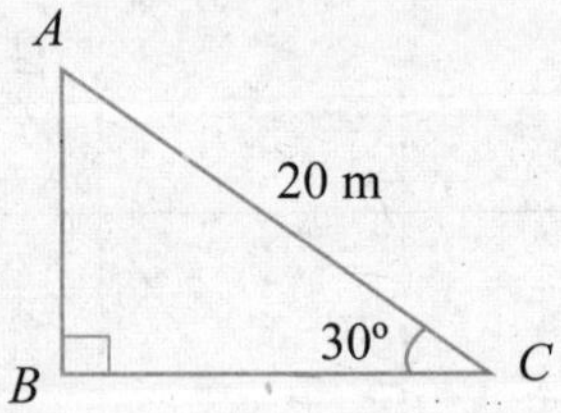

In right ΔABC

$$\sin 30^\circ = \frac{AB}{AC} \Rightarrow \frac{1}{2} = \frac{AB}{20} \Rightarrow AB = \frac{20}{2} = 10\text{m}$$ *(1 M)*

Thus, the height of the pole is 10m. *(1 M)*

4. **The ratio of the length of a vertical rod and the length of its shadow is $1:\sqrt{3}$. Find the angle of elevation of the sun at that moment?** **(*Ap*)**

Sol. $\tan\theta = \dfrac{AB}{BC}$

$\Rightarrow \tan\theta = \dfrac{1}{\sqrt{3}}$ $\left[\text{given } \dfrac{AB}{BC} = \dfrac{1}{\sqrt{3}}\right]$ *(1 M)*

$\Rightarrow \tan\theta = \tan 30^\circ \Rightarrow \theta = 30^\circ$ *(1 M)*

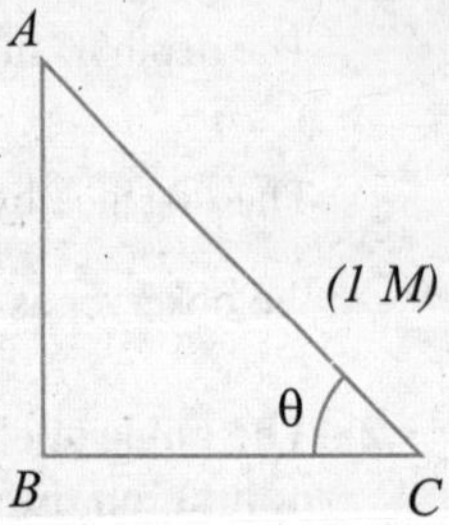

Nailing the Right Answer

Students should carefully draw the angle of elevation in a triangle.

5. **A kite is flying at a height of 60 m above the ground. The string attached to the kite is temporarily tied to a point on the ground. The inclination of the string with the ground is 60°. Find the length of the string, assuming that there is no slack in the string.** **(*Ev*) (NCERT Intext)**

Sol. Let AC be the length of the string.
In ΔABC,

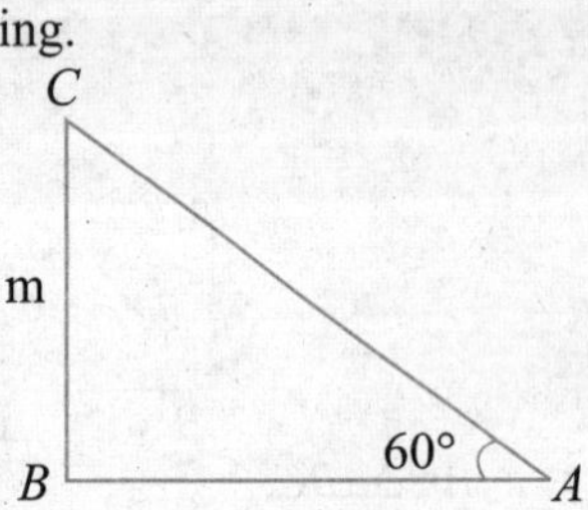

$\sin 60^\circ = \dfrac{BC}{AC}$

$\Rightarrow \dfrac{\sqrt{3}}{2} = \dfrac{60}{AC}$ *(1 M)*

$\Rightarrow AC = \dfrac{120}{\sqrt{3}} \times \dfrac{\sqrt{3}}{\sqrt{3}},$

Hence, $AC = 40\sqrt{3}\text{m}$ *(1 M)*

6. **As shown in the given figure, PQ is a 6 m high pole and CD is a ladder inclined at an angle of 60° to the horizontal and reaches up to a point D of pole. If $PD = 2.54$ m, find the length of the ladder** (use $\sqrt{3} = 1.73$) **(*Un*)**

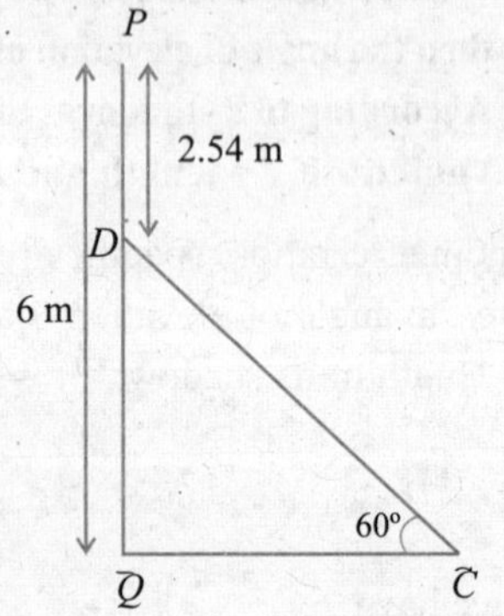

Sol. As, $QD = PQ - PD = 6\text{ m} - 2.54\text{ m} = 3.46\text{ m}$

In right angled ΔDQC,

$\dfrac{QD}{CD} = \sin 60^\circ$ *(1 M)*

$\Rightarrow \dfrac{3.46}{CD} = \dfrac{\sqrt{3}}{2}$ $\left(\because \sin 60^\circ = \dfrac{\sqrt{3}}{2}\right)$

$\Rightarrow CD = 4$ m

Therefore, the length of the ladder is 4 m. *(1 M)*

Short Answer Type Questions (2 or 3 M)

1. **In Figure, the angles of elevation of the top of a tower AB of height 'h' m, from two points P and Q at a distance of x m and y m from the base of the tower respectively and in the same straight line with it, are 60° and 30°, respectively. Prove that $h^2 = xy$.** **(*An*) (CBSE, 2022)**

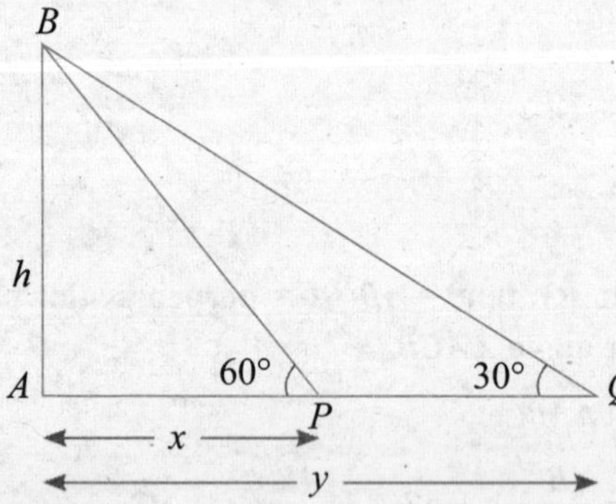

Sol. In ΔABP:

$\tan 60^\circ = \dfrac{AB}{AP} \Rightarrow \sqrt{3} = \dfrac{h}{x} \Rightarrow h = x\sqrt{3}$ ...(*i*) *(1 M)*

In ΔABQ:

$\tan 30^\circ = \dfrac{AB}{AP+PQ} \Rightarrow \dfrac{1}{\sqrt{3}} = \dfrac{h}{y} \Rightarrow h = \dfrac{y}{\sqrt{3}}$ ...(*ii*) *(1 M)*

From equation (*i*) and (*ii*)

$h(h) = \left(x\sqrt{3}\right) \times \dfrac{y}{\sqrt{3}} \Rightarrow h^2 = xy$

Hence proved *(1 M)*

2. **The angle of elevation of the top of a building from the foot of the tower is 30° and the angle of elevation of the top of the tower from the foot of the building is 60°. If the tower is 50 m high, find the height of the building.** **(*Un*) (NCERT Intext)**

Sol. Let us suppose PQ be the height of the tower, AB be the height of the building, BP be the distance between the foot of the building and the tower. Also angle of elevation is 30° and 60° from the tower and the building respectively.

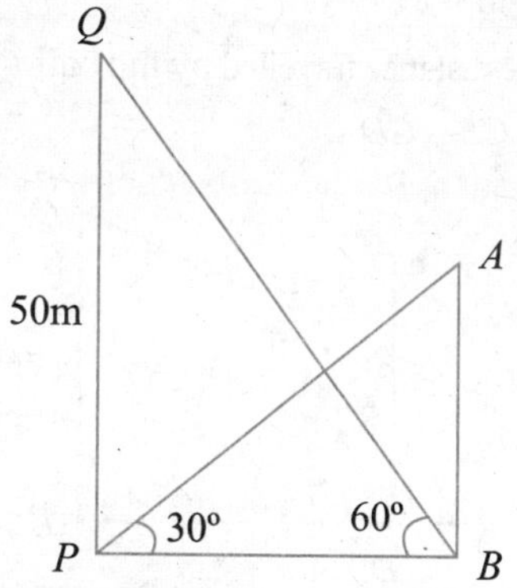

(1 M)

In right angled ΔBPQ,

$$\tan 60° = \frac{PQ}{BP}$$

$$\sqrt{3} = \frac{50}{BP} \qquad \left(\because \tan 60° = \sqrt{3}\right)$$

$$BP = \frac{50}{\sqrt{3}} \qquad \textit{(1 M)}$$

In right ΔABP,

$$\tan 30° = \frac{AB}{BP}$$

$$\Rightarrow \frac{1}{\sqrt{3}} = \frac{AB}{BP} \qquad \left(\because \tan 30° = \frac{1}{\sqrt{3}}\right)$$

$$AB = \frac{50}{3} \qquad \left(\because BP = \frac{50}{\sqrt{3}}\right)$$

Therefore, the height of the building is $\frac{50}{3}$ m. *(1 M)*

3. **Two boats are sailing in the sea 80 m apart from each other towards a cliff AB. The angle of depression of the boats from the top of the cliff are 30° and 45° respectively, as shown in Fig. Find the height of the cliff.** **(*Re*)**

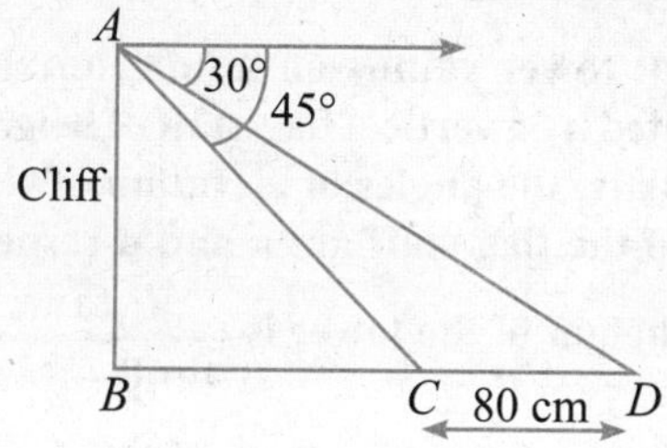

Sol. Let AB = cliff height = h m.

Let the boats are at C and D and given that the angle of depression from B to C and D are 30° and 45° respectively. It is also given that CD = 80 m

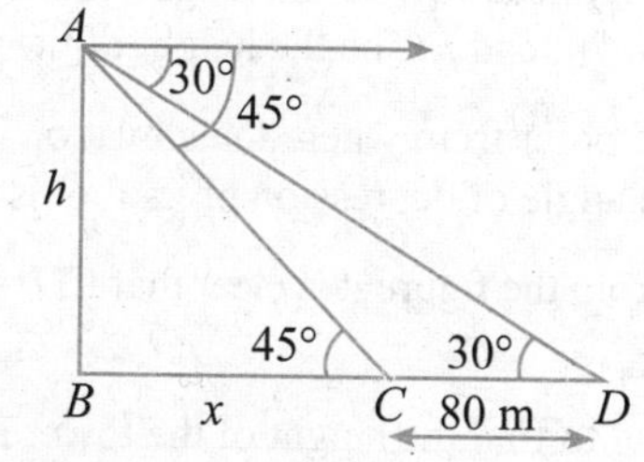

Let assume that $BC = x$ m

Now, In right-angle triangle ABD

$$\tan 30° = \frac{AB}{BD} \Rightarrow \frac{1}{\sqrt{3}} = \frac{h}{80+x} \qquad \textit{(1 M)}$$

$$\Rightarrow \frac{1}{\sqrt{3}} = \frac{h}{80+h} \Rightarrow 80 + h = \sqrt{3}\,h \qquad [\because h = x]$$

$$\Rightarrow 80 = (\sqrt{3} - 1)h \Rightarrow h = \frac{80}{\sqrt{3}-1} \qquad \textit{(1 M)}$$

$$\Rightarrow h = \frac{80}{\sqrt{3}-1} \times \frac{\sqrt{3}+1}{\sqrt{3}+1}$$

$$h = \frac{80(\sqrt{3}+1)}{(\sqrt{3})^2 - (1)^2} \Rightarrow h = \frac{80(\sqrt{3}+1)}{3-1} \Rightarrow h = \frac{80(\sqrt{3}+1)}{2}$$

$$h = 40(\sqrt{3}+1) \Rightarrow h = 40(1.732 + 1)$$

$$h = 40 \times 2.732 \Rightarrow h = 109.28 \text{ m} \qquad \textit{(1 M)}$$

Topper's Explanation ***(CBSE 2020)***

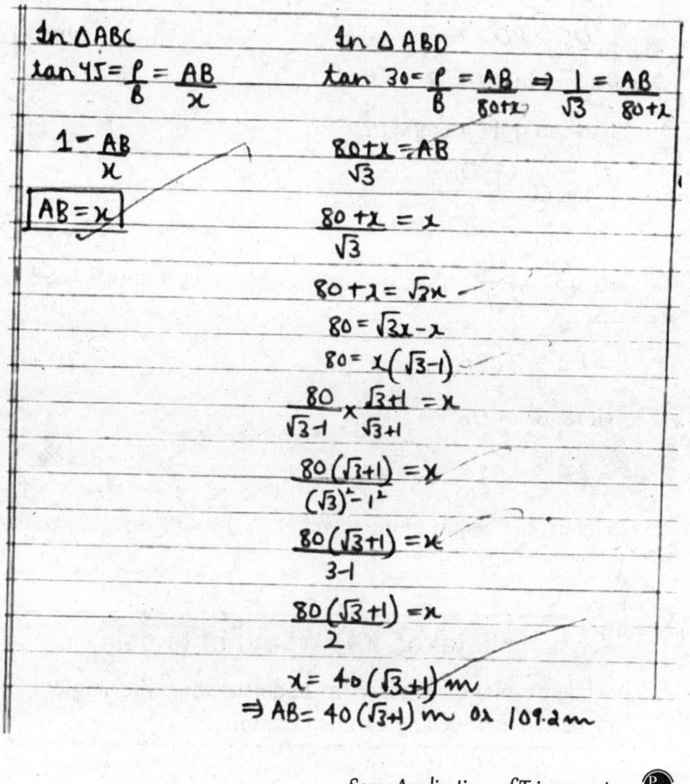

4. From the top of a 7 m high building, the angle of elevation of the top of a cable tower is 60° and the angle of depression of its foot is 45°. Determine the height of the tower. (*Un*) (NCERT Intext)

Sol. Let us suppose PQ be the height of the building which is equal to 7m and EC be the height of the tower.

P is the point from where the elevation of the tower is 60° and the angle of depression of its foot is 45°.

Also, from the figure it is clear that $CD = PQ = 7$ m and $QC = PD$. (½ M)

We need to find the height of the tower i.e., EC.

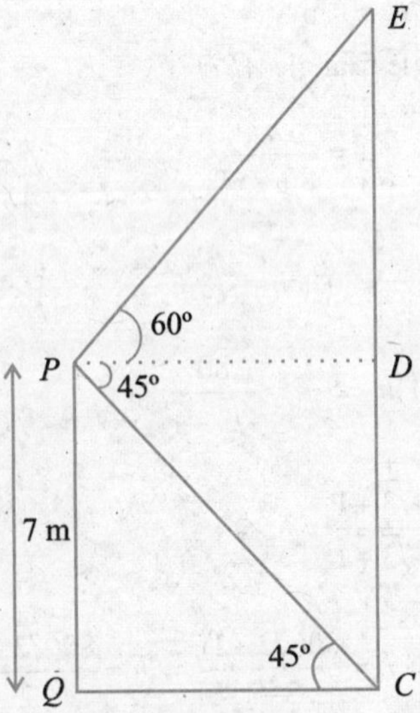

(1 M)

In right angled ΔPQC,

$\tan 45° = \frac{PQ}{QC}$, $1 = \frac{7}{QC}$ ($\because \tan 45° = 1$)

$QC = 7$

$\because QC = PD$ [given]

Therefore, $PD = 7$ (½ M)

Now, in right triangle PDE,

$\tan 60° = \frac{DE}{PD}$

$\sqrt{3} = \frac{DE}{7}$ $\left(\because \tan 60° = \sqrt{3}\right)$

$\Rightarrow DE = 7\sqrt{3}m$ (½ M)

Here, $EC = DE + CD$

$= (7\sqrt{3} + 7) = 7(\sqrt{3} + 1)$

Hence, the height of the tower is $7(\sqrt{3} + 1)$ m. (½ M)

Mistakes 101 : What not to do!

Students make mistakes in understanding the angle of elevation and the angle of depression.

5. A 1.2 m tall girl spots a balloon moving with the wind in a horizontal line at a height of 88.2 m from the ground. The angle of elevation of the balloon from the eyes of the girl at any instant is 60°. After some time, the angle of elevation reduces to 30° (see Fig). Find the distance travelled by the balloon during the interval.

(*Ev*) (NCERT Intext)

Sol. Let us suppose the initial position of the balloon be P and the final position be Q.

Height of balloon above the girl height

$= 88.2 \text{ m} - 1.2 \text{ m} = 87 \text{ m}$ (½ M)

We need to find the distance travelled by the balloon i.e., DE

$\Rightarrow$ $DE = CE - CD$

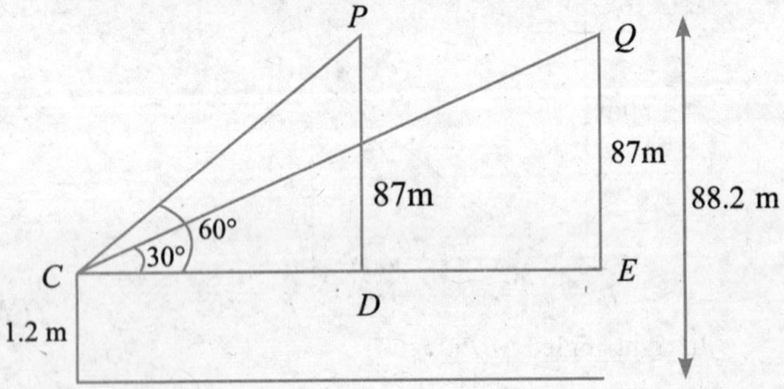

(1 M)

In right angled ΔQEC,

$\tan 30° = \frac{QE}{CE}$

$\frac{1}{\sqrt{3}} = \frac{87}{CE}$ $\left(\because \tan 30° = \frac{1}{\sqrt{3}}\right)$

$CE = 87\sqrt{3}$ ... (*i*)

In right angled ΔPDC, (½ M)

$\tan 60° = \frac{PD}{CD}$

$\sqrt{3} = \frac{87}{CD}$ $\left(\because \tan 60° = \sqrt{3}\right)$

$CD = \frac{87}{\sqrt{3}} = 29\sqrt{3}$ ... (*ii*) (½ M)

As, $DE = CE - CD$ ... (*iii*)

On putting (*i*) and (*ii*) in (*iii*), we get

$DE = (87\sqrt{3} - 29\sqrt{3}) = 58\sqrt{3}$ (½ M)

Therefore, the distance travelled by the balloon is $58\sqrt{3}$ m.

6. A vertical tower stands on a horizontal plane and is surmounted by a vertical flag-staff of height *h*. At a point on the plane, the angles of elevation of the bottom and the top of the flag-staff are α and β respectively. Prove that the height of the tower is $\frac{h \tan\alpha}{\tan\beta - \tan\alpha}$.

(*Ap*) (NCERT Exemplar)

Sol. Let us suppose, $MN = H$ be the height of the tower and $MR = h$ is the height of the flag-staff.

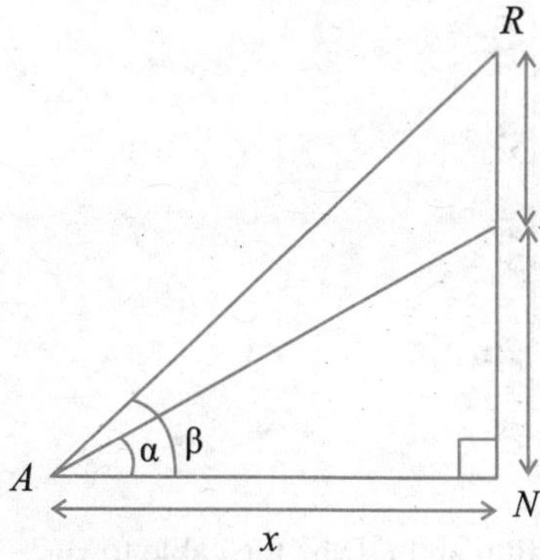

(1 M)

$\angle MAN = \alpha$ and $\angle RAN = \beta$.

Let, $AN = x$

In ΔMAN, $\frac{H}{x} = \tan\alpha$

$\Rightarrow H = x\tan\alpha$ ... (i) (½ M)

In ΔRAN, $\frac{H+h}{x} = \tan\beta$

$\Rightarrow H + h = x\tan\beta$ ... (ii) (½ M)

On dividing equation (ii) by (i), we have

$\frac{H+h}{H} = \frac{\tan\beta}{\tan\alpha} \Rightarrow H\tan\alpha + h\tan\alpha = H\tan\beta$ (½ M)

$\Rightarrow H(\tan\beta - \tan\alpha) = h\tan\alpha$

$\Rightarrow H = \frac{h\tan\alpha}{\tan\beta - \tan\alpha}$. Hence proved. (½ M)

7. From a point on a bridge across a river, the angles of depression of the banks on opposite sides of the river are 30° and 45° respectively. If the bridge is at a height of 3m from the banks, then find the width of the river.

***(Un)* (NCERT Intext)**

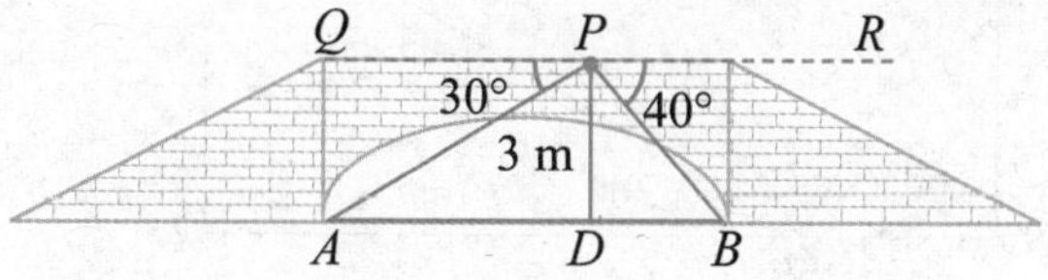

Sol. Let the width of the river = AB

And the bridge is at a height of 3 m from the banks,

So, DP = 3 metre

Angle of depression of the banks on opposite sides of the river are 30° and 45° respectively.

So, $\angle QPA = 30°$ and $\angle RPB = 45°$ (½ M)

Now, $\angle PAD = \angle QPA$ (Alternate Angles)

$\Rightarrow \angle PAD = 30°$ (½ M)

Also, $\angle PBD = \angle RPA$ (Alternate Angles)

$\Rightarrow \angle PBD = 45°$ (½ M)

In ΔAPD, we have,

$\tan 30° = \frac{PD}{AD}$

$AD = \frac{PD}{\tan 30°}$

$AD = 3\sqrt{3}\,m$ (½ M)

In ΔPDB, we have,

$\tan 45° = \frac{PD}{DB}$

$DB = PD$

$DB = 3\text{m}$ (½ M)

Now $AB = AD + DB = 3 + 3\sqrt{3}$

$AB = 3\left(\sqrt{3}+1\right)m$

Therefore, width of the river is $3\left(\sqrt{3}+1\right)m$ (½ M)

Nailing the Right Answer

Students, when tackling this problem, first note the provided angles, then form right triangles, apply trigonometry (tangent), and determine river width.

Long Answer Type Questions (4 or 5 M)

1. From the top of a 7m high building, the angle of elevation of the top of a cable tower is 60° and the angle of depression of its foot is 45°. Determine the height of the tower. ***(An)* (CBSE, 2023)**

Sol. (1 M)

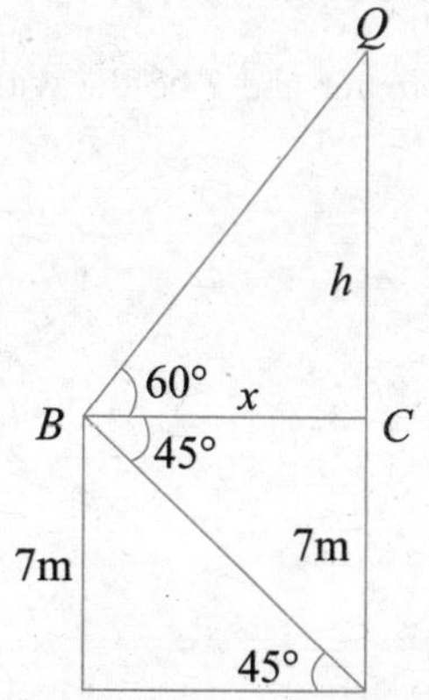

In ΔABP, $\tan 45° = \frac{7}{x} \Rightarrow x = 7$ (1½ M)

In ΔBCQ, $\tan 60° = \frac{h}{x} \Rightarrow h = \sqrt{3}x$ (1½ M)

$\Rightarrow h = 7\sqrt{3}$ m (½ M)

$\therefore$ Height of tower = $PQ = 7 + h$

$= 7 + 7\sqrt{3} = 7\left(1+\sqrt{3}\right)$m (½ M)

2. A TV tower stands vertically on a bank of a canal. From a point on the other bank of a canal. From a point on the other bank directly opposite the tower, the angle of elevation of the top of the tower is 60° from a point 20 m away from this point on the same bank the angle of elevation of the top of the tower is 30°.

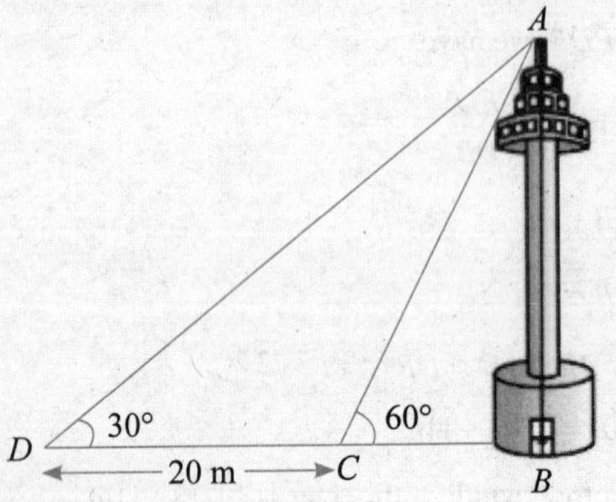

(i) Find the height of the tower

(ii) Find the width of the canal

(*An*) (CBSE, 2022)

Sol. (*1 M*)

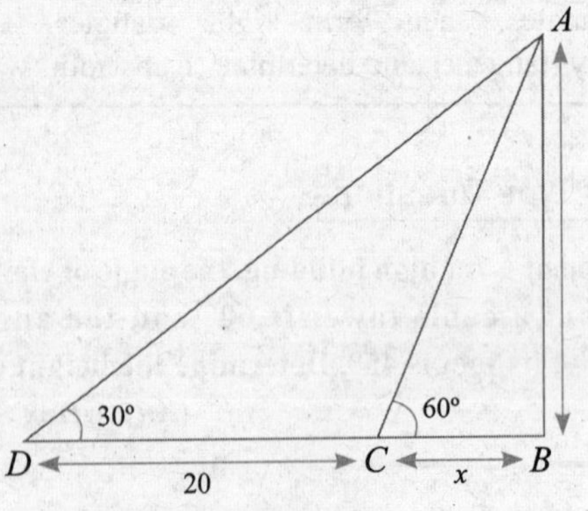

Let 'h' (AB) be the height of tower and x be the width of the river

In $\Delta ABC, \frac{h}{x} = \tan 60^\circ$

$\Rightarrow h = \sqrt{3}x$ ...(*i*) (*½ M*)

In $\Delta ABD, \frac{h}{x+20} = \tan 30^\circ$

$\Rightarrow h = \frac{x+20}{\sqrt{3}}$ ...(*ii*) (*½ M*)

Equating (i) and (ii), we get

$\sqrt{3}x = \frac{x+20}{\sqrt{3}} \Rightarrow 3x = x + 20 \Rightarrow 2x = 20 \Rightarrow x = 10$ m (*1 M*)

Put $x = 10$ in (*i*), $h = \sqrt{3}x \Rightarrow h = 10\sqrt{3}$ m (*1 M*)

3. From the top of a 7m high building, the angle of elevation of the top of a cable tower is 60°, and the angle of depression of its foot is 45°. Find the height of the tower. Given that $\sqrt{3} = 1.732$. **(*An*) (CBSE, 2020)**

Sol. (*1 M*)

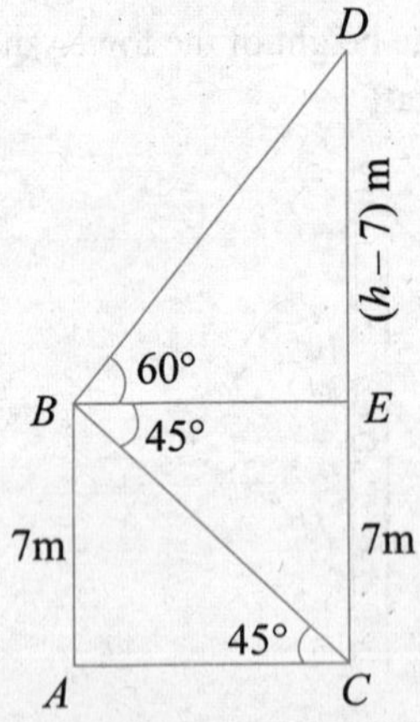

Let AB be the building and CD be the cable tower.

Draw $BE \perp CD$. Let $CD = h$ metres.

Then, $CE = AB = 7$m and $DE = (h-7)$m. (*1 M*)

From right ΔCAB, we have

$\frac{AC}{AB} = \cot 45^\circ \Rightarrow \frac{AC}{7\text{m}} = 1 \Rightarrow AC = 7$

$\therefore BE = AC = 7$m (*1 M*)

From right ΔBED, we have

$\frac{DE}{BE} = \tan 60^\circ = \sqrt{3} \Rightarrow \frac{h-7}{7} = \sqrt{3}$

$\therefore h = 7\sqrt{3} + 7 = 7\left(\sqrt{3}+1\right) = 7(1.732+1)$

$\Rightarrow h = (7 \times 2.732) = 19.12$ m (*1 M*)

4. Two poles of equal heights are standing opposite each other on either side of the road, which is 80 m wide. From a point between them on the road, the angles of elevation of the top of the poles are 60° and 30° respectively. Find the height of the poles and the distances of the point from the poles. **(*Re*) (NCERT Intext)**

Sol.

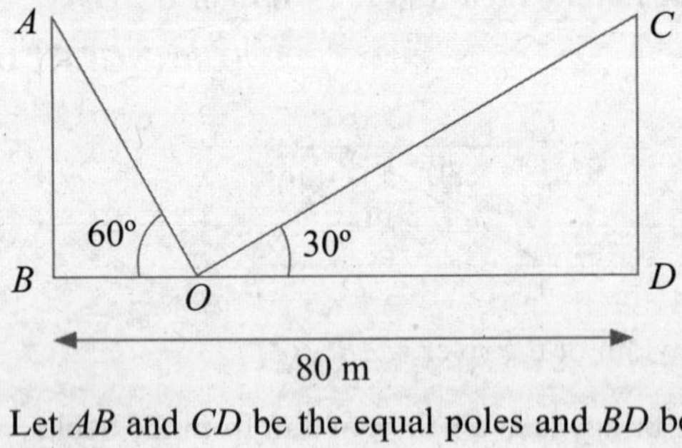

(*1 M*)

Let AB and CD be the equal poles and BD be the width of the road.

We have,

$\angle AOB = 60^\circ$ and $\angle COD = 30^\circ$

In ΔAOB,

$\tan 60^\circ = \frac{AB}{BO} \Rightarrow \sqrt{3} = \frac{AB}{BO} \Rightarrow BO = \frac{AB}{\sqrt{3}}$ (*½ M*)

Now, in ΔCOD,

$\tan 30^\circ = \frac{CD}{DO} \Rightarrow \frac{1}{\sqrt{3}} = \frac{CD}{DO} \Rightarrow DO = \sqrt{3}CD$ (*½ M*)

As, $BD = 80$

$BO + DO = 80$

$\Rightarrow \frac{AB}{\sqrt{3}} + \sqrt{3}CD = 80$ (½ M)

$\Rightarrow \frac{AB}{\sqrt{3}} + \sqrt{3}AB = 80$ (Given: $AB = CD$)

$\Rightarrow AB\left(\frac{1}{\sqrt{3}} + \sqrt{3}\right) = 80 \Rightarrow AB = \frac{80\sqrt{3}}{4}$

$\Rightarrow AB = 20\sqrt{3}\text{m}$ (½ M)

Also, $BO = \frac{AB}{\sqrt{3}} = \frac{20\sqrt{3}}{\sqrt{3}} = 20$ m (½ M)

So, $DO = 80 - 20 = 60$ m

Hence, the height of each pole is $20\sqrt{3}$m and point P is at a distance of 20 m from left pole and 60 m from the right pole.

(½ M)

5. **From the top of a 75 m high lighthouse from the sea level, the angles of depression of two ships are 30° and 45°. If the ships are on the opposite sides of the lighthouse, then find the distance between the two ships.**

(*Ev*) (CBSE, 2020)

Sol. (1 M)

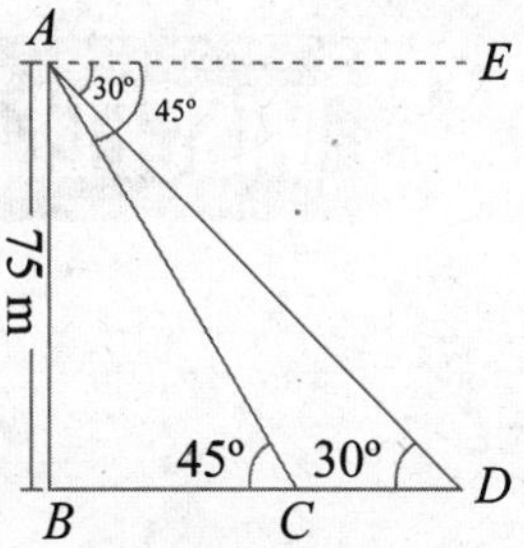

Let AB be the lighthouse and the two ships be at point C and D respectively.

In ΔABC,

$\Rightarrow \tan 45° = \frac{AB}{BC} \Rightarrow 1 = \frac{75}{BC}$

$\therefore BC = 75$ m (1 M)

In ΔABD,

$\Rightarrow \tan 30° = \frac{AB}{BD} \Rightarrow \frac{1}{\sqrt{3}} = \frac{75}{BC + CD}$

$\Rightarrow \frac{1}{\sqrt{3}} = \frac{75}{75 + CD} \Rightarrow 75\sqrt{3} = 75 + CD$ (1 M)

$\therefore CD = 75(\sqrt{3} - 1)m = 75(1.73 - 1) = 75 \times 0.73$

$\therefore CD = 54.75$ m

$\therefore$ The distance between the two ships is 54.75m. (1 M)

MISCELLANEOUS EXERCISE

Multiple Choice Questions (1 M)

1. If the length of the shadow of a pole is increasing, then the angle of elevation of the sun
(a) First increase then decrease
(b) Is decreasing
(c) Remains unaffected
(d) Is increasing

2. If the height of the tower is equal to the length of its shadow, then the angle of elevation of the sun is ______.
(CBSE SQP, 2023)
(a) 30° (b) 45°
(c) 60° (d) 90°

3. An observer 1.5 meters tall is 20.5 meters away from a building 22 meters high. Determine the angle of elevation of the top of the building from the eye of the observer.
(a) 120° (b) 45°
(c) 60° (d) 90°

4. The angles of elevation of the top of a pole from two points distant s and t from its foot and in the same straight line with it are complementary. Then the height of the pole is

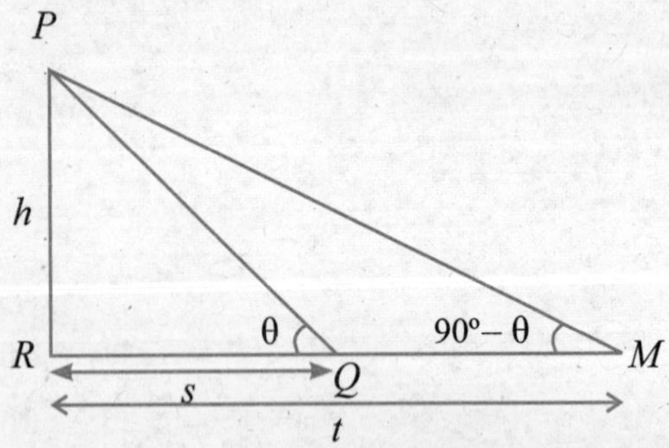

(a) st^2 (b) $\frac{\sqrt{s}}{t}$
(c) $\sqrt{st}$ (d) $\frac{s}{t}$

5. The angle formed by the line of sight with the horizontal when the point being viewed is above the horizontal level is known as
(a) Angle of elevation (b) Angle of depression
(c) Line of sight (d) None of the these

6. The angle of elevation of the top of an unfinished tower at a point distant 100 m from its base is 45°, how much higher must the tower be raised so that its angle of elevation at the same point may be 60°? (Use $\sqrt{3}$ = 1.73)
(a) 120 m (b) 72 m
(c) 80 m (d) 73 m

7. From a window (9 m above the ground) of a house in a street, the angles of elevation and depression of the top and foot of another house on the opposite side of the street are 30° and 60° respectively. Then the width of the street is
(a) $\frac{3}{\sqrt{3}}$ m (b) $3\sqrt{3}$ m
(c) $9\sqrt{3}$ m (d) None of these

8. A pole subtends an angle of 30° at a point on the same level as its foot. At a second point h meters above the first, the depression of the foot of the pole is 60°. The height of the pole is
(a) $\frac{\sqrt{h}}{2}$ m (b) $\sqrt{2h}$ m
(c) $\frac{h}{3}$ m (d) $\frac{h}{\sqrt{3}}$ m

9. In the given figure, length NC is equal to

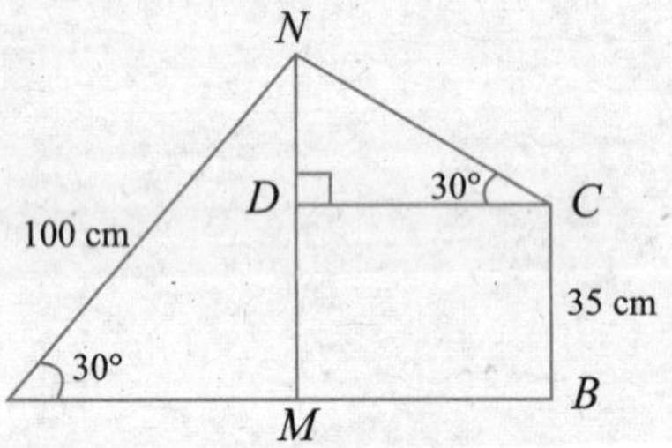

(a) 30 cm (b) $10\sqrt{3}$ cm
(c) $13\sqrt{2}$ cm (d) $5\sqrt{2}$ cm

10. If the height of a pole and the distance of the point of observation from the foot of pole, both are increased by 10%, then the angle of elevation of its top;
(a) Increases
(b) Decreases
(c) Remains unchanged
(d) First increase then decrease

11. If the angle of elevation of the top of a vertical tower from a point on the ground is 60° and from another point which is 10 m vertically above the first, its angle of elevation is 45°, then the height of the tower is
(a) $5(\sqrt{3}+3)$ m (b) $(\sqrt{3}+3)$ m
(c) $(\sqrt{3}-3)$ m (d) $5(\sqrt{3}-3)$ m

Assertion and Reason (1 M)

Direction: **In the following questions, a statement of Assertion (A) is followed by a statement of Reason (R). Mark the correct choice as:**

(*a*) Both Assertion (A) and Reason (R) are true and Reason (R) is the correct explanation of Assertion (A).

(*b*) Both Assertion (A) and Reason (R) are true but Reason (R) is not the correct explanation of Assertion (A).

(*c*) Assertion (A) is true but Reason (R) is false.

(*d*) Assertion (A) is false but Reason (R) is true.

1. **Assertion (A):** If the length of shadow of a vertical pole is equal to its height, then the angle of elevation of the sun is 45°.
   Reason (R): According to pythagoras theorem, $H^2 = P^2 + B^2$, where H = hypotenuse, P = perpendicular and B = base
2. **Assertion (A):** Trigonometry is used to determine the distance between two objects or locations that cannot be directly measured.
   Reason (R): By measuring the angles of elevation or depression of the objects or locations from two different points at a known distance apart, the distance between the objects or locations can be calculated using trigonometric ratios.
3. **Assertion (A):** The angle of elevation of an object viewed, is the angle formed by the line of sight with the horizontal when it is above the horizontal level.
   Reason (R): The angle of depression of an object viewed, is the angle formed by the line of sight with the horizontal when it is below the horizontal level.
4. **Assertion (A):** As shown in the figure, if $QR = 20$ m, then height PQ is 11.56 m.

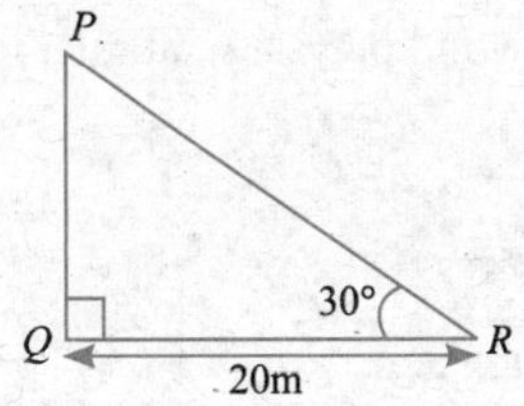

   Reason (R): $\tan\theta = \dfrac{PQ}{QR} = \dfrac{\text{Perpendicular}}{\text{Base}}$, where θ is the $\angle PRQ$.
5. **Assertion (A):** If the angle of elevation of Sun, above a perpendicular line (tower) decreases, then the length of shadow of the tower increases.
   Reason (R): It is due to decrease in slope of the line of sight

Subjective Questions

Very Short Answer Type Questions (1 or 2 M)

1. A balloon is connected to a meteorological station by a cable of length 200 m, inclined at 60° to the horizontal. Find the height of the balloon from the ground. Assume that there is no slack in the cable. (Use $\sqrt{3}$ = 1.732)
2. In Figure, the angle of elevation of the top of a tower AC from a point B on the ground sis 60°. If the height of the tower is 20 m, find the distance of the point from the foot of the tower. **(CBSE, 2020)**

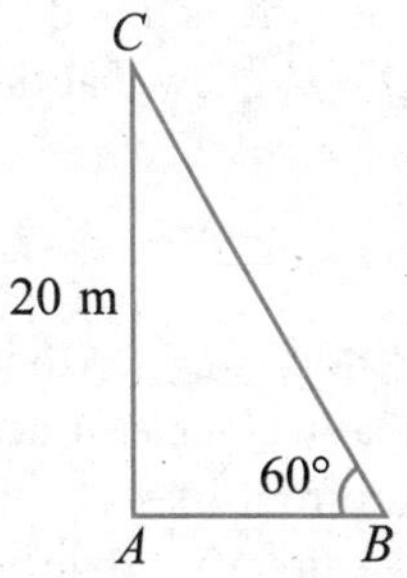

3. An observer on the ground sees a bird in flight at an angle of elevation of 45°. If the bird is flying at a height of 50 meters, how far away is the bird from the observer?
4. A 12-meter tall pole is placed on top of a building. From a point on the ground, the angle of elevation to the top of the pole is 30°. If the building is 20 meters tall, how far away is the point from the foot of the building?
5. A person having height 1.5 m is standing on the top of a tower that is 50 meters tall. The person looks down and sees a car on the road at an angle of depression of 45°. How far away is the car from the base of the tower?

Short Answer Type Questions (2 or 3 M)

1. At a point on level ground, the angle of elevation of a vertical tower is, found to be α such that $\tan\alpha = \dfrac{1}{3}$. After walking 100 m towards the tower, the angle of elevation β becomes such that $\tan\beta = \dfrac{3}{4}$. Find the height of the tower. **(CBSE, 2022)**
2. A man standing on the deck of a ship, which is 10 m above the water level, observes the angle of elevation of the top of a cliff as 60° and the angle of depression of the base of the cliff as 30°. Calculate the distance of the cliff from the ship and the height of the cliff. (Use $\sqrt{3}$ = 1.73)
3. The height of a building is h and the angle of elevation of the building is α. On moving a distance $\dfrac{h}{2}$ towards the building, the angle of elevation becomes β. What is the value of (cot α – cot β)?
4. The angle of elevation of the top of a tower at a point on the level ground is 30°. After walking a distance of 100 m towards the foot of the tower along the horizontal line through the foot of the tower on the same level ground the angle of elevation to the top of the tower is 60°, find the height of the tower. **(CBSE, 2022)**
5. A balloon of radius γ makes an angle α at the eye of an observer and the angle of elevation of its centre is β. Find the height of its centre from the ground. **(NCERT Exemplar)**

6. A boat is being rowed away from a hill 150 m high. Find the speed of the boat if the angle of depression of the boat from the top of the hill changes from 60° to 45° in 2 minutes.

7. The angle of elevation of the top of a pole from a point M due south of the pole is α and from Q due east of the tower is β. If $MQ = d$, show that the height of the pole is $\dfrac{d}{\sqrt{\cot^2 \alpha + \cot^2 \beta}}$.

8. The pilot of an aircraft flying horizontally at a speed of 1200 km/hr observes that the angle of depression of a point on the ground changes from 30° to 45° in 15 seconds. Find the height at which the aircraft is flying. **(CBSE, 2022)**

Long Answer Type Questions (4 or 5 M)

1. The two palm trees are of equal heights are standing opposite to each other on either side of the river, which is 80 m wide. From a point O between them on the river the angles of elevation of the top of the trees are 60° and 30°, respectively. Find the height of the trees and the distances of the point O from the trees.

2. The angles of depression of the top and bottom of a building 50 m high are observed from the top of a tower are 30° and 60° respectively. Find the height of the tower, and also the horizontal distance between the building and the tower.

3. Determine the height of a mountain if the elevation of its top at an unknown distance from the base is 30° and at a distance 10 km further off from the mountain, along the same line, the angle of elevation is 15°. (Use, $\tan 15° = 0.23$)

4. The angle of elevation of the top of a vertical tower from a point on the ground is 60°. From another point 10 m vertically above the first, its angle by elevation is 45°. Find the height of the tower.

5. The angles of depression of the top and bottom of a 50 m height building from the top of a tower are 45° and 60° respectively. Find the height of the tower and horizontal distance between the tower and the building.

6. A bird is sitting on the top of a 80 m high tree. From a point on the ground the angle of elevation of the bird is 45°.

   The bird fly away horizontally in such a way that it remained at a constant height from the ground. After 2 seconds the angle of elevation of the bird from the same point is 30°. Find the speed of flying of the bird.

7. A bird is sitting on the top of a 80 m high tree. From a point on the ground, the angle of elevation of the bird is 45°. The bird flies away horizontally in such a way that it remained at a constant height from the ground. After 2 seconds, the angle of elevation of the bird from the same point is 30°. Find the speed of flying of the bird.

8. A ladder set against a wall at an angle 45° to the ground. If the foot of the ladder is pulled away from the wall through a distance of 4m, its top slides a distance of 3m down the wall making an angle 30° with the ground. Find the final height of the top of the ladder from the ground and length of the ladder.

Case Based Questions

Case Based-I: A boy is standing on the top of light house. He observed that boat P and boat Q are approaching the light house from opposite directions. He finds that angle of depression of boat P is 45° and angle of depression of boat Q is 30°. He also knows that height of the light house is 100 m.

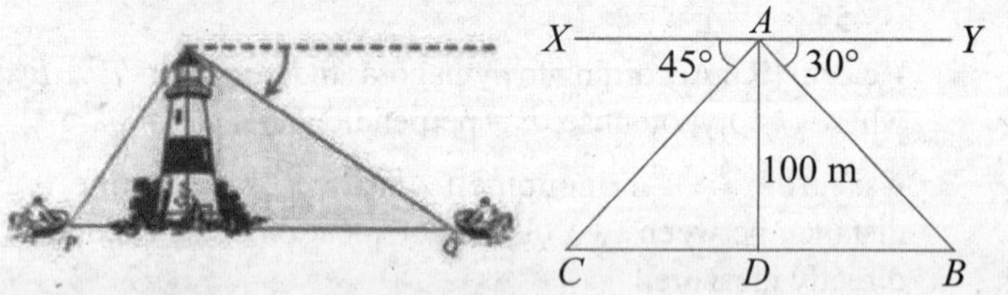

Based on the above information, answer the following questions.

(*i*) What is the measure of $\angle ACD$?

(*ii*) If $\angle YAB = 30°$, then $\angle ABD$ is also 30°, Why?

(*iii*) Find length of CD.

OR

Find length of BD. **(CBSE SQP, 2023)**

Case Based-II: Aviation has revolutionized the life of man. Planes operate between a dense network of major world cities, ferrying people and cargo to their destinations in a very short span of time. Many upgradations have been evolved in the aviation technology in the last few years. Speed, direction and distance as well as other features of the flight have also been considered in this technology. The wind plays a vital role, when a flight travels.

Suppose an airplane flying at 1500 m height from the earth has an angle of elevation 60° from the airport.

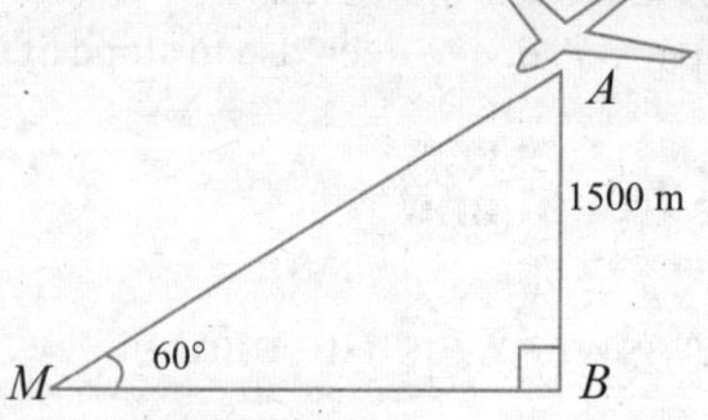

(*i*) If the point M moves towards the point B, then the angle of elevation will increase / decrease.

(*ii*) Find the distance of point M to the object.

OR

Find the distance of point M to B.

(*iii*) If the point M moves away the point B, then the angle of elevation will increase/decrease.

Case Based-III: Ritu went to Noida for the first time with his family and surprised to see tall building and towers of Physics Wallah. From the base of his hotel building, she observed the top of the tower of Physics Wallah and in the same evening from the foot of the tower of Physics Wallah, he observed the top of his hotel building. The angle of elevation of top of a hotel building from the foot of the tower of Physics Wallah is 30° and angle of elevation of top of tower of Physics Wallah from the foot of the hotel building is 60° and height of tower of Physics Wallah is 50 m.

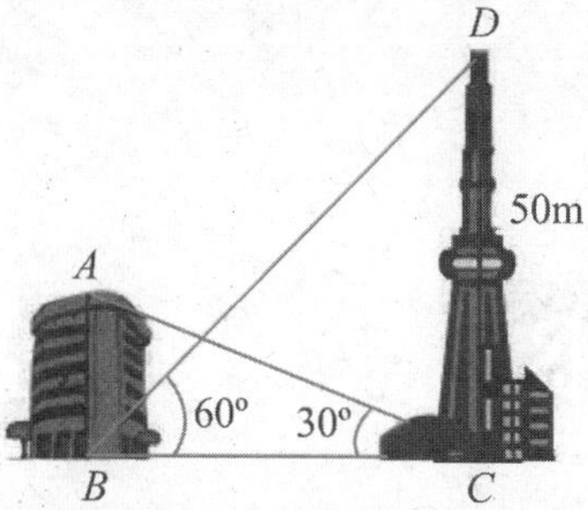

(*i*) The distance between the tower and the hotel building is

(*a*) 80 m (*b*) $\frac{50}{\sqrt{3}}$m (*c*) $50\sqrt{3}$m (*d*) 100 m

(*ii*) The distance between the foot of hotel building and the top of tower of Physics Wallah is

(*a*) $\frac{100}{\sqrt{3}}$m (*b*) $\frac{50}{3}$m (*c*) 100 m (*d*) 300 m

(*iii*) The height of the hotel building is

(*a*) 50 m (*b*) $\frac{50}{3}$m (*c*) $\frac{50}{\sqrt{3}}$m (*d*) $50\sqrt{3}$m

(*iv*) If Raj is standing on the road in between the tower of Physics Wallah and the hotel building and from that point he observed the angle of elevation of the top of the hotel building is 45°, then find his distance from the foot of the hotel building.

(*a*) 20 m (*b*) 42 m (*c*) $\frac{50}{3}$m (*d*) 50 m

(*v*) The difference between the height of a hotel building and the tower of physics wallah is

(*a*) $\frac{100}{3}$m (*b*) $\frac{200}{3}$m (*c*) 50 m (*d*) 100 m

Case Based-IV: A radio station was built near village Baghour for the better transmission of signals and there were two sections, section –x and section-y upon which tower was built. Engineers have observed that the angle of elevation of top of section –X is 30°, when engineers were at a distance of 24 m from the base of radio station and angle of elevation of top of section – Y is 45°. (Use $\sqrt{3}$ = 1.73)

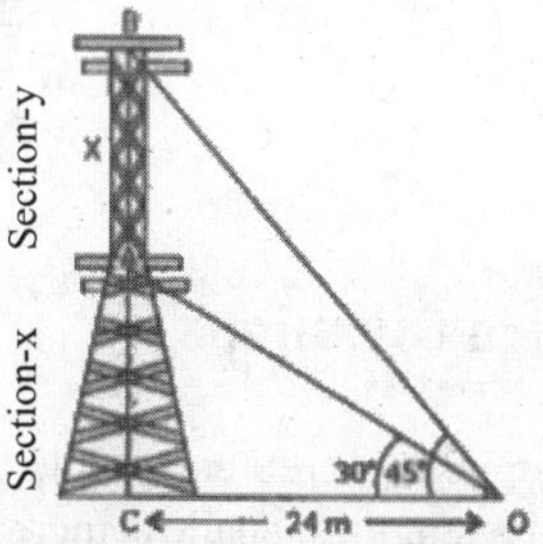

(*i*) Find the total height of the radio station from the ground.

(*ii*) Find the height of section-*x*.

OR

Find the height of section-*y*.

(*iii*) A wire is lied from top of the radio station (from point-*R*) to a point *A* on the ground for additional support. Find the length of the wire.

ANSWER KEYS

Multiple Choice Questions

1. (*b*) **2.** (*b*) **3.** (*b*) **4.** (*c*) **5.** (*a*) **6.** (*d*) **7.** (*b*) **8.** (*c*) **9.** (*a*) **10.** (*c*)
11. (*a*)

Assertion and Reason

1. (*b*) **2.** (*a*) **3.** (*b*) **4.** (*a*) **5.** (*a*)

Case Based Questions

Case Based-III

(*i*) (*b*) (*ii*) (*a*) (*iii*) (*b*) (*iv*) (*c*) (*v*) (*a*)

HINTS & EXPLANATIONS

Multiple Choice Questions

1. (*b*) Let us suppose, P represents the position of the sun, therefore as the length of shadow increases from SR to SQ, the angle of elevation decreases from 60° to 30° respectively.

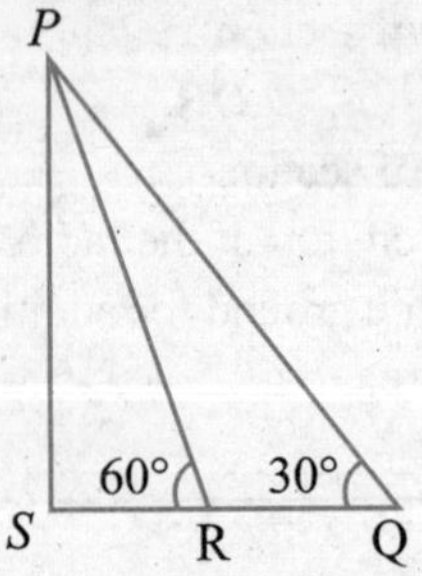

2. (*b*)

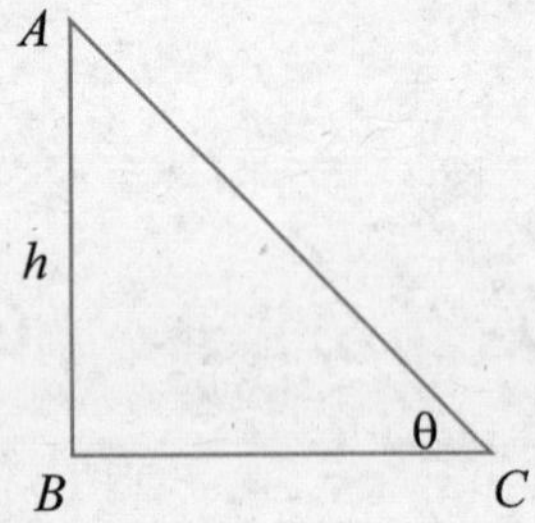

In right angle ΔABC, AB represents the tower and BC represents its shadow on the ground. θ represents angle of elevation of the sun.

$$\tan\theta = \frac{h}{x}$$

But length of shadow = height of the tower, i.e. $h = x$.

$$\tan\theta = \frac{h}{h} = 1$$

$\tan\theta = \tan 45°$

$\theta = \tan 45°$

Thus, angle of elevation of the sun = 45°

3. (*b*) Let PQ be an observer of height 1.5 m which is 20.5 m away from a building MN of height 22 meters.

$PQ = 1.5$m, $NQ = 20.5$m and $MN = 22$m

From P, draw $PA \perp MN$, then $APQN$ is a rectangle.

$AM = MN - AN$

$= MN - PQ$ ($\because$ opposite sides of rectangle are equal)

$= 22 - 1.5 = 20.5$

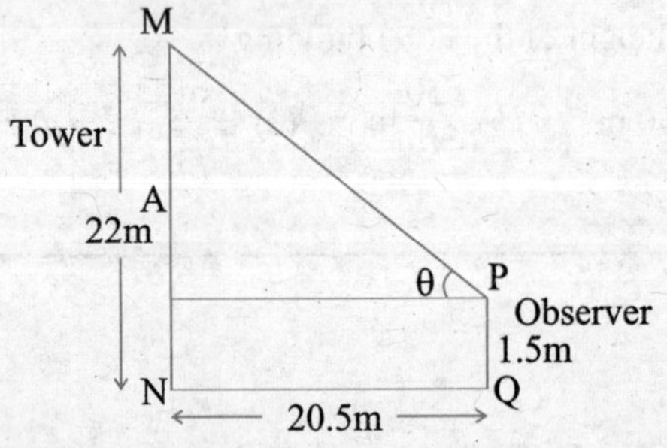

$$\tan\theta = \frac{MA}{PA} \Rightarrow \tan\theta = \frac{20.5}{20.5} \Rightarrow \tan\theta = 1 \Rightarrow \theta = 45°$$

Therefore, the angle of elevation of the top of the building from the eye of the observer is 45°.

4. (*c*) Let us suppose, $PR = h$ be the height of the pole,

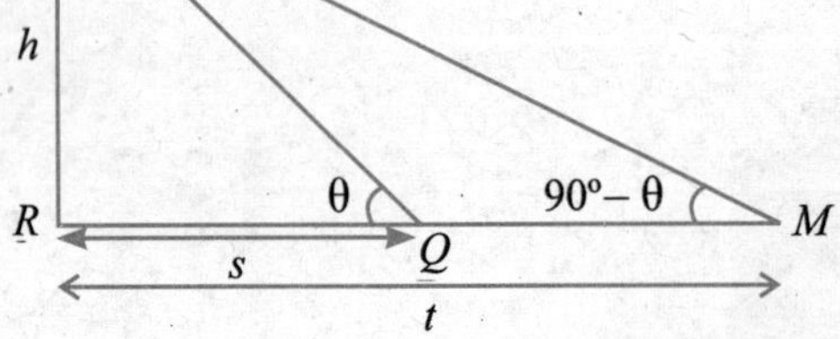

In right ΔPRQ,

$$\tan\theta = \frac{PR}{QR} \Rightarrow \tan\theta = \frac{h}{s} \quad \dots (i)$$

In right ΔPRM, $\angle M = 90° - \theta$ then $\angle RPM = \theta$ using sum of angles of triangle.

$$\therefore \cot\theta = \frac{h}{t} \quad \dots (ii)$$

On multiplying equation (*i*) and (*ii*), we get

$$\tan\theta \times \cot\theta = \frac{h}{s} \times \frac{h}{t}$$

$$\Rightarrow 1 = \frac{h^2}{st} \Rightarrow h = \sqrt{st} \quad \left(\because \cot\theta = \frac{1}{\tan\theta}\right)$$

5. (*a*) The angle formed by the line of sight with the horizontal when the point being viewed is above the horizontal level is known as angle of elevation.

6. (*d*)

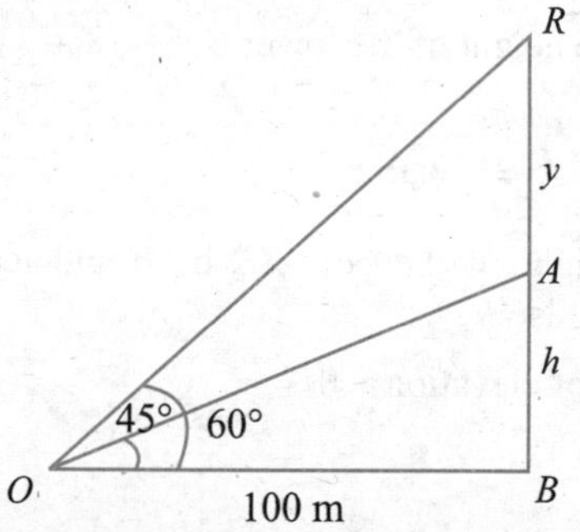

Let us suppose, $AB = h$ be the height of the unfinished tower.
It is given that,
$\angle AOB = 45°$
and $OB = 100$ m
Let the required height to be raised be $AR = y$ meters
In right ΔOAB,

$$\tan 45° = \frac{AB}{OB} \Rightarrow \frac{h}{100} = \tan 45° \Rightarrow h = 100$$

In right ΔOBR,

$$\tan 60° = \frac{BR}{OB}$$

$$\Rightarrow \frac{h+y}{100} = \tan 60° \Rightarrow h + y = 100\sqrt{3} \Rightarrow y = 100\sqrt{3} - 100$$

$$\Rightarrow y = 100 \times 1.73 - 100 \Rightarrow y = 73 \text{ m}$$

Therefore, the height of the tower required to be raised is 73 m.

7. (*b*) Let us suppose, *MN* be the window of height 9 m and *AC* be the height of another house. Let *NC* be the street of width *y*.

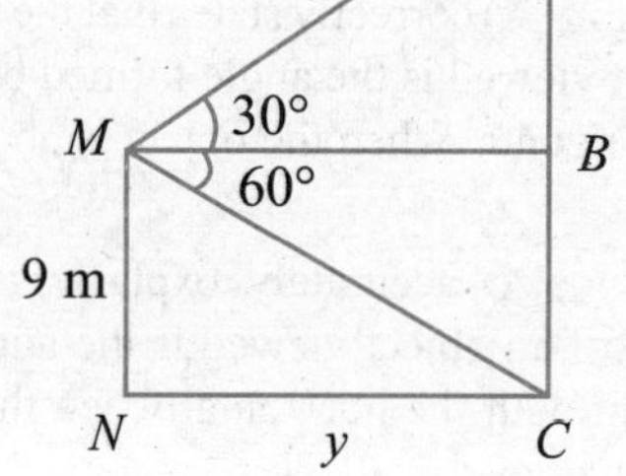

It is given that, $\angle AMB = 30°$ and $\angle CMB = 60°$.

In right ΔCBM,

$$\frac{CB}{BM} = \tan 60° \Rightarrow \frac{9}{y} = \sqrt{3} \quad (\because CN = BM)$$

$$\Rightarrow y = 3\sqrt{3}m \quad \dots (i)$$

8. (*c*)

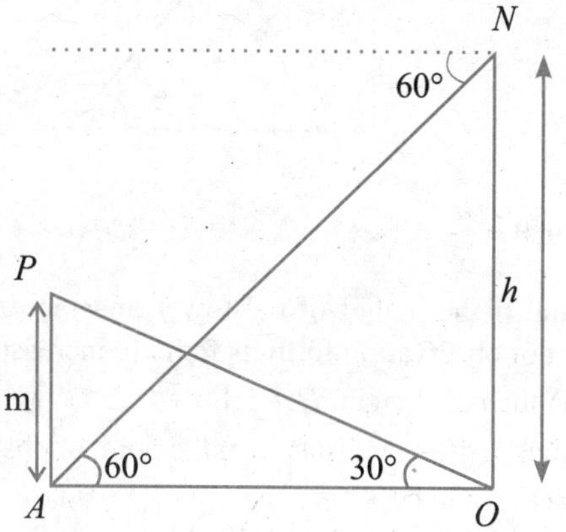

Let us suppose, $PA = l$ be the height of the pole.

In ΔPAO,

$$\tan 30° = \frac{AP}{AO} \Rightarrow \tan 30° = \frac{l}{AO} \Rightarrow l = AO \times \tan 30° \quad \dots (i)$$

In ΔNOA,

$$\tan 60° = \frac{ON}{OA} \Rightarrow \tan 60° = \frac{h}{AO}$$

$$\Rightarrow AO = \frac{h}{\sqrt{3}}m$$

On putting the value of *AO* in eq. (*i*), we get

$$\Rightarrow l = \frac{h}{\sqrt{3}} \times \frac{1}{\sqrt{3}}m = \frac{h}{3}m$$

Therefore, the height of the pole is $\frac{h}{3}$ meters.

9. (*a*) In ΔANM,

$$\sin 30° = \frac{NM}{AN} \Rightarrow \sin 30° = \frac{NM}{100}$$

$$\Rightarrow \frac{1}{2} = \frac{NM}{100} \quad \left(\because \sin 30° = \frac{1}{2}\right)$$

$$\Rightarrow NM = 50 \text{ cm}$$

Also,

$$BC = 35 \text{ cm} \Rightarrow MD = 35 \text{ cm}$$

$$\therefore ND = 15 \text{ cm} \quad (\text{As, } ND = NM - MD)$$

In ΔNDC,

$$\sin 30° = \frac{ND}{NC} \Rightarrow NC = 2ND \Rightarrow NC = 30 \text{ cm.}$$

10. (*c*) Let the height of the pole be *h* and the distance of the point of observation from the foot of the pole be *x*.

Let the angle of elevation = θ

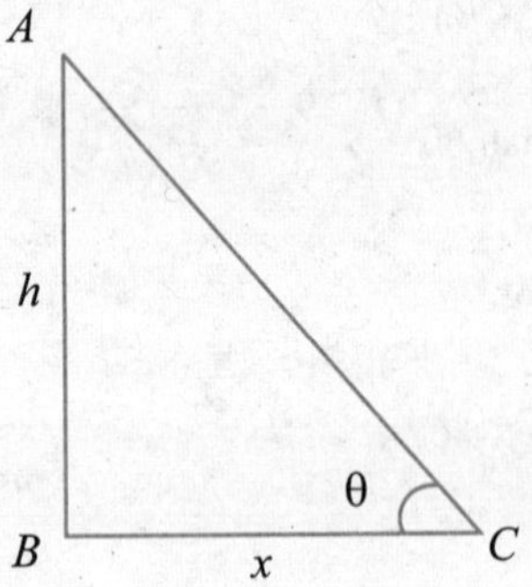

$\therefore \tan\theta = \frac{h}{x}$ ... (*i*)

Again, if the height of the tower and the distance of the point of observation form its foot are increased by 10%.

Then the new height, $H = 1.1\,h$

Similarly, the new distance of the point of observation from its foot, $x = 1.1\,x$

Let the new angle of elevation be ϕ.

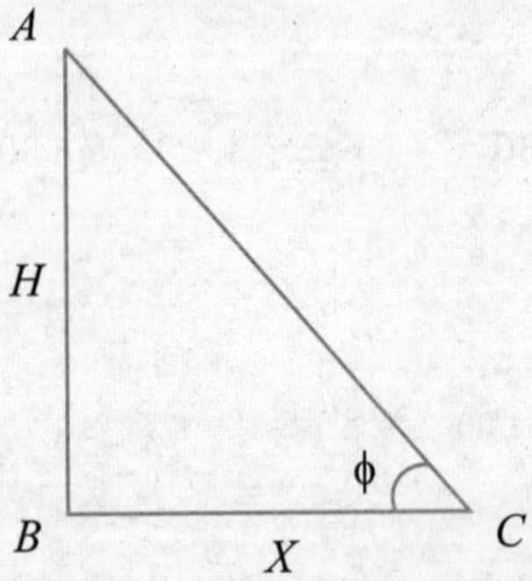

$\therefore \tan\phi = \frac{H}{X} = \frac{1.1\,h}{1.1\,x} = \frac{h}{x} = \tan\theta$ ... from (*i*)

If both are increased by 10%, then the angle will remain unchanged.

11. (*a*) Using given instructions, a figure is drawn as follows:

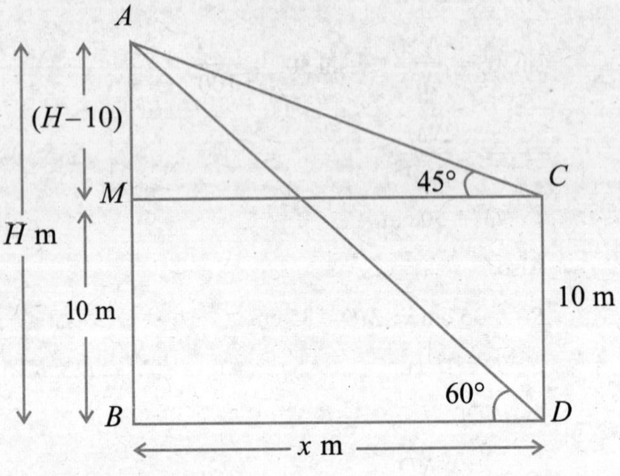

Let $AB = H$ and $BD = x$

In ΔABD,

$\tan 60° = \frac{AB}{DB} \Rightarrow \sqrt{3} = \frac{H}{x}$ $\left(\because \tan 60° = \sqrt{3}\right)$

$\Rightarrow x = \frac{H}{\sqrt{3}}$ ... (*i*)

In ΔAMC,

$\tan 45° = \frac{AM}{MC} \Rightarrow \tan 45° = \frac{H-10}{x}$ $[\because MC = BD = x]$

$\Rightarrow x = H - 10$ ... (*ii*)

From eq. (*i*) and (*ii*), we get

$\frac{H}{\sqrt{3}} = H - 10 \Rightarrow H - \frac{H}{\sqrt{3}} = 10$

On solving for *H*, we get

$\Rightarrow H = \frac{10\sqrt{3}}{\sqrt{3}-1} \Rightarrow H = \frac{10\sqrt{3}}{\sqrt{3}-1} \times \frac{\sqrt{3}+1}{\sqrt{3}+1}$

$\Rightarrow H = 5(\sqrt{3}+3)\,m$

Therefore, the height of the tower is $5\left(\sqrt{3}+3\right)m$.

Assertion and Reason

1. (*b*) If the height of the pole *AB* be *h* and length of its shadow *CB* is also *h*.

Let the angle of elevation = θ

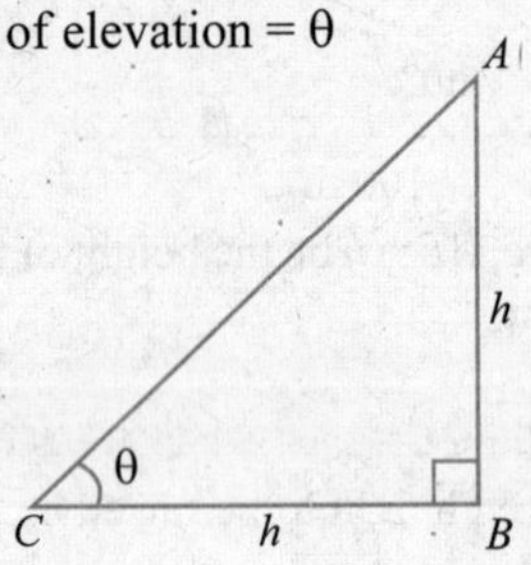

$\tan\theta = \frac{AB}{BC} \Rightarrow \tan\theta = \frac{h}{h}$

$\Rightarrow \tan\theta = 1 \Rightarrow \theta = 45°$ $(\because \tan 45° = 1)$

Reason is also correct as it states Pythagoras Theorem but not the correct explanation of assertion.

2. (*a*)

- Trigonometry indeed plays a crucial role in calculating distances indirectly when direct measurement is not feasible, such as measuring the height of a mountain or the distance between two ships at sea.
- The Reason accurately explains how trigonometric ratios, when combined with measurements of angles, can be used to calculate distances between objects or locations.

Therefore, both Assertion (A) and Reason (R) are true, and Reason (R) is the correct explanation for Assertion (A)

3. (*b*) Assertion (A) correctly states that the angle of elevation of an object viewed is the angle formed by the line of sight with the horizontal when the object is above the horizontal level.s

Reason (R) also accurately explains that the angle of depression of an object viewed is the angle formed by the line of sight with the horizontal when the object is below the horizontal level.

Therefore, both Assertion (A) and Reason (R) are true, and Reason (R) is not the correct explanation for Assertion (A).

4. (*a*) In right ΔPQR,

$$\tan 30^\circ = \frac{PQ}{QR} = \frac{PQ}{20} \Rightarrow PQ = \frac{1}{\sqrt{3}} \times 20 = \frac{20}{1.73} = 11.56 \text{ m}$$

Therefore, height PQ is 11.56 m.
Reason is true and correct explanation of assertion.

5. (*a*) Assertion is correct as the angle of elevation of the sun decreases, Sunlight becomes more horizontal, causing the tower's shadow to lengthen.

Reason (R) supports this, explaining that the decrease in angle leads to a shallower line of sight, extending the shadow away from the tower. Hence, Both Assertion and Reason are correct, Reason is correct explanation of Assertion.

Subjective Questions

Very Short Answer Type Questions

1. Let us suppose M be the position of the balloon and AM be the vertical height. Let C be the meteorological station and CM be the length of the cable.

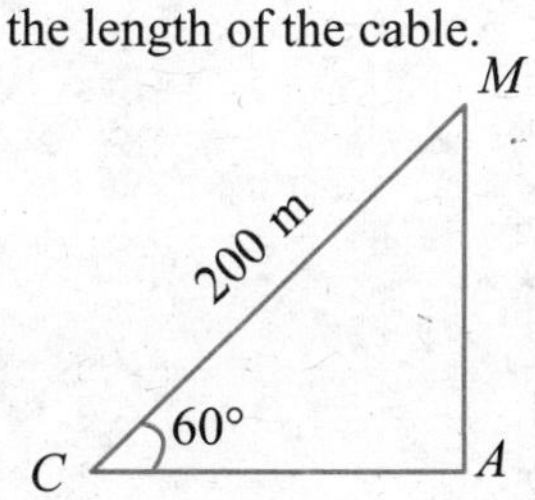

(1 M)

In right angled ΔMAC,

$$\frac{AM}{MC} = \sin 60^\circ$$

$$\Rightarrow \frac{AM}{200} = \frac{\sqrt{3}}{2} \qquad \left(\because \sin 60^\circ = \frac{\sqrt{3}}{2}\right)$$

$$\Rightarrow AM = \left(\frac{200 \times \sqrt{3}}{2}\right) \text{ m} = 173.2 \text{ m.}$$ (1 M)

Therefore, the height of the balloon from the ground is 173.2 m.

2. In ΔABC

$$\tan 60^\circ = \frac{AC}{AB}$$

$$\Rightarrow \sqrt{3} = \frac{20}{AB}$$

$$\Rightarrow AB = \frac{20}{\sqrt{3}}$$

$$\Rightarrow AB = 11.54 \text{ m}$$

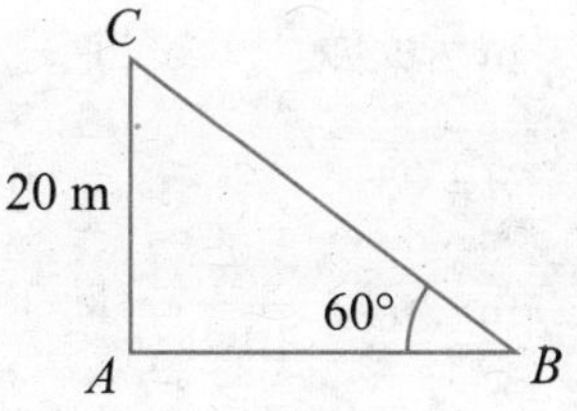

(1 M)

3. 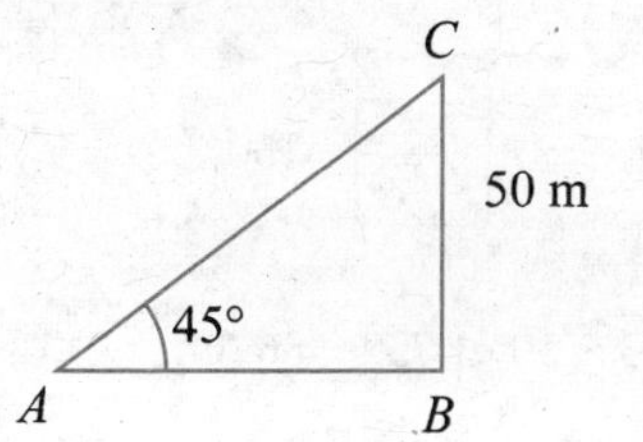

(1 M)

Here, A represents an observer and C represent a bird.
In right ΔABC,

$$\sin 45^\circ = \frac{BC}{AC}, \quad AC = 50\sqrt{2}m$$

Hence, distance of a bird from an observer is $50\sqrt{2}$ m. *(1 M)*

4. 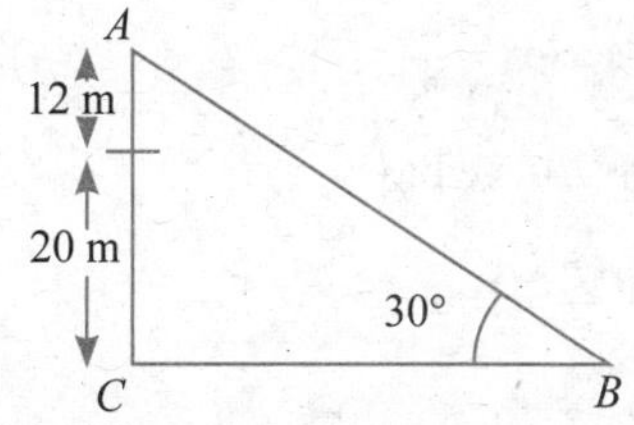

(1 M)

Let AB represents the pole and BC represents the building.
In right ΔACD,

$$\tan 30^\circ = \frac{AC}{CD} \Rightarrow \frac{1}{\sqrt{3}} = \frac{AB + BC}{CD}$$

$$\Rightarrow CD = (20 + 12)\sqrt{3} \Rightarrow CD = 32\sqrt{3} \text{ m.}$$ (1 M)

5. 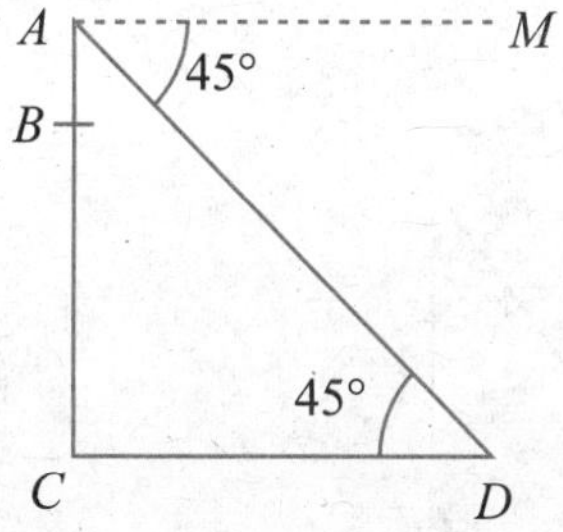

Let BC be the tower of height 50m m and AB be the person of height 1.5 m.

$\angle MAD = CDA$ [Alternate angles]

$\Rightarrow \angle CDA = 45^\circ$ (1 M)

In right ΔACD,

$$\tan 45^\circ = \frac{AC}{CD}$$

$\Rightarrow CD = AB + BC$ $[\because AC = AB + BC]$

$\Rightarrow CD = 1.5 + 50 = 51.5$ m (1 M)

Short Answer Type Questions

1. Let the height of the tower be h m.

Given, $\tan\alpha = \frac{1}{3}$ and $\tan\beta = \frac{3}{4}$

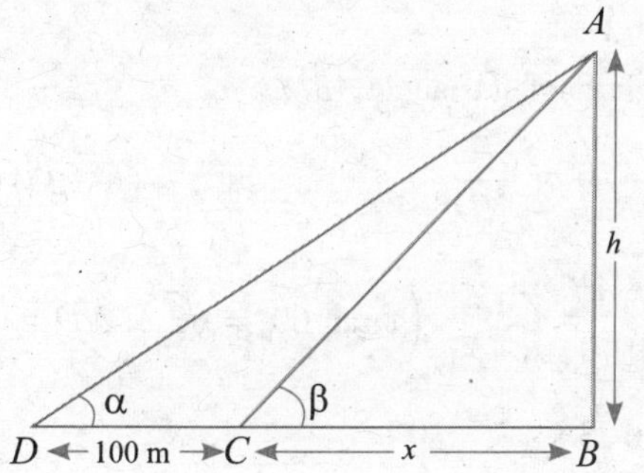

Now, In ΔABD, $\angle D = \alpha$, $\angle B = 90°$

$$\tan\alpha = \frac{AB}{DB} \Rightarrow \frac{1}{3} = \frac{h}{100+x} \Rightarrow 100 + x = 3h$$

$\Rightarrow x = 3h - 100$ ...(*i*) (1 M)

In ΔABC, $\angle C = \beta$, $\angle B = 90°$

$$\tan\beta = \frac{AB}{BC} \Rightarrow \frac{3}{4} = \frac{h}{x} \Rightarrow x = \frac{4h}{3}$$ ...(*ii*) (1 M)

From equations (*i*) and (*ii*), we have

$$3h - 100 = \frac{4h}{3} \Rightarrow 3h - \frac{4h}{3} = 100$$

$$\Rightarrow \frac{5h}{3} = 100 \Rightarrow h = 60 \text{ m}$$

Hence, the height of the tower is 60m. (1 M)

2. In the figure below, let *M* represents the position of the man on the deck of the ship, *A* represents the top of cliff and *D* represents the base of cliff.

Here, lines *MB* and *ND* are parallel and *MD* is transversal.

$\angle NDM = \angle BMD$ [alternate angles]

So, $\angle NDM = 30°$ (½ M)

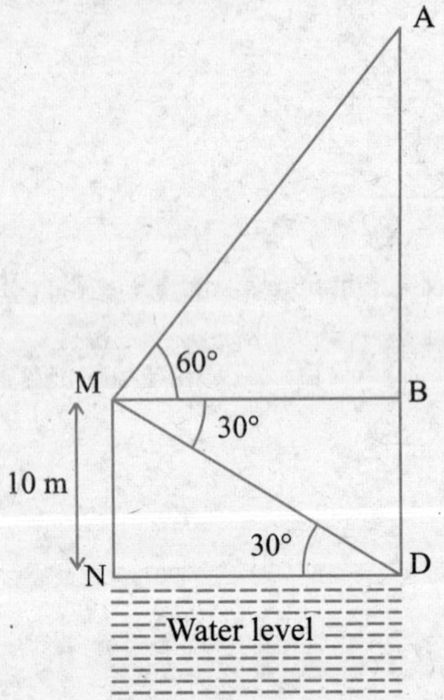

(1 M)

In right-angled triangle *MND*,

$$\tan 30° = \frac{10}{ND} \Rightarrow ND = \frac{10}{\tan 30°}$$

$$\Rightarrow ND = \frac{10}{\frac{1}{\sqrt{3}}} = 10\sqrt{3} = 17.3m \quad \left(\because \tan 30° = \frac{1}{\sqrt{3}}\right)$$ (½ M)

And, in right-angled triangle *ABM*,

$$\tan 60° = \frac{AB}{BM} \text{ or } \frac{AB}{ND}$$ [As, BM = ND]

$$\Rightarrow \sqrt{3} = \frac{AB}{10\sqrt{3}} \quad (\because \tan 60° = \sqrt{3} \text{ \& } ND = 10\sqrt{3})$$

$\Rightarrow AB = 10\sqrt{3} \times \sqrt{3} = 30\ m$ (½ M)

As, $AD = AB + BD = 30\text{m} + 10\text{m} = 40\text{m}$ (½ M)

Hence, the distance of the cliff from the ship is 17.3 m and the height of the cliff is 40 m.

3. In ΔACM, $\tan\beta = \dfrac{h}{CM}$

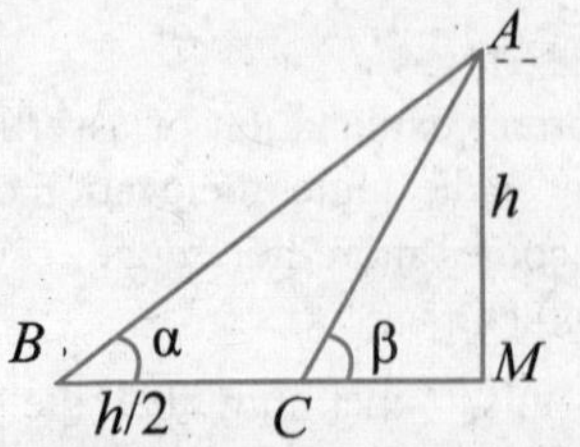

(1 M)

$\Rightarrow CM = h\cot\beta$ ... (*i*) $\left(\because \dfrac{1}{\tan\beta} = \cot\beta\right)$ (½ M)

And in ΔAMB,

$$\tan\alpha = \frac{h}{\frac{h}{2} + CM}$$

$\dfrac{h}{2} + CM = h\cot\alpha$ ... (*ii*) (½ M)

On putting equation (*i*) in (*ii*), we get

$\dfrac{h}{2} + h\cot\beta = h\cot\alpha$ (½ M)

$$h\cot\alpha - h\cot\beta = \frac{h}{2}$$

$$h(\cot\alpha - \cot\beta) = \frac{h}{2}$$

$\therefore \cot\alpha - \cot\beta = \dfrac{1}{2}$ (½ M)

4.

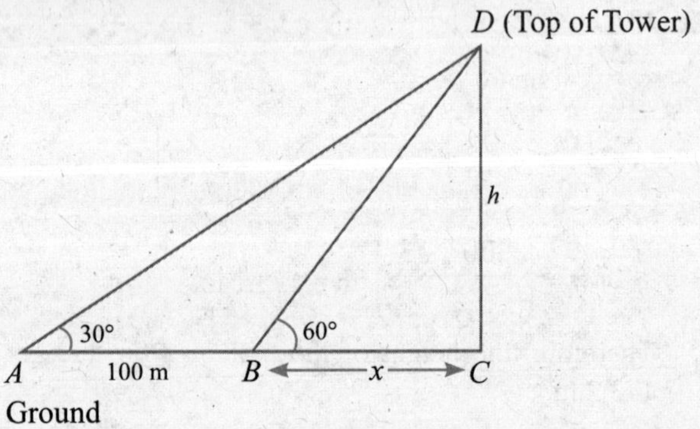

In ΔBCD, $\dfrac{h}{x} = \tan 60° \Rightarrow \dfrac{h}{x} = \sqrt{3}$ $(BC = x)$

$h = \sqrt{3}x$ ...(*i*) (1 M)

In ΔACD, $\dfrac{h}{10+x} = \tan 30° \Rightarrow \dfrac{h}{10+x} = \dfrac{1}{\sqrt{3}}$

$\Rightarrow h\sqrt{3} = 100 + x \Rightarrow h\sqrt{3} = 100 + \dfrac{h}{\sqrt{3}}$ (1 M)

$$\Rightarrow h\left[\sqrt{3} - \frac{1}{\sqrt{3}}\right] = 100 \Rightarrow h\left[\frac{3-1}{\sqrt{3}}\right] = 100$$

$\Rightarrow h = \dfrac{100\sqrt{3}}{2} = 50\sqrt{3} = 50 \times 1.732 = 86.6\text{m}$ (1 M)

5. Let O be the position of the observer at the horizontal line OA and C be the centre of the balloon. Let OP and OQ be the tangents to the balloon such that $\angle POQ = \alpha$, $\angle AOC = \beta$ and $CP = CQ = \gamma$.

In $\Delta\, OPC$ and $\Delta\, OQC$

$OC = OC$ (common)

$\angle OPC = \angle OQC = 90°$ (tangent is $\perp$ to the radius)

$CQ = CP$ (radius of the balloon)

$\therefore \Delta\, OPC \cong \Delta\, OQC$ (SAS congruence rule) *(½ M)*

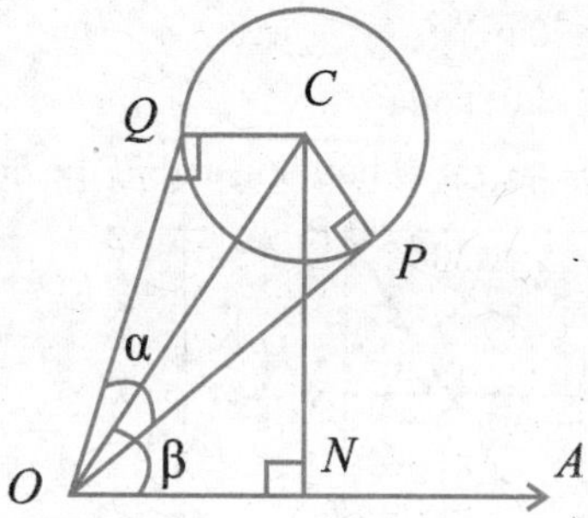

(1 M)

Therefore, $\angle POC = \angle QOC = \dfrac{\alpha}{2}$.

Let $CN \perp OA$

In right angled ΔCPO,

$$\frac{OC}{CP} = \text{cosec}\,\frac{\alpha}{2} \Rightarrow OC = \gamma\,\text{cosec}\,\frac{\alpha}{2} \quad \ldots (i)\ (½\ M)$$

In right angled ΔCNO,

$$\frac{CN}{OC} = \sin\beta$$

$$\Rightarrow CN = OC\sin\beta \quad \ldots (ii)\ (½\ M)$$

Putting eq. (*i*) in (*ii*), we get

$$CN = \gamma\,\text{cosec}\,\frac{\alpha}{2}\,\sin\beta$$

Therefore, the height of the centre of balloon from the ground level is $\gamma\,\text{cosec}\,\dfrac{\alpha}{2}\,\sin\beta$. *(½ M)*

6. Let us suppose, PQ be the height of the hill and C and D be the two positions of the ship. It is given that $PQ = 150$ m. $\angle PCQ = 60°$ and $\angle PDQ = 45°$.

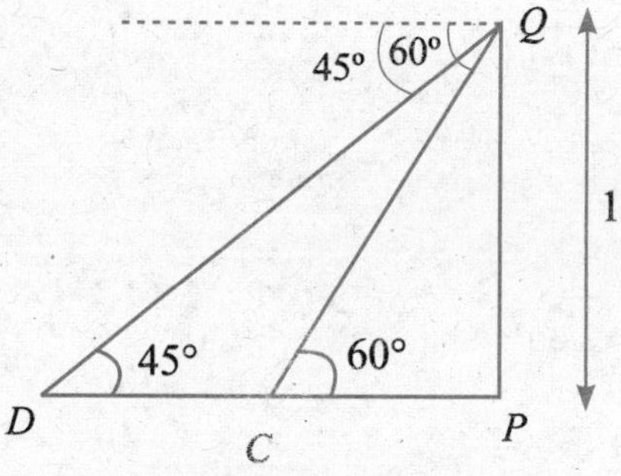

(1 M)

In right angled ΔQPD,

$$\frac{PD}{PQ} = \cot 45° = 1 \Rightarrow \frac{PD}{150} = 1 \Rightarrow PD = 150 \text{ m.}$$

In right angled ΔQPC, *(½ M)*

$$\frac{PC}{PQ} = \cot 60° = \frac{1}{\sqrt{3}} \Rightarrow \frac{PC}{150} = \frac{1}{\sqrt{3}}$$

$$\Rightarrow PC = \frac{150}{\sqrt{3}} = 50\sqrt{3} = 86.6 \text{ m.} \quad (½\ M)$$

As, $CD = PD - PC$

$= (150 - 86.6)$ m

$= 63.4$ m *(½ M)*

Distance travelled by the boat from pt. C to pt. D in 2 minutes $= CD$

$$\text{Speed} = \frac{\text{Distance}}{\text{Time}}$$

$$\text{Speed} = \frac{63.4}{2}$$

Speed = 31.7 m/min *(½ M)*

7. Let us suppose that $OP = h$ be the height of the pole and let M and Q be two points due south and east respectively of the pole such that $\angle OMP = \alpha$ and $\angle OQP = \beta$.

In ΔOMP,

$$\tan\alpha = \frac{h}{OM}$$

$$\Rightarrow OM = h\cot\alpha \quad \ldots (i)\ (½\ M)$$

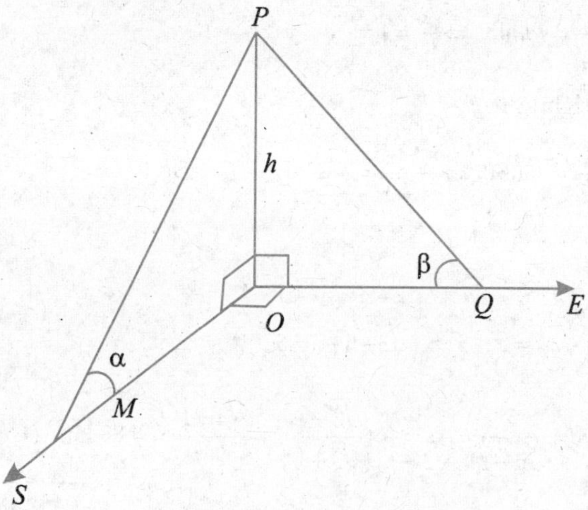

(1 M)

In ΔOQP, we have

$$\tan\beta = \frac{h}{OQ}$$

$$\Rightarrow OQ = h\cot\beta. \quad \ldots (ii)\ (½\ M)$$

As, OMQ is a right angled triangle

Therefore, $MQ^2 = OM^2 + OQ^2$ *(½ M)*

Using eq. (*i*) and (*ii*) we get,

$$\Rightarrow d^2 = h^2\cot^2\alpha + h^2\cot^2\beta \quad (\because MQ = d)$$

$$\Rightarrow h = \frac{d}{\sqrt{\cot^2\alpha + \cot^2\beta}} \quad (½\ M)$$

Nailing the Right Answer

For understanding the figure of the given question, remember that main directions are taken in a horizontal plane and height of pole is taken in vertical plane.

8. Distance covered in 15 seconds = AB

Speed = 1200 km/hr.

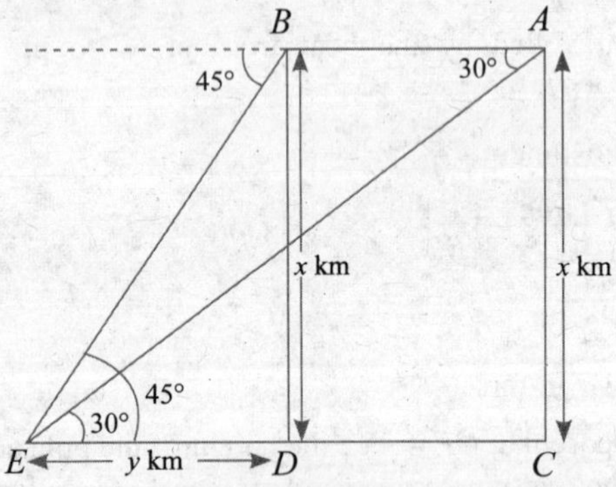

$$\therefore AB = 1200 \times \frac{15}{3600} = 5\text{km} \quad (1\ M)$$

$AB = DC = 5$ km

Let height $= 5$ km

In right ΔBDE,

$$\frac{BD}{ED} = tan45^\circ \Rightarrow \frac{x}{y} = 1 \Rightarrow x = y \quad (1\ M)$$

In right ΔACE,

$$\frac{AC}{EC} = \tan30^\circ \Rightarrow \frac{x}{y+5} = \frac{1}{\sqrt{3}} \quad [\because AB = DC]$$

$$\Rightarrow \frac{x}{x+5} = \frac{1}{\sqrt{3}}$$

$$\Rightarrow \sqrt{3}x = x + 5 \Rightarrow \left(\sqrt{3}-1\right)x = 5$$

$$\therefore x = \frac{5}{\sqrt{3}-1} = \frac{5}{\sqrt{3}-1} \times \frac{\sqrt{3}+1}{\sqrt{3}+1} = \frac{5(\sqrt{3}+1)}{2} = 6.83 \text{ km} \quad (1\ M)$$

Long Answer Type Questions

1. Let, BD be river.

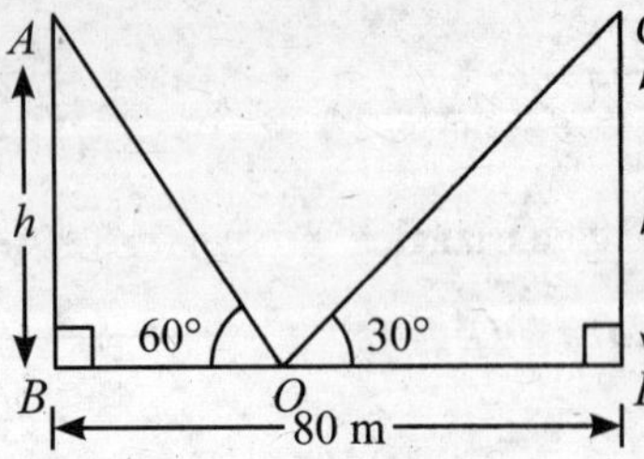

(½ M)

$AB = CD =$ palm trees $= h$

$BO = x$, $OD = 80 - x$ (½ M)

In ΔABO, $\tan 60^\circ = \dfrac{h}{x}$

$$\sqrt{3} = \frac{h}{x} \Rightarrow h = \sqrt{3}x \quad ...(i)\ (1\ M)$$

In ΔCDO, $\tan 30^\circ = \dfrac{h}{80-x}$

$$\frac{1}{\sqrt{3}} = \frac{h}{80-x} \quad ...(ii)\ (1\ M)$$

From Eqn. (*i*) and (*ii*), we get

$x = 20$, $h = \sqrt{3}x = 34.6$ (1 M)

Hence, the height of tree $= h = 34.6$ m

$BO = x = 20$ m

$DO = 80 - 20 = 60$ m (1 M)

2. Let, AB be height of building and RT be the height of tower.

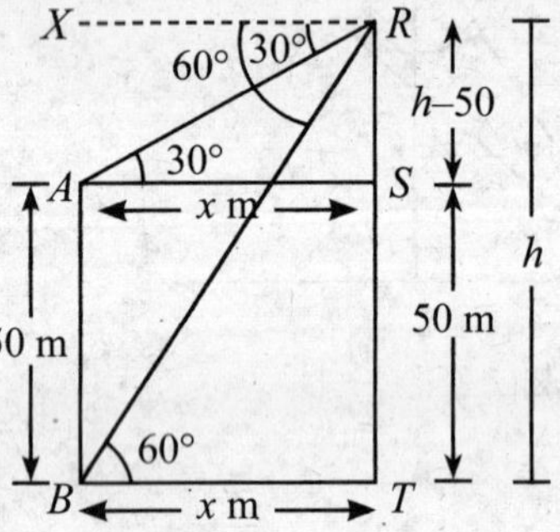

(1 M)

Now, In ΔARS,

$$\tan 30^\circ = \frac{RS}{AS} \Rightarrow \frac{1}{\sqrt{3}} = \frac{h-50}{x} \quad ...(i)\ (1\ M)$$

$$\text{In } \Delta RBT, \tan 60^\circ = \frac{RT}{BT} \Rightarrow \sqrt{3} = \frac{h}{x} \quad ...(ii)\ (1\ M)$$

From Eqn. (*i*) and (*ii*), we get $h = 75$ m.

$$x = \frac{h}{\sqrt{3}} = \frac{75}{\sqrt{3}} = 25\sqrt{3} \text{ m} \quad (1\ M)$$

Hence, the height of the tower $= h = 75$ m.

Distance between the building and the tower $= 25\sqrt{3}$ m $=$ 43.25 m (1 M)

3.

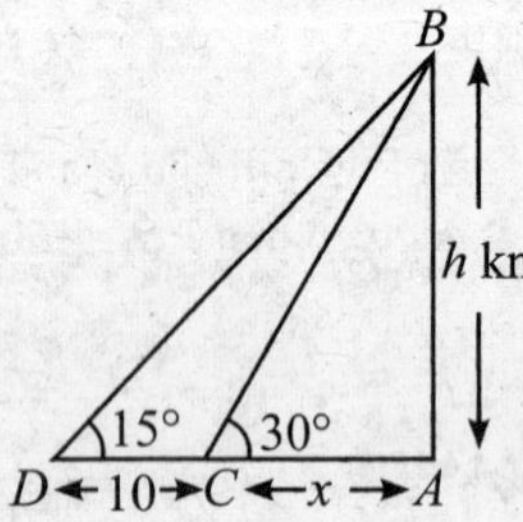

In ΔCAB,

$$\tan 30^\circ = \frac{AB}{AC} \quad (½\ M)$$

$$\frac{1}{\sqrt{3}} = \frac{h}{x} \Rightarrow x = \sqrt{3}h \quad ...(i) \quad (1\ M)$$

In ΔDAB

$$\tan 15^\circ = \frac{AB}{AD} \quad (½\ M)$$

$$0.27 = \frac{h}{x+10} \Rightarrow h = (x+10)(0.27) \quad ...(ii) \quad (1\ M)$$

Put eqn. (*i*) in eqn. (*ii*), we get

$\Rightarrow h = (\sqrt{3}h + 10)\ (0.27)$ (1 M)

$\Rightarrow h = \dfrac{2.7}{0.54} = 5$

Hence, height of the mountain is 5 km. (1 M)

4. Let, height of the vertical tower $OT = H$ and $OP = AB = x$ m (½ M)

Given; $AP = 10$ m

Now, In ΔTPO

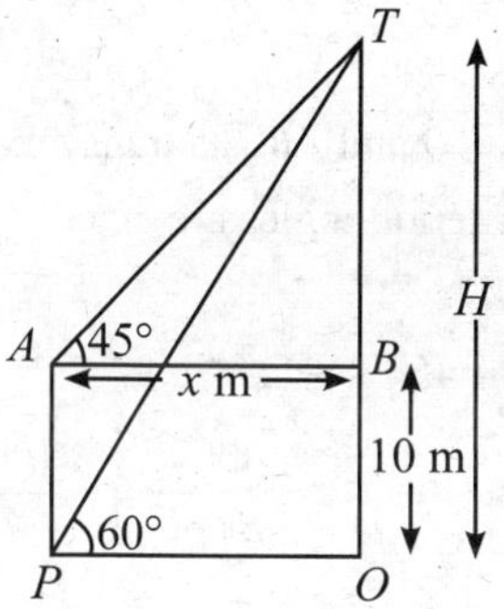

$\tan 60° = \dfrac{OT}{OP} = \dfrac{H}{x}$ (1 M)

$\sqrt{3} = \dfrac{H}{x} \Rightarrow x = \dfrac{H}{\sqrt{3}}$ ...(*i*) (1 M)

In ΔTAB,

$\tan 45° = \dfrac{TB}{AB} = \dfrac{H-10}{x}$ (1 M)

$1 = \dfrac{H-10}{x} \Rightarrow x = H - 10$ (½ M)

$\dfrac{H}{\sqrt{3}} = H - 10 \Rightarrow \dfrac{10\sqrt{3}}{\sqrt{3}-1}$

$H = \dfrac{10\sqrt{3}}{\sqrt{3}-1} \times \dfrac{\sqrt{3}+1}{\sqrt{3}+1} \Rightarrow H = 5(\sqrt{3}+1)$ m. (1 M)

5. (1 M)

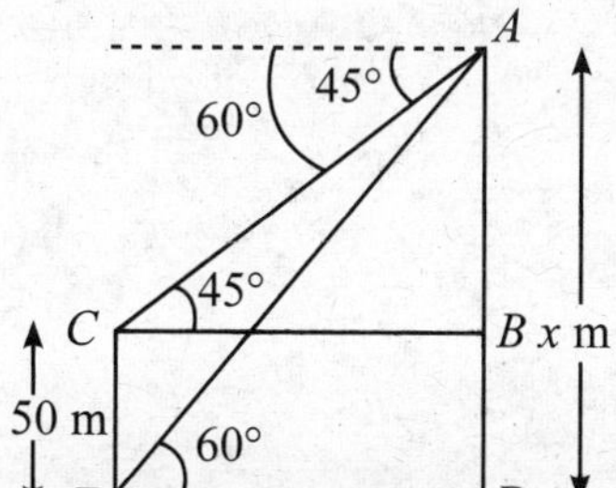

Let $AD = x$ m be the tower and CE be the building.

Let $DE = BC = y$ m, be the distance between the foot of the tower and the bottom of the building and $CE = BD = 50$ m be the height of the building. (1 M)

Then, $AB = AD - BD$

$AB = (x - 50)$ m

In right triangle *ABC*, we have

$\because \tan 45° = \dfrac{AB}{BC} \Rightarrow 1 = \dfrac{AB}{BC} \Rightarrow AB = BC$ (1 M)

$\Rightarrow y = (x - 50)$ m ...(i)

In right triangle *ADE*, we have,

$\because \tan 60° = \dfrac{AD}{DE} \Rightarrow \sqrt{3} = \dfrac{x}{y} \Rightarrow y = \dfrac{x}{\sqrt{3}}$ ...(ii) (1 M)

from (*i*) and (*ii*), we get $\Rightarrow x = \sqrt{3}x - 50\sqrt{3}$

$\Rightarrow x = \dfrac{50\sqrt{3}}{\sqrt{3}-1} \times \left(\dfrac{\sqrt{3}+1}{\sqrt{3}+1}\right) = 25\ (3 + 1.73) = 118.25$ m

Substituting the value of *x* in eqn (i).

We get, $AB = 118.25 - 50 = 68.25$ m (1 M)

6. Let *B* and *C* be the two positions of the bird as observed from a point *A* on the ground.
Let *APQ* be the horizontal line through *A*.

Let *C* be the position of the bird after 2 second.

It is given that the angle of elevation of a bird in two positions *B* and *C* as observed from the point *A* are 45° and 30° respectively. (1 M)

$\therefore \angle BAP = 45°$ and $\angle CAQ = 30°$ and $BP = CQ = 80$ m

Let $AP = x$ m + $PQ = y$ m

$AQ = (x + y)$ m

In right triangle *APB*, we have

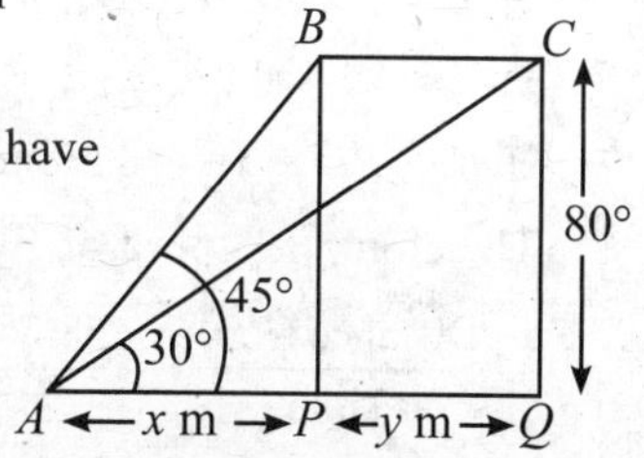

$\tan 45° = \dfrac{BP}{AP}$

$\Rightarrow 1 = \dfrac{80}{x} \Rightarrow x = 80$ m

In right triangle *AQC*, we have (1 M)

$\because \tan 30° = \dfrac{CQ}{AQ}$ (1 M)

$\Rightarrow \dfrac{1}{\sqrt{3}} = \dfrac{80}{x+y} \Rightarrow x + y = 80\sqrt{3}$

$\Rightarrow 80 + y = 80\sqrt{3} \Rightarrow y = 80\sqrt{3} - 80$ (1 M)

$\Rightarrow y = 80\ (1.73 - 1) = 58.4$ m.

Distance covered by a bird is 2 sec = 58.4 m

Speed of bird = $\dfrac{\text{Distance}}{\text{time}} = \dfrac{58.4}{2} = 29.2$ m/sec. (1 M)

7. Let us suppose, *PQ* is 80 m high tree.

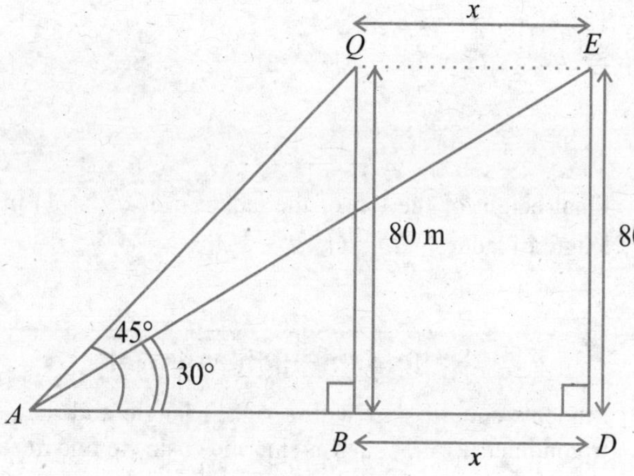

(1 M)

Let the position of bird be E after 2 seconds. (½ M)

Assume, $QE = x$

In right ΔQPA,

$$\frac{PQ}{AP} = \tan 45° \quad (½\ M)$$

$$\Rightarrow \frac{80}{AP} = 1 \quad (\because \tan 45° = 1)$$

$\Rightarrow AP = 80$ m (½ M)

In right ΔEDA,

$$\frac{ED}{AD} = \tan 30° \quad (½\ M)$$

$$\Rightarrow \frac{80}{AP+PD} = \frac{1}{\sqrt{3}}$$

[Since, $AP = 80$ m] ($\because ED = PQ$) (½ M)

$$\Rightarrow \frac{80}{80+x} = \frac{1}{\sqrt{3}} \Rightarrow 80\sqrt{3} = 80 + x \Rightarrow x = 80\sqrt{3} - 80$$

$$\Rightarrow x = 80(\sqrt{3}-1) \Rightarrow x = 80(1.732 - 1)$$

$$\Rightarrow x = 80 \times 0.732 \Rightarrow x = 58.56 \text{ m}$$

Hence, $PD = x = 58.56$ m (½ M)

Therefore, the speed of flying of the bird

$$= \frac{\text{Distance } (PD)}{\text{Time}} = \frac{58.56}{2} = 29.28 \text{ m/s} \quad (1\ M)$$

8.

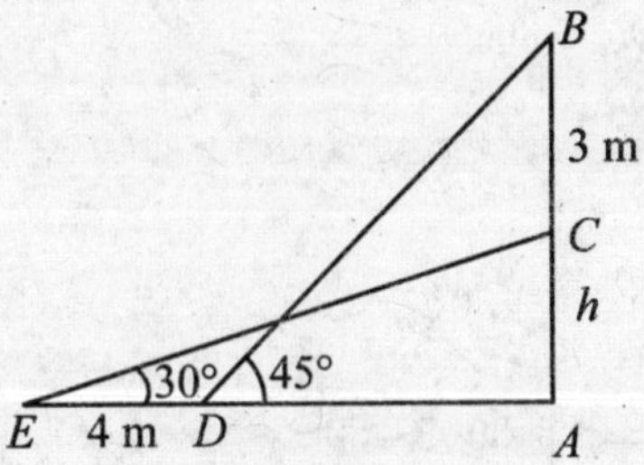

$$\sin 45° = \frac{AB}{BD} = \frac{h+3}{BD} \Rightarrow BD = (h+3)\sqrt{2} \quad \text{...(i)}$$

(1 M)

$$\sin 30° = \frac{1}{2} = \frac{h}{CE} \Rightarrow CE = 2h \quad \text{...(ii)} \quad (1\ M)$$

Length of ladder remains same.

Therefore $BD = CE$

$$\Rightarrow (h+3)\sqrt{2} = 2h \quad (1\ M)$$

$$\Rightarrow h = \frac{3\sqrt{2}}{2-\sqrt{2}} = 3(\sqrt{2}+1) \quad (1\ M)$$

Final height of the top of the ladder = $3(\sqrt{2} + 1)$ m and length of ladder = $2h = 6(\sqrt{2} + 1)$ m (1 M)

Nailing the Right Answer

Students should start with a right triangle and then use trigonometric ratios such as sine and cosine to find missing values.

Case Based Questions

Case Based-I

(i) $XY \parallel CD$ and AC is transversal.

$\angle ACD = \angle CAX$ (alt. int $\angle$S)

$\angle ACD = 30°$

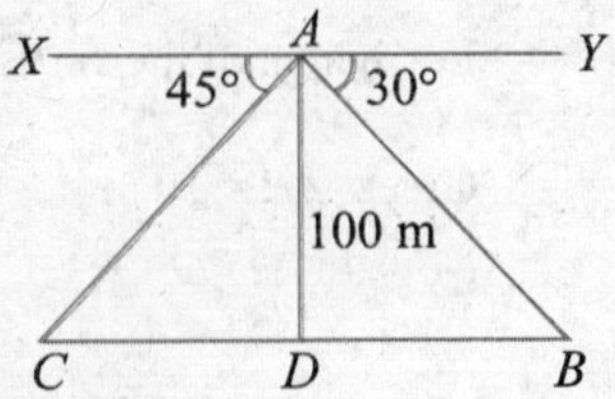

(ii) $\angle YAB = 30°$

$\angle ABD = 30°$

Because $XY \parallel CD$ and AB is a transversal

So alternate interior angles are equal

$\angle YAB = \angle ABD$

(iii) In ΔADC, $\theta = 45°$

$$\tan\theta = \frac{P}{B} \Rightarrow \tan 45° = \frac{100}{B} \Rightarrow 1 = \frac{100}{B}$$

$B = 100$ m

$CD = 100$ m

OR

In ΔABD, $\theta = 30°$

$$\tan\theta = \frac{P}{B} \Rightarrow \tan 30 = \frac{100}{BD}$$

$$\Rightarrow \frac{1}{\sqrt{3}} = \frac{100}{BD} \Rightarrow BD = 100\sqrt{3} \text{ m}$$

Case Based-II

(i) As point M moves towards point B, then the angle of elevation increases.

(ii) In right ΔABM,

We need to find the distance of plane from the point M.

$$\sin 60° = \frac{AB}{AM} = \frac{1500}{AM}$$

$$\frac{\sqrt{3}}{2} = \frac{1500}{AM} \quad \left(\because \sin 60° = \frac{\sqrt{3}}{2}\right)$$

$$AM = \frac{3000}{\sqrt{3}} = 1000\sqrt{3}\ m.$$

OR

In right ΔABM,

We need to find the distance BM.

$$\tan 60° = \frac{AB}{BM} = \frac{1500}{BM}$$

$$\sqrt{3} = \frac{1500}{BM} \Rightarrow BM = \frac{1500}{\sqrt{3}} \quad \left(\because \tan 60° = \sqrt{3}\right)$$

$$\Rightarrow BM = \frac{1500}{\sqrt{3}} \times \frac{\sqrt{3}}{\sqrt{3}} = 500\sqrt{3}\ m.$$

(iii) As point M moves away point B, then the angle of elevation decreases.

Case Based-III

(i) (b)

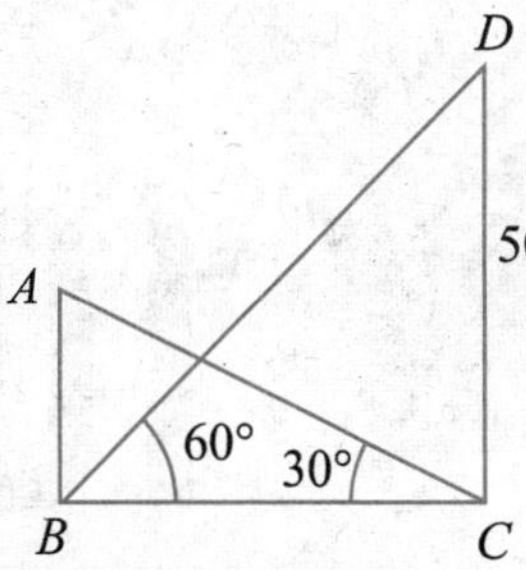

Let CD be the tower having height 50 m and AB be the hotel building.

In right ΔBCD

$$\tan 60° = \frac{CD}{BC}$$

$$BC = \frac{50}{\sqrt{3}}$$

$$BC = \frac{50\sqrt{3}}{3}$$

Hence, the distance between the tower and hotel building is $\frac{50\sqrt{3}}{3}$ m.

(ii) (a) Again in right ΔBCD

$$\sin 60° = \frac{CD}{BD}$$

$$\frac{\sqrt{3}}{2} = \frac{50}{BD}$$

$$BD = \frac{100\sqrt{3}}{3} m$$

(iii) (b) In right ΔABC,

$$\tan 30° = \frac{AB}{BC}$$

$$\frac{1}{\sqrt{3}} = \frac{AB}{\frac{50\sqrt{3}}{3}}$$

$$AB = \frac{50}{3} \text{ m}$$

(iv) (c)

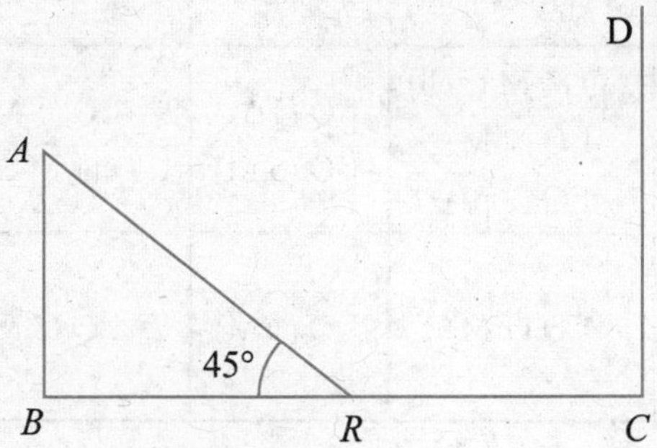

Let Raj is at point R.

In ΔABR

$$\tan 45° = \frac{AB}{BR}$$

$$BR = AB = \frac{50}{3} m$$

Hence, Raj is at a distance of $\frac{50}{3}$ m from the hotel building.

(v) (a) Difference of height of hotel building and the tower of Physics Wallah is $50 - \frac{50}{3} = \frac{100}{3}$ m.

Case Based-IV

(i)

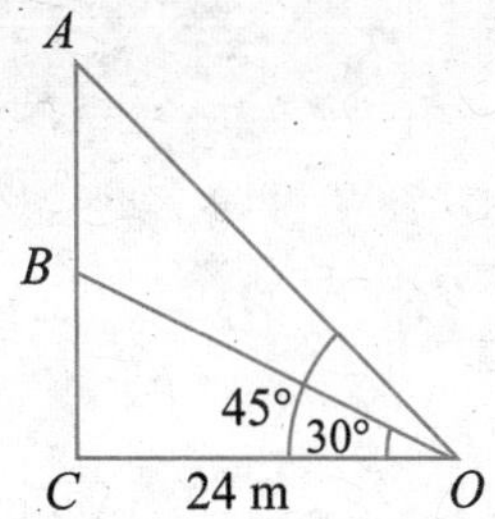

In right ΔAOC,

$$\tan 45° = \frac{AC}{OC}$$

$AC = OC = 24$m

Hence, the total height of radio sation is 24 m.

(ii) Now, we find the height of section-x.

In right ΔBOC

$$\tan 30° = \frac{BC}{OC}$$

$$BC = \frac{24}{\sqrt{3}}$$

$$BC = 8\sqrt{3}$$

Hence, the height of section-x is $8\sqrt{3}$ m.

OR

Height of section $y = AC - BC$

$= 24 - 8\sqrt{3}$

$= 10.16$ m

(iii) In right ΔAOC

$$\cos 45° = \frac{OC}{OA}$$

$$OA = 24\sqrt{2}$$

Hence, the length of wire is $24\sqrt{2}$ m.

CIRCLES

10

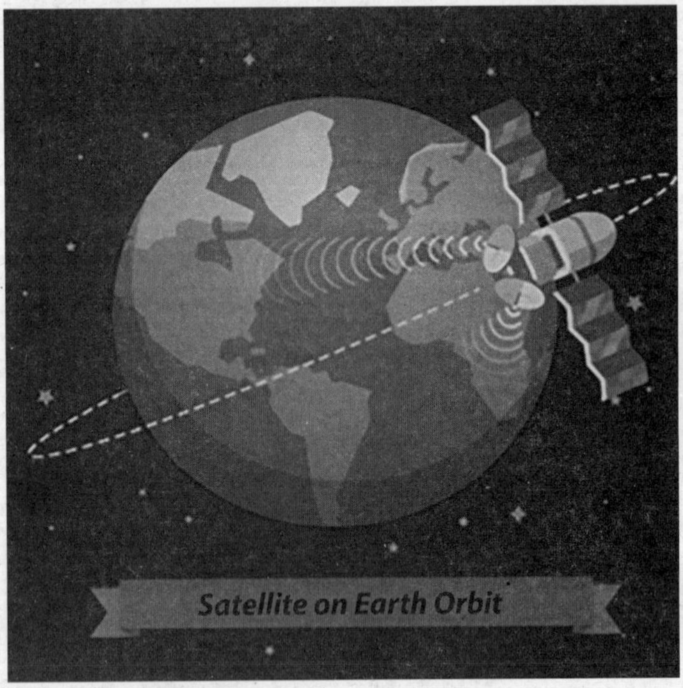

"Circles are used to describe the paths, or orbits, that satellites follow around the Earth. These circular orbits help satellites stay at the same height, which is important for tasks like broadcasting TV, reporting weather, and helping with GPS navigation. Understanding these orbits helps people keep track of satellites and ensure they function properly."

SYLLABUS & WEIGHTAGE

List of Concept Names	Years				
	2021	2022	2023	2024	2025
Tangent to a Circle (The tangent at any point of a circle is perpendicular to the radius through the point of contact)	Exam was not Conducted	1 Q (2 M) 1 Q (4 M)	2 Q (1 M each) 1 Q (2 M) 1 Q (3 M)	1 Q (1 M) 1 Q (5 M)	1 Q (5 M) 2 Q (1 M each)
Number of Tangents from a Point on a Circle (The length of tangent from an external point to a circle are equal, Number of tangents from a point to a circle)		–	1 Q (1 M)	1 Q (1 M)	1 Q (5 M)

CONCEPT MAP

To Access One Shot Revision Video Scan This QR Code

Circles

Number of tangents

- There are no tangent to a circle passing through a point lying inside the circle.

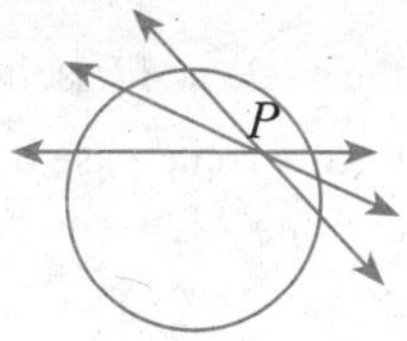

- There is one and only one tangent to a circle passing through a point lying on the circle.

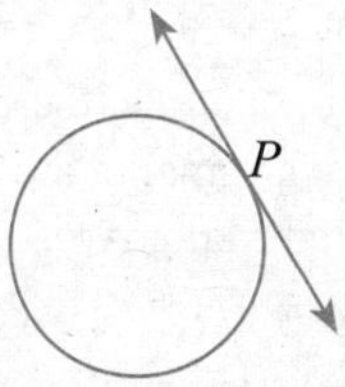

- There are exactly two tangents to a circle through a point lying outside the circle.

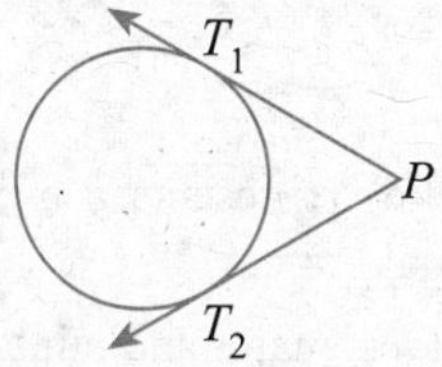

Definition

The locus of a point that is equidistant from a fixed point is known as a circle. The fixed point is called centre and the distance between the fixed point and the point on the circle is called radius.

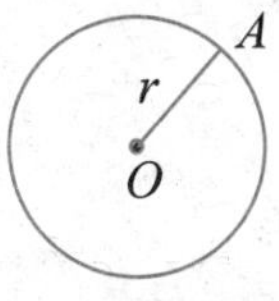

Theorem 1

The tangent at any point of a circle is perpendicular to the radius through the point of contact.

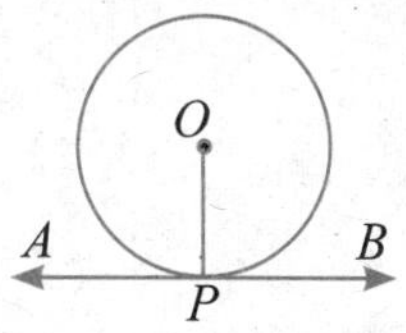

Theorem 2

The lengths of tangents drawn from an external point to a circle are equal.

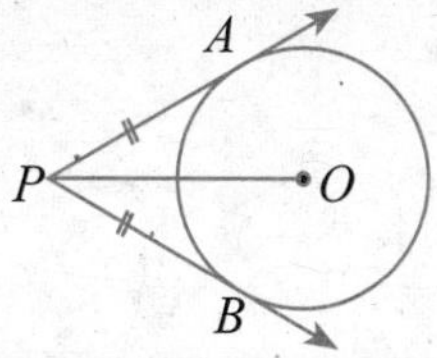

Tangent

A line intersecting a circle at only one point is known as tangent and the intersecting point is known as point of contact.

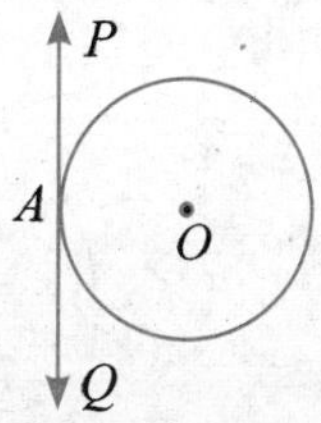

Secant

A line intersecting a circle at two different points is known as secant.

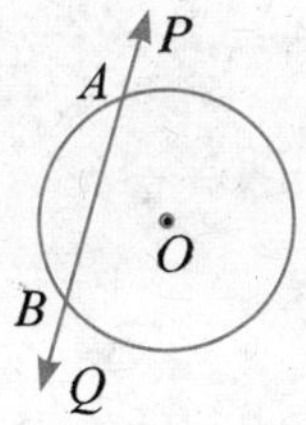

Terms Related to Circle:

1. Chord
2. Arc
3. Sector
4. Segment
   (a) Minor segment
   (b) Major segment

1 TANGENT TO A CIRCLE

Important Terms

- **Circle:** The collection of all the points whose distance from a fixed point is constant is known as a circle.

  Here, the fixed point is called the Centre of the circle, and the distance between the fixed point (centre) and any point on the circle is called the Radius of the circle.

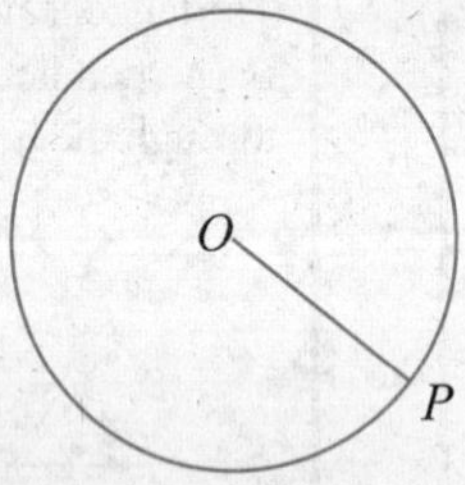

  Here, O is the fixed point or the Centre of the Circle and OP is the radius of the circle.

- **Chord:** A line segment joining any two different points on a circle is called the Chord of the circle.

  If a chord passes through the centre of a circle then the chord is known as the Diameter of the circle.

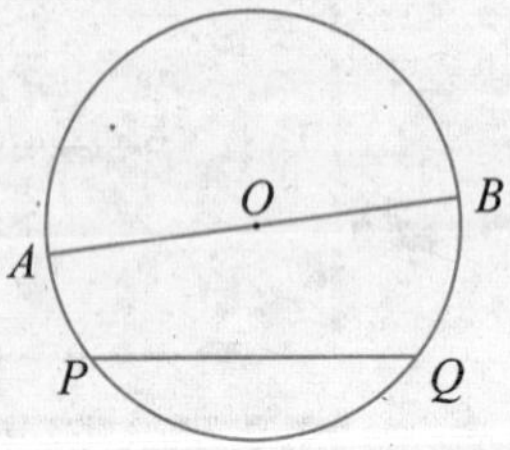

  In the figure, PQ is a chord of the circle, and AOB, or simply AB is the diameter of the circle.

- **Secant:** A line that intersects a circle at two different points is called a Secant of that circle.

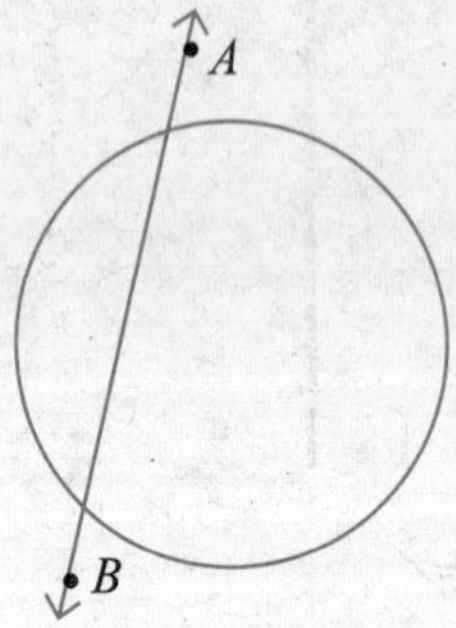

  In the figure, AB is secant to the circle.

- **Tangent:** A line that touches the circle at a point (or intersects the circle at only one point) is called a Tangent to the circle.

  The point at which the tangent touches a circle is called the Point of Contact.

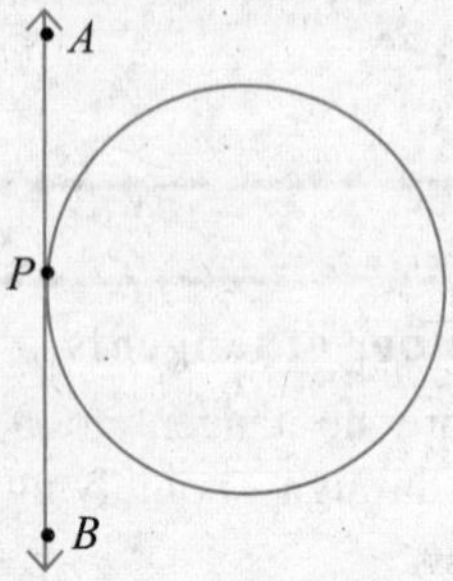

  Here, APB is tangent to the circle and P is the point of contact.

- **Note:** (*i*) Tangent is a special case of secant when the two endpoints of its corresponding chord coincide.

  (*ii*) At any point on a circle, only one tangent can be drawn.

- **Arc:** A piece of a circle between any two different points is called an Arc of that circle.

  Between any two points on a circle, there are two arcs. One is smaller than the other. The smaller arc is known as Minor Arc and the larger is called Major Arc.

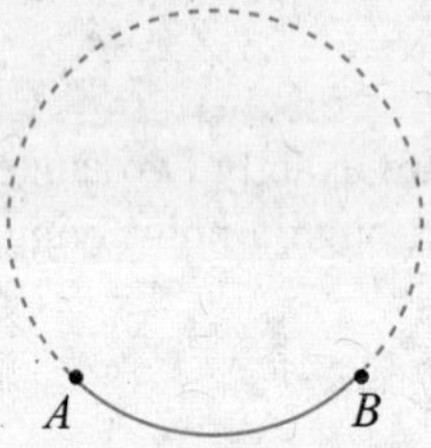

  In the figure, AB (solid) represents a minor arc and AB (dotted) represents a major arc.

  Note: When both the arcs, major and minor, are equal then each is called Semicircle.

- **Circumference:** The length of the whole circle is known as Circumference.

- **Segment:** In a circle, the region between a chord and an arc is called a Segment of the circle.

  As in the case of arc, there are two types of segments.

  - **Minor Segment:** The region between a chord and a minor arc is called Minor Segment.
  - **Major Segments:** The region between a chord and a major arc is called Major Segment.

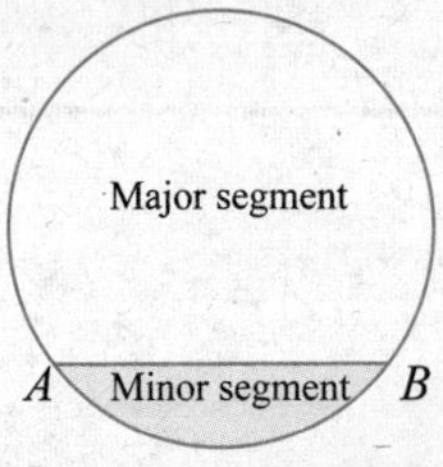

- **Sector:** A sector of a circle is the region between an arc and two radii, joining the endpoints of the arc and the centre.
  - **Minor Sector:** The region between a minor arc and two radii, joining the endpoints of the arc and the centre, of a circle is known as the Minor Sector of the circle.
  - **Major Sector:** The region between a major arc and two radii, joining the endpoints of the arc and the centre, of a circle is known as the Major Sector of the circle.

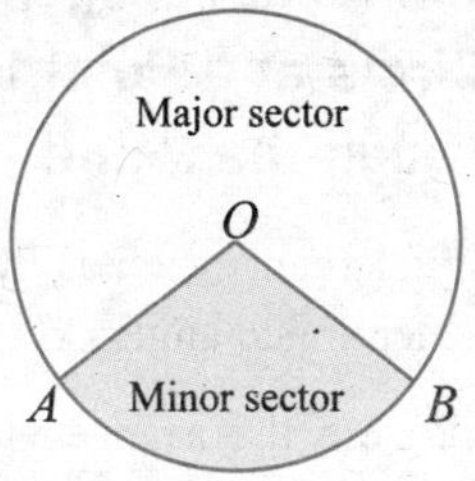

Important Derivations

- **Theorem 1: The tangent at any point of a circle is perpendicular to the radius through the point of contact.**

The tangent at any point of a circle is perpendicular to the radius through the point of contact.

Given: A circle with centre O and a tangent XY at a point P of the circle. **(CBSE, 2016)**

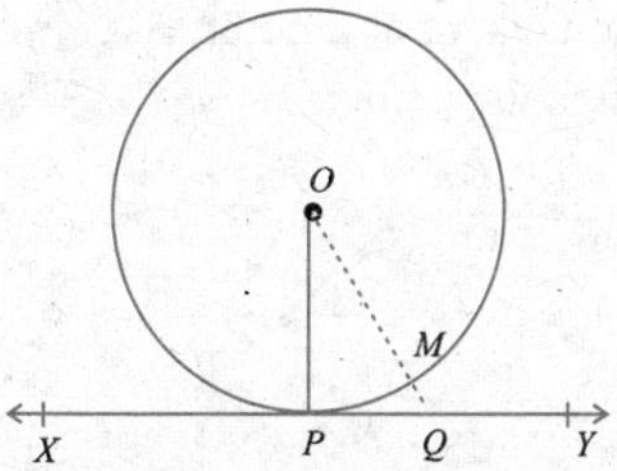

To prove: $OP \perp XY$.

Construction: Other than P, take a point Q, on XY and join OQ.

Proof: Q is a point on the tangent XY, other than the point of contact P. Hence Q lies outside the circle.

Let OQ intersect the circle at M.

Then, $OM < OQ$ [$\because$ a part (OM) of line segment (OQ) is less than the whole line segment (OQ)] ... (*i*)

But, $OP = OM$ [radii of the same circle]. ... (*ii*)

From equation (*i*) and (*ii*), we get

$OP < OQ$

Therefore, OP is shorter than any other line segment drawn from O to any point on XY, except P.

Or, we can say that, OP is the shortest distance between the point O and the line XY.

And also we know that the shortest distance of a point from the given line is the perpendicular distance.

Therefore, $OP \perp XY$. Hence, proved.

Note: Converse of the above theorem is also valid and is given as- **A line drawn through the end of a radius of a circle and perpendicular to the radius is tangent to the circle.**

Topper's Explanation ***(CBSE 2016)***

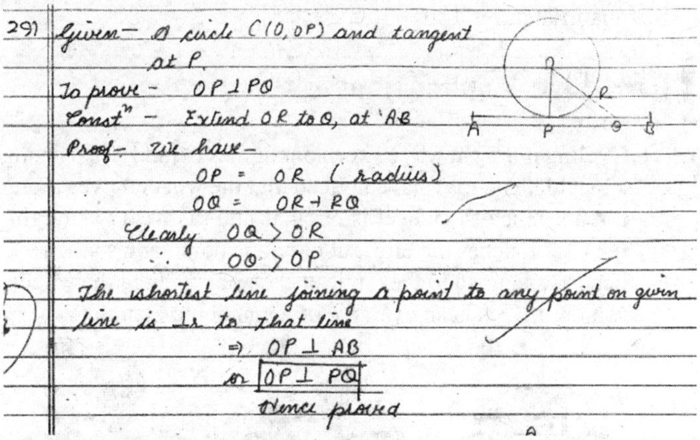

Important Concepts

Some important concepts related to a circle are given below:

- Equal chords of a circle subtend equal angles at the centre.
- The perpendicular from the centre of a circle to a chord bisects the chord.
- The perpendicular distances of equal chords of a circle (or of congruent circles) are equal from the centre (or centres).
- Congruent arcs (or equal arcs) of a circle subtend equal angles at the centre.
- The angle subtended by an arc at the centre is double the angle subtended by it at any point on the remaining part of the circle.i.e., $\angle POQ = 2\angle PAQ$

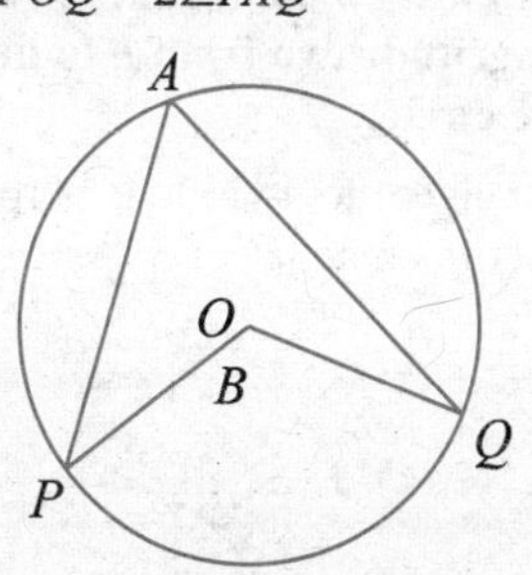

- Angles in the same segment of a circle are equal.

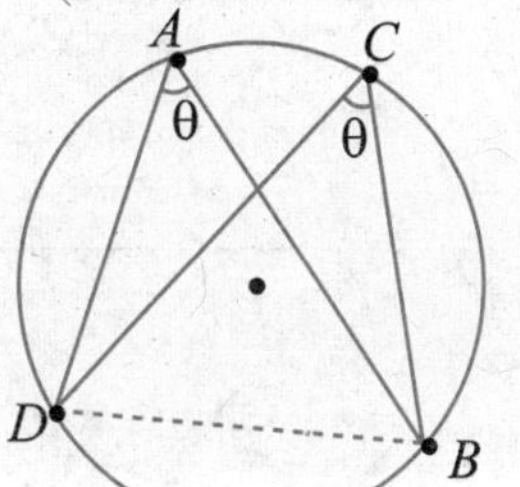

- An angle in a semicircle is a right angle.

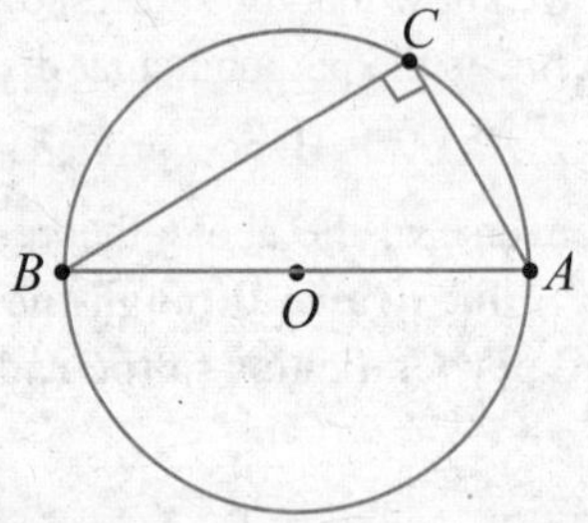

- The sum of either pair of opposite angles of a cyclic quadrilateral is 180°.

Real Life Applications

- Cycling is a great way to keep our bodies fit, and when riding a bicycle, you may have noticed that the wheel moves along a road. Since the wheel is circular and the road is straight, the road touches the circle at only one point, and so the road becomes tangent to the circle at each point where the wheels roll on it. This is an example of a tangent to a circle.

Different Problem Types

Type I: On Finding the Length of the Tangent or Radius of a Circle:

Step I: Identify circle-related lengths and points.

Step II: Recognize tangent's perpendicularity to the radius.

Step III: Formulate a right triangle with radius, tangent, and line to the center.

Step IV: Apply Pythagoras theorem.

Step V: Solve for radius or tangent length.

Example: A point P is 13 cm from the centre of the circle. The length of the tangent drawn from P to the circle is 12 cm. Find the radius of the circle.

Solution: Since tangent to a circle is perpendicular to the radius through the point of contact.

$$\therefore \angle OTP = 90°$$

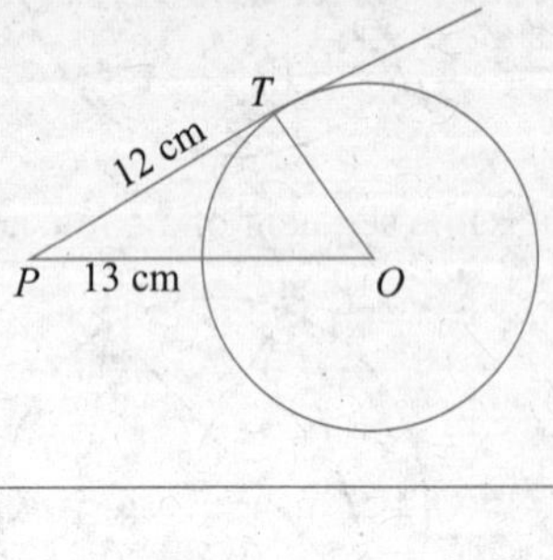

In right triangle OTP, we have

$$OP^2 = OT^2 + PT^2$$

$$\Rightarrow 13^2 = OT^2 + 12^2$$

$$\Rightarrow OT^2 = 13^2 - 12^2 = (13 - 12)(13 + 12) = 25$$

$$\Rightarrow OT = 5.$$

Hence, radius of the circle is 5 cm.

TYPE II: Question Based on the Result that the Tangent to a Circle at a Point is Perpendicular to the Radius through the Point:

Step I: Identify key elements such as the circle's center, tangent segments, and any mentioned angles.

Step II: Apply the property that a tangent to a circle is perpendicular to the radius, forming a 90° angle at the point of tangency.

Step III: Recognize that in a cyclic quadrilateral, opposite angles sum to 180°, indicating the quadrilateral is cyclic.

Step IV: Utilize the tangent property to establish 90° angles between tangent segments and radii. Then, use angle sum properties to confirm the sum of opposite angles is 180°.

Example: In the given figure, O is the centre of the circle. PA and PB are tangent segments. Show that the quadrilateral $AOBP$ is cyclic.

Solution: Since tangent at a point to a circle is perpendicular to the radius through the point.

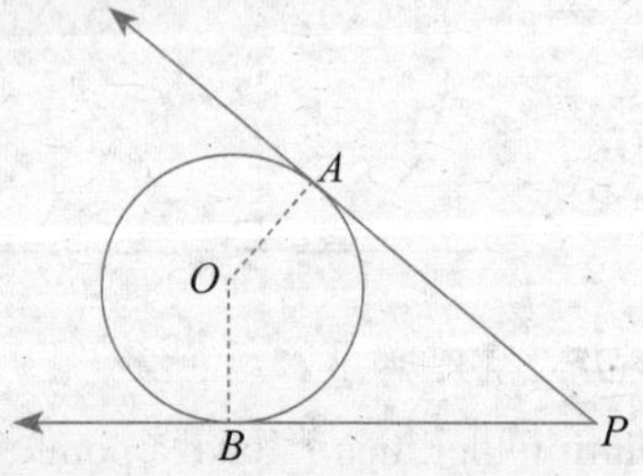

$$\therefore OA \perp AP \text{ and } OB \perp BP$$

$$\Rightarrow \angle OAP = 90° \text{ and } \angle OBP = 90°$$

$$\Rightarrow \angle OAP + \angle OBP = 90° + 90° = 180°$$

In quadrilateral $OAPB$, we have

$$\angle OAP + \angle APB + \angle AOB + \angle OBP = 360°$$

$$\Rightarrow (\angle APB + \angle AOB) + (\angle OAP + \angle OBP) = 360°$$

$$\Rightarrow \angle APB + \angle AOB + 180° = 360°$$

$$\Rightarrow \angle APB + \angle AOB = 180°$$

We can say that the quadrilateral $AOBP$ is cyclic.

COMPETENCY BASED SOLVED EXAMPLES

Multiple Choice Questions (1 M)

1. In Fig. 1, O is the centre of circle. PQ is a chord and PT is tangent at P which makes an angle of 50° with PQ. ∠POQ is (*Un*) (CBSE, 2020)

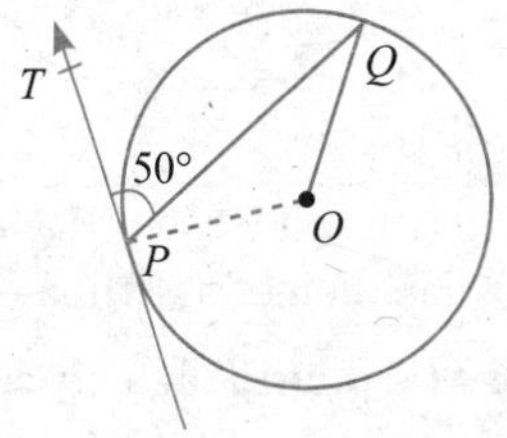

(*a*) 130° (*b*) 90°

(*c*) 100° (*d*) 75°

Sol. Radius from the centre makes an angle of 90° at the point where the tangent meets the circle.

$\angle OPQ = (90 - 50)° = 40°$ $\angle OPQ = \angle OQP = 40°$

(Triangle *OPQ* is isosceles)

By Angle sum property of triangle we get,

$\angle POQ = (180 - 80)° = 100°$

2. In the figure, *AB* is a chord of the circle and *AOC* is its diameter such that ∠*ACB* = 50°. If *AT* is the tangent to the circle at the point *A*, then ∠*BAT* is equal to (*Re*) (NCERT Exemplar)

(*a*) 65° (*b*) 60° (*c*) 50° (*d*) 40°

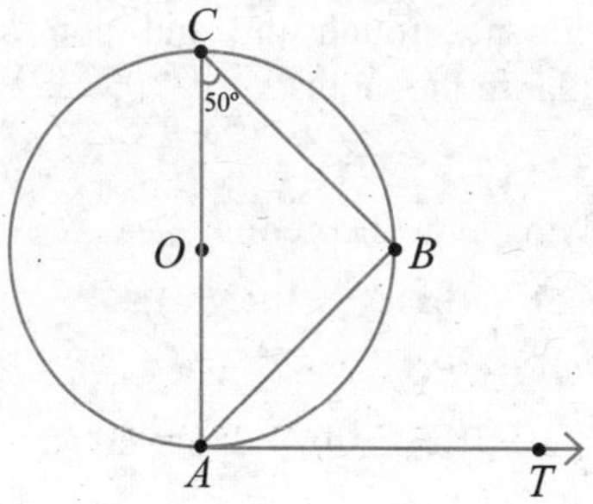

Sol. Since, the angle in a semicircle is 90°.

So, $\angle ABC = 90°$

In ΔACB,

$\angle A + \angle B + \angle C = 180°$ [Angle sum property]

$\Rightarrow \angle A + 90° + 50° = 180°$ [$\angle C = 50°$]

$\Rightarrow \angle A = 180° - 140° = 40° \Rightarrow \angle A$ or $\angle OAB = 40°$

Since tangent to a circle is perpendicular to the radius drawn through the point of contact.

So, *OA* is perpendicular to *AT*.

$\Rightarrow \angle OAT = 90° \Rightarrow \angle OAB + \angle BAT = 90°$

$\Rightarrow \angle BAT = 90° - 40° = 50°$ [Since, $\angle OAB = 40°$]

3. At one end *A* of a diameter *AB* of a circle of radius 5 cm, tangent *XAY* is drawn to the circle. The length of the chord *CD* parallel to *XY* and at a distance 8 cm from *A* is (*Un*) (NCERT Exemplar)

(*a*) 4 cm (*b*) 5 cm (*c*) 6 cm (*d*) 8 cm

Sol.

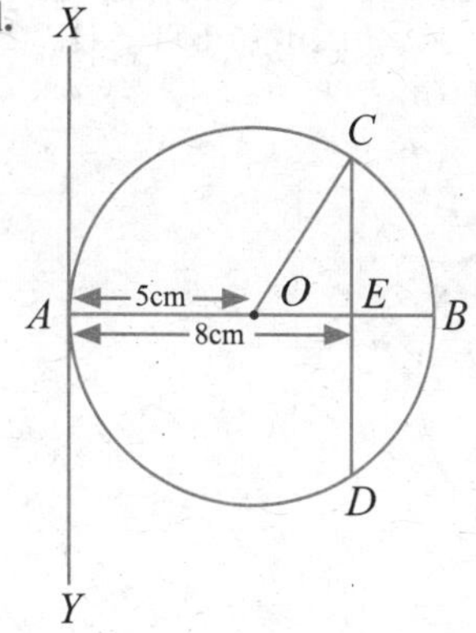

Since, $XY \parallel CD$

$\Rightarrow CD \perp AO \Rightarrow CD \perp AE \Rightarrow \angle OEC = 90°$

$\therefore$ In $\angle OEC$,

$CE^2 = OC^2 - OE^2$ [By Pythagoras theorem]

$\Rightarrow CE^2 = 5^2 - 3^2 = 25 - 9 = 16$

$\therefore CE = 4 \text{ cm} \Rightarrow CD = 2 \times 4 = 8 \text{ cm}$

> **Mistakes 101 : What not to do!**
>
> Students misinterpret that all chords drawn in a circle are equal in length, overlooking variations in chord lengths based on their positions relative to the centre.

4. In the given figure, *TA* is a tangent to the circle with centre *O* such that *OT* = 4 cm, ∠*OTA* = 30°, then length of *TA* is: (*An*)

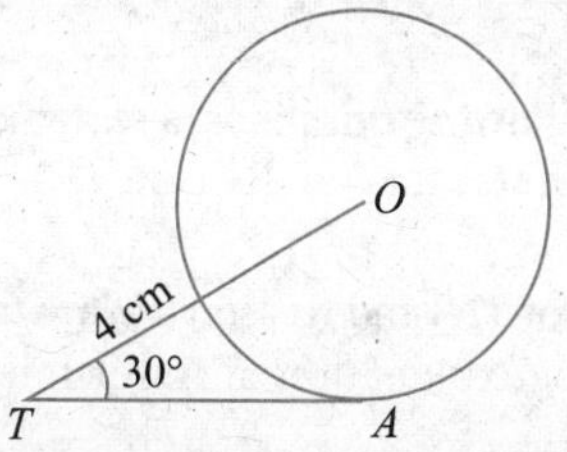

(*a*) $2\sqrt{3}$ cm (*b*) 2 cm (*c*) $2\sqrt{2}$ cm (*d*) $\sqrt{3}$ cm

Sol. We know tangent makes 90° with the Radius.

Given $\angle ATO = 30°$ & $OT = 4$ cm

$\cos 30° = \frac{AT}{OT} = \frac{AT}{4} \Rightarrow \frac{\sqrt{3}}{2} = \frac{AT}{4}$

$\Rightarrow AT = 4 \times \frac{\sqrt{3}}{2} = 2\sqrt{3}$ cm

Mistakes 101 : What not to do!

Students may incorrectly apply properties related to tangents, such as the angle between a tangent and a radius being 90°. They might forget to consider the subtended angle or misinterpret the angle formed by a tangent and a chord.

5. In figure, if TP and TQ are the two tangents to a circle with centre O so that $\angle POQ = 110°$, then $\angle PTQ$ is equal to *(Ap)* **(CBSE SQP, 2023)**

(*a*) 60° (*b*) 70°

(*c*) 80° (*d*) 90°

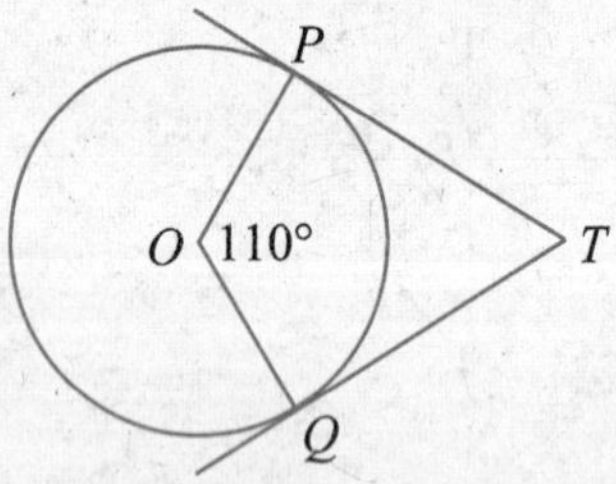

Sol. Given, $\angle POQ = 110°$

We know,

$\angle OPT = \angle OQT = 90°$ (Angle between the tangent and the radial line at the point of intersection of the tangent at the circle)

Now, in quadrilateral $POQT$

Sum of angles = 360°

$\Rightarrow \angle OPT + \angle OQT + \angle PTQ + \angle POQ = 360°$

$90° + 90° + \angle PTQ + 110° = 360°$

$\Rightarrow \angle PTQ = 360° - 290°$

$\Rightarrow \angle PTQ = 70°$

Answer Key

1. (*c*) 2. (*c*) 3. (*d*) 4. (*a*) 5. (*b*)

Assertion and Reason (1 M)

Direction: In the following questions, a statement of Assertion (A) is followed by a statement of Reason (R). Mark the correct choice as:

(*a*) Both Assertion (A) and Reason (R) are true, and Reason (R) is the correct explanation of Assertion (A).

(*b*) Both Assertion (A) and Reason (R) are true, but Reason (R) is not the correct explanation of Assertion (A).

(*c*) Assertion (A) is true, but Reason (R) is false.

(*d*) Assertion (A) is false, but Reason (R) is true.

1. Assertion (A): If in a circle with centre *O*, the radius of the circle is 3 cm and distance of a point *P*, from the centre of a circle is 5 cm, then length of tangent *PQ*, where *Q* is a point on the circle, will be 4 cm.

Reason (R): (hypotenuse)^2 = (base)^2 + (height)^2 *(Cr)*

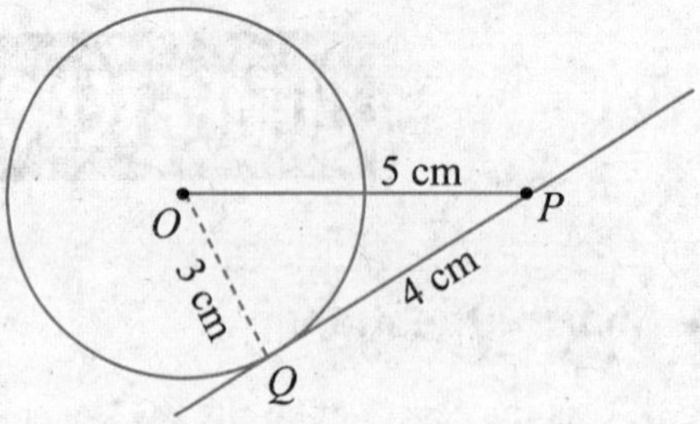

Sol. In the given figure.

$(OP)^2 = (OQ)^2 + (PQ)^2$

$25 = 9 + 16$

$25 = 25$

Hence L.H.S = R.H.S

$\therefore$ Both assertion (A) and reason (R) is true and reason (R) is the correct explanation of assertion (A).

2. Assertion (A): At a point *P* of a circle with centre *O* and radius 12 cm, a tangent *PQ* of length 16 cm is drawn. Then, *OQ* = 20 cm.

Reason (R): The tangent at any point of a circle is perpendicular to the radius through the point of contact. *(Cr)*

Sol.

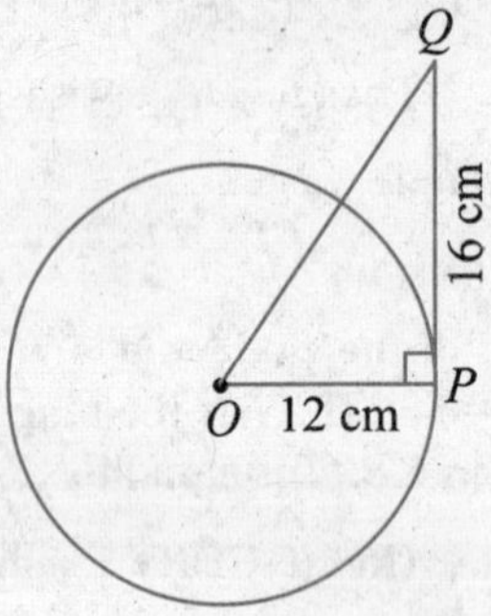

$PQ = 16$ cm and $OP = 12$ cm

Tangent drawn through the end point of a radius is perpendicular to the radius.

So, $OP \perp PQ$

Now, by Pythagoras theorem

(hypotenuse)^2 = (base)^2 + (height)^2

$\Rightarrow OQ^2 = OP^2 + PQ^2$

$\Rightarrow OQ^2 = 12^2 + 16^2 = 144 + 256 = 400$

$\Rightarrow OQ = \sqrt{400} = 20$ cm

Assertion is true.

Reason is also true by theorem.

As we used a theorem to prove assertion.

So, reason is correct explanation of the assertion

Nailing the Right Answer

Always draw accurate diagrams representing the given information in the problem. Pay attention to the positions of points, lines, and circles, and use a ruler and compass if necessary to ensure precision.

3. **Assertion (A): If the radii of two concentric circles are 4 cm and 5 cm, then the length of each chord of one circle which is tangent to the other circle is 3 cm.**

Reason (R): The tangent at any point of a circle is perpendicular to the radius through the point of contact. *(Re)*

Sol.

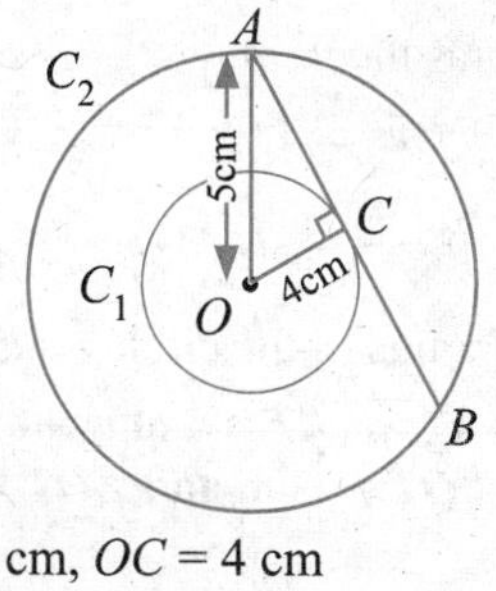

We have, $AO = 5$ cm, $OC = 4$ cm

and $OC \perp AC$ (By theorem 1)

$\therefore AC^2 = AO^2 - OC^2$

$= 5^2 - 4^2 = 25 - 16 = 9 \Rightarrow AC = 3$

Also, in C_2, as the line passing through the centre and $\perp$ to a chord, bisects the chord.

$\therefore$ Length of the required chord $= AB = 2 \times AC = 2 \times 3 = 6$ cm

So, assertion is False.

Reason is true by theorem 1.

Thus, assertion is false and reason is true.

Key Takeaways

Apply the Pythagoras as theorem and properties of right triangles in problems involving tangent-secant or secant-secant intersections.

Answer Key

1. (a) 2. (a) 3. (d)

Subjective Questions

Very Short Answer Type Questions (1 or 2 M)

1. **Two concentric circles are of radii 5 cm and 3 cm. Find the length of the chord of larger circle whcih touches the smaller circle.** *(Ev)* **(CBSE, 2020)**

Sol.

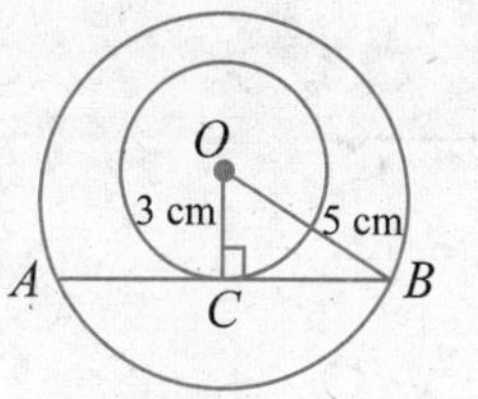

(½ M)

In ΔOCB

$BC = \sqrt{5^2 - 3^2} = 4\text{cm}$ *(1 M)*

$AB = 2 \times BC = 8$ cm *(½ M)*

2. **Two concentric circles are of radii 5 cm and 3 cm. Find the length of the chord of the larger circle which touches the smaller circle.** *(Cr)*

Sol. Given: Two concentric circles are of radii 5 cm and 3 cm.

To find: The length of the chord of the larger circle which touches the smaller circle.

PQ is chord of a larger circle and tangent of a smaller circle.

As, tangent is perpendicular to the radius at the point of contact S.

$\therefore \angle OSP = 90°$ *(½ M)*

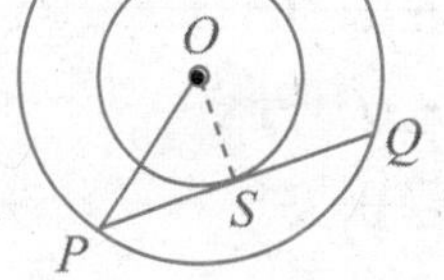

In ΔOSP (Right angled triangle) using Pythagoras Theorem, we get

$OP^2 = OS^2 + SP^2 \Rightarrow 5^2 = 3^2 + SP^2$ *(½ M)*

$\Rightarrow SP^2 = 25 - 9 = 16 \Rightarrow SP = \pm 4$

SP is length of tangent and cannot be negative

$\therefore SP = 4$ cm. *(½ M)*

$QS = SP$ (Perpendicular from center bisects the chord considering the larger circles)

Therefore, $QS = SP = 4$ cm

Length of the chord, $PQ = QS + SP = 4 + 4 = 8$ cm

Therefore, the length of the chord of the larger circle is 8 cm. *(½ M)*

3. **PQ is a tangent drawn from an external point P to a circle with centre O and QOR is the diameter of the circle. If $\angle POR = 120°$, What is the measure of $\angle OPQ$?** *(An)*

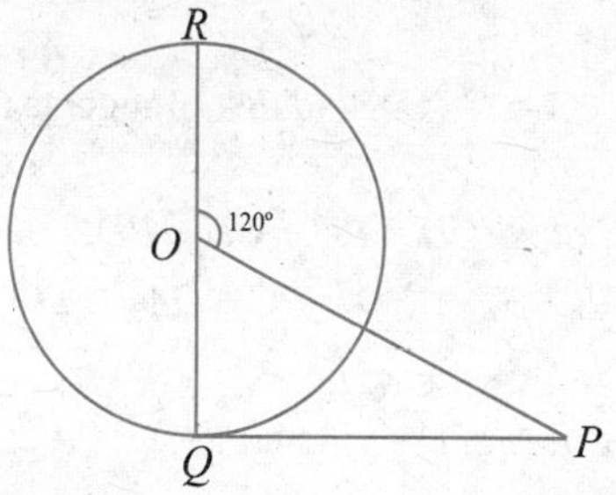

Sol. $\because OQ \perp QP$ (By Theorem 1)

So, $\angle OQP = 90°$

Also,

$\because \angle ROP + \angle QOP = 180°$ (Supplementary angles)

$\Rightarrow 120° + \angle QOP = 180°$

$\Rightarrow \angle QOP = 180° - 120° = 60°$ *(1 M)*

$\because$ In ΔOQP,

$\angle QOP + \angle OQP + \angle OPQ = 180°$

$\Rightarrow 60° + 90° + + \angle OPQ = 180°$

$\Rightarrow \angle OPQ = 180° - 60° - 90° = 30°$ *(1 M)*

4. The length of a tangent from a point A at distance 5 cm from the centre of the circle is 4 cm. Find the radius of the circle. (*Ev*) **(CBSE SQP, 2023)**

Sol.

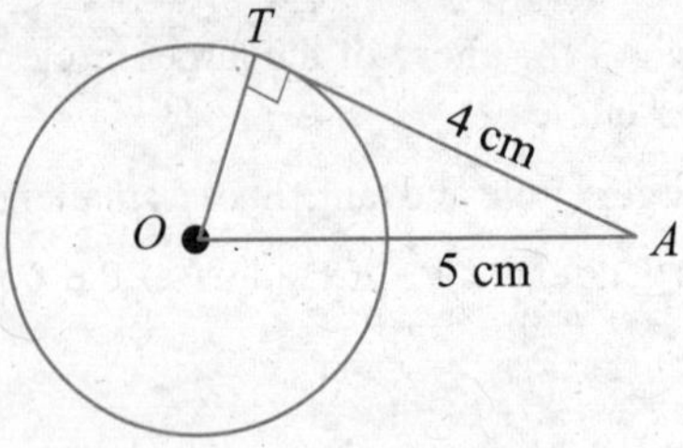

(½ *M*)

In ΔOTA, $\angle OTA = 90°$ (½ *M*)

By Pythagoras theorem

$\Rightarrow OA^2 = OT^2 + AT^2$ (½ *M*)

$\Rightarrow (5)^2 = OT^2 + (4)^2$

$\Rightarrow 25 - 16 = OT^2$

$\Rightarrow 9 = OT^2$

$\Rightarrow OT = 3\text{cm}$

$\Rightarrow$ Radius of circle = 3 cm (½ *M*)

Short Answer Type Questions (2 or 3 M)

1. From an external point *P*, two tangents, *PA* and *PB* are drawn to a circle with centre *O*. At a point *E* on the circle, a tangent is drawn to intersect *PA* and *PB* at *C* and *D*, respectively. If *PA* = 10 cm, find the perimeter of ΔPCD. (*Ap*)

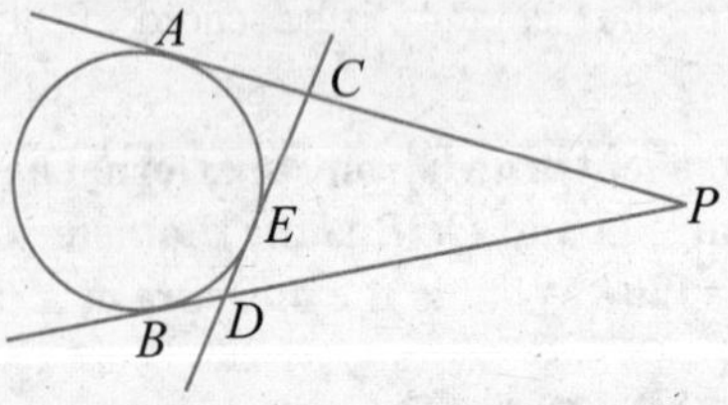

Sol. $PA = PB$; $CA = CE$; $DE = DB$ [Tangents to a circle] (½ *M*)

Perimeter of $\Delta PCD = PC + CD + PD$

$= PC + CE + ED + PD = PC + CA + BD + PD$

$= PA + PB$ (1 *M*)

Perimeter of $\Delta PCD = PA + PA = 2PA = 2(10) = 20$ cm (½ *M*)

2. In the figure, *O* is the centre of the circle and *PT* is the tangent drawn from the point *P* to the circle. Secant *PAB* passes through the centre *O* of the circle. If *PT* = 6 cm and *PA* = 3 cm, then find the radius of the circle. (*Cr*)

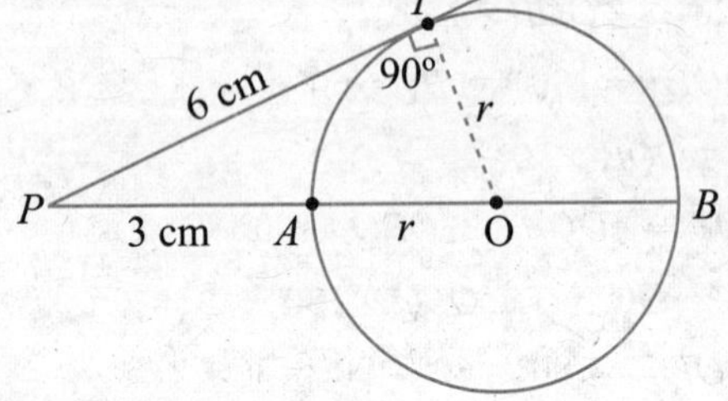

Sol. In the figure *AB* is diameter of the circle and $OA = r$ (radius of the circle)

Join *OT*.

$\therefore \Delta OTP = 90°$.

[$\because$ Radius is $\perp$ to tangent at the point of contact] (½ *M*)

In right angled ΔOTP, $OP = OA + PA = (r + 3)$ cm (½ *M*)

By Pythagoras theorem,

$OP^2 = OT^2 + PT^2 \Rightarrow (r + 3)^2 = r^2 + (6)^2$ (½ *M*)

$\Rightarrow r^2 + 6r + 9 = r^2 + 36 \Rightarrow 6r = 27 \Rightarrow r = \frac{9}{2} = 4.5$

Hence, the radius of the circle = 4.5 cm. (½ *M*)

3. In the given figure, *AT* is a tangent to the circle with centre '*O*' such that *OT* = 4 cm and $\angle OTA = 30°$. Find *AT*. (*Un*)

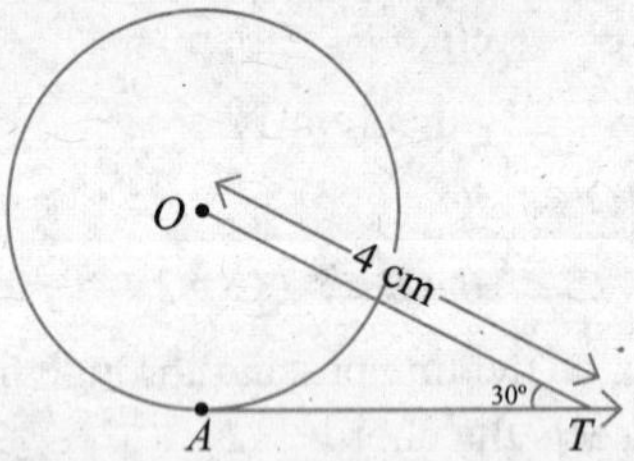

Sol. Join *OA*.

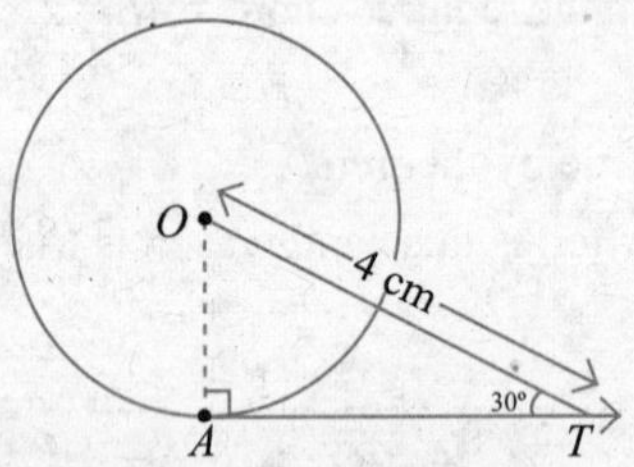

(½ *M*)

$\because OA \perp AT$ [Radius is $\perp$ ar to tangent at the point of contact]

$\Rightarrow \angle OAT = 90°$ (½ *M*)

Now, in ΔOAT, $\cos 30° = \frac{AT}{OT}$ (½ *M*)

$\Rightarrow AT = \cos 30° \times OT = \frac{\sqrt{3}}{2} \times 4 = 2\sqrt{3}$ cm (½ *M*)

4. The length of a tangent from a point *A* at distance 5 cm from the centre of the circle is 4 cm. Find the radius of the circle. (*An*) **(NCERT Intext)**

Sol. $\because$ Radius, *OB*, is $\perp$ to the tangent, *BA*, at the point of contact *B*.

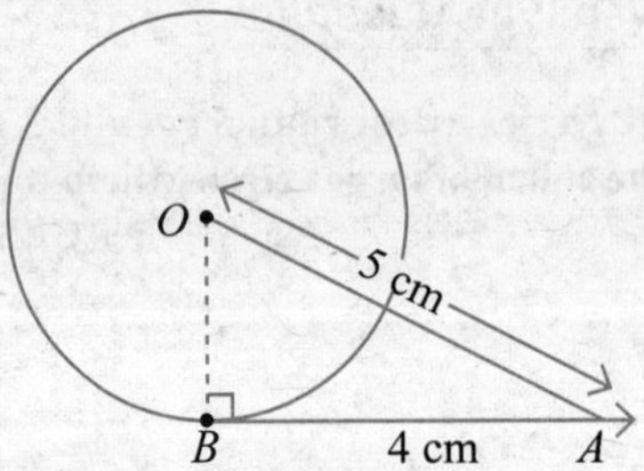

(½ *M*)

So, $\angle OBA = 90°$ (½ *M*)

Now, by Pythagoras Theorem,

$OB = \sqrt{OA^2 - BA^2}$ (½ *M*)

$= \sqrt{5^2 - 4^2} = \sqrt{25 - 16} = \sqrt{9} = 3$

$\therefore$ Radius, $OB = 3$ cm (½ *M*)

5. Two tangents PQ and PR are drawn from an external point to a circle with centre O. Prove that $QORP$ is a cyclic quadrilateral. **(*Cr*) (NCERT Exemplar)**

Sol. Since, Radius ⊥ Tangent

So, $OR \perp PR$

Therefore, $\angle ORP = 90°$ *(½ M)*

Similarily,

Since, Radius ⊥ Tangent

So, $OQ \perp PQ$

Therefore, $\angle OQP = 90°$ *(½ M)*

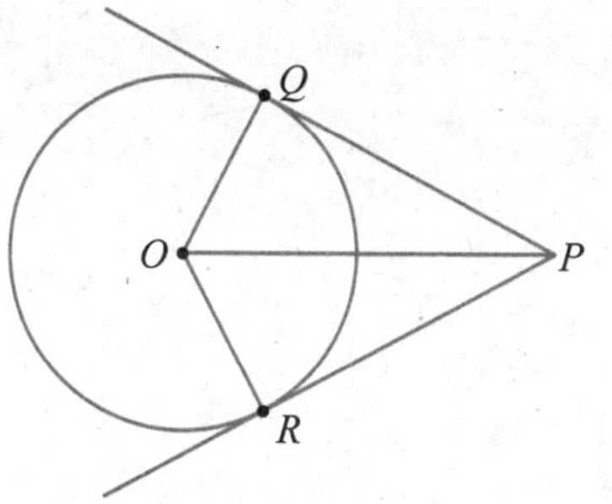

Now, in quadrilateral $ORPQ$,

Sum of all interior angles = 360°

$\angle ORP + \angle RPQ + \angle PQO + \angle QOR = 360°$ *(1 M)*

$\Rightarrow 90° + \angle RPQ + 90° + \angle QOR = 360°$

So, $\angle QOR + \angle RPQ = 180°$ *(½ M)*

Since sum of opposite angles in the quadrilateral is 180°

So, $PROQ$ is a cyclic quadrilateral. *(½ M)*

6. Prove that a diameter AB of a circle bisects all those chords which are parallel to the tangent at the point A. **(*An*) (NCERT Exemplar)**

Sol. Let AB be the a diameter of the circle.

Draw a tangent MN at point A.

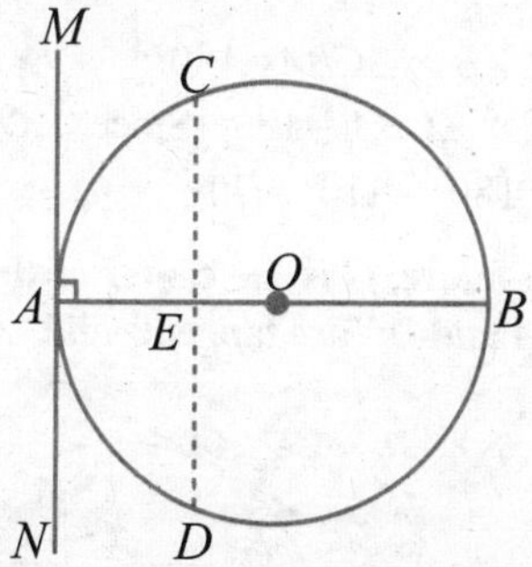

Draw a chord CD parallel to the tangent MN.

Therefore, CD is a chord of the circle and OA is radius of the circle. *(1 M)*

Now,

$\angle MAO = 90°$ [Since tangent at any point of a circle is perpendicular to the radius through the point of contact] *(½ M)*

Also, $\angle CEO = \angle MAO$ [Corresponding angles]

Therefore, $\angle CEO = 90°$ *(½ M)*

Since, a perpendicular line drawn through the centre of the circle to a chord bisects the chord.

So, OE bisects CD or AB bisects CD.

Hence, diameter AB bisects all chords which are parallel to the tangent at the point A. *(1 M)*

7. Prove that in two concentric circles, the chord of the larger circle, which touches the smaller circle, is bisected at the point of contact. **(*Re*)**

Sol. Given: Two concentric circles with centre O and let AB is a chord of the larger circle touching the smaller circle at C.

To Prove: $AC = BC$.

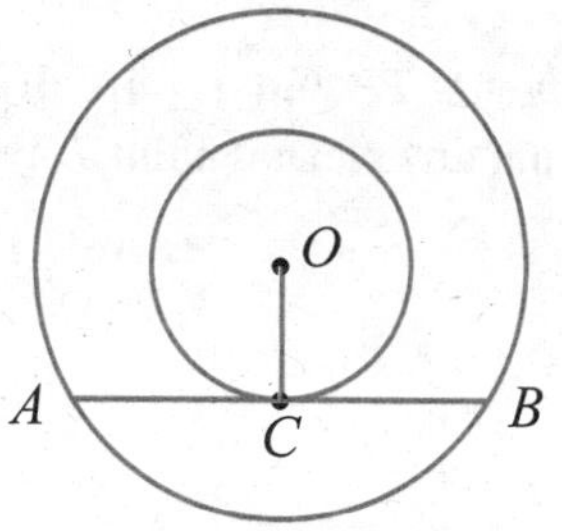

(1 M)

Construction: Join OC.

Proof: AB is a tangent to the smaller circle at the point C and OC is the radius through the point of contact C.

$\therefore OC \perp AB$. *(1 M)*

But, the perpendicular drawn from the centre of a circle to a chord bisects the chord and AB is the chord of the larger circle.

So, OC bisects AB *(½ M)*

Hence, $AC = BC$. *(½ M)*

> **Key Takeaways**
>
> In two concentric circles, the chord of the larger circle that touches the smaller circle is bisected at the point of contact.

8. PA and PB are tangents drawn to a circle of centre O from an external point P. Chord AB makes an angle of 30° with the radius at the point of contact.
If length of the chord is 6 cm, find the length of the tangent PA and the length of the radius OA. **(*Un*)**

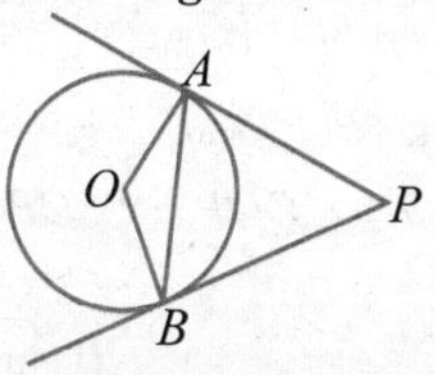

Sol. $\angle OAB = 30°$

$\angle OAP = 90°$ [Angle between the tangent and the radius at the point of contact]

$\angle PAB = 90° - 30° = 60°$ *(½ M)*

$AP = BP$ [Tangents to a circle from an external point]

$\angle PAB = \angle PBA$ [Angles opposite to equal sides of a triangle] *(½ M)*

In ΔABP, $\angle PAB + \angle PBA + \angle APB = 180°$ [Angle Sum Property]

$60° + 60° + \angle APB = 180°$

$\angle APB = 60°$ (½ M)

$\therefore \Delta ABP$ is an equilateral triangle, where $AP = BP = AB$.

$PA = 6$ cm (½ M)

In Right ΔOAP, $\angle OPA = 30°$

$$\tan 30° = \frac{OA}{PA}$$

$$\frac{1}{\sqrt{3}} = \frac{OA}{6}$$ (½ M)

$$OA = \frac{6}{\sqrt{3}} = 2\sqrt{3} \text{ cm}$$ (½ M)

9. In the figure, two tangents *TP* and *TQ* are drawn to a circle with centre *O* from an external point *T*. Prove that $\angle PTQ = 2\angle OPQ$. (*Cr*)

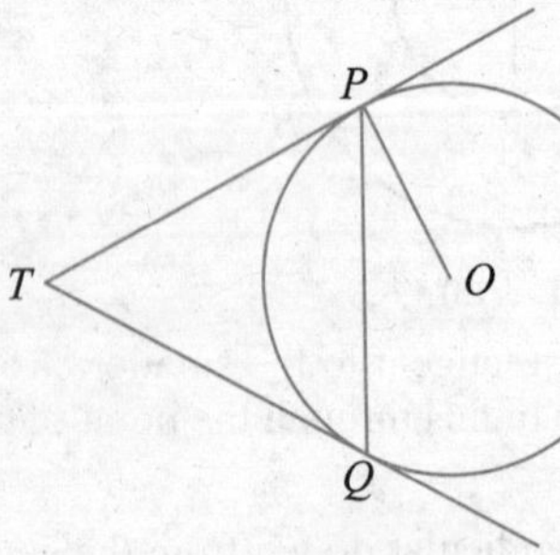

Sol. Join *OQ*.

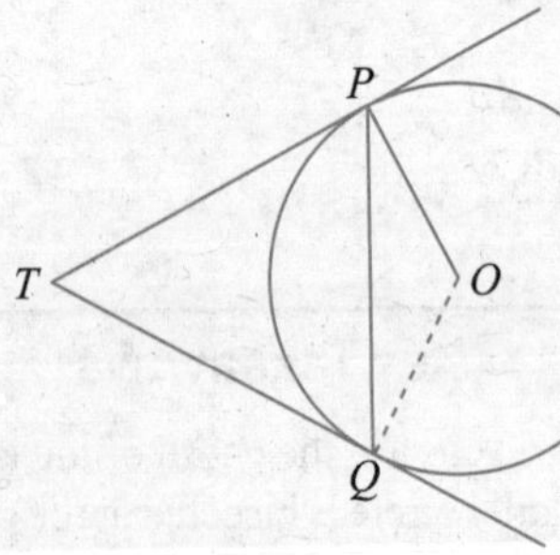

In ΔPOQ,

$\angle POQ + \angle OQP + \angle OPQ = 180°$

[Sum of all angles of triangle = 180°]

$\because PO = QO$ [Radii of circle]

$\Rightarrow \angle OPQ = \angle OQP$ (½ M)

$\therefore \angle POQ + 2\angle OPQ = 180°$ ... (*i*) (½ M)

In quadrilateral, *TPOQ*

$\angle PTQ + \angle TQO + \angle QOP + 2\angle OPQ + \angle TPO = 360°$ ...(*ii*)

(Using Angle sum property)

$TP \perp OP$ & $TQ \perp OQ$ [$\because$ Tangent $\perp$ Radius] (½ M)

$\Rightarrow \angle TPO = \angle TQO = 90°$

$\therefore$ from (*ii*)

$\angle PTQ + \angle QOP = 360° - 90° - 90° = 180°$ ...(*iii*) (½ M)

From (*i*) and (*iii*)

$\angle PTQ + \angle POQ = \angle POQ + 2\angle OPQ$

$\Rightarrow \angle PTQ = 2\angle OPQ$ (1 M)

Hence, proved

Long Answer Type Questions (4 or 5 M)

1. The tangent at a point *C* of a circle and a diameter *AB* when extended intersect at *P*. If $\angle PCA = 110°$, find $\angle CBA$

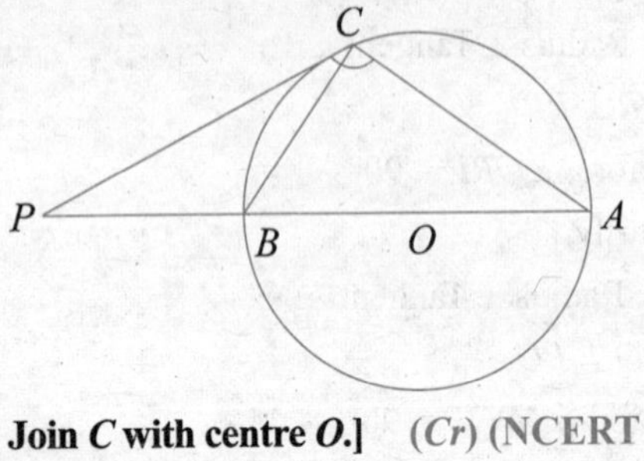

[Hint: Join *C* with centre *O*.] (*Cr*) (NCERT Exemplar))

Sol.

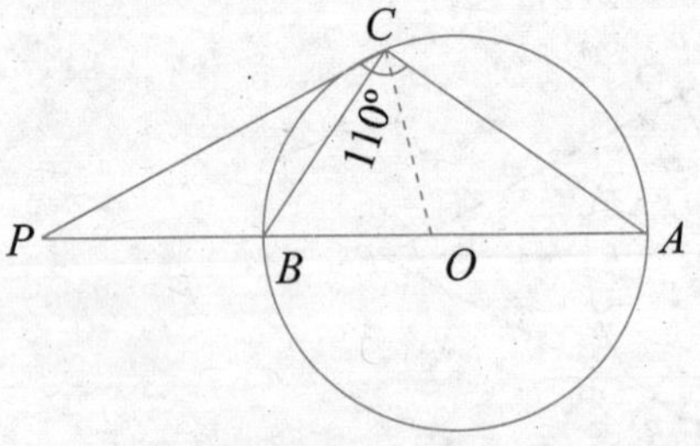

Join *C* with centre *O*. (½ M)

In this, *OC* is the radius.

Since the tangent at any point of a circle is perpendicular to the radius through the point of contact.

Therefore, *OC* perpendicular to *PC*

$\Rightarrow \angle PCO = 90°$ (½ M)

Now, $\angle PCA = 110°$ [Given]

$\Rightarrow \angle PCO + \angle OCA = 110°$ (½ M)

$\Rightarrow 90° + \angle OCA = 110°$ (½ M)

$\Rightarrow \angle OCA = 20°$ (½ M)

Also, $OC = OA$ [Radii of the circle]

Therefore, $\angle OCA = \angle OAC = 20°$ (½ M)

[angles opposite to equal sides are equal]

Now, since the angle in a semicircle is 90°.

So, $\angle BCA = 90°$ (½ M)

In ΔBCA,

$\angle BCA + \angle CAB + \angle CBA = 180°$ (½ M)

$\Rightarrow 90° + 20° + \angle CBA = 180°$ [Since, $\angle OAC = CAB$] (½ M)

$\Rightarrow \angle CBA = 180° - 110° = 70°$ (½ M)

2. In the given figure, *O* is the center of the circle. Determine $\angle APC$, if *DA* and *DC* are tangents and $\angle ADC = 50°$. (*Re*)

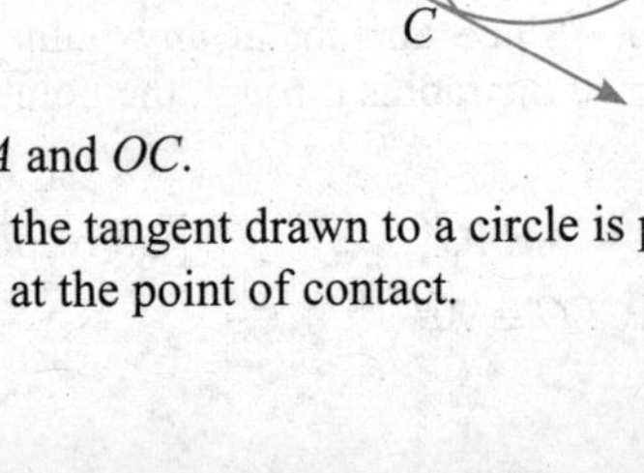

Sol. Join *OA* and *OC*.

Since, the tangent drawn to a circle is perpendicular to the radius at the point of contact.

So, $\angle OAD = \angle OCD = 90°$ *(½ M)*

In quadrilateral $OADC$,

$\Rightarrow \angle OAD + \angle ADC + \angle OCD + \angle AOC = 360°$ *(½ M)*

[Angle sum property of quad.]

$\Rightarrow 90° + 50° + 90° + \angle AOC = 360°$

[Given $\angle ADC = 50°$] *(1 M)*

$\Rightarrow 230° + \angle AOC = 360°$

$\therefore \angle AOC = 130°$ *(½ M)*

Since, the angle subtended by an arc at the centre is double than the subtended angle at any part of the circle.

So, Angle subtended by major arc AC at the centre = 2 (Angle subtended by major arc AC at P) *(1 M)*

$\Rightarrow$ Reflex of $\angle AOC = 2\ \angle APC$

$\Rightarrow \angle APC =$ (Reflex of $\angle AOC$)/2 *(½ M)*

$= (360° - \angle AOC)/2 = (360° - 130°)/2 = 230°/2 = 115°$ *(1 M)*

3. *AB* is a diameter and *AC* is a chord of a circle with centre *O* such that $\angle BAC = 30°$. The tangent at *C* intersects extended *AB* at a point *D*. Prove that *BC* = *BD*. **(Re)**

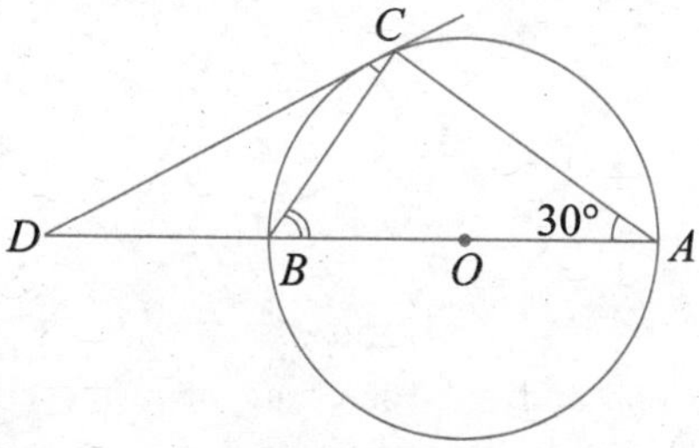

Sol. Given: A tangent at C to a circle having centre O and diameter AB.

A chord AC is that $\angle BAC = 30°$

To prove: $BC = BD$ *(½ M)*

Proof :

Since, DC is a tangent and BC is a chord.

So, $\angle BCD = \angle CAB$ [By alternate segment theorem]

$\therefore \angle BCD = 30°$ ...*(i)* [$\angle CAB = 30°$ is given] *(1 M)*

Since, angle in a semicircle is right angle

$\therefore \angle ACB = 90°$ *(½ M)*

In triangle ABC,

$\angle ABC + \angle BCA + \angle CAB = 180°$

[Angle sum property of Δ]

$\Rightarrow \angle ABC + 90° + 30° = 180°$

$\Rightarrow \angle ABC = 180° - 120° = 60°$ ...*(ii)* *(1 M)*

Now, $\angle CBA + \angle CBD = 180°$ [Linear pair]

$\Rightarrow \angle CBD = 180° - 60° = 120°$ [from *(ii)*] *(½ M)*

Now, in triangle CBD,

$\angle CBD + \angle BDC + \angle DCB = 180°$ [Angle sum property of Δ]

$\Rightarrow 120° + \angle BDC + 30° = 180°$ [From *(i)*]

$\Rightarrow \angle BDC = 30°$ ... *(iii)* *(½ M)*

From equations. *(i)* and *(iii)*,

$\angle BCD = \angle BDC \Rightarrow BC = BD$

[Since, sides opposite to equal angles are equal) *(1 M)*

Hence proved.

2 NUMBER OF TANGENTS FROM A POINT ON A CIRCLE

Important Terms

- **Length of a tangent:** The length of the segment of a tangent from an external point (on the tangent) to the point of contact is known as the length of the tangent to the circle.

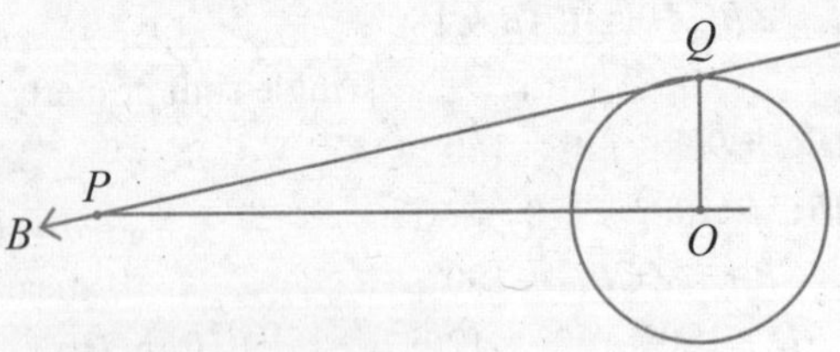

Here, PQ is the length of the tangent AB.

Important Derivations

- **Theorem 2: The lengths of tangents drawn from an external point to a circle are equal.**

Given: Two tangents PQ and PR are drawn from a point P to a circle having centre O.

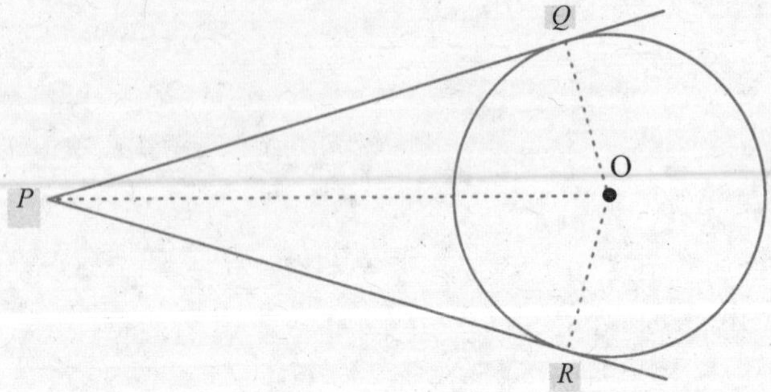

To prove: $PQ = PR$

Construction: Join OP, OQ and OR.

Proof: PQ is a tangent at Q and OQ is the radius.

$\therefore OQ \perp PQ$ [tangent is $\perp$ to the radius]

Similarly, $OR \perp PR$

In the right triangle OPQ and OPR, we have

$OQ = OR$	[radii of the same circle]
$OP = OP$	[common]
$\angle OQP = \angle ORP$	[90° each]
$\therefore \Delta OPQ \cong \Delta OPR$	[by RHS-congruence]
Hence, $PQ = PR$.	[by C.P.C.T]

Important Concepts

- **Number of tangents to a circle from a point:**

Case 1: When the point lies inside the circle

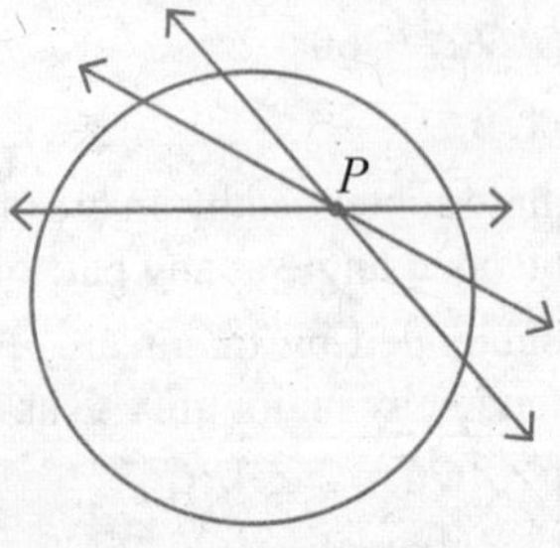

There are no tangents to the circle, passing through the point.

Case 2: When the point lies on the circle:

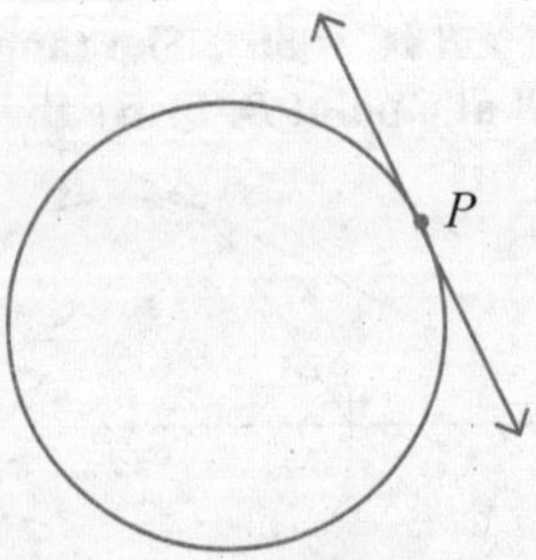

There is one and only one tangent to the circle, passing through the point.

Case 3: When the point lies outside the circle:

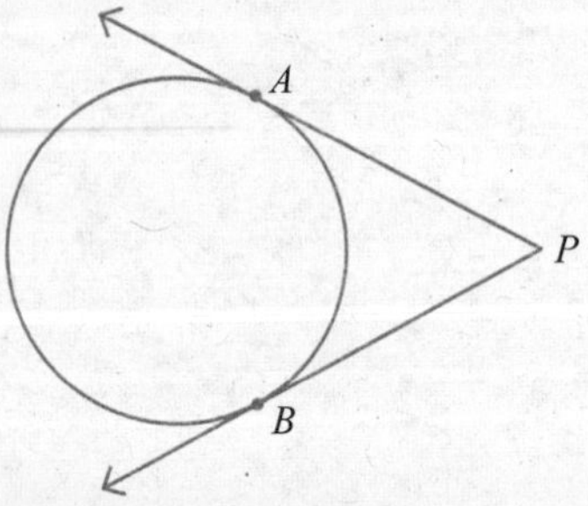

There are exactly two tangents (PA and PB) to the circle, passing through the point (P).

- When two tangents are drawn to the circle from an external point P then,

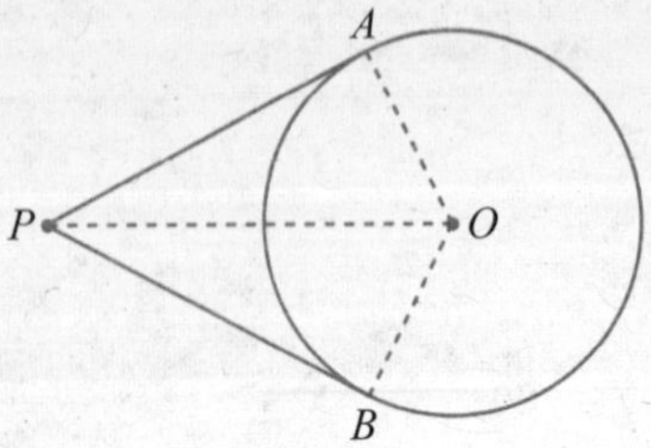

  - The angles subtended by the circles at the centre are equal.
    i.e., $\angle AOP = \angle BOP$
  - The tangents are equally aligned to the line segment joining the centre to the external point.
    i.e., $\angle OPB = \angle OPA$

- ❑ If two chords of a circle intersect each other, then the products of the lengths of their segments are equal.

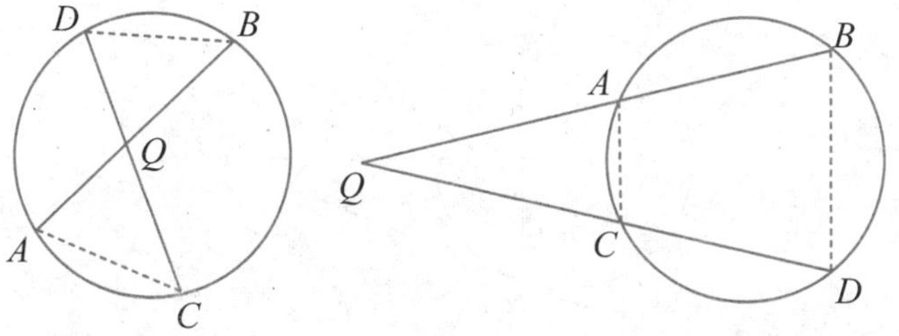

- ❑ If PAB be a secant from an external point P to a circle, which intersects the circle at point A and B and PT is a tangent to the circle having point of contact T, then $PA.PB = PT^2$.

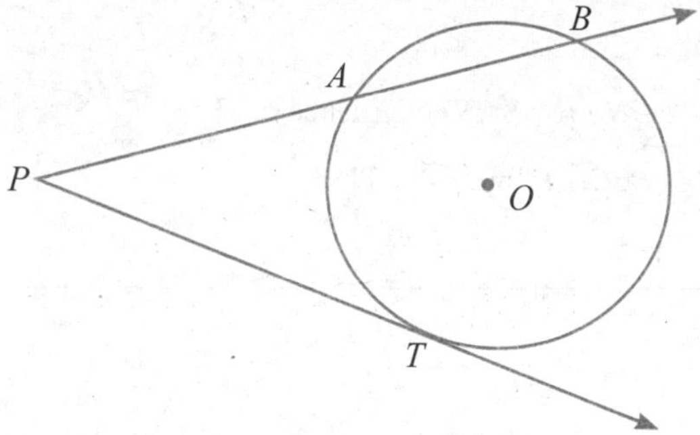

- ❑ If two tangents are parallel to each other, then the line segments joining their point of contact is a diameter of the circle.

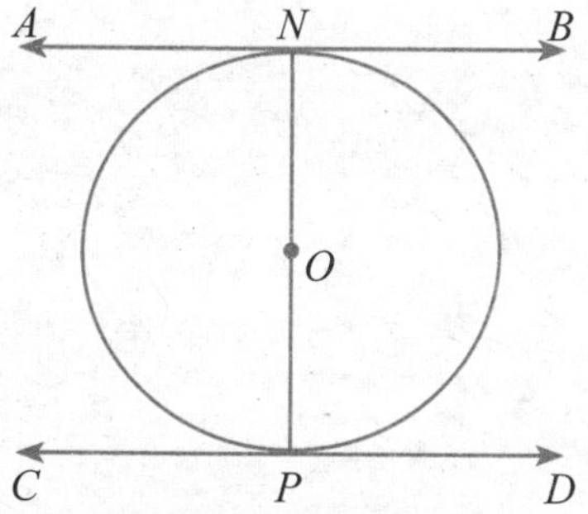

Real Life Applications

- ❑ A simple practical example where the tangent to a circle at an exterior point is equal is if a person is standing outside a round fountain and trying to get the water. A person can extend their arms in two directions, and the point where the arms touch the fountain is the point of contact. Since human arms are of the same length, the two tangents are also of the same length.

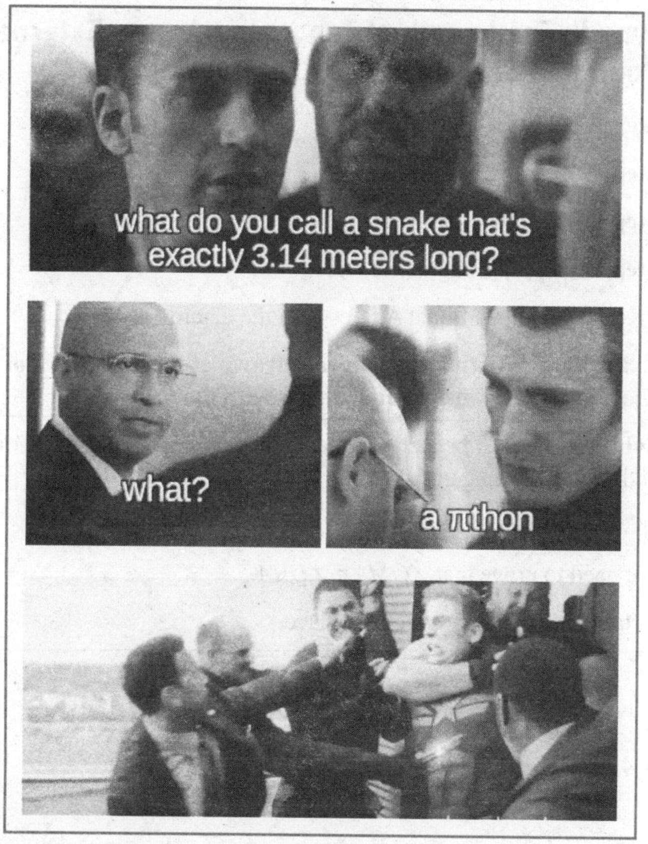

Different Problem Types

Type I: Length of a Tangent

Step I: Understand the given information.

Step II: Draw the circle and label points.

Step III: Form Right Triangle and Apply Pythagoras Theorem.

Step IV: Calculate the length of tangent.

Example: In a circle with radius 10 cm, a tangent is drawn from an external point at a distance of 12 cm from the circle's center. Find the length of the tangent.

Solution: Radius of the circle (r) = 10 cm

Distance from the center to the external point (OA) = 12 cm

Using the Pythagorean theorem:

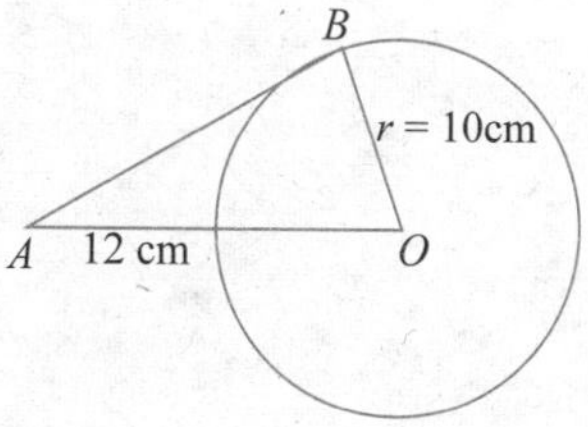

$$OB^2 + AB^2 = OA^2$$

$$10^2 + AB^2 = 12^2$$

$$100 + AB^2 = 144$$

$$AB^2 = 44$$

$$AB = \sqrt{44}$$

$$AB = 2\sqrt{11} \text{ cm (exact length)}$$

Type II: The Length of Tangents from an External Point to a Circle are Equal.

Step I: Draw the Diagram

Step II: Prove Equal Angles

Step III: Establish Triangle Congruence

Step IV: Apply Congruence Rule

Step V: Conclude Equal Angles with the Chord

Example: Prove that the tangents drawn at the end points of a chord of a circle make equal angles with the chord.

Solution: Let MN be a chord of a circle with centre O and let MQ and NQ be the tangents at M and N respectively.

Join OQ and let OQ intersects MN at point A.

We need to prove that $\angle QMA = \angle QNA$.

In triangles QAM and QAN, we have

$QM = QN$ (Tangents from same point Q)

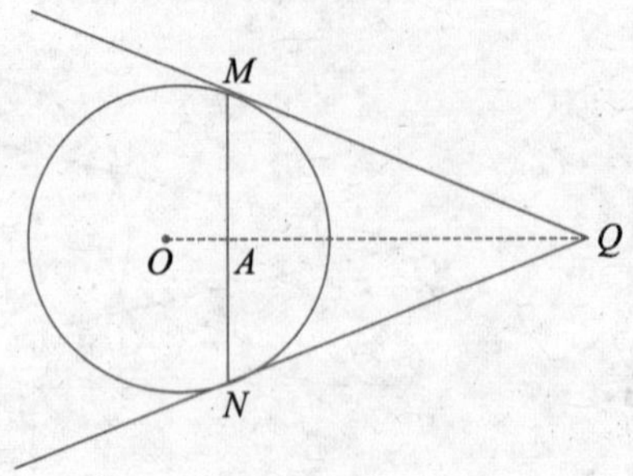

$\angle MQA = \angle NQA$ [$\because$ QM and QN are equally inclined to OQ] and $QA = QA$ [Common]

Therefore,

$\Delta\ QMA \cong \Delta QNA$ [by SAS congruence rule]

$\therefore \angle QMA = \angle QNA$. [by C.P.C.T]

Hence proved

COMPETENCY BASED SOLVED EXAMPLES

Multiple Choice Questionc

(1 M)

1. **In the given figure, PA and PB are tangents from external point P to a circle with centre C and Q is any point on the circle. Then the measure of $\angle AQB$ is:** (*Un*)

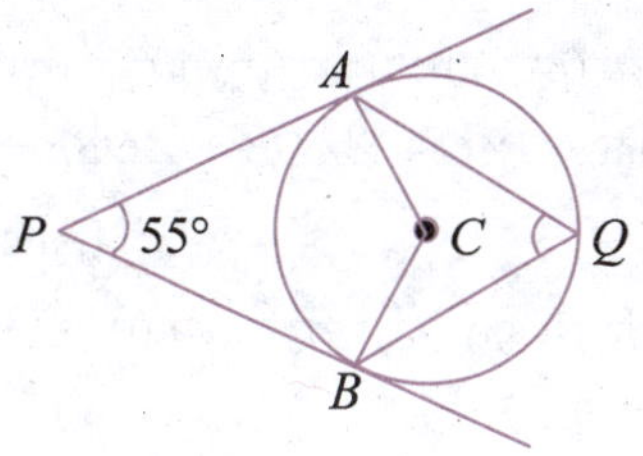

(*a*) $62\frac{1}{2}°$ (*b*) 125° (*c*) 55° (*d*) 90°

Sol. Given, $\angle APB = 55°$

Also, $\angle PAC = \angle PBC = 90°$ [Tangent is $\perp$ to radius]

Now, in quadrilateral $PACB$

$\angle APB + \angle PAC + \angle PBC + \angle ACB = 360°$

[$\because$ Sum of interior angles in quadrilateral = 360°]

$\therefore 55° + 90° + 90° + \angle ACB = 360° \Rightarrow \angle ACB = 125°$

As we know, that the angle subtended by an arc at the centre is double the angle subtended by an arc at the remaining part of the circle.

$\therefore \angle ACB = 2\angle AQB \Rightarrow \angle AQB = \frac{125°}{2} = 62\frac{1}{2}°$

Key Takeaways

Remember that the angle subtended by a chord at the center is twice the angle subtended by it at any point on the circumference.

2. **If two tangents are drawn to a circle from an external point, and the angle between the tangents is 60°, then the ratio of the lengths of the tangents is:** (*Un*)

(*a*) 1:1 (*b*) 1:2 (*c*) 2:1 (*d*) 3:1

Sol. $\because$ Length of tangents to a circle drawn from an external point are equal.

So, ratio of lengths of tangent is 1 : 1.

3. **In the figure below, ΔPXY is formed using three tangents to a circle centred at O.**

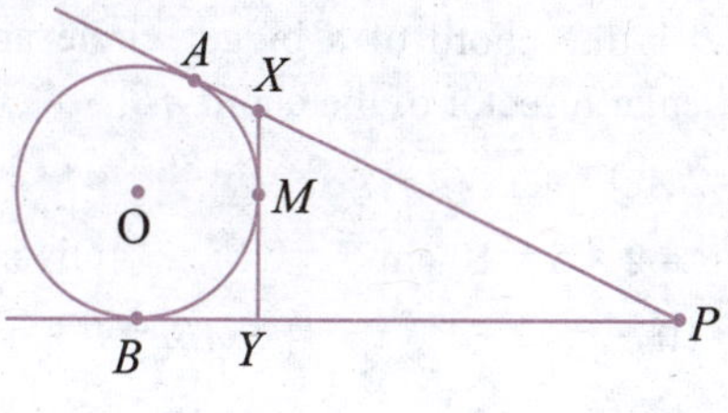

Based on the construction, the sum of the tangents PA and PB is _______ the perimeter of ΔPXY.

(*Cr*) (CBSE CFPQ, 2023)

(*a*) lesser than

(*b*) greater than

(*c*) equal to

(*d*) cannot be answered without knowing the tangent

Sol. We know that if from one external point, two tangents are drawn to a circle, then they have equal tangent segments. Therefore,

$XA = XM$ ...(*i*)

$XM = YB$ ...(*ii*)

Now, the perimeter of $\Delta PXY = PX + XY + YP$

$= PX = (XM + YM) + YP$

$= PX = (XA + YB) + YP$ (From equation (*i*) and (*ii*))

$= (PX + XA) + (YB + YP)$

$= PA + PB$ (Tangents to a circle drawn from an external point are equal)

Hence, the sum of the tangents PA and PB is equal to the perimeter of ΔPXY.

4. **In the given circle in Fig, number of tangents parallel to tangent PQ is** (*Re*) (CBSE, 2020)

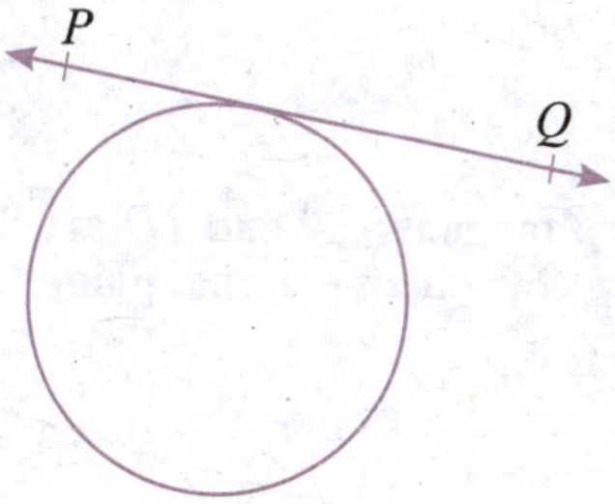

(*a*) 0 (*b*) many

(*c*) 2 (*d*) 1

Sol. For a given tangent, we can draw only one parallel tangent.

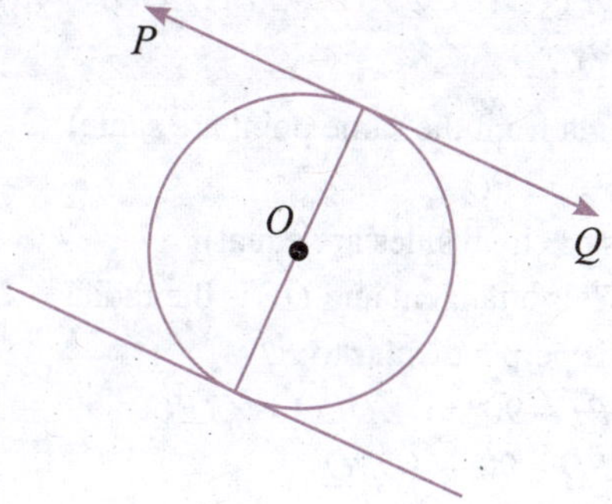

5. In the given figure, AP, AQ and BC are tangents to the circle. If $AB = 5$ cm, $AC = 6$ cm and $BC = 4$ cm then the length of AP is ***(Cr)***

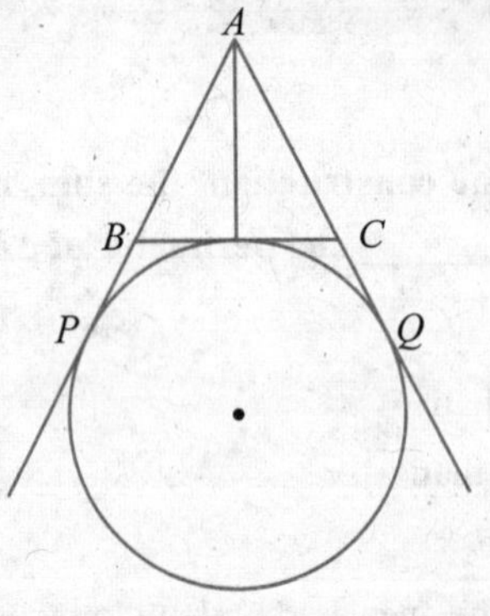

(*a*) 7.2 cm (*b*) 7.5 cm (*c*) 8.5 cm (*d*) 9.2 cm

Sol. Let the point where BC touches the circle is R.

$\because$ Tangents drawn from an external point to a circle are equal.

So, $AP = AQ$

$BP = BR$ ... (*i*)

$CQ = CR$ ... (*ii*)

Now, $AP = AQ$

$\Rightarrow AB + BP = AC + CQ$

$\Rightarrow 5 + BR = 6 + CR$ [From (*i*) and (*ii*)]

$\Rightarrow CR = BR - 1$ ... (*iii*)

Now,

$BC = 4$ cm [Given]

$\Rightarrow BR + CR = 4$

$\Rightarrow BR + BR - 1 = 4$ [From (*iii*)]

$\Rightarrow 2BR = 5$cm

$\Rightarrow BR = 2.5$ cm

$\Rightarrow BP = BR = 2.5$ cm [From (*iv*)]

$\therefore AP = AB + BP = 5 + 2.5 = 7.5$ cm

6. In Fig., two tangents TP and TQ are drawn to a circle with centre O from an external point T. Then $\angle PTQ$ is ***(Re)***

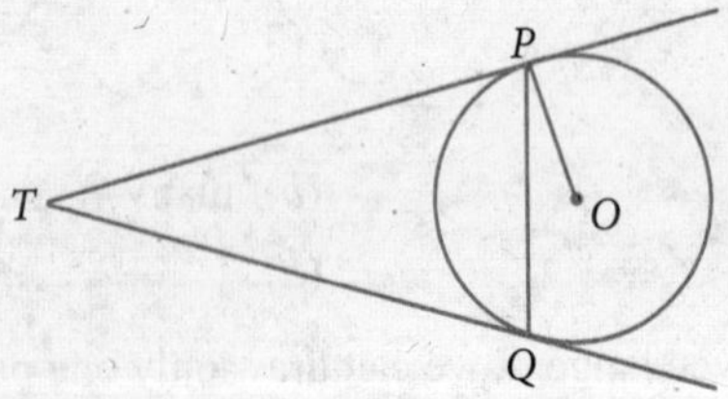

(*a*) $\angle OPQ$ (*b*) $2\angle OPQ$ (*c*) $\angle OQP$ (*d*) $2\angle OQP$

Sol. $TP = TQ$ ... (*i*)

(Tangents from the same point are same)

$\angle TQP = \angle TPQ$ ... (*ii*)

(angles of equal sides are equal)

Now TP is a tangent and OP is the radius.

$\therefore$ OP is perpendicular to PT.

$\therefore \angle OPT = 90° \Rightarrow \angle OPQ + \angle TPQ = 90°$

$\Rightarrow \angle TPQ = 90 - \angle OPQ$ ... (*iii*)

In ΔPTQ

$\angle TPQ + \angle PQT + \angle QTP = 180°$

[$\because$ sum of interior angle of a triangle is 180°]

From equation (*ii*) and (*iii*)

$\Rightarrow 2(90° - \angle OPQ) + \angle QTP = 180°$

$\Rightarrow 180° - 2\angle OPQ + \angle QTP = 180°$

$\Rightarrow 2\angle OPQ = \angle QTP$

7. If tangents PA and PB from a point P to a circle with centre O are inclined to each other at angle of 80°, then $\angle POA$ is equal to ***(Un)***

(*a*) 50° (*b*) 60° (*c*) 70° (*d*) 80°

Sol. We know that $\angle PAO + \angle AOB + \angle OBP + \angle BPA = 360°$

[Angle sum property]

$\Rightarrow 90° + \angle AOB + 90° + \angle BPA = 360°$

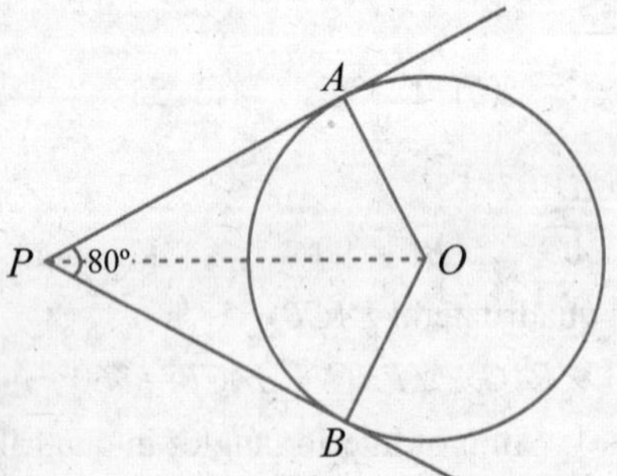

$\Rightarrow \angle AOB + 80° = 180°$

$\Rightarrow \angle AOB = 180° - 80° = 100°$

$\angle POA = \frac{1}{2} \times 100° = 50°$

8. In Fig., there are two concentric circles with centre O. If ARC and AQB are tangents to the smaller circle from the point A lying on the larger circle, what is the length of AC, if $AQ = 5$ cm? ***(Ev)***

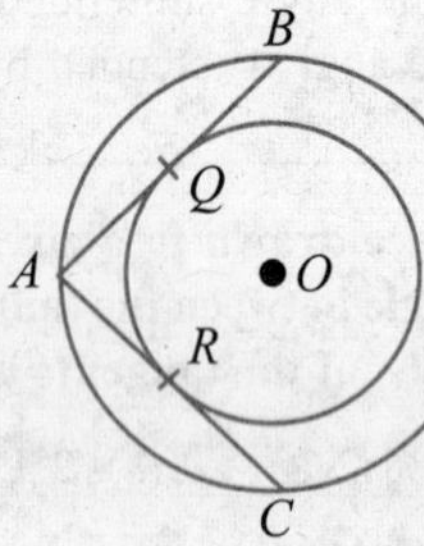

(*a*) 40 cm (*b*) 20 cm (*c*) 15 cm (*d*) 10 cm

Sol. Here AC and AB are tangents from external point A to the smaller circle.

$\therefore AC = AB$

Now, AB is the chord of a bigger circle and OQ is the perpendicular bisector of the chord AB.

or $AB = 2\,AQ$

Now, $AB = 2 \times 5 = 10$ cm {Given $AQ = 5$ cm}

$\therefore AC = 10$ cm {$\because AB = AC$}

Answer Key

1. (a) 2. (a) 3. (c) 4. (d) 5. (b)
6. (b) 7. (a) 8. (d)

Assertion and Reason **(1 M)**

Direction: In the following questions, a statement of Assertion (A) is followed by a statement of Reason (R). M the correct choice as.

(*a*) Both Assertion (A) and Reason (R) are true, and Reason (R) is the correct explanation of Assertion (A).

(*b*) Both Assertion (A) and Reason (R) are true, but Reason (R) is not the correct explanation of Assertion (A).

(*c*) Assertion (A) is true, but Reason (R) is false.

(*d*) Assertion (A) is false, but Reason (R) is true.

1. Assertion (A): If one angle in a cyclic quadrilateral is 40°, then the opposite angle is 140°.

Reason (R): Sum of opposite angles in a cyclic quadrilateral is 360°. ***(Re)***

Sol. $\because$ Sum of opposite angles in a cyclic quadrilateral is 180°.

$\therefore$ Angle + 40° = 180°

$\Rightarrow$ Angle = 180° – 40° = 140°

$\therefore$ Assertion is true.

Reason is false as the sum of opposite angles of cyclic quadrilateral = 180°.

Hence, Assertion (A) is true but reason (R) is false.

2. Assertion (A): If length of a tangent from an external point to a circle is 6 cm, then length of the other tangent from the same point is 6 cm.

Reason (R): Length of the tangents drawn from an external point to a circle are equal. ***(Re)***

Sol. The reason is correct. According to the properties of tangents to a circle, the lengths of the tangents drawn from an external point to a circle are equal.

Both assertion (A) and reason (R) is true and reason (R) is the correct explanation of assertion (A).

3. Assertion (A): If a chord *AB* subtends an angle of 60° at the centre of a circle, then the angle between the tangents at *A* and *B* is also 60°.

Reason (R): The length of the tangent from an external point *P* on a circle with centre *O* is always less than *OP*. ***(Re)***

Sol. Assertion is false due to the fact that the angle subtended by a chord at the center is twice the angle subtended by the same chord at any point on the circumference.

Reason is correct because it refers to the fundamental property drawn fron external point to a circle.

Hence, Assertion is false and reason is true.

Answer Key

1. (c) 2. (a) 3. (d)

Subjective Questions

Very Short Answer Type Questions **(1 or 2 M)**

1. In Fig., *BC* is tangent to the circle at point *B* of circle centred at *O*. *BD* is a chord of the circle so that *BAD* = 55°. Find $m\angle DBC$. **(*Un*) (CBSE, 2022)**

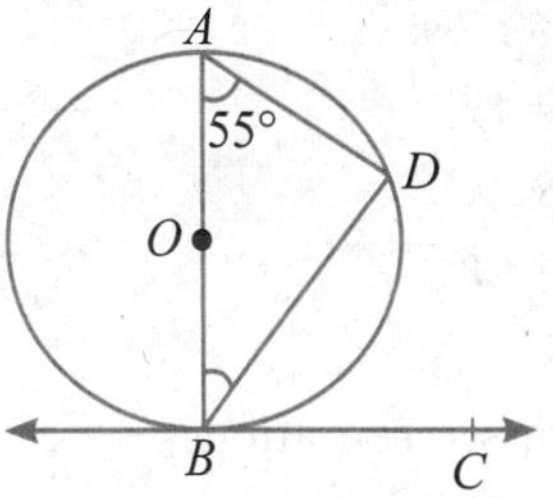

Sol. Since, *AB* is diameter therefore $\angle D = 90°$ (½ M)

$\Rightarrow \angle ABD = 35°$ (½ M)

Also, $AB \perp BC \Rightarrow \angle DBC = 90° - 35° = 55°$ (1 M)

2. In Fig. 4, a circle touches all the four sides of a quadrilateral *ABCD*. If *AB* = 6 cm, *BC* = 9 cm and *CD* = 8 cm, then find the length of *AD*. **(*Ev*) (CBSE 2020)**

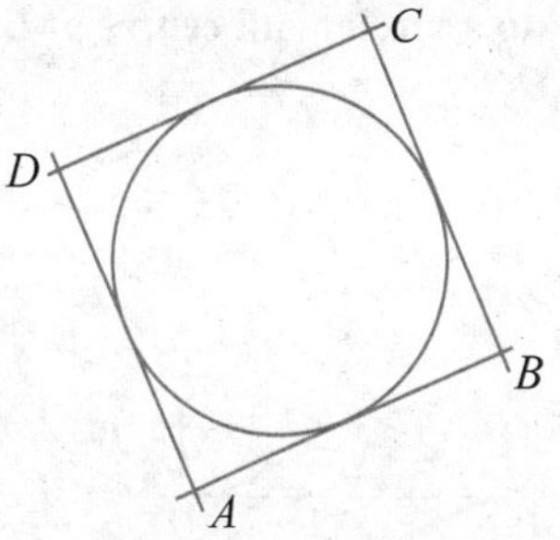

Sol. The figure given in the question is below.

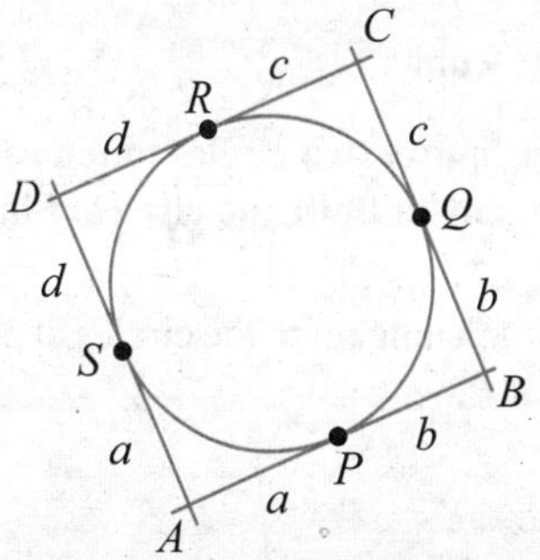

From the property of tangents we know that, the length of two tangents drawn from the same extemal point will be equal. Therefore we have the following:

$SA = AP$, $PB = BQ$, $QC = CR$, $DR = DS$ (½ M)

For our convenience, let us represent *SA* and *AP* by *a*, *PB* and *BQ* by *b*, *QC* and *CR* by *c* and *DR* and *DS* by *d*.

It is given in the problem that, *AB* = 6 Observing the figure, we can rewrite the above equation as follows:

$AP + PB = 6$

$\Rightarrow a + b = 6$

$\Rightarrow b = 6 - a$ (½ M)

$BC = 9$ (Given)

Since, $BQ + QC = BC$

Therefore,

$\Rightarrow BQ + QC = 9$

$\Rightarrow b + c = 9$

$\Rightarrow 6 - a + c = 9$

$\Rightarrow c = a + 3$ (½ M)

Also, $CD = 8$ (Given)

$\Rightarrow CR + RD = 8$

$\Rightarrow c + d = 8$

$\Rightarrow a + 3 + d = 8$

$\Rightarrow a + d = 5$

As per our representations, we can write the above equation as follows:

$SA + DS = 5$

Observing the figure, we can write the following,

$SA + DS = AD$

Comparing with the above equation we found that the length of side AD is 5 cm. (½ M)

3. In Fig., find the length of the tangent PQ drawn from the point P to a circle with centre at O, given that OP = 12 cm and OQ = 5cm. *(Ap)* **(CBSE, 2020)**

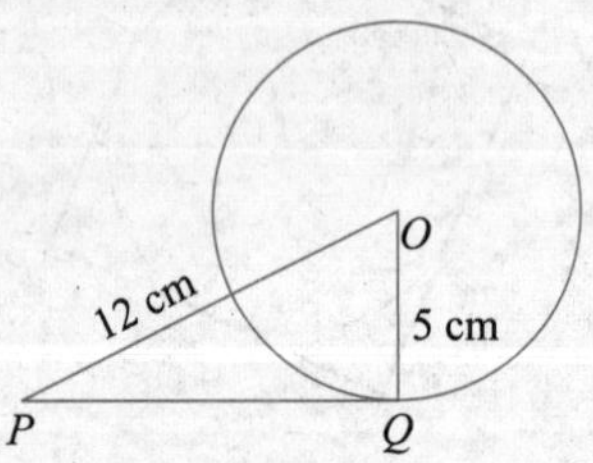

Sol. $PQ^2 = 144 - 25 = 119$ (½ M)

$\therefore PQ = \sqrt{119}$ units (½ M)

4. In the given figure, two circles touch each other at C and AB is a tangent to both the circles. Find the measure of $\angle ACB$. *(Un)*

Sol. Draw a common tangent to the circles at point C meeting the tangent AB at P.

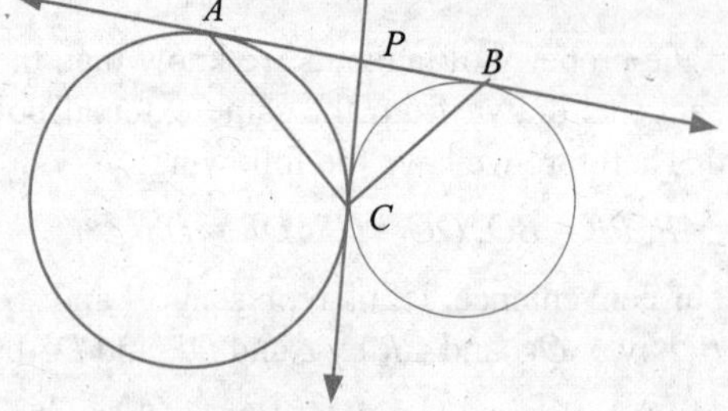

$\because$ The lengths of tangents drawn from an external point to a circle are equal.

$\therefore PA = PC$ and $PB = PC$.

$\Rightarrow \angle PAC = \angle PCA$ [$\because$ Angles opposite to equal sides are equal]

and $\angle PBC = \angle PCB$ (1 M)

$\therefore \angle PAC + \angle PBC = \angle PCA + \angle PCB = \angle ACB$

$\Rightarrow \angle PAC + \angle PBC + \angle ACB = 2\angle ACB$

$\Rightarrow 180^\circ = 2\angle ACB \Rightarrow \angle ACB = 90^\circ$ (1 M)

[By angle sum property]

Mistakes 101 : What not to do!

In problems involving multiple circles, students may forget to consider the possibility of common tangents between the circles.

Misapplying the theorems of tangents and chords, especially in cases where points lie inside the circle.

Forgetting to consider common tangents between multiple circles.

5. Prove that a pair of tangents to a circle are equally inclined to the line joining to centre of the circle to the external point. *(Ev)*

Sol. Given: Let AP and BP are two tangents, from external point P, to a circle with centre O.

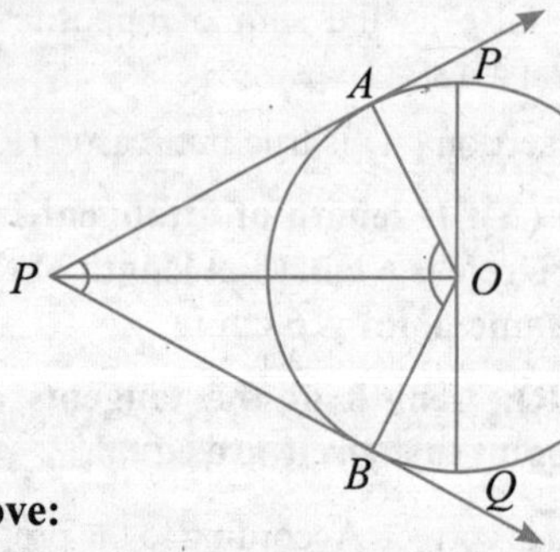

To prove:

$\angle APO = \angle BPO$ (½ M)

Proof: In ΔAPO and ΔBPO

$OA = OB$ (radii)

$AP = BP$ (The length of tangents drawn to a circle are equal to each other.)

$OP = OP$ (common)

$\therefore \Delta APO \cong \Delta BPO$ (by *SSS* congruency) (½ M)

$\angle APO = \angle BPO$ (By CPCT)

Hence, they are equally inclined (1 M)

Nailing the Right Answer

Students should know which congruency criteria to use while proving congruence of triangles

Short Answer Type Questions (2 or 3 M)

1. A quadrilateral *ABCD* is drawn to circumscribe a circle. Prove that *AB* + *CD* = *AD* + *BC*. **(*Un*)(CBSE, 2020)**

Sol.

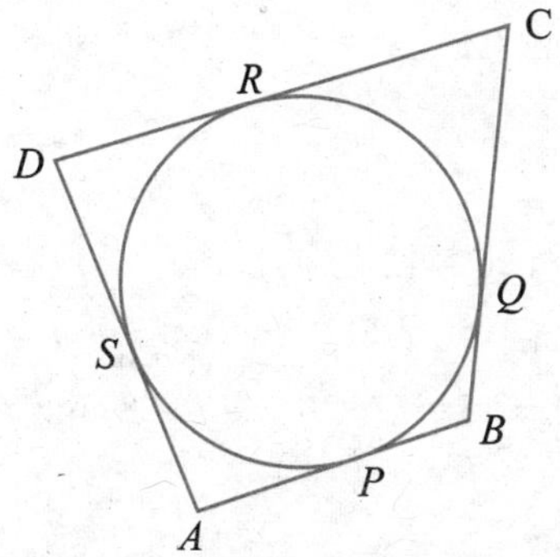

(½ M)

Proof: $AP = AS$

$BP = BQ$

$CR = CQ$

$DR = DS$ (1 M)

By adding,

$\Rightarrow AP + BP + CR + DR = AS + BQ + CQ + DS$ (½ M)

$\Rightarrow AB + CD = AD + BC$ (1 M)

2. Prove that the tangents drawn at the end points of a chord of a circle make equal angles with the chord. **(*Un*)**

Sol. Let *MN* be a chord of a circle with centre *O* and let *MQ* and *NQ* be the tangents at *M* and *N* respectively.

Join *OQ* and let *OQ* intersects *MN* at point *A*. (½ M)

We need to prove that $\angle QMA = \angle QNA$.

In triangles *QAM* and *QAN*, we have

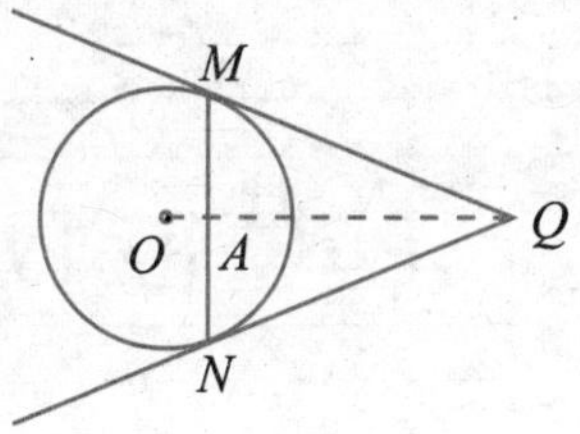

(1 M)

$QM = QN$ (Tangents from same point *Q*)

$\angle MQA = \angle NQA$ (½ M)

[∵ *QM* and *QN* are equally inclined to *OQ*]

and $QA = QA$ [Common]

Therefore,

$\Delta QMA \cong \Delta QNA$ [by *SAS* congruency rule] (½ M)

$\therefore \angle QMA = \angle QNA$. [by C.P.C.T] (½ M)

Hence proved

3. *A* is a point at a distance 13 cm from the centre *O* of a circle of radius 5 cm. *AP* and *AQ* are the tangents to the circle at *P* and *Q*. If a tangent *BC* is drawn at a point *R* lying on the minor arc *PQ* to intersect *AP* at *B* and *AQ* at *C*, find the perimeter of the Δ*ABC*.

(*Un*) (NCERT Exemplar)

Sol. Since, tangent at any point of a circle is perpendicular to the radius through the point of contact

So, $OPA = 90°$ (½ M)

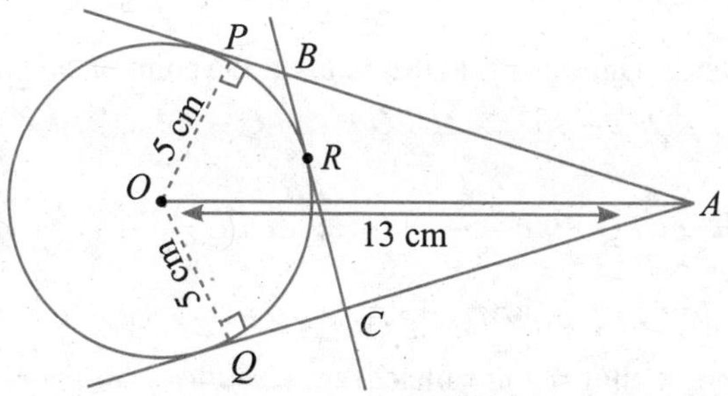

(½ M)

Now, in ΔOAP,

$OA^2 = OP^2 + PA^2$

$\Rightarrow 169 = 25 + PA^2$

$\Rightarrow PA = \sqrt{144} = 12$ cm (½ M)

Now, the perimeter of $\Delta ABC = AB + BC + CA$

$= AB + BR + RC + CA = (AB + BR) + (RC + CA)$ (½ M)

Since, tangents from an external point to a circle are equal so

$BR = BP$, $RC = CQ$ and $AP = AC$

Therefore, perimeter of $\Delta ABC = (AB + BR) + (RC + CA)$

$= (AB + BP) + (CQ + CA)$

$= AP + AQ = 2AP$ (½ M)

[Since, $AP = AQ$]

$= 2 \times 12 = 24$ cm

Hence, the required perimeter of $\Delta ABC = 24$ cm. (½ M)

4. Two tangents *TP* and *TQ* are drawn to a circle with centre *O* from an external point *T*. Prove that ∠*PTQ* = 2∠*OPQ*. **(*Re*)**

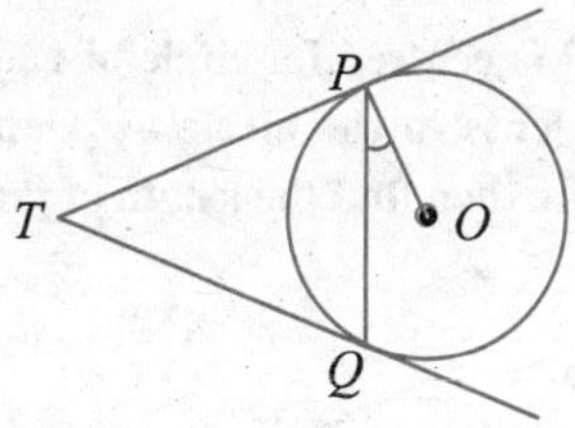

Sol. Given: *TP* and *TQ* are the tangents to a circle having centre *O*. (½ M)

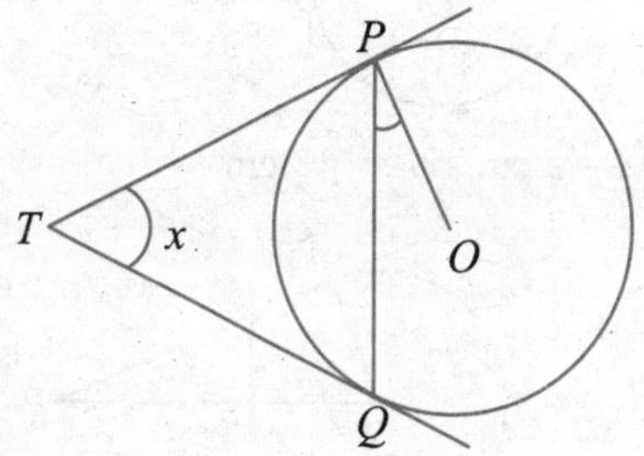

To prove: $\angle PTQ = 2\angle OPQ$ (½ M)

Proof: We know that the tangents drawn from an external point are equal.

$\therefore PT = TQ \Rightarrow \angle TPQ = \angle TQP$ (½ M)

[Equal sides have equal opposite angles]

In ΔPTQ, $\angle PTQ + \angle TPQ + \angle TQP = 180°$

[Sum of interior angles of a triangle]

$\Rightarrow x° + \angle TPQ + \angle TPQ = 180° \Rightarrow 2\angle TPQ = 180° - x°$

$\Rightarrow \angle TPQ = 90° - \dfrac{x}{2}$ ...(i) (½ M)

Since, tangent is $\perp$ to the radius at the point of contact.

$\therefore \angle OPT = 90° \Rightarrow \angle OPQ + \angle TPQ = 90°$

$\Rightarrow \angle OPQ + 90° - \dfrac{x}{2} = 90° \Rightarrow \angle OPQ = \dfrac{x}{2}$ (½ M)

$\Rightarrow 2\angle OPQ = \angle PTQ$ $[\because \angle PTQ = x]$ (½ M)

5. Prove that the parallelogram circumscribing a circle is a rhombus. ***(Un)* (CBSE, 2023)**

Sol.

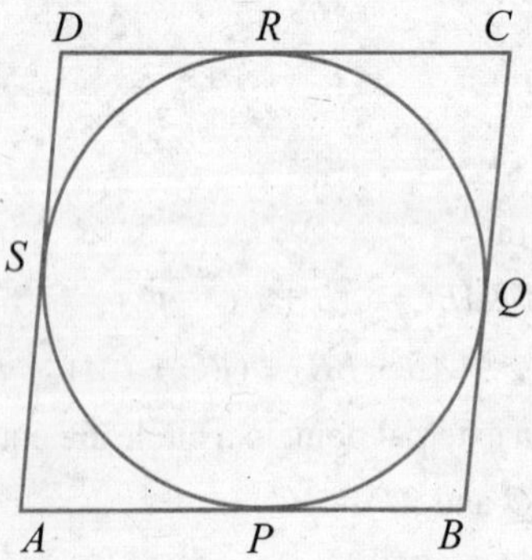

(½ M)

$AP = AS$
$BP = BQ$
$CQ = CR$
$DR = DS$

Tangents from external point (1 M)

$AB + DC = AP + PB + DR + RC$

$= AS + BQ + DS + CQ = AD + BC$ (1 M)

Since, $ABCD$ is a llgm, $AB = DC$, $AD = BC$

$2AB = 2AD \Rightarrow AB = AD \Rightarrow ABCD$ is a rhombus (½ M)

6. In Figure, *O* is centre of a circle of radius 5 cm. *PA* and *BC* are tangents to the circle at *A* and *B* respectively. If *OP* = 13 cm, then find the length of tangents *PA* and *BC*. ***(An)***

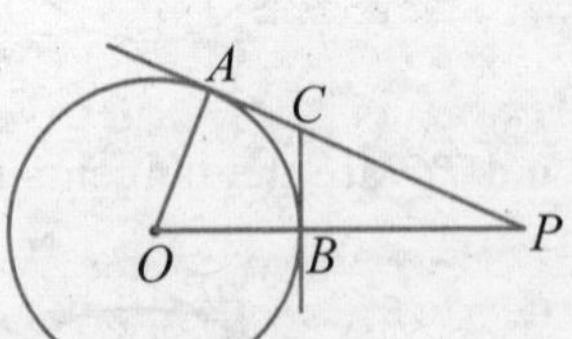

Sol. Given $OA = 5$ cm, $OP = 13$ cm

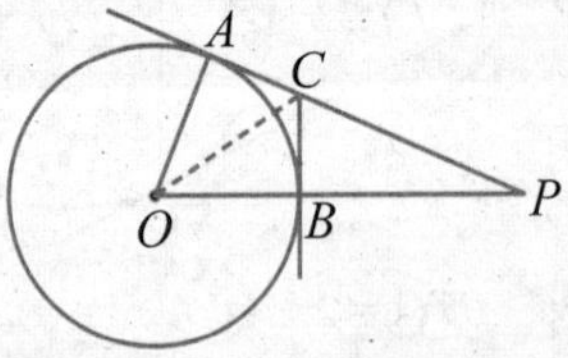

We know that tangents is perpendicular to the radius of a circle

So $\angle OAP = 90°$

In ΔAOP by pythagoras theorem

$(OP)^2 = (OA)^2 + (PA)^2 \Rightarrow 13^2 = 5^2 + (PA)^2$

$\Rightarrow (PA)^2 = 144 \Rightarrow PA = 12$ cm (1 M)

Now

C is a point on tangent PA

So, $PA = CA + PC$

Let $CA = x$ cm then.

$\Rightarrow 12 = x + PC \Rightarrow PC = 12 - x$

Now $AC = BC = x$ cm

Also $OP = OB + PB \Rightarrow 13 = 5 + PB \Rightarrow PB = 8$ cm (1 M)

In ΔPCB, $\angle B = 90°$

$(PC)^2 = (BC)^2 + (PB)^2$

$\Rightarrow (12 - x)^2 = x^2 + 8^2 \Rightarrow 144 + x^2 - 24x = x^2 + 64$

$\Rightarrow 24x = 144 - 64 \Rightarrow 24x = 80 \Rightarrow x = \dfrac{80}{24} = \dfrac{10}{3}$ cm

then $BC = x = \dfrac{10}{3}$ cm, $PA = 12$ cm (1 M)

Topper's Explanation ***(CBSE 2020)***

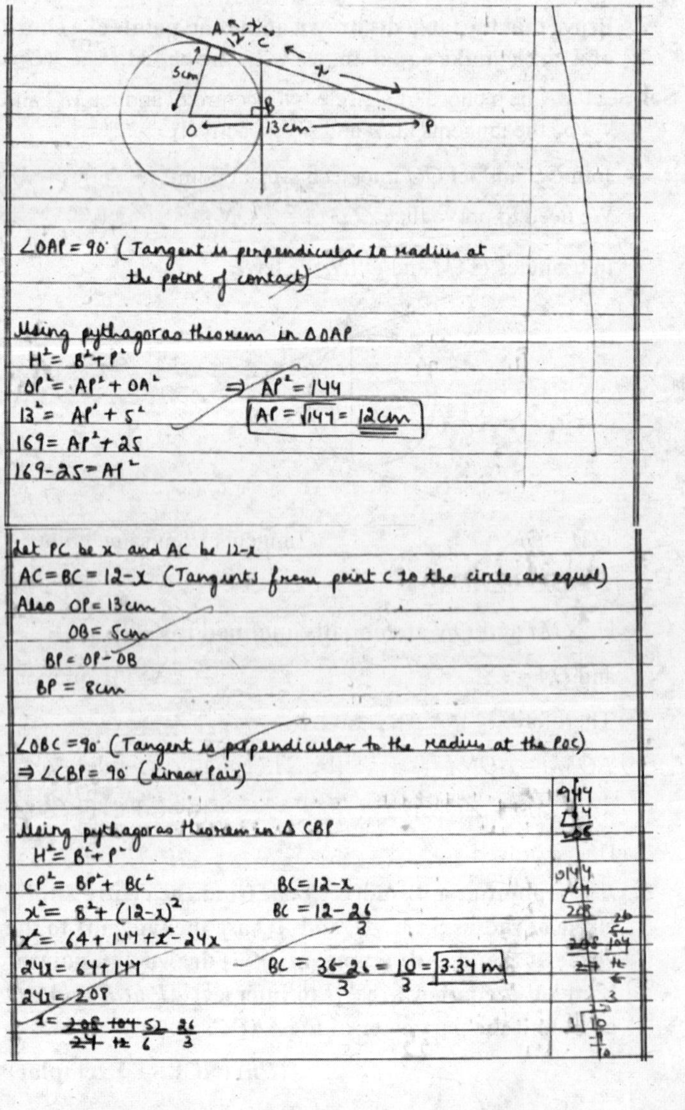

Long Answer Type Questions (4 or 5 M)

1. In Figure, *PQ* and *RS* are two parallel tangents to a circle with centre *O* and another tangent *AB* with point of contact *C* intersecting *PQ* at *A* and *RS* at *B*. Prove that $\angle AOB = 90^{\circ}$. ***(An)***

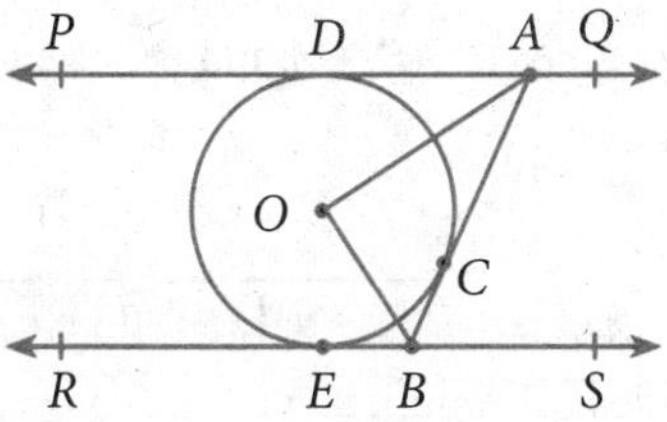

Sol. Join *O* and *C*

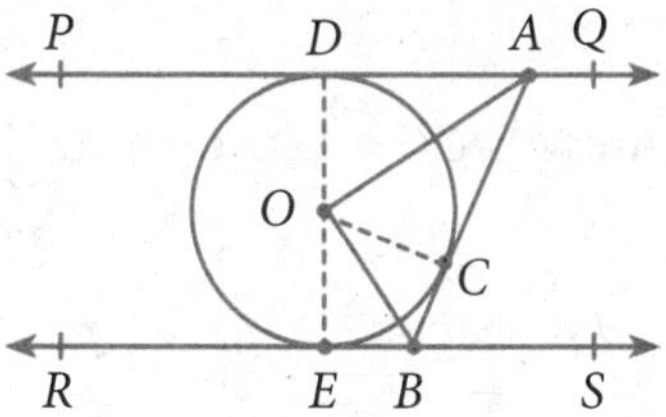

(1 M)

Now, In ΔADO & ΔACO,

$AO = AC$ (tangent drawn from same external point) *(1 M)*

$AO = AO$ (common)

$DO = CO$ (radius)

$\Delta ADO \cong \Delta ACO$ (SSS cong.) *(1 M)*

$\angle AOD = \angle AOC$ (By CPCT) ... *(i)*

Similarly, $\angle BOE = \angle BOC$ ... *(ii)*

Also given, $PQ \parallel RS$

DE is diameter hence it is straingt line *(1 M)*

$\angle AOD + \angle AOC + \angle BOC + \angle BOE = 180^{\circ}$

$2(\angle AOC + \angle BOC) = 180^{\circ}$

$\angle AOB = 90^{\circ}$ Proved *(1 M)*

Mistakes 101 : What not to do!

In a congruent triangle, Students might misidentify congruent parts, using incorrect congruence criteria, and neglecting corresponding angles and sides.

2. In Figure, *PQ* is a chord of length 8 cm of a circle of radius 5 cm. The tangents at *P* and *Q* meet at a point *T*. Find the length of *TP*. ***(Un)***

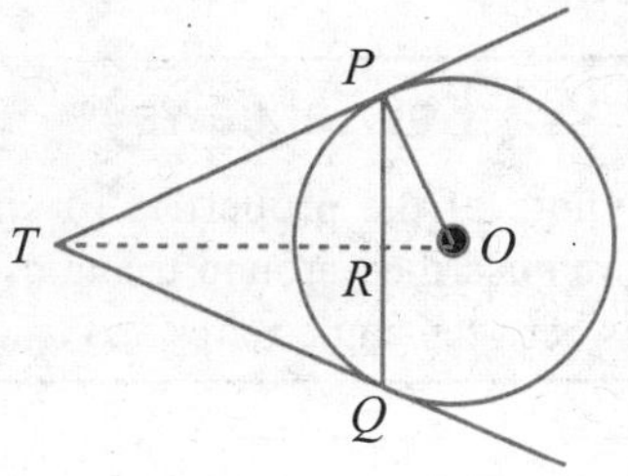

Sol. Join *OT*.

Let it meets *PQ* at the point *R*.

Then ΔTPQ is isosceles triangle, *TO* is the angle bisector of $\angle PTO$.

[$\because TP = TQ$ = Tangents from *T* upon the circle] *(1 M)*

$\therefore OT \perp PQ$

$\therefore$ *OT* bisects *PQ*. *(½ M)*

$PR = RQ = 4$ cm

Now, $OR = \sqrt{OP^2 - PR^2} = \sqrt{5^2 - 4^2} = 3$ cm *(1 M)*

Now, $\angle TPR + \angle RPO = 90^{\circ}$ ($\because TPO = 90^{\circ}$) *(½ M)*

$\angle TPR + \angle PTR$ ($\because TRP = 90^{\circ}$)

$\angle RPO = \angle PTR$ *(1 M)*

$\therefore$ Right triangle *TRP* is similar to the right triangle *PRO* [By *A–A* rule of similar triangles]

$\therefore \dfrac{TP}{PO} = \dfrac{RP}{RO} \Rightarrow \dfrac{TP}{5} = \dfrac{4}{3} \Rightarrow TP = \dfrac{20}{3}$ cm *(1 M)*

Nailing the Right Answer

Use the concept of similarity to solve problems involving circles and their elements.

3. In the figure given below, *O* is the centre of a circle of radius 5 cm, *T* is a point such that *OT* = 13 cm and *OT* intersects the circle at *E*. If *AB* is the tangent to the circle at *E*, find the length of *AB*. ***(Cr)***

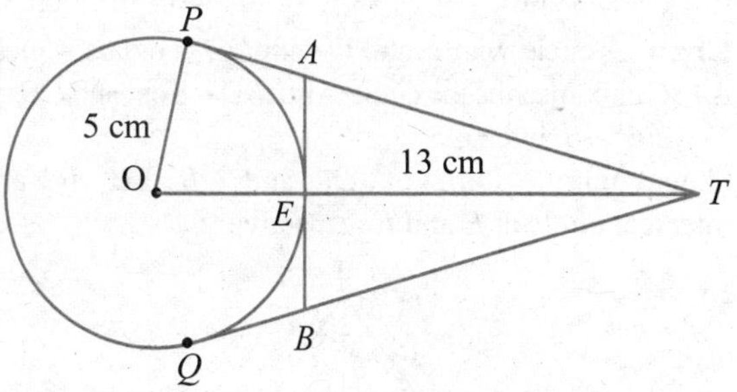

Sol. Since, tangent is perpendicular to the radius drawn through the point of contact.

So, *OP* is perpendicular to *PT*.

$\Rightarrow \angle OPT = 90^{\circ}$ *(½ M)*

In ΔOPT,

$OT^2 = OP^2 + PT^2$ [By Pythagoras Theorem]

$\Rightarrow PT^2 = OT^2 - OP^2 = 13^2 - 5^2 = 169 - 25 = 144$

So $PT = 12$ cm *(½ M)*

Since, the length of pair of tangents from an external point *T* is equal.

So, $QT = PT = 12$ cm

Now, $TA = PT - PA = 12 - PA$ ...*(i)* *(½ M)*

and $TB = QT - QB = 12 - QB$ ...*(ii)* *(½ M)*

Also, $PA = AE$ and $QB = EB$ ...*(iii)*

[Since, pair of tangents are equal]

$ET = OT - OE = 13 - 5 = 8$ cm

[Since, 5 cm = radius](½ M)

Now, OE is perpendicular to AB

[Since, tangent is perpendicular to radius]

$\Rightarrow \angle OEA = 90°$ (½ M)

Now, $\angle AET = 180° - \angle OEA = 90°$

[Linear pair] (½ M)

Now, in right-angled ΔAET,

$AT^2 = AE^2 + ET^2$ [by Pythagoras theorem]

$\Rightarrow (12 - PA)^2 = PA^2 + 8^2 \Rightarrow 144 + PA^2 - 24PA = PA^2 + 64$

$\Rightarrow 24PA = 80 \Rightarrow 3PA = 10$ So, $3AE = 10 \Rightarrow AE = 10/3$ (½ M)

Now, join O and Q,

Similarly, $3BE = 10 \Rightarrow BE = 10/3$ (½ M)

Hence, $AB = AE + BE = 10/3 + 10/3 = 20/3$ cm (½ M)

4. A triangle ABC is drawn to circumscribe a circle of radius 4 cm such that the segments BD and DC into which BC is divided by the point of contact D are of lengths 8 cm and 6 cm respectively (see. Fig.). Find the sides AB and AC

(Re)

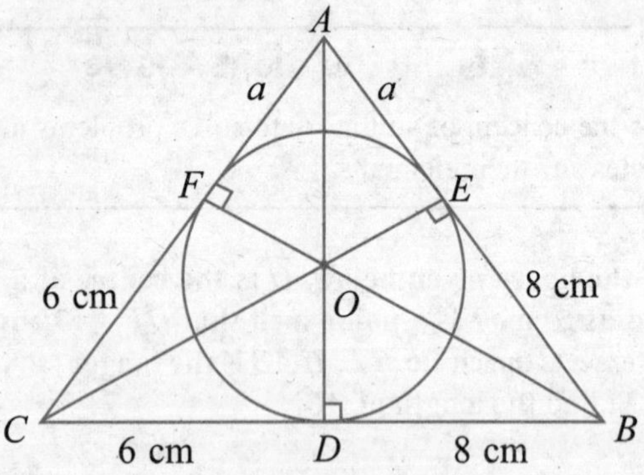

Sol. Given: A circle with centre O with OD = radius = 4 cm. Let ΔABC circumscribe the circle. Also, $BD = 8$ cm and $CD = 6$ cm.

To find: AB and AC

Construction: Join OA, OC and OB. Let AC and AB intersect circle at E and F respectively.

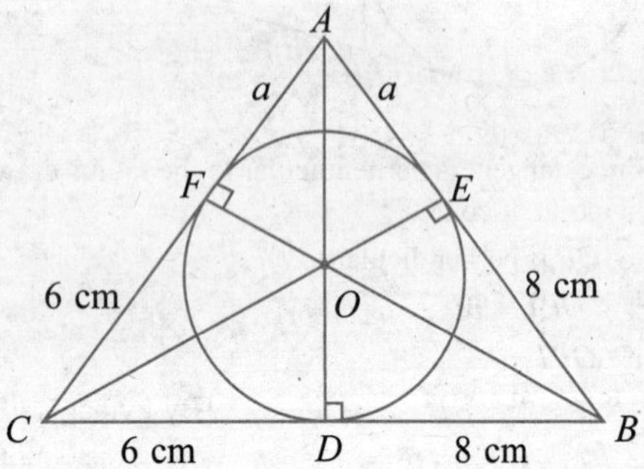

Consider the triangle ABC,

As we already know that the lengths sof any two tangents which are drawn from the same point to the circle are equal.

Therefore,

(i) $CF = CD = 6$ cm

(ii) $BE = BD = 8$ cm

(iii) Let $AE = AF = a$ (½ M)

So,

(i) $AB = EB + AE = 8 + a$

(ii) $CA = CF + FA = 6 + a$

(iii) $BC = DC + BD = 6 + 8 = 14$ (½ M)

Now the semi perimeter "s" of ΔABC can be calculated as:

$\Rightarrow 2s = AB + CA + BC$

On putting values of AB, CA and BC, we get

$2s = 28 + 2a$

$\Rightarrow s = 14 + a$ (½ M)

$\therefore$ Area of $\Delta ABC = \sqrt{s(s-a)(s-b)(s-c)}$, where a, b and c are the sides of triangle.

On solving this, we get

$= \sqrt{(14+a)48a}$ ... (i) (½ M)

Also, Area $[\Delta ABC]$ = Area $[\Delta AOC + \Delta AOB + \Delta COB]$ (½ M)

$= \frac{1}{2} \times AC \times OF + \frac{1}{2} \times AB \times OE + \frac{1}{2} \times BC \times OD$

$= \frac{1}{2} \times (6 + a) \times 4 + \frac{1}{2} \times (8 + a) \times 4 + \frac{1}{2} \times 14 \times 4$ (½ M)

[$\because OF = OD = OE = 4$ cm (radius of circle)]

$= 2(6 + a) + 2(8 + a) + 28$

$= 12 + 2a + 16 + 2a + 28 = 4a + 56$ ...(ii)(½ M)

Now from (i) and (ii) we obtain,

$\sqrt{(14+a)48a} = 56 + 4a$ (½ M)

Now on squaring both the sides, we get

$(14 + a)48a = (56 + 4a)^2 \Rightarrow 48a(14 + a) = 4^2(14 + a)^2$

$\Rightarrow 48a = 16(14 + a) \Rightarrow 3a = 14 + a \Rightarrow 2a = 14$

$\therefore a = 7$ cm. (½ M)

Therefore, $AB = 8 + a = 8 + 7 = 15$ cm

and $CA = a + 6 = 13$ cm. (½ M)

Nailing the Right Answer

In addition to geometric methods, consider using algebraic methods such as coordinate geometry and formulas associated with Triangles.

Key Takeaways

Make a keynote of the properties of circles inscribed within or circumscribed around triangles, especially the relationships between angles, arcs and tangents.

MISCELLANEOUS EXERCISE

Multiple Choice Questions (1 M)

1. In given Fig. the length PB = ________ cm.

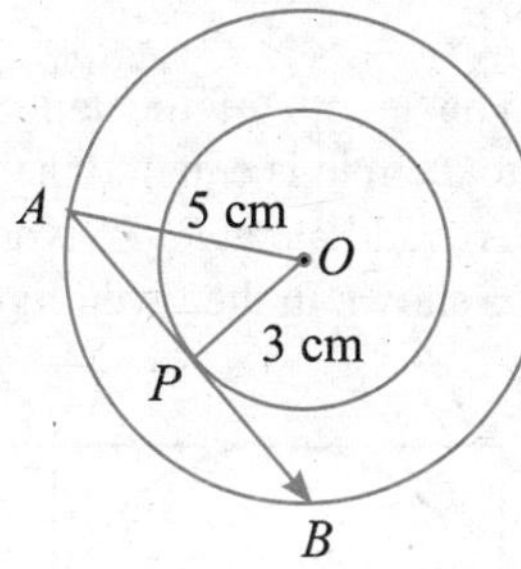

(*a*) 9 cm (*b*) 4 cm

(*c*) 15 cm (*d*) 7 cm

2. A circle has a centre O and radii OQ and OR. Two tangents, PQ and PR, are drawn from an external point, P.

In addition to the above information, which of these must also be known to conclude that the quadrilateral $PQOR$ is a square? **(CBSE CFPQ, 2023)**

(*i*) OQ and OR are at an angle of 90°.

(*ii*) The tangents meet at an angle of 90°.

(*a*) only (*i*)

(*b*) only (*ii*)

(*c*) either (*i*) or (*ii*)

(*d*) both (*i*) and (*ii*)

3. In the figure, if O is the centre of a circle, PQ is a chord and the tangent PR at P makes an angle of 50° with PQ, then $\angle POQ$ is equal to **(NCERT Exemplar)**

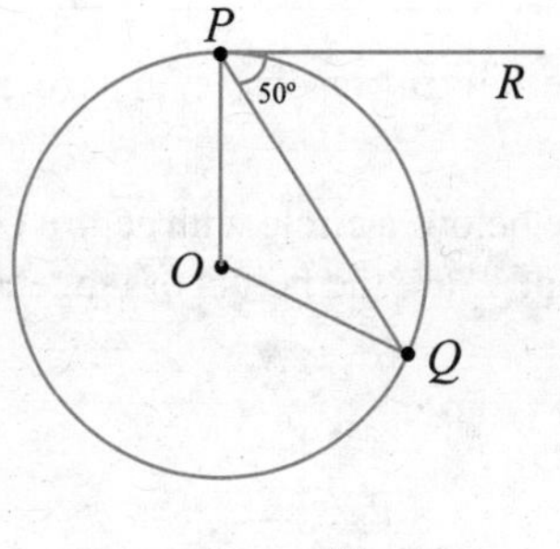

(*a*) 100° (*b*) 80°

(*c*) 90° (*d*) 75°

4. In the figure, AT is a tangent to the circle with centre O such that OT = 4 cm and $\angle OTA$ = 30°. Then AT is equal to **(NCERT Exemplar)**

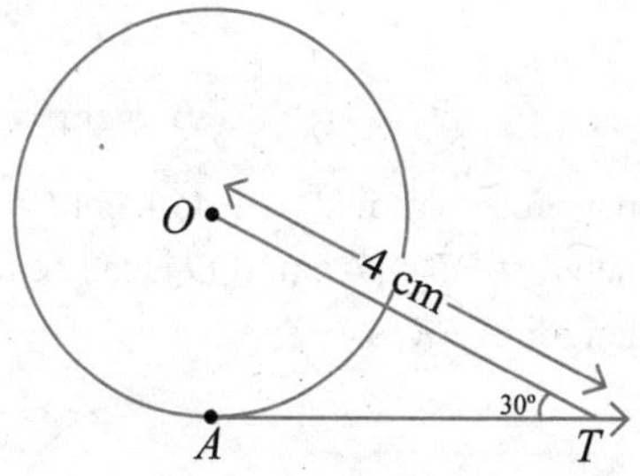

(*a*) 4 cm (*b*) 2 cm

(*c*) $2\sqrt{3}$ cm (*d*) $4\sqrt{3}$ cm

5. In the given figure, AB and AC are tangents to a circle with centre O and radius 8 cm, If OA = 17 cm, then the length of AC (in cm) is:

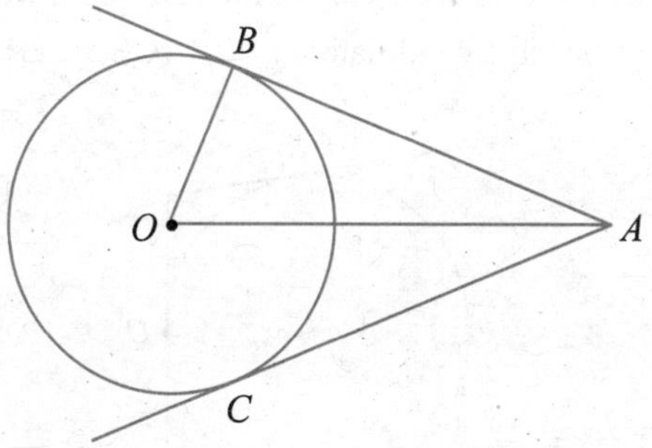

(*a*) 9 cm (*b*) 15 cm

(*c*) $\sqrt{353}$ cm (*d*) 25 cm

6. In fig., PA and PB are two tangents drawn from an external point P to a circle with centre C and radius 4 cm. If $PA \perp PB$, then the length of each tangent is:

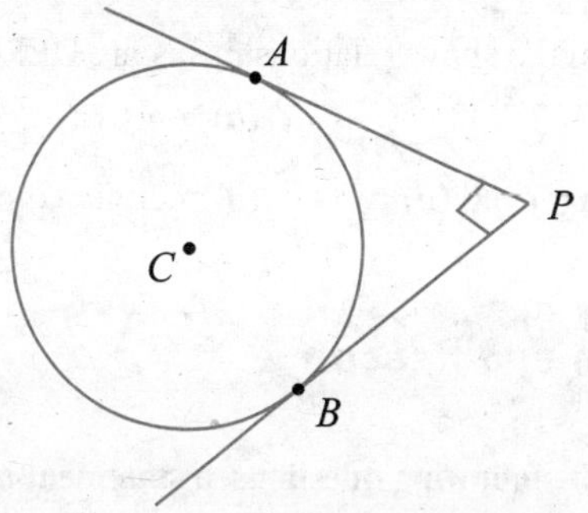

(*a*) 3 cm (*b*) 4 cm

(*c*) 5 cm (*d*) 6 cm

7. From a point P which is at a distance of 13 cm from the centre O of a circle of radius 5 cm, the pair of tangents PQ and PR to the circle are drawn. Then the area of the quadrilateral $PQOR$ is: **(NCERT Exemplar)**

(*a*) 60 cm^2 (*b*) 65 cm^2

(*c*) 30 cm^2 (*d*) 32.5 cm^2

8. If the two tangents inclined at an angle of 60° are drawn to a circle of radius 3 cm, then the length of each tangent is: **(CBSE, 2020)**

(*a*) 3 cm (*b*) $\frac{3\sqrt{3}}{2}$ cm

(*c*) $3\sqrt{3}$ cm (*d*) 6 cm

9. In Fig., on a circle of radius 7 cm, tangent *PT* is drawn from a point *P* such that $PT = 24$ cm. If *O* is the centre of the circle, then the length of *PR* is **(CBSE, 2020)**

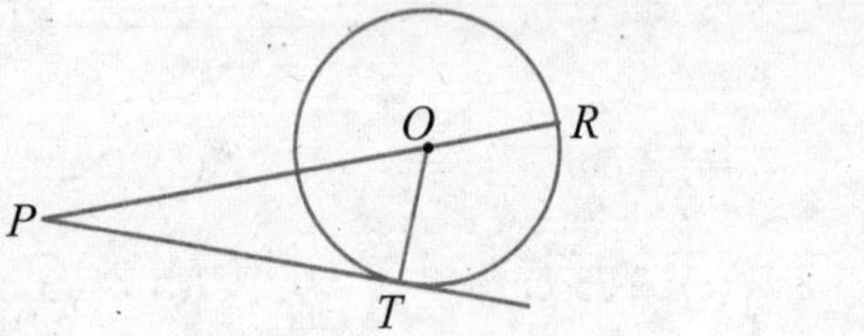

(*a*) 30 cm (*b*) 28 cm

(*c*) 32 cm (*d*) 25 cm

10. Raghav drew the following figure on a board where a circle is inscribed in a quadrilateral. **(CBSE CFPQ, 2023)**

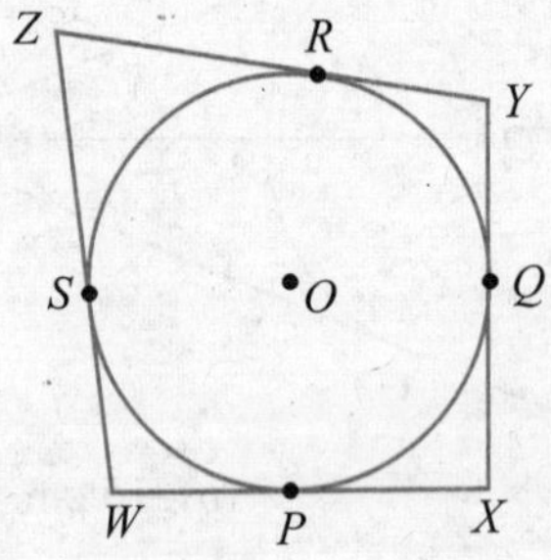

(Note: The figure is not to scale.)

Then he wrote the following relationships.

(*i*) $ZW + WX = XY + YZ$

(*ii*) $ZY + WX = ZW + YX$

Which of the above relationships is/are DEFINITELY true?

(*a*) only (*i*) (*b*) only (*ii*)

(*c*) both (*i*) and (*ii*) (*d*) neither (*i*) nor (*ii*)

Assertion and Reason (1 M)

Direction: In the following questions, a statement of Assertion (A) is followed by a statement of Reason (R). Mark the correct choice as:

(*a*) Both Assertion (A) and Reason (R) are true and Reason (R) is the correct explanation of Assertion (A).

(*b*) Both Assertion (A) and Reason (R) are true but Reason (R) is not the correct explanation of Assertion (A).

(*c*) Assertion (A) is true but Reason (R) is false.

(*d*) Assertion (A) is false but Reason (R) is true.

1. Assertion (A): The length of the tangent drawn from a point 8 cm away from the centre of circle of radius 6 cm is $2\sqrt{7}$ cm.

Reason (R): If the angle between two radii of a circle is 130°, then the angle between the tangents at the end points of radii at their point of intersection is 50°.

2. Assertion (A): If the distance between a point outside a circle and the center of the circle is greater than the radius of the circle, then two tangents can be drawn from the point to the circle.

Reason (R): The length of the tangent drawn from an external point to a circle is equal to the radius of the circle.

3. Assertion (A): A quadrilateral *PQRS* is drawn to circumscribe a given circle as shown in the given figure, then

$PQ + QR = PS + SR$.

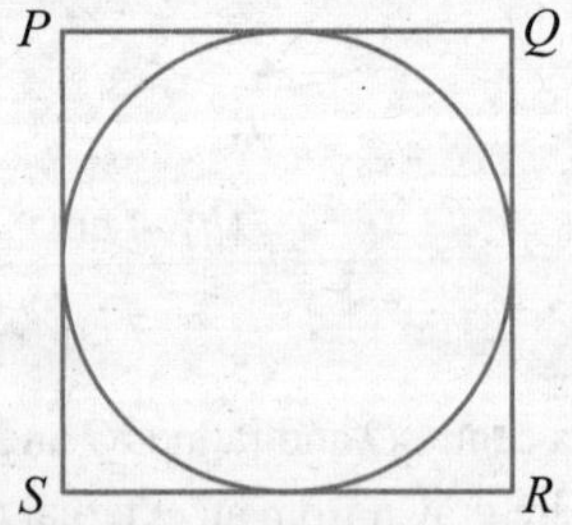

Reason (R): In two concentric circles, the chord of the larger circle, which touches the smaller circle, is bisected at the point of contact.

4. Assertion (A): *PQ* is a tangent to a circle with centre *O* at point *P*. If ΔOPQ is an isosceles triangle, then $\angle PQO = 45°$.

Reason (R): If two tangents inclined at 60° are drawn to a circle of radius 3 cm, then the length of each tangent is $3\sqrt{3}$ cm.

5. Assertion (A): A tangent to a circle is perpendicular to the radius through the point of contact.

Reason (R): The lengths of tangents drawn fron an external point to a circle are equal.

Subjective Questions

Very Short Answer Type Questions (1 or 2 M)

1. A line intersecting a circle in two points is called a __________. **(CBSE, 2020)**

2. In the figure below, a circle with centre *O* is inscribed inside ΔLMN. *A* and *B* are the points of tangency.

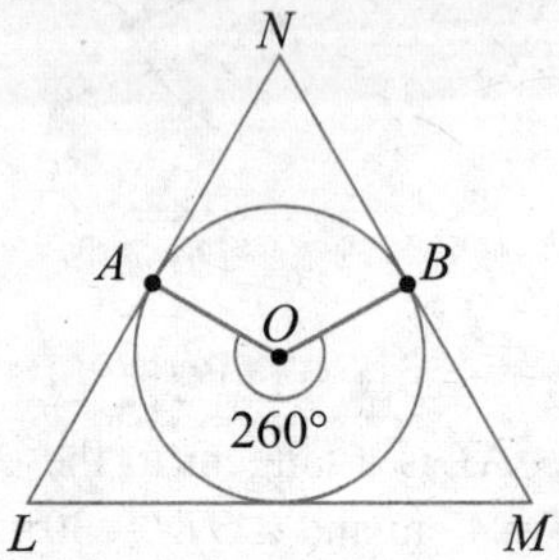

Find $\angle ANB$. Show your steps. **(CBSE CFPQ, 2023)**

3. In Fig., a circle is inscribed in a ΔABC, touching BC, CA and AB at P, Q and R respectively. If $AB = 10$ cm, $AQ = 7$ cm and $CQ = 5$ cm then find the length of BC.

(CBSE, 2020)

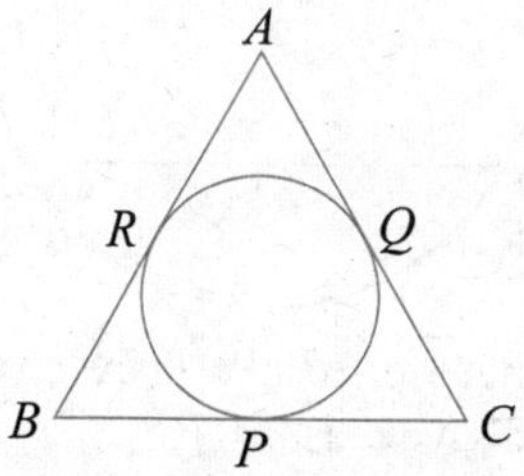

4. A point is 25 cm from the centre of a circle of radius 15 cm. Find the length of the tangent from the point to the circle. Show your steps. **(CBSE CFPQ, 2023)**

5. In the following figure, O is the centre of the circle and PQ and PS are tangents to the circle at points Q and S respectively.

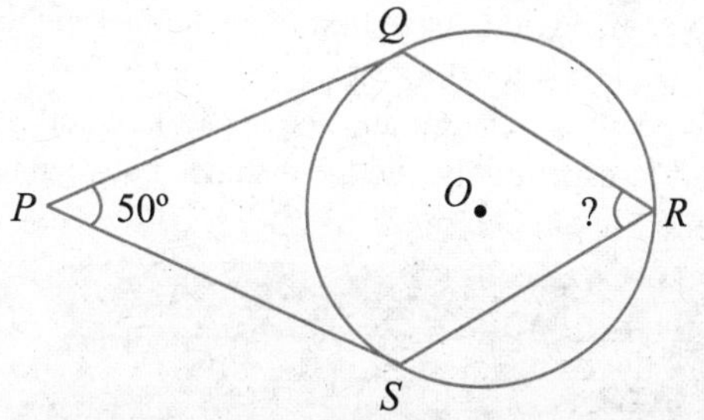

What is the measure of $\angle QRS$? Show your work.

(CBSE CFPQ, 2023)

6. In the given figure, common tangents AB and CD to the two circles with centres O_1 and O_2 intersect at E. Prove that $AB = CD$.

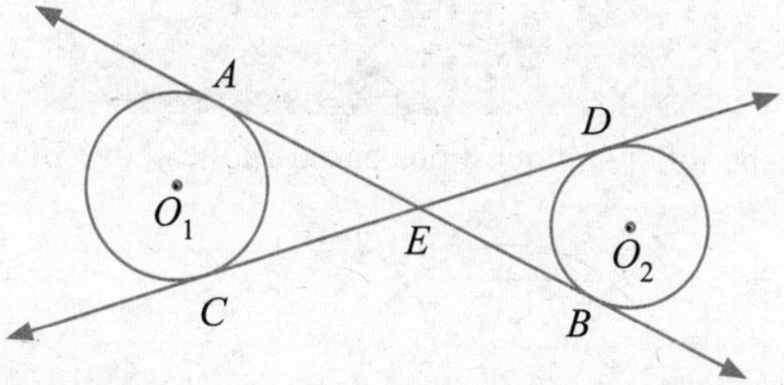

7. Shown below is a circle with centre O and three tangents drawn at points A, E and C. AE is a diameter of the circle. The tangents intersect at points B and D.

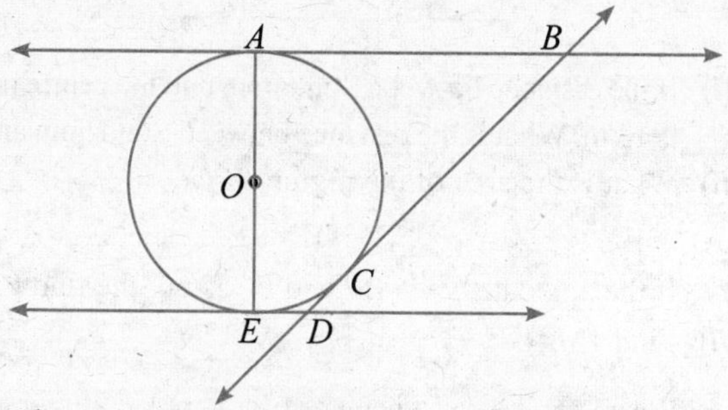

Based on the above information, evaluate whether the following statement is true or false. Justify your answer.
Atleast one pair of opposite sides of $AEDB$ is parallel.

Short Answer Type Questions

(2 or 3 M)

1. Prove that the angle between the two tangents drawn from an external point to a circle is supplementary to the angle subtended by the line-segment joining the points of contact at the center. **(NCERT Intext)**

2. A circle touches all the four sides of quadrilateral $ABCD$. Prove that $AB + CD = AD + DA$.

(CBSE SQP, 2023)

3. In Fig., perimeter of ΔPQR is 20 cm. Find the length of tangent PA. **(CBSE 2022)**

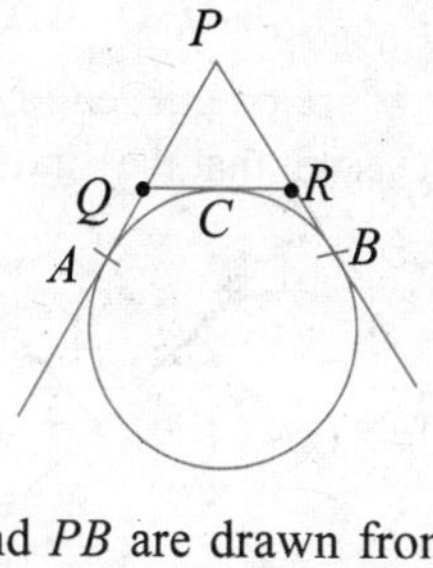

4. Tangents PA and PB are drawn from an external point P to two concentric circles with centre O and radii 8 cm and 5 cm respectively, as shown in the figure. If $AP = 15$ cm then find the length of BP.

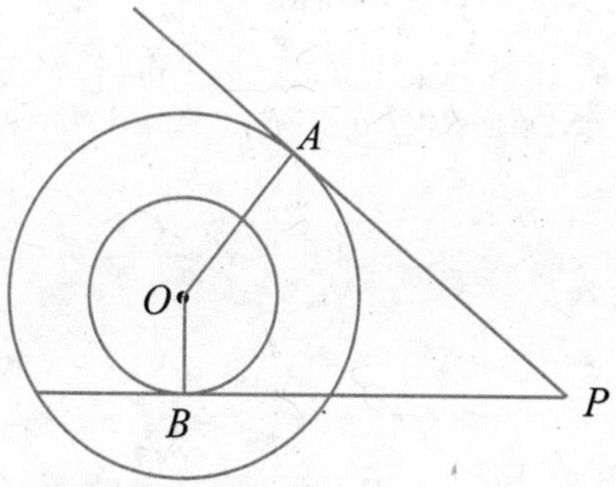

5. In the figure given below, PA is a tangent to the circle with centre O and PCB is a straight line.

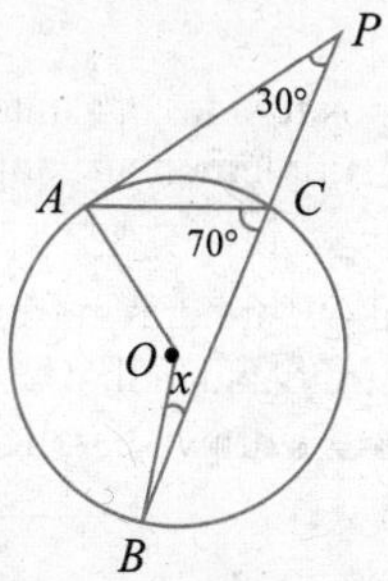

Find the measure of $\angle OBC$. Show your steps and give valid reasons. **(CBSE CFPQ, 2023)**

6. In the figure $PO \perp QO$. The tangents to the circle with centre O at P and Q intersect at a point T. Prove that PQ and OT are right bisectors of each other.

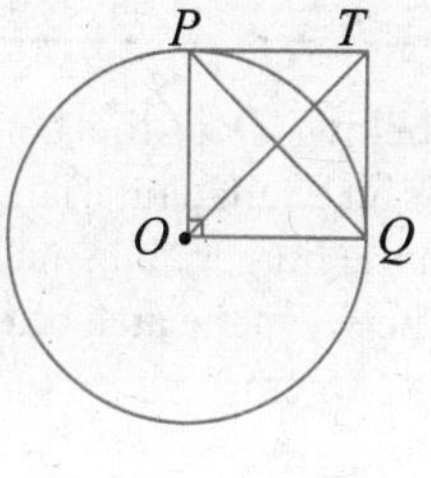

7. Shown below is a circle with centre O and tangents PQ and PR.

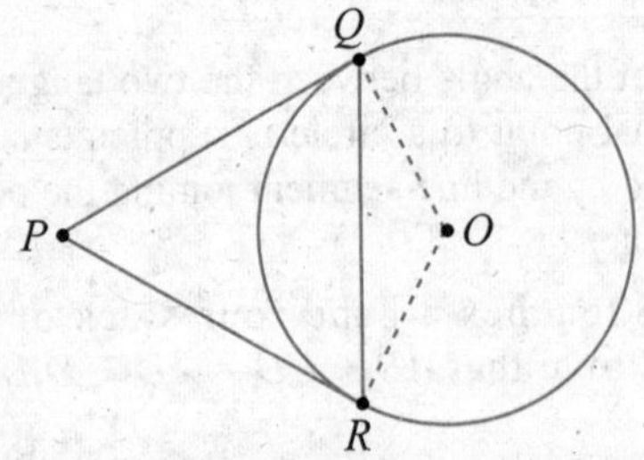

Using triangles QOR and PQR, and without doing any extra constructions, prove that the tangents PQ and PR are equal in length. **(CBSE CFPQ, 2023)**

8. Shown below is a circle with centre O. Tangents are drawn at points A and C, such that they intersect at point B.

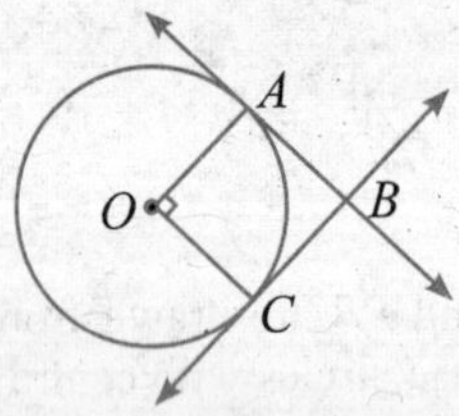

If $OA \perp OC$, then show that quadrilateral $OABC$ is a square.

Long Answer Type Questions (4 or 5 M)

1. In Fig., if a circle touches the side QR of ΔPQR at S and extended sides PQ and PR at M and N, respectively, then

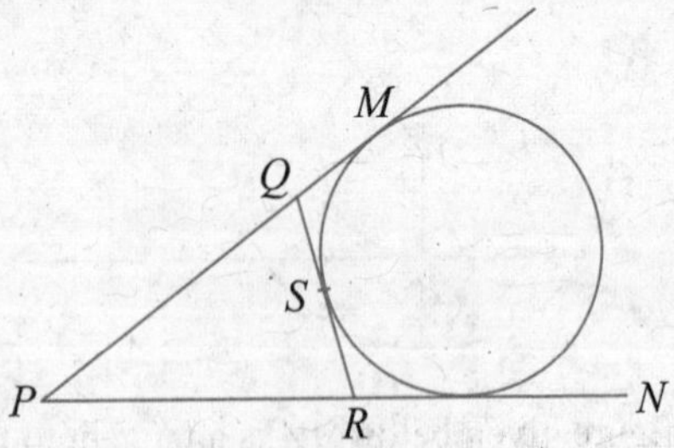

prove that $PM = \frac{1}{2}(PQ + QR + PR)$

2. Prove that the opposite sides of a quadrilateral circumscribing a circle subtend supplementary angles at the centre of the circle.

3. Tangents QA and QB are drawn from an external point Q to a circle with centre O, such that $\angle AQB = 30°$, as shown in figure. A chord BC is drawn parallel to the tangent QA, find $\angle BAC$.

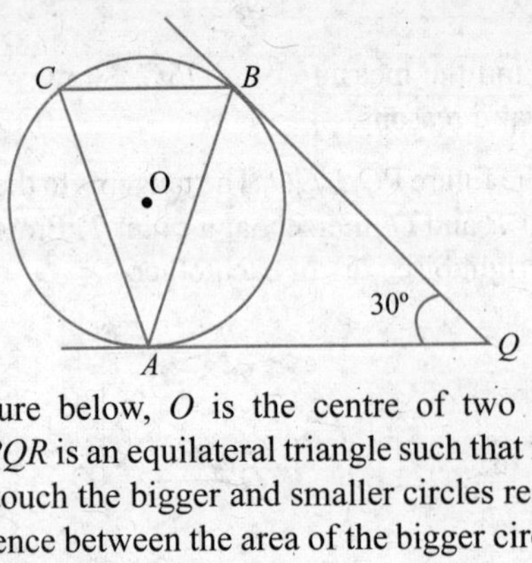

4. In the figure below, O is the centre of two concentric circles. ΔPQR is an equilateral triangle such that its vertices and sides touch the bigger and smaller circles respectively. The difference between the area of the bigger circle and the smaller circle is 616 cm^2.

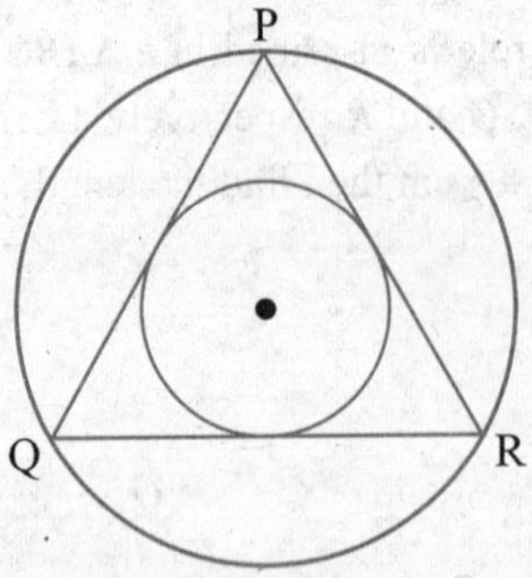

Find the perimeter of ΔPQR. Draw a rough diagram, show your work and give reasons.

(Note: Take π as $\frac{22}{7}$.) **(CBSE CFPQ, 2023)**

Case Based Questions

Case Based-I: Raman, Shyam, Rakhi, and Sundaram go to a maze near his school on a holiday. The shape of the maze is circular. No one wanted to go inside the maze first. After some time Sundaram entered the maze and later the rest of them entered the maze. At an instant, the positions of Raman, Shaym, Rakhi, and Sundaram are A, B, C and P respectively and the distance between the centre of the maze and Shyam is 5 m.

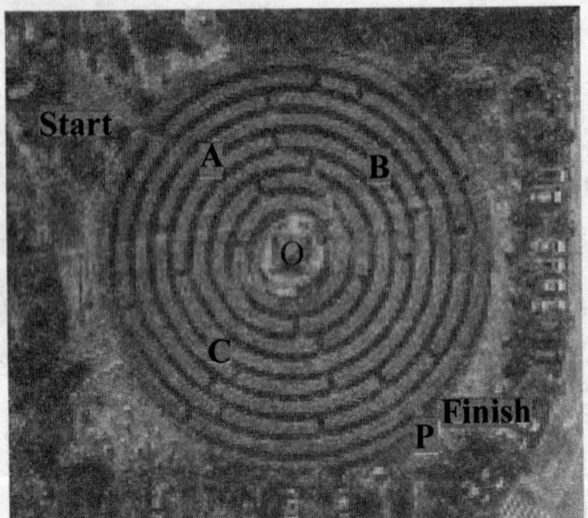

Answer the following questions based on the above situation.

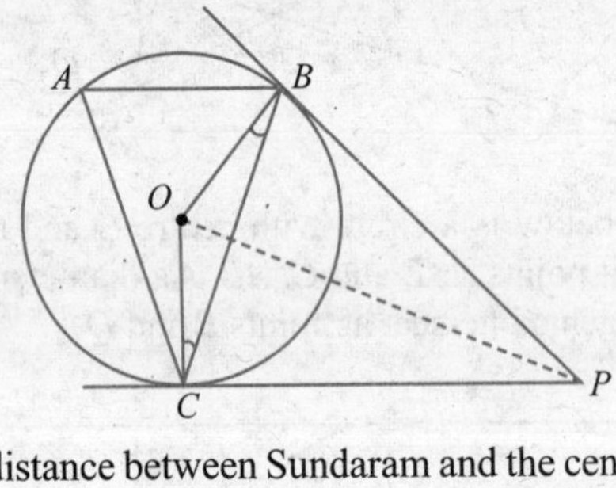

(*i*) If the distance between Sundaram and the centre of the maze is 13 m. What is the distance between Sundaram and Shyam?

(*ii*) What is the area of the region $BPCO$.

OR

If the angle between BP and PC is 60° the find $\angle BOC$.

(*iii*) Find $\angle BAC$.

Case Based-II: Ferris wheels are a popular attraction at fairs and amusement parks all over the world. They offer a unique and exciting experience for people of all ages. It is a large amusement ride consisting of a rotating upright wheel with passenger cars attached to the rim. The wheel is rotated by a motor and gears, and the cars rotate with the wheel. The cars are typically enclosed, and they have seats for riders.

Ravi with his four friends went to a fair and there they decided to enjoy the ride of the Ferris wheel. Due to the fear of the height, Ravi and one of his friends decided not to join them. They came out of the crowd and started observing their friends who were enjoying the ride. Ravi forms the figure as given below where the distance between P and Q is 50 m.

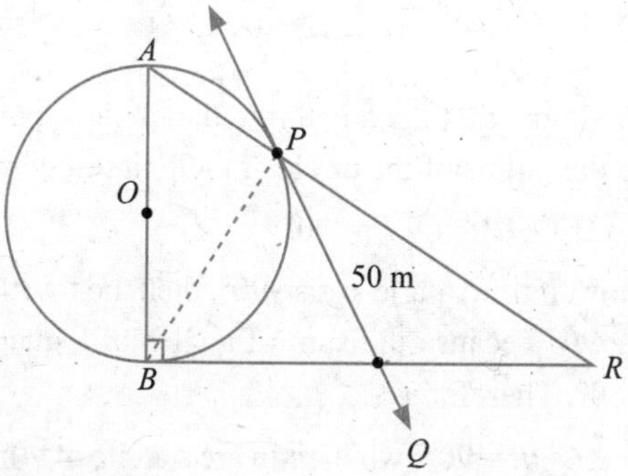

(*i*) Find the $\angle APB$.

(*ii*) Find the distance between B and Q.

OR

Find the distance between Q and R.

(*iii*) If the radius of the Ferris wheel is 10 m, then find the distance between A and R.

Case Based-III: The founders of Physics Wallah launched an event 'PW Sports Maniac', a mass health awareness campaign across PW Vidyapeeth and Pathshala. They planned a variety of sports activities to cater to different interests including, cricket, football, badminton, race, etc.

The centre of attraction of this sport event is a race as it was open to all students, regardless of their age or skill level. It was a great way to promote physical fitness and healthy competition among the students. The track for the race is shown in the figure below.

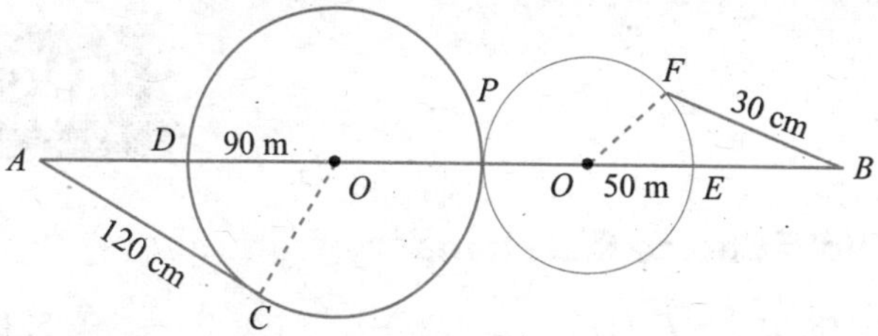

On the basis of the above information, answer the following questions.

(*i*) Find the length of the path OA.

(*ii*) Find the length of the path AD.

OR

Find the length of the path $O'B$.

(*iii*) Find the length of the line segment AB.

Case Based-IV: Running is a great way to improve your health. It is a low-impact activity that can be done by people of all ages and fitness levels. Running can help you to lose weight, improve your cardiovascular health, improve your mental health and reduce your risk of developing chronic diseases such as heart disease, stroke, and diabetes. It can also help to improve your sleep quality and boost your energy levels.

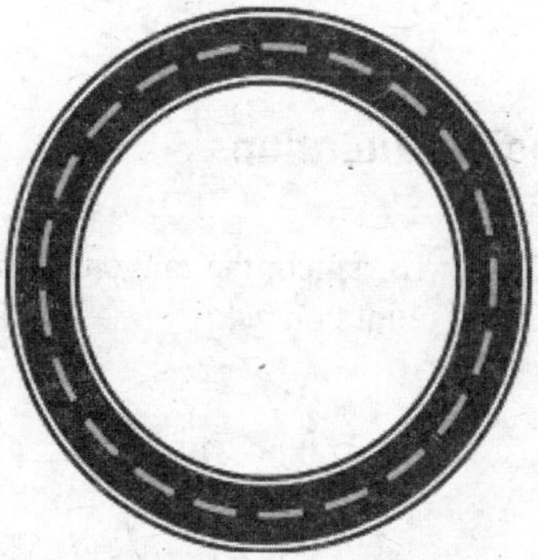

There is a circular track with an inner radius of 60 m and an outer radius of 100 m. Four boys were running on this circular track whose positions are represented by A, B, C, and D in the diagram represented below. On the basis of the above information answer the questions given below.

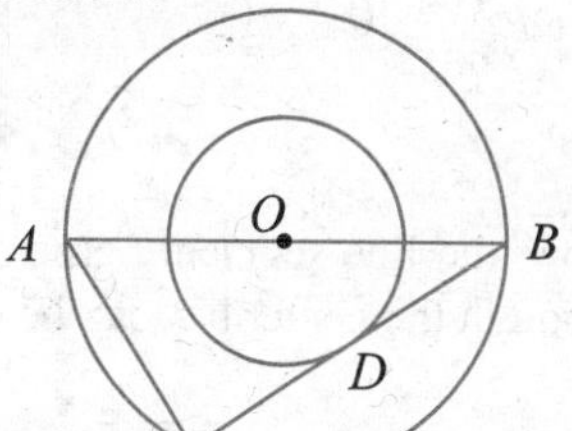

(*i*) Value of the $\angle ODB$ is

(*a*) 90° (*b*) 80° (*c*) 60° (*d*) 45°

(*ii*) The distance between D and B is

(*a*) 100 m (*b*) 80 m (*c*) 60 m (*d*) 160 m

(*iii*) The distance between C and B is

(*a*) 120 m (*b*) 100 m (*c*) 160 m (*d*) 200 m

(*iv*) Value of the $\angle ACB$ is

(*a*) 90° (*b*) 80° (*c*) 60° (*d*) 45°

(*v*) The distance between A and C is

(*a*) 120 m (*b*) 100 m (*c*) 160 m (*d*) 200 m

ANSWER KEYS

Multiple Choice Questions

1. (*b*) 2. (*c*) 3. (*a*) 4. (*c*) 5. (*b*) 6. (*b*) 7. (*a*) 8. (*c*) 9. (*c*) 10. (*b*)

Assertion and Reason

1. (*b*) 2. (*c*) 3. (*d*) 4. (*b*) 5. (*a*)

Case Based Questions

Case Based-IV

(*i*) (*a*) (*ii*) (*b*) (*iii*) (*c*) (*iv*) (*a*) (*v*) (*a*)

HINTS & EXPLANATIONS

Multiple Choice Questions

1. (*b*) Here, $OP \perp AB$, since, the tangent is perpendicular to the radius at point contact

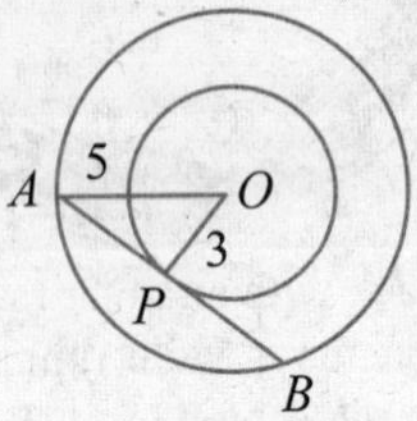

Now, in ΔOAP;

$AP = \sqrt{OA^2 - OP^2} = \sqrt{(5)^2 - (3)^2} = \sqrt{25 - 9}$

$= \sqrt{16} = 4\text{cm}$

Now, we know, the line segment perpendicular to a chord & passing through the center bisects the chord

$\therefore AP = PB$

$\therefore PB = 4$ cm

2. (*c*) Given that a circle has a centre *O* and radii *OQ* and *OR*. Two tangents, *PQ* and *PR*, are drawn from an external point *P* as shown below.

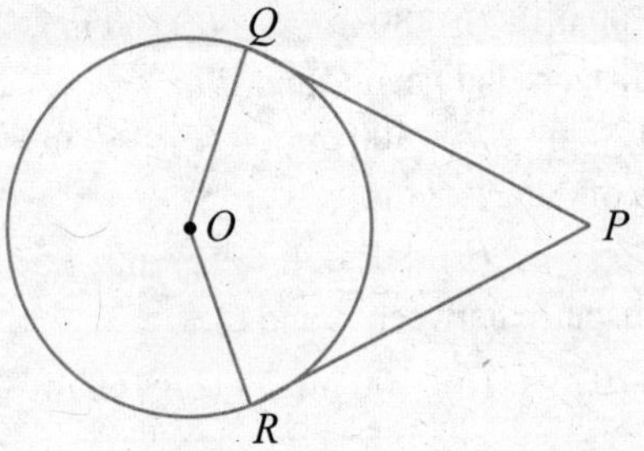

We know that the tangent to the circle is perpendicular to the radius of the circle at the point of contact.

So, $\angle OQP = ORP = 90°$

Now, if third angle is also 90°, then the fourth angle will be 90° because the sum of angles of a quadrilateral is 360°. Therefore,

If $\angle QOR = 90°$ (when radii are a angle of 90°) or $\angle QPR = 90°$ (when the tangents meet on angle of 90°), then the quadrilateral *PQOR* is a square.

Hence, either (i) or (ii) information must be known.

3. (*a*) Since, the tangent at any point of a circle is perpendicular to the radius through the point of contact.

$\therefore \angle OPR = 90°$

$\Rightarrow \angle OPQ + \angle QPR = 90°$

$\Rightarrow \angle OPQ = 90° - 50° = 40°$ $[\because \angle QPR = 50°]$

Now, $OP = OQ$ [radii of the circle]

$\therefore \angle OQP = \angle OPQ = 40°$

[Angle opposite to equal sides are equal]

In ΔOPQ,

$\angle POQ + \angle OPQ + \angle OQP = 180°$

[Angle sum property]

$\Rightarrow \angle POQ = 180° - (40° + 40°)$

[Since, $\angle OQP = \angle OPQ = 40°$]

$= 180° - 80° = 100°$

4. (*c*) Join *OA*.

We have,

$AT \perp OA$ [$\because$ Tangent $\perp$ Radius]

$\Rightarrow \angle OAT = 90°$

$\therefore \Delta OAT$ is a right-angled triangle.

$\therefore$ In ΔOAT,

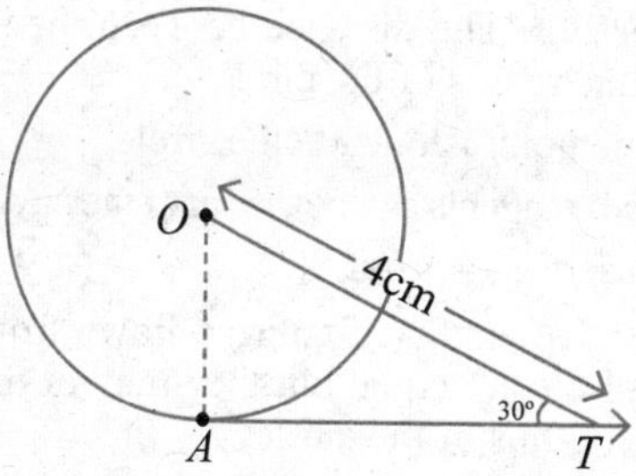

$$\cos 30° = \frac{AT}{OT}$$

$$\Rightarrow AT = \cos 30° \times OT = \frac{\sqrt{3}}{2} \times 4 = 2\sqrt{3}\text{cm}$$

5. (*b*) We know that the radius and tangent are perpendicular at their point of contact

$\therefore \angle ABO = 90°$

Now, by using Pythagoras theorem

$\Rightarrow OA^2 = AB^2 + OB^2$

$\Rightarrow 17^2 = AB^2 + 8^2$ [$\because$ OB is radius]

$\Rightarrow AB^2 = 17^2 - 8^2 = 289 - 64 = 225$

$\Rightarrow AB = 15$ cm

$\because$ The tangents drawn from the external point are equal.

$\therefore AB = AC$

Therefore, the length of AC is 15 cm.

6. (*b*) Join AC and BC.

We have,

$CA \perp AP$ and $CB \perp BP$ [$\because$ Tangent $\perp$ Radius]

$\Rightarrow \angle CAP = \angle CBP = 90°$

Also, $\angle APB = 90°$

$\Rightarrow \angle ACB = 90°$

Also, $AC = BC$ [Radii]

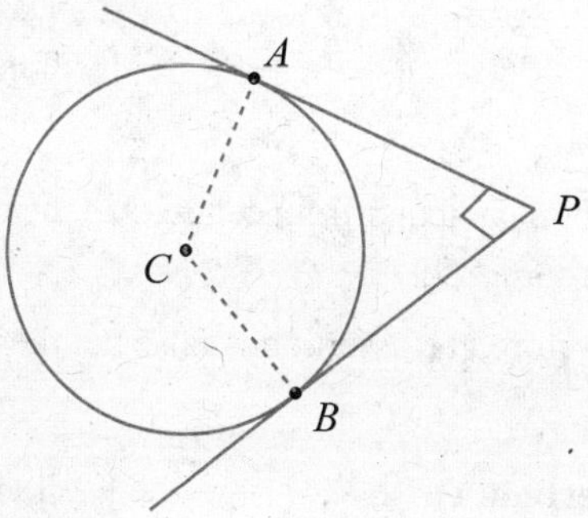

and $AP = PB$ [Tangents from external point P]

So, $BPAC$ is a square

$\Rightarrow AP = PB = BC = CA = 4$ cm [$\because$ radius = 4 cm]

So, length of tangents are 4 cm each.

7. (*a*) We have,

$PQ \perp OQ$ [$\because$ Tangent $\perp$ Radius]

$\Rightarrow \angle PQO = 90°$

Now,

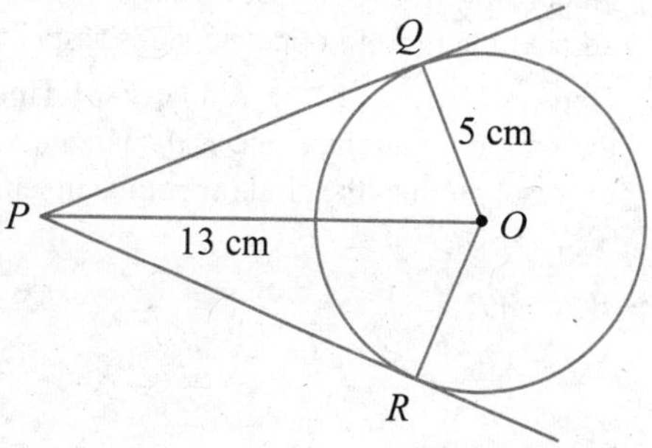

$$PQ = \sqrt{OP^2 - OQ^2} = \sqrt{13^2 - 5^2} = 12 \text{ cm}$$

[By Pythagoras Theorem]

$\because$ Tangents drawn from an external point are equal.

So, $PQ = PR$

$\Rightarrow PR = 12$ cm

Also, $\because$ radius = 5 cm

$\therefore OQ = OR = 5$ cm

Area of quadrilateral $PQOR$

= area of ΔPOQ + area of ΔPOR

$$= \frac{1}{2} \times PQ \times OQ + \frac{1}{2} \times PR \times OR$$

$$\Rightarrow \frac{1}{2} \times 12 \times 5 + \frac{1}{2} \times 12 \times 5$$

$\Rightarrow 30 + 30 = 60$ cm^2

8. (*c*)

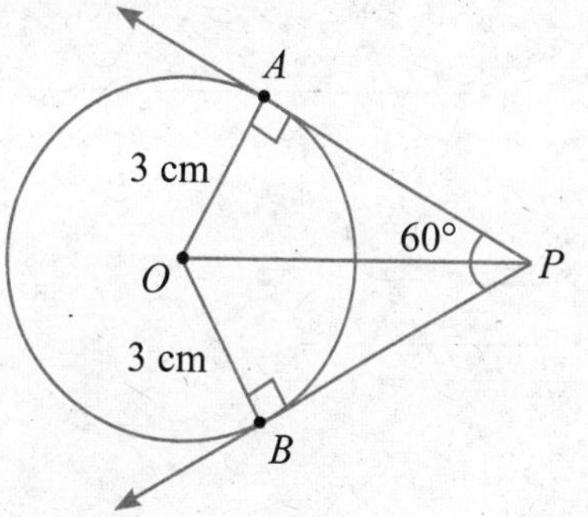

$$\therefore \angle APO = \angle BPO = \frac{1}{2} \times \angle APB = \frac{1}{2} \times 60° = 30°$$

Also, $OA \perp AP$ and $OB \perp BP$ (radius $\perp$ tangent at point of contact)

In right ΔOAP,

$$\tan 30° = \frac{3}{PA} \Rightarrow \frac{1}{\sqrt{3}} = \frac{3}{PA} \Rightarrow PA = 3\sqrt{3}$$

Therefore, $PA = PB = 3\sqrt{3}$ cm

9. (*c*) Clearly PT is a tangent and OT is radius

$\therefore \angle OTP = 90°$

$\Rightarrow \Delta OTP$ is a right angled triangle

Using Pythagoras Theorem, we get

$QP^2 = QT^2 + PT^2$

$\Rightarrow OP^2 = 7^2 + 24^2 = 625$

$\Rightarrow OP = 25$ cm

Now, $PR = OP + OR = 25 + 7 = 32$ cm

10. (*b*) According to the relationships, Raghav added the adjacent sides and opposite sides respectively

Here, we can use the property of tangents from an external point to the circle as the tangents drawn from an external point to the circle are equal in length. Therefore,

$ZS = ZR$ ... (*i*)

$WS = WP$ ... (*ii*)

$XQ = XP$ ... (*iii*)

$YQ = YR$ ... (*iv*)

By adding equations (*i*), (*ii*), (*iii*) and (*iv*)

$ZS + WS + XQ + YQ = ZR + WP + XP + YR$

$\Rightarrow (ZS + WS) + (XQ + YQ) = (ZR + YR) + (WP + XP)$

$\Rightarrow ZW + YX = ZY + WX$

Thus, our relationship is matched with the (*ii*) relationship of Raghav.

Hence, only (*ii*) relationship is definitely correct.

Assertion and Reason

1. (*b*) **Assertion:**

$\because$ Tangent drawn at a point on the centre is $\perp$ar to the radius through the point of contact.

i.e. $AP \perp OA$

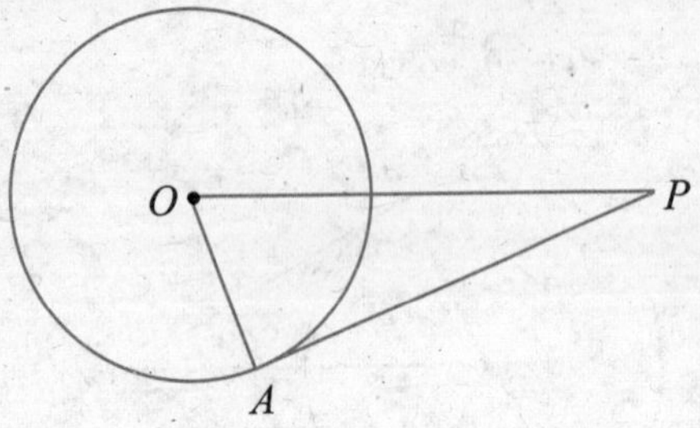

$\Rightarrow AP = \sqrt{OP^2 - OA^2}$

$= \sqrt{28} = 2\sqrt{7}$ cm

$\therefore$ Assertion is true

Reason: We have,

$\angle OAP = \angle OBP = 90°$ [$\because$ Tangent $\perp$ Radius]

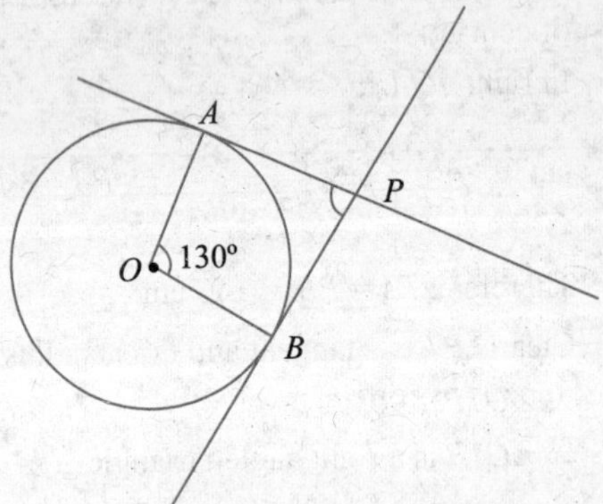

Now, $\angle OAP + \angle OBP + \angle AOB + \angle APB = 360°$

[$\because$ Sum of all angles of a quadrilateral is 360°]

$\Rightarrow 90° + 90° + 130° + \angle APB = 360°$

[$\because \angle AOB = 130°$ is given]

$\Rightarrow \angle APB = 360° - 180° - 130° = 50°$

$\therefore$ Reason is true.

But Reason is not correct explanation of the Assertion.

2. (*c*) **Assertion:** The distance between the points is greater than the radius of the circle.

So, the point is outside the circle.

So, two tangents can be drawn to the circle from the point.

$\therefore$ Assertion is true.

Reason: Lengths of tangent drawn from external point to a circle are equal but they may or may not be equal to the radius of the circle.

So, the reason is false

3. (*d*) **Assertion:** Let the circle touches the quadrilateral at points *ABCD* as shown in the figure.

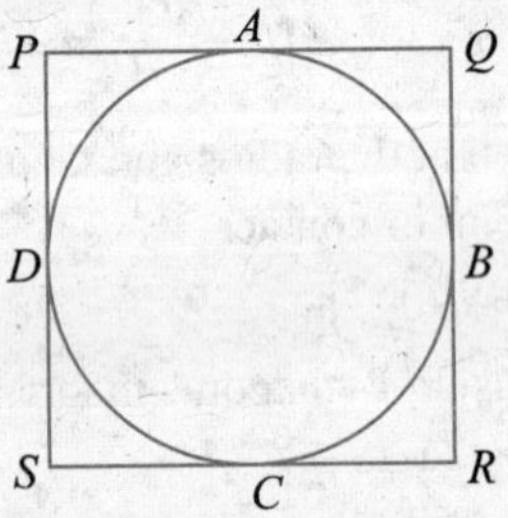

$\because$ Tangents drawn from an external points are equal.

$\therefore (PA + AQ) + (SC + CR) = (PD + SD) + (QB + BR)$

$\Rightarrow PQ + SR = PS + QR$

But, according to the assertion $PQ + QR = PS + SR$

So, the assertion is false.

Reason:

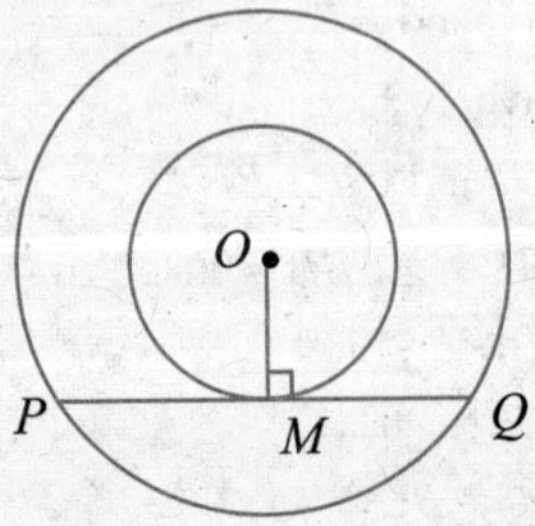

$OM \perp PQ$ [$\because$ Tangent $\perp$ Radius]

$\therefore PM = MQ$

[$\because$ Perpendicular from centre O to the chord PQ bisect the chord PQ]

Therefore, the assertion is false but the reason is true.

4. (*b*) We have

Assertion: $OP \perp PQ$ [$\because$ Tangent $\perp$ Radius]

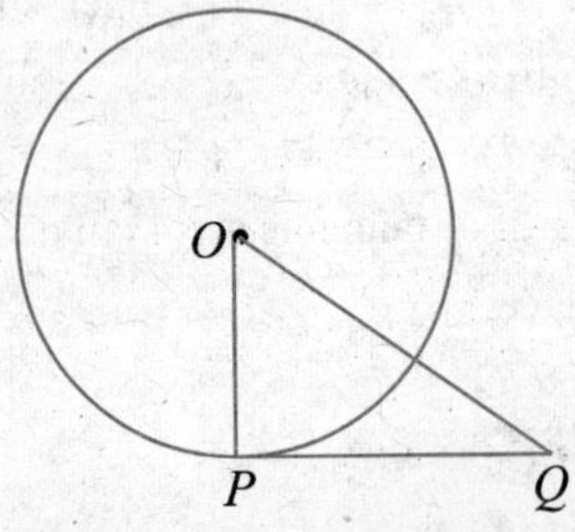

$\angle OPQ + \angle POQ + \angle PQO = 180°$

[Angle sum property]

$\Rightarrow 90° + 2\angle PQO = 180°$ [$\angle POQ = \angle PQO$]

$\Rightarrow 2\angle PQO = 180° - 90° = 90° \Rightarrow \angle PQO = 45°$

Thus, the assertion is true.

Reason: We have,

$OA \perp AP$ [$\because$ Tangent $\perp$ Radius]

$\Rightarrow \angle OAP = 90°$

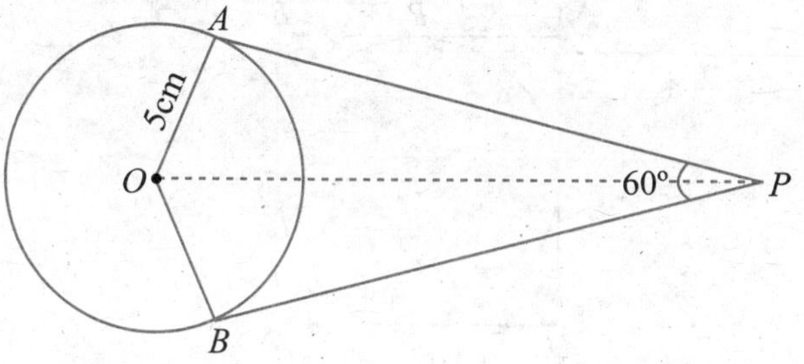

$\angle OPA = \angle OPB$, (PO divides $\angle P$ in two equal parts)

Now,

$\angle APB = 60°$ [Given]

$\Rightarrow \angle OPA + \angle OPB = 60°$

$\Rightarrow 2\angle OPA = 60° \Rightarrow \angle OPA = 30°$

In ΔOPA,

$$\tan 30° = \frac{OA}{AP} \Rightarrow AP = \frac{OA}{\tan 30°} = \frac{3}{\frac{1}{\sqrt{3}}} = 3\sqrt{3} \text{ cm}$$

$\because$ tangents drawn from an external point are equal

So, $AP = BP$

$\therefore$ Length of each tangent is $3\sqrt{3}$ cm

$\therefore$ Reason is also true.

But Reason is not correct explanation of the assertion.

5. (*a*) **Assertion:** It explains the property that "A tangent to a circle is perpendicular to the radius through the point of contact.

Also reason is true as the lengths of two tangents are equal because they are opposite sides of congruent triangle

Also, reason is the correct explanation of Assertion.

Subjective Questions

Very Short Answer Type Questions

1. A line intersecting a circle in two points is called a "secant". (1 M)

2. Given, major $\angle AOB = 260°$

Minor $\angle AOB = 360° - 260° = 100°$ (½ M)

We know that radius and tangent are perpendicular. So,

$\angle NAO = \angle NBO = 90°$ (½ M)

In a quadrilateral $NAOB$.

$\angle NAO + \angle AOB + \angle NBO + \angle ANB = 360°$

$90° + 100° + 90° + \angle ANB = 360°$ $\angle ANB = 360° - 280°$ (½ M)

$\Rightarrow \angle ANB = 80°$

Hence, the value of $\angle ANB$ is 80° (½ M)

3. $AQ = AR = 7$ cm (½ M)

$BR = AB - AR = 10 - 7 = 3$ cm (½ M)

$BC = BP + PC = BR + CQ = 3 + 5 = 8$ cm (1 M)

4. Given, radius = 15 cm

Let OB be radius and PB is a tangent.

Now we know that radius is perpendicular to point of contact

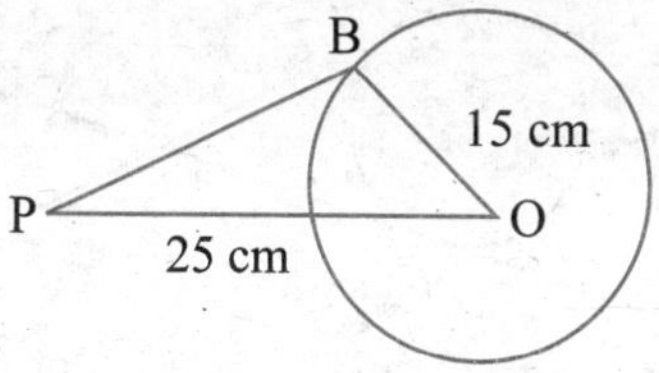

OB is perpendicular to PB

Hence, $\angle PBO = 90°$ (½ M)

Consider $\angle PBO$

Using Pythagoras theorem

$PB^2 + OB^2 = PO^2$ (½ M)

$PB^2 + 15^2 = 25^2$

$PB^2 + 225 = 625$

$PB^2 = 625 - 225$

$PB^2 = 400$

$PB = \sqrt{400}$

$PB = 20$ cm

Hence, the length of the tangent from the point to the circle is 20 cm. (1 M)

5. Given that O is the centre of the circle and PQ and PS are tangents to the circle at points Q and S respectively, and we draw the radii (OQ and OS) of the circle as shown below:

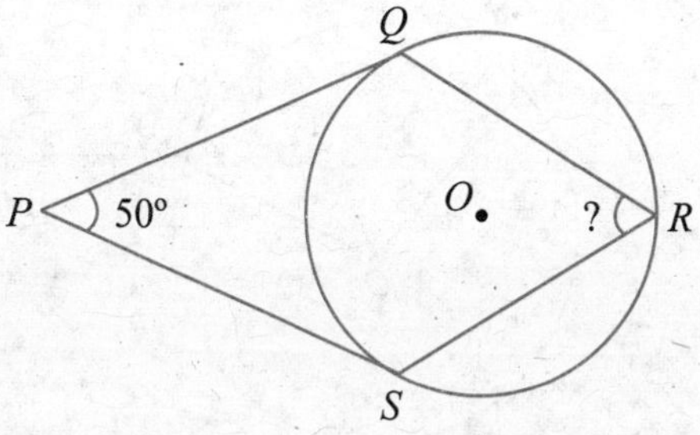

We know that the tangent to the circle is perpendicular to the radius of the circle at the point of contact. (½ M)

So, $\angle OQP = OSP = 90°$ (½ M)

By using angle sum property in quadrilateral $PQOS$

$\angle QOS = 360° - (50° + 90° + 90°) = 360° - 230° = 130°$ (½ M)

As the angle subtended by an arc at the centre is double the angle subtended by it at any point on the remaining part of the circle.

Therefore,

$$\angle QOS = 2\angle QRS \Rightarrow \angle QRS = \frac{\angle QOS}{2} = \frac{130°}{2} = 65°$$

Hence, $\angle QRS = 65°$ (½ M)

6. Tangents drawn to a circle from an external point are equal.

So, $AE = CE$ ... (i)

and $DE = BE$ ... (ii) (1 M)

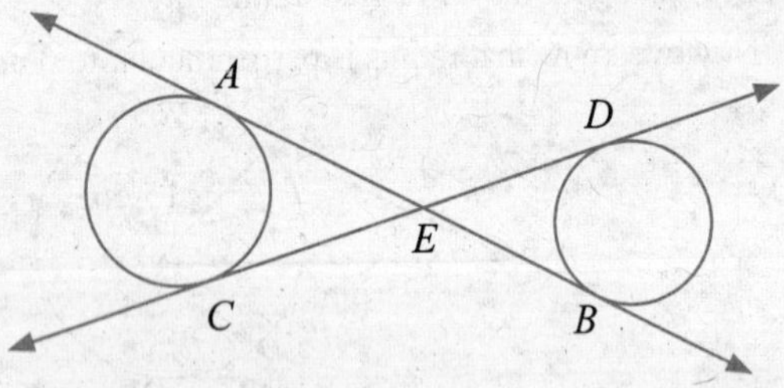

Now, $AB = AE + EB = CE + DE = CD$

Hence, $AB = CD$. (1 M)

7. The statement is true. (½ M)

For example, as tangents are drawn at A and E, $\angle OAB = \angle OED = 90°$. (½ M)

Since these are adjacent interior angles, and are supplementary, $AB \parallel ED$. Hence, at least one pair of opposite sides of $AEDB$ is parallel. (1 M)

Short Answer Type Questions

1. **Given:** A circle with centre O. Tangents NQ and MQ drawn from external point Q.

To prove: $\angle MQN + \angle NOM = 180°$. (½ M)

Construction: Join NM

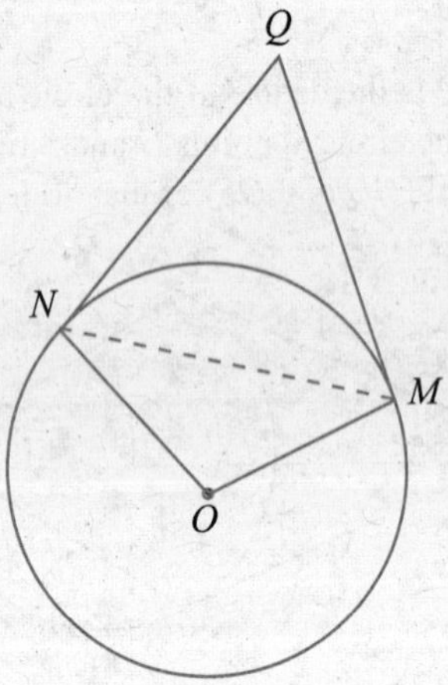

(½ M)

Proof: It is clear from the above diagram that the line segments OM and QM are perpendicular to each other as tangent is perpendicular radius

Therefore, $\angle OMQ = 90°$ (½ M)

Similarly, the line segments $ON \perp QN$ and so, $\angle ONQ = 90°$ (½ M)

Now, in the quadrilateral $OMQN$,

$\angle MQN + \angle OMQ + \angle QNO + \angle NOM = 360°$ (since the sum of all interior angles of a quadrilateral is 360°) (½ M)

$\Rightarrow \angle MQN + 180° + \angle NOM = 360°$ [$\because \angle OMQ = 90°$]

So, $\angle MQN + \angle NOM = 180°$ (½ M)

Hence proved.

2. Given circle touching sides of $ABCD$ at P, Q, R and S

To prove- $AB + CD = AD + DA$

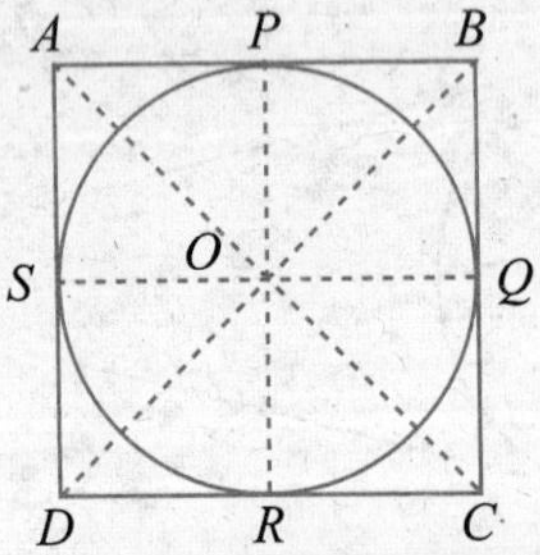

(1 M)

Proof:

$AP = AS$ ...(i) tangents from same point

$PB = BQ$ ...(ii) to a circle are equal in length

$DR = DS$ ...(iii)

$CR = CQ$ ...(iv) (1 M)

Adding eq^n (1), (2), (3) and (4)

$\Rightarrow AP + BP + DR + CR = AS + DS + BQ + CQ$

$\Rightarrow AB + DC = AD + BC$ (1 M)

3. Here, $QC = QA$ and $RC = RB$ (½ M)

Therefore $PA + PB = PQ + QA + PR + RB$

$= PQ + QC + PR + RC$ (½ M)

$\Rightarrow 2PA = PQ + QR + PR = 20$ cm ($PA = PB$) (½ M)

$\Rightarrow PA = 10$ cm (½ M)

4. We have,

$OA \perp AP$ and $OB \perp BP$ [$\because$ Tangent $\perp$ Radius]

$\Rightarrow \angle OAP = \angle OBP = 90°$ (½ M)

Now, Join OP.

In right ΔOAP, we have

$OA = 8$ cm, $AP = 15$ cm

$\therefore OP^2 = OA^2 + AP^2$ [by Pythagoras' theorem]

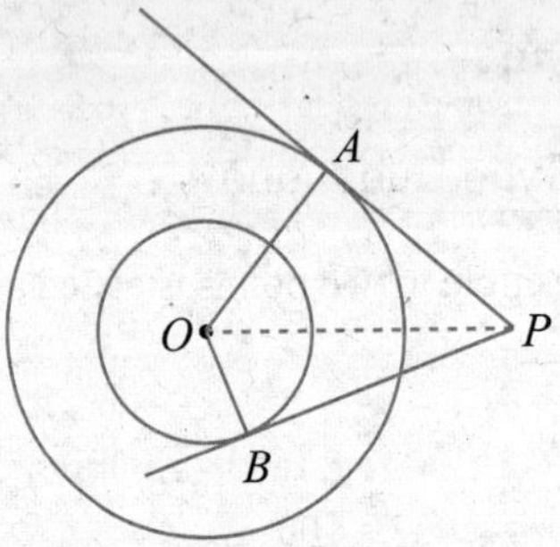

(1 M)

$\Rightarrow OP = \sqrt{OA^2 + AP^2} = \sqrt{8^2 + 15^2} = \sqrt{289} = 17$ cm. (½ M)

In right ΔOBP, we have

$OB = 5$ cm, $OP = 17$ cm.

$\therefore OP^2 = OB^2 + BP^2$ [by Pythagoras' theorem]

$\Rightarrow BP = \sqrt{OP^2 - OB^2} = \sqrt{17^2 - 5^2}$ cm $= \sqrt{264}$ cm

Therefore, $BP = \sqrt{264}$ cm *(1 M)*

5. 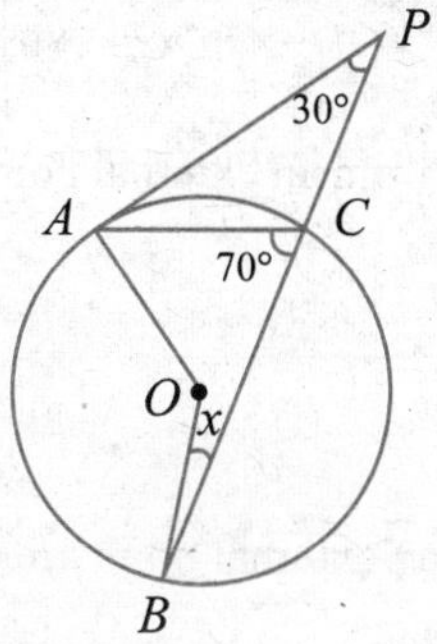

$\angle BCA + \angle PCA = 180°$

$\because$ PCB is a straight line

$70° + \angle PCA = 180°$

$\angle PCA = 180° - 70° = 110°$ *(1 M)*

In $\angle ACP$,

$30° + 110° + \angle PAC = 180°$

$\angle PAC = 180° - 140°$

$\angle PAC = 40°$

We know that radius is perpendicular to the tangent,

So, $\angle OAP = 90°$

$\therefore \angle OAC = 90° - 40°$

$\Rightarrow \angle OAC = 50°$ *(1 M)*

Join OC

In ΔOAC, $OA = OC$

$\angle OAC = \angle OCA = 50°$

$\therefore \angle OCB = 70° - 50° = 20°$

In ΔOBC, $OC = \text{OB}$

$\angle OCB = \angle OCB = 20°$

$\therefore x = 20°$ *(1 M)*

6. We have,

$PO \perp QO$

$\Rightarrow \angle POQ = 90°$ *(½ M)*

Now,

$\Rightarrow PO \perp PT$ and $OQ \perp TQ$ [$\because$ Tangent $\perp$ Radius]

$\Rightarrow \angle OPT = \angle OQT = 90°$ *(½ M)*

Now,

$\because \angle OPT + \angle OQT + \angle POQ + \angle PTQ = 360°$

[Angle sum property]

$\Rightarrow 90° + 90° + 90° + \angle PTQ = 360°$

$\Rightarrow \angle PTQ = 360° - 270° = 90°$

Thus, $\angle OPT = \angle PTQ = \angle TQO = \angle QOP = 90°$

So, $PTQO$ is a rectangle ... (*i*) *(½ M)*

Now, $PO = OQ$ ... (*ii*)

[Radii]

and $PT = TQ$ ... (*iii*) *(½ M)*

[Tangents drawn from an external point to a circle are equal in length]

$\because$ Perpendicular distance from two parallel straight line between any two point are equal.

So, for parallel lines PO and TQ [$\because$ $PTQO$ is a rectangle]

$PT = OQ$ ... (*iv*) *(½ M)*

From (*ii*), (*iii*) and (*iv*)

$PO = OQ = QT = PT$

$\Rightarrow$ $PTQO$ is a square with diagonals PQ and OT.

Therefore, PQ and OT are right bisector of each other.

(½ M)

7. 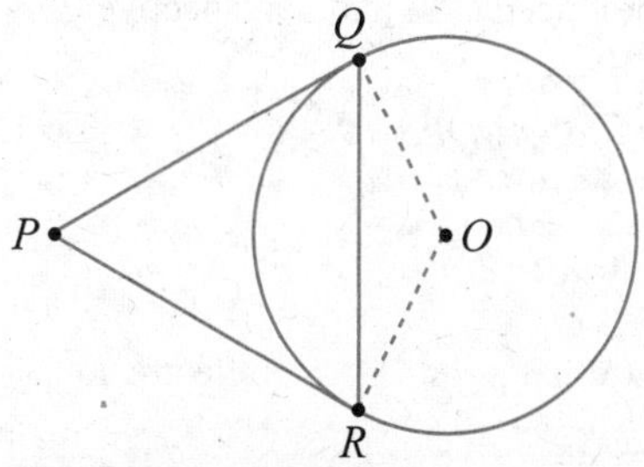

As $OQ = OR$ (radii of the circle) so, ΔOQR is an isosceles triangle. Therefore,

$\angle OQR = \angle ORQ$ *(1 M)*

Let $\angle OQR = \angle ORQ = \theta$

We know that the tangent to the circle is perpendicular to the radius of the circle at the point of contact. So, $\angle OQR = \angle ORP = 90°$ *(½ M)*

From the figure

$\angle PQR = \angle OQP - \angle OQR = 90° - \theta$ ... (*i*)

Similarly, $\angle PRQ = \angle ORP - \angle ORQ = 90° - \theta$ ... (*ii*)

From equation (*i*) and (*ii*)

$\angle PQR = \angle PRQ$ *(½ M)*

So, ΔPRQ is an isosceles triangle. Therefore,

$PQ = PR$ *(1 M)*

Hence, proved.

8. Write that $AB = BC$, as they are tangents from an external point to a circle.

Note that $OA = OC$ as they are radii. *(½ M)*

Write that $\angle BAO = \angle BCO = 90°$ as AB and BC are tangents. *(½ M)*

Note that $OA \parallel BC$ *as* $\angle AOC + \angle OCB = 180°$ (adjacent interior angles)

Note that $OC \parallel AB$ *as* $\angle AOC + \angle OAB = 180°$ (adjacent interior angles) *(½ M)*

Concludes that $OABC$ is a parallelogram. *(½ M)*

Write that, as opposite sides in a parallelogram are equal, $OA = BC$ and $OC = AB$.

Also, as opposite angles in a parallelogram are equal, $\angle AOC = \angle ABC = 90°$ *(½ M)*

Concludes that $OABC$ is a square as all of its angles are 90°, and $OA = AB = BC = OC$. *(½ M)*

Long Answer Type Questions

1. **Given,** A circle is touching a side QR of ΔPQR at point S.

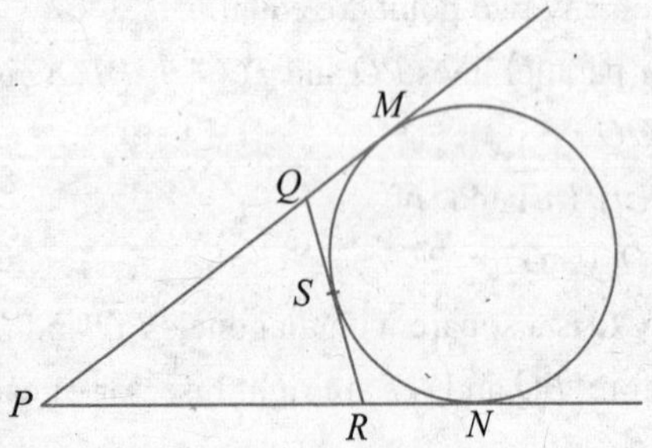

PQ and PR are produced at M and N respectively.

To prove $PM = \frac{1}{2}(PQ + QR + PR)$ *(1 M)*

Proof,

$PM = PN$ ... (*i*)

(tangents from external point P to a circle are equal) *(1 M)*

Similarly, $QM = QS$ ... (*ii*)

(tangents from external point Q to a circle are equal)

and, $RS = RN$ ... (*iii*)

(tangents from external point R to a circle are equal)

Now, $2\,PM = PM + PM$

$= PM + PN$ [from eqn (*i*)]

$= PQ + QM + PR + RN$

$= PQ + QS + PR + RS$ [from eqn (*ii*), (*iii*)] *(1 M)*

$= PQ + PR + QS + SR$

$\Rightarrow 2\,PM = PQ + QR + PR$

$\Rightarrow PM = \frac{1}{2}(PQ + QR + PR)$ Proved *(1 M)*

2. Let $ABCD$ is quadrilateral which circumscribes a circle having centre O. The quadrilateral touches the circle at points R, Q, P and S as shown in the figure. *(½ M)*

To Prove: $\angle AOB + \angle COD = 180°$ and $\angle AOD + \angle BOC = 180°$.

Construction: Join OP, OQ, OR and OS. *(½ M)*

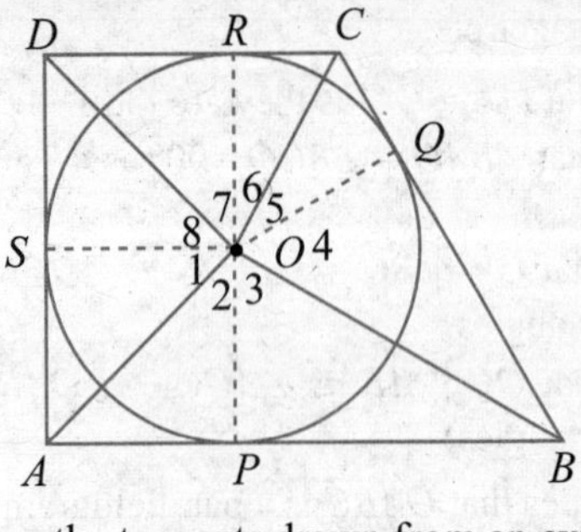

(1 M)

Proof: Since, the tangents drawn from an external point of a circle subtend equal angles at the centre.

So, $\angle 1 = \angle 2$, $\angle 3 = \angle 4$, $\angle 5 = \angle 6$ and $\angle 7 = \angle 8$. *(½ M)*

And $\angle 1 + \angle 2 + \angle 3 + \angle 4 + \angle 5 + \angle 6 + \angle 7 + \angle 8 = 360°$

[$\because$ Angle at a point is 360°] *(½ M)*

$\Rightarrow 2(\angle 2 + \angle 3 + \angle 6 + \angle 7) = 360°$ and

$\Rightarrow 2(\angle 1 + \angle 4 + \angle 5 + \angle 8) = 360°$ *(½ M)*

$\Rightarrow \angle 2 + \angle 3 + \angle 6 + \angle 7 = 180°$ and

$\Rightarrow \angle 1 + \angle 8 + \angle 4 + \angle 5 = 180°$ *(½ M)*

$\Rightarrow \angle AOB + \angle COD = 180°$ and $\angle AOD + \angle BOC = 180°$.

(1 M)

3. Tangents QA and QB are drawn from an external point Q to a circle with centre O.

Also, $\angle AQB = 30°$

Join OB and OA. *(½ M)*

Now, $QB = QA$ *(½ M)*

[$\because$ Tangents drawn from an external point are equal]

$\Rightarrow \angle QBA = \angle QAB$ *(½ M)*

[Angles opposite to equal sides are equal]

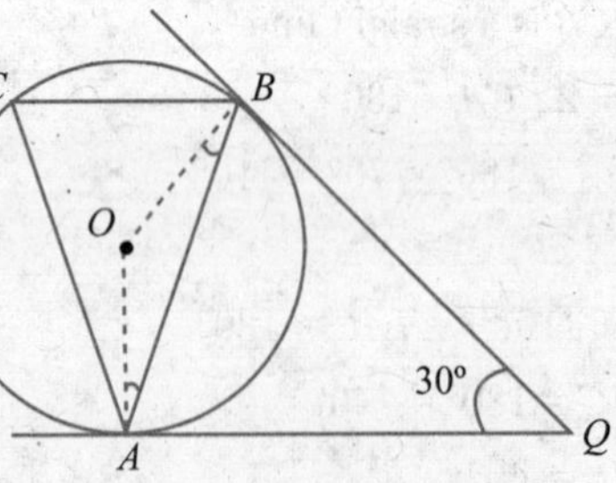

In ΔQAB,

$\angle QBA + \angle BQA + \angle QAB = 180°$

[Sum of angles of a triangle is 180°]

$\Rightarrow 30° + 2\angle QAB = 180°$

$\Rightarrow \angle QAB = \frac{(180 - 30)°}{2} = 75°$ *(½ M)*

Also, $CB \parallel AQ$ and AB is a transversal line.

$\Rightarrow \angle CBA = \angle QAB$ [Alternate interior angle]

$\therefore \angle CBA = 75°$ *(½ M)*

$\Rightarrow \angle OBQ = 90°$ [$\because$ Tangent $\perp$ radius]

$\therefore \angle OBQ = \angle OBA + \angle ABQ$

$\Rightarrow 90° = \angle OBA + 75°$ [$\because \angle ABQ = \angle QAB = 75°$]

$\angle OBA = 90° - 75° = 15°$ *(½ M)*

Similarly, $\angle BAO = 15°$ *(½ M)*

In ΔAOB,

$\angle AOB + \angle ABO + \angle OAB = 180°$

[Sum of angles of a triangle is 180°]

$\therefore \angle AOB + 15° + 15° = 180°$

$\Rightarrow \angle AOB = 180° - 30° = 150°$

$\Rightarrow \angle ACB = \frac{1}{2}\angle AOB$

$\Rightarrow \angle ACB = \frac{150°}{2} = 75°$ *(1 M)*

[$\because$ The angle made by a chord at the centre is double than the angle made anywhere on the circle]

In ΔBCA,

$\angle BCA + \angle ABC + \angle BAC = 180°$

[Sum of angles of a triangle is 180°]

$\Rightarrow 75° + 75° + \angle BAC = 180°$

$\Rightarrow \angle BAC = 180° - 150° = 30°$ (½ M)

4. Given that the difference between the area of larger circle and smaller circle is 616 cm^2

Join from the centre O to point P and S. (½ M)

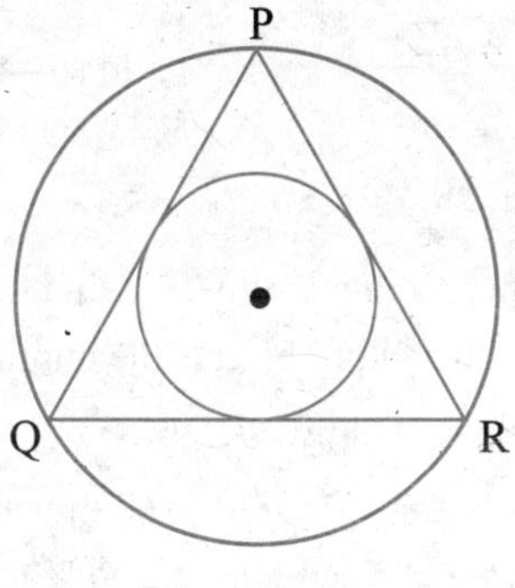

$\therefore \pi(OP^2 - OS^2) = 616$ (½ M)

$\Rightarrow OP^2 - OS^2 = \frac{616}{\pi} = 196\ cm^2$ (½ M)

In ΔOPS, using Pythagoras theorem we get

$OP^2 - OS^2 = PS^2$ (½ M)

$\therefore PS^2 = 196$ PS = 14 cm (½ M)

We know that a perpendicular from the centre of a circle bisects the chord. (½ M)

$\Rightarrow PR = 2 \times$ PS = 28 cm (1 M)

Given that ΔPQR is an equilateral triangle.

Perimeter = 3 × side length (½ M)

$\Rightarrow 3 \times 28 \Rightarrow 84$ cm

Hence, the required perimeter is 84 cm. (½ M)

Case Based Questions

Case Based-I

(*i*) Since, centre of the maze is at O and Sundaram is at P and distance between the centre of the maze and Sundaram = 12 m

$\therefore OP = 13$ m

$\because$ Shyam is at B.

$\because$ So, we have to find PB.

$\because$ Distance between centre of the maze and Shyam = 5 m [Given]

$\therefore OB = 5$m [$\because$ Tangent $\perp$ Radius]

Now, $PB \perp OB \Rightarrow \angle PBO = 90°$

Now, In ΔOBP,

$PO^2 = OB^2 + PB^2$ [By Pythagoras Theorem]

$\Rightarrow PB^2 = PO^2 - OB^2 = 13^2 - 5^2 = 169 - 25 = 144$

$\therefore PB = 12$m

$\therefore$ Required distance = 12 m

(*ii*) $\because$ Tangent drawn from an external point to a circle are equal in length.

So, $PC = PB = 12$ cm.

Also, $OC = OB = 5$m [Radii]

Also, $PC \perp OC \Rightarrow \angle PCO = 90°$

$\therefore$ Area of $BPCO$ = Area of right ΔOPB + Area of right ΔOPC

$= \frac{1}{2} \times OB \times PB + \frac{1}{2} \times OC \times PC = \frac{1}{2} \times 5 \times 12 + \frac{1}{2} \times 5 \times 12$

$= 5 \times 12 = 60\ m^2$

OR

We have,

$\angle PBO + \angle PCO + \angle BPC + \angle BOC = 360°$

$\Rightarrow 90° + 90° + 60° + \angle BOC = 360°$

[$\because \angle PBO = \angle PCO = 90°$ *and* $\angle BPC = 60°$]

$\Rightarrow \angle BOC = 360° - 180° - 60° = 120°$

(*iii*) $\because$ Angle made by a chord at the centre is double the angle made by the chord anywhere on the circle.

$\therefore \angle BAC = \frac{1}{2} \angle BOC = \frac{1}{2} \times 120° = 60°$

Case Based-II

(*i*) Since, we know that angle in a semicircle is 90°.

$\therefore \angle APB = 90°$

(*ii*) Since, the length of tangents drawn from an external point to a circle are equal.

So, tangents PQ and BQ from point Q are equal.

$\because PQ = 50$ m [Given]

$\therefore BQ = PQ = 50$ m

OR

$\because \angle APB + \angle BPR = 180°$

$\Rightarrow \angle BPR = 180° - 90° = 90°$ ... (*i*) [$\because \angle APB = 90°$]

Now, In ΔBPR,

$\angle BPR + \angle PRB + \angle PBR = 180°$

$\Rightarrow \angle PRB + \angle PBR = 180° - 90° = 90°$ [$\because \angle BPR = 90°$]

Also, $\because \angle BPR = 90° \Rightarrow \angle BPQ + \angle QPR = 90°$ ... (*ii*)

From (*i*) and (*ii*)

$\angle PRB + \angle PBR = \angle BPQ + \angle QPR$

$\Rightarrow \angle PRB = \angle QPR$ [$\because \angle PBR = \angle BPQ$ because $BQ = PQ$]

$\Rightarrow PQ = QR$ [$\because$ sides opposite to equal angles are equal]

$\Rightarrow QR = 50$ m [$\because PQ = 50$ m]

(*iii*) $\because AB \perp BR$ [Radius $\perp$ Tangent]

$\Rightarrow \angle ABR = 90°$

$\therefore \Delta ABR$ is right angled triangle.

$\because$ Radius of the ferris wheel is 5m.

$\therefore AB = 2 \times$ radius $= 2 \times 5 = 10$ m

Also, $BR = BQ + QR = 50 + 50 = 100$ m

$\therefore$ By Pythagoras Theorem,

In ΔABR,

$AR^2 = AB^2 + BR^2 = 10^2 + 100^2 = 100 + 10000 = 10100$

$\therefore AR = \sqrt{10100}\text{ m} = 10\sqrt{101}\text{ m}$

Case Based-III

(*i*) Since, tangent to a point on a circle is perpendicular to the radius through the point of contact.

So, $AC \perp OC \Rightarrow \quad \angle ACO = 90^\circ$

$\Rightarrow OA^2 = AC^2 + OC^2$ [By Pythagoras Theorem]

$\Rightarrow OA = \sqrt{AC^2 + OC^2} = \sqrt{AC^2 + OD^2}$

[$\because$ *OC* and *OD* are radii ot the circle]

$= \sqrt{120^2 + 90^2} = \sqrt{14400 + 8100} = \sqrt{22500} = 150\text{ m}$

[$\because OD = 90$ m and $AC = 120$ m]

(*ii*) $\because OA = OD + DA \Rightarrow 150 = 90 + DA$

$\therefore \quad AD = 150 - 90 = 60$ m

OR

We have,

$BF \perp OF$ [$\because$ Tangent $\perp$ Radius]

$\Rightarrow \angle O'FB = 90^\circ \Rightarrow O'B^2 = O'F^2 + BF^2$

$\Rightarrow O'B = \sqrt{O'F^2 + BF^2} = \sqrt{O'E^2 + BF^2}$

[$\because$ *O'D* and *O'E* are radii of the circle and hence equal]

$= \sqrt{50^2 + 30^2}$ [$\because O'E = 50$ m & $BF = 30$ m]

$= \sqrt{2500 + 900} = \sqrt{3400} = 10\sqrt{34}$ m

(*iii*) We have,

$AB = OA + OP + O'P + O'B = OA + OD + O'E + O'B$

$= 150 + 90 + 50 + 10\sqrt{34} = 290 + 10\sqrt{34}$ m

Case Based-IV

(*i*) (*a*) $\because$ Tangent to a circle is perpendicular to the radius through point of contact.

$\therefore DB \perp OD$

$\Rightarrow \angle ODB = 90^\circ$

(*ii*) (*b*) In ΔODB, by Pythagoras Theorem,

$OB^2 = OD^2 + DB^2$

$\Rightarrow DB^2 = OB^2 - OD^2$

$\Rightarrow DB = \sqrt{OB^2 - OD^2}$

$= \sqrt{100^2 - 60^2}$ [$\because$ Inner radius $= OD = 60$ m and outer radius $= OB = 100$ m]

$= \sqrt{10000 - 3600} = \sqrt{6400} = 80\text{ m}$

(*iii*) (*c*) Since, a perpendicular line, passing through the centre of the circle, to a chord bisects the chord.

So, *BC* is bisected by *OD*.

$\therefore BC = 2 \times DB = 2 \times 80 = 160$ m

(*iv*) (*a*) Since, angle in a semicircle is 90°.

$\therefore \angle ACB = 90^\circ$

(*v*) (*a*) $\because$ Outer radius = 100 m

$\therefore AB = 2 \times$ outer radius = 200 m

Also, $BC = 160$ m. [From Q. *iii*]

Now, by Pythagoras theorem in ΔACB,

$AB^2 = AC^2 + BC^2 \Rightarrow AC^2 = AB^2 - BC^2$

$\Rightarrow AC = \sqrt{AB^2 - BC^2} = \sqrt{200^2 - 160^2}$

$= \sqrt{40000 - 25600} = \sqrt{14400} = 120\text{ m}$

❑❑❑

AREAS RELATED TO CIRCLES

11

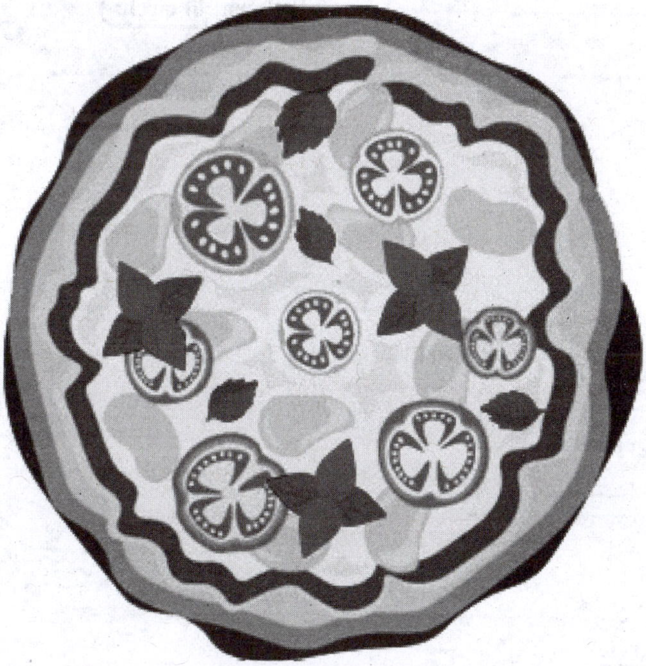

"Pizzas are usually round like a circle, and understanding circle areas helps us know how much pizza we are getting. By figuring out the area, you can compare different pizza sizes to see which is a better deal. This is useful when you want to choose the right size pizza for your group without ordering too much or too little."

SYLLABUS & WEIGHTAGE

List of Concept Name	Years				
	2021	2022	2023	2024	2025
Areas Related to Circles (Area of sectors and segments of a circle. Problems based on areas and perimeter/circumference of the above said plane figures. (In calculating area of segment of a circle, problems should be restricted to a central angle of 60°, 90° and 120° only).	Exam not Conducted	–	2 Q (1 M each) 1 Q (3 M)	1 Q (1 M) 1 Q (4 M)	1 Q (1 M) 1 Q (3 M)

CONCEPT MAP

To Access One Shot Revision Video Scan This QR Code

Areas Related to Circles

Sector of circle

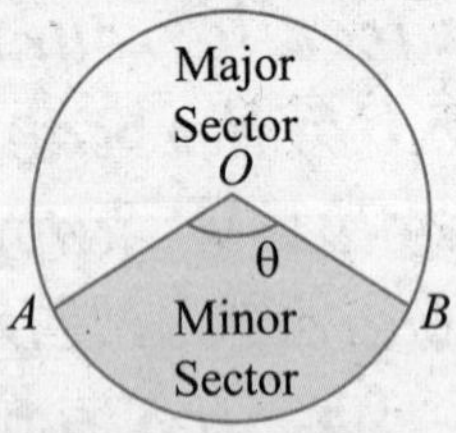

Length of arc $(AB) = \dfrac{\theta}{360^\circ} \times 2\pi r$

Perimeter of sector $(OAB) = 2r +$ length of arc

Area of sector $= \dfrac{\theta}{360^\circ} \times \pi r^2$

Circle

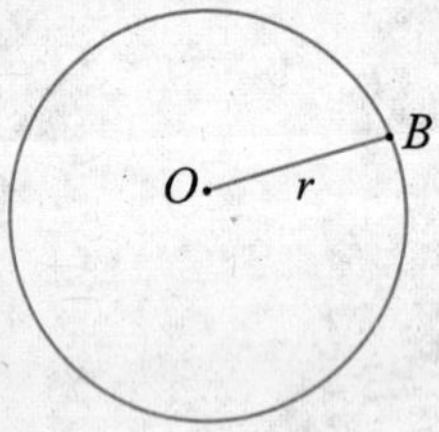

Circumference of the circle $= 2\pi r$

Area of the circle $= \pi r^2$

Segment of circle

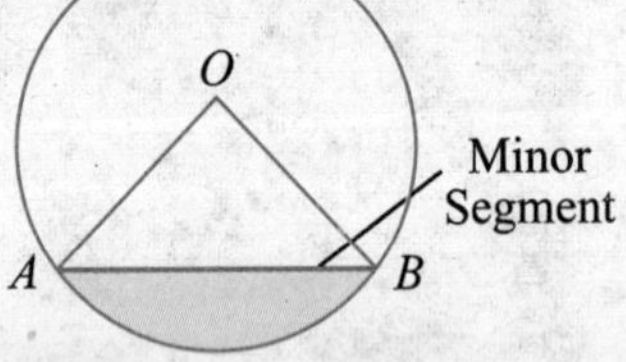

Length of chord $(AB) = 2r\sin\left(\dfrac{\theta}{2}\right)$

Area of segment = Area of sector (OAB) – Area of $\Delta\, OAB$

$= \dfrac{\theta}{360^\circ} \times \pi r^2 - \dfrac{1}{2} r^2 \sin\theta$

Semi-Circle

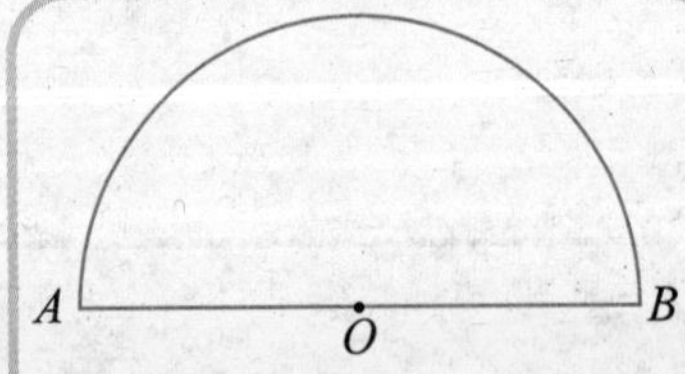

Perimeter of the semi-circle $= \pi r + 2r$

Area of the semi-circle $= \dfrac{1}{2}\pi r^2$

1 AREAS RELATED TO CIRCLES

Important Terms

- **Circle:** A circle is a closed two-dimensional shape consisting of all points on a plane that are equidistant from a fixed point called the center.
- **Chord:** A chord of a circle is a line segment that connects two points on the circle.
- **Diameter:** The diameter of the circle is any straight line segment that passes through the center of the circle and whose endpoints lie on the circumference of a circle.

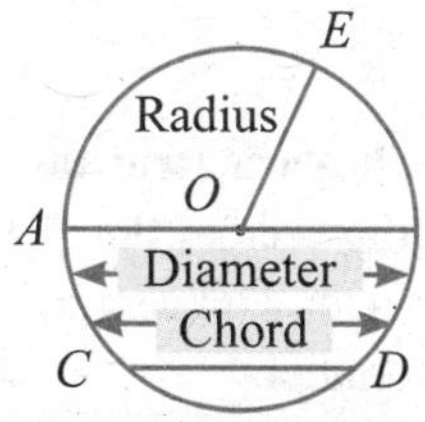

- **Radius:** The radius of a circle is the distance from the center of a circle to any point on the circle. It is denoted by r.
- **Semi-circle:** A diameter of circle divides a circle into two equal parts, each part known as a semi-circle.

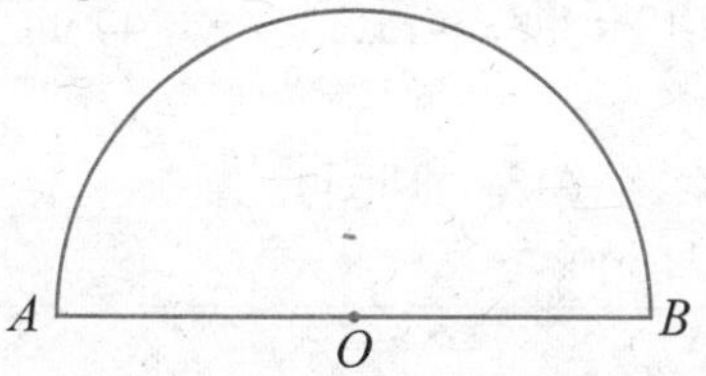

- **Circumference:** The distance covered by travelling once around a circle is its perimeter or circumference.
- **Pi (π):** Pi is the ratio of the circumference of a circle to its diameter. It is approximately equal to 3.14159
- **Area:** The area of a circle is the amount of space inside the circle.
- **Concentric Circles:** Circles having the same centre but different radii are known as concentric circles.

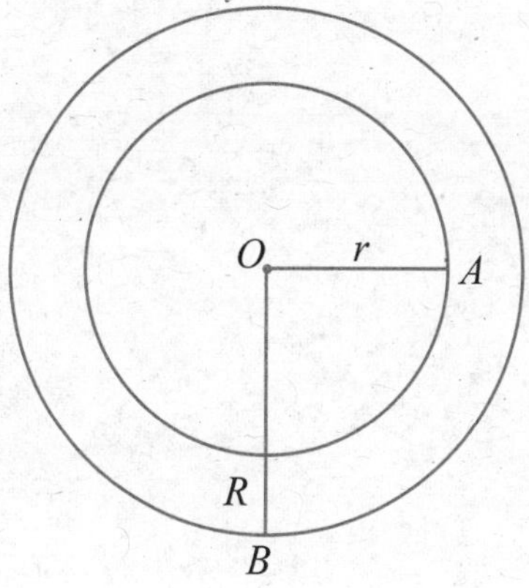

Important Concepts

Angle subtended at the circle by a diameter is always a right angle.

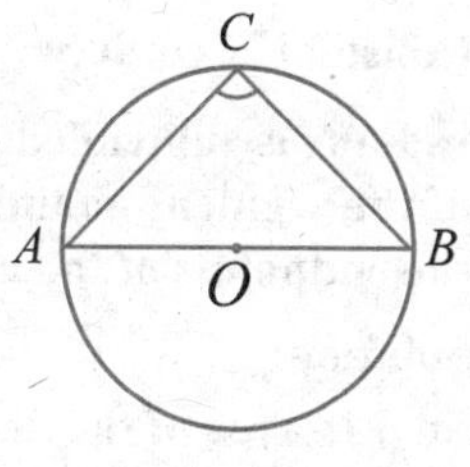

- Angle described by minute hand in 60 minutes is 360°.
- Angle described by hour hand in 12 hours is 360°.

Real Life Applications

- **Pie charts:** A pie chart is a circular chart that is divided into sectors, each of which represents a portion of the whole. The size of each sector corresponds to the proportion of the data it represents. This is a common way to display data in business presentations, market research reports, and scientific studies.

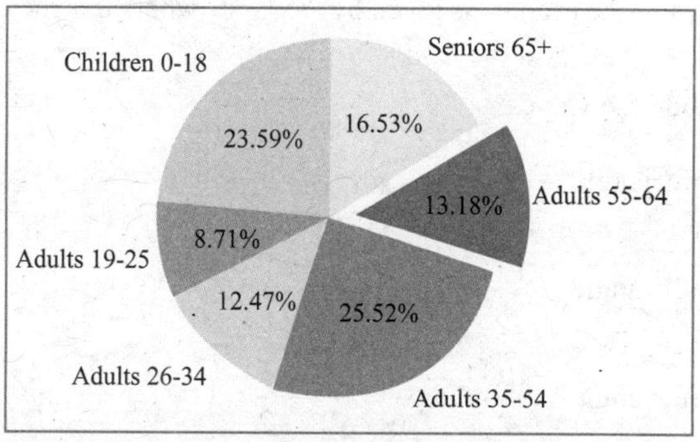

- **Cutting tools:** The cutting tools used in machining operations, such as lathes and milling machines, often have circular shapes with a sector or segment removed. The area of the sector or segment determines the amount of material that is removed during the machining process. Engineers use these calculations to optimize the cutting tool design and ensure that the material is removed efficiently and accurately.

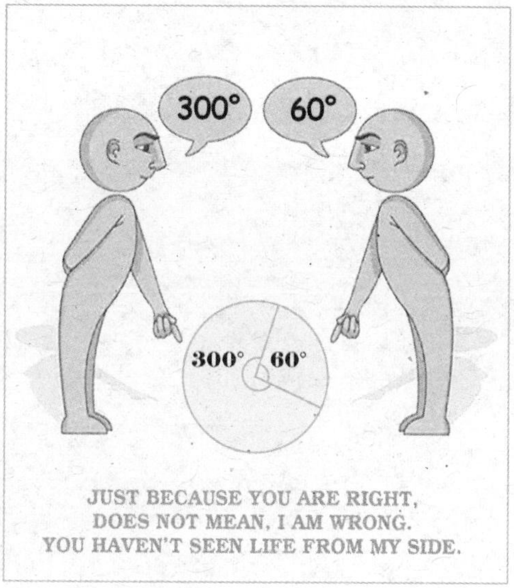

Different Problem Types

Type I: Circle Sector Area and Arc Length with Central Angle Constraint

Consider a circle with radius 10 cm. A central angle of $\frac{5\pi}{6}$ radians is subtended at the center of the circle. Find the area of the segment bounded by the arc and the chord connecting the endpoints of the arc.

Solution:

Step I: Area of the Sector

The area of a sector $= \frac{1}{2}r^2\theta$.

Substitute the values:

$$\text{Area} = \frac{1}{2}\times(10)^2\times\frac{5\pi}{6} \Rightarrow \text{Area} = \frac{250\pi}{6} \Rightarrow \text{Area} = \frac{125\pi}{3}\text{ cm}^2$$

Step II: Area of the Segment

To find the area of the segment, we subtract the area of the triangle formed by the chord and two radii from the area of the sector.

The area of the triangle is given by $\frac{1}{2}r^2\sin\theta$, where θ is the central angle.

Substitute the values:

$$\text{Area of triangle} = \frac{1}{2}\times(10)^2\times\sin\left(\frac{5\pi}{6}\right)$$

$$\text{Area of triangle} = \frac{1}{2}\times 100\times\sin\left(\pi-\frac{\pi}{6}\right)$$

$$\text{Area of triangle} = \frac{100}{2}\times\sin\frac{\pi}{6} = \frac{100}{2}\times\frac{1}{2}$$

Area of triangle = 25 cm^2

Now, subtract the area of the triangle from the area of the sector:

$$\text{Area of segment} = \frac{125\pi}{3} - 25$$

$$\text{Area of segment} = 25\left(\frac{5\pi}{3}-1\right)\text{ cm}^2$$

Example 1: A pendulum swings through an angle of 60° and describes an arc of length 4.4 cm. Find the length of the pendulum.

Solution: It is given that, length of arc

$l = 4.4$ cm and $\theta = 60°$.

$$\therefore l = \frac{\theta}{360}\times 2\pi r \Rightarrow 4.4 = \frac{60°}{360°}\times 2\times\frac{22}{7}\times r$$

$$\Rightarrow r = \frac{4.4\times 3\times 7}{22} = 4.2\text{ cm}$$

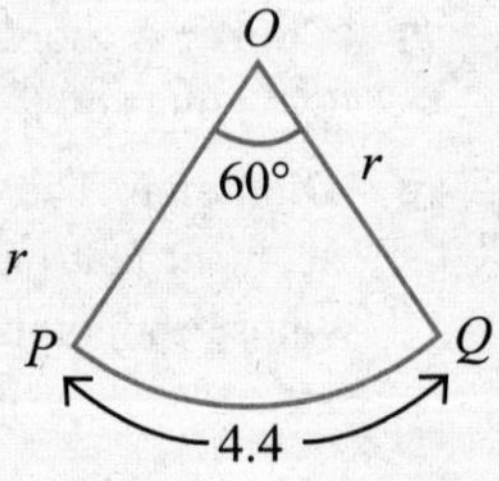

Example 2: A pizza slice has a central angle of 45° and a radius of 12 inches. Calculate the area of this pizza slice.

Solution: The area of a sector with central angle θ in degrees and radius r is given by the formula:

$$\text{Area} = \frac{\theta}{360°}\times\pi r^2$$

Given that the central angle is 45° and the radius r = 12 inches, we can substitute these values into the formula:

$$\text{Area} = \frac{45°}{360°}\times\pi(12\text{ in})^2 \Rightarrow \text{Area} = \frac{1}{8}\times\pi\times 144\text{ in}^2$$

$$\text{Area} = \frac{144}{8}\pi\text{ in}^2 \Rightarrow \text{Area} = 18\pi\text{ in}^2$$

COMPETENCY BASED SOLVED EXAMPLES

Multiple Choice Questions

(1 M)

1. **Area of a sector of angle p (in degrees) of a circle with radius R is** *(Re)* (NCERT Intext)

(a) $\frac{p}{180°}\times 2\pi R$ (b) $\frac{p}{180°}\times \pi R^2$

(c) $\frac{p}{360°}\times 2\pi R$ (d) $\frac{p}{720°}\times 2\pi R^2$

Sol. We know that Area of the sector $= \frac{\theta}{360°}\times \pi r^2$

$= \frac{p}{360°}\times \pi R^2 = \frac{p}{720°}\times 2\pi R^2$

Nailing the Right Answer

Students should remember the area of a sector, which has a theta (θ) angle.

2. **A circle has a circumference of 12π cm. What is its radius?** *(Ap)* (NCERT Intext)

(a) 12 cm (b) 6 cm

(c) 4 cm (d) 2 cm

Sol. We know that the circumference of the circle $= 2\pi r$

$\therefore\ 12\pi = 2\pi r \Rightarrow r = 6$ cm

Key Takeaways

Circumference of circle $= 2\times\pi\times r$

3. **The perimeter of the sector with radius 10.5 cm and sector angle 60°, is:** *(Un)*

(a) 32 cm (b) 31 cm

(c) 34 cm (d) 23 cm

Sol. Given, $r = 10.5$ cm and $\theta = 60°$

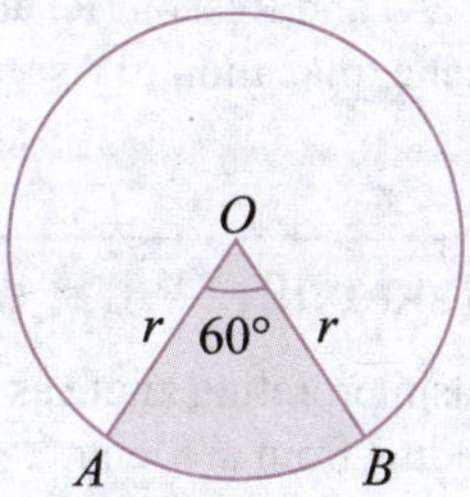

Perimeter of the sector $= 2r + \frac{\theta}{360°}\times 2\pi r$

$= 2\times 10.5 + \frac{60°}{360°}\times 2\times\frac{22}{7}\times 10.5 = 21 + 11 = 32$ cm

4. **If the length of an arc of a sector of angle 60 degrees in a circle is 8 cm, then radius of the circle is:** *(Ev)*

(a) $8/\pi$ cm (b) $24/\pi$ cm

(c) 8π cm (d) 16π cm

Sol. Given $\theta = 60°$ and length of an arc = 8 cm,

we know that the length of an arc $= \frac{\theta}{360°}\times 2\pi r$

$\Rightarrow 8\text{ cm} = \frac{60°}{360°}\times 2\times\pi\times r \Rightarrow r = \frac{24}{\pi}$.

Key Takeaways

Length of an arc $= \frac{\theta}{360°}\times 2\pi r$

5. **If the length of an arc of a segment of angle θ in a circle of radius r is π cm and the angle of the segment is 120°, then radius of the circle is:** *(Ap)*

(a) $2/\pi$ cm (b) 2 cm

(c) $2\pi/3$ cm (d) 3/2 cm

Sol. Given length of the arc is π cm and $\theta = 120°$ and radius $= r$

We know that,

length of arc $= \frac{\theta}{360°}\times 2\pi r \Rightarrow \pi = \frac{120°}{360}\times 2\pi r$

$\Rightarrow 3 = 2r \Rightarrow r = \frac{3}{2}$ cm.

Mistakes 101 : What not to do!

Students often make mistakes when calculating the circumference of a sector of a circle.

6. **If the length of an arc of a segment of angle 90° in a circle is 6π cm, what is the radius of the circle?** *(Ev)*

(a) 6 cm (b) 12 cm

(c) 18 cm (d) 24 cm

Sol. Given $\theta = 90°$ and

We know that, length of an arc $= \frac{\theta}{360°}\times 2\pi r$

$\Rightarrow 6\pi = \frac{90°}{360°}\times 2\pi r$

$\Rightarrow 6 = \frac{1}{2}r$

$\Rightarrow r = 12$ cm.

7. **The radius of a circle is same as the side of a square. Their perimeters are in the ratio.** **(*Ev*) (CBSE SQP, 2023)**

(*a*) 1 : 1 (*b*) 2 : π
(c) π : 2 (*d*) $\sqrt{\pi}$: 2

Sol. Given that,

Radius of circle = Side of square

Let radius of circle be x

⇒ Radius of circle = Side of square = x

$$\text{Ratio of perimeters} = \frac{\text{Perimeter of circle}}{\text{Perimeter of square}} = \frac{2\pi x}{4x} = \frac{\pi}{2}$$

8. **If the perimeter and the area of a circle are numerically equal, then the radius of the circle is** **(*Ev*)**

(*a*) 2 units (*b*) π units
(c) 4 units (*d*) 7 units

Sol. Let's denote the radius of the circle as r.

The perimeter (circumference) of a circle is given by the formula:

$P = 2\pi r$

The area of a circle is given by the formula:

$A = \pi r^2$

According to the problem, the perimeter and the area of the circle are numerically equal, so we have:

$2\pi r = \pi r^2$

To solve for r, we can divide both sides by πr

$$\frac{2\pi r}{\pi r} = \frac{\pi r^2}{\pi r} \Rightarrow r = 2$$

Therefore, the radius of the circle is $r = 2$.

Nailing the Right Answer

Students should remember all the basic formulas related to area of a circle.

Answer Key

1. (d) 2. (b) 3. (a) 4. (b) 5. (d)
6. (b) 7. (c) 8. (a)

Assertion and Reason **(1 M)**

Direction: In the questions number 1 and 3, a statement of Assertion (A) is followed by statement of Reason (R). Choose the correct option:

(*a*) Both Assertion (A) and Reason (R) are true, and Reason (R) is the correct explanation of Assertion (A).

(*b*) Both Assertion (A) and Reason (R) are true, and Reason (R) is not the correct explanation of Assertion (A).

(*c*) Assertion (A) is true, but Reason (R) is false

(*d*) Assertion (A) is false, but Reason (R) is true.

1. **Assertion (A): In a circle of radius 6 cm, the angle of a sector 60°. Then the area of the sector is $18\frac{6}{7}$ cm²**

Reason (R): Area of the circle with radius r is πr^2. **(*Un*)**

Sol. $\text{Area of the sector} = \frac{\theta}{360°} \times \pi r^2 = \frac{60°}{360°} \times \frac{22}{7} \times 6 \times 6$

$= \frac{132}{7} = 18\frac{6}{7}\ \text{cm}^2.$

Assertion is true.

Area of the circle = πr^2

Reason is true.

Both Assertion (A) and Reason (R) are true but Reason (R) is not the correct explanation of Assertion (A).

2. **Assertion (A): If the circumference of a circle is 176 cm, then its radius is 28 cm.**

Reason (R): Circumference of the circle is $2\pi r$. **(*Un*)**

Sol. $\text{Circumference} = 2 \times \frac{22}{7} \times r = 176$

$\Rightarrow r = \frac{176 \times 7}{2 \times 22} = 28\ \text{cm}$

Assertion is true.

Circumference of the circle = $2\pi r$

Reason is true.

Both Assertion (A) and Reason (R) are true and Reason (R) is the correct explanation of Assertion (A).

3. **Assertion (A): The length of the minute hand of a clock is 7cm. Then the area swept by the minute hand in 5 minutes is $12\frac{5}{6}$ cm²**

Reason (R): The length of an arc of a sector of angle and radius r is given by $l = \frac{\theta}{360°} \times 2\pi r$ **(*An*)**

Sol. Area swept by minute hand in 5 minutes

$= \frac{\theta}{360°} \times \pi r^2 = \frac{30°}{360°} \times \frac{22}{7} \times 7 \times 7$

(Angle in 5 minutes by minute hand is 30°)

$= \frac{77}{6} = 12\frac{5}{6}\text{cm}^2$

Both Assertion (A) and Reason (R) are true but Reason (R) is not the correct explanation of Assertion (A).

Mistakes 101 : What not to do!

Students can misinterpreting angle as degrees, not radians, when finding radius from arc length.

Answer Key

1. (b) 2. (a) 3. (b)

Subjective Questions

Very Short Answer Type Questions (1 or 2 M)

1. A chord of a circle of radius 10 cm subtends a right angle at the centre. Find area of minor segment. (Use $\pi = 3.14$) *(Un)* **(CBSE SQP, 2023)**

Sol. r of circle = 10cm, $\theta = 90°$

A of minor segment $= \dfrac{\theta}{360°}\pi r^2 - \text{A of } \Delta$ *(½ M)*

$= \dfrac{\theta}{360°} \times \pi r^2 - \dfrac{1}{2} \times b \times h$ *(½ M)*

$= \dfrac{90°}{360°} \times 3.14 \times 10 \times 10 - \dfrac{1}{2} \times 10 \times 10 = \dfrac{314}{4} - 50$ *(½ M)*

$= 78.5 – 50 = 28.5 \text{ cm}^2$

A of segment $= 28.5 \text{ cm}^2$ *(½ M)*

2. The perimeter of a sector of a circle of radius 14 cm is 68 cm. Find the area of the sector. *(Cr)* **(CBSE, 2020)**

Sol. $P = s + 2r$

Given $P = 68$ cm and $r = 14$ cm, we can find s:

$\Rightarrow 68 = s + 2(14)$

$\Rightarrow 68 = s + 28$

$\Rightarrow s = 68 - 28$

$\Rightarrow s = 40$ cm *(½ M)*

Angle of sector $= \dfrac{20}{\pi} \times 360°$

$A = \dfrac{\text{angle of sector}}{360°} \times \pi r^2 \Rightarrow A = \dfrac{7200}{\pi} \times \dfrac{1}{360} \times \pi (14)^2$

$\Rightarrow A = \dfrac{7200}{\pi} \times \dfrac{1}{360} \times 196\pi \Rightarrow A = \dfrac{7200}{360} \times 14$

$\Rightarrow A = 20 \times 14 \Rightarrow A = 280 \text{ cm}^2$ *(½ M)*

3. In fig., $\widehat{PQ}$ and $\widehat{AB}$ are two arcs of concentric circles of radii 7 cm and 3.5 cm resp., with centre O. If $\angle POQ = 30°$, then find the area of shaded region. *(Ev)* **(CBSE, 2020)**

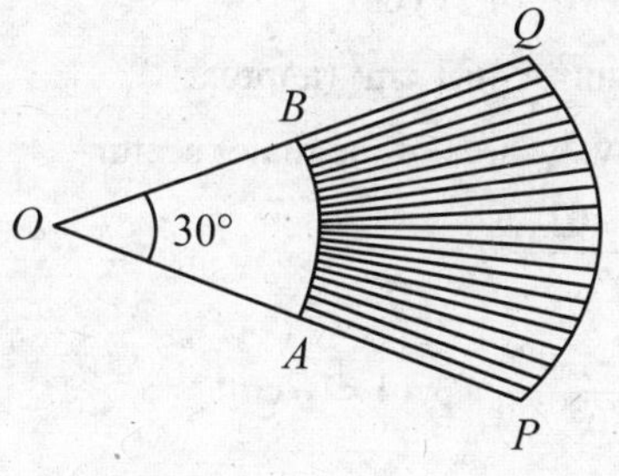

Sol. Area of shaded region $= \dfrac{22}{7} \times \dfrac{\theta}{360°}(7^2 - (3.5)^2) = 9.625 \text{cm}^2$ *(1 M)*

Short Answer Type Questions (2 or 3 M)

1. The perimeter of a sector of a circle with radius 6.5 cm is 31 cm, then find the area of the sector. *(Cr)* **(CBSE, 2020)**

Sol.

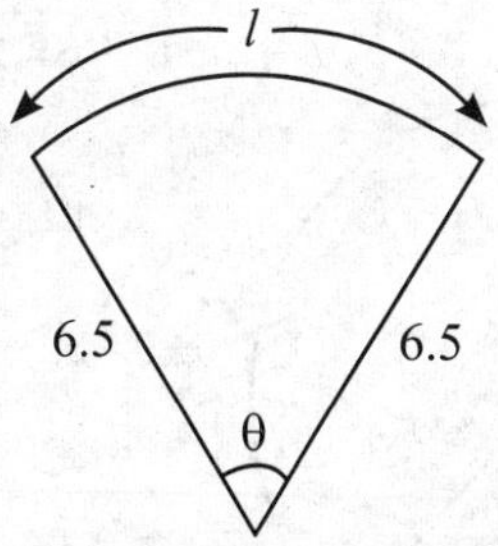

The given sector of a circle has radius (r) = 6.5 cm

Its perimeter is given to be 31 cm.

$\Rightarrow 2r + l = 31 \Rightarrow 2(6.5) + l = 31 \Rightarrow l = 18$ *(1 M)*

Now the area of the sector is given by

$\dfrac{1}{2} \times r \times l = \dfrac{1}{2} \times \dfrac{13}{2} \times 18 = 58.5 \text{cm}^2$ *(1 M)*

2. Find the area of a quadrant of a circle whose circumference is 22 cm. *(An)* **(NCERT Intext)**

Sol. Circumference of the circle, C = 22 cm (given)

It should be noted that a quadrant of a circle is a sector that is making an angle of 90°.

Let the radius of the circle be r

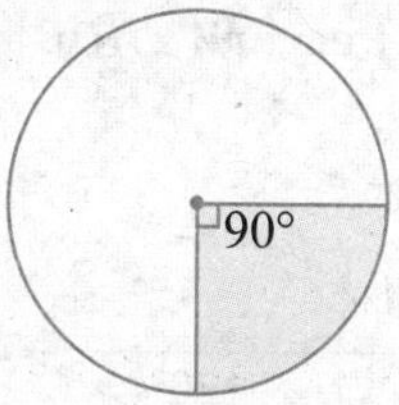

$\therefore 2\pi r = 22$ *(1 M)*

$\Rightarrow 2 \times \dfrac{22}{7} \times r = 22 \Rightarrow r = \dfrac{7}{2}$ cm *(½ M)*

$\therefore$ Area of the quadrant $= \dfrac{90°}{360°} \times \pi r^2$ *(½ M)*

$= \dfrac{1}{4} \times \dfrac{22}{7} \times \dfrac{7}{2} \times \dfrac{7}{2} = \dfrac{77}{8} \text{ cm}^2$ *(1 M)*

3. Find the area of the sector of a circle of radius 7 cm and of central angle 90°. Also, find the area of corresponding major sector. *(Ev)* **(CBSE, 2023)**

Sol. $r = 7$ cm, $\theta = 90°$

Area of sector $= \dfrac{\pi r^2 \theta}{360} = \dfrac{22}{7} \times 7 \times 7 \times \dfrac{90}{360}$ *(1 M)*

$= \dfrac{77}{2} \text{cm}^2$ or 38.5 cm^2 *(½ M)*

Area of circle $= \pi r^2 = \dfrac{22}{7} \times 7 \times 7 = 154 \text{ cm}^2$ *(1 M)*

Area of major sector $= 154 - 38.5 = 115.5 \text{ cm}^2$ *(½ M)*

Long Answer Type Questions (4 or 5 M)

1. In the given figure, AB is a chord of a circle of radius 7 cm and centred at O. Find the area of the shaded region if AOB = 90°. Also, find length of minor are AB.

(*Cr*) (CBSE, 2023)

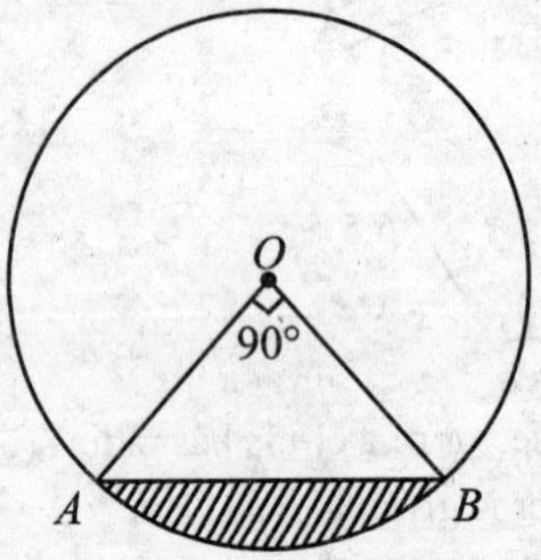

Sol. Area of sector AOB = $\frac{22}{7}\times 7\times 7\times\frac{90}{360}=\frac{77}{2}\text{cm}^2$ *(1½ M)*

Area of $\Delta AOB=\frac{1}{2}\times 7\times 7=\frac{49}{2}\text{cm}^2$ *(1 M)*

$\therefore$ Shaded area = $\frac{77}{2}-\frac{49}{2}=\frac{28}{2}=14\text{cm}^2$ *(1 M)*

Length of arc $AB=2\times\frac{22}{7}\times 7\times\frac{90}{360}$ = 11 cm *(1½ M)*

2. Find the area of the segment *AYB* shown in Fig., if radius of the circle is 21 cm and $\angle AOB$ = 120°. (Use $\pi=\frac{22}{7}$)

(Un)

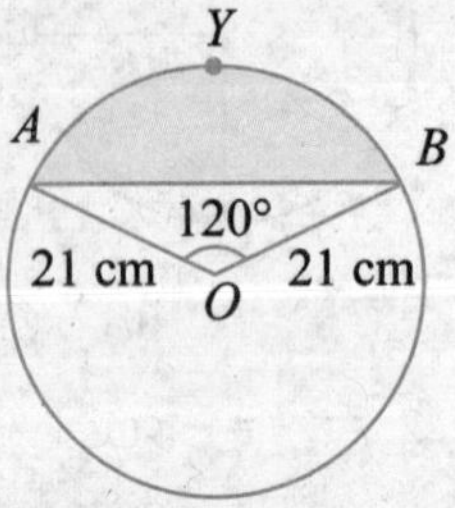

Sol. Area of the segment *AYB*

= Area of sector *OAYB* – Area of ΔOAB … (*i*) *(½ M)*

Now, area of the sector *OAYB*

$=\frac{120^\circ}{360^\circ}\times\frac{22}{7}\times 21\times 21\text{ cm}^2$ = 462 cm² … (*ii*) *(½ M)*

For finding the area of ΔOAB, draw $OM\perp AB$ as shown in Fig.

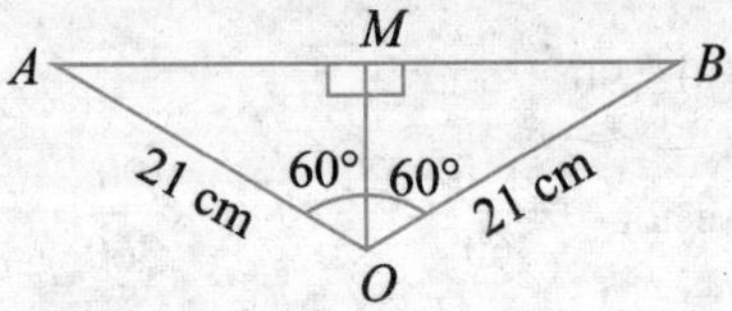

Note that *OA* = *OB*. Therefore, by *RHS* congruence, $\Delta AMO=\Delta BMO$.

So, *M* is the mid-point of *AB* and

$\angle AOM=\angle BOM=\frac{1}{2}\times 120^\circ=60^\circ$. *(½ M)*

Let *OM* = *x* cm

So, from Δ *OMA*, $\frac{OM}{OA}=\cos 60^\circ$ *(½ M)*

or, $\frac{x}{21}=\frac{1}{2}\Rightarrow x=\frac{21}{2}$

So, $OM=\frac{21}{2}$ cm *(1 M)*

Also, $\frac{AM}{OA}=\sin 60^\circ=\frac{\sqrt{3}}{2}$

So, $AM=\frac{21\sqrt{3}}{2}$ cm *(½ M)*

Therefore, $AB=2\,AM=\frac{2\times 21\sqrt{3}}{2}\text{cm}=21\sqrt{3}\text{ cm}$ *(½ M)*

So, area of $\Delta OAB=\frac{1}{2}AB\times OM$

$=\frac{1}{2}\times 21\sqrt{3}\times\frac{21}{2}\text{cm}^2=\frac{441}{4}\sqrt{3}\text{ cm}^2$ … (*iii*)

Therefore, area of the segment *AYB* = $\left(462-\frac{441}{4}\sqrt{3}\right)\text{cm}^2$ [From (*i*), (*ii*) and (*iii*)]

$=\frac{21}{4}(88-21\sqrt{3})\text{cm}^2$ *(1 M)*

3. Find the area of the sector of a circle with radius 4 cm and of angle 30° Also, find the area of the corresponding major sector (Use π = 3.14). **(*Un*) (NCERT Intext)**

Sol. Given sector is *OAPB* (see Fig.).

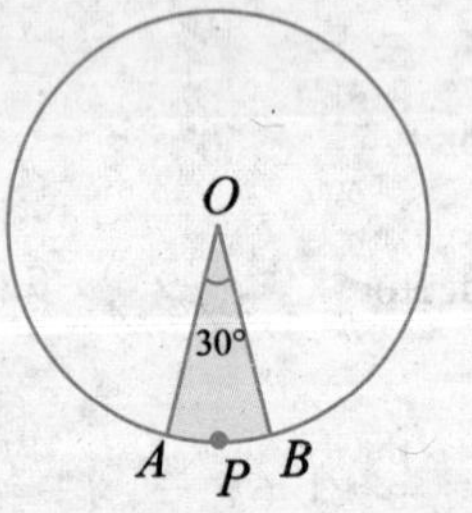

Area of the sector = $\frac{\theta}{360}\times\pi r^2=\frac{30^\circ}{360^\circ}\times 3.14\times 4\times 4\text{ cm}^2$

$=\frac{12.56}{3}\text{cm}^2=4.19\text{ cm}^2$ (approx). *(1 M)*

Area of the corresponding major sector

= πr^2 – area of sector *OAPB* *(1 M)*

= (3.14 × 16 – 4.19) cm²

= 46.05 cm² = 46.1 cm² (approx.) *(1 M)*

Alternatively, area of the major sector

$=\frac{(360^\circ-\theta)}{360^\circ}\times\pi r^2$ *(1 M)*

$=\left(\frac{360^\circ-30^\circ}{360^\circ}\right)\times 3.14\times 16\text{ cm}^2$

$=\frac{330^\circ}{360^\circ}\times 3.14\times 16\text{ cm}^2=46.06\text{ cm}^2$

= 46.1 cm² (approx.) *(1 M)*

Key Takeaways

Area of the major sector = $\frac{(360° - \theta)}{360°} \times \pi r^2$

Nailing the Right Answer

Students should understand formula, plug values, and calculate sector area accurately for major sector.

4. A horse is tied to a peg at one corner of a square shaped grass field of side 15 m by means of a 5 m long rope (see Fig.). Find

(i) the area of that part of the field in which the horse can graze.

(ii) the increase in the grazing area if the rope were 10 m long instead of 5 m. (Use $\pi = 3.14$)

(*Cr*) (NCERT Intext)

Sol. From the figure, it can be observed that the horse can graze a sector of 90° in the circle of 5m radius.

(*i*) The area that can be grazed by the horse when length of the rope is 5m

$= \frac{90°}{360°} \times \pi r^2$ (*1 M*)

$= \frac{90°}{360°} \times 3.14 \times 5 \times 5$ (*½ M*)

$= \frac{1}{4} \times \frac{314}{100} \times 5 \times 5 = \frac{157}{8} = 19.625 \text{ cm}^2$ (*1 M*)

(*ii*) If the rope is increased to 10 m, then the area that can be grazed by horse will be

$= \frac{90°}{360°} \times \pi \times r^2$ (*1 M*)

$= \frac{90°}{360°} \times \frac{314}{100} \times 10^2 = \frac{1}{4} \times 314$ (*½ M*)

$= 78.5 \text{ m}^2$

$\therefore$ Increase in the grazing area

$= 78.5 \text{ m}^2 - 19.625 \text{ m}^2 = 58.875 \text{ m}^2$ (*1 M*)

5. A chord of a circle of radius 20 cm subtends an angle of 90° at the centre. Find the area of the corresponding major segment of the circle. (Use $\pi = 3.14$).

(*Un*) (NCERT Exemplar)

Sol. Let AB be the chord of a circle of radius 10 cm, with O as the centre of the circle (see Fig.).

Here, $\angle AOB = 90°$ and we have to find the area of the major segment (which is shaded). As $\angle AOB = 90°$, therefore angle of the major sector = 360° – 90° = 270° (*1 M*)

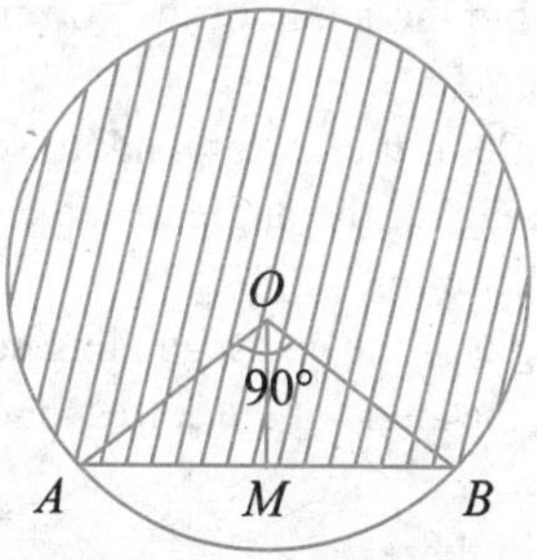

So, area of the major sector $= \frac{270°}{360°} \times \pi \times (10)^2 \text{ cm}^2$ (*1 M*)

$= \frac{3}{4} \times 3.14 \times 100 \text{ cm}^2 = 75 \times 3.14 \text{ cm}^2 = 235.5 \text{ cm}^2$ (*1 M*)

The Area of ΔOAB

As, $\angle AOB = 90°$,

Therefore, area of $\Delta OAB = \frac{1}{2} OA \times OB$

$= \frac{1}{2} \times 10 \times 10 \text{cm}^2 = 50 \text{cm}^2$ (*1 M*)

Therefore, the area of the required major segment

$= 235.5 \text{ cm}^2 + 50 \text{ cm}^2 = 285.5 \text{ cm}^2$ (*1 M*)

Mistakes 101 : What not to do!

Students might error by forgetting to convert angles to radians, misapplying the sector area formula, or miscalculating the major sector area..

MISCELLANEOUS EXERCISE

Multiple Choice Questions

(1 M)

1. If the area of a sector of a circle is one-sixth that of the complete circle, then the angle of the sector is

(*a*) 180° (*b*) 45°
(*c*) 60° (*d*) 90°

2. If the length of an arc of sector of a circle of radius *r* is equal to that of an arc of sector of a circle of radius 2*r*, then

(*a*) the angle of the corresponding sector of the first circle is double the angle of the corresponding sector of the other circle.
(*b*) the angle of the corresponding sector of the first circle is one-eighth the angle of the corresponding sector of the other circle.
(*c*) the angle of the corresponding sector of the first circle is half the angle of the corresponding sector of the other circle.
(*d*) None of these

3. If the angle of the sector is 60°, then the area of a sector of a circle with a radius of 6 cm is

(*a*) 142/7 (*b*) 127/7
(*c*) 132/7 (*d*) 122/7

4. In a circle of radius 21 cm, an arc subtends an angle of 60° at the centre. The length of the arc is

(*a*) 14 cm (*b*) 21 cm
(*c*) 22 cm (*d*) 25 cm

5. In the adjoining figure, *OPRQ* is a quadrant of a circle of radius 7 cm. The perimeter of the quadrant is

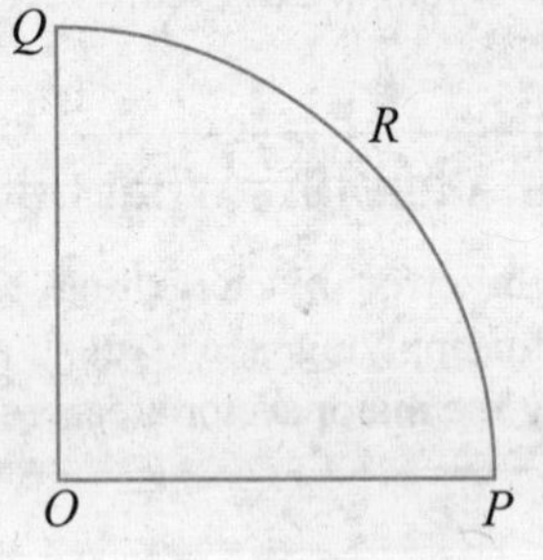

(*a*) 9 cm (*b*) 18 cm
(*c*) 25 cm (*d*) 36 cm

6. The area of the circle is 154 cm². The radius of the circle is **(CBSE SQP, 2023)**

(*a*) 7 cm (*b*) 14 cm
(*c*) 3.5 cm (*d*) 17.5 cm

7. If the radius of a circle is diminished by 10%, then its area is diminished by

(*a*) 14% (*b*) 19%
(*c*) 36% (*d*) 20%

8. If the area of a sector of a circle is 3π cm² with a central angle of 120°, then the length of the corresponding arc of this sector is

(*a*) 5.8 cm (*b*) 4.8 cm
(*c*) 6.3 cm (*d*) 6.8 cm

9. The minute hand of a clock is 10 cm long. The area of the face of the clock described by the minute hand between 10 A.M. and 10:35 A.M. is

(*a*) 183.4 cm² (*b*) 84 cm²
(*c*) 185 cm² (*d*) 184.5 cm²

10. The area of a sector of angle α(in degrees) of a circle with radius *R* is: **(CBSE, 2023)**

(*a*) $\frac{\alpha}{180}\times 2\pi R$ (*b*) $\frac{\alpha}{360}\times 2\pi R$

(*c*) $\frac{\alpha}{180}\times \pi R^2$ (*d*) $\frac{\alpha}{360}\times \pi R^2$

11. If the area of a semi-circular field is 15400 m², then the perimeter of the field is

(*a*) $160\sqrt{2}$ m (*b*) $560\sqrt{2}$ m
(*c*) $360\sqrt{2}$ m (*d*) $460\sqrt{2}$ m

12. A buffalo is tied with a rope of length 14 m at the corner of a rectangular field of dimensions 20m × 16m, then the area of the field in which the buffalo can graze is

(*a*) 154 m² (*b*) 156 m²
(*c*) 168 m² (*d*) 160 m²

13. Two concentric circles of radii 3.5 cm and 7 cm. Third concentric circle is drawn outside the 7 cm circle, such that the area each enclosed between it and the 7 cm circle is same as that between the two inner circles. The radius of the third circle correct to one decimal place O is

(*a*) 9.26 cm (*b*) 8.26 cm
(*c*) 6.26 cm (*d*) 10.26 cm

Assertion and Reason

(1 M)

Direction: In the questions number 1 and 3, a statement of Assertion (A) is followed by statement of Reason (R). Choose the correct option:

(*a*) Both Assertion (A) and Reason (R) are true, and Reason (R) is the correct explanation of Assertion (A).
(*b*) Both Assertion (A) and Reason (R) are true, and Reason (R) is not the correct explanation of Assertion (A).
(*c*) Assertion (A) is true, but Reason (R) is false
(*d*) Assertion (A) is false, but Reason (R) is true.

1. **Assertion (A):** A wire is looped in the form of a circle of radius 28 cm. If it is bent into a form of a square, then the area of the square is 1400 cm^2.

   Reason (R): Minute hand of a clock describes 360° in 60 minutes.

2. **Assertion (A):** If the outer and inner radius of a circular path is 5 m and 3 m, then area of the path is 16π m^2.

   Reason (R): If R and r be the radius of outer and inner circular path then area of the path = $\pi(R^2 - r^2)$

3. **Assertion (A):** If the circumference of two circles are in the ratio 2 : 3, then the ratio of their areas is 4 : 9.

   Reason (R): The circumference of a circle of radius r is $2\pi r$ and its area is πr^2.

Subjective Questions

Very Short Answer Type Questions (1 or 2 M)

1. The areas of two circles are in the ratio 9 : 4, then what is the ratio of their circumferences? **(CBSE, 2020)**
2. The circumference of a circle is 39.6 cm. Find its area. **(CBSE, 2020)**
3. The length of the minute hand of a clock is 14 cm. What is the angle made by the minute hand in 5 minutes?
4. What is the diameter of a circle whose area is equal to the sum of the areas of two circles of radii 40 cm and 9 cm? **(CBSE SQP, 2023)**
5. Find the area of a circle whose circumferences is 44 cm. **(CBSE, 2020)**

Short Answer Type Questions (2 or 3 M)

1. In the given figure, two concentric circles with centre O are shown. Radii of the circles are 2 cm and 5 cm respectively. Find the area of the shaded region.

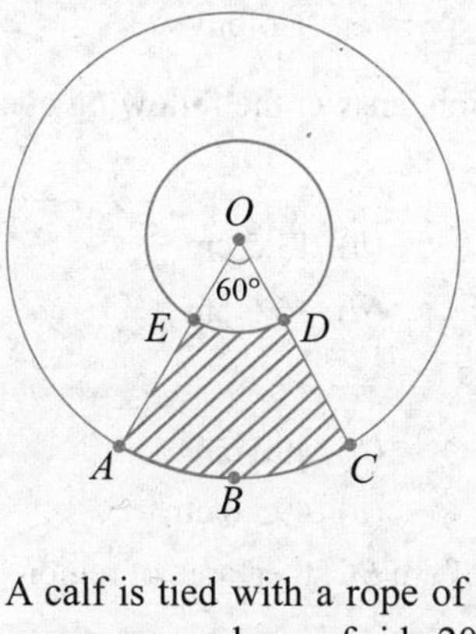

(CBSE, 2023)

2. A calf is tied with a rope of length 6 m at the corner of a square grassy lawn of side 20 m. If the length of the rope is increased by 5.5 m, find the increase in area of the grassy lawn in which the calf can graze. **(NCERT Exemplar)**
3. The minute hand of a clock is 21 cm long. Calculate the area swept by it and the distance travelled by its tip in 20 minutes. **(CBSE, 2020)**
4. A cow is tied at one of the corners of a square shed. The length of the rope is 22 m. The cow can only eat the grass outside the shed as shown below.

   What is the area that the cow can graze on? Show your steps. (Note: Give the answer in terms of π.) **(CBSE CFPQ, 2023)**

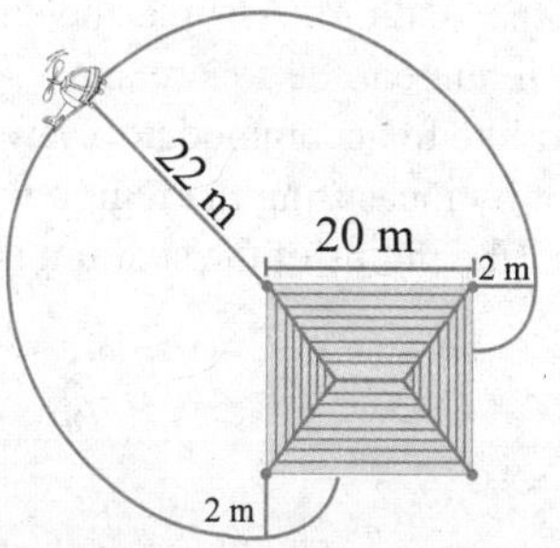

(**Note:** The Figure is not to scale.)

Long Answer Type Questions (4 or 5 M)

1. A chord of a circle of radius 12 cm subtends an angle of 120° at the centre. Find the area of the corresponding segment of the circle. (Use $\pi = 3.14$ and $\sqrt{3} = 1.73$)
2. A brooch is made with silver wire in the form of a circle with a diameter 35 mm. The wire is also used in making 5 diameters which divide the circle into 10 equal sectors as shown in Fig. Find:

   (*i*) the total length of the silver wire required.

   (*ii*) the area of each sector of the brooch.

3. A round table cover has six equal designs as shown in Fig. If the radius of the cover is 28 cm, find the cost of making the designs at the rate of ₹ 0.35 per cm^2. (Use $\sqrt{3} = 1.7$)

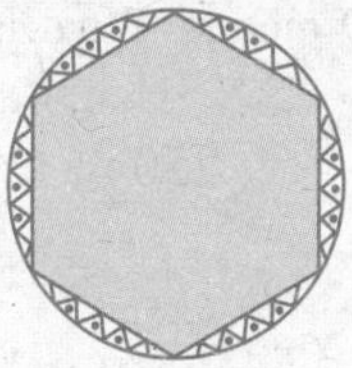

4. An elastic belt is placed around the rim of a pulley of radius 5 cm. From one paint C on the belt, the elastic belt is pulled directly away from O, the centre of the pulley until it is at P, 10 cm from the paint O. Find the length of the belt that is still in contact with the pulley Also find the shaded area.

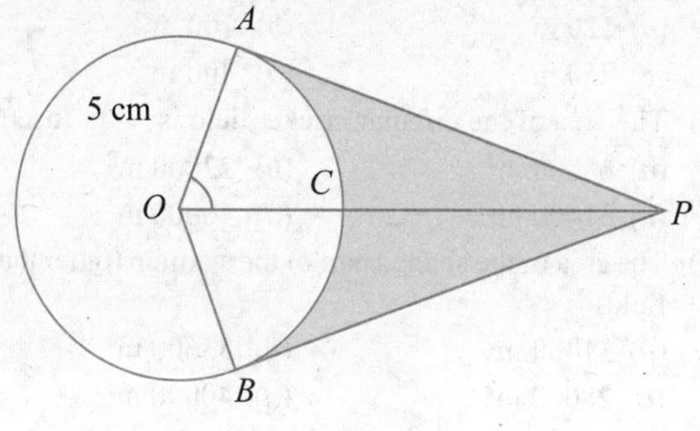

Case Based Questions

Case Based-I: A stadium is in a circular shape. As shown in the figure, some areas have been allotted for a hockey court and a javelin range in the stadium. Assume the shape of the hockey court and the javelin range to be square and triangle, respectively. The curators would like to accommodate a few more sports in the stadium. Help them by measuring the region which is not allotted within the stadium. (the radius of the stadium is 200 metres).

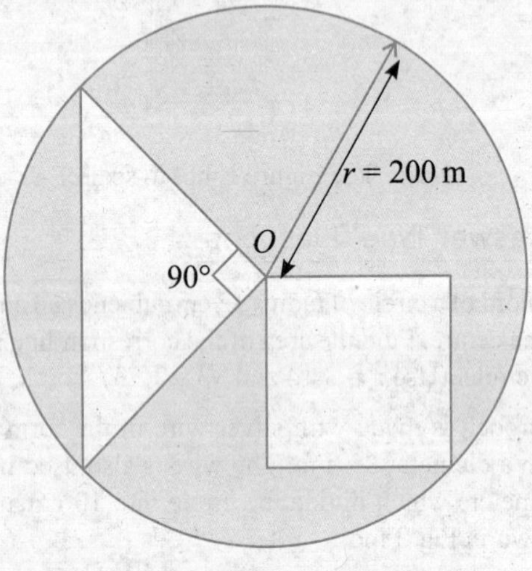

(*i*) Find the area of the circular stadium. (Use $\pi = 3.14$)

(*ii*) Find the area of the hockey court (square).

OR

Find the area of the Javelin Range.

(*iii*) Find the ratio of the areas of the Javelin Range and Circular field.

Case Based-II: Rohit and his friends went to the city. He visited a cricket stadium which is in the shape of a trapezium. A circular green ground for playing cricket is inscribed in a trapezium-shaped stadium with a height of 200 metres and parallel sides of 250 metres and 400 metres. What is the area of the shaded region?

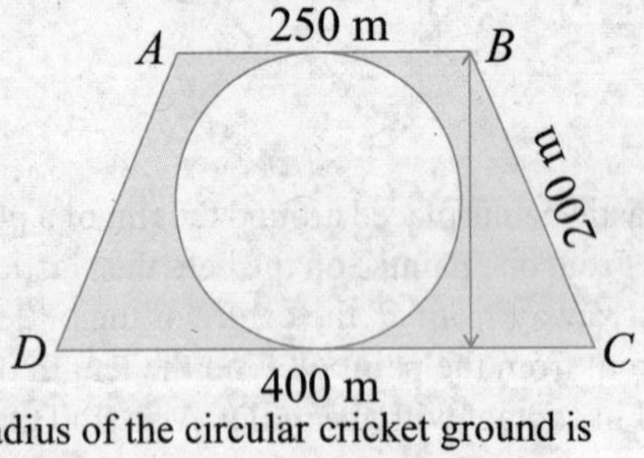

(*i*) The radius of the circular cricket ground is

(*a*) 120 m (*b*) 100 m

(*c*) 250 m (*d*) 400 m

(*ii*) The area of the circular cricket field is (use $\pi = 3.14$)

(*a*) 65000 m^2 (*b*) 22000 m^2

(*c*) 31400 m^2 (*d*) 40000 m^2

(*iii*) The area of the shaded part of the stadium (other than cricket field) is

(*a*) 31400 m^2 (*b*) 33600 m^2

(*c*) 28000 m^2 (*d*) 40000 m^2

(*iv*) The area of circular cricket field excluding pitch whose dimension is 22 m × 3 m is (use $\pi = 3.14$)

(*a*) 31400 m^2 (*b*) 28600 m^2

(*c*) 31334 m^2 (*d*) 40000 m^2

Case Based-III: Pooja wants to change the design of the floor of her living room which is of dimensions 6 m × 4 m and it is covered with circular tiles of diameters 50 cm each, as shown in the figure.

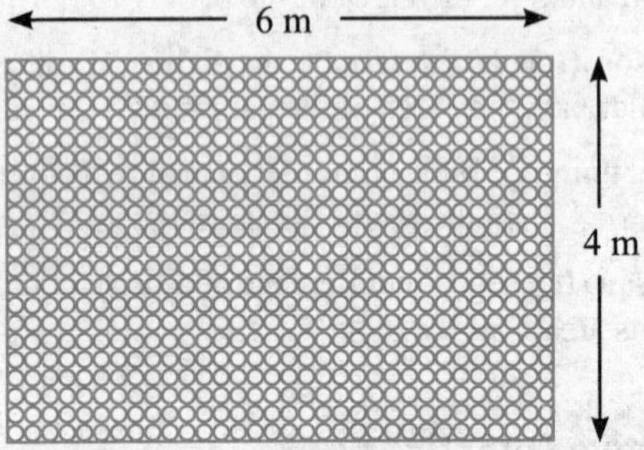

Based on the above information, answer the following questions.

(*i*) Find the number of circular tiles along length of room.

(*ii*) Find the number of circular tiles along breath of room.

OR

Find the area covered by each circular tile.

(*iii*) Find the area of rectangular floor.

Case Based-IV: To find the polluted region in different areas of Dwarka (a part of Delhi represented by the circle given below) a survey was conducted by the students of class X. It was found that the shaded region is the polluted region, where O is the centre of the circle.

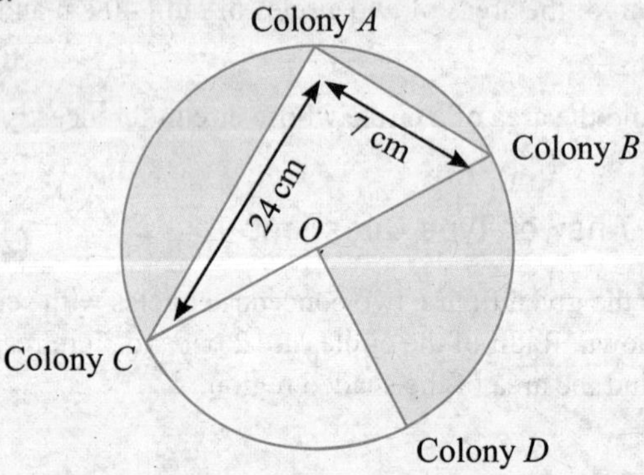

Based on the above information, answer the following questions.

(*i*) The radius of the circle is

(*a*) 12.5 cm (*b*) 13.5 cm

(*c*) 15 cm (*d*) 16.5 cm

(*ii*) The area of the circle is

(*a*) 481.7 cm^2 (*b*) 490 cm^2

(*c*) 491.07 cm^2 (*d*) 495.6 cm^2

(*iii*) If D lies in the middle of arc BC, then area of region COD is

(*a*) 121 cm^2 (*b*) 122.76 cm^2

(*c*) 126 cm^2 (*d*) 129.8 cm^2

(*iv*) Area of the ΔBAC is

(*a*) 77 cm^2 (*b*) 79 cm^2

(*c*) 81 cm^2 (*d*) 84 cm^2

Case Based-V: Director of a company select a round glass trophy for awarding their employees on annual function. Design of each trophy is made as shown in the figure, where its base *ABCD* is golden plated from the front side at the rate of 6 per cm².

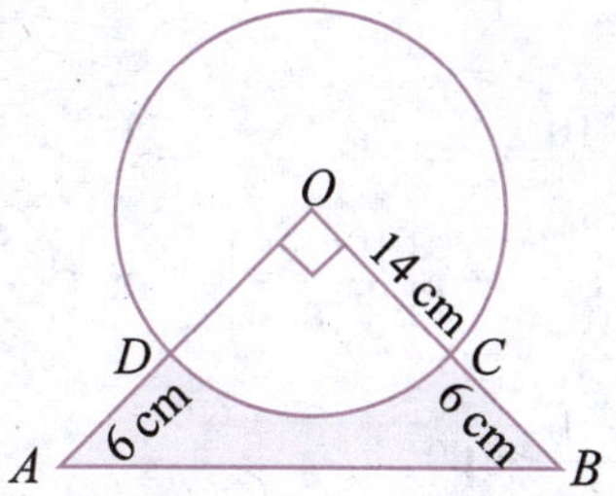

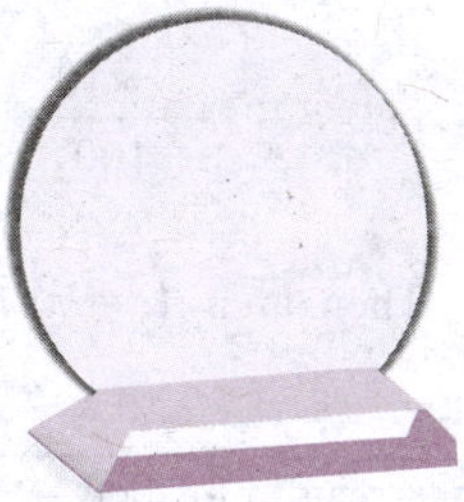

(*i*) The area of sector *ODCO*

(*a*) 154 cm² (*b*) 155 cm²

(*c*) 156 cm² (*d*) 157 cm²

(*ii*) The area of ΔAOB

(*a*) 150 cm² (*b*) 200 cm²

(*c*) 250 cm² (*d*) 300 cm²

(*iii*) The total cost of golden plating

(*a*) 276 (*b*) 280

(*c*) 284 (*d*) 200

(*iv*) The area of major sector formed in the given figure

(*a*) 400 cm² (*b*) 450 cm²

(*c*) 462 cm² (*d*) 472 cm²

ANSWER KEYS

Multiple Choice Questions

1. (*c*) 2. (*a*) 3. (*c*) 4. (*c*) 5. (*c*) 6. (*a*) 7. (*b*) 8. (*c*) 9. (*a*) 10. (*d*)
11. (*c*) 12. (*a*) 13. (*a*)

Assertion and Reason

1. (*d*) 2. (*a*) 3. (*a*)

Case Based Types Questions

Case Based-II

(*i*) (*b*) (*ii*) (*c*) (*iii*) (*b*) (*iv*) (*c*)

Case Based-IV

(*i*) (*a*) (*ii*) (*c*) (*iii*) (*b*) (*iv*) (*d*)

Case Based-V

(*i*) (*a*) (*ii*) (*b*) (*iii*) (*a*) (*iv*) (*c*)

HINTS & EXPLANATIONS

Multiple Choice Questions

1. (*c*) According to question,

$$\therefore \frac{\theta}{360°} \times \pi r^2 = \frac{1}{6}\pi r^2 \Rightarrow \theta = \frac{360°}{6} = 60°$$

2. (*a*) According to the given condition,

$$\frac{\theta_1}{360°} \times 2\pi r_1 = \frac{\theta_2}{360°} \times 2\pi r_2$$

$$\Rightarrow \frac{2\pi}{360°}[\theta_1 r_1] = \frac{2\pi}{360°}[\theta_2 r_2] \Rightarrow \theta_1 r_1 = \theta_2 r_2$$

$$\Rightarrow \theta_1 r = \theta_2(2r) \Rightarrow \theta_1 = 2\theta_2$$

Hence, the angle of the corresponding sector of the first circle is double the angle of the corresponding sector of the other circle.

3. (*c*) Given: Angle of the sector = 60°

Radius of circle = 6 cm

Area of sector = $\frac{\theta}{360°} \times \pi r^2$

$\therefore$ Area of the sector with angle 60° = $\frac{60°}{360°} \times \pi r^2$

$= \frac{1}{6} \times \pi \times (6)^2 = 6 \times \frac{22}{7}\text{ cm}^2 = \frac{132}{7}\text{ cm}^2$

4. (*c*) It is given that, the radius of a circle = 21 cm

Length of an arc = $\left(\frac{\theta}{360°}\right) \times (2\pi r)$

$\therefore$ Length of an arc = $\left(\frac{60°}{360°}\right) \times 2 \times \frac{22}{7} \times 21$

[Given, θ = 60°, *r* = 21 cm]

$= \left(\frac{1}{6}\right) \times 2 \times \left(\frac{22}{7}\right) \times 21$

Hence, length of the arc = 22 cm

5. (*c*) Perimeter of quadrant of circle = $\frac{1}{4} \times 2\pi r + 2r$

$= \left(\frac{1}{2} \times \frac{22}{7} \times 7 + 2 \times 7\right)\text{cm} = 25\text{ cm}$

6. (*a*) Area of circle = 154 cm²

$\Rightarrow \pi r^2 = 154\text{ cm}^2$

$\Rightarrow \frac{22}{7} \times r^2 = 154$

$\Rightarrow r^2 = 154 \times \frac{22}{7}$

$\Rightarrow r^2 = 7 \times 7 = 49$

$\therefore r = \sqrt{49} = 7\text{cm}$

7. (*b*) Let us suppose, *r* be the radius of the circle.

$\therefore$ Area of circle, $A_1 = \pi r^2$

When *r* is diminished by 10%,

i.e., $r = r - \frac{r \times 10}{100} = r - \frac{r}{10}$

Then, area $A_2 = \pi\left(r - \frac{r}{10}\right)^2 = \pi\left[\frac{10r - r}{10}\right]^2 = \pi r^2\left(\frac{81}{100}\right)$

Area diminished = $\frac{A_1 - A_2}{A_1} \times 100$

$$= \frac{\pi r^2 - \pi r^2\left(\frac{81}{100}\right)}{\pi r^2} \times 100 = \frac{\pi r^2\left[1 - \frac{81}{100}\right]}{\pi r^2} \times 100$$

$$= \left[1 - \frac{81}{100}\right] \times 100 = \frac{19}{100} \times 100 = 19\%$$

8. (*c*) Given angle is 120° and area is 3π

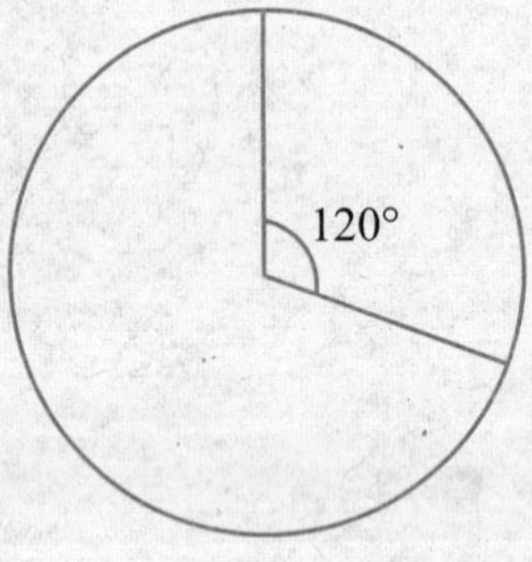

As known area of a sector $= \frac{\theta}{360°} \times \pi r^2$

$\Rightarrow 3\pi = \pi \times r^2 \times \frac{120°}{360°} \Rightarrow r^2 = 9$

$\Rightarrow r = \sqrt{9} \Rightarrow r = 3$

Length of the arc. $l = \frac{\theta}{360°} \times 2\pi r = \frac{120°}{360°} \times 2\pi \times 3 = 2\pi = 6.3$

Thus, length of the arc is 6.3 cm.

9. (*a*) We know that the area *A* of a sector of circle at an angle θ of radius *r* is given by

$A = \frac{\theta}{360°} \times \pi r^2$

We have,

Angle described by the minute hand in one minute = 6°

So, Angle described by the minute hand in 35 minute = 6° × 35 = 210°

$\therefore$ Required area $= \frac{210°}{360°} \times \frac{22}{7} \times (10)^2 = 183.4\text{ cm}^2$

10. (*d*) $A = \frac{\alpha}{360°} \times \pi R^2$

Where:

- α is the angle of the sector in degrees
- R is the radius of the circle

11. (c) Given, Area of the semi-circle = 15400 m^2

Area = $\frac{\pi r^2}{2} \Rightarrow \frac{\pi r^2}{2} = 15400$

$\Rightarrow r^2 = \frac{15400 \times 2 \times 7}{22} \Rightarrow r^2 = 9800$

$\Rightarrow r = \sqrt{9800} = 70\sqrt{2}$ m $\Rightarrow$ Perimeter = $\pi r + 2r$

$= \frac{22}{7} \times 70\sqrt{2} + 2 \times 70\sqrt{2} = 220\sqrt{2} + 140\sqrt{2}$

$= \sqrt{2}(220 + 140)$

Perimeter = $360\sqrt{2}$ m

12. (a) Figure can be represented as:

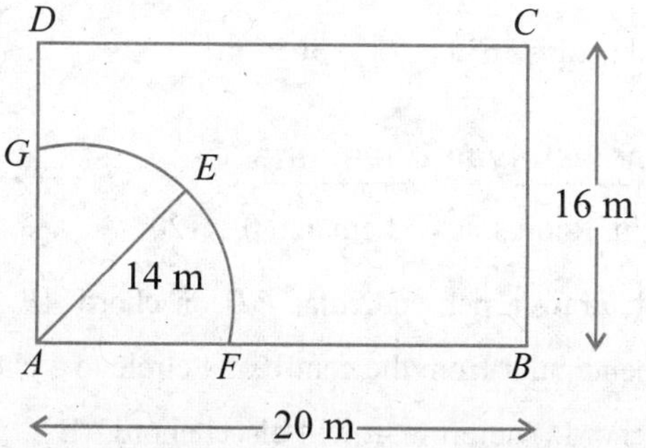

Area of the field in which buffalo can graze

= Area of a sector $AGEF$

$= \left(\frac{\theta}{360°}\right) \times \pi r^2 = \left(\frac{90°}{360°}\right) \times \pi(14)^2$

$= \left(\frac{1}{4}\right) \times \left(\frac{22}{7}\right) \times 196 = 154 \text{ m}^2$

Hence, the area of the field in which buffalo can graze = 154 m^2

13. (a) The area enclosed between the two circles of radii 3.5 cm and 7 cm

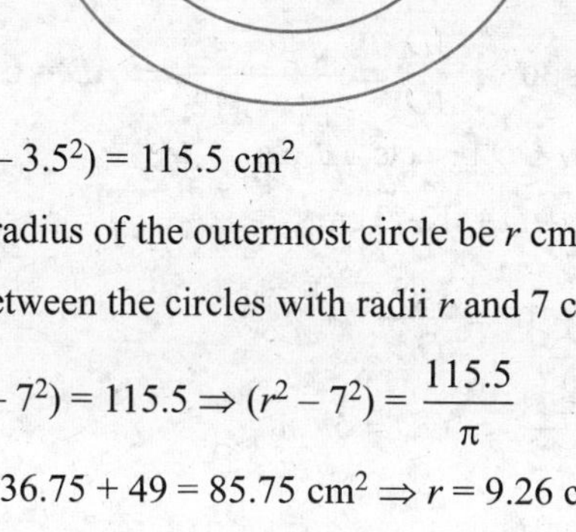

$= \pi(7^2 - 3.5^2) = 115.5 \text{ cm}^2$

Let us radius of the outermost circle be r cm.

Area between the circles with radii r and 7 cm

$= \pi(r^2 - 7^2) = 115.5 \Rightarrow (r^2 - 7^2) = \frac{115.5}{\pi}$

$\Rightarrow r^2 = 36.75 + 49 = 85.75 \text{ cm}^2 \Rightarrow r = 9.26$ cm

Assertion and Reason

1. (d) Length of wire = $2\pi r = 2 \times \frac{22}{7} \times 28 = 176$ cm

According to the question,

Perimeter of square = 176 $\Rightarrow 4a = 176 \Rightarrow a = 44$

Therefore,

Area of square = $(44)^2 = 1936 \text{ cm}^2$

Assertion (A) is false but Reason (R) is true.

2. (a) It is given that,

The outer radius of circular path = 5 m

The inner radius of circular path = 3 m

Therefore,

Area of path = $\pi[(5)^2 - (3)^2]$

$= \pi(25 - 9) = 16\pi \text{ m}^2$

Both Assertion (A) and Reason (R) are true and Reason (R) is the correct explanation of Assertion (A).

3. (a) It is given that,

$\frac{C_1}{C_2} = \frac{2}{3} \Rightarrow \frac{2\pi r_1}{2\pi r_2} = \frac{2}{3}$

$\Rightarrow \frac{r_1}{r_2} = \frac{2}{3}$

Now, the ratio of their areas = $\frac{\pi r_1^2}{\pi r_2^2} = \frac{r_1^2}{r_2^2} = \left(\frac{2}{3}\right)^2 = \frac{4}{9}$

Hence, the ratio of their areas is 4 : 9.

Both Assertion (A) and Reason (R) are true and Reason (R) is the correct explanation of Assertion (A).

Subjective Questions

Very Short Answer Type Questions

1. Given: Ratio of the areas of the two circle is 9 : 4.

Let the areas of the two circles be A_1 and A_2.

Hence,

$\frac{A_1}{A_2} = \frac{9}{4}$ ...(i)

Let the radii of the two circles be r_1 and r_2.

$= \frac{\text{Area of the first circle}}{\text{Area of the second circle}} = \frac{\pi r_1^2}{\pi r_2^2}$

$\Rightarrow \frac{\pi r_1^2}{\pi r_2^2} = \frac{9}{4}$ [From (i)]

$\Rightarrow \frac{r_1}{r_2} = \frac{3}{2}$ ...(ii) (½ M)

Let the circumferences of the two circles be C_1 and C_2.

$$\frac{C_1}{C_2}=\frac{2\pi r_1}{2\pi r_2} \Rightarrow \frac{C_1}{C_2}=\frac{r_1}{r_2} \Rightarrow \frac{C_1}{C_2}=\frac{3}{2} \quad \text{[From (ii)]}$$

The ratio of their circumference is 3 : 2. (½ M)

2. $r=\dfrac{39.6}{2\pi}$ (½ M)

$\Rightarrow A=\dfrac{392.04}{\pi}$ or $124.74\,\text{cm}^2$ $\quad (\because A=\pi r^2)$ (½ M)

3. The minute hand of the clock completes one rotation (*i.e,* 360° angle) in 60 minutes or 1 hour.

$\therefore$ In 60 mins, the minute hand makes angle 360°. (1 M)

$\Rightarrow$ In 1 min, it makes, $\dfrac{360°}{60}=6°$

$\Rightarrow$ In 5 min, it makes $= 5 \times 6° = 30°$

$\Rightarrow$ Required angle = 30°. (1 M)

4. Area of the circle = sum of areas of 2 circles

$\Rightarrow \pi R^2 = \pi(40)^2 + \pi(9)^2$ (½ M)

$\Rightarrow \pi R^2 = \pi \times (40^2 + 9)^2$

$\Rightarrow R^2 = 1600 + 81$ (½ M)

$\Rightarrow R^2 = 1681 \Rightarrow R = 41$ cm

Diameter of given circle = 41 × 2 = 82 cm (1 M)

5. $2\pi r = 44 \Rightarrow r = 7$ cm (1 M)

Area of circle $=\dfrac{22}{7}\times 7\times 7=154\,\text{cm}^2$ (1 M)

Short Answer Type Questions

1. Area of sector $OABC=\dfrac{\pi\times 5^2\times 60°}{360°}=\dfrac{25\pi}{6}\text{cm}^2$ (1 M)

Area of sector $OED=\dfrac{\pi\times 2^2\times 60°}{360°}=\dfrac{4\pi}{6}\text{cm}^2$ (1 M)

Area of shaded region$=\dfrac{25\pi}{6}-\dfrac{4\pi}{6}=\dfrac{21}{6}\times\dfrac{22}{7}=11\,\text{cm}^2$ (1 M)

2. Let the calf be tied at the corner A of the square lawn (see Fig.)

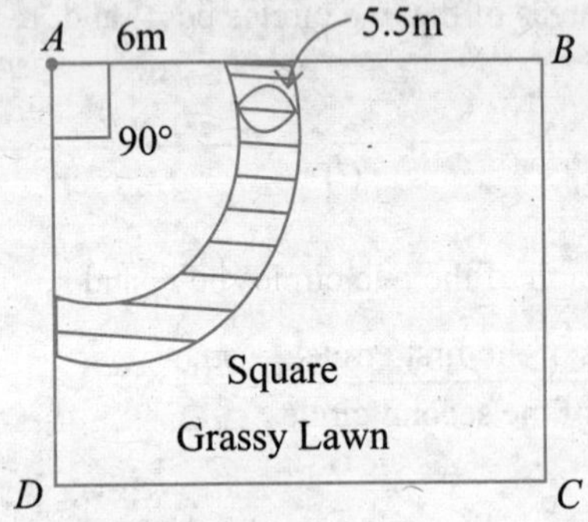

Given length of the rope = 6 m and increased length of the rope = 5.5 m

$\therefore$ Total length of the rope = 11.5 m (1 M)

So, required increase in area

$$=\left[\frac{90°}{360°}\times\pi\times(11.5)^2-\frac{90°}{360°}\pi\times 6^2\right]\text{m}^2 \quad (1\text{ M})$$

$$=\frac{\pi}{4}\times(11.5+6)(11.5-6)\,\text{m}^2$$

$$=\frac{22}{7\times 4}\times 17.5\times 5.5\,\text{m}^2=75.625\,\text{m}^2. \quad (1\text{ M})$$

3. Angle in 20 min = 120° (½ M)

Area $=\dfrac{22}{7}\times\dfrac{120°}{360°}\times(21)^2=462\,\text{cm}^2$ (1½ M)

Distance $=\dfrac{120°}{360°}\times 2\pi r=44$ cm (1 M)

4. Total area = (3 × quarters sector with radius 22 m) + (2 × one-quarter sector with radius 2 m) (1 M)

Total area $=\left(\dfrac{3}{4}\times\pi\times 22^2\right)+\left(2\times\dfrac{1}{4}\times\pi\times 2^2\right)$ (1 M)

Total area = $363\pi + 2\pi = 365\pi$ m² (1 M)

Long Answer Type Questions

1. Given, Radius, r = 12 cm and θ = 120°

Now, draw a perpendicular OD on chord AB. Since, the perpendicular from the centre of a circle to a chord bisects the chord. Therefore, it will bisect chord AB.

So, $AD = DB$

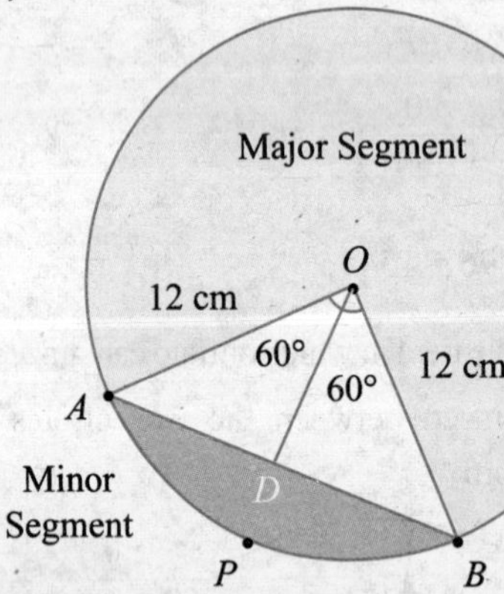

(1 M)

Now, the area of the minor sector $=\dfrac{\theta}{360°}\times\pi r^2$

$=\dfrac{120°}{360°}\times 3.14\times 12\times 12=150.72\,\text{cm}^2$ (1 M)

Consider ΔAOD,

$\angle OAB = 180° - (90° + 60°) = 30°$

Now, $\cos 30°=\dfrac{AD}{AO}\Rightarrow\dfrac{\sqrt{3}}{2}=\dfrac{AD}{12}\Rightarrow AD=6\sqrt{3}$ cm (1 M)

We know OD bisects AB. So,

$AB = 2 \times AD = 12\sqrt{3}$ cm

Now, $\sin 30°=\dfrac{OD}{OA}$

$\Rightarrow\dfrac{1}{2}=\dfrac{OD}{12}\Rightarrow OD=6$ cm (½ M)

So, the area of $\Delta AOB = \frac{1}{2}$ × base × height

$= \frac{1}{2} \times AB \times OD = \frac{1}{2} \times 12\sqrt{3} \times 6 = 36\sqrt{3} = 62.28 \text{ cm}^2$ (½ M)

∴ Area of the corresponding minor segment $APBD$

= Area of the minor sector $OAPB$ – Area of ΔAOB

= 150.72 cm² – 62.28 cm² = 88.44 cm² (1 M)

2. Given, the diameter of the circle = 35 mm

∴ Radius (r) $= \frac{35}{2}$ mm (½ M)

Total number of diameters to be considered = 5

Now, the total length of 5 diameters would be

= 35 × 5 = 175 (½ M)

Circumference of the circle = $2\pi r$

$= 2 \times \frac{22}{7} \times \frac{35}{2}$ mm $= 110$ mm (1 M)

Area of the circle $= \pi r^2 = \left(\frac{22}{7}\right) \times \left(\frac{35}{2}\right)^2 = \frac{1925}{2} \text{mm}^2$ (1 M)

(*i*) Total length of silver wire required

= Circumference of the circle + Length of 5 diameters

= 110 + 175 = 285 mm (½ M)

(*ii*) Total Number of sectors in the brooch = 10

So, the area of each sector = total area of the circle/ number of sectors (½ M)

∴ Area of each sector $= \frac{1925}{2} \times \frac{1}{10} = \frac{385}{4} \text{ mm}^2$ (1 M)

3.

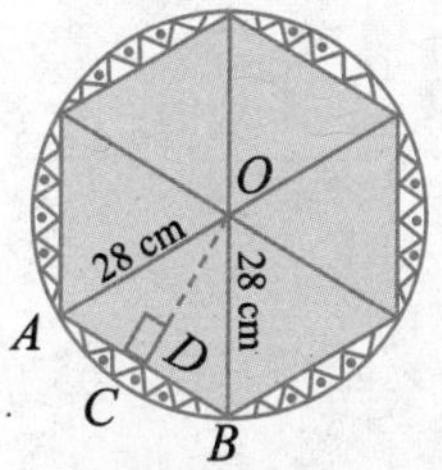

Total number of equal designs = 6

∴ Sector angle, $\theta = \frac{360^o}{6} = 60^o$ (½ M)

So, Area of each sector $= \frac{\theta}{360°} \times \pi r^2$ (½ M)

$= \frac{60^o}{360^o} \times \frac{22}{7} \times 28 \times 28 = \frac{1}{6} \times 22 \times 4 \times 28$

$= \frac{44 \times 28}{3} = 410.67 \text{ cm}^2$ (1 M)

In ΔAOB, $\angle AOB = 60°$, $OA = OB = 28$ cm

∴ $\angle OAB = \angle OBA$ [Equal sides have equal opposite angles]

∴ Area of equilateral $\Delta AOB = \frac{\sqrt{3}}{4} \times 28^2 = 333.2 \text{ cm}^2$ (1 M)

So, area of a single design

= area of sector ACB – area of ΔAOB

= 410.66 cm² – 333.2 cm² = 77.47 cm² (1 M)

∴ Area of 6 designs = 6 × 77.47 cm² = 464.76 cm²

Cost of making design = ₹ 0.35 per cm²

So, total cost of making 6 designs

= 464.76 cm² × ₹ 0.35 per cm² = ₹ 162.68 (1 M)

4. In $\angle AOP, \cos\theta = \frac{5}{10} = \frac{1}{2}$.

$\Rightarrow \theta = 60°$

∴ Reflex $\angle AOB = 240°$ (½ M)

∴ Length of belt in contact with pulley

$= \frac{\theta}{360°} \times 2\pi r = \frac{240°}{360°} \times 2\pi \times 5 = 20.93$ cm. (1 M)

Now, $\frac{AP}{OA} = \tan\theta = \tan 60°$

$\Rightarrow AP = 5\sqrt{3}$ cm $= BP$.

(Tangents from an enteral point are equal) (½ M)

Area ($\Delta OAP + \Delta OBP$)

$= 2 \times \left(\frac{1}{2} \times 5 \times 5\sqrt{3}\right) = 43.25 \text{ cm}^2$ (1 M)

Area of sector $OACB = \frac{120°}{360°} \times \frac{22}{7} \times (5)^2 = 26.17 \text{ cm}^2$

(As $\angle AOB = 2 \times 60° = 120°$) (1 M)

Shaded area = (43.25 – 26.17) cm² = 17.08 cm² (1 M)

Case Based Questions

Case Based-I

Radius of the circular stadium = 200 m

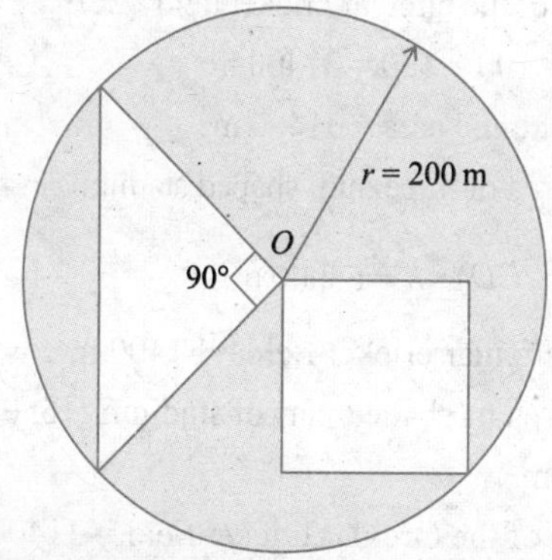

(*i*) Area of circular stadium = πr^2

= 3.14 × 200² = 125600 m²

(*ii*) Radius of the circular stadium = Diagonal of the square of hockey court.

Hence, the sides of the hockey court will be $a = \frac{r}{\sqrt{2}}$

Therefore, the area of the square = a^2

$= \left(\frac{r}{\sqrt{2}}\right)^2 = \frac{(200)^2}{2} = 20000 \text{ m}^2$

OR

Shape of the Javelin Range is a right-angled triangle

Area of the right triangle $= \frac{1}{2} \times r \times r$

$= \frac{1}{2} \times 200 \times 200 = 20000 \text{ m}^2$ [$\because r = 200$ m (given)]

(iii) As, Area of Javelin Range = 20000 m^2.

Area of circular field = 125600 m^2.

Hence, Ratio $= \frac{20000}{125600} = \frac{25}{157}$

Hence, required ratio = 25 : 157

Case Based-II

Given, height of the trapezium = 200 m.
and parallel sides are 250 m and 400 m.

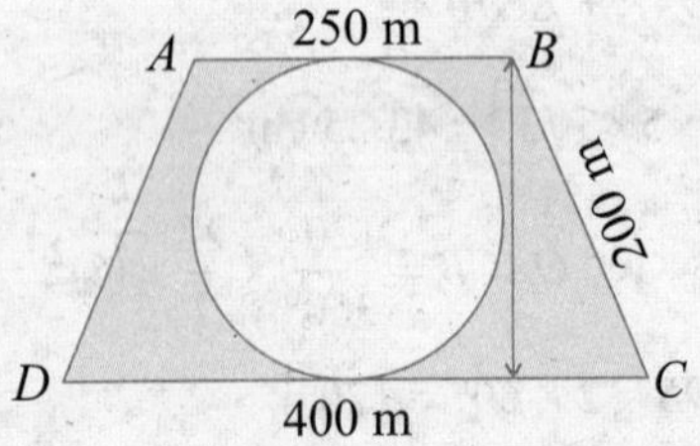

(i) (*b*) Here, diameter = 200 m

As, radius $= \frac{\text{Diameter}}{2}$

$\therefore$ Radius $= \frac{1}{2} \times 200 = 100$ m

(ii) (*c*) Area of the circular cricket field $= \pi r^2$

$= (3.14) \times 100 \times 100 = 31400 \text{ m}^2$

Hence, required area = 31400 m^2

(iii) (*b*) As, area of trapezium shaped stadium

$= \frac{1}{2}(AB + CD) \times h = 65000 \text{ m}^2$.

Area of circular cricket field = 31400 m^2.

Hence, area of shaded part of stadium = 65000 – 31400

= 33600 m^2.

(iv) (*c*) Area of the circular cricket field = 31400 m^2.

Area of pitch = 22 × 3 = 66 m^2.

Hence, area of circular cricket field excluding pitch

= 31400 – 66 = 31334 m^2.

Hence, required area = 31334 m^2

Case Based-III

(i) Number of circular tiles along length of room $= \frac{600}{50} = 12$

(ii) Number of circular tiles along breadth of room $= \frac{400}{50} = 8$

$\therefore$ Total number of circular tiles = 12 × 8 = 96

OR

Area covered by each circular tile $= \pi(25)^2$

$= \frac{22}{7} \times 25 \times 25 = 1964.28 \text{ cm}^2$

(iii) Area of rectangular floor = 600 × 400 = 240000 cm^2

Case Based-IV

(i) (*a*) Since BOC is the diameter and $\angle BAC = 90°$

$\therefore \quad BC^2 = AB^2 + AC^2 = 7^2 + 24^2 = 625$

$\Rightarrow BC = 25$ cm

$\therefore$ Radius of circle $= \frac{25}{2}$ cm = 12.5 cm

(ii) (*c*) Area of circle $= \pi(12.5)^2 = \frac{22}{7} \times 12.5 \times 12.5$

$= 491.07 \text{ cm}^2$

(iii) (*b*) Clearly, $\angle COD = 90°$

[$\because \angle COB = 180°$ and equal arcs subtends equal angles at the centre]

Area of region $COD = \frac{90°}{360°} \times \pi r^2$

$= \frac{1}{4}(491.07) = 122.76 \text{ cm}^2$

(iv) (*d*) Area of $\Delta BAC = \frac{1}{2} \times AB \times AC$

$= \frac{1}{2} \times 7 \times 24 = 84 \text{ cm}^2$

Case Based-V

(i) (*a*) Area of sector $ODCO = \frac{1}{4}\pi r^2$

$= \frac{1}{4} \times \frac{22}{7} \times 14 \times 14 = 154 \text{ cm}^2$

(ii) (*b*) Area of $\Delta AOB = \frac{1}{2} \times OA \times OB = \frac{1}{2}(20 \times 20) = 200 \text{ cm}^2$

(iii) (*a*) Area of region which is golden plated = area of ΔOAB – area of sector $ODCO$ = 200 – 154 = 46 cm^2

$\therefore$ Total cost of golden plating = ₹(6 × 46) = ₹276

(iv) (*c*) Area of major sector = area of circle – area of minor sector

$= \pi r^2 - \frac{1}{4}\pi r^2 = \frac{3\pi r^2}{4} = \frac{3}{4} \times \frac{22}{7} \times 14 \times 14 = 462 \text{ cm}^2$

□□□

SURFACE AREAS AND VOLUMES

12

"Civil engineers use knowledge about surface area and volume to design and build structures like bridges, roads, and buildings. They calculate surface area to figure out how much material, like paint or concrete, is needed to cover surfaces. They use volume to understand how much space structures will fill or how much material is required to build them."

SYLLABUS & WEIGHTAGE

List of Concept Names	Years				
	2021	2022	2023	2024	2025
Surface Areas (Surface Areas of combinations of any two of the following: cubes, cuboids, spheres, hemispheres and right circular cylinders/cones)	Exam not Conducted	1 Q (4 M)	–	1 Q (3 M)	1 Q (1 M) 1 Q (4 M)
Volumes (Volumes of combinations of any two of the following: cubes, cuboids, spheres, hemispheres and right circular cylinders/cones)		1 Q (4 M)	1 Q (4 M)	1 Q (1 M) 1 Q (3 M)	1 Q (1 M)

CONCEPT MAP

To Access One Shot Revision Video Scan This QR Code

Surface Areas and Volumes

- **Volume** → The capacity occupied by a 3-D solid shape
- **Surface Area** → Surface area is the space which is occupied by a solid
- **Combination of Solids**
- **Formula**

Name of Solid	Volume (V)	Curved Surface Area (C.S.A)	Total Surface Area (T.S.A)
Cube	a^3	$4a^2$	$6a^2$
Cuboid	$l \times b \times h$	$2h\,(l+b)$	$2\,(lb+bh+hl)$
Sphere	$\frac{4}{3}\pi r^3$	$4\pi r^2$	$4\pi r^2$
Hemisphere	$\frac{2}{3}\pi r^3$	$2\pi r^2$	$3\pi r^2$
Right Circular Cylinder	$\pi r^2 h$	$2\pi rh$	$2\pi r\,(h+r)$
Right Circular Hollow Cylinder ($R > r$)	$\pi(R^2-r^2)h$	$2\pi(R+r)h$	$2\pi(R+r)(h+R-r)$
Cone	$\frac{1}{3}\pi r^2 h$	πrl	$\pi r\,(l+r)$

T.S.A = $(\text{C.S.A})_{\text{Cylinder}} + (\text{C.S.A})_{\text{Cone}} + (\text{Base Area})_{\text{Cylinder}}$

Volume = $(\text{Volume})_{\text{Cone}} + (\text{Volume})_{\text{Cylinder}}$

T.S.A = $(\text{C.S.A})_{\text{Cone}} + (\text{C.S.A})_{\text{Hemisphere}}$

Volume = $(\text{Volume})_{\text{Cone}} + (\text{Volume})_{\text{Hemisphere}}$

T.S.A = $(\text{T.S.A})_{\text{Cube}} + (\text{C.S.A})_{\text{Hemisphere}} - (\text{Base Area})_{\text{Hemisphere}}$

Volume = $(\text{Volume})_{\text{Cube}} + (\text{Volume})_{\text{Hemisphere}}$

T.S.A = $(\text{T.S.A})_{\text{Cube}} + (\text{T.S.A})_{\text{Cylinder}} - (\text{Base Area})_{\text{Cylinder}}$

Volume = $(\text{Volume})_{\text{Cube}} + (\text{Volume})_{\text{Cylinder}}$

T.S.A = $(\text{T.S.A})_{\text{Cube}} + (\text{C.S.A})_{\text{Cone}} - (\text{Base Area})_{\text{Cone}}$

Volume = $(\text{Volume})_{\text{Cone}} + (\text{Volume})_{\text{Cube}}$

1 SURFACE AREAS

Important Terms

- **Surface Area:** Surface area is the space which is occupied by a Solid.
- **Cube:** Cube shape is a closed 3*d* figure which is enclosed by 6 square faces. The shape of the cube is shown in the below figure. Let us suppose, a be the length of each edge of a cube.

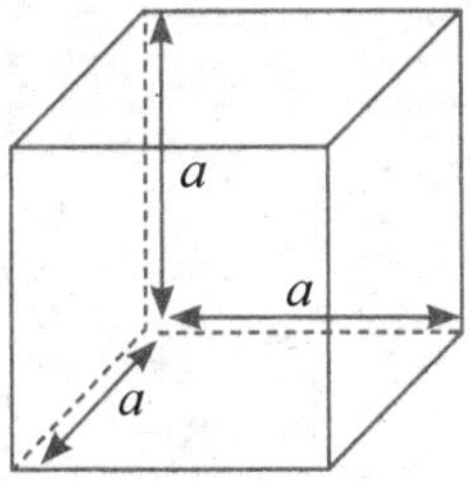

Cube

- **Cuboid:** Cuboid shape is a closed 3*d* figure which is enclosed by 6 rectangular faces. The shape of the cuboid is shown in the below figure.
  Let us suppose, l, b and h be the length, breadth and height of the cuboid respectively.

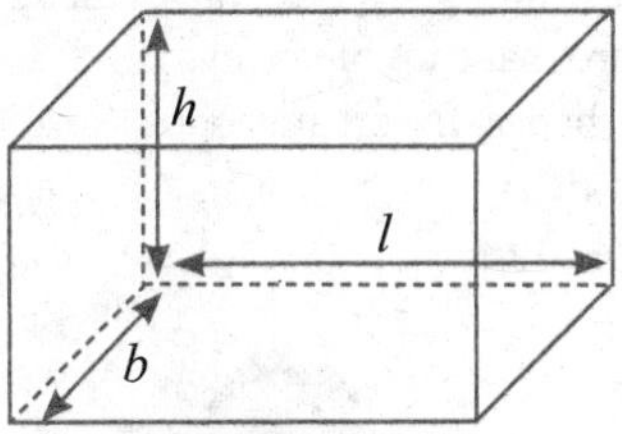

Cuboid

- **Sphere:** A sphere is defined in three-dimensional space. A sphere is a three-dimensional object with a surface and a volume. Like a circle, each point is the same distance from the center.

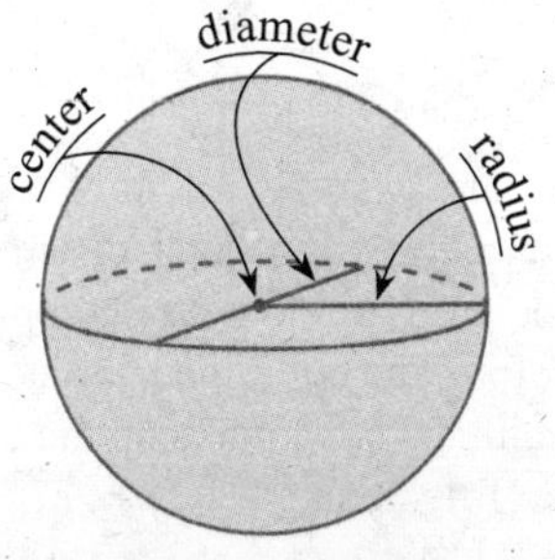

Parts of a Sphere

- **Center:** The center is a unique point which is equidistant from all the points of the sphere.
- **Radius:** The straight line from the center to any point of the sphere is known as radius.
- **Diameter:** The straight line which passes through the center from one point to the other point of the sphere.
- **Surface Area of the Sphere:** The surface area is the space which is occupied by a sphere.

- **Hemisphere:** Hemisphere is also a 3D shape, which is just half of the sphere. When a plane cuts the sphere in two equal halves, we get a hemisphere.

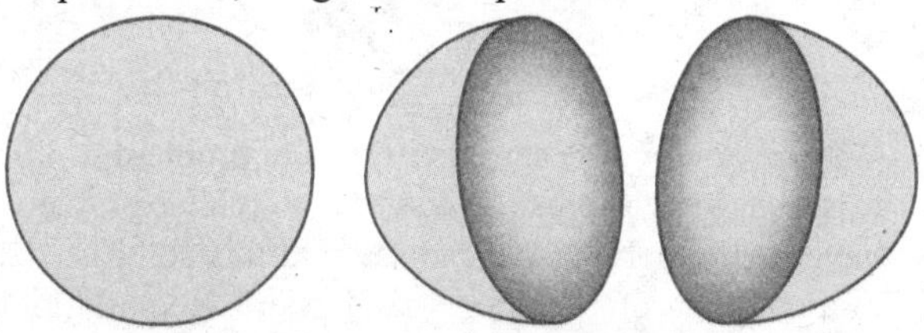

Sphere Hemisphere

- **Right Circular Cylinder:** A cylinder is a 3-dimensional solid with two identical and equal bases connected by curved surfaces.

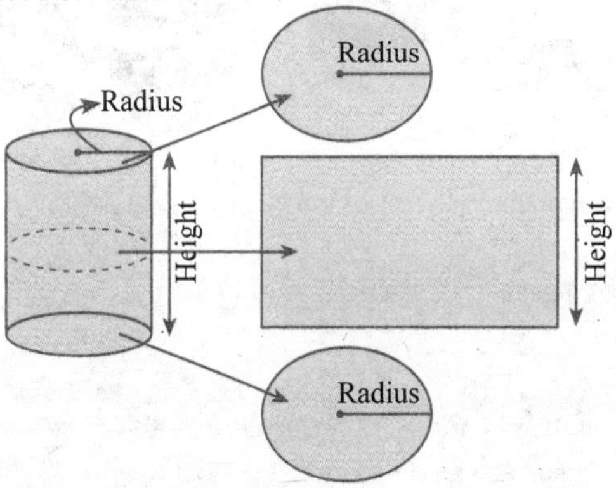

- **Right Circular Hollow Cylinder:** Here, R be the external and r be the internal radii of a hollow right circular cylinder of height h.

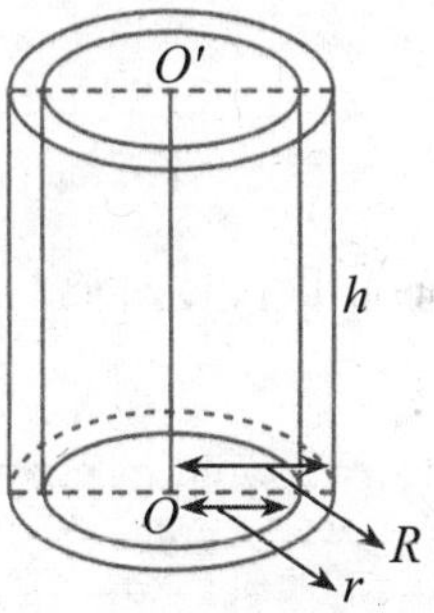

- **Cone:** A cone is a shape formed by using a set of line segments, which connect a common point, called the vertex, to all the points of a circular base.

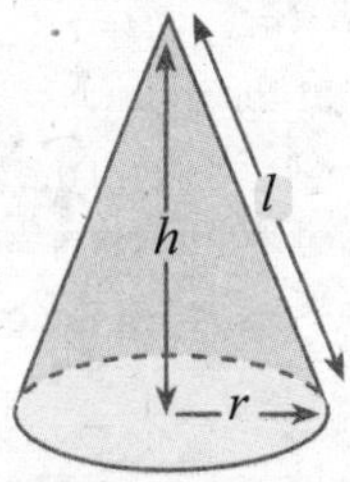

- **Slant Height (l):** The slant height of the right circular cone is the distance from the vertex to the point on the outer line of the circular base of the cone.
- **Height (h):** The distance from the vertex of the cone to the base is called the height of the cone.

- **Surface Area of a Combination of Solids:** Let us consider the toy as shown in the below figure.

Whenever we come across this type of problem, we first try to see if we can break it down into smaller problems, we have earlier solved. We can see that this solid is made up of a circular cone with one hemisphere. It would look like what we have in Fig., after we put the pieces all together.

Therefore, Total surface area of the toy = C.S.A of hemisphere + C.S.A of cone.

Important Formulas

Cube

- Area of four walls = Lateral surface area = $4a^2$
- Total surface area (T.S.A) of the cube = $6a^2$
- Length of diagonal of the cube = $\sqrt{3}a$

Cuboid

- Area of four walls of a room = Lateral surface area = $2h\ (l + b)$
- Total surface area (T.S.A) of the cuboid = $2\ (lb + bh + lh)$
- Length of diagonal of the cuboid = $\sqrt{l^2 + b^2 + h^2}$

Sphere

- Surface area (S.A.) of the sphere = $4\pi r^2$

Hemisphere

- Curved surface area (C.S.A.) of the hemisphere = $2\pi r^2$
- Total surface area (T.S.A.) of the hemisphere = $3\pi r^2$

Right Circular Cylinder

- Area of each end of the cylinder = πr^2
- Curved surface area (C.S.A) of the cylinder = (circumference of circle × height of cylinder) = $2\pi rh$
- Total surface area (T.S.A) of the cylinder = $2\pi r\ (h + r)$

Cone

- Slant Height $(l) = \sqrt{(r^2 + h^2)}$
- Curved surface area (C.S.A.) of cone = πrl
- Total surface area (T.S.A) of cone = $\pi r(r + l)$ $= \pi r(r + \sqrt{(h^2 + r^2)})$

Real Life Applications

- All of us had our homes painted for Diwali, so you must have noticed that when you hire a painter to paint any room in your home, the painter first determines the space's area,so that he can determine how much paint will be needed to paint a room.

Its surface area determines how much paint is needed in that space. Any object's surface area is the space that it occupies.

- In your daily life, you must have encountered a variety of forms that are made up of various solids that each have one or more basic shapes. Ice cream cones, capsules, tents, structures and tankers delivering petrol in the shape of capsules are a few of the most relevant examples of a mixture of solids.

We can use the example of an ice-cream cone, which consists of a cone with a layer of ice cream in the shape of a half-sphere on top, to better comprehend the fusion of solids. Therefore, the combined curved surface areas of the hemisphere and the cone make up the entire surface area of the ice-cream filled cone.

Different Problem Types

Type I: Surface Area of Combined or Modified Geometric Solids

An ice cream cone consists of a right circular cone for the cone part and a hemisphere for the scoop of ice cream. The cone has a diameter of 8 centimeters and a height of 12 centimeters. The hemisphere has the same diameter as the base of the cone.

Calculate the total surface area of the ice cream.

Solution:

Step I: Understand the combined solid. Since the ice cream is formed by combining a cone and a hemisphere.

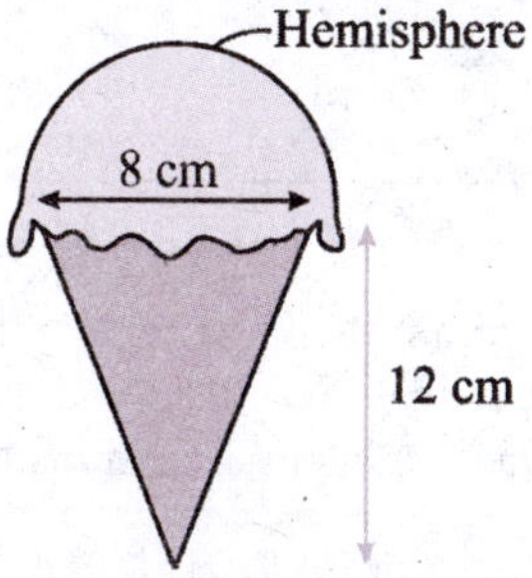

Step II: Identify given values for the cone:

Diameter of base $d_c = 8$ centimeters

Height $h_c = 12$ centimeters

Step III: Calculate surface area of cone first.

$$r_c = \frac{d_c}{2} = \frac{8}{2} = 4 \text{ centimeters}$$

$$l_c = \sqrt{r_c^2 + h_c^2}$$

$$= \sqrt{4^2 + 12^2} = \sqrt{16+144} = \sqrt{160}$$

$$= 4\sqrt{10} \text{ centimeters}$$

Surface Area of Cone $(SA)_{cone} = \pi r_c(rc + lc) = \pi \times 4 \times (4 + 4\sqrt{10}) = 66.6\pi$ square centimeters

Step IV: Calculate Surface Area of Hemisphere. Since the hemisphere has the same diameter as the cone's base, its radius is also $r_c = 4$ centimeters.

Surface area of hemisphere $(SA)_{Hemisphere}$

$= 2\pi r^2 = 2\pi \times 4^2 = 32\pi$ square centimeters

Step V: Total surface area (TSA) of the ice cream:

$TSA = SA_{cone} + SA_{Hemisphere}$

$= 66.6\pi + 32\pi = 98.6\pi$ square centimeters

Example 1: A toy is in the shape of a cylinder surmounted by a hemisphere. The height of the toy is 25 cm. Find the total surface area of the toy if its common diameter is 12 cm.

Solution: Height of the toy (cylinder) $= h_{Cyl} = (25 - 6)$ cm $= 19$ cm

Common diameter = 12 cm

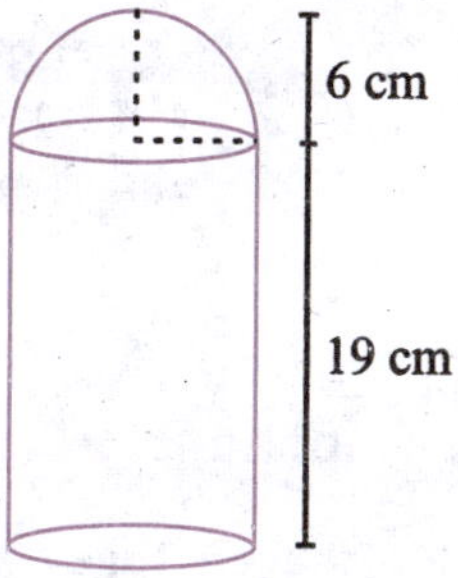

Radius of the cylinder and hemisphere $= r_{Cyl} = \frac{12}{2} = 6$cm

Surface area of a cylinder: $SA_{Cyl} = \pi r_{Cyl}(r_{Cyl} + 2h_{Cyl})$

$SA_{Cyl} = \pi \times 6 \times (6 + 2 \times 19) = \pi \times 6 \times 44 = 264\pi \text{ cm}^2$

Surface area of a hemisphere: $SA_{Hemisphere} = 2\pi r^2$

$SA_{Hemisphere} = \frac{1}{2} \times 4\pi \times 6^2 = 72\pi \text{ cm}^2$

Total surface area of the toy: $TSA = SA_{Cyl} + SA_{Hemisphere} = 264\pi + 72\pi = 336\text{cm}^2$

Example 2: A hemispherical section is cut out from one face of cubical block (see figure) the such that the diameter of the hemisphere is equal to the side length of the cube. Determine the surface area of the remaining solid.

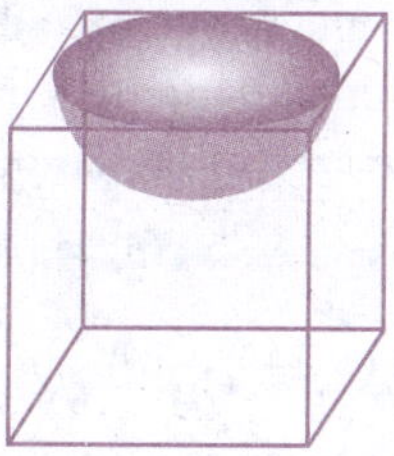

Solution: Let r be the radius of the hemisphere.

Given that, diameter of the hemisphere = side of the cube = a

Radius of the hemisphere = $a/2$

T.S.A of the remaining solid = Surface area of the cubical part + C.S.A. of the hemispherical part – Area of the base of the hemispherical part

$= 6 \times (\text{Edge})^2 + 2\pi r^2 - \pi r^2$

$= 6 \times (\text{Edge})^2 + \pi r^2$

$= 6 \times (a)^2 + \pi\left(\frac{a}{2}\right)^2 = \frac{1}{4}(24+\pi)a^2$

Total surface area of the remaining solid $= \frac{1}{4}(24+\pi)a^2$ sq. units

COMPETENCY BASED SOLVED EXAMPLES

Multiple Choice Questions (1 M)

1. Two cubes each with 6 cm edge are joined end to end. The surface area of the resulting cuboid is *(Un)*

(*a*) 180 cm^2 (*b*) 360 cm^2

(*c*) 300 cm^2 (*d*) 260 cm^2

Sol. If two cubes of edges 6 cm are joined face to face it will take the shape of a cuboid whose length, breadth and height are (6 + 6) cm, 6 cm and 6 cm

i.e. 12 cm, 6 cm and 6 cm respectively.

Thus, total surface area of the cuboid = $2(lb + bh + lh)$

$= 2(12 \times 6 + 6 \times 6 + 12 \times 6)$

$= 2(72 + 36 + 72)$

$= 2 \times 180\ cm^2$

$= 360\ cm^2$

2. A solid right circular cone of radius *r* and height *h* is placed over a solid cylinder of same height and radius. The total surface area of the shape so formed is: *(Cr)*

(*a*) $4\pi rh + 4\pi r^2$ (*b*) $4\pi rh + \pi r^2$

(*c*) $\pi r\left(\sqrt{r^2+h^2}+2h+r\right)$ (*d*) $\pi r^2\left(\sqrt{r^2+h^2}+2h+r\right)$

Sol. T.S.A. of the shape = C.S.A of cone + C.S.A of cylinder + Area of the base of a cylinder

$= \pi r\sqrt{r^2+h^2} + 2\pi rh + \pi r^2$

$= \pi r\left(\sqrt{r^2+h^2}+2h+r\right)$

3. If *d* is the diameter of the sphere, then the surface area of the sphere is given by *(An)*

(*a*) $\frac{4}{3}\pi d^2$ (*b*) $4\pi d^2$ (*c*) πd^2 (*d*) $3\pi d^2$

Sol. If *d* is the diameter of the sphere, then the surface area of the sphere is given by $4\pi r^2 = 4\pi(d/2)^2 = \pi d^2$.

4. Find the curved surface area of a right circular cone (in *sq. cm*), if the radius of the cone is 4 *cm* and height of the cone is 3 *cm*. *(Re)*

(*a*) $16\pi\ cm^2$ (*b*) $18\pi\ cm^2$ (*c*) $20\pi\ cm^2$ (*d*) $4\pi\ cm^2$

Sol. It is given that,

Radius of cone (r) = 4 *cm*

Height of cone (h) = 3 *cm*

Therefore, slant height (l) = $\sqrt{r^2+h^2}$

$= \sqrt{(4)^2+(3)^2} = \sqrt{25} = 5\ cm$

Now,

C.S.A. of cone = $\pi \times r \times l = \pi \times 4 \times 5 = 20\pi\ cm^2$.

Key Takeaways

Utilize Pythagoras' theorem for right triangles to find missing side lengths or diagonals, especially when calculating slant heights in three-dimensional shapes..

5. If the radius and height of a right circular cone are '*r*' and '*h*' respectively, the slant height of the cone is: *(Un)*

(*a*) $(h^2+r^2)^{1/3}$ (*b*) $(h+r)^{1/3}$

(*c*) $(h^2+r^2)^{1/2}$ (*d*) (h^2+r^2)

Sol. It is given that, r is radius and h is the height of the cone.

Therefore, slant height (l) = $\sqrt{h^2+r^2}$

$\Rightarrow l^2 = h^2 + r^2$

$\Rightarrow l = \left(h^2+r^2\right)^{1/2}$

6. If a cylinder is covered by two hemispherical lid having same radius as of cylinder, then the total curved surface area of the new object will be: *(Cr)*

(*a*) $4\pi rh + 2\pi r^2$ (*b*) $3\pi rh - \pi r^2$

(*c*) $2\pi rh + 4\pi r^2$ (*d*) $2\pi rh + 4\pi r$

Sol. As, cylinder is covered by two hemispherical shaped lid of equal shape.

Therefore,

Total curved surface area of new object

= C.S.A of cylinder + 2 × (C.S.A of hemisphere)

$= 2\pi rh + 2(2\pi r^2)$

$= 2\pi rh + 4\pi r^2$

7. There are two cylinders of radius '*R*' and '*r*' and having the same height. Find the ratio of their lateral surface areas. *(Un)*

(*a*) 2 : 3 (*b*) *H* : *h*

(*c*) *R* : *r* (*d*) None of these

Sol. Given, h is the height of both cylinders.

Let R be the radius of 1st cylinder and r be the radius of 2nd cylinder.

$\frac{(\text{C.S.A})_1}{(\text{C.S.A})_2} = \frac{2\pi Rh}{2\pi rh} = \frac{R}{r} = R : r$

8. The total area of the sheet required to make a closed hollow cone of height 24 *cm* and radius 7 *cm* is *(An)*

(*a*) 704 cm^2 (*b*) 304 cm^2

(*c*) 814 cm^2 (*d*) 107 cm^2

Sol. It is given that,

Radius of cone (r) = 7 *cm*

Height of cone (h) = 24 *cm*

Therefore, slant height $(l) = \sqrt{r^2 + h^2} = \sqrt{7^2 + 24^2}$ $= 25\ cm$

Total surface area (T.S.A) $= \pi r(r + l)$

$= \frac{22}{7} \times 7(7 + 25) = \frac{22}{7} \times 7 \times 32 = 704\ cm^2$

Answer Key

1. (*b*) 2. (*c*) 3. (*c*) 4. (*c*) 5. (*c*) 6. (*c*) 7. (*c*) 8. (*a*)

Assertion and Reason (1 M)

Direction: In the following questions, A statement of Assertion (A) is followed by a statement of Reason (R). Mark the correct choice as.

(*a*) Both Assertion (A) and Reason (R) are true, and Reason (R) is the correct explanation of Assertion (A).

(*b*) Both Assertion (A) and Reason (R) are true, but Reason (R) is not the correct explanation of Assertion (A).

(*c*) Assertion (A) is true, but Reason (R) is false.

(*d*) Assertion (A) is false, but Reason (R) is true.

1. Assertion (A): If the surface area of a ball which is in the shape of a sphere is 221.76 cm^2, then its diameter is 8.4 *cm*.

Reason (R): If *r* be the radius of the sphere, then surface area, $S = 4\pi r^2$, i.e. $r = \frac{1}{2}\sqrt{\frac{S}{\pi}}$. (*Re*)

Sol. It is given, C.S.A. of sphere = 221.76 cm^2

$\therefore 4\pi r^2 = 221.76\ cm^2$

$\Rightarrow r = \frac{1}{2}\sqrt{\frac{221.76}{(22/7)}}$

$\Rightarrow r = 4.2\ cm$

Therefore, diameter $= 2r = 8.4\ cm.$

$\therefore$ Both assertion and reason are true and reason is the correct explanation of assertion.

2. Assertion (A): If two identical solid cube of side 5 *cm* are joined end to end, then total surface area of the resulting cuboid is 300 cm^2.

Reason (R): Total surface area of a cuboid is 2 $(lb + bh + hl)$. (*Un*)

Sol. A cuboid will be formed when two cubes are joined end to end.

So, $l = 2 \times 5 = 10\ cm$, $b = 5\ cm$ and $h = 5\ cm$

Now, total surface area (T.S.A) of cuboid formed

$= 2(lb + bh + lh)$

$= 2(10 \times 5 + 5 \times 5 + 10 \times 5)$

$= 2(50 + 25 + 50)$

$= 2 \times 125 = 250\ cm^2$

$\therefore$ Assertion is false but Reason is true.

Answer Key

1. (*a*) 2. (*d*)

Subjective Questions

Very Short Answer Type Questions (1 or 2 M)

1. 3 cubes each of 8 cm edge are joined end to end. Find the total surface area of the cuboid so formed.

(*An*) (CBSE, 2022)

Sol. The dimensions of the cuboid so formed are:

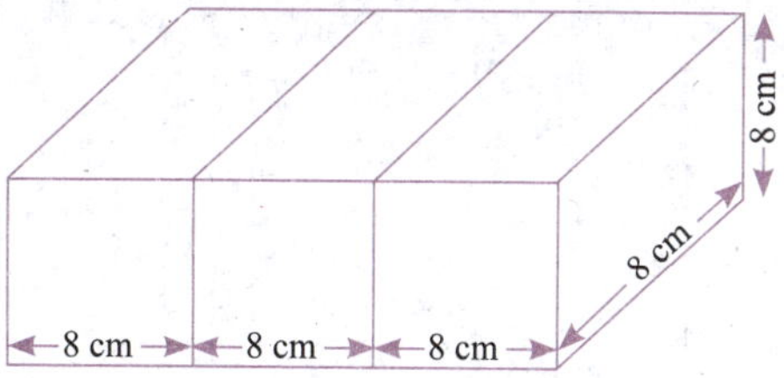

Length, $l = 24$ cm

Breadth, $b = 8$ cm

Height, $h = 8$ cm

Since, surface area of cuboid $= 2(lb + bh + lh)$ (1 M)

$= 2(24 \times 8 + 8 \times 8 + 24 \times 8) = 2(192 + 64 + 192)$

$= 2 \times 448 = 896$ sq cm. (1 M)

2. Find the total surface area of the cone whose radius and slant height are 7 *cm* and 12 *cm* respectively.

(*Cr*) (NCERT Intext)

Sol. $\because$ Given, $r = 7$cm

$h = 12$ cm

Since, total surface area of the cone $= \pi r(r + l)$ (1 M)

$= \frac{22}{7} \times 7(7+12) = 418\ cm^2$ (1 M)

3. A paint roller is a paint application tool used for painting large flat surfaces rapidly and efficiently. One such roller is shown below, which is 26 cm long with an outer diameter of 7 cm.

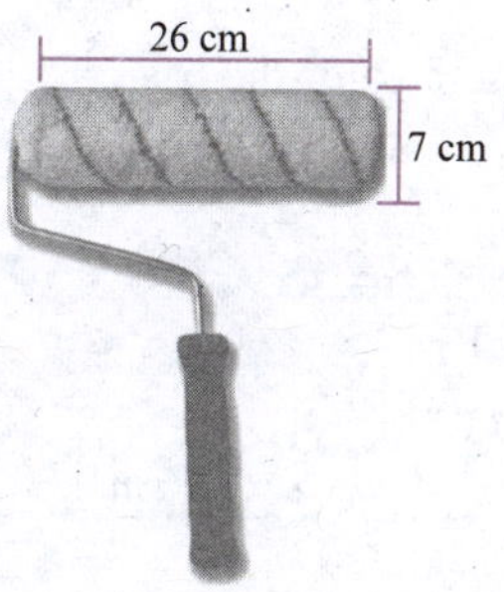

Find the maximum area of the surface that gets painted when the roller makes 6 complete rotations vertically. Show your work. (*Un*) (CBSE CFPQ, 2023)

(Note: Take $\pi = \frac{22}{7}$.)

Sol. Given,

A cylindrical shaped roller with height = 26 cm and diameter = 7 cm.

We know,

Curved surface area of cylinder = $2\pi rh$

Therefore, we get:

CSA of the paint roller = $2\times\frac{22}{7}\times\frac{7}{2}\times 26 = 572$ cm

i.e., Area covered after one rotation = 572 cm^2

$\therefore$ Area covered after 6 rotations= 3432 cm^2

4. Find the area of the unshaded region shown in the given figure. (*Cr*)

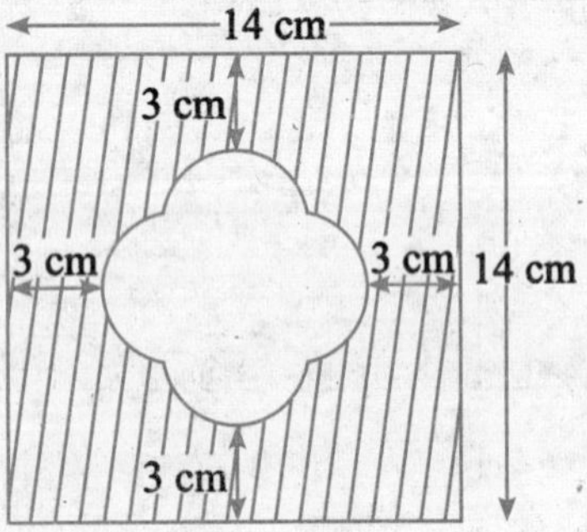

Sol. Area of Shaded Region = Area of a square of side a + 4 (Area of a semi-circle of diameter 'a') (½ *M*)

The horizontal/vertical extent of the white region = 14 – 3 – 3 = 8 cm

Radius of the semi-circle + side of a square + Radius of the semi-circle = 8 cm (½ *M*)

2 (radius of the semi-circle) + side of a square = 8 cm

$2a = 8$ cm $\Rightarrow$ $a = 4$ cm (½ *M*)

Area of the unshaded region

= Area of a square of side 4 cm + 4 (Area of a semi-circle of diameter 4 cm)

$= (4)^2 + 4\times\frac{1}{2}\pi(2)^2 = (16 + 8\pi)$ cm^2 (½ *M*)

5. The area of the base of a right circular cylinder is 154 *cm*² and its height is 15 *cm*. Find the C.S.A of the cylinder. (*An*)

Sol. It is given that, area of the base = 154 cm^2 and height (h) = 15 *cm*

$\therefore \pi r^2 = 154$ (½ *M*)

$\Rightarrow \frac{22}{7}r^2 = 154$

$\Rightarrow r^2 = \frac{7\times 154}{22} = 49 \Rightarrow r = 7\ cm$

As, we know

C.S.A = $2\pi rh$ (½ *M*)

$= 2\times\frac{22}{7}\times 7\times 15$

= 660 cm^2 (1 *M*)

6. A cubical block of side 7 cm is surmounted by a hemisphere of largest possible diameter as shown in Fig. Find the total surface area of the solid. (*Un*) (CBSE, 2022)

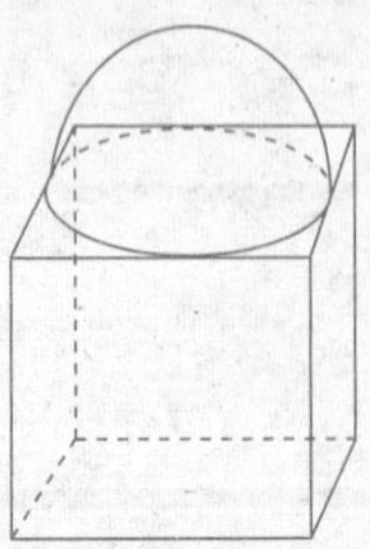

Sol. The diameter of the hemisphere = the side of the cube = 7 cm

Total Surface Area of the solid = Total Surface Area of cube - Area of base of hemisphere + Curved Surface Area of hemisphere

$\Rightarrow$ TSA of solid = $6\times 7^2 + \pi\times(3.5)^2 + 2\times\pi\times(3.5)^2$ (1 *M*)

$\Rightarrow$ TSA = $6\times 7^2 + \pi\times(3.5)^2$

$\Rightarrow$ TSA = 332.465 cm^2 (1 *M*)

Short Answer Type Questions (2 or 3 M)

1. Mayank made a bird-bath for his garden in the shape of a cylinder with a hemispherical depression at one end. The height of the cylinder is 1.45 *m* and its radius is 30 *cm*. Find the total surface area of the bird-bath. (Take π = 22/7) (*Re*) (NCERT Intext)

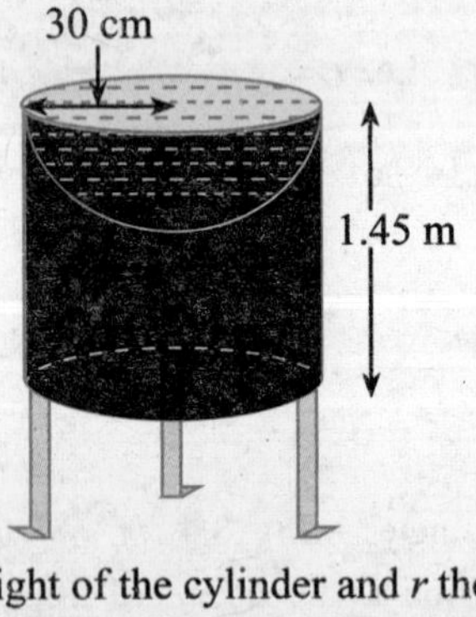

Sol. Let h be height of the cylinder and r the common radius of the cylinder and hemisphere. Then, the total surface area of the bird-bath = C.S.A of cylinder + C.S.A of hemisphere

$= 2\pi rh + 2\pi r^2 = 2\pi r(h + r)$ (1 *M*)

$= 2\times\frac{22}{7}\times 30(145+30)\ cm^2$ [$\because r = 30cm, h = 145\ cm$] (1 *M*)

= 33000 cm^2 = 3.3 m^2 (1 *M*)

Mistakes 101 : What not to do!

In surface area and volume-based questions the unit plays a very important role.

2. A wooden article was made by scooping out a hemisphere from each end of a solid cylinder, as shown in Fig. If the height of the cylinder is 10 *cm*, and its base is of radius 3.5 *cm*, find the total surface area of the article. (*Cr*)

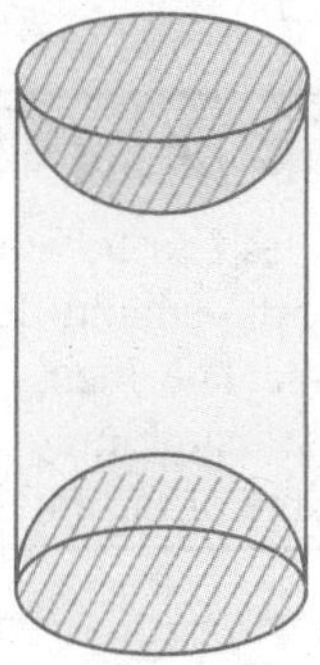

Sol. Given, $r = 3.5\ cm$, $h = 10\ cm$

T.S.A. of the article = 2 × C.S.A. of the hemispherical part + C.S.A. of the cylindrical part

$= 2 \times 2\pi r^2 + 2\pi rh$ *(1 M)*

$= 2\pi r(2r + h)$

$= 2 \times \frac{22}{7} \times 3.5 \times (2 \times 3.5 + 10)$ *(1 M)*

$= \frac{22}{3.5} \times 3.5 \times (7 + 10) = 22 \times 17$

$= 374\ cm^2$ *(1 M)*

Thus, the total surface area of the article is 374 cm^2.

3. A tent is in the shape of a cylinder surmounted by a conical top. If the height and diameter of the cylindrical part are 2.1 *m* and 4 *m* respectively, and the slant height of the top is 2.8 *m*, find the area of the canvas used for making the tent. Also, find the cost of the canvas of the tent at the rate of ₹ 500 per m^2. (Note that the base of the tent will not be covered with canvas.)

(*Un*) (NCERT Intext)

Sol. The diagram can be shown as:

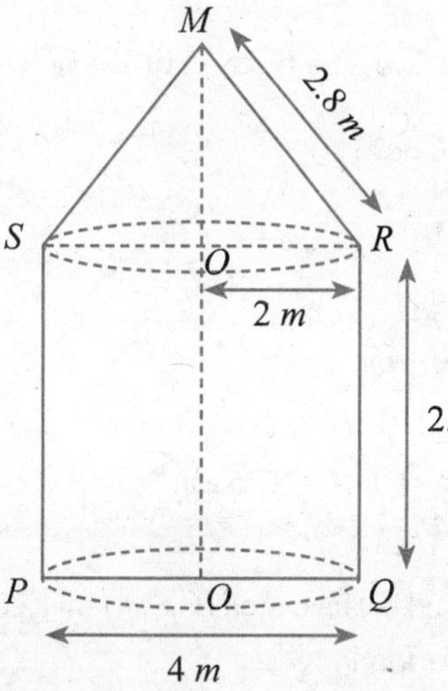

(1 M)

It is given that,

Diameter (D) = 4 m

Slant height (l) of the cone = 2.8 m

Therefore, radius of the cone (r) = radius of cylinder (r) $= \frac{D}{2}$

$= \frac{4}{2} = 2\ m$ *(½ M)*

Also, height of the cylinder (h) = 2.1 m

Hence, the required surface area of tent

= lateral surface area of cone+lateral surface area of cylinder

$= \pi rl + 2\pi rh$ *(½ M)*

$= \pi r(l + 2h)$

$= \frac{22}{7} \times 2(2.8 + 2 \times 2.1) = \frac{22}{7} \times 2 \times 7$

$= \frac{44}{7} \times 7 = 44\ m^2$

Now, the cost of the canvas of the tent

= Surface area of canvas × cost of canvas per m^2

= 44 × 500 = ₹ 22000

Hence, the cost of the canvas of the tent is ₹ 22,000. *(1 M)*

Nailing the Right Answer

Students should check the units, and use formulas while putting values in them carefully.

4. A right circular cylinder and a cone have equal bases and equal heights. If their curved surface areas are in the ratio 8 : 5, then find the ratio between the radius of their bases to their heights **(*Re*)**

Sol. Let the radius and height of cylinder and cone be r and h

Let slant height of cone be l

Curved surface area of cylinder = $2\pi rh$ *(½ M)*

Curved surface area of cone = πrl *(½ M)*

$\frac{\text{CSA of cylinder}}{\text{CSA of cone}} = \frac{2\pi rh}{\pi rl} = \frac{8}{5}$ *(½ M)*

$\Rightarrow \frac{h}{l} = \frac{4}{5}$

Squaring on both sides, we get

$\frac{h^2}{l^2} = \frac{16}{25}$ *(½ M)*

$l^2 = \left(\frac{25}{16}\right)h^2$

$h^2 + r^2 = \left(\frac{25}{16}\right)h^2$ *(½ M)*

$r^2 = \left(\frac{9}{16}\right)h^2$

$\left(\frac{r}{h}\right)^2 = \left(\frac{3}{4}\right)^2, \frac{r}{h} = \frac{3}{4}$

Hence ratio of radius to height is 3 : 4 *(½ M)*

Long Answer Type Questions (4 or 5 M)

1. A toy is in the form of a cone of radius 3.5 *cm* mounted on a hemisphere of same radius. The total height of the toy is 15.5 *cm*. Find the total surface area of the toy.

(*Cr*) (NCERT Intext)

Sol. The diagram can be shown as:

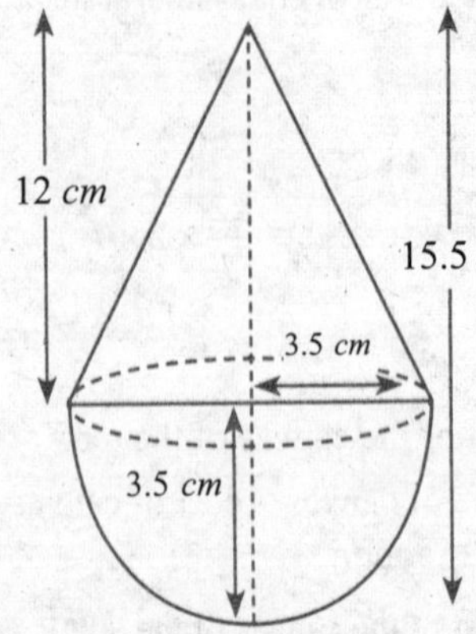

(1 M)

It is given that the radius of the cone and the hemisphere, $(r) = 3.5\ cm$ or $\frac{7}{2}\ cm$

And, the total height of the toy = 15.5 *cm*.

Therefore, the height of the cone $(h) = 15.5 - 3.5 = 12cm$ (½ M)

Now, slant height of the cone $(l) = \sqrt{h^2 + r^2}$ (½ M)

$\Rightarrow l = \sqrt{12^2 + (3.5)^2}$

$\Rightarrow l = \sqrt{12^2 + \left(\frac{7}{2}\right)^2}$

$\Rightarrow l = \sqrt{144 + \frac{49}{4}}$

$= \sqrt{\frac{576+49}{4}} = \sqrt{\frac{625}{4}}$

$\Rightarrow l = \frac{25}{2}\ cm$ (½ M)

The curved surface area (C.S.A) of conical part = πrl

$\Rightarrow \frac{22}{7} \times \frac{7}{2} \times \frac{25}{2} = \frac{275}{2}\ cm^2$ (½ M)

And, the curved surface area (C.S.A) of the hemispherical part = $2\pi r^2$

$\Rightarrow 2 \times \frac{22}{7} \times \left(\frac{7}{2}\right)^2$

$\Rightarrow 2 \times \frac{22}{7} \times \frac{7}{2} \times \frac{7}{2}$

$= 77\ cm^2$ (½ M)

Total surface area (T.S.A) of the toy

= C.S.A of conical part + C.S.A of hemispherical part (½ M)

$= \frac{275}{2} + 77\ cm^2$

$= \frac{275+154}{2}\ cm^2$

$= \frac{429}{2}\ cm^2 = 214.5\ cm^2$

Hence, the total surface area (T.S.A) of the toy is 214.5 cm^2. (1 M)

Nailing the Right Answer

Many complex shapes can be broken down into simpler components. Students should learn to identify these components and calculate their individual surface areas and volumes before combining them to find the total surface area or volume of the entire shape.

Key Takeaways

For composite shapes, break them down into simpler geometric shapes whose surface areas and volumes can be calculated individually. Then, sum up the results to find the total surface area or volume.

2. A factory manufactures 1,20,000 pencils daily. The pencils are cylindrical in shape, each of length 25 *cm* and circumference of base as 1.5 *cm*. Determine the cost of colouring the curved surfaces of the pencils manufactured in one day at ₹0.05 per dm^2.

(*An*) (NCERT Exemplar)

Sol. Given, shape of the pencils is cylindrical and length of each pencil $(h) = 25\ cm$

Let radius of base of the pencil be *r*.

Now, circumference of base = 1.5 *cm*

$\Rightarrow 2\pi r = 1.5$ (½ M)

$\Rightarrow r = \frac{1.5}{2\pi}$

Curved surface area (C.S.A) of 1 pencil = $2\pi rh$

$= 2 \times \pi \times \frac{1.5}{2\pi} \times 25$

$= 37.5\ cm^2$ (1 M)

We know that

$1\ cm = 0.1\ dm$

$\Rightarrow 1\ cm^2 = 0.01\ dm^2$

$\therefore\ 37.5\ cm^2 = 0.01 \times 37.5\ dm^2$

$= 0.375\ dm^2$ (½ M)

Now, curved surface area (C.S.A) of 1,20,000 pencils

$= 0.375 \times 120000$

$= 45000\ dm^2$. (1 M)

Since, cost of colouring 1 dm^2 of area of pencils

= ₹0.05 (½ M)

Cost of colouring 45000 dm^2 of area of pencils

= ₹0.05 × ₹45000 = ₹2250 (½ M)

Hence, the cost of colouring the curved surface of pencils is ₹2250. (1 M)

Mistakes 101 : What not to do!

Sometimes, when solving problems, students make mistakes by using the wrong formulas and getting confused when they need to change the units or measurements.

3. A tent is in the shape of a cylinder surmounted by a conical top. If the height and radius of the cylindrical part are 3 m and 14 m respectively, and the total height of the tent is 13.5 *m*, find the area of the canvas required for making the tent, keeping a provision of 26 m^2 of canvas for stitching and wastage. Also, find the cost of the canvas to be purchased at the rate of ₹500 per m^2. *(Ap)* (CBSE SQP, 2023)

Sol. Radius of the cylindrical tent (r) = 14 m

Total height of the tent = 13.5 m

Height of the cylinder = 3 m

Height of the Conical part = 10.5 m *(½ M)*

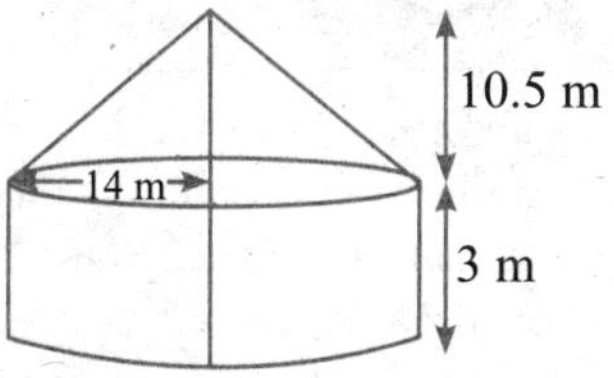

Slant height of the cone (l) = $\sqrt{h^2 + r^2}$

$= \sqrt{(10.5)^2 + (14)^2} = \sqrt{110.25 + 196}$ *(1 M)*

$= \sqrt{306.25} = 17.5$

Curved surface area of cylindrical portion = $2\pi rh$

$= 2 \times \frac{22}{7} \times 14 \times 3$ *(1 M)*

$= 264 \text{ m}^2$

Curved surface area of conical portion = πrl

$= \frac{22}{7} \times 14 \times 17.5$ *(1 M)*

$= 770 \text{ m}^2$ *(½ M)*

Total curved surface area = $264 \text{ m}^2 + 770 \text{ m}^2 = 1034 \text{ m}^2$

Provision for stitching and wastage = 26 m^2

Area of canvas to be purchased = 1060 m^2 *(½ M)*

Cost of canvas = Rate × Surface area *(½ M)*

= 500 × 1060 = ₹5,30,000

Nailing the Right Answer

Recognize that surface area involves two dimensions (length and width) for flat surfaces and three dimensions (length, width, and height) for solids.

2 | VOLUMES

Important Terms

- **Volume:** The capacity occupied by a three-dimensional solid shape is defined as volume.

Important Formulas

- Volume of the cube = a^3
- Volume of the cuboid = Area of the base × height = $l \times b \times h$
- Volume of a sphere = $\frac{4}{3}\pi r^3$
- Volume of a hemisphere = $\frac{2}{3}\pi r^3$
- Volume of a cylinder = $\pi r^2 h$

This is why it's called 'pizza'

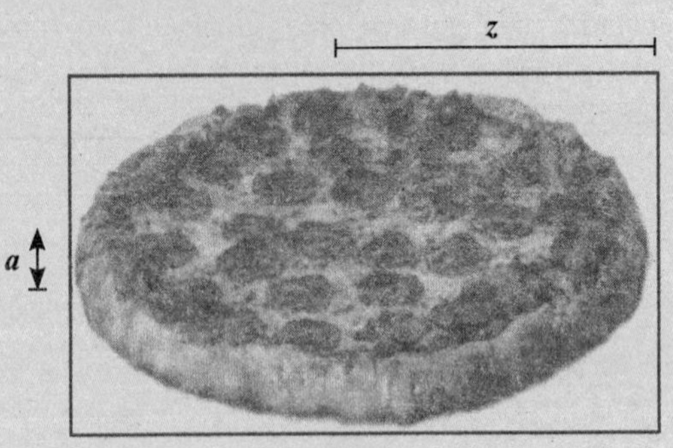

Thickness = a

Radius = z

Volume = $\pi z^2 a$

Volume = $pi\ (zz)\ a$

- Volume of a cone = $\frac{1}{3}\pi r^2 h$

Real Life Applications

- We can use the example of your lunchbox that you bring to school to better comprehend the amount of solid figures. Your lunch box's volume determines how much food it can contain. The quantity of space that a thing has is known as its volume.

- You must have noticed the cylindrical cottage. The cylindrical hut, which consists of a cylinder and a conical-shaped top, is an example of a combination of solids.

The hut's volume is how much room it has within. The volume of the hut is the same as the sum of the volumes of the cylinder and the cone. You may obtain the volume of various solid combinations in a similar way. Basically, solids that can separate into two or more different solids are considered to be a combination of solids. Now let's determine the volume of a mixture of solids.

Different Problem Types

Type I: Volume of a Combination of Solids

A juice seller was serving his customers using glasses as shown in Fig. below. The inner diameter of the cylindrical glass was 4 cm, but the bottom of the glass had a hemispherical raised portion which reduced the capacity of the glass. If the height of a glass was 7 cm, find the apparent capacity of the glass and its actual capacity. (Use $\pi = 3.14$.)

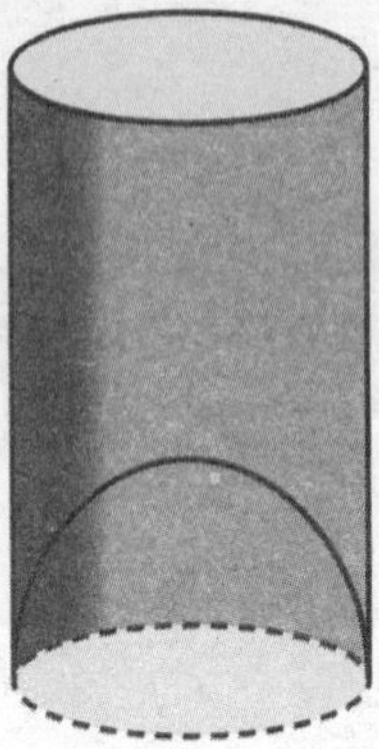

Solution:

Step I: Understand the Given Information:

Since the inner diameter of the glass = 2 cm and height = 7 cm,

Step II: Recall the formulas for calculating the volume of the individual shapes involved.

The apparent capacity of the glass = $\pi r^2 h$

$= \frac{22}{7} \times 2 \times 2 \times 7 cm^3 = 88 cm^3$

Volume of the hemisphere, $\left(\frac{2}{3}\pi r^3\right) = \frac{2}{3} \times \frac{22}{7} \times 2 \times 2 \times 2$ cm^3 = 16.76 cm^3

Step III: Combine the volumes of all individual shapes to find the total volume.

The actual capacity of the glass is less by the volume of the hemisphere at the base of the glass.

So, the actual capacity of the glass = Apparent capacity of glass – Volume of the hemisphere

= (88 – 16.76) cm^3

= 71.24 cm^3

Example 1: A vessel is shaped like a hemispherical bowl with a hollow cylindrical structure mounted on top. The vessel has a diameter of 14 cm and a total height of 13 cm. Calculate the capacity (volume) of the vessel.

Solution:

Cylinder: radius r = 7 cm

Hemisphere: height h = 6 cm, radius r = 7 cm

Volume of the vessel = Volume of cylinder + volume of hemisphere

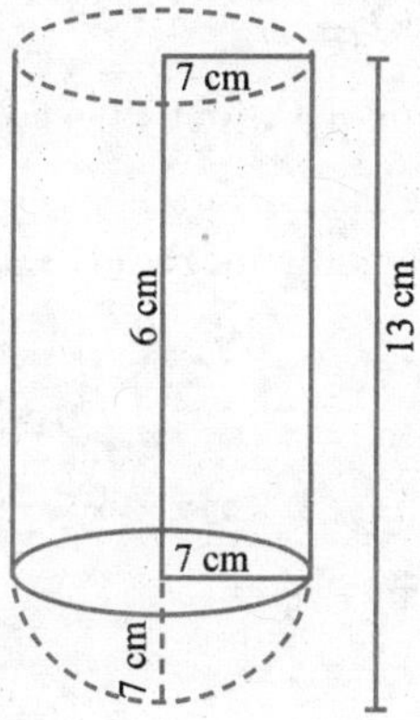

$= \pi r^2 h + \frac{2}{3}\pi r^3 = \pi r^2\left(h + \frac{2r}{3}\right)$

$= \frac{22}{7} \times 7 \times 7\left(6 + \frac{2}{3} \times 7\right) cm^3$

$= 154\left(\frac{14+14}{3}\right) cm^3 = 154 \times \frac{32}{3} cm^3$

= 1642.67 cm^3

Example 2: Ram, a budding engineer, has crafted a unique model consisting of a cylinder with two cones attached at each end. The model's diameter measures 3 cm, and its length spans 12 cm. The height of each cone is 2 cm. Determine the volume of Ram's innovative model.

Solution:

Cylinder: radius $R = \frac{3}{2}$ cm, height H = 8 cm

Cone: radius $r = \frac{3}{2}$ cm, height h = 2 cm

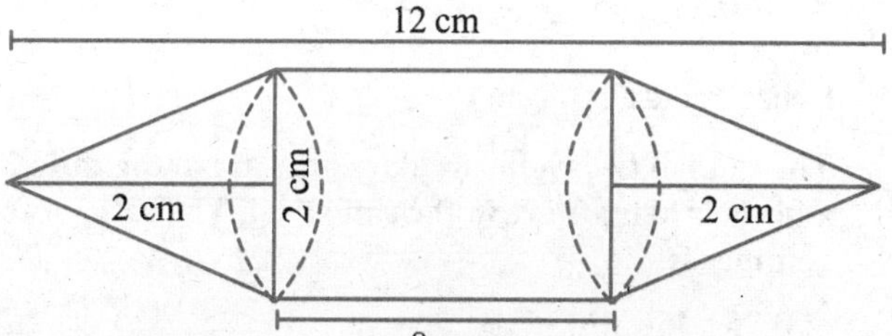

Volume of the model = Volume of cylinder + 2 × volume of cone

$= \pi R^2 H + 2 \times \frac{1}{3}\pi r^2 h$

$= \pi\left[R^2 H + \frac{2}{3} r^2 h\right]$

$= \pi\left[\frac{3}{2} \times \frac{3}{2} \times \frac{8}{1} + \frac{2}{3} \times \frac{3}{2} \times \frac{3}{2} \times 2\right] = \frac{22}{7}[18+3]$

= 22 × 3 = 66 cm^3

COMPETENCY BASED SOLVED EXAMPLES

Multiple Choice Questions (1 M)

1. A rectangular sheet of paper 40 cm × 22 cm, is rolled to form a hollow cylinder of height 40 cm. The radius of the cylinder (in cm) is: *(Ap)* **(CBSE SQP, 2023)**

(*a*) 3.5 (*b*) 7

(*c*) $\frac{80}{7}$ (*d*) 5

Sol. According to question,

Height of cylinder = 40 cm

Let radius of cylinder be r

And circumference of base = 22 cm

$\Rightarrow 2\pi r = 22$ cm

$\Rightarrow 2 \cdot \frac{22}{7} \cdot r = 22 \Rightarrow r = \frac{7}{2}$ cm

Hence, radius = 3.5 cm

2. The radii of two right circular cones are in the ratio 2 : 3 and their heights are in the ratio 5 : 4. The ratio of their volumes is: ***(Un)***

(*a*) 25 : 36 (*b*) 5 : 9 (*c*) 36 : 25 (*d*) 9 : 25

Sol. Let us suppose, $2r$ and $3r$ be the radii of two right circular cones respectively. Their heights be $5h$ and $4h$ respectively.

Let V_1 and V_2 be their volumes.

$$V_1 = \frac{1}{3}\pi \times (2r)^2 \times 5h = \frac{20}{3}\pi r^2 h$$

$$V_2 = \frac{1}{3}\pi \times (3r)^2 \times 4h = 12\pi r^2 h$$

$$\frac{V_1}{V_2} = \frac{20}{3} \times \frac{1}{12} = \frac{5}{9}$$

3. The volume of a largest sphere that can be cut off from a cylindrical log of wood of base radius 1 *m* and height 4 *m*, is: ***(Cr)***

(*a*) $\frac{5}{3}\pi\, m^3$ (*b*) $\frac{8}{3}\pi\, m^3$

(*c*) $\frac{4}{3}\pi\, m^3$ (*d*) $\frac{10}{3}\pi\, m^3$

Sol. Radius of largest sphere which can be cut off from cylinder = 1 *m*

$$\therefore \text{ Volume of sphere} = \frac{4}{3}\pi r^3 = \frac{4}{3}\pi(1)^3 = \frac{4}{3}\pi\, m^3$$

4. A sphere of maximum volume is cut out from a solid hemisphere of radius 7 cm. Then the ratio of the volume of the original hemisphere to that of the cut-out sphere is ***(Re)***

(*a*) 2 : 1 (*b*) 16 : 1 (*c*) 3 : 1 (*d*) 4 : 1

Sol. $r = 7$ cm

$$\text{Volume of the hemisphere} = \frac{2}{3}\pi r^3$$

$$\text{Volume of biggest Sphere} = \frac{4}{3}\pi\left(\frac{r}{2}\right)^3 = \frac{1}{6}\pi r^3$$

$$\therefore \text{ Required ratio} = \frac{\frac{2}{3}\pi r^3}{\frac{1}{6}\pi r^3} = \frac{\frac{2}{3}\times 7\times 7\times 7}{\frac{1}{6}\times 7\times 7\times 7} = \frac{2}{3}\times\frac{6}{1} = \frac{4}{1}$$

5. The radius of a piece of wire is decreased to one-half. If volume remains the same, then its length will increase by ***(Re)***

(*a*) 2 times (*b*) 8 times (*c*) 4 times (*d*) 5 times

Sol. Let us suppose, r and h be the radius and length of a wire.

$\therefore$ New radius = $\frac{1}{2}r$ and new length of a wire be h_1

Now, according to the question, volume remains the same.

$$\therefore \pi r^2 h = \pi\left(\frac{r}{2}\right)^2 h_1 \Rightarrow h_1 = 4h$$

Hence, the length of a wire will increase by 4 times to keep the volume the same.

6. The volume of cylinder of radius 3.5 cm and height 10 cm is ________ ***(Re)***

(*a*) 385 cm³ (*b*) 384 cm³

(*c*) 383 cm³ (*d*) None of these

Sol. Given, $r = 3.5 \text{ cm} = \frac{7}{2}$ cm

$h = 10$ cm

$V = \pi r^2 h$

$$V = \frac{22}{7}\times\frac{7}{2}\times\frac{7}{2}\times 10 = 11 \times 35 = 385 \text{ cm}^3$$

Answer Key

1. (*a*) 2. (*b*) 3. (*c*) 4. (*d*)
5. (*c*) 6. (*a*)

Assertion and Reason (1 M)

Direction: In the following questions, A statement of Assertion (A) is followed by a statement of Reason (R). Mark the correct choice as.

(*a*) Both Assertion (A) and Reason (R) are true, and Reason (R) is the correct explanation of Assertion (A).

(*b*) Both Assertion (A) and Reason (R) are true, but Reason (R) is not the correct explanation of Assertion (A).

(*c*) Assertion (A) is true, but Reason (R) is false.

(*d*) Assertion (A) is false, but Reason (R) is true.

1. Assertion (A): Total surface; area of the cylinder having radius of the base 14 *cm* and height 30 *cm* is 3872 cm^2.

Reason (R): If r be the radius and h be the height of the cylinder, then total surface area = $(2\pi rh + 2\pi r^2)$. *(Re)*

Sol. Reason (R): Total surface area of the cylinder is $2\pi r(r + h)$ i.e., $(2\pi rh + 2\pi r^2)$ where r and h are radius and height of the cylinder respectively.

$\therefore$ Reason is true.

Assertion (A) Radius of the base $(r) = 14$ *cm*, height $(h) = 30$ *cm*

T.S.A. of the cylinder $= 2\pi rh + 2\pi r^2 = 2\pi r(r + h)$

$$= 2\times\frac{22}{7}\times 14\times(44) = 3872\ cm^2$$

$\therefore$ Assertion is true & Reason is the correct explanation of Assertion.

2. Assertion (A): If the radius of a cone is halved and volume is not changed, then height remains same.

Reason (R): If the radius of a cone is halved and volume is not changed then height must become four times of the original height. *(Cr)*

Sol. Since, volume of cone $= \frac{1}{3}\pi r^2 h$

Given, $r_2 = \frac{r_1}{2}$ and $V_2 = V_1$

Hence, $\frac{V_1}{V_2} = \frac{\frac{1}{3}\pi r_1^2 h_1}{\frac{1}{3}\pi\left(\frac{r_1}{2}\right)^2 h_2} = \frac{4h_1}{h_2}$

$\because V_1 = V_2$

$\therefore h_2 = 4h_1$

Therefore, if radius is halved, then height must become four times of the original height.

Hence, assertion is false and reason is true.

Answer Key

1. (*a*) 2. (*d*)

Subjective Questions

Very Short Answer Type Questions (1 or 2 M)

1. A cylindrical bucket, 32 cm high and with radius of base 14 cm, is filled completely with sand. Find the volume fo the sand. $\left(\text{Use } \pi = \frac{22}{7}\right)$ *(Un)* (CBSE, 2020)

Sol. Radius of cylinder = 18 cm, height = 32 cm

Height of cone = 24 cm

Volume of cylinder $= \pi r^2 h = \pi \times 18^2 \times 32$

Volume of cone = Volume of cylinder

Volume of cone $= \frac{1}{3}\pi r^2 \times 24$ *(1 M)*

Hence, radius of cone can be calculated as follows:

$$= r^2 = \frac{3\times\pi\times 18^2\times 32}{\pi\times 24}$$

Or $r^2 = 18^2 \times 2^2$

Or, $r = 36$ cm

Now, slant height of conical heap can be calculated as follows:

$$l = \sqrt{h^2 + r^2} = \sqrt{24^2 + 36^2}$$

$$= \sqrt{576 + 1296} = \sqrt{1872} = 12\sqrt{13}\text{ cm}$$ *(1 M)*

2. Find the volume of the cone if $r = 7$ cm and $h = 5$ *cm*. *(Ap)*

Sol. Given, $r = 7$ *cm*, $h = 5$ *cm*

$\because$ Volume of a cone $(V) = \frac{1}{3}\times\pi r^2 h$ *(1 M)*

$\therefore V = \frac{1}{3}\times\frac{22}{7}\times 7^2\times 5$

Hence, $V = 256.67\ cm^3$ *(1 M)*

> **Mistakes 101 : What not to do!**
>
> **Rounding errors:** In calculations involving multiple steps, rounding errors can accumulate and lead to significant discrepancies in the final answer if not managed carefully.

3. Two cones have their heights in the ratio 1 : 4 and radii in the ratio 4 : 1. What is the ratio of their volumes? *(Ap)*

Sol. Given, ratio of heights of cone, $\frac{h_1}{h_2} = \frac{1}{4}$

Ratio of radii, $\frac{r_1}{r_2} = \frac{4}{1}$

We know, volume of cone $(V) = \frac{1}{3}\pi r^2 h$

Now, ratio of volume of two cones $\frac{V_1}{V_2} = \frac{\frac{1}{3}\pi r_1^2 h_1}{\frac{1}{3}\pi r_2^2 h_2}$ *(1 M)*

$$= \left(\frac{r_1}{r_2}\right)^2 \times \left(\frac{h_1}{h_2}\right) = \left(\frac{4}{1}\right)^2 \times \left(\frac{1}{4}\right) = \frac{16}{4} = \frac{4}{1}$$

Hence, the required ratio is 4 : 1. *(1 M)*

Short Answer Type Questions (2 or 3 M)

1. A heap of rice is in the form of a cone of base diameter 24 *m* and height 3.5 *m*. Find the volume of the rice. How much canvas cloth is required to just cover the heap? *(Ap)*

Sol. Given that a heap of rice is in the form of a cone

Diameter = $d = 24\ m$

$\therefore$ Radius $= r = \dfrac{d}{2} = 12\ m$

Height $= h = 3.5\ m$

Volume of a cone $= V = \dfrac{\pi r^2 h}{3}$ *(1 M)*

$V = \dfrac{\frac{22}{7} \times 12^2 \times 3.5}{3}$

$V = \dfrac{\frac{22}{7} \times 144 \times 3.5}{3}$

$V = 528\ m^3$ *(½ M)*

Given that canvas cloth is required to just cover the heap. It covered the only curved surface area of cone

Slant height of cone $= l = \sqrt{h^2 + r^2}$ *(½ M)*

$= \sqrt{3.5^2 + 12^2}\ m = \sqrt{156.25}\ m = 12.5\ m$

Curved surface area of cone (C.S.A) $= \pi rl$

$\text{C.S.A} = \dfrac{22}{7} \times 12 \times 12.5$

$\text{C.S.A} = 471.42\ m^2$ *(1 M)*

Key Takeaways

The slant height refers to the distance from the vertex of a cone or pyramid to any point on the perimeter of its base, measured along the lateral surface.

2. Shown below is a solid made of a cone, a cylinder and a hemisphere.

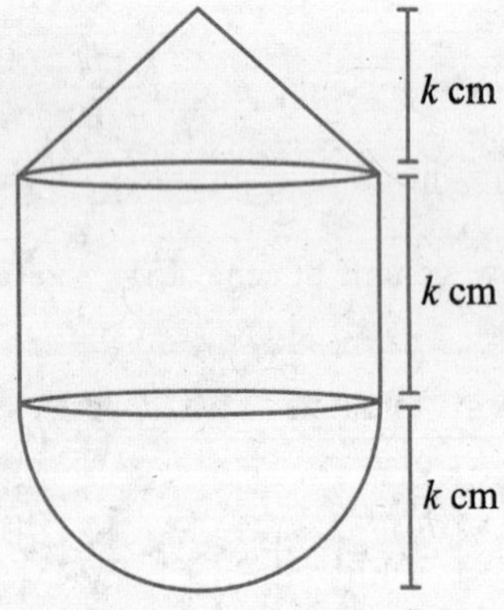

Prove that the total volume of the solid is twice the volume of the cylinder. ***(Re)* (CBSE CFPQ, 2023)**

Sol. Given,

We know,

Volume of cylinder $= \pi r^2 h$

Volume of cone $= \pi r^2 \dfrac{h}{3}$

Here, $h = k$, $r = k$

Therefore, we get:

Volume of cylinder $= \pi k^2 \times k = \pi k^3$ cm^3 *(½ M)*

Volume of cone $= \dfrac{1}{3}\pi k^2 \times \dfrac{k}{3} = \dfrac{\pi k^3}{3}$ cm^3 *(½ M)*

Volume of hemisphere $= \dfrac{2}{3}\pi \times k^3 = \dfrac{2\pi k^3}{3}$ cm^3 *(½ M)*

Total volume of solid $= \pi\left(k^3 + \dfrac{k^3}{3} + \dfrac{2k^3}{3}\right)$ cm^3

$= \pi\left(\dfrac{3k^3 + k^3 + 2k^3}{3}\right) = \pi\dfrac{6k^3}{3} = 2\pi k^3$ cm^3 ... *(i)* *(1 M)*

Volume of cylinder $= \pi k^3$ cm^3 ... *(ii)*

Comparing both *(i)* and *(ii)*, we get:

The volume of Solid = 2 × volume of cylinder

Hence, proved. *(½ M)*

3. A solid is in the form of a cylinder with hemispherical ends. The total height of the solid is 20 cm and the diameter of the cylinder is 7 cm. Find the total volume of the solid. (Use $\pi = \dfrac{22}{7}$) ***(Ap)***

Sol. Total volume = Volume of cylinder + Volume of 2 hemispherical

Height of cylinder = 20 – 7 = 13 *(1 M)*

Total volume $= \pi R^2 h + \dfrac{4}{3}\pi R^3$ *(1 M)*

$= \dfrac{22}{7} \times \dfrac{7}{2} \times \dfrac{7}{2} \times 13 + \left(\dfrac{4}{3} \times \dfrac{22}{7} \times \dfrac{7}{2} \times \dfrac{7}{2} \times \dfrac{7}{2}\right)$

$= 500.5 + 179.6 = 680.66$ cm^3 *(1 M)*

Long Answer Type Questiona (4 or 5 M)

1. A solid is in the shape of a cone surmounted on a hemisphere. The radius of each of them being 3.5 cm and the total height of the solid is 9.5 cm. Find the volume of the solid. ***(Un)* (CBSE, 2020)**

Sol.

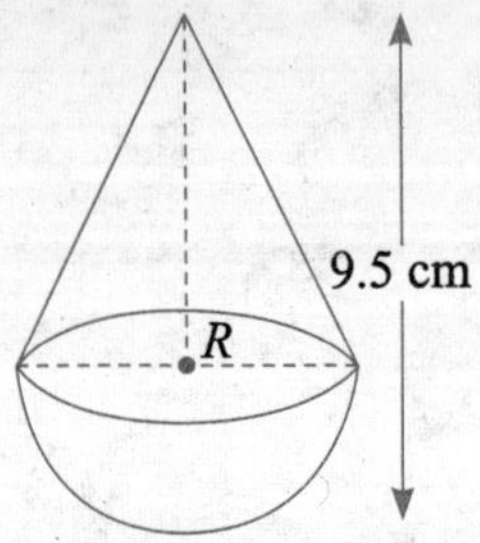

(1 M)

Radius = 3.5 cm

$\therefore$ Height of the cone

$h = 9.5 - 3.5 = 6$ cm *(1 M)*

$\therefore$ Volume of cone + Volume of Hemisphere

$= \frac{1}{3}\pi R^2 h + \frac{2}{3}\pi R^3$ *(1 M)*

$= \frac{1}{3}\pi \times (3.5)^2 \times 6 + \frac{2}{3}\pi \times (3.5)^3$

$= \frac{1}{3} \times \frac{22}{7} \times (3.5)^2 (13) = 166.83 \text{cm}^3$ *(1 M)*

2. A cone of height 24 *cm* and radius of base 6 *cm* is made up of modeling clay. A child reshapes it in the form of a sphere. Find the radius of the sphere. *(Cr)*

Sol. For cone: Height (h) = 24 *cm*, radius (r) = 6 *cm* *(½ M)*

The volume of cone = $\frac{1}{3}\pi r^2 h = \frac{1}{3} \times \pi \times 6 \times 6 \times 24\ cm^3$ *(1 M)*

If r is the radius of the sphere, then its volume is $\frac{4}{3}\pi r^3$. *(½ M)*

Since the volume of clay in the form of the cone and the sphere remains the same, we have, *(1 M)*

$\frac{4}{3}\pi r^3 = \frac{1}{3} \times \pi \times 6 \times 6 \times 24$ *(1 M)*

$r^3 = 3 \times 3 \times 24 = 3^3 \times 2^3$

So, $r = 3 \times 2 = 6\ cm$

Therefore, the radius of the sphere is 6 *cm*. *(1 M)*

3. A solid toy is in the form of a hemisphere surmounted by a right circular cone. The height of the cone is 2 *cm*, and the diameter of the base is 4 *cm*. Determine the volume of the toy. If a right circular cylinder circumscribes the toy, find the difference between the volumes of the cylinder and the toy. (Take π = 3.14) ***(Un)* (NCERT Intext)**

Sol.

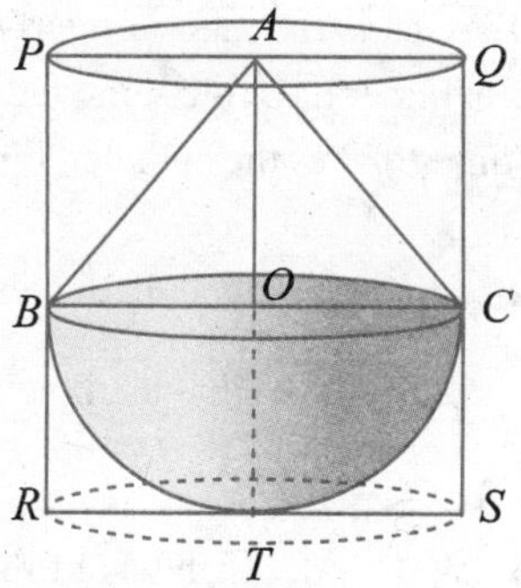

(1 M)

Let BTC be the hemisphere and ABC be the cone standing on the base of the hemisphere as shown in the above figure.

The radius BO of the hemisphere (as well as of the cone) =

$r = \frac{1}{2} \times 4\ cm = 2\ cm.$ *(½ M)*

Given, height of the cone (h) = 2 *cm*

So, volume of the toy = $\frac{2}{3}\pi r^3 + \frac{1}{3}\pi r^2 h$ *(1 M)*

$= \frac{2}{3} \times 3.14 \times 2^3 + \frac{1}{3} \times 3.14 \times 2^2 \times 2$

$= 25.12\ cm^3$ *(1 M)*

Now, let the right circular cylinder $PQRS$ circumscribes the given solid.

The radius of the base of the right circular cylinder = RT = BO = 2 *cm*, and its height is

$PR = AO + OT = (2 + 2)\ cm = 4\ cm$ *(½ M)*

So, required difference between volumes of the cylinder and the toy = volume of the right circular cylinder – the volume of the toy

$= (3.14 \times 2^2 \times 4 - 25.12)\ cm^3 = 25.12\ cm^3$

Hence, the required difference between the two volumes $= 25.12\ cm^3$ *(1 M)*

Mistakes 101 : What not to do!

Using incorrect values for constants: Some shapes involve constants like pi (π) or square roots, and students may use incorrect or approximated values for these constants, leading to inaccuracies in the final result.

Key Takeaways

Develop the ability to visualize three-dimensional shapes. Visualization helps in understanding the problem and selecting the appropriate formulas.

MISCELLANEOUS EXERCISE

Multiple Choice Questions (1 M)

1. Find the ratio of the volume of two cylinders having radii 'R' and 'r' and are of the same height.

   (a) $H^2 : R^2$ (b) $R : r$

   (c) $R^2 : r^2$ (d) None of these

2. The ratio of the volumes of two cones with same radii and height h_1 and h_2 is

   (a) $h_1 : h_2$ (b) $r^2 : h^2$

   (c) $r_1 : r_2$ (d) None of these

3. If the radius and slant height of a cone are in the ratio 4 : 7 and its curved surface area is 792 cm^2, then its radius is (take π as 22/7)

   (a) 18 cm (b) 8 cm (c) 12 cm (d) 9 cm

4. Three cubes each of side 15 cm are joined end to end. The total surface area of the cuboid is

   (a) 3150 cm^2 (b) 1575 cm^2

   (c) 1012.5 cm^2 (d) 576.4 cm^2

5. If the radius of a sphere is increased by 100%, the volume of the corresponding sphere is increased by

   (a) 200% (b) 500%

   (c) 700% (d) 800%

6. The curved surface area of a right circular cone of height 15 cm and base diameter 16 cm is

   (a) 120π cm^2 (b) 60π cm^2

   (c) 68π cm^2 (d) 136π cm^2

7. A medicine-capsule is in the shape of a cylinder of radius 0.25 cm with two hemispheres stuck to each of its ends. The length of the entire capsule is 2 cm. Then the total surface area of the capsule is

   (a) 3.14 cm^2 (b) 2.7475 cm^2

   (c) 0.98125 cm^2 (d) 0.785 cm^2

8. Two cones of equal heights have their radii in the ratio 3 : 2. The ratio of their volumes will be equal to:

   (a) 3 : 2 (b) 9 : 4 (c) 27 : 8 (d) 81 : 16

Assertion and Reason (1 M)

Direction: In the following questions, A statement of Assertion (A) is followed by a statement of Reason (R). Mark the correct choice as.

(a) Both Assertion (A) and Reason (R) are true, and Reason (R) is the correct explanation of Assertion (A).

(b) Both Assertion (A) and Reason (R) are true, but Reason (R) is not the correct explanation of Assertion (A).

(c) Assertion (A) is true, but Reason (R) is false.

(d) Assertion (A) is false, but Reason (R) is true.

1. **Assertion (A):** The volume and surface area of a sphere are related to each other by radius.

   Reason (R): Relation between Surface area S and Volume V is $S^3 = 36\pi V^2$.

2. **Assertion (A):** If the volumes of two spheres are in the ratio 27 : 8, then their surface areas are in the ratio 3 : 2.

   Reason (R): Volume of the sphere $= \frac{4}{3}\pi r^3$ and its surface area = $4\pi r^2$

Subjective Questions

Very Short Answer Type Questions (1 or 2 M)

1. Two cones have their heights in the ratio 1 : 3 and radii in the ratio 3 : 1. What is the ratio of their volumes?
2. A cone and a cylinder have the same radii but the height of the cone is 3 times that of the cylinder. Find the ratio of their volumes.
3. The volume of a right circular cylinder with the height equal to the radius is $25\frac{1}{7}$ cm^3. Find the height of the cylinder.
4. The water in a rectangular reservoir having a base 80 m × 60 m, is 6.5 m deep. In what time can the water be emptied by a pipe of which the cross section is a square of side 20 cm, if water runs through the pipe at the rate of 10 km/hr?

Short Answer Type Questions (2 or 3 M)

1. Water in a canal, 6 m wide and 1.5 m deep, is flowing with a speed of 10 km/hr. How much area will it irrigate in 30 minutes; if 8 cm standing water is needed?
2. If r, h, c, v are radius, height, curved surface area and volume of a cone respectively, then prove that $3\pi vh^3 - c^2h^2 + 9v^2 = 0$.
3. If the total surface area of a solid hemisphere is 462 cm², find its volume. $\left[\text{Take } \pi = \frac{22}{7}\right]$

4. A solid is composed of a cylinder with hemispherical ends. If the whole length of the solid is 100 cm and the diameter of the hemispherical ends is 28 cm. Find the cost of polishing the surface of the solid at the rate of 5 paise per sq. cm

Long Answer Type Questions (4 or 5 M)

1. Rachel, an engineering student, was asked to make a model shaped like a cylinder with two cones attached at its two ends by using a thin aluminium sheet. The diameter of the model is 3 *cm* and its length is 12 *cm*. If each cone has a height of 2 *cm*, find the volume of air contained in the model that Rachel made. (Assume the outer and inner dimensions of the model to be nearly the same.) **(NCERT Intext)**
2. A gulab jamun, contains sugar syrup up to about 30% of its volume. Find approximately how much syrup would be found in 45 gulab jamuns, each shaped like a cylinder with two hemispherical ends with length 5 cm and diameter 2.8 cm (See figure). **(NCERT Intext)**

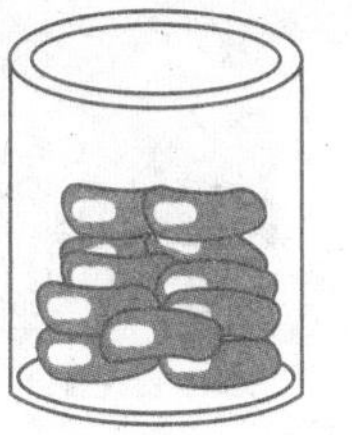

3. From a solid cylinder, whose height is 2.4 cm and diameter 1.4 cm, a conical cavity of the same height and same diameter is hollowed out. Find the total surface area of the remaining solid. **(CBSE, 2022)**
4. A vessel is in the form of an inverted cone. Its height is 8 *cm* and the radius of its top, which is open, is 5 *cm*. It is filled with water up to the brim. When lead shots, each of which is a sphere of radius 0.5 *cm* are dropped into the vessel, one-fourth of the water flows out. Find the number of lead shots dropped in the vessel. **(NCERT Intext)**
5. A solid consisting of a right circular cone of height 120 *cm* and radius 60 *cm* standing on a hemisphere of radius 60 *cm* is placed upright in a right circular cylinder full of water such that it touches the bottom. Find the volume of water left in the cylinder, if the radius of the cylinder is 60 *cm* and its height is 180 *cm*. **(NCERT Intext)**

Case Based Questions

Case Based-I: A 'circus' is a company of performers who put on shows of acrobats, clowns etc. to entertain people started around 250 years back, in open fields, now generally performed in tents.

One such 'Circus Tent' is shown below.

The tent is in the shape of a cylinder surmounted by a conical top. If the height and diameter of cylindrical part are 9 m and 30 m respectively and height of conical part is 8 m with same dsiameter as that of the cylindrical part, then find:

(*i*) What is the radius of conical part?

(*ii*) The area of the canvas used in making the tent.

OR

Find the slant height of the cone.

(*iii*) The cost of the canvas bought for the tent at the rate ₹200 per sqm, if 30 sq *m* canvas was wasted during stitching.

Case Based-II: A school mathematics teacher took her class x students on an educational trip to show Gol Gumbaz. The teacher had an interest in history as well. She told children about the history of Gol Gumbaz. Gol Gumbaz is the tomb of king Muhammad Adil Shah. The construction of this tomb was started in 1626 and completed in 1656. The teacher then stated that this monument contains a combination of solid figures. She pointed that there are a cubical bases and a hemispherical dome is at the top.

(*i*) If one side of the cubical portion is 23 *m*, then what is the diagonal of the cubic portion of the Gol Gumbaz?

(*ii*) A block of Gol Gumbaz is in the shape of a cylinder of diameter 0.5 cm with two hemispheres stuck to each of its ends. The length of the shape is 2 *cm*. What is the volume of the block? (Use $\pi = 3.14$)

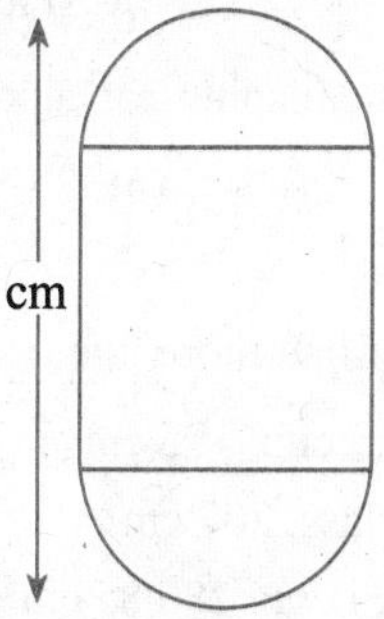

OR

Find the total surface area of Gol Gumbaz.

(*iii*) What is the curved surface area of the new solid formed by joining two solid hemispheres of same radii r along their bases?

Case Based-III: Adventure camps are the perfect place for the children to practice decision making for themselves without parents and teachers guiding their every move. Some students of a school reached for adventure at Sakleshpur. At the camp, the waiters served some students with a welcome drink in a cylindrical glass and some students in a hemispherical cup whose dimensions are shown below. After that they went for a jungle trek. The jungle trek was enjoyable but tiring. As dusk fell, it was time to take shelter. Each group of four students was given a canvas of area $551 m^2$. Each group had to make a conical tent to accommodate all the four students. Assuming that all the stitching and wasting incurred while cutting, would amount to $1 m^2$, the students put the tents. The radius of the tent is 7m. **(CBSE QB)**

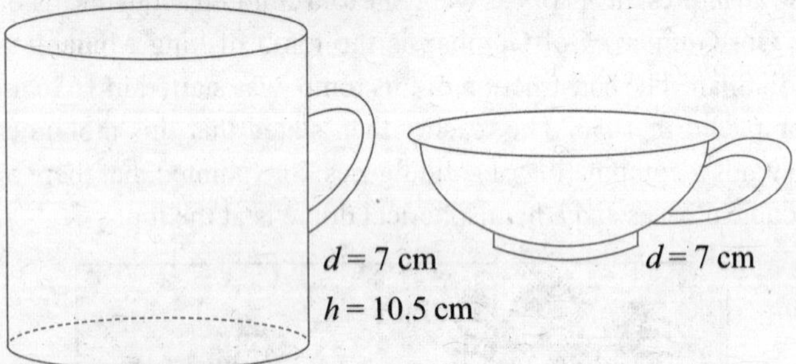

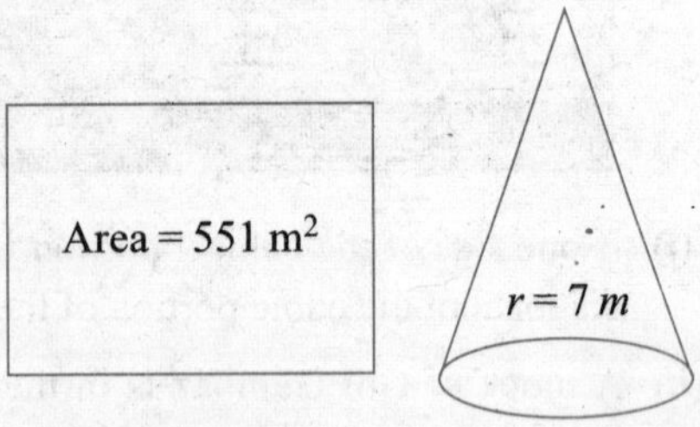

(i) The volume of cylindrical cup is

(a) 295.75 cm^3 (b) 7415.5 cm^3
(c) 384.88 cm^3 (d) 404.25 cm^3

(ii) The volume of hemispherical cup is

(a) 179.67 cm^3 (b) 89.83 cm^3
(c) 172.25 cm^3 (d) 210.60 cm^3

(iii) Which container had more juice and by how much?

(a) Hemispherical cup, 195 cm^3
(b) Cylindrical glass, 207 cm^3
(c) Hemispherical cup, 280.85 cm^3
(d) Cylindrical glass, 314.42 cm^3

(iv) The height of the conical tent prepared to accommodate four students is

(a) 18 m (b) 10 m
(c) 24 m (d) 14 m

(v) How much space on the ground is occupied by each student in the conical tent?

(a) 54 m^2 (b) 38.5 m^2
(c) 86 m^2 (d) 24 m^2

Case Based-IV: The Great Stupa at Sanchi is one of the oldest stone structures in India, and an important monument of Indian Architecture. It was originally commissioned by the emperor Ashoka in the 3rd century BC. Its nucleus was a simple hemispherical brick structure built over the relics of the Buddha. .It is a perfect example of combination of solid figures. A big hemispherical dome with a cuboidal structure mounted on it. $\left(\text{Take } \pi = \frac{22}{7}\right)$ **(CBSE QB)**

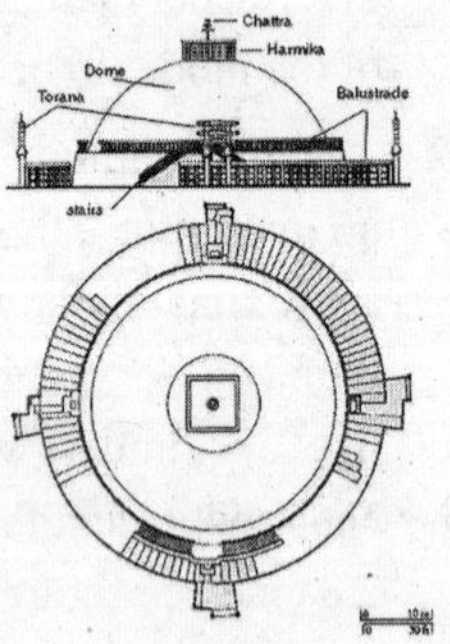

(i) Calculate the volume of the hemispherical dome if the height of the dome is 21 m.

(a) 19404 cu.m (b) 2000 cu.m
(c) 15000 cu.m (d) 19000 cu.m

(ii) The formula to find the Volume of Sphere is

(a) $\frac{2}{3}\pi r^3$ (b) $\frac{4}{3}\pi r^3$
(c) $4\pi r^2$ (d) $2\pi r^2$

(iii) The cloth required to cover the hemispherical dome if the radius of its base is 14m, is

(a) 1222 sq.m (b) 1232 sq.m
(c) 1200 sq.m (d) 1400 sq.m

(iv) The total surface area of the combined figure i.e. hemispherical dome with radius 14m and cuboidal shaped top with dimensions 8m × 6m × 4m is

(a) 1200 sq.m (b) 1232 sq.m
(c) 1392 sq.m (d) 1932 sq.m

(v) The volume of the cuboidal shaped top with dimensions mentioned in question (iv) above, is

(a) 182.45 m^3 (b) 282.45 m^3
(c) 292 m^3 (d) 192 m^3

ANSWER KEYS

Multiple Choice Questions

1. (*c*) 2. (*a*) 3. (*c*) 4. (*a*) 5. (*c*) 6. (*d*) 7. (*a*) 8. (*b*)

Assertion and Reason

1. (*a*) 2. (*d*)

Case Based Questions

Case Based-III

(*i*) (*d*) (*ii*) (*b*) (*iii*) (*d*) (*iv*) (*c*) (*v*) (*b*)

Case Based-IV

(*i*) (*a*) (*ii*) (*b*) (*iii*) (*b*) (*iv*) (*c*) (*v*) (*d*)

HINTS & EXPLANATIONS

Multiple Choice Questions

1. (*c*) It is given that both the cylinders have the same height and their radii are 'R' and 'r'.

$$\therefore \frac{V_1}{V_2} = \frac{\pi R^2 h}{\pi r^2 h} = \frac{R^2}{r^2}$$

Hence, $V_1 : V_2 = R^2 : r^2$

2. (*a*) It is given that both cones have the same radii

Therefore,

$$\frac{V_1}{V_2} = \frac{\frac{1}{3}\pi r^2 h_1}{\frac{1}{3}\pi r^2 h_2} = \frac{h_1}{h_2}$$

Hence, $V_1 : V_2 = h_1 : h_2$

3. (*c*) It is given that,

$$\frac{r}{l} = \frac{4}{7}$$

$$\Rightarrow 4l = 7r$$

$$\Rightarrow l = \frac{7r}{4} \quad \ldots(i)$$

It is also given that, C.S.A of cone = 792 cm^2

$$\therefore \frac{22}{7} \times r \times l = 792$$

$$\frac{22}{7} \times r \times \frac{7r}{4} = 792 \quad \text{(using eq. } (i))$$

$$\Rightarrow r^2 = \frac{792 \times 4}{22}$$

$\Rightarrow r^2 = 144\ cm \Rightarrow r = 12\ cm$

Hence, the radius of cone is 12 *cm*.

4. (*a*) The dimensions of the cuboid are 45 *cm* × 15 *cm* × 15 *cm*

So, total surface area of the cuboid = $2(lb + bh + hl)$

$= 2(675 + 225 + 675)\ cm^2$

$= 3150\ cm^2$

5. (*c*) Let r be the original radius of the sphere.

When, radius is increased by 100% then its becomes twice of its original value i.e., $r' = 2r$

So, new volume $(V') = \frac{4}{3}\pi(r')^3$

$= \frac{4}{3}\pi(2r)^3$ s

$= 8 \times \frac{4}{3}\pi r^3$

$= 8V$

So, increase in volume $= \frac{V' - V}{V} \times 100\%$

$= \frac{8V - V}{V} \times 100 = \frac{7V}{V} \times 100$

$= 700\%$

6. (*d*) Curved surface area (C.S.A) of a cone = πrl

Given, Diameter $(D) = 16cm$ and $h = 15cm$

$\therefore$ Radius $(r) = \frac{D}{2} = \frac{16}{2} = 8\ cm$

$\because\ l = \sqrt{r^2 + h^2} = \sqrt{8^2 + 15^2} = \sqrt{64 + 225} = \sqrt{289} = 17\ cm$

$\therefore$ C.S.A. = πrl

$= \pi(8)(17)$

$= 136\pi\ cm^2$

7. (*a*) It is given that

Radius of cylinder (r) = Radius of hemisphere (r) = 0.25 *cm*

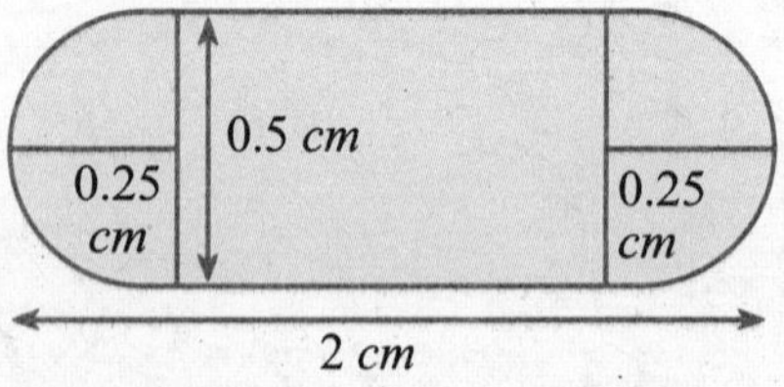

Total length of capsule = 2 *cm*

Here, the length of cylindrical part of capsule (h) = length of capsule – radius of both hemispheres = 2 – (2 × 0.25) = 2 – 0.5 = 1.5 *cm*

∴ Total surface area of capsule = C.S.A of cylindrical part + 2 × C.S.A of hemisphere

∵ C.S.A of cylinder = $2\pi rh$

∵ C.S.A of hemisphere = $2\pi r^2$

Substituting the values of r and h, we obtain

$= 2\pi rh + 2(2\pi r^2)$

$= 2\pi(rh + 2r^2)$

$= 2\times\frac{22}{7}[0.375+0.125] = 2\times\frac{22}{7}[0.5]$

$= 3.14\ cm^2$

8. (*b*) For cone:

Given that, $h_1 = h_2$ and $\frac{r_1}{r_2} = \frac{3}{2}$

The ratio of their volume is given by

$$\frac{V_1}{V_2} = \frac{\frac{1}{3}\pi r_1^2 h_1}{\frac{1}{3}\pi r_2^2 h_2} = \left(\frac{3}{2}\right)^2 = \frac{9}{4}$$

Assertion and Reason

1. (*a*) ∵ Volume of sphere $= \frac{4}{3}\pi r^3$

$\Rightarrow V = \frac{4}{3}\pi r^3$

$\Rightarrow \frac{3V}{4\pi} = r^3$

$\Rightarrow r = \left(\frac{3V}{4\pi}\right)^{1/3}$

Also, $S = 4\pi r^2$

$\Rightarrow S = 4\pi\left(\frac{3V}{4\pi}\right)^{2/3}$

$\Rightarrow S^3 = \frac{64\pi^3 9V^2}{(16\pi^2)} = 36\pi V^2$

Which proves that assertion is true.

Therefore, Both assertion and reason are true and reason is the correct explanation of assertion.

2. (*d*) According to the question,

$\frac{V_1}{V_2} = \frac{27}{8}$

$\therefore \frac{\frac{4}{3}\pi R^3}{\frac{4}{3}\pi r^3} = \frac{27}{8}$

$\Rightarrow \frac{R^3}{r^3} = \frac{27}{8} \Rightarrow \frac{R}{r} = \frac{3}{2}$

Now, ratio of surface areas

$= \frac{4\pi R^2}{4\pi r^2} = \frac{R^2}{r^2} = \left(\frac{3}{2}\right)^2 = \frac{9}{4}$ $\left(\because \frac{R}{r} = \frac{3}{2}\right)$

∴ Assertion is false but reason is true.

Subjective Questions

Very Short Answer Type Questions

1. Let the heights of the two cones be h and $3h$ and their radii be $3r$ and r.

We know, volume of cone $(V) = \frac{1}{3}\pi r^2 h$

Then, $V_1 : V_2 = \frac{1}{3}\pi(3r)^2(h) : \frac{1}{3}\pi(r)^2(3h)$

$= 9 : 3$ i.e., $3 : 1$

Hence, the ratio of their volumes is 3 : 1. *(1 M)*

2. Let r be the radii of the cone as well as the cylinder both.

Let h be the height of the cylinder. Then, the height of the cone will be $3h$

Now, V_1 (Volume of cone): V_2 (Volume of cylinder)

$= \frac{1}{3}\pi r^2(3h) : \pi r^2 h$

$= 1 : 1$

Hence, the ratio of their volumes is 1 : 1. *(1 M)*

3. Let the height of the cylinder be *h cm.*

According to the question,

$r = h$

$\because V = \pi r^2 h$

$V = \pi(h)^2(h) = 25\frac{1}{7}$

$\Rightarrow \frac{22}{7}h^3 = \frac{176}{7}$

$\Rightarrow h^3 = 8$

$\Rightarrow h = 2$

Thus, the height of the cylinder is 2 *cm*. *(1 M)*

4. The given dimensions of the rectangular reservoir are 80 *m*, 60 *m* and 6.5 *m* respectively. Hence,

∵ Volume of water in the reservoir = $l \times b \times h$

= (80 × 60 × 6.5) m^3 = 31200 m^3

Now, area of cross section of the pipe = (side)^2

$= \left(\frac{20}{100}\times\frac{20}{100}\right)m^2 = \frac{1}{25}m^2$ *(1 M)*

As, rate of flow of water = 10 *km/hr* = 10,000 *m/hr*.

So, volume of water emptied in 1 *hr* = Speed × Area of the cross-section

$$= \left(10000 \times \frac{1}{25}\right) m^3 = 400\, m^3$$ (½ M)

Therefore, time taken to empty the reservoir

$$= \frac{\text{Volume of tank}}{\text{Volume of water emptied in 1 } hr.}$$

$$= \frac{31200}{400} = 78$$

Hence, time taken to empty the tank will be 78 hours.

(½ M)

Short Answer Type Questions

1. Given, depth of water in a canal = 1.5 *m*

Width = 6 *m*

Speed of canal = 10 *km/hr*

Length of canal in 30 minutes

$$= \frac{30}{60} \times 10 = 5\ km = 5000\ m$$ [∵ 1 *km* = 1000 *m*] (½ M)

Height = 8 *cm* = 0.08 *m* [1 *m* = 100 *cm*]

Volume of canal = length × breadth × height

= 1.5 × 6 × 5000 = 45000 m^3 (½ M)

$$\therefore \text{Area} = \frac{\text{Volume}}{\text{Height}} = \frac{45000}{0.08} = 562500\ m^2$$ (1 M)

$$\therefore \text{Area irrigated} = \frac{562500}{10000} \text{ hectares}$$

Hence, area irrigated = 56.25 hectares (1 M)

2. It is given that *r, h, c* and *v* are the radius, height, curved surface area and volume of a cone respectively. Now, let us suppose, *l* be the slant height of cone.

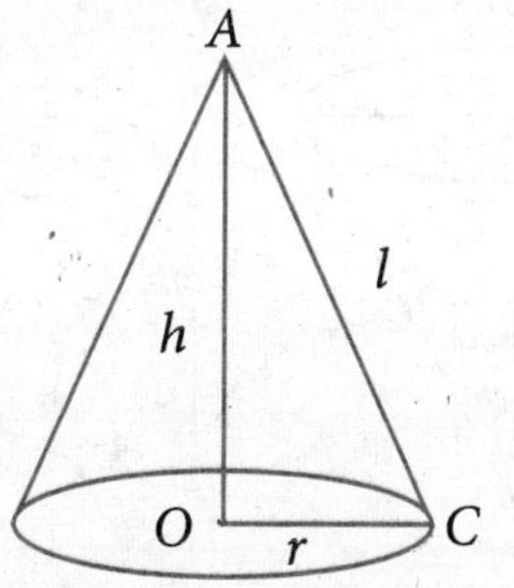

$$l = \sqrt{r^2 + h^2},\ v = \frac{1}{3}\pi r^2 h$$

$$c = \pi r l = \pi r\sqrt{r^2 + h^2}$$ (1 M)

Now, taking L.H.S of the question, i.e., $3\pi v h^3 - c^2h^2 + 9v^2$ and putting the values, we get

$$3\pi \times \left[\frac{1}{3}\pi r^2 h\right] \times h^3 - \pi^2 r^2\left(r^2 + h^2\right)h^2 + 9 \times \left[\frac{1}{3}\pi r^2 h\right]^2$$ (1 M)

$$= \pi^2 r^2 h^4 - \pi^2 r^4 h^2 - \pi^2 r^2 h^4 + 9 \times \frac{1}{9}\pi^2 r^4 h^2$$

$$= \pi^2 r^2 h^4 - \pi^2 r^4 h^2 - \pi^2 r^2 h^4 + \pi^2 r^4 h^2$$

= 0 = R.H.S. (1 M)

Hence proved.

3. Given, total surface area of solid hemisphere = 462 cm^2

$$\Rightarrow 3r^2 = 462\ cm^2$$

$$\Rightarrow 3 \times \frac{22}{7} \times r^2 = 462$$

$$\Rightarrow r^2 = 49 \Rightarrow r = 7 \text{ cm}$$ (1 M)

$$\text{Volume of solid hemisphere} = \frac{2}{3}\pi r^3 = \frac{2}{3} \times \frac{22}{7} \times 7 \times 7 \times 7$$

= 718.67 cm^3 (1 M)

4. we have

$$r = \text{radius of cylinder} = \text{radius of hemispherical ends} = \frac{28}{2} \text{ cm}$$

h = height of the cylinder = 100 – 2 × 14 = 100 – 28 = 72 cm.

Total surface area

= curved surface area of cylinder + 2 × surface area of hemispherical ends (1 M)

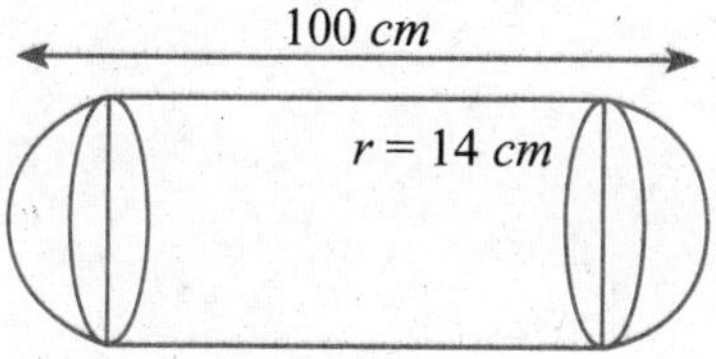

$$= 2\pi rh + 2 \times (2\pi r^2)$$

$$= 2\pi rh + 4\pi r^2 = 2\pi r\,(h + 2r)$$

$$= 2 \times \frac{22}{7} \times 14(72 + 28)$$

$$= 2 \times \frac{22}{7} \times 14 \times 100 = 8800 \text{ cm}^2$$ (1 M)

Rate of polishing = 5 paise per sq. cm.

$$\text{Cost of polishing the surface} = \frac{8800 \times 5}{100} = ₹440$$ (1 M)

Long Answer Type Questions

1. Volume of air contained in model = Total volume solid

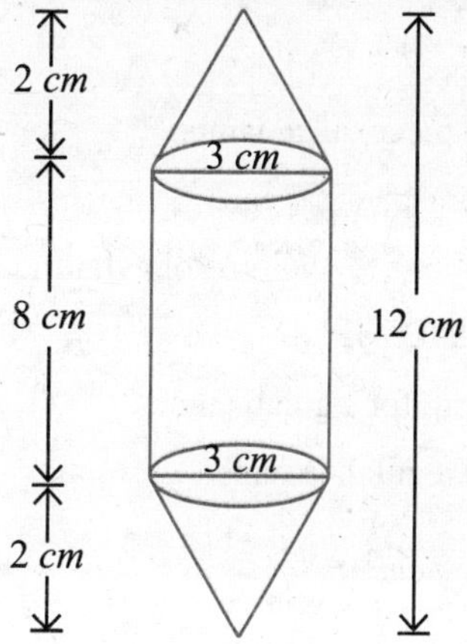

(1 M)

Diameter of base of cone (D) = 3 cm

$\therefore$ Radius of base of cone (r) = $\frac{3}{2}$ cm

Height of cone (h) = 2 cm

Volume of a cone = $\frac{1}{3}\pi r^2 h = \frac{1}{3}\pi\left(\frac{3}{2}\right)^2 \times 2$

$= \frac{1}{3}\pi\frac{9\times 2}{4} = \frac{3}{2}\pi\ cm^3$ (1 M)

$\therefore$ Volume of both cones = $2\times\frac{3}{2}\pi = 3\pi\ cm^3$ (1 M)

Volume of cylindrical portion = $\pi r^2 h$

$= \pi\left(\frac{3}{2}\right)^2 \times 8 = \frac{\pi\times 9\times 8}{4} = 18\pi\ cm^3$ (1 M)

Volume of air contained in the model

= Total volume of solid = $3\pi + 18\pi$

$= 21\pi = \frac{21\times 22}{7} = 66\ cm^3$ (1 M)

2. Radius of hemispherical portion (r) = $\frac{2.8}{2} = 1.4\ cm$

Volume of hemispherical ends

$= \frac{2}{3}\pi r^3 = \frac{2}{3}\times\frac{22}{7}(1.4)^3$

$= \frac{2}{3}\times\frac{22}{7}\times 1.4\times 1.4\times 1.4$

$= \frac{2\times 22\times 2\times 14\times 14}{3\times 10\times 10\times 10} = 5.74\ cm^3$ (1 M)

Volume of both hemispherical ends = 2 × 5.74 = 11.48 cm^3

Height of cylindrical portion

= (Total height) – (Radius of both hemispherical ends)

= 5 – 2 (1.4) = 5 – 2.8 = 2.2 cm (1 M)

Radius of cylindrical portion (r) = 1.4 cm

volume of cylindrical portion of gulab jamun

$= \pi r^2 h = \frac{22}{7}\times(1.4)^2\times 2.2$

$= \frac{22\times 1.4\times 1.4\times 2.2}{7} = 13.55\ cm^3$ (1 M)

Total volume of one piece gulab jamun

= Volume of two hemispherical ends

+ Volume of cylindrical portion

= 11.48 + 13.55 = 25.03 cm^3 (½ M)

Volume of sugar syrup for a gulab jamun

= 30% of volume of a gulab jamun

$= \frac{30}{100}\times 25.03 = 7.50\ cm^3$ (½ M)

Volume of sugar syrup in 45 gulab jamuns

= 45 (volume of one gulab jamun) = 45 × 7.50

= 337.5 = 338 cm^3 approx. (1 M)

3.

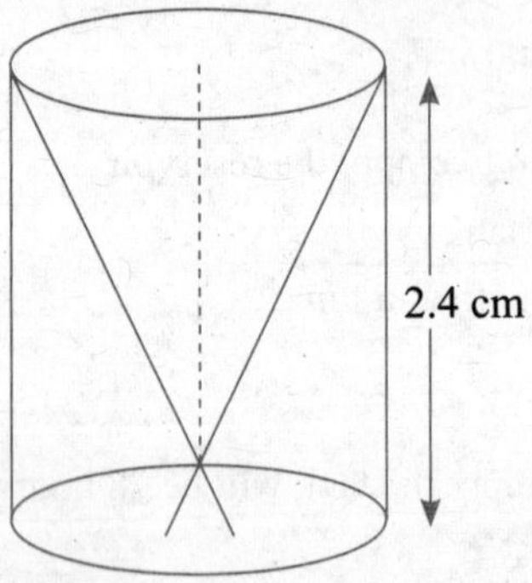

Given:

Height (h) of the conical part = Height (h) of the cylindrical part = 2.4 cm Diameter of the cylindrical part = 1.4 cm

Radius = $\frac{\text{Diameter}}{2}$

Radius (r) of the cylindrical part = 0.7 cm (1 M)

Slant height (l) of conical part = $\sqrt{r^2 + h^2}$

$= \sqrt{0.7^2 + 2.4^2} = \sqrt{0.49 + 5.76} = \sqrt{6.25} = 2.5$ (1 M)

Total surface area of the remaining solid = CSA of cylindrical part + CSA of conical part + Area of cylindrical base

$= 2\pi rh + \pi rl + \pi r^2$

$= 2\times\frac{22}{7}\times 0.7\times 2.4 + \frac{22}{7}\times 0.7\times 2.5 + \frac{22}{7}\times 0.7\times 0.7$ (1 M)

= 4.4 × 2.4 + 2.2 × 2. + 2.2 × 0.7

= 10.56 + 5.50 + 1.54 = 17.60 cm^2

The total surface area of the remaining solid to the nearest cm^2 is 18 cm^2 (1 M)

4. Given, height of the cone (h) = 8 cm

Radius of the cone (r) = 5 cm

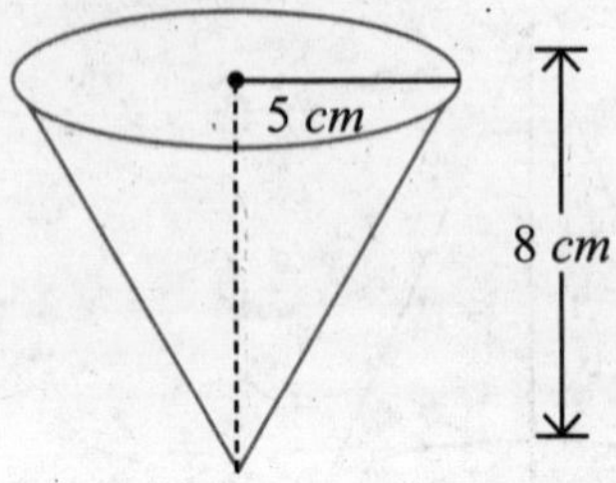

(1 M)

$\therefore$ Volume of cone = $\frac{1}{3}\pi r^2 h$

$= \frac{1}{3}\pi(5)^2 8 = \frac{200}{3}\pi\ cm^3$ (1 M)

Radius of one spherical lead shot = 0.5 cm

$\therefore$ Volume of one spherical lead shot $= \frac{4}{3}\pi r^3$

$= \frac{4}{3}\pi(0.5)^3 = \frac{4\times 0.125}{3}\pi = \frac{0.5}{3}\pi\ cm^3$ (1½ M)

When spherical lead are dropped in the vessel, one fourth of water flows out

Let number of lead shots be n

Volume of n spherical shots = $\frac{1}{4}$ volume of conical vessel

$$\Rightarrow n\left(\frac{0.5}{3}\pi\right) = \frac{1}{4}\left(\frac{200}{3}\pi\right) \Rightarrow n(0.5) = 50$$

$$\Rightarrow n = \frac{50 \times 10}{5} = 100 \qquad (1½ M)$$

5. Radius of hemisphere (r) = 60 cm

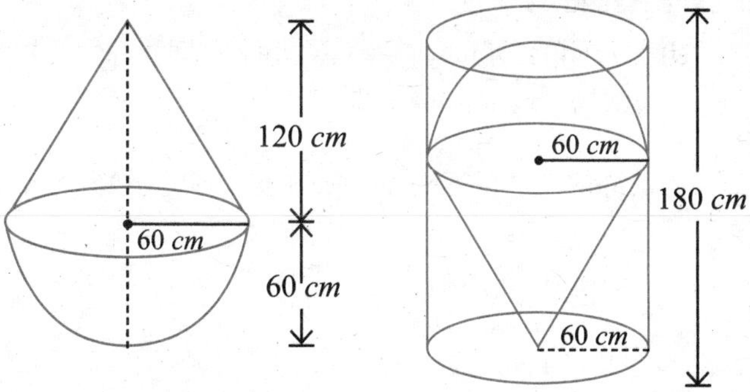

(1 M)

Volume of hemisphere = $\frac{2}{3}\pi(60)^3\ cm^3$

Radius of conical base (r) = 60 cm

Height of conical portion (h) = 120 cm

Volume of conical portion = $\frac{1}{3}\pi r^2 h$

$$= \frac{1}{3}\pi(60)^2 \times 120\ cm^3 \qquad (1 M)$$

Total volume of hemisphere and conical solid

= Volume of hemisphere + Volume of conical portion

$$= \frac{2}{3}\pi(60)^3 + \frac{1}{3}\pi(60)^2 \times 120$$

$$= \frac{1}{3}\pi(60)^2[2(60)+120]$$

$$= \frac{1}{3}\pi \times 60 \times 60 \times 240 = \pi(60)^2 \times 80\ cm^3 \qquad (1 M)$$

Volume of cylindrical solid = $\pi r^2 h = \pi(60)^2 \times 180\ cm^3$

[Where r = 60 cm and h =180 cm] (1 M)

When (hemisphere + conical) solid kept in cylindrical solid then Volume of water left in cylinder = Volume of cylinder – (Volume of hemisphere + Volume of cone) = $[\pi(60)^2 \times 180 - \pi(60)^2 \times 80] = \pi(60)^2\ (180-80) = \pi \times 3600 \times 100$ = 1130400 cm^3 = 1.130 m^3 (1 M)

Case Based Questions

Case Based-I

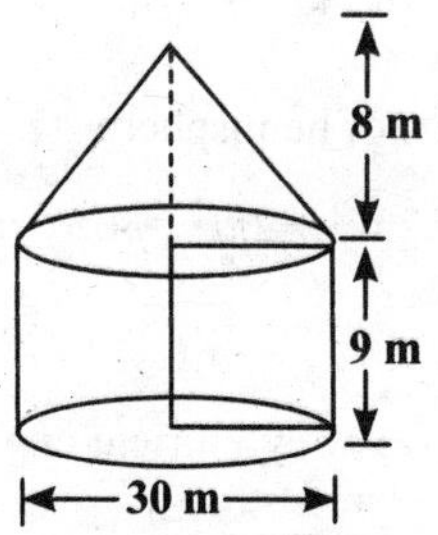

(*i*) Radius of conical part = Radius of cylindrical part = 15 m is the radius of conical part also.

(*ii*) The area of the canvas used in making the tent

= Curved surface area of cone + Curved surface area of cylinder

$$= \pi rl + 2\pi rh = \frac{22}{7} \times 15 \times 17 + 2 \times \frac{22}{7} \times 15 \times 9$$

$$= \frac{22}{7} \times 15(17+18) = \frac{22}{7} \times 15 \times 35 = 1650\ m^2$$

OR

Here we have

Total canvas bought for the tent = 1650 + 30 = 1680 m^2

∴ cost of canvas for the tent

= 1680 × 200 = ₹3,36,000

(*iii*) Radius of conical part = Radius of cylindrical part

$$= \frac{30}{2} = 15 m = r (say)$$

Given height of conical = 8 m and height of cylindrical part = 9 m

$$\therefore l = \sqrt{(15)^2 + 8^2} = \sqrt{225 + 64} = \sqrt{289} = 17\ m$$

Case Based-II

(*i*) It is given that, side of cubical portion (a) = 23 m

As, diagonal of cubic portion = $a\sqrt{3}$

Hence, diagonal = $23\sqrt{3}m$.

(*ii*) ∵ Radius of cylinder (r) = radius of hemisphere (r) = $\frac{0.5}{2} cm = 0.25\ cm$

Height of the cylinder (h) = (2 – 0.25 – 0.25) = 1.5 cm

∴ Volume of the block = Volume of a cylinder + Volume of 2 hemispheres

$$= \pi r^2 h + 2 \times \left(\frac{2}{3}\pi r^3\right) = \pi r^2\left(h + \frac{4}{3}r\right)$$

$$= 3.14 \times (0.25)^2\left(1.5 + \frac{4}{3} \times 0.25\right) = 3.14 \times (0.25)^2 \times \frac{5.5}{3}$$

$$= 3.14 \times 0.0625 \times \frac{5.5}{3} = 0.36\ cm^3\ \text{(approx)}$$

OR

Total surface area of gol gumbaz = $2\pi rh$

$= 2\times\frac{22}{7}\times\frac{1}{4}\times 2 = 3.14\ \text{cm}^2$

(iii) It is given that, radius of hemisphere = r

CSA of new solid = $2\pi r^2 + 2\pi r^2 = 4\pi r^2$

Case Based-III

(i) (*d*) We have, radius (r) of cylindrical cup $= \frac{7}{2}$ cm

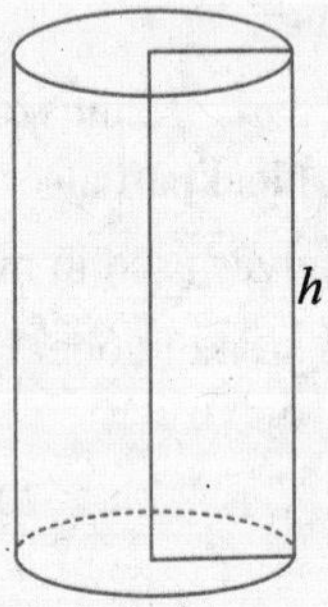

and its height (h) = 10.5 cm

$\therefore$ Volume of cylindrical cup = $\pi r^2 h$

$= \frac{22}{7}\times\left(\frac{7}{2}\right)^2\times 10.5$

$= 404.25\ \text{cm}^3$

(ii) (*b*) We have, radius (r) of hemispherical cup $= \frac{7}{2}$ cm

$\therefore$ Volume of hemispherical cup $= \frac{2}{3}\pi r^3$

$= \frac{2}{3}\times\frac{22}{7}\times\left(\frac{7}{2}\right)^3$

$= \frac{2}{3}\times\frac{22}{7}\times\frac{7\times7\times7}{2\times2\times2} = 89.83\ \text{cm}^3$

(iii) (*d*) Cylindrical glass has more juice by $(404.25 - 89.83)\ \text{cm}^3$
$= 314.42\ \text{cm}^3$

(iv) (*c*) We have cloth given of area 551 m^2 and waste is 1 m^2

$\therefore$ Curved surface area of conical tent = 551 – 1 = 550 m^2

$\therefore\ \pi rl = 550 \Rightarrow \frac{22}{7}\times 7\times l = 550$

$\Rightarrow\ l = 25\ \text{cm} \Rightarrow l^2 = 625 \Rightarrow r^2 + h^2 = l^2$

$\Rightarrow\ (7)^2 + h^2 = 625 \Rightarrow h^2 = 625 - 49 = 576$

$\Rightarrow\ h = \sqrt{576} \Rightarrow h = 24\ \text{m}$

$\therefore$ Height of the tent is 24 m.

(v) (*b*) Space occupied by each student $= \frac{\pi r^2}{4} = \frac{22}{7}\times\frac{(7)^2}{4}$
$= 38.5\ \text{m}^2$

Case Based-IV

(i) (*a*) Height of the dome = Radius of the dome = 21 m

i.e., $h = r = 21$ m

Volume of the hemispherical dome $= \frac{2}{3}\pi r^3$

$= \frac{2}{3}\times\frac{22}{7}\times 21\times 21\times 21$

= 19404 cu. m

(ii) (*b*) Volume of sphere $= \frac{4}{3}\pi r^3$

(iii) (*b*) The cloth require to cover the hemispherical dome

= Curved surface area of dome = $2\pi r^2$

$= 2\times\frac{22}{7}\times 14\times 14 = 1232$ sq. m

(iv) (*c*) Total surface area of the combined dome with cuboidal shaped top

= C.S.A of dome + $2(lb + bh + lh) - l\times b$

= 1232 + 2(48 + 24 + 32) – 48

= 1392 sq. m

(v) (*d*) Volume of the cuboidal shaped top = $l\times b\times h$

$= 8\times 6\times 4 = 192\ \text{m}^3$

STATISTICS

13

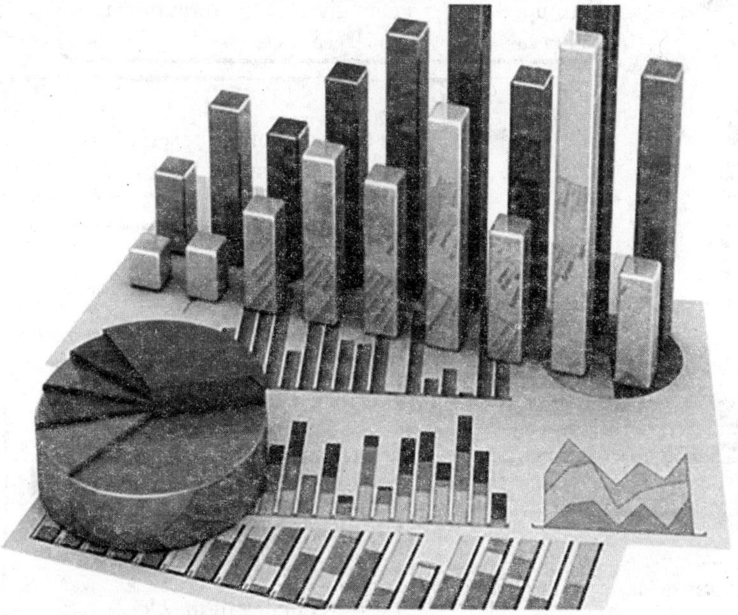

"Statistics is like a tool that helps us make decisions, guess what might happen, and see patterns in information by looking at data. It gives us important ideas that help us make things better in many different areas."

SYLLABUS & WEIGHTAGE

List of Concept Names	Years				
	2021	2022	2023	2024	2025
Mean and its Grouped Data (Mean of grouped data)	Exam not Conducted	1 Q (3 M)	–	1 Q (1 M)	–
Mode and its Grouped Data (Mode of grouped data (bimodal situation to be avoided))		1 Q (2 M)	1 Q (1 M)	–	1 Q (1 M)
Median and its Grouped Data (Median of grouped data)		1 Q (3 M)	1 Q (4 M)	1 Q (1 M) 1 Q (5 M)	1 Q (5 M)

CONCEPT MAP

To Access One Shot Revision Video Scan This QR Code

Statistics

Data:
Facts, observations and information that come from investigations are known as data.

Grouped data:
Grouped data is a data given in the form of class intervals 0–5, 5–10, 10–15,...etc.

$$\text{Class width} = \frac{\text{Lower limit} + \text{Upper limit}}{2}$$

Mode:
Mode is the value of the observation having the maximum frequency.

Modal Class:
Class having maximum frequency called modal class.

$$\text{Mode} = l + \left(\frac{f_1 - f_0}{2f_1 - f_0 - f_2}\right) \times h$$

f_1 = frequency of the modal class
f_0 = frequency of the class preceding the modal class
f_2 = frequency of the class succeeding the modal class
h = size of class internal
l = lower limit of the modal class

Mean:
The arithmetic mean is the sum of the values of all the observations divided by total number of observations.

$$\bar{x} = \frac{x_1 + x_2 + x_3 + \ldots + x_n}{n}$$

- **Direct Method**

$$\text{Mean } \bar{x} = \frac{\sum_{i=1}^{n} f_i x_i}{\sum_{i=1}^{n} f_i}$$

- **Assumed mean method**

$$\bar{x} = a + \frac{\sum f_i d_i}{\sum f_i}$$

- **Step-deviation method**

$$\bar{x} = a + \frac{\sum f_i u_i}{\sum f_i} \times h$$

Median:
The middle most value of the given data set when it is arranged in either ascending or descending order of magnitude is called median.

Median:

- If total number of observations is odd, say n. Then,

$$\text{Median} = \text{value of } \left(\frac{n+1}{2}\right)^{th} \text{ observation.}$$

- If total number of observations is even, say n. Then,

$$\text{Median} = \frac{\text{Value of } \left(\frac{n}{2}\right)^{\text{th}} \text{ term} + \text{Value of } \left(\frac{n}{2}+1\right)^{\text{th}} \text{ term}}{2}$$

Median Class:
Median class is just greater than $\frac{N}{2}$ is called median class where N is sum of frequencies i.e. $N = \Sigma f_i$

$$\text{Median} = l + \left(\frac{\frac{N}{2} - Cf}{f}\right) \times h$$

l = lower limit of median class interval
Cf = Cumulative frequency preceding to the median
f = frequency of the class interval to which median belongs.
h = size of class internal

1 MEAN AND ITS GROUPED DATA

Important Terms

- **Observation:** Each numerical value in the given data is called an observation.
- **Data:** Facts, observations and informations that come from investigations are known as data.
- **Class Marks:** Class mark is defined as the mid-value of each class interval.
- **Frequency:** Number of times a particular information (observation) occurs in a given data is called the frequency of that information.
- **Mean:** The arithmetic mean is the sum of the values of all the observations or variables divided by the total number of observations.

Note: In real-life situations, data is usually so large that to make a meaningful study we need to convert the given ungrouped data into a grouped data and devise some method to find its mean.

The arithmetic mean of grouped data can be calculated by any one of the following methods:

(*a*) Direct method

(*b*) Assumed mean method

(*c*) Step deviation method

Important Formulas

- **Mean:**

$$\overline{X} = \frac{x_1 + x_2 + x_3 + \ldots + x_n}{n} = \frac{1}{n}\left(\sum_{i=1}^{n} x_i\right)$$

Here the symbol $\sum_{i=1}^{n} x_i$ denotes the sum of observation $x_1 + x_2 + x_3 + \ldots + x_n$.

- **Mean of grouped data:**

$$\text{Mean}\left(\overline{X}\right) = \frac{f_1x_1 + f_2x_2 + \ldots + x_nf_n}{f_1 + f_2 + \ldots + f_n} = \frac{\sum_{i=1}^{n} f_ix_i}{\sum_{i=1}^{n} f_i}$$

- **Direct Method:**

$$\text{Mean, } \overline{X} = \frac{\sum_{i=1}^{n} f_ix_i}{\sum_{i=1}^{n} f_i}$$

- **Assumed Mean Method:**

$$\text{Mean: } \overline{X} = a + \frac{\sum_{i=1}^{n} f_id_i}{\sum_{i=1}^{n} f_i}$$

- **Step Deviation Method:**

$$\text{Mean } \overline{X} = a + \frac{\sum_{i=1}^{n} f_iu_i}{\sum_{i=1}^{n} f_i} \times h$$

Important Derivations

- **Mean:** Let $x_1, x_2, x_3, \ldots, x_n$ are n values of a variable X, with respective frequencies $f_1, f_2, f_3, \ldots f_n$ then mean $\overline{X}$ is defined by

$$\text{Mean}\left(\overline{X}\right) = \frac{f_1x_1 + f_2x_2 + \ldots + x_nf_n}{f_1 + f_2 + \ldots + f_n} = \frac{\sum_{i=1}^{n} f_ix_i}{\sum_{i=1}^{n} f_i}$$

- **Mean of grouped data**

Direct Method: The following steps must be followed for finding the arithmetic mean of grouped data using direct method.

Step I: Prepare the table in such a way that it consists of columns of the class interval, mid-point or class-marks, and of corresponding frequencies. We can find the mid-point or class mark (x_i) of each class using,

$$x_i = \frac{\text{lower class limit} + \text{upper class limit}}{2}$$

Step II: Calculate the f_ix_i for each row.

Class-interval	Class mark (x_i)	Class mark Frequency (f_i)	Class mark f_ix_i
$b_0 - b_1$	$x_1 = \frac{b_0 + b_1}{2}$	f_1	f_1x_1
$b_1 - b_2$	$x_2 = \frac{b_1 + b_2}{2}$	f_2	f_2x_2
$b_2 - b_3$	$x_3 = \frac{b_2 + b_3}{2}$	f_3	f_3x_3
⋮	⋮	⋮	⋮
$b_n - b_{n+1}$	$x_n = \frac{b_n + b_{n+1}}{2}$	f_n	f_nx_n
		$\text{Total} = \sum_{i=1}^{n} f_i = N$	$\text{Total} = \sum f_ix_i$

Step III: Now use the formula to find the mean,

$$\overline{X} = \frac{\sum_{i=1}^{n} f_i x_i}{\sum_{i=1}^{n} f_i}$$

- **Assumed Mean Method:** In this method Mean is calculated

In some cases, especially when the magnitude of the class-mark is large finding the mean using the direct method can be quite lengthy. In such cases, we can use the assumed mean method to find the mean of given observations.

In this method, we choose an arbitrary constant 'a' (also called the assumed mean) and subtract it from each of the value of the class-mark (x_i). The reduced value ($x_i - a$) is called the deviation and is denoted by d_i.

Note: The assumed mean should be one of the central values, when x_i are arranged in ascending or descending order.

The following steps should be followed to find the arithmetic mean of grouped data by the Assumed mean method.

Step I: Prepare the table in such a way that it consists of columns of the class interval, mid-point or class-marks, and of corresponding frequencies.

Step II: Choose a number 'a' (preferably among the central values of class-mark column), that will be our assumed mean.

Step III: Obtain deviations d_i by subtracting 'a' from x_i i.e. ($x_i - a$). Write these deviations against the corresponding frequencies in the fourth column.

Step IV: Multiply the frequencies with corresponding deviations d_i to prepare a fifth column of $f_i d_i$.

Step V: Find the sum of all the entries of fifth column to obtain $\Sigma f_i d_i$ and also find the sum of all the frequencies to obtain Σf_i.

Class-interval	Frequency (f_i)	Class-mark (x_i)	Deviation ($d_i = x_i - a$)	$f_i \cdot d_i$
$b_0 - b_1$	f_1	x_1	$d_1 = x_1 - a$	$f_1 d_1$
$b_1 - b_2$	f_2	x_2	$d_2 = x_2 - a$	$f_2 d_2$
$b_2 - b_3$	f_3	x_3	$d_3 = x_3 - a$	$f_3 d_3$
⋮	⋮	⋮	⋮	⋮
$b_n - b_{n+1}$	f_n	x_n	$d_n = x_n - a$	$f_n d_n$
	Total $= \sum_{i=1}^{n} f_i = N$			$\Sigma f_i d_i$

Step VI: Use the formula to find the mean:

$$\overline{X} = a + \frac{\sum_{i=1}^{n} f_i d_i}{\sum_{i=1}^{n} f_i}$$

- **Step Deviation Method:** This method can be calculated When the values of both x_i and f_i are large, the calculation by the above methods becomes quite lengthy. In that case, we use Step-deviation method also known as shortcut method for computing the mean.

In this method, the reduced values of deviation i.e., ($x_i - a$) are divided by a constant 'h', where h is the length of the class-interval in the frequency table.

Thus, we define $u_i = \dfrac{x_i - a}{h}$ where $h = b_{n+1} - b_n$ = Difference between class-interval

The following steps should be followed to find the arithmetic mean of grouped data by Step deviation method.

Step I: Prepare the table in such a way that it consists of columns of the class interval, mid-point or class-marks, and of corresponding frequencies.

Step II: Choose a number 'a' from the central values of x_i (mid-values)

Step III: Calculate length of the class interval i.e., $h = b_{n+1} - b_n$.

Step IV: Obtain $u_i = \dfrac{x_i - a}{h}$ or $\dfrac{x_i - a}{b_{n+1} - b_n}$ or $\dfrac{d_i}{h}$

Step V: Multiply the frequency f_i with the corresponding u_i to get $f_i u_i$.

Step VI: Find the sum of all $f_i u_i$, i.e., $\Sigma f_i u_i$

Class-interval	Frequency (f_i)	Class-mark (x_i)	Deviation ($d_i = x_i - a$)	$u_i = \dfrac{x_i - a}{h}$	$f_i u_i$
$b_0 - b_1$	f_1	x_1	$d_1 = x_1 - a$	$u_1 = \dfrac{x_1 - a}{h}$	$f_1 u_1$
$b_1 - b_2$	f_2	x_2	$d_2 = x_2 - a$	$u_2 = \dfrac{x_2 - a}{h}$	$f_2 u_2$
$b_2 - b_3$	f_3	x_3	$d_3 = x_3 - a$	$u_3 = \dfrac{x_3 - a}{h}$	$f_3 u_3$
⋮	⋮	⋮	⋮	⋮	⋮
$b_n - b_{n+1}$	f_n	x_n	$d_n = x_n - a$	$u_n = \dfrac{x_n - a}{h}$	$f_n u_n$
	Σf_i				$\Sigma f_i u_i$

Step VII: Use the formula to find the mean $\overline{X} = a + \dfrac{\Sigma f_i u_i}{\Sigma f_i} \times h$

Important Concepts

- If $\overline{X}$ is the mean of n observations $x_1, x_2, ..., x_n$, then the mean of the observations $x_1 + a, x_2 + a, ..., x_n + a$ is ($\overline{X} + a$) i.e. if each observation is increased by a, then the mean will also be increased by a.
- If $\overline{X}$ is the mean of $x_1, x_2, ... x_n$ then the mean of $ax_1, ax_2, ... ax_n$ is equal to ($a\overline{X}$). Where a is any number different from zero i.e. if each observation is multiplied by a non-zero number a, then the mean will also be multiplied by a, ($a \neq 0$)

- If $\overline{X}$ is the mean of n observations $x_1, x_2, x_3..., x_n$, then the mean of $\frac{x_1}{a}, \frac{x_2}{a}, \frac{x_3}{a}, ..., \frac{x_n}{a}$ is $\left(\frac{\overline{X}}{a}\right)$, $a \neq 0$ where a is any non-zero number.
- If $\overline{X}$ is the mean of n observations $x_1, x_2 ..x_n$, then the mean of $x_1 - a, x_2 - a, ..., x_n - a$ is $(\overline{X} - a)$, where a is any real number.

Real Life Applications

In the real life, mean is used to find the average age of students of a class, we have to add the age of individual students present in the class and then divide the sum by the total number of students present in the class.

Suppose, in a data table, the price values of 10 clothing materials are mentioned. If we have to find the mean of the prices, then add the prices of each clothing material and divide the total sum by 10. It will result in an average value.

Different Problem Types

Type I: Calculate the Mean of Ungrouped Data

Suppose a group of students took a mathematics test, and their scores (out of 100) are as follows: 85, 92, 78, 89, 98, 82, 88, 90, 87, and 91. Find the mean score of the students.

Solution: To find the mean score without grouped data, we'll add up all the scores and then divide by the total number of scores.

Step I: Sum of Scores

Scores 85, 92, 78, 89, 95, 82, 88, 90, 87, 91

Total sum = 85 + 92 + 78 + 89 + 95 + 82 + 88 + 90 + 87 + 91 = 887

Step II: Calculate Mean

$$\text{Mean} = \frac{\text{Total Sum of Scores}}{\text{Number of Scores}}$$

$$\text{Mean} = \frac{85+92+78+89+95+82+88+90+87+91}{10}$$

$$\text{Mean} = \frac{877}{10} = 87.7$$

Example: A group of students participated in a science quiz, and their scores (out of 50) are as follows: 40, 35, 42, 48, 39, 44, 46, 41, 37, and 43. Find the mean score of the students.

Solution: To find the mean score without detailed steps, we can use the formula for mean:

$$\text{Mean Score} = \frac{\text{Sum of Scores}}{\text{Number of Scores}}$$

Given scores: 40, 35, 42, 48, 39, 44, 46, 41, 37, and 43

Sum of Scores = 40 + 35 + 42 + 48 + 39 + 44 + 46 + 41 + 37 + 43 = 415

Number of Scores = 10 (since there are 10 scores)

$$\text{Mean Score} = \frac{415}{10} = 41.5$$

Therefore, the mean score of the students in the science quiz is 41.5 out of 50

Type II: Calculate the Mean of Grouped Data

Given the following grouped data:

Class Interval	Frequency
10 – 20	5
20 – 30	8
30 – 40	12
40 – 50	7
50 – 60	4

Calculate the mean (average) of the data.

Solution:

Step I: Calculate Midpoints (m)

Use the formula $m = \frac{\text{Lower limit} + \text{Upper limit}}{2}$

Midpoint of 10 – 20: $m_1 = \frac{10+20}{2} = 15$

Midpoint of 20 – 30: $m_2 = \frac{20+30}{2} = 25$

Midpoint of 30 – 40: $m_3 = \frac{30+40}{2} = 35$

Midpoint of 40 – 50: $m_4 = \frac{40+50}{2} = 45$

Midpoint of 50 – 60: $m_5 = \frac{50+60}{2} = 55$

Step II: Calculate $f \cdot m$ for Each Class:

$$f_1 \cdot m_1 = 5 \cdot 15 = 75$$
$$f_2 \cdot m_2 = 8 \cdot 25 = 200$$
$$f_3 \cdot m_3 = 12 \cdot 35 = 420$$
$$f_4 \cdot m_4 = 7 \cdot 45 = 315$$
$$f_5 \cdot m_5 = 4 \cdot 55 = 220$$

Step III: Calculate Mean

Add the products $f \cdot m$ to get $\sum f \cdot m = 75 + 200 + 420 + 315 + 220 = 1230$.

Add all the frequencies to get $\sum f = 5 + 8 + 12 + 7 + 4 = 36$.

Use the formula Mean $= \frac{\sum_{i=1}^{5} f_i m_i}{\sum_{i=1}^{5} f_i}$

$$\text{Mean} = \frac{1230}{36} = 34.17$$

Example: In a survey conducted in a school, the following data represents the distribution of students according to their heights in cm:

Height Range (cm)	Number of Students
120-130	5
130-140	12
140-150	18
150-160	15
160-170	10

Calculate the mean height of the students in the survey.

Solution:

Midpoint of 120 – 130 range: $m_1 = \frac{120+130}{2} = 125\text{cm}$

Midpoint of 130 – 140 range: $m_2 = \frac{130+140}{2} = 135\text{cm}$

Midpoint of 140 – 150 range: $m_3 = \frac{140+150}{2} = 145\text{cm}$

Midpoint of 150 – 160 range: $m_4 = \frac{150+160}{2} = 155\text{cm}$

Midpoint of 160 – 170 range: $m_5 = \frac{160+170}{2} = 165\text{cm}$

$$\text{Mean} = \frac{\sum_{i=1}^{5} f_i m_i}{\sum_{i=1}^{5} f_i}$$

$$\text{Mean} = \frac{(125\times5)+(135\times12)+(145\times18)+(155\times15)+(165\times10)}{5+12+18+15+10}$$

$$\text{Mean} = \frac{625+1620+2610+2325+1650}{60} = \frac{8830}{60} = 147.17\text{cm}$$

Hence, the mean height of the students in the survey is approximately 147.17 cm.

Type III: Calculate the Mean using Step Deviation Method

In a survey conducted among students regarding their daily study hours, the following data represents the distribution:

Class Interval	Frequency
0-2	10
2-4	15
4-6	20
6-8	12
8-10	8

Using the Step Deviation Method, calculate the mean daily study hours of the students.

Solution:

Step I: Assumed Mean (*a*) Calculation

Let assumed mean $(a) = 5$, class size $(h) = 2$

So, $u_1 = \frac{x_1 - a}{h} = \frac{x_1 - 5}{2}$

Step II: Multiply Frequency (f_i) with u_i for Each Class

Class Interval	Frequency (f_i)	Class Mark	$u_i = \frac{x_i - 5}{2}$	$f_i u_i$
0 – 2	10	1	–2	–20
2 – 4	15	3	–1	–15
4 – 6	20	5	0	0
6 – 8	12	7	1	12
8 – 10	8	9	2	16
Total	$\Sigma f_i = 65$			$\Sigma f_i u_i = -7$

Step III: Calculate Mean using Step Deviation Method

$$\text{Mean}\left(\overline{X}\right) = a + \frac{\Sigma f_i u_i}{\Sigma f_i} \times h = 5 + \left(\frac{-7}{65}\right) \times 2 = 5 - \frac{14}{65} = 4.78$$

Therefore, the mean daily study hours of the students using the Step Deviation Method is approximately 4.78 hours.

Example: In a survey conducted during the COVID-19 pandemic, the following data represents the daily new cases of a particular region for a week:

Class Interval (Number of Cases)	Frequency
0 – 100	5
100 – 200	8
200 – 300	12
300 – 400	10
400 – 500	5

Using the Step Deviation Method, calculate the mean daily new cases of COVID-19 in the region for the week.

Solution:

Assumed Mean $(a) = 250$

Class Size $(h) = 100$

Class Interval	Frequency (f_i)	Class Mark	$u_i = \frac{x_i - 250}{100}$	$f_i u_i$
0 – 100	5	50	–2	–10
100 – 200	8	150	–1	–8
200 – 300	12	250	0	0
300 – 400	10	350	1	10
400 – 500	5	450	2	10
Total	$\Sigma f_i = 40$			$\Sigma f_i u_i = 2$

$$\text{Mean}\left(\overline{X}\right) = a + \frac{\Sigma f_i u_i}{\Sigma f_i} \times h = 250 + \left(\frac{2}{40}\right) \times 100$$

$$= 250 + \frac{200}{40} = 250 + 5 = 255$$

Therefore, the mean daily new cases of COVID-19 in the region for the week using the Step Deviation Method is approximately 255 cases.

COMPETENCY BASED SOLVED EXAMPLES

Multiple Choice Questions

(1 M)

1. If $x_1, x_2, x_3, ... x_n$ are the observations of a given data. Then the mean of the observations will be: *(Re)*

(*a*) Sum of observations/Total number of observations

(*b*) Total number of observations/Sum of observations

(*c*) Sum of observations + Total number of observations

(*d*) None of the above

Sol. The mean or average of observations will be equal to the ratio of sum of observations and total number of observations.

$$\text{Mean}(\overline{X}) = \frac{x_1 + x_2 + x_3 + \ldots + x_n}{n}$$

$$\because \text{ Mean} = \frac{\text{Sum of observations}}{\text{Total number of observations}}$$

Key Takeaways

$$\text{Mean}(\overline{X}) = \frac{x_1 + x_2 + x_3 + \ldots + x_n}{n}$$

2. If the mean of frequency distribution is 7.5 and $\Sigma f_i x_i = 120 + 3k$, $\Sigma f_i = 30$, then k is equal to: *(Ap)*

(*a*) 40 (*b*) 35

(*c*) 50 (*d*) 45

Sol. We know

$$\text{mean, } \overline{X} = \frac{\sum f_i x_i}{\sum f_i}$$

$$\Rightarrow 7.5 = \frac{(120 + 3k)}{30}$$

$\Rightarrow 7.5 \times 30 = 120 + 3k$

$\Rightarrow 3k = 225 - 120$

$\Rightarrow 3k = 105 \quad \Rightarrow k = 35$

Key Takeaways

$$\text{Mean, } \overline{X} = \frac{\sum f_i x_i}{\sum f_i}$$

3. The mean of following distribution is: *(An)*

x_i	11	14	17	20
f_i	3	6	8	7

(*a*) 15.6 (*b*) 17

(*c*) 14.8 (*d*) 16.4

Sol.

x_1	f_1	$f_1 x_1$
11	3	33
14	6	84
17	8	136
20	7	140
	$\Sigma f_i = 24$	$\Sigma f_i x_i = 393$

$$\text{We know mean, } \overline{X} = \frac{\sum f_i x_i}{\sum f_i} = \frac{393}{24} = 16.4$$

4. The method used to find the mean of a given data is(are): *(Re)*

(*a*) direct method

(*b*) assumed mean method

(*c*) step deviation method

(*d*) all the above

Sol. Methods used to find the mean of a given data include the direct method, the assumed mean method, and the step deviation method.

5. Mean of n numbers $x_1, x_2, ... x_n$ is m. If x_n is replaced by x, then new mean is *(Un)*

(*a*) $m - x_n + x$ (*b*) $\frac{nm - x_n + x}{n}$

(*c*) $\frac{(n-1)m + x}{n}$ (*d*) $\frac{m - x_n + x}{n}$

Sol. $\text{Mean} = \frac{x_1 + x_2 + x_3 + \ldots + x_n}{n} = m$

$\Rightarrow x_1 + x_2 + ... + x_n = nm$

$\Rightarrow x_1 + x_2 + ... + x_{n-1} + x_n = nm$

$\Rightarrow x_1 + x_2 + ... + x_{n-1} = nm - x_n$

New sum $= x_1 + x_2 + ... + x_{n-1} + x$

$$\text{New mean} = \frac{x_1 + x_2 + x_3 + \ldots + x_n}{n} = \frac{nm - x_n + x}{n}$$

6. The mean of x, x+1, x+2, x+3, x+4, x+5 and x+6 is *(Ap)*

(*a*) x (*b*) $x + 4$

(*c*) 3 (*d*) $x + 3$

Sol. $\text{Mean} = \frac{x + (x+1) + (x+2) + (x+3) + (x+4) + (x+5) + (x+6)}{7}$

$= \frac{7x + 21}{7} = x + 3$

7. The mean of first 5 prime numbers is: *(Ev)*

(*a*) 5.5 (*b*) 5.6

(*c*) 5.7 (*d*) 5

Sol. First time prime number is 2, 3, 5, 7, 11.

$\therefore$ Mean $= \dfrac{28}{5} = 5.6$

8. The mean of the first 10 multiples of 6 is *(Ap)*

(*a*) 3.3 (*b*) 33

(*c*) 34 (*d*) None of these

Sol. Observation is 6, 12, 18, 24, 30, 36, 42, 48, 54, 60

$$\text{Mean} = \frac{6+12+18+24+30+36+42+48+54+60}{10}$$

$$= \frac{330}{10} = 33$$

Mistakes 101 : What not to do!

Students may make errors in calculating mean by omitting data points, misinterpreting instructions, or miscalculating averages.

9. If the mean of the frequency distribution is 6 and $\Sigma f_i x_i$ = 90, then Σf_i = *(Ev)*

(*a*) 12 (*b*) 13

(*c*) 15 (*d*) None of these

Sol. $\text{Mean} = \dfrac{\sum f_i x_i}{\sum f_i} \Rightarrow \sum f_i = \dfrac{\sum f_i x_i}{\text{Mean}} \Rightarrow \sum f_i = \dfrac{90}{6} = 15$

Answer Key

1. (*a*) 2. (*b*) 3. (*d*) 4. (*d*) 5. (*b*)
6. (*d*) 7. (*b*) 8. (*b*) 9. (*c*)

Assertion and Reason (1 M)

Direction: In the following questions, a statement of Assertion (A) is followed by a statement of Reason (R). Mark the correct choice as.

(*a*) Both Assertion (A) and Reason (R) are true, and Reason (R) is the correct explanation of Assertion (A).

(*b*) Both Assertion (A) and Reason (R) are true, but Reason (R) is not the correct explanation of Assertion (A).

(*c*) Assertion (A) is true, but Reason (R) is false.

(*d*) Assertion (A) is false, but Reason (R) is true.

1. Assertion (A): Mean of *n* observations = Sum of observations / Number of observations

Reason (R): If the mean of five observations *x*, *x* + 2, *x*+4, *x*+6, *x*+8 is 11 , then mean of last three observations is 8 *(Ev)*

Sol. Assertion (A):

$$\text{Mean} = \frac{\text{Sum of observation}}{\text{Total number of observation}}$$

Reason (R):

$$\text{Mean} = \frac{x(x+2)+(x+4)+(x+6)+(x+8)}{5}$$

$\Rightarrow 11 = \dfrac{5x+20}{5}$

$\Rightarrow 11 = x + 4$

$\Rightarrow x = 7$

$\therefore$ Lost three observation is $x + 4$, $x + 6$, $x + 8 = 7 + 4$, $7 + 6$, $7 + 8 = 11$, 13, 15

$\therefore$ Means of last three observation $= \dfrac{11+13+15}{3} = \dfrac{39}{3} = 13$

$\therefore$ Assertion is true and Reason is false.

2. Assertion (A): The arithmetic mean of the following given frequency distribution table is 13.81.

x	4	7	10	13	16	19
f	7	10	15	20	25	30

Reason (R): $\overline{x} = \dfrac{\Sigma f_i x_i}{\Sigma f_i}$ *(Cr)*

Sol. Assertion (A):

$$\text{Mean} = \frac{4\times7+7\times10+10\times15+13\times20+16\times25+19\times30}{7+10+15+20+25+30}$$

$$= \frac{28+70+150+260+400+570}{107} = \frac{1478}{107} = 13.81$$

Reason (R): $\overline{x} = \dfrac{\sum f_i x_i}{\sum f_i}$

Hence, both assertion and reason are correct and reason is correct explanation of assertion

Answer Key

1. (*c*) 2. (*a*)

Subjective Questions

Very Short Answer Type Questions (1 or 2 M)

1. The mean marks obtained by 30 students in physics test is 19.5. If the marks of Rajesh is excluded, then the mean marks become 19. Find the marks obtained by Rajesh. *(Ap)*

Sol. Sum of marks obtained by a class = 30×19.5 = 585. *(1 M)*

Sum of marks obtained by a class excluding Rajesh's mark = 29 × 19 = 551

Hence, the marks obtained by Rajesh = 585 – 551 = 34 *(1 M)*

2. If the mean of the data; 6, 3 + x, 7, 2, 6 + x, 4 is 9, then find the value of x. *(An)*

Sol. We know that

$$\text{Mean} = \frac{6+(3+x)+7+2+(6+x)+4}{6} \quad (1\ M)$$

$$\Rightarrow 9 = \frac{28+2x}{6} \Rightarrow 54 = 28+2x \Rightarrow 2x = 26 \Rightarrow x = 13 \quad (1\ M)$$

3. Find the, mean of the given data: 7, 8, 4, 9, 6, 5? *(Ev)*

Sol. Mean, $\overline{X} = \frac{7+8+4+9+6+5}{6}$ *(1 M)*

$= \frac{39}{6} = 6.5$ *(1 M)*

4. If the mean of the observation $x, x+4, x+8, x+3$ and $x+10$ is 9, then find the mean of the first three observation. *(Ev)*

Sol. Mean $= \frac{x+(x+4)+(x+8)+(x+3)+(x+10)}{5}$

$\Rightarrow 9 = \frac{5x+25}{5} \quad \Rightarrow x = 4$ *(1 M)*

So, mean of first three observation is

$\overline{X} = \frac{x+(x+4)+(x+8)}{3} = \frac{4+4+4+4+8}{3} = \frac{24}{3} = 8$ *(1 M)*

5. If the mean of the first n natural number is 15 , then find n. *(An)*

Sol. Given $\frac{1+2+3+4+\ldots+n}{n} = 15$ *(1 M)*

$\Rightarrow \frac{\frac{n(n+1)}{2}}{n} = 15 \quad \Rightarrow n^2 + n = 30n$

$\Rightarrow n^2 = 29n \Rightarrow n = 29$ *(1 M)*

Key Takeaways

Sum of n natural number is $\frac{n(n+1)}{2}$.

Short Answer Type Questions (2 or 3 M)

1. Calculate the mean of the following data, using a direct method. *(Ap)*

Class	25–35	35–45	45–55	55–65	65–75
Frequency	6	10	8	12	4

Sol.

Class interval	f_i	Class Mark (x_i)	$f_i x_i$
25-35	6	$\frac{25+35}{2} = 30$	180
35-45	10	$\frac{35+45}{2} = 40$	400
45-55	8	$\frac{45+55}{2} = 50$	400
55-65	12	$\frac{55+65}{2} = 60$	720
65-75	4	$\frac{65+75}{2} = 70$	280
	$\Sigma f_i = 40$		$\Sigma f_i x_i = 1980$

(2 M)

$\therefore$ Direct Method, Mean $\overline{X} = \frac{\sum_{i=1}^{n} f_i x_i}{\sum_{i=1}^{n} f_i} = \frac{1980}{40} = 49.5$

(1 M)

2. If the mean of the following data is 18, then find the value of p. *(An)*

x	10	15	20	25
f	5	10	p	8

Sol.

x_i	f_i	$x_i f_i$
10	5	50
15	10	150
20	p	$20p$
25	8	200
Total	$\Sigma f_i = 23 + p$	$\Sigma x_i f_i = 400 + 20p$

(1 M)

$\overline{x} = \left(\frac{\Sigma x_i f_i}{\Sigma f_i}\right)$ *(1 M)*

$\Rightarrow 18 = \frac{400+20p}{23+p} \Rightarrow 414 + 18p = 400 + 20p$

$\Rightarrow 2p = 14 \Rightarrow p = 7$

Hence the value of p is 7. *(1 M)*

3. Find the mean of the following data:

Class Interval	0–8	8–16	16–24	24–32	32–40
Frequency	6	7	10	8	9

(Ev)

Sol. Since the value of f_i and x_i are small, we will use direct method for finding the mean of this question.

Class interval	Frequency (f_i)	Class mark (x_i)	$f_i x_i$
0-8	6	4	24
8-16	7	12	84
16-24	10	20	200

24-32	8	28	224
32-40	9	36	324
	$\Sigma f_i = 40$		$\Sigma f_i x_i = 856$

(2 M)

$$\therefore \text{ Mean, } \bar{x} = \frac{\sum_{i=1}^{n} f_i x_i}{\sum_{i=1}^{n} f_i} = \frac{856}{40} = 21.4$$ (1 M)

4. If the mean of *n* observations $ax_1, ax_2, ax_3, ..., ax_n$ is a $\bar{X}$, show that (Ev)

$$(ax_1 - a\bar{X}) + (ax_2 - a\bar{X}) + ... + (ax_n - a\bar{X}) = 0$$

Sol. We have

$$a\bar{X} = \frac{ax_1 + ax_2 + ... + ax_n}{n}$$ (1 M)

$$\Rightarrow ax_1 + ax_2 + ... + ax_n = n(a\bar{X})$$ ...(i) (½ M)

Now, $(ax_1 - a\bar{X}) + (ax_2 - a\bar{X}) + ... + (ax_n - a\bar{X})$ (½ M)

$$= (ax_1 + ax_2 + ... + ax_n) - (a\bar{X} + a\bar{X} + ... + a\bar{X})$$

$$= n(a\bar{X}) - n(a\bar{X}) = 0$$ (1 M)

5. The mean of *n* observations $x_1, x_2, ..., x_n$ is $\bar{x}$. If $(a - b)$ is added to each of the observations, show that the mean of the new set of observations is $\bar{x} + (a - b)$ (Un)

Sol. Given, $\bar{x} = \frac{x_1 + x_2 + ... + x_n}{n}$ ...(i) (1 M)

Let $\bar{x}'$, be the mean of $x_1 + (a - b) + x_2 + (a - b) + ... x_n + (a - b)$, then,

$$\bar{x}' = \frac{\{x_1 + (a - b)\} + \{x_2 + (a - b)\} + ... + \{x_n + (a - b)\}}{n}$$ (1 M)

$$\Rightarrow \bar{x}' = \frac{x_1 + x_2 + ... + x_n + n(a - b)}{n} = \bar{x} + (a - b)$$ (1 M)

6. Find the mean of following distribution (Ap)

x_i	12	16	18	20
f_i	3	6	8	7

Sol.

x_i	f_i	$f_i x_i$
12	3	36
16	6	96
18	8	144
20	7	140
	$\Sigma f_i = 24$	$\Sigma f_i x_i = 416$

(2 M)

$$\text{Mean}(x) = \frac{\Sigma f_i x_i}{\Sigma f_i} = \frac{416}{24} = 17.34$$ (1 M)

7. Find the mean for the following distribution:

Class	5–15	15–25	25–35	35–45
Frequency	2	4	3	1

(Ap) (CBSE, 2020)

Sol.

Class interval	f_i	x_i	$f_i x_i$
5-15	2	10	20
15-25	4	20	80
25-35	3	30	90
35-45	1	40	40
Total	10		230

(1 M)

$$\text{Mean } \bar{X} = \frac{\sum f_i x_i}{\sum f_i} = \frac{230}{10} = 23$$ (1 M)

Therefore, mean for the following distribution is 23. (1 M)

8. Find the mean of the following distribution by direct method. (Un)

Class Interval	1–10	11–20	21–30	31–40	41–50
Frequency	3	4	2	5	6

Sol. Find the class-mark of the given interval using the formula:

$$\text{Class-mark} = \frac{\text{upper limit} + \text{lower limit}}{2}$$

Class Interval	Frequency (f_i)	Class Mark (x_i)	$f_i x_i$
1 – 10	3	$\frac{1+10}{2} = 5.5$	16.5
11 – 20	4	$\frac{11+20}{2} = 15.5$	62.0
21 – 30	2	$\frac{21+30}{2} = 25.5$	51.0
31 – 40	5	$\frac{31+40}{2} = 35.5$	177.5
41 – 50	6	$\frac{41+50}{2} = 45.5$	273.0
	$\Sigma f_i = 20$		$\Sigma f x_i = 580$

(2 M)

$$\text{Mean}, \bar{X} = \frac{\Sigma f_i x_i}{\Sigma f_i} = \frac{580}{20} = 29$$ (1 M)

Long Answer Type Questions (4 or 5 M)

1. If the mean of the following frequency distribution is 50, then find the value of missing frequencies f_1 and f_2. (Cr)

Class	0-20	20-40	40-60	60-80	80-100	Total
Frequency	17	f_1	32	f_2	19	120

Sol. We may prepare the table as given below:

Class	Frequency (f)	Class mark (x_i)	$f_i x_i$
0-20	17	10	170
20-40	f_1	30	$30f_1$
40-60	32	50	1600
60-80	f_2	70	$70f_2$
80-100	19	90	1710
$\Sigma f_i = 68 + f_1 + f_2$		$\Sigma f_i x_i = 3480 + 30f_1 + 70f_2$	

(1 M)

$\therefore$ Mean, $\bar{x} = \dfrac{\Sigma f_i x_i}{\Sigma f_i} = \dfrac{3480 + 30f_1 + 70f_2}{68 + f_1 + f_2}$ *(1 M)*

Given, mean = 50

$\therefore \; 50 = \dfrac{3480 + 30f_1 + 70f_2}{68 + f_1 + f_2}$ *(1 M)*

$\Rightarrow 3400 + 50f_1 + 50f_2 = 3480 + 30f_1 + 70f_2$

$\Rightarrow 20f_1 - 20f_2 = 80$

$\Rightarrow f_1 - f_2 = 4$ ...(*i*)

And $\Sigma f_1 = 68 + f_1 + f_2$

$\therefore 120 = 68 + f_1 + f_2$

$\Rightarrow f_1 + f_2 = 52$ .....(*ii*) *(1 M)*

Adding (*i*) and (*ii*), we get $2f_1 = 56$

$\Rightarrow f_1 = 28$

By substituting f_1 in eq. (*i*), we get

$f_2 = 24$

Hence, the missing frequencies f_1 and f_2 are 28 and 24 respectively. *(1 M)*

2. The following frequency distribution shows the marks obtained by 80 students in an examination. Find the mean marks obtained by students. *(Un)*

Marks	No. of Students
Above 0	80
Above 10	77
Above 20	72
Above 30	65
Above 40	55
Above 50	43
Above 60	23
Above 70	16
Above 80	10
Above 90	8
Above 100	0

Sol. The given table is cumulative frequency distribution.

Marks	No. of Students	Class Interval	f_i	Class mark (x_i)	$f_i x_i$
Above 0	80	0-10	3	5	15
Above 10	77	10-20	5	15	75
Above 20	72	20-30	7	25	175
Above 30	65	30-40	10	35	350
Above 40	55	40-50	12	45	540
Above 50	43	50-60	20	55	1100
Above 60	23	60-70	7	65	455
Above 70	16	70-80	6	75	450
Above 80	10	80-90	2	85	170
Above 90	8	90-100	8	95	760
Above 100	0	100-110	0	105	0
			$\Sigma f_i = 80$		$\Sigma f_i x_i = 4090$

(3 M)

$\therefore$ Mean, $\overline{X} = \dfrac{\Sigma f_i x_i}{N} = \dfrac{4090}{80} = 51.125$ *(2 M)*

3. The following frequency distribution shows the salaries of employees of small scale industry. *(Un)*

Salary (in ₹)	4000-5000	5000-6000	6000-7000	7000-8000	8000-9000	9000-10000
Number of employees	20	60	100	50	80	90

Then find the mean salary of the employee?

Sol.

Class-interval	Frequency (f_i)	Midpoint (x_i)	$f_i x_i$
4000-5000	20	4500	90000
5000-6000	60	5500	330000
6000-7000	100	6500	650000
7000-8000	50	7500	375000
8000-9000	80	8500	680000
9000-10000	90	9500	855000
	$\Sigma f_i = 400$		$\Sigma f_i x_i = 2980000$

(3 M)

Therefore mean is:

$\therefore$ Mean, $\overline{X} = \dfrac{\sum f_i x_i}{\sum f_i}$ *(1 M)*

$\Rightarrow \overline{X} = \dfrac{2980000}{400} = 7450$ *(1 M)*

4. **The following distribution shows the daily wages of a workers of a factory. The mean daily wage is ₹180, find the missing frequency *f*.** **(*An*)**

Daily wages of workers (in ₹)	Number of workers
110-130	7
130-150	6
150-170	9
170-190	13
190-210	*f*
210-230	5
230-250	4

Sol. To find out the missing frequency, use the Mean formula.

Daily wages	Number of workers	Class mark (x_i)	$f_i x_i$
110-130	7	120	840
130-150	6	140	840
150-170	9	160	1440
170-190	13	180	2340
190-210	f	200	200f
210-230	5	220	1100
230-250	4	240	960
	$\sum f = 44 + f$		$\sum f x_i = 7520 + 200f$

(2 M)

$$\therefore \text{Mean}, \; \overline{x} = \frac{\sum_{i=1}^{n} f_i x_i}{\sum_{i=1}^{n} f_i} = \frac{7520 + 200f}{44 + f}$$ *(1 M)*

Given, mean = 180

$$\therefore 180 = \frac{7520 + 200f}{44 + f}$$ *(1 M)*

$\Rightarrow 7920 + 180f = 7520 + 200f$

$\Rightarrow 20f = 400 \Rightarrow f = 20$ *(1 M)*

5. **The mean of the following distribution is 18. Find the frequency *f* of the class 19–21.** **(*Ap*)**

Class	11–13	13–15	15–17	17–19	19–21	21–23	23–25
Frequency	3	6	9	13	*f*	5	4

Sol.

Class interval	f_i	x_i	$f_i x_i$
11-13	3	12	36
13-15	6	14	84
15-17	9	16	144
17-19	13	18	234
19-21	*f*	20	20*f*
21-23	5	22	110
23-25	4	24	96
	$\sum f_i = 40 + f$		$\sum f_i x_i = 704 + 20f_2$

(2 M)

$$\text{Mean} = \frac{\sum f_i x_i}{\sum f_i}$$ *(1 M)*

$$\Rightarrow 18 = \frac{704 + 20f}{40 + f}$$ *(1 M)*

$\Rightarrow f = 8$ *(1 M)*

2 MODE AND ITS GROUPED DATA

Important Terms

- **Mode:** Mode is the value of the observation having the maximum frequency.
- **Modal class:** The modal class is the class with the highest frequency.
- **Mode of grouped data:** In the case of **grouped frequency distribution**, it is not possible theory to determine the mode by looking at the frequencies. In such cases, we can only locate the class having maximum frequency called 'modal-class'.

Important Formulas

- **Mode** $= l + \left(\frac{f_1 - f_0}{2f_1 - f_0 - f_2}\right) \times h$

Where,

f_1 is the frequency of the modal class

f_0 is the frequency of the class preceding the modal class

f_2 is the frequency of the class succeeding the modal class

h is the size of the class intervals

l is the lower limit of the modal class

Real Life Applications

People visited a zoo When people go to the zoo, we observed that how many people of different ages come there. The zoo owners charge differently for people of different age groups and allot different area to them. So how do they keep a track that people of which age group are exceeding in number? They do so with the help of Mode. So, first of all their software prepares a data in which it calculates and gives how many people of different ages have bought the tickets and entered the zoo. The one that has the most frequency is the mode . Mode refers to the number in a list that occurs most often. Let us learn move about mode and how is it calculated.

The observation which occurs most frequently among the given set of observation i.e. the value of the observation having the maximum frequency is the mode of the given data.

Sometimes, it is possible that in a given set of data more than one value may have the same maximum frequency.

Such type of data is said to be multi modal.

Different Problem Types

Type I: Statistical Measures - Mode Calculation

A researcher recorded the daily temperatures (in degrees Celsius) for ten consecutive days. The data collected is as follows: 22, 25, 25, 28, 28, 30, 30, 30, 32, 35. Determine the mode of the daily temperatures for these ten days.

Solution:

Step I: Count the frequency of each temperature value

- 22 degrees Celsius: 1 day
- 25 degrees Celsius: 2 days
- 28 degrees Celsius: 2 days
- 30 degrees Celsius: 3 days
- 32 degrees Celsius: 1 day
- 35 degrees Celsius: 1 day

Step II: Identify the temperature value(s) with the highest frequency

- The temperature value 30 degrees Celsius has the highest frequency of 3 days.

Therefore, the mode of the daily temperatures for the ten days is 30 degrees Celsius.

Example: A survey was conducted to record the number of hours spent studying by students in a week. The data collected for 15 students is as follows: 6,6,8,8,8,10,10,12,12,14,14,16,16,18,20. Determine the mode of the number of hours spent studying per week.

Solution:

To find the mode using a table:

Number of Hours	Frequency
6	2
8	3
10	2
12	2
14	2
16	2
18	1
20	1

From the table, we can see that the number of hours with the highest frequency is 8 hours, occurring 3 times. Therefore, the mode of the number of hours spent studying per week is 8 hours.

Type II: Calculate Mode Using Formula with Grouped Data

A survey was conducted among students to determine their weekly study hours. The data collected for a group of 20 students is as follows:

Study Hours (hours)	Number of Students
5 – 10	5
10 – 15	8
15 – 20	10
20 – 25	4
25 – 30	3

Find the mode of the weekly study hours for the students.

Solution:

Step I: **Identify the modal class**

Here, the modal class is "15-20 hours" because it has the highest frequency of 10 students.

Step II: **Determine the values needed for the mode formula:**

- l = Lower boundary of the modal class = 15
- f_0 = Frequency of the class before the modal class = 8
- f_1 = Frequency of the modal class = 10
- f_2 = Frequency of the class after the modal class = 4
- h = Size of the modal class interval = 5

Apply the modal class formula:

$$\text{Mode} = l + \left(\frac{f_1 - f_0}{(f_1 - f_0) + (f_1 - f_2)}\right) \times h$$

Step III: **Substitute the values into the formula**

$$\text{Mode} = 15 + \left(\frac{10-8}{(10-8)+(10-4)}\right) \times 5$$

$$\text{Mode} = 15 + \left(\frac{2}{2+6}\right) \times 5$$

$$\text{Mode} = 15 + \left(\frac{2}{8}\right) \times 5$$

Mode = 15 + (0.25) × 5

Mode = 15 + 1.25

Mode = 16.25

Therefore, the mode of the weekly study hours for the students is approximately 16.25 hours.

Example: **A survey was conducted to determine the favorite colors of students in a school. The data is grouped as follows:**

Color Range	Number of Students
Red (1 – 5)	15
Blue (6 – 10)	20
Green (11 – 15)	25
Yellow (16 – 20)	10

Using the formula for mode with grouped data, find the mode of the favorite colors among the students.

Solution:

f_0 = Frequency of the class before the modal class =20

f_1 = Frequency of the modal class =25

f_2 = Frequency of the class after the modal class =10

h = Size of the modal class interval =5

The formula for mode with grouped data is:

$$\text{Mode} = l + \left(\frac{f_1 - f_0}{(f_1 - f_0) + (f_1 - f_2)}\right) \times h$$

$$\text{Mode} = 11 + \left(\frac{25-20}{(25-20)+(25-10)}\right) \times 5$$

$$\text{Mode} = 11 + \left(\frac{5}{5+15}\right) \times 5$$

$$\text{Mode} = 11 + \left(\frac{5}{20}\right) \times 5$$

Mode = 11 + (0.25) × 5

Mode = 11+ 1.25

Mode = 12.25

Therefore, the mode of the favorite colors among the students is approximately 12.25, which falls within the modal class "Green (11-15)".

COMPETENCY BASED SOLVED EXAMPLES

Multiple Choice Questions

(1 M)

1. The Mode of 12, 14, 11, 16, 15, 14, 11, 13, 14 is *(An)*

(*a*) 14 (*b*) 11 (*c*) 15 (*d*) 16

Sol. Mode is most frequent data

Here, 14 occurs most number of times i.e., 3.

Hence, Mode of given data is 14

Nailing the Right Answer

To determine the mode, students identify the most frequent value or values in the data set.

2. The upper limit of the modal class of the given distribution is: *(An)* (CBSE SQP, 2023)

Height [in cm]	below 140	below 145	below 150	below 155	below 160	below 165
Number of girls	4	11	29	40	46	51

(*a*) 165 (*b*) 160

(*c*) 155 (*d*) 150

Sol. First, let's compute the frequencies for each class interval:

Class interval 140-145: $11 - 4 = 7$

Class interval 145-150: $29 - 11 = 18$

Class interval 150-155: $40 - 29 = 11$

Class interval 155-160: $46 - 40 = 6$

Class interval 160-165: $51 - 46 = 5$

From these calculations, we can see that the class interval 145-150 has the highest frequency (18).

The upper limit of the modal class, therefore, is the upper boundary of this class interval, which is 150 cm.

So, the upper limit of the modal class is 150 cm.

3. The mode of the given data is *(Ap)*

Marks	No. of students
1–5	7
6–10	10
11–15	16
16–20	32
21–25	24
26–30	18
31–35	10
36–40	5
41–45	1

(*a*) 18 (*b*) 32 (*c*) 24 (*d*) 18.66

Sol. Given maximum 32 students in range 16–20

$l = 16, f_1 = 32, f_0 = 16, f_2 = 24, h = 4$

$$\text{mode} = 16 + \frac{32-16}{64-16-24} \times 4$$

mode = 18.66

Key Takeaways

$$\text{mode} = l + \left(\frac{f_1 - f_0}{2f_1 - f_0 - f_2}\right) \times h$$

4. Sweety, Nitesh, and Ashraf visited a hospital for their annual body checkup, which included a blood pressure evaluation. The results of their systolic blood pressure readings are as follows: *(An)*

Sweety: 121 mmHg

Nitesh: 147 mmHg

Ashraf: 160 mmHg

The table below depicts the systolic blood pressure ranges of all the patients who visited the hospital on the same day.

Blood pressure (mmHg)	115-125	125-135	135-145	145-155	155-165
Number of patients	10	9	12	19	10

Who among the three friends have a blood pressure reading that falls in the modal class?

(*a*) Sweety

(*b*) Nitesh

(*c*) Ashraf

(*d*) Both Sweety and Ashraf

Sol. The modal class is the class interval with the highest frequency, which is 145-155mmHg.

- Sweety's blood pressure reading (121mmHg) does not fall in the modal class.
- Nitesh's blood pressure reading (147mmHg) falls in the modal class.
- Ashraf's blood pressure reading (160mmHg) does not fall in the modal class.

Thus, only Nitesh's blood pressure reading falls in the modal class.

5. The mode of the following frequency distribution is

Seconds	51–55	56–60	61–65	66–70
Frequency	2	7	8	4

(An)

(*a*) 61.5 (*b*) 62.5

(*c*) 64.5 (*d*) 63.5

Sol. The interval is not continuous, therefore subtract 0.5 from the lower limit and add 0.5 in the upper limit.

Seconds	50.5–55.5	55.5–60.5	60.5–65.5	65.5–70.5
Frequency	2	7	8	4

Here, modal class = 60.5 – 65.5

$l = 60.5, f_1 = 8, f_0 = 7, f_2 = 4, h = 5$

$$\text{Mode} = 60.5 + \left[\frac{8-7}{2\times 8-7-4}\right]\times 5 = 60.5 + \frac{1}{5}\times 5 = 60.5 + 1 = 61.5$$

6. Below are the results of the students in an exam. Find the mode of given results.

90, 80, 77, 86, 90, 91, 77, 25, 45, 35, 66, 69, 65, 43, 65, 75, 43, 90, 89 *(Ap)*

(*a*) 43 (*b*) 77

(*c*) 65 (*d*) 90

Sol. 90 occurs Maximum numbers of times in the given data. So mode is 90

7. Mode is not affected by *(Re)*

(*a*) Maximum value

(*b*) Minimum value

(*c*) Extreme values

(*d*) All of the above

Sol. The mode of a set of data values is the value that appears most often. It is the value that is most likely to be sampled This means mode is the observations whose frequency is highest. So it does not pay attention to what is the maximum value or the minimum value. So it is not affected either by maximum or minimum values and its not affected by both as well.

8. The mode of observations 7, 12, 8, 5, 6, 4, 9, 10, 8, 9, 7, 9, 6, 5, 9 is *(Un)*

(*a*) 7 (*b*) 8

(*c*) 9 (*d*) 12

Sol. Number 9 occurs 4 times in the given data, So mode is 9.

Mistakes 101 : What not to do!

Students may forget to arrange data in ascending order, causing errors in determining both mode and median.

9. The mode of the given series is 36. Then the value of *k* is

Class Interval	Frequency
0 –10	7
10 –20	6
20 –30	*k*
30 –40	16
40 –50	12
50 –60	8
60 –70	10

(Ev)

(*a*) 10 (*b*) 20

(*c*) 2 (*d*) 30

Sol. Modal class = 30–40

$\therefore l = 30, f_1 = 16, f_0 = k, f_2 = 12, h = 10$

and given Mode = 36

$$\Rightarrow 30 + \left(\frac{16-k}{2\times 16-k-12}\right)\times 10 = 36$$

$$\Rightarrow \frac{(16-k)10}{(20-k)} = 6$$

$$\Rightarrow 160 - 10k = 120 - 6k \Rightarrow 40 = 4k \Rightarrow k = 10$$

Answer Key

1. (a) 2. (d) 3. (d) 4. (b) 5. (a)
6. (d) 7. (d) 8. (c) 9. (a)

Assertion and Reason (1 M)

Direction: In the following questions, A statement of Assertion (A) is followed by a statement of Reason (R). Mark the correct choice as.

(*a*) Both Assertion (A) and Reason (R) are true, and Reason (R) is the correct explanation of Assertion (A).

(*b*) Both Assertion (A) and Reason (R) are true, but Reason (R) is not the correct explanation of Assertion (A).

(*c*) Assertion (A) is true, but Reason (R) is false.

(*d*) Assertion (A) is false, but Reason (R) is true.

1. Assertion (A): Consider the following frequency distribution:

Class Interval	3–6	6–9	9–12	12–15	15–18	18–21
Frequency	2	5	21	23	10	12

The mode of the above data is 12.4.

Reason (R): The value of the variable which occurs most often is the mode. *(Ap)*

Sol. Assertion (A): Modal class = 12 –15

$l = 12, f_1 = 23, f_0 = 21, f_2 = 10$ & $h = 3$

$$\text{Mode} = 12 + \left(\frac{23-21}{2\times 23 - 21 - 10}\right)\times 3$$

$$= 12 + \frac{2}{46-31}\times 3 = 12 + \frac{2}{15}\times 3 = \frac{62}{5} = 12.4$$

Reason (R): Mode is the value of the observation having the maximum frequency or value of variable which occurs most often is the mode.

Both Assertion (A) and Reason (R) are true, but Reason (R) is not the correct explanation of Assertion (A).

2. **Assertion (A): The mode of the call received on 7 consecutive day 11, 13, 13, 17, 19, 23, 25 is 13.**

Reason (R): Mode is the value that appears most frequent; 2 times maximum call received day is 13 *(An)*

Sol. ∴ Mode is 13, Hence Assertion (A) is true and Reason R is also true.

Both Assertion and Reason are correct and reason is correct explanation of assertion.

Answer Key

1. (b) 2. (a)

Subjective Questions

Very Short Answer Type Questions (1 or 2 M)

1. **For what value of x the mode of the following data is 8? 4, 5, 6, 8, 5, 4, 8, 5, 6, *x*, 8, 4** *(Un)*

Sol. Number of 4's = 3

Number of 5's = 3

Number of 6's = 2

Number of 8's = 3 *(1 M)*

But, mode = 8 ⇒ 8 should be maximum number of times

$\therefore x = 8$ *(1 M)*

2. **In a singing competition, the points (maximum being 60) allotted to the 15 participants are 60, 52, 42, 40, 43, 44, 46, 45, 42, 41, 40, 46, 48 and 46. What is the mode of the above data?** *(Cr)*

Sol. Given data are

60, 52, 42, 40, 43, 44, 46, 46, 45, 42, 41, 40, 46, 48 and 46.

Points	Frequency
40	2
41	1
42	2
43	1
44	1
45	1
46	4
48	1
52	1
60	1

(1 M)

Here,

The number 46 comes 4 times in the given data.

∴ Mode of above data is 46. *(1 M)*

Short Answer Type Questions (2 or 3 M)

1. **Calculate the mode of the following data distribution:**

Age (in years)	0.5	5–10	10–15	15–20	20–25	25–30	30–35
Number of patients	6	11	18	24	17	13	5

(Ev)

Sol. Modal class is 15-20,

$l = 15, f_1 = 24, f_0 = 18, f_2 = 17$ & $h = 5$ *(1 M)*

$$\text{Mode} = 15 + \left(\frac{24-18}{2\times 24 - 18 - 17}\right)\times 5$$ *(1 M)*

$$= 15 + \frac{6}{13}\times 5$$

$= 15 + 2.3 = 17.3$ years. *(1 M)*

2. **Calculate the mode of weekly wages from the following frequency distribution:** *(Ev)*

Wages (in ₹)	Number of workers
30–40	10
40–50	20
50–60	40
60–70	16
70–80	8
80–90	6

Sol. Clearly, the modal class is 50 – 60,

$l = 50, f_1 = 40, f_0 = 20, f_2 = 16, h = 10$ *(1 M)*

$$\text{Mode} = l + \left[\frac{f_1 - f_0}{2f_1 - f_0 - f_2}\right]\times h = 50 + \left[\frac{40-20}{2\times 40 - 20 - 16}\right]\times 10$$

(1 M)

$$= 50 + \left(\frac{50}{11}\right)$$

$$= \frac{600}{3} = 54.55 \text{ (approx.)}$$ *(1 M)*

3. **Find the mode of the following frequency distribution.** *(Ap)*

Class	Frequency
0–10	8
10–20	10
20–30	10
30–40	16
40–50	12
50–60	6
60–70	7

Sol. Modal class = 30 – 40

$l = 30, f_1 = 16, f_0 = 10, f_2 = 12, h = 10$ *(2 M)*

$$\text{mode} = 30+\left(\frac{16-10}{2\times16-10-12}\right)\times10 = 30+\frac{6}{10}\times10 = 36$$

(1 M)

4. **For the following distribution:**

Class	Frequency
0–5	10
5–10	15
10–15	12
15–20	20
20–25	9

Find the sum of the lower limit of median class and modal class. *(Ev)*

Sol.

Class	Frequency	Cumulative frequency
0 – 5	10	10
5 – 10	15	25
10 – 15	12	37
15 – 20	20	57
20 – 25	9	66

(1 M)

Here, $\frac{N}{2} = \frac{66}{2} = 33$

Thus 37 is just greater than 33,

∴ The median class is "10–15".

The lower limit of the median class is 10. *(1 M)*

Modal class = class with maximum frequency.

∴ Modal class is 15–20.

The lower limit of the modal class is 15.

Sum of lower limits of median class and modal class = 10 + 15 = 25 *(1 M)*

5. **The following distribution shows the transport expenditure of 100 employees:**

Expenditure (in ₹)	Number of employees
200–400	21
400–600	25
600–800	19
800–1000	23
1000–1200	12

Find the mode of the distribution. *(Cr)***(CBSE, 2020)**

Sol.

Expenditure (in ₹)	Number of employees
200–400	21
400–600	25
600–800	19
800–1000	23
1000–1200	12

From the given data, we have

$l = 400, f_1 = 25, f_0 = 21, f_2 = 19, h = 200$ *(1 M)*

$$\text{Mode} = l+\frac{f_1-f_0}{2f_1-f_0-f_2}\times h$$ *(1 M)*

$$= 400+\left(\frac{25-21}{2\times25-21-19}\right)\times200 = 480$$

Mode of the given data is 480. *(1 M)*

Long Answer Type Questions (4 or 5 M)

1. **If the mode of the following distribution is 57.5, find the value of *x*** *(Cr)*

Class	Frequency
30–40	6
40–50	10
50–60	16
60–70	x
70–80	10
80–90	5
90–100	2

Sol.

Class Interval	Frequency
30–40	6
40–50	10
50–60	16
60–70	x
70–80	10
80–90	5
90–100	2

(2 M)

Mode = 57.5 (given)

Let, Modal class = 50 – 60

$l = 50, f_1 = 16, f_0 = 10, f_2 = x \;\&\; h = 10$

$\therefore$ Mode $= l + \left(\dfrac{f_1 - f_0}{2f_1 - f_0 - f_2}\right) \times h$ (1 M)

$\Rightarrow 57.5 = 50 + \left(\dfrac{16-10}{2\times16-10-x}\right)\times10$

$\Rightarrow 57.5 = 50 + \dfrac{60}{22-x}$ (1 M)

$\Rightarrow 7.5 = \dfrac{60}{22-x} \Rightarrow \dfrac{75}{10} = \dfrac{60}{22-x}$

$\Rightarrow 1650 - 75x = 600$

$\Rightarrow 75x = 1050 \Rightarrow x = 14$ (1 M)

Mistakes 101 : What not to do!

Mistakes may occur if students incorrectly identify the modal class interval without considering frequency distribution.

2. **Find the value of f_1 from the following data, if its mode is 65.** *(Un)*

Class	Frequency
0–20	**6**
20–40	**8**
40–60	f_1
60–80	**12**
80–100	**6**
100–120	**5**

Where frequency 6, 8, f_1, and 12 are in ascending order

Sol.

Class	Frequency
0–20	6
20–40	8
40–60	f_1
60–80	12
80–100	6
100–120	5

(2 M)

Given mode = 65

$\therefore$ modal class = 60 –80 as its frequency is 12

$l = 60, f = 12, f_0 = f_1, f_2 = 6, h = 20$ (1 M)

Mode $= l + \left(\dfrac{f - f_0}{2f - f_0 - f_2}\right) \times h$ (1 M)

$\Rightarrow 65 = 60 + \dfrac{12 - f_1}{2\times12 - f_1 - 6}\times 20 \Rightarrow 5 = \left(\dfrac{12-f_1}{18-f_1}\right)\times 20$

$\Rightarrow 90 - 5f_1 = 240 - 20f_1 \Rightarrow 15f_1 = 150 \Rightarrow f_1 = 10$ (1 M)

3 MEDIAN AND ITS GROUPED DATA

Important Terms

- **Median:** The middle most value of the given data set when it is arranged in either ascending order or descending order of magnitude is called **median**. Median is also called a positional average.
- **Median of grouped data:** In case of **grouped frequency distribution,** the class corresponding to the cumulative frequency (*cf*) which is just greater than $\frac{N}{2}$ is called the median class.

Important Formulas

- $\text{Median} = l + \dfrac{\frac{N}{2} - Cf}{f} \times h$

  where,
  l = lower limit of median class interval
  Cf = cumulative frequency preceding to the median class.
  f = frequency of the class interval to which median belongs
  h = width of the class interval
  $N = \Sigma f$

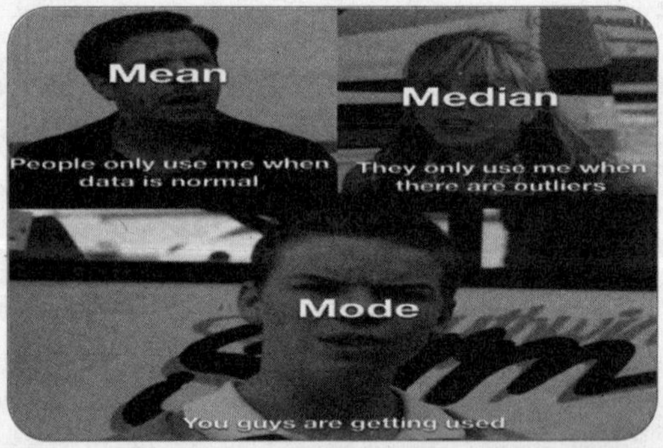

- If total number of observations is odd, say n. Then, Median $= \text{value of} \left(\dfrac{n+1}{2}\right)^{th}$ observation.
- If total number of observations is even, say n. Then,

$$\text{Median} = \frac{\text{Value of} \left(\frac{n}{2}\right)^{\text{th}} \text{term} + \text{Value of} \left(\frac{n}{2}+1\right)^{\text{th}} \text{term}}{2}$$

Important Concepts

- There is a empirical relationship between the three measures of central tendency:

  3 Median = Mode + 2 Mean
- The median of grouped data with unequal class sizes can also be calculated. However, we shall not discuss it here

Real Life Applications

- In finance, the median is used to calculate the middle value of a dataset, which can help investors identify the average return on their investments and make informed decisions about their portfolio.
- In healthcare, the median can be used to determine the typical length of hospital stays for patients with a particular condition, which can help hospitals plan for staffing and resource needs.
- In sports, the median is used to determine the average performance of athletes in a competition, which can help coaches and trainers identify areas for improvement and develop effective training strategies.

Different Problem Types

Type I: Calculate the Median Using Formula with Ungrouped Data

The following data represents the ages of participants in a marathon race: 18, 22, 26, 28, 30, 32, 34, 36, 38, 40, 42, 44

Find the median age of the participants.

Solution:

Step I: Arrange the data in ascending order 18, 22, 26, 28, 30, 32, 34, 36, 38, 40, 42, 44

Step II: Calculate the median for even *n*:

$$\text{Median position } = \frac{n}{2}$$

For this dataset with 12 values, the median position is $\frac{12}{2} = 6$ and $\frac{12}{2} + 1 = 7$.

$$\text{Median } = \frac{X_{\frac{n}{2}} + X_{\frac{n}{2}+1}}{2}$$

In this case, $X_6 = 32$ and $X_7 = 34$.

$$\text{Median } = \frac{32+34}{2} = \frac{66}{2} = 33$$

Therefore, the median age of the participants in the marathon race is 33 years.

Example: The following data represents the test scores of students in a mathematics class: 78, 82, 85, 88, 92, 95, 98, 100, 102, 105

Find the median test score of the students using the median formula for even *n*.

Solution:

To find the median for even n, we use the formula:

$$\text{Medium} = \frac{X_{\frac{n}{2}} + X_{\frac{n}{2}+1}}{2}$$

Arranging the data in ascending order: 78, 82, 85, 88, 92, 95, 98, 100, 102, 105

Since there are 10 data points, the median position is $\frac{10}{2} = 5$ and $\frac{10}{2} + 1 = 6$.

The 5th and 6th terms are 92 and 95, respectively.

$$\text{Median} = \frac{92+95}{2} = \frac{187}{2} = 93.5$$

Therefore, the median test score of the students in the mathematics class is 93.5.

Type II: Calculate the Median Using Formula with Grouped Data

The following data represents the heights (in inches) of students in a class, grouped into intervals:

Height Range	Frequency
0 – 10	2
10 – 20	6
20 – 30	12
30 – 40	18
40-50	10

Find the median height of the students using the formula for the median of grouped data.

Solution:

Step I: Calculate Cumulative Frequencies

Height Range	Frequency	Cumulative Frequency
0 – 10	2	2
10 – 20	6	2 + 6 = 8
20 – 30	12	8 + 12 = 20
30 – 40	18	20 + 18 = 38
40 – 50	10	38 + 10 = 48

Step II: Identify Median Class

Since $\frac{n}{2} = \frac{48}{2} = 24$ falls in the cumulative frequency range of the fourth class (30 – 40), the median class is 30 – 40.

Step III: Use Median Formula for Grouped Data.

$$\text{Median} = l + \left(\frac{\frac{n}{2} - Cf}{f}\right) \times h$$

Where:

$l = 30$ (lower boundary of the median class)

$n = 48$ (total frequency)

$Cf = 20$ (cumulative frequency of the class before the median class)

$f = 18$ (frequency of the median class)

$h = 10$ (size of the class interval)

$$\text{Median} = 30 + \left(\frac{20-20}{18}\right) \times 10$$

$$\text{Median} = 30 + \left(\frac{4}{10}\right) \times 10$$

Median = 30 + (0.222) × 10

Median = 30 + 2.2222

Median = 32.2222

Therefore, the median height of the students in the class is approximately 32.2222 inches.

Example: The following data represents the ages (in years) of participants in a sports event, grouped into intervals:

Age Range	Frequency
10-20	5
20-30	12
30-40	18
40-50	10
50-60	8

Find the median age of the participants using the formula for median of grouped data.

Solution:

First, we calculate the cumulative frequencies:

Age Range	Frequency	Cumulative Frequency
10 – 20	5	5
20 – 30	12	5 + 12 = 17
30 – 40	18	17 + 18 = 35
40 – 50	10	35 + 10 = 45
50 – 60	8	45 + 8 = 53

$\frac{n}{2} = \frac{53}{2} = 26.5$, which falls in the cumulative frequency range of the third class (30 – 40), the median class is 30 – 50.

In out case:

$l = 30$ (lower boundary of the median class)

$n = 53$ (total frequency)

$Cf = 17$ (cumulative frequency of the class before the median class)

$f = 18$ (frequency of the median class)

$h = 10$ (size of the class interval)

$$\text{Median} = 30 + \left(\frac{26.5-17}{18}\right) \times 10$$

$$\text{Median} = 30 + \left(\frac{9.5}{18}\right) \times 10$$

Median = 30 + (0.5278) × 10

Median = 30 + 5.278

Median = 35.78

Therefore, the median age of the participants in the sports event is approximately 35.278 years.

COMPETENCY BASED SOLVED EXAMPLES

Multiple Choice Questions **(1 M)**

1. Shown below is a table representing the percentage distribution of mental health disorders of Asian countries in 2019.

Percentage of citizens with mental health disorders	Number of Asian countries
7.5–10	1
10–12.5	25
12.5–15	11
15–17.5	4
17.5–20	1

Can the median of the above data be greater than 12.5%? Give a valid reason. *(An)* **(CBSE CFPQ, 2023)**

(*a*) No (*b*) Yes

(*c*) can't say (*d*) Data insufficient

Sol. The median of the given data cannot be greater than 12.5% as 10-12.5 is the median class.

Nailing the Right Answer

Students should arrange data in ascending order to easily identify the median and mode.

2. The following frequency distribution shows the weights of new born babies in a hospital.

Weight of new born baby (in kg)	1.4 – 1.8	1.8 – 2.2	2.2 – 2.6	2.6 – 3.0
No of babies	3	15	6	1

Then the median weight is: *(Ap)*

(*a*) 2kg (*b*) 3kg

(*c*) 2.05 kg (*d*) 2.5 kg

Sol. Construct a table as follows:

Class-interval	Frequency (f_i)	Midpoint (x_i)	Cumulative Frequency (Cf)
1.4–1.8	3	1.6	3
1.8–2.2	15	2.0	18
2.2–2.6	6	2.4	24
2.6–3.0	1	2.8	25

Here, $N = 25$. Hence, $\frac{N}{2} = \frac{25}{2} = 12.5$

Median class = 1.8 – 2.2

$\therefore l = 1.8,\ f = 15,\ Cf = 3$ and $h = 0.4$

$$= 1.8 + \left(\frac{12.5-3}{15}\right) \times 0.4 = 1.8 + \frac{9.5}{15} \times 0.4 = 1.8 + 0.25 = 2.05$$

Hence, Median weight of new born baby is 2.05 kg

Key Takeaways

$$\text{Median} = l + \left(\frac{\frac{N}{2} - Cf}{f}\right) \times h$$

3. The median of the observation 8, 72, 19, 13, 54, 63, 35, 49, 27 is *(Un)*

(*a*) 35 (*b*) 49

(*c*) 63 (*d*) 27

Sol. First arrange the term in ascending order 8, 13, 19, 27, 35, 49, 54, 63, 72

Total no. of terms = 9

$= \frac{9+1}{2} = 5^{\text{th}}$ observation

Hence, Median is 35

Key Takeaways

$\therefore \text{Median} = \left(\frac{n+1}{2}\right)^{\text{th}}$ observation where n = odd

4. Table shows the salaries of 100 employees of an Ed-tech firm. *(Ap)*

Candidate Salary (in thousand)	25–35	35–45	45–55	55–65	65–75	75–85
Number of Employees	40	15	8	18	12	7

The median of given data (up to 2 decimals places) is:

(*a*) 39.90 (*b*) 47.14

(*c*) 41.66 (*d*) 43.25

Sol.

Candidate	Number of Employees	Cumulative frequency
25–35	40	40 = *Cf*
35–45	15 = *f*	55
45–55	8	63
55–65	18	81
65–75	12	93
75–85	7	100
	N = 100	

$N/2 = 100/2 = 50$

$\therefore$ The median class is 35–45

So, $l = 35, f = 15, Cf = 40, h = 10$

$\Rightarrow \text{Median} = 35 + \frac{50-40}{15} \times 10$

$\Rightarrow \text{Median} = 35 + \frac{10}{15} \times 10$

$\Rightarrow$ Median = 35 + 6.66 = 41.66

Hence, median = 41.66

Answer Key

1. (*a*) 2. (*c*) 3. (*a*) 4. (*c*)

Assertion and Reason (1 M)

Direction: In the following questions, a statement of Assertion (A) is followed by a statement of Reason (R). Mark the correct choice as.

(*a*) Both Assertion (A) and Reason (R) are true, and Reason (R) is the correct explanation of Assertion (A).

(*b*) Both Assertion (A) and Reason (R) are true, but Reason (R) is not the correct explanation of Assertion (A).

(*c*) Assertion (A) is true, but Reason (R) is false.

(*d*) Assertion (A) is false, but Reason (R) is true.

1. **Assertion (A): If the median of the given data 26, 29, 42, 53, x, $x + 2$, 70, 75, 82, 93 is 65 then the value of x is 64.**

   Reason (R): When the number of observations (n) is odd then the median is the value of the $\left(\frac{n+1}{2}\right)^{th}$ observation. (*An*)

Sol. Assertion: Given no. observation is 10 (even)

$$\text{Median} = \frac{\left(\frac{n}{2}\right)^{th} \text{term} + \left(\frac{n}{2}+1\right)^{th} \text{term}}{2}$$

$$\text{Median} = \frac{x+(x+2)}{2} = \frac{2x+2}{2} = x+1$$

$\Rightarrow 65 = x + 1 \Rightarrow x = 64$

Reason is also true. But reason is not correct explanation of assertion.

2. **Assertion (A): The median of the data 13, 15, 16, 17, 19, 20 is 33/2**

   Reason (R): Median = (16 + 17)/2 = 33/2 (*Ev*)

Sol. Total no. of terms = 6(even)

$$\text{Median} = \frac{\left(\frac{n}{2}\right)^{th} \text{term} + \left(\frac{n}{2}+1\right)^{th} \text{term}}{2}$$

$$= \frac{16+17}{2} = \frac{33}{2}$$

$$\text{and Reason} = \frac{16+17}{2} = \frac{33}{2}$$

Both assertion and reason are correct and reason is correct explanation of assertion.

Answer Key

1. (*b*) 2. (*a*)

Subjective Questions

Very Short Answer Type Questions (1 or 2 M)

1. **The run scored by a cricketer in 10 matches are as follows:**

   47, 58, 96, 1, 6, 52, 6, 78, 102 and 1. Find the median of the data. (*Ap*)

Sol. Arranging the scores in ascending order

1, 1, 6, 6, 47, 52, 58, 78, 96, 102

Here, $x = 10$

$$\therefore \text{Median} = \frac{\left(\frac{n}{2}\right)^{th} \text{term} + \left(\frac{n}{2}+1\right)^{th} \text{term}}{2} \quad (1\ M)$$

$$\text{Median} = \frac{5^{th} \text{term} + 6^{th} \text{term}}{2}$$

$$\text{Median} = \frac{47+52}{2} = \frac{99}{2} = 49.5 \quad (1\ M)$$

2. **The numbers of runs scored by a player in 11 cricket matches are: 5, 19, 42, 11, 50, 30, 21, 0, 52, 36, and 27. Find the median.** (*Ev*)

Sol. Let us arrange the value in ascending order

0, 5, 11, 19, 21, 27, 30, 36, 42, 50, 52 (*1 M*)

As number of observation are odd.

$$\therefore \text{Median} = \left(\frac{n+1}{2}\right)^{th} \text{term} = \left(\frac{11+1}{2}\right)^{th} \text{term}$$

$= 6^{th}$ term

Now 6th value in the data is 27

$\therefore$ Median = 27 runs. (*1 M*)

3. If the median of the observations 9, 13, 15, 20, $x + 2$, $x + 4$, 33, 45, 56, 61 arranged in ascending order is 24. Find the value of x. *(An)*

Sol. Here, the number of observations $n = 10$. Since n is even, therefore

$$\text{Median} = \frac{\left(\frac{n}{2}\right)^{\text{th}} \text{observation} + \left(\frac{n}{2}+1\right)^{\text{th}} \text{observation}}{2}$$ *(1 M)*

$$\Rightarrow 24 = \frac{5^{\text{th}} \text{ observation} + 6^{\text{th}} \text{ observation}}{2}$$

$$\Rightarrow 24 = \frac{(x+2)+(x+4))}{2} \Rightarrow 24 = \frac{2x+6}{2}$$

$$\Rightarrow 24 = x + 3 \Rightarrow x = 21$$ *(1 M)*

4. Find the median of the call received on 7 consecutive days 11, 13, 17, 13, 23, 25, 19 *(Ap)*

Sol. The median is the middle value of the data sets, so first, Arrange the number in ascending order

11, 13, 13, 17, 19, 23, 25

Here, n = number of terms = 7 *(1 M)*

$$\text{Median} = \left(\frac{n+1}{2}\right)^{\text{th}} \text{term} = \left(\frac{7+1}{2}\right)^{\text{th}} = 4^{\text{th}} \text{ term}$$

∴ Median = 17. *(1 M)*

Short Answer Type Questions (2 or 3 M)

1. A sequence $a, ax, ax^2, \ldots ax^n$, has odd number of terms. Find its median. *(Un)*

Sol. Given sequence $a, ax, ax^2, \ldots, ax^n$ has odd numbers of term.

Let N = total terms = $n + 1$

$$\therefore \text{Median} = \left(\frac{N+1}{2}\right)^{\text{th}} \text{term}$$ *(1 M)*

$$= \left(\frac{(n+1)+1}{2}\right)^{\text{th}} \text{term}$$ *(1 M)*

$$= \left(\frac{n+2}{2}\right)^{\text{th}} \text{term}$$

$$= a\left(x^{\left(\frac{n+2}{2}\right)-1}\right) = ax^{\frac{n}{2}}$$ *(1 M)*

2. The weight of 8 students in kgs are 54, 49, 51, 58, 61, 52, 54, 60. Find the median weight. *(Ev)*

Sol. Arranging the given data in ascending order,

We get 49, 51, 52, 54, 54, 58, 60, 61. *(1 M)*

Here, $n = 8$.

$$\text{Median} = \frac{\left(\frac{n}{2}\right)^{\text{th}} \text{terms} + \left(\frac{n}{2}+1\right)^{\text{th}} \text{terms}}{2}$$ *(1 M)*

Hence, median = (54 + 54)/2 = 108/2 = 54.

∴ The median weight is 54 kg. *(1 M)*

3. Calculate the median marks of students from the following distribution. *(An)*

Marks	Number of students
10–20	7
20–30	10
30–40	10
40–50	20
50–60	20
60–70	15
70–80	8

Sol.

Class interval	Number of students (frequency)	Cumulative frequency
10–20	7	7
20–30	10	17
30–40	10	27 = Cf
40–50	20 = f	47
50–60	20	67
60–70	15	82
70–80	8	90

$$\therefore \frac{N}{2} = \frac{90}{2} = 45$$ *(1 M)*

Cumulative frequency greater and nearer to 45 is 47, which lies in the interval 40–50

Median class is 40–50.

Lower limit of the median class = $l = 40$

Class size = $h = 10$

Frequency of the median class = $f = 20$

Cumulative frequency of the class preceding the median class = $Cf = 27$ *(1 M)*

As we know,

$$\text{Median} = l + \left(\frac{\frac{N}{2} - Cf}{f}\right) \times h = 40 + \left(\frac{45-27}{20}\right) \times 10 = 49$$

Hence, the median marks of the students = 49. *(1 M)*

4. The table below shows the salaries of 280 persons:

Salary (In thousand ₹)	No. of Persons
5–10	49
10–15	133
15–20	63
20–25	15
25–30	6
30–35	7

35–40	**4**
40–45	**2**
45–50	**1**

Calculate the median salary of the data. (*Cr*)

Sol.

Salary	Frequency	*Cf*
5–10	49	49 = *Cf*
10–15	133 = *f*	182
15–20	63	245
20–25	15	260
25–30	6	266
30–35	7	273
35–40	4	277
40–45	2	279
45–50	1	280

(*2 M*)

$\frac{N}{2} = \frac{280}{2} = 140$

Modal class = 10 – 15

$\therefore l = 10$ & $h = 5$

Median = $10 + \left(\frac{140-49}{133}\right) \times 5 = 13.42$ thousand (*1 M*)

Nailing the Right Answer

Students should first identify class intervals and their frequencies to determine mode and median.

Long Answer Type Questions (4 or 5 M)

1. **If the median of a distribution given below is 28.5 , then find the value of *x* and *y*.** (*Un*)

Class	Frequency
0–10	**5**
10–20	***x***
20–30	**20**
30–40	**15**
40–50	***y***
50–60	**5**
Total	**60**

Sol. From the given,

Class	Frequency	Commutative frequency
0–10	5	5
10–20	*x*	5 + *x* = *Cf*
20–30	20 = *f*	25 + *x*
30–40	15	40 + *x*
40–50	*y*	40 + *x* + *y*
50–60	5	45 + *x* + *y*
Total	*N* = 60	

(*2 M*)

$\frac{N}{2} = \frac{60}{2} = 30$

Median of the given data = 28.5

Median class = 20 – 30

Lower limit of median class = $l = 20$

Frequency of the median class = $f = 20$

Cumulative frequency of the class preceding the median class = $Cf = 5 + x$

Class size = $h = 10$ (*1 M*)

$$\text{Median} = l + \left(\frac{\frac{N}{2} - Cf}{f}\right) \times h$$

$\Rightarrow 28.5 = 20 + [(30 - 5 - x)/20] \times 10$

$\Rightarrow 28.5 - 20 = (25 - x)/2$

$\Rightarrow 8.5 \times 2 = 25 - x$

$\Rightarrow 17 = 25 - x$

$\Rightarrow x = 25 - 17$

Therefore, $x = 8$ (*1 M*)

Also,

$\Rightarrow 60 = 5 + 20 + 15 + 5 + x + y$

$\Rightarrow 60 = 5 + 20 + 15 + 5 + 8 + y$

$\Rightarrow y = 60 - 53$

$\Rightarrow y = 7$

Therefore, the value of $x = 8$ and $y = 7$. (*1 M*)

2. **The following table give the frequency distribution of married women by age at marriage:** (*Cr*)

Age (in years)	Frequency
15-19	**53**
20-24	**140**
25-29	**98**
30-34	**32**
35-39	**12**
40-44	**9**
45-49	**5**
50-54	**3**
55-59	**3**
60 and above	**2**

Obtain the median and describe what information does it convey?

Sol. As we can see the class intervals are not continuous. There is a gap of 1 between two class intervals. So, we have to add 0.5 to upper class limit and 0.5 from lower class limit of each interval.

Age (in years)	Frequency (f)	Cumulative frequency (Cf)
14.5-19.5	53	53
19.5-24.5	140	193
24.5-29.5	98	291
29.5-34.5	32	323
34.5-39.5	12	335
39.5-44.5	9	344
44.5-49.5	5	349
49.5-54.5	3	352
54.5-59.5	3	355
59.5 and above	2	357
	N=357	

(2 M)

Here. $N = 357$ and hence $\frac{N}{2} = 178.5$

$\therefore$ Median class is 19.5 - 24.5 with cumulative frequency = 193

$l = 19.5, f = 140, Cf = 53$ and $h = 5$ *(1 M)*

$$\therefore \text{Median} = l + \left(\frac{\frac{N}{2} - Cf}{f}\right) \times h$$ *(1 M)*

$$= 19.5 + \left(\frac{178.5 - 53}{140}\right) \times 5 = 19.5 + \frac{125.5}{28} = 23.98$$

Thus, nearly half the women were married between the ages 15 and 24 year. *(1 M)*

3. The following frequency distribution shows the sales of athletic shoes at a online store each day during the past 100 days. *(Un)*

Sales	No. of days (f_i)
0-100	2
100-200	5
200-300	x
300-400	12
400-500	17
500-600	20
600-700	y
700-800	9
800-900	7
900-1000	4
	$N = 100$

Sol. At first we prepare a cumulative frequency distribution table as given below:

Class Interval	Frequency (f)	Cumulative frequency (Cf)
0-100	2	2
100-200	5	7
200-300	x	$7 + x$
300-400	12	$19 + x$
400-500	17	$36 + x$
500-600	20	$56 + x$
600-700	y	$56 + x + y$
700-800	9	$65 + x + y$
800-900	7	$72 + x + y$
900-1000	4	$76 + x + y$
	$N = 100$	

(2 M)

Here, $N = 100$ and hence, $\frac{N}{2} = 50$.

$\therefore 76 + x + y = 100 \Rightarrow x + y = 24$ ...(*i*)

Since the median is 525, Therefore median class is 500-600

$l = 500, f = 20, Cf = 36 + x$ and $h = 100$ *(1 M)*

$$\therefore \text{Median} = l + \left(\frac{\frac{N}{2} - Cf}{f}\right) \times h$$ *(1 M)*

$$\Rightarrow 525 = 500 + \left(\frac{50 - 36 - x}{20}\right) \times 100$$

$$\Rightarrow 25 = (14 - x)5 \Rightarrow x = 9$$

By putting $x = 9$ in (*i*), we get $y = 15$

Hence, the value of x is 9 and y is 15. *(1 M)*

Mistakes 101 : What not to do!

Students may struggle to comprehend the concept of cumulative frequencies, resulting in incorrect calculations.

4. If the median of the following frequency distribution is x and y, if total frequency is 100: *(AP)*

Class	Frequency
0–100	2
100–200	5
200–300	x
300–400	12
400–500	17
500–600	20
600–700	y

700–800	**9**
800–900	**7**
900–1000	**4**

Sol.

Class	Frequency (f)	Cumulative frequency (Cf)
0–100	2	2
100–200	5	7
200–300	x	$x+7$
300–400	12	$x+19$
400–500	17	$x+36=Cf$
500–600	$20=f$	$x+56$
600–700	y	$x+y+56$
700–800	9	$x+y+65$
800–900	7	$x+y+72$
900–1000	4	$x+y+76$
	$N=100$ (given)	

(2 M)

$$\frac{N}{2}=\frac{100}{2}=50$$

Given Median = 525

∴ Median class = 500 – 600

Here $l=500, f=20, Cf=x+36$ and $h=100$ *(1 M)*

Given $x+y+76=100 \Rightarrow x+y=24$ ...(*i*)

Now, Median $= l+\left(\dfrac{\frac{N}{2}-Cf}{f}\right)\times h$ *(1 M)*

$$\Rightarrow 525 = 500+\left(\frac{50-x-36}{20}\right)\times 100$$

$$\Rightarrow 25=(14-x)5 \Rightarrow 25=70-5x \Rightarrow 5x=45 \Rightarrow x=9$$

From eq (*i*)

$y=24-9=15$ *(1 M)*

Nailing the Right Answer

Student should calculate the cumulative frequency to locate the median class interval for finding the median.

5. If the median of the following frequency distribution is 32.5. Find the values of f_1 and f_2. *(Un)*

Class	Frequency
0–10	f_1
10–20	**5**
20–30	**9**
30–40	**12**
40–50	f_2
50–60	**3**
60–70	**2**
Total	**40**

Sol.

Class	Frequency (f)	Cumulative frequency (Cf)
0–10	f_1	f_1
10–20	5	f_1+5
20–30	9	$f_1+14=Cf$
30–40	$12=f$	f_1+26
40–50	f_2	f_1+f_2+26
50–60	3	f_1+f_2+29
60–70	2	f_1+f_2+31
Total	40	

(1 M)

$$\therefore \frac{N}{2}=\frac{40}{2}=20$$

Given Median = 32.5

∴ Class interval = 30 – 40

$l=30, f=12, Cf=f_1+14$, and $h=10$

Here $f_1+f_2+31=40$, $f_1+f_2=9$ ...(*i*) *(1 M)*

We know

Median $= l+\left(\dfrac{\frac{N}{2}-Cf}{f}\right)\times h$ *(1 M)*

$$32.5 = 30+\frac{\{20-(f_1+14)\}}{12}\times 10$$ *(1 M)*

$$\Rightarrow 2.5=\frac{(6-f_1)}{6}\times 5 \Rightarrow 15=30-5f_1 \Rightarrow 5f_1=15 \Rightarrow f_1=3$$

From eqn (i)

$f_2=9-3=6$ *(1 M)*

MISCELLANEOUS EXERCISE

Multiple Choice Questions (1 M)

1. The Median when it is given that mode and mean are 8 and 5 respectively, is:

   (*a*) 8 (*b*) 6 (*c*) 4 (*d*) 9

2. If the ratio of mean and median of a certain data is 5 : 7, then find the ratio of its mode and mean.

   (*a*) 2 : 5 (*b*) 11 : 5
   (*c*) 6 : 5 (*d*) 2 : 3

3. If the difference of mode and median of a data is 36, then the difference of median and mean is:

   (*a*) 18 (*b*) 24
   (*c*) 8 (*d*) 36

4. The median and mode of a frequency distribution are 525 and 500 then mean of same frequency distribution is:

   (*a*) 437 (*b*) 537
   (*c*) 527.5 (*d*) 537.5

5. For a grouped data, modal class is 22 – 29. If $2f_0 = f_1 = 3f_2$ then mode is

   (*a*) 23 (*b*) 24
   (*c*) 25 (*d*) 26

6. The median and mode respectively of a frequency distribution are 26 and 29. Then its mean is. **(CBSE, 2020)**

   (*a*) 27.5 (*b*) 24.5
   (*c*) 28.4 (*d*) 25.8

7. If for a given data median is 125.6 and mean is 128 , find mode.

   (*a*) 120.8 (*b*) 128.0
   (*c*) 108.2 (*d*) 180.2

8. The table below depicts the weight of the students of class 6 of Red Bricks Public School. There are 18 students in the class that weigh above the median weight.

Weight	25-28	28-31	31-34	34-37	37-40
Number of students	6	8	7	10	?

   If there are no students with the same weight as median weight, how many students weigh between the range of 37-40 kgs?

   (*a*) 5 (*b*) 7
   (*c*) 18 (*d*) 31

Assertion and Reason (1 M)

Direction: In the following questions, a statement of assertion (A) is followed by a statement of reason (R). Mark the correct choice as:

(*a*) Both Assertion (A) and Reason (R) are true and Reason (R) is the correct explanation of Assertion (a).

(*b*) Both Assertion (A) and Reason (R) are true but Reason (R) is not the correct explanation of Assertion (A).

(*c*) Assertion (A) is true but Reason (R) is false.

(*d*) Assertion (A) is false but Reason (R) is true.

1. **Assertion (A):** The arithmetic mean of the following given frequency distribution table is 13.81.

x	4	7	10	13	16	19
f	7	10	15	20	25	30

   Reason (R): $\bar{x}$ = value of $\left(\frac{n+1}{2}\right)^{\text{th}}$ observation.

2. **Assertion (A):** If the number of runs scored by 11 players of a cricket team of India are 5, 19, 42, 11, 50, 30, 21, 0, 52, 36, 27, then median is 30.

   Reason (R): Median $= \left(\frac{n+1}{2}\right)^{\text{th}}$ value, if n is odd.

3. **Assertion (A):** If the value of mode and mean is 60 and 66 respectively, then the value of median is 64.

   Reason (R): Median $= \frac{1}{3}$ (mode + 2 mean)

4 **Assertion (A):** The modal class of given frequency distribution is 30-40

Class-Interval	0-10	10-20	20-30	30-40	40-50
Frequency	4	6	5	8	3

   Reason (R): The class corresponding to the maximum frequency is modal-class.

Subjective Questions

Very Short Answer Type Questions (1 or 2 M)

1. Calculate the mean for the following distribution:

Variable	5	6	7	8	9
Frequency	4	10	15	11	3

2. Find the median of first 100 natural number.
3. If the mean of first n natural numbers is 15 , then find n.
4. Construct the cumulative frequency distribution of the following distribution:

Class	Frequency
12.5–17.5	2
17.5–22.5	22
22.5–27.5	19
27.5–32.5	14
32.5–37.5	13

5. Find the mode from the following data:
110, 120, 130, 120, 110, 140, 130, 120, 140, 120.
6. Find the median of the following distribution:
37, 31, 42, 43, 46, 25, 39, 45, 32, 35, 49

Short Answer Type Questions (2 or 3 M)

1. Find the mean of the following frequency distribution by direct Method:

Class Interval	Frequency
10–30	90
30–50	20
50–70	30
70–90	20
90–110	40

2. The frequency distribution of daily rainfall in a town during a certain period is shown below.

Rainfall (in mm)	Number of days
0-20	7
20-40	x
40-60	10
60-80	4

Unfortunately, due to manual errors, the information on the 20-40 mm range got deleted from the data.

If the mean daily rainfall for the period was 35 mm, find the number of days when the rainfall ranged between 20-40 mm. Show your work. **(CBSE CFPQ, 2023)**

3. Find the mode of the following distribution

Height	No. of Plants
above 30	34
above 40	30
above 50	27
above 60	19
above 70	8
above 80	2

4. Find the median of the following data:
25, 34, 31, 23, 22, 26, 35, 28, 20, 24, 32, 33
5. The length of 40 leaves of a plant are measured correct to nearest millimetre, and the data obtained is represented in the following table.

Length [in mm]	118-126	127-135	136-144	145-153	154-162	163-171	172-180
Number of leaves	3	5	9	12	5	4	2

Find the mean length of the leaves. **(CBSE SQP, 2023)**

Long Answer Type Questions (4 or 5 M)

1. The following table gives the distribution of the life time of 400 neon lamps:

Life time (in hours)	Number of lamps
1500-2000	14
2000-2500	56
2500-3000	60
3000-3500	86
3500-4000	74
4000-4500	62
4500-5000	48

Find the average life time of a lamp. **(CBSE, SQP 2023)**

2. If the mean of the distribution given below is 9.2, then find the value of p.

x	4	6	7	$p+4$	12	14
f	5	6	4	10	8	7

3. Find the mean marks from the following data by step deviation method:

Marks	Number of students
Below 10	5
Below 20	9
Below 30	17
Below 40	29
Below 50	45
Below 60	60
Below 70	70
Below 80	78
Below 90	83
Below 100	85

4. The following distribution shows the daily pocket allowance of children of a locality. The mean pocket allowance is Rs 18. Find the missing frequency *f*.

Daily Pocket Allowance(in ₹)	Number of children
11-13	7
13-15	6
15-17	9
17-19	13
19-21	*f*
21-23	5
23-35	4

5. The median of the following data is 50. Find the values of '*p*' and '*q*', if the sum of all frequencies is 90. Also find the mode of the data. **(CBSE SQP, 2023)**

Marks obtained	20–30	30–40	40–50	50–60	60–70	70–80	80–90
Number of students	*p*	15	25	20	*q*	8	10

6. The following distribution gives the state-wise teacher-student ratio in higher secondary schools of India. Find the mode and mean of this data. Interpret the two measures.

No of Students per teacher	Number of states / U.T
15-20	3
20-25	8
25-30	9
30-35	10
35-40	3
40-45	0
45-50	0
50-55	2

7. The following frequency distribution gives the monthly consumption of an electricity of 68 consumers in a locality. Find the median, mean and mode of the data and compare them.

Monthly consumption(in units)	No. of customers
65-85	4
85-105	5
105-125	13
125-145	20
145-165	14
165-185	8
185-205	4

8. The lengths of 40 leaves in a plant are measured correctly to the nearest millimeter, and the data obtained is represented as in the following table:

Length (in mm)	Number of leaves
118-126	3
127-135	5
136-144	9
145-153	12
154-162	5
163-171	4
172-180	2

Find the median length of leaves.

Case Based Questions

Case Based-I: A man is decided to make a playground in various colony parks. They decided to study the age-group of children playing in a park of the particular colony. The classification of children according to their ages, playing in a park is shown in the following table.

Age group of children (in years)	6-8	8-10	10-12	12-14	14-16
Number of children	43	58	70	42	27

Based on the above information, answer the following questions.

(*i*) Which age group has the maximum number of children?

(*ii*) Find frequency of the class succeeding the modal class

OR

Find the mode of the ages of children playing in the park

(*iii*) Find the lower limit of the modal class

Case Based-II: In Delhi, The Nation Highway Authority of India (NHAI) checking in particular toll plaza for toll tax collection.

The following table shows the toll tax paid by drivers and the number of vehicles on that particular day.

Toll tax (in ₹)	30–40	40–50	50–60	60–70	70–80
Number of vehicles	80	110	120	70	40

Based on the above information, answer the following questions.

(*i*) If A is taken as assumed mean, then find the possible value of A.

(*ii*) Find the mean of toll tax received by NHAI by assumed mean method.

OR

Find the average toll tax received by NHAI in a day, from that particular toll plaza,

(*iii*) If x_i's denotes the class marks and d_i's 's denotes the deviation of assumed mean (A) from x_i's, then find the minimum value of $|d_i|$.

Case Based-III: The Kendriya Vidyalaya Sangathan or 'Central School Organisation oversees the functioning of the schools with its headquarters in New Delhi . The chairman of Kendriya Vidyalaya Sangathan is providing a common programme of education.

Chairman of Regional office Delhi preapare a table of the marks obtained of 100 students which is given below

Marks obtained	0–20	20–40	40–60	60–80	80–100
Number of students	15	18	21	29	p

He was told that mean marks of a student is 53 .

(*i*) How many students got marks between 80–100?

(*a*) 21 (*b*) 38
(*c*) 17 (*d*) 26

(*ii*) The lower limit of model class is

(*a*) 20 (*b*) 40
(*c*) 60 (*d*) 80

(*iii*) The value of model marks is

(*a*) 58 (*b*) 62
(*c*) 65 (*d*) 68

(*iv*) The value of median marks is

(*a*) 58 (*b*) 62
(*c*) 65 (*d*) 72

(*v*) The upper limit of median class is

(*a*) 20 (*b*) 40
(*c*) 60 (*d*) 80

Case Based-IV: The COVID-19 pandemic, also known as corona virus pandemic, is an ongoing pandemic of coronavirus disease caused by the transmission of severe acute respiratory syndrome coronavirus 2 (SARS-CoV-2) among humans.

The following table shows the age distribution of case admited during a day in two different hospitals

Table 1:

Age (in years)	5 – 15	15 – 25	25 – 35	35 – 45	45 – 55	55 – 65
No. of cases	6	11	21	23	14	5

Table 2:

Age (in years)	5 – 15	15 – 25	25 – 35	35 – 45	45 – 55	55 – 65
No. of cases	8	16	10	42	24	12

Based on the above information, answer the following questions:

(CBSE QB)

Refer to table 1

(*i*) The average age for which maximum cases occurred is

(*a*) 32.24 (*b*) 34.36
(*c*) 36.82 (*d*) 42.24

(*ii*) The upper limit of modal class is

(*a*) 15 (*b*) 25
(*c*) 35 (*d*) 45

(*iii*) The mean of the given data is

(*a*) 26.2 (*b*) 32.4
(*c*) 33.5 (*d*) 35.4

Refer to table 2

(*iv*) The mode of the given data is

(*a*) 41.4 (*b*) 48.2
(*c*) 55.3 (*d*) 64.6

(*v*) The median of the given data is

(*a*) 32.7 (*b*) 40.2
(*c*) 42.3 (*d*) 48.6

Case Based-V: Electricity energy consumption is the form of energy consumption that uses electric energy. Global electricity consumption continues to increase faster than world population, leading to an increase in the average amount of electricity consumed per person (per capita electricity consumption).

Tariff	:LT - Residential	Bill Number	:384756
Type of Supply	: Single Phase	Connected Load	:3KW
Meter Reading Date	:31-11-13	Meter Reading	:65789
Previous Reading Date	:31-10-13	Previous Meter Reading	:65500
		Units Consumed	:289

A survey is conducted for 56 families of a colony *A*. The following tables gives the weekly consumption of electricity of these families.

Weekly consumption (in units):	No. of Cases
0 – 10	16
10 – 20	12
20 – 30	18
30 – 40	6
40 – 50	4
50 – 60	0

The similar survey is conducted for 80 families of colony *B* and the data is recorded as below:

Weekly consumption (in units):	No. of Cases
0 – 10	0
10 – 20	5
20 – 30	10
30 – 40	20
40 – 50	40
50 – 60	5

Based on the above information, answer the following questions: (CBSE QB)

Refer to data received from colony *A*

(*i*) The median weekly consumption is

(*a*) 12 units (*b*) 16 units
(*c*) 20 units (*d*) None of these

(*ii*) The mean weekly consumption is

(*a*) 19.64 units (*b*) 22.5 units
(*c*) 26 units (*d*) None of these

(*iii*) The modal class of the above data is

(*a*) 0 – 10 (*b*) 10 – 20
(*c*) 20 – 30 (*d*) 30 – 40

Refer to data received from colony *B*

(*iv*) The modal weekly consumption is

(*a*) 38.2 units (*b*) 43.6 units
(*c*) 26 units (*d*) 32 units

(*v*) The mean weekly consumption is

(*a*) 15.65 units (*b*) 32.8 units
(*c*) 38.75 units (*d*) 48 units

ANSWER KEYS

Multiple Choice Questions

1. (*b*) **2.** (*b*) **3.** (*a*) **4.** (*d*) **5.** (*c*) **6.** (*b*) **7.** (*a*) **8.** (*a*)

Assertion and Reason

1. (*c*) **2.** (*d*) **3.** (*a*) **4.** (*a*)

Case Based Type Questions

Case Based-III

(*i*) (*c*) (*ii*) (*c*) (*iii*) (*d*) (*iv*) (*a*) (*v*) (*c*)

Case Based-IV

(*i*) (*c*) (*ii*) (*c*) (*iii*) (*d*) (*iv*) (*a*) (*v*) (*b*)

Case Based-V

(*i*) (*c*) (*ii*) (*a*) (*iii*) (*c*) (*iv*) (*b*) (*v*) (*c*)

HINTS & EXPLANATIONS

Multiple Choice Questions

1. (*b*) As we know,

$$\text{Median} = \frac{\text{Mode} + 2\text{Mean}}{3}$$

$$\text{Median} = \frac{8 + 2 \times 5}{3} = 6$$

2. (*b*) Given: Mean : Median = 5 : 7

We know, Mode = 3 Median – 2 Mean

Let, Mean = $5k$ and median = $7k$

Now, mode = $3 \times 7k - 2 \times 5k = 11k$

$$\frac{\text{mode}}{\text{mean}} = \frac{11k}{5k} = \frac{11}{5}$$

∴ Mode : mean = 11 : 5

3. (*a*) We have, Mode – Median = 36

As we know, Mode = 3 (Median) – 2 Mean

Mode – Median = 2 Median – 2 Mean

36 = 2 (Median – Mean)

Median – Mean = 18

4. (*d*) As we know,

Mode = 3 Median - 2 Mean

$$\therefore \quad \text{Mean} = \frac{3\text{Median} - \text{Mode}}{2}$$

$$\text{Mean} = \frac{3(525) - 500}{2} = 537.5$$

5. (*c*) Given: $2f_0 = f_1 = 3f_2$

Modal class = 22 – 29

$l = 22$ $h = 7$

$$\text{Mode} = l + \left(\frac{f_1 - f_0}{2f_1 - f_0 - f_2}\right)h$$

$$= 22 + \left(\frac{2f_0 - f_0}{4f_0 - f_0 - \frac{2}{3}f_0}\right)7$$

$$= 22 + \left(\frac{1}{3 - \frac{2}{3}}\right)7 = 22 + \left(\frac{3}{7}\right)7 = 22 + 3$$

Mode = 25

6. (*b*) The empirical relationship between mean, median and mode is

Mode = 3 Median – 2 Mean

⇒ 2 Mean = 3 Median – Mode

⇒ 2 Mean = 3 × 26 – 29

$$\Rightarrow \text{Mean} = \frac{49}{2} = 24.5$$

7. (*a*) **Hint:** Mode = 3 Median – 2 Mean

8. (*a*) Given that there are 18 students above the median weight, and the total number of studsents in the class is 18, the median weight falls within the 10th student's weight.

Weight	No of Students	Cumulative Frequency
25 – 28	6	6
28 – 31	8	6 + 8 = 14
31 – 34	7	14 + 7 = 21
34 – 37	10	21 + 10 = 31
37 – 40	x	31 + x

$$\frac{31 + x}{2} = 18 \Rightarrow x = 34 - 31 \Rightarrow x = 5$$

Assertion and Reason

1. (*c*) As, we know, Mean $(\bar{x})$ is given by

$$\bar{x} = \frac{\Sigma f_i x_i}{\Sigma f_i} = \frac{28 + 70 + 150 + 260 + 400 + 570}{107} = 13.81$$

Assertion (A) is true but reason (R) is false.

2. (*d*) By arranging the terms in ascending order,

0, 5, 11, 19, 21, 27, 30, 36, 42, 50, 52

$$\text{Median value} = \left(\frac{11+1}{2}\right)^{\text{th}} = 6^{\text{th}} \text{ value} = 27$$

Assertion (A) is false but reason (R) is true.

3. (*a*) Assertion: $\text{Median} = \frac{1}{3}(\text{mode} + 2\text{ mean})$

$$= \frac{1}{3}(60 + 2 \times 66) = 64$$

Both assertion (A) and reason (R) are true but reason is the correct explanation of assertion.

4. (*a*) As the maximum frequency is 8 and the class corresponding to it i.e.,30-40 is the modal-class.

Both assertion (A) and reason (R) are true and reason is the correct explanation of the assertion.

Subjective Questions

Very Short Answer Type Questions

1.

x	f	fx
5	4	20
6	10	60
7	15	105
8	11	88
9	3	27
Total	$N = \Sigma f_i = 43$	$\Sigma f_i x_i = 300$

(1 M)

$\therefore$ Mean $= \frac{\Sigma f_i x_i}{\Sigma f_i} = \frac{300}{43} = 6.976$ *(1 M)*

2. Required median =

$$\frac{\left(\frac{100}{2}\right)^{th} \text{term} + \left(\frac{100}{2}+1\right)^{th} \text{term}}{2} = \frac{50+51}{2} = 50.5$$ *(2 M)*

3. We know that the sum of first n natural numbers $= \frac{n(n+1)}{2}$

(1 M)

Mean of the first n natural numbers = Sum of first n natural numbers/n

$$= \frac{\left[\frac{n(n+1)}{2}\right]}{n} = \frac{(n+1)}{2}$$ *(½ M)*

According to the given question,

$$\Rightarrow \frac{(n+1)}{2} = 15 \Rightarrow n + 1 = 30 \Rightarrow n = 29$$ *(½ M)*

4. The cumulative frequency distribution of the given distribution is

Class	Frequency	Cumulative frequency
12.5–17.5	2	2
17.5–22.5	22	24
22.5–27.5	19	43
27.5–32.5	14	57
32.5–37.5	13	70

(2 M)

5. Arranging the data in the form of a frequency table, we have

Value	Tally	Frequency
110	||	2
120	||||	4
130	||	2
140	||	2

(1 M)

Since the value 120 occurs maximum number of times i.e. 4. Hence, the modal value is 120. *(1 M)*

6. Arranging the data in ascending order, we have 25, 31, 32, 35, 37, 39, 42, 43, 45, 46, 49.

Here, the number of observations $n = 11$ (odd) *(1 M)*

$\therefore$ Median = Value of $\left(\frac{11+1}{2}\right)^{th}$ observation= Value of 6th observation = 39.

Hence, The median of the given data is 39. *(1 M)*

Short Answer Type Questions

1. In order to find the mean value, we will use direct method.

Class-mark $(x_i) = \frac{\text{upper limit} + \text{lower limit}}{2}$

Class Interval	f_i	Class Mark (x_i)	$f_i x_i$
10 – 30	90	$\frac{10+30}{2} = 20$	1800
30 – 50	20	$\frac{30+50}{2} = 40$	800
50 – 70	30	$\frac{50+70}{2} = 60$	1800
70 – 90	20	$\frac{70+90}{2} = 80$	1600
90 – 110	40	$\frac{90+110}{2} = 100$	4000
	$\Sigma f_i = 200$		$\Sigma f_i x_i = 10000$

(2 M)

Mean $(\overline{X}) = \frac{\Sigma f_i x_i}{\Sigma f_i} = \frac{10000}{200} = 50$ *(1 M)*

2. Completes the frequency distribution table as:

Rainfall (in mm)	Number of days / Frequency (f)	Class-mark (x)	(fx)
0-20 mm	7	10	70
20-40 mm	X	30	$30X$
40-60 mm	10	50	500
60-80 mm	4	70	280
Total	$21 + X$		$850 + 30X$

(2 M)

The equation for mean as:

$$\frac{850+30X}{21+X} = 35 \Rightarrow 850 + 30X = 735 + 35X$$

$\Rightarrow 5X = 115 \Rightarrow X = 23$ *(1 M)*

3. To convert the given data into frequency distribution, we can write above 30 as 30-40, above 40 as 40-50 and so on. Whereas corresponding frequencies (f_i) can be found by subtracting the next number of plants from the current number of plants.

Height (in cm)	No. of Plants
30–40	34 – 30 = 4
40–50	30 – 27 = 3
50–60	27 – 19 = 8
60–70	19 – 8 = 11
70–80	8 – 2 = 6
80–90	2

(1 M)

$\therefore$ Modal class is 60-70 because it is having maximum frequency that is 11.

Here, $l = 60, f_1 = 11, f_0 = 8, f_2 = 6$ and $h = 10$. *(1 M)*

$\therefore$ Mode

$$= l + \frac{f_1 - f_0}{2f_1 - f_0 - f_2} \times h = 60 + \frac{11-8}{22-8-6} \times 10$$

$$= 60 + \frac{3 \times 10}{22 - 14} = 60 + 3.75 = 63.75$$

Hence, modal value is 63.75. *(1 M)*

4. Arranging the data in ascending order, we get 20, 22, 23, 24, 25, 26, 28, 31, 32, 33, 34, 35

Here, the number of observations $n = 12$ (even). *(1 M)*

$\therefore$ Median

$$= \frac{\text{Value of} \left(\frac{12}{2}\right)^{th} \text{observation} + \text{Value of} \left(\frac{12}{2}+1\right)^{th} \text{observation}}{2}$$

(1 M)

$$\Rightarrow \text{Median} = \frac{\text{Value of } 6^{th} \text{ obervation} + \text{Value of } 7^{th} \text{ observation}}{2}$$

$$\therefore \text{Median} = \frac{26 + 28}{2} = 27$$

Hence, median of the given data is 27. *(1 M)*

5.

Length [in mm]	Number of leaves (f)	C.I	Mid x	d	fd
118–126	3	117.5 – 126.5	122	–27	–81
127–135	5	126.5 – 135.5	131	–18	–90
136–144	9	135.5 – 144.5	140	–9	–81
145–153	12	144.5 – 153.5	$a = 149$	0	0
154–162	5	153.5 – 162.5	158	9	45
163–171	4	162.5 – 171.5	167	18	72
172–180	2	171.5 – 180.5	176	27	54

(2 M)

Here $a = 149$

$$\text{Mean} = a + \frac{\Sigma fd}{\Sigma f} = 149 + \frac{-8}{40}$$ *(½ M)*

$= 149 - 2.025 = 146.975$

Average length of the leaves = 146.975 *(½ M)*

Long Answer Type Questions

1.

Life time (in hours)	Number of lamps	Mid x	d	fd
1500–2000	14	1750	-1500	-21000
2000–2500	56	2250	-1000	-56000
2500–3000	60	2750	-500	-30000
3000–3500	86	3250	0	0
3500–4000	74	3750	500	37000
4500–4500	62	3750	1000	62000
4500–5000	48	4250	1500	72000
	400			64000

(2 M)

$$\text{Mean } a + \frac{\Sigma fd}{\Sigma f}$$ *(½ M)*

$a = 3250$ *(½ M)*

$$\text{Mean} = 3250 + \frac{64000}{400} = 3250 + 160 = 3410$$ *(1 M)*

Average life of lamp is 3410 hr *(1 M)*

2. In order to find the value of p, we will use direct method.

x_i	f_i	$f_i x_i$
4	5	20
6	6	36
7	4	28
$p + 4$	10	$(p+4)(10) = 10p + 40$
12	8	96
14	7	98
Total	$\Sigma f_i = 40$	$\Sigma f_i x_i = 318 + 10p$

(2 M)

As we know, Mean $\bar{x} = \frac{\Sigma f_i . x_i}{\Sigma f_i} = \frac{318 + 10.p}{40}$ *(1 M)*

$\therefore 9.2 = \frac{318 + 10.p}{40} \Rightarrow 318 + 10.p = 368 \Rightarrow 10p = 50$ *(1 M)*

$\Rightarrow p = 5$ *(1 M)*

3. To convert the given data into frequency distribution, we can write below 10 as 0-10, below 20 as 10-20 and so on. Whereas corresponding frequencies (f_i) can be found by subtracting the previous number of students from the current number of students.

Find the class-mark using the formula: *(1 M)*

$$\text{Class} - \text{mark}(x_i) = \frac{\text{lower class limit} + \text{upper class limit}}{2}$$

Let us assumed mean, $a = 55$

Class interval	Frequency (f_i)	Class-mark (x_i)	$u_i = \frac{x_i - 55}{10}$	$f_i u_i$
0 – 10	5	5	$\frac{5-55}{10} = -5$	–25
10 – 20	9 – 5 = 4	15	$\frac{15-55}{10} = -4$	–16
20 – 30	17 – 9 = 8	25	$\frac{25-55}{10} = -3$	–24
30 – 40	29 – 17 = 12	35	$\frac{35-55}{10} = -2$	–24
40 – 50	45 – 29 = 16	45	$\frac{45-55}{10} = -1$	–16
50 – 60	60 – 45 = 15	$a = 55$	$\frac{55-55}{10} = 0$	0
60 – 70	70 – 60 = 10	65	$\frac{65-55}{10} = 1$	10
70 – 80	78 – 70 = 8	75	$\frac{75-55}{10} = 2$	16
80 – 90	83 – 78 = 5	85	$\frac{85-55}{10} = 3$	15
90 –100	85 – 83 = 2	95	$\frac{95-55}{10} = 4$	8
Total	$\sum f_i = 85$			$\sum f_i u_i = -56$

(2 M)

Here, $a = 55$, $h = 10$, $\Sigma f_i = 85$, $\Sigma f_i u_i = -56$ *(1 M)*

$$\text{Mean } (\bar{x}) = a + \frac{\sum f_i u_i}{\sum f_i} \times h = 55 + \frac{-56}{85} \times 10$$

$= 55 - 6.59 = 48.41$

Hence, mean mark = 48.41. *(1 M)*

4. To find out the missing frequency, use the direct mean formula.

Given, mean $\bar{x} = 18$

Class interval	Number of children (f_i)	Mid-point (x_i)	$f_i x_i$
11–13	7	12	84
13–15	6	14	84
15–17	9	16	144
17–19	13	$18 = \bar{x}$	234
19–21	f	20	$20f$
21–23	5	22	110
23–25	4	24	96
Total	$\Sigma f_i = 44 + f$		$\Sigma f_i x_i = 752 + 20f$

(2 M)

The mean $\bar{x}$ of the given data is given by:

$$= \bar{x} = \frac{\sum f_i x_i}{\sum f_i} = \frac{(752 + 20f)}{(44 + f)} \quad (1\ M)$$

Now substitute the values and equate to find the missing frequency (f)

$$\Rightarrow 18 = \frac{(752 + 20f)}{(44 + f)}$$

$\Rightarrow 18(44 + f) = (752 + 20f)$ *(1 M)*

$\Rightarrow 792 + 18f = 752 + 20f \Rightarrow 792 - 752 = 20f - 18f$

$\Rightarrow 40 = 2f \Rightarrow f = 20$

So, the missing frequency, $f = 20$. *(1 M)*

5.

Marks obtained	Number of students	Cumulative frequency
20 – 30	p	p
30 – 40	15	$p + 15$
40 – 50	25	$p + 40$
50 – 60	20	$p + 60$
60 – 70	q	$p + q + 60$
70 – 80	8	$p + q + 68$
80 – 90	10	$p + q + 78$
	90	

(1 M)

Here, $p + q + 78 = 90$ *(½ M)*

$p + q = 12$

$$\text{Median} = l + \left(\frac{\frac{N}{2} - Cf}{f}\right) \times h \quad (½\ M)$$

$$50 = 50 + \frac{45 - (p + 40)}{20}.10 \quad (½\ M)$$

$$\Rightarrow \frac{45 - (p + 40)}{20}.10 = 0 \quad (½\ M)$$

$\Rightarrow 45 - (p + 40) = 0 \Rightarrow p = 5$ *(½ M)*

$\Rightarrow 5 + q = 12 \Rightarrow q = 7$ *(½ M)*

$$\text{Mode} = l + \frac{f_1 - f_0}{2f_1 - f_0 - f_2}.h = 40 + \frac{25 - 15}{2(25) - 15 - 20}.10$$

$$= 40 + \frac{100}{15} = 40 + 6.67 = 46.67 \quad (1\ M)$$

6. Here, the greatest frequency is 10.

Modal class = 30 – 35,

$l = 30$,

Class size (h) = 5,

$f_1 = 10, f_0 = 9$ and $f_2 = 3$ *(1 M)*

Mode Formula:

$$\text{Mode} = l + \left[\frac{(f_1 - f_0)}{(2f_1 - f_0 - f_2)}\right] \times h$$

Substitute the values in the given formula

$$\text{Mode} = 30 + \left(\frac{(10-9)}{20-9-3}\right) \times 5$$

$$\text{Mode} = 30 + \left(\frac{5}{8}\right) = 30 + 0.625 = 30.625$$ *(1 M)*

Therefore, the mode of the given data = 30.625

Calculate the Mean:

The class mark using the formula,

$$x_i = \frac{\text{upper limit + lower limit}}{2}$$

Let us assumed mean, $a = 32.5$ and class size $h = 5$

Class interval	Frequency (f_i)	Class mark	$u_i = \frac{x_i - a}{h}$	$f_i u_i$
15–20	3	17.5	–3	-9
20–25	8	22.5	–2	–16
25–30	9	27.5	–1	–9
30–35	10	32.5=a	0	0
35–40	3	37.5	1	3
40–45	0	42.5	2	0
45–50	0	47.5	3	0
50–55	2	52.5	4	8
	$\Sigma f_i = 35$			$\Sigma f_i u_i = -23$

(2 M)

$$\text{Mean} = a + \left(\frac{\sum f_i u_i}{\sum f_i}\right) \times h$$

$$= 32.5 + \left(\frac{-23}{35}\right) \times 5 = 32.5 - \frac{23}{7} = 29.22$$

Therefore, mean = 29.22 *(1 M)*

7. The cumulative frequency of the given data as follows:

Class Interval	Frequency (f)	Cumulative frequency (Cf)
65–85	4	4
85–105	5	4 + 5 = 9
105–125	13	9 + 13 = 22
125–145	20	22 + 20 = 42
145–165	14	42 + 14 = 56
165–185	8	56 + 8 = 64
185–205	4	64 + 4 = 68
	$N = 68$	

(1 M)

From the table, it is observed that, $N = 68$ and hence $\frac{N}{2} = 34$

Hence, the median class is 125–145 with cumulative frequency = 42

lower limit (l) of median class interval = 125

cumulative frequnecy (Cf) preceding to the median class frequency = 22

frequency (f) of the class interval to which median belongs = 20

Class size, $h = 20$

$$\text{Median} = l + \left(\frac{\frac{N}{2} - Cf}{f}\right) \times h = 125 + \left(\frac{(34-22)}{20}\right) \times 20 = 137$$

Therefore, median = 137

To calculate the mode:

Modal class = 125 – 145,

$f_1 = 20, f_0 = 13, f_2 = 14$ & $h = 20$

$$\therefore \quad \text{Mode} = l + \left[\frac{(f_1 - f_0)}{(2f_1 - f_0 - f_2)}\right] \times h$$

$$= 125 + \left(\frac{(20-13)}{(40-13-14)}\right) \times 20 = 125 + \left(\frac{140}{13}\right) = 135.77$$

Therefore, mode = 135.77 *(1 M)*

Calculate the Mean:

Class Interval	f_i	x_i	$d_i = x_i - a$	$u_i = \frac{d_i}{h}$	$f_i u_i$
65–85	4	75	–60	–3	–12
85–105	5	95	–40	–2	–10
105–125	13	115	–20	–1	–13
125–145	20	135=a	0	0	0
145–165	14	155	20	1	14
165–185	8	175	40	2	16
185–205	4	195	60	3	12
	$\Sigma f_i = 68$				$\Sigma f_i u_i = 7$

(2 M)

$$\therefore \bar{x} = a + h\frac{\sum f_i u_i}{\sum f_i} = 135 + 20\left(\frac{7}{68}\right) = 135 + 2.05 = 137.05$$

In this case, mean, median and mode are more/less equal in this distribution. *(1 M)*

8. As we can see the class intervals are not continuous. There is a gap of 1 between two class intervals.

So, we have to reduce 0.5 from the lower limit and add 0.5 in the upper limit.

Class Interval	Frequency (f)	Cumulative frequency (Cf)
117.5–126.5	3	3
126.5–135.5	5	8
135.5–144.5	9	17
144.5–153.5	12	29
153.5–162.5	5	34
162.5–171.5	4	38
171.5–180.5	2	40

(2 M)

So, the data obtained are:

$N = 40$ i.e., $\frac{N}{2} = 20$

$\therefore$ Median class = 144.5 – 153.5, $l = 144.5$, $Cf = 17$, $f = 12$ & $h = 9$ (1 M)

$\therefore$ Median $= l + \left(\frac{\frac{N}{2} - Cf}{f}\right) \times h$ (1 M)

$= 144.5 + \left(\frac{(20-17)}{12}\right) \times 9 = 144.5 + \left(\frac{9}{4}\right) = 146.75$ mm

Therefore, the median length of the leaves = 146.75 mm. (1 M)

Case Based Questions

Case Based-I

(i) The highest frequency = 70

$\therefore$ Maximum number of student the age group = 10 – 12

(ii) Here $f_1 = 70, f_0 = 58$ and $f_2 = 42$

Succeeding class of the modal class = 42

OR

Here $f_1 = 70, f_0 = 58, f_2 = 42$ and $h = 2$

$$\text{Mode} = 10 + \left(\frac{70-58}{2\times70-58-42}\right)\times 2$$

$$= 10 + \frac{12}{40}\times 2 = 10 + 0.6 = 10.6 \text{ years}$$

(iii) Modal class = 10 – 12

$\therefore$ lower limit = 10

Case Based-II

(i)

Class interval	(f_i)	x_i	$d = x_i - a$	$f_i d_i$
30–40	80	35	–20	–1600
40–50	110	45	–10	–1100
50–60	120	55 = a	0	0
60–70	70	65	10	700
70–80	40	75	20	800
	$\Sigma f_i = 420$			$\Sigma f_i d_i = -1200$

$a = 55$ (Let)

(ii) Mean $= a + \frac{\sum f_i d_i}{\sum f_i} = 55 - \frac{1200}{420} = 55 - 2.86 = 52.14$

OR

By a vehicle received average toll tax = ₹ 52.14

Total number of vehicles = 420

$\therefore$ Average toll tax received in a day

= 52.14 × 420 = ₹ 21898.80.

(iii) The value of $d_i = -20, -10, 0, 10, 20$

$\therefore |d_i|_{\min} = 0$

Case Based-III

(i) (c) Since numbers of students are 100,

$15 + 18 + 21 + 29 + p = 100$

$\Rightarrow 83 + p = 100 \Rightarrow p = 100 - 83 = 17$

(ii) (c) Class 60 – 80 has the maximum frequency 29, therefore this is modal class. Lower limit of this class is 60.

(iii) (d) Here, $l = 60, f_1 = 29, f_0 = 21, f_2 = 17$ and $h = 20$

$$\text{Mode} = l + \left(\frac{f_1 - f_0}{2f_1 - f_0 - f_2}\right)\times h$$

$$= 60 + \left(\frac{29-21}{2\times29-21-17}\right)\times 20 = 60 + \left(\frac{8}{58-38}\right)\times 20$$

$$= 60 + \frac{8}{20}\times 20 = 68$$

(iv) (a) Given Mean = 53

$$\text{Median} = \frac{\text{Mode} + 2\,\text{Mean}}{3}$$

$$= \frac{68 + 2\times 53}{3} = \frac{68+106}{3} = \frac{174}{3} = 58$$

(v) (c) Since median is 58 and corresponding class is 40–60. Upper limit of this class is 60.

Case Based-IV

(i) (c) We have for table 1

Age (in years)	No. of Cases
5 – 15	6
15 – 25	11
25 – 35	21
35 – 45	23
45 – 55	14
55 – 65	5

Since 23 is the maximum frequency, therefore 35 – 45 is the modal class.

$\therefore$ Mode $= l + \dfrac{f_1 - f_0}{2f_1 - f_0 - f_2} \times h$

$= 35 + \dfrac{23-21}{2\times 23 - 21 - 14} \times 10 = 35 + \dfrac{20}{11} = 35 + 1.82 = 36.82$

(ii) (c) Modal class is 35 – 45.

$\therefore$ Upper limit is 45.

(iii) (d) We have,

Age (in years)	No. of cases (f_i)	Mid value (x_i)	f_ix_i
5 – 15	6	10	60
15 – 25	11	20	220
25 – 35	21	30	630
35 – 45	23	40	920
45 – 55	14	50	700
55 – 65	5	60	300
Total	**80**		**2830**

$\therefore$ Average age $= \dfrac{\Sigma f_ix_i}{\Sigma f_i} = \dfrac{2830}{80} = 35.38 \approx 35.4$

(iv) (a) We have for table 2

Age (in years)	No. of cases	cf
5 – 15	8	8
15 – 25	16	24
25 – 35	10	34
35 – 45	42	76
45 – 55	24	100
55 – 65	12	112
Total	**112**	

We have, 42 is the maximum frequency, therefore 35 – 45 is the modal class.

$\therefore$ Mode $= l + \dfrac{f_1 - f_0}{2f_1 - f_0 - f_2} \times h$

$= 35 + \dfrac{42-10}{2\times 42 - 10 - 24} \times 10 = 35 + \dfrac{320}{50} = 35 + 6.4 = 41.4$

(v) (b) We have, $N = 112 \Rightarrow \dfrac{N}{2} = 56$

$\therefore$ 76 is just greater than 56 in cumulative frequency.

$\therefore$ 35 – 45 is the median class.

$\therefore$ Median $= l + \dfrac{\frac{N}{2} - cf}{f} \times h = 56$

$= 35 + \dfrac{56-34}{42} \times 10 = 56 = 35 + \dfrac{220}{42} = 40.23 \approx 40.2$

Case Based-V

(i) (c) From colony A, we have

Weekly consumption (in units)	No. of families (f_i)	cf
0 – 10	16	16
10 – 20	12	28
20 – 30	18	46
30 – 40	6	52
40 – 50	4	56
50 – 60	0	56

We have, $N = 56 \Rightarrow \dfrac{N}{2} = 28$

$\therefore$ 20 – 30 is the median class.

$\therefore$ Median $= l + \dfrac{\frac{N}{2} - Cf}{f} \times h = 20 + \dfrac{28-28}{18} \times 10 = 20$

(ii) (a) From colony A

Class	Frequency (f_i)	Mid value (x_i)	f_ix_i
0 – 10	16	5	80
10 – 20	12	15	180
20 – 30	18	25	450
30 – 40	6	35	210
40 – 50	4	45	180
50 – 60	0	55	0
Total	**56**		**1100**

$\therefore$ Mean $= \dfrac{\Sigma f_ix_i}{\Sigma f_i} = \dfrac{1100}{56} = 19.64$

(iii) (c) Since 18 is the maximum frequency in the given table, therefore 20 – 30 is the modal class.

(iv) (b) From the given table for colony B, we have

Weekly Consumption (in units)	No. of families
0 – 10	0
10 – 20	5
20 – 30	10
30 – 40	20
40 – 50	40
50 – 60	5

Since 40 is the maximum frequency, therefore 40 – 50 is the modal class.

$\therefore$ Mode $= l + \dfrac{f_1 - f_0}{2f_1 - f_0 - f_2} \times h = 40 + \dfrac{40-20}{80-20-5} \times 10$

$= 40 + \dfrac{200}{55} = 40 + 3.63 = 43.63 \approx 43.6$

(v) (c) We have,

Class	Frequency (f_i)	Mid value (x_i)	f_ix_i
0 – 10	0	5	0
10 – 20	5	15	75
20 – 30	10	25	250
30 – 40	20	35	700
40 – 50	40	45	1800
50 – 60	5	55	275
Total	**80**		**3100**

$\therefore$ Mean $= \dfrac{\Sigma f_ix_i}{\Sigma f_i} = \dfrac{3100}{80} = 38.75$

❑❑❑

PROBABILITY

14

"Probability is used by quantitative traders to guess if stocks will go up or down. They use math to make these guesses and decide which stocks to buy. It's a way of picking stocks that could make money, like choosing the right card in a game. This helps them make good choices and try to earn more money from their investments."

SYLLABUS & WEIGHTAGE

List of Concept Names	Years				
	2021	2022	2023	2024	2024
Probability (Classical definition of Probability, Simple problems on finding the probability of an event.)	Exam not Conducted	–	2 Q (1 M each) 1 Q (3 M)	2 Q (1 M each) 1 Q (2 M)	3 Q (1 M each) 1 Q (2 M)

CONCEPT MAP

To Access One Shot Revision Video Scan This QR Code

Complementary Event

When there are two events such that one event can occur if and only if the other does not take place then such events are known as complementary events in probability. The sum of the probability of complementary events will always be equal to 1. The complement of A is denoted by $\overline{A}$.

Compound Event

An event which has more than one elementary event is called a compound event.

For example, the probability of rolling an even number on a die, then tossing a head on a coin.

Impossible Event

The events whose probability is zero are called impossible events.

For example, the event of drawing a black ball from a bag containing three red and four white balls is an impossible event.

Elementary Event

An event having only one outcome or any single outcome of an experiment is called an elementary event.

For example, the probability of getting a 3 when a die is tossed.

- Sum of probability of all elementary events is 1.

Event

A desired outcome of the random experiment is known as an event of the random experiment e.g., Getting a tail on tossing a coin, getting a red card when a card is drawn from a pack of 52 cards.

Sure or Certain Event

The events whose probability is one are called sure/certain events.

For example, the event of drawing a black ball from a bag containing ninety red balls is a sure event.

Experiment: An experiment refers to a specific action or process that produces an outcome. For example, tossing a coin, rolling a die, or selecting a card from a deck.

Probability

Definition: Probability is the branch of mathematics that deals with the study of random events or outcomes. It is the measure of the likelihood or chance that an event will occur.

Theoretical Probability

The theoretical (or classical) probability of an event E is given by

$$P(E) = \frac{\text{Number of outcomes favourable to } E}{\text{Number of all possible outcomes of the experiment}}$$

Experimental Probability

The experimental (or empirical) probability of an event E is given by

$$P(E) = \frac{\text{Number of trials in which the event happened}}{\text{Total number of trials}}$$

1 PROBABILITY

Important Terms

- **Probability:** Probability is the branch of mathematics that deals with the study of random events or outcomes. It is the measure of the likelihood or chance that an event will occur.
- **Experimental Probability:** The experimental or empirical probability of an event is based on result of actual experiments.
- **Theoretical Probability:** In the theoretical probability, we predict the results without actually performing the experiment on the basis of certain assumptions.
- **Experiment:** An experiment is any process or activity which produces some well-defined outcomes. There are two types of experiment
  - (i) Random Experiment
  - (ii) Deterministic Experiment
- **Random experiment:** An experiment is said to be a random experiment:
  - (i) If the experiment has more than 1 outcome.
  - (ii) If it is not possible to predict the outcomes of an experiment in advance.

    e.g., tossing a coin, throwing a dice, selecting a card, selecting an object etc.
- **Deterministic Experiment:** The experiments which have only one possible result or outcome i.e. whose result is certain or unique are called deterministic or predictable experiments. E.g., tossing a coin having either head or tail on both sides, as it gives the same result while tossing the coin any number of times.
- **Sample Space:** All possible outcomes of a random experiment form the sample space of the random experiment. For example, if a coin is tossed twice the possible outcomes are *HH*, *HT*, *TH* and *TT*. These four possible outcomes form the sample space of this random experiments.
- **Event:** A desired outcome of the random experiment is known as an event of the random experiment e.g., Getting a tail on tossing a coin, getting a red card when a card is drawn from a pack of 52 cards.
- **Elementary Event:** An event having only one outcome or any single outcome of an experiment is called an elementary event. e.g., In the experiment of tossing a coin, the possible outcomes are *H* and *T*. Any one outcome like *H* is called an elementary event.
- **Compound Event:** An event which has more than one elementary event is called a compound event. For example, if we toss two coins simultaneously, then the probability of getting at least one head is a compound event as it contains three elementary events i.e. *HH*, *HT*, *TH*.
- **Equally likely events:** Those events are said to be equally likely in which the chances of happening of all the outcomes of an experiment are equal. For example, In rolling a dice the probability of getting 1, 2 or any other number are equally likely events, since the probabilities of each event are equal.
- **Complementary events:** When there are two events such that one event can occur if and only if the other does not take place then such events are known as complementary events in probability. The sum of the probability of complementary events will always be equal to 1.
- **Sure Events:** The events whose probability is one are called sure/certain events.
- **Impossible Events:** The events whose probability is zero are called impossible events.

Important Formulas

- The experimental (or empirical) probability of an event E is given by

$$P(E)=\frac{\text{Number of trials in which the event happened}}{\text{Total number of trials}}$$

- The theoretical (or classical) probability of an event E is given by

$$P(E)=\frac{\text{Number of outcomes favourable to } E}{\text{Number of all possible outcomes of the experiment}}$$

- For an event $E, P(\bar{E})=1-P(E)$, where the event $\bar{E}$ representing 'not E' is the complement of the event E.

Doctor: "Sir, the surgery has a 50% survival rate, but don't worry, my last 20 patients have all survived"

Normal People **Mathematician**

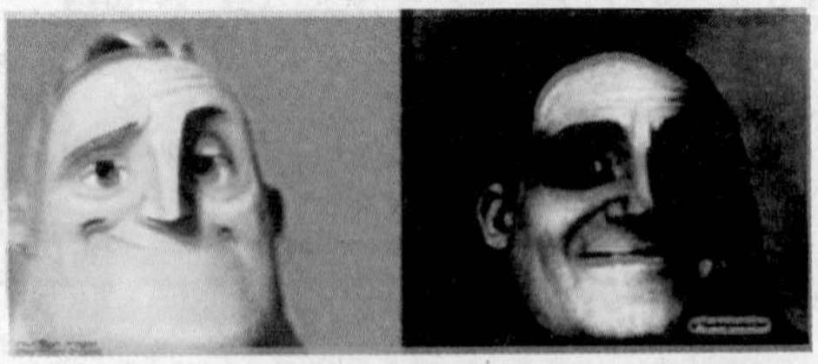

Important Concepts

- The experimental probability of an event approaches to its theoretical probability, if the number of trials of an experiment is very large.
- The sum of the probabilities of all the elementary events of an experiment is 1.

- ❑ Probability of an event can never be negative.
- ❑ Probability of happening of an event always lies between 0 and 1.
- ❑ In case of one-coin, possible outcomes are *H* and *T*.
- ❑ In case of two coins, possible outcomes are *HH*, *HT*, *TH* and *TT*.
- ❑ In case of three coins, possible outcomes are *HHH*, *HHT*, *HTH*, *HTT*, *THH*, *THT*, *TTH*, *TTT*.

Virat Kohli after losing 5 consecutive tosses

Kohli to toss: Are you defying the laws of probability?

- ❑ A deck of playing cards consists of 52 cards which are divided into 4 suits of 13 cards each: spades (♠), hearts (♥), diamonds (♦) and clubs (♣). Clubs and spades are of black colour, while hearts and diamonds are of red colour.
- ❑ Each suit consists of an ace, one king, one queen, one jack and 9 other cards numbered from 2 to 10.
- ❑ King, Queen and Jack are face cards i.e., each suite has 3 face cards.
- ❑ In case of a die, possible outcomes are 1, 2, 3, 4, 5 and 6.
- ❑ In case of two dice, possible outcomes are

  (1, 1) (1, 2) (1, 3) (1, 4) (1, 5) (1, 6)
  (2, 1) (2, 2) (2, 3) (2, 4) (2, 5) (2, 6)
  (3, 1) (3, 2) (3, 3) (3, 4) (3, 5) (3, 6)
  (4, 1) (4, 2) (4, 3) (4, 4) (4, 5) (4, 6)
  (5, 1) (5, 2) (5, 3) (5, 4) (5, 5) (5, 6)
  (6, 1) (6, 2) (6, 3) (6, 4) (6, 5) (6, 6)

Real Life Applications

- ❑ Have you ever seen weather forecast reports in television? How do you think they are able to predict the weather?

  The weather forecast deals by Meteorological Department. They use specific tools and techniques to measure daily maximum and minimum temperatures, direction and speed of wind, air pressures, relative humidity, patterns of cloud formation and other meteorological variables daily at weather stations across the world. Then, they look at all the other historical databases of the days, which have similar characteristics of temperature, wind speed, air pressure, etc. Suppose they find out that 45 out of 100 similar days in the past, it had rained. By using these reports, the weather forecaster will announce on television and radio that there is a 45% chance that rain may occur. Hence, we can say that weather forecasting is completely based on probability.

- ❑ Traffic on roads is affected by things like how many vehicles are on the road, how the roads are shaped, and how people drive. Traffic experts use special models that use probability (chance) to guess how traffic will behave. These models can predict things like where traffic jams might happen and how long it might take to get somewhere. By using these models, engineers and planners can make roads work better, time traffic lights better, and make rules that keep people safer on the roads.

Different Problem Types

Type I: Calculating the Probability of Events

A standard deck of playing cards contains 52 cards, including 4 suits (hearts, diamonds, clubs, spades), with each suit having 13 cards (Ace through King). If a card is randomly selected from the deck, what is the probability that it is a face card (Jack, Queen, or King)?

Solution:

Step I: Understand the problem and identify the sample space when a card is selected from the deck, the possible outcomes are the 52 cards in the deck. Sample Space (S): {Ace of Hearts, 2 of Hearts,..., King of Spades}

Step II: Determine the favourable outcomes here, we are interested in the probability of selecting a face card (Jack, Queen, or King). Favorable Outcome (F): {Jack of Hearts, Queen of Hearts, King of Hearts, ..., King of Spades} There are a total of 12 face cards in the deck (3 in each suit).

Step III: Probability (P) is calculated as the ratio of favourable outcomes to the total possible outcomes.

$$P = (\text{Face Card}) = \frac{\text{Number of face Cards}}{\text{Total number of cards}} = \frac{12}{52}$$

Example 1: Find the probability of rolling an even number on a fair six-sided die.

Solution: A fair six-sided die has 6 possible outcomes (numbers 1 through 6). Out of these, there are 3 even numbers (2, 4, and 6).

$$\text{Probability of rolling an even number} = \frac{\text{Total no. of even number}}{\text{Total possible outcomes}}$$

$$\text{Probability} = \frac{3}{6} = \frac{1}{2} = 0.5$$

Therefore, the probability of rolling an even number on a fair six-sided die is $\frac{1}{2}$ or 0.5, which is equivalent to 50%.

Example 2: A bag contains 5 red balls, 3 blue balls, and 2 green balls. If a ball is randomly selected from the bag, what is the probability that it is blue?

Solution: Total number of balls in the bag = 5(red) + 3 (blue) + 2 (green) = 10 balls

$$P(\text{Blue}) = \frac{\text{Number of blue balls}}{\text{Total number of balls}} = \frac{3}{10} = 0.3$$

So, the probability of selecting a blue ball from the bag is 0.3 or 30%.

Example 3: A fair coin is flipped three times. What is the probability of getting exactly two heads?

Solution: Total number of possible outcomes when flipping a coin three times = 2^3 = 8 outcomes (HHH, HHT, HTH, THH, HTT, THT, TTH, TTT)

Number of outcomes with exactly two heads = 3 (HHT,HTH,THH)

$$P(\text{Two Heads}) = \frac{\text{Number of favorable outcomes}}{\text{Total outcomes}} = \frac{3}{8} = 0.375$$

So, the probability of getting exactly two heads when flipping a fair coin three times is 0.375 or 37.5%

Example 4: A box contains 4 black socks, 3 white socks, and 2 grey socks. If two socks are drawn at random without replacement, what is the probability that both socks are white?

Solution: Total number of socks in the box = 4 (black) + 3 (white) + 2 (grey) = 9 socks Probability of drawing a white sock on the first draw = P(White on first draw) $= \frac{3}{9} = \frac{1}{3}$ Probability of drawing a white sock on the second draw, given that the first was white and not replaced = P (White on second draw) $= \frac{2}{8} = \frac{1}{4}$

Probability of both socks being white = P (Both White) = P (White on first draw) × P (White on second draw)

$$= \frac{1}{3} \times \frac{1}{4} = \frac{1}{12} \approx 0.083$$

So, the probability of drawing two white socks from the box is approximately 0.083 or 8.3%.

COMPETENCY BASED SOLVED EXAMPLES

Multiple Choice Questions

(1 M)

1. When a die is thrown, the probability of getting an even number less than 4 is *(Cr)* (CBSE SQP, 2023)

(a) $\frac{1}{4}$ (b) 0

(c) $\frac{1}{2}$ (d) $\frac{1}{6}$

Sol. We have,

Even number less than 4 = {2}

Probability of getting an even number less than 4 = $\frac{1}{6}$

2. One ticket is drawn at random from a bag containing tickets numbered 1 to 40. The probability that the selected ticket has a number which is a multiple of 5 is *(Cr)* (NCERT Exemplar)

(a) $\frac{1}{5}$ (b) $\frac{3}{5}$ (c) $\frac{4}{5}$ (d) $\frac{1}{3}$

Sol. Total no. of outcomes = 40

No. of favourable outcomes which are multiple of 5 are 5, 10, 15, 20, 25, 30, 35 and 40.

Thus, $P(\text{getting a multiple of 5}) = \frac{\text{No. of multiples of 5}}{\text{Total outcomes}}$

$= \frac{8}{40} = \frac{1}{5}$

3. If a pair of dice is thrown once, then what is the probability of getting a sum of 8? *(Ap)* (CBSE, 2020)

(a) $\frac{5}{36}$ (b) $\frac{7}{36}$ (c) $\frac{1}{36}$ (d) $\frac{1}{6}$

Sol. Favorable outcomes = {(2, 6), (3, 5), (4, 4), (5, 3), (6, 2)}

Thus, P(sum of 8 with two dice) = $\frac{5}{36}$

Therefore the probability that we get the sum as 8 when two dice are thrown = $\frac{5}{36}$

4. A school has five houses *A*, *B*, *C*, *D* and *E*. A class has 23 students, 4 from house *A*, 8 from house *B*, 5 from house *C*, 2 from house *D* and rest from house *E*. A single student is selected at random to be the class monitor. The probability that the selected student is not from *A*, *B* and *C* is *(Un)* (NCERT Exemplar)

(a) $\frac{4}{23}$ (b) $\frac{6}{23}$ (c) $\frac{8}{23}$ (d) $\frac{17}{23}$

Sol. Total number of students, $n(S) = 23$

Number of students in houses *A*, *B* and *C*

$= 4 + 8 + 5 = 17$

$\therefore$ Remaining students = 23 – 17 = 6

Hence, $n(E) = 6$

So, probability that the selected students is not from *A*, *B* and *C is*

$P(E) = \frac{6}{23}$

5. Two coins are tossed simultaneously. The probability of getting at most one head is *(Ev)* (CBSE, 2020)

(a) $\frac{1}{4}$ (b) $\frac{1}{2}$ (c) $\frac{2}{3}$ (d) $\frac{3}{4}$

Sol. Two coin tossed

Total sample space = {*HH, HT, TH, TT*}

Sample space for getting atmost one head = {*TT, TH, HT*}

$P(S) = \frac{3}{4}$.

6. Two dices are thrown simultaneously. The probability of getting a sum of 9 is *(An)*

(a) $\frac{1}{10}$ (b) $\frac{1}{12}$ (c) $\frac{1}{9}$ (d) $\frac{4}{9}$

Sol. Total cases = 36

Total cases in which sum of 9 can be obtained are:

(5, 4), (4, 5), (6, 3), (3, 6) = 4

$\therefore P\text{ (sum of 9)} = \frac{4}{36} = \frac{1}{9}$

7. At a party, there is one last pizza slice and two people who want it. To decide who gets the last slice, two fair six-sided dice are rolled. If the largest number in the roll is:

- **1, 3 or 6, Ananya would get the last slice, and**
- **2, 4 or 5, Pranit would get it.**

In a random roll of dice, who has a higher chance of getting the last pizza slice? *(Un)* (CBSE CFPQ, 2023)

(Note: If the number on both the dice is the same, then consider that number as the large number.)

(a) Ananya

(b) Pranit

(c) Both have an equal chance

(d) cannot be answered without knowing the exact numbers in a roll.

Sol. S = {1.1, 1.2, 1.3, 1.4, 1.5, 1.6, 2.2, 2.3, 2.4, 2.5, 2.6, 3.3, 3.4, 3.5, 3.6, 4.4, 4.5, 4.6, 5.5, 5.6, 6.6)

Let *A* be the event of getting the largest number in the roll of Ananya's number

A = 1.1, 1.3, 2.3, 3.3, 1.6, 2.6, 3.6, 4.6, 5.6, 6.6

$\Rightarrow n(A) = 10$

Let B be the event of getting the largest number in the roll of Pranit's number.

$B = \{1.2, 2.2, 1.4, 2.4, 3.4, 4.4, 1.5, 2.5, 3.5, 4.5, 5.5)$

$\Rightarrow n(B) = 11$

$\because n(A) < n(B)$

So, the chances of event B is more

Hence, Pranit has a higher chance of getting the last pizza slice

8. A card is drawn at random from a well shuffled deck of 52 playing cards. The probability of getting a face card is: *(Cr)*

(a) $\frac{1}{2}$ (b) $\frac{3}{13}$ (c) $\frac{4}{13}$ (d) $\frac{1}{13}$

Sol. Total number of outcomes = 52

No. of face card = 12

$P(\text{getting a face card}) = \frac{12}{52} = \frac{3}{13}$

9. One card is drawn at random from a well-shuffled deck of 52 cards. What is the probability of getting a Jack? *(Re)* **(CBSE, 2020)**

(a) $\frac{3}{26}$ (b) $\frac{1}{52}$ (c) $\frac{1}{13}$ (d) $\frac{3}{52}$

Sol. Favourable number of outcomes i.e., numbers of jack cards = 4

Total number of outcomes = 52

Thus, probability $= \frac{4}{52} = \frac{1}{13}$

10. A single letter is selected at random from the word "COMMUNICATIONS". The probability that the selected letter is a vowel is *(Un)*

(a) $\frac{2}{14}$ (b) $\frac{6}{13}$ (c) $\frac{3}{7}$ (d) $\frac{1}{2}$

Sol. Total number of alphabets = 14

Number of favourable outcomes = 6

$\therefore$ Required probability $= \frac{6}{14} = \frac{3}{7}$

11. A two digit number is to be formed using the digits 3, 4, 7, 8 and 2 without repetition. The probability that it is an odd number is *(Ap)*

(a) $\frac{2}{5}$ (b) $\frac{9}{20}$ (c) $\frac{1}{2}$ (d) $\frac{3}{5}$

Sol. Total number of two digit numbers formed are 34, 37, 38, 32, 43, 47, 48, 42, 73, 74, 78, 72, 83, 84, 87, 82, 23, 24, 27 and 28

Number of favourable outcomes i.e., odd numbers = 8

$\therefore$ Required probability $= \frac{8}{20} = \frac{2}{5}$

12. One card is selected from a well shuffled pack of cards, what is probability that it is black face card? *(Cr)*

(a) $\frac{3}{26}$ (b) $\frac{2}{13}$ (c) $\frac{1}{13}$ (d) $\frac{9}{13}$

Sol. Number of black face card = 6

$\therefore$ Required probability $= \frac{6}{52} = \frac{3}{26}$

Key Takeaways

There are 13 cards of each (Spade, Club, Diamond, Heart) in a deck of cards.

13. A bag contains 12 good mobiles and some defective mobiles. If the probability of drawing a good mobile is three times of a defective mobile, then the number of defective mobiles in the bag are *(Re)*

(a) 3 (b) 18

(c) 4 (d) 6

Sol. Let there be x defective phones in a bag.

and total number of phones $= x + 12$

Let P_1 be the probability of drawing a defective phone $= \frac{x}{x+12}$

And P_2 be the probability of drawing a good phone $= \frac{12}{x+12}$

According to the question,

$P_2 = 3P_1$

$\frac{12}{x+12} = 3\left(\frac{x}{x+12}\right)$

$\Rightarrow x = 4$

Hence, number of defective phones in a bag are 4.

14. A box contains 54 marbles each of which is blue, green or white. The probability of selecting a blue marble at random from the box is $\frac{1}{3}$ and the probability of selecting a green marble at random is $\frac{4}{9}$. The number of white marbles in the box are *(Un)*

(a) 10 (b) 12

(c) 14 (d) 16

Sol. Let the number of blue marbles be 'b', number of green marbles be 'g' and number of white marbles be 'w'.

Then, $b + g + w = 54$ ... (i)

Hence, $P(\text{selecting } a \text{ blue marble}) = \frac{b}{54}$

According to the question,

$\frac{b}{54} = \frac{1}{3} \Rightarrow b = 18$

Also, $P(\text{selecting a green marble}) = \frac{g}{54}$

Hence, $\frac{g}{54} = \frac{4}{9}$

$\Rightarrow g = 24s$

On substituting the values of b and g in Eq. (*i*), we get

$18 + 24 + w = 54$

$w = 54 - 42 = 12$

15. The probability of an impossible event is

***(Re)* (CBSE, 2020)**

(*a*) 1 (*b*) $\frac{1}{2}$

(*c*) not defined (*d*) 0

Sol. The probability of an impossible event is 0.

Nailing the Right Answer

Students may forget to use the complement rule when calculating probabilities, leading to incorrect results.

16. A coin is tossed twice. Find the probability of getting head both the times. ***(An)* (CBSE, 2020)**

(*a*) $\frac{1}{2}$ (*b*) $\frac{1}{4}$ (*c*) $\frac{3}{4}$ (*d*) 1

Sol. The sample space of two tossed coins is:

S: {(H, H), (H, T), (T, H), (T, T)}

Probability = (No. of favourable outcomes)/(Total no. of outcomes)

Here, from the sample space,

P(getting 2 heads when a coin is tossed twice) = $\frac{1}{4}$

Mistakes 101 : What not to do!

Students may leave fractions in improper form without simplifying, leading to errors in probability calculations.

17. A dice is rolled twice. The probability that 5 will not come up either time is ***(Ap)***

(*a*) $\frac{11}{36}$ (*b*) $\frac{1}{3}$ (*c*) $\frac{13}{36}$ (*d*) $\frac{25}{36}$

Sol. All possible events are written below:

(1, 1)	(1, 2)	(1, 3)	(1, 4)	(1, 5)	(1, 6)
(2, 1)	(2, 2)	(2, 3)	(2, 4)	(2, 5)	(2, 6)
(3, 1)	(3, 2)	(3, 3)	(3, 4)	(3, 5)	(3, 6)
(4, 1)	(4, 2)	(4, 3)	(4, 4)	(4, 5)	(4, 6)
(5, 1)	(5, 2)	(5, 3)	(5, 4)	(5, 5)	(5, 6)
(6, 1)	(6, 2)	(6, 3)	(6, 4)	(6, 5)	(6, 6)

Total events = 36

Out of the events in which 5 will not come up either time are {(1, 1) (1, 2) (1, 3) (1, 4) (1, 6) (2, 1) (2, 2) (2, 3) (2, 4) (2, 6) (3, 1) (3, 2) (3, 3) (3, 4) (3, 6) (4, 1) (4, 2) (4, 3) (4, 4) (4, 6) (6, 1) (6, 2) (6, 3) (6, 4) (6, 6)}.

No. of required events = 25

$\therefore$ Required probability = $\frac{25}{36}$

Nailing the Right Answer

Clearly define the sample space, which includes all possible outcomes of the experiment or situation being described in the question.

Answer Key

1. (d)	2. (a)	3. (a)	4. (b)	5. (d)
6. (c)	7. (b)	8. (b)	9. (c)	10. (c)
11. (a)	12. (a)	13. (c)	14. (b)	15. (d)
16. (b)	17. (d)			

Assertion and Reason

(1 M)

Direction: **In the following questions, a statement of Assertion (A) is followed by a statement of Reason (R). Mark the correct choice as:**

(*a*) Both Assertion (A) and Reason (R) is true and Reason (R) is the correct explanation of Assertion (A)

(*b*) Both Assertion (A) and Reason (R) is true but Reason (R) is not the correct explanation of Assertion (A).

(*c*) Assertion (A) is true but Reason (R) is false.

(*d*) Assertion (A) is false but Reason (R) is true.

1. Assertion (A): **The probability of getting a bad egg in a lot of 400 is 0.035. The number of good eggs in the lot is 386.**

Reason (R): **If the probability of an event is p, the probability of its complementary event will be 1-p**

Sol. Assertion: Here, total number of eggs = 400

Probability of getting a bad egg = 0.035

$\Rightarrow \frac{\text{Number of bad eggs}}{\text{Total number of eggs}} = 0.035$

$\Rightarrow \frac{\text{Number of bad eggs}}{400} = 0.035$

$\therefore$ Number of bad eggs = $0.035 \times 400 = 14$

Reasan is true.

Hence, Both Assertion (A) and Reason (R) is true but Reason (R) is not the correct explanation of assertion (A).

2. Assertion (A): **A bag has 3 red balls and 5 green balls. If we take a ball from the bag, then probability of getting red balls only is 3/8.**

Reason (R): **Probability of getting red balls = number of red balls/total number of balls** ***(Un)***

Sol. Given, a bag has 3 red balls and 5 green balls.

Hence, total number of balls = 8

Therefore, Probability (drawing a red ball) = number of red balls / total number of balls = 3/8

Hence, both assertion and reason are true and reason is the correct explanation of assertion

3. Assertion (A): **The probability that a leap year has 53 Sundays is $\frac{2}{7}$.**

Reason (R): **The probability that a non-leap year has 53 Sundays is $\frac{5}{7}$.** *(Cr)*

Sol. The leap year has 366 days i.e., 52 weeks and 2 days.

These two days can be; Sun-Mon, Mon-Tue, Tue-Wed, Wed-Thu, Thu-Fri, Fri-Sat, Sat-Sun.

Thus, the probability of 53 Sundays = $\frac{2}{7}$

So, Assertion (A) is true.

Now, the non-leap year has 365 days i.e., 52 weeks and 1 day.

Thus, the probability of 53 Sundays = $\frac{1}{7}$

So, Reason(R) is false.

Answer Key

1. (b) 2. (a) 3. (c)

Subjective Questions

Very Short Answer Type Questions (1 or 2 M)

1. **The probability of selecting a rotten apple randomly from a heap of 900 apples is 0.18. What is the number of rotten apples in the heap?** *(Cr)*

Sol. Total no. of apples = 900

Let the no. of rotten apples be = x

$$\text{Probability of selecting a rotten apple} = \frac{\text{No. of rotten apples}}{\text{Total no. of apples}}$$

$$= \frac{x}{900} = 0.18 \quad (1\ M)$$

$\Rightarrow x = 900 \times 0.18 \Rightarrow x = 9 \times 18 \Rightarrow x = 162$ *(1 M)*

Mistakes 101 : What not to do!

Students may inappropriately use approximations or rounding in their calculations, leading to inaccurate results, especially when dealing with small probabilities or large numbers.

2. **If a fair coin is tossed twice, find the probability of getting 'atmost one head'.** *(Cr)*

Sol. When a coin is tossed twice, the possible outcomes are {*TT, HH, TH, HT*} *(½ M)*

Number of possible outcomes = 4

Favourable outcomes = {*TT, HT, TH*} *(½ M)*

Number of favourable outcomes = 3

$\therefore$ Probability of getting atmost one head $= \frac{3}{4}$ *(1 M)*

3. **A bag contains 5 red balls and some blue balls. If the probability of drawing a blue ball at random from the bag is three times that of a red ball, find the number of blue balls in the bag.** *(Un)*

Sol. Let the number of blue balls be x.

Number of red balls = 5

Total number of balls = $x + 5$

P (getting a red ball) = $\frac{5}{x+5}$

P (getting a blue ball) = $\frac{x}{x+5}$ *(½ M)*

Given that, $2\left(\frac{5}{x+5}\right) = \frac{x}{x+5}$

10(x + 5) = x2 + 5x

$x^2 - 5x - 50 = 0$ *(½ M)*

$(x - 10)(x + 5) = 0$

Either $x - 10 = 0$ or $x + 5 = 0$

$x - 10$ or $x = -5$

However, the number of balls cannot be negative.

Hence, number of blue balls = 10 *(1 M)*

4. **Among Minal and Shreya, who has a higher chance of landing on the Goan restaurant in their next? Show your steps.** *(An)* (CBSE CFPQ, 2023)

Sol. Find the probability of Minal landing on the Goan restaurant as $\frac{5}{36}$. *(1 M)*

Find the probability of Shreya landing on the Goan restaurant as $\frac{4}{36}$.

Hence, concludes that Minal has a higher chance of landing on the Goan restaurant. *(1 M)*

5. **In a medical centre, 780 randomly selected people were observed to find if there is a relationship between age and the likelihood of getting a heart attack. The following results were observed.** *(An)* (CBSE CFPQ, 2023)

	Younger than or equal to 55	Older than 55	Total
Number of persons who have had a heart attack	29	75	104
Number of persons who have never had a heart attack	401	275	676
Total	430	350	780

(i) **Based on this table, what is the probability that a randomly chosen person from the same sample is younger than or equal to 55 years and has had a heart attack?**

(ii) **Looking at the data in the table, Giri says "if a person is randomly chosen, then the probability that the person have had a heart attack is about 12.5%".**

Is the statement true or false? Justify your reason.

Sol. (i) Calculate the probability as $\frac{29}{780}$ or any equivalent number. *(1 M)*

(ii) Explain that the statement is true and gives the justification that the probability that a random person have had a heart attack is $\frac{104}{780}$ which is approximately $\frac{1}{8}$ or 12.5% *(1 M)*

6. Shown below is a square dart board with circular rings inside.

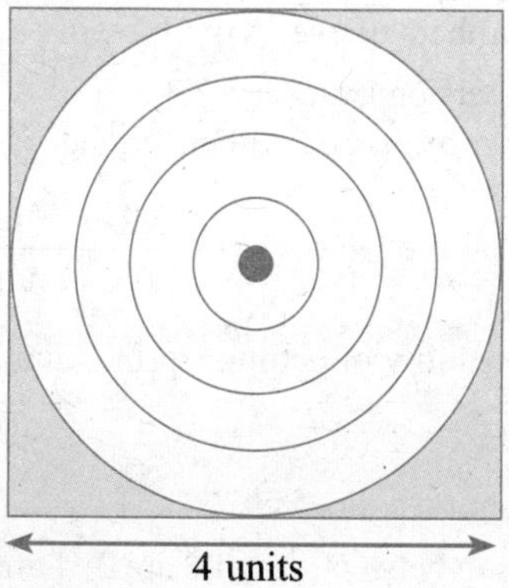

4 units

(Note: The figure is not to scale.)

Find the probability that a dart thrown at random lands on the shaded area. Show your steps.

(An) **(CBSE CFPQ, 2023)**

Sol. The area of the square dartboard as $4^2 = 16$ sq units. *(½ M)*

The area of the outer circular ring with radius 2 units as $\pi(2)^2 = 4\pi$ sq units. *(½ M)*

The probability that a dart thrown at random lands on the shaded area as $\frac{16-4\pi}{16} = \frac{4-\pi}{4}$. *(1 M)*

7. A 4-sided fair die is numbered 1 – 4. Nikhil and Pratik are playing with such a die each. They roll their dice once at the same time. A player wins only if they get a number larger than the other player.

What is the probability of Pratik winning the game? Show your work. *(An)* **(CBSE CFPQ, 2023)**

Sol. Identify the total number of outcomes as 16 and the probable outcomes to win the game as 6. *(1 M)*

Find the probability of Pratik winning the game as $\frac{6}{16}$ or $\frac{3}{8}$. *(1 M)*

Short Answer Type Questions (2 or 3 M)

1. Apoorv throws two dice once and computes the product of the numbers appearing on the dice. Peehu throws one die and squares the number that appears on it. Who has the better chance of getting the number 36?

(Re) **(NCERT Exemplar)**

Sol. Apoorv throws two dice once.

So, total number of outcomes = 36

Number of outcomes for getting product 36 = 1 i.e., (6 × 6)

$\therefore$ Probability for Apoorv $= \frac{1}{36}$ *(1 M)*

Also, Peehu throws one die

So, total number of outcomes = 6

Number of outcomes for getting square 36 = 1

$\therefore$ Probability for Peehu $= \frac{1}{6} = \frac{6}{36}$ *(1 M)*

Hence, Peehu has a better chance of getting the number 36. *(1 M)*

2. On a particular day, Vidhi and Unnati couldn't decide on who would get to drive the car. They had one coin each and flipped their coins exactly three times. The following was agreed upon:

- **If Vidhi gets two heads in a row, she would drive the car.**
- **If Unnati gets a head immediately followed by a tail, she would drive the car.**

Who has more probability to drive the car that day? List all outcomes and show your steps.

(Cr) **(CBSE CFPQ, 2023)**

Sol. Let S be the sample space

Since, one coin is tossed three times.

$S = \{HHH, HHT, HTH, HTT, THH, THT, TTH, TTT)$

So, $n(S) = 8$

Let A be an event that the Vidhi drives the car.

Vidhi drives the car only if she gets heads in a row.

$\therefore A = HHH, HHT, THH$

$\Rightarrow n(A) = 3$

$\therefore P(A) = \frac{n(A)}{n(S)} = \frac{3}{8}$ ... (i) *(1 M)*

Let B be an event that the Unnati drives the car.

Unnati drives the car only if she gets a head immediately followed by a tail.

$\therefore B = HHT, HTH, THT, HTT$

$\Rightarrow n(B) = 4$

$\therefore P(B) = \frac{n(B)}{n(S)} = \frac{4}{8} = \frac{1}{2}$ ... (ii) *(1 M)*

Using equations (i) and (ii),

$P(A) > sP(B)$

If they flipped their coins exactly three times, Unnati is more likely to drive the car that day. *(1 M)*

3. A bag contains 15 white and some black balls. If the probability of drawing a black ball from the bag is thrice that of drawing a white ball, find the number of black balls in the bag. *(Un)*

Sol. No. of white balls = 15

Let, the no. of black balls be 'x'

Then, total no. of balls = $15 + x$

Now,

P(drawing a white ball) $= \frac{15}{15+x}$ *(1 M)*

And, P(drawing a black ball) $= \frac{x}{15+x}$ *(1 M)*

As per the question,

$\frac{x}{15+x} = \frac{3\times15}{15+x} \Rightarrow x = 3 \times 15$

$\Rightarrow x = 45$

Therefore, there are 45 black balls in the bag. *(1 M)*

4. Two different dices are tossed together. Find the probability:

(i) of getting a doublet

(ii) of getting a sum 10, of the numbers on the two dice. ***(An)***

Sol. Possible outcomes are

{(1, 1), (1, 2), (1, 3), (1, 4), (1, 5), (1, 6)
(2, 1), (2, 2), (2, 3), (2, 4), (2, 5), (2, 6)
(3, 1), (3, 2), (3, 3), (3, 4), (3, 5), (3, 6)
(4, 1), (4, 2), (4, 3), (4, 4), (4, 5), (4, 6)
(5, 1), (5, 2), (5, 3), (5, 4), (5, 5), (5, 6)
(6, 1), (6, 2), (6, 3), (6, 4), (6, 5), (6, 6)}

Total elementary events = 36 *(1 M)*

(*i*) Outcomes of doublet = {(1, 1), (2, 2), (3, 3), (4, 4), (5, 5), (6, 6)}, i.e. 6

P (getting a doublet) $= \frac{6}{36} = \frac{1}{6}$ *(1 M)*

(*ii*) Outcomes of getting a sum 10 = {(4, 6), (5, 5), (6, 4)}, i.e. 3

P (getting a sum 10) $= \frac{3}{36} = \frac{1}{12}$ *(1 M)*

Mistakes 101 : What not to do!

Students may make mistakes when figuring out the total outcomes and the favourable outcomes when calculating Probability.

5. An integer is chosen at random between 1 and 100 . Find the probability that it is:

(i) divisible by 8.

(ii) not divisible by 8. ***(Re)***

Sol. (*i*) The integers divisible by 8 between 1 and 100 are 8, 16, 24, 32, 40, 48, 56, 64, 72, 80, 88, 96, i.e. 12 *(1 M)*

Total outcomes = 98

P(divisible by 8) $= \frac{12}{98} = \frac{6}{49}$ *(1 M)*

(*ii*) P(not divisible by 8) $= \frac{98-12}{98} = \frac{86}{98} = \frac{43}{49}$ *(1 M)*

6. A game consists of tossing a coin 3 times and noting the outcome each time. If getting the same result in all the tosses is a success, find the probability of losing the game. ***(Cr)***

Sol. The outcomes associated with the experiment in which a coin is tossed thrice:

HHH, HHT, HTH, THH, TTH, HTT, THT, TTT

Therefore, total number of outcomes = 8 *(1 M)*

Number of favourable outcomes (same result in all the tosses) = 6 *(1 M)*

Hence, required probability $= \frac{6}{8} = \frac{3}{4}$ *(1 M)*

7. A die is thrown once. Find the probability of getting a number which ***(Un)*** **(NCERT Intext)**

(i) is a prime number.

(ii) lies between 2 and 6.

Sol. We have,

Possible numbers of events on throwing a dice = 6

(*i*) Prime numbers on a dice are 2,3,5.

Total number of prime numbers on dice is 3

We know that probability $= \frac{\text{Number of favourable event}}{\text{Total number of event}}$

Hence, probability of getting a prime number $= \frac{3}{6} = \frac{1}{2}$

(1½ M)

(*ii*) Total number on a dice is 6.

Number lying between 2 and 6 are 3, 4 and 5

Total number of number lying between 2 and 6 is 3

We know that;

Probability $= \frac{\text{Number of favourable event}}{\text{Total number of event}}$

Hence, probability of getting a number lying between 2 and 6 is $\frac{3}{6} = \frac{1}{2}$ *(1½ M)*

8. Find the probability that 5 Sundays occur in the month of November of a randomly selected year. ***(Ev)*** **(CBSE, 2020)**

Sol. We know that

November has 30 days, which means 4 weeks and 2 days.

Now, 4 weeks will contain 4 Sunday.

The remaining 2 days may be:

1. Sunday and Monday
2. Monday and Tuesday
3. Tuesday and Wednesday
4. Wednesday and Thursday
5. Thursday and Friday
6. Friday and Saturday
7. Saturday and Sunday

Total number of possible outcomes =7 *(1 M)*

Now, favourable outcomes are: Sunday and Monday, Saturday and Sunday Number of favourable outcomes = 2

Required probability (P) = Number of favourable outcomes/ Total number of possible outcomes

$P=\frac{2}{7}$ *(1 M)*

9. A lot of 20 bulbs contain 4 defective ones. One bulb is drawn at random from the lot.

(*i*) What is the probability that this bulb is defective?

(*ii*) Suppose the bulb drawn in (*i*) is not defective and is not replaced. Now one bulb is drawn at random from the rest. What is the probability that this bulb is not defective? **(*Un*) (NCERT Intext)**

Sol. (*i*) Number of defective bulbs = 4

Total number of bulbs = 20

$\therefore$ Probability of getting a defective bulb

$= P$ (defective bulb) $=\frac{4}{20}=\frac{1}{5}$ *(1½ M)*

(*ii*) Since 1 non-defective bulb is drawn, then the total number of bulbs left are 19.

So, the total number of events (or outcomes) = 19

Number of non-defective bulbs = 19 – 4 = 15

So, the probability that the bulb is not defective = $\frac{15}{19}$

(1½ M)

10. A die is thrown once. Find the probability of getting a number which (*i*) is a prime number (*ii*) lies between 2 and 6. **(*Un*)**

Sol. (*i*) We know, when a die is thrown, total possible outcomes = 6

$\because$ Prime numbers are 2, 3 and 5

$\therefore$ Total number of prime numbers = 3

$\therefore$ *P*(getting a prime number)

$=\frac{\text{Total no. of favourable outcomes}}{\text{Total no. of possible outcomes}}=\frac{3}{6}=\frac{1}{2}$ *(1½ M)*

(*ii*) Since, numbers between 2 and 6 are 3, 4, and 5

$\therefore$ Total number between 2 and 6 = 3

$\therefore$ *P*(Getting a number between 2 and 6) $=\frac{3}{6}=\frac{1}{2}$ *(1½ M)*

11. A bag contains 6 red balls and 4 black balls. A ball is drawn at random from the bag. What is the probability that the ball drawn is

(*i*) red? (*ii*) not red? **(*An*) (CBSE, SQP 2023)**

Sol. Red color balls = 6

Black color balls = 4

Total ball = 10 *(½ M)*

$P(S)=\frac{\text{Favourable out comes}}{\text{Total no of out comes}}$ *(½ M)*

$P(\text{getting } C)=\frac{6}{10}=\frac{3}{5}$ *(1 M)*

$\text{P(Not Red)}=1-\frac{3}{5}=\frac{5-3}{5}=\frac{2}{5}$ *(1 M)*

12. A die is thrown once. What is the probability of getting a number less than 3?

Sol. Number of total outcomes = (1, 2, 3, 4, 5, 6) = 6

Number which is less than 3 i.e. 1, 2 *(1 M)*

Then, number of favorable outcomes = 2

Therefore, probability of getting a number less than 3 is $\frac{2}{6}=\frac{1}{3}$ *(1 M)*

Long Answer Type Questions (4 or 5 M)

1. Two different dice are thrown together. Find the probability that the numbers obtained have **(*Re*)**

(*i*) even sum, and

(*ii*) even product.

Sol. Total number of possible outcomes = 6^2 = 36 *(1 M)*

(*i*) Let *A* be the event of getting an even sum.

Favourable outcome for event A

= (1, 1), (1, 3), (1, 5),

(2, 2), (2, 4), (2, 6),

(3, 1), (3, 3), (3, 5),

(4, 2), (4, 4), (4, 6),

(5, 1), (5, 3), (5, 5),

(6, 2), (6, 4), (6, 6), *(1 M)*

So, there are 18 favourable outcomes. Therefore,

$P(A)=\frac{18}{36}=\frac{1}{2}$

Hence, the probability of getting an even sum is $\frac{1}{2}$. *(1 M)*

(*ii*) Let *B* be the event of getting an even product

Favourable outcomes for event B

= (1, 2), (1, 4), (1, 6),

(2, 1), (2, 2), (2, 3), (2, 4), (2, 5), (2, 6),

(3, 2), (3, 4), (3, 6),

(4, 1), (4, 2), (4, 3), (4, 4), (4, 5), (4, 6),

(5, 2), (5, 4), (5, 6),

(6, 1), (6, 2), (6, 3), (6, 4), (6, 5), (6, 6), *(1 M)*

So, there are 27 favourable outcomes. Therefore,

$P(B)=\frac{27}{36}=\frac{3}{4}$

Hence, the probability of getting an even product is $\frac{3}{4}$.

(1 M)

2. A box contains 12 balls out of which *x* are black. If one ball is drawn at random from the box, what is the probability that it will be a black ball? If 6 more black balls are put in the box, the probability of drawing a black ball is now double of what it was before. Find *x* **(*Un*)**

Sol. Total number of black balls = *x*

Total number of balls = 12

P (getting black balls) $=\frac{x}{12}$ ... (*i*) *(1 M)*

Now, when 6 more black balls are added,

Total balls become = 18 *(1 M)*

$\therefore$ Total number of black balls = $x + 6$

Now, P (getting black balls) = $\dfrac{(x+6)}{18}$ ... *(ii)* *(1 M)*

It is given that, the probability of drawing a black ball after adding 6 black balls now is double of what it was before

$\therefore \quad \dfrac{(x+6)}{18} = 2 \times \dfrac{x}{12}$ *(1 M)*

$\Rightarrow x + 6 = 3x \Rightarrow 2x = 6$

$\therefore x = 3$ *(1 M)*

Nailing the Right Answer

Clearly show all steps of your solution, including any calculations, formulas used, and reasoning applied. This will help you and others understand your thought process.

3. A box contains 90 discs which are numbered from 1 to 90. If one disc is drawn at random from the box, find the probability that it bears *(Un)* (NCERT Intext)

(i) a two-digit number

(ii) a perfect square number

(iii) a number divisible by 5.

Sol. The total numbers of discs = 90

$$P(E) = \frac{\text{Number of favourable outcomes}}{\text{Total number of outcomes}}$$

(i) Total number of discs having two digit numbers = 81

(Since 1 to 9 are single digit numbers and so, total 2 digit numbers are 90 – 9 = 81)

P (getting a two-digit number) = $\dfrac{81}{90} = \dfrac{9}{10}$ *(1 M)*

(ii) Total number of perfect square numbers = 9

i.e., 1, 4, 9, 16, 25, 36, 49, 64 and 81 *(1 M)*

P (getting a perfect square number) = $\dfrac{9}{90} = \dfrac{1}{10}$ *(1 M)*

(iii) Total numbers which are divisible by 5 = 18

i.e., 5, 10, 15, 20, 25, 30, 35, 40, 45, 50, 55, 60, 65, 70, 75, 80, 85 and 90 *(1 M)*

P (getting a number divisible by 5) = $\dfrac{18}{90} = \dfrac{1}{5}$ *(1 M)*

4. 14 defective bulbs are accidentally mixed with 98 good ones. It is not possible to just look at the bulb and tell whether it is defective or not. One bulb is taken out at random from this lot. Determine the probability that the bulb taken out is a good one. *(Ev)* (CBSE, 2020)

Sol. Number of defective bulbs = 14

Number of good bulbs = 98 *(1 M)*

Total number of outcomes = 98 + 14 = 112 *(1 M)*

Probability of getting a good bulbs

$$= \frac{\text{Number of favourable outcomes}}{\text{Total no. of Outcomes}} = \frac{98}{112} = \frac{7}{8}$$ *(2 M)*

Hence, the probability that Shweta will get a prize is $\dfrac{3}{10}$

(1 M)

Topper's Explanation **(CBSE 2020)**

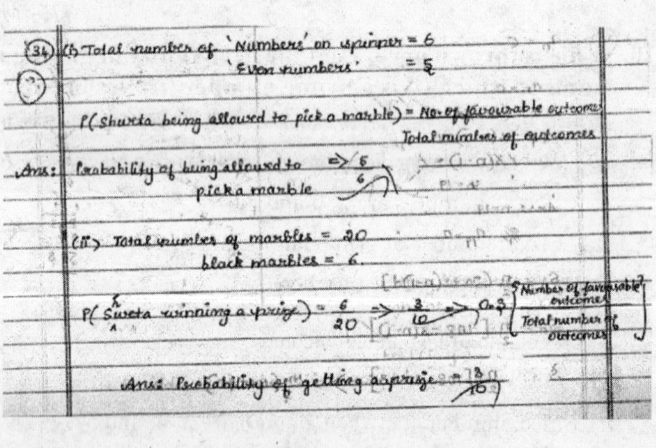
(34) (i) Total numbers of 'Numbers' on spinner = 6
'Even numbers' = 5
P(Shweta being allowed to pick a marble) = No. of favourable outcomes / Total numbers of outcomes
Ans: Probability of being allowed to pick a marble => 5/6
(ii) Total number of marbles = 20
black marbles = 6.
P(Shweta winning a prize) = 6/20 => 3/10 => 0.3 {Number of favourable outcomes / Total number of outcomes}
Ans: Probability of getting a prize = 3/10

MISCELLANEOUS EXERCISE

Multiple Choice Questions

(1 M)

1. A girl calculates that the probability of her winning the first prize in a lottery is 0.08. If 6000 tickets are sold, how many tickets has she bought? **(NCERT Exemplar)**

   (a) 40 (b) 240
   (c) 480 (d) 750

2. One ticket is drawn at random from a bag containing tickets numbered 1 to 40. The probability that the selected ticket has a number which is a multiple of 5 is **(NCERT Exemplar)**

   (a) $\frac{1}{5}$ (b) $\frac{3}{5}$ (c) $\frac{4}{5}$ (d) $\frac{1}{3}$

3. 2 cards of hearts and 4 cards of spades are missing from a pack of 52 cards. A card is drawn at random from the remaining pack. What is the probability of getting a black card? **(CBSE SQP, 2023)**

   (a) $\frac{22}{52}$ (b) $\frac{22}{46}$
   (c) $\frac{24}{52}$ (d) $\frac{24}{46}$

4. A number x is chosen at random from the numbers –2, –1, 0, 1, 2. Then the probability that $x^2 < 2$ is?

   (a) $\frac{1}{5}$ (b) $\frac{2}{5}$
   (c) $\frac{3}{5}$ (d) 1

5. If $P(E) = 0.34$, then what is the probability of 'not E'?

   (a) 0.66 (b) 0.34
   (c) 0.64 (d) 0.90

6. The probability that the month of April has exactly 5 Mondays is

   (a) $\frac{3}{7}$ (b) $\frac{5}{30}$
   (c) $\frac{2}{15}$ (d) $\frac{2}{7}$

7. If a vowel is chosen at random from the vowels of English alphabet, then the probability that it is a vowel of the word 'DELHI' is

   (a) $\frac{2}{5}$ (b) $\frac{1}{26}$
   (c) $\frac{5}{26}$ (d) $\frac{2}{26}$

8. Two numbers are selected randomly from {1, 2, 3, 4, 5, 6}, one after another without replacement.

   Then the probability that the smaller value among the two numbers is less than 4 is

   (a) $\frac{4}{5}$ (b) $\frac{23}{30}$ (c) $\frac{2}{5}$ (d) $\frac{8}{15}$

9. Cards marked with numbers 2 to 101 are placed in a box and mixed thoroughly. One card is randomly drawn from the box. The probability that the number on drawn card is a perfect square

   (a) $\frac{9}{101}$ (b) $\frac{9}{100}$
   (c) $\frac{9}{10}$ (d) $\frac{19}{100}$

10. A game consists of tossing a one rupee coin 3 times and noting its outcome each time. Aryan wins if all the tosses give the same result i.e. three heads or three tails and loses otherwise. Then the probability that Aryan will lose the game.

    (a) $\frac{3}{4}$ (b) $\frac{5}{8}$
    (c) 1 (d) $\frac{1}{4}$

11. A number is selected at random from first 50 natural numbers. Then the probability that it is a multiple of 3 and 4 is:

    (a) $\frac{7}{50}$ (b) $\frac{16}{50}$
    (c) $\frac{1}{25}$ (d) $\frac{2}{25}$

12. The probability of getting a defective mobile in a lot of 400 mobiles is 0.0375. The number of defective mobile in the lot is

    (a) 35 (b) 15
    (c) 21 (d) 28

13. There are 1000 sealed envelopes in a box. 10 of them contain a cash prize of ₹100 each, 100 of them contain a cash prize of ₹50 each and 200 of them contain a cash prize of ₹10 each and rest do not contain any cash prize. If they are well-shuffled and an envelope is picked, then the probability of getting a cash prize more than ₹10 is

    (a) 0.31 (b) 0.11
    (c) 0.54 (d) 0.69

14. A letter is chosen at random from the letters of the word 'MISSISSIPPI'. If the probability of selecting a vowel is $\frac{4}{3x-1}$, then x is equal to:

(*a*) 5 (*b*) 4 (*c*) 7 (*d*) 8

15. A number x is selected from the numbers 1, 2, 3 and then a second number y is randomly selected form the numbers 1, 4, 9 then the probability that the product xy of the two numbers will be less than 9 is

(*a*) $\frac{3}{7}$ (*b*) $\frac{4}{9}$

(*c*) $\frac{5}{9}$ (*d*) $\frac{7}{9}$

16. Two numbers b and c are chosen at random with replacement from the numbers 1, 2, 3, 4, 5 and 6. The probability that $x^2 + bx + c = 0$ has non real roots is:

(*a*) $\frac{17}{36}$ (*b*) $\frac{15}{36}$

(*c*) $\frac{17}{25}$ (*d*) None of these

17. At a fare, cards bearing numbers 1 to 3500, one number on one card, are put in a box. Each player selects one card at random and that card is not replaced. If the selected card has a perfect cube number greater than 500, the player wins a prize. The probability that the first player wins is:

(*a*) $\frac{2}{875}$ (*b*) $\frac{10}{3500}$

(c) 0.997 (*d*) $\frac{36}{3500}$

Assertion and Reason (1 M)

Direction: In the following questions, a statement of Assertion (A) is followed by a statement of Reason (R). Mark the correct choice as:

(*a*) Both Assertion (A) and Reason (R) is true and Reason (R) is the correct explanation of Assertion (A)

(*b*) Both Assertion (A) and Reason (R) is true but Reason (R) is not the correct explanation of Assertion (A).

(*c*) Assertion (A) is true but Reason (R) is false.

(*d*) Assertion (A) is false but Reason (R) is true.

1. **Assertion (A): The probability of getting a prime number when a dice is thrown once is $\frac{2}{3}$.**

   Reason (R): Prime numbers on a dice are 2, 3, 5.

2. **Assertion (A): Card numbered as 1, 2, 3 .... 15 are put in a box and mixed thoroughly, one card is then drawn at random. The probability of drawing a perfect square number is $\frac{4}{15}$**

   Reason (R): For any event E, we have $0 \le P(E) \le 1$

3. **Assertion (A): The probability of winning a game is 0.4, then the probability of losing it is 0.6**

   Reason (R): $P(E) + P(\text{not } E) = 1$

4. **Assertion (A): In a simultaneous throw of a pair of dice, the probability of getting a doublet is $\frac{1}{6}$.**

   Reason (R): Probability of an event can never be negative.

5. **Assertion (A): When two coins are tossed simultaneously then the probability of getting atleast one tail is $\frac{1}{4}$.**

   Reason (R): The probability of getting a head (i.e., no tail) in one toss of a coin is $\frac{1}{2}$.

Subjective Questions

Very Short Answer Type Questions (1 or 2 M)

1. A bag has 3 red balls and 5 green balls. If we take a ball from the bag, then what is the probability of getting red balls only?
2. A bag has 11 green marbles, 4 black marbles and 7 purple marbles. If one marble is drawn out randomly, then what is the probability of not getting a purple marble?
3. If we throw two coins in the air, then what is the probability of getting both tails?
4. One card is drawn from a well shuffled deck of 52 cards. Find the probability of getting a red colour face card.
5. Find the probability of getting a number greater than 2 in a single throw of a die.
6. Out of one digit prime numbers, one number is selected at random, then what is the probability of selecting an even prime number?
7. A selection committee interviewed some people for the post of CEO. So, they called male and female candidates in the ratio 5 : 6. What is the probability of a male candidate being selected?
8. It is given that in a group of 6 students, the probability of 2 students not having the same birthday is 0.867. What is the probability that the same 2 students have the same birthday?
9. It is known that a box of 600 electric bulbs contains 12 defective bulbs one bulb is taken out at random from this box. What is the probability that it is a non- defective bulb?
10. Two dice are thrown at the same time and the product of numbers appearing on them is noted. Find the probability that the product is less than 9.

Short Answer Type Questions (2 or 3 M)

1. A jar contains 24 marbles. Some are red and others are white. If a marble is drawn at random from the jar, the probability that it is red is 2/3, then find the number of white marbles in the jar.

2. Two dice are numbered 1, 2, 3, 4, 5, 6 and 1, 1, 2, 2, 3, 3 respectively. They are thrown and the sum of numbers on them is noted. Then, find the probability of getting an even sum. **(NCERT Exemplar)**

3. A dart is thrown at a circular dartboard and lands randomly over the area of the dartboard. What is the probability that it lands closer to the center i.e., at the distance of $\frac{r}{2}$ from the centre?

4. Five cards the two, jack, queen, king and ace of diamonds, are well- shuffled with their faces downward. One card is then picked up at random.
   (*i*) What is the probability that the card is the king?
   (*ii*) If the king is drawn and put aside, what is the probability that the second card picked up is
   (*a*) a face card?
   (*b*) a king?

5. A box contains cards numbered 3, 5, 7, 9, 11,..., 35, 37, 39. a card is drawn at random from the box. Find the probability that the number on the drawn card is a prime number.

6. Naima is playing a game and has two identical 6-sided dice. The faces of the dice have 3 even numbers and 3 odd numbers.
   She has to roll the two dice simultaneously and has two options to choose from before rolling the dice. She wins a prize if:
   Option 1: The sum of the two numbers appearing on the top of the two dice is odd.
   Option 2: The product of the two numbers appearing on top of the two dice is odd.
   Which option should Naima choose so that her chances of winning a prize is higher? Show your work.

7. A bag contains 14 green cards and some blue cards. If the probability of drawing a green card is double than that of a blue card, determine the number of blue cards in the bag.

8. A bag contains 5 black, 7 red and 3 white balls. A ball is drawn from the bag at random. Find the probability that the ball drawn is:
   (*i*) red
   (*ii*) black or white
   (*iii*) not black

9. A lot consists of 48 mobile phones of which 42 are good, 3 have only minor defects and 3 have major defects. Customer will buy a phone, if it is good but the trader will only buy a mobile, if it has no major defect. One phone is selected at random from the lot. The probability if chosen phone is acceptable to the customer is $\frac{x}{8}$. Find x. **(NCERT Exemplar)**

Long Answer Type Questions (4 or 5 M)

1. In fig. a disc on which a player spins an arrow twice. The fraction $\frac{a}{b}$ is formed, where '*a*' is the number of sector on which the arrow stops on the first spin and '*b*' is the number of the sector in which the arrow stops on the second spin, On each spin, each sector has an equal chance of selection by the arrow.
   Find the probability that the fraction $\frac{a}{b} > 1$.

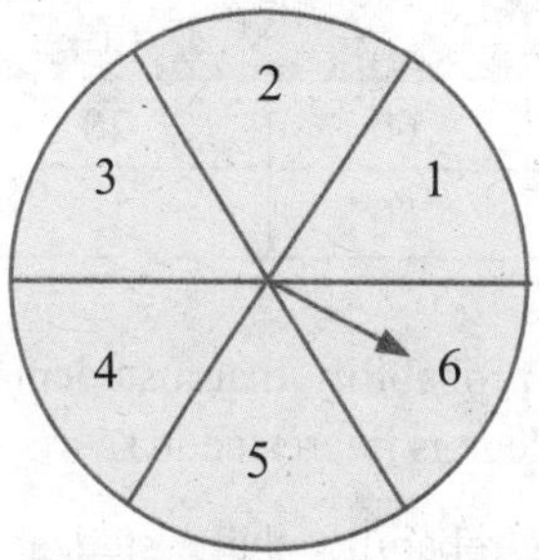

2. A box contains 20 balls bearing numbers 1, 2, 3,........,19, 20 respectively. A ball is drawn at random from the box. Find the probability that the number on the ball is:
   (*i*) a prime number.
   (*ii*) an even number.
   (*iii*) divisible by 3 or 5.
   (*iv*) neither divisible by 3 nor by 5.

3. At a fete, cards bearing numbers 1 to 1000, one number on one card, are put in a box. Each player selects one card at random and that card is not replaced. If the selected card has a perfect square greater than 500, the player wins a prize. What is the probability that
   (*i*) the first player wins a prize?
   (*ii*) the second player wins a prize, if the first has won?

4. A bag contains 3 red, 5 black and 7 white balls. A ball is drawn from the bag at random. Find the probability that the ball drawn is:
   (*i*) white
   (*ii*) red
   (*iii*) not black
   (*iv*) red or white
   (*v*) Black or Red

Case Based Questions

Case Based-I

A survey was conducted in a college to find out how many students were interested in sports and music. The following table gives the result of the survey.

	Sports only	Music only	Both Sports and Music	Neither Sports nor Music
Boys	40	60	20	30
Girls	30	50	15	35

(*i*) What is the probability that a student selected at random from the college is interested in sports only?

(*ii*) What is the probability that a student selected at random from the college is interested in neither sports nor music?

OR

What is the probability that a student selected at random from the college is a girl who is interested in music only?

(*iii*) What is the probability that a student selected at random from the college is a boy who is interested in either sports or music?

Case Based-II

A manufacturer produces two types of TV sets, Type-A and Type-B. The following table gives the result of a quality control check of a day's production.

Type-A

Type-B

	Type A	Type B
Defective	20	30
Non-defective	180	270

(*i*) What is the probability that a TV set selected at random from the production is defective?

(*ii*) If a TV set is defective, what is the probability that it is of Type A?

OR

If a TV set is non-defective, what is the probability that it is of Type B?

(*iii*) If a customer buys a TV set at random, what is the probability that the TV set is of Type B and non defective?

Case Based-III

"Eight Ball" is a game played on a pool table with 15 balls numbered 1 to 15 and a "cue ball" that is solid and white. Of the 15 numbered balls, eight are solid (non-white) coloured and numbered 1 to 8 and seven are striped balls numbered 9 to 15.

The 15 numbered pool balls (no cue ball) are placed in a large bowl and mixed, then one ball is drawn out at random.

Based on the above information, answer the following questions:

(*i*) What is the probability that the drawn ball bears number 8?

(*ii*) What is the probability that the drawn ball bears an even number?

OR

What is the probability that the drawn ball bears a number, which is a multiple of 3?

(*iii*) What is the probability that the drawn ball is a solid coloured and bears an even number?

Case Based-IV

Ramesh goes to a supermarket to purchase soap cartons for his shop. The store has 100 cartons of Moisturizing soap, 150 cartons of Antibacterial soap, 85 cartons of Natural soap and 115 cartons of Chemical-free soap. If Ramesh chooses a carton at random, then answer the following questions.

(*i*) The probability that the selected carton is of moisturizing soap is

(*a*) $\frac{4}{9}$ (*b*) $\frac{7}{11}$ (*c*) $\frac{3}{13}$ (*d*) $\frac{2}{9}$

(*ii*) The probability that the selected carton is not of natural soap is

(*a*) $\frac{14}{25}$ (*b*) $\frac{61}{90}$

(*c*) $\frac{73}{90}$ (*d*) None of these

(*iii*) The probability of selecting a carton of Chemical-free soap is

(*a*) $\frac{13}{90}$ (*b*) $\frac{15}{37}$ (*c*) $\frac{16}{31}$ (*d*) $\frac{23}{90}$

(*iv*) If the super market storekeeper bought 15 more cartons of anti-bacterial soap, then the probability of selecting a carton of anti-bacterial soap from the super market is

(*a*) $\frac{33}{59}$ (*b*) $\frac{11}{31}$

(*c*) $\frac{75}{101}$ (*d*) None of these

Case Based-V

Spinning wheel games are popular activity at birthday parties. They are a fun and easy way to add some excitement to the party, and they can be enjoyed by people of all ages. There are many different spinning wheel games that can be played at a birthday party.

Spin the wheel and win a prize: This is a simple game where the player spins the wheel and then wins a prize that the wheel lands on. The prizes can be anything from small toys to candy to gift cards.

Rohit organized his birthday party and invited all his friends for the same. He also arranges the game Spin the wheel and wins a prize for fun. On the basis of the above information, answer the following questions.

(*i*) If Ashok spins the wheel, then find the probability that he gets a cricket kit.

(*ii*) If Anita spins the wheel, then find the probability of getting no prize.

OR

If Anshu spins the wheel, then find the probability that the wheel stops at soccer ball.

(*iii*) Find the probability of winning a volley ball.

ANSWER KEYS

Multiple Choice Questions

1. (*c*) **2.** (*a*) **3.** (*b*) **4.** (*c*) **5.** (*a*) **6.** (*d*) **7.** (*a*) **8.** (*a*) **9.** (*b*) **10.** (*a*)
11. (*d*) **12.** (*b*) **13.** (*b*) **14.** (*b*) **15.** (*c*) **16.** (*a*) **17.** (*a*)

Assertion and Reason

1. (*d*) **2.** (*d*) **3.** (*a*) **4.** (*b*) **5.** (*d*)

Case Based Questions

Case Based-IV

(*i*) (*d*) (*ii*) (*c*) (*iii*) (*d*) (*iv*) (*b*)

HINTS & EXPLANATIONS

Multiple Choice Questions

1. (*c*) Given, total number of sold tickets = 6000

Let she bought x tickets.

Then, probability of her winning the

$$\text{first prize} = \frac{x}{6000} = 0.08 \qquad \text{....[Given]}$$

$$x = 0.08 \times 6000$$

$$\therefore \quad x = 480$$

Hence, she bought 480 tickets.

2. (*a*) Total no. of outcomes = 40

No. of favourable outcomes which are multiples of 5 = 8 (5, 10, 15, 20, 25, 30, 35, 40)

$$\because \quad \text{Probability} = \frac{\text{Favourable outcomes}}{\text{Total outcomes}}$$

$$\text{Probability} = \frac{8}{40} = \frac{1}{5}$$

3. (*b*)

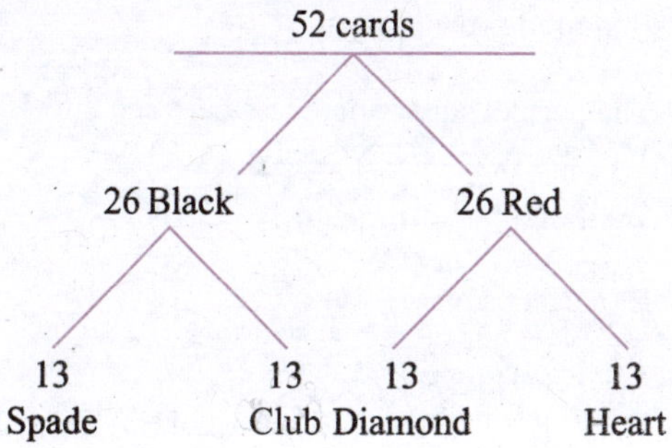

$$P = \frac{\text{Favourable outcomes}}{\text{Total outcomes}}$$

$$= \frac{26-4}{52-6} = \frac{22}{46}$$

4. (*c*) The square of the given numbers (–2, –1, 0, 1, 2) are (4, 1, 0, 1, 4).

Therefore, number of favourable outcomes are 3.

$$P(x^2 < 2) = \frac{3}{5}$$

5. (*a*) $P(E) + P(\text{not } E) = 1$

So, $P(\text{not } E) = 1 - P(E)$

Or, $P(\text{not } E) = 1 - 0.34$ $(\because P(E) = 0.34)$

$\therefore P(\text{not } E) = 0.66$

6. (*d*) We know that

Total number of days in the month of April = 30.

Now, 30 days = 4 weeks + 2 days.

Now 4 weeks will surely contain 4 Mondays.

The remaining two days may be

(1) Sunday and Monday
(2) Monday and Tuesday
(3) Tuesday and Wednesday
(4) Wednesday and Thursday
(5) Thursday and Friday
(6) Friday and Saturday
(7) Saturday and Sunday

Total number of possible outcomes = 7

Now, favourable outcomes are: Sunday & Monday and Monday and Tuesday

Number of favourable outcomes = 2

∴ Required probability

$$= \frac{\text{No. of favourable outcomes}}{\text{Total no. of possible outcomes}} = \frac{2}{7}$$

7. (*a*) The English alphabet has 5 vowels in all. The word 'DELHI' has 2 vowels, so the number of favourable outcomes is 2

$\therefore$ Required probability $= \frac{2}{5}$

8. (*a*) Total number of events = 6 × 5 = 30

(i.e., (1, 2), (1, 3).... (6, 4) (6, 5))

Unfavourable outcomes = (4, 5), (4, 6), (5, 4), (5, 6), (6, 4), (6, 5)

∴ Number of favourable outcomes = 30 – 6 = 24

Required probability $= \frac{24}{30} = \frac{4}{5}$.

9. (*b*) The perfect square numbers between 2 to 101 are: 4, 9, 16, 25, 36, 49, 64, 81, 100

Total numbers from 2 to 101 = 100

$$P\text{ (perfect square)} = \frac{9}{100}$$

10. (*a*) Total outcomes are:

HHH, HHT, HTH, THH, HTT, THT, TTH, TTT

Favourable outcomes for losing game are

HHT, HTH, THH, HTT, THT, TTH

$$P\text{ (Losing the game)} = \frac{6}{8} = \frac{3}{4}$$

11. (*d*) To find the multiples of 3 and 4, first we need to find the L.C.M of 3 and 4 i.e., 12.

So common multiples of 3 and 4 are 12, 24, 36, 48.

$$P\text{ (multiple of 3 and 4)} = \frac{4}{50} = \frac{2}{25}$$

12. (*b*) Let the number of defective mobiles be x.

$$P\text{(defective mobiles)} = \frac{x}{400}$$

$$0.0375 = \frac{x}{400} \Rightarrow x = 400 \times 0.0375 = 15$$

∴ Number of defective mobiles in a lot is 15.

13. (*b*) Total number of envelopes in the box = 1000

Number of envelopes containing cash prize more than ₹10 = 10 + 100 = 110

Hence, Required probability $= \frac{110}{1000} = 0.11$

14. (*b*) There are 11 letters in the word 'MISSISSIPPI'

Hence, Total number of outcomes = 11

There are 4 vowels in the word 'MISSISSIPPI',

So, there are 4 ways of selecting a vowel.

∴ Required probability $= \frac{4}{11}$

According to question,

$$\frac{4}{11} = \frac{4}{3x-1}$$

$\Rightarrow 3x - 1 = 11$

$\Rightarrow x = 4$

15. (*c*) Two numbers x and y can be selected in 9 ways as listed below:

(1, 1), (1, 4), (1, 9), (2, 1), (2, 4), (2, 9), (3, 1), (3, 4), (3, 9)

The product xy will be less than 9, if x and y are chosen in one of the following ways:

(1, 1), (1, 4), (2, 1), (2, 4), (3, 1)

Hence, favourable number of elementary events = 5

∴ Required probability $= \frac{5}{9}$

16. (*a*) Since, b and c both can be selected from 1 to 6. So, total number of ways of choosing b and c is:

6 × 6 = 36

Now, for having non real roots of the equation

$x^2 + bx + c = 0$, Discriminant < 0, *i.e.*, $b^2 - 4ac < 0$

$\Rightarrow b^2 < 4c$ $[\because a = 1]$

The following table shows the possible values of b and c for which $b^2 - 4c < 0$

Value of b	$b^2 < 4c$	Possible value of c	Total
1	$1 < 4c \Rightarrow \frac{1}{4} < c$	1, 2, 3, 4, 5, 6	6
2	$4 < 4c \Rightarrow 1 < c$	2, 3, 4, 5, 6	5
3	$9 < 4c \Rightarrow \frac{9}{4} < c$	3, 4, 5, 6	4
4	$16 < 4c \Rightarrow 4 < c$	5, 6	2
5	$25 < 4c \Rightarrow \frac{25}{4} < c$	Not possible	0
6	$36 < 4c \Rightarrow 9 < c$	Not possible	0
			17

So, favourable number of elementary events = 17

Hence, Required probability = $\frac{17}{36}$

17. (*a*) Let E_1 = Event that the first player wins the prize
= player selects a card which is a perfect cube greater than 500.
= {512, 729, 1000, 1331, 1728, 2197, 2744, 3375}
So, Number of Outcomes favourable to $E_1 = 8$
∴ Required probability

$$= \frac{\text{Number of outcomes favourable to } E_1}{\text{Number of total outcomes}} = \frac{8}{3500} = \frac{2}{875}$$

Assertion and Reason

1. (*d*) When a die is thrown once, total possible outcomes = 6 and prime numbers in it are {2, 3, 5}.
Total possible outcomes = 3
Probability of getting a prime = $\frac{3}{6} = \frac{1}{2}$
Hence, Assertion (A) is false but Reason (R) is true.

2. (*d*) Total possible outcomes = 15
Total favourable outcomes are 1, 4, 9
Probability of drawing a perfect square number = $\frac{3}{15}$
$= \frac{1}{5}$
Hence, Assertion (A) is false but Reason (R) is true.

3. (*a*) We have, $P(E) = 0.4$,
where E = event of winning
$P(\text{Not } E) = 1 - P(E) = 1 - 0.4 = 0.6$
Hence, Both Assertion (A) and Reason (R) is true and Reason (R) is the correct explanation of Assertion (A).

4. (*b*) When two dice are tossed, total possible outcomes = 36 and favourable outcomes (doublet)
= {(1, 1), (2, 2), (3, 3), (4, 4), (5, 5), (6, 6)}
Probability = $\frac{6}{36} = \frac{1}{6}$ and,
We know that $0 \le P(E) \le 1$.
Hence, Both Assertion (A) and Reason (R) are true but Reason (R) is not the correct explanation of Assertion (A).

5. (*d*) Probability of getting atleast one tail = $\frac{3}{4}$ when two coins are tossed simultaneously.
As we know that the probability of getting a head in single throw of a coin is $\frac{1}{2}$
Hence, Assertion (A) is false but Reason (R) is true.

Subjective Questions

Very Short Answer Type Questions

1. Number of red balls = 3
Number of green balls = 5
Total balls in bag = 3 + 5 = 8 (1 M)
Probability of getting red balls = $\frac{3}{8}$ (1 M)

2. Total number of purple marbles = 7
Total number of marbles in bag = 11 + 4 + 7 = 22
Probability of getting purple marbles = $\frac{7}{22}$ (1 M)
Hence, the probability of not getting purple marbles
$= 1 - \frac{7}{22} = \frac{15}{22}$ (1 M)

3. When two coins are tossed, the total outcomes will be 4 i.e., (H, H), (H, T), (T, H) and (T, T) (1 M)
Hence, the probability of getting both tails = $\frac{1}{4}$ (1 M)

4. Total number of cards = 52
Number of red face cards = 6 (1 M)
The probability of getting red face card = $\frac{6}{52} = \frac{3}{26}$
(1 M)

5. Favourable outcomes are 3, 4, 5 and 6. (1 M)
∴ Required probability = $\frac{4}{6} = \frac{2}{3}$ (1 M)

6. One digit prime numbers are 2, 3, 5, 7. Out of these numbers, only the number 2 is even prime. (1 M)
∴ Required probability = $\frac{1}{4}$ (1 M)

7. The ratio in which male and female candidates are called is 5 : 6.
Let the number of males be $5x$
and the number of females be $6x$
Total number of candidates = $5x + 6x = 11x$ (1 M)
Probability of male candidate being selected

$$= \frac{\text{Number of males}}{\text{Total number of candidates}} = \frac{5x}{11x} = \frac{5}{11}$$ (1 M)

8. Probability of 2 students not having the same birthday $P(\bar{E}) = 0.867$

Probability of same 2 students having the same birthday $P(E)$ $= 1 - P(\bar{E})$ (1 M)

$= 1 - 0.867$

$= 0.133$ (1 M)

9. The number of non-defective bulbs in the box = 600 – 12 = 588. (1 M)

So, probability of taking out a non-defective bulb $= \frac{588}{600} = \frac{49}{50}$

(1 M)

10. Number of total outcomes = 36

When product of numbers appearing on them is less than 9, then favourable outcomes are (1, 1), (1, 2), (1, 3), (1, 4), (1, 5), (1, 6), (2, 1), (2, 2), (2, 3), (2, 4), (3, 1), (3, 2), (4, 1), (4, 2), (5, 1), and (6, 1). (1 M)

Number of favourable outcomes = 16

$\therefore$ Required probability $= \frac{16}{36} = \frac{4}{9}$. (1 M)

Short Answer Type Questions

1. Let the number of red marbles be x.

$P(\text{red marble}) = \frac{x}{24}$ (1 M)

$\Rightarrow \frac{2}{3} = \frac{x}{24} \Rightarrow x = 16$ (1 M)

$\therefore$ No. of white marbles $= 24 - x = 8$ (1 M)

2. Total number of outcomes = 6 × 6 = 36

Possible sum of two numbers on the two dice are 2, 3, 4, 5, 6, 7, 8, 9 (1 M)

Let, E = Event of getting even sum i.e., 2, 4, 6, 8

i.e. outcomes favourable to event are :

(1, 1),(1,1), (2, 2), (2, 2), (3, 1), (3, 1), (1, 3) (1, 3), (3, 3), (3, 3), (4, 2), (4, 2), (5, 1), (5, 1), (5, 3) (5, 3), (6, 2), (6, 2). (1 M)

Hence, $P(E) = \frac{\text{Number of outcomes favourable to } E}{\text{Number of total outcomes}}$

$= \frac{18}{36} = \frac{1}{2}$ (1 M)

3. All possible outcomes are the points which lie on the area of the circle $= \pi r^2$, where r is the radius of dart board.

And, the point closer to centre of circle lies on area having radius $\frac{r}{2}$. (1 M)

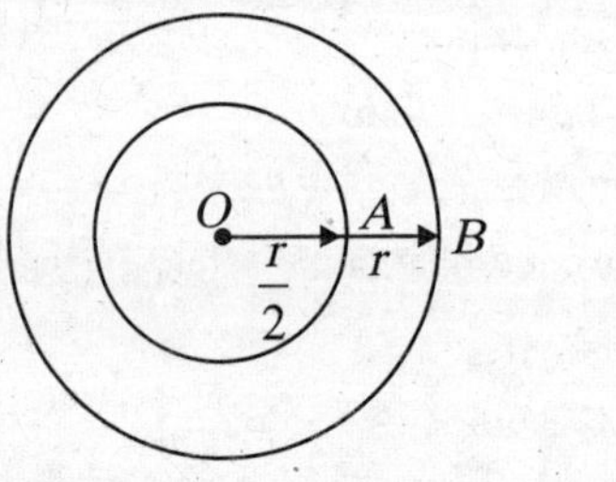

So, closer area $= \pi\left(\frac{r}{2}\right)^2 = \frac{\pi r^2}{4}$ (1 M)

so, Probability (closer to center) $= \frac{\pi r^2/4}{\pi r^2} = \frac{1}{4}$ (1 M).

4. There are five cards – the two, jack, queen, king and ace of diamond.

(*i*) Let A = event of getting a king. There is only one king out of the five cards.

$\therefore P(\text{getting a king}) = \frac{1}{5}$ (1 M)

(*ii*) When a king is drawn and put aside, four cards- the two, jack, queen and ace are left. Therefore,

(*a*) required probability = P(getting face card) $= \frac{2}{4} = \frac{1}{2}$ (1 M)

(*b*) required probability = P(getting a king) $= \frac{0}{4} = 0$

(1 M)

5. Here, 3, 5, 7, 9, 11, ..., 35, 37, 39 form an A.P. with first term 3 and common difference 2.

$\therefore a_n = a + (n-1)d$ (½ M)

$\Rightarrow 39 = 3 + (n-1)\,2$ (½ M)

$\Rightarrow 36 = 2n - 2$

$\Rightarrow 38 = 2n$

$\Rightarrow n = 19$ (½ M)

So, there are 19 elementary events in the sample space.

Prime numbers are 3, 5, 7, 11, 13, 17, 19, 23, 29, 31, 37, i.e., these are 11 in number. (½ M)

$\therefore$ Required probability $= \frac{11}{19}$. (1 M)

6. The sum of the two numbers on the dice is one of these:

odd + odd = even (1 M)

odd + even = odd

even + odd = odd

even + even = even

Then the probability of getting an odd number as the sum on rolling the two dice as $\frac{1}{2}$. (½ M)

and the product of the two numbers on the dice is one of these:

odd × odd = odd (1 M)

odd × even = even

even × odd = even

even × even = even

Then the probability of getting an odd number as the product on rolling the two dice as $\frac{1}{4}$.

Hence, concludes that Naima should choose option 1 (½ M)

7. Let the number of blue cards be x.

Let E_1 = event of getting a green card

And E_2 = event of getting a blue card

$P(E_1) = P(\text{getting a green card}) = \frac{14}{x+14}$ (1 M)

$P(E_2) = P(\text{getting a blue card}) = \frac{x}{x+14}$ (1 M)

According to the question,

$P(E_1) = 2P(E_2)$

$\Rightarrow \frac{14}{x+14} = 2\left(\frac{x}{x+14}\right) \Rightarrow x = 7$

Hence, required number of blue cards is 7. (1 M)

8. Total number of balls = 5 + 7 + 3 = 15.

(*i*) Number of red balls = 7.

$\therefore P(\text{drawing a red ball}) = \frac{7}{15}$. (1 M)

(*ii*) Number of black or white balls = 5 + 3 = 8.

$\therefore P(\text{drawing a black or white ball}) = \frac{8}{15}$. (1 M)

(*iii*) Number of balls which are not black = 15 – 5 = 10.

$\therefore P(\text{drawing a ball that is not black}) = \frac{10}{15} = \frac{2}{3}$. (1 M)

9. Given, total number of mobile phones = 48

∴ Number of favourable outcomes = 42 (1 M)

Let E_1 = Event that customer will buy a mobile phone

$P(E_1) = \frac{42}{48} = \frac{7}{8}$ (1 M)

Hence, the value of x is 7. (1 M)

Long Answer Type Questions

1. For $\frac{a}{b} > 1$, when $a = 1$, b can not take any value,

$a = 2$, b can take 1 value, (½ M)

$a = 3$, b can take 2 values, (½ M)

$a = 4$, b can take 3 values (½ M)

When $a = 5$, b can take 4 values, (½ M)

$a = 6$, b can take 5 values. (½ M)

Total possible outcomes = 36 (½ M)

$\therefore\ p\left(\frac{a}{b} > 1\right)$ (1 M)

$= \frac{1+2+3+4+5}{36} = \frac{15}{36}$ or $\frac{5}{12}$ (1 M)

2. Total number of balls in the box = 20

∴ number of all possible outcomes = 20 (1 M)

(*i*) Let A_1 = event of getting a prime number. Then, the favourable outcomes are 2, 3, 5, 7, 11, 13, 17, 19.

Number of favourable outcomes = 8 (½ M)

$\therefore P(\text{getting a prime number}) = P(A_1) = \frac{8}{20} = \frac{2}{5}$ (½ M)

(*ii*) Let A_2 = event of getting an even number. Then, the favourable outcomes are 2, 4, 6, 8, 10, 12, 14, 16, 18, 20.

Number of favourable outcomes = 10. (½ M)

Hence, required probability = P (getting an even Number) $= P(A_2) = \frac{10}{20} = \frac{1}{2}$ (½ M)

(*iii*) Let A_3 = event of getting a number divisible by 3 or 5.

Then, the favourable outcomes are 3, 5, 6, 9, 10, 12, 15, 18, 20.

∴ Number of favourable outcomes = 9 (½ M)

P (getting a number divisible by 3 or 5) $= P(A_3) = \frac{9}{20}$ (½ M)

(*iv*) Let A_4 = event of getting a number neither divisible by 3 nor by 5.

P (getting a number neither divisible by 3 nor by 5)

= 1 – P(getting a number either divisible by 3 or 5) (½ M)

$= 1 - \frac{9}{20} = \frac{11}{20}$ (½ M)

3. Total number of outcomes are $n(S) = 1000$. If the selected card has a perfect square greater than 500, then player wins a prize.

(*i*) Let E_1 = Event first player wins a prize = Player select a card which is a perfect square greater than 500

= {529, 576, 625, 676, 729, 784, 841, 900, 961}

$= \{(23)^2, (24)^2, (25)^2, (26)^2, (27)^2, (28)^2, (29)^2, (30)^2, (31)^2\}$

$\therefore n(E_1) = 9$ (1 M)

So, required probability $= \frac{n(E_1)}{n(S)} = \frac{9}{1000} = 0.009$ (1 M)

(*ii*) First, has won i.e., one card is already selected, greater than 500, has a perfect square.

Since, repetition is not allowed. So, one card is removed out of 1000 cards. (1 M)

Total number of remaining outcomes, $n(S') = 999$

Let E_2 = Event the second player wins a prize, if the first has won.

= Remaining cards has a perfect square greater than 500 are 8.

$n(E_2) = 9 - 1 = 8$ (1 M)

So, required probability $= \frac{n(E_2)}{n(S')} = \frac{8}{999}$ (1 M)

4. (*i*) $P(\text{a white ball}) = \frac{n\{\text{white ball}\}}{n\{\text{total balls}\}} = \frac{7}{3+5+7} = \frac{7}{15}$ (1 M)

(*ii*) $P(\text{red ball}) = \frac{n\{\text{red balls}\}}{n\{\text{total balls}\}} = \frac{3}{15} = \frac{1}{5}$ (1 M)

(*iii*) $P(\text{notblack}) = 1 - P(\text{black}) = 1 - \frac{n\{\text{black}\}}{n\{\text{total}\}} = 1 - \frac{5}{15} = \frac{10}{15} = \frac{2}{3}$ (1 M)

(*iv*) $P(\text{Red or White}) = \frac{3+7}{15} = \frac{10}{15} = \frac{2}{3}$ (1 M)

(*v*) $P(\text{Black or Red})$

$= \frac{5}{15} + \frac{3}{15} = \frac{8}{15}$ (1 M)

Case Based Questions

Case Based-I

(*i*) Total number of boys = 40 + 60 + 20 + 30 = 150

Total number of girls = 30 + 50 + 15 + 35 = 130

∴ Total number of students = 280

Let E_1 = event of getting a student interested in sports only. Then, the number of favourable outcome = 40 + 30 = 70

$$P(E_1) = \frac{70}{280} = \frac{1}{4}$$

(*ii*) Let E_2 = event of getting a student who is interested neither in sports nor music. Then, the number of favourable outcome = 30 + 35 = 65

$$P(E_2) = \frac{65}{280} = \frac{13}{56}$$

OR

Let E_3 = event of selecting a girl who is interested in music. Then, the number of favourable outcome = 50

$$P(E_3) = \frac{50}{280} = \frac{5}{28}$$

(*iii*) Let E_4 = event of selecting a boy who is interested in sports or music. Then, the number of favourable outcome = 40 + 60 = 100

$$P(E_4) = \frac{100}{280} = \frac{5}{14}$$

Case Based-II

(*i*) Total no. of defective TV sets = 50

Total no. of non-defective TV sets = 450

∴ Total no. of TV sets = 500

Let E_1 denotes an event that selected TV set is defective. Then, no. of favourable outcome = 50

$$P(E_1) = \frac{50}{500} = \frac{1}{10}$$

(*ii*) Let E_2 denotes an event that defective TV set is of type A. Then, no. of favourable outcomes = 20

$$P(E_2) = \frac{20}{50} = \frac{2}{5}$$

OR

Let E_3 denotes the event that the non-defective TV set is of type B. Then, no. of favourable outcomes = 270

$$P(E_3) = \frac{270}{450} = \frac{3}{5}$$

(*iii*) Let E_4 denotes an event that the selected TV set is of Type B and non defective. Then, no. of favourable outcomes = 270

$$P(E_4) = \frac{270}{500} = \frac{27}{50}$$

Case Based-III

(*i*) Total number of balls = 15

Number of ball bears numbers 8 = 1

$$P(\text{drawing a ball bears number 8}) = \frac{1}{15}$$

(*ii*) Even number balls are 2, 4, 6, 8, 10, 12 and 14

Total number of even balls = 7

$$P(\text{drawing a ball bears an even number}) = \frac{7}{15}$$

OR

Number of ball bears a number which is a multiple of 3 are 3, 6, 9, 12 and 15

∴ Total number of ball bears a number, which is a multiple of 3 = 5.

P(drawing a ball bears a number having a multiple of 3) $= \frac{5}{15} = \frac{1}{3}$

(*iii*) Number of solid coloured balls = 8

Number of solid coloured balls having an even number = 4

P(drawing a solid coloured and bears an even number ball) $= \frac{4}{15}$

Case Based-IV

(*i*) (*d*) Total number of cartons in the store

= 100 + 150 + 85 + 115 = 450

$$P(\text{choosing a moisturizing soap carton}) = \frac{100}{450} = \frac{2}{9}$$

(*ii*) (*c*) $P(\text{choosing a natural soap carton}) = \frac{85}{450} = \frac{17}{90}$

$$\therefore P(\text{choosing not a natural soap carton}) = 1 - \frac{17}{90} = \frac{73}{90}$$

(*iii*) (*d*) $P(\text{choosing a chemical-free soap carton}) = \frac{115}{450} = \frac{23}{90}$

(*iv*) (*b*) Number of cartons he bought = 14

∴ Total number of cartons are with storekeeper now = 450 + 15 = 465

So, P(selecting a carton of anti-bacterial soap carton from store)

$$= \frac{150+15}{465} = \frac{165}{465} = \frac{33}{93} = \frac{11}{31}$$

Case Based-V

(*i*) Total number of possible outcomes = 10

$$P(\text{getting cricket kit}) = \frac{1}{10}$$

(*ii*) $P(\text{getting no prize}) = \frac{3}{10}$

OR

$$P(\text{getting a soccer ball}) = \frac{2}{10} = \frac{1}{5}$$

(*iii*) $P(\text{getting a volley ball}) = \frac{2}{10} = \frac{1}{5}$

❑❑❑

MOCK TEST PAPER-1

Time allowed : 3 hours | **Maximum Marks : 80**

GENERAL INSTRUCTIONS:

Read the following instructions very carefully and follow them:

(i) *This question paper contains **38** questions. **All** questions are compulsory.*

(ii) *Question Paper is divided into 5 Sections-**Section A, B, C, D and E.***

(iii) *In **Section A question number 1 to 18 are** Multiple Choice Questions **(MCQs)** and question number **19 & 20** are Assertion-Reason based **questions of 1 mark each.***

(iv) *In **Section-B question number 21 to 25 are** Very Short Answer (VSA) type **questions of 2 marks each.***

(v) *In **Section-C question number 26 to 31 are** Short Answer (SA) type **questions carrying 3 marks each.***

(vi) *In **Section-D question number 32 to 35 are** Long Answer (LA) type **questions carrying 5 marks each.***

(vii) *In **Section-E question number 36 to 38 are** Case Study based questions **carrying 4 marks each. Internal choice is provided in 2 marks question in each case-study.***

(viii) ***There is no overall choice. However, an internal choice has been provided in 2 questions in Section B, 2 questions in Section C, 2 questions in Section D and 3 questions in Section E.***

(ix) ***Draw neat figures wherever required. Take π = 22/7 wherever required if not stated.***

(x) ***Use of calculators is NOT allowed.***

SECTION - A

Section - A consists of Multiple Choice type questions of 1 mark each.

1. The least number that is divisible by all the natural numbers from 1 to 10 (both inclusive) is
   (*a*) 10 (*b*) 100 (*c*) 504 (*d*) 2520

2. If the zeroes of the quadratic polynomial $ax^2 + bx + c$, $c \neq 0$ are equal, then
   (*a*) c and a have opposite signs (*b*) c and b have same sign
   (*c*) c and a have same sign (*d*) c and b have opposite sign

3. The given pair of linear equations $x + 2y - 5 = 0$ and $-3x - 6y + 15 = 0$ have
   (*a*) Exactly one solution (*b*) Exactly two solutions
   (*c*) Infinitely many solutions (*d*) No solution

4. If $ax^2 + bx + c = a(x - p)^2$, the relation among a, b and c is:
   (*a*) $abc = 1$ (*b*) $a + c - 2b = 0$
   (*c*) $b^2 - ac = 0$ (*d*) $b^2 = 4ac$

5. If the numbers $n - 2$, $4n - 1$ and $5n + 2$ are in AP then value of n is
   (*a*) 1 (*b*) 4 (*c*) –4 (*d*) –2

6. The points which divides the line segment of points $A(-1, 7)$ and $B(4, -3)$ in ratio of 2 : 3 is

(a) (–1, 3) (b) (2, 4) (c) (–2, –4) (d) (1, 3)

7. The point on x-axis which is equidistant from the points $P(-2, 3)$ and $Q(5, 4)$ is

(a) (0, 4) (b) (2, 0) (c) (8, 0) (d) (– 2, 0)

8. D and E are the mid points of side AB and AC of ΔABC respectively and $BC = 6$ cm. If $DE \parallel BC$ then the length (in cm) of DE is:

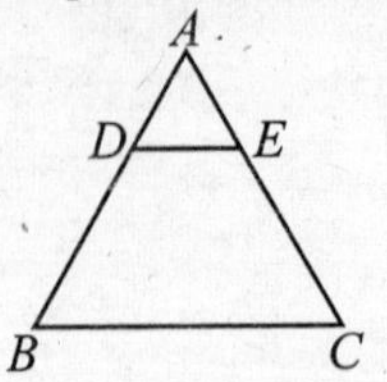

(a) 2.5 cm (b) 3 cm (c) 5 cm (d) 6 cm

9. If $\angle OPQ$ is an isosceles triangle such that PQ is tangent to a circle with centre O at point P, then $\angle OQP$ is

(a) 30° (b) 60° (c) 45° (d) 90°

10. A tangent AB at a point A of a circle of radius 5 cm meets a line through the centre O at a point B. Such that $OB = 13$ cm. Length of AB is

(a) 8.5 cm (b) 10 cm (c) 12 cm (d) $2\sqrt{119}$ cm

11. Given that $\tan\theta = \frac{a}{b}$, then $\sin\theta$ is

(a) $\frac{a}{\sqrt{a^2+b^2}}$ (b) $\frac{b}{\sqrt{a^2+b^2}}$ (c) $\frac{b}{a}$ (d) $\frac{\sqrt{a^2+b^2}}{a}$

12. The value of $\cos^2\theta + \frac{1}{1+\cot^2\theta}$ is

(a) $\sqrt{3}$ (b) 1 (c) 0 (d) $\frac{1}{2}$

13. If the ratio of length of a pole and its shadow is $1:\sqrt{3}$, then angle of elevator of sun is

(a) 120° (b) 45° (c) 30° (d) 90°

14. If the perimeter and area of a circle on numerically equal, then the radius of the circle is

(a) 2 units (b) π units (c) 4 units (d) 7 units

15. A right circular cylinder of radius r cm and height h cm ($h > 2r$) just encloses a sphere of diameter. Then diameter is

(a) r cm (b) $2r$ cm (c) h cm (d) $2h$ cm

16. Two dice are thrown simultaneously. The probability of getting a sum of 9 is

(a) $\frac{1}{10}$ (b) $\frac{3}{36}$ (c) $\frac{1}{9}$ (d) $\frac{4}{9}$

17. A bag has 11 green marbles, 4 black marbles and 7 purple marbles. One marble is drawn out randomly. The probability of not getting a purple marble is

(a) 0.5 (b) 0.56 (c) 0.75 (d) 0.68

18. The median and mean of frequency distribution is 7 and 8 respectively. Then the mode is

(a) $\frac{1}{13}$ (b) 4 (c) 5 (d) 33

DIRECTIONS: In the question number **19** and **20**, a statement of **Assertion (A)** is followed by a statement of **Reason (R)**. Choose the correct option out of the following:

(a) Both Assertion (A) and Reason (R) are true and Reason (R) is the correct explanation of Assertion (A).

(b) Both Assertion (A) and Reason (R) are true but Reason (R) is not the correct explanation of Assertion (A).

(c) Assertion (A) is true but Reason (R) is false.

(d) Assertion (A) is false but Reason (R) is true.

19. **Assertion (A):** If surface area of ball is $221.76\ cm^2$, then its diameter is 8.4 cm

Reason (R): If S is the surface area of sphere, then its radius i.e., $r = \frac{1}{2}\sqrt{\frac{S}{\pi}}$

20. **Assertion (A):** If $a_n - a_{n-1}$ is not independent of n, then given sequence is A.P.

Reason (R): Common difference $d = a_n - a_{n-1}$ is constant.

SECTION - B

Section - B consists of Very Short Answer (VSA) type questions of 2 marks each.

21. Explain why $7 \times 11 \times 13 + 13$ and $7 \times 6 \times 5 \times 4 \times 3 \times 2 \times 1 + 5$ are composite numbers.

22. In the given figure, $LM \parallel RQ$ if $PM = 4x - 3$, $MQ = 3x - 1$, $PL = 8x - 7$, $LR = 5x - 3$, then find the value of x.

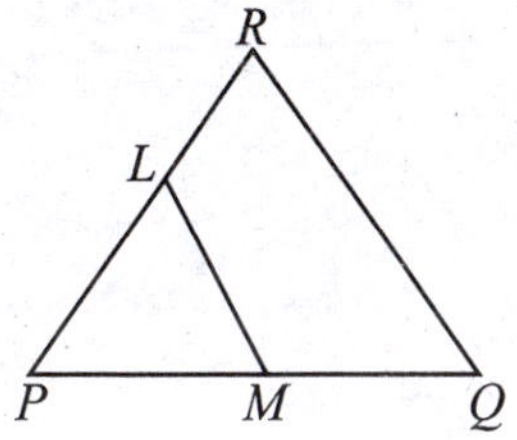

23. In the given figures, $PA = 7$ cm $= PQ$ if $RA = 8$ cm, find SR.

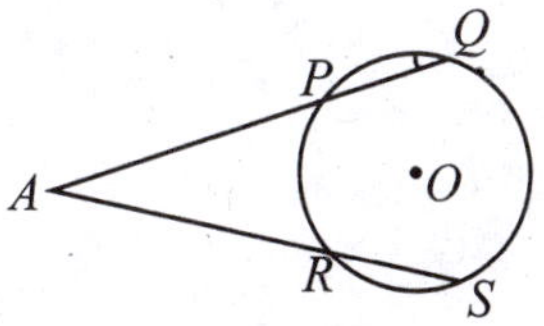

24. (*a*) Show that $\sec^4\theta - \sec^2\theta = \tan^4\theta + \tan^2\theta$.

OR

(*b*) Prove that: $\frac{2\cos^3\theta - \cos\theta}{\sin\theta - 2\sin^3\theta} = \cot\theta$

25. (*a*) In the given figure 'O' is the centre of a circle. The area of sector $OPMQ$ is $\frac{5}{18}$ of the area of the circle. Then, find the value of x.

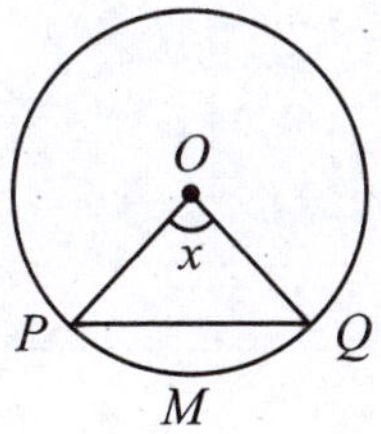

OR

(*b*) A pendulum describes an arc 8.8 cm in length when it swings through an angle of 30°. Find the length of the pendulum.

SECTION - C

Section - C consists of Short Answer (SA) type questions of 3 marks each.

26. Two different dices are tossed together. Find the probability:

(*i*) of getting a doublet

(*ii*) of getting a sum 10, of the numbers on the two dice.

27. Find the value of $\frac{1}{(a\alpha + b)} + \frac{1}{(a\beta + b)}$ where α and β are the roots of equation $ax^2 + bx + c = 0$

28. (*a*) There are some students in the two examination halls A and B. To make the number of students equal in each hall, 10 students are sent from A to B. But if 20 students are sent from B to A, the number of students in A becomes double the number of students in B. Find the number of students in the two halls.

OR

(*b*) The sum of numerator and denominator of a fraction is 3 less than twice the denominator. If each of the numerator and denominator is decreased by 1, the fraction becomes $\frac{1}{2}$. Find the fraction.

29. Find the distance of point M from the circle, if radius of the circle be 5 and length of a tangent from point M is $5\sqrt{3}$.

30. If $\frac{\cos\alpha}{\cos\beta} = p$ and $\frac{\cos\alpha}{\sin\beta} = q$, then prove that $(p^2 + q^2)\cos^2\alpha = q^2p^2$

31. (*a*) An army contingent of 616 members is to march behind an army band of 32 members in a parade. The two groups are to march in the same number of columns. What is the maximum number of columns in which they can march?

OR

(*b*) There is a circular path around a sports field. Monika takes 18 minutes to drive one round of the field, while Rohit takes 12 minutes for the same. Suppose they both start at the same point and at the same time, and go in the same direction. After how many minutes will they meet again at the starting point?

SECTION - D

Section - D consists of Long Answer (LA) type questions of 5 marks each.

32. (*a*) One day, the National Museum of India, New Delhi admitted 321 people (adults and children) and collected ₹1590. The price of admission is ₹ 6 for an adult and ₹4 for a child. How many adults and how many children were admitted to the museum on the day.

OR

(*b*) The present age of a father is three years more than three times the age of his son. Three years hence the father's age will be 10 years more than twice the age of the son. Determine their present ages.

33. If AD and PM are medians of triangles ABC and PQR, respectively where $\Delta ABC \sim \Delta PQR$, prove that $\frac{AB}{PQ} = \frac{AD}{PM}$.

34. (*a*) A spherical glass vessel has a cylindrical neck 8 cm long, 2 cm in diameter; the diameter of the spherical part is 8.5 cm. By measuring the amount of water it holds, a child finds its volume to be 345 cm^3. Check whether she is correct, taking the above as the inside measurements, and $\pi = 3.14$.

OR

(*b*) The water in a rectangular reservoir having a base 80 m × 60 m, is 6.5 m deep. In what time can the water be emptied by a pipe of which the cross section is a square of side 20 cm, if water runs through the pipe at the rate of 10 km/hr?

35. The following table shows the ages of patients admitted in a hospital during a year:

Age is years	5–15	15–25	25–35	35–45	45–55	55–65
No. of patients	6	11	21	23	14	5

Find the mode of the data given above.

SECTION - E

Section - E consists of three Case Based questions of 4 marks each.

36. A radio station was built near village Baghour for the better transmission of signals and there were two sections, section –*x* and section-y upon which tower was built. Engineers have observed that the angle of elevation of top of section –*X* is 30°, when engineers were at a distance of 24 *m* from the base of radio station and angle of elevation of top of section – *Y* is 45°.

(Use $\sqrt{3}$ = 1.73)

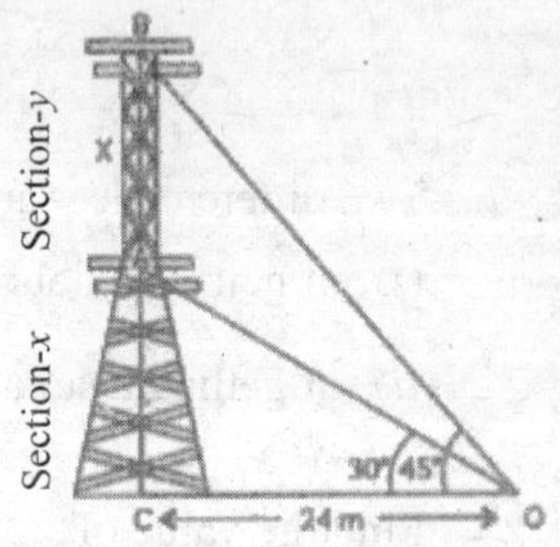

(*i*) Find the total height of the radio station from the ground. 1

(*ii*) Find the height of section-*x*. 2

OR

Find the height of section-*y*.

(*iii*) A wire is lied from top of the radio station (from point-*R*) to a point *A* on the ground for additional support. Find the length of the wire. 1

37. A group of Class X students went to picnic during summer holidays. There were three different slides and three friends, Rahul, Rohit and Mohit an sliding in three slides. The position of three friends shown by A, B and C in three different slides are given below

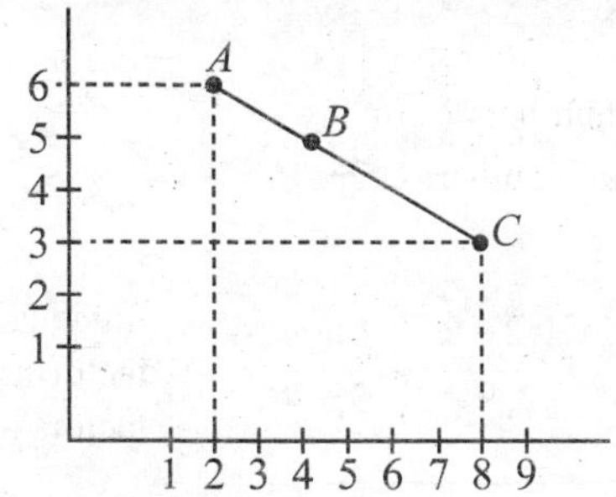

(*i*) Find co-ordinates of point 'B' which divides the line segment AC in ratio 1 : 2 internally. **1**

(*ii*) Find the coordinates of point on x-axis which is at equal distance from A and B. **2**

OR

Find the coordinates of point on y-axis which is at equal distance from A and B.

(*iii*) Find the distance AC. **1**

38. In a factory, the production of TV sets increases uniformly by a fixed number every year, it produced 16000 sets in 6th year and 22600 in 9th year.

(*i*) What is production during 8th year? **1**

(*ii*) What is production during I^{st} year? **2**

OR

Find total production of TV sets during I^{st} 4 years.

(*iii*) What is production during 6th year? **1**

HINTS & EXPLANATIONS

1. (*d*) The least number divisible by all the numbers from 1 to 10 will be the L.C.M of the following number: 1, 2, 3, 4, 5, 6, 7, 8, 9 & 10.

Prime factorisation of these numbers are $1 = 1, 2 = 2, 3 = 3, 4 = 2 \times 2, 5 = 5, 6 = 2 \times 3, 7 = 7, 8 = 2 \times 2 \times 2, 9 = 3 \times 3, 10 = 2 \times 5$

So, the L.C.M of these number is

$1 \times 2 \times 2 \times 2 \times 3 \times 3 \times 5 \times 7 = 2520$ *(1 M)*

Key Takeaways

Check that the correct option should be divisible by all the natural numbers 1–10 as the L.C.M is the lowest common multiple.

2. (*c*) Given polynomial $ax^2 + bx + c, c \neq 0$

In quadratic polynomial. Coefficient of x^2 and constant term have the same sign i.e. 'c' and 'a' have the same sign. While 'b', coefficient of x can be positive or negative but not zero. *(1 M)*

3. (*c*) Given, $x + 2y - 5 = 0$ and $-3x - 6y + 15 = 0$

Here, $a_1 = 1, \quad b_1 = 2, \quad c_1 = -5$

$a_2 = -3, \quad b_2 = -6 \quad c_2 = 15$

Now, $\frac{a_1}{a_2} = -\frac{1}{3}, \frac{b_1}{b_2} = -\frac{1}{3}, \frac{c_1}{c_2} = -\frac{1}{3}$

It implies that

$$\frac{a_1}{a_2} = \frac{b_1}{b_2} = \frac{c_1}{c_2}$$

So, given pair of linear equation have infinitely many solution. *(1 M)*

4. (*d*) We have, $ax^2 + bx + c = a(x - p)^2$

$ax^2 + bx + c = ax^2 + ap^2 - 2apx$

On comparing coefficients, we get $-2ap = b$

$\Rightarrow p = -\frac{b}{2a}$ ... (*i*)

and $c = ap^2$ ... (*ii*)

from equation (*i*) and (*ii*), we get

$\Rightarrow c = a\frac{b^2}{4a^2} \Rightarrow b^2 = 4ac$

Nailing the Right Answer

Students should start to identify the quadratic equation's key components: the coefficient of the squared term (a), the linear term (b), and the constant term (c).

Mistakes 101 : What not to do!

Students may forget common factors or skip steps while factoring quadratic expressions, which results the incorrect factors and solutions.

5. (*a*) Let, $a = n - 2; b = 4n - 1; c = 5n + 2$

Since the terms are in AP,

$\therefore\ 2b = a + c \Rightarrow 2(4n - 1) = n - 2 + 5n + 2$

$\Rightarrow 8n - 2 = 6n \Rightarrow 8n - 6n = 2 \Rightarrow n = 1$

Therefore, the value of n is 1. *(1 M)*

6. (*d*) We know that coordinates of the point dividing the line segment joining the points (x_1, y_1) and (x_2, y_2) in ratio $m : n$ then

$$(x, y) = \left(\frac{mx_2 + nx_1}{m+n}, \frac{my_2 + ny_1}{m+n}\right)$$

Now, Given, $x_1 = -1, \quad y_1 = 7, \quad m = 2$

$x_2 = 4, \quad y_2 = -3 \quad n = 3$

$$\text{Now, } (x, y) = \left(\frac{2\times4+3\times(-1)}{2+3}, \frac{2\times(-3)+3\times7}{2+3}\right)$$

$$(x, y) = \left(\frac{5}{5}, \frac{15}{5}\right)$$

Hence, $(x, y) = (1, 3)$ *(1 M)*

7. (*b*) Let the point on x-axis be $A(x, 0)$

Given, $P(-2, 3), Q(5, 4)$

Now, according to question

$PA = QA$

$\Rightarrow\ PA^2 = QA^2$

$\Rightarrow\ (x - (-2))^2 + (0 - 3)^2 = (x - 5)^2 + (0 - 4)^2$

$\Rightarrow\ x^2 + 4 + 4x + 9 = x^2 + 25 - 10x + 16$

$\Rightarrow\ 14x = 28 \Rightarrow x = 2$

So, coordinate on x-axis is (2, 0) *(1 M)*

8. (*b*) From the given condition D and E are midpoint of AB and AC and $DE \parallel BC$.

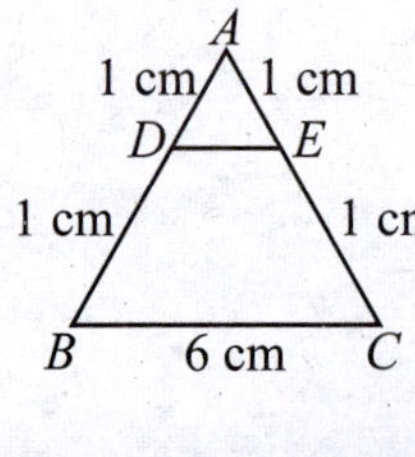

We can say that $\Delta ABC \sim \Delta ADE$

So, $\frac{AD}{AB} = \frac{DE}{BC}$

$\Rightarrow \frac{1}{2} = \frac{DE}{6} \Rightarrow DE = 3$ cm (1 M)

9. (c)

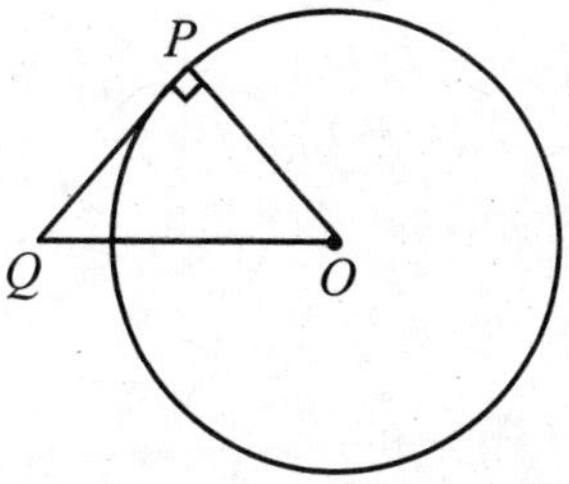

In $\angle OPQ$,

$PO \perp PQ \Rightarrow \angle P = 90^\circ$ ...(i)

$\because$ tangent is $\perp$ar to the radius passing through the point of contact. Also, $\angle PQO$ is an isosceles triangle.

So, $\angle Q = \angle O$ ...(ii)

Now, $\angle P + \angle Q + \angle O = 180^\circ$

$\Rightarrow 2\angle Q + 90^\circ = 180^\circ$ (From (i) and (ii))

$\Rightarrow 2\angle Q = 90^\circ$

$\therefore \angle Q = 45^\circ$ (1 M)

10. (c)

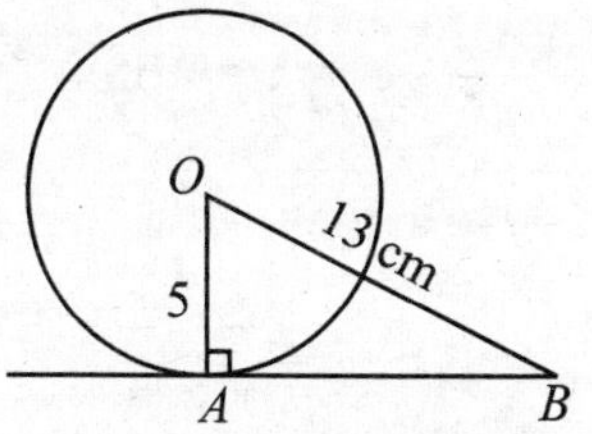

In ΔAOB, $\angle OAB = 90^\circ$

By Pythagoras theorem,

$\Rightarrow (OB)^2 = (OA)^2 + (AB)^2 \Rightarrow (13)^2 = (5)^2 + (AB)^2$

$\Rightarrow (AB)^2 = 169 - 25 \Rightarrow (AB)^2 = 144$

$\Rightarrow AB = 12$ cm (1 M)

11. (a) Given, $\tan\theta = \frac{a}{b}$

Perp. = ak, base = bk

Now, by Pythagoras theorem

$\Rightarrow (\text{Hypo.})^2 = (\text{Perp.})^2 + (\text{base})^2$

$\Rightarrow (\text{Hypo.})^2 = (ak)^2 + (bk)^2$

$\Rightarrow (\text{Hypo.})^2 = a^2k^2 + b^2k^2$

$\Rightarrow (\text{Hypo.}) = \sqrt{(a^2+b^2)k^2}$

$\Rightarrow \text{Hypo.} = \sqrt{(a^2+b^2)}k$

Now, $\sin\theta = \frac{\text{Perp.}}{\text{Hypo.}} = \frac{ak}{\sqrt{a^2+b^2}\cdot k}$

$\therefore \sin\theta = \frac{a}{\sqrt{a^2+b^2}}$ (1 M)

12. (b) $\cos^2\theta + \frac{1}{1+\cot^2\theta}$

$= \cos^2\theta + \frac{1}{1+\frac{\cos^2\theta}{\sin^2\theta}}$

$= \cos^2\theta + \frac{1}{\frac{\sin^2\theta+\cos^2\theta}{\sin^2\theta}}$

$= \cos^2\theta + \frac{\sin^2\theta}{\sin^2\theta+\cos^2\theta}$

$= \cos^2\theta + \sin^2\theta$ $[\because \sin^2\theta + \cos^2\theta = 1]$

$= 1$ (1 M)

13. (c) Let the length of pole be AB and length of shadow be AC

Now, $\tan\theta = \frac{AB}{AC}$

$\Rightarrow \tan\theta = \frac{1}{\sqrt{3}} \Rightarrow \tan\theta = \tan 30^\circ \Rightarrow \theta = 30^\circ$ (1 M)

14. (a) We know, Perimeter of circle = $2\pi r$

Area of circle = πr^2

Now, according to question

Perimeter = Area

$\Rightarrow 2\pi r = \pi r^2 \Rightarrow r = 2$ units (1 M)

15. (b) Radius of cylinder = r

Height = $h > 2r$

Since the sphere is enclosed by a cylinder, the radius of the cylinder will be the radius of the sphere. Therefore, diameter of sphere = $2r$ cm. (1 M)

16. (c) Two dice are thrown than maximum possible outcomes = 36.

Let A be the event of getting a sum of 9.

= {(3, 6) (4, 5) (5, 4) (6, 3)}

$\therefore n(A) = 4$

Now, Probability $= \frac{n(A)}{n(S)} = \frac{4}{36} = \frac{1}{9}$ (1 M)

17. (d) S = Total number of marbles in bag = 11 + 4 + 7

$\therefore n(S) = 22$

Number of marbles other than purple = 11 + 4 = 15

Probability $= \frac{15}{22} = 0.68$ (1 M)

18. (*c*) Given, median = 7, mean = 8

We know, mode = 3 × median – 2 × mean

$= 3 \times 7 - 2 \times 8 = 21 - 16 = 5$ (1 M)

19. (*a*) Given surface area, $S = 221.76\text{ cm}^2$

We know, surface area, $S = 4\pi r^2$

$\Rightarrow r = \frac{1}{2}\sqrt{\frac{S}{\pi}}$

$\Rightarrow r = \frac{1}{2}\sqrt{\frac{221.76 \times 7}{22}}$

$\Rightarrow r = 4.2$ cm

$\therefore$ Diameter $(d) = 2r = 8.4$ cm

Both (A) and (R) are true and Reason (R) is correct explanation of A. (1 M)

20. (*d*) Reason: Common difference is difference between two consecutive terms which is same throughout the sequence, so R is true.

Now, Assertion:

Here, $a_n - a_{n-1} = d$ which is independent of n.

So, A is false. (1 M)

21. It can be observed that

$7 \times 11 \times 13 + 13 = 13 \times (7 \times 11 + 1) = 13 \times (77 + 1)$

$= 13 \times 78 = 13 \times 13 \times 6$ (½ M)

The given expression has 6 and 13 as its factors. Therefore, it is a composite number.

$7 \times 6 \times 5 \times 4 \times 3 \times 2 \times 1 + 5 = 5 \times (7 \times 6 \times 4 \times 3 \times 2 \times 1 + 1)$

$= 5 \times (1008 + 1) = 5 \times 1009$ (½ M)

1009 cannot be factorised further. Therefore, the given expression has 5 and 1009 as its factors. Hence, it is a composite number. (1 M)

22. $LM \parallel RQ$

By Thales theorem

In ΔPLM and ΔPRQ

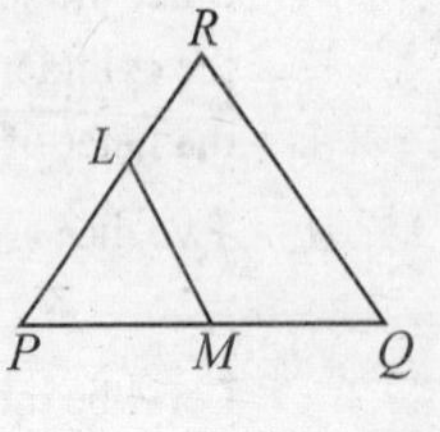

$\frac{PL}{LR} = \frac{PM}{MQ}$

[in accordance to converse *BPT*]

$\Rightarrow \frac{8x-7}{5x-3} = \frac{4x-3}{3x-1}$ (1 M)

$\Rightarrow (8x-7)(3x-1) = (4x-3)(5x-3)$

$\Rightarrow 24x^2 - 29x + 7 = 20x^2 - 27x + 9$

$\Rightarrow 4x^2 - 29x + 27x + 7 - 9 = 0$

$\Rightarrow 4x^2 - 2x - 2 = 0$

$\Rightarrow 2x^2 - x - 1 = 0 \Rightarrow 2x^2 - 2x + x - 1 = 0$

$\Rightarrow 2x(x-1) + 1(x-1) = 0 \Rightarrow (2x+1)(x-1) = 0$

$\therefore x = 1, -\frac{1}{2}$ (1 M)

23. $AR \times AS = AP \times AQ$ [$\because AQ = AP + PQ$

$\Rightarrow 8 \times AS = 7 \times 14$ $= 7 + 7 = 14$ cm]

$\Rightarrow AS = \frac{7 \times 14}{8}$ (1 M)

$\Rightarrow AS = \frac{49}{4}$ cm

$RS = AS - AR = \frac{49}{4} - \frac{8}{1} = \frac{49-32}{4} = \frac{17}{4}$ cm. (1 M)

24. (*a*) $\text{L.H.S} = \sec^4\theta - \sec^2\theta = \sec^2\theta(\sec^2\theta - 1) = \sec^2\theta \times \tan^2\theta$ (1 M)

$\text{R.H.S} = \tan^4\theta + \tan^2\theta = \tan^2\theta(1 + \tan^2\theta) = \tan^2\theta \times \sec^2\theta$ (1 M)

Hence, L.H.S = R.H.S Proved

OR

(*b*) $\text{L.H.S} = \frac{2\cos^3\theta - \cos\theta}{\sin\theta - 2\sin^3\theta}$

$= \frac{\cos\theta\,(2\cos^2\theta - 1)}{\sin\theta\,(1 - 2\sin^2\theta)} = \cot\theta \frac{(\cos^2\theta + \cos^2\theta - 1)}{(1 - \sin^2\theta - \sin^2\theta)}$

[$\because 1 - \sin^2\theta = \cos^2\theta$ and $1 - \cos^2\theta = \sin^2\theta$] (1 M)

$= \cot\theta \frac{(\cos^2\theta - \sin^2\theta)}{\cos^2\theta - \sin^2\theta} = \cot\theta = \text{RHS}$ (1 M)

Hence, L.H.S = R.H.S Proved

Topper's Explanation ***(CBSE 2020)***

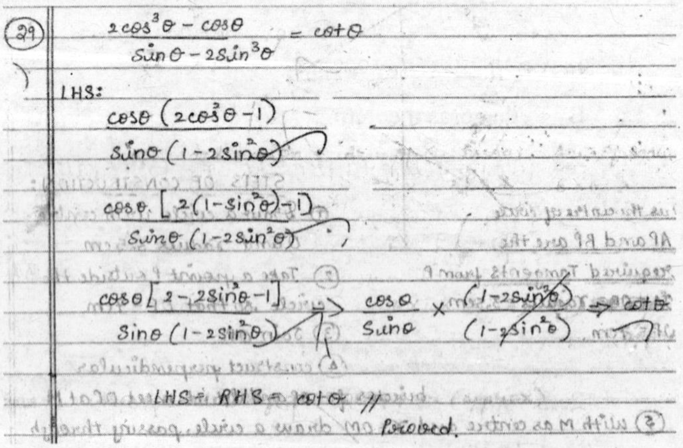

25. (*a*) Area of sector $OPMQ = \frac{x}{360°} \times \pi r^2$ $(\theta = x)$

According to the questions,

Area of sector $OPMQ = \frac{5}{18} \times \pi r^2$ (1 M)

$\Rightarrow \frac{x}{360°} \times \pi r^2 = \frac{5}{18} \times \pi r^2 \Rightarrow x = \frac{5 \times 360°}{18} = 100°$

Hence, the value of x is 100°. (1 M)

OR

(*b*) It is given that, length of arc $l = 8.8$ cm and $\theta = 30°$

Given length of arc (l) = 8.8 cm

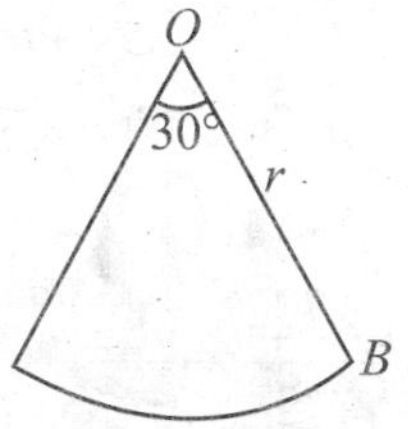

$\therefore$ We know, $l = \dfrac{\theta}{360°} \times 2\pi r$

$\Rightarrow \quad 8.8 = \dfrac{30°}{360°} \times 2 \times \dfrac{22}{7} \times r$ *(1 M)*

$\Rightarrow \quad r = \dfrac{8.8 \times 6 \times 7}{22} = 16.8$ cm *(1 M)*

26. Possible outcomes are

{(1, 1), (1, 2), (1, 3), (1, 4), (1, 5), (1, 6)
(2, 1), (2, 2), (2, 3), (2, 4), (2, 5), (2, 6)
(3, 1), (3, 2), (3, 3), (3, 4), (3, 5), (3, 6)
(4, 1), (4, 2), (4, 3), (4, 4), (4, 5), (4, 6)
(5, 1), (5, 2), (5, 3), (5, 4), (5, 5), (5, 6)
(6, 1), (6, 2), (6, 3), (6, 4), (6, 5), (6, 6)}

Total elementary events = 36 *(1 M)*

(*i*) Outcomes of doublet = {(1, 1), (2, 2), (3, 3), (4, 4), (5, 5), (6, 6)}, i.e. 6

P (getting a doublet) = $\dfrac{6}{36} = \dfrac{1}{6}$ *(1 M)*

(*ii*) Outcomes of getting a sum 10 = {(4, 6), (5, 5), (6, 4)}, i.e. 3

P (getting a sum 10) = $\dfrac{3}{36} = \dfrac{1}{12}$ *(1 M)*

Mistakes 101 : What not to do!

Students may make mistakes while figuring out the total outcomes and the favourable outcomes while calculating Probability.

27. Given equation $ax^2 + bx + c = 0$

Sum of roots = $\alpha + \beta = \dfrac{-b}{a}$

and Product of roots = $\alpha\beta = \dfrac{c}{a}$ *(1 M)*

Now, $\dfrac{1}{a\alpha + b} + \dfrac{1}{a\beta + b}$

$= \dfrac{a\beta + b + a\alpha + b}{(a\alpha + b)(a\beta + b)} = \dfrac{a(\alpha + \beta) + 2b}{a^2\alpha\beta + ab(\alpha + \beta) + b^2}$ *(1 M)*

$= \dfrac{-\dfrac{b}{a} \times a + 2b}{a^2 \times \dfrac{c}{a} - \dfrac{b}{a} \times ab + b^2} = \dfrac{b}{ac - b^2 + b^2} = \dfrac{b}{ac}.$ *(1 M)*

28. (*a*) Let the number of students in A and B be x and y respectively. *(½ M)*

Now, according to the question,

$x - 10 = y + 10 \Rightarrow \quad x - y = 20$ ...(*i*) *(½ M)*

Also,

$x + 20 = 2(y - 20) \Rightarrow \quad x - 2y = -60$ ...(*ii*) *(½ M)*

Subtracting eqn (*ii*) from eqn (*i*) we get,

$(x - y) - (x - 2y) = 20 - (-60)$

$\Rightarrow \quad -y + 2y = 80 \Rightarrow \quad y = 80$ *(½ M)*

$\Rightarrow \quad x - 80 = 20$ [From eqn (*i*)]

$\Rightarrow \quad x = 20 + 80 = 100$ *(½ M)*

Thus, the number of students in hall A and B are 100 and 80 respectively. *(½ M)*

OR

(*b*) Let the numerator be x and denominator be y and the fraction be $\dfrac{x}{y}$.

Now, $x + y + 3 = 2y \Rightarrow x = y - 3$ ...(*i*)

Also, $\dfrac{(x-1)}{(y-1)} = \dfrac{1}{2}$ *(1 M)*

$\Rightarrow \quad x - 1 = \dfrac{y-1}{2} \Rightarrow x = \dfrac{y-1}{2} + 1$ ...(*ii*)

From Eqn. (*i*) and (*ii*) we get

$\Rightarrow \quad y - 3 = \dfrac{y - 1 + 2}{2}$ *(1 M)*

$\Rightarrow \quad 2(y - 3) = y + 1 \Rightarrow 2y - 6 = y + 1 \Rightarrow y = 7$

Put the value of y in Eqn (*i*), we get $x = 7 - 3$

$\Rightarrow \quad x = 4$ *(1 M)*

Hence, the fraction is $\dfrac{4}{7}$.

29.

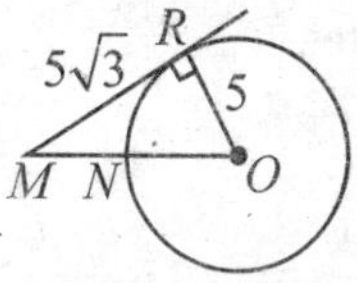

(1 M)

We have, $OM^2 = OR^2 + RM^2$ *(1 M)*

$= 5^2 + (5\sqrt{3})^2 = 25 + 25 \times 3 = 100$

$OM^2 = 100 \Rightarrow OM = 10$ cm.

Distance M from circle = $MN = OM - ON = 10 - 5 = 5$ cm *(1 M)*

30. L.H.S. = $(p^2 + q^2)\cos^2\alpha$

$= \left(\dfrac{\cos^2\alpha}{\cos^2\beta} + \dfrac{\cos^2\alpha}{\sin^2\beta}\right)\cos^2\alpha$ *(½ M)*

$= \cos^4\alpha\left[\dfrac{1}{\sin^2\beta} + \dfrac{1}{\cos^2\beta}\right] = \cos^4\alpha\left(\dfrac{\sin^2\beta + \cos^2\beta}{\sin^2\beta\cos^2\beta}\right)$

$= \dfrac{\cos^4\alpha}{\sin^2\beta\cos^2\beta}$ [$\because \sin^2\beta + \cos^2\beta = 1$]

R.H.S. = q^2p^2 *(1 M)*

$= \dfrac{\cos^2\alpha}{\sin^2\beta} \times \dfrac{\cos^2\alpha}{\cos^2\beta}$ *(½ M)*

$= \dfrac{\cos^4\alpha}{\sin^2\beta\cos^2\beta}$

Hence, L.H.S. = R.H.S. proved *(1 M)*

31. (a) Given:

Number of members in army contingent = 616

Number of members in army band = 32

If the two groups have to march in the same number of columns, we need to find out the highest common factor (HCF) between the two groups. *(1 M)*

We shall find the H.C.F, 616 is greater than 32, therefore

$616 = 32 \times 19 + 8$

$32 = 8 \times 4 + 0$ *(1 M)*

Now, we have obtained zero as remainder. Therefore, HCF (616, 32) = 8.

Hence, the maximum number of columns in which the two groups can march is 8. *(1 M)*

OR

(b) It is given that the time taken by Sonia is more than Ravi to complete one round.

We need to find the number of minutes after which they will meet again at the starting point. For this, there will be a smallest number that is divisible by both 18 and 12 and that will be the time when both meet again at the starting point. To find this we have to take LCM of both numbers. *(2 M)*

Therefore, LCM (18, 12) = $2 \times 3 \times 3 \times 2 \times 1 = 36$

Hence, Monika and Rohit will meet again at the starting point after 36 minutes. *(1 M)*

32. (a) Let the number of adults be x

Let the number of children be y *(1 M)*

$\Rightarrow x + y = 321$ ...(*i*)

and $6x + 4y = 1590$ ...(*ii*) *(1 M)*

Multiplying 4 in eqn. (*i*) and subtracting from (*ii*) we get

$4x + 4y = 1284$ *(1 M)*

$\Rightarrow 6x + 4y = 1590$

$\quad - \quad - \quad -$

$-2x \quad = -306$

$\Rightarrow x = 153$ *(1 M)*

put x in eqn. (*i*)

$\Rightarrow 153 + y = 321, y = 321 - 153 = 168$

Hence, number of adults and children are 153 and 168 respectively. *(1 M)*

OR

(b) Let, present age of son = x

And, present age of father = $3x + 3$ *(1 M)*

3 years later, age of son = $x + 3$

Age of father = $3x + 3 + 3 = 3x + 6$ ...(*i*) *(1 M)*

According to the given condition,

Age of father = $10 + 2(x + 3)$ *(1 M)*

$\therefore 3x + 6 = 10 + 2(x + 3) \Rightarrow 3x + 6 = 10 + 2x + 6$

$\Rightarrow 3x - 2x = 10 + 6 - 6 \Rightarrow x = 10$ *(1 M)*

$\therefore$ Present age of son = 10 years

Present age of father = $3x + 3 = 3 \times 10 + 3 = 33$ years *(1 M)*

Topper's Explanation *(CBSE 2020)*

(30) Let the Present age of Father = x years

son = y years

$x = 3y + 3$

$x - 3y - 3 = 0 \rightarrow (1)$

$x + 3 = 2(y + 3) + 10$

$x + 3 = 2y + 6 + 10$

$x - 2y = 16 - 3$

$x - 2y - 13 = 0 \rightarrow (2)$

Solving (1) and (2), $x - 3y - 3 = 0$

$-x + 2y + 13 = 0$

$-y + 10 = 0$

$y = 10$

$x = 33$

Ans: Present age of father = 33 years

son = 10 years

33. Given: $\Delta ABC \sim \Delta PQR$

We have to prove that $\frac{AB}{PQ} = \frac{AD}{PM}$

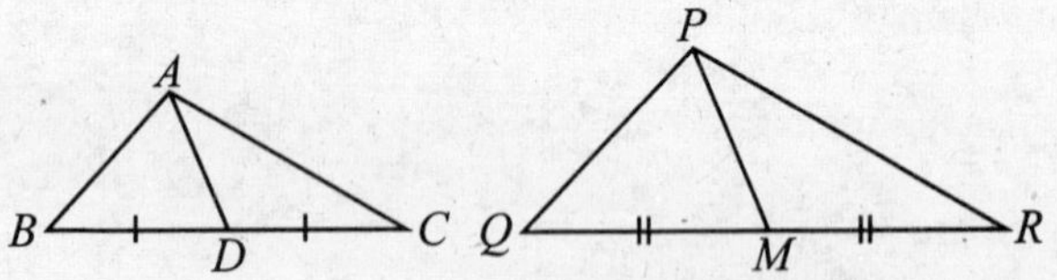

(1 M)

Proof: $\Delta ABC \sim \Delta PQR$

We know that the corresponding sides of similar triangles are in proportion.

$\therefore \frac{AB}{PQ} = \frac{AC}{PR} = \frac{BC}{QR}$ ...(*i*) *(1 M)*

Also, $\angle A = \angle P, \angle B = \angle Q, \angle C = \angle R$ ...(*ii*)

Since AD and PM are medians,

$\therefore BD = \frac{BC}{2}$ and $QM = \frac{QR}{2}$ ...(*iii*) *(1 M)*

From equations (*i*) and (*iii*), we get

$$\frac{AB}{PQ} = \frac{BD}{QM} \qquad ...(iv)$$

In ΔABD and ΔPQM,

$\angle B = \angle Q$ [using eq. (*ii*)] *(1 M)*

From equation (*iv*), we have, $\frac{AB}{PQ} = \frac{BD}{QM}$

$\therefore \Delta ABD \sim \Delta PQM$ (SAS similarity criterion)

$\Rightarrow \frac{AB}{PQ} = \frac{BD}{QM} = \frac{AD}{PM}$ (by definition of similarity)

$\frac{AB}{PQ} = \frac{AD}{PM}$ *(1 M)*

Hence proved

34. (*a*) Given, for the cylinder part, height $(h) = 8\ cm$ and radius $(R) = \left(\frac{2}{2}\right)\ cm = 1\ cm$ *(1 M)*

For the spherical part, radius $(r) = \left(\frac{8.5}{2}\right)\ cm = 4.25\ cm$

(1 M)

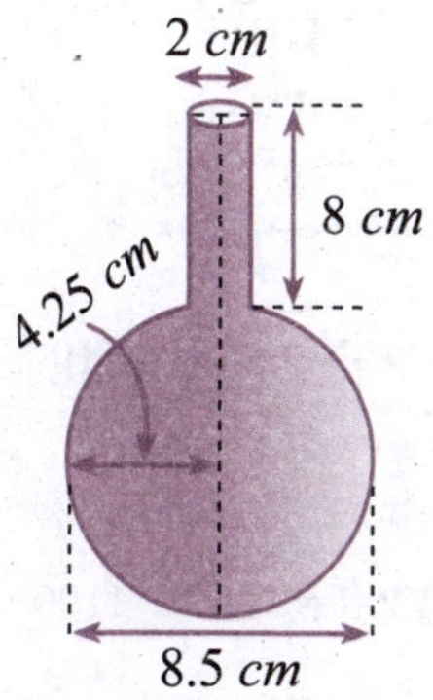

(1 M)

Now, the volume of this vessel = Volume of the cylinder + Volume of a sphere

$= \pi R^2 h + \frac{4}{3}\pi r^3$ *(1 M)*

$= \pi \times (1)^2 \times 8 + \frac{4}{3}\pi(4.25)^3$

$= 25.12 + 321.39$

$= 346.51\ cm^3$ *(1 M)*

OR

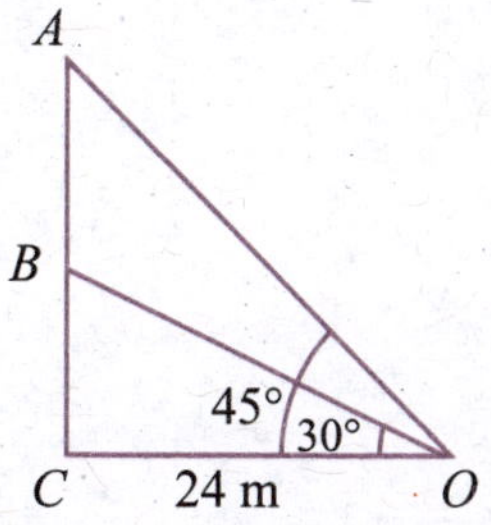

(*b*) The given dimensions of the rectangular reservoir are 80 *m*, 60 *m* and 6.5 *m* respectively. Hence,

$\because$ Volume of water in the reservoir $= l \times b \times h$

$= (80 \times 60 \times 6.5)\ m^3 = 31200\ m^3$ *(1 M)*

Now, area of cross section of the pipe = $(\text{side})^2$

$= \left(\frac{20}{100} \times \frac{20}{100}\right) m^2 = \frac{1}{25} m^2$ *(1 M)*

As, rate of flow of water = 10 *km/hr* = 10,000 *m/hr*.

So, volume of water emptied in 1 *hr* = Speed × Area of the cross-section $= \left(10000 \times \frac{1}{25}\right) m^3 = 400\ m^3$ *(1 M)*

Therefore, time taken to empty the reservoir

$= \frac{\text{Volume of tank}}{\text{Volume of water emptied in 1 } hr.}$ *(1 M)*

$= \frac{31200}{400} = 78$

Hence, the time taken to empty the tank will be 78 hours.

(1 M)

35. To find modal class, let us consider class interval with high frequency.

Greatest frequency = 23, modal class = 35–45

Lower limit of modal class. $l = 35$ *(1 M)*

Class size $(h) = 15 - 5 = 10$

Frequency of modal class, $f_1 = 23$

Frequency of class preceding the modal class $f_0 = 21$

Frequency of class succeeding the modal class $f_2 = 14$ *(1 M)*

$$\text{Mode} = l + \left[\frac{f_1 - f_0}{2f_1 - f_0 - f_2}\right] \times h \qquad (1\ M)$$

$$\Rightarrow \text{Mode} = 35 + \left[\frac{23-21}{46-21-14}\right] \times 10 = 35 + \frac{20}{11} = 36.8 \qquad (1\ M)$$

$\Rightarrow$ Mode = 36.8. *(1 M)*

36. (*i*) In right ΔAOC,

$$\tan 45° = \frac{AC}{OC}$$

$AC = OC = 24\text{m}$

Hence, the total height of radio sation is 24 m. *(1 M)*

(***ii***) Now, we find the height of section-*x*.

In right ΔBOC

$$\tan 30° = \frac{BC}{OC} \Rightarrow BC = \frac{24}{\sqrt{3}} \Rightarrow BC = 8\sqrt{3} \qquad (1\ M)$$

Hence, the height of section-*x* is $8\sqrt{3}$ m. *(1 M)*

OR

Height of section $y = AC - BC$ *(1 M)*

$= 24 - 8\sqrt{3} = 10.16$ m *(1 M)*

(***iii***) In right ΔAOC

$$\cos 45° = \frac{OC}{OA}$$

$OA = 24\sqrt{2}$

Hence, the length of wire is $24\sqrt{2}$ m. *(1 M)*

37. (*i*) Co-ordinate of $A = (2, 6)$

Co-ordinate of $C = (8, 3)$

Coordinate of $B = \left(\frac{1\times8+2\times2}{1+2}, \frac{1\times3+2\times6}{1+2}\right)$

$= \left(\frac{12}{3}, \frac{15}{3}\right) = (4, 5)$ *(1 M)*

(*ii*)

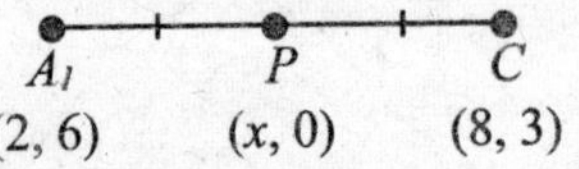

Let X be the point

On x-axis

Given $PA = CP$

$\sqrt{(x-2)^2+(0-6)^2} = \sqrt{(x-8)^2+(0-3)^2}$ *(1 M)*

$\Rightarrow\ x^2 + 4 - 4x + 36 = x^2 + 64 - 16x + 9$

$\Rightarrow\ 12x = 64 + 9 - 4 - 36 \Rightarrow 12x = 33 \Rightarrow x = \frac{33}{12} = \frac{11}{4}$

$\therefore$ Coordinate of point P on x-axis is $\left(\frac{11}{4}, 0\right)$ *(1 M)*

OR

Let $Q(0, y)$ be the coordinates on y-axis

Coordinate of $A = (2, 6)$ and $B(4, 5)$

Given $QA = QB$

$\sqrt{(2-0)^2(6-y)^2} = \sqrt{(4-0)^2+(5-y)^2}$ *(1 M)*

$\Rightarrow\ 4 + 36 + y^2 - 12y = 16 + 25 + y^2 - 10y$

$\Rightarrow\ 2y = -1 \Rightarrow y = -\frac{1}{2}$

$\therefore$ Coordinate of $Q(0, y) = \left(0, -\frac{1}{2}\right)$ *(1 M)*

(*iii*) Distance $AC = \sqrt{(8-2)^2+(3-6)^2}$

$= \sqrt{36+9} = \sqrt{45}$ *(1 M)*

38. (*i*) Production during 8th year $= a + 7d$

$= 5000 + 7 \times 2200 = 5000 + 15400 = 20400.$ *(1 M)*

(*ii*) Production in 6th year $= 16000$

$a + 5d = 16{,}000$ ...(*i*)

Production in 9th year $= 22600$

$a + 8d = 22600$ ...(*ii*)

Subtracting (*ii*) from (*i*)

$a + 5d = 16000$

$a + 8d = 22600$

$-\quad -\quad -$

$-3d = -6600$ *(1 M)*

$\Rightarrow\ d = \frac{6600}{3} = 2200 \Rightarrow a + 5 \times 2200 = 16000$

$\Rightarrow\ a + 11000 = 16000 \Rightarrow a = 5000$

Production in Ist year $= 5000$ *(1 M)*

OR

Total production of TV sets

During Ist 4 years $= \frac{n}{2}[2a+(n-1)d]$ *(1 M)*

$= \frac{4}{2}[2 \times 5000 + 3 \times 2200] = 2[10000 + 6600] = 33200.$ *(1 M)*

(*iii*) Production during 6th year $= a + 5d$

$= 5000 + 5 \times 2200 = 5000 + 11000 = 16000$ *(1 M)*

❑❑❑

MOCK TEST PAPER-2

Time allowed : 3 hours **Maximum Marks : 80**

GENERAL INSTRUCTIONS:

Read the following instructions very carefully and follow them:

(i) *This question paper contains* ***38*** *questions.* ***All*** *questions are compulsory.*

(ii) *Question Paper is divided into 5 Sections-****Section A, B, C, D and E.***

(iii) *In* ***Section A question number 1 to 18 are*** *Multiple Choice Questions* ***(MCQs)*** *and question number* ***19 & 20*** *are Assertion-Reason based* ***questions of 1 mark each.***

(iv) *In* ***Section-B question number 21 to 25 are*** *Very Short Answer (VSA) type* ***questions of 2 marks each.***

(v) *In* ***Section-C question number 26 to 31 are*** *Short Answer (SA) type* ***questions carrying 3 marks each.***

(vi) *In* ***Section-D question number 32 to 35 are*** *Long Answer (LA) type* ***questions carrying 5 marks each.***

(vii) *In* ***Section-E question number 36 to 38 are*** *Case Study based questions* ***carrying 4 marks each. Internal choice is provided in 2 marks question in each case-study.***

(viii) ***There is no overall choice. However, an internal choice has been provided in 2 questions in Section B, 2 questions in Section C, 2 questions in Section D and 3 questions in Section E.***

(ix) ***Draw neat figures wherever required. Take π = 22/7 wherever required if not stated.***

(x) ***Use of calculators is NOT allowed.***

SECTION - A

Section - A consists of Multiple Choice type questions of 1 mark each.

1. The HCF and the LCM of 12, 21, 15 respectively are

(*a*) 3, 140 (*b*) 12, 420 (*c*) 3, 420 (*d*) 420, 3

2. If $p-1, p+1$ and $2p+3$ are in A.P., then the value of p is

(*a*) –2 (*b*) 4 (*c*) 0 (*d*) 2

3. If α, β are zeroes of a polynomial $p(x) = 2x^2 - x - 1$ then $\alpha^2 + \beta^2$ is equal to

(*a*) $\frac{-3}{4}$ (*b*) $\frac{5}{4}$ (*c*) $\frac{1}{4}$ (*d*) $\frac{3}{4}$

4. The distance between the points $(0, 2\sqrt{5})$ and $(-2\sqrt{5}, 0)$ is

(*a*) $2\sqrt{10}$ units (*b*) $4\sqrt{10}$ units (*c*) $2\sqrt{20}$ units (*d*) 0

5. $A(5, 1)$, $B(1, 5)$ and $C(-3, -1)$ are the vertices of ΔABC. Then the length of median AD is

(*a*) $\sqrt{37}$ units (*b*) $\sqrt{17}$ units (*c*) $\sqrt{45}$ units (*d*) $\sqrt{27}$ units

6. In the given figure, PQ is tangent to the circle centered at O. If $\angle AOB = 95°$ then the measure of $\angle ABQ$ is

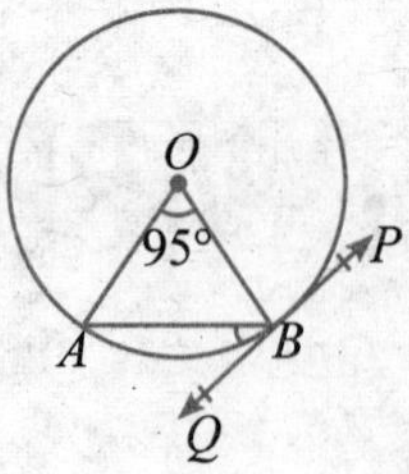

(a) 47.5° (b) 42.5° (c) 85° (d) 95°

7. If $2 \tan A = 3$, then the value of $\dfrac{4\sin A + 3\cos A}{4\sin A - 3\cos A}$ is

(a) $\dfrac{7}{\sqrt{13}}$ (b) $\dfrac{1}{\sqrt{13}}$ (c) 3 (d) does not exist

8. $\left[\dfrac{5}{8}\sec^2 60° - \tan^2 60° + \cos^2 45°\right]$ is equal to

(a) $\dfrac{-5}{3}$ (b) $\dfrac{-1}{2}$ (c) 0 (d) $\dfrac{-1}{4}$

9. The zeroes of $x^2 - 2x - 8$ are

(a) (2, –4) (b) (4, –2) (c) (–2, –2) (d) (–4, –4)

10. If $f(t) = 2t^2 - 8 - 8t$ and m, n are the zeroes of the polynomial, then the value of $m^2 - 2mn + n^2$ is

(a) 0 (b) 32 (c) 4 (d) 16

11. Curved surface area of a cylinder of height 5 cm is 94.2 cm^2. Radius of the cylinder is (Take $\pi = 3.14$)

(a) 2 cm (b) 3 cm (c) 2.9 cm (d) 6 cm

12. If d is the diameter of the sphere, then the surface area of the sphere is given by

(a) $\dfrac{4}{3}\pi d^2$ (b) $4\pi d^2$ (c) πd^2 (d) $3\pi d^2$

13. If the radius and height of a right circular cone are 'r' and 'h' respectively, the slant height of the cone is

(a) $(h^2 + r^2)^{1/3}$ (b) $(h + r)^{1/3}$ (c) $(h^2 + r^2)^{1/2}$ (d) $(h^2 + r^2)$

14. The radii of two right circular cones are in the ratio 2 : 3 and their heights are in the ratio 5 : 4. The ratio of their volumes is

(a) 25 : 36 (b) 5 : 9 (c) 36 : 25 (d) 9 : 25

15. If the mean of frequency distribution is 7.5 and $\Sigma f_i x_i = 120 + 3k$, $\Sigma f_i = 30$, then k is equal to

(a) 40 (b) 35 (c) 50 (d) 45

16. A girl calculates that the probability of her winning the first prize in a lottery is 0.08. If 6000 tickets are sold, how many tickets has she bought ?

(a) 40 (b) 240 (c) 480 (d) 750

17. The mode of observations 7, 12, 8, 5, 6, 4, 9, 10, 8, 9, 7, 9, 6, 5, 9 is

(a) 7 (b) 8 (c) 9 (d) 12

18. The mode and mean is given by 7 and 8 , respectively. Then the median is

(a) $\dfrac{1}{13}$ (b) $\dfrac{13}{3}$ (c) $\dfrac{23}{3}$ (d) 33

DIRECTIONS: In the question number **19** and **20**, a statement of **Assertion (A)** is followed by a statement of **Reason (R)**. Choose the correct option out of the following:

(a) Both Assertion (A) and Reason (R) are true and Reason (R) is the correct explanation of (A).

(b) Both Assertion (A) and Reason (R) are true but Reason (R) is not the correct explanation of Assertion (A).

(c) Assertion (A) is true but Reason (R) is false.

(d) Assertion (A) is false but Reason (R) is true.

19. **Assertion (A)** : Point $P(0, 2)$ is the point of intersection of y-axis with the line $3x + 2y = 4$.
Reason (R): The distance of point $P(0, 2)$ from x-axis is 2 units.

20. **Assertion:** The probability of getting a prime number when a die is thrown once is $\dfrac{2}{3}$.
Reason: Prime numbers on a die are 2,3,5.

SECTION - B

Section - B consists of Very Short Answer (VSA) type questions of 2 marks each.

21. If the HCF of 408 and 1032 is expressible in the form $1032 \times 2 + 408 \times p$, then find the value of p.

22. (a) The area of the base of a right circular cylinder is 154 cm^2 and its height is 15 cm. Find the C.S.A of the cylinder.

OR

(b) Find the height of a cylinder whose radius is 7 cm and the total surface area is 968 cm^2.

23. E is a point on the side AD produced of a parallelogram $ABCD$ and BE intersects CD at F. Show that $\Delta ABE \sim \Delta CFB$.

24. (a) If $\sin\theta + \sin^2\theta = 1$, then prove that $\cos^2\theta + \cos^4\theta = 1$

OR

(b) If $\sin\alpha = \frac{1}{\sqrt{2}}$ and $\cot\beta = \sqrt{3}$, then find the value of $\operatorname{cosec}\alpha + \operatorname{cosec}\beta$.

25. Find the mode of the following distribution:

Marks	0–10	10–20	20–30	30–40	40–50	50–60
Number of Students	4	6	7	12	5	6

SECTION - C

Section - C consists of Short Answer (SA) type questions of 3 marks each.

26. Prove that $\sqrt{3}$ is an irrational number.

27. Solve $2x + 3y = 11$ and $2x - 4y = -24$ and hence find the value of 'm' for which $y = mx + 3$.

28. Find the roots of the quadratic equation $\sqrt{2}x^2 + 7x + 5\sqrt{2} = 0$, by factorisation method.

29. Find the ratio in which the y-axis divides the line segment joining the points (6, –4) and (–2, –7). Also find the point of intersection.

30. (a) In the figure, if $PQ \parallel RS$, prove that & $\Delta POQ \sim \Delta SOR$

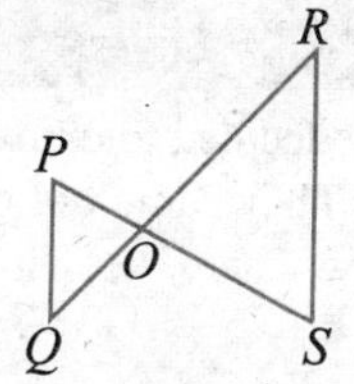

OR

(b) From an external point PA, tangents PA and PB are drawn to a circle with centre O. If $\angle PAB = 50°$, then find $\angle AOB$.

31. (a) Prove that $\frac{\tan\theta + \sec\theta - 1}{\tan\theta - \sec\theta + 1} = \frac{1 + \sin\theta}{\cos\theta}$

OR

(b) Prove that $(\operatorname{cosec}A - \sin A)(\sec A - \cos A) = \frac{1}{\cot A + \tan A}$

SECTION - D

Section - D consists of Long Answer (LA) type questions of 5 Marks each.

32. The sum of four consecutive numbers in an A.P is 32 and the ratio of the product of the first and the last term to the product of two middle terms is 7 : 15. Find the numbers.

33. Two taps running together can fill a tank in $3\frac{1}{13}$ hours. If one tap takes 3 hours more than the other to fill the tank, then how much time will each tap take to fill the tank?

34. (a) If a line is drawn parallel to one side of a triangle to intersect the other two sides at distinct points, prove that the other two sides are divided in the same ratio.

OR

(b) In the given figure, $\frac{PS}{SQ} = \frac{PT}{TR}$ and $\angle PST = \angle PRQ$. Prove that PQR is an isosceles triangle.

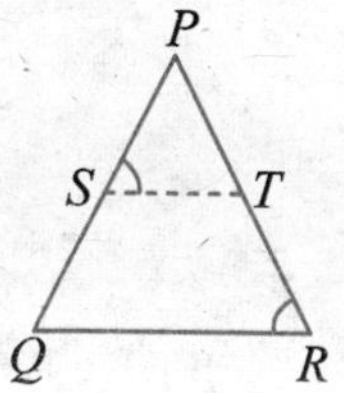

35. (*a*) A ladder set against a wall at an angle 45° to the ground. If the foot of the ladder is pulled away from the wall through a distance of 4m, its top slides a distance of 3m down the wall making an angle 30° with the ground. Find the final height of the top of the ladder from the ground and length of the ladder.

OR

(*b*) A spherical balloon of radius *r* subtends an angle of 60° at the eye of an observer. If the angle of elevation of its centre is 45° from the same point, then prove that height. of the centre of the balloon is $\sqrt{2}$ times its radius.

SECTION - E

Section - E consists of three Case Study Based questions of 4 marks each.

36. Ferris wheels are a popular attraction at fairs and amusement parks all over the world. They offer a unique and exciting experience for people of all ages. It is a large amusement ride consisting of a rotating upright wheel with passenger cars attached to the rim. The wheel is rotated by a motor and gears, and the cars rotate with the wheel. The cars are typically enclosed, and they have seats for riders.

Ravi with his four friends went to a fair and there they decided to enjoy the ride of the Ferris wheel. Due to the fear of the height, Ravi and one of his friends decided not to join them. They came out of the crowd and started observing their friends who were enjoying the ride. Ravi forms the figure as given below where the distance between *P* and *Q* is 50 m.

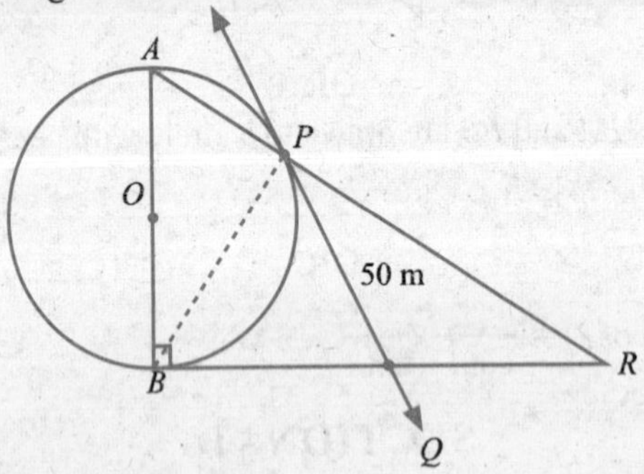

Based on the above information, answer the following questions.

(*i*) Find the $\angle APB$. **1**

(*ii*) Find the distance between *B* and *Q*. **2**

OR

Find the distance between *Q* and *R*.

(*iii*) If the radius of the Ferris wheel is 10 m, then find the distance between *A* and *R*. **1**

37. A 'circus' is a company of performers who put on shows of acrobats, clowns etc. to entertain people started around 250 years back, in open fields, now generally performed in tents.

One such 'Circus Tent' is shown below.

The tent is in the shape of a cylinder surmounted by a conical top. If the height and diameter of cylindrical part are 9 m and 30 m respectively and height of conical part is 8 m with same dsiameter as that of the cylindrical part.

Based on the above information, answer the following questions.

(*i*) What is the radius of conical part? **1**

(*ii*) The area of the canvas used in making the tent. **2**

OR

find the slant height of the cane.

(*iii*) The cost of the canvas bought for the tent at the rate ₹200 per sqm, if 30 sq *m* canvas was wasted during stitching. **1**

38. A man is decided to make a playground in various colony parks. They decided to study the age-group of children playing in a park of the particular colony. The classification of children according to their ages, playing in a park is shown in the following table.

Age group of children (in years)	6-8	8-10	10-12	12-14	14-16
Number of children	43	58	70	42	27

Based on the above information, answer the following questions.

(*i*) Which age group has the maximum number of children? **1**

(*ii*) Find frequency of the class succeeding the modal class **2**

OR

Find the mode of the ages of children playing in the park

(*iii*) Find the lower limit of the modal class **1**

HINTS & EXPLANATIONS

1. (*c*) Prime factor of given number is
$12 = 2 \times 2 \times 3$
$15 = 3 \times 5$
$21 = 3 \times 7$
H.C.F = Product of smallest power of each common prime factor $= 3 \times 1 = 3$
L.C.M = Product of greatest power of each prime factor $= 2^2 \times 3 \times 5 \times 7 = 4 \times 3 \times 5 \times 7 = 420$
Hence the H.C.F and L.C.M are 3 and 420 respectively. (1 M)

2. (*c*) Given:
$p-1, p+1, 2p+3$ are in A.P.
$\therefore 2(p+1) = p-1+2p+3$
$\Rightarrow 2p+2 = 3p+2 \Rightarrow p = 0$ (1 M)

3. (*b*) Here, the polynomial is $2x^2 - x - 1$
Comparing given polynomial with the general form $ax^2 + bx + c$, we get $a = 2; b = -1; c = -1$
Then, $\alpha + \beta = \frac{-b}{a} = \frac{1}{2}$
$\alpha\beta = \frac{c}{a} = \frac{-1}{2}$
Therefore,
$\alpha^2 + \beta^2 = (\alpha+\beta)^2 - 2\alpha\beta$
$= \left(\frac{1}{2}\right)^2 - 2\left(\frac{-1}{2}\right) = \frac{5}{4}$ (1 M)

4. (*a*) Here, $x_1 = 0, y_1 = 2\sqrt{5}$ and $x_2 = -2\sqrt{5}, y_2 = 0$
$d = \sqrt{(x_2-x_1)^2 + (y_2-y_1)^2}$
$\therefore$ Distance between the points $(0, 2\sqrt{5})$ and $(-2\sqrt{5}, 0)$
$\sqrt{(-2\sqrt{5}-0)^2 + (0-2\sqrt{5})^2}$
$= \sqrt{20+20} = \sqrt{40} = 2\sqrt{10}$ Units (1 M)

5. (*a*)

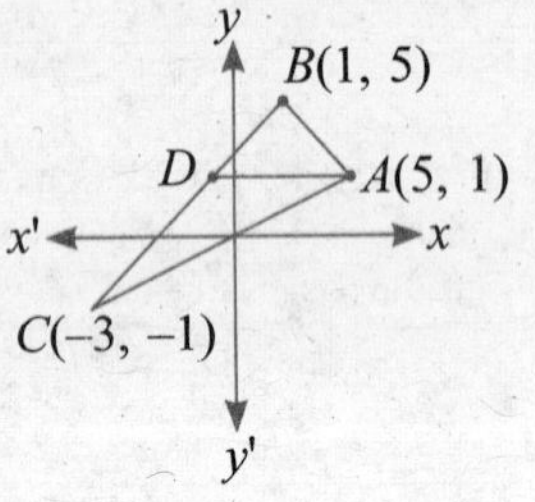

In this fig., D is the mid-point of BC
Then, the coordinates of D
$= \left(\frac{1-3}{2}, \frac{5-1}{2}\right) = (-1, 2)$
$\therefore AD = \left|\sqrt{(5+1)^2 + (1-2)^2}\right|$
$= \left|\sqrt{(36+1)}\right| = \left|\sqrt{37}\right|$
Therefore, the length of AD is $\sqrt{37}$ units (1 M)

6. (*a*) Given $\angle AOB = 95°$
In ΔAOB
$\angle AOB + \angle OAB + \angle OBA = 180°$
$\Rightarrow 95° + x + x + 180°$ [$OA = OB$ (radius)]
$\Rightarrow 2x = 85° \Rightarrow x = 42.5°$
$OB \perp PQ$
$\Rightarrow \angle OBA + \angle ABQ = 90° \Rightarrow 42.5° + \angle ABQ = 90°$
$\therefore \angle ABQ = 47.5°$ (1 M)

7. (*c*) Given: $2\tan A = 3 \Rightarrow \tan A = \frac{3}{2}$
$\frac{4\sin A + 3\cos A}{4\sin A - 3\cos A}$
On dividing by $\cos A$ in Numerator and Denominator, we get
$$= \frac{4\frac{\sin A}{\cos A}+3}{\frac{\sin A}{\cos A}-3} = \frac{4\tan A+3}{4\tan A-3} = \frac{4\times\left(\frac{3}{2}\right)+3}{4\times\left(\frac{3}{2}\right)-3} = \frac{9}{3} = 3$$
(1 M)

8. (*c*) $\frac{5}{8}\sec^2 60° - \tan^2 60° + \cos^2 45°$
$= \frac{5}{8}(2)^2 - (\sqrt{3})^2 + \left(\frac{1}{\sqrt{2}}\right)^2 = \frac{5}{8}\times 4 - 3 + \frac{1}{2} = 0$ (1 M)

9. (*b*) Comparing given polynomial with the general form $ax^2 + bx + c$, we get $a = 1, b = -2$ and $c = -8$
We have $x^2 - 2x - 8 = x^2 - 4x + 2x - 8$
$= x(x-4) + 2(x-4) = (x+2)(x-4)$
Equating this to 0, we will get the zeroes of the polynomial.
$(x-4)(x+2) = 0 \Rightarrow x = 4$ or $x = -2$
$\Rightarrow -2$ and 4 are the two zeroes of the given polynomial. (1 M)

10. (*b*) Given $f(t) = 2t^2 - 8t - 8$
$\therefore m + n = \frac{-(-8)}{2} = 4$
and $mn = \frac{-8}{2} = -4$
$(m-n)^2 = (m+n)^2 - 4mn = 16 + 16 = 32$
$\therefore m^2 - 2mn + n^2 = (m-n)^2 = 32$ (1 M)

11. (*b*) Given, $h = 5$ cm, Let radius $= r$
$\therefore$ Curved Surface Area = 94.2
$2\pi rh \Rightarrow 94.2 = 2 \times 3.14 \times r \times 5$
$\Rightarrow r = 3$ cm (1 M)

12. (*c*) If d is the diameter of the sphere, then the surface area of the sphere is given by $4\pi r^2 = 4\pi(d/2)^2 = \pi d^2$.

13. (*c*) It is given that r is radius and h is the height of the cone.
Therefore, slant height $(l) = \sqrt{h^2 + r^2}$
$\Rightarrow l^2 = h^2 + r^2 \Rightarrow l = (h^2 + r^2)^{1/2}$ (1 M)

14. (*b*) Let us suppose, $2r$ and $3r$ be the radii of two right circular cones respectively. Their heights be $5h$ and $4h$ respectively.

Let V_1 and V_2 be their volumes.

$$V_1 = \frac{1}{3}\pi \times (2r)^2 \times 5h = \frac{20}{3}\pi r^2 h$$

$$V_2 = \frac{1}{3}\pi \times (3r)^2 \times 4h = 12\pi r^2 h$$

$$\frac{V_1}{V_2} = \frac{20}{3} \times \frac{1}{12} = \frac{5}{9}$$ *(1 M)*

15. (*b*) We know

$$\text{mean, } \bar{X} = \frac{\sum f_i x_i}{\sum f_i} \Rightarrow 7.5 = \frac{(120+3k)}{30}$$

$\Rightarrow 7.5 \times 30 = 120 + 3k \Rightarrow 3k = 225 - 120$

$\Rightarrow 3k = 105 \quad \Rightarrow k = 35$ *(1 M)*

16. (*c*) Given, total number of tickets = 6000

Probability of her winning = 0.08

Total number of tickets she bought = 6000 × 0.08 = 480

(1 M)

17. (*c*) Number 9 occurs 4 times in the given data, So mode is 9.

(1 M)

Mistakes 101 : What not to do!

Students may forget to arrange data in ascending order, which results errors in determining both mode and median.

18. (*c*) Mode =3 Median –2 Mean

$\Rightarrow$ 3 Median = Mode + 2 Mean

$$\Rightarrow \text{Median} = \frac{(\text{Mode} + 2\text{ Mean})}{3}$$

$$\Rightarrow \text{Median} = \frac{[7+2(8)]}{3} = \frac{(7+16)}{3} = \frac{23}{3}$$ *(1 M)*

19. (*b*) y-axis $\Rightarrow x = 0$ ...(*i*)

$3x + 2y = 4$ ...(*ii*)

Put equation (*i*) in equation (*ii*), we get

$\Rightarrow 3 \times 0 + 2y = 4 \Rightarrow y = 2$

Point of intersection = (0, 2) *(½ M)*

Assertion is true.

$d = \sqrt{(0-0)^2 + (0-2)^2} = \sqrt{4} = 2$ Reason is true

(½ M)

Both Assertion (A) & Reason (R) are true, but Reason (R) is not the correct explanation of Assertion (A).

20. (*d*) The correct probability of getting a prime number when a die is thrown once is $\frac{1}{2}$, not $\frac{2}{3}$.

This is because a die has six faces numbered from 1 to 6 and only three of them are prime, which are 2, 3, and 5. Therefore, the probability of getting a prime number when a die is thrown once is $\frac{3}{6}$ or $\frac{1}{2}$.

Hence, Assertion (A) is false but Reason (R) is true. *(1 M)*

21. HCF of 408 and 1032 is 24.

$1032 \times 2 + 408 \times (p) = 24 \Rightarrow 408p = 24 - 2064$ *(1 M)*

$\therefore p = -5$ *(1 M)*

22. (*a*) It is given that, area of the base = 154 cm² and height (h) = 15 cm

$\therefore \pi r^2 = 154$ *(½ M)*

$$\Rightarrow \frac{22}{7}r^2 = 154 \Rightarrow r^2 = \frac{7 \times 154}{22} = 49 \Rightarrow r = 7 \text{ cm}$$

As, we know

C.S.A = $2\pi rh$ *(½ M)*

$= 2 \times \frac{22}{7} \times 7 \times 15$

$= 660$ cm² *(1 M)*

OR

(*b*) Let height of the cylinder = h, radius = r = 7cm

Total surface area = $2\pi r(h + r)$ *(1 M)*

$$\Rightarrow \quad \text{TSA} = 2 \times \frac{22}{7} \times 7 \times (7 + h) = 968 \Rightarrow h = 15 \text{ cm}$$

(1 M)

23. **Given:** E is a point on the side AD produced of a parallelogram $ABCD$ and BE intersects CD at F.

To prove: $\Delta ABE \sim \Delta CFB$

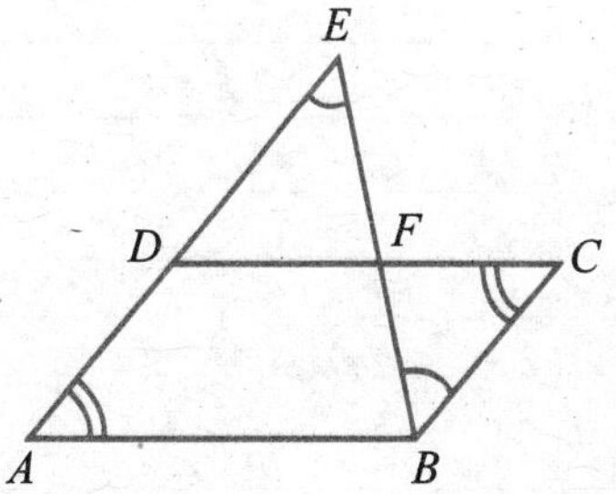

Proof: In ΔABE and ΔCFB, *(1 M)*

$\angle A = \angle C$ (Opposite angles of a parallelogram)

$\angle AEB = \angle CBF$ (Alternate interior angles as $AE \parallel BC$)

By AA similarity criterion, we have

$\Delta ABE \sim \Delta CFB$. *(1 M)*

24. (*a*) $\sin\theta + \sin^2\theta = 1$

$\Rightarrow \sin\theta = 1 - \sin^2\theta = \cos^2\theta$ *(1 M)*

$\therefore \cos^2\theta + \cos^4\theta = \cos^2\theta(1 + \cos^2\theta)$

$= \sin\theta\,(1 + \sin\theta) = \sin\theta + \sin^2\theta = 1$ *(1 M)*

OR

(*b*) $\text{cosec}\,\alpha = \frac{1}{\sin\alpha} = \sqrt{2}$

$\text{cosec}\,\beta = \sqrt{1 + \cot^2\beta} = \sqrt{1+3} = 2$ *(1 M)*

$\Rightarrow \text{cosec}\,\alpha + \text{cosec}\,\beta = \sqrt{2} + 2$ or $\sqrt{2}\,(\sqrt{2} + 1)$

(1 M)

25.

Marks	Number of Students (f)
0 – 10	4
10 – 20	6
20 – 30	$7 \rightarrow f_0$
30 – 40	$12 \rightarrow f_1$
40 – 50	$5 \rightarrow f_2$
50 – 60	6

(1 M)

Modal class $= 30 - 40$

$h = 10, f_0 = 7, f_1 = 12, f_2 = 5, l = 30$

$\therefore$ Mode $= l + \dfrac{f_1 - f_0}{2f_1 - f_0 - f_2} \times h$

$= 30 + \dfrac{12-7}{2\times12-7-5} \times 10 = 34.17\text{(Approx)}$ *(1 M)*

Topper's Explanation ***(CBSE 2020)***

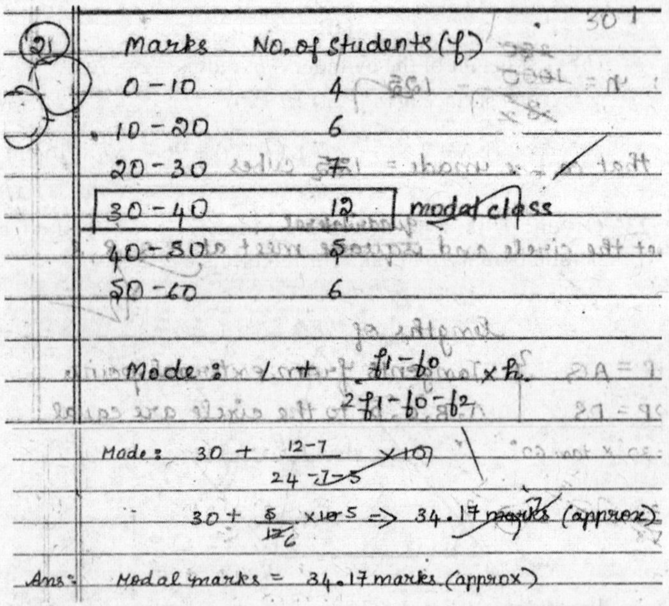

Marks	No. of Students (f)
0-10	4
10-20	6
20-30	7
30-40	12
40-50	5
50-60	6

modal class: 30-40

Mode: $l + \dfrac{f_1 - f_0}{2f_1 - f_0 - f_2} \times h$

Mode: $30 + \dfrac{12-7}{24-7-5} \times 10$

$30 + \dfrac{5}{12} \times 10 \Rightarrow 34.17$ (approx)

Ans: Modal marks = 34.17 marks (approx)

26. Let us make an assumption on the contrary that $\sqrt{3}$ is a rational number. Therefore, there must exist positive integers a and b for which $\sqrt{3} = \dfrac{a}{b}$ where, a and b, are co-prime i.e., their H.C.F is 1

Now, $\sqrt{3} = \dfrac{a}{b} \Rightarrow 3 = \dfrac{a^2}{b^2} \Rightarrow 3b^2 = a^2$ *(1 M)*

$\Rightarrow$ 3 divides a^2 [$\because$ 3 divides $3b^2$]

$\Rightarrow$ 3 divides a ... (i)

$\Rightarrow a = 3c$ for some integer c

$\Rightarrow a^2 = 9c^2 \Rightarrow 3b^2 = 9c^2 \Rightarrow b^2 = 3c^2$ *(1 M)*

$\Rightarrow$ 3 divides b^2 [$\because$ 3 divides $3c^2$]

$\Rightarrow$ 3 divides b ... (ii)

Therefore, a and b have at least 3 as a common factor.

But this contradicts the fact that a and b do not have a common factor other than 1.

This contradiction has arisen because of our wrong assumption that $\sqrt{3}$ is a rational number.

Thus, $\sqrt{3}$ is an irrational number. *(1 M)*

Topper's Explanation ***(CBSE 2019)***

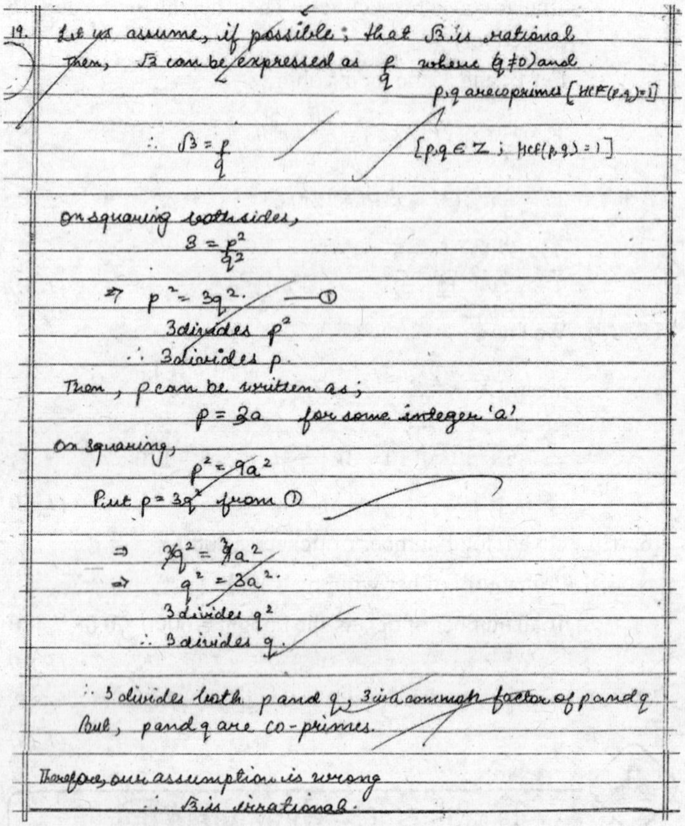

19\. Let us assume, if possible; that $\sqrt{3}$ is rational

Then, $\sqrt{3}$ can be expressed as $\frac{p}{q}$ where $(q \neq 0)$ and p, q are co-primes [HCF(p,q) = 1]

$\therefore \sqrt{3} = \frac{p}{q}$ [p, q ∈ Z; HCF(p,q) = 1]

On squaring both sides,

$3 = \frac{p^2}{q^2}$

$\Rightarrow p^2 = 3q^2$ —— ①

3 divides p^2

$\therefore$ 3 divides p.

Then, p can be written as;

p = 3a for some integer 'a'

On squaring,

$p^2 = 9a^2$

Put $p = 3q^2$ from ①

$\Rightarrow 3q^2 = 9a^2$

$\Rightarrow q^2 = 3a^2$

3 divides q^2

$\therefore$ 3 divides q.

$\therefore$ 3 divides both p and q, 3 is a common factor of p and q.

But, p and q are co-primes.

Therefore, our assumption is wrong

$\therefore \sqrt{3}$ is irrational.

27. $2x + 3y = 11$ ... (i)

$2x - 4y = -24$ ... (ii)

From equation (i), we obtain

$x = \dfrac{11-3y}{2}$ ... (iii) *(½ M)*

Substituting this value in equation (ii), we obtain

$2\left(\dfrac{11-3y}{2}\right) - 4y = -24$ *(½ M)*

$11 - 3y - 4y = -24 \Rightarrow -7y = -35$

$y = 5$ ... (iv) *(1 M)*

Putting this value of y in equation (iii), we obtain

$x = \dfrac{11-3\times5}{2} = -\dfrac{4}{2} = -2$ *(½ M)*

Hence, $x = -2,\ y = 5$

Also, $y = mx + 3 \Rightarrow 5 = -2m + 3 \Rightarrow -2m = 2 \Rightarrow m = -1$ *(½ M)*

28. Given, equation is:

$\sqrt{2}x^2 + 7x + 5\sqrt{2}$

Here, $a = \sqrt{2}, b = 7, c = 5\sqrt{2}$

Then,

$a \times c = \sqrt{2} \times 5\sqrt{2} = 10 = 5 \times 2 = (p \times q)$ *(1 M)*

and $a + c = 5 + 2 = (p + q) = 7 = b$ *(½ M)*

$\therefore \sqrt{2}x^2 + 5x + 2x + 5\sqrt{2} = 0$

$\Rightarrow x\left(\sqrt{2}x + 5\right) + \sqrt{2}\left(\sqrt{2}x + 5\right) = 0$ *(½ M)*

$\Rightarrow (x+\sqrt{2})(\sqrt{2}x+5)=0 \Rightarrow x+\sqrt{2}=0$ or $\sqrt{2}x+5=0$

$\Rightarrow x=-\sqrt{2}$ or $x=\dfrac{-5}{\sqrt{2}}$

Hence, the required roots are $-\sqrt{2}$ or $\dfrac{-5}{\sqrt{2}}$. *(1 M)*

Nailing the Right Answer

Evaluate which method (factorisation, or quadratic formula) would be most efficient and appropriate for solving the given quadratic equation.

29. Point dividing the line in ratio 1 : k by joining (x_1, y_1) and (x_2, y_2) is given by

$x=\dfrac{kx_1+x_2}{1+k},\ y=\dfrac{ky_1+y_2}{1+k}$ *(1 M)*

Let the point on y-axis be $(0, y)$

$0=\dfrac{k(6)+(-2)}{1+k} \Rightarrow k=\dfrac{1}{3}$ *(1 M)*

So y-axis divides the line in the ratio of 3:1

$$y=\frac{-4k-7}{1+k}=\frac{-4\left(\frac{1}{3}\right)-7}{1+\left(\frac{1}{3}\right)}=\frac{\frac{-25}{3}}{\frac{4}{3}}=\frac{-25}{4}$$

Hence the point of intersection $\left(0, \dfrac{-25}{4}\right)$ *(1 M)*

Topper's Explanation ***(CBSE 2020)***

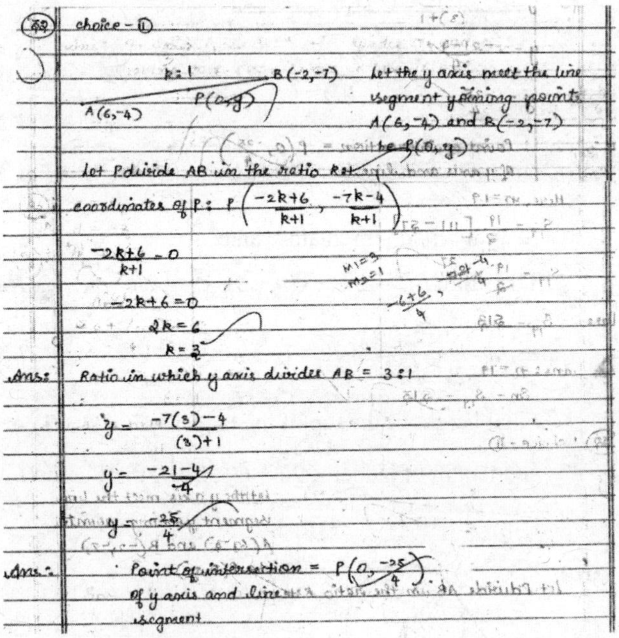

29) choice - ①

k : 1

A (6, -4) P(0, y) B (-2, -7)

Let the y axis meet the line segment joining points A(6, -4) and B(-2, -7) be P(0, y)

Let P divide AB in the ratio k : 1

coordinates of P : P$\left(\dfrac{-2k+6}{k+1}, \dfrac{-7k-4}{k+1}\right)$

$\dfrac{-2k+6}{k+1}=0$

$-2k+6=0$

$2k=6$

$k=3$

Ans: Ratio in which y axis divides AB = 3 : 1

$y=\dfrac{-7(3)-4}{(3)+1}$

$y=\dfrac{-21-4}{4}$

$y=\dfrac{-25}{4}$

Ans: Point of intersection of y axis and line segment = P$\left(0, \dfrac{-25}{4}\right)$

30. (*a*) Given,

$PQ \parallel RS$

$\angle P=\angle S$ (Alternate angles) *(1 M)*

and $\angle Q=\angle R$

Also, $\angle POQ=\angle SOR$ (Vertically opposite angles) *(1 M)*

Therefore, $\Delta POQ \sim \Delta SOR$ (by AAA similarity criterion)

Hence proved. *(1 M)*

OR

(*b*) $PA=PB$

...(Tangent drawn from external point are equal) *(½ M)*

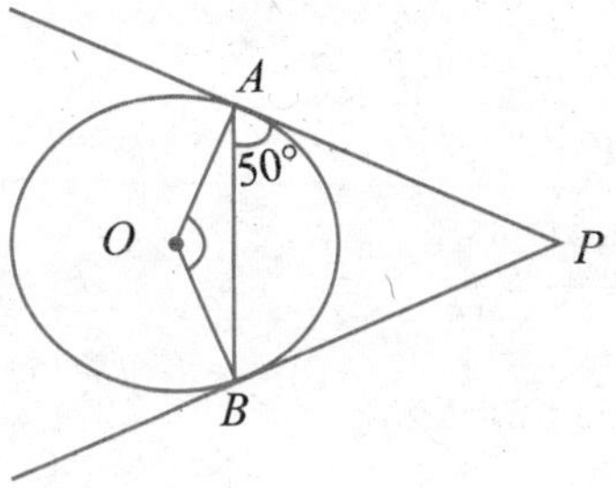

$\angle PBA=\angle PAB=50°$

(Angles equal to opposite sides) *(½ M)*

In ΔABP, $\angle PBA+\angle PAB+\angle APB=180°$

(Angle-sum-property of a Δ)

$\Rightarrow 50°+50°+\angle APB=180°$ *(1 M)*

$\Rightarrow \angle APB=180°-50°-50°=80°$

In cyclic quadrilateral $OAPB$

$\Rightarrow \angle AOB+\angle APB=180°$ (Sum of opposite angles of a cyclic quadrilateral is 180°)

$\Rightarrow \angle AOB+80°=180° \Rightarrow \angle AOB=180°-80°=100°$ *(1 M)*

31. (*a*) L.H.S $=\dfrac{(\tan\theta+\sec\theta)-(\sec^2\theta-\tan^2\theta)}{\tan\theta-\sec\theta+1}$ *(1 M)*

$=\dfrac{(\tan\theta+\sec\theta)(1-\sec\theta+\tan\theta)}{\tan\theta-\sec\theta+1}=\tan\theta+\sec\theta$ *(1 M)*

$=\dfrac{1+\sin\theta}{\cos\theta}=$ R.H.S

Hence, L.H.S = R.H.S proved *(1 M)*

OR

(*b*) L.H.S $=\left(\dfrac{1}{\sin A}-\sin A\right)\left(\dfrac{1}{\cos A}-\cos A\right)$ *(1 M)*

$=\dfrac{1-\sin^2 A}{\sin A}\times\dfrac{1-\cos^2 A}{\cos A}=\sin A\cos A$ *(½ M)*

R.H.S $=\dfrac{1}{\dfrac{\cos A}{\sin A}+\dfrac{\sin A}{\cos A}}=\dfrac{\sin A\cos A}{\sin^2 A+\cos^2 A}$

$=\sin A\cos A$ *(1 M)*

Hence, L.H.S = R.H.S proved *(½ M)*

32. Let the 4 numbers which are in AP be

$a-3d, a-d, a+d, a+3d$ ... (*i*) (½ M)

Given, the sum of these terms = 32

$\Rightarrow (a-3d)+(a-d)+(a+d)+(a+3d)=32$ (½ M)

$\Rightarrow 4a = 32 \Rightarrow a = 8$ (½ M)

Given, the ratio of the product of the first and the last term to the product of two middle terms is 7 : 15

$\frac{(a-3d)(a+3d)}{(a-d)(a+d)} = \frac{7}{15}$ (½ M)

$\frac{a^2-9d^2}{a^2-d^2} = \frac{7}{15}$ (½ M)

$15a^2 - 135d^2 = 7a^2 - 7d^2$ (½ M)

$8a^2 = 128d^2$

$128d^2 = 512$ $(\because a = 8)$

$d^2 = 4$

$d = \pm 2$ (1 M)

Putting the value $d = \pm 2$ and $a = 8$ in (*i*) we get the required number as 2, 6, 10, 14 (1 M)

33. Let time taken by 1st tap to fill the tank = *x hrs*

Time taken by 2nd tap = $(x+3)$*hrs*

Together they fill in $3\frac{1}{13} = \frac{40}{13}$ *hrs* (1 M)

Now, $\Rightarrow \frac{1}{x} + \frac{1}{x+3} = \frac{13}{40} \Rightarrow \frac{x+3+x}{x(x+3)} = \frac{13}{40}$

$\Rightarrow \frac{2x+3}{x^2+3x} = \frac{13}{40}$ (1 M)

$\Rightarrow 13x^2 + 39x = 80x + 120 \Rightarrow 13x^2 - 41x - 120 = 0$

$\Rightarrow 13x^2 - 65x + 24x - 120 = 0$ (1 M)

$\Rightarrow 13x(x-5) + 24(x-5) = 0 \Rightarrow (x-5)(13x+24) = 0$

Either $x - 5 = 0$ or $13x + 24 = 0$

$\Rightarrow x = 5$ or $x = -\frac{24}{13}$ [Rejected] (1 M)

So, 1st tap fill the tank in 5 *hrs* and 2nd tap fill the tank in $(5+3)$*hrs* = 8 *hrs* (1 M)

34. (*a*) Given: $DE \parallel BC$

To prove that: $\frac{EC}{AE} = \frac{BD}{AD}$

Proof:

$\angle AED = \angle ACB$ (Corresponding angles) (1 M)

$\angle ADE = \angle ABC$ (Corresponding angles) (1 M)

$\angle EAD$ is common to both the triangles

$\Rightarrow \Delta AED \sim \Delta ACB$ by AAA similarity (½ M)

$\Rightarrow \frac{AC}{AE} = \frac{AB}{AD}$ (1 M)

$\Rightarrow \frac{AE+EC}{AE} = \frac{AD+BD}{AD} \Rightarrow \frac{EC}{AE} = \frac{BD}{AD}$ (1 M)

Hence Proved (½ M)

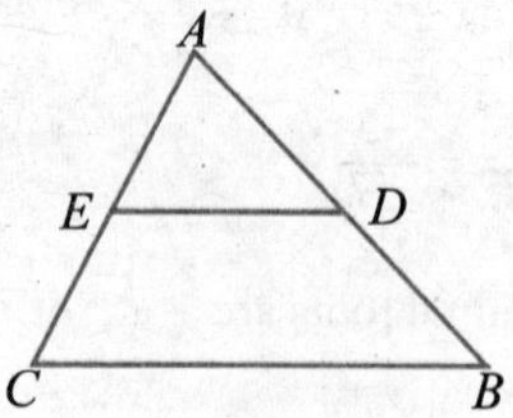

OR

(*b*) Given $\frac{PS}{SQ} = \frac{PT}{TR}$

We know that if a line divides any two sides of a triangle in the same ratio, then the line is parallel to the third side.

Therefore, $ST \parallel QR$ (1 M)

And $\angle PST = \angle PQR$ (Corresponding angles) ...(*i*) (1 M)

Also, given, $\angle PST = \angle PRQ$ ...(*ii*) (1 M)

From (*i*) and (*ii*),

$\angle PRQ = \angle PQR$ (½ M)

Therefore, $PQ = PR$ (sides opposite the equal angles) (1 M)

Hence, *PQR* is an isosceles triangle. (½ M)

35. (*a*)

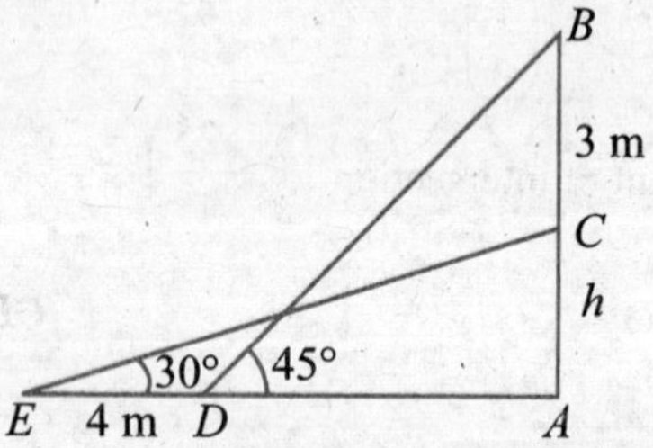

$\sin 45° = \frac{AB}{BD} = \frac{h+3}{BD} \Rightarrow BD = (h+3)\sqrt{2}$ ...(*i*) (1 M)

$\sin 30° = \frac{1}{2} = \frac{h}{CE} \Rightarrow CE = 2h$ ...(*ii*) (1 M)

Length of ladder remains same.

Therefore $BD = CE \Rightarrow (h+3)\sqrt{2} = 2h$ (1 M)

$\Rightarrow h = \frac{3\sqrt{2}}{2-\sqrt{2}} = 3(\sqrt{2}+1)$ (1 M)

Final height of the top of the ladder = $3(\sqrt{2}+1)$ m

and length of ladder = $2h = 6(\sqrt{2}+1)$ m (1 M)

OR

(*b*)

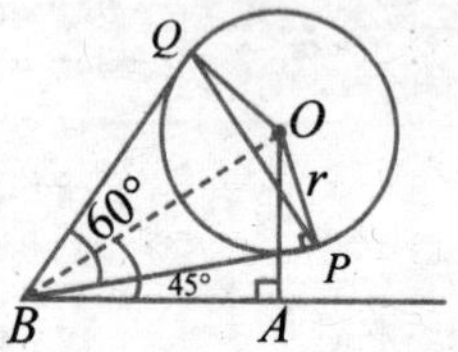

Let Point *B* represents the observer.

$\therefore \angle QBP = 60°; \angle ABO = 60°$ (1 M)

Using geometry $\angle PBO = \frac{1}{2} \times 60° = 30°$ (½ M)

Now, $\frac{r}{OB} = \sin 30° = \frac{1}{2} \Rightarrow OB = 2r$ ...(i) (1 M)

Also $\frac{OA}{OB} = \sin 45° = \frac{1}{\sqrt{2}} \Rightarrow OB = OA\sqrt{2}$ ...(ii)

(1 M)

Using (i) and (ii) $OA = \sqrt{2}\,r$ (1 M)

Or height of center of balloon $\sqrt{2}\,r$ units (½ M)

36. (i) Since, we know that angle in a semicircle is 90°.

$\therefore \angle APB = 90°$ (1 M)

(ii) Since, the length of tangents drawn from an external point to a circle are equal.

So, tangents PQ and BQ from point Q are equal.(1 M)

$\because PQ = 50$ m [Given]

$\therefore BQ = PQ = 50$ m (1 M)

OR

$\because \angle APB + \angle BPR = 180°$

$\Rightarrow \angle BPR = 180° - 90° = 90°$ ... (i) [$\because \angle APB = 90°$]

Now, In ΔBPR,

$\angle BPR + \angle PRB + \angle PBR = 180°$ (½ M)

$\Rightarrow \angle PRB + \angle PBR = 180° - 90° = 90°$

[$\because \angle BPR = 90°$]

Also, $\because \angle BPR = 90° \Rightarrow \angle BPQ + \angle QPR = 90°$ ... (ii)

From (i) and (ii)

$\angle PRB + \angle PBR = \angle BPQ + \angle QPR$ (½ M)

$\Rightarrow \angle PRB = \angle QPR$ [$\because \angle PBR = \angle BPQ$ because $BQ = PQ$]

$\Rightarrow PQ = QR$

[$\because$ sides opposite to equal angles are equal]

$\Rightarrow QR = 50$ m [$\because PQ = 50$ m] (1 M)

(iii) $\because AB \perp BR$ [Radius $\perp$ Tangent]

$\Rightarrow \angle ABR = 90°$

$\therefore \Delta ABR$ is right angled triangle.

$\because$ Radius of the ferris wheel is 5m.

$\therefore AB = 2 \times$ radius $= 2 \times 5 = 10$ m

Also, $BR = BQ + QR = 50 + 50 = 100$ m

$\therefore$ By Pythagoras Theorem,

In ΔABR,

$AR^2 = AB^2 + BR^2 = 10^2 + 100^2 = 100 + 10000 = 10100$

$\therefore AR = \sqrt{10100}$ m $= 10\sqrt{101}$ m (1 M)

37.

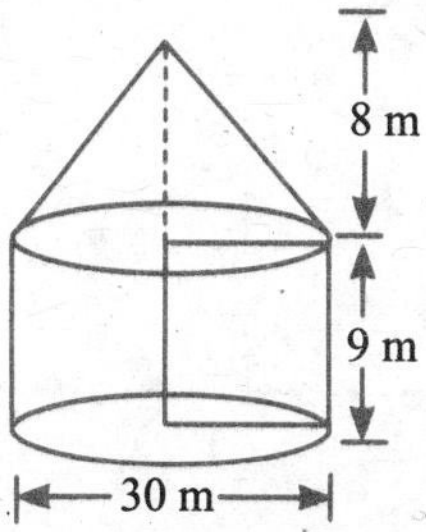

(i) Radius of conical part = Radius of cylindrical part ⇒ 15 m is the radius of conical part also. (1 M)

(ii) The area of the canvas used in making the tent

= Curved surface area of cone + Curved surface area of cylinder

$= \pi rl + 2\pi rh = \frac{22}{7} \times 15 \times 17 + 2 \times \frac{22}{7} \times 15 \times 9$ (1 M)

$= \frac{22}{7} \times 15(17+18) = \frac{22}{7} \times 15 \times 35 = 1650 \text{ m}^2$

(1 M)

OR

Here we have

Total canvas bought for the tent $= 1650 + 30 = 1680 \text{ m}^2$

(1 M)

$\therefore$ cost of canvas for the tent

$= 1680 \times 200 =$ ₹3,36,000 (1 M)

(iii) Radius of conical part = Radius of cylindrical part

$= \frac{30}{2} = 15 \text{m} = \text{r(say)}$

Given height of conical = 8 m and height of cylindrical part = 9 m

$\therefore l = \sqrt{(15)^2 + 8^2} = \sqrt{225 + 64} = \sqrt{289} = 17$ m (1 M)

38. (i) The highest frequency = 70

$\therefore$ Maximum number of student the age group = 10 – 12

(1 M)

(ii) Here $f_1 = 70, f_0 = 58$ and $f_2 = 42$ (1 M)

Succeeding class of the modal class = 42 (1 M)

OR

Here $f_1 = 70, f_0 = 58, f_2 = 42$ and $h = 2$

Mode $= 10 + \left(\frac{70-58}{2 \times 70 - 58 - 42}\right) \times 2$ (1 M)

$= 10 + \frac{12}{40} \times 2$

$= 10 + 0.6 = 10.6$ (1 M)

(iii) Modal class = 10 – 12

$\therefore$ lower limit = 10 (1 M)

❑❑❑

Notes